Defending posses

eighth edition

Jan Luba QC is a circuit judge. He was formerly a barrister in the housing team at Garden Court Chambers in London. He was called to the Bar in 1980 and was made Queen's Counsel in 2000. Jan is co-author of a number of housing law titles including *Repairs: tenant's rights* (LAG, 5th edn, 2016) and *Housing Allocations and Homelessness* (Jordans, 4th edn, 2016), and he writes, with Nic Madge, the monthly series 'Recent developments in housing law' in *Legal Action*.

Nic Madge is a circuit judge. He was formerly a district judge and head of the housing department at Bindman and Partners, London. Nic is co-author, with Sam Madge-Wyld, of *Housing Law Casebook* (LAG, 7th edn, 2016), a member of the senior editorial board of *Civil Procedure* (the White Book) (Sweet & Maxwell) and co-authors, with Jan Luba, 'Recent developments in housing law' in *Legal Action*. He is a founder member of the Housing Law Practitioners Association and is a member of the tutor team of the Judicial College. His personal website is www.nicmadge.co.uk.

Derek McConnell is a solicitor at South West Law in Bristol. Since 1978 he worked in a number of law centres, and then in private practice, specialising in housing law. He writes the regular 'Owner-occupier' updates in *Legal Action*.

John Gallagher is Principal Solicitor with Shelter, and has specialised in housing and homelessness law for over 25 years. He previously worked at SHAC (the London Housing Aid Centre), at Nottingham Law Centre and in private practice in Liverpool.

Sam Madge-Wyld is a barrister practising from Arden Chambers. He specialises in housing, real property and local government law. Sam is co-author of *Quiet enjoyment* and *Housing Law Casebook* (both LAG). He is also a contributor to the *Local Government Encyclopaedia* (on the Human Rights Act 1998) and an assistant editor of *Local Government Finance: law and practice* (both Sweet and Maxwell). Sam also regularly lectures and teaches solicitors, tenants, landlords and letting agents on housing law.

Available as an ebook at www.lag.org.uk/ebooks

The purpose of the Legal Action Group is to promote equal access to justice for all members of society who are socially, economically or otherwise disadvantaged. To this end, it seeks to improve law and practice, the administration of justice and legal services.

Defending possession proceedings

EIGHTH EDITION

Jan Luba QC, Nic Madge, Derek McConnell, John Gallagher and Sam Madge-Wyld

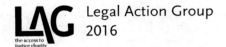
Legal Action Group
2016

This edition published in Great Britain 2016
by LAG Education and Service Trust Limited
National Pro Bono Centre, 48 Chancery Lane, London WC2A 1JF
www.lag.org.uk

First edition 1987
Second edition 1989
Third edition 1993
Fourth edition 1997
Fifth edition 2002
Sixth edition 2006
Sixth edition reprinted 2009
Seventh edition 2010

While every effort has been made to ensure that the details in this text are
correct, readers must be aware that the law changes and that the accuracy of
the material cannot be guaranteed and the author and the publisher accept no
responsibility for any losses or damage sustained.

British Library Cataloguing in Publication Data
a CIP catalogue record for this book is available from the British Library.

Crown copyright material is produced with the permission of the Controller of
HMSO and the Queen's Printer for Scotland.

This book has been produced using Forest Stewardship Council
(FSC) certified paper. The wood used to produce FSC certified
products with a 'Mixed Sources' label comes from FSC certified
well-managed forests, controlled sources and/or recycled
material.

Print ISBN   978 1 908407 64 1
ebook ISBN   978 1 908407 68 9

Typeset by Regent Typesetting, London
Printed by Hobbs the Printers, Totton, Hampshire

Preface

The task of advisers and lawyers helping those facing possession proceedings has become increasingly difficult in the 29 years since the first edition of this book was written. In 2015, a total of 173,547 claims for possession were started in county courts throughout England and Wales, of which 19,853 were mortgage-related. A total of 132,545 possession orders were made. There were 5,585 repossessions by court bailiff in mortgage cases, and 42,710 repossessions in respect of rented residential premises. Although the figures relating to mortgage possession are the lowest annual figures in the series, which covers the period from 1987, the number of repossessions in respect of rented accommodation is the highest annual figure in the series, which covers the period from 2000.[1]

The economic stringency of the times is one obvious explanation for the growth in repossessions in the rented sector. Since the last edition of this book was published, the Government's welfare reform agenda has produced the application to housing benefit claims of the social sector size criteria, whereby a person's eligible rent for benefit purposes is reduced by 14 per cent or 25 per cent if he or she is considered to be under-occupying the home by one or two bedrooms respectively;[2] and a benefit cap applied to the total amount of benefits received by a household, which is implemented through reducing

---

1   Compiled from *Mortgage and landlord possession statistics*: Ministry of Justice statistics bulletins for 2015, obtainable at www.gov.uk/government/collections/mortgage-and-landlord-possession-statistics.
2   Housing Benefit Regulations 2006 SI No 213 reg B13, inserted by the Housing Benefit (Amendment) Regulations 2012 SI No 3040. Similar deductions are made where the occupier is in receipt of the housing element of universal credit. See paras 16.15–16.19 and 16.61–16.63.

housing benefit by the amount by which the household's total entitlement exceeds the amount of the cap.[3]

The aim of *Defending possession proceedings* is to assist advice workers, solicitors, barristers and others called upon to help defendants or potential defendants to possession claims. This book is not, and could not be, a treatise on all the relevant law of tenancies and mortgages. There are other weighty volumes which fulfil that function. *Defending possession proceedings* is essentially a practical book. We concentrate on matters of practice and procedure and relevant substantive law. We have aimed to write it in a user-friendly way so that it contains information which is of use to the most experienced legal practitioners, yet is still understandable to the least experienced housing advisers.

In recent years, the law has become more and more complex – demonstrated by the fact that this eighth edition is more than four times longer than the first edition. In the last six years alone, the primary statutes – Housing Act 1985 Part IV (secure tenancies); Housing Act 1988 Part I (rented accommodation: assured tenancies); and Housing Act 1996 Parts III (Landlord and Tenant) and V (Conduct of Tenants) – have been, or are about to be, substantially amended by the: Localism Act 2011; Anti-social Behaviour, Crime and Policing Act 2014; Deregulation Act 2015; Immigration Acts 2014 and 2016; and Housing and Planning Act 2016, such that the amended Acts are now unrecognisable in comparison with their original incarnations. The Housing and Planning Act 2016, in particular, contains over 20 pages of amendments to Housing Acts 1985 and 1996.[4] Housing law has become shamefully inaccessible to those who need it most.

This state of affairs brings to mind the words of Baroness Hale:

> *Legislation designed to protect residential tenants should be clear, simple and consistent in its effects, not dubious, complex and arbitrary.*[5]

Nothing could be further from the condition of English housing law in 2016. Too often, housing law is anything but clear, simple and consistent. The sole beacon in housing law reform has come from

3 Welfare Reform Act 2012 s96(1); Housing Benefit Regulations 2006 SI No 213 regs 75A–75G, inserted by the Benefit Cap (Housing Benefit) Regulations 2012 SI No 2994 reg 2(5). Similar deductions are made where the occupier is in receipt of the housing element of universal credit. See paras 16.20–16.21 and 16.67–16.68.

4 Housing and Planning Act 2016 Sch 7 and 8.

5 In *Austin v London Borough of Southwark* [2010] UKSC 28, [2010] HLR 38 at para [53].

Wales, where the Renting Homes (Wales) Act 2016 was passed on 18 January 2016 and is expected to come into force in 2017/18. This Act is based on the work of the Law Commission[6] and consists of a 'root and branch' codification of housing law based on the concept of the 'occupation contract'. While English housing law is continually required to absorb still further layers of complexity, the Welsh legislation shows the way.

This book does not cover the Renting Homes (Wales) Act 2016. Until that Act comes into force, this book applies to Wales, except where expressly indicated in the text.[7] From the commencement date of the new regime of housing law in the 2016 Act, Parts I, II and III of this book will cease to apply to Wales (apart from chapter 16 and some elements of chapters 19 and 20). In Part IV, Chapters 24–27 will still apply in Wales, but it is not yet known whether and to what extent the chapters on court procedure will be applicable, with modifications, to the new occupation contracts. Part V will still apply in Wales (apart from the fact that the provisions of the Mortgage Repossessions (Protection of Tenants etc) Act 2010[8] will not apply in their current form).

The complexity of the law in England is increasing at a time when, under the Legal Aid, Sentencing and Punishment of Offenders Act 2012, legal aid has been drastically restricted and the number of legal aid providers is declining. Possession proceedings remain within scope of legal aid[9] for those who are financially eligible, but legal aid has disappeared for advice on preventative work such as assisting clients with negotiations under the Protocols, and for assistance with welfare benefits. A stark but familiar illustration of the problem occurs where a tenant has fallen into rent arrears because he or she has not received the welfare benefits to which he or she is entitled, whether housing benefit or the housing element of universal credit. In the event of possession action being taken against such a tenant, the fact that he or she is not receiving his or her full benefits entitlement is at the heart of the case, but legal aid is no longer available to fund the work required to resolve the benefits issue. As a result, occupiers face eviction from their homes needlessly and unjustifiably, for the want of assistance in resolving their benefits problems.

6   *Renting Homes* (Law Com No 297), Cm 6781, May 2006.
7   See, for example, in relation to assured shorthold tenancies, paras 10.103–10.104.
8   See paras 37.67–37.68.
9   Legal Aid, Sentencing and Punishment of Offenders Act 2012 Sch 1 para 33 (Loss of Home). See chapter 24.

Clearly, tenants and borrowers need at least to have ready access to the judicial system, yet the current programme of court closures will deprive many occupiers of their local court and, in some cases, will require them to travel considerable distances to attend the hearings at which their homes are at stake.

This edition of *Defending possession proceedings* is published at a time when the rights of occupiers in the social rented sector in England are at the lowest ebb since the introduction of security of tenure in that sector in 1980. Security of tenure in the private rented sector vanished long ago, except for those with historic entitlement.[10] The erosion of social tenants' rights began in earnest with the Localism Act 2011, which introduced the fixed-term 'flexible tenancy' for tenants of local housing authorities, whereby authorities could opt to grant a fixed-term tenancy for a minimum of two years. At the same time, housing associations and other private registered providers of social housing (in England) are encouraged to grant fixed term tenancies for a minimum of two years: such providers already have a mechanism for doing so, namely, the assured shorthold tenancy.

The Housing and Planning Act 2016, when in force, will require new secure tenancies, granted by local housing authorities in England after the date of commencement, to be fixed-term tenancies of between two and ten years (except that, where a tenant's family includes a child under nine years of age, the fixed term may extend until the child's 19th birthday).[11] When the fixed term expires, the local housing authority will need to decide whether or not to renew the tenancy. If it decides not to do so, and seeks possession of the property, it will be necessary to consider whether the tenant may be able to invoke a public law or human rights defence (see chapters 25 and 26).

Certain other developments which have occurred since the last edition deserve particular comment. As that edition went to press, the appeal in the case of *Manchester City Council v Pinnock*[12] was being heard by the Supreme Court. The Supreme Court's judgments in that case, and in *Hounslow LBC v Powell*,[13] resolved the tension which had arisen between decisions of the Strasbourg court and the domestic courts over the question whether an alleged breach of an

---

10 See chapter 12 (Rent Act regulated tenants) and chapter 11 paras 11.3–11.4 (assured tenants).

11 See para 1.89.

12 [2010] UKSC 45, [2011] HLR 7

13 [2011] UKSC 45, [2011] HLR 23.

occupier's rights under Human Rights Act 1998 Sch 1 Article 8 could be raised as a defence in a county court possession claim. In *Pinnock*, the Supreme Court held that if UK law was to be compatible with Article 8, 'the court must have the power to assess the proportionality of making the order, and, in making that assessment, to resolve any relevant dispute of fact'.[14] Since then, defendants in a number of other cases have sought both to explore the boundaries of the 'human rights' defence and to assert a public law defence where the claimant public body has arguably acted unlawfully on administrative law principles in bringing the possession claim. More recently, the Supreme Court has declined to extend the benefit of a proportionality review in possession proceedings to homeless persons placed in temporary accommodation under Housing Act 1996 s188,[15] or to the assured shorthold tenant of a private landlord.[16]

Since the last edition was published, the Equality Act 2010 has superseded a number of earlier statutes, each of which dealt with discrimination on the basis of what is now a 'protected characteristic' under the 2010 Act (such as the Disability Discrimination Act 1995). The 2010 Act establishes the possibility of a defence to possession proceedings where the decision to bring the possession claim amounts to discrimination on the basis of a protected characteristic, or specifically, in cases involving disability, where the reason for the unfavourable treatment, ie the decision to evict, is 'something arising in consequence of [the defendant's] disability', where the landlord cannot show that the treatment is a proportionate means of achieving a legitimate aim.[17] In *Akerman-Livingstone v Aster Communities Limited*[18] the Supreme Court has held that the correct approach to be taken by the courts in considering Equality Act defences at the first hearing is not the same as that which must be taken in respect of 'human rights' defences to possession claims. In Equality Act cases, the court is required to make a careful evaluation at the initial stage

---

14 [2010] UKSC 45, [2011] HLR 7 at [49].

15 *R (ZH and CN) v Newham LBC and Lewisham LBC* [2014] UKSC 62, [2015] HLR 6.

16 *McDonald v McDonald and others* [2016] UKSC 28, [2016] HLR 28.

17 Equality Act 2010 s15(1). This provision overturned the effect of the decision of the House of Lords in *London Borough of Lewisham v Malcolm* [2008] 1 AC 1399, [2008] HLR 41 in which it was held that the Council's action in seeking possession of a tenant's flat for reasons which were arguably related to his disability did not amount to 'less favourable treatment' under the Disability Discrimination Act 1995. See paras 27.11–27.12.

18 [2015] UKSC 15, [2015] HLR 20.

as to whether, in the terms of CPR 55.8(2), the claim is genuinely disputed on grounds which appear to be substantial.[19]

This edition of the book has involved a major restructuring of the main chapters in Parts I and II, dealing with rented accommodation. Instead of considering the secure and assured tenancy regimes separately, as we have done in previous editions, we have divided the types of occupancy into the social rented sector (Part I) and the private rented sector (Part II). We believe that this division more closely reflects the reality of rental occupation. It also allows us to give unified consideration to those grounds for possession which are common to both regimes or similar, together with the ways in which the court exercises its discretion (where permitted by the relevant Act) in deciding whether it is reasonable to make a possession order.

As ever, we are very grateful to those colleagues who have written to us with suggestions and comments on earlier editions. We have taken them into account where possible. Comments on this edition (addressed to us c/o Legal Action Group) are warmly welcomed.

Many of the issues dealt with in this book are the subject of regular discussions at the bi-monthly meetings of the Housing Law Practitioners' Association (see www.hlpa.org.uk). In addition, the material in this book can be updated by reference to Nic Madge and Jan Luba's 'Recent developments in housing law', a monthly column in *Legal Action*, and to Derek McConnell's annual review 'Owner-occupiers: recent developments' which also appears in *Legal Action* in April each year.

In this edition we welcome to the writing team Sam Madge-Wyld. Sam was a reader for the last edition, but this time we are delighted to have him on board. We are grateful to Kathy Meade, professional support lawyer at Shelter, who devised the flowcharts for section 21 defences and tenancy deposit issues which are reproduced at paras 10.105–10.107; and to Desmond Rutledge of Garden Court Chambers, who read and commented on chapter 16 (Welfare benefits).

This edition has been a long time in the making. We would still be working on it ten years hence if it were not for the incomparable skills, dedication and wells of patience of our editor at LAG, Esther Pilger, to whom we owe a deep and heartfelt debt of gratitude. We are immensely grateful to Lesley Exton at Regent Typesetting, who has once again done the impossible in assimilating major additions and updating at page proof stage; and to the entire team at LAG, but especially to Lucy Logan-Green, who has acted as a reader, and provided

19 See paras 27.26–27.32.

editorial support to Esther by assisting with citations and proof corrections. Their contributions, as always, have been incalculable. Any mistakes are ours.

The law in England and Wales is stated as at 1 September 2016.

Jan Luba QC,
Nic Madge,
Derek McConnell,
John Gallagher
and
Sam Madge-Wyld

How to use this book

Since the first edition was published in January 1987, *Defending possession proceedings* has been a practical reference handbook dealing with all aspects of the law and practice relating to possession proceedings pursued against occupiers of *residential* property. It seeks to guide occupiers and their advisers in dealing with possession claims. It traces the court process from the initial notice given to the occupier to the aftermath of the bailiff's eviction. The main content of the book deals with three principal types of occupier, namely, the social housing tenant, the private tenant and the mortgage borrower.

The starting point for making best use of this book is to establish what form of right to occupation of the property the occupier enjoys (if any). For owner-occupiers, the reader needs to go straight to Part V except in relation to shared ownership leaseholders (see chapter 9) or rental purchasers (chapter 13). If the occupier has, at the other end of the spectrum, no legal right of occupation at all; go to chapter 23. In between ownership and trespass, the most common form of occupation will be under a tenancy. To make best use of this book in those cases, the type of tenancy will first need to be identified.

Part I of this book deals with tenants and other occupiers in the *social rented sector*. Chapter 1 deals with the dominant kinds of tenancy available to social landlords, namely the secure tenancy (granted by local housing authorities) and the *assured* (or *assured shorthold*) tenancy (granted by housing associations). Chapters 2 to 4 deal with the statutory procedures for recovery of possession of such tenancies, the grounds of possession for each kind of tenancy, and the preparation of a defence.

A particular difficulty can be to identify the correct form of occupation of a resident of social housing because of the different kinds of tenancy which may be available in the social rented sector, particularly where the landlord is a local housing authority. Chapters 5 to 8 deal with occupiers of social sector accommodation who do not qualify for secure, assured or assured shorthold status. Chapter 5 deals with *introductory and starter* tenancies; chapter 6, with demoted tenancies; chapter 7, with *family intervention* tenancies; and chapter 8, with social sector licensees, sub-tenants and other special cases.

Clarity has not been assisted by the descriptions now given to the particular types of social housing provider known loosely as 'housing associations' or by the different arrangements for the regulation of those providers. The book uses the statutory terms 'private registered provider of social housing' (PRPSH) for non-local authority social landlords in England and 'registered social landlords' (RSL) for those same landlords in Wales.

Part II of the book deals with tenants and other occupiers in the *private rented sector*. Relatively few private tenants are still protected by the Rent Acts (see chapter 12). The great majority are *assured shorthold* tenants (chapter 10). Assured shorthold tenants have no security of tenure, and, subject to the terms of their agreement, can be required to leave on two months' notice given under Housing Act 1988 s21. There are a number of possible defences to claims for possession based on 'section 21' notices. It is hoped that the flowcharts in chapter 10 may assist in providing an aide-memoire in relating the circumstances in which those defences apply, together with the sanctions which are available against landlords who fail to follow the statutory procedures for protecting their tenants' deposits. Chapter 11 deals with other private sector occupiers, including certain tenants with full assured status; tenants excluded from the assured tenancy scheme; and licensees.

Where the type of tenancy which an occupier has is clear, then reference should be made to the relevant part or chapter of the book. However, where it is unclear, the brief introduction to the types of tenancy, found at the beginning of each of Parts I and II, may assist in locating the relevant section of the book.

Part III of the book deals with other tenancy issues which can apply to tenancies in both the social and the private rented sectors. Chapter 14 deals with the termination of *contractual* tenancies, including by notice to quit, surrender and forfeiture, while chapter 15 covers the limited protection available to *wholly unprotected* tenants and licensees. The text also covers the critical related issues that may trigger or affect possession claims. The subjects of *welfare benefits for tenants* and termination of accommodation linked to *employment* are covered in chapters 16 and 17 respectively. Chapter 18 deals with *death* of the occupier, while chapter 19 tackles *bankruptcy*. Chapter 20 deals with *relationship breakdown* in a rented home.

Part IV of the book addresses possession procedure and related points as they affect residential tenants and other occupiers. Chapter 24 deals with *legal aid* for defendants. Part IV also contains three chapters which consider the relatively 'modern' defences to possession claims based on: (1) *public law principles*; or (2) *human rights*; or (3) *disability discrimination*. These are described in chapters 25, 26 and 27 respectively.

Part V deals with mortgages, possession procedure, the powers of the court, the regulation of mortgage lenders and other issues as they affect mortgage borrowers. In particular, chapter 33 considers the lender's right to possession, while chapter 34 explains the court's powers to allow borrowers to remain in their homes. Chapter 35 deals with regulation of mortgage lending by the Financial Conduct Authority. Chapter 36 discusses steps that may be taken to prevent the lender from obtaining possession. Chapter 37 covers procedure and tactics in mortgage possession cases.

The remaining chapters in Part V concern various issues which impact on residential mortgages and the homes which are subject to them. Chapter 38 deals with *tenants* of borrowers; chapter 39, with *domestic relationship breakdown* in the owner-occupied home. Chapter 40 considers *Islamic property finance*; chapter 41, the rights of *equitable owners*; and chapter 42, *undue influence*. Chapter 43 discusses *sale* of the security, while chapter 44 covers possession claims by *unsecured creditors*.

The appendices contain the various statutory notices and a set of precedents which practitioners might find useful. An instructions checklist is provided as an aide-memoire. Also included in the appendices are the texts of the two Protocols: for possession claims by social landlords; and for claims based on mortgage arrears; the text of the Civil Procedure Rule governing possession cases – CPR Part 55 – and the practice directions to it; and Schedule 2A to the Housing Act 1985 – the meaning of 'serious offence' for the purposes of the absolute grounds for possession for anti-social behaviour.

Contents

Table of cases

Table of statutes

Table of statutory instruments

Table of European legislation

Abbreviations

ABCPA	Anti-social Behaviour, Crime and Policing Act 2014
AJA	Administration of Justice Acts
BC	Borough Council
BRMA	Broad rental market area
CA	Court of Appeal
CC	City Council
CCA	Consumer Credit Act 1974
CCMS	Client and cost management system
CCR	County Court Rules
ChD	Chancery Division
CLA	Criminal Law Act 1977
CLRA	Commonhold and Leasehold Reform Act 2002
CML	Council of Mortgage Lenders
CPR	Civil Procedure Rules
DC	District Council
DCLG	Department for Communities and Local Government
DHP	Discretionary housing payments
DoE	Department of the Environment
DRO	Debt relief orders
DWP	Department for Work and Pensions
EA	Equality Act 2010
ECHR	European Convention on Human Rights
ECtHR	European Court of Human Rights
EPC	Energy Performance Certificate
FCA	Financial Conduct Authority
FOS	Financial Ombudsman Service
FSMA	Financial Services and Markets Act 2000
H&RA	Housing & Regeneration Act 2008
HA	Housing Acts
HAT	Housing action trust
HB Regs	Housing Benefit Regulations 2006 SI No 213
HCA	Homes and Communities Agency
HL	House of Lords
HMO	House in multiple occupation
HPA	Housing and Planning Act 2016
HRA	Human Rights Act 1998
IA	Immigration Act 2014

IA	Insolvency Act 1986
IPO	Interim possession order
IS Regs	Income Support (General) Regulations 1987 SI No 1967
ISA	Individual savings account
JSA Regs	Jobseeker's Allowance Regulations 1996 SI No 207
LAA	Legal Aid Agency
LASPO	Legal Aid, Sentencing and Punishment of Offenders Act 2012
LBC	London Borough Council
LHA	Local housing allowance
LPA	Law of Property Act 1925
LRA	Land Registration Act 2002
LSVT	Large Scale Voluntary Transfer scheme
LTA	Landlord and Tenant Acts
LVT	Leasehold Valuation Tribunal
MAPPA	Multi-agency Public Protection Arrangements
MBC	Metropolitan Borough Council
MCOB	Mortgage: conduct of business sourcebook
NSP	Notice Seeking Possession
OFT	Office of Fair Trading
PCOL	Possession Claims Online
PEA	Protection from Eviction Act 1977
PERG	Perimeter Guidance Manual
PIP	Personal independence payment
PRPSH	Private registered provider of social housing
PSED	Public sector equality duty
RA	Rent Act
RSC	Rules of the Supreme Court
RSL	Registered social landlord
SMI	Support for mortgage interest
TLATA	Trusts of Land and Appointment of Trustees Act 1996
UTCC Regs	Unfair Terms in Consumer Contracts Regulations 1999

Tenants of social housing

Introduction to Part I

I.1   Part I of this book is concerned with defending possession proceedings brought against occupiers of social housing. Its main focus is on tenants of housing associations (which are now the main providers of social housing) and on tenants of those local housing authorities in England and Wales which retain and manage their own housing stock (or which have retained ownership but have contracted-out the management of the stock to 'arms-length management organisations' [ALMOs] or others). For the purposes of this book, both housing associations and council landlords are described as 'social landlords'.[1]

I.2   Most tenants of social housing will not only have the benefit of the contractual terms of their periodic or fixed-term tenancy but they will also enjoy security of tenure in their homes under one of two statutory regimes.

I.3   Tenants of housing associations are usually assured tenants. Their protection is provided by Housing Act (HA) 1988 Part 1. In contrast, most council tenants are *secure* tenants. They are protected by Housing Act 1985 Part 4. Both these statutory regimes prevent social landlords from ending the tenancies or recovering possession except by proving, to a county court judge, the particular grounds for possession as set out in the respective Housing Acts. In most cases, the tenant is further protected by a discretion the court exercises as to whether the particular circumstances justify the making of any possession order. On paper, therefore, these tenants have considerable protection against loss of their homes.

---

1 The term will also be used when referring to other social or public bodies which rent-out housing accommodation, eg housing societies, trusts and charities.

I.4   The first chapter in Part I of this book provides a short summary of how security of tenure works in the social housing sector and deals briefly with the situations in which that security of tenure can be lost otherwise than by the making of a possession order. Chapter 2 outlines the procedures a social landlord must follow in order to recover possession. The third chapter deals with the grounds for possession that apply to proceedings against assured or secure tenants and chapter 4 deals with the preparation of defences.

I.5   Although tenants of social housing normally have the benefit of the highest level of security of tenure available in the rented sector, this statutory protection has not led to any perceptible containment of social landlords' attempts to recover possession. The county courts in England and Wales deal with tens of thousands of possession claims brought against tenants of social housing each year. Research has repeatedly shown that these social housing possession cases can receive insufficiently thorough attention in some county courts. Researchers have suggested that in some parts of the country the speed with which possession cases are heard indicates little regard for security of tenure and, rather, an emphasis on quick disposal.

I.6   Despite the security of tenure that social housing tenants enjoy, possession orders are made in the majority of cases and thousands of tenants are actually evicted each year as a result. Research has emphasised the need for more tenants to attend court, for better access to advice and representation and more consistent handling of housing possession cases by the courts.[2]

I.7   Most of the claims for possession brought against social housing tenants are – in reality – 'debt collecting' actions. The main function of the proceedings is to threaten repossession on the ground of rent arrears unless the tenant resumes regular and full payment of their rent. This happens notwithstanding the UK Government's repeated exhortations to social landlords to see possession proceedings only as the last resort in recovering arrears.[3] Social landlords presumably regard possession proceedings as a 'bigger stick' to wield against defaulting tenants than other available recovery procedures.

---

2 C Hunter et al, *The exercise of judicial discretion in rent arrears cases,* Department of Constitutional Affairs, Research Series 6/05, 2005; and S Bright et al, *Information, Advice & Representation in Housing Possession Cases,* Oxford Legal Studies Research Paper No 25/2014, 2014.

3 *The use of possession actions and evictions by social landlords,* ODPM, June 2005, Guide on Effective Rent Arrears Management, DCLG, August 2006 and see too Pawson et al, *Rent arrears management practices in the housing association sector,* TSA, February 2010.

This practice, which might appear to some to verge on an abuse of the process of the court, received critical scrutiny from Lord Woolf's review of civil justice,[4] but appears not to have abated. It was hoped that the introduction of a new '*Rent Arrears Pre-action Protocol*' (now amended and re-named the *Pre-action Protocol for possession claims by social landlords*: see paras 3.77–3.80) in October 2006 would lead to a reduction in the overall number of possession proceedings and a sharper focus on the statutory criteria limiting the circumstances in which possession orders can be made. But after an initial post-protocol 'blip', the numbers of possession claims brought by social landlords have since increased again.

1.8   Concern that security of tenure makes it too difficult for social landlords to recover possession, and in effect gives tenants a 'home for life', has led to the creation of an increasing number of exceptions to full protection. For example, following a very effective lobbying campaign by council landlords, the Housing Act 1996 introduced a new reduced form of security of tenure for most new council tenants who would otherwise have been secure. As a result, since 1997 local housing authorities have had power to elect to put these new tenants 'on probation' for their first year – now extendable to 18 months – by the grant of 'introductory tenancies'. In parallel, housing associations were allowed by their then regulator to grant tenancies with less than the full assured status as 'starter tenancies'. Possession claims against these reduced-status social housing tenants are considered in chapter 5.

1.9   But these were merely the initial inroads into full security of tenure in the social housing sector. Since June 2004, social landlords have been able to apply to the courts for 'demotion orders', whereby the security of tenure of an assured or secure tenant can be removed by the county court and the tenancy reduced to probationary status for a period of one year. These demoted tenancy arrangements are described in chapter 6.

1.10   The Housing and Regeneration Act 2008 introduced yet another form of social housing tenancy which does not enjoy security of tenure – the family intervention tenancy. The defence of possession proceedings brought against those tenants is discussed in chapter 7.

1.11   Although they remain in the significant majority, tenants of social landlords are not the only occupiers of social housing. There are many people living in social housing in a variety of other circumstances. Some, for example those provided with accommodation by

4 Woolf, *Access to Justice: Final Report*, HMSO, 1996, ch 16.

a social landlord who are also employees of the landlord, may have a licence rather than a tenancy. Others will be living in social housing as the subtenant of the social landlord's tenant. Yet others will be occupying in even more unusual situations. The circumstances of the whole range of these special cases are described in chapter 8.

I.12   Finally, this Part deals in chapter 9 with the situation of those occupying social housing under part-rent, part-buy arrangements ('shared ownership').

CHAPTER 1

Tenants with security of tenure

continued

Notice to the absent tenant under Part 3 of the Housing and Planning Act 2016

1.193   The tenant assigns

Introduction

1.1   Since 1980, tenants of social housing (mainly tenants of local housing authorities and housing associations), have, save for some limited exceptions, had 'security of tenure'. This meant that even though
the vast majority were weekly periodic tenants their landlord could
not simply recover possession by serving a notice to quit.

1.2   Unlike the Rent Acts, which always allowed a landlord to determine the contractual tenancy, a tenant's security of tenure under both
the Housing Act (HA) 1985 and Housing Act 1988 acts as a 'cloak' to
protect an ordinary common law tenancy from, among other things,
being determined by the landlord in the ordinary way.[1] Under those
ordinary rules, a tenancy granted for a fixed period simply ended on
expiry of its term. Or, if the tenancy was a periodic tenancy, a landlord
could bring it to an end by notice to quit. Security of tenure operates
by way of a statutory overlay on those rules to prevent them operating in the usual way. To put that another way, security of tenure for
a social housing tenant arises because the Housing Acts have 'added
statutory incidents to that tenancy which overrode some of the contractual terms. These overriding provisions include the provisions
which prevent it from being terminated except by an order of the
court on the statutory grounds'.[2]

1.3   The landlord, to recover possession, must serve a notice that complies with the statutory provisions, prove a ground for possession,
that is of application to the tenant, and then satisfy the court that the
other (if any) statutory conditions are satisfied, eg it is reasonable
to make a possession order or that suitable alternative accommodation is made available to the tenant. Although a lot has changed in
the last 36 years, with even more change to come,[3] at the time of
going to press the vast majority of social tenants that have occupied
their homes for more than 18 months still have this form of security
tenure.

1.4   The 'cloak' affording protection under both HA 1985 and HA 1988
is the highest form of security of tenure for tenants of social housing.
The scheme for *assured* tenants is contained in HA 1988 Pt 1 and it

---

1   'In the graphic words of Mr Luba, it is a contractual tenancy "cloaked" with
statutory protection': *Sheffield City Council v Wall (No 2)* [2010] EWCA Civ 922,
[2010] HLR 47, CA at [57].

2   *Birmingham City Council v Walker* [2007] UKHL 22, [2007] HLR 38 at para [3].

3   See below paras 1.87–1.96 for the position for secure tenants whose tenancies
were granted after the coming into force of Housing and Planning Act 2016
Sch 7.

mainly applies to tenants of housing associations. The scheme for *secure* tenants, who are mainly the tenants of local authorities, is contained in HA 1985 Pt 4.

1.5　This chapter deals first with the numerically most common social housing tenancy – the assured tenancy – and then with secure tenancies. As there is a degree of overlap between the two tenures the principles that are relevant to both will be considered in detail insofar as they relate to assured tenancies and, when considering the position of secure tenants, cross-references will refer back to the relevant principles. The chapter then concludes with a brief review of the circumstances in which both assured and secure tenants can lose their security of tenure other than by a landlord's successful claim for a possession order.

Assured tenants

1.6　HA 1988 s1(1) provides that:

> A tenancy under which a dwelling-house is let as a separate dwelling is for the purposes of this Act an assured tenancy if and so long as –
> (a) the tenant or, as the case may be, each of the joint tenants is an individual; and
> (b) the tenant or, as the case may be, at least one of the joint tenants occupies the dwelling-house as his only or principal home; and
> (c) the tenancy is not one which, by virtue of subsection (2) or subsection (6) below, cannot be an assured tenancy.

'A tenancy'

1.7　There must be a 'tenancy'. A licensee cannot have security of tenure under HA 1988. The case-law that developed under the Rent Acts governing the distinction between tenancies and licenses is therefore of crucial importance. In *Street v Mountford*,[4] Lord Templeman held that, other than in special circumstances, exclusive possession at a rent for a term, coupled with the intention to create legal relations, will give rise to a tenancy. The parties' subjective intentions, or the fact that the agreement is called a licence, are irrelevant if the three hallmarks of a tenancy are present.[5] A joint tenancy does not arise where a number of occupiers share accommodation under separate

4　[1985] AC 809, [1985] 2 All ER 289, HL.
5　*Street v Mountford* [1985] AC 809, HL; *Kirby v Lynch* [2010] EWHC 297 (QB). Cf *Eastleigh BC v Walsh* [1985] AC 809, in which an occupier was found to be

agreements granted at different times.[6] The grant of one room with exclusive occupation, within a shared house, in consideration of a periodic payment does create a tenancy.[7] Where a couple have entered into two separate licence agreements to live in a flat comprising one bedroom they hold as joint tenants despite the 'label' on their agreements.[8]

1.8   A tenancy may even be granted by a person who does not own the land, as freehold or leaseholder, and is merely a licensee[9] or even by a person with no interest in the land at all.[10] In such cases, the landlord is estopped from denying that he or she has title to grant the tenancy. It has been held that a tenancy by estoppel attracts security of tenure.[11] The person who has an immediate right of possession as against the landlord can, however, recover possession from a tenant as a trespasser.[12]

1.9   A minor, ie anyone under the age of 18, cannot hold a legal estate in land.[13] A minor who succeeds to a tenancy under either HA 1985 or HA 1988 will, however, hold the tenancy in equity with the protection of either Act.[14] A landlord, however, who purports to grant a tenancy to anyone under the age of 18 does not create a legal estate; rather the grant operates as a declaration that the land is held on trust for the minor.[15] The minor's right to occupy the property therefore arises in equity under the trust and not under an equitable tenancy.[16]

a tenant where he had signed an agreement that referred to 'conditions of tenancy'.

6   *AG Securities v Vaughan* [1990] 1 AC 417, [1988] 3 WLR 1205, HL.

7   *Curl v Angelo* [1948] 2 All ER 189, CA.

8   *Antoniades v Villiers* [1990] 1 AC 417, [1988] 3 WLR 1205, HL.

9   *Bruton v London and Quadrant Housing Trust* [2000] 1 AC 406, [1999] 3 WLR 1205, HL.

10   *Stratford v Syrett* [1958] 1 QB 107, CA.

11   *Lewis v Morelli* [1948] 2 All ER 1021; *Mackley v Nutting* [1949] 2 KB 55, CA; *Whitmore v Lambert* [1955] 1 WLR 495, CA; *Stratford v Syrett* [1958] 1 QB 107, CA.

12   *Bruton v London and Quadrant HT* [2000] 1 AC 406, [1999] 3 WLR 150, HL.

13   Law of Property Act 1925 s1(6).

14   *Kingston upon Thames RLBC v Prince* (1999) 31 HLR 794, CA. HA 1988 s45 defines a tenancy as including 'an agreement for a tenancy', which is the definition of an equitable tenancy: *Walsh v Lonsdale* (1882) 21 Ch D 9, CA.

15   Trusts of Land and Appointment of Trustees Act 1996 s2(6) and Sch 1 para 1(1). *Hammersmith & Fulham LBC v Alexander-David* [2009] EWCA Civ 259, [2009] HLR 39.

16   One effect of this is that the purported landlord, who is in fact the trustee, is unable to terminate the agreement as to do so is inconsistent with the trust continuing and is likely to amount to a breach of the trustee's duties under the

Exclusive possession

1.10   Ordinarily, granting someone the right to reside or live in a dwelling will give rise to the inference that it is to be occupied with exclusive possession unless there are other circumstances that point to the contrary. One such circumstance is where, under the agreement, the owner of residential accommodation provides services or attendance and *retains possession for that purpose*, in which case the occupier is a lodger and the agreement creates a licence.[17] It is not enough that the landlord provides the tenant with services or attendance; he or she must need possession of the premises to do so.

1.11   The most obvious example of a licence will be where the provider cleans the room, changes bedding or provides breakfast in a hotel.[18] An agreement that gives the provider a right to enter, on short or no notice, to provide such services will also point towards the agreement being a licence. The fact that the services are not in fact provided is not relevant provided that the occupier could, under the agreement, have demanded that the services be provided.[19] Similarly, a provision in an agreement that entitles the provider to move the occupier into a different room will point against the occupier having exclusive possession.[20]

1.12   However, advisers should be careful to watch out for sham agreements, ie an agreement 'which [is] intended ... to give to third parties or to the court the appearance of creating between the parties legal rights and obligations different from the actual legal rights and obligations (if any) which the parties intend to create'.[21] Agreements which, on their face, require a landlord to provide certain services, but which were never intended to be provided and are not in fact provided, will create tenancies.[22] In practice, unless the agreement is obviously absurd it will be difficult to prove that an agreement is a sham without other evidence to demonstrate that the agreement was not what the parties intended.

trust: *Hammersmith & Fulham LBC v Alexander-David* [2009] EWCA Civ 259, [2009] HLR 39 and see *Croydon LBC v Tando* June 2012 *Legal Action* 35.

17 *AG Securities v Vaughan* [1990] 1 AC 417, [1988] 3 WLR 1205, HL.

18 *Brillouet v Landless* (1996) 28 HLR 836, CA.

19 *Huwyler v Ruddy* (1996) 28 HLR 550, CA.

20 *Westminster City Council v Clarke* [1992] AC 288, [1992] 24 HLR 360; *Brennan v Lambeth LBC* (1998) 30 HLR 481, CA.

21 *Snook v London and West Riding Investments Ltd* [1967] 2 QB 786, CA.

22 *Street v Mountford* [1985] AC 809, HL; *Aslan v Murphy (No 2)* [1990] 1 WLR 766, CA; *Crancour Ltd v Da Silvaesa* (1986) 18 HLR 265, CA.

At a rent

1.13   While the existence of the payment of rent is a hallmark of a tenancy it is possible to create a tenancy at no rent.[23] A tenancy at no rent is, however, incapable of being an assured tenancy.[24]

For a term

1.14   A grant that is not for a term or for an uncertain term cannot take effect as a tenancy.[25] An agreement that gives rise to a periodic arrangement, which is determinable by either party, will create a valid tenancy.[26] The payment of rent, which gives rise to a periodic tenancy, will therefore cause there to be a valid tenancy.[27] An agreement that prevents one party from determining a periodic tenancy does create a tenancy as the term is uncertain. However, such an agreement still takes effect as a tenancy, albeit for a term of 90 years determinable on the death of the tenant.[28]

Service occupiers

1.15   In *Street v Mountford*,[29] Lord Templeman held that, in addition to circumstances in which the parties did not intend to enter into legal relations (see below paras 1.18–1.19), it:

> ... sometimes may appear from the surrounding circumstances that the right to exclusive possession is referable to a legal relationship other than a tenancy. Legal relationships to which the grant of exclusive possession might be referable and which would or might negative the grant of an estate or interest in the land include occupancy under a contract for the sale of the land, *occupancy pursuant to a contract of employment or occupancy referable to the holding of an office*. [emphasis added.][30]

23   *Ashburn Anstalt v Arnold* [1989] Ch 1, [1988] 2 All ER 147, CA.
24   HA 1988 Sch 1 para 3. See para 1.37 below. In any event, where there is not a written agreement specifying the term, in the absence of rental payments it will be difficult, without other evidence as to the parties' intentions at the time the occupation was entered into, to identify the term.
25   *Prudential Insurance Company Ltd v London Residuary Body* [1992] 2 AC 386, [1992] 3 WLR 279, HL.
26   *Mexfield Housing Co-operative Ltd v Berrisford* [2011] UKSC 52, [2012] HLR 15.
27   *Javad v Aqil* [1991] 1 WLR 1007, CA.
28   *Mexfield Housing Co-operative Ltd v Berrisford* [2011] UKSC 52, [2012] HLR 15.
29   [1985] AC 809, [1985] 2 WLR 877, HL.
30   [1985] AC 809, [1985] 2 WLR 877 at 823–824.

1.16 An employee who occupies premises with exclusive possession will do so as a service occupier, as opposed to a tenant, in two circumstances:

- it is an express term of the employment contract that he or she occupy the premises and by doing so he or she can better perform his or her duties to a material degree, or
- it is essential to the performance of the duties of the occupying employee that he or she should live in the premises, ie if he or she did not live in the premises he or she would be unable to perform his or her duties.[31]

1.17 The grant of exclusive occupation in return for the provision of services, rather than for the purpose of performing them, will ordinarily give rise to occupation as tenant.[32] The distinction between such a tenant, commonly referred to as a service tenant, and a service occupier is that the service tenant's occupation results from their employment, ie as a reward, whereas a service occupier's occupation is necessary for the performance of their employment.

No intention to create legal relations and other exceptions

1.18 The classic example of a relationship that is not intended to create legal relations is where, absent any other unusual circumstances, the agreement is between family members,[33] although not every agreement between family members will necessarily negate a tenancy.[34]

1.19 Other examples of relationships that were not intended to create legal relations were where:

- an individual had remained in occupation of the premises to complete his exams after an intermediate lease had ended;[35]
- an individual occupied two rooms of a house in exchange 'for rent' while caring for the occupier, who occupied the property under a trust;[36]

---

31 *Glasgow Corporation v Johnstone* [1965] AC 609; *Hughes v Greenwich LBC* [1994] 1 AC 170.
32 *Hughes v Chatham Overseers* 134 ER 479; *Royal Philanthropic Society v County* (1986) 18 HLR 83, (1985) 276 EG 106, CA.
33 *Errington v Errington* [1952] 1 KB 290, CA; *Marcroft Wagons Ltd v Smith* [1951] 2 KB 496; *Meynell Family Properties Ltd v Meynell*, June 1998 *Legal Action* 12, CA.
34 *Nunn v Dalrymple* (1989) 21 HLR 569, CA; *Ward v Warnke* (1990) 22 HLR 496, CA.
35 *Vaughan-Armatrading v Sarsah* (1995) 27 HLR 631, CA.
36 *Vesely v Levy* [2007] EWCA Civ 367, [2008] L&TR 9.

- an unlawful occupier had previously been told to leave the premises but had, in error, been given a rent book and had rent accepted from the owner of the property;[37] and
- an individual had occupied premises pending their sale after the owner had taken pity on him.[38]

Subtenancies

1.20   A tenancy includes a subtenancy, as well as an agreement for a subtenancy (ie an equitable subtenancy).[39] However, where two persons move into residential premises together under a tenancy granted to one but not the other, each occupying a bedroom or bedrooms and the remainder of the premises being shared between them, the court will be slow to infer a common intention that the one who is not the tenant shall be the subtenant of the one who is.[40]

1.21   Where an assured subtenant's landlord's interest in the property is brought to an end by a surrender, the subtenant will become the head landlord's tenant.[41] Likewise, where the subtenant's landlord's tenancy or lease comes to an end, eg by forfeiture, notice to quit or effluxion of time, the subtenant will become the assured tenant of the head landlord provided that the subtenant's landlord was not prohibited from granting the subtenancy under the former tenancy and, by the nature of the head landlord, the tenancy is not excluded from being assured by HA 1988 Sch 1.[42]

---

37 *Westminster CC v Basson* (1991) 23 HLR 225, CA. Although cf with *Tower Hamlets LBC v Ayinde* (1994) 26 HLR 631, CA, where the landlord accepted rent from occupiers after already being aware that the former tenants had surrendered their tenancy.

38 *Sharp v McArthur* (1987) 19 HLR 364, CA.

39 HA 1988 s45(1).

40 *Monmouth BC v Marlog* (1995) 27 HLR 30, CA.

41 *Parker v Jones* [1910] 2 KB 32, KBD. Cf the position for licensees; a licence is terminated on the surrender of the intermediate licensor's interest: *Kay v Lambeth LBC* [2004] HLR 56, CA.

42 HA 1988 s18(1) and(2).

'Under which a dwelling-house is let'

1.22   The term 'dwelling-house' is not a term with a general legal meaning.[43] In a case concerned with deciding whether a particular letting
had been on an assured tenancy, Lord Bingham said:

> Save that a dwelling-house may be a house or part of a house (HA
> 1988 s45(1)), no statutory guidance is given on the meaning of this
> now rather old-fashioned expression. But the concept is clear enough:
> it describes a place where someone dwells, lives or resides. In decid-
> ing in any given case whether the subject-matter of a letting falls
> within that description it is proper to have regard to the object of the
> legislation, directed as it is to giving a measure of security to those
> who make their homes in rented accommodation at the lower end of
> the housing market.[44]

1.23   A 'dwelling' is 'the place where [an occupier] lives and to which he
returns and which forms the centre of his existence ... No doubt he
will sleep there and usually eat there; he will often prepare at least
some of his meals there'.[45] However, there is no legislative requirement that cooking facilities must be available for premises to qualify
as a dwelling.

1.24   In deciding whether an occupant has security of tenure as an
assured tenant 'The first step is to identify the subject-matter of the
tenancy agreement. If this is a house or part of a house of which the
tenant has exclusive possession with no element of sharing, the only
question is whether, at the date when proceedings were brought, it
was the tenant's home. If so, it was his dwelling ... The presence or
absence of cooking facilities in the part of the premises of which the
tenant has exclusive occupation is not relevant'.[46]

1.25   The 'dwelling-house' does not, however, include structures that
are chattels or that are not sufficiently attached to the land to form
part of the tenancy. This includes a house that is designed so as to be
removable even if it is connected to water and electricity and has to

---

43 For example, the words 'dwelling' and 'dwelling-house' may have different
meanings in certain provisions of the Protection from Eviction Act 1977: see
R (ZH and CN) v Newham LBC and Lewisham LBC [2014] UKSC 62, [2015]
HLR 6.

44 *Uratemp Ventures Ltd v Collins and Carrell* [2001] UKHL 43, [2002] 1 AC 301 at
[10].

45 *Uratemp Ventures Ltd v Collins and Carrell* [2001] UKHL 43, [2002] 1 AC 301 at
[31].

46 *Uratemp Ventures Ltd v Collins and Carrell* [2001] UKHL 43, [2002] 1 AC 301 at
[31].

be removed in separate pieces.[47] Likewise, a caravan,[48] a houseboat[49] and a chalet[50] have been held not to be dwelling-houses.

'As a separate dwelling'

1.26   This connotes two requirements: first, the letting must have been a letting of the premises 'as' a separate dwelling and, second, the premises let must actually be a 'separate' dwelling.

1.27   Premises that are let for mixed residential and business use are not 'let' as a separate dwelling and therefore are incapable of attracting security of tenure under HA 1988 (nor HA 1985).[51] For example, in *Webb v Barnet LBC*,[52] the council let a house, yard, workshop and associated buildings for use by a motor repair business. The tenant used them in this way until retirement and continued in occupation of the house once the business had closed. It was held that the tenancy was not secure. The original letting had been for commercial use, not for use 'as' a separate dwelling.

1.28   Likewise, in *Tomkins v Basildon DC*,[53] the tenant had a lease of a bungalow and kennels. The authorised use of the premises was for the training of greyhounds, and the letting was accordingly a business tenancy under the Landlord and Tenant Act (LTA) 1954 Part II. Eventually, commercial activity ceased and the premises were used only as a residence. On the expiry of the lease, the tenant continued to live in the bungalow and claimed housing benefit in respect of the rent. However, the property had not been let 'as' a separate dwelling and the tenancy was not, therefore, a secure tenancy. The landlord had been content not to enforce the tenant's covenant for business use, but this was not sufficient to amount to an agreed variation of the letting condition.

1.29   The tenant must also occupy the dwelling-house separately from adjoining premises. A tenant who occupies two sets of adjoining premises under a single tenancy, but only occupies one as a dwelling-

47   *Elitestone Ltd v Morris* [1997] 1 WLR 687, HL.
48   *R v Rent Officer of Nottingham Registration Area ex p Allen* (1985) 17 HLR 481, QBD.
49   *Chelsea Yacht and Boat Co Ltd v Pope* [2000] EWCA Civ 425, [2000] 1 WLR 1941, CA; *Mew v Tristmire Ltd* [2011] EWCA Civ 912, [2012] 1 WLR 852.
50   *Spielplatz Ltd v Pearson* [2015] EWCA Civ 804, [2015] HLR 40.
51   *Tan v Sitowski* [2007] EWCA Civ 30, [2007] 1 WLR 1628.
52   (1989) 21 HLR 288, CA.
53   [2002] EWCA Civ 876, [2003] L&TR 7.

house is not an assured tenant.[54] Usually this condition is satisfied because the tenant and his or her household are the only intended occupiers of the property concerned. If, however, parts of a building are shared with other tenants this does not affect security unless the sharing is of living accommodation (ie kitchen,[55] lounge, dining room or bedroom).[56] Such sharing means that the tenant has not been let a 'separate' dwelling. In the case of an ordinary residential house or flat, a tenant of a single bedroom in a building who shares the kitchen, living room, etc, with the occupiers of the other bedrooms will not have a 'separate dwelling' for these purposes.[57] Therefore, where an occupier shares facilities in a shared house, and each occupier has a separate agreement, the house will not be occupied as a separate dwelling.[58]

1.30　　However, HA 1988 s3 provides that if a tenant enjoys exclusive occupation of some rented accommodation, with a right to share other accommodation with other people, apart from the landlord, the mere fact that the other accommodation is shared does not prevent the tenant from occupying the accommodation which is not shared 'as a separate dwelling'.

'The tenant is an individual'

1.31　　Only an individual, ie an actual rather than legal person, can be an assured tenant. In the case of a joint tenancy all of the tenants must be individuals. Security of tenure is only provided for a letting to a person or to several people as joint tenants.

54　*Kavanagh v Lyroudias* [1985] 1 All ER 560, CA. A tenant who occupied two sets of adjoining premises as a dwelling would, however, satisfy the test: *Jenkins v Renfrew DC* 1989 SLT (Lands Tr) 41.

55　Note the important distinction for these purposes between the shared occupation of a kitchen and the sharing of limited use of a kitchen (eg, to wash up or cook) described in *Uratemp Ventures Ltd v Collins* [2001] UKHL 43, [2002] 1 AC 301 at [58] of the judgment.

56　See *Kensington and Chelsea RLBC v Haydon* (1984) 17 HLR 114, CA on the effect of sharing with a hostel worker, and generally *Thomson v Glasgow CC* 1986 SLT (Lands Tr) 6, noted at December 1986 *Legal Action* 165, Lands Tr.

57　*Parkins v Westminster CC* (1998) 30 HLR 894, [1998] 1 EGLR 22, CA and *Smith v Hackney LBC* August 1998 *Legal Action* 21, CA.

58　*St Catherine's College v Dorling* [1980] 1 WLR 66, CA. Obviously, security of tenure is not lost just because living accommodation is shared by the tenant with other members of the tenant's own household or with the tenant's lodgers.

1.32   A tenancy that is purportedly let to a company is incapable of being an assured tenancy.[59] Tenancies that are let to companies will therefore not be assured tenancies and may only be terminated by the landlord forfeiting the fixed term or exercising a break clause. If the fixed term has ended, unless a fresh periodic tenancy has arisen, the landlord may, however, simply recover possession by issuing a claim.[60] If a periodic tenancy has arisen, the landlord must serve a notice to quit.

'Only or principal home'

1.33   The tenant or – if there are joint tenants – at least one of them, must occupy the premises as his or her only or principal home. This is the same wording as used in relation to secure tenants by HA 1985 s81. It is a more restrictive definition than the comparable provision in Rent Act (RA) 1977 s2(1)(a).[61]

1.34   Although it is possible for tenants to occupy more than one home at the same time, a tenancy can only continue to be assured if it is a tenancy of the tenant's principal home.

1.35   There is no reason why an assured tenant should not be temporarily absent from the rented property, eg for holidays, stays in hospital or working abroad, provided that the property remains his or her main home.[62] If an assured tenant moves out permanently, the tenancy becomes unprotected and, provided it is a periodic tenancy, can be terminated by a landlord's notice to quit. The landlord does not have to prove any ground for possession in such circumstances. For the difficulties which arise from extended absences, see the discussion at paras 1.150–1.192.

1.36   If a spouse or civil partner is a sole assured tenant, but moves out, occupation by the other spouse or civil partner as his or her only or principal home can preserve the assured tenancy. This is provided for by Family Law Act 1996 s30(4) as amended by Civil Partnership Act 2004 Sch 9.

---

59   *Hiller v United Dairies* [1934] 1 KB 57, CA; *Hilton v Plustitle Ltd and Rose* [1989] 1 WLR 149, CA; *Kaye v Massbetter Ltd and Kanter* (1992) 24 HLR 28, CA and *Eaton Square Properties Ltd v O'Higgins* (2001) 33 HLR 68, CA.

60   *Cobb v Stokes* (1807) 103 ER 380, KBD.

61   For more detailed consideration of these issues, see chapter 12.

62   *Crawley BC v Sawyer* (1987) 20 HLR 98, CA; *Sutton LBC v Swann* (1985) 18 HLR 140, CA; *Hussey v Camden LBC* (1995) 27 HLR 5, CA; *Hammersmith & Fulham LBC v Clarke* [2000] EWCA Civ 3032, (2001) 33 HLR 77 and *Amoah v Barking and Dagenham LBC* March 2001 *Legal Action* 28, Ch D.

Exceptions to assured tenancy status

1.37   A tenancy cannot be an assured tenancy if any of the exceptions listed in HA 1988 Sch 1 apply. They include:

- tenancies at a high rent (ie more than £100,000 per annum[63]), and, if granted before 1 April 1990, tenancies of premises with high rateable values (ie, over £1,500 in Greater London and over £750 elsewhere);[64]
- tenancies under which no rent is payable;[65]
- tenancies at a low rent (ie at a rent of less than £1,000 per annum in London or less than £250 per annum elsewhere, or, if granted before 1 April 1990, at a rent less than two-thirds of the rateable value);[66]
- business premises which are protected under the LTA 1954 Pt 2;
- licensed premises such as public houses;
- agricultural land or holdings;
- lettings to students by specified educational institutions;[67]
- holiday lettings where the tenant merely has 'the right to occupy the dwelling-house for a holiday';[68]
- lettings by resident landlords;[69]

---

63 HA 1988 Sch 1 para 2(1)(b), amended in England by Assured Tenancies (Amendment) (England) Order 2010 SI No 908 and in Wales by the Assured Tenancies (Amendment of Rental Threshold) (Wales) Order 2011 SI No 1409.

64 HA 1988 Sch 1 para 2A, inserted by the References to Rating (Housing) Regulations 1990 SI No 434, and HA 1988 Sch 1 paras 14–16.

65 HA 1988 Sch 1 para 3. Under the Rent Acts rent was held to denote rent in money only; it does not cover services provided by the tenant to the landlord, unless the rent is monetarily quantified and it is agreed that it will be paid, in part or in full, by the provision of services: *Montagu v Browning* [1954] 1 WLR 1039 and *Barnes v Barratt* [1970] 2 QB 657. While these cases concerned the Rent Acts there is no reason to doubt that they apply equally to HA 1988 as HA 1988 has a similar, if not identical, mechanism for regulating a tenant's rent. The mechanism cannot operate if the rent is not monetarily quantified: see *Barnes*.

66 HA 1988 Sch 1 paras 3A–3C inserted by the References to Rating (Housing) Regulations 1990 SI No 434.

67 The educational institutions specified for this purpose are listed in the Assured and Protected Tenancies (Lettings to Students) Regulations 1998 SI No 1967 as amended.

68 But note *Buchmann v May* [1978] 2 All ER 993, 7 HLR 1, CA and *R v Rent Officer for Camden ex p Plant* (1980) 7 HLR 15, QBD (where tenancies which were not genuine holiday lets were found to be protected tenancies). Even a working holiday may be a 'holiday' for this purpose: *McHale v Daneham* (1979) 249 EG 969.

69 HA 1988 Sch 1 paras 10 and 17–22.

- crown tenancies,[70] but not tenancies of premises managed by the Crown Estate Commissioners;
- tenancies granted by fully mutual housing associations (see paras 8.20 to 8.26);[71]
- tenancies granted by local authorities and other prescribed public bodies' (if this exception applies, the tenancy may be a secure tenancy: see paras 1.53–1.96 below);
- tenancies granted under statutory provisions for accommodating asylum seekers or certain displaced persons;
- tenancies which are secure tenancies, protected tenancies old-style 'housing association tenancies' or agricultural protected occupancies;
- family intervention tenancies (see chapter 7); and
- accommodation for asylum-seekers.[72]

1.38   A further exception provides that tenancies granted by private landlords under arrangements made by local housing authorities in accordance with their functions under HA 1996 ss188, 190, 200 or 204(4) (limited duties towards the homeless) within 12 months of the date of notification of the local authority's decision on the homelessness application or the determination of any HA 1996 s202 review or section 204 appeal, unless the landlord notifies the tenant that the tenancy is to be an assured shorthold tenancy. Note that there is no similar general exception from assured tenancy status where the accommodation is provided to enable the local authority to perform the main housing duty (HA 1996 s193). See paras 8.12–8.17.

1.39   If any one of these exceptions applies, the tenant has no security of tenure as an assured tenant and the social landlord does not need to prove a reason or ground for possession. Once a notice to quit has been served and has expired, the tenant has no statutory protection, except, in some cases, under the Protection from Eviction Act (PEA) 1977 s3 which provides that it is unlawful for a landlord to evict such a tenant without taking court proceedings. The landlord only has to prove that the contractual tenancy has been terminated in order to obtain a possession order. In some circumstances, it may not even

---

70 Note that an attempt to challenge this exception was made, but not addressed by the Court of Appeal, in *Nicholas v Secretary of State for Defence* [2015] EWCA Civ 53, [2015] HLR 25.

71 HA 1988 Sch 1 para 12(1)(h). This exception is subject to a transitional provision for tenancies pre-dating HA 1988: see s1(5).

72 HA 1988 Sch 1 paras 12A and 12B.

be necessary to serve a notice to quit if a fixed term has expired by effluxion of time.[73]

Security of tenure under assured tenancies

1.40   Security of tenure for assured tenants is provided in one of two ways. If the assured tenancy is a *periodic* tenancy, it cannot be ended by a landlord's notice to quit but only by execution of a possession order. If it is a *fixed-term* assured tenancy, when it expires or is otherwise determined a periodic tenancy is created by statute to take its place.

1.41   The central provision which achieves these effects is HA 1988 s5 which provides that:

(1) An assured tenancy cannot be brought to an end by the landlord except by –
   (a) obtaining –
      (i) an order of the court for possession of the dwelling-house under section 7 or 21, and
      (ii) the execution of the order,
   (b) obtaining an order of the court under section 6A (demotion order), or
   (c) in the case of a fixed-term tenancy which contains power for the landlord to determine the tenancy in certain circumstances, by the exercise of that power,
   and, accordingly, the service by the landlord of a notice to quit is of no effect in relation to a periodic assured tenancy.
(1A) Where an order of the court for possession of the dwelling-house is obtained, the tenancy ends when the order is executed.
(2) If an assured tenancy which is a fixed-term tenancy comes to an end otherwise than by virtue of –
   (a) an order of the court of the kind mentioned in subsection (1)(a) or (b) or any other order of the court, or
   (b) a surrender or other action on the part of the tenant,
   then, subject to section 7 and Chapter II ... the tenant shall be entitled to remain in possession of the dwelling-house let under that tenancy and, subject to subsection (4) below, his right to possession shall depend upon a periodic tenancy arising by virtue of this section.
[(3)–(6) omitted]
(7) Any reference in this Part of this Act to a statutory periodic tenancy is a reference to a periodic tenancy arising by virtue of this section.

73 *Cobb v Stokes* (1807) 103 ER 380, KBD.

Periodic assured tenancies

1.42   HA 1988 s5 provides that a periodic assured tenancy can be brought
        to an end – by a landlord – only by means of execution of an order of
        the court. HA 1988 s5(1) makes it clear that notices to quit served by
        landlords have no effect upon periodic assured tenancies. However,
        a notice to quit served by a tenant on the landlord terminates both
        the assured tenancy and the tenant's security of tenure.[74] In short, a
        social landlord seeking to end a periodic assured tenancy needs to
        bring a possession claim and then obtain and execute an order for
        possession.

Fixed-term assured tenancies

1.43   HA 1988 s5 has the effect that if a contractual, fixed-term assured
        tenancy comes to an end, other than by an order of a court or by sur-
        render, (so either by the simple expiry of the term or by the landlord
        giving a break notice in accordance with the terms of the agreement),
        a periodic assured tenancy (called a 'statutory periodic tenancy') will
        generally come into existence immediately after the fixed-term ten-
        ancy ends. In some ways this is similar to the old statutory tenancy
        under the Rent Acts,[75] but there are significant differences. The most
        important of these is the provision for fixing the terms of the statu-
        tory periodic tenancy.[76] The basic rule is that the terms will be the
        same as for the former contractual assured tenancy.[77] However, HA
        1988 s6 provides a mechanism by which landlords and tenants may
        propose new terms.

1.44   If the social landlord seeks to recover possession during the fixed
        term, it will need to bring a claim for possession relying on one
        of the statutory grounds for possession and can only utilise those
        grounds if: (1) they are listed in HA 1988 s7(6)(a); and (2) the fixed-
        term tenancy agreement expressly provides for termination on the
        relevant ground.[78]

---

74 For a discussion of termination by a tenant's notice to quit see paras 1.115–
    1.133.
75 RA 1977 s2.
76 HA 1988 s5(3).
77 HA 1988 s5(3)(d) and (e).
78 HA 1988 s7(6) and see *Artesian Residential Developments Ltd v Beck* [2000] QB
    541, (1999) 31 HLR 107, CA.

1.45   Once the fixed term has ended and there is a statutory periodic assured tenancy, a social landlord wishing to terminate it must bring a possession claim and then obtain and execute an order for possession.

Assured shorthold tenancies in the social housing sector

1.46   Most tenancies granted by private registered providers of social housing (PRPSHs) and registered social landlords (RSLs) are likely to be assured tenancies carrying the security of tenure described above. It is increasingly common, however, for such landlords to grant assured shorthold tenancies, which carry a reduced level of security of tenure and which have become the default tenancy in the private rented sector (see chapter 5). This is a result of two modern policy developments. The first was the notion that social tenants should serve an initial trial period before obtaining full security of tenure. That policy was achieved for council landlords by permitting them to grant introductory rather than secure tenancies. The like effect is achieved for housing associations by granting 'probationary' or 'starter' tenancies on an assured shorthold basis. This type of 'starter tenancy' is discussed more fully in chapter 5. The second policy development was the move to granting new social housing tenants fixed-term tenancies rather than 'life-time' periodic tenancies. That would not work if the fixed-term tenancies were full assured tenancies because (as explained above) when they ended, statutory periodic assured tenancies would spring up carrying full security of tenure. But if the tenancies are assured shorthold fixed-term tenancies, social landlords have the facility to recover possession at the end of the term as easily as private landlords would (albeit with additional obligations in relation to notice).[79] Special additional provision has been made for assured shorthold tenancies to be granted following demoted or family intervention tenancies.[80]

1.47   The only legal constraint on a wholesale shift by social landlords from letting on full assured tenancies to letting on periodic or short fixed-term assured shorthold tenancies is the regulatory guidance

---

79 See HA 1988 s21(1A) and(1B) and generally, Jon Holbrook, 'In a fix (2)?' [2012] NLJ 930.
80 See HA 1988 ss20C and 20D. See paras 6.64–6.70 for further detail.

issued by the regulators of social housing in England and Wales respectively. In England, that guidance provides first that:

> Where registered providers use probationary tenancies, these shall be for a maximum of 12 months, or a maximum of 18 months where reasons for extending the probationary period have been given and where the tenant has the opportunity to request a review.[81]

and second that:

> Registered providers must grant general needs tenants a periodic ... assured (excluding periodic assured shorthold) tenancy, or a tenancy for a minimum fixed term of five years, or exceptionally, a tenancy for a minimum fixed term of no less than two years, in addition to any probationary tenancy period.[82]

1.48   In Wales, the regulator's expected 'Delivery Outcome' is that social landlords are able to say: 'We can demonstrate that: We use the most secure form of tenancy compatible with the purpose of the housing'.[83]

1.49   In practice, the grant of an assured shorthold tenancy is only avoided by the social landlord serving notice on the prospective tenant, before the tenancy is entered into, indicating that the tenancy is not to be an assured shorthold tenancy but rather a full assured tenancy.[84] The notice must state that the tenancy is not to be an assured shorthold tenancy as opposed to stating that the tenancy is assured.[85]

Secure tenancies

1.50   Most council tenants are secure tenants although some other social landlords may have secure tenants. However, it is always important to check that all the hallmarks of a secure tenancy, as set out at paras 1.53–1.69 below, are present in each case.

1.51   Secure tenancies are created and governed by the provisions of HA 1985 Pt 4.

---

81 *Tenancy Standard* (Homes and Communities Agency, 31 March 2015), para 2.2.2.

82 *Tenancy Standard* (Homes and Communities Agency, 31 March 2015), para 2.2.4.

83 *The Regulatory Framework For Housing Associations Registered in Wales* (Welsh Government, December 2011) p20.

84 HA 1988 Sch 2A para 1.

85 *Andrews v Cunningham* [2007] EWCA Civ 762, [2008] HLR 13.

1.52   Once Housing and Planning Act (HPA) 2016 Sch 7 para 4 comes into force, in England, there will be two types of secure tenancies: those granted before the day on which HPA 2016 Sch 7 comes into force and those granted afterwards. The position concerning old secure tenancies will be considered first.

Old secure tenancies granted before Housing and Planning Act 2016 came into force

Definition of a 'secure tenancy'

1.53   A secure tenancy exists at any time when the conditions set out in HA 1985 ss79–81 are *all* satisfied. The general conditions are given in section 79. Section 80 contains a 'landlord condition' and section 81 a 'tenant condition'. Combining the three provisions produces the following list of requirements for a 'secure' tenancy:

- the property is a 'dwelling-house';
- the landlord is a prescribed social landlord;
- the tenant is an individual;
- the tenant occupies the property as his or her only or principal home;
- the property was let 'as a separate dwelling'; and
- the tenancy is not in an excluded category.

1.54   Each of these requirements is discussed in turn below.

'A tenancy'

1.55   Unlike under HA 1988, the protection to tenants afforded under Part 4 also applies to licences.[86] It follows that the distinction between a tenancy and a licence is irrelevant in relation to 'secure' status.

'The property is a dwelling house'

1.56   The term 'dwelling-house' covers both houses and parts of houses[87] and extends to any land let together with the dwelling-house, other than agricultural land exceeding two acres.[88] Neither of the words

---

86   HA 1985 s79(3).
87   HA 1985 s112(1).
88   HA 1985 s112(2).

'house' or 'dwelling-house' is further defined in HA 1985 Part 4. The phrase 'part of a house' is sufficiently broad to include flats, rooms, apartments and bed-sitting rooms and possibly accommodation in some hostels.

1.57   See also paras 1.22–1.25 for meaning of 'dwelling-house', a term used for the same purposes in HA 1988.

'The landlord is a prescribed landlord'

1.58   The 'landlord condition' for the tenancy to be secure is that the land-lord must be one of the authorities or bodies within the list set out in HA 1985 s80, as amended. If there are joint landlords they must *all* be in the statutory list.[89] Unfortunately, the section has been rendered long and complex by multiple amendments, which makes it difficult to set out in detail. The following landlords who granted tenancies on or after 15 January 1989 will satisfy the landlord condition:[90]

- local authorities;
- development corporations;[91]
- housing action trusts;
- housing co-operatives governed by an agreement made under:
  - Housing Rents and Subsidies Act 1975 Sch 1 para 9,
  - HA 1980 Sch 20, or
  - HA 1985 s27 (if before 7 January 1987);[92]
- a co-operative housing association that has ceased to be an PRPSH or RSL;[93] and
- the Homes and Communities Agency, Greater London Authority and Welsh Ministers where the criteria specified within HA 1985 s80(2A)–(2E) are satisfied.

1.59   Certain tenants of landlords who are not on that list, eg housing asso-ciations, will, however, also be secure tenants where HA 1988 Sch 14 para 4 applies (see below paras 1.62–1.64).

---

89 *R v Plymouth CC and Cornwall CC ex p Freeman* (1987) 19 HLR 328, CA.
90 HA 1985 s80 and HA 1988 Sch 18 para 4.
91 Established by an order made under the New Towns Act 1981, Local Government, Planning and Land Act 1980 Pt XVI and Localism Act 2011 Pt 8.
92 HA 1985 s80(4) and HA 1985 s27B.
93 HA 1985 s80(3).

Local authorities

1.60   Secure tenants are most commonly tenants of a 'local authority'.
That term is widely defined by HA 1985 s4(1)(e) to include a whole
range of local government bodies and statutory authorities.[94] It is not
limited to local housing authorities.

Housing action trusts

1.61   'Housing action trusts' (HATs) were set up to take over, revitalise,
improve and regenerate specific areas of run-down local authority housing. The statutory basis of their operation is to be found in
HA 1988 Part 3. Only six[95] have been created, owing in part to the
substantial finances that needed to be raised for them to be able to
undertake their work successfully. The sixth and last – Stonebridge
HAT – was wound down and dissolved in 2007.[96]

Housing associations

1.62   It is a common misconception that tenants of housing associations
can no longer be secure tenants. In fact, some tenants of housing
associations who were granted secure tenancies *before* 15 January 1989 retain their secure status[97] and such landlords may grant
some new secure tenancies but only in very narrowly-defined circumstances,[98] ie:

- where a possession order is made against a secure tenant on the
grounds that suitable alternative accommodation will be provided
and the landlord of such accommodation is a housing association;[99] and

---

94 A county, county borough, district or London borough council, the Common
Council of the City of London or the Council of the Isles of Scilly, the Broads
Authority, a police and crime commissioner, a joint authority established by
Local Government Act 1985 Pt 4, an economic prosperity board, a combined
authority and the London Fire and Emergency Planning Authority.

95 North Hull HAT, Waltham Forest HAT, Liverpool HAT, Castle Vale HAT,
Tower Hamlets HAT and Stonebridge HAT.

96 The Stonebridge Housing Action Trust (Dissolution) Order 2007 SI No 1862.

97 HA 1988 s35(4).

98 HA 1988 s35(4).

99 HA 1988 Sch 18 para 14 and HA 1985 s35(4)(e). Such a tenant will continue to
be a secure tenant if he or she is subsequently granted a tenancy by the same
landlord: HA 1988 s35(4)(d).

- where the tenancy was entered into pursuant to a contract formed before 15 January 1989[100] and the tenancy is granted pursuant to an obligation under HA 1985 s554(2A).[101]

These changes reflect the general policy intention that most *modern* lettings (ie those made since 15 January 1989) by housing associations, housing trusts and other such social landlords should *not* come within the secure tenancy regime but should be assured tenancies.

1.63   Where the interest of the landlord under a secure tenancy is transferred to a social landlord which is not in the section 80 list, for example, by the sale of council property into the private sector or to a housing association,[102] any sitting secure tenants lose secure status although they may become 'assured' tenants under provisions described earlier in this chapter.[103] All sitting tenants will have ceased to be secure tenants on completion of the sale of their council landlord's stock.[104] For the circumstances in which a social landlord of a secure tenant may seek to recover possession before such a sale, in order to sell with vacant possession, see paras 3.313–3.316.

Former Rent Act tenants who become tenants of housing associations

1.64   Surprisingly, it is still possible for a non-secure tenancy held from such a landlord to 'become' secure automatically. This occurs when a housing association acquires property with sitting Rent Act tenants[105] or if the transitional provisions in HA 1988 Sch 18 para 4 are activated by some change in the landlord's status.[106]

'The tenant is an individual'

1.65   The tenant must be an individual person[107] or a group of individuals holding as joint tenants. Therefore, a tenancy cannot be secure if the

---

100 HA 1988 Sch 18 para 14 and HA 1988 s35(4)(c).
101 HA 1988 Sch 18 para 14 and HA 1988 s35(4)(f).
102 See HA 1985 ss32–44 for disposals of council housing.
103 HA 1988 s38.
104 *Knowles Housing Association Limited v Miller*, 2001 SLT 1326, Court of Session (Extra Division) and *McAllister v Queen's Cross Housing Association Limited* 22 November 2001, LTS/TR/2001/5, Lands Tribunal (Scotland).
105 HA 1988 s35(5).
106 *Bhai v Black Roof Community Housing Association* [2000] EWCA Civ 276, (2001) 33 HLR 607, CA.
107 HA 1985 s81.

tenant is a company,[108] a charity, a short-life housing association,[109] a co-operative, a statutory authority or a statutory corporation. The sub-tenants of such bodies may of course themselves be secure tenants as against their immediate landlords.

The 'only or principal home' rule

1.66   The 'tenant condition' is that the tenant must occupy the property as his or her only *or* principal home.[110] As with assured tenants, secure tenants may, therefore, have more than one home but can have a 'secure' tenancy only in relation to the principal one.[111] See above para 1.33 and below paras 1.150–1.183 for further discussion. Where there are joint tenants, at least one of them must occupy as his or her only or principal home in order to retain the 'secure' status.[112]

1.67   If an absent secure tenant is married or has a registered civil partner and the home has been their shared home, his or her spouse or civil partner can preserve the security of the tenancy by continuing in occupation during the secure tenant's absence.[113] There is no equivalent automatic provision for cohabitants or other family members to be deemed to be preserving the absent tenant's security of tenure, but if a cohabitant or former cohabitant successfully applies for an 'occupation order' under the Family Law Act 1996 s36(1) he or she will be treated as satisfying the 'only or principal home' rule on behalf of the absentee tenant (see chapter 20).[114]

'Let as a separate dwelling'

1.68   This requirement has three components: first, the property subject to the tenancy must be a dwelling (see above paras 1.56–1.57), second, the letting must have been a letting of the premises 'as' a separate

---

108 *City of London Corp v Ukpoma* (1996) 1 L&T Rev D8; September 1996 *Legal Action* 11. And see n59 above for further cases noted to the similar condition for assured tenancies.

109 *Camden LBC v Shortlife Community Housing Ltd* (1993) 25 HLR 330, HC and *Kay and others v Lambeth LBC* [2006] UKHL 10, [2006] 2 AC 465.

110 HA 1985 s81.

111 *Islington LBC v Boyle* [2011] EWCA Civ 1450, [2012] HLR 18.

112 HA 1985 s81.

113 Family Law Act 1996 s30(4)(b), amended by Civil Partnership Act 2004 Sch 9 para 1.

114 Family Law Act 1996 s36(13) and see *Gay v Sheeran and Enfield LBC* [2000] 1 WLR 673, (2000) 32 HLR 1126, CA.

dwelling (see above paras 1.27–1.28) and, third, the premises let must factually be a 'separate' dwelling (see above paras 1.29–1.30).[115]

Exceptions to secure tenancy status

1.69   Some tenancies are excluded from the full security of tenure provided by 'secure' status. They are:

- Tenancies in one of the classes exempted from protection by HA 1985 Sch 1, as amended.[116] Detailed consideration of each of the classes set out in the Schedule is beyond the scope of this work, but the categories may be broadly summarised as:
  - long tenancies (defined in HA 1985 s115);[117]
  - introductory tenancies (see chapter 5);
  - demoted tenancies (see chapter 6);
  - family intervention tenancies (see chapter 7);
  - premises occupied in connection with employment;[118]
  - tenancies of land acquired for development;[119]
  - accommodation provided for homeless people in performance of certain statutory functions (see paras 8.1–8.11);[120]
  - temporary accommodation for people taking up employment;[121]

---

115 HA 1985 s79(1).
116 HA 1985 s79(2)(a).
117 HA 1985 Sch 1 para 1.
118 HA 1985 Sch 1 para 2; *Hughes v Greenwich LBC* [1994] 1 AC 170, (1994) 26 HLR 99, HL; *Elvidge v Coventry CC* [1994] QB 241, (1994) 26 HLR 281, CA; *South Glamorgan DC v Griffiths* (1992) 24 HLR 334, [1992] 2 EGLR 232, CA; *Surrey CC v Lamond* (1999) 31 HLR 1051, CA; *Brent LBC v Charles* (1997) 29 HLR 876, CA and *Greenfield v Berkshire CC* (1996) 28 HLR 691, CA. For modern illustrations see: *Lee v Neath & Port Talbot CC* June 1998 *Legal Action* 10; *Coleman v Ipswich BC* [2001] EWCA 852, August 2001 *Legal Action* 23; *Godsmark v Greenwich LBC* [2004] EWHC 1286 (Ch), [2004] HLR 53, ChD; *Holmes v South Yorkshire Police Authority* [2008] EWCA Civ 51, [2008] HLR 32; and *Wragg v Surrey CC* [2008] EWCA Civ 19, [2008] HLR 30.
119 HA 1985 Sch 1 para 3; *Attley v Cherwell DC* (1989) 21 HLR 613, CA; *Harrison v Hyde Housing Association Ltd* (1991) 23 HLR 57, [1991] 1 EGLR 51, CA; *London & Quadrant Housing Trust v Robertson* (1991) unreported, but noted at September 1991 *Legal Action* 15 and *Lillieshall Road Housing Co-operative v Brennan* (1992) 24 HLR 195, [1991] EGCS 132, CA.
120 HA 1985 Sch 1 para 4.
121 HA 1985 Sch 1 para 5; *Campbell v Western Isles Island Council* 1989 SLT 602, CS, noted at December 1989 *Legal Action* 13.

- 'private sector leasing' accommodation (see paras 8.12–8.17);[122]
- temporary accommodation provided during works to a tenant's home;[123]
- tenancies of agricultural holdings;[124]
- licensed premises;[125]
- student lettings by educational institutions;[126]
- LTA 1954 Part II tenancies (business tenancies);[127]
- almshouses;[128]
- accommodation provided to asylum-seekers;[129] and
- temporary accommodation for displaced persons.[130]
- Tenancies which ceased to be secure after the death of the secure tenant[131] (see paras 1.137–1.149).
- Tenancies which ceased to be secure following assignment, parting with possession or full subletting (see paras 1.153–1.160).
- Tenancies at will.[132]

Security of tenure under secure tenancies

1.70   Security of tenure for secure tenants is provided in one of two ways. If the secure tenancy is a *periodic* tenancy, it cannot be ended by a landlord's notice to quit but only by execution of a possession order. If it is a *fixed-term* secure tenancy, the normal rule[133] is that when it expires or is otherwise determined, a periodic tenancy is created by statute to take its place (but see 'flexible' and 'new English' fixed-term secure tenancies discussed at paras 1.74–1.77 and 1.89–1.94). The central provision which achieves these effects is HA 1985 s82 which provides that:

122 HA 1985 Sch 1 para 6.
123 HA 1985 Sch 1 para 7.
124 HA 1985 Sch 1 para 8.
125 HA 1985 Sch 1 para 9.
126 HA 1985 Sch 1 para 10.
127 HA 1985 Sch 1 para 11.
128 HA 1985 Sch 1 para 12.
129 HA 1985 Sch 1 para 4A inserted by Immigration and Asylum Act 1999 Sch 14 para 81.
130 HA 1985 Sch 1 para 4B inserted by the Displaced Persons (Temporary Protection) Regulations 2005 SI No 1379.
131 HA 1985 s79(2)(b).
132 *Banjo v Brent LBC* [2005] EWCA Civ 287, [2005] 37 HLR 32.
133 HA 1985 s86.

(1) A secure tenancy which is either –
    (a) a weekly or other periodic tenancy, or
    (b) a tenancy for a term certain but subject to termination by the landlord,
cannot be brought to an end by the landlord except as mentioned in subsection (1A).
(1A) The tenancy may be brought to an end by the landlord
    (a) obtaining –
        (i) an order of the court for the possession of the dwelling-house, and
        (ii) the execution of the order,
    (b) obtaining an order under subsection (3), or
    (c) obtaining a demotion order under section 82A.
(2) In the case mentioned in subsection (1A)(a), the tenancy ends when the order is executed.
(3) Where a secure tenancy is a tenancy for a term certain but with a provision for re-entry or forfeiture, the court shall not order possession of the dwelling-house in pursuance of that provision, but in a case where the court would have made such an order it shall instead make an order terminating the tenancy on a date specified in the order and section 86 (periodic tenancy arising on termination of fixed term) shall apply.
(4) Section 146 of the Law of Property Act 1925 (restriction on and relief against forfeiture), except subsection (4) (vesting in under-lessee), and any other enactment or rule of law relating to forfeiture, shall apply in relation to proceedings for an order under subsection (3) of this section as if they were proceedings to enforce a right of re-entry or forfeiture.

Periodic secure tenancies

1.71   As noted above, HA 1985 s82 provides that a periodic secure tenancy can normally be brought to an end by a landlord only by means of execution of an order of the court. HA 1985 s82(1)(a) makes it clear that notices to quit served by landlords have no effect upon periodic secure tenancies. However, a notice to quit served by a secure tenant on the landlord terminates both the tenancy and the tenant's security of tenure.[134]

---

134 For a discussion of termination by a tenant's notice to quit see paras 1.115–1.133.

Fixed-term secure tenancies

1.72   As is clear from the terms of HA 1985 ss82(3), 82(4) and 86, tenancies granted for fixed terms can be secure tenancies.

1.73   If a fixed-term secure tenancy comes to an end, other than by an order of a court or by surrender, either by the simple expiry of the term or by the landlord relying on a forfeiture clause under the terms of the tenancy and obtaining an order under HA 1985 s82(3), a periodic secure tenancy (called a 'statutory periodic secure tenancy') will generally come into existence immediately after the fixed-term tenancy ends.[135] In some ways this is similar to a Rent Act statutory tenancy,[136] but there are significant differences. The most important of these is the provision for fixing the terms of the statutory periodic secure tenancy. The basic rule is that the terms and parties will be the same as for the former contractual secure tenancy.

Flexible secure tenancies

1.74   The Localism Act 2011 introduced a new type of fixed-term secure tenancy known as the 'flexible tenancy' by inserting section 107A into the Housing Act 1985.[137] This form of tenancy is only available in England and not Wales. The policy intention is that, when they expire, these new flexible tenancies will not automatically run-on as secure periodic tenancies (see above para 1.73). Instead, a social landlord will be free to grant another fixed-term tenancy or a normal periodic secure tenancy or to obtain possession based on the simple fact of expiry of the fixed term.

1.75   The basic form of flexible tenancy is made when a local housing authority (or other landlord who can grant secure tenancies) in England grants a tenant a secure tenancy with a fixed term of not less than two years and, before it is granted, the landlord serves a written notice on the prospective tenant stating that the tenancy will be a flexible tenancy.[138] Similar notices can be served to create flexible secure

---

135   HA 1985 s86.
136   RA 1977 s2.
137   Note that once HPA 2016 Sch 7 para 4 is brought into force s107A will be repealed and replaced – in identical form – by HA 1985 s115B. All references given below are therefore to both provisions with the post-HPA 2016 references in brackets.
138   HA 1985 s107A(2) (HA 1985 s115B(2)).

tenancies to follow-on from introductory tenancies,[139] demoted tenancies[140] or family intervention tenancies.[141]

1.76   The prospective tenant served with a notice that the tenancy is to be a fixed-term flexible secure tenancy can ask the prospective landlord to review its decision.[142] But the only ground on which review can be sought is that the length of the fixed term should be different from that proposed.[143] The procedure to be followed on such a review is set out in regulations.[144] The main reference point for determining such a review will be the local housing authority's tenancy strategy (which will set out the periods for which social landlords in the area should be granting fixed-term tenancies).[145] The Regulatory Framework issued by the regulator of social housing in England requires that: 'Registered providers must grant general needs tenants a periodic secure ... tenancy, or a tenancy for a minimum fixed term of five years, or exceptionally, a tenancy for a minimum fixed term of no less than two years, in addition to any probationary tenancy period'.[146]

1.77   For the basis on which possession can be claimed from a flexible secure tenant, see chapter 2. A flexible tenancy that simply comes to an end, without the landlord having complied with the requirements within HA 1985 s107D entitling it to recover possession, will become a secure weekly periodic tenancy.[147]

Replacement secure tenancies

1.78   The 'replacement' secure tenancy is a historical anomaly. It was created by statute to address the situation of 'thousands of occupiers of council housing who were in a state of limbo as a result of the mak-

139 HA 1985 s107A(6)(a) (HA 1985 s115B(6)(a)) and HA 1996 s137A.

140 HA 1985 s107A(6)(b) (HA 1985 s115B(6)(b)) and HA 1996 s143MA.

141 HA 1985 ss107A(3), (4) (HA 1985 s115B(3)).

142 HA 1985 s107B. Once HPA 2016 Sch 7 is brought into force HA 1985 s107B will be repealed. The right to request a review as to the length of a flexible tenancy will arise from HA 1985 s81D. The post-HPA 2016 references are set out below in brackets.

143 HA 1985 s107B(3) (HA 1985 s81D(2)).

144 HA 1985 s107B(6) (HA 1985 s81D(4) and (5)) and the Flexible Tenancies (Review Procedures) Regulations 2012 SI No 695.

145 Localism Act 2011 s150(1)(c).

146 *Tenancy Standard* (Homes & Communities Agency, March 2015) para 2.2.2, p3.

147 HA 1985 s86(1).

ing of an old, but unenforced, possession order'.[148] Most tenants who have a replacement secure tenancy would not know that they do so and most staff who manage such tenancies do not know that they are doing so. Yet, on 20 May 2009, hundreds of thousands of occupiers of social housing in England and Wales became replacement tenants of their homes on the commencement of the Housing and Regeneration Act (H&RA) 2008 s299 and Sch 11 and a good many of them remain in occupation.[149]

1.79   The creation of these replacement tenancies happened 'automatically' in the sense that it required no action on the part of either the social landlord or the tenant and in most cases there was no new document reflecting the fact that a replacement tenancy had arisen. The H&RA 2008 simply provides that, if certain conditions were fulfilled, a replacement tenancy relationship arose between the parties on or after 20 May 2009.[150]

1.80   Most replacement tenants are likely to be council tenants who have been in continuous occupation of their homes since before 2009. They will be tenants who lost their old secure tenancies because their landlords obtained possession orders against them but those orders were not enforced by an eviction. Commonly, the possession order will have been made at a time when the tenant was in arrears of rent but there was no eviction because the arrears were later cleared.

1.81   Social landlords were 'strongly encouraged to issue former tolerated trespassers with a document confirming the terms of the new tenancy on commencement of these provisions'[151] but many did not do so.

1.82   A replacement tenancy arises by virtue of statute rather than by grant between landlord and tenant. There is unlikely to be any document expressly stating that the tenancy is a replacement tenancy. Accordingly, a first step for anyone advising a longstanding council tenant about defending possession proceedings is to identify whether there is in fact a replacement tenancy and, if so, the type of replacement tenancy that it is and the terms on which it is held.

---

148 *Francis v Brent Housing Partnership Ltd* [2013] EWCA Civ 912, [2013] HLR 47 at [49]. They were referred to as tolerated trespassers.

149 Housing and Regeneration Act 2008 (Commencement No 5) Order 2009 SI No 1261.

150 The Department for Communities and Local Government (DCLG) produced non-statutory guidance on the operation of the replacement tenancy regime *Tolerated Trespassers: guidance for social landlords*, May 2009.

151 *Tolerated Trespassers: guidance for social landlords* (DCLG, May 2009) at para [37].

1.83   In summary, there will be a replacement secure tenancy only if all
of the following conditions are satisfied:[152]

- the tenant was formerly a secure tenant under an earlier secure
  tenancy;
- that earlier tenancy was ended (before 20 May 2009) by a possession order;[153]
- the ex-tenant was not evicted;
- on 20 May 2009 the ex-landlord was still the owner of the
  property;
- the ex-tenant was still using the property as his or her only or
  principal home and had been so using it throughout the termination period.[154] (If the old tenancy was a joint tenancy, the occupation condition will have been fulfilled if at least one former joint
  tenant was still using the property as his or her only or principal
  home on 20 May 2009 and had been so using it throughout the
  termination period[155]); and
- no new tenancy agreement was entered into between the ex-tenant and the landlord before 20 May 2009.

1.84   An extraordinary feature of the replacement tenancy regime is that,
although replacement secure tenancies are new tenancies created on
or after 20 May 2009, they remain subject to the terms of possession
orders made before they commenced. By definition, there is only a
replacement tenancy if there was a possession order that ended the
occupier's old tenancy. That order continues to have a 'life' in respect
of the new tenancy.

1.85   Therefore a landlord of a replacement tenant who wishes to recover possession does not usually need to bring fresh possession proceedings. The possession order which brought the old tenancy to an
end is treated, so far as practicable, as applying to the replacement
secure tenancy.[156] Any other court orders made in connection with
or in consequence of the possession order (for example, an order for
stay or suspension of a possession warrant) are likewise to be treated,

---

152 H&RA 2008 Sch 11 para 16.
153 H&RA 2008 Sch 11 para 15.
154 H&RA 2008 Sch 11 paras 16(1)(a)(i) and 16(2) discussed in *Francis v Brent
     Housing Partnership Ltd* [2013] EWCA Civ 912, [2013] HLR 47, CA. Any period
     during which the occupier was out of possession by virtue of a warrant for
     possession which was subsequently set aside is ignored: H&RA 2008 Sch 11
     para 16(6).
155 H&RA 2008 Sch 11 para 21.
156 H&RA 2008 Sch 11 para 20(1).

so far as practicable, as applying to the replacement tenancy.[157] However, CPR 83.2(3)(a) provides that permission is needed to obtain a warrant where more than six years have elapsed since the making of the possession order. Over six years have elapsed since 2009 and so an application for permission to enforce an old possession order against a replacement tenant will always have to be made. As the years pass, it will become increasingly unlikely for courts to give such permission and the norm will be for landlords to begin new possession claims.

1.86   Any adviser who finds themselves dealing with a replacement secure tenancy is directed to chapter 10 of the seventh edition (2010) of this book which treats the subject in detail. Given the rarity with which replacement secure tenancies are actually identified as such, a fuller treatment cannot be justified in this edition.

Secure tenancies granted after the Housing and Planning Act 2016 came into force

1.87   Once HPA 2016 Sch 7 para 4 comes into force, in England, save for some limited exceptions, it will no longer be possible for landlords to grant 'old-style' secure tenancies, ie secure periodic or fixed-term tenancies, which were not flexible tenancies, that were granted before the day on which HPA 2016 Sch 7 para 4 came into force.[158] In short, as a general rule all new secure tenancies that are granted after HPA 2016 comes into force will be 'new English' secure tenancies (which are flexible tenancies by another name). Landlords will therefore no longer have the choice over whether to grant life-time or flexible tenancies.

1.88   By and large the existing conditions that must be satisfied (see above paras 1.53–1.69) for a 'new-style' secure tenancy to be granted are the same. Any differences are set out below. The changes made by HPA 2016 Sch 7 to HA 1985 concern the length of the fixed term and the statutory pre-conditions that must be satisfied before the grant of an introductory tenancy or the demotion of a secure tenancy (see chapters 5 and 6).

157   H&RA 2008 Sch 11 para 20(2).
158   HA 1985 s115C.

New-style English secure tenancies

1.89   A landlord who intends to grant a secure or introductory tenancy[159] must grant the tenancy for a fixed term of at least two years and no more than ten years, unless the landlord has been notified in writing that a child aged under nine will live in the dwelling-house. Where the landlord is notified that a child under nine will live in the dwelling-house, the landlord may grant a term that expires on the day on which the child will reach the age of 19.[160] In all other cases, ie where a landlord purports to grant a periodic tenancy or a term that is either less than two years or greater than the permitted maximum, the fixed term is deemed to be for five years unless one of a limited number of exceptions applies.[161]

1.90   In fixing the term, the landlord must have regard to any guidance given by the Secretary of State.[162] There is no requirement that the tenancy agreement must be made by deed.[163]

1.91   A tenant who is offered a secure or introductory tenancy can ask the prospective landlord, within 21 days of the tenancy being offered, for a review of the length of the fixed term offered.[164] The procedure to be followed on such a review will be set out in regulations, but the review decision must contain the landlord's reasons if its decision is to grant the term that was originally offered.[165] The main reference point for determining such a review will be whether the decision is in accordance with the local housing authority's policy as to the length of tenancy it will grant and in what circumstances.[166]

When can an old-style secure tenancy be granted?

1.92   An old-style tenancy may be granted by a landlord:

- in circumstances specified in regulations made by the Secretary of State;[167]

---

159   The prohibition on the grant of a fixed-term introductory tenancy has been removed.
160   HA 1985 s81A(1)–(3); HA 1996 s124A(1)–(3).
161   HA 1985 s81A(4); HA 1996 s124A(4).
162   HA 1985 s81A(5) and (6); HA 1996 s124A(5).
163   Law of Property Act 1925 s52(dc) and (dd).
164   HA 1985 s81D(2) and (3); HA 1996 s124B(2) and (3).
165   HA 1985 s81D(4) and (5); HA 1996 s124B(4) and (5).
166   HA 1985 s81D(2); HA 1996 s124B(2).
167   HA 1985 s81B(1). At the time of going to press no regulations had been made.

- where the tenancy is offered as a replacement for an old-style secure tenancy of some other dwelling-house and the tenant has not made an application to move (ie where the landlord has initiated a transfer);[168]
- if a tenant, who previously had an assured or old-style secure tenancy, was granted the tenancy after an application for a mutual-exchange under Localism Act 2011 s158 which was made before HPA 2016 s121 came into force.[169]

What happens when the fixed term of a new-style English secure tenancy expires?

1.93   Where the fixed term comes to an end, a new-style English secure tenancy will arise.[170] The term will either be that which the landlord offered the tenant (whether it was accepted or not) or, in default of a term being offered, for a further five-year fixed term.[171] However, the landlord may recover possession of the new five-year fixed-term tenancy provided that it has complied with all of the requirements of HA 1985 s86A to HA 1985 s86C.[172]

1.94   The terms of the new tenancy are the same as those of the tenancy that it replaces.[173]

Exemptions to secure tenancies granted after the Housing and Planning Act 2016 came into force

1.95   The list set out at para 1.69 above applies to tenancies that were entered into on or after the day on which HPA 2016 Sch 7 para 4 came into force. In addition, tenancies that are granted after that date, which were not introductory or secure tenancies at the date of their grant, and are periodic tenancies or for a fixed term of less than two years or more than five years are incapable of becoming secure tenancies irrespective of whether the other conditions are satisfied.[174] In such circumstances, the landlord must, within 28 days, make the

---

168 HA 1985 s81B(1) and (2).
169 HA 1985 s81B(1).
170 HA 1985 s86D(2).
171 HA 1985 s86D(3) and (4).
172 HA 1985 s86E(4). See paras 2.80–2.99.
173 HA 1985 s86D(5).
174 HA 1985 Sch 1 para 1ZA.

tenant a written offer to surrender the existing tenancy in exchange for a written offer of a secure tenancy.[175]

1.96   This is, presumably, designed to prevent landlords from avoiding the prohibition on granting weekly periodic tenancies to tenants who do not immediately meet the requirements for security of tenure, eg they do not occupy the property as their only principal home. This provision prevents such tenancies from becoming secure.

Going in and out of assured or secure status

1.97   HA 1988 s1(1) provides that a tenancy is assured '... if and so long as ...' all the conditions set out at para 1.6 above are satisfied. HA 1985 s79(1) accords a contractual tenancy secure status '... at any time when ...' all the conditions set out at para 1.53 above are satisfied.

1.98   These 'temporal' elements in the definitions of these forms of tenancy mean that a tenancy may lose assured or secure status for want of satisfaction of one of the conditions but later become assured or secure again on its subsequent fulfilment. The statutes are aptly described as having 'ambulatory' effect.[176]

1.99   Therefore, if a social landlord seeks possession on the basis that the tenancy has lost protection and the contractual tenancy has been determined by a notice to quit, break clause or is forfeited, it is crucial to consider whether the tenancy was in or out of the protection of the relevant Housing Act at the date of expiry of that notice.[177] If the tenancy was assured or secure at the date the break clause was operated, the fixed term forfeited or at the expiry of the notice to quit, the tenancy will continue.

Termination of an assured or secure tenancy by the tenant

1.100   The main focus of this part of this book is on possession claims brought against tenants of social housing in which the landlord seeks a possession order to end the tenancy. But a possession claim may

---

175 HA 1985 s81C.
176 *Basingstoke & Deane BC v Paice* (1995) 27 HLR 433, [1995] 2 EGLR 9, CA; *Manchester CC v Finn* [2002] EWCA Civ 1998, [2003] HLR 41 at [32] and *Islington LBC v Boyle* [2011] EWCA Civ 1450, [2012] PTSR 1093 at [66].
177 *Hussey v Camden LBC* (1995) 27 HLR 5, CA.

commonly be brought on the basis that the tenancy has been ended by the tenant and that they have become a trespasser.

1.101   Nothing in HA 1985 or HA 1988 restricts the ability of an assured or a secure tenant to determine their own tenancy. Termination can be achieved by either surrender or by notice. These are considered in turn.

Surrender

1.102   An assured or secure tenant may end his or her own fixed-term or periodic tenancy by *surrender*. Surrender is the termination of a tenancy by mutual agreement between landlord and tenant. If the tenancy is a joint tenancy, all the joint tenants must agree to the surrender.[178]

1.103   Agreement between landlord and tenant to a termination of the tenancy is best demonstrated by a deed of surrender.[179]

1.104   If there is no deed, surrender can be achieved by operation of the common law. A surrender by operation of law arises where the tenant acts in such a way that there can be no doubt that he or she is offering the landlord possession (for example, by emptying the property and returning the keys) and the landlord responds by accepting possession (for example, by acknowledging that the tenancy is over, closing the rent account, taking steps to clear the property and re-let). The conduct of the parties creates an estoppel preventing either of them from asserting the continuation of the tenancy. The concept of surrender by operation of law in the general landlord and tenant context is more fully described in paras 14.36–14.45.[180]

1.105   Several cases have illustrated the surrender of social housing tenancies by operation of law. In *Brent LBC v Sharma and Vyas*,[181] the tenant wrote to her landlord stating that she was no longer living in the property and would not be returning. The landlord responded by closing the rent account. This was held to amount to a concluded surrender by operation of law. In *Camden LBC v Alexandrou*,[182] the tenant moved out of his flat. He wrote to the landlord that he was

---

178 *Leek and Moorlands Building Society v Clark* [1952] 2 QB 788, [1952] 2 All ER 492, CA.

179 Law of Property Act 1925 ss52–53.

180 For a useful modern statement of the law of 'surrender by operation of law' see *QFS Scaffolding Ltd v Sable* [2010] EWCA Civ 682, [2010] L&TR 30 and *Obichukwu v Enfield LBC* [2015] UKUT 64 (LC).

181 (1993) 25 HLR 257, CA.

182 (1998) 30 HLR 534, CA.

unable to pay for the upkeep and considered it no longer his responsibility. Acting on that, the landlord granted a tenancy of the flat to
the tenant's estranged wife. The Court of Appeal refused permission
to appeal from a finding that the husband's tenancy had ended by
surrender.

1.106   However, in order to establish a surrender, the party asserting it
must demonstrate both unequivocal conduct of the tenant in offering up the tenancy and unequivocal conduct on the part of the landlord in accepting that offer. In *R v Hammersmith & Fulham LBC ex p
Quigley,*[183] the judge summarised the law in these terms:

> The court must, adopting an objective approach, ask itself the follow-
> ing two questions. First, does the conduct of the tenant on his or her
> part drive the court objectively to the conclusion that he or she has
> surrendered his or her tenancy and ... is it demonstrated, on the other
> hand, that the landlord for his or their part has unequivocally accepted
> that act of surrender?[184]

1.107   Ms Quigley's partner fled his flat, abandoning their children there.
The council claimed that his tenancy had been determined by surrender at that point. The assertion of surrender failed because the
council's conduct in later serving a notice to quit and beginning
possession proceedings (contending that the tenancy had continued
until expiry of the notice) was inconsistent with unequivocal acceptance of the implied offer of surrender.

1.108   In *Hackney LBC v Ampratum,*[185] a tenant left her family in occupation of her home when she was deported. During her six-year absence,
the council consented to the assignment of her tenancy to someone
else. A claim that the tenancy had been surrendered by operation of
law prior to the assignment was rejected. The fact that the tenant was
absent by reason of her deportation was not unequivocal conduct on
her part demonstrating that she was treating her tenancy as at an
end.

1.109   Likewise, in *Sanctuary HA v Baker,*[186] the acts of a tenant in leaving a property, ceasing to pay the rent and handing in the keys to her
landlord were not sufficient to amount to unequivocal evidence of
surrender because those acts were all consistent with her belief that
the tenancy had been assigned to an assignee (who had been a secure
tenant) who was to collect the keys from the landlord.

---

183 (2000) 32 HLR 379, QBD.
184 (2000) 32 HLR 379, QBD at 383.
185 September 2003 *Legal Action* 25, Central London Civil Trial Centre, Bell J.
186 (1998) 30 HLR 809, CA.

1.110   In *Newham LBC v Phillips*,[187] Miss Phillips had become a sole
secure tenant by succession on the death of her mother. She later
agreed that her sister's name could be added to the rent book provided that she remained the sole successor tenant. The council subsequently argued that this amounted to the surrender of the sole
tenancy and grant of a joint tenancy. The Court of Appeal held that
the express statement by Miss Phillips that she wished to remain the
sole successor tenant was inconsistent with the assertion that there
had been an unequivocal act of surrender of that tenancy by her.

1.111   Exceptionally, it may be possible to imply a surrender from circumstances in which the tenant abandons the premises and the landlord, finding them empty, simply secures them (see further paras
1.178–1.180). A social landlord relying on what seems to be such an
implied offer of surrender by a tenant must, however, expect to exercise some caution, given that a tenancy of social housing is a valuable
asset not likely to be given up lightly by some informal act of the
tenant. For example, in *Zionmor v Islington LBC*,[188] the tenant – in an
attempt to gain relief from harassment by his neighbours – posted
on a communal notice-board a notice that he had ceased to reside in
his flat. He then went away for a while, leaving a friend in occupation. The council, on finding the flat apparently empty, changed the
locks. It was held that: (1) the tenant's leaving a friend in possession was inconsistent with a suggestion that he wished to bring the
tenancy to an end; and (2) changing the locks and boarding-up were
not unequivocal acts by the landlord of acceptance of surrender: they
might equally well be explained by an intention to protect the council's stock during the tenant's temporary absence. On the facts, there
had been no surrender.

1.112   Particular difficulties can arise in applying the concept of surrender by operation of law where the tenant's alleged unequivocal conduct is departure from the premises but where the tenant's spouse or
former partner is left in occupation. The courts have historically been
reluctant to permit surrender[189] to be used as a device to overcome
'home rights', that is, the rights of occupation of a spouse or civil
partner (arising under the Family Law Act 1996 as amended by the
Civil Partnership Act 2004[190]).

---

187 (1998) 30 HLR 859, CA.
188 (1997) 30 HLR 822, CA. Note that HPA 2016 s57 (Recovering abandoned
     premises) only applies to private sector landlords of assured shorthold tenants.
     See para 1.188 below.
189 See *Hoggett v Hoggett* (1980) 39 P&CR 121, CA.
190 Sch 9 para 1, amending Family Law Act 1996 s30.

1.113   If the sole tenant spouse or civil partner has purported to surrender, it may be argued by the non-tenant spouse or civil partner that
there can have been no termination by operation of law because the
tenant cannot give possession so long as he or she remains in residence. However, a surrender effective to terminate a sole secure tenancy was identified in *Sanctuary Housing Association v Campbell*.[191] In
that case the wife – a sole secure tenant – left the property, taking her
children, and was rehoused. Her husband remained in possession.
The Court of Appeal found that the tenancy had been determined
by the wife's unequivocal conduct in writing to inform the landlords
that she was leaving, that she would not be paying the rent and that
she was returning the keys. She had done all she could, short of taking proceedings against her husband, to give back vacant possession.
The landlords impliedly accepted that position by treating the tenancy as terminated and seeking possession against the husband.

1.114   Similarly, in *Ealing FHA v McKenzie*,[192] a sole secure tenant left
her home but her husband remained in occupation. The council
agreed to rehouse her on condition that she would give up her tenancy. On being rehoused, she gave notice to quit her former home and
the council treated the tenancy as ended by closing the rent account
of the former home and opening a rent account for the new one.
Although the notice to quit was invalid, the Court of Appeal found
the conduct of landlord and tenant sufficient to amount to a surrender of the secure tenancy of the former home.

Tenant's notice

1.115   A periodic tenant can end a tenancy of social housing by giving the
landlord appropriate notice. Weekly periodic tenants may end their
tenancy by the service of a notice to quit.[193]

1.116   The tenant will be assumed to have the mental capacity to give
such a notice.[194] Any contention that the tenant did not have capacity
must be made good by the person asserting it.[195] If the tenant does
lack capacity to terminate their tenancy by notice (or by surrender,
see above) an application would need to be made to the Court of Pro-

---

191 [1999] 1 WLR 1279, (2000) 32 HLR 100, CA.
192 [2003] EWCA Civ 1602, [2004] HLR 21.
193 See para 1.121 onwards.
194 Mental Capacity Act 2005 s1.
195 *Beech v Birmingham City Council* [2014] EWCA Civ 830, [2014] HLR 38.

tection for a declaration that it would be in their best interests for the tenancy to be ended.[196]

1.117   It is unclear whether the person who receives a notice to quit from a person who lacks capacity must know of the person's incapacity for the notice to quit to be set aside. The point appears to be free from authority.[197]

1.118   Sometimes, the suggestion of giving a tenant's notice terminating a tenancy of social housing will come from the social landlord itself.[198] In *Beech v Birmingham CC* the tenant moved into a residential care home. She was visited there by a housing officer employed by the landlord and she gave him a notice to quit. It was suggested that the notice had been procured by undue influence and had, in effect, been elicited by the landlord. Rejecting that contention, the Chancellor said:

> I do not accept that the giving of the Notice to Quit by Mrs Warren was an unusual or unexpected transaction or that, for the purposes of presumed undue influence, it calls for an explanation for any other reason. So far as concerned the interests of the Council, it was guardian of the stock of social housing and was concerned to make the best use of that stock in the public interest. Mrs Warren's tenancy had ceased to be a secure tenancy because it had ceased to be her home. ... The Council considered that the Property was too large for the needs of Mrs Howell and Mr Beech. The Council was, therefore, entitled to bring the tenancy to an end and to obtain possession and it was perfectly predictable that it would seek to do so.[199]

1.119   In the case of a *fixed-term* tenancy of social housing, the tenant may bring the tenancy to an end by giving such notice as may be required by any *break clause* in the contractual tenancy agreement. Unless the tenancy agreement provides to the contrary, a fixed-term joint tenancy can only be ended within that term by a notice given by *all* the

---

196 *Islington LBC v QR* [2014] EWCOP 26, (2014) 17 CCLR 344.

197 The current editors of *Megarry and Wade's The Law of Real Property* note in a footnote (fn 102 at 36-025) that the principle that a party must know of the incapacity of the other before a disposition can be set aside should 'in principle be equally applicable to dispositions'. In *Tadema Holdings Ltd v Ferguson* (2000) 32 HLR 866, the Court of Appeal held that a statutory notice served by a landlord on a tenant who lacked capacity would still be valid if the landlord was unaware that the tenant lacked capacity.

198 See, for example, the circumstances of *McCann v UK* (2008) 47 EHRR 40, [2008] HLR 40 in which the European Court of Human Rights found that 'the local authority chose to bypass the statutory scheme by requesting Mrs McCann to sign a common law notice to quit, the effect of which was immediately to terminate the applicant's right to remain in the house' at [52].

199 *Beech v Birmingham City Council* [2014] EWCA Civ 830, [2014] HLR 38 at [71].

joint tenants. Once the term has expired, any periodic joint tenancy arising can be terminated by notice given by any one of the joint tenants (see para 1.121).

1.120   Flexible tenants and new English secure tenants may also determine their tenancies, irrespective of when the fixed term is due to come to an end, by giving the landlord notice in writing stating that the tenancy will be terminated after the end of a period of four weeks beginning with the date on which the notice is served.[200] Although a defect in the notice may be waived by the landlord, the tenancy will only determine if the tenant does not owe any arrears of rent and the tenant is not otherwise materially in breach of a term of the tenancy.[201]

1.121   *Periodic* tenancies of social housing can be ended by the tenant's service on the landlord of a valid *notice to quit*. Such a notice operates unilaterally and brings to an end both any security of tenure and the tenancy itself. To be effective, any such notice must be in writing and meet contractual,[202] common law and statutory requirements.[203] For example, the tenancy agreement may:

- specify a minimum amount of notice;
- stipulate that any notice to be given must expire on a particular day or date; or
- require service by delivery of the notice to a particular address.

A valid notice to quit will end the tenancy on expiry.

1.122   At common law, the minimum period of notice is a period of the tenancy and the notice must expire on the first or last day of such a period.[204] The primary statutory requirement, contained in PEA 1977 s5, is that at least 28 days' notice in writing must be given.

1.123   An invalid notice can also operate to determine the tenancy on expiry if the parties agree to waive the invalidity. For example, in *Hackney LBC v Snowden*,[205] the tenant gave a notice to quit expressed to take effect only three days later. The council acted on the notice, rehoused the former tenant, sought no further rent for the property and voided the rent account. The Court of Appeal held that the ten-

---

200 HA 1985 s107C(1)–(3) (HA 1985 s86F(1)–(3) when HPA 2016 Sch 7 comes into force).
201 HA 1985 s107C(4) and (5) (HA 1985 s86F(4) and (5) when HPA 2016 Sch 7 comes into force).
202 *Community Housing Association v Hoy* December 1988 *Legal Action* 18.
203 The main statutory requirements are contained in PEA 1977 s5, reproduced at para 14.8.
204 *Crate v Miller* [1947] KB 946, [1947] 2 All ER 45, CA.
205 (2001) 33 HLR 554, [2001] L&TR 60, CA.

ancy had terminated on expiry of the notice because the council had agreed to waive non-compliance with the requirements of PEA 1977 s5. Once a landlord has accepted and acted upon an invalid notice to quit, and treated the tenancy as at an end, it will be too late for the tenant to assert the invalidity in support of an argument that the tenancy is continuing.[206]

1.124   However, in *Hounslow LBC v Pilling*,[207] the invalid notice to quit had been given by a joint tenant. The Court of Appeal held that such a notice could determine the tenancy but only if both the landlord and the other joint tenant(s) were prepared to waive the invalidity. This is because the service and acceptance of an invalid notice to quit acts as a surrender and both joint tenants must assent to a surrender.

1.125   A sole tenant is free to end his or her tenancy by notice to quit irrespective of the concerns or interests of other occupiers or any family members. This may cause particular difficulties if the property has been the matrimonial home, the non-tenant spouse or civil partner remains in occupation, and a consequence of the termination is to render that person a trespasser in what had been their home. The courts have historically been reluctant to uphold notices[208] which are being used as devices to overcome 'home rights', that is, the rights of occupation of a spouse or civil partner (arising under the Family Law Act 1996 as amended by the Civil Partnership Act 2004[209]) in this way, but most modern statutory schemes enabling the family courts to regulate the disposal, occupation or use of the family home require that a tenancy is still extant when the jurisdiction comes to be exercised.

1.126   If a sole tenant has given notice to quit in these circumstances, the non-tenant spouse or civil partner may be able to show that there is still a tenancy by asserting the invalidity of the notice, for example, if it can be shown that the notice failed to comply with the contractual, common law or statutory requirements (see paras 1.121–1.122 above). However, in such a case the landlord could waive a deficiency in the notice and thus restore its validity.[210]

1.127   If the notice given by a sole tenant is in a valid form and is effective to end the tenancy, the non-tenant spouse or civil partner is not

---

206 *Lewisham LBC v Lasisi-Agiri* [2003] EWHC 2392 (Ch), [2003] 45 EGCS 175.
207 [1993] 1 WLR 1242, (1993) 25 HLR 305, CA.
208 See *Griffiths v Renfree* (1989) 21 HLR 338, [1989] 2 EGLR 46, CA.
209 Sch 9 para 1, amending Family Law Act 1996 s30.
210 *Hackney LBC v Snowden* (2001) 33 HLR 49, [2001] L&TR 60, CA.

able to apply in family proceedings for it to be set aside.[211] The giving of a notice to quit is not a 'disposal' for the purposes of statutes addressing family property.[212] Everything will therefore turn on the ability of the non-tenant to restrain the sole tenant from actually giving notice to quit (see para 1.132 below).

1.128   The position is broadly the same if there is a *joint tenancy*. If one joint tenant to a *periodic* tenancy gives a valid notice to quit to the landlord, the whole tenancy determines on its expiry even if the effect will be to leave the other joint tenant as a trespasser in the former home.[213] It has been suggested that this rule (sometimes referred to as 'the rule in *Monk*') might fall foul of the terms of Human Rights Act 1998 Sch 1 which provide for respect for a home (Article 8) and the prevention of arbitrary interference with property rights (Article 1 of Protocol 1).[214] But these arguments have now been rejected by the Supreme Court.[215]

1.129   Attempts to establish that the rule in *Monk* can operate only where one joint tenant has at least *consulted* the other(s) before giving notice have also failed.[216] At present, the law remains that one joint tenant can give notice to quit entirely unilaterally with the effect that, if the notice is valid, the whole tenancy ends. Indeed, a joint tenant is free to give such a notice to quit even if he or she is the subject of an order of the court not to 'exclude' the other tenant(s).[217]

1.130   One joint tenant may be able to demonstrate that the tenancy subsists if the notice given by another joint tenant was invalid due to failure to comply with contractual, common law or statutory requirements (see paras 1.121–1.122). For example, the notice is ineffective if given in respect of a weekly tenancy for a shorter period than the

---

211   Matrimonial Causes Act 1973 s37 and see, generally, chapter 20.
212   *Newlon Housing Trust v Al-Sulaimen* [1999] 1 AC 313, (1998) 30 HLR 1132, HL.
213   *Hammersmith & Fulham LBC v Monk* [1992] 1 AC 478, (1992) 24 HLR 207, HL, approving *Greenwich LBC v McGrady* (1982) 6 HLR 36, 81 LGR 288, CA.
214   As to human rights generally, see chapter 26.
215   *Sims v Dacorum BC* [2014] UKSC 63, [2015] HLR 7.
216   See *Crawley BC v Ure* [1996] QB 13, (1995) 27 HLR 524, CA and *Notting Hill Housing Trust v Brackley* [2001] EWCA Civ 601, [2002] HLR 10.
217   *Harrow LBC v Johnstone* [1997] 1 WLR 459, (1997) 29 HLR 475, HL.

four weeks prescribed by PEA 1977 s5[218] or if it fails to provide for expiry at the end of a period of a periodic tenancy.[219]

1.131   But again, the service of a valid notice by a joint tenant causes particular difficulty in the context of relationship breakdown where the effect is to leave family members as trespassers in the former family home. If the notice is valid, the other joint tenant, even if a spouse or civil partner, is not able to apply in family law proceedings for the setting aside of disposal of the home in this way.[220] This is again because the giving of a notice is not a 'disposal' of family assets.[221]

1.132   An occupier who believes that a notice to quit may be about to be given by his or her (former) partner would be best advised to make a 'without notice' application for an injunction to restrain the giving of such notice (see chapter 20). It has been suggested that such an injunction may be granted under the court's inherent jurisdiction in matrimonial matters or in proceedings brought under the Matrimonial Causes Act 1973 s37[222] (or the Children Act 1989 Sch 1 where there are children of the family).[223] Alternatively and additionally, it may be possible to apply for a transfer of the tenancy from sole to joint names and to seek an injunction in those proceedings.[224] See further chapter 20.

1.133   Once the notice to quit validly given by a sole (or a joint) tenant has expired, the former landlord can physically retake possession if the premises are empty. Otherwise, straightforward possession proceedings can be taken against anyone left in occupation (such as any partner or former joint tenant). They will be trespassers at common law and will have no defence to the possession claim unless exceptionally it may be seriously arguable that the social housing provider has acted unlawfully in bringing the possession proceedings (see chapter 25) or that the making of a possession order would amount

---

218 *Hounslow LBC v Pilling* [1993] 1 WLR 1242, [1994] 1 All ER 432, CA. See too
     Fletcher v Brent LBC [2006] EWCA Civ 960, [2007] HLR 12, in which a joint
     secure tenant gave a notice expressed to take effect on that day or 'on the first
     Monday after that date being at least four clear weeks after service'. The Court
     of Appeal treated it as having been validly given.

219 *Camden LBC v Lahouasnia* March 1998 *Legal Action* 12, Central London
     County Court (the notice given by one joint tenant and held to be invalid
     simply said 'I hereby give notice of 28 days that I am relinquishing my
     tenancy').

220 Matrimonial Causes Act 1973 s37.

221 *Newlon Housing Trust v Al-Sulaimen* [1999] 1 AC 313, (1998) 30 HLR 1132, HL.

222 *Bater v Greenwich LBC* [1999] 4 All ER 944, (2000) 32 HLR 127, CA.

223 *Re F (Minors)* [1994] 1 WLR 370, (1993) 26 HLR 354, CA.

224 Family Law Act 1996 s53 and Sch 7.

to a breach of the defendant's Convention rights (see chapter 26),[225] or that bringing the proceedings for possession was an act of unlawful discrimination,[226] or that a new tenancy has been granted.

How security of tenure may be lost

1.134   A tenant of social housing will have the best prospects of resisting a claim for possession if he or she is an assured or secure tenant. However, a tenant who has had that status may lose it – at any time – by failing to satisfy the necessary conditions for assured or secure status that are described earlier in this chapter.

1.135   Therefore, in a wide variety of situations, the social landlord may be able to proceed on the basis that security of tenure has been lost. It will terminate the tenancy by serving a notice to quit or determining the fixed term while the tenancy is without security of tenure. Indeed, in some situations, a statutory provision may have been triggered to deprive the tenant of their assured or secure status irretrievably.

1.136   The remaining paragraphs of this chapter review the most common of these situations.

The tenant dies[227]

1.137   As explained in chapter 18, the death of a tenant will not usually end a tenancy. That is as true in respect of social housing tenancies as across the whole rented sector. But there are circumstances in which security of tenure can be lost by reason of a death.

1.138   If one *joint tenant* dies, and the other remains in occupation, the social housing tenancy devolves by survivorship and the last remaining joint tenant becomes a sole tenant by operation of law.[228] The tenancy retains its security of tenure as long as the conditions described earlier in this chapter remain fulfilled.

1.139   If a *sole tenant* (or the last remaining joint tenant) dies, neither the tenancy itself nor security of tenure automatically ends.[229] If there is

---

225 eg *Beech v Birmingham City Council* [2014] EWCA Civ 830, [2014] HLR 38.
226 *Aster Communities Ltd v Akerman-Livingstone* [2015] UKSC 15, [2015] HLR 20 and see chapter 27.
227 See also chapter 18 (death of a tenant).
228 *Solihull MBC v Hickin* [2012] UKSC 39, [2012] HLR 40.
229 Unless, unusually, the tenancy agreement expressly provides otherwise: *Youngmin v Heath* [1974] 1 WLR 135, [1974] 1 All ER 461, CA.

a person in occupation entitled to succeed the tenant, the tenancy automatically vests in the successor.[230]

1.140   The detailed rules concerning succession are beyond the scope of this book. In general terms, however, where there is no person entitled to succeed, what happens to security of tenure will depend on what form of secure or assured tenancy the late social housing tenant had:

- *A periodic or fixed-term assured tenancy:* the tenancy will pass by will or intestacy as part of the deceased's estate. If it remains an assured tenancy (eg because the person to whom it devolves occupies the dwelling as his or her only or principal home) the landlord can seek possession under ground 7 (a mandatory ground) (see paras 3.368–3.371).[231]
- *A periodic secure tenancy:* the tenancy ceases to be secure either (1) when it is vested or otherwise disposed of in the course of the administration of the tenant's estate (unless the vesting or other disposal is in pursuance of one of a prescribed list of family court orders) or (2) when it is known that when the tenancy is so vested or disposed of it will not be in pursuance of such an order.[232]
- *A fixed-term secure tenancy:* the tenancy remains a secure tenancy until it is vested or otherwise disposed of in the course of the administration of the tenant's estate (but there are some circumstances in which such vesting or disposal may maintain security of tenure[233]) or it is known that when it is so vested or disposed of it will not be a secure tenancy.[234]

1.141   If security of tenure has been lost following the tenant's death, the newly unprotected contractual tenancy vests in the estate of the deceased. Thereafter it will be disposed of in the administration of the estate, usually by being surrendered to the landlord by the executors or administrator. If the deceased tenant did not leave a will, the tenancy vests in the Public Trustee until such time as letters of

---

230 HA 1985 s89(1A) and (2) (secure tenancies); HA 1988 s17(1)–(1C) (assured tenancies).
231 HA 1988 Sch 2 ground 7 as amended by Localism Act 2011.
232 HA 1985 s89(3). In *Austin v Southwark LBC* [2009] EWCA Civ 66, [2010] HLR 1 Arden LJ said at [10]: 'Where there is no successor, the tenancy does not automatically cease to be a secure tenancy at the death of the tenant. If there is no person who is qualified to succeed to the tenancy, it does not cease to be secure until that time specified in section 89(3) arrives. When it ceases to be a secure tenancy, it becomes a contractual tenancy only'.
233 HA 1988 s90(3).
234 HA 1988 s90.

administration are taken out by the next of kin: see chapter 18.[235] However, special provision is made to deal with the situation which arises if a court exercising family law jurisdiction has earlier ordered what is to happen to a secure tenancy in the event of the tenant's death.[236] Similar orders may have been made in respect of assured tenancies but no special provision is made for them in HA 1988.

1.142   In the event that other occupiers remain in possession, a social landlord cannot simply rush into proceedings on the basis that it has a right to possession against the alleged trespasser (see chapter 23). An occupier who is able to show, in such proceedings, that the deceased tenant's tenancy has not been properly determined (for example, by service of notice on the executor/administrator or the Public Trustee[237]) has a complete defence to the action.[238]

1.143   Where the tenancy was for a fixed term , the landlord will be unable to determine the unprotected tenancy by serving a notice to quit. Instead, the landlord will be required to bring the tenancy to an end by forfeiting the term. Consideration should therefore be given to whether the landlord is entitled to forfeit the term. For example, the landlord may not have a right of re-entry arising from the death of the tenant.[239] In such circumstances, the landlord will be unable to recover possession of the property until the fixed term has expired or an unrelated right to forfeit arises, eg through non-payment of rent.

1.144   Once the social landlord has served an effective notice to quit on the person responsible for the deceased tenant's estate it may, if there is no occupier, simply take possession or, in the case of a fixed term, peaceably re-enter (if such a right exists under the tenancy).

1.145   Commonly, following the death of a tenant of social housing, a dispute may arise between the landlord and an occupier about whether the occupier is entitled to succeed to the tenancy. In such cases, if the landlord is satisfied that there has been no statutory succession, it will purport to determine the tenancy either by forfeiting the fixed term or by notice (by service of such notice on the executor or

235 Administration of Estates Act 1925 s9 as substituted by Law of Property (Miscellaneous Provisions) Act 1994 s14.
236 HA 1985 ss89(3) (periodic secure tenancies) and 90(3) (fixed-term secure tenancies).
237 See the Public Trustee (Notices Affecting Land) (Title on Death) Regulations 1995 SI No 1330. As to service of such notice, see *Practice Direction (Probate: Notice to Quit)* [1995] 1 WLR 1120.
238 *Wirral BC v Smith and Cooper* (1982) 4 HLR 81, (1982) 43 P&CR 312, CA.
239 See chapter 14 for further discussion on forfeiture.

administrator or the Public Trustee[240]) and, once notice has expired, start ordinary possession proceedings against the occupier on the basis that they have no right to occupy. (It would be unusual for the social landlord to serve a notice seeking possession while asserting that the occupier has not become the tenant by succession but such a notice might be served without prejudice to the notice to quit.) Non-statutory guidance is available to social landlords on the process of recovering possession from those considered to be 'unauthorised successors'.[241]

1.146　　In these circumstances, the occupier may defend the claim on the basis that he or she is the current tenant, having properly 'succeeded' the deceased tenant. In such a case, an adjournment of what appear to be straightforward possession proceedings may be necessary.[242] The burden of proof is on the occupier to establish the right to succeed, including any requirement that he or she lived with the deceased tenant at the date of death or, where relevant, throughout the 12-month period before the death.[243]

1.147　　An occupier claiming to have succeeded would be well advised to put aside sums equivalent to the rent, or to make a claim for housing benefit because, if he or she is successful in establishing succession, he or she will be liable to pay the rent from the date of death.

1.148　　More unusually, those in occupation following the death of a social housing tenant may defend on the basis that, since the death of the tenant, they have been accepted as tenants of the property in their own right. However, the making and acceptance of payments while a disputed issue of succession is resolved are insufficient, on their own, to show an intention on the landlord's part to create a new tenancy.[244]

1.149　　Alternatively, it may be possible for the occupier to defend the claim if he or she can show that it is seriously arguable that the decision to take possession proceedings was reached in breach of

240　See the Public Trustee (Notices Affecting Land) (Title on Death) Regulations 1995 SI No 1330. As to service of such notice, see *Practice Direction (Probate: Notice to Quit)* [1995] 1 WLR 1120.

241　*Tackling unlawful subletting and occupancy: Good practice guidance for social landlords* (Communities and Local Government, November 2009), pp69–72.

242　*Camden LBC v Hall* March 1998 *Legal Action* 11, CA.

243　*Peabody Donation Fund Governors v Grant* (1982) 6 HLR 41, (1982) 264 EG 925, CA.

244　See *Hammersmith & Fulham LBC v Jastrzebska* May 2001 *Legal Action* 22, ChD and *Hammersmith & Fulham LBC v Jastrzebski* [2001] EWCA Civ 431.

public law principles (see chapter 25)[245] or of human rights (see chapter 26).

The tenant is absent

1.150   An assured or secure tenant's absence from the property, however lengthy, does not of itself bring the *tenancy* to an end. However, the *security of tenure* of such a tenant may be placed in jeopardy by a long-term absence.

1.151   That is because, as already mentioned above (paras 1.133–1.136 and 1.66–1.67), an assured or secure tenancy retains security of tenure only for so long as the tenant (or one of the joint tenants) 'occupies the dwelling-house as his only or principal home'.[246] A very prolonged absence may indicate that the tenant no longer occupies the property as a home and thus the security of tenure may lapse. A social landlord may then serve, provided the tenancy is periodic, a notice to quit to bring to an end the unprotected tenancy. For the requirements of a valid landlord's notice to quit, see paras 14.8–14.26. (The landlord may face considerable difficulties in *serving* the true tenant with notice to quit – see paras 1.185–1.187.) Even a notice to quit expressed to expire only one day short of the necessary minimum period will be invalid and insufficient to end an unprotected tenancy.[247] Where the period is a fixed term it may be determined by a break clause or forfeited provided there is a clause that permits the landlord to re-enter where the tenant is no longer occupying the premises as his only or principal home.

1.152   There are several possible variations on the scenario of the absentee tenant of social housing. They are reviewed in the following paragraphs.

The tenant has sublet, or otherwise parted with possession of, the whole property

1.153   In these circumstances, the security of tenure of the tenancy is brought to an end not only by the tenant's own failure to occupy but also by the specific provision that subletting or parting with possession of

---

245   As in *Leicester City Council v Shearer* [2013] EWCA Civ 1467, [2014] HLR 8 where a secure tenant had died, his partner and their children moved in and the council sought possession without considering, under its own procedures, whether to grant a fresh tenancy to the partner.

246   HA 1985 s81 (secure tenancies) and HA 1988 s1 (assured tenancies).

247   *Southwark LBC v Jackson* April 2009 *Legal Action* 18, Lambeth County Court.

the whole of the property causes loss of security.[248] Security may even be lost inadvertently by the unintentional creation of what is later held to be a true subtenancy of the whole property.[249]

1.154   This loss of security cannot be repaired by the tenant ousting the subtenants and returning to the property because the statutes provide that the tenancy cannot again become an assured or secure tenancy.[250] The suggestion that this statutory provision is incompatible with the tenant's human rights because it operates in the absence of a consideration of whether the tenant has behaved reasonably has been rejected by the Court of Appeal.[251]

1.155   Whether there has been a subletting of the whole will be a matter for determination by a court on the evidence. In one case where there was evidence that all the rooms in a property were occupied by persons other than the tenant or her family, and most doors had separate locks, the court was entitled to conclude that there had been an unlawful subletting of the whole of the premises.[252] In another, a tenant's advertisement of their home to let had provided powerful evidence of subletting.[253]

1.156   In some cases the judge will need to resolve a conflict of evidence between the tenant and the occupier as to whether there was a true subletting or a simple temporary licence.[254] It seems particularly common for secure tenancies to be sublet in the run-up to a right to buy purchase.[255]

1.157   If there has been a true subletting of the whole, then security is plainly lost.[256] But it does not necessarily follow that, just because the tenant is absent and others are in occupation, security has been lost

---

248 HA 1985 s93(2) (secure tenancies) and HA 1988 s15A(1) (assured tenancies).
249 *Brent LBC v Cronin* (1998) 30 HLR 43, CA.
250 HA 1985 s93(2) (secure tenancies) and HA 1988 s15A(2) (assured tenancies). See *Merton LBC v Salama* (1989) *Independent* 20 March, June 1989 *Legal Action* 25, CA.
251 *Delson v Lambeth LBC* [2002] EWCA Civ 1894.
252 *Lambeth LBC v Vandra* [2005] EWCA Civ 1801, [2006] HLR 19.
253 *Luton BC v Menni* [2006] EWCA Civ 1850.
254 *Brent LBC v Smart* [2005] EWCA Civ 434.
255 As in *Sutton LBC v Swann* (1985) 18 HLR 140, (1985) *Times* 30 November, CA; *Muir Group Housing Association Ltd v Thornley* (1993) 25 HLR 89, [1993] 10 EG 144, CA; *Jennings v Epping Forest DC* (1993) 25 HLR 241 and *Lewisham LBC v Malcolm* [2008] UKHL 43, [2008] 1 AC 1399.
256 *Muir Group Housing Association Ltd v Thornley* (1993) 25 HLR 89, [1993] 10 EG 144, CA.

by 'parting with possession'.[257] It may be that those in occupation are mere 'house-sitters' or other licensees simply taking care of the premises pending the return of the tenant and there has been no parting with possession at all.[258]

1.158   As already noted, even subletting the whole does not bring the tenancy to an end – only security of tenure is lost. If the social land-lord considers that there has been a parting with possession or sub-letting of the whole it may serve an ordinary notice to quit on the true tenant to determine that tenancy[259] and, once that has expired, start possession proceedings to recover possession against both the true tenant and the actual occupiers. (The landlord may, where the ten-ancy agreement does not provide for service of notices to be effected by leaving them at the property, face considerable difficulties in serv-ing the true tenant with notice to quit – see paras 1.185–1.187.)

1.159   Of course, the landlord will be unable to serve a notice to quit on a fixed-term former secure or assured tenant, ie a new English secure tenant, a flexible tenant or fixed-term assured shorthold ten-ant, because the tenancy, by its nature, will not be periodic. Instead, the landlord will have to rely on a forfeiture clause that gives the landlord the right to re-enter the premises once security of tenure has been lost or the right to serve a break clause. In the absence of either of these clauses the landlord will not be able to recover posses-sion until the term has expired by effluxion of time.

1.160   If there is simply a suspicion that the tenant may have sublet, a letter before action seeking information about the true position may protect the landlord in costs if it is later unsuccessful in establishing full subletting.[260]

The tenant is absent for a long period (but intends to return)

1.161   Many tenants of social housing are temporarily away from their homes from time to time – on holiday, receiving medical treat-ment, working away from home, and such like. Some tenants may

---

257 *Hussey v Camden LBC* (1995) 27 HLR 5, CA. For a modern restatement of the law on breach of an obligation not to 'part with possession', see *Clarence House Ltd v National Westminster Bank plc* [2009] EWCA Civ 1311, [2010] 1 WLR 1230.

258 *Basildon DC v Persson* September 1995 *Legal Action* 13 and *Islington LBC v LaMarque* September 1991 *Legal Action* 14.

259 Some landlords react to such situations by serving a notice seeking possession as well as ordinary notice to quit, each expressed to be without prejudice to the other.

260 *Brent LBC v Aniedobe* January 2000 *Legal Action* 25, CA.

be absent for long periods, perhaps many years, through working abroad, being imprisoned, travelling, visiting relatives overseas, or otherwise. In such cases, furniture and other belongings are usually left in the property and, in the case of prolonged absence, an informal 'caretaker' (usually a friend or relative) may have been let into occupation to take care of the property and to ensure that the rent is paid.

1.162   However, long absences may give rise to the inference that security of tenure has been lost because the tenant is no longer occupying the property as his or her principal home.

1.163   After a review of all the previous authorities, the Court of Appeal[261] has held that the relevant principles to be applied in determining whether a tenant continues to occupy a dwelling as his or her only or principal home are as follows:

> *First,* absence by the tenant from the dwelling may be sufficiently continuous or lengthy or combined with other circumstances as to compel the inference that, on the face of it, the tenant has ceased to occupy the dwelling as his or her home. In every case, the question is one of fact and degree.

> *Secondly,* assuming the circumstances of absence are such as to give rise to that inference: (1) the onus is on the tenant to rebut the presumption that his or her occupation of the dwelling as a home has ceased; (2) in order to rebut the presumption the tenant must have an intention to return; (3) while there is no set limit to the length of absence and no requirement that the intention must be to return by a specific date or within a finite period, the tenant must be able to demonstrate a 'practical possibility' or 'a real possibility' of the fulfilment of the intention to return within a reasonable time; (4) the tenant must also show that his or her inward intention is accompanied by some formal, outward and visible sign of the intention to return, which sign must be sufficiently substantial and permanent and otherwise such that in all the circumstances it is adequate to rebut the presumption that the tenant, by being physically absent from the premises, has ceased to be in occupation of it.

> *Thirdly,* two homes cases, that is to say where the tenant has another property in which he or she voluntarily takes up full-time residence, must be viewed with particular care in order to assess whether the tenant has ceased to occupy as a home the place where he or she formerly lived.

> *Fourthly,* whether or not a tenant has ceased to occupy premises as his or her home is a question of fact. [Emphasis added.]

261 *Islington LBC v Boyle* [2011] EWCA Civ 1450, [2012] HLR 18 at [55].

1.164 In *Crawley BC v Sawyer*,[262] a tenant was away from his home for over a year. The gas and electricity were disconnected. The tenant had moved in with his girlfriend and they intended to buy a property together. The council served a notice to quit. The couple's relationship broke down and the tenant moved back to his home. The county court judge held that the council property had throughout remained his principal home and the tenant had always intended to return to it. The Court of Appeal did not interfere with that finding.

1.165 In contrast, in *Jennings v Epping Forest DC*,[263] the tenants, an elderly couple in failing health, left their council home and took a flat near to their daughter's home. Once there, the husband's health deteriorated and he was admitted to a residential care home. His wife stayed in the new flat to be near him. The trial judge (the point not being in issue in the appeal) had no difficulty in finding that security of tenure had been lost. There was no prospect of, or intention to, return to the original home.

1.166 In *Lewisham LBC v Robinson*,[264] the tenant was not at home on repeated visits by housing staff. On each occasion the property was found to be occupied by persons who said that they paid rent to Mr Robinson who lived elsewhere. Upholding an appeal by the council against a refusal to grant possession, the Court of Appeal said:

> The judge was ... required to consider whether, given that he may have continued to have occupation of No 50, that occupation was either as his main or as his principal home. The mere fact, as the judge found, that Mr Robinson kept keys to the property, that he had clothing in the property and that he had never given up a bedroom of his own in the property does not answer that enquiry.

1.167 The overwhelming evidence of long-term residence by other occupiers who had claimed to be tenants, the absence of the tenant and his residence elsewhere and the judge's finding that the tenant was a dishonest and unbelievable witness, should have led the judge to find that he was no longer occupying as his only or principal home. The appeal was allowed.

1.168 The most common situations of long-term absence arise from: tenants going abroad for indeterminate periods to visit relatives or to travel; tenants serving terms of imprisonment; tenants receiving

---

262 (1988) 20 HLR 98, (1988) 86 LGR 629, CA.
263 (1993) 25 HLR 241, CA.
264 [2003] EWHC 2630 (Ch).

long-term hospital treatment;[265] and tenants moving into residential care or nursing homes.[266]

1.169   The case of the social housing tenant who is sentenced to *imprisonment* is relatively straightforward because he or she can be promptly located, will have left belongings at the property and usually asserts an intention to return even when serving a lengthy term.[267]

1.170   The case of a very elderly or mentally ill tenant in a *caring institution* is more problematic, as it can be difficult to establish that he or she has both the intention and the prospect of returning to resume occupation. There may well be difficulties with 'fleeting changes of mind' in such cases, which make a focus on the real or 'enduring' intention of the tenant all the more important.[268]

1.171   The tenant loses security of tenure if his or her home in social housing is neither his nor her *only* or *principal* home.[269] It is a question of fact, in relation to secure tenants with two homes, which of them is the principal home.[270] The Court of Appeal, having reviewed the earlier authorities, has recently set out the following principles applicable to determining which is the principal home of a two-home tenant:[271]

> *First*, the length or other circumstances of the tenant's absence may raise the inference that the dwelling which is the subject of the proceedings ceased to be the tenant's principal home so as to cast on the tenant the burden of proving the contrary.
>
> *Secondly*, in order to rebut that presumption, it is not sufficient for the tenant to prove that at the material time it was his or her subjective intention and belief that the dwelling remained the principal home. The objective facts must bear out the reality of that belief and intention both in the sense that the intention and belief are or were genuinely held and also that the intention and belief themselves reflect reality. The reason for the absence, the length and other circumstances of the absence and (where relevant) the anticipated future duration of the

---

265 See *McLoughlin's Curator Bonis v Motherwell DC* 1994 SLT (Lands Tr) 31.

266 *Hammersmith & Fulham LBC v Clarke* (2001) 33 HLR 77, CA and *Braintree DC v Vincent* [2004] EWCA Civ 415.

267 See *Notting Hill Housing Trust v Etoria* April 1989 *Legal Action* 22; *Oldham MBC v Walker* January 1999 *Legal Action* 26 and *Amoah v Barking and Dagenham LBC* (2001) 81 P&CR D12, March 2001 *Legal Action* 28, ChD.

268 *Hammersmith & FulhamLBC v Clarke* (2001) 33 HLR 77, CA and see *McLoughlin's Curator Bonis v Motherwell DC* 1994 SLT (Lands Tr) 31.

269 HA 1985 s81 and HA 1988 s1 (see paras 1.33–1.36).

270 See Thompson, 'The two-home tenant' (1986) 83 LS Gaz 2073 and the case-law on the two-home tenant under the Rent Acts discussed at para 16.14.

271 *Islington LBC v Boyle* [2011] EWCA Civ 1450, [2012] HLR 18 at [65].

absence, as well as statements and conduct of the tenant, will all be relevant to that objective assessment.

Thirdly, the court's focus is on the enduring intention of the tenant, which, depending on the circumstances, may not be displaced by fleeting changes of mind.

Fourthly, the issue is one of fact to be determined in the light of the evidence as a whole ... [Emphasis added.]

1.172   In *Sutton LBC v Swann*,[272] the tenant of a council flat purchased another home. At the other home, he registered as a residential customer with the telephone company, gave that address to his bank and mortgage lenders, gave that address as his residence to the local police and had the address on his firearms certificate changed to that address. The trial judge's finding that his council flat had ceased to be his 'principal' home was not disturbed by the Court of Appeal.

1.173   A landlord not satisfied that the tenant remains in occupation of the property as his or her principal home and wishing to recover possession may serve an ordinary notice to quit on the absentee tenant (on the basis that security has lapsed) and physically recover possession – if there is no one in occupation – or start possession proceedings. (The landlord may, where the tenancy agreement does not provide for service of notices to be effected by leaving them at the property, face considerable difficulties in serving the true tenant with notice to quit – see paras 1.185–1.187.)

1.174   The landlord will not, however, be able to serve a notice to quit on a fixed-term tenant, eg a flexible or fixed-term assured shorthold tenant, for the same reasons as set out above at para 1.159.

1.175   A tenant who can show that, notwithstanding prolonged 'temporary' absence, he or she continues to occupy the property as his or her principal home (see above), retains security of tenure and may successfully defend the action or secure reinstatement.

The tenant has 'disappeared'

1.176   It is not unusual, particularly in serious rent arrears cases, for the social landlord to find that the tenant has abandoned the premises, leaving them vacant or with 'unauthorised' occupiers in possession. The social landlord will want to regularise the position quickly and to re-let.

1.177   However, if the landlord commences proceedings to recover possession against the 'trespassers' (see chapter 23) too hastily, without

272 (1985) 18 HLR 140, CA.

first determining the tenancy at common law, the occupiers will have a complete defence to the action on the basis that the social landlord does not have an immediate right to possession.[273] (The landlord may, where the tenancy agreement does not provide for service of notices to be effected by leaving them at the property, face considerable difficulties in serving the true tenant with notice to quit – see paras 1.185–1.187.)

1.178   In certain limited circumstances, it may be possible for the social landlord to show that the tenant has, by his or her action, surrendered the tenancy, thus entitling the landlord to recover possession (see paras 1.101–1.114). In order for this to be established, the court must be satisfied that, at the very least, 'a tenant had left owing a very substantial sum of money and had been absent for a substantial time'.[274] The burden of proof is on the social landlord.

1.179   The courts have varied in their approach as to whether a simple abandonment is sufficient, on the particular facts, to amount to an offer by the tenant to surrender the tenancy. In *Preston BC v Fairclough*[275] the tenants had left another family in occupation but there was no evidence of the tenants' own date of departure or the amount of rent in arrears, if any. The court held that surrender was not established.

1.180   In *R v Croydon LBC ex p Toth*,[276] the premises had been left empty for several weeks, all furniture had been removed and £488 rent was outstanding. It was held that termination by surrender was made out when the landlord simply took possession of the empty flat.

1.181   If the social landlord deals with a case of 'abandonment' by serving notice to quit, it may recover possession of a vacant property on expiry or commence proceedings for possession against any occupiers. The difficulties of serving notice on the absentee tenant are discussed at paras 1.85–1.87. The landlord will not, however, be able to serve a notice to quit on a fixed-term tenant, ie a new English, a flexible or fixed-term assured shorthold tenant, for the same reasons as set out at para 1.159 above.

---

273 *Preston BC v Fairclough* (1982) 8 HLR 70, CA and *Braintree DC v Vincent* [2004] EWCA Civ 415, [2004] All ER (D) 167 (Mar).

274 *Preston BC v Fairclough* (1982) 8 HLR 70, CA, per Griffiths LJ at 73. See too, *R v Croydon LBC ex p Toth* (1988) 20 HLR 576, CA.

275 (1982) 8 HLR 70, CA.

276 (1988) 20 HLR 576, CA.

The tenant has left a non-tenant spouse/civil partner/cohabitant in occupation

1.182   During a tenant's temporary absence, or following a permanent departure, the presence of a spouse or registered civil partner in the property makes good the tenant's failure to occupy and is treated as occupation by him or her (see paras 1.182–1.18).[277] That situation continues for so long as the parties are married or their civil partnership subsists and lasts up to decree absolute or dissolution order.

1.183   Other cohabitants – whether heterosexual or same sex – may also be able to claim that their partner's tenancy remains secure. Depending on the specific facts, they may argue that their occupation is indicative of the tenant's intention to return and thereby the security of the absent tenant's tenancy is preserved (see paras 1.161–1.175). Otherwise, former spouses and cohabitants can apply under the Family Law Act 1996 for court orders permitting them to occupy. Any such order works as a 'deemed' occupation by the departed tenant (see, generally, chapter 21).[278]

Notice to the absent tenant

1.184   If security of tenure has been lost in any of the circumstances described above, provided the tenancy was not a fixed-term secure, flexible, assured or assured shorthold tenancy, the landlord may end the tenancy by service of a valid notice to quit.

1.185   At common law, such a notice is proved to have been served only if the landlord can establish personal delivery (to the tenant, his wife or 'servant') or that the notice has otherwise actually come to the attention of the tenant.

1.186   This can prove difficult if the whereabouts of the absent tenant are unknown. If the tenancy agreement expressly makes provision for service of notice by simple delivery to the premises or in some other way, then such notice may be effectively given in that way.[279]

1.187   If there is no such provision in the agreement, there is at present no alternative statutory basis for even a local authority landlord to

---

277   Matrimonial Homes Act 1983 s1(6), as amended by Housing (Consequential Provisions) Act 1985 Sch 2 para 56(2), and Family Law Act 1996 s30(4)(b), as amended by Civil Partnership Act 2004 Sch 9 para 1.

278   Family Law Act 1996 ss35(13)(a) and 36(13)(a), as amended by Civil Partnership Act 2004 Sch 9 para 6, and *Gay v Enfield and Sheeran* [2000] 1 WLR 673, (1999) 31 HLR 1126, CA.

279   *Wandsworth LBC v Atwell* (1995) 27 HLR 536, CA and *Lambeth LBC v Davies* March 1998 *Legal Action* 11.

serve such a notice to quit other than in one of the ways sufficient at common law.[280]

Notice to absent tenant under Part 3 of the Housing and Planning Act 2016

1.188　When HPA 2016 Part 3 is brought into force, a social landlord in England which is unable to grant secure tenancies[281] may give a tenant a notice bringing an *assured shorthold tenancy* to an end on the day on which the notice is given if –

- the tenancy relates to premises in England,
- the unpaid rent condition is met,[282]
- the landlord has given the warning notices under s59, and
- no tenant, named occupier or deposit payer has responded in writing to any of those notices before the date specified in the warning notices.

1.189　The landlord must have given three warning notices before the notice under HPA 2016 s57 can bring the tenancy to an end. The first two warning notices must be given to the tenant, any named occupiers, and any deposit payers by:

(a) leaving it at, or sending it to, the premises to which the tenancy relates,

(b) leaving it at, or sending it to, every other postal address in the United Kingdom that the tenant, named occupier or deposit payer has given the landlord as a contact address for giving notices,

(c) sending it to every email address that the tenant, named occupier or deposit payer has given the landlord as a contact address for giving notices, and

(d) in the case of a tenant, leaving it at or sending it to every postal address in the United Kingdom of every guarantor, marked for the attention of the tenant.[283]

1.190　The third warning notice must be given by fixing it to some conspicuous part of the premises to which the tenancy relates.[284]

1.191　　　Each warning notice must explain –

280　*Enfield LBC v Devonish and Sutton* (1997) 29 HLR 691, (1996) *Times* 12 December, CA.

281　This therefore plainly includes private registered providers of social housing such as housing associations.

282　At least eight weeks' or two months' rent is unpaid on the date that the notice is served: HPA 2016 s58.

283　HPA 2016 ss59(2) and 61(3).

284　HPA 2016 s59(3).

(a) that the landlord believes the premises to have been abandoned,

(b) that the tenant, a named occupier or a deposit payer must respond in writing before [the day after the end of the period of 8 weeks beginning with the day on which the first warning notice is given to the tenant] if the premises have not been abandoned, and

(c) that the landlord proposes to bring the tenancy to an end if no tenant, named occupier or deposit payer responds in writing before that date.[285]

1.192   The first warning notice may be given even if the unpaid rent condition is not yet met. The second warning notice may be given only once the unpaid rent condition has been met and must be given at least two weeks, and no more than four weeks, after the first warning notice. The third warning notice must be given before the period of five days ending with the date specified in the earlier warning notices.[286]

The tenant assigns

1.193   'Assignment' is the legal word for a transfer of a tenancy from the current tenant to a different person. If the tenancy is transferred by an *assignment* there is no subletting and no parting with possession which would otherwise put security of tenure in jeopardy in the ways described above.[287]

1.194   However, HA 1985 s91 provides that, except in prescribed cases, a *secure* tenancy is not capable of assignment *at all*. The three prescribed cases are:

- assignment by way of mutual exchange (in these circumstances the strict provisions of HA 1985 s92 and Sch 3 must be complied with);
- assignment pursuant to a property transfer order made under specified family law statutes; and
- assignment to a person who would have been qualified to succeed to the tenancy if the tenant had died immediately before the assignment.

---

285 HPA 2016 s59(4) and (5).

286 HPA 2016 s59(6)–(9).

287 *Clarence House Ltd v National Westminster Bank plc* [2009] EWCA Civ 1311, [2010] 1 WLR 1230.

1.195 The prohibition is one of substance rather than legal form. Where two joint secure tenants purport, by deed of release, to transfer the tenancy from joint names into the sole name of one of them, that will be an attempted assignment and will fail.[288] If an assignment takes place in one of the three prescribed circumstances, the assignee receives the full secure tenancy (notwithstanding any prohibition on assignment in the tenancy agreement itself).[289] The landlord can then obtain possession only by serving a notice seeking possession on the new secure tenant and commencing possession proceedings on one of the grounds applicable to a secure tenant.

1.196 In *Peabody Donation Fund Governors v Higgins,*[290] the tenant assigned the tenancy to his daughter, who was his potential successor. The landlord claimed possession on the basis that the assignment was in breach of a specific clause in its tenancy agreement which prohibited assignment without the landlord's consent. While accepting that the secure tenancy had been transferred to the assignee, the Court of Appeal left open whether the assignment would give rise to a ground for possession on the basis of a breach of obligation of the tenancy.

1.197 However, there is considerable doubt whether it is open to a landlord to grant a secure tenancy subject to a covenant against entering into any one of the three classes of statutorily permitted assignment, since such a covenant arguably offends Consumer Rights Act 2015 Pt 2.[291] In any event, it is unlikely that the court would consider it

288 *Burton v Camden LBC* [2000] 2 AC 399, (2000) 32 HLR 625, HL.
289 *Peabody Donation Fund Governors v Higgins* [1983] 1 WLR 1091, [1983] 3 All ER 122, (1983) 10 HLR 82, CA.
290 *Peabody Donation Fund Governors v Higgins* [1983] 1 WLR 1091, [1983] 3 All ER 122, (1983) 10 HLR 82, CA.
292 There are good arguments to support the proposition that the Consumer Rights Act applies to tenancies, although there is nothing in the Act which explicitly states this and there are no relevant authorities on the new Act. However, in relation to unfair terms, there was nothing in the former Unfair Terms in Consumer Contracts Regulations 1999 SI No 2083 either which referred to tenancies or interests in land, but it was clear that they did apply to land: *R (Khatun) v Newham LBC* [2004] EWCA Civ 55, [2004] HLR 29. Also, by way of confirmation in relation to the Directive, there is *Brusse and de Man Garabito v Jahani BV,* C-488/11, [2013] HLR 38, which also relates to unfair terms. Since the UTCCR appear to have been substantially imported into the 2015 Act, it is assumed that the new provisions do apply to tenancies. Further, section 66 provides that (1) section 65 does not apply to ... (b) any contract so far as it relates to the creation or transfer of an interest in land. (Section 65 prohibits exclusion clauses restricting liability for death or personal injury resulting from negligence.) The Competition and Market Authority Guidance for Lettings Professionals (June 2014) proceeds on the assumption that

reasonable to enforce a tenancy condition which appears to be at variance with the statutory purpose of permitting three forms of assignment.

1.198   If the assignment is not made within the permitted three classes[292] or the purported assignment is ineffective (for example, because no deed of assignment was used),[293] the tenancy is not transferred.

1.199   In respect of *assured* periodic tenancies, HA 1988 s15(1)(a) provides that it is a term of the tenancy that the tenant shall not assign except with the consent of the landlord. If the tenancy is assigned with consent, the assignee will have an assured tenancy if they can fulfil the ordinary conditions for assured status (see para 1.6 above). If no consent was sought or given, while the assignment is effective, the social landlord can seek possession against the assignee on the ground that a term of the tenancy has been breached.[294]

1.200   If the true tenant has left and the assignment was ineffective, eg because it was not made by deed,[295] the assignee will be without any right to occupy. He or she will be able to remain only until the landlord has taken the appropriate steps to recover possession. The landlord must first determine properly the tenancy of the original tenant (usually by service of a valid notice to quit, since the tenancy will no longer be secure or assured) and then take proceedings for possession against the assignee as a trespasser. Where the tenancy was not periodic, eg it was a fixed-term assured shorthold tenancy, the landlord will be required to rely on a forfeiture clause or break notice to bring the tenancy to an end.

for the purpose of the Consumer Protection in Unfair Trading Regs 2008 (as well as the UTCCR), a tenancy is a consumer contract. Para 3.7 states: 'For the purpose of this guidance, the CMA proceeds on the basis that: most residential tenants are consumers, most letting and managing agents are acting in the course of a business'. See too the Unfair Contract Terms Guidance (Competition and Markets Authority), 31 July 2015.

292 *Croydon LBC v Bustin and Triance* (1991) 24 HLR 36, CA; *Newham LBC v Bennett* [1984] CLY 1960 (both cases of ineffective transfer from mother to son) and *Crago v Julian* [1992] 1 WLR 372, CA (spouse to spouse).

293 *Crago v Julian* [1992] 1 WLR 372, (1992) 24 HLR 306, CA.

294 *Paul v Nurse* (1828) 8 B&C 486; HA 1988 Sch 2 ground 12. See para 3.253.

295 *Crago v Julian* [1992] 1 WLR 372, (1992) 24 HLR 306, CA.

CHAPTER 2

Procedure for recovery of possession from a tenant with security of tenure

continued

Introduction

2.1 Landlords of social housing tenants[1] with security of tenure must, save in a number of limited circumstances,[2] recover possession by obtaining and executing a court order for possession. In almost all cases, the first step of the process is either to determine the tenancy or to serve a statutory notice. The form of notice required depends upon the type of tenancy or licence that the landlord is seeking to end. This chapter considers the procedure for:

1) assured periodic tenancies,
2) assured fixed-term tenancies,
3) assured shorthold fixed-term tenancies,
4) old-style English and Welsh secure periodic tenancies,
5) old-style English and Welsh secure fixed-term tenancies,
6) new English secure and flexible tenancies.

2.2 The procedure for recovering possession of tenancies that lack, or have limited, security of tenure (eg introductory, starter, demoted, family intervention and other non-secure tenancies and licences) granted by social landlords is considered within chapters 5, 6, 7 and 8 respectively.

2.3 Chapter 3 will consider the next step in the process, namely the grounds and conditions for possession that must be satisfied before the court can make an order for possession.

Assured periodic tenancies

2.4 HA 1988 s8 provides, so far is material, that:

(1) The court shall not entertain proceedings for possession of a dwelling-house let on an assured tenancy unless –

   (a) the landlord or, in the case of joint landlords, at least one of them has served on the tenant a notice in accordance with this section and the proceedings are begun within the time limits stated in the notice in accordance with subsections (3) to (4B) below; or

   (b) the court considers it just and equitable to dispense with the requirement of such a notice.

(2) The court shall not make an order for possession on any of the grounds in Schedule 2 to this Act unless that ground and par-

---

1 Including secure licencees.
2 See paras 1.101–1.114.

ticulars of it are specified in the notice under this section; but the grounds specified in such a notice may be altered or added to with the leave of the court.

(3) A notice under this section is one in the prescribed form informing the tenant that –

(a) the landlord intends to begin proceedings for possession of the dwelling-house on one or more of the grounds specified in the notice; and

(b) those proceedings will not begin earlier than a date specified in the notice in accordance with subsections (3A) to (4B) below ; and

(c) those proceedings will not begin later than twelve months from the date of service of the notice.

(3A) If a notice under this section specifies in accordance with subsection (3)(a) ground 7A in Schedule 2 to this Act (whether with or without other grounds), the date specified in the notice as mentioned in subsection (3)(b) is not to be earlier than –

(a) in the case of a periodic tenancy, the earliest date on which, apart from section 5(1), the tenancy could be brought to an end by a notice to quit given by the landlord on the same date as the date of service of the notice under this section;

(b) in the case of a fixed-term tenancy, one month after the date on which the notice was served.

(4) If a notice under this section specifies in accordance with subsection (3)(a) above ground 14 in Schedule 2 to this Act (whether without other grounds or with any ground other than ground 7A), the date specified in the notice as mentioned in subsection (3)(b) above shall not be earlier than the date of the service of the notice.

(4A) If a notice under this section specifies in accordance with subsection (3)(a) above, any of grounds 1, 2, 5 to 7, 9 and 16 in Schedule 2 to this Act (whether without other grounds or with any ground other than ground 7A or 14, the date specified in the notice as mentioned in subsection (3)(b) above shall not be earlier than –

(a) two months from the date of service of the notice; and

(b) if the tenancy is a periodic tenancy, the earliest date on which, apart from section 5(1) above, the tenancy could be brought to an end by a notice to quit given by the landlord on the same date as the date of service of the notice under this section.

(4B) In any other case, the date specified in the notice as mentioned in subsection (3)(b) above shall not be earlier than the expiry of the period of two weeks from the date of the service of the notice.

(4C) A notice under this section that specifies in accordance with subsection (3)(a) ground 7A in Schedule 2 to this Act (whether with or without other grounds) must be served on the tenant within the time period specified in subsection (4D), (4E) or (4F).

(4D) Where the landlord proposes to rely on condition 1, 3 or 5 in ground 7A, the notice must be served on the tenant within –

    (a) the period of 12 months beginning with the day of the conviction, or

    (b) if there is an appeal against the conviction, the period of 12 months beginning with the day on which the appeal is finally determined or abandoned.

(4E) Where the landlord proposes to rely on condition 2 in ground 7A, the notice must be served on the tenant within –

    (a) the period of 12 months beginning with the day on which the court has made the finding, or

    (b) if there is an appeal against the finding, the period of 12 months beginning with the day on which the appeal is finally determined, abandoned or withdrawn.

(4F) Where the landlord proposes to rely on condition 4 in ground 7A, the notice must be served on the tenant within –

    (a) the period of 3 months beginning with the day on which the closure order was made, or

    (b) if there is an appeal against the making of the order, the period of 3 months beginning with the day on which the appeal is finally determined, abandoned or withdrawn.

(5) The court may not exercise the power conferred by subsection (1)(b) above if the landlord seeks to recover possession on ground 7A or 8 in Schedule 2 to this Act. ...

Forms

2.5   Any notice served under section 8 must be in the prescribed form.[3] The prescribed form is contained within Schedule 1 to the Assured Tenancies and Agricultural Occupancies (Forms) (England) Regulations 2015[4] and a copy of the current prescribed notice is contained within appendix A. The notice was last changed on 6 April 2016.

2.6   Any notice that is not in the prescribed form will be invalid unless it is in a 'form substantially to the same effect'.[5] It is therefore important to check that the correct notice has been used. The use of delegated legislation in this way to save otherwise faulty notices has been held to be within the relevant powers of the secretary of state.[6] It is likely that a notice that does not include all of the information contained within the prescribed form will not be substantially to the same effect. For example, a notice would differ in substance if the

---

3 HA 1988 s8(3).

4 SI No 620.

5 SI No 620 reg 2.

6 *Dudley MBC v Bailey* (1990) 22 HLR 424, CA.

'Notes for Guidance' contained in the body of the prescribed form were omitted from the notice actually served.[7] Alternatively, a notice that paraphrases all of the information, or replicates the information in a different order, is more likely to be substantially to the same effect.

2.7   It should be noted that the words 'Notice of Seeking Possession' and the statutory reference at the head are themselves important parts of the prescribed form. They enable the tenant to identify the statutory power under which it is alleged the notice has been given. On the other hand, simple 'slips' such as the omission of a manuscript signature above the typescript job title of the officer authorising the giving of the notice, will not prevent the form being substantially to the same effect as the prescribed form and thus valid.[8]

Name of tenant

2.8   Where there are joint tenants the notice must be served on all of the tenants.[9] All must therefore be named in the notice even if some are no longer in residence.[10] Practical difficulties may arise over the misspelling of names or the use of former names where the tenant has changed his or her name following marriage or otherwise. To guard against this difficulty most landlords will use the name as it appears on the original tenancy agreement. It is unlikely that this practice will render the notice defective even if the name of the tenant has changed.

Ground

2.9   The notice must specify the ground(s) of possession that the landlord intends to rely on in a claim for possession.[11] This does not necessarily mean that the full text of the ground needs to be set out within the notice. However, the words used must set out fully the substance of the ground so that the notice is adequate to achieve the legislative purpose of the provision, ie to give the tenant sufficient information to enable the tenant to consider what he or she should do and, with or without advice, to do that which is in her power and which will best

---

7   See *Manel v Memon* (2001) 33 HLR 24, CA.
8   *City of London v Devlin* (1997) 29 HLR 58, CA.
9   HA 1988 s45(3).
10   *Newham LBC v Okotoro* March 1993 *Legal Action* 11.
11   HA 1988 s8(2).

protect a tenant against the loss of the home.[12] In *Malih v Yousaf*,[13] the Court of Appeal held that a notice which set out ground 8 without including the words 'rent means rent lawfully due from the tenant' was not defective as the substance of the ground had been given (rent could not be in arrear if it was lawfully due from the tenant) and the tenant had sufficient information to know what to do to avoid a possession order being made.

2.10   If a different ground for possession is made out at trial from that shown in the notice seeking possession, the proceedings must be dismissed[14] unless the court gives permission for an alternative ground to be read into the notice seeking possession by alteration or addition, or the court exercises a discretion to dispense with the requirement of notice altogether.[15]

Particulars

2.11   The particulars must give the tenant sufficient details of the circumstances that the landlord relies upon in asserting that a ground for possession is made out, since the function of the notice is to fire a 'warning shot' telling the tenant what the complaint is against him or her so as to enable the tenant to rectify it.[16] Clearly, the simple statement 'arrears of rent' is an insufficient particular,[17] but the notice need not state the actual sum owing provided the particulars give the tenant sufficient information to ascertain the true level of the arrears, eg no rent has been paid since a certain date or four months of arrears are due.[18] Similarly 'various acts of nuisance' or 'instances of dilapidation' would be inadequate.[19] In a nuisance case, the Court of Appeal described the following particulars as 'obviously' insufficient:[20]

---

12 *Mountain v Hastings* (1993) 25 HLR 427, CA.

13 [2014] EWCA Civ 234, [2014] HLR 27.

14 See *Midlothian DC v Tweedie* 1993 GWD 1068, Sh Ct.

15 HA 1988 s8(1) and (2) and see *Gedling BC v Brener* September 2001 *Legal Action* 23.

16 *Torridge DC v Jones* (1986) 18 HLR 107, [1985] 2 EGLR 54, CA. See too *Marath v MacGillivray* (1996) 28 HLR 484, CA.

17 *Torridge DC v Jones* (1986) 18 HLR 107, [1985] 2 EGLR 54, CA.

18 *Marath v MacGillivary* (1996) 28 HLR 484, CA.

19 *South Buckinghamshire DC v Francis* [1985] CLY 1900 and *Slough BC v Robbins* [1996] CLY 3832, December 1996 *Legal Action* 13.

20 *Camden LBC v Oppong* (1996) 28 HLR 701, CA at 703.

The tenant frequently disturbs his neighbour, and on one occasion has threatened his neighbour with physical violence.

2.12   Likewise, the use of the simple words 'major refurbishment scheme' (in a claim for possession under HA 1988 ground 6) is deficient,[21] as is the bare repetition of the terms of a tenancy agreement where the ground alleged is breach of those terms.[22] Neither can simple repetition of the text of the statutory ground amount to 'particulars'.

2.13   The court can give the landlord permission to amend the notice seeking possession for the purpose of improving the particulars,[23] but it should not be assumed that the discretion will be exercised in favour of such an amendment if application is made at a late stage in the proceedings.[24] However, permission is more likely to be granted where the deficiency has been cured by detailed particulars being given in the form of the particulars of claim accompanying the claim form.[25]

2.14   If particulars are given but they are *inaccurate*, the court may (according to the degree of inaccuracy) permit the claim to proceed or allow amendment of the notice seeking possession. For example, if the notice gives particulars that the 'arrears of rent are £X' and it is shown at trial that the landlord has innocently and in error included in that figure amounts which are not arrears of rent, the action can proceed, but the judge will take into account the nature and extent of the error in determining whether possession should be given.[26]

Dates

2.15   A notice is not in the prescribed form, or in a form to substantially the same effect, if a material date has either been omitted[27] or incorrectly stated.[28]

2.16   A notice under section 8 must give two dates: (1) the date before which proceedings may not be issued and (2) the date after which proceedings may not be issued.[29] In all cases, the second date given in

---

21   *Waltham Forest LBC v England* March 1994 *Legal Action* 11.
22   *East Devon DC v Williams* December 1996 *Legal Action* 13.
23   HA 1988 s8(2); *Camden LBC v Oppong* (1996) 28 HLR 701, CA.
24   *Merton LBC v Drew* July 1999 *Legal Action* 22.
25   *Bryant v Portsmouth CC* (2000) 32 HLR 906, CA.
26   *Dudley MBC v Bailey* (1990) 22 HLR 424, CA.
27   *Patel v Rodrigo* June 1997 *Legal Action* 23.
28   *Panayi v Roberts* (1993) 25 HLR 421, CA.
29   HA 1988 s8(3).

the notice must be 12 months from the date of service of the notice.[30] No proceedings can be brought in respect of a notice that has lapsed unless the court is able to, and does, dispense with the service of the notice.[31] Arguably, a notice should be treated as 'spent' once it has been used to found a claim for possession and a court should be unlikely to allow a second set of proceedings to be issued within the period of validity of a single notice.[32]

2.17   The first date depends on the grounds relied upon in the notice. A claim for possession cannot be brought until the day of the specified date unless the court is able to, and does, dispense with the service of the notice.[33]

2.18   For these purposes, the proceedings 'begin' on the date the county court issues the claim.[34]

Grounds 3, 4, 8, 10–13, 14ZA, 14A, 15, 17

2.19   Where either grounds 3, 4, 8, 10, 11, 12, 13, 14ZA, 14A or 15 are relied upon, the date is two weeks from the date of the service of the notice.[35]

Ground 7A (conviction for a serious offence, etc)

2.20   Where ground 7A is relied upon, the date is the earliest date on which, apart from section 5(1), the tenancy could be brought to an end by a notice to quit given by the landlord on the date that the section 8 notice is served.[36] In the case of a weekly periodic tenancy which began on a Monday, the date will be either the Sunday or Monday that is at least four weeks after the notice is served.[37] However, where rent is payable on a different day, eg a Wednesday, the notice to quit must expire on the Tuesday or Wednesday unless there are clear words within the tenancy agreement to the contrary.[38]

30 HA 1988 s8(3)(c).
31 HA 1988 s8(1).
32 See *Shaftesbury HA v Rickards* December 2005 *Legal Action* 20.
33 HA 1988 s8(1).
34 *Shepping v Osada* (2001) 33 HLR 13, CA.
35 HA 1988 s8(4B).
36 HA 1988 s8(3A)(a).
37 *Sidebotham v Holland* [1895] QB 378; *Lemon v Lardeur* [1946] KB 613 and *Crate v Miller* [1947] KB 946. Cf *Harler v Calder* (1989) 21 HLR 214, in which the Court of Appeal held that the common law rule was that a notice to quit must expire on a 'rent day'. The better view is that there is no choice and the landlord must serve the notice to quit to expire at the beginning or end of a new period.
38 *Harley v Calder* (1989) 21 HLR 214.

Ground 14 (nuisance)

2.21   Where ground 14 is relied upon, the date is the date on which the notice is served.[39] This means that proceedings may be begun as soon as the notice has been served.

All other grounds

2.22   In all other cases, including cases in which any of the other grounds (save for ground 7A) are relied upon, the date is two months from the date of the service of the notice or, where longer, the earliest date on which, apart from section 5(1), the tenancy could be brought to an end by a notice to quit given by the landlord.[40]

Served on the tenant

2.23   The notice must be served on the tenant or in the case of joint tenants on all of the tenants.[41] It has been held that 'serve' is an ordinary English word connoting the delivery of a document to a particular person.[42] For the rules on acceptable service developed by the courts in relation to methods of service of notices to quit (in summary: personal service on the tenant, service on a wife of the tenant or service on the servant of the tenant), see para 14.24.[43]

2.24   In the absence of an express admission by the tenant of service of the notice seeking possession, the burden of proof is on the landlord to show that the notice was properly served. The Law of Property Act 1925 s196 does not apply to notices served under HA 1988; it follows that the mere fact that the landlord has posted the document to the tenant by first class post will not mean that the tenant has in fact been served. However, a landlord can grant a tenancy with a clause in the tenancy agreement expressly incorporating LPA 1925 s196 or providing that all notices that are sent by first class post to the tenant are deemed served on the second day after posting. Otherwise, the common law rules apply and the landlord must prove that the notice has been brought to the attention of the tenant.[44] Other than where the landlord has personally served the tenant, a landlord who cannot

---

39   HA 1988 s8(4).
40   HA 1988 s8(4A).
41   HA 1988 s8(1)(a).
42   *Tadema Holdings v Ferguson* (2000) 32 HLR 866 at 873.
43   See *Enfield LBC v Devonish and Sutton* (1997) 29 HLR 691, CA.
44   *Wandsworth LBC v Atwell* (1995) 27 HLR 536, CA.

prove that the notice has come to the attention of the tenant will not be able to rely on the section 8 notice.

Ground 7A: served within a specified period

2.25 Where ground 7A (conviction for a serious offence, etc) is relied upon, unlike the other grounds, the notice must also be served within a specified period. Where conditions 1, 3 or 5 (see paras 3.212, 3.232 and 3.238) are relied upon, the notice must be served within the period of 12 months beginning with the day of the conviction or, if there is an appeal against the conviction, the period of 12 months beginning with the day on which the appeal is finally determined or abandoned.[45] Where condition 2 (see para 3.233) is relied upon, the notice must be served within the period of 12 months beginning with the day on which the court has made the finding, or if there is an appeal against the finding, the period of 12 months beginning with the day on which the appeal is finally determined, abandoned or withdrawn.[46] Where condition 4 (see para 3.233) is relied upon, the notice must be served within the period of three months beginning with the day on which the closure order was made, or if there is an appeal against the making of the order, the period of three months beginning with the day on which the appeal is finally determined, abandoned or withdrawn.[47]

Ground 14A: additional requirements

2.26 Where ground 14A (domestic violence) is relied upon in a HA 1988 section 8 notice, and the partner who has left the dwelling-house as mentioned in that ground (see para 2.4) is not a tenant of the dwelling-house, the court shall not, unless it considers it just and equitable to dispense with the notice requirements, entertain proceedings for possession of the dwelling-house unless the landlord or, in the case of joint landlords, at least one of them has served on the partner who has left a copy of the notice or has taken all reasonable steps to serve a copy of the notice on that partner.[48]

2.27 Where proceedings have already begun, and the court gives the landlord permission to amend the HA 1988 section 8 notice so as to

---

45 HA 1988 s8(4D).
46 HA 1988 s8(4E).
47 HA 1988 s8(4F).
48 HA 1988 s8A(1).

rely on ground 14A, and the partner who has left the dwelling-house as mentioned in that ground is not a party to the proceedings, the court shall not, unless it considers it just and equitable to dispense with the requirement to serve a notice, continue to entertain the proceedings unless the landlord or, in the case of joint landlords, at least one of them has served on the partner who has left a notice, or has taken all reasonable steps to serve such a notice, which must:

(a) state that proceedings for the possession of the dwelling-house have begun;
(b) specify the ground or grounds on which possession is being sought; and
(c) give particulars of the ground or grounds.[49]

Dispensing with notice

2.28   Other than where a landlord is seeking to recover possession under grounds 7A or 8 (conviction for a serious offence, etc or eight weeks' rent arrears), the court may dispense with the requirements to serve a notice under section 8 where it considers it just and equitable to do so.[50] An application to dispense should not be entertained by the court if the tenant has not been given full notice of it and of the basis on which the exercise of the power is sought.[51]

2.29   A court when exercising the discretion must have regard to the fact that the discretion should be exercised exceptionally,[52] weigh all the factors before it and take all circumstances into account both from the view of the tenant and the landlord. The fact that a tenant has not been given an opportunity to avoid the ground being satisfied is likely to be significant. As would the tenant being aware, through other sources, of what it is necessary to do in order to avoid the ground being satisfied and the risks of not doing so.[53]

2.30   In ground 14 (nuisance) cases, where proceedings can be begun immediately after the service of a notice, provided that detailed particulars accompany the claim form, and the tenant is advised of the right to seek legal advice, it is hard to envisage circumstances in which it would not be just and equitable to dispense with the notice.

---

49   HA 1988 s8A(2) and (3).
50   HA 1988 s8(1)(b) and (5).
51   *Knowsley Housing Trust v Revell; Helena Housing Limited v Curtis* [2003] EWCA Civ 496, [2003] HLR 63.
52   *Braintree DC v Vincent* [2004] EWCA Civ 415.
53   *Kelsey HA v King* (1996) 28 HLR 270, CA.

Review

2.31   There is no statutory obligation on a landlord to consider representations or to review its decision to serve a notice. The landlord may
issue proceedings as soon as the first date in the notice has expired.
However, where a landlord seeks to rely on ground 7A, Home Office
guidance provides that the Secretary of State:

> ... would expect housing associations to offer a similar non-statutory
> review procedure (in the same way that they have done so for starter
> tenancies).[54]

Assured fixed-term tenancies

2.32   A social landlord that wishes to bring an assured fixed-term tenancy
to an end must also serve a notice under section 8.[55] A landlord cannot simply rely on a forfeiture clause to recover possession.[56] A notice
served under section 8 during a fixed-term tenancy which has since
become periodic or relates to events that occurred during a fixed term
is still effective.[57] The same principles, discussed above, are of equal
effect save for a handful of differences described at paras 2.5–2.31.

Right to possession under the tenancy

2.33   First, the tenancy agreement must specify, be it in the form of a provision for re-entry, forfeiture, determination by notice or otherwise,
the grounds on which the landlord may rely in order to bring the
fixed term to an end.[58] Second, the landlord cannot recover possession under grounds 6–7 (see paras 3.359–3.371), 9 or 16 (see paras
3.372–3.398) until the fixed term has come to an end.[59] A section
8 notice therefore cannot specify grounds for possession that are
excluded or not covered by the tenancy agreement. In those cases,
the landlord must wait for the fixed term to come to an end.

---

54 *Anti-social Behaviour, Crime and Policing Act 2014: Reform of anti-social
behaviour powers Statutory guidance for frontline professionals* (Home Office), July
2014, p62. See paras 3.252–3.254 for further discussion.

55 HA 1988 s8(1).

56 *Artesian Residential Investments Ltd v Beck* [2000] QB 541, (2000) 32 HLR 107,
CA. This also means that the law concerning relief from forfeiture does not
apply.

57 HA 1988 s8(6).

58 HA 1988 s7(6)(b).

59 HA 1988 s7(6)(a).

Dates

2.34   The same requirements as to dates (see above paras 2.15–2.18) apply, save that where ground 7A is relied upon, the notice must state that proceedings may not be begun until one month after the date on which the notice was served.[60]

Assured shorthold fixed-term tenancies

2.35   An assured shorthold fixed-term tenancy is also an assured fixed-term tenancy. It follows that if the landlord wishes to bring the tenancy to an end during the fixed term the same principles set out at paras 2.32–2.34 above apply.

2.36   At the end of the fixed term, the landlord may bring the tenancy to an end by serving the tenant with a notice under HA 1988 s21 (see paras 10.18–10.24 for further discussion on section 21). Where, however, the fixed term was for a period of two years or more in respect of a dwelling-house in England, and the tenancy was granted by a private registered provider of social housing, the court may not make an order for possession under section 21 unless the landlord has given to the tenant not less than six months' notice in writing:

a) stating that the landlord does not propose to grant another tenancy on the expiry of the fixed-term tenancy, and

b) informing the tenant of how to obtain help or advice about the notice and, in particular, of any obligation of the landlord to provide help or advice.[61]

2.37   Although there is no statutory requirement for private registered providers of social housing to undertake a review of a decision not to grant another tenancy on the expiry of the fixed-term tenancy, the Tenancy Standard,[62] produced by the Homes and Communities Agency[63] and which contains the outcomes that all registered providers of social housing are expected to achieve, requires providers to have a policy that includes provision for 'the way in which a tenant or prospective tenant may appeal against or complain about the length of fixed-term tenancy offered and the type of tenancy offered, and against a decision not to grant another tenancy on the expiry of the

---

60 HA 1988 s8(3A)(b).
61 HA 1988 s21(1A) and (1B).
62 *Tenancy Standard* (Homes and Communities Agency, 31 March 2015).
63 The current regulator of social housing providers in England.

fixed term'.[64] The Tenancy Standard therefore plainly envisages that tenants should have the right to appeal or review against a decision not to renew the fixed-term tenancy. Although it will be for the individual landlord to decide the appeal or review procedure, the failure to offer the tenant an opportunity to review the decision is likely to give rise to an arguable public law or proportionality defence (see chapter 25).

Old-style English and Welsh secure periodic tenancies

2.38 There are now two separate notice requirements for Welsh and old-style English secure periodic tenancies, ie those granted in England before HPA 2016 Sch 7 para 4 came into force: HA 1985 s84A and HA 1985 s83. The notice requirements are different depending upon the grounds for possession on which the social landlord wants to rely.

Where the landlord intends to rely on other grounds for possession

2.39 In all other cases, before issuing a claim for possession under any of the grounds contained within Schedule 2 to HA 1985 the notice must meet the requirements of HA 1985 s83 which provides, so far as is material:

(A1) This section applies in relation to proceedings for an order mentioned in section 82(1A) other than –
  (a) proceedings for possession of a dwelling-house under section 84A (absolute ground for possession for anti-social behaviour), including proceedings where possession is also sought on one or more of the grounds set out in Schedule 2, or
  (b) proceedings for possession of a dwelling-house under section 107D (recovery of possession on expiry of flexible tenancy).
(1) The court shall not entertain proceedings to which this section applies unless –
  (a) the landlord has served a notice on the tenant complying with the provisions of this section, or
  (b) the court considers it just and equitable to dispense with the requirement of such a notice.

64 Paragraph 2.2.1(f).

(2) A notice under this section shall –
    (a) be in a form prescribed by regulations made by the Secretary of State,
    (b) specify the ground on which the court will be asked to make the order, and
    (c) give particulars of that ground.
(3) Where the tenancy is a periodic tenancy and the ground or one of the grounds specified in the notice is ground 2 in Schedule 2 (nuisance or other anti-social behaviour), the notice –
    (a) shall also –
        (i) state that proceedings for the possession of the dwelling-house may be begun immediately, and
        (ii) specify the date sought by the landlord as the date on which the tenant is to give up possession of the dwelling-house, and
    (b) ceases to be in force twelve months after the date so specified.
(4) Where the tenancy is a periodic tenancy and ground 2 in Schedule 2 is not specified in the notice, the notice –
    (a) shall also specify the date after which proceedings for the possession of the dwelling-house may be begun, and
    (b) ceases to be in force twelve months after the date so specified.
    ...
(5) The date specified in accordance with subsection (3) ,(4) ... must not be earlier than the date on which the tenancy could, apart from this Part, be brought to an end by notice to quit given by the landlord on the same date as the notice under this section.
    ...
(7) Regulations under this section shall be made by statutory instrument and may make different provision with respect to different cases or descriptions of case, including different provision for different areas.

Form

2.40   The notice must usually be in the form prescribed in regulations made by the secretary of state.[65] Those regulations are made by statutory instrument. The current prescribed form of notice is contained in the Secure Tenancies (Notices) Regulations 1987,[66] as amended

---

65 HA 1985 s83(2)(a).
66 1987 SI No 755. The earliest prescribed form was contained in Secure Tenancies (Notices) Regulations 1980 SI No 1339, as amended by SI 1984 No 1224 and upheld in *Wansbeck DC v Charlton* (1981) 79 LGR 523, (1981) 42 P&CR 162, CA. Those regulations were saved for the purposes of the Housing Act 1985 by Housing (Consequential Provisions) Act 1985 s2(2). A revised form was prescribed by Secure Tenancies (Notices) Regulations 1987, which came into force on 13 May 1987.

by the Secure Tenancies (Notices) (Amendment) (England) Regulations 1997,[67] and subsequently by the Secure Tenancies (Notices) (Amendment) (England) Regulations 2004[68] and the Secure Tenancies (Notices) (Amendment) (Wales) Regulations 2005.[69]

2.41 These numerous references to regulations simply serve to demonstrate the importance of checking the actual notice relied on by the landlord against the prescribed form which was required on the date on which the notice was given. As under HA 1988 s8 (see para 2.4), if the notice is *not* in the form prescribed at the date of service it may be ineffective if it is not 'in a form substantially to the same effect'.[70]

Name of tenant

2.42 The prescribed form has a space for the insertion of the tenant's name and the notice must be served on *that tenant*.[71] See above para 2.81 for the similar provision for assured tenants. If the tenancy is a joint tenancy then the reference on the prescribed form to the 'tenant' is a reference to all the joint tenants. All must therefore be named in the notice even if some are no longer in residence.[72]

Ground

2.43 The notice must 'specify the ground on which the court will be asked to make the order'.[73] The ground specified must therefore correspond with the ground that is (1) pleaded in the particulars of claim and (2) relied on in court. Although worded slightly different, the requirements are identical to HA 1988 s8 (see above para 2.9 for further discussion in respect concerning the specification of grounds contained within HA 1988 s8 notices).

---

67 1997 SI No 71.
68 2004 SI No 1627.
69 2005 SI No 1226.
70 Secure Tenancies (Notices) Regulations 1987 reg 2(1).
71 HA 1985 s83(1)(a). See *Enfield LBC v Devonish and Sutton* (1997) 29 HLR 691, CA.
72 *Newham LBC v Okotoro* March 1993 *Legal Action* 11.
73 HA 1985 s83(2)(b).

Particulars

2.44   The notice must, on its face, give 'particulars' of the ground for possession specified in it.[74] This is also an identical requirement to that for HA 1988 s8 notices. See above paras 2.11–2.14 for further discussion on the requirement to give particulars in section 8 notices.

The dates

2.45   The prescribed form contains a space for completion of the specified date and for entry of the date of the notice itself (which should be the date of service). The specified date must be no earlier than the date on which the tenancy or licence could have been brought to an end by notice to quit or notice to determine given by the landlord on the same date that the notice seeking possession was served.[75] In the case of a weekly periodic tenancy which began on a Monday, the date will be either the Sunday or Monday that is at least four weeks after the notice is served.[76] HA 1985 does not give the court power to amend the dates set out in the notice.

2.46   Where the landlord is seeking to rely on ground 2 (nuisance) (see para 3.125), the notice must also state that proceedings for the possession of the dwelling-house may be begun immediately.[77]

2.47   The notice must also state that it ceases to be in force 'twelve months after the date so specified'. This means that the landlord has in effect nearly 13 months to issue a claim for possession after the notice has been served. Where ground 2 is relied upon this is 12 months after the date specified, ie not the date that the notice was served, even though proceedings could have been issued on the same day.

Where the landlord intends to rely on the absolute ground for possession

2.48   Where the landlord wishes to rely on the mandatory ground for possession under HA 1985 s84A it must follow the procedure contained within s83ZA.[78]

74   HA 1985 s83(2)(c).
75   HA 1985 s83(3) and (5).
76   *Sidebotham v Holland* [1895] QB 378; *Lemon v Lardeur* [1946] KB 613 and *Crate v Miller* [1947] KB 946. But see also discussion at footnote 37 in chapter 1.
77   HA 1985 s83(3)(a)(i).
78   HA 1985 s83A(1).

Section 83ZA notices

2.49   The notice need not be in any particular form, but all notices must contain the following information:

a) state that the court will be asked to make an order under HA 1985 s84A for the possession of the dwelling-house,

b) set out the reasons for the landlord's decision to apply for the order (including the condition or conditions in section 84A on which the landlord proposes to rely),

c) inform the tenant of any right that the tenant may have under section 85ZA to request a review of the landlord's decision and of the time within which the request must be made,

d) inform the tenant that, if the tenant needs help or advice about the notice and what to do about it, the tenant should take it immediately to a Citizens' Advice Bureau, a housing aid centre, a law centre or a solicitor,

e) specify the date after which proceedings for the possession of the dwelling-house may be begun (ie 28 days for weekly periodic tenancies and one month for fixed-term flexible tenancies), and

f) that it ceases to be in force 12 months after the date so specified.[79]

2.50   Where the landlord intends to also rely on any grounds under Schedule 2 the notice must also:

a) specify the ground on which the court will be asked to make the order, and

b) give particulars of that ground.[80]

The other requirements of the notice depend on which condition of the absolute ground the landlord intends to rely on. Where the landlord intends to rely on conditions 1, 3 or 5 (ie where the tenant has been convicted of a serious criminal offence, breaching a criminal behaviour order under Anti-social Behaviour, Crime and Policing Act 2014 s30 or an offence under Environmental Protection Act 1990 s80(4) or s82(8)) the notice:

...

(a) must also state the conviction on which the landlord proposes to rely, and

(b) must be served on the tenant within –

79 HA 1985 s83ZA(3), (8), (9) and (10).
80 HA 1985 s83ZA(4).

> (i) the period of 12 months beginning with the day of the conviction, or
>
> (ii) if there is an appeal against the conviction, the period of 12 months beginning with the day on which the appeal is finally determined or abandoned.[81]

2.51   Where the landlord intends to rely on condition 2 (ie breach of an injunction under Anti-social Behaviour, Crime and Policing Act 2014) the notice:

> ...
>
> (a) must also state the finding on which the landlord proposes to rely, and
>
> (b) must be served on the tenant within –
>
> (i) the period of 12 months beginning with the day on which the court has made the finding, or
>
> (ii) if there is an appeal against the finding, the period of 12 months beginning with the day on which the appeal is finally determined, abandoned or withdrawn.[82]

2.52   Where the landlord intends to rely on condition 3 (ie where a closure order has been made under Anti-social Behaviour, Crime and Policing Act 2014 s80) the notice:

> ...
>
> (a) must also state the closure order concerned, and
>
> (b) must be served on the tenant within –
>
> (i) the period of 3 months beginning with the day on which the closure order was made, or
>
> (ii) if there is an appeal against the making of the order, the period of 3 months beginning with the day on which the appeal is finally determined, abandoned or withdrawn.[83]

2.53   Importantly, the court has no power to dispense with the requirements to serve a notice. It follows that if the notice requirements have not been complied with the possession claim, insofar as it only relies on section 84A, must be dismissed.

Right to a review

2.54   Tenants of local housing authorities and housing action trusts may request a review of the landlord's decision to seek an order under section 84A.[84] Any request for a review must be made in writing 'before

81 HA 1985 s83ZA(5).
82 HA 1985 s83ZA(6).
83 HA 1985 s83ZA(7).
84 HA 1985 s85ZA(1).

the end of the period of seven days beginning with the day on which the notice under section 83ZA is served'.[85] For example, if the tenant is served with a notice on a Monday he must request a review before midnight on Sunday.

2.55   Once a tenant has requested a review the landlord must review its decision.[86]

2.56   The Absolute Ground for Possession for Anti-social Behaviour (Review Procedure) (England) Regulations 2014[87] govern the review procedure in England. The Secure Tenancies (Absolute Ground for Possession for Anti-social Behaviour) (Review Procedure) (Wales) Regulations 2014[88] govern the review procedure in Wales.

2.57   The application for a review need not be in any particular form, or even be in writing, but *must* include:

a) the applicant's name and address;
b) a description of the original decision in respect of which the review is sought including the date on which the decision was made;
c) a statement of the grounds on which the review is sought;
d) a statement to the effect that the applicant does, or does not, require the review to be conducted by way of an oral hearing;
e) a statement to the effect that the applicant does, or does not, agree to receive communications relating to the review by email, and if the former, the email address to which such communications should be sent.[89]

While the application does not need to be in writing and may be sent by email or text message, it will be hard to prove that the application complied with the above requirements where it was made orally and was not at least noted down by someone.

2.58   It is unclear whether the landlord is able to treat an application for a review which does not comply with regulation 2 as not having been made. Presumably, that was the intention of the 2014 Regulations, but they do not say that. Tenants' representatives should argue that section 85ZA requires a landlord to carry out a review whenever one has been requested; it does not provide that it need not carry out a review unless regulation 2 has been complied with.

2.59   If the tenant does not request an oral hearing the landlord must send a written notice to the applicant stating that the applicant may

---

85   HA 1985 s85ZA(2).
86   HA 1985 s85ZA(3).
87   SI No 2554.
88   SI No 3278 (W335).
89   2014 Regulations (England) reg 2; 2014 Regulations (Wales) reg 2.

make written representations in support of the application not earlier than five days after the day on which the notice has been *received* by the tenant.[90] If the notice is posted to the tenant it is treated as having been received by the tenant on the second business day after it is sent by first class post. For example, if it is sent on a Friday, it will be treated as being received on the following Tuesday. Otherwise, the notice is treated as being received by the tenant on the date it is sent by email,[91] personally served on the tenant or delivered by hand to the tenant's address.[92] Any representations received by the landlord must be considered by the person conducting the review.[93]

2.60   Where the tenant has requested a hearing the landlord must send a written notice to the applicant stating the date, time and place of the oral hearing. The hearing must not be heard earlier than five days (ten days in Wales) after the day on which the notice of the hearing is *received* by the applicant. The same rules, set out above at para 2.59, governing the service of notices applies. The landlord may, on the tenant's request, postpone the date of the hearing.[94]

2.61   The review, whether oral or not, may be conducted by anyone appointed by the landlord provided they were not involved in making the original decision. If it is an officer or employee of the landlord the person must be of greater seniority than the person who made the original decision.[95]

2.62   At an oral hearing the tenant may:

a) make oral or written representations relevant to the decision to be made on the review;

b) be accompanied or represented by another person appointed by the applicant for the purpose (whether that person is professionally qualified or not);

c) call persons to give evidence on any matter relevant to the decision to be made on the review; and

---

90 2014 Regulations (England) reg 5(1) and (2); 2014 Regulations (Wales) reg 5(1) and (2).
91 A notice may only be sent by email if the tenant has, when making an application for a review, specified that he is willing to receive communications by email: 2014 Regulations (England) reg 4(1); 2014 Regulations (Wales) reg 4(1).
92 2014 Regulations (England) reg 4; 2014 Regulations (Wales) reg 4.
93 2014 Regulations (England) reg 5(3); 2014 Regulations (Wales) reg 5(3).
94 2014 Regulations (England) reg 6; 2014 Regulations (Wales) reg 6.
95 2014 Regulations (England) regs 5 and 7; 2014 Regulations (Wales) regs 5 and 7.

d) put questions to any person who gives evidence at the hearing.[96]

2.63 Where a tenant, or a representative on his behalf, does not attend the hearing the review may proceed in the tenant's absence or adjourn the hearing.[97]

2.64 The person conducting the review must notify the tenant of its decision in writing, including its reasons where the decision is to uphold the decision to seek possession, 'before the day specified in the notice under section 83ZA as the day after which proceedings for the possession of the dwelling-house may be begun.'[98]

2.65 For example, if a weekly periodic tenant is given a notice on Monday 2 January 2017, and the tenant requests a review, the tenant must be notified of the landlord's decision, and if it is to uphold the original decision the reasons for doing so, by Sunday 29 January 2017. This is because the review must be concluded the day before the day after which proceedings may be begun.

2.66 If a landlord fails to comply with any of its obligations under section 85ZA or the 2014 Regulations the claim for possession, insofar as it relies on section 84A, must be dismissed. As the review procedure has a number of procedural requirements and must be completed within a very short time frame (in Wales the review and decision must be completed in less than a week) tenant's representatives should always pay very close attention to whether the landlord has complied with the review procedure; any deficiency should be relied upon to defeat the claim for possession.

Ground 2A: additional requirements

2.67 Where ground 2A (domestic violence) is relied upon in a HA 1985 s83 or s83ZA notice, and the partner who has left the dwelling-house as mentioned in that ground is not a tenant of the dwelling-house, the court shall not entertain proceedings for possession unless the landlord or, in the case of joint landlords, at least one of them has served on the partner who has left a copy of the notice or has taken all reasonable steps to serve a copy of the notice on that partner.[99] Unlike under HA 1988 s8A, the court may not dispense with such requirements unless the landlord has also relied on ground 2 in a

---

96 2014 Regulations (England) reg 7(5); 2014 Regulations (Wales) reg 7(5).
97 2014 Regulations (England) regs 8–9; 2014 Regulations (Wales) regs 8–9.
98 HA 1985 s85ZA(4)–(6); 2014 Regulations (England) reg 10; 2014 Regulations (Wales) reg 10.
99 HA 1985 s83A(3).

notice under HA 1985 s83 or served a notice in accordance with section 83ZA.[100]

2.68   Where proceedings have already begun, and the court gives the landlord permission to amend the HA 1985 s83 or s83ZA notice so as to rely on ground 2A, and the partner who has left the dwelling-house as mentioned in that ground is not a party to the proceedings, the court shall not continue to entertain the proceedings unless the landlord has served on the partner who has left a notice, or has taken all reasonable steps to serve such a notice, which

a)   states that proceedings for the possession of the dwelling-house have begun,
b)   specifies the ground or grounds on which possession is being sought, and
c)   gives particulars of the ground or grounds.[101]

2.69   The requirement to serve a notice under section 83A(4) may only be dispensed with if the landlord has also relied on ground 2 in a notice under HA 1985 s83 or served a notice in accordance with section 83ZA.[102]

Served on the tenant

2.70   The same rules on service of notices, as set out above for assured tenants at paras 2.23–2.24 apply to secure tenancies. Local authority landlords are not assisted in establishing service by the Local Government Act 1972 s233 (which permits service by post or hand delivery of statutory notices to the 'proper address', usually the last known address), because a notice seeking possession is not served by the authority in its capacity as a local authority but rather in the capacity of landlord.[103] To avoid these difficulties, the Court of Appeal has encouraged landlords of secure tenants to ensure that express provision for appropriate methods of service is made in the tenancy agreement itself.[104]

---

100 HA 1985 s83A(5).
101 HA 1985 s83A(4) and (6).
102 HA 1985 s83A(5).
103 See *Chesterfield BC v Crossley* June 1998 *Legal Action* 10 and *Eastbourne BC v Dawson* June 1999 *Legal Action* 23.
104 *Wandsworth LBC v Atwell* (1995) 27 HLR 536, CA and *Enfield LBC v Devonish* (1997) 29 HLR 691, CA.

Dispensing with the notice

2.71   As under HA 1988 s8, the court has the power to dispense with a notice under s83.[105] The court may not dispense with the requirements to serve a notice under s83ZA, ie where the absolute ground for possession is relied upon, or the additional notice requirements for ground 2A where ground 2 has not been relied upon in a notice under HA 1985 s83A or a notice has not been served under HA 1985 s83ZA.[106]

2.72   See above paras 2.28–2.30 for further discussion on the factors to be taken into account by the court when considering whether to dispense with the notice.

Old-style English and Welsh fixed-term tenancies

2.73   A landlord can bring a fixed-term secure tenancy[107] to an end before the term has expired in one of three ways provided that the tenancy itself is 'subject to termination by the landlord'.[108] This means that, in addition to the landlord serving a notice under either HA 1985 ss83, 83ZA or 83A and establishing that a ground is satisfied and that it is reasonable to make a possession order, the tenancy agreement must contain provision for the landlord to determine the fixed term before its expiry.

2.74   Provided this condition is met, the landlord's three options for bringing the fixed term to an end are either to:

a) obtain and execute a possession order,
b) obtain an order under HA 1985 s82(3), or
c) obtain a demotion order under HA 1985 s82A.[109]

2.75   HA 1985 s82(3) provides that the court may terminate the fixed term, with the effect that a secure periodic tenancy will arise on the expiry of the fixed term, in circumstances where it would otherwise have been brought to an end by a provision for re-entry.[110] This termination is, however, subject to Law of Property Act 1925 s146 and any

---

105 HA 1985 s83(1)(b) and (1A) and HA 1985 s84(1).
106 HA 1985 s83A(5).
107 Until the HPA 2016 Sch 7 para 4 came into force this included flexible tenancies: HA 1985 s107A(1) and (2). See paras 1.74–1.77.
108 HA 1985 s82(1)(b).
109 See chapter 6 for the circumstances in which a demotion order may be made.
110 HA 1985 ss82(3) and 86(1).

other enactment or rule of law relating to forfeiture, eg relief from forfeiture and waiver.[111] There are conflicting views as to whether the court has the power to make a possession order, in the same way it would for a periodic tenancy, before the landlord has brought the fixed term to an end under subsection (3).[112] However, the fact that Parliament has, under HPA 2016 s119, amended HA 1985 s82, insofar as it relates to new-style English tenancies, so as to provide expressly that it is unnecessary for a fixed term to be brought to an end before the court can make a possession order, would suggest that the fixed term must be brought to an end before the court has the power to make an order for possession as it would for a periodic tenancy.

New English secure tenancies and flexible tenancies

2.76   There are two circumstances in which a flexible tenancy or a new English secure tenancy can be brought to an end by order of the court: (1) during the fixed term under any of the statutory grounds for possession and (2) at the expiry of the fixed term.

During the fixed term

2.77   The procedure for bringing a flexible tenancy, ie a tenancy that was granted before HPA 2016 Sch 7 para 4 was brought into force,[113] to an end is the same as for old-style fixed-term secure tenancies (see above paras 2.58–2.72).

2.78   In respect of new English secure tenancies, ie those granted after HPA 2016 Sch 7 para 4 was brought into force,[114] the landlord may bring the fixed term *and* the tenancy to an end by obtaining an order of the court for the possession of the dwelling-house and the execution of the order.[115] Unlike, for flexible tenancies, there is no requirement to bring the fixed term to an end under HA 1985 s82(3) first.

---

111 HA 1985 s82(4). See also chapter 14 on forfeiture.
112 J Holbrook, 'In a fix', (2012) 162 NLJ 868 and A Dymond, 'Flexible tenancies and forfeiture' (2014) 17 JHL 4.
113 HA 1985 s115B. See paras 1.74–1.77.
114 HA 1985 s81A. See paras 1.89–1.91.
115 HA 1985 s82(A1), as amended by HPA 2016 s119.

2.79   The procedure for obtaining possession of a new English secure tenancy is no different to the requirements for old-style periodic tenancies, ie the landlord must serve a notice under HA 1985 s83 or s84A, and the court must be satisfied that both the ground and condition are satisfied.[116]

At the end of the fixed term: new English secure tenancies and flexible tenancies where the term does not end within nine months of Housing and Planning Act 2016 coming into force

2.80   A landlord must carry out a review to decide what to do at the end of the fixed term while the term still has six to nine months to run.[117] The landlord, at the conclusion of the review, has one of three options:[118]

1) offer to grant a new secure tenancy of the dwelling-house at the end of the current tenancy;[119]
2) seek possession of the dwelling-house at the end of the current tenancy but offer a secure tenancy of another dwelling-house instead; or
3) seek possession of the dwelling-house.[120]

2.81   The landlord must notify the tenant in writing of the outcome of the review, indicating which option it has decided to take, not later than six months before the end of the current tenancy.[121]

2.82   If the landlord has decided to seek possession of the dwelling-house (in either case) the landlord must inform the tenant that there is a right to a review of that decision under HA 1985 s86C within 21 days of the tenant being notified of the decision.[122]

2.83   The landlord must, on a request by the tenant, reconsider its decision and notify the tenant of its review decision (and give reasons where the decision is to uphold the original decision). In undertaking the review the landlord must, in particular, consider whether the original decision is in accordance with any policy that the landlord

---

116 HA 1985 s84. See para 2.39 above and chapter 3.
117 HA 1985 s86A(1) and (4).
118 HA 1985 s86A(5).
119 Note that this must be of a new English tenancy as opposed to an old-style secure tenancy.
120 In appropriate cases, the landlord may also offer the tenant advice on buying a home or on other housing options: HA 1985 s86A(6).
121 HA 1985 s86B(1)–(3).
122 HA 1985 s86B(4) and HA 1985 s86C(2).

has about the circumstances in which it will grant a further tenancy on the coming to an end of an existing fixed-term tenancy.[123]

2.84   The review procedure is governed by regulations made by the secretary of state.[124]

2.85   Once the fixed term has ended, provided the landlord has carried out a review in accordance with HA 1985 s86A and has not subsequently revised its decision under HA 1985 s86C (para 2.80 above), the landlord may bring proceedings for possession.[125] The court must make a possession order if it is satisfied that:

- the original fixed-term tenancy has ended and that the only fixed term in existence is one that has arisen under HA 1985 s86D(2) (see para 1.131);
- *all* of the requirements within sections 86A–86C have been complied with; and
- the proceedings were commenced within three months beginning with the day on which the tenancy ended unless the court is satisfied that a decision of the landlord not to grant a further fixed term was wrong in law.[126]

2.86   In the event that the court makes a possession order, the fixed-term tenancy, that has arisen under HA 1985 s86D(2), comes to an end once the possession order is executed.[127]

At the end of the fixed term: flexible tenancies where the term ended within nine months of Housing and Planning Act 2016 coming into force

2.87   On the coming to the end of a flexible tenancy, in which the term ended within the period of nine months beginning with the day on which HPA 2016 Sch 7 para 4 came into force, a court must make an order for possession of the dwelling-house if it is satisfied that the landlord has, at the request of the tenant, carried out a review of its decision not to grant another tenancy and the following conditions are met:[128]

123 HA 1985 s86C(3)–(5).
124 HA 1985 s86C(6). At the time of going to press no regulations had been made.
125 HA 1985 s86E(1).
126 HA 1985 s86E(2).
127 HA 1985 s86E(4).
128 HA 1985 s107D(1) and (6). Although repealed by HPA 2016, HA 1985 s107D–107E remain of application in relation to flexible tenancies where the term

1) The fixed term has ended and no tenancy other than a secure periodic tenancy is in existence.[129]
2) The landlord has given the tenant not less than six months' notice in writing –
   (a) stating that the landlord does not propose to grant another tenancy on the expiry of the flexible tenancy,
   (b) setting out the landlord's reasons for not proposing to grant another tenancy, and
   (c) informing the tenant of the tenant's right to request a review of the landlord's proposal and of the time within which such a request must be made.[130]
3) The landlord has, on or before the fixed term came to an end, given the tenant not less than two months' notice in writing stating that the landlord requires possession of the dwelling-house.[131]

2.88   In practice therefore, a flexible tenancy that simply ends will become a weekly periodic tenancy by virtue of HA 1985 s86(1) and cannot be brought to an end under section 107D. To have the benefit of HA 1985 s107D, the landlord must first have served a notice to the tenant that the tenancy will not be renewed. Second, the landlord must then carry out a review of that decision, provided the tenant has requested a review within 21 days of the notice being served on the tenant.[132] Finally, the landlord must give the tenant, before the fixed term has ended, two months' notice in writing stating that the landlord requires possession of the dwelling-house.

The notices

2.89   It is unclear whether the landlord must give the tenant the first notice (see above paragraph 2.87(2)) at a time when there is still more than six months of the fixed term left to run or if the landlord is simply precluded from bringing a claim for possession before six months have elapsed from the notice being served. However, if the words of the section are given their literal meaning it would appear that the landlord may serve a notice with less than six months of the term remaining and still bring a claim for possession.

ended within the period of nine months of HPA 2016 Sch 7 para 4 coming into force.
129 HA 1985 s107D(2).
130 HA 1985 s107D(3).
131 HA 1985 s107D(4) and (5).
132 HA 1985 s107E(1) and (2).

2.90   Likewise, it is also not clear whether the second notice can only be given after the first notice period had expired. It would appear that the landlord must at least wait until the review has concluded before serving the second notice.

The review

2.91   An application for a review must be made in writing and must include:

a) the applicant's name and address;
b) a description of the original decision in respect of which the review is sought including the date on which the decision was made;
c) a statement of the grounds on which the review is sought;
d) a statement to the effect that the applicant does, or does not, require the review to be conducted by way of an oral hearing;
e) a statement to the effect that the applicant does, or does not, agree to receive communications relating to the review by email, and if the former, the email address to which such communications should be sent.[133]

2.92   The review may be conducted by an officer or employee of the landlord, but must be a person who was not involved in making the original decision and is of greater seniority than the person who made the decision.[134]

2.93   Where the tenant has not requested an oral hearing, the landlord must send a written notice to the applicant stating that the applicant may make written representations in support of the application and that such representations must be made within five days of the notice being received.[135]

2.94   Where the tenant has requested an oral hearing, the landlord must send a written notice to the tenant stating the day on which, and the time and place at which it is proposed that the oral hearing is to take place. The date of the hearing must not be earlier than five days after the day on which the notice referred to in that paragraph is received by the tenant.[136] The landlord may adjourn the date of the hearing.[137]

---

133 Flexible Tenancies (Review Procedures) Regulations 2012 SI No 695 reg 2.
134 Flexible Tenancies (Review Procedures) Regulations 2012 SI No 695 regs 5(4)–(6) and 7(1)–(3).
135 2012 SI No 695 reg 5(1)–(3).
136 2012 SI No 695 reg 6(1)–(2).
137 2012 SI No 695 regs 6(3)–(4) and 9.

Where the tenant does not attend the landlord may proceed with the hearing or make other directions.[138]

2.95   At the hearing the tenant and the person who made the original decision may:

a) make oral or written representations relevant to the decision to be made on the review;

b) be accompanied or represented by another person appointed by the applicant for that purpose (whether that person is professionally qualified or not);

c) call persons to give evidence on any matter relevant to the decision to be made on the review; and

d) put questions to any person who gives evidence at the hearing.[139]

2.96   The person who conducted the hearing must make the final decision.[140] In reaching the decision, the reviewing officer must consider, in particular, whether the decision is in accordance with any policy of the landlord as to the circumstances in which it will grant a further tenancy on the coming to an end of an existing flexible tenancy.[141]

2.97   Once the review has concluded, the landlord must notify the tenant in writing of its decision and, where the decision is to uphold the decision not to grant a new tenancy, give the reasons for not doing so.[142]

2.98   Confusingly, HA 1985 s107E(8) requires that the tenant is notified of the outcome of the review before 'the date specified in the notice of proceedings as the date after which proceedings for the possession of the dwelling-house may be begun.' However, there is no requirement that such a date be included within the notice to the tenant that a new tenancy will not be granted.

2.99   Moreover, it is not clear that such a date could be given before the review is concluded because the second notice, ie giving the tenant two months' notice stating that the landlord requires possession, can only be given after the review has been concluded because before that time the landlord has no right to possession.

---

138 2012 SI No 695 reg 8.
139 2012 SI No 695 reg 7(5)–(7).
140 2012 SI No 695 reg 10.
141 HA 1985 s107E(3).
142 HA 1985 s107E(6) and (7).

The effect of not carrying out a review

2.100   If the court is bound to refuse the order for possession because the landlord has failed to carry out a review, it may make directions for there to be a review.[143] Accordingly, it does not follow that the failure to carry out a review will automatically result in the possession claim being dismissed.

---

143 HA 1985 s107D(7).

CHAPTER 3

Grounds and conditions for possession against assured or secure tenants

continued

Grounds and conditions

3.1 Once the court is seised of the substance of the claim for possession (in the sense that all the technical requirements scrutinised in chapter 2 have been met) it must first be satisfied that a *ground* for possession is made out. In respect of secure tenants, Housing Act (HA) 1985 s84(1) provides that:

> The court shall not make an order for the possession of a dwelling-house let under a secure tenancy except on one or more of the grounds set out in Schedule 2.

3.2 Likewise, in respect of assured tenants, HA 1988 s7(1) provides, so far as is material, that:

> The court shall not make an order for possession of a dwelling-house let on an assured tenancy except on one or more of the grounds set out in Schedule 2 to this Act.

3.3 If a ground within either HA 1985 Sch 2 or HA 1988 Sch 2 cannot be established, the proceedings must inevitably be dismissed. Each of the grounds is separately considered below (para 3.11 onwards). The burden of proof is on the landlord throughout to show that the ground is made out on the balance of probabilities.

3.4 While all grounds for possession contained within HA 1985 Sch 2 apply to all secure tenancies, only grounds 2, 7A, 8, 10, 11, 12, 13, 14, 14A, 15 or 17 of the HA 1988 (and ground 7 in England) apply to fixed-term assured tenancies (and then only if the tenancy contains a provision entitling the landlord to rely on that ground).[1]

3.5 Even if the court is satisfied that a ground is made out under HA 1985 in respect of a secure tenant or under HA 1988, possession is not to be ordered unless:

i) the tenancy agreement permits the ground to be relied upon,

ii) the ground has been specified in the notice seeking possession (which was served before the proceedings were commenced) or,

iii) where no notice has been served, and only when possible, a notice seeking possession has been dispensed with.

3.6 The routes available to a social landlord who makes out an alternative ground that has not been specified in a notice is to either:

i) seek permission of the court to amend the notice seeking possession to embrace the new ground;[2] or

---

1 HA 1988 s7(4), (6) and (6A).
2 HA 1985 s84(3); HA 1988 s8(2).

ii) adjourn the proceedings and serve a new notice seeking possession based on the new ground (perhaps with the intention of then
consolidating the new proceedings with the current proceedings);[3] or

iii) seek permission of the court to dispense with the requirement for
a notice seeking possession altogether.[4]

3.7   It does not necessarily follow, however, that a possession order
should be made because a ground for possession, that applies to the
tenancy, has been established. Although there are certain grounds in
respect of which a court has no choice but to make a possession order
once the ground has been satisfied, eg HA 1988 grounds 7A and 8
and HA 1985 ss84A and 90, in respect of other grounds the landlord
must also prove that any relevant conditions are also made out. In
respect of secure tenants HA 1985 s84(2) provides:

(2) The court shall not make an order for possession –
  (a) on the grounds set out in Part I of that Schedule (grounds 1 to
      8), unless it considers it reasonable to make the order,
  (b) on the grounds set out in Part II of that Schedule (grounds 9 to
      11), unless it is satisfied that suitable accommodation will be
      available for the tenant when the order takes effect,
  (c) on the grounds set out in Part III of that Schedule (grounds 12
      to 16), unless it both considers it reasonable to make the order
      and is satisfied that suitable accommodation will be available
      for the tenant when the order takes effect;
  and Part IV of that Schedule has effect for determining whether
  suitable accommodation will be available for a tenant.

3.8   Likewise, in respect of assured tenants HA 1988 s7(4) provides

(4) If the court is satisfied that any of the grounds in Part II of Sched-
    ule 2 to this Act is established, then, subject to subsections (5A)
    and (6) below, the court may make an order for possession if it
    considers it reasonable to do so.

3.9   If a landlord has proved a ground for possession, but cannot show on
the balance of probabilities that it is reasonable to make a possession
order, the court may adjourn (eg generally with liberty to restore or to
a fixed date) or dismiss the claim. If a landlord has proved a ground
for possession, and satisfied the court on the balance of probabilities that it is reasonable to make a possession order, the court may
make an absolute (or outright) order for possession or may make a
suspended or postponed order for possession (see paras 3.92–3.93).

---

3 *City of London Corp v Devlin* (1997) 29 HLR 58, CA.
4 HA 1985 s83(1)(b); HA 1988 s8(1)(b). See paras 2.28–2.30 and 2.71–2.72.

If a landlord has proved a ground for possession, but cannot show on the balance of probabilities that one of the conditions other than reasonableness which is relevant to the particular ground is satisfied, the claim for possession should be dismissed even though the ground has been proved.

3.10 Some of the grounds of possession contained in HA 1985 and HA 1988 are in similar or identical form. It is therefore common for the courts to apply the case-law concerning HA 1985 to cases brought under HA 1988 and vice versa. Therefore, where possible, this chapter will consider the grounds that are common to both Acts together under the following headings:

i) Rent arrears and other charges;
ii) Anti-social and criminal behaviour;
iii) Other breaches of tenancy;
iv) Tenancy obtained by deception or false statement;
v) Waste or the neglect/deterioration of furniture;
vi) Other grounds for possession against secure tenants;
vii) Other grounds for possession against assured tenants.

Rent arrears and other charges

Rent arrears: discretionary (HA 1988 grounds 10 and 11 and HA 1985 ground 1 (first limb))

3.11 The first limb of ground 1 of HA 1985 Sch 2 will be satisfied where the landlord proves that:

Rent lawfully due from the tenant has not been paid.

3.12 Ground 10 of HA 1988 Sch 2 will be satisfied if the landlord proves that:

Some rent lawfully due from the tenant –
(a) is unpaid on the date on which the proceedings for possession are begun; and
(b) except where subsection (1)(b) of section 8 of this Act applies [ie when the requirements of a notice have been dispensed with], was in arrears at the date of the service of the notice under that section relating to those proceedings.

3.13 Ground 11 of HA 1988 Sch 2 will be satisfied if:

Whether or not any rent is in arrears on the date on which proceedings for possession are begun, the tenant has persistently delayed paying rent which has become lawfully due.

3.14   It follows that HA 1985 ground 1 is satisfied whether or not there remain arrears, provided the landlord can prove that there were arrears of rent at the date the claim was issued (see below para 3.61). A landlord of an assured tenant must, however, plead ground 11 if the tenant has cleared the arrears by the date of the possession hearing.

3.15   As all three grounds are discretionary the court must also be satisfied by the landlord that the appropriate condition is met – in this case that it is reasonable to make the order.[5] If satisfied that it is reasonable to make an order, the court must then consider whether to make an immediate or postponed order.

The grounds

3.16   In the usual case, the landlord proves the ground, be it ground 1, 10 or 11, by showing, on the balance of probabilities:

- that rent was payable under the tenancy agreement;
- the particulars of the current rent due; and
- the record of payments made by the tenant.

CPR 55.8(3) provides that this evidence may be provided in the form of a written witness statement other than where the claim is allocated to the fast or multi-track or the court orders otherwise. As witness statements must be filed and served two clear days before a hearing (CPR 55.8(4)) it is hard to see, however, how a landlord can prove the extent of any arrears at a hearing with a witness statement that was drafted three days previously. How can the court be sure that no payments were made in the intervening period?

3.17   For the purpose of preparing a defence to a rent arrears possession claim based on discretionary grounds it is necessary to give careful consideration to the following points:

i) is all of what is being claimed rent?

ii) is the sum being claimed as rent each week, month or quarterly actually due?

iii) are the arrears lawfully due from the tenant or some other person?

iv) is the sum due unpaid?

If a landlord fails to prove grounds 1, 10 or 11, proceedings founded solely on either ground must be dismissed.

---

5   HA 1985 s84(2)(a); HA 1988 s7(4).

'rent'

3.18   The rent in question is the rent due in respect of the relevant property under the secure or assured tenant's tenancy agreement. *'Rent'* is not defined under either the HA 1985 or HA 1988. In addition to collecting basic 'rent', social landlords have a tendency to use the rent payment system to collect a variety of charges from tenants, ranging from fees for communal TV aerials to tenants' association membership subscriptions, and from rent for separate garages to heating charges. This begs the question whether these additional charges are 'rent' for the purposes of grounds 1, 10 or 11?

3.19   Nowadays, rent is defined as being 'a payment which a tenant is bound by his contract to pay to the landlord for the use of his land'.[6]

3.20   Other charges that would not historically be considered as rent, such as service charges, can, depending on the provisions of a tenancy agreement, be classified as rent. For example, in *Escalus Properties Ltd v Robinson*,[7] Nourse LJ held that a lease:

> ... [b]y providing that [the] service charge should be deemed to be sums due by way of additional rent, had the effect of conferring the like attributes on the service charge, an effect confirmed by the further provision that it should be recoverable as rent. To hold thus is to do no more than give full effect to the agreement between the parties ...

3.21   Rent can therefore, potentially, include any of the additional charges set out at para 3.18 above. Indeed, under the Rent Acts it has been held that 'rent' embraces the total monetary payment made to the landlord.[8] The correct position is likely to be that, provided the tenancy agreement is written in a way that requires such charges to be paid as rent or provides that such charges are to be paid in consideration for the tenant to use the land, then they will be payable as 'rent'.

3.22   That is not to say that any charge levied under a tenancy agreement can be characterised as rent merely by an express provision of the agreement; the payment of the charge must itself be an obligation of the tenancy. An obligation will not be an obligation of the tenancy, irrespective of whether it is included within the written agreement, where it is merely a personal obligation on the tenant.[9] In the context of charges, a charge that has no relation to the land

6   *United Scientific Holdings Ltd v Burnley BC* [1978] AC 904 at 934.
7   [1996] QB 231.
8   *Sidney Trading Co v Finsbury Corp* [1952] 1 All ER 460 at 461 and *Markworth v Hellard* [1921] 2 KB 755.
9   *RMR Housing Society v Combs* [1951] 1 KB 486. In *Combs* an obligation to remain in employment was held not be an obligation of the tenancy.

in question is therefore unlikely to be an obligation of the tenancy. It could therefore be argued that overpaid housing benefit, unpaid court costs, unpaid council tax or an administration fee levied at the start of the tenancy are personal obligations rather than obligations that arise from a relationship with the land.

3.23   In any event, in the absence of an express provision in the tenancy agreement, the tenant may argue that any additional charges are not rent.

3.24   In practice, however, provided the tenancy agreement provides for the charge to be payable, it is unlikely to be of any material relevance to a claim for possession brought on discretionary grounds (although cf para 3.102 for the position concerning ground 8 where it is of crucial importance). The second limb of ground 1 (HA 1985) and ground 12 (HA 1988) (considered below paras 3.111–3.120) provide that both grounds are satisfied when an obligation of the tenancy has not been performed. It follows that, provided either ground has been relied upon, the court may still make a possession order where such charges are an obligation of the tenancy agreement (see para 3.22 above) and have not been paid.[10]

'lawfully due'

3.25   Rent must be lawfully due from the tenant. It is therefore open to the tenant to assert in a defence that the rent is not yet payable or has been improperly fixed or increased and that accordingly the amount claimed is not 'lawfully' due. That involves a careful consideration of any statutory bars to recovery of the sum claimed and the contractual provisions for rent and rent increases in the tenancy agreement.

3.26   At common law, rent becomes lawfully due at midnight at the start of the day it is payable, but it is not in arrears until the end of that day.[11] Rent due on a Bank Holiday is not, however, payable until the following day.[12]

Particular issues may arise where a council includes other sums, such as water charges, as rent.[13]

---

10 See for example *Rochdale BC v Dixon* [2011] EWCA Civ 1173, [2012] PTSR 1336, where it was found that HA 1985 ground 1 was satisfied where a tenant refused to pay a charge for the use of water payable under his tenancy.

11 *Aspinall v Aspinall* [1961] Ch 526.

12 Banking and Financial Dealings Act 1971 s1(4).

13 *Jones v Southwark LBC* [2016] EWHC 457 (Ch), 4 March 2016, considered at para 3.119 below.

Set-off

3.27   Where a tenant successfully counterclaims against the landlord, and has pleaded set-off, the damages awarded for the counterclaim will reduce any arrears that are due.[14] A tenant cannot, however, plead set-off in relation to breaches committed by a landlord's predecessor in title unless the current landlord is making a claim for arrears of rent which had accrued prior to assignment.[15]

Statutory bars to recovery

3.28   Landlord and Tenant Act 1987 s48 provides that landlords must furnish tenants with an address in England and Wales at which notices may be served. Failure to provide that information means that any rent or service charges claimed is treated as not being due. A failure to comply with s48 does not extinguish the liability to pay the rent forever; as soon as a landlord provides a compliant notice, the tenant becomes liable to pay the rent and service charges.[16] A landlord can even provide a compliant notice after the point has been taken in a defence by a tenant in proceedings for arrears.[17]

3.29   Rent that is unpaid for more than six years is extinguished by the Limitation Act 1980 s22 and therefore ceases to become due. In practice, however, section 22 is of limited application because the landlord can choose to appropriate future payments of rent to any existing rent arrears unless, when the payment of rent is made, the tenant expressly appropriates the payment to the latest rent due. Moreover, the landlord can elect to appropriate any payments made by the tenant at any time.[18]

Secure periodic tenants

3.30   Where the landlord is a local housing authority there may be an assertion that in breach of its statutory duty the council has not fixed a reasonable rent.[19] Although this is a straightforward assertion to make, it is exceptionally difficult to prove.[20] A successful defence of not 'lawfully' due may be raised if the rent increase was based

14   *Etherington v Burt* [2004] EWHC 95 (QB), [2004] All ER (D) 117.
15   *Muscat v Smith* [2003] EWCA Civ 962, [2004] HLR 6.
16   *Lindsey Trading Properties Inc. v Dallhold Estates (UK) Pty Ltd* (1995) 70 P&CR 332.
17   *Rogan v Woodfield Building Services Ltd* (1995) 27 HLR 78.
18   *Milverton Group Ltd v Warner World Ltd* [1995] 32 EG 70 at 73.
19   HA 1985 s24. See *Wandsworth LBC v Winder (No 1)* [1985] AC 461, (1985) 17 HLR 196, HL.
20   *Wandsworth LBC v Winder (No 2)* (1987) 20 HLR 400, CA.

on some misinterpretation by the landlord of the relevant housing finance legislation (as in *R v Ealing LBC ex p Lewis*[21]). Such an argument will, however, be almost impossible to run without the evidence of an expert in housing finance.

3.31   Similarly, the rent claimed is not lawfully due if the landlord has failed to observe any contractual or statutory requirements as to notice of increase.[22] Such requirements are strictly construed.[23] Furthermore, rent cannot usually be lawfully increased on account of any improvement work by the tenant.[24] In the case of a secure housing association tenant with a registered fair rent, the maximum rent recoverable will be that so registered. Any excess will not be 'lawfully due'.

3.32   Since 1 April 2016, local housing authorities, have, however, been required to reduce the amount of rent paid by their tenants by one per cent per year for the following four years.[25] It is therefore arguable that a rent that is not set in accordance with the 'cut' is not lawfully due and not recoverable.

3.33   When chapter 3 of Part 4 of the Housing and Planning Act (HPA) 2016 comes into force some tenants with high incomes will be required to pay higher rents than other tenants: either the market rate or a proportion of the market rate.[26] The amount that each tenant will have to pay is likely to be the subject of a complicated taper and will be based on information given to the landlord about the tenant's household income. It will therefore be necessary to consider the regulations, when made, to ensure that the rent levied is in accordance with the taper and corresponds to the tenant's household income. Where the rent is set too high it should be argued that the additional rent is not recoverable. It is likely that the regulations will govern the procedure for increasing the rent under the tenancy agreement; if that process has not been complied with, it may be possible to argue that the increased rent is not payable.

---

21   (1992) 24 HLR 484, (1992) 90 LGR 571, CA.

22   HA 1985 s102. For the correct approach to construction of tenancy agreement provisions relating to rent increases see *Riverside HA v White* [2007] UKHL 20, [2007] HLR 31 below paras 3.45–3.46. See too *Rent Lawfully Due* July/August 2014 *Legal Action* 49 and *Housing: Rent Lawfully Due* June 2016 *Legal Action* 38.

23   *Clements & O'Boyle v Brent LBC* March 1990 *Legal Action* 12.

24   HA 1985 s101.

25   Welfare Reform and Work Act 2016 s23(1).

26   HPA 2016 s80.

Fixed-term secure tenancies (flexible tenancies and new English secure tenancies)

3.34   Historically, these were very rare. They are now much more common, and will become increasingly more common, after the gradual abolition of the periodic secure tenancy by HPA 2016.

3.35   HA 1985 s103 does not apply to fixed-term tenancies. The terms of a fixed-term or flexible tenancy may only be varied:

i)   by agreement between the landlord and the tenant; or

ii) to the extent that the variation relates to rent or to payments in respect of rates, council tax or services, by the landlord or the tenant in accordance with a provision in the lease or agreement creating the tenancy, or in an agreement varying it.[27]

3.36   Therefore, in the absence of an agreement with the tenant, the local authority can only vary the rent in accordance with the terms of the tenancy agreement. If the local authority has not followed the procedure set out in the tenancy agreement then it will not have increased the rent and any difference between the previous and increased rent will not be lawfully due.

3.37   The cut in social housing rents from 1 April 2016 (see above para 3.32) does not, however, just apply to periodic tenants. It follows that irrespective of the terms of the tenancy agreement it is arguable that any rent that is not set in accordance with the cut is unlawful and not recoverable. At the very least, it ought not to give rise to a possession claim on the grounds of rent arrears.

3.38   Where the tenant's rent has been increased under chapter 3 of HPA 2016, as with periodic tenancies, consideration should be given as to whether the rent set is in accordance with the regulations (see above para 3.33).

Fixed-term assured shorthold tenants

3.39   HA 1988 does not have a mechanism for increasing a fixed-term assured shorthold tenant's rent unless provision is made for increasing the rent in the tenancy agreement. Accordingly, if the landlord has not followed the procedure provided for in the tenancy agreement any increased rent will not be due.

3.40   However, from 1 April 2016 private registered providers of social housing, in England, have been under an obligation to reduce the amount of rent paid by their tenants by one per cent per year for the

27   HA 1985 s102(1).

following four years.[28] It is therefore arguable, irrespective of what the tenancy agreement provides, that it is unlawful for providers not to make the one per cent cut and that any landlord that does not make the cut should be prevented from relying on the additional rent as founding a claim for possession.

3.41   Private registered providers of social housing have a discretion as to whether to set an increased rent for tenants with high incomes. If the tenant's landlord has adopted a policy to increase the rent consideration should be given as to whether the increased rent is in accordance with the policy and, crucially, whether the tenancy agreement allows for the rent to be increased. As there is no statutory mechanism to increase the rent, any increase in the rent that is not permitted by the tenancy agreement will be unlawful.

Assured periodic tenants

3.42   HA 1988 s13 governs the procedure by which a landlord may lawfully increase the rent of a statutory periodic assured tenant. Rent will therefore not be due if the landlord of an assured tenant has sought to increase the rent and failed to comply with HA 1988 s13.

3.43   To lawfully increase an assured tenant's rent a landlord must comply with the following requirements:

a) serve a notice in the prescribed form; and[29]
b) propose a date for increasing the rent which is:
    i)   at the beginning of a new period of the tenancy,[30]
    ii) at least one month after the date the notice was served,[31]
    iii) at least 52 weeks after the tenancy began,[32] and
    iv) at least 52 weeks after the rent was last increased under section 13.[33]

3.44   HA 1988 s13 does not, however, apply if the tenancy agreement itself governs the procedure by which the landlord may increase the rent under the tenancy.[34] In those circumstances, it will be necessary to check that the landlord has complied with the terms of the tenancy agreement for increasing rent.

---

28 Welfare Reform and Work Act 2016 s23(1). Albeit this does not apply to supported housing until 1 April 2017.
29 HA 1988 s13(2).
30 HA 1988 s13(2).
31 HA 1988 s13(2)(a).
32 HA 1988 s13(2)(b).
33 HA 1988 s13(2)(c).
34 HA 1988 s13(1)(b).

3.45   In *White v Riverside Housing Association Ltd,*[35] the association's tenancy agreement provided that the landlord could increase the rent by giving the tenant four weeks' notice in writing and that the rent payable would take effect from the first Monday in June. The House of Lords held that a proper construction of this agreement meant that the association could only increase the rent once a year on any date from and including the first Monday in June provided the tenant had been given four weeks' written notice.

3.46   This decision was based purely on the construction of the tenancy agreement. The House of Lords did hold, however, that had the tenancy agreement stated that the only date on which the defendants' rent could have been increased had been the first Monday in June then it would have prohibited the association from increasing the rent on any other date.

3.47   As many tenancy agreements do provide that rent may only be increased on a particular date or day, it is important to check that the procedure has been complied with.[36]

3.48   In any event, as for fixed-term assured shorthold tenants, registered providers are under an obligation, from 1 April 2016, to cut the rent by one per cent per year for the following four years.[37]

3.49   If the landlord has decided to charge higher rents for tenants with higher incomes the same considerations as discussed in para 3.33 above apply.

'from the tenant'

3.50   Only the rent due from the tenant is relevant. The importance of this restriction question arises where the tenancy has been transmitted by succession (ie after a tenant's death) or has been assigned.

Succession

3.51   Under the Rent Acts, a successor to a statutory tenancy is not liable for the arrears of the former tenant.[38] One obvious exception to this is where the person succeeding to the tenancy was the deceased's joint tenant as he or she would have been joint and severally liable for the rent. Likewise, if a suspended possession order was made before the death of the former tenant the person entitled to succeed

---

35 [2007] UKHL 20, [2007] HLR 31.

36 See too *Rent Lawfully Due* July/August 2014 *Legal Action* 49 and *Housing: Rent Lawfully Due* June 2016 *Legal Action* 38.

37 Welfare Reform and Work Act 2016 s23(1).

38 *Tickner v Clifton* [1929] 1 KB 207.

to the tenancy takes the tenancy subject to the suspended possession order. While the successor is not personally liable for the arrears, if he or she does not comply with the terms of the suspended possession order the court may order that possession be given.[39] In practice therefore, where a suspended possession order has been made, the successor will have to discharge the arrears to be able to keep the tenancy.

3.52   There is no reason to doubt that the same principles apply to secure and assured tenants.

3.53   If the successor is the executor of the deceased's estate, he or she will be under an obligation to use whatever assets have vested in the deceased's estate (but not his own) to meet any liabilities that existed prior to the deceased tenant's death. This includes rent arrears although such arrears do not take priority over other debts.[40] In the absence of any assets within the estate, however, the executor is not personally liable for the arrears.

3.54   Where there is no one qualified to succeed to the tenancy, an executor or personal representative becomes liable, but only on behalf of the estate and not personally, for the payment of rent from the date of the former tenant's death until the tenancy is determined, irrespective of whether he moves in.[41] Where the tenancy has vested in the Public Trustee – and no one has succeeded to the tenancy – no person is liable to pay the arrears as the Public Trustee takes the property free of any obligations.[42]

Assignment

3.55   Where a lawful assignment is made, an assignee (ie the person who takes over the tenancy) is not liable for a breach of covenant that arose prior to the assignment taking place. This is the case for tenancies that were granted both before and after the implementation of the Landlord and Tenant (Covenants) Act 1995.[43] For example, in *Notting Hill Housing Trust v Jones*,[44] the defendant had received the secure tenancy on its transfer to her from her former husband pursuant to an order made in family proceedings. He owed arrears of rent. The tenant agreed to clear those arrears by instalments. Thereafter,

39   *Sherrin v Brand* [1956] 1 QB 403.
40   *Youngmin v Heath* [1974] 1 WLR 135.
41   *Youngmin v Heath* [1974] 1 WLR 135.
42   Administration of Estates Act 1925 s9.
43   *Parry v Robinson-Wyllie Ltd* (1987) 54 P&CR 187 and Landlord and Tenant (Covenants) Act 1995 s23(1).
44   [1999] L&TR 397.

she paid her current rent but failed to clear the arrears. The housing trust brought possession proceedings based on non-payment
of the old 'arrears'. The Court of Appeal dismissed the proceedings
– the amount outstanding was not rent due from the defendant, the
present tenant.

3.56   In respect of tenancies granted before 1 January 1996, there is
no reason, however, why a landlord may not insist, either within
the tenancy or as a condition of consenting to an assignment of an
assured tenancy, upon the assignee entering into a covenant to pay
any arrears that existed prior to his assignment. It is likely, however,
that where the Landlord and Tenant (Covenants) Act 1995 applies, a
landlord may not insist, either within the tenancy agreement or as a
condition of giving consent, on a covenant that requires the assignee
to meet the assignor's past obligations, eg to pay rent, because such
an agreement would frustrate the application of the Act.[45]

3.57   It is unclear, in the absence of authority, if the principle in *Sherrin
v Brand* (see para 3.51 above) applies to assigned tenancies. It might
be argued, however, that if it frustrates the application of the Landlord and Tenant (Covenants) Act 1995 then it should not.[46]

3.58   Any one of a number of joint tenants may be sued for the whole
rent due from the commencement of their joint tenancy. There is no
legal concept of one joint tenant's 'part' or 'proportion' of the rent.
The whole rent is 'lawfully due' from each of them.

'unpaid' or 'has not been paid'

3.59   If all arrears are cleared before the issue of proceedings, the court is
not able to order possession under ground 1.[47] This is so, even if the
landlord can prove that there were arrears at the date of the notice
seeking possession or that there is a history of poor payment. The
position is different for assured tenants: ground 11 is satisfied if a
tenant has failed persistently to pay rent as and when it has fallen
due.

3.60   The landlord cannot seek to avoid this consequence by refusing to
accept or by returning payments tendered shortly before the issue of
proceedings, even if they are substantially late.[48]

3.61   If arrears were outstanding at the date of issue of the proceedings
but are cleared before the hearing or on the hearing date, while the

45 Landlord and Tenant (Covenants) Act 1995 s25.
46 See too Law of Propeerty Act 1925 s136.
47 *Bird v Hildage* [1948] 1 KB 91, CA.
48 *Bird v Hildage* [1948] 1 KB 91, CA

court may find the ground to be satisfied as a general rule it will be rare for the court to make a possession order.[49] If there were arrears at date of issue, a tenant who produces a cheque before the hearing is taken to have paid the sum provided that the cheque subsequently clears. Accordingly, in circumstances where a tenant provides the landlord with a cheque shortly before the hearing, and insufficient time has passed for it to have cleared into the landlord's account, the proper approach of the court is to adjourn the claim to see whether the cheque would be paid if the sum rendered would have a significant impact on the possession claim.[50]

3.62   In spite of apparent arrears shown on the (often computer-generated) rent account, it may be that there are in fact no true arrears of rent or only a lesser amount than that shown. A number of possibilities should be carefully checked.

3.63   First, the tenant may have made payments not in fact recorded as received. These may either be very recent payments that had not reached the rent account by the date it was printed or earlier payments that the landlord has attributed to the wrong account. Many large social landlords have an account holding substantial amounts in 'unattributed' receipts from current or former tenants.

3.64   Second, the landlord may be charging an incorrect (higher) rent than that actually payable under the tenancy, including sums that are not rent or are arrears from a previous tenant.[51]

3.65   Third, if the tenant has been having deductions made from welfare benefits by the Department for Work and Pensions those monies deducted may have been received by the landlord direct from the DWP, but not yet applied to the account. Such 'direct deductions' are usually paid in a lump sum every four weeks in arrears.

3.66   Fourth, even if there is an amount of rent seemingly owing, that may be matched or exceeded by an amount which the tenant is entitled to set off, for example, the cost of repair work which the tenant has had to undertake because of the landlord's default in undertaking repairs or the damages awarded to the tenant on a counterclaim. Such a set-off will act as a complete defence to the claim for rent if it exceeds or extinguishes the arrears.[52] All these possibilities repay careful consideration.

---

49 *Dellenty v Pellow* [1951] 2 KB 858, CA and *Haringey LBC v Stewart* (1991) 23 HLR 557, CA.

50 *Day v Coltrane* [2003] EWCA Civ 342, [2003] 1 WLR 1379.

51 See paras 3.30–3.49 above.

52 See above para 3.27.

Housing benefit

3.67   The payment of, or entitlement to, housing benefit may also be relevant to what if any rent remains outstanding.

3.68   An entitlement to *housing benefit* does not, of itself, serve to reduce or eliminate liability for rent. It is only when such benefit is awarded by the benefit authority, and (if the rent is not a rebated council rent) actually paid to the landlord, that liability for rent is satisfied (see chapter 16). From that point in time the rent will have been 'paid' even if there is an administrative delay in attributing it to the particular tenant's rent account. If the landlord is the benefit authority itself, 'payment' is made by rebating the rent otherwise payable and showing only a net amount to be paid as rent. It appears from the forms of 'payment' listed in the Social Security Administration Act 1992 s134(2)[53] that the tenant's liability for the rent is satisfied by such a rebate, even if the local authority subsequently decides that there has been an overpayment of housing benefit. If the authority debits the amount of the overpaid housing benefit on the rent account, this sum should not be treated as rent arrears and should be kept separate in the account.[54] However, the council may recover the overpayment by weekly deductions from current housing benefit entitlement, so that the tenant will have to make up the shortfall in the rent from other resources. Where the tenant of a social landlord other than the benefit authority has been overpaid housing benefit and the overpayment has been recovered directly from that landlord by the benefit authority, the landlord may seek to debit the amount of the overpayment to the tenant's rent account, with the result that the tenant will be placed in rent arrears and will be vulnerable to possession proceedings.[55]

Reasonableness

3.69   Even if the court is satisfied that there has been a failure to pay rent lawfully due, it cannot make a possession order of any description (including a 'suspended' or 'postponed' order) unless it is also satisfied that in all the circumstances of the case it would be reasonable to do so.[56] Even if the court is satisfied that it is reasonable to make

---

53   As amended by the Welfare Reform Act 2007.
54   See *R v Haringey ex p Ayub* (1993) 25 HLR 566 and *Complaint against Wychavon DC*, Local Government Ombudsman Investigation 90/B/2514, 23 March 1992.
55   Housing Benefit Regulations 2006 reg 95(2)(b).
56   HA 1985 s84(2)(a); HA 1988 s7(4).

a possession order it must also consider whether it is appropriate, necessary or proportionate to postpone or suspend the execution of the order under HA 1985 s85 or HA 1988 s9 (see below paras 3.92–3.93).

3.70   The court, in assessing reasonableness, is required to have regard to all relevant factors but has a very wide discretion as to what weight and how much weight it applies to each factor.[57] These will include the duration of the tenancy, the age of the tenant, the past rent record of the tenant, compliance with the *Pre-action Protocol for possession claims by social landlords* (see paras 3.77–3.81), whether the failure to pay rent is persistent, whether there have been earlier agreements to clear arrears, the conduct of the landlord in seeking or waiving amounts due and the personal circumstances of the tenant. While all cases turn on their own facts and there are no general rules that ought to be applied in a rigid fashion, the cases set out below are useful illustrations of the correct application of the principles.

3.71   In *Woodspring DC v Taylor*,[58] the Court of Appeal held that a particular decision that it was reasonable to make a possession order was a conclusion that no reasonable judge could reach because, notwithstanding the seriousness of the arrears (circa £700), at the date of the hearing:

i)   the tenant was paying the rent plus a contribution towards the arrears;

ii) the arrears had arisen through no fault of the tenant;

iii) the tenant had a good history of paying the rent; and

iv) the tenant's wife was in ill health.

3.72   Likewise, in *Brent LBC v Marks*,[59] a secure tenant, having earlier fallen into arrears, was receiving housing benefit by way of rent rebate in respect of almost all her rent. The shortfall (water rates), together with a weekly sum of £2.50 in respect of the arrears, were being deducted at source from her welfare benefits and paid over quarterly in arrears to the council landlord. In January 1997 the council served notice seeking possession and claimed possession under ground 1. A judge granted possession, suspended on payment of current rent plus £2.50 per week to meet the arrears of £1,500. On appeal, the Court of Appeal set the order aside and remitted the claim for rehearing. As it was clear that the social security office was paying the deducted

---

57   *Bracknell Forest BC v Green* [2009] EWCA Civ 238, [2009] HLR 38. See too the quotations from *Cumming v Danson* [1942] 2 All ER 653, CA at 3.174 below.

58   (1981–82) 4 HLR 95.

59   (1999) 31 HLR 343.

amounts quarterly in arrears, the terms of the order requiring weekly payment unnecessarily put the tenant at risk of breach of the order. The relevant material about the history of the reduction of the arrears had not been properly put before the judge. As to the retrial, Butler-Sloss LJ indicated that the first main matter for the judge to deal with would be 'whether there should be an order for possession at all'. The council failed to recover its costs both in the county court and in the Court of Appeal.

3.73   In *Second WRVS Housing Society v Blair*,[60] the Court of Appeal set aside an order for possession made against a young, single man who owed £1,200 rent (in 1985) and had been a tenant for only eight years. The judge had not adequately considered: (a) the possibility of arranging direct payment of current rent from the housing benefit authority to the landlord; (b) the possibility of the social security office deducting small amounts from the tenant's welfare benefits and paying them direct to the landlord towards the arrears; and (c) the tenant's medical condition.

A tenant's lack of capacity and mental health may also be a relevant factor that will mean it will not be reasonable to make a possession order. In *Peabody Trust v Evans*, a district judge found that it was not reasonable to make a possession order where the landlord had simply referred the tenant to the welfare benefits team; the tenant suffered from a number of disabilities that had been a factor in giving rise to his arrears.[61]

3.74   In *Sopwith v Stutchbury*,[62] the Court of Appeal overturned an immediate possession order and held that a court should not ordinarily make an immediate possession order where the arrears are not substantial and the tenant's conduct is not such to justify an outright possession order.

3.75   In *Dellenty v Pellow*,[63] the Court of Appeal upheld a decision that it was reasonable to make a possession order in circumstances where the tenant had paid all of the arrears the day before the possession hearing. While as a general rule it would rarely be reasonable to make a possession order where the arrears had been cleared, in this case it was reasonable because the tenant had frequently been in arrears and proceedings had been issued on a number of occasions.

---

60 (1986) 19 HLR 104, CA.
61 September 2014 *Legal Action* 47, Wandsworth County Court.
62 (1985) 17 HLR 50.
63 [1951] 2 KB 858.

3.76 The same result was also reached in *Drew-Morgan v Hamid-Zadeh*.[64] The Court of Appeal held it to be reasonable to make a possession order where the refusal to pay had been 'deliberate and avoidable' and the arrears had not been cleared until the date of the hearing.

Pre-action Protocol for possession claims by social landlords

3.77 A *Protocol for Possession Claims based on Rent Arrears* ('Rent Arrears Protocol') came into force on 2 October 2006. This was updated in April 2015 and re-titled *Pre-action Protocol for possession claims by social landlords*. It includes a new section concerning claims brought on mandatory grounds. The existing section content concerning rent arrears claims brought on discretionary grounds remains substantially unchanged. The protocol is a critical document for both the parties and the court in relation to any action for possession brought by a social landlord on the basis of rent arrears.

3.78 The aim of Part 2 of the Protocol is to encourage more pre-action contact between the parties and to enable court time to be used effectively. The Protocol requires landlords bringing claims under discretionary grounds to:

- contact the tenant as soon as reasonably possible once he or she falls into rent arrears to discuss the cause of the arrears, the tenant's financial circumstances, his or her entitlement to benefits and payment of the arrears;
- attempt to agree an affordable sum for the tenant to pay off the arrears and (where appropriate) assist in arranging for direct payments to be made towards the arrears from the tenant's benefit entitlement;
- provide the tenant with a full rent statement;
- take reasonable steps to ensure that information has been appropriately communicated;
- if appropriate, arrange for arrears to be paid by the DWP from tenants' benefit;
- assist the tenant in connection with his or her claim for housing benefit and establish effective liaison with the housing benefit department;
- refrain from taking possession action where the tenant has a reasonable expectation of eligibility for housing benefit and has provided all the evidence necessary for the claim to be processed;

---

64 (2000) 32 HLR 316.

- if a possession claim must be brought, contact the tenant before the court hearing to discuss the current position with regard to the arrears and housing benefit;
- postpone the court proceedings where the tenant has reached an agreement to pay the current rent and arrears, so long as the tenant keeps to the agreement; and
- encourage the tenant to attend the court hearing.

3.79   If a landlord unreasonably fails to comply with the terms of the Protocol the court may impose a sanction or sanctions in the form of costs and/or adjournment of the proceedings or may strike out or dismiss the claim. If the tenant unreasonably fails to comply with the terms of the Protocol, the court may take such failure into account when considering whether it is reasonable to make a possession order.

3.80   Whether it is reasonable to make a possession order in a rent arrears case may well be influenced by the landlord's conduct both in relation to the Protocol and in the management of the arrears issue in the particular case.

Since 2015, landlords bringing claims under ground 8 have been required to comply with Part 3 of the Protocol. Paragraph 3.2 of the Protocol requires landlords to write to occupants in advance of the claim to explain why they intend to seek possession and to invite the occupiers to, within a specified period, notify the landlord of any personal circumstances or other matters that they wish to be considered. The landlord is then expected to consider those representations before deciding whether to issue a claim for possession. Paragraph 3.3 of the Protocol further requires landlords to, within its particulars of claim or a witness statement, confirm that it has complied with paragraph 3.2 and give brief reasons for deciding to bring the claim. However, unlike under Part 2 of the Protocol, there are no sanctions for non-compliance with the Protocol. In practice therefore, the court will not be entitled to dismiss the claim or postpone an order in the event that Part 3 of the Protocol has not been complied with. It may, however, be more willing to grant an adjournment to allow a defendant to file a public law or human rights defence and, potentially, to award the occupier its costs of the hearing.

Non-statutory good practice guidance

3.81   Extensive good practice guidance on rent recovery by social landlords (although non-statutory) has been published. For example, in 2006, the *Guide on Effective Rent Arrears Management*[65] was published and intended to be read with the (then) new Rent Arrears Protocol. 'The guidance is aimed at social landlords and all levels of a landlord's rent arrears management service ... It sets out clearly the DCLG view ... that social landlords should seek to maintain and sustain tenancies, rather than terminate them and that eviction should be used as a last resort.' In respect of court action for possession based on arrears of rent, it states at para [11]:

- Tenants should never be served with a Notice Seeking Possession (NSP) until the landlord has established personal contact or exhausted all possible means of doing so.
- NSPs should be served on tenants with unresolved Housing Bene-fit claims only where it has been established beyond doubt that the claim remains outstanding due to the tenant's failure to supply requested information or provide requested documents or if the tenant is failing to pay agreed personal contributions.
- Existing regulatory and good practice guidance for registered social landlords stresses that eviction is the last resort.
- Prior to court action landlords should seek a meeting with the tenant and agencies supporting them if appropriate, whilst also reviewing the tenant's personal circumstances and actions taken.
- Landlords taking tenants to court should encourage and assist the tenant to contact agencies providing relevant advice, and/or counselling services, as well as to access legal advice and to attend hearings.
- During court proceedings, and where a repayment agreement has already been struck, it is good practice to seek an adjournment on terms rather than a postponed Possession Order (*note*: following the introduction of an amended possession procedure in July 2006, as a result of the decision in *Harlow DC v Hall*, a possession order where possession is deferred will be called a 'postponed possession order', replacing the previous widely used but incorrect 'suspended possession order' and this replacement term should be read into the guidance).

3.82   The court's attention should be drawn to the guidance where the landlord's practices do not meet these standards or where proceedings have been brought without trying other methods of rent recovery. Particular emphasis might be placed on the three concluding paras of the *Guide* which state:

12. Social landlords should seek to maintain and sustain tenancies and should only seek to terminate a tenancy and evict as a last resort.

---

65 DCLG, August 2006. Available to download at www.gov.uk/government/publications/effective-rent-arrears-management.

13. Landlords should have in place a clear strategy for preventing and managing rent arrears, produce clear guidance for officers and have in place robust systems for prevention and management. They should put in place measures to prevent arrears accruing and seek to maximise rental income.

14. Where arrears have accrued landlords should seek early intervention through personal contact with the tenant, offering support and advice and agreeing a way forward for recovering the arrears. These strategies should be evaluated for cost-effectiveness and overall effectiveness.

Housing benefit

3.83   Historically, if tenants of social housing were unable to afford their rent they would, save for where they were ineligible, be entitled to housing benefit to cover the shortfall. Moreover, it was even possible to make a backdated claim, sometimes for up to six months, for housing benefit to clear any, or at least some, of the arrears that had built up and had caused the possession claim to be issued.

3.84   This meant that a tenant's representative could ordinarily rely on the powerful submission that where there was an apparent entitlement to housing benefit there should be an adjournment to allow an application, accompanied with a backdated claim, for housing benefit to be made or for enquiries to be made as to why the tenant's housing benefit had ceased or been suspended.

3.85   Unfortunately, there are now a number of social housing tenants who struggle to pay their rent because they have one or more spare bedrooms, so that the 'bedroom tax' applies. Or their housing benefit is otherwise cut by the benefit cap. In such cases, the tenant's representative should still seek an adjournment to allow the tenant to make an application for discretionary housing payments (DHPs) which may be able to clear some of the existing arrears) and/or, if appropriate, to make an application to the housing benefit authority to de-classify one or more bedrooms within the property. This is especially the case where the tenant is disabled and his or her disability means that the tenant requires a spare bedroom for other legitimate reasons. It is strongly arguable that the refusal to provide DHPs in such circumstances would amount to unlawful discrimination under Human Rights Act 1998 Sch 1 Articles 8 and 14.[66] Chapter 16 considers the 'bedroom tax', 'benefit cap' and DHPs in more detail.

66 See *Rutherford v Secretary of State for Work and Pensions* [2016] EWCA Civ 29, [2016] HLR 8.

3.86   An adjournment should therefore still be sought if there remains a reasonable prospect that the shortfall will be met and/or some of the arrears cleared. In such cases, it should be argued that a court should delay considering whether or not a possession order should be made until all outstanding housing benefit issues have been resolved. It is not possible to consider whether or not it is reasonable to make a possession order until the court knows the true figure for the arrears and that DHPs will not cover the rent. A proposed application for discretionary housing payments coupled with a disrepair set-off ought to obtain at least an adjournment.

3.87   Where an application for discretionary housing payments and an application to de-classify a bedroom has been made and the tenant is still unable to pay the rent, eg because the applications have been refused or the award of DHPs is insufficient to cover the remaining shortfall, the arguments available to resist a possession order are much more limited. One possible argument is that the tenant is willing to move to a smaller and more affordable property and the tenant's landlord has either refused to move the tenant or unreasonably delayed in processing any such application. Otherwise, public law defences (chapter 25) under the Equality Act 2010 (chapter 27) or the Human Rights Act 1998 (chapter 26) may be available.

3.88   In other cases, where the bedroom tax or benefit cap do not apply, it is arguable that it is not reasonable for a court to make a possession order in circumstances where:

i) the delay by the local housing authority in processing the claim for housing benefit or in considering a tenant's change of circumstances, especially if it is the landlord, has, at least in part, caused the arrears;

ii) the tenant has not been provided with debt advice or with sufficient assistance, by their landlord, with their housing benefit application; or

iii) the landlord has not arranged with the Department for Work and Pensions for the deduction at source of a small amount from the tenant's welfare benefit to pay off the arrears.

3.89   Where housing benefit is in payment and it is covering the rent in full, or if not in full the tenant has demonstrated over a number of weeks a willingness and ability to pay whatever rent remains outstanding, and the tenant is making regular contributions towards the arrears, save for in exceptional cases (eg where the tenant has a particularly poor payment history and the arrears are very high), it is strongly arguable that the court ought to find that it is not reasonable to make a possession order and rather to adjourn the claim on terms that the tenant pay the rent and whatever he or she can afford each week towards the arrears.

Set-off and counterclaims

3.90   Where there are arrears but the tenant has an arguable set-off or counterclaim (see para 3.27), the court will be unable to decide the claim at the first hearing (as it will need to determine first if there is a set-off or counterclaim that reduces or extinguishes the arrears). It can adjourn the claim and give directions.[67] The most common example of an arguable set-off is a claim for disrepair. Another potential set-off may arise where a tenant has repeatedly faced unmeritorious claims for possession based on rent arrears, which have been repeatedly dismissed by the courts and is seeking damages for harassment.[68]

3.91   However, if arrears have arisen because the tenant has *withheld* the rent, he or she should be advised of the need to put the rent aside rather than spend it. In *Haringey LBC v Stewart,*[69] the secure tenant withheld rent on account of alleged disrepair. At trial, his counterclaim for damages for disrepair was dismissed. In relation to the possession claim, the tenant was then unable to repay the withheld rent amounting to over £1,000 (because it had been spent rather than set aside) and made no proposals as to payment of current rent or payment of the arrears. The Court of Appeal declined to interfere with a decision that it was reasonable to make an outright possession order.

Immediate or postponed order?

3.92   Once a court has decided it is reasonable to make a possession order it must decide whether to fix or postpone the date of possession. HA 1985 s85 provides (with the relevant passage emphasised in italics):

> (1) Where proceedings are brought for possession of a dwelling-house let under a secure tenancy on any of the grounds set out in Part I or Part III of Schedule 2 (grounds 1 to 8 and 12 to 16: cases in which the court must be satisfied that it is reasonable to make a possession order), the court may adjourn the proceedings for such period or periods as it thinks fit.

---

67   CPR 55.8(1).
68   *Allen v Southwark LBC* [2008] EWCA Civ 1478.
69   (1991) 23 HLR 557, CA.

(2) On the making of an order for possession of such a dwelling-house on any of those grounds, or at any time before the execution of the order, the court may –
    (a) stay or suspend the execution of the order, or
    (b) *postpone the date of possession,*
    for such period or periods as the court thinks fit.
(3) On such an adjournment, stay, suspension or postponement the court –
    (a) shall impose conditions with respect to the payment by the tenant of arrears of rent (if any) and rent, unless it considers that to do so would cause exceptional hardship to the tenant or would otherwise be unreasonable, and
    (b) may impose such other conditions as it thinks fit.

3.93   Likewise, HA 1988 s9 provides that where a ground for possession is made on a discretionary ground:

(1) ... the court may adjourn for such period or periods as it thinks fit proceedings for possession of a dwelling-house let on an assured tenancy.
(2) On the making of an order for possession of a dwelling-house let on an assured tenancy or at any time before the execution of such an order, the court, subject to subsection (6) below, may –
    (a) stay or suspend execution of the order, or
    (b) *postpone the date of possession,*
    for such period or periods as the court thinks just.
(3) On any such adjournment as is referred to in subsection (1) above or on any such stay, suspension or postponement as is referred to in subsection (2) above, the court, unless it considers that to do so would cause exceptional hardship to the tenant or would otherwise be unreasonable, shall impose conditions with regard to payment by the tenant of arrears of rent (if any) and rent and may impose such other conditions as it thinks fit.

3.94   Once the court has decided that the conduct of the tenant and the level of arrears warrant a possession order, the court should decide whether to make an outright possession order, or whether to fix or postpone the date of possession. The court has a wide discretion. The correct approach is to determine the extent of the rent arrears and how quickly those are likely to be paid. The fundamental purpose of a suspended possession order is to enable the arrears to be paid within a reasonable time.[70]

3.95   In *Laimond Properties Ltd v Raeuchle*,[71] the Court of Appeal held that in circumstances where a tenant had offered to repay the arrears

---

70 *Taj v Ali (No 1)* (2001) 33 HLR 253, CA.
71 (2001) 33 HLR 113.

at a rate which would have seen them cleared within a year, and there was not a history of the tenant breaching earlier orders, the court ought to have made a suspended possession order. In that case, at the date of trial, there were arrears of £511.10 and the tenant had offered to pay £10 per week. Sedley LJ, on granting permission to appeal, said that, in his experience:

> ... it would have been unique to find an outright order made in circumstances such as these, even against a tenant as difficult as this one where there was no history (and there was none) of breaches of the conditions upon which previous orders have been suspended. There was indeed no history of suspended possession orders.

3.96 In *Lambeth LBC v Henry*,[72] the defendant was a secure tenant. The council obtained an order for possession and judgment for arrears and costs of £2,375. The tenant appealed, contending among other things, that the order had been wrong in principle because its terms would involve a suspended order hanging over them for 23 years with the tenancy liable to be lost automatically on any breach.

3.97 The Court of Appeal dismissed the appeal. A suspended possession order (SPO) had been the obvious order to make. Although the court practice was to be merciful to tenants and to give them a realistic opportunity to pay arrears, the question of whether it was appropriate for Ms Henry, who owed substantial arrears, to have the threat of losing her home hanging over her for years was a political question and did not go to the correctness of making the order. The order was fully permitted under HA 1985 as it stood. There were, in any event, cases in which long-term suspension of possession orders was appropriate and this was such a case.

3.98 Landlords often rely on *Taj* (see footnote 70 above) as authority for the proposition that suspended possession orders 'should not extend into the mists of time'. Where, however, the tenancy is in effect a 'lifetime' social housing tenancy a 'reasonable period' can be for a very long time. Indeed, in *Henry*, the Court of Appeal reminded itself that home owners are often given the lifetime of their mortgage to repay arrears (see para 3.96) and there was no reason why a similar length of time could not apply to social housing tenants. Plainly this argument is of less force where the tenancy is for a fixed term of between two and ten years.

A tenant who has been made bankrupt or made subject to a debt relief order (DRO) may not be required, as a condition of a suspended order, to repay any arrears that are covered by the bankruptcy or DRO.

Rent arrears: mandatory (HA 1988 ground 8)

3.99 Ground 8 is satisfied in the case of an assured tenant if:

> Both at the date of the service of the notice under section 8 of this Act relating to the proceedings for possession and at the date of the hearing –
> (a) if rent is payable weekly or fortnightly, at least eight weeks rent is unpaid;
> (b) if rent is payable monthly, at least two months rent is unpaid;
> (c) if rent is payable quarterly, at least one quarter's rent is more than three months in arrears; and
> (d) if rent is payable yearly, at least three months' rent is more than three months in arrears;
> and for the purpose of this ground 'rent' means rent lawfully due from the tenant.

3.100 There is no equivalent to ground 8 in the HA 1985; it only applies to assured tenants. Under ground 8, two months' rent arrears, where rent is lawfully due from the tenant, (or eight weeks' arrears in the case of a weekly tenancy) give a landlord an automatic right to a possession order. It follows that if the tenant does not appear to have a conventional defence, eg rent 'not lawfully due' or a counterclaim, he or she should consider raising an Equality Act 2010 defence (see chapter 27) or a public law defence (see chapter 25) or a human rights defence (see chapter 26). In particular, as a number of registered providers of social housing have policies that prohibit the use of ground 8 other than in limited circumstances, consideration should be given to whether the landlord is in breach of their own policy.

3.101 A possession order cannot be made under ground 8 unless the landlord proves that a valid HA 1988 s8 notice has been served. There is no discretion to dispense with a section 8 notice if ground 8 is relied on.[73]

3.102 The points concerning whether rent is 'payable' and 'due' from the tenant remain of equal, if not of greater, importance under ground 8 (see paras 3.18–3.58). The question of whether a charge is 'rent', however, is of particular importance because, unlike under the discretionary grounds (where the second limb of HA 1985 ground 1 and HA 1988 ground 12 can be relied upon), ground 8 cannot be satisfied if the charge outstanding is not rent.

---

73 HA 1988 s8(5). See para 2.28.

3.103   Money which a defendant has been ordered to pay into court (and has been paid in) to await the outcome is available 'on account of rent arrears' and is treated as though it were rent 'paid' because ignoring such money would lead to an artificial and inequitable result when calculating arrears for the purpose of ground 8.[74]

3.104   At the date of the hearing the landlord must prove that there were eight weeks' or two months' arrears, both at the time when the notice of the landlord's intention to bring proceedings was served and at the date of the hearing. 'The date of the hearing' is the date when the claim is heard. It is not the date fixed for the hearing if, on that date, an adjournment is granted without a hearing taking place at all.[75]

3.105   The court retains jurisdiction to grant an adjournment at any time before it is satisfied that the landlord is entitled to possession. A court may lawfully adjourn a possession hearing where, for example, there is no judge available or because the defendant is prevented by ill health from attending court. Likewise, it may be a proper exercise of discretion to adjourn where there is an arguable claim for damages which can be set off against arrears or where the tenant shows that there is otherwise an arguable defence, eg he or she has paid the rent owed.[76]

3.106   However, it is not legitimate for a court to adjourn the hearing to enable the tenant to pay off arrears and so defeat the ground 8 claim for possession, unless there are exceptional circumstances, eg if a tenant is robbed on the way to court or if a computer failure prevents the housing benefit authority from being able to pay the tenant's housing benefit until the day after the hearing date.[77] However, the fact that arrears are attributable to maladministration on the part of the housing benefit authority is not an exceptional circumstance.[78]

3.107   Once the court has expressed the conclusion that it is satisfied that the landlord is entitled to possession, there is no power to grant an adjournment in any circumstances (see HA 1988 s9(6)). The court cannot be 'satisfied' within the meaning of section 9(6) until the

---

74 *Etherington v Burt* [2004] EWHC 95 (QB), [2004] All ER (D) 117.
75 *North British Housing Association Limited v Matthews* [2004] EWCA Civ 1736, [2005] HLR 17.
76 *North British Housing Association Limited v Matthews* [2004] EWCA Civ 1736, [2005] HLR 17.
77 *North British Housing Association Limited v Matthews* [2004] EWCA Civ 1736, [2005] HLR 17.
78 Ibid and *Marath v MacGillivray* (1996) 28 HLR 484, CA. In cases where arrears have been caused by delays in paying housing benefit, it is worth considering issuing a witness summons to compel the appropriate official to attend at court to explain personally the reason for any delay.

judge has given a judgment and effect is given to that judgment in a perfected order of the court.[79]

3.108   It follows that in practice, where a tenant faces a claim for possession under ground 8, the only way for him or her to obtain time to pay the rent arrears is to apply for an adjournment *before* evidence has been heard. The following are examples, albeit in different contexts, of where the court has exercised its discretion to adjourn a case:

i)   to allow a tenant to obtain legal aid and representation;[80]
ii) to allow a tenant's appeal against a decision to refuse him or her legal aid to be determined;[81] and
iii) pending the outcome of an appeal to the Supreme Court.[82]

3.109   In a case where an outright order for possession was made under HA 1988 Sch 2 ground 8, but the landlord subsequently accepted the tenant's offer to pay rent and £100 per month off arrears, the Court of Appeal held that the landlord had done nothing to affect the legal relations between the parties.[83] No new or different terms were come to. The landlord had no intention to create a new tenancy. The legal relations between the parties were governed by the terms of the order until the landlord took a position inconsistent with the order.

3.110   As ground 8 is mandatory, once the court is satisfied that the ground is proved, there is no power to postpone the date for possession.[84] However, unless it is clear from the face of the order that a possession order was made on mandatory grounds the court should treat a possession order as if made on discretionary grounds.[85]

Sums in addition to rent: discretionary (HA 1988 ground 12 and HA 1985 ground 1 (second limb))

3.111   Ground 1 of HA 1985 Sch 2 further provides that (subject to it being reasonable in all the circumstances to grant possession) an order for possession can be made against a secure tenant if:

an obligation of the tenancy has been broken or not performed.

---

79   Ibid.
80   *Bates v Croydon LBC* [2001] EWCA Civ 134, (2001) 33 HLR 792.
81   *Birmingham CC v Lloyd* [2012] EWCA Civ 744.
82   *Kingcastle Ltd v Owen-Owen* (1999) *Times* 18 March.
83   *Stirling v Leadenhall Residential 2 Ltd* [2001] EWCA Civ 1011, [2002] 1 WLR 499.
84   HA 1988 s9(6).
85   *Capital Prime Plus Plc v Wills* (1999) 31 HLR 926.

3.112   Ground 12 of HA 1988 Sch 2 is satisfied in respect of an assured tenant if:

> Any obligation of the tenancy (other than one related to the payment of rent) has been broken or not performed.

3.113   One of the most common obligations relied on in such cases is an obligation in the tenancy agreement to pay additional sums together with the rent, such as water rates.[86] It is therefore often of limited relevance whether the charge is defined as rent or not.

3.114   Consideration must, however, be given to whether the obligation which is relied on by the landlord arises from an express or implied term of the tenancy agreement itself, and not from some collateral agreement (eg, the separate renting of a garage or a free-standing agreement to clear a previous tenant's arrears of rent[87]). A failure to comply with the condition attached to a separate grant of permission to carry out improvements is, however, specifically brought within HA 1985 ground 1 and HA 1988 ground 12.

3.115   The term breached must be a term of the tenancy itself, not a matter of mere personal obligation on the part of the tenant. Obligations to pay outstanding court costs, administration fees levied at the start of the tenancy or other charges, such as council tax, are unlikely to be terms of the tenancy.

3.116   In preparing the defence, the tenancy terms should be carefully checked to see whether the term relied on by the landlord is in fact a term of the agreement applicable to the tenant's *present* tenancy. Landlords often produce to the court the 'current version' of their standard tenancy agreement. However, the true tenancy agreement is the one originally entered into by the tenant, subject to any statutory or contractual procedure for variation.[88] A variation cannot be achieved simply by sending the tenant a 'fresh' tenancy agreement, even if after having received such a document, the tenant remains in occupation and pays the rent.[89]

3.117   In addition, the term relied on by the landlord should be scrutinised carefully to see whether it is 'fair' for the purposes of Part 2,

---

86   *Lambeth LBC v Thomas* (1998) 30 HLR 89, CA and *Rochdale BC v Dixon* [2011] EWCA Civ 1173, [2012] HLR 6.

87   *Notting Hill Housing Trust v Jones* [1999] L&TR 397, CA.

88   HA 1985 ss102 and 103 for secure tenancies. There is no equivalent statutory procedure for assured tenancies.

89   *Palmer v Sandwell MBC* (1988) 20 HLR 74, CA and *Carolan and Hamnett v Warrington BC* June 2000 *Legal Action* 24.

Consumer Rights Act 2015.[90] Useful guidance as to 'fairness' in this context is provided by the Competition and Markets Authority on what terms are, or might be, unfair.[91] If the term is unfair the court should reject any attempt to rely on it in ground 1 proceedings.[92]

3.118   Where the sum being claimed is in respect of water charges consideration should also be given to whether the landlord is a re-seller of water or merely acting as the water utility company's agent.

3.119   In *Jones v Southwark LBC*,[93] the High Court held that Southwark LBC had, between 2000 and 2010, been a re-seller of water and sewerage services within the meaning of the Water Resale Order 2006 and that it was therefore prevented from charging its tenants a commission for recovering the charges. Southwark was found to be a water re-seller because its agreement with Thames Water contained no reference to: tenants being liable to pay water or sewerage charges to Thames Water; Thames Water authorising Southwark to collect such charges on its behalf; Southwark owing any duty of skill and care; Southwark having any obligation to invoice tenants or in respect of complaints from them. Moreover, the commission paid to Southwark was nothing of the sort. It simply reduced what Southwark had to pay Thames Water and was not conditional on a service being performed. Equally important was the fact that until 2010 it was Southwark that had been liable to pay Thames Water for water charges. It could not therefore have been Thames Water's agent during that time as its tenants were not liable to pay Thames Water.

3.120   The High Court, in *Jones*, distinguished two earlier cases[94] in which the Court of Appeal had held that the local authority was, in the context of those agreements, collecting the water charges as the utility company's agent.

---

90 SI No 2083. See also footnote 291 at para 1.197.
91 *Unfair contract terms guidance; Guidance on the unfair terms provisions in the Consumer Rights Act 2015*, 31 July 2015: www.gov.uk/government/uploads/system/uploads/attachment_data/file/450440/Unfair_Terms_Main_Guidance.pdf.
92 *R (Khatun, Zeb and Iqbal) v Newham LBC* [2005] QB 37, [2004] HLR 29, CA and *Rochdale BC v Dixon* [2011] EWCA Civ 1173, [2012] HLR 6.
93 [2016] EWHC 457 (Ch), [2016] HLR 14.
94 *Rochdale BC v Dixon* [2011] EWCA Civ 1173, [2012] HLR 6 and *Lambeth LBC v Thomas* (1997) 30 HLR 89.

Anti-social and criminal behaviour

3.121   There are now a number of grounds that both local housing authorities and private registered providers of social housing can rely on
to recover possession from tenants or members of their households
who commit acts of anti-social and criminal behaviour. They may
also claim that such conduct amounts to a breach of the tenancy
agreement and so rely on the second limb of ground 1 of HA 1985
and ground 12 of HA 1988. See para 3.255 below. Since the last
edition of this book the Anti-social Behaviour, Crime and Policing
Act 2014 has created three[95] further grounds for possession, one of
which includes a new mandatory ground for possession that has its
own special requirements for notices and reviews.[96]

3.122   Generally, the law governing the provision of notices where a
landlord intends to rely on an anti-social behaviour ground for possession is different from the law governing notice of other grounds.
Claims for possession under HA 1985 grounds 2, 2ZA, 2A and HA
1988 grounds 14, 14ZA and 14A may be begun as soon as a notice
seeking possession has been served, while claims under HA 1985
ground s84A and HA 1988 ground 7A are subject to a statutory and
non-statutory review process (see paras 2.31, 2.54–2.66). In a case of
really serious nuisance or criminality it is not uncommon for a landlord to simply issue proceedings immediately and invite the court to
exercise its power to dispense with notice seeking possession altogether (see paras 2.21 and 2.46). This is not be possible where one of
the new mandatory grounds is relied upon.

3.123   In this part of this chapter the following will be considered:

i)   each of the discretionary grounds;
ii) when it will be reasonable to make a possession order;
iii) when it will be appropriate to make a postponed as opposed to
     immediate order; and
iv) the mandatory grounds for possession.

3.124   It is clear that anti-social behaviour cases involving alleged nuisance
can give rise to difficult issues of fact and law and that the risk of a possession order being made is such that the tenant should have a proper opportunity to prepare a defence and secure representation.[97]

---

95 Two in Wales.
96 See paras 2.25 and 2.49–2.53.
97 *Bates v Croydon LBC* [2001] EWCA Civ 134, (2001) 33 HLR 792.

The grounds

Nuisance or annoyance to a person in the locality of the dwelling-house: discretionary (HA 1988 ground 14 (first limb) and HA 1985 ground 2 (first limb))

3.125　The first limb of ground 2 of HA 1985 Sch 2 and ground 14 of HA 1988 is satisfied where:

> The tenant or a person residing in or visiting the dwelling-house
> (a) has been guilty of conduct causing or likely to cause a nuisance or annoyance to a person residing, visiting or otherwise engaging in a lawful activity in the locality ...

'the tenant or a person residing in or visiting the dwelling house'

3.126　The ground imputes the secure or assured tenant with responsibility for the actions of *any* others living in *or* visiting the property – not just members of the same household. In this sense the ground is one of 'strict liability' – its terms may be satisfied even in a case where the tenant did not know that a co-resident or visitor was causing a nuisance or where, if the tenant had known, he or she would have been powerless to stop it.[98]

3.127　　However, a casual caller to tenant's home, who is guilty of causing nuisance or annoyance, may arguably not be 'visiting the dwelling-house' for the purposes of the ground if his or her visit is uninvited or positively unwelcome to the tenant. Likewise, someone who causes nuisance or annoyance after they have been refused admittance to the property will not satisfy grounds 2 or 14. Otherwise a tenant may be faced with a claim for possession based on the activities of a person coming to the property for the purpose of causing nuisance to him or her, such as a violent ex-partner.

'guilty'

3.128　The use of the term 'guilty' does not impose a requirement that conduct be deliberate or culpable. In *Kensington and Chelsea RLBC v Simmonds*,[99] the tenant's teenage son, who resided with her, had deliberately engaged in conduct amounting to nuisance. He was therefore 'guilty' of such conduct and ground 2 was satisfied. The Court of Appeal rejected the contention that the ground could be satisfied only if there was also some fault on the tenant's part. It did

98　*Portsmouth CC v Bryant* (2000) 32 HLR 906, CA.
99　(1997) 29 HLR 507, CA.

hold that the existence or extent of any personal blame on the tenant's part would be relevant to the question of 'reasonableness' (discussed below at para 3.199). That approach has likewise been applied to the current wording of ground 2 by the Court of Appeal in *Portsmouth CC v Bryant*[100] and again more recently in *Tuitt v Greenwich RLBC*.[101]

3.129   A court cannot, however, treat the fact that a person has been arrested as evidence of either anti-social or criminal behaviour. The trial judge must decide whether or not the behaviour which caused the tenant to be arrested actually happened on the balance of probabilities.[102]

3.130   In *Croydon LBC v Moody*,[103] a point was taken that the defendant tenant was so affected by mental illness as to have been incapable of being 'guilty' of the conduct complained of, which was simply a manifestation of his illness. However, as the conduct was also a breach of a tenancy term and the landlord was relying on ground 1 (which makes no reference to 'guilty' – see para 3.255), as well as ground 2, the issue did not need to be resolved. For a possible defence under the Equality Act 2010 in these circumstances, see chapter 27.

'nuisance or annoyance'

3.131   The meaning of 'nuisance' is not restricted in this context to the narrow legal meaning of the terms 'public nuisance' and 'private nuisance'.[104] Indeed, the words 'or annoyance' add to and broaden the concept of nuisance. Both words are given their ordinary rather than their technical legal meanings. 'Annoyance' has been held to cover anything likely to trouble ordinary sensible persons even though not involving physical interference with their comfort.[105] The necessary 'conduct' to be proved may possibly be constituted by one single act but is more likely to be shown through a number of examples of similar behaviour. The particulars of claim must detail the 'conduct' alleged.[106]

100   (2000) 32 HLR 906, CA. See too, *Bedfordshire Pilgrims HA v Khan* [2007] EWCA Civ 1445.
101   [2014] EWCA Civ 1669, [2015] HLR 10.
102   *Wandsworth LBC v Webb* [2008] EWCA Civ 1643.
103   (1999) 31 HLR 738, CA.
104   *Harlow DC v Sewell* [2000] EHLR 122, February 2000 *Legal Action* 25, CA.
105   *Tod-Heatly v Benham* (1888) 40 ChD 80 at 98, per Bowen LJ.
106   CPR PD 55A para 2.4A.

'likely to cause'

3.132   There is no need for the landlord to prove that any person was actually the victim of nuisance or annoyance – it is sufficient if there is evidence of conduct that was *likely* to cause such nuisance or annoyance (so that no victim need give evidence). The landlord may prove the ground using the evidence of those who simply saw or heard the misconduct complained of, for example, a police officer, an environmental health patrol member, a caretaker or other 'professional' witnesses. If the judge is prepared to give it sufficient weight, even pure hearsay evidence may satisfy the court that the ground is made out.[107]

'to a person residing, visiting or otherwise engaging in a lawful activity in the locality'

3.133   A much wider group of potential victims than simply 'neighbours' is embraced by the ground. It extends to the protection of others living in, visiting or otherwise lawfully conducting themselves in the locality. It is therefore not limited to behaviour that occurs within the dwelling-house, provided it takes place in its locality.[108] The term 'locality' is not defined. It was substituted for the word 'vicinity' which appeared in earlier drafts of the legislation and was thought too narrow. It is an ordinary English word requiring no special elaboration or definition. Any issue as to whether the matters complained of took place within the 'locality' of the dwelling is to be resolved as a question of fact on all the evidence.[109]

3.134   The availability of this wide ground for possession does not mean that a victim can always expect it to be used by a social landlord. Even if its terms are satisfied, the landlord cannot be required to instigate proceedings in reliance on it unless there is an express term in the victim's own tenancy agreement that the landlord will bring such proceedings on request. There is certainly no implied term which requires the landlord to take action under grounds 2 or 14 in the case

---

107 *Leeds City Council v Harte* April 1999 *Legal Action* 27, CA. See also *Solon South West Housing Association Ltd v James* [2004] EWCA Civ 1847, [2005] HLR 24; *Washington Housing Company Ltd v Morson* [2005] EWHC 3407 (Ch) and *Incommunities Ltd v Boyd* [2013] EWCA Civ 756, [2013] HLR 44. On the caution which must be exercised in reliance on hearsay in residential tenancy cases see *Moat Housing v Harris and Hartless* [2005] EWCA Civ 287, [2005] HLR 33.

108 *Northampton BC v Lovatt* (1998) 30 HLR 875, CA.

109 *Manchester City Council v Lawler* (1999) 31 HLR 119, CA.

of neighbour nuisance. The victim cannot compel the landlord to act in the absence of an express agreement to do so.[110]

Nuisance and annoyance directed at a landlord: discretionary ground (HA 1988 ground 14 (second limb) and HA 1985 ground 2 (second limb))

3.135   Ground 2(aa) and ground 14(aa) were inserted into both Schedule 2 to the HA 1985 and Schedule 2 to the HA 1988 by the Anti-social Behaviour, Crime and Policing Act 2014 s98 on 13 May 2014. The purpose of the ground is to cover anti-social behaviour that is directed at a landlord's employee, but which occurs away from the locality, eg at a housing office. The ground is satisfied where:

> The tenant or a person residing in or visiting the dwelling-house – has been guilty of conduct causing or likely to cause a nuisance or annoyance to the landlord of the dwelling-house, or a person employed (whether or not by the landlord) in connection with the exercise of the landlord's housing management functions, and that is directly or indirectly related to or affects those functions.

'the tenant or a person residing in or visiting the dwelling house'

3.136   The same principles as set out at paras 3.126–3.127 apply. The grounds are satisfied if someone other than the tenant, who is residing in or visiting the dwelling-house, is guilty of conduct causing, or likely to cause, a nuisance.

'guilty of conduct causing or likely to cause a nuisance or annoyance'

3.137   The same principles as set out at paras 3.128–3.130 apply.

'to the landlord of the dwelling-house, or a person employed (whether or not by the landlord)'

3.138   Unlike under the first limb, these grounds are satisfied where the behaviour is directed at the landlord. It can, however, include behaviour that is directed at the landlord's employees or other people who are employed but not by the landlord, eg contractors.

---

110 *O'Leary v Islington LBC* (1983) 9 HLR 81, CA; *Hussain v Lancaster City Council* (1999) 31 HLR 164, CA and *Mowan v Wandsworth LBC* (2001) 33 HLR 56, CA.

'in connection with the exercise of the landlord's housing management functions'

3.139   These grounds are, however, limited to behaviour that is directed at employees *in connection* with the landlord's housing management functions. While the behaviour may be committed away from the property, theoretically even in another country, the second limb of the ground would not be satisfied unless the person is employed in *connection* with the landlord's housing management functions. It will therefore presumably cover anti-social behaviour directed at anyone employed to facilitate the landlord's housing management functions. For the meaning of 'housing management functions' see para 6.9.

3.140   It is unclear if this will include behaviour directed at employees when they are off-duty, eg at the weekend in the pub or in the supermarket. It would be surprising, however, if, where the cause of the abuse relates to the landlord's housing management functions, the court did not construe the ground to include this behaviour. If the cause of the behaviour is wholly unrelated to the landlord's housing management functions, ie it is a purely personal dispute, it is arguable that the ground ought not to apply.

3.141   It is also arguable that the use of the word 'employed' does not cover volunteers or people not acting under the direction of another, eg truly self-employed individuals. It is, however, unlikely that this is what Parliament intended.

Domestic violence: discretionary ground (HA 1988 ground 14A and HA 1985 ground 2A)

3.142   Ground 2A and ground 14A were introduced into Schedule 2 to the HA 1985 and Schedule 2 to the HA 1988 by the HA 1996 s145. The grounds have been subsequently amended by the Civil Partnership Act 2004. The grounds can be satisfied where:

> The dwelling-house was occupied (whether alone or with others) by a married couple, a couple who are civil partners of each other, a couple living together as husband and wife or a couple living together as if they were civil partners and –
> (a) one or both of the partners is a tenant of the dwelling-house,
> (b) one partner has left because of violence or threats of violence by the other towards –
>   (i) that partner, or
>   (ii) a member of the family of that partner who was residing with that partner immediately before the partner left, and

(c) the court is satisfied that the partner who has left is unlikely to return.

3.143 The ground is designed to deal with what might be broadly described as 'domestic violence', particularly where this has housing management implications for the landlord. The ground is most commonly relied on where the landlord has re-housed the departed victim of violence, leaving the perpetrator under-occupying the former family home.

3.144   Special requirements concerning service of notices seeking possession apply if possession is to be sought on grounds 2A and 14A (see paras 2.67–2.69 and 2.26–2.27). If the partner who has left is not the tenant (or one of the joint tenants), the landlord must serve a copy of the notice on that partner or show that it has 'taken all reasonable steps' to do so.[111] Likewise, if permission is given to add grounds 2A or 14A to a notice seeking possession after proceedings have started, the landlord must serve a special notice on the departed partner if he or she is not a party in the proceedings, or show that it has 'taken all reasonable steps' to do so.[112] The court cannot entertain a ground 2A claim unless these requirements are met. The notice under s83A can be dispensed with only if (a) the landlord has also specified ground 2 (nuisance – see above) in the notice seeking possession and (b) it is just and equitable to do so.[113] In contrast, in a case relying on ground 14A, the court appears to have a power to dispense with the requirement to serve a notice under HA 1988 s8A where the landlord has not served a notice under s8.[114]

3.145   Presumably, the rationale for providing the departed partner with these copy notices is that in all save the most urgent cases the departed partner should be forewarned that the former family home is at risk so that he or she might make any appropriate application under the Family Law Act 1996 Part IV for occupation or transfer orders before the tenancy is lost (see chapter 20).

'occupied by a ... couple'

3.146 The ground has no application where there is no 'couple' as defined by the ground, ie a married couple, civil partners or a couple living together as husband and wife or as if civil partners. This means that

---

111 HA 1985 s83A(3); HA 1988 s8A(1).
112 HA 1985 s83A(4); HA 1988 s8A(2).
113 HA 1985 s83A(5); HA 1988 s8A.
114 HA 1988 s8A(1)(b).

the ground does not apply where, for example, the violence of a child causes a parent to leave. It must be a partner who leaves. It is not necessary to prove that the couple were living together as a couple at the date that the violence occurred which caused the person to leave the dwelling-house.[115]

In *Southern Housing Group v Nutting*,[116] Evans-Lombe J held that for a person to be treated as living with the tenant as his or her spouse the relationship had to satisfy two tests:

- Is the relationship an emotional one of mutual lifetime commitment rather than simply one of convenience, friendship, companionship or the living together of lovers?
- Is the relationship one which has been presented to the outside world openly and unequivocally so that society considers it to be of permanent intent – the words 'till death us do part' being apposite?

'one or both the partners is a tenant of the dwelling-house'

3.147   One or both of the partners must also be the tenant. Accordingly, the ground does not apply where neither of the partners is the tenant.

'one partner has left because of violence or threats of violence'

3.148   The landlord must prove that one of the partners who left did so because of violence or the threat of violence. Violence, in the context of HA 1996 Part 7, has been held to include, in addition to actual physical violence, other threatening or intimidating behaviour or abuse, provided it is of such a nature and seriousness as to be liable to cause psychological harm.[117] There is no reason why a similar meaning would not apply to the ground under either the HA 1985 or HA 1988.

3.149   It is not necessary for the landlord to establish that the violence was the sole cause of the partner's departure. However, it will not suffice simply to demonstrate that the violent behaviour was one of a number of factors that caused the departed partner to leave. It must be the main, substantive or significant reason why the victim left.[118]

115 *Metropolitan Housing Trust v Hadjazi* [2010] EWCA Civ 750, [2010] HLR 39.
116 [2004] EWHC 2982 (Ch), [2005] HLR 25.
117 *Yemshaw v Hounslow LBC* [2011] UKSC 3, [2011] 1 WLR 433 and *Hussain v Waltham Forest LBC* [2015] EWCA Civ 14, [2015] 1 WLR 2912.
118 *Camden LBC v Mallett* (2001) 33 HLR 20, CA.

'towards that partner or a member of the family of that partner
who was residing with that partner immediately before the partner
left'

3.150   The grounds are satisfied not only where there has been violence or
a threat of violence directed to the departed partner but also where
there has been violence or a threat of violence directed to another
family member that has caused the partner to leave. The term 'member of the family' is defined by HA 1985 s113 and HA 1996 s62.

'he or she is unlikely to return'

3.151   This will be particularly difficult to satisfy if the departed partner
wants to return when the partner remaining is evicted. If the departed partner is him or herself unwilling to give oral evidence the landlord may rely on hearsay evidence as proof that the departed partner
is unlikely to return.

Criminal activity: discretionary (HA 1988 ground 14 (third limb) and HA 1985 ground 2 (third limb))

3.152   A landlord may additionally or alternatively rely on grounds 2 or 14
where:

> The tenant or a person residing in or visiting the dwelling-house ...
> (b) has been convicted of –
>   (i) using the dwelling-house, or allowing it to be used, for immor-
>   al or illegal purposes, or
>   (ii) an indictable offence committed in, or in the locality of, the
>   dwelling-house.

'the tenant or a person residing in or visiting the dwelling house'

3.153   The same principles as set out at paras 3.126–3.127 apply. The
grounds are satisfied if someone other than the tenant who is residing in or visiting the dwelling-house is convicted of an offence.

'convicted'

3.154   A conviction is necessary to satisfy the grounds the mere fact that
someone has been arrested for, or even admitted to having committed, a criminal offence is not enough. For example, a tenant who has
accepted a caution or been arrested and charged (but not convicted)
will not fall within the second part of the grounds (albeit such facts
may satisfy the first part).

'using the dwelling-house, or allowing it to be used, for immoral or illegal purposes'

3.155   In *Raglan Housing Association Ltd v Fairclough*,[119] the Court of Appeal held that this part of the ground would be unlikely to be satisfied if the tenant's, or visitor's, use of the dwelling-house for immoral or illegal purposes was not undertaken during the currency of the tenancy.

3.156   The mere fact that a tenant has been convicted of a crime which took place on the premises may not be sufficient to establish this part of the ground unless it can be shown that the premises have been used for the purpose of committing the crime.[120] Being convicted for the possession of cannabis while present in dwelling-house does not of itself satisfy the grounds unless it can be shown that the dwelling-house is being used to store the cannabis.[121] The use of the premises to grow cannabis would, however, plainly satisfy the grounds.[122] The use of the premises for prostitution also satisfies the grounds.[123]

'an indictable offence committed in, or in the locality of, the dwelling-house'

3.157   The latter part of the third limb of grounds 2 and 14 (conviction of an indictable offence) was an innovation introduced by the Housing Act 1996. It breaks the link between the acts of criminality and use of the dwelling which is the criminal's home. Guidance published by central government at the time of its enactment suggested that it may be particularly useful for a landlord 'which is concerned about drug dealing where the trafficking is taking place in the common parts of the estate rather than in a house or flat'.[124]

3.158   In *Raglan*, (above paras 3.155–3.156), the Court of Appeal held that this part of the ground could be satisfied where the tenant was convicted of an indictable offence in the locality of the dwelling-house before the tenancy was entered into.

3.159   The word 'indictable' replaced 'arrestable' on 1 January 2006.[125] The offence must be indictable. It does not, however, need to be an

---

119 [2007] EWCA Civ 1087, [2008] HLR 21.

120 *Schneiders & Sons v Abrahams* [1925] 1 KB 301 at 311.

121 *Abrahams v Wilson* [1971] 2 QB 88.

122 See for example *Sandwell BC v Hensley* [2007] EWCA Civ 1425, [2008] HLR 22.

123 *Yates v Morris* [1951] 1 KB 77.

124 DoE Circ 2/97 para 28(iii).

125 Substitution made by Serious Organised Crime and Police Act 2005 s111 and Sch 7 Pt 3 para 45.

offence that may only be triable as an indictable offence or one that was in fact tried in the Crown Court. It includes offences that are triable either way where the conviction was obtained in the magistrates' court.

3.160   For the meaning of locality see above para 3.133.

Riot: discretionary (HA 1988 ground 14ZA and HA 1985 ground 2ZA)

3.161   Grounds 2ZA and 14ZA were inserted into Schedule 2 to both the HA 1985 and HA 1988 by the Anti-social Behaviour, Crime and Policing Act 2014 s99 following the summer riots in 2011. As the grounds apply irrespective of where the criminal conduct took place, it is another example of the link between the acts of criminality and use of the dwelling which is the criminal's home as being broken. They only apply in England.

3.162   The grounds provide:

> The tenant or an adult residing in the dwelling-house has been convicted of an indictable offence which took place during, and at the scene of, a riot in the United Kingdom.

3.163   In this ground –

> 'adult' means a person aged 18 or over;
> 'indictable offence' does not include an offence that is triable only summarily by virtue of section 22 of the Magistrates' Courts Act 1980 (either way offences where value involved is small);
> 'riot' is to be construed in accordance with section 1 of the Public Order Act 1986.

3.164   This ground applies only in relation to dwelling-houses in England.

'the tenant or an adult residing in the dwelling-house'

3.165   Unlike under grounds 2 or 14, the criminal conduct must have been committed by either the tenant or by an adult actually residing in the dwelling-house. The ground does not apply to a regular visitor to the dwelling-house. The conviction must also be of an adult; the conviction of a tenant's child, who is under 18 at the date of the conviction, will not therefore satisfy the ground.

'has been convicted'

3.166   It is unclear presently if, for the grounds to be satisfied, the perpetrator must be residing in the dwelling-house at the same time that he or she either committed or was convicted of the offence. Like the third limb of grounds 2 and 14, however, the grounds merely require the tenant to have been convicted. They do not specify that the conviction needs to relate to conduct that took place while the tenancy was in existence. Landlords are therefore likely to argue that the Court of Appeal's decision in *Raglan* (see above paras 3.155–3.156) is of equal application to these grounds.

'indictable offence'

3.167 See paras 3.157–3.160 above for meaning of 'indictable offence'.

'during, and at the scene of, a riot in the United Kingdom'

3.168 Public Order Act 1986 s1 defines the offence of 'riot' as:

> … where 12 or more persons who are present together use or threaten unlawful violence for a common purpose and the conduct of them (taken together) is such as would cause a person of reasonable firmness present at the scene to fear for his personal safety, each of the persons using unlawful violence for the common purpose is guilty of riot.

3.169 Public Order Act 1986 s1 enacts an indictable offence. The tenant need only be convicted of that offence for the grounds to be satisfied. However, the grounds are of equal application where the tenant is not convicted under section 1, but is convicted of another offence (eg robbery or burglary) at the scene of a riot. It will, presumably, be for the court to determine if someone is at the 'scene' of a riot when committing an indictable offence.

3.170 Where the landlord is seeking possession under these grounds and the offence has been committed by another member of the tenant's household away from the locality of the property it could be argued that a tenant should be held responsible for the acts of other adults that are committed away from the property and as such it is not reasonable to make a possession order. While a tenant can take steps to prevent criminal conduct *in* the locality, eg by requiring the perpetrator to leave, it is hard to see how a tenant can prevent another adult from committing a criminal offence in another part of the country.

Reasonableness

3.171   Even if one of the above grounds (2, 2ZA, 2A, 14, 14ZA or 14A) is made out, the landlord must go on to prove that it is reasonable that possession of the tenant's home should be ordered.[126] This is the 'reasonableness condition' and must always be satisfied before an order under any of the above grounds can be made. There may be cases in which a judgment proceeds from a finding that a ground is made out directly to a conditional postponed possession order, thereby missing the vital issue of whether it is reasonable for *any* order to be made. The Court of Appeal has repeatedly emphasised the importance of the judge indicating in the judgment that the question of reasonableness has been expressly considered.[127]

Effect of nuisance on neighbours

3.172   In determining 'reasonableness' in ground 2 or 14 cases, the court is directed by HA 1985 s85A(2) and HA 1988 s9A[128] to consider in particular:

    (a) the effect that the nuisance or annoyance has had on persons other than the person against whom the order is sought;
    (b) any continuing effect the nuisance or annoyance is likely to have on such persons; and
    (c) the effect that the nuisance or annoyance would be likely to have on such persons if the conduct is repeated.

3.173   This provision has the effect of structuring the court's discretion towards the interests of the victims or potential victims of the alleged behaviour, gives statutory effect to the approach of the Court of Appeal in anti-social behaviour cases in recent years (see para 3.176). Although the rubric is of strict application only when the court is considering 'reasonableness', much the same factors will be taken into account in considering whether to postpone any order for possession or stay or suspend execution of the order.[129]

3.174   While the court must give special prominence to the interests of the victims of the behaviour complained of, it nevertheless retains its discretion to consider other factors. The court should always be

---

126 HA 1985 s84(1); HA 1988 s7(4).
127 For an example see *Manchester City Council v Green* January 1999 *Legal Action* 26, CA.
128 Inserted by Anti-social Behaviour Act 2003 ss14 and 16.
129 *Birmingham CC v Ashton* [2012] EWCA Civ 1557, [2013] HLR 8.

reminded of the fact that, in deciding whether it is reasonable to make a possession order:

> the duty of the Judge is to take into account all relevant circumstances as they exist at the date of the hearing. That he must do in what I venture to call a broad common-sense way as a man of the world, and come to his conclusion giving such weight as he thinks right to the various factors in the situation. Some factors may have little or no weight, others may be decisive, but it is quite wrong for him to exclude from his consideration matters which he ought to take into account.[130]

3.175   The court therefore should also be invited to consider, among other issues: the seriousness and frequency of the nuisance; whether it is continuing, persistent or recently abated;[131] the likelihood of the nuisance continuing or re-occurring;[132] warnings issued by the landlord; the tenant's remorse; the relevant personal circumstances of the tenant; and the consequences of making an order for the tenant.[133] The court must, in particular, have regard to any medical evidence of the tenant's mental health and consider if, with treatment, the tenant's behaviour could improve.[134]

3.176   Historically, the Court of Appeal had been unwilling to interfere with the decisions of trial judges on 'reasonableness' issues in nuisance-related cases.[135] But in the context of modern concerns about anti-social behaviour, the Court of Appeal has, in a series of judgments, reversed the decisions of judges who have not been satisfied that it was reasonable to order possession in 'nuisance' cases or who have made only postponed orders rather than outright orders.[136] In practice, where the tenant has been found guilty of anti-social or criminal conduct, unless it was abated some time ago, it will be likely to be difficult to avoid a finding that it is reasonable to make a possession order. Moreover, the court will be used to making possession

---

130 *Cumming v Danson* [1942] 2 All ER 653, CA.
131 *Barking & Dagenham LBC v Bakare* [2012] EWCA Civ 750, [2012] HLR 34.
132 *Accent Peerless Ltd v Kingsdon* [2007] EWCA Civ 1314.
133 *Darlington BC v Sterling* (1997) 29 HLR 309, CA.
134 *Croydon LBC v Moody* (1999) 31 HLR 738, CA.
135 *Ealing LBC v Jama* [2008] EWCA Civ 896, August 2008 *Legal Action* 40.
136 *Woking BC v Bistram* (1993) 27 HLR 1; *Darlington BC v Sterling* (1997) 29 HLR 309; *Bristol City Council v Mousah* (1998) 30 HLR 32; *West Kent Housing Association v Davies* (1999) 31 HLR 415; *Newcastle upon Tyne City Council v Morrison* (2000) 32 HLR 891 and *Birmingham CC v Ashton* [2012] EWCA Civ 1557, [2013] HLR 8.

orders when presented with such behaviour and have in mind the type of conduct that it views as warranting a possession order.

3.177   It is incumbent on the tenant's legal representatives to persuade the court that the circumstances of the case – be it the tenant's vulnerability, the lack of fault on the tenant, the impact on other members of the household – are such that place it outside the norm. Where the tenant is disabled, it is likely that the best prospects of successfully defending the claim will be to advance an Equality Act defence (see chapter 27).

3.178   In certain cases, it may be arguable that the landlord's failure to engage other agencies (eg social services or the community mental health team) or the refusal to use, or failure to consider the use of, alternative remedies (eg acceptable behaviour contracts, injunctions under Anti-social Behaviour, Crime and Policing Act 2014) mean that it is not reasonable to make a possession order. This is an especially powerful submission where the landlord's own policy is to use, or to consider the use of, alternative remedies before bringing a claim for possession.[137]

3.179   HA 1996 s218A[138] requires every landlord of secure tenants to prepare, maintain and keep under review a policy in relation to anti-social behaviour and procedures for dealing with occurrences of anti-social behaviour. Those documents must be published and available at the landlord's offices. A free summary of them must be available on request.[139] The policy and procedures (and any review of them) must have regard to the content of relevant statutory guidance.[140]

3.180   In England, the current regulatory standard[141] provides that all registered providers of social housing must:

> 2.3.1 ... [P]ublish a policy on how they work with relevant partners to prevent and tackle anti-social behaviour (ASB) in areas where they own properties.
>
> 2.3.2 In their work to prevent and address ASB, registered providers shall demonstrate:
>
> (a) that tenants are made aware of their responsibilities and rights in relation to ASB;

---

137 *Barber v Croydon LBC* [2010] EWCA Civ 51, [2010] HLR 26.
138 Inserted by the Anti-social Behaviour Act 2003 s12.
139 HA 1996 s218A(6).
140 HA 1996 s218A(7).
141 *Neighbourhood and Community Standard* (Homes and Communities Agency), April 2012, pp1 and 2.

    (b) strong leadership, commitment and accountability on preventing and tackling ASB that reflects a shared understanding of responsibilities with other local agencies;

    (c) a strong focus exists on preventative measures tailored towards the needs of tenants and their families;

    (d) prompt, appropriate and decisive action is taken to deal with ASB before it escalates, which focuses on resolving the problem having regard to the full range of tools and legal powers available;

    (e) all tenants and residents can easily report ASB, are kept informed about the status of their case where responsibility rests with the organisation and are appropriately signposted where it does not; and

    (f) provision of support to victims and witnesses.

3.181   In Wales, much more detailed provision, which cannot be summarised here, for managing anti-social behaviour is given in *Anti-social behaviour: Policies and procedures – code of guidance for local authorities and housing associations.*[142]

3.182   However, the mere existence of alternative remedies, in the absence of a policy that says they will be used first, is no bar to the landlord seeking possession on an anti-social behaviour ground instead of, or in addition to, seeking other relief.[143]

3.183   The Court of Appeal has, over time, also held that the following factors are all relevant to the consideration of reasonableness:

    i) where the tenant has committed or been convicted of a serious criminal offence in relation to conduct committed at the dwelling-house, absent exceptional circumstances, it will be reasonable to make a possession order;[144]

    ii) where there is an admitted breach of covenant and absence of an intention to cease the breach, possession should only be refused in a very special case;[145]

    iii) although the court should consider what might happen to the tenant if he were to be evicted, it cannot hold that a local housing

---

142 Welsh Assembly, July 2005 (http://gov.wales/desh/publications/housing/antisocial/guidee.pdf?lang=en).

143 *Newcastle upon Tyne City Council v Morrison* (2000) 32 HLR 891, CA.

144 *Bristol CC v Mousah* (1998) 30 HLR 32. Although cf *North Devon Homes Ltd v Batchelor* [2008] EWCA Civ 840, where the Court of Appeal refused to overturn a decision of the trial judge that it was not reasonable to make a possession order despite the fact that the tenant, a 61-year-old woman, had been convicted of being in possession of cannabis and cocaine at the property and in cross examination had admitted that she would continue to use cannabis.

145 *Sheffield CC v Green* (1994) 26 HLR 349.

authority will inevitably find a tenant to have become intentionally homeless so that the tenant has nowhere else to stay;[146]

iv) there is no general rule that it cannot be reasonable to make a possession order when the tenant has not been personally culpable
for the anti-social behaviour;[147]

v) it is in the public interest that necessary and reasonable conditions of tenancy are enforced fairly and effectively;[148] and

vi) the court should only take into account facts that have been
proved, eg it should not take into account the fact that a person
has been arrested without first determining if the tenant committed the conduct that led to the arrest.[149]

3.184   The following are illustrations of decisions that have either been
upheld or reversed by the Court of Appeal. Their apparent inconsist-
encies demonstrate well the principle that each case will turn on its
own facts and that the approach of the Court of Appeal is generally not
to interfere with an order of a lower court unless it is obviously wrong
or the judge failed to take into account a relevant consideration.

3.185   In *Woking BC v Bistram*,[150] the nuisance proved was foul, abusive
and menacing language. The trial judge refused to order possession,
on the basis that such language was commonplace in areas of council housing. The Court of Appeal held that: (a) the finding as to use
of similar language elsewhere was not supported by any evidence;
and (b) as the abuse had been continuing right up to trial it was reasonable for the protection of other tenants to grant possession. In
contrast, in *Brent LBC v Doughan*,[151] the Court of Appeal upheld the
decision of a trial judge not to make a possession order where a finding had been made that the tenant had shouted abusive language and
played loud music while drunk on a handful of occasions. The trial
judge had been entitled to find that the premises were poorly insu-
lated, the noise was no more than what was to be expected in normal
urban conditions and the housing department was at fault for placing an overly sensitive tenant next to Mr Doughan.

---

146 *Bristol CC v Mousah* (1998) 30 HLR 32; *Shrewsbury and Atcham BC v Evans*
(1998) 30 HLR 123 and *Lewisham LBC v Akinsola* (2000) 32 HLR 414. Cf
Croydon LBC v Moody (1999) 31 HLR 738.

147 *Royal Borough of Kensington & Chelsea v Simmonds* (1996) 29 HLR 507 at 511
per Simon Brown LJ.

148 *Sheffield CC v Jepson* (1993) 25 HLR 299.

149 *Wandsworth LBC v Webb* [2008] EWCA Civ 1643.

150 (1995) 27 HLR 1, CA.

151 [2007] EWCA Civ 135, [2007] HLR 28.

3.186   In *Wandsworth LBC v Hargreaves*,[152] the Court of Appeal refused
to overturn a trial judge's decision not to make a possession order
– in circumstances where a visitor to the tenant's flat was found to
have thrown, in the presence of the tenant, petrol bombs from the flat
damaging a car below before setting fire to the flat causing £14,000
worth of damage – on the grounds that there had not been further
allegations of nuisance up until trial. In contrast in both *London and
Quadrant HT v Root*[153] and *New Charter Housing (North) Ltd v Ashcroft*,[154] the Court of Appeal refused to overturn immediate orders
for possession even though the perpetrators of the anti-social behaviour had left the premises, in accordance with an ASBO, or had been
imprisoned.[155]

3.187   If the judge is satisfied that it is reasonable to grant an order for
possession in a ground 2 or ground 14 case, it is not part of his or her
function to require the landlord to set out what arrangements will be
available for the rehousing of the family after eviction.[156]

Immediate or postponed order?

3.188   Tenants and their representatives should be realistic. As has been
said above, by and large, absent circumstances that bring the case
outside the norm, the court is very likely to find it reasonable to make
a possession order where there are serious or repeated instances of
anti-social or criminal conduct.

3.189   It follows that often a tenant's best hope of avoiding an immediate
possession order is to approach the case by accepting that an order
is likely to be made and that the best chance of the tenant retaining
his or her home is to admit the conduct complained of and to show
genuine remorse. While this may inevitably lead to a finding that it
is reasonable to make a possession order it is much more likely to
result in a postponed order being made.

Is there a hope for the future?

3.190   Once a court has found it reasonable to make a possession order it
must then consider whether it is appropriate to postpone the date

152 (1995) 27 HLR 142, CA.
153 [2005] EWCA Civ 43, [2005] HLR 28.
154 [2004] EWCA Civ 310, [2004] HLR 36.
155 Cf *Castle Vale Housing Action Trust v Gallagher* (2001) 33 HLR 72, below para
     3.199.
156 *Watford BC v Simpson* (2000) 32 HLR 901, CA.

of possession of the order under either HA 1985 s85 (see para 3.92) or HA 1988 s9 (see para 3.93). In *Manchester CC v Higgins*,[157] Ward LJ gave helpful guidance. When coupled with guidance given in a number of other cases, can be summarised in the following way:

a) Each case turns on its own facts.

b) The weight to be given to the various relevant factors is for the trial judge and will vary depending on the circumstances.

c) The discretion is unfettered but must be judicially exercised.

d) The fact that anti-social behaviour is serious and persistent enough to justify making an injunction will be strong but not conclusive evidence that the tenant will have forfeited his entitlement to retain possession.

e) In other cases, where the making of an injunction has served its purpose, ie the behaviour has since stopped, it might make it reasonable to make an order yet be appropriate for the order to be postponed.

f) There is a need to support the people that come forward to give evidence against their neighbours;[158] the effect on them and the message it would send, should the court refuse to make an immediate order where there has been serious anti-social conduct, must be considered.[159]

g) The question of whether or not to postpone the execution of an order is a question of the future. There is no point postponing the date for possession on terms if the inevitable outcome is a breach.[160] There must 'always be a sound basis for the hope that the anti-social behaviour will cease'.

h) The factors that point towards an order being complied with are:
   i)   genuine remorse;
   ii) whether an injunction has been complied with;
   iii) the level of support available to a parent who is making proper efforts to control an errant child.

i) Ultimately, given the human right to respect for the tenant's home, the question is whether an immediate possession order is necessary in order to meet the need to protect the rights and freedoms of others – the neighbours – and is proportionate to it.[161]

---

157 [2005] EWCA Civ 1423, [2006] HLR 14.

158 *Canterbury CC v Lowe* (2001) 33 HLR 53, CA.

159 *West Kent Housing Association Ltd v Davies* (1999) 31 HLR 415.

160 *Canterbury CC v Lowe* (2001) 33 HLR 53, CA; *Leeds & Yorkshire HA v Vertigan* [2010] EWCA Civ 1583, [2011] HLR 13.

161 HRA 1998 Sch 1 Art 8.

j) An immediate order should only be made if there is no lesser alternative which would realistically prevent the re-occurrence of the behaviour.[162]

3.191 In *Higgins*, the behaviour of Ms Higgins and her children, especially her son, had been quite intolerable. The son had shown himself unrepentantly anti-social. The mere fact that an ASBO would remain in force until the son attained the age of 16 would not give the neighbours sufficient protection. In the absence of any expression of remorse, or any well-founded expectation of improvement, it was disproportionate not to make an immediate possession order. Ms Higgins was without remorse and totally indifferent to the effect her children's behaviour was having on her neighbours. She had forfeited her right to respect for her home. The recorder should have made an order for possession in 28 days.

3.192 On the other hand, in *Moat Housing Group South Ltd v Harris and Hartless*,[163] where the anti-social behaviour was far less serious, the Court of Appeal considered the absence of any prior warning or complaint by the landlord together with good school reports received by the tenant's children, the absence of any criminal record or any serious record of police involvement with the family, and favourable testimonies which were given about the tenant, and allowed an appeal from the outright possession order made in the county court.

3.193 In *Greenwich LBC v Grogan*,[164] the Court of Appeal held that it was entitled to take into account the wider public interest when deciding whether to overturn an immediate possession order. The tenant – a care leaver – had been convicted of handling stolen goods while he was 17 years old. By the date of the possession claim no further matters of complaint had been made against him. The court accepted that the tenant was genuinely trying to live a life free of crime and that this would be undermined if he were to be evicted. It was appropriate therefore to allow an appeal from an outright order.

Likewise, in *Lincoln City Council v Bird*,[165] while the High Court ordered that the county court had been wrong not make a possession order because it had failed to consider the impact that the tenant's threatening and intimidating behaviour had on his neighbours, it was appropriate to suspend the order because the tenant's behaviour

---

162 *CDS Housing v Bellis* [2008] EWCA Civ 1315.
163 [2004] EWCA Civ 1852, [2005] HLR 33.
164 (2001) 33 HLR 140, CA.
165 [2015] EWHC 843 (QB), [2015] 2 P&CR DG12.

had improved after the court had made an anti-social behaviour injunction.

Serious criminal offence

3.194   In *Sandwell MBC v Hensley*,[166] the Court of Appeal held that where a tenant, or a member of his household, has committed a serious criminal offence the court should only postpone the order if there is cogent evidence which demonstrated a sound basis for the hope that the previous conduct would cease. An absence of offending for a period of time is not, of itself, cogent evidence that the tenant will not re-offend in the future. The fact that a tenant has a number of previous convictions is likely to be a better guide as to the likelihood of his further offending than a recent absence of offending.

3.195   To be 'cogent', the evidence must be more than simply credible: it must be persuasive. The standard is, however, pitched at a realistic level; the tenant does not need to give a cast iron guarantee. The cogent evidence need not even come from the tenant; the court can take into account the likely actions of third parties, eg the provision of medical assistance or evidence that the perpetrator of the criminal behaviour has been imprisoned or left the area. However, where the assurances are coming from the tenant the judge must hear the tenant's evidence so as to be in a position to assess their credibility and cross-check their evidence against other available objective evidence. It is inevitable that if the court has found that the tenant has lied it is likely to result in the court finding that the tenant's evidence is not to be trusted and will therefore be unable to accept the tenant's assurances that his or her behaviour will improve. Each case, however, turns on its own facts and it is always for the judge to decide whether the evidence presented by the tenant is sufficient to persuade the court that the tenant's criminal behaviour will cease. The fact that a tenant has lied cannot of itself lead the court to finding that there is no hope for the future.[167]

3.196   Accordingly, in *City West Housing Trust v Massey and others*, the Court of Appeal upheld a decision of a district judge to suspend a possession order, in a case where the judge had found that the tenant had permitted a third party to grow cannabis in her flat and had lied when she said she was ignorant of the fact, on the condition that she comply with her terms of tenancy, the person responsible for growing cannabis in her flat be prohibited from returning to the flat and

166 [2007] EWCA Civ 1425, [2008] HLR 22.
167 *City West Housing Trust v Massey and others* [2016] EWCA Civ 704.

allowing the housing trust the right to inspect the property on less than two hours' notice. The judge had been entitled to find, on his assessment of her evidence, that there was a sound basis for believing that such an order would prevent further instances of criminal behaviour.[168]

3.197   Likewise, in *Stonebridge Housing Action Trust v Gabbidon*,[169] where the home had been used for dealing in drugs, the judge found it reasonable to grant possession but was persuaded to postpone the order because the female defendant had not personally been involved in the dealing and there was no evidence of recent incidents. The judge also took into account the fact that there was a seven-month-old child in the household. The High Court on appeal refused to interfere with the judge's ruling. The landlord's contention that allowing the family to remain in occupation would set a precedent for other tenants was not supportable.

3.198   In all cases, the tenant's adviser should draw the attention of the court to the increased risk of further offending if a criminal is evicted to live an insecure life on the streets or in transient accommodation as opposed to receiving the benefit of support services (such as that of the probation service), which can be more straightforwardly supplied to those with a fixed address.[170] Alternatively, a critical feature in such cases will often be that the tenant has the capacity to reform and has stated an intention to 'mend [his or her] ways'.[171]

Nuisance caused by other members of household

3.199   Where the nuisance has been caused by another member of the tenant's household the court will need to have regard to a number of factors. First, the fact that the tenant is unable to control the behaviour of their children, or anyone else visiting or residing with them, does not support an argument that a postponed order should be made.[172] Unless the nuisance maker has vacated or will shortly vacate the property, the fact that the tenant is unable to control their children's behaviour is a factor which will point towards the court making an

---

168 [2016] EWCA Civ 704. See also *Hammersmith and Fulham LBC v Forbes* June 2011 *Legal Action* 24, Willesden Crown Court.

169 [2002] EWHC 2091 (Ch), (2003) 100(5) LSG 30.

170 *Greenwich LBC v Grogan* (2001) 33 HLR 140, CA.

171 *Sheffield CC v Shaw* [2007] EWCA Civ 42, [2007] HLR 25.

172 *Portsmouth City Council v Bryant* (2000) 32 HLR 906; *Kensington and Chelsea RLBC v Simmonds* (1997) 29 HLR 507 and *Greenwich RLBC v Tuitt* [2014] EWCA Civ 1669, [2015] HLR 10.

immediate order for possession.[173] Second, the fact that innocent children or siblings will be punished by an eviction may not be a reason to postpone the order.[174] Third, the fact that the children might continue to cause anti-social behaviour in the locality of the property, in the event that their mother were to be evicted, is an irrelevant consideration.[175] Finally, the fact that the perpetrator has moved away from the property may be sufficient to give rise to a hope that the behaviour will not recur.[176]

Serious acts of harassment

3.200   Where there have been serious acts of harassment or intimidation, even a subsequent improvement in the conduct of the tenant's family might not prevent the court from making an outright order where there is a genuine ongoing fear that the behaviour will re-occur.[177]

3.201   This does not equate to a general principle that an immediate possession order must be made wherever the harassment of neighbours is such that the fear and tension cannot be dispelled. While it is a relevant factor, a court is still entitled, in appropriate cases where there is evidence of reform, to make a postponed order.[178]

Anti-social behaviour: mandatory ground (HA 1988 ground 7A and HA 1985 s84A)

3.202   Anti-social Behaviour, Crime and Policing Act (ABCPA) 2014 ss94 and 97 inserted HA 1985 s84A and HA 1988 Sch 2 ground 7A on 21 October 2014.

3.203   The stated purpose of the 'absolute' ground for possession, according to the guidance that accompanied the passing of the 2014 Act, is 'to expedite the eviction of landlords' most anti-social tenants

---

173 *Knowsley HT v Mullen* [2006] EWCA Civ 539, [2006] HLR 43.
174 *Friendship Care and Housing Association v Begum* [2011] EWCA Civ 1807, [2013] HLR 11.
175 *Newcastle upon Tyne CC v Morrison* (2000) 32 HLR 891, CA.
176 *Castle Vale Housing Action Trust v Gallagher* (2001) 33 HLR 72. Although cf *London & Quadrant HT v Root* [2005] EWCA Civ 43, [2005] HLR 28 and *New Charter Housing (North) Ltd v Ashcroft* [2004] EWCA Civ 310, [2004] HLR 36, above para 3.186.
177 *Solon South West Housing Association Ltd v James* [2004] EWCA Civ 1847, [2005] HLR 24 and *Lambeth LBC v Howard* [2001] EWCA Civ 468, (2001) 33 HLR 58.
178 *Sheffield CC v Shaw* [2007] EWCA Civ 42, [2007] HLR 2.

to bring faster relief to victims.'[179] The guidance stresses, however, that:

> The new absolute ground is intended for the most serious cases of anti-social behaviour and landlords should ensure that the ground is used selectively.
>
> ... Landlords should ensure that tenants are aware from the commencement of their tenancy that anti-social behaviour or criminality either by the tenant, people living with them, or their visitors could lead to a loss of their home under the new absolute ground.[180]

3.204   It is hard to see, however, how the new grounds will actually speed up the eviction process. First, for any of the absolute ground's conditions to be satisfied a county court, Crown Court or magistrates' court must first have found that a tenant has undertaken anti-social activity. This will, unless the earlier order or conviction was based on admissions, inevitably involve there being a trial. The absolute ground may replace the need for a possession trial, but it will not replace the need for some form of hearing to take place. Such hearings, whether they are in the county court, magistrates' court or Crown Court, are subject to the same delays that affect the possession claims.

3.205   Second, it was already the case that where another court, be it civil or criminal, had found that a tenant had been guilty of anti-social conduct the landlord could rely on those findings in the possession trial and was not required to prove them again. This already greatly reduces the time estimate of a possession trial in many anti-social behaviour cases.

3.206   In practice, the likely effect of the new grounds will be to increase evictions as the courts will be forced to make immediate possession orders that they might not have made previously.[181]

HA 1985 s84A

3.207   The new grounds under both the HA 1985 s84A and HA 1988 Sch 2 ground 7A, although identical, have different notice and review requirements and so consideration is separately required of each. The following paragraphs deal with HA 1985 s84A. For discussion of HA 1988 ground 7A, see paras 3.249–3.254.

179 *Anti-social Behaviour, Crime and Policing Act 2014: Reform of anti-social behaviour powers. Statutory guidance for frontline professionals*, July 2014, Home Office, pp58–59.

180 Ibid, p59.

181 See more generally Madge-Wyld 'The proposal for a new absolute ground for possession is misjudged' (2013) 157(22) SJ 10–11.

HA 1985 s84A, which applies to secure tenants, provides:

(1) If the court is satisfied that any of the following conditions is met, it must make an order for the possession of a dwelling-house let under a secure tenancy. This is subject to subsection (2) (and to any available defence based on the tenant's Convention rights, within the meaning of the Human Rights Act 1998).

(2) Subsection (1) applies only where the landlord has complied with any obligations it has under section 85ZA (review of decision to seek possession).

(3) Condition 1 is that –
   (a) the tenant, or a person residing in or visiting the dwelling-house, has been convicted of a serious offence, and
   (b) the serious offence –
      (i) was committed (wholly or partly) in, or in the locality of, the dwelling-house,
      (ii) was committed elsewhere against a person with a right (of whatever description) to reside in, or occupy housing accommodation in the locality of, the dwelling-house, or
      (iii) was committed elsewhere against the landlord of the dwelling-house, or a person employed (whether or not by the landlord) in connection with the exercise of the landlord's housing management functions, and directly or indirectly related to or affected those functions.

(4) Condition 2 is that a court has found in relevant proceedings that the tenant, or a person residing in or visiting the dwelling-house, has breached a provision of an injunction under section 1 of the Anti-social Behaviour, Crime and Policing Act 2014, other than a provision requiring a person to participate in a particular activity, and –
   (a) the breach occurred in, or in the locality of, the dwelling-house, or
   (b) the breach occurred elsewhere and the provision breached was a provision intended to prevent –
      (i) conduct that is capable of causing nuisance or annoyance to a person with a right (of whatever description) to reside in, or occupy housing accommodation in the locality of, the dwelling-house, or
      (ii) conduct that is capable of causing nuisance or annoyance to the landlord of the dwelling-house, or a person employed (whether or not by the landlord) in connection with the exercise of the landlord's housing management functions, and that is directly or indirectly related to or affects those functions.

(5) Condition 3 is that the tenant, or a person residing in or visiting the dwelling-house, has been convicted of an offence under section 30 of the Anti-social Behaviour, Crime and Policing Act 2014

consisting of a breach of a provision of a criminal behaviour order prohibiting a person from doing anything described in the order, and the offence involved –

(a) a breach that occurred in, or in the locality of, the dwelling-house, or

(b) a breach that occurred elsewhere of a provision intended to prevent –

    (i) behaviour that causes or is likely to cause harassment, alarm or distress to a person with a right (of whatever description) to reside in, or occupy housing accommodation in the locality of, the dwelling-house, or

    (ii) behaviour that causes or is likely to cause harassment, alarm or distress to the landlord of the dwelling-house, or a person employed (whether or not by the landlord) in connection with the exercise of the landlord's housing management functions, and that is directly or indirectly related to or affects those functions.

(6) Condition 4 is that –

(a) the dwelling-house is or has been subject to a closure order under section 80 of the Anti-social Behaviour, Crime and Policing Act 2014, and

(b) access to the dwelling-house has been prohibited (under the closure order or under a closure notice issued under section 76 of that Act) for a continuous period of more than 48 hours.

(7) Condition 5 is that –

(a) the tenant, or a person residing in or visiting the dwelling-house, has been convicted of an offence under –

    (i) section 80(4) of the Environmental Protection Act 1990 (breach of abatement notice in relation to statutory nuisance), or

    (ii) section 82(8) of that Act (breach of court order to abate statutory nuisance etc.), and

(b) the nuisance concerned was noise emitted from the dwelling-house which was a statutory nuisance for the purposes of Part 3 of that Act by virtue of section 79(1)(g) of that Act (noise emitted from premises so as to be prejudicial to health or a nuisance).

(8) Condition 1, 2, 3, 4 or 5 is not met if –

(a) there is an appeal against the conviction, finding or order concerned which has not been finally determined, abandoned or withdrawn, or

(b) the final determination of the appeal results in the conviction, finding or order being overturned.

(9) In this section –

'relevant proceedings' means proceedings for contempt of court or proceedings under Schedule 2 to the Anti-social Behaviour, Crime and Policing Act 2014;

'serious offence' means an offence which –
- (a) was committed on or after the day on which subsection (3) comes into force,
- (b) is specified, or falls within a description specified, in Schedule 2A at the time the offence was committed and at the time the court is considering the matter, and
- (c) is not an offence that is triable only summarily by virtue of section 22 of the Magistrates' Courts Act 1980 (either-way offences where value involved is small). ...

3.208   In essence, the ground provides that, if s85ZA has been complied with and any one of the conditions is satisfied, the court must make an immediate order for possession unless the tenant is able to raise a successful defence under the Human Rights Act 1998 (see chapter 26). Although the ground does not expressly say so, it must also be subject to a public law defence (see chapter 25) or an Equality Act 2010 defence (see chapter 27) as well.

3.209   The court may not, however, entertain proceedings under section 84A unless the landlord has first served on the tenant a notice that complies with section 83ZA.[182]

'a notice that complies with s83ZA'

3.210   A notice under section 83ZA must be served whenever the landlord wishes to rely on the absolute ground for possession and also applies where the landlord intends to rely on any other grounds under HA 1985 Sch 2.[183] For discussion of the notice requirement see paras 2.49–2.53.

'has complied with any obligations it has under s85ZA'

3.211   A secure tenant may request a review of the landlord's decision to seek an order under section 84A.[184] For discussion of the review requirements, see paras 2.54–2.66.

'Condition 1'

3.212   Condition 1 is satisfied if the tenant, or a person residing in or visiting the dwelling-house, has been convicted of a serious offence provided that the offence was:

---

182 HA 1985 s83ZA(2).
183 HA 1985 s83ZA(1).
184 HA 1985 s85ZA(1).

i) committed (wholly or partly) in, or in the locality of, the dwelling-house; or

ii) committed elsewhere against a person with a right (of whatever description) to reside in, or occupy, housing accommodation in the locality of the dwelling-house; or

iii) committed elsewhere against the landlord of the dwelling-house, or a person employed (whether or not by the landlord) in connection with the exercise of the landlord's housing management functions, and directly or indirectly related to or affected those functions.

3.213 The condition, as with all of the other four conditions, is not met if there is:

a) an appeal against the conviction, finding or order concerned which has not been finally determined, abandoned or withdrawn; or

b) the final determination of the appeal results in the conviction, finding or order being overturned.[185]

'tenant or person residing in or visiting the dwelling-house'

3.214 See above paras 3.126–3.127.

'has been convicted'

3.215 See above para 3.154.

'serious offence'

3.216 A serious offence is one that is:

- committed on or after 21 October 2014;
- an offence that is included within HA 1985 Sch 2A both at the date it was committed and at the date of the hearing at which the court considers whether condition 1 is satisfied; and
- not an offence that is triable only summarily.[186]

3.217 As the offences contained within Schedule 2A can be added to by the Secretary of State or the Welsh Ministers,[187] it is important to check that the offence was prescribed within Schedule 2A at the date it was committed (as opposed to the date of the conviction).

3.218 Schedule 2A includes a number of serious offences covering:

185 HA 1985 s84A(8).
186 HA 1985 s84A(9).
187 HA 1985 s84A(10) and (11).

i) violent and sexual offences;
ii) offensive weapons;
iii) offences against property;
iv) road traffic offences;
v) drug-related offences; and
vi) modern slavery.

3.219   The full schedule is included in appendix C.

'was committed (wholly or partly) in the locality of the dwelling house'

3.220   See above para 3.133 for meaning of 'locality'.

'was committed elsewhere against a person with a right to reside in or occupy accommodation in the locality'

3.221   The mandatory ground applies if the offence was committed against someone outside the locality. The condition is satisfied where a tenant, for example, attacks his or her neighbour while on an overseas holiday.

'was committed elsewhere against the landlord of the dwelling-house'

3.222   This mirrors ground 2(aa). See above para 3.138.

Condition 2

3.223   Condition 2 is satisfied if the the tenant, or a person residing in or visiting the dwelling-house, has breached an injunction made under ABCPA 2014 s1 provided that:

(a) it was not a breach of a requirement to participate in a particular activity, and
(b) the breach occurred in, or in the locality, of the dwelling-house, or
(c) the provision breached was intended to prevent
  (i) conduct that is capable of causing nuisance or annoyance to a person with a right (of whatever description) to reside in, or occupy housing accommodation in the locality of, the dwelling-house;
  (ii) conduct that is capable of causing nuisance or annoyance to the landlord of the dwelling-house, or a person employed (whether or not by the landlord) in connection with the exercise of the

landlord's housing management functions, and that is directly or indirectly related to or affects those functions.

'tenant or person residing in or visiting the dwelling-house'

3.224   See above paras 3.126–3.127.

'has breached an injunction under section 1'

3.225   The injunction must have been made under ABCPA 2014 s1. Condition 2 does not apply to breach of any other injunctions, eg one that has been obtained in a purely contractual claim under the tenancy. It does not apply to undertakings given by the tenant in proceedings for an injunction.[188]

3.226   It does, however, include interim injunctions made under section 1 because ABCPA 2014 s7 provides that injunctions made on an interim basis are made under section 1.

3.227   There is no requirement that the breach has occurred within a particular period of time or be of a particular severity. One breach at any time during the currency of the injunction is potentially sufficient to satisfy condition 2.

'was not in breach of a requirement to participate in a particular activity'

3.228   An injunction made under ABCPA 2014 s1 can include provision that a tenant 'do anything described in the injunction', eg attend a support group for alcohol or drug abuse or even undertake a medical assessment. The failure to comply with these provisions does not, however, satisfy condition 2.

'the breach occurred in, or in the locality of, the dwelling-house'

3.229   For meaning of 'locality' see above para 3.133. Note that the breach can include breach of any condition of the injunction that prohibits the tenant from doing something. It could therefore cover the tenant entering an exclusion zone, contacting another person or breaching a curfew.

---

188   From 23 March 2020 this will also include injunctions that were made under HA 1996 s153A as from that date such injunctions are deemed to have been made under ABCPA 2014 s1: ABCPA 2014 s21(5)(a).

'provision breached was intended to prevent conduct that is capable of causing nuisance or annoyance to a person with a right to reside or occupy housing accommodation in the locality of the dwelling-house'

3.230   This includes circumstances where the tenant has, for example, verbally abused a neighbour in another part of the city. It will also apply to circumstances where a tenant enters an exclusion zone away from the locality where the purpose of the exclusion zone is to protect a person who does live in the locality, eg the tenant enters a neighbouring resident's place of work.

'provision breached was intended to prevent conduct that is capable of causing nuisance or annoyance to the landlord of the dwelling-house'

3.231   This applies to the circumstances covered by ground 2(aa). See above para 3.138. Accordingly, a tenant who abuses a housing officer, in breach of an injunction, while in the housing office will satisfy condition 2.

Condition 3

3.232   Condition 3 is drafted in almost identical terms to condition 2. Where the tenant has breached a criminal behaviour order, ie an order obtained by the police on a person's conviction that prohibits a person from doing certain things, provided that the same provisions in condition 2 are satisfied, then condition 3 is satisfied.

Condition 4

3.233   Condition 4 is satisfied where the dwelling-house is or has been subject to a closure order under ABCPA 2014 s80 and access to the dwelling-house has been prohibited for a continuous period of more than 48 hours.

3.234   A closure order is made, on the application of a local housing authority or the police, by the magistrates' court within 48 hours of a closure notice being served. This has always been a particularly draconian measure, but is even more so now that one of the consequences of a closure order being made is the availability of absolute grounds.

3.235   Where possible the tenant should seek to appeal, under ABCPA 2014 s84, against the making of a closure order. The appeal is to the

Crown Court[189] and is therefore by way of a re-hearing. This means that the tenant can, in effect, have a second chance of defending the application for a closure order. It is likely to be the best chance of avoiding an immediate possession order.

3.236 This will only be possible, however, where the closure order was made less than 21 days previously as there does not appear to be any power to allow an appeal that is not made within 21 days.[190]

3.237 A landlord must serve a notice under HA 1985 s83ZA within three months of the closure order being made (see above para 2.52) as opposed to the 12-month period for the other conditions. This runs from the date of the making of the closure order, not the date that it expired or the date it was extended.

Condition 5

3.238 Condition 5 is satisfied where the tenant or a person residing in or visiting the dwelling-house, has been convicted of an offence under Environmental Protection Act (EPA) 1990 s80(4) or s82(8) and the nuisance, that gave rise to the offence, was noise emitted from the dwelling-house.

'tenant or a person residing in or visiting the dwelling-house'

3.239 See above paras 3.126–3.127.

'convicted'

3.240 See above para 3.154.

'an offence under s80(4) or s82(8)'

3.241 A person who has been served with an abatement notice under EPA 1990 s80(1) commits an offence under section 80(4) if, without reasonable excuse, he or she contravenes or fails to comply with any requirement or prohibition imposed by the notice.

3.242 A person who has been made subject to an order by a magistrate to abate a nuisance or to prohibit the recurrence of a nuisance under EPA 1990 s82(2) commits an offence under section 82(8) if, without reasonable excuse, he or she contravenes any requirement or prohibition imposed by the order.

189 ABCPA 2014 s84(4).
190 ABCPA 2014 s84(5).

'the nuisance concerned was noise emitted from the dwelling-house which was a statutory nuisance'

3.243   The condition is only satisfied if the tenant, or member of or visitor to his household, commits the offence in a manner that is itself a statutory nuisance within the meaning of EPA 1990 s79(1)(g), ie by noise emitted from premises so as to be prejudicial to health or a nuisance.

3.244   It follows that the landlord must not only prove that the offence was committed, but that the act giving rise to the offence was a statutory nuisance.

3.245   The meaning of 'nuisance' under the 1990 Act is the same as at common law.[191] Something will not be a nuisance if the acts are necessary for the common and ordinary use and occupation of land and houses' and are 'conveniently done', ie in consideration to those neighbouring the land.[192]

3.246   The landlord will need the evidence of an environmental health officer, which supported the conviction, to prove that section 79(1)(g) was satisfied.

3.247   It is arguable that unless the evidence in support of the conviction proves that the noise was such as to be prejudicial to health or a nuisance the condition is not satisfied. The landlord should not be able to adduce additional evidence to prove that the noise was prejudicial to health or a nuisance if it has not been found proved in the criminal court. Otherwise the tenant will not have been given the opportunity to challenge it.

Defences

3.248   A tenant has the following defences:

i)   the landlord has not complied with the notice procedure under s83ZA; or

ii)   the landlord has not complied with the review procedure under s85ZA; or

iii) none of the five conditions are satisfied; or

iv) the making of a possession order would amount to a breach of the tenant's Article 8 rights, the Equality Act 2010 or is otherwise made unlawful on judicial review grounds (see chapters 25, 26 and 27).

---

191 *Dennis Rye Limited v Bolsover District Council* [2013] EWHC 1041 (Admin).
192 *Southwark LBC v Mills* [2001] 1 AC 1, [2000] 32 HLR 148.

HA 1988 ground 7A

3.249 The conditions to satisfy HA 1988 ground 7A in respect of an assured tenant are identical to the conditions set out in HA 1985 s84A (above paras 3.207–3.247).

Notice requirements

3.250 The notice requirements are also similar, but not identical to those that apply to secure tenant cases. Before commencing a claim for possession the landlord must serve a notice under HA 1988 s8. It must be in the prescribed form (see para 2.25)

3.251 The requirement to serve a valid notice cannot be dispensed with.[193]

Review procedure

3.252 The landlord of an assured tenant is not required to comply with a statutory review procedure before using ground 7A.[194] However, the Home Office guidance states that the Home Secretary:

> would expect housing associations to offer a similar non-statutory review procedure (in the same way that they have done so for starter tenancies).[195]

3.253 The failure to provide such a non-statutory review, even more so the failure to *consider* providing a review, may give rise to a public law defence to the claim (see chapter 25).

3.254 It will be for the landlord to determine the form and structure of the review. A review process that does not permit a tenant to make representations and/or is conducted by the same person (or someone of equivalent seniority to the person) whose decision it was to bring a claim for possession under ground 7A is unlikely to be fair and may give rise to a public law challenge.

---

193 HA 1988 s8(5).
194 See the position under HA 1985 discussed at paras 2.54–2.66.
195 *Anti-social Behaviour, Crime and Policing Act 2014: Reform of anti-social behaviour powers* Statutory guidance for frontline professionals, July 2014, Home Office, p62.

Other breaches of the tenancy conditions

Breach of tenancy conditions: discretionary (HA 1988 ground 12 and HA 1985 ground 1 (second limb))[196]

3.255   These grounds are concerned with breaches of conditions of tenancy other than payment of rent. They cover breaches of any other term of the tenancy. Their effect can therefore be to provide the potential sanction of eviction for the breach of absolutely any tenancy term. Consideration should always be given to whether the obligation which is relied on by the landlord is a term of tenancy, and not a personal obligation (see above para 3.115), arises from an express or implied term of the tenancy agreement itself, and not from some collateral agreement (see above para 3.114), whether the term relied on by the landlord is a term of the agreement applicable to the tenant's present tenancy (see above para 3.116) and whether the term relied is 'fair' for the purposes of Consumer Rights Act 2015 Part 2 (see above para 3.117).

3.256   Some social landlords have included in their tenancy agreements a requirement to desist from particular activity in the locality of the premises which might amount to a crime, for example, being in possession of controlled drugs in the locality of dwelling-house. This allows possession to be claimed under the second limb of ground 1 or ground 12 even if the tenant is not actually prosecuted for or convicted of an offence (in which case ground 2 above or ground 14 could have been relied on). If it is made out, the usual order would be for possession. Social landlords may bring proceedings for possession arising from any breaches of the tenancy agreement, other than rent arrears, under the second limb of ground 1 or ground 12.

3.257   However, it is arguable that in certain circumstances a landlord should not be permitted to use this limb of ground 1 or ground 12 to obtain possession in reliance on a tenancy term which has been designed to avoid the need to rely on another statutory ground for possession specifically dealing with the issue. For example, the landlord should not be permitted to rely on ground 1 or ground 12 in respect of breach of a covenant not to allow premises to be statutorily overcrowded because there is a specific ground for possession covering overcrowding (see para 3.299 below) and that ground carries an obligation to supply suitable alternative accommodation.[197]

---

196 The full texts of both grounds are set out above at paras 3.111–3.112.
197 *Newham LBC v Anwar Ali* February 2004 *Legal Action* 31, Bow County Court.

3.258   Another common provision in agreements is a prohibition against the keeping of pets or other animals on the premises let.[198] Proceedings under ground 1 or 12 based on this particular breach provide a good illustration of the distinction between the ground for possession and the reasonableness requirement. The tenant may well admit a clear and continuing breach of the agreement by keeping an 'animal companion' but a possession order may be refused where, in the particular circumstances, it would not be reasonable to order possession (notwithstanding that the tenant intends to continue keeping the pet at the premises).[199] This may be the case particularly if there is good medical or social evidence of the effect that loss of the animal companion will have on the tenant.[200] In the absence of any such evidence, however, the court is likely to take the view that it is reasonable to evict a tenant who, despite having entered into a plain 'no pets' agreement, and having been given appropriate notice that the landlord intends to enforce the agreement, will not get rid of the animal.[201] Where the landlord is itself, as a long leaseholder, subject to a covenant not to permit pets within the block and is under the threat of forfeiture proceedings the tenant can have little hope of persuading a court that it would not be reasonable for the landlord to be granted a possession order where the tenant has kept a pet in breach of the tenancy agreement and intends to continue to do so.[202]

3.259   It is, however, no part of the court's function in determining 'reasonableness' to investigate whether the landlord's policy justification for including a particular term in a tenancy agreement is a good or valid one.[203]

3.260   Advisers may find it helpful to draw the attention of the court to the landlord's readily available alternative remedy for breach of the contractual agreement – an order for specific performance to enforce compliance with the agreement or an injunction to restrain further breach.[204] Where a member of the tenant's household is the main party responsible for the conduct amounting to the alleged breach of the tenant's tenancy agreement, it might be suggested that the more

---

198 See Allotments Act 1950 s12.
199 *Bell London and Provincial Properties Ltd v Reuben* [1947] KB 157, CA.
200 *Corporation of London v Prior* (1996) 1 L&T Rev 1 pD8.
201 *Sheffield City Council v Jepson* (1993) 25 HLR 299, CA and *Green v Sheffield City Council* (1994) 26 HLR 349, CA.
202 *Thomas-Ashley v Drum Housing Association* [2010] EWCA Civ 265, [2010] 2 P&CR 17.
203 *Barking and Dagenham LBC v Hyatt* (1992) 24 HLR 406, CA.
204 *Sutton Housing Trust v Lawrence* (1987) 19 HLR 520, CA.

sensible course is for the landlord to seek an injunction or other relief against that person – rendering the grant of possession against the tenant unnecessary. However, tenants' advisers will need to be prepared to tackle the reverse contention – that there are circumstances in which a conditional possession order carrying the sanction of eviction for breach can be more appropriate than an injunction enforceable by committal.[205]

3.261   Those defending assured and secure tenants in these ground 1 or ground 12 cases should always argue against the apparently attractive option of an order postponed on terms (that there be no further breach) as this is likely to give rise to an adverse costs order. It should be argued that it would not be reasonable in the circumstances to make any possession order where the same objective can be met by adjourning the proceedings on terms, giving the landlord liberty to restore in the event of a further alleged breach.

3.262   Those representing secure tenants should argue that a postponed conditional order in a 'breach of obligation' case should, where appropriate, only be made on terms that it is not to be enforced without a prior finding by the court that there has been a breach of the conditions.[206] Without such an express restriction the landlord could obtain a warrant for possession, without a further hearing, simply by alleging breach (albeit even though in such a case the tenant could always apply to set aside the warrant and insist on a hearing to determine if the order has been breached).

Tenancy obtained by deception or false statement

The grounds: HA 1988 ground 17 and HA 1985 ground 5

3.263   HA 1985 Sch 2 ground 5 and HA 1988 Sch 2 ground 17 are satisfied if:

> The tenant is the person, or one of the persons, to whom the tenancy was granted and the landlord was induced to grant the tenancy by a false statement made knowingly or recklessly *by* –
> *(a) the tenant, or*
> *(b) a person acting at the tenant's instigation.* [Emphasis added.]

---

205 See Ralph Gibson LJ in *Sheffield City Council v Jepson* (1993) 25 HLR 299, CA at 303.
206 See *Solon Co-op Housing Services Ltd v Headly* March 1997 *Legal Action* 11 and *Knowsley Housing Trust v McMullen* [2006] EWCA Civ 539, [2006] HLR 43.

3.264 The grounds are basically designed for those cases in which the tenancy has been obtained by deception. They extend not only to the making of false representations known to be false at the time of their making, but also to the 'reckless' making of statements which turn out to be false. Where a person completes an application form for allocation of housing on the basis that he or she will inform the prospective landlord of any changes in circumstances which might affect the need for housing, the subsequent failure to disclose new information to the prospective landlord may amount to a false statement which induces the grant of a tenancy.[207] On the other hand, *the grounds are not available where the landlord's essential complaint is that it would not have granted the tenancy if the tenant had given information for which in fact the landlord had failed to ask.*[208]

3.265 The words in italics were added on 12 February 1997 by HA 1996 s146. Previously, only statements attributable to the *tenant* (or to one of the joint tenants) could satisfy the ground. If a partner induced the landlord to let the accommodation in the sole name of the other partner, the ground could not be relied on. The effect of the amendment is to close that lacuna and enable the landlord to rely on the ground in respect of a representation made by a third party. It is not enough for the landlord just to prove that a third party made the relevant representation – it must additionally be shown that this was done at the instigation of the tenant.[209] Note also that ground 5 and ground 17 are not available where the current tenant is not the person to whom the tenancy was granted (so, for example, it cannot be made out where a tenant obtained the tenancy by deception and then lawfully assigned it to an innocent party).[210]

3.266 In order to prove a ground 5 or ground 17 case the landlord must establish not only a false statement but also that the statement *induced* the grant of the tenancy. It is not necessary for the landlord to produce evidence from the actual decision-maker who granted the tenancy. In *Waltham Forest LBC v Roberts*,[211] the tenant had stated in her application for housing that she did not own any property, whereas she was in fact the joint owner of an undisclosed property. The Court of Appeal held that the correct approach was to ask whether the misstatement was material to the landlord's discharge

207 *North Hertfordshire DC v Carthy* [2003] EWCA Civ 20.
208 *Peterborough CC v Moran* September 1993 *Legal Action* 13.
209 *Merton LBC v Richards* [2005] EWCA Civ 639, [2005] HLR 44.
210 *Islington LBC v Uckac* [2006] EWCA Civ 340, [2006] 1 WLR 1303.
211 [2004] EWCA Civ 940, [2005] HLR 2.

of its social housing functions. Once the materiality of the misstatement had been established, it was a 'fair inference' of fact that the
decision-maker had been influenced by it.

In *Windsor and District HA v Hewitt*,[212] a tenant's statement that
she needed a two-bedroom property to live with her son was found to
be false when she subsequently moved into the property on her own.
A district judge's finding that the ground was not made out because
the tenant had forgotten her earlier representation was unsustainable as she had not asserted that she had forgotten it.

Reasonableness

3.267   Even if the grounds are proved, the landlord must also show that it is
reasonable for possession to be ordered.[213]

3.269   When defending on the issue of 'reasonableness' in such a case, a
tenant's advocate may wish to remind the court that a *local authority*
landlord already has a specific remedy if induced to grant the tenancy
by the deception of an applicant for housing – prosecution under HA
1996 s171 (where the application was made under the housing allocation scheme) or s214 (where application was made under homelessness provisions). The loss of the home, it may be argued, would
be 'excessive punishment' in all but the most exceptional cases.
On the other hand, the argument may itself prompt the landlord to
prosecute.

3.270   In *Rushcliffe BC v Watson*,[214] the tenant recorded on her application form that she had been a lodger in her former home. The landlord subsequently discovered that she had held a housing association
tenancy elsewhere. The entry on the form was unquestionably 'false'
for the purposes of ground 5. The judge was satisfied that all the
other elements of the ground were similarly proven, and ordered
possession. An appeal on the basis, inter alia, that it was not reasonable to render the tenant homeless by repossession was dismissed.

3.271   If it is clear that there has been flagrant and deliberate lying and
deceitfulness, the expectation will be that possession will be ordered.
In such a case it would be 'an affront to those who put forward their
claims honestly, wait patiently and rely on the local housing authority to deal fairly with their claims' if a judge in such a case was not

---

212 [2011] EWCA Civ 735, [2011] HLR 39.
213 HA 1985 s84(2)(a); HA 1988 s7(4).
214 (1992) 24 HLR 124, CA. See also *Camden LBC v Burrell* June 1997 *Legal
      Action* 19.

satisfied that it was reasonable to order possession.[215] Nevertheless, even in a case where the tenant has been successfully prosecuted and received a custodial sentence in respect of the deception, it will not always be reasonable to make a possession order.[216] The possibility that the evicted tenant may be faced with a subsequent finding of intentional homelessness is no impediment to the court holding that it is reasonable to order possession in a ground 5 or ground 17 case.[217]

3.272   The requirements of ground 5 or ground 17 cannot be avoided by the landlord seeking possession on the basis that the tenancy falls to be rescinded on account of fraud or deception.[218] Even if the tenancy was granted to a person who would not have been entitled to be allocated it under the terms of a relevant housing allocation scheme, it will not be ultra vires and therefore void.[219]

3.273   As a result of the launch of a major initiative in November 2009 to address social housing fraud in England, the number of claims brought under grounds 5 and 17 has increased. As part of that initiative, social landlords in England were supplied with non-statutory guidance designed to assist with evidence gathering and case preparation in ground 5 and ground 17 cases.[220]

Waste or the neglect/deterioration of furniture

Deterioration in condition/waste or neglect: discretionary (HA 1988 ground 13 and HA 1985 ground 3)

3.274   HA 1985 Sch 2 ground 3 and HA 1988 Sch 2 ground 13 provide a ground for possession where:

> The condition of the dwelling-house or any of the common parts has deteriorated owing to acts of waste by, or the neglect or default of, the tenant or a person residing in the dwelling-house and, in the case of an act of waste by, or the neglect or default of, a person lodging with the tenant or a sub-tenant of his, the tenant has not taken such steps

---

215 *Shrewsbury and Atcham BC v Evans* (1998) 30 HLR 123, CA.
216 *Southwark LBC v Erekin* [2003] EWHC 1765 (Ch).
217 *Lewisham LBC v Akinsola* (2000) 32 HLR 414, CA.
218 *Islington LBC v Uckac* [2006] EWCA Civ 340, [2006] 1 WLR 1303.
219 *Birmingham CC v Qasim* [2009] EWCA Civ 1080, [2010] HLR 19.
220 *Tackling unlawful subletting and occupancy: Good practice guidance for social landlords* (CLG, November 2009).

as he ought reasonably to have taken for the removal of the lodger or sub-tenant.

3.275   The grounds are subject to the condition that an order for possession may be made only if it would be reasonable to do so.[221]

3.276   Useful guidance on the construction of these grounds can be derived from cases on the Rent Act 1977 Sch 15 Case 3 (see para 17.23). However, unlike the Rent Act Cases, grounds 3 and 13 embrace deterioration in the condition of 'common parts'. This phrase is defined[222] as meaning:

> ... any part of a building comprising the dwelling-house and any other premises which the tenant is entitled under the terms of the tenancy to use in common with the occupiers of other dwelling-houses let by the landlord ...

and the ground may therefore cover the situation in which the tenant or another person residing in the dwelling-house has been responsible for damaging the lifts, stairways, rubbish chutes, communal lighting, etc, in the block of flats of which the dwelling-house forms part. The acts or omissions must be proved on the balance of probabilities to have been the responsibility of the tenant or co-resident.

3.277   The grounds may apply even though there has been no breach of any term of the tenancy or of any common law duty.[223] The court should, however, take into account only neglect or waste which has taken place since the tenant became tenant of the premises. For example, in a Rent Act case where a son who was living with aged parents became a statutory tenant by succession after their death, it was wrong for the court to take into account his failure to do any works in the garden before their death.[224]

3.278   Note that the wording of grounds 3 and 13 has not been enlarged to make tenants responsible for damage caused by 'visitors' (although it does cover visitors who can properly be considered to be 'residing in' the dwelling or 'lodging with the tenant').

Both grounds are subject to the condition that, even if the terms of the grounds are established, an order may only be granted if it would be reasonable in all the circumstances.[225]

---

221 HA 1985 s84(2)(a); HA 1988 s7(4).

222 HA 1985 s116; HA 1988 Sch 2 ground 13.

223 *Lowe v Lendrum* (1950) 159 EG 423, where it was also said that 'neglect' is used in the context of tenant-like conduct.

224 *Holloway v Povey* (1984) 15 HLR 104, CA.

225 HA 1988 s7(4); HA 1985 s84(2)(a).

Deterioration of furniture: discretionary (HA 1988 ground 15 and HA 1985 ground 4)

3.279 HA 1985 Sch 2 ground 4 provides:

> The condition of furniture provided by the landlord for use under the tenancy, or for use in the common parts, has deteriorated owing to ill-treatment by the tenant or a person residing in the dwelling-house and, in the case of ill-treatment by a person lodging with the tenant or a sub-tenant of his, the tenant has not taken such steps as he ought reasonably to have taken for the removal of the lodger or sub-tenant.

3.280 HA 1988 Sch 2 ground 15 is almost identical save for the fact that it does not include 'furniture in the common parts'.

3.281 Although they have power to provide furniture for tenants,[226] local authoritiy landlords rarely do so. Most social housing is let unfurnished. However, as HA 1985 ground 4 extends to furniture provided by the landlord in the common parts of the property, given the extended definition of 'common parts' in HA 1985 s116 (set out at para 3.276 above), this would embrace vandalism by the tenant or co-resident in such places as the communal laundry or children's playing area.

3.282 Note that the wording of grounds 4 and 15 has not been enlarged to make tenants responsible for damage caused by 'visitors' although they will extend to those 'lodging with' the tenant.

3.283 Ground 4 and ground 15 are subject to the condition that, even if the terms of the ground are established, an order may be granted only if it would be reasonable in all the circumstances.[227]

Other grounds for possession: secure tenants

HA 1985 ground 6: payment of a premium (discretionary)

3.284 HA 1985 permits assignment by way of exchange of tenancies between secure occupiers[228] but payment of a premium as part of such a transaction renders both parties to the exchange exposed to possible possession proceedings based on HA 1985 Sch 2 ground 6. This applies where:

226 HA 1985 s10.
227 HA 1985 s84(2)(a); HA 1988 s7(4).
228 HA 1985 s92, and in some cases between secure occupiers and other tenants of social housing: see para 1.194.

The tenancy was assigned to the tenant, or to a predecessor in title of his who is a member of his family and is residing in the dwelling-house, by an assignment made by virtue of section 92 (assignments by way of exchange) and a premium was paid either in connection with that assignment or the assignment which the tenant or predecessor himself made by virtue of that section. In this paragraph the word 'premium' means any fine or other like sum and any other pecuniary consideration in addition to rent.

3.285   The wide definition of 'premium' was presumably intended to catch not only those tenants who are induced to agree to 'swap' their homes by outright cash payments but also those offered other financial inducements by the other party to the swap – such as the purchase (at inflated values) of curtains and carpets left behind or the payment of removal expenses.

3.286   The ground is met whichever party to the assignment pays a premium and extends to the current tenant where the assignment was carried out by a predecessor in title. In the latter case, the predecessor must be a member of the tenant's family still living in the tenant's home. If a notice seeking possession is served relying on this latter aspect of the ground, the claim can be defeated if the family member responsible moves permanently out of residence prior to the issue of proceedings.

3.287   Those defending tenants should carefully examine whether the mutual exchange in relation to which a premium was paid or received was in fact achieved by way of assignment under HA 1985 s92 at all. Many social landlords still undertake exchanges by inviting each tenant to surrender his or her existing tenancy in order to take a fresh tenancy of his or her exchange-partner's home.[229] Such an exchange would plainly not be within the reach of this ground at all. Nor can it be relied on where, although the administrative records of the landlord appear to show an assignment by way of mutual exchange, there is – as a matter of fact – no assignment at all.[230]

3.288   In order to recover possession, the landlord must, in addition to proving the ground, show that it would be reasonable for an order for possession to be made.[231]

---

229 As in *Merton LBC v Richards* [2005] EWCA Civ 639, [2005] HLR 44.
230 *Birmingham CC v Qasim* December 2008 *Legal Action* 24, Birmingham County Court. Not appealed on this point: see *Birmingham CC v Qasim* [2009] EWCA Civ 1080, [2010] HLR 19.
231 HA 1985 s84(2)(a).

HA 1985 ground 7: non-housing accommodation (discretionary)

3.289　HA 1985 Sch 2 ground 7 makes very specific provision for recovery of possession from those secure tenants residing in non-housing accommodation (for example, in a social services or educational facility) who are guilty of inappropriate conduct. It is met where:

> The dwelling-house forms part of, or is within the curtilage of, a building which, or so much of it as is held by the landlord, is held mainly for purposes other than housing purposes and consists mainly of accommodation other than housing accommodation, and –
>
> (a) the dwelling-house was let to the tenant or a predecessor in title of his in consequence of the tenant or predecessor being in the employment of the landlord, or of –
>> a local authority,
>> a development corporation,
>> a housing action trust,
>> a Mayoral development corporation,
>> an urban development corporation,
>> ... or
>> the governors of an aided school,
>
> and
>
> (b) the tenant or a person residing in the dwelling-house has been guilty of conduct such that, having regard to the purpose for which the building is used, it would not be right for him to continue in occupation of the dwelling-house.

3.290　The cases that Parliament presumably had in mind were of 'misbehaviour' by resident staff (or their successors) accommodated within the buildings or grounds of schools, colleges and residential homes.

3.291　The misconduct must be related to the purpose for which the main building is generally used. The dwelling occupied by the tenant must either be within the same building as the workplace or be within the 'curtilage' of that building. It is not sufficient simply to show that the tenanted dwelling is within the same grounds as that building.[232]

3.292　Whether the dwelling is within the 'curtilage' of another building is largely an issue of fact. Advisers will find helpful guidance in the case-law relating to applications for exercise of the right to buy which

---

232 *Dyer v Dorset CC* [1989] QB 346, (1988) 20 HLR 490, CA and *Burns v Central Regional Council* 1988 SLT (Lands Tr) 46.

turn on whether the property sought to be purchased is within the curtilage of another.[233]

3.293   Likewise, assistance may be derived from judicial consideration of the term 'curtilage' in planning cases.[234]

3.294   If the accommodation has been provided to an employee who is required to occupy it for the better performance of his or her duties, the tenancy or licence may not be secure at all.[235]

3.295   Possession may be ordered under ground 7 only if in all the circumstances it is reasonable for an order to be made.[236]

HA 1985 ground 8: temporary accommodation (discretionary)

3.296   Occasionally, landlords temporarily rehouse secure tenants while works of repair or improvement are in progress at their homes. If the secure tenant is offered and accepts an alternative secure tenancy or licence of such accommodation while work is in progress, HA 1985 Sch 2 ground 8 deals with the situation if that tenant or his or her successor refuses to return 'home' once the work is completed. The ground will be satisfied where:

> The dwelling-house was made available for occupation by the tenant (or a predecessor in title of his) while works were carried out on the dwelling-house which he previously occupied as his only or principal home and –
> (a) the tenant (or predecessor) was a secure tenant of the other dwelling-house at the time when he ceased to occupy it as his home,
> (b) the tenant (or predecessor) accepted the tenancy of the dwelling-house of which possession is sought on the understanding that he would give up occupation when, on completion of the works, the other dwelling-house was again available for occupation by him under a secure tenancy, and
> (c) the works have been completed and the other dwelling-house is so available.

3.297   Note that ground 8 is not concerned with requiring the tenant to move *out* for works to be undertaken – that is covered by ground 10 (see paras 3.304–3.312). Ground 8 concerns the scenario of a

---

233 HA 1985 Sch 5 para 5. See, in particular, *Barwick v Kent CC* (1992) 24 HLR 341, CA.
234 See, eg, *Skerritts of Nottingham Ltd v Secretary of State for the Environment* [2001] QB 59, CA and *Morris v Wrexham BC* December 2001 *Legal Action* 22.
235 HA 1985 Sch 1 para 2 (see para 1.69 above).
236 HA 1985 s84(2)(a).

tenant refusing to move *back* to the former home when the work on that home is completed. It must be shown both that the tenant had agreed to move back (the term 'understanding' is used in the ground) and that the works have been completed. For an example of the factual circumstances in which ground 8 could have been (but was not) deployed, see *Lambeth LBC v Gent*.[237] The ground can be satisfied only if the tenant will be returning to the former home which is to be let under a secure tenancy. Therefore, it cannot apply if, after the tenant was temporarily decanted, the former home was subject of a sale or a transfer to a landlord incapable of granting a secure tenancy (see paras 1.58–1.64). Of course, if the tenant's current temporary home is so transferred, the tenant will no longer be a secure tenant and the ground cannot be relied upon at all.

In *Francis v Brent Housing Partnership*,[238] Ms Francis occupied her home as a tolerated trespasser. In 2004, Brent decided that they needed to move Ms Francis into temporary accommodation to carry out repairs to the property. The parties entered into a decant agreement so that the Brent could, in the event that Ms Francis refused to return to her home, rely on Ground 8. In doing so, the agreement recorded that Ms Francis was the secure tenant of her home and it would continue to be secure when she moved back to it. The Court of Appeal held that the effect of this agreement was to grant Ms Francis a secure tenancy of her home.

3.298   The ground is subject to the condition that the grant of an order must be reasonable in all the circumstances.[239] Relevant factors on reasonableness will include: the circumstances under which the tenant was initially required to move; the terms of any understanding reached at that time with the landlord; and the length of time the tenant has been in the present property. The court may be particularly reluctant to disturb the tenant if works at the former home were scheduled to take a few months and were only completed some years later.

HA 1985 ground 9: overcrowding (mandatory)

3.299   Housing Act 1985 Sch 2 ground 9 will be made out where:

> The dwelling-house is overcrowded, within the meaning of Part X, in such circumstances as to render the occupier guilty of an offence.

---

237 July 2001 *Legal Action* 32.
238 [2013] EWCA Civ 912, [2013] HLR 47.
239 HA 1985 s84(2)(a).

3.300   'Overcrowding', for these purposes, is defined by HA 1985 Part 10 which provides:

324 *Definition of overcrowding*

A dwelling is overcrowded for the purposes of this Part when the number of persons sleeping in the dwelling is such as to contravene –

(a) the standard specified in section 325 (the room standard), or

(b) the standard specified in section 326 (the space standard).

325 *The room standard*

(1) The room standard is contravened when the number of persons sleeping in a dwelling and the number of rooms available as sleeping accommodation is such that two persons of opposite sexes who are not living together as husband and wife must sleep in the same room.

(2) For this purpose –

    (a) children under the age of ten shall be left out of account, and

    (b) a room is available as sleeping accommodation if it is of a type normally used in the locality either as a bedroom or as a living room.

326 *The space standard*

(1) The space standard is contravened when the number of persons sleeping in a dwelling is in excess of the permitted number, having regard to the number and floor area of the rooms of the dwelling available as sleeping accommodation.

(2) For this purpose –

    (a) no account shall be taken of a child under the age of one and a child aged one or over but under ten shall be reckoned as one-half of a unit, and

    (b) a room is available as sleeping accommodation if it is of a type normally used in the locality either as a living room or as a bedroom.

(3) The permitted number of persons in relation to a dwelling is whichever is the less of –

    (a) the number specified in Table I in relation to the number of rooms in the dwelling available as sleeping accommodation, and

    (b) the aggregate for all such rooms in the dwelling of the numbers specified in column 2 of Table II in relation to each room of the floor area specified in column 1.

No account shall be taken for the purposes of either Table of a room having a floor area of less than 50 square feet.

TABLE I

Number of persons	Number of rooms
1	2
2	3
3	5
4	7½
5 or more	2 for each room

TABLE II

Number of persons	Floor area of room
110 sq ft or more	2
90 sq ft or more but less than 110 sq ft	1½
70 sq ft or more but less than 90 sq ft	1
50 sq ft or more but less than 70 sq ft	½

(4) The Secretary of State may by regulations prescribe the manner in which the floor area of a room is to be ascertained for the purpose of this section; and the regulations may provide for the exclusion from computation, or the bringing into computation at a reduced figure, of floor space in a part of the room which is of less than a specified height not exceeding eight feet.

(5) Regulations under subsection (4) shall be made by statutory instrument which shall be subject to annulment in pursuance of a resolution of either House of Parliament.

(6) A certificate of the local housing authority stating the number and floor areas of the rooms in a dwelling, and that the floor areas have been ascertained in the prescribed manner, is prima facie evidence for the purposes of legal proceedings of the facts stated in it.

Responsibility of occupier

327 *Penalty for occupier causing or permitting overcrowding*

(1) The occupier of a dwelling who causes or permits it to be overcrowded commits a summary offence, subject to subsection (2).

(2) The occupier is not guilty of an offence –

(a) if the overcrowding is within the exceptions specified in section 328 or 329 (children attaining age of 10 or visiting relatives), or

(b) by reason of anything done under the authority of, and in accordance with any conditions specified in, a licence granted by the local housing authority under section 330.

(3) A person committing an offence under this section is liable on conviction to a fine not exceeding level 2 on the standard scale and to a further fine not exceeding one-tenth of the amount corresponding to that level in respect of every day subsequent to the date on which he is convicted on which the offence continues.

328   *Exception: children attaining age of 1 or 10*

(1) Where a dwelling which would not otherwise be overcrowded becomes overcrowded by reason of a child attaining the age of one or ten, then if the occupier –
  (a) applies to the local housing authority for suitable alternative accommodation, or
  (b) has so applied before the date when the child attained the age in question,

he does not commit an offence under section 327 (occupier causing or permitting overcrowding), so long as the condition in subsection (2) is met and the occupier does not fail to take action in the circumstances specified in subsection (3).

(2) The condition is that all the persons sleeping in the dwelling are persons who were living there when the child attained that age and thereafter continuously live there, or children born after that date of any of those persons.

(3) The exception provided by this section ceases to apply if –
  (a) suitable alternative accommodation is offered to the occupier on or after the date on which the child attains that age, or, if he has applied before that date, is offered at any time after the application, and he fails to accept it, or
  (b) the removal from the dwelling of some person not a member of the occupier's family is on that date or thereafter becomes reasonably practicable having regard to all the circumstances (including the availability of suitable alternative accommodation for that person), and the occupier fails to require his removal.

329   *Exception: visiting family member*

Where the persons sleeping in an overcrowded dwelling include a member of the occupier's family who does not live there but is sleeping there temporarily, the occupier is not guilty of an offence under section 327 (occupier causing or permitting overcrowding) unless the circumstances are such that he would be so guilty if that member of his family were not sleeping there.

3.301   Overcrowding is generally prohibited by HA 1985 Part 10, but not all overcrowding renders the occupier guilty of an offence. In particular, overcrowding caused by visiting family members[240] or by a

---

240 HA 1985 s329.

natural growth in family size[241] is excepted and a local council may, in any event, license what would otherwise be illegal overcrowding[242] to prevent the occupier being liable to conviction. However, a council which places secure tenants in overcrowded property may itself be liable to conviction.[243]

3.302 If this ground is made out, the landlord need not also satisfy the court on 'reasonableness' but must show that suitable alternative accommodation will be available to the tenant if an order is made.[244] HA 1985 Sch 2 Part IV para 3 makes special provision as to what is 'suitable alternative accommodation' for those against whom possession is sought on overcrowding grounds, in the following terms:

> 3. Where possession of a dwelling-house is sought on ground 9 (overcrowding such as to render occupier guilty of offence), other accommodation may be reasonably suitable to the needs of the tenant and his family notwithstanding that the permitted number of persons for that accommodation, as defined in section 326(3) (overcrowding: the space standard), is less than the number of persons living in the dwelling-house of which possession is sought.

3.303 Of course, the accommodation must also be suitable in the other respects referred to in HA 1985 Sch 2 Part IV (see para 3.355).

HA 1985 ground 10: landlord's works (mandatory)

3.304 Possession proceedings may be brought on HA 1985 Sch 2 ground 10 where:

> The landlord intends, within a reasonable time of obtaining possession of the dwelling-house –
> (a) to demolish or reconstruct the building or part of the building comprising the dwelling-house, or
> (b) to carry out work on that building or on land let together with, and thus treated as part of, the dwelling-house,
> and cannot reasonably do so without obtaining possession of the dwelling-house.

3.305 See also the commentary to HA 1988 ground 6 below (paras 3.359– 3.367). The landlord must not simply intend to carry out substantial work but, in order to satisfy this ground, must also show that the work *cannot* be carried out without obtaining possession of the dwell-

---

241 HA 1985 s328.
242 HA 1985 s330.
243 See *DPP v Carrick DC* (1985) 31 *Housing Aid* 5.
244 HA 1985 s84(2)(b).

ing-house. The landlord needs to establish that legal possession of the property and termination of the tenancy is necessary, not simply access to, or temporary occupation of, the premises by the landlord's contractors.[245]

3.306   Unless the case is one of prospective complete demolition, it must be proved that either the tenant has refused to co-operate with the landlord's proposals for temporary displacement to other accommodation or that the landlord does not have and cannot supply any accommodation to provide a temporary dwelling for the tenant while works are in progress. That is because the ground cannot be made out if the tenant demonstrates a willingness to move out of the premises (for example, to stay with relatives or in temporary accommodation supplied by the landlord) while work is in progress.

3.307   On the other hand, there will be cases in which the proposed works are so extensive as to amount to reconstruction, in which circumstances the recovery of possession seems sensible and the ground will be satisfied.

3.308   The Court of Appeal has held that in order to establish ground 10, the landlord must be in a position to: (a) identify specifically the proposed works and (b) show why it is necessary to recover possession in order for the works to be carried out.[246]

3.309   Even if the ground is made out, possession cannot be ordered unless suitable alternative accommodation is available to the tenant and his or her family.[247] There is, however, no requirement that the landlord also prove 'reasonableness', whether in the sense that it is reasonable for the landlord to want to carry out the particular works or that it is reasonable for the particular tenant to be compulsorily moved.

3.310   If the tenant is forced to give up possession, he or she will usually seek to move to permanent suitable alternative accommodation rather than to negotiate an 'understanding' with the landlord for return to the original accommodation once work is completed because such an understanding opens the way to later proceedings under ground 8 (see paras 3.296–3.298).

---

245 See *Sugarwhite v Afridi* [2002] CLY 3013, Central London Civil Justice Centre (where possession was unsuccessfully sought from an assured tenant on a similarly worded ground) and the discussion of *Heath v Drown* [1973] AC 498, at para 3.365.

246 *Wansbeck DC v Marley* (1988) 20 HLR 247, CA.

247 HA 1985 s84(2)(b). See para 3.7.

3.311   Tenants displaced as a result of ground 10 proceedings may be entitled to home loss payments.[248] A check should also be made to see if there is any specific provision in the tenancy agreement about the compensation which may be payable.[249]

3.312   Before the introduction of HA 2004, a tenant attached to his or her home in its present condition could frustrate the landlord's intentions for demolition or reconstruction by exercising the statutory right to buy. If the application to buy reached the stage at which the tenant would be enabled to compel completion by injunction, the tenant would be entitled to complete the purchase if the application for the injunction was heard before the trial of any claim for possession under ground 10.[250] If the injunction application and trial were listed on the same date, it would be for the judge to decide which matter to take first.[251] However, in order to prevent the purchase of properties obviously scheduled for future redevelopment, the right to buy provisions have now been extensively modified in such cases by HA 2004 ss182–183.

HA 1985 ground 10A: landlord seeking to sell with vacant possession (mandatory)

3.313   The Housing and Planning Act 1986 s5 inserted ground 10A into HA 1985 Sch 2.[252] It assists landlords who want to achieve vacant possession and thereafter sell property for redevelopment. Ground 10A provides that a court may order possession if suitable alternative accommodation is available to the secure tenant (see paras 3.7 and 3.351–3.357) and:

> The dwelling-house is in an area which is the subject of a redevelopment scheme approved by the Secretary of State[253] or the Regulator

---

248 Land Compensation Act 1973 s29, as amended by Housing and Planning Act 1986 s5(3).
249 *Borg v Southwark LBC* June 1987 *Legal Action* 19, CA.
250 *Dance v Welwyn Hatfield DC* [1990] 22 HLR 339, CA.
251 *Bristol City Council v Lovell* [1998] 1 WLR 446, [1998] 1 All ER 775, HL.
252 Housing and Planning Act 1986 (Commencement) (No 5) Order 1987 SI No 754. Effective date 13 May 1987; see DoE Circ 14/87.
253 Functions of the secretary of state, so far as exercisable in relation to Wales, were transferred to the National Assembly for Wales, by the National Assembly for Wales (Transfer of Functions) Order 1999 SI No 672 art 2 and Sch 1.

of Social Housing[254] or Scottish Homes in accordance with Part V of this Schedule and the landlord intends within a reasonable time of obtaining possession to dispose of the dwelling-house in accordance with the scheme.

or

Part of the dwelling-house is in such an area and the landlord intends within a reasonable time of obtaining possession to dispose of that part in accordance with the scheme and for that purpose reasonably requires possession of the dwelling-house.

3.314　In order for the ground to become available, the dwelling must be in a 'redevelopment' area. HA 1985 Sch 2 Part V sets out the terms under which the secretary of state, the regulator of social housing or the Welsh Assembly Government may designate such an area. The procedure requires an element of prior consultation with tenants[255] and allows the secretary of state, the regulator or the Welsh Assembly Government to require information from the relevant landlord,[256] take into account a variety of factors[257] and grant conditional or outright approval.[258] If the scheme is approved conditionally, the landlord may rely on a notice seeking possession served on ground 10A even though the conditions are not satisfied at the date of service, so long as they are fulfilled at the date of the hearing.[259] Where the landlord is a local housing authority or private registered provider of social housing, the HA 1985 Part V functions fall on the new regulator of social housing.[260]

3.315　In order to obtain possession on ground 10A, the landlord need not satisfy the court that an order is reasonably required. The only relevant condition is that suitable alternative accommodation is available.

3.316　Tenants displaced as a result of ground 10A proceedings may be entitled to home loss payments.[261] A check should also be made to

---

254　From 1 April 2010 the Regulator of Social Housing replaced the Housing Corporation for these purposes: Housing and Regeneration Act 2008 (Consequential Provisions) Order 2010 SI No 866 Sch 2 para 37(2). The regulator in England is the Homes and Community Agency.
255　HA 1985 Sch 2 Pt V para 2.
256　HA 1985 Sch 2 Pt V para 3(2).
257　HA 1985 Sch 2 Pt V para 3(1).
258　HA 1985 Sch 2 Pt V para 5(1).
259　HA 1985 Sch 2 Pt V para 5(3).
260　HA 1985 Sch 2 Pt V para 6.
261　Land Compensation Act 1973 s29, as amended by Housing and Planning Act 1986 s5(3).

see if there is any specific provision in the tenancy agreement about the compensation which may be payable.[262]

HA 1985 ground 11: charitable landlords (mandatory)

3.317 Housing Act 1985 Sch 2 ground 11 provides that a ground for possession arises where:

The landlord is a charity and the tenant's continued occupation of the dwelling-house would conflict with the objects of the charity.

3.318 The condition which the landlord must also satisfy is that suitable alternative accommodation is available to the tenant[263] (see paras 3.7 and 3.351–3.357). However, the landlord need not also show that it is reasonable to require the tenant to move.

3.319 If the conflict with the objects of the charity is caused by the tenant's breach of the tenancy agreement, the tenant runs the risk that the landlord may in the alternative rely on ground 1 and secure possession without being required to provide alternative accommodation (see para 3.255).

3.320 In other cases, the ground is likely to be satisfied as a result of a change in the tenant's circumstances (for example, where the charity's object is the provision of accommodation for single people and the tenant marries or has children) or by a change in the charity's objects.

HA 1985 s90: recovery of fixed-term tenancy after secure tenant dies (mandatory)

3.321 HA 1985 s90 provides that a landlord may recover possession of a fixed-term tenancy of a dwelling-house in England that has ceased to be secure on the death of the secure tenant and has been vested or otherwise disposed of in the administration of the secure tenant's estate.[264] In those circumstances, the landlord may apply to the court for an order for possession of the dwelling-house let under the tenancy and the court must make a possession order provided:

- the landlord has served a notice in writing on the tenant (ie the tenant's estate or the person or body who has succeeded to the fixed-term tenancy) stating that the landlord requires possession of the dwelling-house, and specifying a date, which must be more

---

262 *Borg v Southwark LBC* June 1987 *Legal Action* 19, CA.
263 HA 1985 s84(2)(b).
264 HA 1985 s90(5).

than four weeks after the notice is served on the tenant, after which
proceedings for an order for possession may be begun, and
- the notice has expired without the tenant giving up possession of
  the dwelling-house.[265]

The ground is aimed at preventing a fixed-term tenancy from passing
to a person who is not qualified to succeed to the tenancy under HA
1985 s89. Otherwise, that person will be able to inherit a fixed-term
secure tenancy which may have many years left to run. This had previously been unnecessary as almost all secure tenancies were periodic and could be determined by a notice to quit when they ceased to
be secure.

As it is a mandatory ground for possession the tenant's sole means
of defending the claim will be to argue that the notice is invalid or
to raise a public law, human rights or Equality Act 2010 defence
(see chapters 25, 26 and 27). The tenancy ends when the order is
executed.[266]

HA 1985 ground 12: tied accommodation (discretionary)

3.322   HA 1985 Sch 2 ground 12 relates to what might be described as 'tied'
or 'employment-related' accommodation. It requires the landlord to
prove that:

> The dwelling-house forms part of, or is within the curtilage of, a build-
> ing which, or so much of it as is held by the landlord, is held mainly
> for purposes other than housing purposes and consists mainly of
> accommodation other than housing accommodation, or is situated in
> a cemetery, and –
> (a) the dwelling-house was let to the tenant or a predecessor in title
>   of his in consequence of the tenant or predecessor being in the
>   employment of the landlord or of –
>   a local authority,
>   a development corporation,
>   a housing action trust,
>   a Mayoral development corporation,
>   an urban development corporation,
>   ..., or
>   the governors of an aided school,
>   and that employment has ceased,
> and

265 HA 1985 s90(6)–(9).
266 HA 1985 s90(10).

(b) the landlord reasonably requires the dwelling-house for occupation as a residence for some person either engaged in the employment of the landlord, or of such a body, or with whom a contract
for such employment has been entered into conditional on housing being provided.

The ground is not restricted to the situation in which the same body
is both landlord and employer. It expressly incorporates situations
where the landlord is a prescribed social landlord (see para 1.58) and
the tenant is an employee of another or different authority of the type
mentioned in the body of the ground.

3.323 It is not sufficient that the tenant (or the person from whom the
tenant derived title) is an ex-employee of the landlord. The original
letting must have been 'in consequence' of that employment. See the
discussion on the similar Rent Act ground (para 12.62) and generally
chapter 17 (Premises occupied by employees). For the meaning of
'within the curtilage of' see paras 3.291–3.292.

3.324 The landlord must already be employing the next person for
whom the property is required or have a contract for the employment of that person. The property must also be 'reasonably required'
by the landlord.[267]

3.325 In addition, the landlord must satisfy the dual conditions that: (a)
there will be suitable alternative accommodation (see para 3.203) for
the tenant and any family and (b) it is reasonable to order possession
in all the circumstances of the case.[268]

3.326 In considering whether it would be reasonable to order possession,
the court should have regard to issues including: the ex-employee's
age; his or her length of service; other accommodation possibilities
for the new employee; and the nature of the accommodation of which
possession is sought.

HA 1985 ground 13: accommodation for the disabled (discretionary)

3.327 Special provision is made for the recovery of premises adapted for
the disabled. HA 1985 Sch 2 ground 13 applies where:

The dwelling-house has features which are substantially different
from those of ordinary dwelling-houses and which are designed to
make it suitable for occupation by a physically disabled person who

267 Compare with Rent Act 1977 Sch 15 Case 8 discussed at para 12.62.
268 HA 1985 s84(2)(c).

requires accommodation of a kind provided by the dwelling-house and –

(a) there is no longer such a person residing in the dwelling-house, and

(b) the landlord requires it for occupation (whether alone or with members of his family) by such a person.

3.328   Note that the special features must be 'substantially' different from those of an ordinary dwelling and they must have been 'designed' (in the technical sense) for the special needs of the physically disabled. A simple additional ground-floor lavatory does not fulfil those requirements.[269]

3.329   The ground is not available where the premises are adapted for use by a *mentally* disabled tenant (recovery of possession in such cases would be sought under grounds 14 or 15 discussed below). Furthermore, the landlord must show that possession is required for a new prospective tenant who is a physically disabled person with requirements for all or any of the particular special features presently provided.

3.330   If the ground is made out, the landlord must prove, in addition, that: (a) suitable alternative accommodation is available (see parsa 3.351–3.357); and (b) it would be reasonable for a possession order to be made.[270]

HA 1985 ground 14: special needs accommodation provided by housing associations and trusts (discretionary)

3.331   HA 1985 Sch 2 ground 14 applies where:

The landlord is a housing association or housing trust which lets dwelling-houses only for occupation (whether alone or with others) by persons whose circumstances (other than merely financial circumstances) make it especially difficult for them to satisfy their need for housing, and –

(a) either there is no longer such a person residing in the dwelling-house or the tenant has received from a local housing authority an offer of accommodation in premises which are to be let as a separate dwelling under a secure tenancy, and

(b) the landlord requires the dwelling-house for occupation (whether alone or with members of his family) by such a person.

---

269 *Freeman v Wansbeck DC* (1983) 10 HLR 54, [1984] 2 All ER 746, CA.
270 HA 1985 s84(2)(c).

3.332 Note that the limbs of paragraph (a) are expressed in the alternative. The second limb makes special provision for those reluctant to move on from 'half-way' houses or 'bridging' accommodation into secure social housing sector tenancies. That limb cannot be satisfied by the association or trust making available a secure or an assured tenancy with the same or another association or trust – only a local authority secure tenancy (and not an introductory tenancy) satisfies the provision. Whichever limb is relied on, the landlord must also show that a person with the appropriate special housing need would take the tenant's place.

3.333 In order to succeed in recovering possession in reliance on this ground, the landlord must show that both the 'suitable alternative accommodation' (see paras 3.351–3.357) and 'reasonableness' conditions are satisfied.[271]

HA 1985 ground 15: special needs accommodation (discretionary)

3.334 Provision is made by HA 1985 Sch 2 ground 15 for recovery of possession of one of a group of dwellings let to those with special needs.

3.335 It applies where:

The dwelling-house is one of a group of dwelling-houses which it is the practice of the landlord to let for occupation by persons with special needs and –

(a) a social service or special facility is provided in close proximity to the group of dwelling-houses in order to assist persons with those special needs,

(b) there is no longer a person with those special needs residing in the dwelling-house, and

(c) the landlord requires the dwelling-house for occupation (whether alone or with members of his family) by a person who has those special needs.

3.336 The special needs dwellings must be in a 'group' within the ordinary meaning of that term. It is suggested that this requirement would not be met where the relevant dwellings said by the landlord to comprise the 'group' were spread throughout the area of the landlord's ordinary housing stock.[272]

3.337 Limbs (a), (b) and (c) must all be satisfied. In order to succeed in recovering possession the landlord must also show that 'suitable

271 HA 1985 s84(2)(c).
272 *Martin v Motherwell DC* 1991 SLT (Lands Tr) 4, noted at September 1991 *Legal Action* 15.

alternative accommodation is available' (see paras 3.351–3.357) and that the making of an order would be reasonable in all the circumstances.[273]

HA 1985 ground 15A (ground 16 in Wales):[274] under-occupation on death of tenant (discretionary)

3.338   No ground for possession is available to the landlord in HA 1985 Sch 2 simply on the basis that the original tenant no longer requires such extensive accommodation as was needed at the date of the original letting. Extensive non-statutory guidance is available to help landlords encourage secure tenants to move voluntarily from under-occupied homes.[275]

3.339   However, if the present tenant has become a secure tenant on a statutory succession (as described at para 1.140 above) and was not the deceased tenant's spouse or registered civil partner, grounds 15A and 16 make limited provision for recovery of the property by the landlord where:

> The accommodation afforded by it is more extensive than is reasonably required by the tenant and –
> (a) the tenancy vested in the tenant by virtue of section 89 (succession to periodic tenancy) or 90 (devolution of term certain) in a case where the tenant was not the previous tenant's spouse or civil partner, and
> (b) notice of the proceedings for possession was served under section 83 (*or, where no such notice was served, the proceedings for possession were begun*) more than six months but less than twelve months after the relevant date.

> For this purpose 'the relevant date' is –
> (a) the date of the previous tenant's death, or
> (b) if the court so directs, the date on which, in the opinion of the court, the landlord (or, in the case of joint landlords, any one of them) became aware of the previous tenant's death.

> The matters to be taken into account by the court in determining whether it is reasonable to make an order on this ground include –
> (a) the age of the tenant,

---

273 HA 1985 s84(2)(c).

274 The ground is now 15A in England and 16 in Wales despite being in identical form.

275 *Overcrowding and under-occupation: Self-assessment for social landlords* (TSA, November 2009) and *Managing underoccupation: A guide to good practice in social housing* (DETR, April 2001).

(b) the period (if any) during which the tenant has occupied the dwelling-house as the tenant's only or principal home, and

(c) any financial or other support given by the tenant to the previous tenant.

3.340 Note therefore that grounds 15A and 16 do not provide for recovery of possession from a widow or widower or surviving civil partner of the deceased tenant who is under-occupying. Nor do they apply to the under-occupying successor to a fixed-term tenancy.[276]

3.341 They can also be avoided if the late tenant had sufficient foresight to assign the tenancy to the successor in advance of his or her death rather than leaving it to be transmitted on death.[277] In such a case, the new assignee tenant cannot be ousted under ground 15A or 16 (although ground 1 may be applicable if the assignment was made in breach of a prohibition against assignment: but see para 1.197 on the possible unfairness of such a restriction).[278]

3.342 Grounds 15A and 16 set a specific timetable for action by the landlord. The notice seeking possession must be served no earlier than six months from the date of death of the former tenant. The Localism Act 2011 s162 amended HA 1985 Sch 2 by introducing ground 15A for England and amending ground 16 in Wales. The wording of both grounds are, however, identical. Ground 15A and the amended ground 16 provide that the notice may now either be served within one month after the death of the tenant or, if the court so directs, the date on which, in the opinion of the court, the landlord became aware of the previous tenant's death. This reverses the decision of the Court of Appeal in *Newport CC v Charles*.[279] The court held that the notice had to be given within 12 months of the tenant's death irrespective of when the landlord learnt of it.

3.343 In the event that the landlord still serves the notice out of time, the requirement cannot be avoided by the landlord inviting the court to dispense with a notice altogether[280] because the grounds provide that where no notice is served, the proceedings for possession must still have been commenced within the same six-month 'window'.

3.344 The words italicised in ground 15A/16 were added by HA 1996 s147(3). It seems difficult to envisage a case in which the court could

276 HA 1985 s90.
277 HA 1985 s91(3)(c).
278 *Peabody Donation Fund Governors v Higgins* [1983] 3 All ER 122, (1983) 10 HLR 82, CA.
279 [2008] EWCA Civ 1541, [2009] HLR 18.
280 HA 1985 s83(1).

be persuaded in a ground 16 situation to exercise its discretion and dispense with a notice seeking possession when no notice had been given to the bereaved successor at all. More likely the new words will be relied on by a landlord which is found to have served a technically defective notice but has nevertheless brought the claim in time.

3.345   The grounds require the landlord to prove that the dwelling *is* more extensive than *is* reasonably required. It is not sufficient to show that the dwelling was more extensive than the successor reasonably required at the date of succession. The question is to be addressed by the judge on the facts as the date of the hearing.[281]

3.346   The landlord must not only satisfy each limb of the relevant ground but also show that: (a) suitable alternative accommodation is available (see paras 3.351–3.357) and (b) it would be reasonable for an order to be made.[282] Indeed, the fact that suitable alternative accommodation is available to the tenant is a factor that goes to the 'reasonableness' of making an order in this class of case.[283]

3.347   As to (a), because the present tenant is a successor, he or she will take the fresh secure tenancy of alternative accommodation also as a successor unless the landlord can be persuaded to agree otherwise.[284] The possibility of such an agreement may be raised in negotiations designed to achieve a compromise in ground 15A and 16 cases where the defence is not strong and the successor is attracted by the offer of alternative accommodation which is not only suitable but which will (if agreement can be reached) also provide the opportunity for a further succession within the family. Alternative accommodation will usually be suitable if, like the secure tenant's present tenancy, it will offer the opportunity to exercise the right to buy. Whether it can be a suitable alternative at all where the tenant will lose the right to buy was canvassed in, but not resolved by, the Court of Appeal in *Manchester CC v Benjamin*.[285]

3.348   As to (b), the reasonableness test, note that the second paragraph of the grounds makes specific provision for identified factors to be taken into account by the court. In addition, the successor tenant may argue that account should be taken of his or her rights under HRA 1998 Sch 1 to respect for home, family and private life in relation to what may have been a lifetime home (see chapter 26).

---

281 *Wandsworth LBC v Randall* [2007] EWCA Civ 1126, [2008] 1 WLR 359.
282 HA 1985 s84(2)(c).
283 *Bracknell Forest BC v Green* [2009] EWCA Civ 238, [2009] HLR 38.
284 HA 1985 s88(4).
285 [2008] EWCA Civ 189, [2009] 1 All ER 798.

3.349　　It has been held that if the successor tenant has claimed a right to buy, the court, in considering reasonableness, should take into account the reasons why the landlord wishes to recover possession and the fact that the tenant may have established a right to purchase.[286] For the specific factors which the court should consider in weighing the legitimate claim by a tenant to exercise the right to buy against the landlord's well-founded claim for possession, see *Kensington and Chelsea RLBC v Hislop*[287] and *Basildon DC v Wahlen*.[288] Both cases were reviewed and discussed by the Court of Appeal in *Manchester CC v Benjamin*.[289] Ultimately, it is a matter for the judge who has heard the evidence to balance the various factors.

3.350　　More commonly, the issues on reasonableness will come down to a fine balance between the tenant's understandable desire to remain in what may have been their lifetime home against the housing needs of others on the landlord's waiting list who could fully utilise the presently under-occupied accommodation. The classic example is provided by *Bracknell Forest BC v Green*.[290] In that case, the Court of Appeal said that:

> Taking into account all the factors relevant to the reasonableness of making a possession order, the Recorder was entitled to conclude that the combination of factors relied on by the council, including the offer of suitable accommodation, was outweighed by the length of Mr Green's occupation of the house, his personal and family circumstances, his age and the permanently destabilising effect of a possession order on him. (at [35])

and that

> The judicial process of balancing the circumstances, some pointing one way and some the other way, is for the lower court, not for the council nor for this court on an appeal. The terms of the 1985 Act expressly contemplate cases in which the tenant's personal circumstances, such as Mr Green's age and his unusually long period of occupation, may outweigh the pressures on public housing and other factors. (at [37])

For example, judges in the county court have refused to order possession where there is medical evidence which shows that the tenant's mental or physical health would deteriorate if they were required to

---

286 *Enfield LBC v McKeon* [1986] 2 All ER 730, (1986) 18 HLR 330, CA.
287 [2003] EWHC 2944 (Ch), [2004] HLR 26.
288 [2006] EWCA Civ 326, [2006] HLR 34.
289 [2008] EWCA Civ 189, [2008] HLR 38.
290 [2009] EWCA Civ 238, [2009] HLR 38.

move.[291] Possession orders have also been refused where the evidence was that the tenant had lived in the property for most of his life and spent many years caring for his mother.[292]

Suitable alternative accommodation

3.351   In any proceedings based on grounds 9 to 16 the landlord must show that suitable alternative accommodation will be available to the tenant and his or her family if a possession order is made.[293]

3.352   Where the landlord is not the local housing authority, the obligation is satisfied by production of a certificate issued by the local housing authority to the effect that it will provide suitable accommodation before a specified date.[294]

3.353   Where the landlord is the local housing authority or there is no certificate, the landlord must prove at the hearing of the claim that suitable accommodation within the terms of HA 1985 Sch 2 Part IV paras 1 and 2 is going to be available to the tenant if a possession order is made. There is no requirement that an offer of accommodation is made before the date of the trial or that the accommodation is available at the date of the hearing. The court need only be satisfied that suitable accommodation will be available once the possession order is executed.[295] Tenants' representatives should ensure, however, that where a possession order has been made without suitable accommodation having been identified, it is not enforceable until the landlord has in fact provided or identified such accommodation and that the tenant has liberty to apply to the court in circumstances where it is contended that the accommodation is not suitable.

3.354   It also follows that earlier offers of other accommodation are irrelevant save possibly to any consideration of 'reasonableness'.[296]

---

291 *Greenwich LBC v McMullan* May 2012 *Legal Action* 31, Woolwich County Court; *Redbridge LBC v West* May 2013 *Legal Action* 35, Bow County Court; *Wandsworth LBC v Matty* June 2016 *Legal Action* 41, County Court at Wandsworth; *Governors of Peabody v Lawrence* February 2016 *Legal Action* 43, County Court at Central London.

292 *Hackney LBC v Sheehan* May 2012 *Legal Action* 32, Clerkenwell and Shoreditch County Court.

293 HA 1985 s84(2)(b) and (c).

294 HA 1985 Sch 2 Pt IV para 4. As to such certificates see para 3.375.

295 *Reading BC v Holt* [2013] EWCA Civ 641, [2013] HLR 40.

296 *Wandsworth LBC v Randall* [2007] EWCA Civ 1126, [2008] HLR 24.

3.355   HA 1985 Sch 2 Part IV paras 1 and 2 provide:

1) For the purposes of section 84(2)(b) and (c) (case in which court is not to make an order for possession unless satisfied that suitable accommodation will be available) accommodation is suitable if it consists of premises –

   (a) which are to be let as a separate dwelling under a secure tenancy, or

   (b) which are to be let as a separate dwelling under a protected tenancy, not being a tenancy under which the landlord might recover possession under one of the Cases in Part II of Schedule 15 to Rent Act 1977 (cases where court must order possession), or

   (c) *which are to be let as a separate dwelling under an assured tenancy which is neither an assured shorthold tenancy, within the meaning of the Housing Act 1988, nor a tenancy under which the landlord might recover possession under any of Grounds 1 to 5 in Schedule 2 to that Act*

   and, in the opinion of the court, the accommodation is reasonably suitable to the needs of the tenant and his family.

2) In determining whether the accommodation is reasonably suitable to the needs of the tenant and his family, regard shall be had to –

   (a) the nature of the accommodation which it is the practice of the landlord to allocate to persons with similar needs;

   (b) the distance of the accommodation available from the place of work or education of the tenant and of any members of his family;

   (c) its distance from the home of any member of the tenant's family if proximity to it is essential to that member's or the tenant's well-being;

   (d) the needs (as regards extent of accommodation) and means of the tenant and his family;

   (e) the terms on which the accommodation is available and the terms of the secure tenancy;

   (f) if furniture was provided by the landlord for use under the secure tenancy, whether furniture is to be provided for use in the other accommodation, and if so the nature of the furniture to be provided.

3.356   The words in italics were added by HA 1988 Sch 17 para 65. On the quality of security offered by an assured tenancy, compared with the secure status that the tenant enjoys, see chapter 12.

3.357   In applying these provisions, note that:

- 'Family' is defined broadly in HA 1985 Part 4.[297]
- If family members have different or conflicting views about the suitability of the alternative accommodation offered, the court should grant permission for them to be joined as parties to the proceedings in addition to the tenant.[298]
- The list of factors set out in paragraph 2 is not exhaustive.[299]
- The listed factors are not identical to those set out for Rent Act tenants in similar circumstances (although case-law developed in the Rent Act jurisdiction may provide useful aids to construction (see para 12.34), the Rent Act authorities must be approached with some caution).[300]
- Nor are the listed factors identical to those set out for the recovery of possession against assured tenants in similar circumstances (although case-law developed in that jurisdiction may provide useful aids to construction (see paras 3.372–3.398)).
- It may be helpful to invite the judge to view the present home and the alternative accommodation offered.
- If the alternative accommodation will be provided by a different landlord, and that landlord is a housing association or other private registered provider of social housing, the court should be invited to direct that the tenancy of the accommodation be a secure rather than an assured tenancy.[301]
- Paragraph 2(a) has no parallel in the grounds for possession against Rent Act or assured tenants. It allows the court to consider the landlord's usual allocation policy for families of the same size etc as that of the tenant. It will be open to the landlord to suggest in the case of a single person that its usual policy is to provide a small flat or bedsitter. The defence for a tenant faced with such an assertion relies on showing that it is an unreasonable rule or that an exception should be made.
- Where the alternative accommodation is council housing and that local authority landlord has elected to operate an introductory tenancy regime, it will be necessary for the tenant's adviser

---

297 HA 1985 s113, as amended by Civil Partnership Act 2004 Sch 8 para 27; and see *Stonebridge HAT v McKay* June 2006 *Legal Action* 37 (in which accommodation was held not to be suitable because it did not enable the tenant's grandchildren to stay with her).

298 *Wandsworth LBC v Fadayomi* [1987] 3 All ER 474, (1987) 19 HLR 512, CA.

299 *Enfield LBC v French* (1984) 17 HLR 211, CA.

300 *Enfield LBC v French* (1984) 17 HLR 211, CA at 216–217.

301 HA 1988 s35(4)(e).

to ensure that the new tenancy is secure rather than introductory (see HA 1996 s124(2)).

Other grounds for possession: assured tenants

3.358   The following grounds contained in HA 1988 Sch 2 are of potential relevance to tenants of private registered providers of social housing letting an assured tenancy. A careful check should be made to see whether use of all or any of the grounds would be a breach of the tenancy by the landlord.

HA 1988 ground 6: Demolition or reconstruction (mandatory)

3.359   HA 1988 ground 6 is available where the landlord seeking possession[302] intends to demolish or reconstruct the whole or a substantial part of the dwelling-house or to carry out substantial works on the dwelling-house or any part thereof or any building of which it forms part and the following conditions are fulfilled:

(a)   the intended work cannot reasonably be carried out without the tenant giving up possession of the dwelling-house because –

(i)   the tenant is not willing to agree to such a variation of the terms of the tenancy as would give such access and other facilities as would permit the intended work to be carried out, or

(ii)   the nature of the intended work is such that no such variation is practicable, or

(iii) the tenant is not willing to accept an assured tenancy of such part only of the dwelling-house (in this sub-paragraph referred to as 'the reduced part') as would leave in the possession of his landlord so much of the dwelling-house as would be reasonable to enable the intended work to be carried out and, where appropriate, as would give such access and other facilities over the reduced part as would permit the intended work to be carried out, or

(iv)   the nature of the intended work is such that such a tenancy is not practicable; and

---

302   Or, if that landlord is a non-profit registered provider of social housing, registered social landlord or charitable housing trust or, (where the dwelling-house is social housing within the meaning of Part 2 of the Housing and Regeneration Act 2008) a profit-making registered provider of social housing, a superior landlord.

(b) either the landlord seeking possession acquired his interest in the dwelling-house before the grant of the tenancy or that interest was in existence at the time of that grant and neither that landlord (or, in the case of joint landlords, any of them) nor any other person who, alone or jointly with others, has acquired that interest since that time acquired it for money or money's worth; and

(c) the assured tenancy on which the dwelling-house is let did not come into being by virtue of any provision of Schedule 1 to the Rent Act 1977, as amended by Part I of Schedule 4 to this Act or, as the case may be, section 4 of the Rent (Agriculture) Act 1976, as amended by Part II of that Schedule.

For the purposes of this ground if, immediately before the grant of the tenancy, the tenant to whom it was granted or, if it was granted to joint tenants, any of them was the tenant or one of the joint tenants of the dwelling-house concerned under an earlier assured tenancy or, as the case may be, under a tenancy to which Local Government and Housing Act 1989 Sch 10 applied, any reference in paragraph (b) above to the grant of the tenancy is a reference to the grant of that earlier assured tenancy, or as the case may be, to the grant of the tenancy to which Schedule 10 applied.

For the purposes of this ground 'registered social landlord' has the same meaning as in the HA 1985 (see section 5(4) and (5) of that Act) and 'charitable housing trust' means a housing trust, within the meaning of Housing Associations Act 1985, which is a charity, within the meaning of the Charities Act 1993.

3.362   This ground is available to a landlord who 'intends to demolish or reconstruct the whole or a substantial part of the dwelling-house or to carry out substantial works'. It is very similar to the LTA 1954 s30(1)(f), which allows landlords of business tenants to oppose the grant of a new tenancy in similar circumstances.

3.363   It has been held that 'reconstruction' means 'a substantial interference with the structure of the premises and then a rebuilding, in probably a different form, of such part of the premises as has been demolished by reason of the interference with the structure'.[303]

3.364   The landlord must show that the intention to demolish or reconstruct will be fulfilled shortly after the date of the hearing.[304] There are two elements to the concept of intention: first, a genuine desire that the result will come about and, second, a reasonable prospect of

---

303 *Joel v Swaddle* [1957] 1 WLR 1094, [1957] 3 All ER 325 at 329 (removal of internal walls and replacement with reinforced steel joists amounted to reconstruction of a substantial part). See also *Barth v Pritchard* [1990] 20 EG 65 and *Cook v Mott* (1961) 178 EG 637, CA.

304 *Betty's Cafes Ltd v Phillips Furnishing Stores Ltd (No 1)* [1959] AC 20, HL.

bringing about that result. For example, in *Edwards v Thompson*,[305] the landlord failed to prevent the grant of a new tenancy because she had not found a developer at the time of the hearing and 'there was a real possibility that [she] would not be in a position to carry out the entire development on the termination of the current tenancy ... She had failed to show that she had the means and ability; she had not established the necessary intention'. A landlord's case is stronger if planning permission has been obtained in advance of the institution of possession proceedings, but this is not essential if it can be shown that there is a reasonable prospect of getting planning consent.[306]

3.365 The landlord must also show that, because of one of four specified reasons, the intended work cannot reasonably be carried out without the tenant giving up possession of the premises. 'Possession' means 'putting an end to legal rights of possession' and not merely access. For example, in *Heath v Drown*,[307] a business tenant successfully defeated the landlord's claim even though the front wall of the premises had to be entirely rebuilt and it would not be possible to occupy the premises while such work was carried out. It is not enough for the landlord to say that access is required, since most tenancies contain an express or implied[308] right of access to carry out repairs. The landlord must show that the work cannot be carried out while the tenancy still exists.

3.366 This ground for possession is not available to a social landlord which has acquired its interest in the property by purchasing it after the grant of the tenancy.[309]

3.367 When a possession order is made under this ground the landlord must pay a sum equal to the tenant's reasonable removal expenses.[310]

HA 1988 ground 7: Death of the tenant (mandatory)

3.368 HA 1988 Sch 2 ground 7 is satisfied where:

> The tenancy is a periodic tenancy (including a statutory periodic tenancy), *or a fixed-term tenancy of a dwelling-house in England,* which

---

305 (1990) 60 P&CR 222, CA. See also *Capocci v Goble* (1987) 284 EG 230, CA.

306 *Gregson v Cyril Lord* [1963] 1 WLR 41, [1962] 3 All ER 907, CA.

307 [1972] 2 WLR 1306, CA and, for an example in the county court, *Sugarwhite v Afridi* [2002] CLY 3013, Central London Civil Justice Centre. See too HA 1988 s16.

308 HA 1988 s16.

309 See discussion in relation to HA 1988 ground 1(b), paras 11.6–11.8.

310 HA 1988 s11(1).

has devolved under the will or intestacy of the former tenant and the proceedings for the recovery of possession are begun not later than twelve months after the death of the former tenant or, if the court so directs, after the date on which, in the opinion of the court, the landlord or, in the case of joint landlords, any one of them became aware of the former tenant's death.

For the purposes of this ground, the acceptance by the landlord of rent from a new tenant after the death of the former tenant shall not be regarded as creating a new tenancy, unless the landlord agrees in writing to a change (as compared with the tenancy before the death) in the amount of the rent, the period or length of term of the tenancy, the premises which are let or any other term of the tenancy.

This ground does not apply to a fixed term tenancy that is a lease of a dwelling-house–

(a) granted on payment of a premium calculated by reference to a percentage of the value of the dwelling-house or of the cost of providing it, or

(b) under which the lessee (or the lessee's personal representatives) will or may be entitled to a sum calculated by reference, directly or indirectly, to the value of the dwelling-house.

3.370   The words in italics were added by Localism Act 2011 s162(5) on 1 April 2012. Although an assured tenancy may pass by will or on intestacy after the death of the tenant, the landlord may obtain possession using the ground if proceedings are brought within 12 months of the death of the tenant or the date on which the landlord became aware of the death. 'Proceedings' means the issue of a court claim, not merely the service of a notice seeking possession.[311] No other reason for seeking possession on this ground need be given.

3.371   This ground does not apply if a spouse or civil partner, or person living with the tenant 'as his or her wife or husband or civil partner' succeeds to the tenancy as a result of the statutory succession provisions in HA 1988 s17. The Act specifies that acceptance of rent after the death of the former tenant should not be regarded as creating a new tenancy unless the landlord has agreed in writing to a change in the terms of the tenancy, such as an increase in rent.

In England, the ground does not apply to a fixed-term tenancy that is a lease of a dwelling-house either granted on payment of a premium calculated by reference to a percentage of the value of the dwelling-house or of the cost of providing it or under which the lessee (or the lessee's personal representatives) will or may be entitled to a sum calculated by reference, directly or indirectly, to the value of

311 *Shepping v Osada* (2001) 33 HLR 13, [2000] 30 EG 125, CA. See also *Tunbridge and Malling Housing Association v Reed* September 2001 *Legal Action* 24.

the dwelling-house. In Wales, the ground does not apply where the deceased tenant had a fixed-term tenancy.

HA 1988 ground 9: Suitable alternative accommodation (mandatory)

3.372   HA 1988 Sch 2 ground 9 provides a ground for possession:

> if suitable alternative accommodation is available for the tenant or will be available for him when the order for possession takes effect.

3.373   The availability of suitable alternative accommodation, either at the time of the hearing or when the order is to take effect, will satisfy this ground for possession. HA 1988 Sch 2 Part III[312] gives further clarification of the matters to be taken into account when determining whether or not accommodation is 'suitable'. It states:

1   For the purposes of Ground 9 above, a certificate of the local housing authority for the district in which the dwelling-house in question is situated, certifying that the authority will provide suitable alternative accommodation for the tenant by a date specified in the certificate, shall be conclusive evidence that suitable alternative accommodation will be available for him by that date.

2   Where no such certificate as is mentioned in paragraph 1 above is produced to the court, accommodation shall be deemed to be suitable for the purposes of ground 9 above if it consists of either –

(a) premises which are to be let as a separate dwelling such that they will then be let on an assured tenancy, other than –

(i) a tenancy in respect of which notice is given not later than the beginning of the tenancy that possession might be recovered on any of Grounds 1 to 5 above, or

(ii) an assured shorthold tenancy, within the meaning of chapter II of Part 1 of this Act, or

(b) premises to be let as a separate dwelling on terms which will, in the opinion of the court, afford to the tenant security of tenure reasonably equivalent to the security afforded by chapter I of Part I of this Act in the case of an assured tenancy of a kind mentioned in sub-paragraph (a) above,

and, in the opinion of the court, the accommodation fulfils the relevant conditions as defined in paragraph 3 below.

3(1) For the purposes of paragraph 2 above, the relevant conditions are that the accommodation is reasonably suitable to the needs of the tenant and his family as regards proximity to place of work, and either –

---

312 Cf RA 1977 Sch 15 Pt IV. HA 1988 Sch 2 Pt III is very similar to the comparable Rent Act provisions, although the alternative accommodation should be let on an assured tenancy, rather than on a protected tenancy.

(a) similar as regards rental and extent to the accommodation afforded by dwelling-houses provided in the neighbourhood by any local housing authority for persons whose needs as regards extent are, in the opinion of the court, similar to those of the tenant and his family; or

(b) reasonably suitable to the means of the tenant and to the needs of the tenant and his family as regards extent and character; and

that if any furniture was provided for use under the assured tenancy in question, furniture is provided for use in the accommodation which is either similar to that so provided or is reasonably suitable to the needs of the tenant and his family.

(2) For the purposes of subparagraph (1)(a) above, a certificate of a local housing authority stating –

(a) the extent of the accommodation afforded by dwelling-houses provided by the authority to meet the needs of tenants with families of such number as may be specified in the certificate, and

(b) the amount of the rent charged by the authority for dwelling-houses affording accommodation of that extent,

shall be conclusive evidence of the facts so stated.

4   Accommodation shall not be deemed to be suitable to the needs of the tenant and his family if the result of their occupation of the accommodation would be that it would be an overcrowded dwelling-house for the purposes of Part X of the Housing Act 1985.

5   Any document purporting to be a certificate of a local housing authority named therein issued for the purposes of this Part of this Schedule and to be signed by the proper officer of that authority shall be received in evidence and, unless the contrary is shown, shall be deemed to be such a certificate without further proof.

6   In this Part of this Schedule 'local housing authority' and 'district' in relation to such an authority, have the same meaning as in the Housing Act 1985.

Local authority certificate that accommodation will be made available

3.375   HA 1988 Sch 2 Part III para 1 provides that a certificate from a local housing authority confirming that it will provide suitable alternative accommodation for the tenant is conclusive evidence that suitable alternative accommodation will be available[313] at the date specified in the certificate. The certificate must be from the local housing authority for the area in which the relevant premises are situated, otherwise it is ineffective.[314] It seems that there is no requirement that the

---

313 *Wallasey v Pritchard* (1936) 3 LJNCCR 35.
314 *Sills v Watkins* [1956] 1 QB 250, CA.

certificate provide details of the address or size of the suitable alternative accommodation. If, after issuing a certificate, a local housing authority failed to provide suitable alternative accommodation, the court would have power under HA 1988 s9(2) to stay execution of the order on an application by the tenant. There is no requirement that the certificate be in any particular form: a signed letter will suffice.

3.376   In view of the shortage of local authority accommodation, it is extremely rare for local authorities to provide certificates under paragraph 1. Accordingly, whether or not suitable accommodation is available is usually decided in the light of the guidelines in HA 1988 Sch 2 Part III paras 2–6.

No local authority certificate that accommodation will be made available

3.377   If there is no local authority certificate the landlord must prove that the requirements set out below are satisfied (see HA 1988 Sch 2 Part III paras 2–4).

3.378   **Equivalent security of tenure**

> 2 ... (a) ... premises which are to be let as a separate dwelling ... on an assured tenancy, other than [one under which] possession might be recovered on any of Grounds 1 to 5 above, or ... an assured shorthold tenancy ... or ... premises ... let as a separate dwelling on terms which will ... afford to the tenant security of tenure reasonably equivalent to ... an assured tenancy ...

3.379   It is clear from the Rent Act cases referred to below that the accommodation offered must be in a single building. Accommodation offered in two separate houses cannot be suitable.[315] Similarly, the requirement is not satisfied if the premises offered consist of two separate parts of a building which are separated by another flat[316] or if the alternative accommodation involves sharing a kitchen.[317]

3.380   HA 1988 Sch 2 Part III para 2(b) provides that accommodation may be suitable even if it is not let on an assured tenancy, if the security of tenure provided is 'reasonably equivalent' to that provided by HA 1988 Part 1 chapter I. In determining whether this condition is satisfied it is necessary to look carefully at the rights which the landlord of the alternative accommodation has to terminate the tenancy and not at common practice or the assurances given by the

---

315 *Sheehan v Cutler* [1946] KB 339.
316 *Selwyn v Hamill* [1948] 1 All ER 70, CA.
317 *Cookson v Walsh* (1954) 163 EG 486.

new landlord.[318] What is 'reasonably equivalent' security will depend on the facts. In one Rent Act case an unprotected fixed-term tenancy of 16 years was held to provide reasonably equivalent security.[319] In another, an unprotected fixed-term tenancy of ten years offered to a tenant aged 57 and her husband aged 58 was held to provide reasonably equivalent security.[320] It is not necessary for the alternative accommodation to be let by the same landlord. It is enough that it is available and suitable.

3.381   If the tenant against whom possession is sought occupies premises as a sole tenant, a joint tenancy or even joint ownership of a house cannot be suitable alternative accommodation since the other joint tenant or joint owner may unilaterally terminate the tenancy or force a sale.[321] It is not clear whether other premises owned by the tenant can amount to suitable alternative accommodation.[322]

3.382   ## Closeness to workplace

3. (1) ... the accommodation is reasonably suitable to the needs of the tenant and his family as regards proximity to place of work ...

3.383   A 'place of work' need not be a factory or an office. It can be an area or the location in which the tenant's work is based.[323] The court should consider not only distance from work, but also the time which it would take to travel, the means of transport available and any inconvenience which would be caused.[324] The work may be unpaid.[325]

---

318   eg, *Sills v Watkins* [1956] 1 QB 250, CA, where the offer of alternative accommodation was a council tenancy with no security of tenure (prior to the advent of secure tenancies introduced by HA 1980). Although in practice the council did not evict tenants without reason, this offer did not comply with the statutory requirements.

319   *Fulford v Turpin* [1955] CLY 2324.

320   *Edwards v Cohen* (1958) 108 LJ 556.

321   *Barnard v Towers* [1953] 1 WLR 1203, [1953] 2 All ER 877, CA; *Greenwich LBC v McGrady* (1982) 6 HLR 36, CA; *Hammersmith and Fulham LBC v Monk* [1992] 1 AC 478, (1992) 24 HLR 206, HL and *Notting Hill Housing Trust v Brackley* [2001] EWCA Civ 601, [2002] HLR 10.

322   See the conflicting dicta in *Barnard v Towers* [1953] 1 WLR 1203, [1953] 2 All ER 877, CA and *Standingford v Probert* [1950] 1 KB 377, CA.

323   *Yewbright Properties Ltd v Stone* (1980) 40 P&CR 402, CA.

324   *Yewbright Properties Ltd v Stone* (1980) 40 P&CR 402, CA. See also *Minchburn Ltd v Fernandez* (1987) 19 HLR 29, May 1985 *Legal Action* 66, CA, where alternative accommodation was held not to be suitable because it would have doubled the tenant's 30-minute walk to work to one hour. The needs of the particular tenant count, not those of a reasonable tenant.

325   *Dakyns v Pace* [1948] 1 KB 22.

3.384   When considering the workplaces of other members of the tenant's family, the court can consider only those members actually
residing with the tenant. 'Member of the family' is given the ordinary
meaning as understood by an ordinary person.[326] It has been held
to include a son, daughter-in-law[327] and mother-in-law.[328] It will also
now include a long-term gay or lesbian partner.[329] It is possible that a
lodger may be counted as a member of the family.[330]

3.385   **Rental and size**

    3. (1) ... the accommodation is... (a) similar as regards rental and
    extent to the accommodation afforded by dwelling-houses provided in
    the neighbourhood by any local housing authority for persons whose
    needs as regards extent are ... similar to those of the tenant and his
    family; or (b) reasonably suitable to the means of the tenant and to the
    needs of the tenant and his family as regards extent and character ...

3.386   The landlord can satisfy this test in either of two ways. First, the landlord may produce a certificate from the local authority for the area
in which the tenant rents his or her current accommodation setting
out the kind of accommodation which would be provided for people
of similar needs. The certificate should probably state the number
of rooms which would be provided and give some indication of the
dimensions of such rooms.[331] A certificate which stated that local
authority rents would be more than twice as high as the alternative
accommodation offered did not show that the accommodation offered
was similar as regards rental.[332] It is for a judge to decide, after considering the certificate, whether or not the accommodation offered
is similar to that which the local authority would provide. In *Jones v
Cook*,[333] the Court of Appeal set aside a possession order where a judge
had simply accepted the contents of a certificate which had stated that

---

326 *Standingford v Probert* [1950] 1 KB 377, CA and *Scrace v Windust* [1955] 1 WLR
     475, CA. See also, in another context, *Fitzpatrick v Sterling Housing Association*
     [2001] 1 AC 27, (2000) 32 HLR 178, HL and *Ghaidan v Godin-Mendoza* [2004]
     UKHL 30, [2004] HLR 46.
327 *Standingford v Probert* [1950] 1 KB 377, CA.
328 *Scrace v Windust* [1955] 1 WLR 475, CA.
329 *Fitzpatrick v Sterling Housing Association* [2001] 1 AC 27, (2000) 32 HLR 178
     and *Ghaidan v Godin-Mendoza* [2004] UKHL 30, [2004] HLR 46.
330 *Standingford v Probert* [1950] 1 KB 377, CA, cf *Stewart v Mackay* 1947 SLT 250.
331 Per Edmund Davies LJ in *Macdonnell v Daly* [1969] 1 WLR 1482, CA, cf
     Wallasey v Pritchard (1936) 3 LJNCCR 35.
332 *Turner v Keiller* 1950 SC 43 and *Robert Thackeray's Estate Ltd v Kaye* (1989) 21
     HLR 160, CA.
333 (1990) 22 HLR 319, CA.

the property offered by the landlord was 'similar in extent to council-owned dwelling-houses which may be provided in the neighbourhood for families consisting of husband, wife and three children'.

3.387   If there is no local authority certificate (and it is rare for a land-lord to obtain such a certificate), the court should consider whether the property offered is reasonably suitable. Accommodation may be suitable even though it is inferior to the accommodation currently occupied by the tenant.[334] It may also be suitable even though it is considerably smaller.[335] Part only of the accommodation currently rented by the tenant may amount to suitable alternative accommodation if at the time of the hearing the tenant is not occupying all of the accommodation let (for example, because part is sublet[336]) or because it is larger than the tenant requires.[337]

3.388   When the court considers the 'needs' of the tenant and the tenant's family, it should primarily consider their housing needs and not incidental advantages, such as the use of a stable and paddock.[338] The court may, however, take into account a tenant's professional needs, such as an artist using a room as a studio[339] or the need for a tenant to entertain business associates.[340] Accommodation may be unsuitable if it:

- is too large;[341]
- is in disrepair;[342]

334 Per Lord Asquith in *Warren v Austen* [1947] 2 All ER 185, CA.

335 *Quick v Fifield* (1982) 132 NLJ 140 (less than half the size) and *Hill v Rochard* [1983] 1 WLR 478, CA.

336 *Parmee v Mitchell* [1950] 2 KB 199, CA; *Thompson v Rolls* [1926] 2 KB 426, [1926] All ER 257 and *Yoland v Reddington* (1981–82) 5 HLR 41, (1982) 263 EG 157, CA.

337 *Macdonnell v Daly* [1969] 1 WLR 1482, CA (two out of three rooms) and *Mykolyshyn v Noah* [1970] 1 WLR 1271, CA (current accommodation less sitting room).

338 *Hill v Rochard* [1983] 1 WLR 478, CA, although such matters will be relevant when considering reasonableness. See also *Montross Associated Investments v Stone* March 2000 *Legal Action* 29, CA ('magnificent views' overlooking Hyde Park). On tenants' 'needs' generally, see H W Wilkinson, 'What does a tenant need?' (1985) 135 NLJ 933, where there is a summary of the facts of some of the cases noted in the following footnotes.

339 *Macdonnell v Daly* [1969] 1 WLR 1482, CA.

340 *De Markozoff v Craig* (1949) 93 SJ 693, CA. Cf *Stewart v Mackay* 1947 SLT 250 (tenant's inability to take in lodgers); *Wilcock v Booth* (1920) 122 LT 678 (loss of off-licence) and *Warren v Austen* [1947] 2 All ER 185, CA (unreasonable to make order where alternative accommodation not large enough to enable tenant to continue to take lodgers).

341 *Islington LBC v Metcalfe and Peacock* August 1983 *LAG Bulletin* 105.

342 If there is any question of disrepair in the alternative accommodation it is always wise for the tenant to obtain a full survey report.

- lacks a bathroom and toilet;[343]
- means the tenant living with his estranged wife;[344] or
- does not have a garden in which the tenant's children can play.[345]

Accommodation in a shared house may be unsuitable for a tenant currently living alone.[346]

3.389   The court should take into account environmental factors. For example, in *Redspring Limited v Francis*,[347] the alternative accommodation was on a busy traffic thoroughfare, had no garden, was next door to a fish shop and was near to a hospital, cinema and public house with the result that there were people 'coming and going' at all hours of the day and night, whereas the tenant's current accommodation was in a quiet and secluded residential street. However, environmental factors can be taken into account only so far as they relate to the character of the property. The proximity of the tenant's friends and cultural interests are not relevant here, although they clearly are relevant when the court comes to consider reasonableness.[348]

3.390   **Furniture**

3. (1) ... if any furniture was provided for use under the assured tenancy in question, furniture is provided for use in the accommodation which is either similar to that so provided or is reasonably suitable to the needs of the tenant and his family ...

3.391   **Availability**

... accommodation is available for the tenant or will be available for him when the order in question takes effect (see ground 9).

3.392   The suitable alternative accommodation must be available for the particular tenant.[349] In determining whether it is available, accommodation which was previously available is completely irrelevant,[350] although refusals by the tenant of previous offers of other

---

343   *Esposito v Ware* (1950) 155 EG 383.
344   *Heglibiston Establishments v Heyman* (1977) 246 EG 567, CA.
345   *De Markozoff v Craig* (1949) 93 SJ 693, CA, cf in the public sector, *Enfield LBC v French* (1984) 17 HLR 211, CA; *Watford Community HT v Personal Representatives of Elizabeth Chalmers* April 2011 *Legal Action* 29, Watford County Court.
346   *Barnard v Towers* [1953] 1 WLR 1203, [1953] 2 All ER 877, CA.
347   [1973] 1 WLR 134. See also *Dawncar Investments Ltd v Plews* (1993) 25 HLR 639, CA.
348   *Siddiqu v Rashid* [1980] 1 WLR 1018, CA.
349   *Topping v Hughes* [1925] NI 90.
350   *Kimpson v Markham* [1921] 2 KB 157.

accommodation may be considered when the court decides the question of reasonableness and may be relevant when the court considers costs. It is sufficient for the landlord to show that such accommodation is available even if it is to be rented from another person. It need not have been available when the HA 1988 section 8 notice was served or when proceedings were issued, although such circumstances would no doubt be relevant to costs.

3.393 **Overcrowding**

> 4. Accommodation shall not be deemed to be suitable to the needs of the tenant and his or her family if the result of their occupation of the accommodation would be that it would be an overcrowded dwelling-house for the purposes Part X of the Housing Act 1985.

3.394 For the definition of overcrowding, see para 3.300.

Reasonableness

3.395 It should be remembered that even if the court is satisfied that suitable alternative accommodation exists, the court must still consider whether it is reasonable to make a possession order. Failure to do this makes the possession order a nullity.[351]

3.396 The correct approach to reasonableness in this context was considered by the Court of Appeal in the Rent Act case of *Whitehouse v Loi Lee*.[352] Here, the landlord wished to obtain possession and sell the property in order to fund her pension. The tenant did not wish to move as she had lived in her home for 45 years and had many associations with the immediate locality. A county court judge made a possession order. However, the Court of Appeal held that:

> the decision ... required the judge to look at the question from all angles, in particular by considering the effect on the parties if an order was made and also if an order was not made.

Although the judge had considered the effects on both parties of making an order, he had only considered the effect on the tenant of making no order. The judge had accepted that the landlord was financially secure and there was no suggestion she would suffer financial hardship if she were unable to sell the flat with vacant possession. Consequently, considering the effects on both parties if an order was

---

351 *Minchburn Estates v Fernandez (No 2)* (1986) 19 HLR 29, CA; *Treismann v Cotterell* September 1996 *Legal Action* 14 and *Hildebrand v Constable* September 1996 *Legal Action* 14.
352 [2009] EWCA Civ 375, [2010] HLR 11.

made, and also if an order was not made, it was not reasonable to make an order for possession.

When a possession order is made under this ground, the landlord must pay a sum equal to the tenant's reasonable removal expenses.[353]

HA 1988 ground 16: Premises let to employees (discretionary)

3.397 HA 1988 Sch 2 ground 16 is met if:

> The dwelling-house was let to the tenant in consequence of his employment by the landlord seeking possession or a previous landlord under the tenancy and the tenant has ceased to be in that employment.

3.398 This ground for possession is wider than Case 8, the comparable Rent Act ground (see para 12.62). It applies whether or not the employer requires the premises for another employee. Unlike under HA 1985 ground 12 (see para 3.321), the ground is only satisfied once the tenant's employment has ceased. Usually, the employer and the landlord have to be the same person. However, if health service employees are employed by a health service body (for example, a health authority) but live in premises owned by the Department of Health, the secretary of state, when bringing possession proceedings, may rely on ground 16.[354]

353 HA 1988 s11(1).
354 National Health Service and Community Care Act 1990 s60(7) and Sch 8 para 10.

Preparing the defence

General preparation

4.1   The preparation of a defence to the possession claim for a secure or assured tenant[1] should take place at the earliest possible opportunity. If the reader has been instructed *at the last minute* for such a tenant, go immediately to para 4.30.

4.2   If instructed *well in advance* of any prospective or actual court hearing date, an adviser will need to take full instructions from the tenant (see the instructions checklist at appendix D).

4.3   In addition to taking the client's statement and assembling background material relating to the particular possession proceedings, the adviser will wish to gather together:

- the claim form and particulars of claim;
- a copy of the tenancy agreement;
- a copy of the notice seeking possession – if any;
- the rent book/rent account/schedule of any arrears; and
- other relevant documents.

4.4   An early opportunity might usefully be taken to inspect the tenant's housing management file as held by the landlord, in order to secure copies of the above and any other relevant documents. In the case of a local authority landlord an application for such access should:

- be made in writing;
- make reference to the Data Protection Act 1998;
- enclose a signed authority from the client;
- enclose a cheque for £10 (being the maximum fee currently payable for access).

4.5   Most local authority landlords will respond to such a request either by simply forwarding a photocopy of the entire file or by making it available at their offices with a copying facility. Other social landlords make similar provision for tenants (or their advisers) to inspect housing files. If the possession proceedings have already started (and will proceed beyond the first hearing), such documents would in any event eventually be obtained in the course of disclosure.[2] If the proceedings have not yet started but are contemplated, early disclosure of the documents would certainly accord with the principles of the

---

1 References in this chapter to a 'secure tenant' should be treated as including a 'secure licensee' (see para 1.55) unless the contrary is stated.
2 CPR Part 31.

Practice Direction on Pre-Action Protocols[3] and, in a rent arrears case, with the *Pre-Action Protocol for possession claims by social landlords.*

4.6   Depending on the issues which arise in the client's statement, and after consideration of the documents, it may be necessary to undertake a housing benefit (or general welfare benefit) assessment and/or obtain an expert's report on the condition of the property.

4.7   Many defendants will qualify for initial advice under the Legal Help and Legal Help at Court schemes (see chapter 24) but a full certificate for publicly funded legal representation should be applied for immediately if: the tenant or licensee has a defence; the proportionality test is met; and there is a need for representation in all the circumstances of the case, including the nature and complexity of the issues.[4]

4.8   If the adviser is instructed only a few days prior to the hearing, an emergency certificate for legal representation should be granted under powers devolved to the adviser by the Legal Aid Agency (see chapter 24).

4.9   If a defence is to be submitted this should be in the appropriate variant of the defence form (N11), filed with the court, and properly served on the landlord in advance of the hearing date (see chapter 21 for possession procedure and appendix B for a precedent defence). The adviser instructed at a late stage will simply have to pass a copy to the landlord at court (if it has been possible to prepare a defence at all) or apply for an extension of time in which to file a defence. In the latter case, it would be sensible to have an outline or early draft of the defence available at court.

Defences

Status of occupation incorrect

4.10   The first consideration should always be whether the occupier's status of occupation has been correctly identified. If the landlord's pleaded case is wrong on this point then it is likely to found a complete defence to the claim. For example, if the landlord has asserted that the tenant is a starter or introductory tenant and is seeking to recover possession on that basis and in fact the tenant is secure or assured then the claim must be dismissed.

---

3   See para 4 of the CPR Practice Direction on Pre-Action Conduct and Protocols.
4   Civil Legal Aid (Merits Criteria) Regulations 2013 regs 39 and 61.

4.11   An occupier's adviser must therefore first ascertain whether:

i)   the occupier is a tenant or licensee (see paras 1.17–1.21), and
ii) what type of tenancy or licence they hold, ie unprotected (see chapter 8), old-style secure (see paras 1.53–1.68), flexible (see paras 1.74–1.77), new English secure (see paras 1.187–1.194), introductory (chapter 5), demoted (chapter 6), family intervention (chapter 7), assured (see paras 1.6–1.36), fixed-term assured shorthold (see para 1.46) or periodic assured shorthold (see paras 10.4–10.6).

Notice defective

4.12   Once the tenant's status of occupation has been identified, the next issue to consider is whether the landlord has (a) brought the tenancy or licence to an end or (b), if the tenancy or licence has not been terminated, served the correct notice giving the landlord a right to bring proceedings for possession. Unless it is obvious that the notice will be dispensed with (eg the claim for possession is on the grounds of serious nuisance) and there are no other grounds for defending the claim, the fact that the notice is defective should always be taken as it will amount to a complete defence to the claim.

4.13   Detailed consideration of the notice requirements for:

• old-style secure, flexible, new English secure, assured and assured shorthold is provided in chapter 2;
• unprotected tenancies or licences are covered in chapter 8;
• introductory tenancies in chapter 5;
• demoted tenancies in chapter 6; and
• family intervention tenancies in chapter 7.

4.14   Where the tenancy is for a fixed term, and is or has become unprotected, a notice will not be effective to determine the term. Instead the term will need to be brought to an end by the landlord forfeiting the lease. Consideration must be given as to whether the landlord is entitled to forfeit the term or whether the right has been waived. See chapter 14 for further discussion of forfeiture.

Review process not undertaken correctly

4.15   In the case of flexible or new English secure tenant, where the term has ended, an introductory or demoted tenant, the landlord must also have complied with the statutory review procedure. Detailed consideration of each review process is contained within chapters 5 and 6 and paras 2.82–2.84. Failure to have carried out the requisite review procedure correctly may provide a defence to the claim.

Grounds not made out

4.16   Where the tenant has true security of tenure, ie as an assured tenant or secure tenant, the adviser should consider whether the landlord's pleaded case will satisfy, on the balance of probabilities, any of the grounds for possession set out within HA 1985 Sch 2 or HA 1988 Sch 2. Particular consideration needs to be given to the precise wording of each ground, because the grounds often require a number of factors to be satisfied (see chapter 3). For example, a claim against a secure tenant under ground 1 – for breach of an obligation – may appear, without further investigation, to be satisfied. However, on a closer inspection of the term of the tenancy agreement it may be arguable that the term is unfair and unenforceable under the Consumer Rights Act 2015[5] or that a sum due under the agreement that the tenant has not paid, for example for water rates, is not recoverable by the landlord.

4.17   Where the claim is for unpaid rent or other sums of money, a counterclaim for disrepair may provide a complete defence to an action for possession. It may result in damages equal to or greater than the amount the landlord has claimed and be set off against that claim. Reliance should not be placed solely on a defence by way of set-off which requires a successful counterclaim, because there is never a guarantee that the counterclaim will succeed.[6]

4.18   Where the landlord's pleaded case does not even plead or raise an arguable case that a ground has been satisfied, the tenant should make an application to strike out the claim once the defence has been filed.

4.19   If the landlord's pleaded case does rely on a ground, which is more than likely, the tenant's adviser must ascertain whether the allegations are admitted or denied by the tenant. Detailed instructions ought to be taken from the tenant which explain why the facts relied upon by the landlord are incorrect.

Reasonableness test not satisfied

4.20   The second line of defence for a tenant with full security of tenure, assuming that the landlord has proved (or the tenant admits) that a ground has been made out, is to demonstrate that there is

5   See footnote 291 at para 1.197.
6   *Haringey LBC v Stewart* (1991) 23 HLR 557, CA.

insufficient evidence to establish on the balance of probabilities that any necessary condition is satisfied. The conditions are discussed in chapter 3 together with the respective grounds to which they relate. The most common condition is that it is reasonable to order possession. It is for the landlord to satisfy the court that it would be reasonable to make a possession order. The defence may take the point that this condition (where applicable) is not made out and that the claim should be dismissed.

Public law/human rights/Equality Act 2010 defences

4.21   Where the tenant lacks security of tenure, and the procedural requirements have been satisfied, a public law, human rights or Equality Act 2010 defence may be available (see chapters 25, 26, 27). In all cases, irrespective of whether the tenant has security of tenure or not, such defences should be considered.

Claim for possession defective

4.22   The usual rules on drafting claims in civil litigation apply to possession proceedings (see chapter 21). Common technical deficiencies in landlords' claims for possession include:
- failure to join all joint tenants;
- failure to set out the landlord's title;
- failure to refer to the notice seeking possession;
- insufficient particulars given (particularly of 'reasonableness');[7] and
- failure to restrict the claim to the ground in the notice seeking possession.

4.23   The claim for possession must be brought in accordance with the provisions of CPR 55 and the Practice Directions to that rule (each of which is reproduced in appendix F). The particulars of claim in possession proceedings must contain prescribed basic information about the premises and the tenancy agreement.[8] If the claim is on the ground of non-payment of rent the particulars of claim should be in the relevant court form[9] and must contain prescribed particulars concerning the arrears and the circumstances of the parties.[10]

---

7 See *Midlothian DC v Brown* 1990 SCLR 765 and *Renfrew DC v Inglis* 1991 SLT (Sh Ct) 83.
8 CPR PD 55A para 2.1.
9 Form N119.
10 CPR PD 55A paras 2.1–2.4A.

4.24   Because landlords can generally apply for and obtain permission to amend, reliance on defects in the claim form will rarely provide a long-term defence.[11]

Action improperly brought

4.25   If the possession proceedings have been improperly brought (for example, the decision to bring them has been motivated by bad faith, abuse of power or malice by landlord), the county court may be invited to strike out the action as an abuse of process or the tenant could set up the unlawful action of the landlord by way of defence to the claim.[12] Some cases in this category may provide a public law defence (see chapter 25).

No arguable defence

4.26   Where the tenant has true security of tenure even if there does not appear to be an arguable defence to a possession order being made it is still likely that an immediate possession order can be avoided if the tenant can put forward a case that supports the making of a postponed order for possession.

4.27   See chapter 3, in particular in the part concerning rent arrears (paras 3.92–3.98) and nuisance (paras 3.188–3.201) for a detailed discussion on when the court is likely to make such an order.

4.28   Tactically it may be preferable to try to negotiate a postponed possession order after a defence has been filed, eg where there is a risk that an immediate order will be made and little hope of avoiding some form of possession order. Although the concept of a 'consent order' is not applicable in the case of assured or secure tenants or secure licensees,[13] and a possession order obtained 'by consent' in

---

11   See for example *Hounslow LBC v Cumar* [2012] EWCA Civ 1426, [2013] HLR 17, in which permission was given to substitute the claimant for another party where an ALMO had issued a claim for possession in its own name rather than the name of the landlord.

12   The repeated issue of unjustified proceedings may even amount to 'harassment': *Allen v Southwark LBC* [2008] EWCA Civ 1478, January 2009 *Legal Action* 25.

13   *Wandsworth LBC v Fadayomi* (1987) 19 HLR 512, [1987] 3 All ER 474, CA and see *R v Bloomsbury and Marylebone County Court ex p Blackburne* (1984) 14 HLR 56, (1985) 2 EGLR 157, CA. Even where specific admissions have been made as to the facts necessary to found a ground for possession, the issue of reasonableness must be specifically considered: see *Cobalt Housing Ltd v Devine* January 2005 *Legal Action* 28, Liverpool County Court.

such cases should be set aside,[14] it does not follow that there must be a contested hearing to obtain a possession order.

4.29 In practice, it is common for tenants to agree to the making of possession orders (commonly in cases concerning rent arrears or anti-social behaviour). Such orders may be made lawfully provided that the order is not called a 'consent order' and records in the preamble that:

i) the tenant has admitted that a notice seeking possession has been served and admits facts (or a fact) which satisfy the ground for possession;

ii) the court is satisfied that the admission(s) satisfy the ground for possession;

iii) the court is satisfied that it is reasonable to make a possession order, but that it is appropriate and proportionate for the date of possession to be suspended on terms; and

iv) the parties attend a hearing to put the order before a judge for approval. A court could refuse to make the order sought, but this is rare.

'Duty advocate' plan

4.30 Almost every county court now has a 'duty representation scheme' available to a tenant who attends court unrepresented on the date fixed for the hearing of a possession claim. Such schemes are funded by the Legal Aid Agency[15] or operated by volunteers. This section of this chapter illustrates how an adviser on such a scheme might respond to the type of possession case which occurs with greatest frequency – a claim based on rent arrears – and where instructions are received *at the door of the court.*

4.31 The proper preparation of a defence in a rent arrears possession case usually requires careful consideration. In particular, all the documents must be examined, statements taken and negotiations with the landlord pursued. Where appropriate, a fully pleaded defence should be filed (possibly including a counterclaim).

4.32 If instructed at 'the door of the court' the adviser should avoid the temptation of immediately negotiating or advocating for a postponed conditional possession order requiring payment of current rent and a modest level of weekly payment off the arrears. After all, closer

14 *Hounslow LBC v McBride* (1999) 31 HLR 143, CA.
15 For details of the Legal Aid Agency funded schemes see chapter 24.

examination may establish that there are in fact no arrears at all or (if there are arrears) that the tenant has a defence as described earlier in this chapter.

4.33   If instructions are received literally at the last moment, the adviser should make an initial application for the case to be put back in the list of cases awaiting hearing and then take some brief particulars from the client. Although the court list may contain dozens of cases, it does not always follow that there will be the opportunity to have a lengthy discussion – these cases can be processed very quickly in some courts.

4.34   The adviser should try to take a preliminary statement from the tenant covering the duration of the tenancy, the personal circumstances of the tenant, the circumstances surrounding the 'arrears', details of income and details of housing benefit received (see appendix D for a useful checklist).

4.35   If the tenant has any documents with him or her, or if copies can be obtained from the landlord's representative at court, the adviser should inspect:

- the notice seeking possession or notice to quit;
- the claim form and the particulars of claim (see paras 4.22–4.24);
- the rent account schedule; and
- any correspondence or other relevant documents.

4.36   If it emerges that the arrears are disputed, or there is disrepair which may sustain a counterclaim, or simply that more time is needed to ensure that the defence can be put fairly, the immediate objective should be to secure an adjournment to another date. Before returning to court to make such an application in court the adviser should be prepared to deal with:

- the likely eventual defence;
- the tenant's circumstances;
- the possibility of an agreement to pay current rent during the adjournment;
- the possibility of an agreement to pay something off the alleged arrears during that time (without prejudice to any contention that nothing, or not the amount claimed, is owed);
- the reason why advice was not sought earlier; and
- the minimum case management directions necessary to achieve the next stage in the claim (for example, a date by which a defence should be served).

4.37   The adviser may then indicate to the landlord's representative that a request for an adjournment will be made. If the application is opposed, the adviser may need to explain to the court that:

- he or she has just been instructed;
- those instructions reveal that the client has an arguable defence (for example, that the arrears are disputed or that it would not be reasonable to order possession and/or that the tenant has a potential counterclaim and defence by way of set-off based on disrepair or failure to pay housing benefit, etc);
- the tenant will immediately be directed to a legal adviser to draft the defence; and
- an adjournment is sought for that purpose.

4.38   It is usually helpful to be able to indicate that the tenant will submit to a condition that current rent be paid throughout the period of the adjournment.[16] The court may be tempted to impose a requirement for additional modest payments towards the arrears but (where appropriate) the adviser may respond that further conditions would be unreasonable or would cause excessive hardship.[17] The adviser should invite the making of directions for a defence to be filed within (say) 21 days and for such other directions as may be appropriate, for example, disclosure, experts' reports, etc. The court should be addressed on the proper order as to the costs of the adjournment.

4.39   In most cases, the above procedure ought to achieve an adjournment. If not, the adviser has to do his or her best to defend successfully on the day and obtain permission to appeal against any adverse order made. In an appropriate case, an appeal may be entered against the refusal to adjourn, in addition to an appeal against the order made.[18]

4.40   Once the adjournment has been secured, the adviser should make the necessary arrangements for full legal representation to be obtained and for all technical and substantive defences and counterclaims to be considered. If the matter is to be conducted by a legal aid provider, advisers should bear in mind the possible delays in obtaining a full funding certificate for legal representation and the importance of not exceeding the time allowed by the court for filing and service of the defence.

16 HA 1985 s85(3); HA 1988 s9(3).
17 HA 1985 s85(3)(a); HA 1988 s9(3).
18 See *Janstan Investments Ltd v Corregar* (1973) 21 November, unreported, CA; *Spitaliotis v Morgan* [1986] 1 EGLR 51, (1985) 277 EG 750, CA and *Bates v Croydon LBC* [2001] EWCA Civ 134, (2001) 33 HLR 70.

CHAPTER 5

Introductory and starter tenancies

Introductory tenancies

Background

5.1   In 1995 the concerted efforts of some local authority landlords produced a commitment from central government to increase legal powers available to those landlords to deal with errant tenants guilty of
'anti-social' behaviour towards others.[1] The result was an array of new
measures and amendments to existing housing law enacted in Housing Act (HA) 1996 Pt 5, which bears the title 'Conduct of Tenants'.

5.2   Chapter I of HA 1996 Part V set out the arrangements for a new
regime of 'introductory tenancies'. It was brought into force on 12
February 1997. It has been amended by the Housing and Planning
Act (HPA) 2016. This chapter will consider the position for introductory tenancies granted before and after HPA 2016 came into
force. The introductory tenancy regime is not of universal application – each local housing authority in England and Wales is free to
choose whether to apply its provisions in its area. Voluntary adoption
of the provisions by a local housing authority allows it to offer all its
lettings to new tenants on a 'probationary' or 'trial' basis. If the tenancy endures for 12 months (or for 18 months where the trial period
has been extended – see para 5.24), it becomes a 'secure' tenancy if it
otherwise fulfils the requirements for attracting that status.

5.3   In the 'probationary' or 'trial' period, the introductory tenant has
limited security of tenure and only modified statutory rights. The
tenancy can be ended by a process which starts with the landlord
giving a notice. Once that has expired, possession can be recovered
virtually 'as of right'. The underlying intention of the provisions is to
enable local authority landlords to 'nip in the bud' anti-social behaviour among new tenants.

5.4   In the event, there is nothing in HA 1996 Pt 5 chapter I (save
its title) which confines the operation of the introductory tenancy
scheme to a context of nuisance or nuisance-related issues. A local
authority landlord may perfectly lawfully adopt the introductory
scheme for other reasons (for example, to achieve quicker possession
against new tenants in early default with rent) and may seek possession during the trial or probationary period for any reason at all. Not
all local authorities have elected to adopt the introductory tenancy
regime but the majority have done so.

---

1 Department of the Environment, *Anti-social behaviour on council estates*, April
1995.

5.5   To accompany the introduction of HA 1996 Pt 5, considerable guidance was prepared about the operation of introductory tenancy schemes for those authorities choosing to adopt them. Just before their amalgamation into the Local Government Association, the representative associations for local authorities published *Introductory tenancies: guidance for local authorities*,[2] with the intention of assisting those councils which had decided to operate introductory tenancies with practical matters of implementation. That guidance was expressly endorsed by central government (the then Department of the Environment (DoE)) in its own circular[3] outlining the new provisions. The circular does not appear to have been withdrawn or superseded and may usefully be referred to by an adviser asked to assist an introductory tenant.

5.6   This chapter does not purport to offer a description of every facet of the introductory tenancy, the specific rights that attach to it, or the more general rights of introductory tenants.[4] Its aim is to provide assistance in those circumstances where a person alleged to be an introductory tenant is faced with the prospect of repossession by his or her landlord. All references are to sections of HA 1996, unless otherwise stated.

5.7   The introductory tenancy scheme, by its very nature, creates the opportunity for discrimination in local authority housing. Two tenants of identical houses in the same street and paying the same rent may hold very different tenancies from their council landlord – one may have long-term security of tenure as a 'secure' tenant, the other may be (for an initial 12, or possibly 18, months) at risk of dispossession as an introductory tenant. The argument that this discrimination is in unlawful breach of Human Rights Act 1998 Sch 1 Article 14 has, however, been rejected by the courts.[5]

5.8   The adviser faced with a prospective or actual claim for possession against a person alleged to be an introductory tenant should consider first whether the tenancy is 'introductory' at all and (if it is), second, how best to use the procedures available to delay or prevent repossession. What steps to take should then be determined by the results of

---

2 AMA/ADC/ALG, February 1997.
3 DoE Circ 2/97, *Introductory tenancies and repossession for secure tenancies*, 31 January 1997.
4 Although the term 'tenancy' is used throughout this chapter it is possible to have an 'introductory licence' to which the provisions described in the chapter apply with like effect: HA 1996 s126.
5 *R (McLellan) v Bracknell Forest DC* [2001] EWCA Civ 1510, (2001) 33 HLR 86 at para 104.

that consideration. Finally, consideration should be given to whether there is an Equality Act 2010 (chapter 27), public law (chapter 25) or human rights (chapter 26) defence.

Is the tenancy 'introductory'?

5.9   First, the tenant's adviser needs to establish whether the tenancy really is 'introductory', if that is the description being used by the landlord. Working through the following headings should enable that issue to be resolved. If this 'checking process' gives rise to an issue as to whether the tenancy is introductory, that could be resolved by proceedings issued by the tenant in the county court.[6] Such proceedings may take so long to resolve that the alleged introductory tenant remains in possession beyond the expiry of the trial period and moves into secure status by default (but see para 5.33 on the effect of the landlord starting possession proceedings before the expiry date).

The landlord

5.10   Only a local housing authority may operate an introductory tenancy regime.[7] If the landlord claiming possession is a housing association or any other form of landlord,[8] the tenancy cannot be 'introductory' at all (although it may be some other form of tenancy enjoying reduced statutory protection, such as an assured shorthold tenancy).[9] If a housing association or other social landlord acquires council stock with sitting introductory tenants, the tenancies will cease to have that status.

The election

5.11   The landlord must have 'elected' to operate the introductory tenancy regime.[10] That requires a decision of the authority's executive (ie not full council) in accordance with its constitution.[11] No such election

---

6   HA 1996 s138.
7   HA 1996 s124(1).
8   It is possible for a housing action trust (HAT) to operate an introductory tenancy regime but the six HATs previously operating have been wound up (see para 1.12) and there are no plans to introduce new ones.
9   See below paras 5.64–5.85 for the position of 'starter' tenants of private registered providers of social housing.
10 HA 1996 s124(1).
11 Local Government Act 2000 s13(2) and Local Authorities (Functions and Responsibilities) (England) Regulations 2000 SI No 2853.

can have been made before 12 February 1997 when the statutory provisions were commenced and, accordingly, the fact of the making of an election and the date of the election should be identified and checked.

5.12   A tenancy can be introductory only if it is granted by that council *after* the election and at a date when the election is still in force. An election can be revoked at any time and can even be adopted again later.[12] In *Gorman v Newark and Sherwood DC*,[13] the Court of Appeal held that the decision of the authority to 'implement introductory tenancies on a trial basis for one year to be monitored by the Housing Managing sub-committee' did not mean that the election ceased after the year; the election had not been revoked and so continued.

5.13   If it can be shown that the election was made improperly or is otherwise invalid or has been revoked, that would provide a complete defence to any assertion that the tenant is an introductory tenant.[14]

5.14   A tenancy entered into (or adopted) *before* the date of the election cannot be an introductory tenancy.[15] For these purposes a tenancy is 'adopted' if the council becomes the landlord under the tenancy following a disposal or surrender to it of the former landlord's interest.[16]

The tenant

5.15   A tenant who is a secure tenant (whether periodic or for a fixed term) at the date of any election to operate an introductory tenancy regime retains that status. Indeed, a secure tenant will not become an introductory tenant of the same landlord on subsequently moving to alternative accommodation, by way of a transfer, after the election.[17]

5.16   Those becoming new tenants of a local authority landlord which has adopted an introductory regime will also not be introductory tenants if, immediately before the new tenancy is entered into (or

---

12 HA 1996 s124(5).

13 [2015] EWCA Civ 764, [2015] HLR 42.

14 Any argument by the authority that an election that has been made improperly can be subsequently ratified retrospectively, in accordance with the principle in *Tachie v Welwyn Hatfield BC* [2013] EWHC 3972 (QB), [2014] PTSR 662, should be resisted on the grounds that at the time that the tenancy was granted the election was not effective and so the tenancy must therefore have been secure and it cannot subsequently become introductory.

15 HA 1996 s124(3).

16 HA 1996 s124(4).

17 HA 1996 s124(2)(a).

adopted), they were secure or flexible tenants of another landlord or assured tenants (not assured shorthold) of another social landlord.[18]

5.17   If any one of several joint tenants satisfies any of the above conditions then the new tenancy will not be an introductory tenancy.[19]

The tenancy

5.18   Both periodic tenancies and periodic licences can be introductory.[20] A fixed-term tenancy or licence cannot be introductory unless, it was granted in England after HPA 2016 Sch 7 para 4 came into force. In that case it will be for a fixed term of at least two years,[21] but introductory only for a year.

5.19   The tenancy is only an introductory tenancy if it would otherwise have been a *secure* tenancy but for the extant election to operate the introductory scheme.[22] Thus, the landlord and tenant conditions of HA 1985[23] must be satisfied and the tenancy must not come within any of the exceptions to secure tenancy status in that Act.[24] For the prerequisites of 'secure' status see chapter 1.

5.20   Similarly, if an event occurs which would cause a secure tenancy to lose its status as such (for example, subletting the whole – see paras 1.153–1.160), any introductory tenancy loses that status and reverts to being a bare contractual tenancy.[25] In contrast to the position with secure tenants, introductory tenants cannot pass in and out of introductory status (see the 'ambulatory' nature of protection for secure occupiers described at para 1.98 above). Once a tenancy has lost introductory status that status cannot apply to it again later.[26]

The trial period

5.21   A tenancy usually remains an introductory tenancy only until the end of the 'trial period' of one year. At the end of the trial period it will become a secure tenancy without the need for further action by landlord or tenant (but see para 5.33). An introductory tenancy will, however, become a flexible tenancy (see paras 1.74–1.77) if the tenancy

18   HA 1996 s124(1A) and (2) and s124A.
19   HA 1996 s124(2).
20   HA 1996 s126.
21   HA 1996 s124(2).
22   HA 1996 s124(2).
23   HA 1985 ss80–81; see also paras 1.58–1.65.
24   HA 1985 s79(4) and Sch 1; see also para 1.69.
25   HA 1996 s125(5)(a).
26   HA 1996 s125(6).

was granted before HPA 2016 Sch 7 para 4 came into force and the landlord, before the introductory tenancy was granted, served a written notice on the prospective tenant

a) stating that, on ceasing to be an introductory tenancy, the tenancy would become a secure tenancy that would be a flexible tenancy for a term certain of the length specified in the notice,

b) specifying a period of at least two years as the length of the term of the tenancy, and

c) setting out the other express terms of the tenancy.[27]

5.22   It is therefore crucial to establish the date on which the one year starts to run. In the case of a tenancy which was granted by the council itself, the period begins with whichever is the later of:

- the date on which the tenancy was entered into; or
- the date on which the tenant was first entitled to possession under the tenancy.[28]

5.23   Thus, if a tenancy agreement is signed on 14 August 2016 which entitles the tenant to possession on 20 August 2016, the trial period runs from the latter date and expires on 19 August 2017. If on 14 August 2016 the tenant not only signs the agreement but also moves in (for example, to start decorating and installing furniture), the trial period runs from that date even if the first rent payable under the agreement is expressed to be due from 20 August 2016.[29]

5.24   The landlord has a power to extend the trial period by a further six months.[30] Where the landlord wishes to exercise this power, presumably because there has been some breach of tenancy obligations but the landlord is prepared to give the tenant a chance to remedy the situation, it must serve a notice of extension on the tenant at least eight weeks before the original one-year anniversary date. The notice must set out the reasons for the landlord's decision and inform the tenant of his or her right to request a review of that decision and the time allowed for making the request. The request must be made within 14 days beginning with the day when the notice of extension is served. The procedure on review is similar to that on review of a decision to seek possession (see paras 5.43–5.47). The review is to be carried out – and the tenant notified of the review decision – before the original one-year expiry date.

27 HA 1996 s137A.
28 HA 1996 s125(2).
29 *Salford City Council v Garner* [2004] EWCA Civ 364, [2004] HLR 35.
30 HA 1996 s125A, inserted by HA 2004 s179.

5.25   Where the tenancy was granted on or after HPA 2016 Sch 7 para 4 came into force, the new expiry date (ie the date to which the introductory tenancy will be extended) must be before the last nine months of the fixed term,[31] eg if the original fixed term was for two years, the introductory tenancy cannot be extended for more than an additional three months because it must expire when there are at least nine months of the fixed term remaining.

5.26   An introductory tenant may of course be offered a further introductory tenancy by the same or another council before the initial year expires (for example, as a result of a successful early request for a transfer). In such circumstances the time served under the former tenancy counts towards the trial period of the new tenancy, providing that the former tenancy ended immediately before the grant of the new one.[32]

5.27   If a tenant has held more than two successive introductory tenancies then each period counts towards the trial period providing that:

- the most recently completed period ended immediately before the new introductory tenancy was entered into (or was adopted); and
- each period succeeded the other without interruption.[33]

5.28   Where the new introductory tenancy is held by joint tenants, time towards the trial period is calculated by reference to the tenant who has been an introductory tenant, without interruption, for the longest period.[34]

5.29   A housing association's assured shorthold tenant might successfully apply for a transfer to a local authority which is operating the introductory tenancy regime. Providing the housing association is a registered social landlord (RSL) or private registered provider of social housing (PRPSH), the time served under the assured shorthold tenancy counts towards the trial period so long as the former assured shorthold tenancy ends immediately before the grant of the new tenancy.[35]

Loss of introductory status

5.30   An introductory tenancy ceases to be an introductory tenancy, even before the end of the trial period, if one of the following occurs:

31 HA 1996 s125A(3A)–(3B).
32 HA 1996 s125(3).
33 HA 1996 s125(3)(b).
34 HA 1996 s125(4).
35 HA 1996 s125(3).

- the circumstances are or become such that the tenancy could not otherwise be secure;
- the landlord ceases to be a local authority;
- the election in force when the tenancy was entered into (or adopted) is revoked; or
- the tenant dies and there is no one qualified to succeed.[36]

5.31 In any of these circumstances (other than revocation of the election), the tenancy itself continues but only as a bare contractual tenancy and it cannot later resume introductory status.[37] Where the election is revoked, the tenancy may become secure (or flexible if notice was served – see above para 5.21 – and it was granted before HPA 2016 Sch7 para 4 came into force).

5.32 However, if by the date of the occurrence of one of these developments listed in para 5.30 the landlord has already started possession proceedings, the tenancy has a deemed introductory status until those proceedings are concluded.[38]

5.33 Of course, the most common cause for the loss of introductory status is automatic conversion into a secure or flexible tenancy at the end of the one-year trial period or 18-month extended trial period. The landlord can only prevent that happening by the actual *issue* of possession proceedings before the trial period expires. The date when the proceedings are issued by the court is crucial, and this will often be a few days later than the date when the landlord lodged the claim form with the court.[39] The issue of proceedings serves to preserve introductory status until the proceedings are determined.[40]

The possession procedure

5.34 Assuming that consideration of the above factors has shown that the tenancy is indeed 'introductory', it will be necessary next for the adviser to check for proper observance by the landlord of the prescribed steps for recovery of possession. Those steps should be examined in turn and carefully scrutinised for error which may be relied on in defence of any proceedings. Particular care is needed if the tenant is vulnerable. Local authorities have been advised by central government that:

36 HA 1996 s125(5).
37 HA 1996 s125(6).
38 HA 1996 s130(1)(b).
39 *Salford City Council v Garner* [2004] EWCA Civ 364, [2004] HLR 35.
40 HA 1996 s130(1)(a).

Landlords should ensure that introductory tenancies can never be used as a weapon against vulnerable individuals and ensure that there are safeguards to protect such tenants ... It is essential that landlords are fully alive to the special needs of vulnerable tenants and their relationship with the community as a whole.[41]

5.35   Where problems have arisen between a vulnerable tenant and neighbours, eviction may not necessarily be the most appropriate action to take.[42]

Preliminary notice

5.36   Before issuing possession proceedings, the landlord must serve a HA 1996 s128 notice on the tenant. The reference to 'service' would suggest that only a written notice suffices. Without service of such a notice the landlord cannot bring proceedings for possession and there is no jurisdiction in the court to dispense with service of such a notice or waive any defect in it.[43]

5.37   No form of notice is prescribed but the notice must:[44]

- state that the court will be asked to make a possession order;
- set out the reasons for the landlord's decision to apply for such an order;
- specify a date after which possession proceedings may be begun;
- inform the tenant of the right to request a review of the decision to seek an order;
- inform the tenant of the time within which such a request must be made; and
- inform the tenant that, if he or she needs help or advice about the notice, and what to do about it, he or she should take it immediately to a citizen's advice bureau, a housing aid centre, a law centre or a solicitor.

In the county court, it has been held that the notice must contain all of the information specified in section 128(7). The fact that information

---

41 See Department of the Environment Circular 2/97 paras 10–15. See also the joint DoH/DoE guidance *Housing and community care: establishing a strategic framework*, January 1997.
42 Department of the Environment Circular 2/97 paras 10–15. See also the joint DoH/DoE guidance *Housing and community care: establishing a strategic framework*, January 1997.
43 HA 1996 s128(1).
44 HA 1996 s128(2)–(7).

had been provided in documents accompanying the notice was not sufficient.[45]

5.38   A notice which informed a tenant that she should (as opposed to 'must') complete a form in writing in order to request a review is not defective.[46]

Reasons

5.39   A notice with no reasons at all is plainly defective. Generally, a statutory duty to give reasons is construed to mean that the reasons given must be proper, intelligible and adequate.[47] The government circular on introductory tenancies advises landlords to give a 'full statement of reasons' which should include 'a case history of the sequence of events'.[48]

5.40   It is strongly arguable that where unintelligible, or inadequate reasons or plainly wrong reasons are given, the notice is invalid and the court cannot entertain the possession proceedings.[49] The basis for such an argument is that the tenant needs to know why the landlord has decided to bring the introductory tenancy to an end so that this can be challenged in a review. By way of an example, in *Lambeth LBC v Dearie*,[50] a possession order granted against an introductory tenant was set aside by a district judge. The reasons given in the notice were 'the tenant has failed to pay the rent due'. The court held this to be insufficient. These reasons did not enable the tenant to know precisely what had to be done to rectify the position or to exercise properly the right to review which was referred to in the notice. Likewise, a notice which simply said that possession was being sought 'because you have proved an unsatisfactory tenant' may also be held invalid for non-compliance with the statutory requirement to give reasons.

---

45   *Islington LBC v Giama* May 2015 *Legal Action* 44, Central London County Court.
46   *Wolverhampton CC v Shuttleworth* February 2013 *Legal Action* 34, 27 November 2012, High Court. Cf *Hammershith and Fulham LBC v Patterson* May 2016 *Legal Action* 40, County Court at Willesden, where the notice stated that a request for a view must be made in writing.
47   Per Megaw J in *Re Poyser and Mills' Arbitration* [1964] 2 QB 467, [1963] 2 WLR 1309, approved by the House of Lords in *Save Britain's Heritage v Number 1 Poultry Ltd* [1991] 1 WLR 153, HL.
48   DoE Circ 2/97 para 16. It also advises (para 17) that an explanation in a covering letter is not an adequate substitute.
49   See by analogy *Torridge DC v Jones* (1986) 18 HLR 107, CA and *Dudley MBC v Bailey* (1990) 22 HLR 424, CA.
50   April 2001 *Legal Action* 20.

Dates

5.41   The date stated in the notice as the date after which possession proceedings may be begun must, in the case of a periodic tenancy, not be earlier than the date on which the tenancy could, if it were not an introductory tenancy, be brought to an end by notice to quit given on the same date as the notice of proceedings.[51] For a weekly periodic tenancy, the earliest date is a date at least 28 days after service and that date must be the first or last day of a period of the tenancy.[52] The notice must also comply with any express terms of the tenancy as to the period of notice.

5.42   In the case of a fixed-term tenancy, ie a flexible tenancy or a tenancy granted after HPA 2016 Sch 7 para 4 came into force, the date in the notice must not be earlier than the end of a period of six weeks beginning with the date on which the notice of proceedings is served.[53]

The request for review

5.43   Within 14 days of being served with the notice, the tenant may request that the landlord reviews the decision to seek possession. The request need not be made in writing (although it would be sensible to ensure it was recorded in writing). There is no prescribed form, and no requirement to make the request in any particular manner.[54] There is no requirement to give grounds for seeking a review.

5.44   The period of 14 days begins with the day on which the notice is served.[55] If the notice is served on a Thursday the request for a review must be made by a week next Wednesday.[56] This 14-day time period cannot be extended by the landlord nor on application to a county court because a court has no discretion to extend a statutory time limit.[57]

---

51   HA 1996 s128(4)(a).
52   *Crate v Miller* [1947] KB 946; Protection from Eviction Act 1977 s5.
53   HA 1996 s128(4)(b).
54   *R (Chelfat) v Tower Hamlets LBC* [2006] EWHC 313 (Admin), April 2006 *Legal Action* 32.
55   HA 1996 s129(1).
56   *Trow v Ind Coope (West Midlands) Ltd* [1967] 2 QB 899, [1967] 3 WLR 633.
57   *Honig v Lewisham LBC* (1958) 122 JPJ 302, CA.

Timing and procedure on review

5.45 The review must be dealt with speedily. It must be concluded (which includes notification of the result to the tenant) within the period between the service of the notice and the date specified in it for earliest commencement of proceedings.[58] That may be as short as 28 days. If the landlord misses this window, the chance to seek possession may be lost – possibly for good if the trial year (or 18-month period) has meantime expired. If it has not expired, the landlord can start again with a new notice. However, failure to conclude a review within the statutory period may not be fatal to the council's case. In *R (Chelfat) v Tower Hamlets LBC*,[59] the court in its discretion refused relief where the council had not conducted a review within the prescribed timescale because the tenant's request for a review had been directed to the housing benefits section of the council and not to the housing officer named in the notice. The council had subsequently agreed to a warrant of possession being suspended by consent to enable a review to be carried out, and against that background it would have been wholly unjust to allow the tenant's application for judicial review.

5.46 Since HA 1996 s129(6) is silent as to the consequences of any failure to carry out a review within the time specified, the question of whether such a delay was fatal to the council's claim for possession would turn on the facts. If the failure was due to a genuine oversight capable of being remedied, there would seem to be no good reason to prevent a landlord from remedying the position and bringing a possession claim. In particular, if the reason that the time limit for completion of the review has been exceeded is because the landlord acceded to a tenant's request to adjourn or postpone a review hearing, it is unlikely that a court would hold that the landlord had thereby lost the possibility of proceeding with a possession claim.

5.47 The Introductory Tenants (Review) Regulations 1997[60] are concerned with the procedure that is to be followed on a review. In summary:

- Regulation 2 provides that there is to be no oral hearing unless one has been expressly requested by the tenant within 14 days of the service of the notice of intention to seek possession. There is no power to extend that time limit. That notice need not advise

---

58 HA 1996 s129(6).
59 [2006] EWHC 313 (Admin), April 2006 *Legal Action* 32.
60 SI No 72.

the tenant of this right to request an oral hearing (see the actual requirements at para 5.37). The request for an oral hearing need not be made in writing.

- Regulation 3 provides that the review is to be carried out by a person who was not involved in the decision to apply for possession and if that person is an officer the reviewer must be a person senior to the officer who took the decision to serve the notice of intention to seek possession.

- Regulation 4 provides that, if no oral hearing has been requested in time, the tenant has a right to submit written representations within a fixed period of being notified of that right. This is based on the premise, therefore, that on receipt of a request for review the landlord will acknowledge it and invite written representations by a fixed date which must not be earlier than five clear days from the date the tenant receives this notice of the right to make representations.

- Regulations 5 and 6 deal with oral hearings. Where a request for an oral hearing has been made in time, the landlord must give the tenant notice of the date, time and place of the hearing, which cannot be less than five days after the landlord receives the tenant's request. If the notice is defective or short then the hearing may only proceed with the consent of the tenant or his or her representative. At a hearing the tenant has a right to:
  - be heard and to be accompanied and represented by another person (professional or otherwise);
  - call people to give evidence;
  - put questions to any person who gives evidence; and
  - make written representations.

  The tenant should be given sufficient opportunity to read any written material relied on by the council and to prepare his or her own case.[61]

- Regulations 7 to 10 deal with such matters as adjournments, postponements and non-attendance.

5.48   As is apparent from this description of the statutory review scheme, and of the regulations which flesh it out, the scheme makes no pretence of 'independence'. The review is carried out by the very landlord that has decided to give notice of intention to claim possession. In *R (McLellan) v Bracknell Forest BC*,[62] it was contended that the review

---

61   *R (McDonagh) v Salisbury DC* [2001] EWHC 567 (Admin), September 2001 *Legal Action* 23.

62   [2001] EWCA Civ 1510, (2001) 33 HLR 86.

scheme was incompatible with the right to a fair and impartial determination of civil rights guaranteed by Human Rights Act 1998 Sch
1 Article 6(1). The Court of Appeal decided that the requirements of
Article 6 were met because the Administrative Court's judicial review
jurisdiction could be invoked to cure any deficiency in the review
process in any particular case.

Outcome of the review

5.49   After the review has been completed, the landlord must notify the
tenant of its decision and, if the decision to take possession proceedings still stands, then the landlord must give reasons for that decision.[63] The use of the word 'notify' would suggest that the notice and
the reasons both have to be in writing.

5.50   Where the landlord decides, following a review, to uphold the decision to seek possession but to allow the tenant an opportunity to remedy any breach of tenancy obligations, but the tenant does not do so,
the landlord may take proceedings for possession without the need
to serve a fresh notice. In *Cardiff City Council v Stone*,[64] the tenant
had fallen into rent arrears. The council issued a notice of intention
to take proceedings for possession. Following a review, the tenant
was informed that proceedings would not be taken if she cleared the
arrears at the rate of £3 per week. The arrears later increased, and the
council claimed possession on the basis of the original notice. The
Court of Appeal rejected the argument that a second notice should
have been served: this might deter a landlord from taking a humane
'wait and see' approach before issuing proceedings. In these circumstances, the landlord should make it clear that on the review it
has upheld the decision to seek possession and is merely deferring
proceedings to give the tenant a further chance to save his or her
home.[65]

5.51   In contrast, in *Camden LBC v Stafford*,[66] the Court of Appeal
upheld a decision to dismiss a possession claim where the reviewing
panel had failed to uphold the landlord's decision to seek possession and had instead suggested that alternative measures be adopted
but the landlord had issued proceedings, without issuing a second
notice, when such measures failed.

---

63 HA 1996 s129(5).
64 [2002] EWCA Civ 298, [2003] HLR 47.
65 *R (Forbes) v Lambeth LBC* [2003] EWHC 222 (Admin), [2003] HLR 49.
66 [2012] EWCA Civ 839, [2012] HLR 39.

5.52   Where the landlord serves a notice of intention to seek possession and the tenant then commits breaches of a different nature from those specified in the notice, the landlord will usually be required to serve a second notice and hold a further review (if requested). This requirement may, however, be waived if the landlord has acted fairly and the tenant has suffered no prejudice.[67]

Possession proceedings

5.53   The landlord can only bring an introductory tenancy to an end (while it is an introductory tenancy) by obtaining a possession order and then executing that order.[68]

5.54   Before commencing possession proceedings the landlord does *not* need to serve a notice to quit or a notice seeking possession (under HA 1985) – the notice procedure described at para 5.37 above substitutes for those requirements. The landlord should use the usual procedure for possession in the county court set out in CPR Part 55 (see chapter 21). It has been held in the county court that the landlord cannot issue a claim for possession by using Possession Claims Online ('PCOL') because CPR 55B PD 5.1 provides that any claim must be brought solely on the grounds of rent. A claim for possession of an introductory tenancy is not brought solely on the grounds of rent. Its use is therefore an abuse of process and any claim should be struck out.[69]

5.55   A landlord is also required to comply with Part 3 of the *Pre-action Protocol for possession claims by social landlords*. Although the title of the protocol suggests that it only applies to claims based on rent arrears, the Protocol explains that Part 3 applies to all claims where the court's discretion to postpone possession is limited by HA 1980 s89(1), ie where the court is not required to consider whether it is reasonable to make a possession order.

Paragraph 3.2 of the Protocol requires landlords to write to occupants in advance of the claim to explain why they intend to seek possession and to invite the occupiers to, within a specified period, notify the landlord of any personal circumstances or other matters that they wish to be considered. The landlord is then expected to consider those representations before deciding whether to issue a claim

---

67 *R (Laporte) v Newham LBC* [2004] EWHC 227 (Admin), [2004] 2 All ER 874.
68 HA 1996 s127(1) and (1A), as substituted by Housing and Regeneration Act 2008 s299 and Sch 11 Pt 1 paras 10 and 11(1) and (2), on 20 May 2009.
69 *Crosby v Birmingham City Council*, County Court at Birmingham, 8 March 2016, HHJ Worster.

for possession. Paragraph 3.3 of the Protocol further requires land-lords to, within its particulars of claim or a witness statement, con-firm that it has complied with paragraph 3.2 and give brief reasons for deciding to bring the claim. However, unlike under Part 2 of the Protocol, there are no sanctions for non-compliance with the Proto-col. In practice therefore, the court will not be entitled to dismiss the claim in the event that Part 3 of the Protocol has not been complied with. It may, however, be more willing to grant an adjournment to allow a defendant to file a public law or human rights defence and, potentially, to award the occupier its costs of the hearing

Defending the proceedings

5.56   The court shall not make an order for possession unless satisfied that the provisions of HA 1996 s128 apply.[70] To meet that requirement the landlord needs to prove that:

- the tenancy was an introductory tenancy at the time when posses-sion proceedings were begun; and
- a valid HA 1996 s128 notice (para 5.37) has been served; and
- the proceedings were begun after the date specified in that notice (paras 5.41–5.42).

If the landlord can prove the three above-mentioned matters on the balance of probabilities, possession *must* be granted.

5.57   This apparently mandatory ground is, however, subject to certain caveats. The court must, if the issue is raised by the tenant, refuse to order possession where the tenant's eviction would amount to a disproportionate interference with the tenant's human rights.[71] The same principle applies equally where the tenant establishes a defence that the decision to seek possession unlawfully discriminates against the tenant under the Equality Act 2010 or is flawed on public law grounds.[72] See chapters 25, 26 and 27 respectively for further discus-sion on such defences.

5.58   HA 1996 s128 does not require the landlord to prove that the post-notice review procedure has been properly observed or completed in order to recover possession, the failure to carry out a review or a failure to comply with the review procedure is likely to give rise to an arguable public law defence (see below and chapter 26) if it is raised by the tenant.

---

70 HA 1996 s127(2).
71 *Hounslow LBC v Powell* [2011] UKSC 8, [2011] 2 AC 186.
72 *Hounslow LBC v Powell* [2011] UKSC 8, [2011] 2 AC 186.

5.59   Advisers will want to explore the possibilities of running defences based on either or any of the following:

- the tenancy was not 'introductory' at the date the proceedings were issued (see paras 5.11–5.14);
- the HA 1996 s128 notice is defective or was not served (see paras 5.36–5.42);
- the proceedings were begun prematurely (see paras 5.41–5.42);
- the proceedings were begun too late (ie after the trial period had expired) (see para 5.33);[73] or
- the decision to seek possession is a breach of the Equality Act 2010 (see chapter 27), is a disproportionate interference with the tenant's human rights under Article 8 (see chapter 26) or is flawed on public law grounds (see chapter 25).

5.60   For example, in *Southend on Sea v Armour*,[74] an introductory tenant successfully resisted a claim for possession on the grounds that his eviction was not proportionate.[75] The result of which was that he became a secure tenant. Likewise, in *Southwark LBC v Hyacienth*,[76] in the county court, a claim for possession was dismissed as the landlord had failed to follow and apply its own policy on arrears management and the review panel had not identified this failing.

5.61   If any of these defences succeeds, the proceedings should be dismissed, usually with costs. There are two exceptions to this rule: (1) where a court dealing with a human rights or discrimination defence makes a finding that the immediate eviction would be disproportionate, but that the proportionate outcome is to give the tenant a period of up to six weeks to leave; or (2) where a public law defence is successful, but the court decides that it ought not to prevent the landlord from recovering possession as it is a case in which relief would have been refused had the defence been brought as a claim for judicial review.[77]

---

73 *Salford CC v Entwhistle* October 2002 *Legal Action* 28 and *Salford CC v Garner* [2004] EWCA Civ 364, [2004] HLR 35.
74 [2014] EWCA Civ 231, [2014] HLR 23.
75 See paragraph 26.98.
76 May 2012 *Legal Action* 32, Lambeth County Court.
77 *Barnsley MBC v Norton* [2011] EWCA Civ 834, [2011] HLR 46. See also *R (Swindells) v Greenwich LBC* [2008] EWCA Civ 244, June 2008 *Legal Action* 31, in which the Court of Appeal upheld the dismissal of a claim for judicial review (see [2007] EWHC 2131 (Admin)) on the grounds that, notwithstanding flaws in the decision making process, there was a lack of merit in the tenant's application.

The possession order

5.62 If the court makes a possession order against an introductory tenant it cannot postpone the date for giving of possession for more than 14 days unless:

- possession by that date would cause exceptional hardship, in which case the postponement can be for up to six weeks;[78] or
- the landlord consents to a longer period.

Except by consent, there is no scope for the making of other forms of possession orders.

5.63 The court has no discretion to stay or suspend execution of the possession order beyond the periods mentioned above.[79] This even applies where the court finds that it is proportionate to make a possession order, but finds that it would be disproportionate for it to be executed until a date that is after six weeks. In such cases, the court must dismiss the claim.[80]

5.64 The introductory tenancy will only come to an end with the eviction of the tenant on execution of the possession order. This means that an introductory tenancy can in theory continue indefinitely if the authority chooses not to execute the possession order, eg because the tenant complies with a repayment plan to clear rent arrears or their behaviour improves.

Starter tenancies

5.65 'Starter' or 'probationary' tenancies for tenants of PRPSHs and RSLs are not statutorily defined. There is no statute which sets out the circumstances in which a starter tenancy can be granted, makes provision for its length or identifies the means by which it can be terminated.

5.66 Many PRPSHs and RSLs grant tenancies which are, by default, assured shorthold tenancies. They only convert them to full assured tenancies after initial 'starter' or probationary periods. Provided the tenancy agreement has not specified that the tenancy is to be a full assured tenancy, all new tenancies granted by a PRPSH or an RSL will be assured shorthold tenancies provided that the conditions for being an assured tenancy are otherwise satisfied, ie the tenancy is

78 HA 1980 s89.
79 HA 1980 s89 and *Plymouth CC v Hill* January 2010 *Legal Action* 31.
80 *Hounslow LBC v Powell* [2011] UKSC 8, [2011] 2 AC 186.

of a dwelling-house let as a separate dwelling to an individual and it is not otherwise excluded by HA 1988 Sch 1.[81] Starter tenancies can either be fixed-term or periodic assured shorthold tenancies.

5.67   To recover possession of the property from such an assured secure tenant, the landlord must rely on a HA 1988 s21 notice (see paras 10.7–10.14) or one of the grounds for possession contained within HA 1988 Sch 2. As with introductory tenancies, the landlord must comply with Part 3 of the *Pre-action Protocol for possession claims by social landlords* (see above para 5.55) before entering a claim.

5.68   There are, however, a limited number of other considerations that will only apply to so-called 'starter' or 'probationary' tenancies granted by PRPSHs and RSLs.

Has the assured shorthold tenancy become assured?

5.69   HA 1988 s19A provides that an assured tenancy that is entered into on or after 28 February 1997 will be an assured shorthold tenancy unless one of the exceptions within HA 1988 Schedule 2A applies.

5.70   HA 1988 Sch 2A paras 1–2 provide that what would otherwise be an assured secure tenancy will be a full assured tenancy if it is:

1(1) An assured tenancy in respect of which a notice is served as mentioned in sub-paragraph (2) below.

(2) The notice referred to in sub-paragraph (1) above is one which –
  (a) is served before the assured tenancy is entered into,
  (b) is served by the person who is to be the landlord under the assured tenancy on the person who is to be the tenant under that tenancy, and
  (c) states that the assured tenancy to which it relates is not to be an assured shorthold tenancy.

2(1) An assured tenancy in respect of which a notice is served as mentioned in sub-paragraph (2) below.

(2) The notice referred to in sub-paragraph (1) above is one which –
  (a) is served after the assured tenancy has been entered into,
  (b) is served by the landlord under the assured tenancy on the tenant under that tenancy, and
  (c) states that the assured tenancy to which it relates is no longer an assured shorthold tenancy.

5.71   Ordinarily, the tenancy agreement will specify the circumstances in which the tenancy will cease to be an assured shorthold tenancy so as to satisfy Schedule 2A para 2. Normally, the agreement will provide

---

81 See paras 1.6–1.36 for further discussion on the conditions necessary for a tenancy to be assured.

that after 12 months, or 18 months if extended, the agreement will cease to be an assured shorthold tenancy. Although a well-drafted agreement is likely to provide that the tenancy will not become assured once proceedings for possession have been issued, it does not, unlike for introductory tenancies, automatically follow and so consideration should always be given to whether conditions specified within the tenancy agreement have been satisfied.

5.72　　However, a landlord can also, through the provision of a notice after the tenancy has been granted, and sometimes inadvertently, notify the tenant that the tenancy is no longer an assured shorthold tenancy. In *Saxon Weald Homes Ltd v Chadwick*,[82] a letter, which was sent to a tenant in error after proceedings for possession had been begun for the recovery of a starter tenancy and stated that the tenant's assured shorthold tenancy had become an assured tenancy, was construed to be a notice for the purposes of Schedule 2A. The result of which was that the tenant became an assured tenant and the claim for possession based on section 21 was dismissed.

5.73　　The notice must, however, state that the tenancy is no longer an assured shorthold tenancy or that the assured shorthold tenancy has become an assured tenancy. A letter which mistakenly refers to a tenant as an assured tenant will not constitute a notice for the purposes of Schedule 2A.[83]

Retaliatory eviction

5.74　　Deregulation Act 2015 s33 prohibits landlords, in England, from serving HA 1988 s21 notices in certain specified circumstances where the tenant has complained about the condition of the premises.[84] This prohibition does not, however, apply to tenancies where the landlord is a PRPSH.[85] It is therefore not a defence available to a starter tenant.

Prescribed information

5.75　　The Deregulation Act 2015 introduced a prohibition on landlords, in England, from serving a HA 1988 s21 notice if they had not, before

---

82　[2011] EWCA Civ 1202, [2012] HLR 8.
83　*Andrews v Cunningham* [2007] EWCA Civ 762, [2008] HLR 13. See also *Wandsworth LBC v Tompkins* [2015] EWCA Civ 846, [2015] HLR 44.
84　See paras 10.92–10.102.
85　Deregulation Act 2015 s34(6).

serving the notice, provided the tenant with prescribed information. The Assured Shorthold Tenancy Notices and Prescribed Requirements (England) Regulations 2015[86] specifies that landlords, in order to meet this requirement, must give tenants the document 'How to rent: the checklist for renting in England'. This requirement does not, however, apply to tenancies where the landlord is a PRPSH[87] and is therefore not a defence that is available to starter tenants.

Potential defences that are particular to starter tenancies in England

5.76   The Tenancy Standard,[88] in England, regulates the use of assured shorthold tenancies by RPSHs. The Tenancy Standard provides:

> 2.2.2 Registered providers must grant general needs tenants a periodic secure or assured (excluding periodic assured shorthold) tenancy, or a tenancy for a minimum fixed term of five years, or exceptionally, a tenancy for a minimum fixed term of no less than two years, in addition to any probationary tenancy period.
>
> ...
>
> 2.2.4 Where registered providers use probationary tenancies, these shall be for a maximum of 12 months, or a maximum of 18 months where reasons for extending the probationary period have been given and where the tenant has the opportunity to request a review.
>
> ...

5.77   While a county court that is asked to make a possession order in respect of an assured shorthold tenancy that has persisted for more than 18 months will not have the power to convert the tenancy into a fully assured tenancy, it would, provided the provider was found to be a public authority for the purposes of judicial review, be able to consider a public law defence that the decision to seek possession was one that no reasonable registered provider would have taken as it is in direct contradiction to the statutory guidance. In the event that the defence succeeded the court would have the power to dismiss the claim. See chapter 25 on public law defences. The dismissal of the claim would not, of itself, turn the assured shorthold tenancy into an assured tenancy.

5.78   Likewise, similar public law defences could be run where the landlord has failed to provide the tenant with an opportunity to request

---

86   SI No 1646.
87   Reg 3(5)(a).
88   *Tenancy Standard* (Homes and Communities Agency, 31 March 2015).

a review of the decision not to grant a fully assured tenancy or to extend the probationary period to 18 months.

5.79   The Tenancy Standard also requires RPSHs 'to develop and provide services that will support tenants to maintain their tenancy and prevent unnecessary evictions'.[89]

5.80   It may therefore also be argued that where a PRPSH has failed to provide such services to support tenants in maintaining their tenancies that it is unreasonable, in the public law sense, for a landlord to seek possession of a starter tenancy.

5.81   Finally, the Tenancy Standard also requires that the landlord have policies, that are accessible to the tenant, which set out:

1) The circumstances in which they may or may not grant another tenancy on the expiry of the fixed term,[90]

2) The way in which a tenant or prospective tenant may appeal against or complain about a decision not to grant another tenancy on the expiry of the fixed term,[91]

3) Their policy on taking into account the needs of those households who are vulnerable by reason of age, disability or illness, and households with children, including through the provision of tenancies which provide a reasonable degree of stability,[92] and

4) The advice and assistance they will give to tenants on finding alternative accommodation in the event that they decide not to grant another tenancy.[93]

5.82   Accordingly, the fact that a landlord has failed to adhere to any of its policies, which relate to the termination of the starter tenancy or to the services provided to a vulnerable tenant during the tenancy, may also give rise to a public law defence.

5.83   An example of a successful public law defence by a starter tenant was in *Eastlands Homes Partnership Ltd v Whyte*.[94] The tenant successfully defended the claim where the landlord failed to follow its own policy in relation to rent arrears; offered an appeal against its decision but failed to disclose the evidence put before the appeal panel

---

89 Para 2.2.7.
90 Para 2.2.1(e). While this appears to apply to fixed-term assured shorthold tenancies as opposed to starter periodic tenancies, there is no reason why this does not equally apply to the circumstances in which the landlord opts to bring a starter tenancy to an end.
91 Para 2.2.1(f).
92 Para 2.2.1(g).
93 Para 2.2.1(h).
94 [2010] EWHC 695 (QB).

and/or broadened the matters considered on appeal beyond the case summary it had prepared; and, having stated that it would offer a second or further appeal, failed to do so. For further discussion on the availability of other public law defences see chapter 25.

5.84   Consideration should, as for any other tenants with limited security of tenure, also be given to whether an Equality Act 2010 or human rights defence will be available. Unlike for introductory tenants,[95] there are presently no reported examples of successful human rights defences brought by starter tenants. In both *West Kent v Haycraft*[96] and *Riverside Group Ltd v Thomas*,[97] the court found that it would not be disproportionate to evict starter tenants who had been guilty of anti-social behaviour (see paras 26.142 to 26.146). For further discussion on the principles governing such defences see chapters 26 and 27. Other than for defences under the Equality Act 2010, particular consideration will need to be given to whether the private registered provider is a public authority (see paras 25.34 to 25.43).

Potential defences that are particular to starter tenancies in Wales

5.85   The guidance for Welsh registered social landlords in Wales is less prescriptive and therefore affords less of an opportunity for tenants to show that it has not been complied with. Although the guidance provides that landlords must 'use the most secure form of tenancy compatible with the purpose of the housing',[98] it does not follow from this statement that landlords ought not to grant starter tenancies. Indeed, it could be legitimately argued that a starter tenancy is the appropriate form of security for a new tenant.

5.86   While there is no equivalent provision for reviews, the guidance does require landlords to

> support tenants to prevent arrears of rent and service charges arising and act quickly to avoid arrears building up. We recover any arrears fairly and effectively, whilst helping tenants to meet their due payments,

and to be

---

95 See above para 5.60.
96 [2012] EWCA Civ 276; [2012] HLR 23.
97 [2012] EWHC 169 (QB).
98 *The Regulatory Framework For Housing Associations Registered in Wales* (Welsh Government, December 2011) p20.

[R]esponsive to people's individual housing support needs and help them to sustain their tenancies.[99]

5.87 As in England, consideration should be given to whether an Equality Act 2010, public law or human rights defence will be available. See chapters 27, 25 and 26 respectively.

99 *The Regulatory Framework For Housing Associations Registered in Wales* (Welsh Government, December 2011) p20.

CHAPTER 6

Demoted tenancies

Background

6.1   The Anti-social Behaviour Act (ASBA) 2003 introduced a new weapon in the armoury of social landlords to deal with serious nuisance behaviour. ASBA 2003 s14 gave some social landlords the power to ask courts to 'demote' secure or assured tenancies to 12-month probationary tenancies.[1] If during that year the social landlord has cause for complaint about the tenant's behaviour, the tenancy can be terminated by court order following a notice of proceedings, but without the need to prove a ground for possession.

6.2   A local authority, a registered social landlord (RSL) or a private registered provider of social housing (PRPSH) can apply to a county court for a demotion order, under:

- Housing Act (HA) 1985 s82A (where the tenancy is a secure tenancy);[2] or
- HA 1988 s6A (where the tenancy is an assured tenancy).[3]

6.3   Demotion involves the court making an order that:

- ends an existing secure or assured tenancy; and
- replaces it with a new tenancy which gives the tenant reduced security of tenure for a fixed period of time; and
- carries forward any rent arrears or credits from the old rent account on to the new rent account.[4]

6.4   This chapter deals with the rules on demotion of both secure and assured tenancies. While the grounds for demotion are identical in respect of both types of tenancy, there are major differences in the nature of the demoted tenancy which is created in each case.

---

1   The provisions were brought into effect in England from 30 June 2004 and in Wales from 30 September 2004. See generally Jon Holbrook and Dean Underwood, 'Defending demoted tenancy claims' September 2004 *Legal Action* 27 and October 2004 *Legal Action* 23 and Christopher Baker, 'Demoting tenancies: innovation or exasperation?' (Part 1 and 2) [2004] 7(5) JHL 72–76 and [2004] 7(6) JHL 85–89.

2   This includes a flexible tenancy as it is a fixed-term secure tenancy: HA 1985 s107A (HA 1985 s115B).

3   Both sections were inserted in the respective Acts by Anti-social Behaviour Act 2003 s14(2).

4   HA 1985 s82A(3); HA 1988 s6A(3).

'Relevant landlord'

6.5 Demotion can only be sought by a relevant landlord. Only a local housing authority, a RSL or a PRPSH is a 'relevant landlord' for these purposes, ie, one which can apply to demote a secure or assured tenancy.[5] No private sector landlord can apply for a demotion order and not all of the various types of landlord that can grant a secure tenancy (see paras 1.58–1.64) can apply for demotion.[6]

Grounds for a demotion order

6.6 The court must not make a demotion order unless it is satisfied that: (1) the tenant or a person residing in or visiting the tenant's home has engaged in or threatened to engage in conduct which falls within *either* of the limbs set out below; *and* (2) it is reasonable to make the order.[7] The same two-stage test applies in all cases.

The first limb: nuisance and annoyance

6.7 This limb relates to conduct. The landlord must show that the tenant or a person residing in or visiting the dwelling-house has engaged or threatened to engage in conduct that:

a) is capable of causing nuisance or annoyance;
b) to some person (who need not be a particular identified person); and
c) that conduct directly or indirectly relates to or affects the landlord's housing management function.[8]

6.8 This is the same meaning given to 'anti-social behaviour' under Anti-social Behaviour, Crime and Policing Act (ABCPA) 2014 s2(1)(c).

6.9 The definition is widely drafted. It captures conduct committed by any visitor to the tenant's dwelling-house anywhere and against

5 HA 1985 s82A(1); HA 1988 s6A(1) (in each case amended by Housing and Regeneration Act 2008 (Consequential Provisions) Order 2010 SI No 866 art 5 and Sch 2).
6 Although housing action trusts are a type of landlord capable of applying for demotion of a secure tenancy under HA 1985 s82A(1), all the housing action trusts have now been wound up.
7 HA 1985 s82A(4) in respect of secure tenancies; HA 1988 s6A(4) in respect of assured tenancies.
8 HA 1985 s82A(4)(a)(i) in respect of secure tenancies; HA 1988 s6A(4)(a)(i) in respect of assured tenancies.

any person, whether or not it was directed against that person or not. However, there must be a connection between the conduct and the landlord's 'housing management functions'. ABCPA 2014 s2(4) defines 'housing management functions' as being:

(a) functions conferred by or under an enactment;
(b) the powers and duties of the housing provider or local authority as the holder of an estate or interest in housing accommodation.

6.10   Clearly, any behaviour which adversely affects tenants of the landlord or their household members or visitors, or the landlord's staff, relates to housing management functions even if it occurs far away from the property. Despite the reference to conduct which affects functions conferred by any enactment, it is suggested that the scope of this provision does not extend to the non-housing functions of a local authority, for example, in its capacity as highways authority. However, the phrase has been given the widest possible interpretation by the courts. In *Swindon BC v Redpath*,[9] Rix LJ said that the tenant's conduct had to be viewed as a whole:

> Viewed as a whole ... the council's housing management functions easily embrace its sense of responsibility to its continuing tenants and also to owner-occupiers [in the same street] for the conduct of its former tenant, ... who has pursued his vendetta against his former neighbours irrespective of the loss of his tenancy. (para 55)

Lord Neuberger said that it was clear that the definition was intended 'to have a broad sweep' (para 62). He said that 'housing related' conduct

> can clearly be engaged in by someone who is not a tenant or an occupier of property owned by the relevant landlord; equally, it can be engaged in by someone who neither resides nor works within the area in which the conduct occurs. (para 64)

The second limb: use of premises for unlawful purposes

6.11   Under this limb the landlord must establish that the tenant or a person residing in or visiting the dwelling-house has engaged or threatened to engage in conduct that consists of or involves using housing accommodation owned or managed by the landlord for an unlawful purpose.[10]

---

9   [2009] EWCA Civ 943, [2010] HLR 13.
10   HA 1985 s82A(4)(a)(ii) in respect of secure tenancies; HA 1988 s6A(4)(a)(ii) in respect of assured tenancies.

6.12   It is not necessary to prove a conviction for the unlawful use of the accommodation (in contrast with the third limb of the comparable ground for possession for secure and assured tenancies – see paras 3.152–3.160).

Reasonableness

6.13   The court cannot grant a demotion order unless it is satisfied that it is reasonable to do so.[11] The court has a broad exercise of judgment to undertake in assessing reasonableness, and some guidance may be derived from case-law under the 'nuisance or annoyance' ground for possession in relation to secure and assured tenancies (see paras 3.171–3.187). In *Washington Housing Company Ltd v Morson*,[12] the landlord sought a demotion order based on evidence of the misconduct of the tenant's children. Refusing permission to appeal against a finding that it was reasonable to make the order, the appeal court said that the order was 'a reasonable way of balancing the parents' right and entitlement to a secure home with the public interest in preventing this sort of behaviour in future'.[13] See para 6.38 for further discussion on when it will be reasonable to make an order.

New English secure tenancies granted after the Housing and Planning Act 2016 came into force

6.14   The court may not make a demotion order in relation to a secure tenancy of a dwelling-house in England if the landlord is a local housing authority or housing action trust and the fixed term has less than one year and nine months to run.

6.15   This prohibition was added by Housing and Planning Act (HPA) 2016 to ensure that when any demotion period comes to an end, after a year, the landlord has sufficient time to conduct a review (under HA 1985 s86A) to determine whether to grant another fixed-term tenancy or to recover possession.

---

11 HA 1985 s82A(4)(b) in respect of secure tenancies; HA 1988 s6A(4)(b) in respect of assured tenancies.

12 *Washington Housing Company Ltd v Morson* [2005] EWHC 3407 (Ch).

13 *Washington Housing Company Ltd v Morson* [2005] EWHC 3407 (Ch) at [67].

Notice of intention to apply for a demotion order

6.16   Before applying for a demotion order, the landlord must serve a notice of its intention to do so. The procedure differs according to whether the tenancy is a secure tenancy or an assured tenancy.

Demotion notices and secure tenants

6.17   The landlord must first serve a notice in the prescribed form.[14] Where the landlord also intends to seek possession, in the alternative to a demotion order, there is no need for two separate notices to be served. The notice of seeking possession and the notice seeking demotion can be given in a single notice and the prescribed form has been adapted to accommodate that possibility.[15]

6.18   The notice of intended demotion must contain particulars of the conduct which has caused the landlord to seek to demote the tenancy. In respect of secure periodic tenancies, it must also specify a date after which proceedings may be begun.[16] That date must not be earlier than the date on which a notice to quit would expire.[17] Since most secure tenants are weekly periodic tenants, a notice to quit would need to give at least 28 days following the date of service and expire on the first or last day of a tenancy period.[18] Where the tenancy is for a fixed term (ie a flexible or new English secure tenancy), the notice does not need to specify a date after which proceedings may be begun.[19]

6.19   There is no provision allowing proceedings to be begun immediately after service of the notice, as there is with regard to possession claims on nuisance grounds, but there is provision for the court to dispense with notice altogether.[20]

---

14   HA 1985 s83(2), as amended by ASBA 2003 s14(3). See also Secure Tenancies (Notices) (Amendment) (England) Regulations 2004 SI No 1627 and Secure Tenancies (Notices) (Amendment) (Wales) Regulations 2005 SI No 1226.

15   See Secure Tenancies (Notices) (Amendment) (England) Regulations 2004 SI No 1627 and Secure Tenancies (Notices) (Amendment) (Wales) Regulations 2005 SI No 1226.

16   HA 1985 s83(4A)(a).

17   HA 1985 s83(5).

18   Protection from Eviction Act 1977 s5.

19   HA 1985 s83(6).

20   HA 1985 s83(1)(b).

6.20   The notice has a 'life span' of 12 months beginning with the date specified in it.[21] During that calendar year, proceedings may be issued based on the notice. After that period, a fresh notice must be issued, unless the court agrees to dispense with the notice requirement if it considers it 'just and equitable' to do so.

Demotion notices and assured tenants

6.21   In the case of an assured tenant, the landlord must serve a notice of intention to apply for demotion before the court can entertain proceedings,[22] but there is no prescribed form of notice. However, the notice must:

- give particulars of the conduct complained of;
- state that proceedings will not begin before the date specified in the notice; and
- state that proceedings will not begin later than 12 months after the date of service.[23]

6.22   The notice period is shorter than that for secure tenancies: the date specified in the notice must be at least two weeks from the date of service of the notice and the specified date need not be the first or last day of a tenancy period.[24] The 'life span' of the notice dates from the date of service, not from the date specified.

6.23   The court may dispense with the notice requirements in an assured tenancy case if it considers it just and equitable to do so.[25]

6.24   The same procedure applies to assured shorthold tenancies in England that were granted by a PRPSH for a fixed term of not less than two years.[26] The result of any demotion order is that the fixed term comes to an end and an assured shorthold weekly periodic tenancy takes its place.[27]

---

21 HA 1985 s83(4A)(b).
22 HA 1988 s6A(5).
23 HA 1988 s6A(6).
24 HA 1988 s6A(7).
25 HA 1988 s6A(5)(b).
26 HA 1988 ss6A and 20C(1)(c).
27 HA 1988 s6A(9).

Applying for a demotion order

6.25   A landlord can seek a demotion order in possession proceedings as an alternative to a possession order, in which case the landlord should use the claim form N5 (for possession). The claim will then be governed by CPR Part 55 and the procedure described in chapter 21.

6.26   Alternatively, a landlord may make a free-standing application for a demotion order without seeking possession. In this situation the landlord should use form N6 (claim form for demotion of a tenancy) and specific particulars of claim (form N122). The conduct of these stand-alone claims is governed by CPR 65 Part III and the associated Practice Direction 65 Part III. The procedure is described in paras 6.27–6.33.

6.27   Claims for demotion may be issued in any county court hearing centre, but will be sent to the hearing centre which serves the address where the property is situated. Landlords should consider the potential delay which may arise if an application is not made to the appropriate hearing centre in the first instance.[28]

6.28   The claim form seeking demotion and the form of defence sent with it must be in the forms set out in the relevant Practice Direction.[29] Particulars of claim in form N122 must be filed and served with the claim form.[30] The particulars of claim must:

- state whether the demotion claim is made under HA 1985 s82A(2) or HA 1988 s6A(2);
- state whether the claimant is a local housing authority, RSL or PRPSH;
- identify the property to which the claim relates;
- provide details about the tenancy, including the parties, the period of the tenancy, the rent, the dates on which the rent is payable and any statement of express terms of the tenancy served on the tenant; and
- state details of the conduct alleged.[31]

6.29   Courts should fix hearing dates when they issue the claim forms. The hearing date should be not less than 28 days from the date of

---

28 CPR 65.12 and PD 65 para 6.1.
29 PD 65 para 6.2 and PD 4 Table 1. The forms are N6 and N11D.
30 CPR 65.15.
31 PD 65 para 7.1. See too PD 65 para 9.1, which provides that each party should wherever possible include all the evidence he or she wishes to present in his or her statement of case, verified by a statement of truth.

issue of the claim form. The standard period between the issue of the claim form and the hearing should be not more than eight weeks. Defendants must be served with claim forms and particulars of claim not less than 21 days before the hearing date.[32] Courts may extend or shorten these times.[33] Particular consideration should be given to abridging time between service and the hearing if:

- the defendant has assaulted or threatened to assault the claimant, a member of the claimant's staff or another resident in the locality;
- there are reasonable grounds for fearing such an assault; or
- the defendant has caused serious damage or threatened to cause serious damage to the property or to the home or property of another resident in the locality.[34]

6.30 Defendants should file defences within 14 days after service of the particulars of claim, but they may still take part in any hearing even if they do not do so. However, courts may take such a failure to do so into account when deciding what order to make about costs.[35] It is not possible for a landlord to enter judgment in default if a tenant fails to file a defence.[36]

6.31 At the hearing, the court may decide the demotion claim, or give case management directions. Where the demotion claim is genuinely disputed on grounds which appear to be substantial, case management directions should be given. They should include the allocation of the demotion claim to a track or directions to enable it to be allocated.[37]

6.32 Any fact that needs to be proved by the evidence of witnesses may be proved by evidence in writing unless the demotion claim has been allocated to the fast or multi-track or the court directs otherwise.[38] The claimant's evidence should include details of the conduct alleged.[39] All witness statements should be filed and served at least two days before the hearing.

32 CPR 65.16.
33 CPR 3.1(2)(a).
34 PD 65 para 8.2.
35 CPR 65.17(1).
36 CPR 65.17(2); cf CPR Pt 12.
37 CPR 65.18(1).
38 CPR 65.18(3). See too CPR 32.2.
39 PD 65 para 6. See too *Washington Housing Company Ltd v Morson* [2005] EWHC 3407, ChD.

6.33   District judges have jurisdiction to try demotion claims.[40]

Defending the proceedings

6.34   The court shall not make an order for demotion unless satisfied that
the provisions of HA 1985 s82A(4) (in the case of secure tenancies)
or HA 1988 s6A(4) (in the case of assured tenancies) are satisfied.
Accordingly, the landlord needs to prove that:

- the proper notice of intention to bring proceedings has been
served (or the court agrees to dispense with such a notice);
- the proceedings were begun after the specified date and within
the appropriate 12-month period;
- the tenant or a person residing in or visiting the dwelling has
engaged or has threatened to engage in conduct which falls within one of the statutory limbs – see paras 6.7–6.12 above; and
- it is reasonable for a demotion order to be made.

6.35   Advisers should initially check that the form of the notice complies
with the statutory requirements, that it was properly served and that
the proceedings were not begun prematurely. Any irregularity in any
of these respects may provide sufficient defence to the claim.

Substantive defences

6.36   Assuming that none of the more technical defences mentioned above
is available, it may be open to the tenant to defend the claim on the
basis that neither limb of the statutory ground has been made out on
the evidence and on the balance of probabilities.

6.37   The first line of defence is to test the evidence concerning the
alleged misconduct. As in possession proceedings based on anti-
social behaviour, the adviser will need to take detailed instructions
from the tenant and any other witnesses on every allegation particularised in the landlord's statement of case, and prepare the defence
and witness statements accordingly. In practice, bare denials are
unlikely to suffice; tenant's advisers should, where possible, put a
case that proves, or at least casts doubt, that the behaviour could
not have been committed by the tenant or a member of the tenant's
household.

40 PD 2B para 11.1(b).

6.38   The second line of defence, assuming that the landlord has proved (or the tenant admits) that one of the limbs has been made out, is to assert that it is not reasonable to order demotion. It is for the landlord to satisfy the court that it would be reasonable to grant a demotion order. In applying the 'reasonableness' test, the court is required to have regard to all relevant factors. The defence and the witness statements should deal in detail with the tenant's own personal circumstances, including any health problems or other life experiences which have contributed to the present situation. Where the tenant accepts general responsibility for the behaviour complained of, he or she should make the necessary admissions, explain any mitigating factors and emphasise his or her willingness to change his or her behaviour. Where the tenant has not personally been responsible for the nuisance but the conduct is that of a household member or visitor, the tenant should clearly set out the steps that he or she has taken to address the problem, including co-operating with any statutory or other agencies involved. In practice, however, unless the perpetrator has left the property or demonstrated that they are willing and able to change their behaviour, it is likely to be difficult to avoid a finding that is reasonable to make a demotion order.

6.39   In deciding whether to make an order, the court will be influenced by the tenor of Court of Appeal decisions in relation to the 'nuisance' ground for possession and anti-social behaviour injunctions, and in particular the need to consider the interests of those affected by the behaviour. Even so, the objective will be to convince the court that demotion would be unnecessary and disproportionate, and that alternative measures – such as an undertaking to the court, or a willingness to engage in an acceptable behaviour contract – are sufficient to deal with the situation. Where the tenant, or the perpetrator of the behaviour, is disabled, the best defence is likely to be under the Equality Act 2010 (see chapter 27).

6.40   Assuming that the tenant is financially eligible, he or she may be able to obtain a public funding (legal aid) certificate for legal representation in defending the proceedings. See generally chapter 24.

6.41   Where the application for demotion is made in possession proceedings, it will be one of the options which the court is considering at the conclusion of the evidence. In some cases, the range of choices will effectively be between a demotion order and a postponed possession order. A demotion order may be presented by the landlord as a less drastic alternative to a postponed possession order. In such a case, the tenant should point out that the effect of a demoted order is more serious than a postponed order as once a demoted order has been made the court lacks discretion to suspend the execution order, a discretion which it would retain if a possession order had been postponed. In *Manchester CC v Pinnock*, the Court of Appeal said:

> 27. ... A demotion order is a drastic measure: it deprives the tenant of his security of tenure for the period of the demotion order and, as will be seen, removes from the county court the jurisdiction to examine whether the making of an order evicting the tenant, if it comes to that, is reasonable or proportionate. It is a far more drastic step than the making of a suspended possession order, following which the county court retains supervision of the landlord's claim, and may vary the conditions of the order or in due course discharge or rescind the order: section 85 of the 1985 Act.[41]

6.42   Another judge has said of demotion orders:[42]

> Although that is obviously a Draconian sanction, it is not as Draconian as an immediate order for possession ...

The effect of a demotion order

6.43   A demotion order – whether made in respect of a secure, assured tenancy or assured shorthold fixed-term tenancy – has the following effects:

- the former tenancy is terminated with effect from the date specified in the order;
- if the tenant remains in occupation of the dwelling after that date, a demoted tenancy is created with effect from that date;
- it is a term of the demoted tenancy that any rent in arrears or rent paid in advance at the termination of the secure or assured tenancy becomes payable or is credited under the demoted tenancy;[43] and
- the parties to, and period of, the tenancy, the amount of the rent and the dates on which rent is payable are the same as under the former tenancy.[44]

6.44   The nature of the demoted tenancy is different depending on whether the former tenancy was secure, assured or fixed-term assured shorthold. When a secure tenancy is demoted and the landlord is a local

---

41   [2009] EWCA Civ 852, [2010] HLR 7 at [27]. These comments were not disapproved on appeal.
42   *Washington Housing Company Ltd v Morson* [2005] EWHC 3407 (Ch) at [67].
43   HA 1985 s82A(3); HA 1988 s6A(3).
44   HA 1985 s82A(5); HA 1988 s6A(8).

authority,[45] it becomes a *demoted tenancy* governed by HA 1996 ss143A–143P.[46] When an assured tenancy, a secure tenancy with a non-local authority social landlord, or a fixed-term assured shorthold tenancy is demoted, it becomes a *demoted assured shorthold tenancy* governed by HA 1988 s20B.

Demoted tenancies (old-style periodic, flexible and new English secure tenancies)

6.45   The framework for demoted tenancies inserted at HA 1996 ss143A–143P follows much the same model as the introductory tenancy provisions in Part V of the same Act. The two statutory schemes are very similar, as the demoted tenancy scheme has been closely modelled on the introductory tenancy regime. The statutory framework also deals with matters such as succession, assignment, the right to carry out repairs and the provision of information in respect of demoted tenancies.

6.46   The demoted tenancy will start on the date specified in the demotion order. In the case of a fixed-term tenancy, the effect of the demotion order is to bring the fixed-term tenancy to an end.[47] The new tenancy will only remain a demoted tenancy if the landlord's interest remains held by a local housing authority *and* the tenant continues to occupy the premises as his or her only or principal home.[48]

6.47   What happens to the tenancy after the year has concluded will depend on the type of tenancy that existed before the demotion order was made.

Old-style periodic secure tenancy

6.48   If, after one year from the date specified in the demotion order, the landlord has not given notice of proceedings for possession, the tenancy will cease to be a demoted tenancy and will become a secure tenancy again.[49] Before the HPA 2016 came into force this meant that the tenancy became a weekly periodic tenancy. In the absence of any provision to the contrary, it must follow that this remains the case.

---

45   HA 1996 s143A(2).
46   Inserted by ASBA 2003 Sch 1.
47   HA 1985 s82(A1)(b).
48   HA 1996 s143A.
49   HA 1996 s143B.

New-style English secure tenancy

6.49   If, after one year from the date specified in the demotion order, the landlord has not given notice of proceedings for possession, the tenancy will cease to be a demoted tenancy and will become a secure tenancy again.[50]

6.50   The amendments made by HPA 2016 do not specifically state that upon the demoted tenancy expiring the fixed term of the new English secure tenancy will be revived so that it continues until the original date of expiry. While this is plainly what was intended, the position is complicated by the fact that the effect of the demotion order is to terminate the fixed term.[51] Curiously, unlike for the position of the flexible tenancy that was granted before HPA 2016 (see below para 6.51), there is no deeming provision that the revived tenancy will be for any particular term. Accordingly, in the absence of a fixed term, it is arguable that the tenancy will be periodic. While the amendments made by HPA 2016 prohibit the grant of an old-style periodic tenancy,[52] it is arguable that a deeming provision, under HA 1996 s143B does not equate to a landlord granting a new tenancy.

Flexible secure tenancy granted before Housing and Planning Act 2016 came into force

6.51   If, after one year from the date specified in the demotion order, the landlord has not given notice of proceedings for possession, the tenancy will become a flexible tenancy again provided that the landlord has served a notice before the end of the demoted tenancy:

1) stating that, on ceasing to be a demoted tenancy, the tenancy will become a secure tenancy that is a flexible tenancy for a term certain of at least two years, and

2) set out the express terms of the tenancy.[53]

In the latter case, the tenancy will become a flexible tenancy for the period specified in the notice, but must be no longer than ten years unless the landlord has been notified in writing that a child aged under nine will live in the dwelling-house, in which case the fixed term may expire on the day on which the child will reach the age of 19.[54]

---

50   HA 1996 s143B.
51   HA 1985 s82(A1)(b).
52   HA 1985 s81A(4).
53   HA 1996 s143MA.
54   HA 1996 s143MA(3A)–(4).

6.52 Where the landlord fails to serve such a notice, and the tenancy has come to an end after the HPA 2016 came into force, the tenancy will become a secure tenancy for a fixed term of five years.[55]

Possession claims against demoted tenants

6.53 The landlord may give notice of possession proceedings against a demoted tenant for any reason. There is no prescribed form, but the notice of proceedings must:

- state that the court will be asked to make an order for possession;
- set out the landlord's reasons for seeking the order;
- specify the date after which possession proceedings may begin; and
- inform the tenant of his or her right to request a review of the landlord's decision and the time within which the request must be made (ie within 14 days from the date of service).[56]

6.54 Although the basis for the demotion order in the first place lay in the anti-social behaviour of the tenant, the landlord's reasons for seeking possession of the demoted tenancy need not be related to such behaviour. They can relate to any breach of the tenancy conditions, such as rent arrears, or indeed to any other factor, such as under-occupation.

6.55 The date specified in the notice must not be earlier than the date on which the tenancy could be brought to an end by a notice to quit or, where the demoted tenancy is a fixed-term new English secure tenancy, must not be earlier than the end of the period of six weeks beginning with the date on which the notice of proceedings is served.[57] In the usual case of a weekly tenancy, the earliest date will be the first or last day of a tenancy period which follows a period of 28 days from the date of the notice. The notice must also advise the tenant to take the notice immediately to a citizen's advice bureau, housing aid centre, law centre or solicitor if he or she needs help or advice.[58]

6.56 Where a landlord serves a notice of proceedings for possession on a demoted tenant, the tenancy will continue as a demoted tenancy

55 HA 1996 s143MB.
56 HA 1996 s143E(2).
57 HA 1996 s143E(3).
58 HA 1996 s143E(5).

even if the 12-month anniversary of the start date goes by, until any of the following events occur:

- the notice of proceedings is withdrawn by the landlord;
- the proceedings are determined in favour of the tenant;
- a period of six months has gone by since the notice was served and no proceedings for possession have been brought;[59] or
- the proceedings are determined in favour of the landlord (when the tenancy will come to an end on the date on which the possession order is executed[60]).

6.57   The effective extension of the demotion period by six months is achieved solely by the service of a valid notice of intended proceedings and is not dependent (as in the case of introductory tenancies) on the service of a special notice of extension.

6.58   The tenant has 14 days beginning with the date of service of the notice to ask the landlord to review its decision[61] (the fourteenth day effectively being two calendar weeks less one day). If a tenant so requests, the landlord must carry out a review of the decision to seek an order for possession and notify the tenant of the outcome along with its reasons for the decision on review. The review must take place, and the decision must be notified, before the date specified in the notice as the date after which proceedings may be begun.[62] The decision on review must be made by a person of appropriate seniority who was not involved in the original decision, and the review must be conducted in accordance with the Demoted Tenancies (Review of Decisions) (England) Regulations 2004[63] or the Demoted Tenancies (Review of Decisions) (Wales) Regulations 2005.[64] In particular, the tenant may request an oral hearing. This procedure does not provide an independent or impartial consideration of the decision to seek possession but the Court of Appeal has held that it does not infringe the Human Rights Act 1998 Sch 1 Articles 6 or 8 (see chapter 26).[65]

6.59   If the tenant does not request a review within the 14-day period, or if the landlord on review decides to confirm its decision to seek possession, the landlord may thereafter start possession proceedings.

---

59 HA 1996 s143B(4).
60 HA 1996 s143D(1A), inserted by Housing and Regeneration Act 2008 s299 and Sch 11 Pt 1 paras 10 and 13(1) and (3).
61 HA 1996 s143F(1).
62 HA 1996 s143F(6).
63 SI No 1679.
64 SI No 1228.
65 *R (Gilboy) v Liverpool City Council* [2008] EWCA Civ 751, [2009] HLR 11.

6.60   The court must make an order for possession unless it thinks that the procedure relating to either the notice of proceedings or the review 'has not been followed'.[66] In *Pinnock v Manchester CC*,[67] Lord Neuberger, giving the judgment of the Supreme Court, held that:

> 77. ... If the procedure laid down in section 143E or 143F has not been lawfully complied with, either because the express requirements of that section have not been observed or because the rules of natural justice have been infringed, the tenant should be able to raise that as a defence to a possession claim under section 143D(2).

> 78. ... [Moreover], an occupier who is the defendant in possession proceedings in the county court and who claims that it would be incompatible with his Article 8 convention rights for him to be put out of his home must be able to rely on those rights in defending those proceedings.

> 79. ... [Accordingly], section 143D(2) should be read as allowing the court to exercise the powers which are necessary to consider and, where appropriate, to give effect to, any Article 8 defence which the defendant raises in the possession proceedings.

6.61   A demoted tenant may therefore have a defence to the claim for possession if:

- the notice of proceedings did not contain the requisite information;
- the notice was not served on the tenant;
- the period of the notice was insufficient;
- proceedings were started before the specified date;
- the landlord has not held a review despite the fact that the tenant requested one within the 14-day period allowed;
- the review has not been conducted by a person of appropriate seniority;
- there has been some other material breach of the review regulations;[68]
- the tenant has some other public law defence (see chapter 26);
- the tenant has a human rights defence (see chapter 28);
- the tenant has an Equality Act 2010 defence (see chapter 27).

---

66 HA 1996 s143D(2).
67 [2010] UKSC 45, [2011] 2 AC 104.
68 In *Brighton & Hove CC v Knight* June 2009 *Legal Action* 33, Brighton County Court, the notice of outcome of a review was given one day outside the time limit prescribed by HA 1996 s143F and the court dismissed the possession claim against the demoted tenant.

6.62   Where the court makes an order for possession, it cannot postpone the date for giving of possession for more than 14 days unless:

- possession by that date would cause exceptional hardship, in which case the postponement can be for up to six weeks;[69] or
- the landlord consents, in the preamble to the order, not to enforce the order for a specified period.

6.63   The court has no power to suspend a possession order or the execution of it beyond those periods unless the landlord consents. The demoted tenancy ends on the date on which the order is executed by the bailiffs.

Demoted assured shorthold tenancies

6.64   Before issuing a claim for possession a landlord must to comply with Part 3 of the *Pre-action Protocol for possession claims by social landlords*. Although the title of the Protocol suggests that it only applies to claims based on rent arrears, the Protocol explains that Part 3 applies to all claims where the court's discretion to postpone possession is limited by HA 1980 s89(1), ie where the court is not required to consider whether it is reasonable to make a possession order.

6.65   Paragraph 3.2 of the Protocol requires landlords to write to occupants in advance of the claim to explain why they intend to seek possession and to invite the occupiers to, within a specified period, notify the landlord of any personal circumstances or other matters that they wish to be considered. The landlord is then expected to consider those representations before deciding whether to issue a claim for possession. Paragraph 3.3 of the Protocol further requires landlords to, within its particulars of claim or a witness statement, confirm that it has complied with paragraph 3.2 and give brief reasons for deciding to bring the claim. However, unlike under Part 2 of the Protocol, there are no sanctions for non-compliance with the Protocol. In practice therefore, the court will not be entitled to dismiss the claim in the event that Part 3 of the Protocol has not been complied with. It may, however, be more willing to grant an adjournment to allow a defendant to file a defence raising a public law or human

---

69   HA 1980 s89(1). In *Powell v Hounslow LBC* [2011] UKSC 8, [2011] 2 AC 186, Lord Phillips held that s89 could not be 'read down' so as to provide tenants who raise a successful human rights or public law defence with more time. The court must either dismiss the claim or postpone the execution of the order for a period not exceeding six weeks.

rights defence and, potentially, to award the occupier its costs of the hearing.

6.66   Former *secure* tenants of RSLs or PRPSHs (demoted under HA 1985 s82A), former *assured* tenants and former *fixed-term assured shorthold* of such landlords (demoted under HA 1988 s6A) will have demoted assured shorthold tenancies governed by HA 1988 s20B. This form of tenancy is in most respects similar to a standard assured shorthold tenancy: see chapter 10.

6.67   The demoted assured shorthold tenancy will start on the date specified in the demotion order. If within one year from that date the landlord has not given notice of proceedings for possession, the tenancy will cease to be an assured shorthold tenancy.[70] The tenancy will then, subject to one exception considered below, become *assured*, even where the original tenancy was a secure tenancy.

6.68   The exception is where the original tenancy was a fixed-term assured shorthold tenancy that was granted for a term of not less than two years by a PRPSH in England and, before the expiry of the demoted assured shorthold tenancy, the landlord served the tenant with a notice:

1) stating that on ceasing to be a demoted assured shorthold tenancy the tenancy will become an assured shorthold tenancy for a specified term of at least two years; and

2) setting out the express terms of the tenancy.[71]

6.69   Where notice of proceedings has been given within the one-year demotion period, the tenancy continues to be a demoted assured shorthold tenancy even after the 12-month anniversary of the start date has gone by, and will remain such, until one of the following events occurs:

- the landlord withdraws the notice of proceedings;
- the proceedings are determined in favour of the tenant (for example, where the possession claim is dismissed because the landlord has served an invalid notice);
- a period of six months from the date of the notice has gone by and no proceedings for possession have been brought;[72] or
- the proceedings result in a possession order in favour of the landlord (as they usually will).

---

70 HA 1988 s20B(2).
71 HA 1988 s20C.
72 HA 1988 s20B(4).

Possession claims against demoted assured shorthold tenants

6.70   Where the landlord wishes to bring a demoted assured shorthold tenancy to an end, it must serve a notice requiring possession. The landlord should also comply with Part 3 of the *Pre-action Protocol for possession claims by social landlords* (see above, paras 6.64–6.65). The procedure governing such notices is much less regulated than that governing notices served on demoted tenants of local authorities. The notice given to a demoted assured shorthold tenant will be a two months' notice under HA 1988 s21: see para 10.7. Moreover, the landlord is not obliged to offer the demoted assured shorthold tenants a right to a review of its decision to seek possession. In practice, it is to be expected that landlords will in fact offer a review in order to provide at least a sufficiently fair procedure to avoid a possible public law defence (see chapter 25) or a human rights defence (see chapter 26).

6.71   Where the landlord brings proceedings for possession of a demoted assured shorthold tenancy, the court's role is restricted to examining the validity of the HA 1988 s21 notice and, if satisfied on that matter, it must make an order for possession unless the PRPSH or RSL bringing the claim is a public authority (for the purposes of the Human Rights Act 1998 or for judicial review) and the tenant has a possible public law or human rights defence (see chapters 25 and 26). Irrespective of whether the PRPSH or RSL is a public authority, the tenant may also raise an Equality Act 2010 defence (see chapter 27).

6.72   Where the court makes an order for possession, it cannot postpone the date for giving possession for more than 14 days unless:

- possession by that date would cause exceptional hardship, in which case the postponement can be for up to six weeks;[73] or
- the landlord consents, in the preamble to the order, not to enforce the order for a specified period.

---

73 HA 1980 s89(1). In *Powell v Hounslow LBC* [2011] UKSC 8, [2011] 2 AC 186, Lord Phillips held that s89 could not be 'read down' so as to provide tenants who raise a successful Article 8 or public law defence more time. The court must either dismiss the claim or postpone the execution of the order for a period not exceeding six weeks.

CHAPTER 7

Family intervention tenancies

Introduction

7.1   Since 1 January 2009 it has been possible for social landlords in England to grant a new form of tenancy – the family intervention tenancy. This is a non-secure non-assured, usually periodic, social housing tenancy. A family intervention tenancy gives no long term security of tenure and can be terminated by simple notice to quit given by the social landlord (or by the tenant). Although the description contains the word 'family', the tenancies can be granted to an individual or individuals. There need not be a family (in the sense of dependent children) at all.

7.2   The new form of tenancy has been created by legislation in a somewhat indirect fashion. Both the Housing Act (HA) 1985 (which deals with secure tenancies) and HA 1988 (which deals with assured tenancies) contain a list – in Schedule 1 – of those tenancies which are not, respectively, 'secure' or 'assured' despite fulfilling all the usual requirements for such tenancies. In each case Schedule 1 was amended on 1 January 2009 by the Housing and Regeneration Act (H&RA) 2008 s297 to add family intervention tenancies as a further type of tenancy which is not 'secure' or 'assured'.[1] The new paragraph inserted in each schedule fleshes out the detailed requirements for family intervention tenancies – discussed in turn below. But the provisions regulating termination of a family intervention tenancy are to be found in the body of H&RA 2008 itself.[2] Although those provisions expressly apply only to family intervention tenancies granted by local housing authorities, the expectation is that they will also be voluntarily applied by other social landlords when they are terminating family intervention tenancies.

7.3   Family intervention tenancies are designed to be granted to tenants who are to be provided with 'behaviour support services' after entering into agreements to receive such support.[3] Those services are intended to help people who have previously been evicted from their homes (or who face the prospect of eviction) as a result of their anti-social behaviour. Such services are usually provided by, or in

---

1   In HA 1985, provision is made by Sch 1 para 4ZA. In HA 1988, it is Sch 1 para 12ZA.

2   H&RA 2008 s298.

3   See Jill Morgan, 'Family intervention tenancies: the de(marginalisation) of social tenants' [2010] 32 *Journal of Social Welfare Law* 37.

association with, local family intervention projects.[4] As Government guidance has made clear,

> Family Intervention Tenancies are usually offered to residents in specialist or purpose built accommodation, and are likely to be located away from the tenant's previous home. Distance between old and new homes is necessary to establish a new start and remove links with previous surrounding factors that may have encouraged the family's anti-social behaviour, such as friends, peer groups and local connections.[5]

7.4 The policy intention is that the behaviour support services will help address the root causes of such past anti-social behaviour. At the end of the period of support, it is hoped that the tenant will no longer be inclined towards anti-social behaviour and will be ready to move on to other social housing[6] or to an alternative long-term home. The family intervention tenancy can then be ended by surrender. If the period of support is disrupted by the tenant or is unproductive, the tenancy can be ended for those – or any other – reasons by the landlord.

7.5 The Government has issued non-statutory guidance to social landlords covering the grant and termination of family intervention tenancies.[7] The guidance contains a useful set of appendices reproducing the legislation, statutory instruments and a glossary.

7.6 The intention is that a tenant will occupy under a family intervention tenancy for only a temporary short-term period while engaged in

---

4   An early evaluation of the effectiveness of family intervention projects (FIPs) reported that 60% of families surveyed were subject to one or more housing enforcement actions when they started working with a FIP but that this had reduced to 18% for families leaving the schemes. The results of research into intensive family support projects, which seek to provide families at risk of eviction because of anti-social behaviour with intensive support to address their often multiple and complex needs, suggest that 70% of families using the schemes had managed to sustain or achieve positive change with no further complaints about their behaviour: *CLG Housing Research Summary 240* Communities and Local Government (CLG), January 2008. See also *Momitoring and evaluation of family intervention services and projects between February 2007 and March 2011* DCLG, December 2011.

5   *Tackling anti-social behaviour: tools and powers – toolkit for social landlords* DCLG, April 2010, para 4.134.

6   If an occupier is moving from a family intervention tenancy to a new home in social housing, the usual rules for allocation of social housing are disapplied: Allocation of Housing (England) (Amendment) (Family Intervention Tenancies) Regulations 2008 SI No 3015. The policy intention is that unfettered access to offers of social housing – without having to go through the usual housing allocation scheme procedure – will ensure that social housing can be available at the earliest time when the tenant is ready to move on.

7   *Guidance on the use of family intervention tenancies* DCLG, January 2009.

the behaviour support programme. Although the tenancy will often be a periodic (usually, weekly) tenancy, 'the typical length of tenancy would be expected to be between six months and a year or possibly longer'.[8] However, a social landlord can at any time convert a family intervention tenancy into a secure, flexible or assured tenancy, or a fixed-term assured shorthold tenancy, as appropriate, by serving a notice to that effect on the tenant in writing.[9]

Preliminaries to claiming possession

7.7   Family intervention tenancies are simply unprotected contractual tenancies. To end them, social landlords need to serve a notice to quit. Once the notice to quit has expired, if the former tenant does not leave the property, the social landlord can seek possession in court proceedings but need not prove any specific grounds for possession.

7.8   However, there are special additional preliminary requirements before notice to quit can be served.

Local housing authorities

7.9   If the family intervention tenant's landlord is a local housing authority then, before it can give notice to quit, it must first serve a 'minded-to' notice.[10] There is no prescribed form of that notice.

7.10   The notice must be in writing and state:[11]

- that the local housing authority has decided to serve a notice to quit on the tenant;
- the effect of serving a notice to quit;
- the reasons for the local housing authority's decision;
- when the local housing authority is intending to serve the notice to quit; and

---

8   *Guidance on the use of family intervention tenancies* DCLG, 2009, para 15.

9   HA 1985 Sch 1 para 4ZA(2); HA 1988 Sch 1 para 12ZA(2). From the date that the HPA 2016 came into force, any such notices must also state the fixed term that is to apply. The term may not be for less than two years and no more than ten unless the landlord is notified that a child under nine is to occupy the property, in which case the fixed term may expire on the day that the child turns 19.

10   H&RA 2008 s298(1)(a).

11   H&RA 2008 s298(2).

- that the tenant has the right to request, within the period of 14 days beginning with the service of the notice, a review of the local housing authority's decision.

7.11 The 'minded-to' notice must also contain advice to the tenant about how the tenant may be able to obtain assistance in relation to the notice.[12]

7.12 After the 'minded-to' notice has been served, a notice to quit cannot be served until either:

- 14 days have elapsed without the tenant requesting a review; or
- any such review request has been withdrawn; or
- the requested review has been completed and notice of the review decision has been served on the tenant.

7.13 If the tenant exercises the right to seek a review (by a request – which need not be made in writing – received by the authority within 14 days of service of the minded-to notice),[13] the local housing authority must conduct a review of the decision to serve a notice to quit.[14] The outcome of the review must be given by service of a written notice containing reasons for the review decision.[15] The review must be conducted in keeping with a procedure laid down in regulations.[16] The regulations[17] stipulate that:

- the reviewer must be a person who was not involved in the decision to serve a notice to quit;[18]
- if the tenant requests that the review be by way of an oral hearing, the detailed procedure set out in Schedule 1 to the regulations must be followed;[19] and
- if the tenant does not request that the review be by way of an oral hearing, the detailed procedure set out in Schedule 2 to the regulations must be followed.[20]

12 H&RA 2008 s298(7).
13 H&RA 2008 s298(3).
14 H&RA 2008 s298(4)(a).
15 H&RA 2008 s298(4)(b).
16 H&RA 2008 s298(5).
17 Family Intervention Tenancy (Review of Local Authority Decisions) (England) Regulations 2008 SI No 3111.
18 Family Intervention Tenancy (Review of Local Authority Decisions) (England) Regulations 2008 reg 3.
19 Family Intervention Tenancy (Review of Local Authority Decisions) (England) Regulations 2008 reg 4.
20 Family Intervention Tenancy (Review of Local Authority Decisions) (England) Regulations 2008 reg 5.

7.14   There is no right of appeal to any court or tribunal against the decision to serve a minded-to notice or against the decision made on review. Any challenge would need to be brought by way of judicial review (but see paras 7.39–7.41 below).

Other social landlords

7.15   Although the obligations to serve a 'minded-to' notice and to undertake a review (if requested) are imposed only on local housing authorities, other social landlords are encouraged to take broadly the same steps. The guidance states that 'the Tenant Services Authority[21] would expect registered social landlords to operate a similar termination and review procedure to that required under the Act by local authorities (as outlined above)'.[22] Indeed, the guidance stresses that 'there is a clear regulatory expectation of fairness. Eviction should be the last resort and only after due process. ... RSLs [are expected] to offer a review process which closely parallels that offered by local authorities.'[23]

Reasons

7.16   There is no limitation on the reasons for which a landlord might end a family intervention tenancy. However, the non-statutory guidance strongly suggests that reasons would usually be limited to non-compliance with the support programme or a breach of the tenancy agreement. It states:[24]

> Where eviction is sought we would expect this would normally be justified on the basis that a family had wilfully refused to accept support as defined through the Behaviour Support Agreement (having been given opportunities to address any breaches) and that there was no significant improvement in their behaviour.

> There may be cases where a landlord (in consultation with partner agencies) might decide it is appropriate to terminate the tenancy and take possession proceedings against a family for reasons other than breaching the terms of their support agreement (for example rent arrears). Although we anticipate that this would be extremely rare in cases where families are undergoing resource intensive support programmes, landlords should ensure they have considered other

---

21 Now the Homes and Communities Agency.
22 *Guidance on the use of family intervention tenancies* CLG, 2009, para 22.
23 *Guidance on the use of family intervention tenancies* CLG, 2009, para 49.
24 *Guidance on the use of family intervention tenancies* CLG, 2009, paras 37–38.

reasonable steps before deciding that possession is the appropriate response.

Defending a possession claim

7.17   Where possession is claimed on the basis that the defendant has been a tenant under a family intervention tenancy and that the tenancy has been terminated, five possible lines of defence should be explored:

1) the alleged family intervention tenancy is not, in fact, a family intervention tenancy at all but a social housing tenancy which is either secure or assured; or

2) the family intervention tenancy has not been lawfully terminated; or

3) the claim for possession amounts to a breach of the Equality Act 2010;[25] and/or

4) the claim for possession is the result of an unlawful decision to serve the notice to quit or to bring or continue the proceedings;[26] and/or

5) the grant of possession would not infringe the former tenant's human rights.[27]

7.18   The third, fourth and fifth lines of defence are explored fully elsewhere in this book. The remainder of this chapter is concerned primarily with the first two.

Defence (1): the tenancy is not a family intervention tenancy at all

7.19   If a tenant can succeed in showing that the tenancy was not in fact a family intervention tenancy, the possession claim should be dismissed. That is because the tenancy (subject to all other conditions having been satisfied) would be a secure or assured tenancy. Such a tenancy cannot be determined by the notice to quit on which the claimant is relying in seeking possession against an occupier under an alleged family intervention tenancy.

25 See chapter 27.
26 See chapter 25.
27 See chapter 26.

7.20   Four conditions must be satisfied before what would have been an assured or secure tenancy can instead be a family intervention tenancy. They are (in summary) that:

1) the letting must have commenced on or after 1 January 2009;
2) the tenant under the family intervention tenancy is a person against whom a possession order was made or could have been made on ground of anti-social behaviour in respect of the former home;
3) the purpose of the letting was the provision of behaviour support services; and
4) a notice in appropriate form was given *before* the tenant entered into the tenancy.

7.21   If the defendant to the possession claim can demonstrate that any one or more of those four conditions is not met then the tenancy cannot have been a family intervention tenancy. The detailed provisions in respect of each condition are as follows.

7.22   **Condition 1**: the special provisions for a family intervention tenancy do not apply to any tenancy granted before 1 January 2009.[28] Any purported grant of a family intervention tenancy before that date, even with a later tenancy commencement date, failed to create a valid family intervention tenancy.

7.23   **Condition 2**: the tenant under the family intervention tenancy must be a person against whom an earlier possession order in respect of another dwelling-house either –

- had been made, in relation to a secure tenancy, on HA 1985 Sch 2 ground 2, 2ZA or 2A or s84A or in relation to an assured tenancy on HA 1988 Sch 2 ground 7A, 14, 14ZA or 14A; or
- could, in the opinion of the social landlord, have been so made in relation to such a tenancy; or
- could, in the opinion of the social landlord, have been so made if the person had held such a tenancy prior to the grant of the family intervention tenancy.[29]

7.24   Some family intervention tenancies may have been granted to former tenants who were actually evicted for their anti-social behaviour on

---

28 H&RA 2008 ss297(3) and 298(10) and Housing and Regeneration Act 2008 (Commencement No 2 and Transitional, Saving and Transitory Provisions) Order 2008 SI No 3068 art 4(11).

29 HA 1985 Sch 1 para 4ZA(3)(a) and (12) and HA 1988 Sch 1 para 12ZA(3)(a). In Wales, the second condition is not satisfied by the mandatory grounds for possession is made out (ie ss84A and 7A).

one of the statutory grounds. Others may have been granted to tenants who would have faced eviction on those grounds but agreed to surrender their tenancies when offered the option of a behaviour support programme and a family intervention tenancy. Yet others may have previously been tenants who would have faced eviction on the stipulated grounds had they been secure or assured tenants at that time.

7.25 **Condition 3**: the purpose of the letting must have been to provide 'behaviour support services'.[30] This term means: 'relevant support services' to be provided by any person to –

- the new tenant, or
- any person who is to reside with the new tenant

for the purpose of addressing the kind of behaviour which led to the new tenant falling within the 'behaviour' condition described above.

7.26 The phrase 'relevant support services' means support services of a kind identified in a behaviour support agreement and designed to meet such needs of the recipient as are identified in the agreement.[31]

7.27 It follows that with every family intervention tenancy there must be a tailor-made behaviour support agreement. Such an agreement must be in writing and be made between the parties who are the landlord and the tenant under the family intervention tenancy.[32] Additionally, if the landlord is not a local housing authority, the local housing authority for the area in which the property to be occupied under a family intervention tenancy is situated must also be a party to the behaviour support agreement.[33] The behaviour support agreement should be separate from, but probably referred to in, the tenancy agreement for the family intervention tenancy itself.

7.28 **Condition 4**: the landlord must have served the tenant with a pre-letting notice before the tenant entered into the family intervention tenancy.[34] This notice is intended to ensure that the prospective tenant is made fully aware of the nature of the decision he or she is being asked to make, in order that he or she might properly reflect on it before reaching a decision to accept a family intervention tenancy.[35]

30 HA 1985 Sch 1 para 4ZA(3)(b) and HA 1988 Sch 1 para 12ZA(3)(b).
31 HA 1985 Sch 1 para 4ZA(12) and HA 1988 Sch 1 para 12ZA(12).
32 HA 1985 Sch 1 para 4ZA(12) and HA 1988 Sch 1 para 12ZA(12).
33 HA 1988 Sch 1 para 12ZA(12).
34 HA 1985 Sch 1 para 4ZA(4) and HA 1988 Sch 1 para 12ZA(4).
35 *Guidance on the use of family intervention tenancies* DCLG, 2009, para 27.

The form of notice is not prescribed. But what it must contain is pre-scribed.[36] It must set out:

(a) the reasons for offering the tenancy to the new tenant;

(b) the dwelling-house in respect of which the tenancy is to be granted;

(c) the other main terms of the tenancy (including any requirements on the new tenant in respect of behaviour support services);

(d) the reduced security of tenure available under the tenancy and any loss of security of tenure which is likely to result from the new tenant agreeing to enter into the tenancy;

(e) that the new tenant is not obliged to enter into the tenancy or (unless otherwise required to do so) to surrender any existing ten-ancy or possession of a dwelling-house; and

(f) any likely action by the social landlord if the new tenant does not enter into the tenancy or surrender any existing tenancy or posses-sion of a dwelling-house.

It must also contain advice to the prospective tenant as to how he or she may be able to obtain assistance in relation to the notice.[37]

7.29   Note that the notice must be given *before* the family intervention tenancy is entered into. That requirement cannot be complied with by giving the notice at the same time as the agreement is made, or at some point between sign-up and the first day of the commencement of tenancy, or after the tenant has taken up occupation.

7.30   Given the importance of the pre-tenancy notice and the likelihood that some vulnerable tenants may be among those entering into fam-ily intervention tenancies, the guidance suggests that 'efforts should be made to ensure any information is presented in a user-friendly format ... If a landlord is aware that the tenant has difficulty in read-ing or understanding printed information, the landlord should take reasonable steps to address this. This should include consideration of mental capacity and the [Equality Act 2010]'.[38]

7.31   A regulation-making power enables the secretary of state to change, add to or remove the required contents of the pre-tenancy notice but that power has not been exercised.[39]

7.32   If the defendant demonstrates that the claimant in the possession claim cannot make out all four of the conditions, the claim should be dismissed.

---

36 HA 1985 Sch 1 para 4ZA(5) and HA 1988 Sch 1 para 12ZA(5).

37 HA 1985 Sch 1 para 4ZA(7) and HA 1988 Sch 1 para 12ZA(7).

38 *Guidance on the use of family intervention tenancies* DCLG, 2009, para 30. The Equality Act 2010 was passed after the guidance was issued.

39 HA 1985 Sch 1 para 4ZA(6) and HA 1988 Sch 1 para 12ZA(6).

7.33   A landlord can, at any time after the tenancy has been granted, serve the tenant with a notice that the tenancy is to become a secure or assured tenancy.[40] In that case, the landlord cannot rely on a notice to quit.

Defence (2): the family intervention tenancy has not been lawfully terminated

7.34   If the tenancy is (or is found by the court to be) a family intervention tenancy, the second available line of defence is that the family intervention tenancy has not been lawfully terminated.

7.35   The termination must have been by service of a valid notice to quit.

7.36   If the landlord was a local housing authority, the minded-to notice procedure above must have been complied with (and the requirements in relation to review must have been complied with) before notice to quit was given.[41]

7.37   In addition to the usual checks to see whether the form and content of the notice to quit are in order, the notice given by a local housing authority landlord should be examined to see whether it contains 'advice to the tenant as to how the tenant may be able to obtain assistance in relation to the notice.'[42] If it does not, it is invalid. The expectation is that such advice should be a good deal fuller than the detail already required by the prescribed information[43] which any notice to quit must contain. Otherwise the special statutory provision will have achieved nothing. There is a reserve power to make regulations about the type of advice that a notice to quit must contain when given in respect of a family intervention tenancy but it has not been exercised.[44]

---

40 HA 1985 Sch 1 para 4ZA(2); HA 1988 Sch1 para 12ZA(2). From the date that the HPA 2016 came into force, any such notices must also state the fixed term that is to apply. The term may not be for less than two years and no more than ten unless the landlord is notified that a child under nine is to occupy the property, in which case the fixed term may expire on the day that the child turns 19.

41 H&RA 2008 s298(1).

42 H&RA 2008 s298(7).

43 Protection from Eviction Act 1977 s5 and the regulations made thereunder. See para 14.8.

44 H&RA 2008 s298(8).

7.38   If the notice to quit was given by a local housing authority, it will be invalid if served prematurely, ie before the dates mentioned in para 7.12.

Other defences

7.39   If a tenant considers that the landlord under the family intervention tenancy has not lawfully complied with the requirements for a review of the decision to give a notice to quit that point can be raised as a public law defence (see chapter 25). Likewise, a tenant of a local housing authority may also challenge the validity of a notice to quit where either the tenant has not been notified of the review decision or the review decision does not contain reasons for serving the notice to quit. In either case the notice would be invalid.

7.40   As explained in chapters 25 and 26 respectively on public law and human rights defences and in chapter 27 on Equality Act defences, there may be other circumstances in which a tenant may wish to challenge the legality of the notice to quit and/or the review decision. In such circumstances reference should be made to the advice given in those chapters.

7.41   Where such a defence is raised, reference may be usefully made to para 7.16 and to the further non-statutory guidance which advises landlords under family intervention tenancies that a 'key consideration in any decision to terminate the tenancy is what will happen to the family afterwards. The local authority homelessness and housing options teams need to be involved at or before the point at which the [landlord] decides to terminate the tenancy.'[45]

---

45 *Guidance on the use of family intervention tenancies* DCLG, 2009, para 47.

CHAPTER 8

Tenants and licensees of social landlords without security of tenure

Tenancies granted pursuant to Housing Act 1996 Pt 7 and Housing (Wales) Act 2014 Pt 2 (Homelessness)

Placement in council-owned accommodation

8.1   There are six common situations in which a local authority landlord in England might be providing temporary accommodation for homeless people in its own housing stock where they have applied to that authority for homelessness assistance under the provisions of the Housing Act (HA) 1996 Pt 7 (Homelessness):

1) while enquiries are being conducted to establish the circumstances of an applicant who is apparently homeless and may have a priority need;[1]

2) while an applicant who became homeless intentionally, but is in priority need, is being given an opportunity to secure his or her own accommodation;[2]

3) pending the outcome of a referral of the application to another local housing authority;[3]

4) as a matter of discretion pending the outcome of a review or appeal;[4]

5) when the local housing authority has accepted an obligation to house the applicant because he or she is eligible, in priority need and not intentionally homeless;[5] and

6) when the local housing authority exercises its discretion to accommodate an eligible person not in priority need who did not become homeless intentionally.[6]

8.2   In Wales, as in England, an occupier provided with accommodation by a local authority in performance of its obligations under Housing (Wales) Act (H(W)A) 2014 Pt 2, whether as a tenant or licensee, cannot enjoy 'introductory or secure status' in respect of the council accommodation he or she occupies unless and until the local authority concerned gives notice that the occupancy is to be secure.[7]

---

1   HA 1996 s188.
2   HA 1996 s190(2)(a).
3   HA 1996 s200.
4   HA 1996 ss188(3) and 204(4).
5   HA 1996 s193.
6   HA 1996 s192(3), as inserted by the Homelessness Act 2002.
7   HA 1985 Sch 1 para 4, as modified by H(W)A 2014 Sch 3(1) para 1.

8.3 The circumstances in which a local authority in Wales may provide accommodation under H(W)A 2014 Pt 2 are as follows:

1) where the authority has a reason to believe, but is not yet satisfied, that an applicant is homeless, eligible and has a priority need for accommodation;[8]

2) where the duty under H(W)A 2014 s73 has come to an end and the authority is under an obligation to secure accommodation for an applicant that has a priority need, has become homeless intentionally and the duty under H(W)A 2014 s75 does not apply;[9]

3) pending the outcome of a referral of the application to another local housing authority;[10]

4) as a matter of discretion pending the outcome of a review or appeal;[11]

5) where the authority is satisfied that the applicant is homeless and eligible – whether or not they have a priority need – and is providing the applicant with accommodation for 56 days in which to obtain alternative accommodation;[12] and

6) where the duty under H(W)A 2014 s73 has come to an end and the authority is under an obligation to provide accommodation to the applicant because it is satisfied that the applicant has a priority need and, save for in certain prescribed circumstances, has not become homeless intentionally.[13]

The occupier provided with such accommodation by the local authority, whether as a tenant or licensee, cannot enjoy 'introductory or secure status' in respect of the council accommodation he or she occupies unless and until the local authority concerned gives notice that the occupancy is to be secure.[14] Because such notification counts as an 'allocation' of social housing,[15] it is unlikely to be given unless and until the occupier achieves priority under the local authority's housing allocation scheme. For example, in *Wandsworth LBC v Tompkins*,[16] the Court of Appeal held that a tenancy, which was provided under Housing Act 1996 Pt 7 and mistakenly stated it to be an

---

8   H(W)A 2014 s68(2).
9   H(W)A 2014 ss 68 and 69.
10 H(W)A 2014 s82.
11 H(W)A 2014 s69 and s88(5).
12 H(W)A 2014 ss73 and 74.
13 H(W)A 2014 s75.
14 HA 1985 Sch 1 para 4, as substituted by HA 1996 Sch 17 para 3.
15 HA 1996 s159(3).
16 [2015] EWCA Civ 846, [2015] HLR 44.

introductory tenancy, was not construed as the grant of a secure tenancy; using the wrong form of agreement did not alter the statutory function which was being exercised and the form of words used was not any form of notification by the council whether for the purposes of paragraph 4 or otherwise.

Some applicants for homelessness assistance may be placed in short-life council accommodation which is awaiting redevelopment, and so are excepted from secure status for that reason also (see para 1.69).

8.4   As there is no security of tenure, the council landlord can determine the non-secure tenancy in the usual way by service of notice to quit and then recover possession by proceedings.[17] Any notice given to determine a non-secure licence or tenancy has to

i)   be in writing;
ii) contain the prescribed information; and
iii) be given not less than four weeks before it takes effect.[18]

8.5   If the tenancy (or licence) is not properly determined (for example, because the notice given is defective) it continues, and possession cannot be ordered until proper notice is given and expires and fresh proceedings are issued.[19]

8.6   If the notice to quit is valid and the local authority claims possession based on it, the occupier could defend the proceedings by raising a human rights, Equality Act 2010 or public law defence (see chapters 25, 26 and 27). Several tenants provided with non-secure council accommodation in performance of homelessness duties have been able to defeat or delay possession claims in that way.[20]

8.7   If the accommodation has been provided in a local authority hostel[21] on a licence, the Protection from Eviction Act (PEA) 1977 does not apply.[22] Likewise, the Supreme Court has held that the PEA 1977 does not apply to licences granted to occupiers in pursuance of the duty to provide interim accommodation under HA 1996 s188.[23]

---

17 *Restormel BC v Buscombe* (1984) 14 HLR 91, CA.
18 PEA 1977 s5(1B), as inserted by HA 1988 s32(2).
19 *Eastleigh BC v Walsh* [1985] AC 809, (1985) 17 HLR 392, HL.
20 See, eg *McGlynn v Welwyn Hatfield DC* [2009] EWCA Civ 285, [2010] HLR 10 and *Croydon LBC v Barber* [2010] EWCA Civ 51, [2010] HLR 26.
21 Defined in HA 1985 s622 and see *Rogerson v Wigan MBC* [2004] EWHC 1677 (QB), [2005] HLR 10.
22 PEA 1977 s3A(8)(a) and see *Brennan v Lambeth LBC* (1998) 30 HLR 481, CA and *Rogerson v Wigan MBC* [2004] EWHC 1677 (QB), [2005] HLR 10.
23 *R (ZH and CN) v Lewisham LBC* [2014] UKSC 62, [2015] AC 1259.

However, it has been suggested[24] that where the accommodation has been provided as a temporary home following the authority's acceptance of the main housing duty under HA 1996 s193, the occupier will be entitled to basic protection from eviction, ie the service of a formal notice to quit[25] and the right not to be evicted without a court order.[26] This point was not considered or decided in *R (CN and ZH) v Newham LBC and Lewisham LBC*.[27]

8.8 An unprotected licence can be determined by the giving of contractual or reasonable notice.[28] On the notice period expiring, the landlord can recover possession without a court order. In *R (CN and ZH) v Newham LBC and Lewisham LBC*,[29] the Supreme Court held that this meant that the authority was entitled to give no more than a night's or day's notice as that is what was provided for in the agreement.

8.9 Where the agreement is silent as to the notice period, reasonable notice must still be given. What is a reasonable time depends on all the circumstances of the case and where the licence has been to occupy premises for residential purposes the reasonable time has reference to enabling the licensee to have an opportunity of taking his effects away from the property.[30]

8.10 If the licence is not determined in accordance with the agreement or the occupier is not given reasonable notice, that may give rise to a defence (or a right to claim injunctive relief preventing the eviction from taking place if proceedings are not issued) that longer notice should have been given and that the notice relied on is insufficient. Any steps to recover possession, eg the changing of the locks or bringing proceedings, on the basis that the licensee has become a trespasser (see chapter 23) can be started only after the contractual notice or reasonable notice period has expired.[31]

8.11 All authorities are under a public law duty to act reasonably in terminating accommodation.[32] In *R v Newham LBC ex p Ojuri (No 5)*,[33] it was held that the giving of one day's notice to terminate

24 *Rogerson v Wigan MBC* [2004] EWHC 1677 (QB), [2005] HLR 10.
25 Under PEA 1977 s5.
26 Under PEA 1977 s3: see para 14.11.
27 [2014] UKSC 62, [2015] HLR 6.
28 *Minister of Health v Bellotti* [1944] KB 298, CA.
29 [2014] UKSC 62, [2015] HLR 6.
30 *GLC v Jenkins* [1975] 1 All ER 354 at 357C per Diplock LJ.
31 *GLC v Jenkins* [1975] 1 All ER 354 at 357C per Diplock LJ.
32 *R v Secretary of State for the Home Department ex p Shelter* [1997] COD 49, QBD.
33 (1999) 31 HLR 631, QBD.

accommodation that was occupied by a homeless applicant, where the authority had decided that no duty under Part 7 was owed, was not reasonable notice. In contrast in *R v Newham LBC ex p Lumley*,[34] it was held that a notice period of six days was lawful.

Placement in non council-owned accommodation

8.12   Under arrangements made by the local housing authorities to whom they have applied for assistance under HA 1996 Pt 7 or H(W)A 2014 Pt 2, many homeless households are placed temporarily in the private rented sector in hostels, hotels or bed and breakfast accommodation. Where such accommodation is provided by way of interim accommodation pending the authority's decision on the household's application for accommodation[35] or under one of the authority's other duties or powers to provide temporary accommodation,[36] it does not attract the protection of the PEA 1977.[37]

8.13   Under similar arrangements, a private landlord may provide self-contained accommodation to the homeless person in a house or flat. The general rule is that accommodation provided to homeless people under such arrangements in any of the situations described in the first four paragraphs in paras 8.1 and 8.3 does not attract security of tenure as 'assured' or even, at least for the first 12 months, as 'assured shorthold'.[38] A letting in the circumstances described in the last two paragraphs in para 8.1 will be an assured shorthold tenancy.[39]

8.14   As an alternative, the local authority may itself be the homeless person's 'landlord' of the privately owned accommodation. It is now widespread practice for local housing authorities to acquire

---

34   [2000] EWHC 285 (Admin), (2001) 33 HLR 11.

35   Under HA 1996 s188(1) or H(W)A 2014 s68(2).

36   eg under HA 1996 ss188(3), 190(2), 200(1) or 204(4) and H(W)A 2014 ss68(3), 82 or 88(5).

37   *Mohamed v Manek and Kensington and Chelsea RLBC* (1995) 27 HLR 439, CA, approved by a majority in *Desnousse v Newham LBC* [2006] EWCA Civ 547, [2006] HLR 692 and *R (CN and ZH) v Newham LBC and Lewisham LBC* [2014] UKSC 62, [2015] HLR 6, at least in respect of accommodation provided on a licence rather than a tenancy.

38   HA 1996 s209(2), as substituted by Homelessness Act 2002, and H(W)A 2014 s92.

39   This includes 'private rented sector offers' under HA 1996 s193(7AA) and H(W)A 2014 s76(3)(b), ie where the authority brings its duty to under HA 1996 s193 or H(W)A 2014 s75(1) to an end by offering the homeless applicant with an assured shorthold tenancy, as well as circumstances where the authority performs its duty under HA 1996 s193(2) or H(W)A 2014 s75(1) by arranging private sector accommodation.

short-term leases of accommodation from private landlords. These properties are then let to homeless applicants by the local housing authority as a means of meeting the temporary accommodation needs of homeless households. Under this route, a local authority may take a lease or licence of vacant privately owned property for use as temporary accommodation for the homeless. The council may then install – as its subtenant – the homeless applicant. HA 1985 Sch 1 para 6 exempts from 'secure' and 'introductory' status the tenancy granted to the homeless person, irrespective of the period for which it continues or the reasons why the homeless household is being accommodated.[40] The homeless person, at best, holds a non-secure subtenancy of the leased property.

8.15   Although HA 1985 Sch 1 para 6 is very narrowly drawn, and even if the local authority is in difficulty showing that it is satisfied, the tenancy will nevertheless usually be non-secure if the accommodation has been provided in performance of a duty under HA 1996 Part 7 (Homelessness) by virtue of Schedule 1 para 4.[41] For example, in *Wandsworth LBC v Tompkins,*[42] the Court of Appeal held that a tenancy, which was provided under Housing Act 1996 Pt 7 and mistakenly stated it to be an introductory tenancy, was not construed as the grant of a secure tenancy; using the wrong form of agreement did not alter the statutory function which was being exercised and the form of words used was not any form of notification by the council whether for the purposes of paragraph 4 or otherwise.

8.16   Under another variant, the lease or licence from the private landlord is taken by a housing association or other social landlord. It then sublets to a homeless person nominated by the local authority in any of the situations described in the first four paragraphs in para 8.1. Again, the homeless person has no security of tenure for a year unless the landlord notifies the tenant that the tenancy is to be regarded as an assured (or assured shorthold) tenancy.[43] A letting in the circumstances described in the last two paragraphs in para 8.1 will be an assured shorthold tenancy.

8.17   Where the tenant's immediate landlord is a housing association which has taken a lease or licence of the property from a local authority, even if the tenant is a secure tenant of the housing association, he

---

40 Provided that the statutory conditions for the exception to secure status are strictly complied with: *Hickey v Haringey LBC* [2006] EWCA Civ 373, [2006] HLR 36.

41 *Westminster CC v Boraliu* [2007] EWCA Civ 1339, [2008] HLR 42.

42 [2015] EWCA Civ 846, [2015] HLR 44.

43 HA 1996 s209, as substituted by Homelessness Act 2002.

or she will have no right to remain in possession when the housing association's interest ends. In *Kay v Lambeth LBC*,[44] the council had granted a licence of a group of 'short-life' properties to a housing association. That was later replaced by individual leases of the properties. Eventually, the council exercised a 'break clause' and terminated the leases. It was acknowledged that the occupiers had been secure tenants of the housing association. However, as soon as the housing association's interest came to an end, so also did the secure subtenancies.

Licensees and other tenants of registered providers of social housing or registered social landlords without security of tenure

8.18   Licensees of private registered providers (PRPSHs) of social housing (or, in Wales, registered social landlords (RSLs)) cannot have security of tenure because the HA 1988 does not confer security of tenure on licensees.[45] Some PRPSHs and RSLs grant contractual licences of accommodation in supported housing schemes for vulnerable adults and young people. In such cases, it is important to ascertain whether the agreement actually is for a licence rather than a tenancy.[46] If the agreement confers a tenancy, ie exclusive possession for a term for the payment of rent, the agreement will in all likelihood be for an assured shorthold tenancy that can be determined by execution of a possession order based on a notice served under HA 1988 s21.

If the agreement is for a licence, the occupier may still be able to raise a human rights, public law or Equality Act 2010 defence. In *Riverside Housing Group Ltd v Ahmed*,[47] a licensee of a room in a hostel for persons with psychiatric, alcohol and drug problems successfully argued that it would be disproportionate to evict him where he had been found to throw a cup at a member of staff.

8.19   Generally, where a *tenancy* is granted by a PRPSH or RSL it will be either an assured or assured shorthold tenancy and will only cease to be assured if the requirements of HA 1988 are no longer met (see

---

44 [2006] UKHL 10, [2006] 2 AC 465 and see also *Bruton v London and Quadrant Housing Trust* [2000] 1 AC 406, HL.

45 See above para 1.7.

46 See discussion above at paras 1.7–1.21 on the distinction between tenancies and licences.

47 November 2013 *Legal Action* 30, Lambeth County Court.

paras 1.6–1.36 above). Family intervention tenancies (considered in chapter 7) are likely to be the only exception, contained within HA 1988 Sch 1, that will apply to prevent a tenancy, that otherwise meets the requirement of HA 1988 s1, from being assured.

Fully mutual housing associations

8.20 A fully mutual housing association is a housing association whose rules restrict membership to persons who are tenants or prospective tenants of the association and preclude the granting or assignment of tenancies to persons other than members.[48] Tenants of fully mutual housing associations are not assured or assured shorthold tenants,[49] nor are they secure tenants.[50] In Wales, however, a tenant of a fully mutual housing association may be an assured or assured shorthold tenant if, before the tenancy was granted, the landlord served the prospective tenant with a notice stating that the tenancy is to be exempted from HA 1988 Sch 1 para 12(1) and the tenancy agreement also states that the normal exclusion does not apply.[51]

8.21 It follows that the only protection afforded to such tenants is that provided by PEA 1977 ss3 and 5, ie the tenancy must be determined by a notice to quit that gives at least 28 days' notice and contains the prescribed information and any eviction must follow a possession order being made.

8.22 As a result, many tenancy agreements granted by fully mutual housing associations contain provisions that limit the circumstances in which the association can bring a tenancy to an end, eg stating that possession will be sought only when there are arrears or the tenant has otherwise breached the terms of the agreement. In *Mexfield Housing Co-operative Ltd v Berrisford*,[52] Ms Berrisford's tenancy contained a clause that limited the circumstances in which Mexfield could bring it to an end to the exercise of a right of re-entry on default by the tenant. The Supreme Court held that, notwithstanding the fact that the tenancy was described as being from month to month, the restriction on the landlord recovering possession, coupled with the lack of fixed term, meant that the agreement was incapable of being

---

48 Housing Associations Act 1985 s1(2).
49 HA 1988 Sch 1 para 12(1)(h).
50 HA 1985 s80.
51 HA 1988 Sch 1 para 12(3).
52 [2011] UKSC 52, [2012] HLR 15.

a tenancy as it was not for a certain term. However, an agreement for an uncertain term, that would otherwise be a tenancy, is deemed by Law of Property Act 1925 s149(6) to be a tenancy for a fixed term of 90 years. This meant that Mexfield could not determine the tenancy by serving a notice to quit. As this is how Mexfield had purported to end the tenancy, its claim for possession was dismissed.

8.23   That does not mean, however, that Mexfield could never have recovered possession of the property before the 90-year term had expired. Rather than serving a notice to quit Mexfield could have exercised its right of re-entry to forfeit the lease.

8.24   It follows that those advising tenants of fully mutual housing associations must always check the terms of the tenancy agreement before settling a defence to the claim. If the tenancy is periodic, ie it does not contain a clause that limits the circumstances in which the agreement can be brought to an end, the landlord is entitled to serve a notice to quit.[53] In those circumstances, the scope of any defence is likely to be limited to whether the notice to quit was valid and whether a defence under the Equality Act 2010 can be pursued (see chapter 27). In some instances, it might be possible, depending on the terms of the tenancy agreement, to defend the claim if the landlord has not terminated the tenant's membership of the co-operative.[54]

8.25   Neither a human rights nor a public law defence is likely to be available (see chapters 25 and 26). This is because in *Joseph v Nettleton Road Housing Co-operative Ltd,*[55] the Court of Appeal held, albeit after a concession made by the tenant, that the fully mutual association in that case was not a 'public authority' for the purposes of the Human Rights Act 1998 s6 (and therefore, by implication was also not amenable to judicial review and public law challenges).

8.26   Where the agreement tenancy purports to restrict the landlord's right to bring it to an end, it is likely to be for a fixed term of 90 years. In that case, the law on forfeiture will apply. This means that consideration will need to be given to:

- whether the agreement gives the landlord a right to re-enter;
- the circumstances in which the right to re-enter may be exercised;
- whether those circumstances have arisen;

53 In *Mexfield*, the tenancy could not be periodic because Mexfield were precluded from determining the tenancy by serving a notice to quit unless certain conditions were satisfied.

54 *Sterling v Cyron Housing Co-Operative* Ltd [2013] EWHC 4445 (QB).

55 [2010] EWCA Civ 228, [2010] HLR 30.

- whether the right is exercisable (ie has a determination been obtained that there has been a breach of the lease under HA 1996 s81 or Commonhold and Leasehold Reform Act 2002 s168);
- whether there is a need for a Law of Property Act 1925 s146 notice to be served;[56]
- whether such a notice has expired or been complied with; and
- whether the right to forfeit has been waived.

Even if the lease is capable of being forfeit, or has even already been forfeited, the court retains a wide discretion to grant relief from forfeiture: County Courts Act 1984 s138 and Law of Property Act 1925 s146.[57]

Crown tenancies

8.27   A tenant whose landlord is the Crown or a government department (or where the landlord's interest in the land is held in trust for the Crown for the purpose of a government department) is not an assured or assured shorthold tenant.[58] Nor is it a secure tenancy.[59] It follows that any such tenancies lack security of tenure and may be determined by a notice to quit, albeit tenants of such landlords can raise human rights, public law or Equality Act 2010 defences (see chapters 26, 25 and 27 respectively).[60]

Subtenants/licensees of tenants of social landlords

8.28   It is common for local housing authorities, private registered providers of social housing and private social landlords to bring claims for possession against secure or assured tenants on the grounds that they are no longer secure or assured tenants because they have sublet

---

56 A s146 notice does not need to be served where there are arrears of rent (s146(11)) or where service or other charges are expressed to be recoverable or reserved as rent: *Escalus Properties Ltd v Robinson* [1996] QB 231, CA.

57 See chapter 14 for more detailed consideration of the law of forfeiture.

58 HA 1988 Sch 1 para 11. A challenge to this provision, on the grounds that it unlawfully discriminated against tenants of government departments under Human Rights Act 1998 Sch 1, was rejected by the Court of Appeal in *Nicholas v Secretary of State for Defence* [2015] EWCA Civ 53, [2015] 1 WLR 2116.

59 HA 1985 s80.

60 See for example *R (JL) v Secretary of State for Defence* [2013] EWCA Civ 449, [2013] PTSR 1014.

the premises to a third party.[61] In such cases it is necessary to identify correctly the true legal status of those persons living in the tenant's property and the terms of the secure or assured tenant's tenancy agreement. That is because it does not necessarily follow that the presence of a third party within the property means that security of tenure has been lost.

Subtenants and lodgers of secure tenants

8.29   It is a term of every secure tenancy that the tenant may allow lodgers in the dwelling-house (see para 8.30) but will not, without the written consent of the landlord, sublet or part with possession of *part* of the dwelling-house.[62] A secure tenant who sublets or parts with possession of the *whole* of the dwelling-house ceases to be a secure tenant.[63] See paras 8.37–8.39 for subletting of part and see paras 8.40–8.43 for subletting of the whole property.

Lodgers of secure tenants

8.30   An occupier is a lodger in the secure tenant's home if he or she has not been provided with any exclusive part of the tenant's home for his or her own use. Even if the occupier does have his or her 'own room', he or she is a lodger if the secure tenant provides services which require unrestricted access to the occupier's room (such as changes of bed-linen, cleaning, removing refuse, etc).[64] Where the tenant exercises a high degree of control over the occupier's use of the room – for example, regarding decoration or visitors – this will also point towards a lodging situation. A true lodger is not a sub-tenant because he or she has no exclusive occupation of any property – such 'exclusive possession' is one of the key hallmarks of a (sub)tenancy.[65] In law, the lodger is a mere licensee of the tenant.

8.31   The secure tenant may have allowed visiting family members to come and stay in his or her home or have had such people sharing with him or her from the outset of the tenancy. None of these

---

61   See paras 1.153–1.160 above.
62   HA 1985 s93(1).
63   HA 1985 s93(2).
64   *Huwyler v Ruddy* (1996) 28 HLR 550, CA. See also *Aslan v Murphy (No 2)* [1990] 1 WLR 766, [1989] 3 All ER 130, CA and *Crancour v Da Silvaesa* (1986) 18 HLR 265, CA.
65   See paras 1.7–1.21 above on discussion between distinction between tenancy and licence.

occupiers has a subtenancy. That is either because they do not have exclusive possession (a prerequisite of tenancy – see above) or because there has been no intention to create a legal relationship,[66] or both.

8.32 The true lodger's position is precarious. He or she is liable to exclusion by the tenant at the end of any period of lodging without the need for a formal notice in any prescribed form. For example, a lodger allowed to 'stay for a week' can be turned out at the end of the week and a lodger staying on a weekly basis can be given as little as a week's notice. This results from the exclusion of the lodger from the scope of PEA 1977 and is a consequence of the lodger sharing use of the premises with his or her licensor, the true tenant.[67]

8.33 In *Monmouth BC v Marlog*,[68] a woman and her two children moved into a council house with its new tenant and she paid him £20 per week. She and her children had two of the three bedrooms, the tenant had his own bedroom and the use of the other rooms was shared. The Court of Appeal refused to disturb the county court judge's finding that the woman was only a licensee. The court described as 'ludicrous' any suggestion that the parties might have intended the creation of a subtenancy.

8.34 The lodger's right to remain is subsidiary to the tenant's own continuing tenancy and, as a result, the lodger cannot be ousted by the head landlord for as long as that tenancy remains in place. For example, in *Braintree DC v Vincent*,[69] the secure tenant left the premises and went to live in a nursing home. The tenant's sons, her licensees, remained in occupation. The council claimed possession against the sons and the judge granted a possession order on the basis that the tenant was no longer fulfilling the tenancy condition (see para 1.65) and so was no longer a secure tenant. The Court of Appeal held that to have been an error because nothing had been done – by notice to quit or otherwise – to end the mother's non-secure tenancy. Only if and when that tenancy was determined would the licensees become trespassers capable of being ousted by the council.

8.35 Once the secure tenant's interest is determined, eg by notice to quit or by a possession order, the lodger's right to remain will also end because it is conditional on the tenant having a proprietary right to occupy the premises.[70] If the secure tenant has left the premises

---

66 *Errington v Errington* [1952] 1 KB 290, [1952] 1 All ER 149, CA. See also paras 1.18–1.19.
67 PEA 1977 s3A(2)(a).
68 (1995) 27 HLR 30, CA.
69 [2004] EWCA Civ 415.
70 *Pennell v Payne* [1995] QB 192, CA.

after serving a notice to quit, the landlord can bring a claim against the former lodger as a trespasser as soon as the notice to quit expires.[71] Moreover, unlike the position for subtenants,[72] a lodger will not become the lodger of the local housing authority landlord where the secure tenant surrenders the tenancy.[73]

8.36   Where the secure tenant's tenancy has been brought to an end by the execution of a possession order, there is no requirement that the landlord issue a fresh claim against a lodger who remains in occupation, even where the lodger was not named as a party to the possession claim. The landlord may enforce the possession order against anyone in occupation of the premises.[74]

Subtenants of part of the premises

8.37   Secure tenants are free to sublet parts of their homes with the written consent of their landlord.[75] In practice, many do not seek or obtain such consent even though it may not be unreasonably withheld.[76] That may expose a secure tenant to a claim for possession for breach of an obligation (to seek consent before subletting) of his or her own tenancy under the second limb of ground 1: see paras 3.255–3.262. However, whether or not consent of the head landlord has been obtained, any subletting is valid and enforceable as between the secure tenant and the subtenant.

8.38   Such a true subletting does not usually give the subtenant any security of tenure or protection under the PEA 1977 because the 'landlord' (the secure tenant) will be resident in the part not sublet and will therefore be sharing living accommodation with the tenant.[77]

8.39   The subtenant's interest comes to an end when the secure tenant's tenancy determines unless the secure tenant's tenancy has been surrendered. In that case, provided the subtenant is occupying the property as a separate dwelling and as his only or principal home, he will become the secure tenant of the premises as against the local

---

71   *Moore Properties v McKeon* [1976] 1 WLR 1278, CA.

72   *Parker v Jones* [1910] 2 KB 32.

73   *Kay v Lambeth LBC* [2004] EWCA Civ 926, [2005] QB 352 (the principle was neither questioned nor overturned by the House of Lords on appeal).

74   *R v Wandsworth County Court ex p Wandsworth LBC* [1975] 1 WLR 1314, CA and *Thompson v Elmbridge BC* [1987] 1 WLR 1425, (1987) 19 HLR 526, CA.

75   HA 1985 s93(1)(b).

76   HA 1985 s94.

77   PEA 1977 s3A(2)(a).

housing authority landlord irrespective of whether the head landlord consented to the subtenancy.[78] The most difficult of the conditions for the subtenant of part of the secure tenant's former home to establish will be that he or she occupies a dwelling which 'was let as a separate dwelling'.[79]

Subtenants of the whole

8.40 It is not uncommon for secure tenants to move out of their homes and put others in exclusive occupation on long-term or short-term arrangements. Even if the secure tenant intends to return and resume occupation at a later date, security of tenure is lost by the subletting or parting with possession of the whole and cannot be regained.[80] In such circumstances, therefore, little is to be achieved by the tenant displacing the subtenant and attempting to regain occupation. It simply follows automatically, from any subletting of the whole, that secure status is lost and with it the secure tenant's statutory rights which flow from that status (such as the right to buy).[81]

8.41 In any dispute with the secure tenant, it is for the social landlord to prove the subletting of the whole. It does not follow simply from the fact of occupation by a third party that the tenant has sublet or otherwise parted with possession of the whole.[82] For further discussion of the effect of subletting on the position of the secure tenant see paras 1.153–1.160.

8.42 As between the secure tenant and the subtenant, the letting is valid and enforceable and, if made after 28 February 1997, is more than likely to be an assured shorthold tenancy.

8.43 In the unlikely event that the social landlord, rather than serving a notice to quit on the secure tenant, agrees for the contractual tenancy to be surrendered the subtenant will become the landlord's secure tenant.[83]

---

78 *Parker v Jones* [1910] 2 KB 32.
79 W Birtles, 'Sub-tenants: Problems for local authorities when properties are surrendered' *Local Government Chronicle* 18 September 1987, p12.
80 HA 1985 s93(2) and the discussion of the consequences for the secure tenant of subletting the whole at paras 1.153–1.160.
81 *Merton LBC v Salama* June 1989 *Legal Action* 25, CA; *Jennings v Epping Forest DC* (1993) 25 HLR 241, CA and *Muir Group Housing Association v Thornley* (1993) 25 HLR 89, CA, all discussed at para 1.157 above.
82 *Hussey v Camden LBC* (1995) 27 HLR 5, CA, but see *Brent LBC v Cronin* (1998) 30 HLR 43, September 1997 *Legal Action* 13, CA and the cases discussed at paras 1.155–1.156.
83 *Parker v Jones* [1910] 2 KB 32.

Subtenants and licensees of assured tenants

8.44   HA 1988 s15(1) provides that it is an implied term of every assured or assured shorthold tenancy that the tenant must not, without the consent of the landlord, sublet or part with possession of the whole or any part of the dwelling-house that is subject to the tenancy agreement. Such consent may be unreasonably withheld.[84] This means that the landlord can refuse consent without giving any reasons.[85] However, any express term contained within the tenancy agreement will take precedence over the implied term.

8.45   This has two important consequences. First, if an express term provides that a tenancy may be sublet with consent then such a term is subject to the qualification that consent is not to be unreasonably withheld.[86] Second, if the express term contains an absolute prohibition on subletting then the landlord does not even need to consider a request to sublet.

Lodgers of assured tenants

8.46   The position of lodgers of assured tenants is very similar to that of secure tenants (see above paras 8.30–8.36). The provision of a spare room to a person by an assured tenant does not amount to subletting or parting with possession provided that the occupier of the room is a lodger and not a tenant.[87] The lodger will be an excluded licensee under PEA 1977 and may be removed from the premises at short notice by the co-resident assured tenant,[88] albeit such notice must be in accordance with the lodging agreement or at least be reasonable. The lodger's interest will also end when the assured tenant's interest ends.[89]

---

84   HA 1988 s15(2).
85   This does not mean that the landlord can necessarily refuse consent for any reason. If the reasons given amount to unlawful discrimination within the meaning of Equality Act 2010 then it is likely that the decision would give the tenant an entitlement to damages and an injunction requiring that consent be given (or at least a new decision taken).
86   Landlord and Tenant Act 1988 s1; *R (McIntyre) v Gentoo Group Ltd* [2010] EWHC 5 (Admin).
87   *Segal Securities Ltd v Thoseby* [1963] 1 QB 887. See above para 8.18 and paras 1.7–1.21 for discussion on the distinction between tenants and licensees.
88   See above para 8.32.
89   See above paras 8.35–8.36.

Subtenants of part of the premises

8.47   If the assured tenant has been given permission to sublet part of the premises then the subtenant's status will depend upon whether the assured tenant continues to live in the premises. If only part of the premises is sublet then the assured tenant is likely to be a resident landlord, which will mean that the subtenancy is excluded from the protection of the HA 1988. The assured tenant will be a resident landlord if:

i)   the dwelling-house, over which the subtenancy has been granted, forms part of a building or part of a flat, and

ii)   the assured tenant who granted the tenancy occupied another part of the building or flat as his only or principal home at the time that the tenancy was granted and at all times during the tenancy.[90]

8.48   In that case, it is also likely that the tenancy will be excluded by the PEA 1977 provided that the assured tenant shares part of the premises with the subtenant, eg kitchen or bathroom.[91] In such cases, the subtenant is in not much better position than a lodger. The subtenant without security of tenure is in a better position, however, if the assured tenant surrenders his tenancy to the head landlord. In that case, the subtenant will become the direct tenant of the former assured tenant's landlord.[92] This will likely be as an assured shorthold tenant provided that the conditions are satisfied.[93]

Subtenants of the whole

8.49   If an assured tenant, in breach of an express or implied term of their own tenancy, sublet the whole property, their assured status is lost and cannot be restored: HA 1988 s15A(2). If an assured tenant of a PRP or RSL has been given permission[94] to sublet the whole of the premises then, provided the subtenant is an individual and occupies the dwelling-house as his or her only or principal home, he or she is likely to be an assured shorthold tenant of the assured tenant. More-

---

90   HA 1988 Sch 1 para 10.
91   PEA 1977 s3A(2) and (4).
92   *Parker v Jones* [1910] 2 KB 32.
93   See paras 1.6–1.36.
94   This is likely to be very rare, but unlike for secure tenants, provided the tenancy agreement permits the subletting of the whole, the assured tenancy does not automatically cease to be assured by virtue of it: HA 1988 s15A(1). It will cease to be assured because the assured tenant is no longer occupying as his or her home.

over, provided the subtenancy has been granted by the assured tenant in accordance with the terms of the tenancy agreement granted by the PRPSH or RSL, the subtenancy will not end when the assured tenant's interest ends, eg by order of the court, surrender or notice to quit. In such circumstances, the subtenant will become the direct tenant of the PRPSH or RSL.[95] This is likely to be an assured shorthold tenancy provided that the conditions are satisfied.[96]

8.50   It is unclear how HA 1988 s18 operates where the social landlord obtains a possession order against its assured tenant. The assured tenancy cannot be brought to an end until the possession order is executed.[97] However, as soon as the possession order is executed the lawful subtenant becomes the assured shorthold tenant of the head landlord. In practice, this presumably means that on the date of an eviction the social landlord will, in attendance with the bailiff, change the locks of the premises, thereby securing possession, but then be required to hand a set of keys to the subtenant immediately.

95   HA 1988 s18.
96   Above paras 1.6–1.36.
97   HA 1988 s5(1)(b).

CHAPTER 9

Shared ownership of social housing

9.1   The last three decades have seen attempts to blur the edges between owner-occupation and renting. There is every reason to believe that the blurring will continue. Great efforts have been made to ease people into owner-occupation by use of shared ownership schemes operated by social landlords. These usually allow occupiers progressively to buy tranches of the homes that they occupy until the property is owned outright, or at least owned subject to a mortgage.

9.2   There are particular problems which face occupiers under such schemes, the principal one being that where part is owned subject to a mortgage and part is rented, there are potentially two separate claims for possession if the occupier defaults. It will be necessary to service both debts (ie the liabilities for both mortgage payments and rental payments) simultaneously in order to retain possession.

9.3   Under a typical shared ownership scheme (for a worked example, see the end of this chapter), a freeholder agrees to grant a long lease to the occupier in return for a premium representing, for example, a quarter or half of the capital value of the property. If the prospective occupier cannot raise the money, the premium is raised by way of a mortgage from an institutional lender, or even from the freeholder. The occupier moves into the property and pays rent calculated by reference to the outstanding element not yet purchased.

9.4   In the above example, the occupier will usually be an assured tenant since none of the exceptions in the Housing Act (HA) 1988 Sch 1 is likely to apply. Shared ownership leases were also excluded from Rent Act protection.[1] It is likely that if the freeholder is a housing association it will have specifically granted an assured tenancy which is not an assured shorthold tenancy. Only where the rent payable

---

1   See the Housing Association Shared Ownership Leases (Exclusion from Leasehold Reform Act 1967 and Rent Act 1977) Regulations 1987 SI No 1940.

under the tenancy is over £100,000 or below £250 per annum (£1,000 per annum in London) would the tenancy fall outside the HA 1988 assured tenancy regime on grounds of rent level (see para 1.37). Like any other assured tenant, the tenant is at risk of possession proceedings under any of the grounds in HA 1988 Sch 2.

9.5   In *Richardson v Midland Heart Ltd*,[2] the court made a possession order on the basis that the occupying 'shared owner' was an assured tenant and, on the basis of rent arrears, was liable to eviction under HA 1988 Sch 2 ground 8. The court rejected the argument that the housing association held the freehold or the lease on trust for the tenant. She was simply an assured tenant under a 99-year lease and none of the exemptions took the tenancy outside the assured tenancy regime.[3]

9.6   In addition, where in purchasing the lease the purchaser executed a legal charge, there is also a risk of mortgage possession proceedings in the event of default under that agreement.

9.7   Occupiers under shared ownership agreements which fall within the scope of the assured tenancy regime in HA 1988 and the Administration of Justice Acts (which enable the courts to assist defaulting mortgage borrowers) will be entitled to claim protection under either legislative regime in the event of possession proceedings except where proceedings are brought relying on HA 1988 Sch 2 ground 8.

9.8   Advisers will need to consider the particular agreement entered into by the individual being advised, as there are many differing forms of shared ownership agreement.

9.9   If there is a mortgage and, in default of rent or service charge payments, the freeholder threatens to forfeit the lease, the lender will often meet those payments (to protect its security) and add the payment made to the outstanding debt owed by the mortgage borrower. Advisers will need to be alert to assess whether payments made by the mortgage lender to the landlord in such circumstances are validly made. It is common for lenders to pay over money to the landlord simply because the landlord says that there are rent arrears and hence the risk of forfeiture. Such payments may be recorded as mortgage arrears and, in turn, put the borrower/tenant at risk of eviction by the lender. The assertion that the borrower is in mortgage arrears should be tested in correspondence and in possession proceedings

2   [2008] L&TR 31, County Court. See also *Jasmine Ker v Optima Community Association* [2013] EWCA Civ 579.
3   For an analysis of the issues see S Bright, 'Low cost home ownership: legal issues of the shared ownership lease' [2009] 73 Conv 337.

if the borrower has ceased to pay rent to the landlord for legitimate reasons. It is clear that a mortgage lender has the right to seek relief against forfeiture if the freeholder seeks to forfeit the shared owner-ship lease.[4]

9.10   The Homes and Communities Agency, the Council of Mortgage Lenders and the National Housing Federation have issued joint guid-ance about shared ownership properties, including repossession: *Shared ownership: joint guidance for England*.[5]

Example of a simple shared ownership arrangement

P agrees to buy a one-third share of a 99-year lease on a flat renovated by a housing association which has a market value of £180,000. The market rent for the flat is £1,200 per month. P takes a 99-year lease and borrows £60,000 from a bank (to meet the value of one-third of the market price), secured by way of legal charge on the leasehold title. P then makes mortgage repay-ments on the £60,000 borrowed and pays rent at the rate of £800 per month (represents two-thirds of the rental value). Subse-quently P agrees to purchase a further one-third share. P borrows an additional £60,000, and as a result the rent paid to the associa-tion is reduced to £400 per month but the mortgage repayments double. On buying the last third for a further £60,000, P will then cease paying rent to the association and will continue to pay the mortgage repayments until the end of the term agreed with the bank at the time of the taking of the loan.

---

4   *Sinclair Gardens Investments (Kensington) Ltd v Walsh* [1996] QB 231, (1996) 28 HLR 338, CA. See para 14.6 onwards on relief from forfeiture.
5   November 2012.

PART II

Private sector tenants

Introduction to Part II

II.1   Outside the local authority sector, almost all new residential tenancies created on or after 15 January 1989 are assured or assured shorthold tenancies.[1] In practice, private sector landlords invariably wish to create assured shorthold tenancies, whereas fully assured tenancies are more likely to be found in the social rented sector. Following the implementation of Housing Act (HA) 1988 s19A on 28 February 1997, most new private sector tenancies created on or after that date will automatically be assured shorthold tenancies unless the landlord elects to create a fully assured tenancy (see para 10.6). However, between 15 January 1989 and 27 February 1997 inclusive, some private sector landlords inadvertently created assured tenancies because they failed to comply with the requirements in HA 1988 s20 (see para 10.4).

II.2   Part II of this book is expressed to deal with private sector tenants. However, it is important to note that housing associations may grant fixed-term assured shorthold tenancies. In practice, social landlords such as housing associations or other 'private registered providers of social housing' (PRPSHs) or, in Wales, registered social landlords (RSLs) continue to grant assured tenancies with security of tenure. However, many PRPSHs and RSLs grant assured shorthold tenancies in respect of temporary accommodation or initially as probationary tenancies (often referred to as 'starter tenancies').[2] In addition, the policy purpose of the recent changes introduced by the Localism Act 2011 was to encourage PRPSHs in England to let on fixed-term assured shorthold tenancies of at least two years (see para 10.25).

---

1   For tenancies granted by local authorities, see para 1.50 onwards. Occupiers of agricultural accommodation may enjoy 'assured agricultural occupancy' status. See para 17.8.

2   See paras 1.46–1.49 and 5.64–5.85.

Chapter 10 therefore applies (except where otherwise stated) equally to PRPSH and RSL assured shorthold tenancies, as well as to private sector assured shorthold tenancies. For this reason, it is necessary to consider briefly the means of regulation of PRPSHs.

II.3   Housing associations and other PRPSHs in England are regulated by the Homes and Communities Agency (HCA). The HCA has published a number of standards which registered providers (including for some purposes local housing authorities) are required to meet.[3] The regulatory standards contain the outcomes that providers are expected to achieve. Housing associations' boards of management and local authority councillors are responsible for meeting the standards and determining the policies which seek to ensure that the regulator's expectations are satisfied. The standards are of two kinds: economic and consumer. The three economic standards – the Governance and Financial Viability Standard; the Value for Money Standard; and the Rent Standard – apply to all private registered providers, but not to local authorities. The four consumer standards apply to all registered providers including local authorities: the Tenant Involvement and Empowerment Standard; the Home Standard; the Tenancy Standard; and the Neighbourhood and Community Standard.

II.4   In Wales, housing associations and other RSLs are regulated by the Welsh Ministers and are subject to the Regulatory Framework established by the Welsh Government.[4] Regulation is undertaken by the Housing Regulation Team, which is part of the Government's Housing Division. The Regulatory Board for Wales, an advisory body set up by the Welsh Government, monitors the operation of the Regulatory Framework and oversees the work of the Housing Regulation Team.

---

3   The regulatory framework for social housing in England with effect from 1 April 2015 consists of the regulatory requirements, together with codes of practice and regulatory guidance. See *What is the Regulatory Framework?*, HCA, April 2015. The approach of the HCA to regulation is explained in *Regulating the Standards* (July 2016) and in *Guidance on the regulator's approach to intervention, enforcement and use of powers* (May 2016).

4   See the *Regulatory Framework for Housing Associations Registered in Wales*, Welsh Government, 2 December 2011. The Regulatory Board for Wales is supported by a Tenant Advisory Panel, comprising housing association tenant representatives from across Wales.

Transitional provisions under the Housing Act 1988

II.5 Tenancies granted before 15 January 1989 by private sector landlords either enjoyed security of tenure under the Rent Act 1977 or lacked long-term security of tenure. There are still many thousands of Rent Act protected or statutory tenants (see chapter 12).[5] HA 1988 s34 provides that no new Rent Act regulated tenancies can be created after 15 January 1989, except in limited circumstances, notably where a new tenancy is granted to an existing regulated tenant by the same landlord (see para 12.7). In the same way, the standard form of tenancy granted by housing associations before 15 January 1989 was a hybrid: such tenancies were both secure tenancies under the HA 1985 and, for the purposes of rent control, they were 'housing association tenancies' under Rent Act 1977 Part VI (which brought them within the system of fair rent registration). HA 1988 s35 provides that no new secure or housing association tenancies can be created by PRPSHs or RSLs on or after 15 January 1989, except in limited circumstances, notably where a new tenancy is granted to an existing secure tenant by the same landlord (see para 1.62).

---

5 See *Cadogan Estates Ltd v McMahon* [2001] 1 AC 378, [2000] 3 WLR 1555, HL, per Lord Millett.

Assured shorthold tenancies

continued

Introduction

10.1   The assured shorthold tenancy is the standard form of tenancy in the private rented sector. Assured shorthold tenancies provide no long-term security of tenure and are subject to minimal rent control. Although, legally, they are a kind of assured tenancy,[1] the lack of security of tenure means that, from a tenant's point of view, the adjective 'assured' is something of a misnomer. The assured shorthold tenancy is also available to housing associations and other private registered providers of social housing and registered social landlords. Many housing associations use assured shortholds for a fixed term of 12 months as probationary tenancies (sometimes called 'starter tenancies'), with the intention of converting them into fully assured tenancies at the end of that period, assuming that the tenant has complied with tenancy conditions. In the wake of the Localism Act 2011, private registered providers in England may also grant fixed-term tenancies of at least two years on the basis that at the end of that period the landlord will make a decision whether to grant a fully assured tenancy or grant a further fixed-term tenancy, or recover possession[2] (see para 10.25). For details of the application of this chapter to Wales see paras 10.103–10.104.

10.2   Most private sector lettings since 15 January 1989 have been assured shorthold tenancies. Until 28 February 1997, when amendments introduced by the Housing Act (HA) 1996 ss96–100 came into force, a landlord who wished to create an assured shorthold tenancy had to serve on the prospective tenant a notice under HA 1988 s20 before the tenancy began, informing him or her that the tenancy being offered was to be an assured shorthold tenancy. Failure to serve such notices, or service of invalid notices, resulted in the creation of fully assured tenancies. However, since 28 February 1997 the section 20 requirement has been abolished and, subject to the exceptions set out at para 10.6 below, all new tenancies created since that date are assured shorthold tenancies. This is the case whether they are granted in writing or orally, and whether they are fixed-term or periodic tenancies. When advising, it is vital to determine when the tenancy was granted or, if there has been a succession of tenancies, when the first tenancy was granted.

---

1 See paras 1.6–1.49.
2 See, further, in relation to assured shorthold tenancies in the social rented sector, paras 1.46–1.49 and 5.75–5.85.

10.3   The Court of Appeal has held that the assured shorthold regime does not breach Human Rights Act 1998 Sch 1 Article 8 (right to respect for private and family life and for the home).[3] In *McDonald v McDonald*,[4] the Supreme Court further decided that it is not open to a tenant facing possession proceedings brought by a private landlord to require the court to consider the proportionality of the order for possession where the landlord's contractual rights entitle him or her to possession.

Tenancies granted before 28 February 1997

10.4   HA 1988 s20 stipulated four requirements for the creation of an assured shorthold tenancy:

- It must have been granted for a fixed term of not less than six months.[5]
- It must not have contained any provision enabling the landlord to terminate the tenancy within six months of the beginning of the tenancy. HA 1988 s45(4) provides that a power of re-entry or forfeiture for breach of condition does not count as a provision enabling the landlord to determine the tenancy for this purpose.[6]
- Notice in the prescribed form must have been served[7] before the commencement of the tenancy stating that the tenancy would be an assured shorthold tenancy. A court had no power to dispense with service of this notice.[8] The form of the notice was prescribed by the Assured Tenancies and Agricultural Occupancies (Forms) Regulations 1988.[9] The omission of certain words from the prescribed form or the inclusion of incorrect details might render the notice invalid.[10] However, in view of the purposive approach

---

3 *Poplar HARCA v Donoghue* [2001] EWCA Civ 595, [2002] QB 48; *McDonald v McDonald* [2014] EWCA Civ 1049, [2014] HLR 43.

4 [2016] UKSC 28.

5 *Bedding v McCarthy* [1994] 41 EG 151, (1995) 27 HLR 103, CA. A tenancy granted for 'a term certain of one year ... and ... thereafter from month to month' is a tenancy granted for a term certain within the meaning of s20(1)(a) which was capable of being an assured shorthold tenancy: *Goodman v Evely* [2001] EWCA Civ 104, [2002] HLR 53.

6 See *Maryland Estates v Bar-Joseph* [1999] 1 WLR 83, [1998] 3 All ER 193, CA.

7 See *Yenula Properties Ltd v Naidu* [2002] EWCA Civ 719, [2003] HLR 18.

8 *Panayi v Roberts* (1993) 25 HLR 421, [1993] 28 EG 125, CA.

9 SI No 2203.

10 *Panayi v Roberts* (1993) 25 HLR 421, [1993] 2 EGLR 51 (notice failed to state date); *Clickex Ltd v McCann* (2000) 32 HLR 324, [1999] 30 EG 6, CA (dates

adopted and sanctioned in *Manel v Memon*[11] and *Mannai Invest-ment Co Ltd v Eagle Star Life Assurance Co Ltd*,[12] a notice is likely to be valid if, notwithstanding any errors or omissions, it was substantially to the same effect as the prescribed form, that is, it accomplished the statutory purpose of informing the proposed tenant of the special nature of an assured shorthold tenancy.[13]

- It would be an assured tenancy but for the above requirements being satisfied. See para 1.6.

A further tenancy (or tenancies[14]) of the same or substantially the same premises granted before 28 February 1997 to a former assured shorthold tenant is also an assured shorthold tenancy even if any of the first three requirements above was not satisfied.

10.5   By virtue of HA 1988 s20(3), where, before 28 February 1997, a landlord granted a new tenancy to someone who, immediately before the grant of that tenancy, was already a fully assured tenant (alone or jointly with others) of the same landlord, the new tenancy could not be an assured shorthold tenancy and so would be a fully assured tenancy. This is the case even if the premises in question were differ-ent. Where a new tenancy is entered into between the same parties on or after 28 February 1997, the provisions of HA 1996 Sch 2A para 7 apply, but in most cases the outcome will be the same and the new tenancy will be a fully assured tenancy: see para 10.6 below.

---

in notice in conflict with dates in tenancy agreement); *London and Quadrant Housing v Robertson* September 1991 *Legal Action* 17; *Lomas v Atkinson* September 1993 *Legal Action* 16 (notice failed to include information about how to seek advice); *Mistry v Dave* June 1995 *Legal Action* 19 (notice gave no date for the end of the tenancy); *Symons v Warren* [1995] CLW 33/95 (failure to identify landlord properly and incorrect date); *Stevens v Lamb* March 1996 *Legal Action* 12 (failure to include landlord's name, address and telephone number); *Smith v Willson* November 1999 *Legal Action* 28 (error in date and use of notice of *protected* shorthold (HA 1980 s52)) and *Charalambous v Pesman* January 2001 *Legal Action* 26 (name and address of landlord omitted).

11   (2001) 33 HLR 235, [2000] 33 EG 74, CA (omission of bullet points, exhortation to take legal advice and statement that tenant was not committed to take the tenancy).

12   [1997] AC 749, [1997] 3 All ER 352, HL.

13   *Ravenseft Properties Ltd v Hall; White v Chubb; Kasseer v Freeman* [2001] EWCA Civ 2034, [2002] HLR 33. See too *Osborn and Co Ltd v Dior* [2003] EWCA Civ 281, [2003] HLR 45 (even if the particulars of the landlord are absent, a notice is still substantially to the same effect where the agent has signed and given its particulars), cf *York and Ross v Casey* (1999) 31 HLR 209, [1998] 30 EG 110, CA.

14   *Lower Street Properties Ltd v Jones* (1996) 28 HLR 877, [1996] 48 EG 154, CA.

Tenancies granted on or after 28 February 1997

10.6   By virtue of HA 1988 s19A and Sch 2A,[15] all new tenancies entered into on or after 28 February 1997, which would otherwise have been assured tenancies, are automatically assured shorthold tenancies lacking long-term security of tenure. This applies whether the tenancy is granted orally or by a written agreement, or whether it is a fixed-term or periodic tenancy. From that date, the requirement of an HA 1988 s20 notice (informing the tenant that the tenancy would be an assured shorthold tenancy) was abolished. There are, however, several exceptions which are set out in HA 1988 Sch 2A. A tenancy will not be an assured shorthold tenancy where one of the following applies:

- the new tenancy was granted pursuant to a contract made before 28 February 1997;[16]
- the landlord serves a notice before entering into the tenancy stating that the tenancy is not to be an assured shorthold tenancy;[17]
- the landlord serves a notice after the grant of the tenancy stating that the tenancy is no longer an assured shorthold tenancy;[18]
- there is a provision in the tenancy agreement stating that the tenancy is not an assured shorthold tenancy;[19]
- the tenancy is an assured tenancy by succession, ie where a member of the family of a deceased protected or statutory tenant under the Rent Act 1977 or the Rent (Agriculture) Act 1976 became an assured tenant after the death of the former tenant;[20]
- the tenancy was formerly a secure tenancy and became an assured tenancy, for example, on transfer of housing stock from a local housing authority to a housing association or other landlord;[21]

15   Introduced by HA 1996 s96 and Sch 7.

16   HA 1988 s19A(a).

17   HA 1988 Sch 2A para 1. In *Andrews and Andrews (Executors of W Hodges deceased) v Cunningham* [2007] EWCA Civ 762, [2008] HLR 13, it was held that the use of a rent book bearing the words 'Assured tenancy' on the cover was not sufficient to convert the tenancy from an assured shorthold tenancy to a fully assured tenancy. The words 'assured tenancy' were not a statement 'that the assured tenancy to which [the notice] relates is not to be an assured shorthold tenancy' within HA 1988 Sch 2A para 1(2)(c) because an assured shorthold tenancy was itself a type of assured tenancy.

18   HA 1988 Sch 2A para 2. See *Saxon Weald Homes Ltd v Chadwick* [2011] EWCA Civ 1202, [2012] HLR 8.

19   HA 1988 Sch 2A para 3.

20   Rent Act 1977 s2(1)(b) and Sch 1, HA 1988 s39 and HA 1988 Sch 2A para 4, as amended by Civil Partnership Act 2004 Sch 8.

21   HA 1985 Pt IV, HA 1988 s38 and HA 1988 Sch 2A para 5.

- the assured tenancy came into existence on the ending of a long residential tenancy;[22]
- the tenancy is granted to a person (alone or jointly with others) who immediately before its grant was a fully assured tenant (or, in the case of joint tenants, one of the tenants) and is granted by the person who was the landlord under the old tenancy;[23]
- the tenancy is a statutory periodic tenancy arising after the expiry of a non-shorthold fixed-term assured tenancy;[24] and
- in some cases, the tenancy or licence is an assured agricultural occupancy.[25]

Recovery of possession of assured shorthold tenancies: the section 21 procedure

10.7   HA 1988 s21 enables a landlord to recover possession of premises let on an assured shorthold tenancy on the basis only of two months' notice requiring possession. It must be stressed that neither service nor expiry of a 'section 21 notice' operates to end the tenancy. If the tenant does not leave on the date required by the notice, the landlord will need to obtain a court order for possession.

HA 1988 s21, as amended, provides:

Recovery of possession on expiry or termination of assured shorthold tenancy

21(1) Without prejudice to any right of the landlord under an assured shorthold tenancy to recover possession of the dwelling-house let on the tenancy in accordance with Chapter I above, on or after the coming to an end of an assured shorthold tenancy which was a fixed-term tenancy, a court shall make an order for possession of the dwelling-house if it is satisfied –

(a) that the assured shorthold tenancy has come to an end and no further assured tenancy (whether shorthold or not) is for

---

22   Landlord and Tenant Act 1954 Pt I, Local Government and Housing Act 1989 s186 and Sch 10 and HA 1988 Sch 2A para 6.

23   HA 1988 Sch 2A para 7. The tenancy may be of a different property as long as it is granted to the same tenant by the same landlord. There is an exception in para 7(1)(c) and 7(2), where the tenant serves a notice in a prescribed form on the landlord before the tenancy begins, stating that the new tenancy is to be an assured shorthold tenancy.

24   HA 1988 Sch 2A para 8.

25   Rent (Agriculture) Act 1976, HA 1988 s24 and Sch 3 and HA 1988 Sch 2A para 9.

  the time being in existence, other than an assured shorthold periodic tenancy (whether statutory or not); and

 (b) the landlord or, in the case of joint landlords, at least one of them has given to the tenant not less than two months' notice in writing stating that he requires possession of the dwelling-house.

(1A) Subsection (1B) applies to an assured shorthold tenancy of a dwelling-house in England if –

 (a) it is a fixed-term tenancy for a term certain of not less than two years, and

 (b) the landlord is a private registered provider of social housing.

(1B) The court may not make an order for possession of the dwelling-house let on the tenancy unless the landlord has given to the tenant not less than six months' notice in writing –

 (a) stating that the landlord does not propose to grant another tenancy on the expiry of the fixed-term tenancy, and

 (b) informing the tenant of how to obtain help or advice about the notice and, in particular, of any obligation of the landlord to provide help or advice.

 (2) A notice under paragraph (b) of subsection (1) above may be given before or on the day on which the tenancy comes to an end; and that subsection shall have effect notwithstanding that on the coming to an end of the fixed-term tenancy a statutory periodic tenancy arises.

 (3) Where a court makes an order for possession of a dwelling-house by virtue of subsection (1) above, any statutory periodic tenancy which has arisen on the coming to an end of the assured shorthold tenancy shall end (without further notice and regardless of the period) in accordance with section 5(1A).

 (4) Without prejudice to any such right as is referred to in subsection (1) above, a court shall make an order for possession of a dwelling-house let on an assured shorthold tenancy which is a periodic tenancy if the court is satisfied –

 (a) that the landlord or, in the case of joint landlords, at least one of them has given to the tenant a notice in writing stating that, after a date specified in the notice, being the last day of a period of the tenancy and not earlier than two months after the date the notice was given, possession of the dwelling-house is required by virtue of this section; and

 (b) that the date specified in the notice under paragraph (a) above is not earlier than the earliest day on which, apart from section 5(1) above, the tenancy could be brought to an end by a notice to quit given by the landlord on the same date as the notice under paragraph (a) above.

(4ZA) In the case of a dwelling-house in England, subsection (4)(a) above has effect with the omission of the requirement for the date specified in the notice to be the last day of a period of the tenancy.

(4A) Where a court makes an order for possession of a dwelling-house by virtue of subsection (4) above, the assured shorthold tenancy shall end in accordance with section 5(1A).

(4B) A notice under subsection (1) or (4) may not be given in relation to an assured shorthold tenancy of a dwelling-house in England –

    (a) in the case of a tenancy which is not a replacement tenancy, within the period of four months beginning with the day on which the tenancy began, and

    (b) in the case of a replacement tenancy, within the period of four months beginning with the day on which the original tenancy began.

(4C) Subsection (4B) does not apply where the tenancy has arisen due to section 5(2).

(4D) Subject to subsection (4E), proceedings for an order for possession under this section in relation to a dwelling-house in England may not be begun after the end of the period of six months beginning with the date on which the notice was given under subsection (1) or (4).

(4E) Where –

    (a) a notice under subsection (4) has been given in relation to a dwelling-house in England, and

    (b) paragraph (b) of that subsection requires the date specified in the notice to be more than two months after the date the notice was given,

proceedings for an order for possession under this section may not be begun after the end of the period of four months beginning with the date specified in the notice.

(5) Where an order for possession under subsection (1) or (4) above is made in relation to a dwelling-house let on a tenancy to which section 19A above applies, the order may not be made so as to take effect earlier than –

    (a) in the case of a tenancy which is not a replacement tenancy, six months after the beginning of the tenancy, and

    (b) in the case of a replacement tenancy, six months after the beginning of the original tenancy.

(5A) Subsection (5) above does not apply to an assured shorthold tenancy to which section 20B (demoted assured shorthold tenancies) applies.

(6) In subsections (4B)(b) and (5)(b) above, the reference to the original tenancy is –

    (a) where the replacement tenancy came into being on the coming to an end of a tenancy which was not a replacement tenancy, to the immediately preceding tenancy, and

    (b) where there have been successive replacement tenancies, to the tenancy immediately preceding the first in the succession of replacement tenancies.

(7) For the purposes of this section, a replacement tenancy is a tenancy –
   (a) which comes into being on the coming to an end of an assured shorthold tenancy, and
   (b) under which, on its coming into being –
      (i) the landlord and tenant are the same as under the earlier tenancy as at its coming to an end, and
      (ii) the premises let are the same or substantially the same as those let under the earlier tenancy as at that time.
(8) The Secretary of State may by regulations made by statutory instrument prescribe the form of a notice under subsection (1) or (4) given in relation to an assured shorthold tenancy of a dwelling-house in England.
(9) A statutory instrument containing regulations made under subsection (8) is subject to annulment in pursuance of a resolution of either House of Parliament.

10.8   Subsections 21(1)(b) and 21(4)(a) were amended by HA 1996 s98(2) and (3) to make it clear that notices under this section must be in writing. Subsections (1A) and (1B) were added by Localism Act 2011 s164(1). Subsection (3) was amended and subsection (4A) inserted by Housing and Regeneration Act 2008 Sch 11 para 9(2) and 9(3), with the effect that, upon the court making an order for possession under section 21(1) or section 21(4), the tenancy shall end only when the order is executed. Subsection (4ZA) was added by Deregulation Act 2015 s35, and subsections (4B) to (4E) by Deregulation Act 2015 s36(2). Subsections (5)–(7) were added by HA 1996 s99. Subsection (5A) was added by Anti-social Behaviour Act 2003 s15(2). Subsection (6) was amended by Deregulation Act 2015 s36(3). Subsections (8) and (9) were added by Deregulation Act 2015 s37.[26]

10.9   The essence of section 21 is that it gives the landlord an automatic right to possession on giving two months' notice, where a tenancy is a periodic tenancy (whether statutory or contractual). However,

26 The provisions of Deregulation Act 2015 ss33–41 came into force on 1 October 2015: Deregulation Act 2015 (Commencement No 1 and Transitional and Saving Provisions) Order 2015 SI No 994 art 11. See also the Assured Shorthold Tenancy Notices and Prescribed Requirements (England) Regulations 2015 SI No 1646 and the Assured Shorthold Tenancy Notices and Prescribed Requirements (England) (Amendment) Regulations 2015 SI No 1725. These provisions apply to all assured shorthold tenancies granted on or after 1 October 2015, other than statutory periodic tenancies which arose on or after 1 October 2015 on the expiry of a fixed-term tenancy which was granted before that date: Deregulation Act 2015 s41(2). The provisions also apply to any assured shorthold tenancy which is in existence on 1 October 2018, irrespective of when it began: s41(3).

in respect of tenancies which began prior to 1 October 2015,[27] there are two different notice procedures under section 21: one under section 21(1), which applies where there has been a fixed-term tenancy which has expired; and the other under section 21(4), which applies where the tenancy is a contractual periodic tenancy.[28] The two notice procedures will be examined below. However, for tenancies which began on or after 1 October 2015, and for all assured shorthold tenancies in existence on 1 October 2018,[29] there are few differences between the two forms of notice: see paras 10.38–10.40. As the following paragraphs indicate there are now a number of restrictions on giving a valid section 21 notice. It is hoped that the flowchart at para 10.105 will assist in determining whether there is a defence to a possession claim based on a section 21 notice.

10.10   A section 21 notice will be of no effect if a new contractual tenancy is subsequently granted to the tenant since it is clearly superseded by the new agreement.

10.11   Where a landlord has served a valid section 21 notice, he or she can issue proceedings to recover possession on the basis of the section alone, and without the need to show a ground or reason for possession. A section 21 notice will not be valid if at the time the notice is given the landlord has failed to comply with statutory conditions relating to the protection of tenants' deposits and with any relevant licensing requirements (see paras 10.56–10.91). For tenancies that began on or after 1 October 2015[30] (other than statutory periodic tenancies) there are additional restrictions relating to retaliatory eviction and non-compliance with other statutory obligations.[31] Subject to these restrictions, however, if landlords comply with the relevant notice requirements, they are automatically entitled to possession. The court has no power to prevent possession orders from having virtually immediate effect. HA 1980 s89(1) provides that orders for possession must take effect no later than 14 days after the court order is made unless exceptional hardship would be caused, in which case

---

27 Except where a pre-1 October 2015 tenancy is still in existence on 1 October 2018, whereupon the differences between the two subsections cease to have any significance: see para 10.38.

28 Since 28 February 1997 landlords have been able to grant assured shorthold tenancies that are periodic from the outset.

29 Deregulation Act 2015 s41(3).

30 And for all assured shorthold tenancies in existence on 1 October 2018: Deregulation Act 2015 s41(3).

31 See paras 10.43–10.53 and 10.92–10.102.

the maximum period which may be allowed is six weeks. See para 28.1.

10.12   Until the Deregulation Act 2015 came into force, a section 21 notice was not required to be in a particular form, although it was required to be in writing.[32] However, Deregulation Act 2015 s37 gave the Secretary of State power to make regulations prescribing the form of notice to be used for the purposes of section 21(1) or section 21(4). For tenancies commencing on or after 1 October 2015[33] (other than statutory periodic tenancies) the prescribed form is now mandatory: see para 10.41.

10.13   There is no power in the court to dispense with service of a section 21 notice. A section 21 notice may be given by only one of two or more joint landlords.[34]

10.14   The ability of a landlord to recover possession, and the procedure to be used, depends on the kind or phase of tenancy involved – whether fixed-term or statutory periodic or contractual periodic. The following paragraphs consider each in turn.

During a fixed-term tenancy

10.15   If the assured shorthold tenancy is for a fixed term which has not yet expired, a landlord cannot rely on HA 1988 s21 (automatic right to possession on giving two months' notice) in order to claim possession, unless there is a contractual 'break clause' in the tenancy allowing the landlord to recover possession before the expiry of the term.[35] If there is such a break clause in an assured shorthold tenancy, which permits the landlord to terminate the tenancy on giving notice within the fixed term, service of a HA 1988 s21 notice may of itself be sufficient to activate the break clause.[36]

10.16   However, most of the usual grounds for possession against assured tenants set out in HA 1988 Sch 2 are available during the fixed term (see para 3.4). For a landlord to regain possession during a fixed-term tenancy on the basis of a ground for possession:

- the tenancy must contain a term allowing the landlord to re-enter or terminate the tenancy for breach of any condition in the tenancy

---

32 HA 1988 s21(1)(b) and s21(4)(a), as amended by HA 1996 s98.
33 And for all assured shorthold tenancies in existence on 1 October 2018: Deregulation Act 2015 s41(3).
34 HA 1988 s21(1)(b) and s21(4)(a).
35 *Gloucestershire HA v Phelps* May 2003 *Legal Action* 35, Gloucester County Court.
36 *Aylward v Fawaz* (1997) 29 HLR 408, (1996) *Times* 15 July, CA.

or where one of the grounds for possession against assured tenants exists;[37]

- the landlord must serve notice of proceedings for possession in accordance with HA 1988 s8 (see para 2.4); and
- the landlord must prove the existence of any of the following grounds for possession, namely, 2, 7A, 7B,[38] 8, 10, 11, 12, 13, 14, 14A, 15 or 17 (ie, essentially 'tenant's default' grounds), and, except in relation to grounds 2, 7, 7A and 8, prove that it is reasonable for an order to be made.[39]

10.17　The tenant cannot apply for relief from forfeiture. HA 1988 s5(1) sets out the only routes for bringing an assured tenancy to an end.[40] If the landlord is prepared to wait until the end of the fixed term to claim possession, he or she may rely on a section 21 notice served during the currency of the term (see para 10.21 below), subject to the various restrictions on the giving of a valid section 21 notice imposed by HA 2004 ss75 and 98 (licensing requirements), HA 2004 s215 (tenancy deposit protection) and the Deregulation Act 2015 ss33–41 (see paras 10.42–10.102).

At the end of a fixed-term tenancy or during a statutory periodic tenancy

10.18　A landlord may grant an assured shorthold tenancy for a fixed term, such as six or 12 months, but then allow the tenant to 'hold over' after the end of that period. In those circumstances, if the tenant continues to occupy the premises as his or her only or principal home, a *statutory periodic tenancy* arises, but it remains an assured shorthold tenancy and lacks security of tenure.

10.19　Where the tenancy is or has been a fixed-term tenancy, the landlord may rely on a notice under section 21(1). Section 21(1) requires a landlord who wishes to recover possession to:

- prove that any fixed-term tenancy has come to an end and that no new tenancy has been granted (other than a periodic tenancy, whether contractual or statutory);

37　HA 1988 s7(6)(b).
38　Not in force until the commencement of Immigration Act 2016 s41(2). See para 11.18.
39　HA 1988 s7(6)(a).
40　See para 2.32. See also *Artesian Residential Investments Ltd v Beck* [2000] QB 541, [2000] 2 WLR 357, CA.

- give at least two months' notice in writing to the tenant stating that the landlord requires possession; and
- take court proceedings.

Where an initial fixed-term tenancy (normally of 12 months' duration) has been granted as a 'starter tenancy' by a housing association or other private registered provider of social housing or registered social landlord, see paras 5.75–5.85 for potential defences which are particular to starter tenancies. Special rules apply where a tenancy was granted in England for a fixed term of two years or more by a housing association or other private registered provider of social housing: see para 10.25.

10.20 Under section 21(1), there is no need to specify a date, provided that the notice is two calendar months long.[41] A notice is not 'given' until it is received, and the period of two months therefore runs from the date of receipt. Landlords who send notices by post should therefore allow an adequate period for postal delivery.

10.21 Section 21(2) provides that a section 21(1) notice 'may be given before or on the day on which the tenancy comes to an end'. A landlord may therefore serve notice within the fixed term or at its expiry. The subsection does not in terms require that a valid notice should not expire earlier than the last day of the fixed term, and subsection (1)(b) provides only that two months' notice must be given. It is, however, arguable that a notice which expires within the fixed term is not a proper notice, even though proceedings are not started until after the end of the fixed term. Such a notice cannot have been intended to operate on the date on which it purports to require possession.

10.22 In *Spencer v Taylor*,[42] the Court of Appeal held that a section 21(1) notice may also be used where a tenancy has become a statutory periodic tenancy following the expiry of a fixed term, and that it was not necessary for the landlord to use the more complex notice provisions relating to periodic tenancies in section 21(4) (see para 10.26). The Court considered that the words of section 21(2) were permissive, not prescriptive. A landlord may therefore serve a notice

41 A 'month' means a calendar month (Interpretation Act 1978 Sch 1). This is defined in Halsbury's Laws, 3rd ed, vol 37 as follows: 'When the period prescribed is a *calendar month* running from any arbitrary date the period expires with the day in the succeeding month immediately preceding the day corresponding to the date upon which the period starts: save that, if the period starts at the end of a calendar month which contains more days than the next succeeding month, the period expires at the end of the latter month'.

42 [2013] EWCA Civ 1600, [2014] HLR 9.

requiring possession under section 21(1) during a statutory periodic
tenancy which has arisen at the end of a fixed-term tenancy.

10.23　　Some fixed-term tenancies provide for their own continuance as
periodic tenancies after the end of the fixed term, for example, where
the tenancy is expressed to be 'for a term of twelve months and thereafter from month to month'. Such tenancies continue as contractual
periodic tenancies at the expiry of the fixed term, and not as statutory
periodic tenancies. It is uncertain whether such continuation periodic tenancies may also be terminated following a notice under section
21(1) or whether they require a section 21(4) notice. The contractual
periodic tenancy which follows the fixed term is part and parcel of
the same tenancy and the original tenancy has not therefore 'come to
an end' within the meaning of section 21(1). On that basis, it is likely
that a section 21(4) notice would be necessary for such a tenancy in
its periodic phase. For tenancies which began after 1 October 2015,[43]
the point will be largely academic in view of the substantial align-
ment between section 21(1) and section 21(4) notices and the introduction of a prescribed form for section 21 notices (see para 10.41).

10.24　　Where, as a result of the service of a notice under section 21, the
tenancy is brought to an end before the end of a period of the tenancy, and the tenant has paid rent in advance for that period, and
the tenant was not in occupation for one or more whole days of that
period, the tenant is entitled to a proportionate repayment of rent
from the landlord.[44]

At the end of a housing association tenancy in England for a fixed term of at least two years

10.25　　An additional, and longer, form of notice is required where an assured
shorthold tenancy was granted for a fixed term of two years or more
by a housing association or other private registered provider of social
housing in England and that landlord seeks to rely on a section 21
notice to recover possession. In this case, section 21(1B)[45] requires
that, in addition to a notice requiring possession under section 21(1),
the landlord must also have given the tenant at least six months'
written notice (a) stating that it does not propose to renew the tenancy when the fixed term expires, and (b) informing the tenant how

43　And for all assured shorthold tenancies in existence on 1 October 2018: see
　　Deregulation Act 2015 s41(3).
44　Housing Act 1988 s21C, inserted by Deregulation Act 2015 s40. See para 10.54.
45　Inserted by Localism Act 2011 s164(1).

to obtain help or advice about the notice and, in particular, of any obligation of the landlord to provide help or advice. These requirements resemble the procedure for recovery of possession of flexible tenancies by local authorities under HA 1985 s107D[46] (see para 2.87), although there is no obligation for housing associations to state their reasons for non-renewal of the tenancy and the assured shorthold tenant has no right to a review of the decision to seek possession.[47] Tenants facing a claim for possession in these circumstances may in certain cases be able to raise a public law or human rights defence (see chapters 25 and 26).

During a contractual periodic tenancy

10.26   HA 1988 s21(4) deals with the kind of notice requiring possession which is necessary in relation to 'an assured shorthold tenancy which is a periodic tenancy'. Since the decision of the Court of Appeal in *Spencer v Taylor*,[48] it is no longer necessary for the landlord to use a section 21(4) notice where the tenancy is a *statutory* periodic tenancy (however long ago the fixed term may have ended). As a result, section 21(4) now applies only:

- where the tenancy originates as a contractual periodic tenancy; or
- where a tenancy provides for its own continuance as a periodic tenancy after the end of the fixed term; or
- where a landlord and tenant enter into a new agreement for a contractual periodic tenancy following the expiry of a fixed term.

This is one of the surprising outcomes of the decision in *Spencer v Taylor*, because between 15 January 1989 and 28 February 1997 (when it was a condition of an assured shorthold tenancy that it should be for a fixed term of at least six months) it was not possible for an assured shorthold tenancy to begin life as a contractual periodic tenancy.

10.27   A section 21(4) notice is therefore necessary where a tenancy commenced as a contractual periodic tenancy and has continued as

---

46   Inserted by Localism Act 2011 s154. Note that this procedure will be replaced, for flexible tenancies where the term ends nine months or more after the Housing and Planning Act (HPA) 2016 comes into force, by the procedure under new HA 1985 ss86A–86E, inserted by HPA 2016 Sch 7 para 10 (see para 2.80 onwards).

47   In contrast with the flexible tenant, who has such a right under HA 1985 s107E.

48   [2013] EWCA Civ 1600, [2014] HLR 9.

such. However, as a result of changes made by the Deregulation Act 2015, section 21(4) now operates in two different ways. The original, more complex section 21(4) still applies to tenancies in England which began before 1 October 2015.[49] This transitional provision in England lasts until 1 October 2018, when the modified section 21(4)[50] will thereafter apply to all assured shorthold tenancies in England which are in existence at that time. The application of the original form of section 21(4) to these 'older' tenancies will therefore be dealt with under the heading 'Contractual periodic tenancies in England granted before 1 October 2015 where notice is given before 1 October 2018'. The application of the modified section 21(4) will be dealt with under the heading 'Contractual periodic tenancies in England granted on or after 1 October 2015 and all other contractual periodic assured shorthold tenancies still in existence on 1 October 2018'. The end of the transitional period on 1 October 2018 has no application to Wales. In the meantime, however, housing law in Wales is expected to undergo radical change on commencement of the Renting Homes (Wales) Act 2016.[51]

Contractual periodic assured shorthold tenancies in England granted before 1 October 2015 where notice is given before 1 October 2018

10.28   In these cases,[52] the original form of notice under section 21(4), which is significantly more prescriptive than a section 21(1) notice or a notice under the modified section 21(4), must be used. This type of section 21(4) notice must comply with the following conditions.

10.29   *The notice must give at least two months' notice.*[53] No actual date need be specified, provided that 'the tenant knows or can easily ascertain the date referred to'. ('The word 'specified' ... means no more

---

49 Including statutory periodic tenancies which arose on or after 1 October 2015 on the expiry of a fixed-term tenancy which was granted before that date: Deregulation Act 2015 s41(2).

50 In accordance with new s21(4ZA), inserted by Deregulation Act 2015 s35 (see para 10.38).

51 See paras 10.103–10.104.

52 This class of tenancies also includes contractual periodic assured shorthold tenancies in Wales, whenever granted, pending commencement of the Renting Homes (Wales) Act 2016.

53 *Symons v Warren* [1995] CLW 33/95. See also *Mundy v Hook* (1998) 30 HLR 551, [1997] 3 CL 388.

than 'made clear'.'[54]) It is open to landlords to use a formula which produces the correct date: see para 10.33.

10.30   A section 21(4) notice should state that possession is required 'after', rather than 'on', the date in question. In *Notting Hill Housing Trust v Roomus*,[55] the Court of Appeal held that a section 21 notice which stated 'Possession is required (by virtue of section 21(4) of the Housing Act 1988) of [the property] which you hold as tenant at the end of the period of your tenancy which will end after expiry of two months from the service upon you of this notice' was valid because the phrase 'at the end of a tenancy' in this context meant the same as 'after the end of the tenancy' and so the notice complied with the requirements of section 21(4)(a).

10.31   *The date specified in the notice must be 'the last day of a period of the tenancy'*. In contrast with section 21(1)(b), which merely provides that the landlord must give the tenant 'not less than two months' notice stating that he requires possession of the dwelling-house', section 21(4)(a) in its application to 'older' tenancies provides that the date specified in a notice relating to 'a periodic tenancy' shall be 'the last day of a period of the tenancy'.

10.32   This requirement under section 21(4) is illustrated by the decision in *Fernandez v McDonald*,[56] in which tenants occupied under a periodic tenancy from the 4th of each month to the 3rd of the following month.[57] On 24 October 2002, the landlord gave them a notice stating 'I give you notice that I require possession of the dwelling house known as ... on 4th January 2003'. The Court of Appeal held that the notice did not comply with section 21(4)(a) and was defective: its expiry date should have been the last day of a period of the tenancy, ie the 3rd of the month.[58]

10.33   In order to avoid the pitfalls of specifying the wrong date in a section 21(4) notice, landlords may serve notices containing a rider which provides that the notice may expire on a date produced by a

---

54   *Lower Street Properties Ltd v Jones* [1996] 48 EG 154, (1996) 28 HLR 877, CA.

55   [2006] EWCA Civ 407, [2006] 1 WLR 1375. See too *Elias v Spencer* [2010] EWCA Civ 246.

56   [2003] EWCA Civ 1219, [2004] 1 WLR 1027.

57   The tenancy was in fact a statutory periodic tenancy, which had arisen at the end of a fixed-term tenancy. Before the decision in *Spencer v Taylor* [2013] EWCA Civ 1600, (2014) HLR 9 it was generally accepted that a section 21(4) notice was required in respect of a statutory periodic tenancy.

58   See too *Gracechurch International SA v Tribhovan and Abdul* (2001) 33 HLR 28, CA.

formula or 'saving clause'. In *Spencer v Taylor*,[59] the notice gave an incorrect expiry date followed by a saving clause in the alternative.[60] Such saving clauses have been upheld,[61] in spite of the confusion caused to tenants, who may be presented with two different dates after which possession is required.

10.34 The last day of a period of the tenancy will usually be the day before rent is due, but this is not necessarily the case because the period of the tenancy does not always run from the rent day.[62] A tenancy may provide for payment of rent on a day which is not the first day of a period. In *Salford CC v Garner*,[63] Chadwick LJ said:

> There is ... no conceptual difficulty in an obligation which requires a tenant to pay, on the Monday, rent for a period of seven days which commenced on the previous Friday. When the rent is paid is simply a matter of accounting convenience for the landlord.

10.35 *The date specified 'is not earlier than the earliest day on which ... the tenancy could be brought to an end by a notice to quit given by the landlord on the same date as the notice ...'* (section 21(4)(b)). Accordingly, more than two months' notice is required where there is an express provision requiring a longer period of notice or the rental period is longer than two months; for example, where there is a quarterly tenancy, three months' notice must be given.

10.36 *The section 21(4) notice must include reference to section 21 itself.* Section 21(4) provides that the court must be 'satisfied ... that the landlord ... has given ... notice ... stating that ... possession ... is required *by virtue of this section*' (emphasis added). A district judge, dismissing a possession claim, has held that a notice which failed to do this was defective.[64]

10.37 *Proceedings have not been commenced before the date specified in the notice.* The claim for possession in *Lower Street Properties Ltd v Jones*[65] was dismissed because proceedings were started the day before the section 21 notice expired. Schiemann LJ stated that it 'is implicit that

59 [2013] EWCA Civ 1600, [2014] HLR 9.
60 The saving clause stipulated that possession was required 'at the end of your period of tenancy which will end next after the expiration of two months from the service upon you of this notice'.
61 See also *Bradford Community Housing Ltd v Hussain* [2009] EWCA Civ 763, [2010] HLR 16.
62 See, eg, *Baynes v Hall and Thorpe* November 2005 *Legal Action* 21, 29 June 2005, Dewsbury County Court.
63 [2004] EWCA Civ 364, [2004] HLR 35.
64 *Adamson v Mather* November 2004 *Legal Action* 25, Harrogate County Court.
65 (1996) 28 HLR 877, [1996] 2 EGLR 67.

the landlord cannot bring proceedings until after [the date specified in the notice]', although Kennedy LJ reached his decision on the ground that the notice served stated that the 'landlord cannot apply for such an order before the notice has run out', and left open whether, with a different wording, proceedings could have been begun before expiry. It would, however, be surprising if it were open to a landlord to commence proceedings prematurely, before the notice has run its course, since at the date of issue of proceedings the landlord could not claim to be entitled to possession.

Contractual periodic assured shorthold tenancies in England granted on or after 1 October 2015 and all other contractual periodic assured shorthold tenancies still in existence on 1 October 2018

10.38   In respect of these tenancies, HA 1988 s21(4ZA)[66] has the effect of simplifying the section 21(4) process. Section 21(4ZA) provides:

> In the case of a dwelling-house in England, subsection (4)(a) above has effect with the omission of the requirement for the date specified in the notice to be the last day of a period of the tenancy.

10.39   A section 21(4) notice given in respect of these tenancies therefore need not specify a date which is the last day of a period of the tenancy. It is sufficient for the notice to be two calendar months in duration, the same length as a section 21(1)(b) notice, unless the periods of the tenancy are longer than one month, eg in the case of a quarterly tenancy, since the date specified must not be earlier than the earliest day on which a notice to quit could expire. In relation to a quarterly, six-monthly or yearly tenancy, subject to a contrary provision in the agreement, the length of the notice must still therefore be a full period of the tenancy (except that in the case of a yearly tenancy, the notice period is six months) ending on the first or last day of a period of the tenancy.

10.40   Strictly, there are still minor differences between the modified section 21(4) notice and the still simpler notice under section 21(1)(b). Under the modified section 21(4), the notice must still 'specify' a particular date 'after' which possession is required. The notice must state that possession of the dwelling-house is required by virtue of section 21. But these discrepancies are academic, since for tenancies

66   Inserted by Deregulation Act 2015 s35.

beginning on or after 1 October 2015[67] (and for all tenancies in existence on 1 October 2018) it is now mandatory to use a prescribed form of notice. The prescribed form (see para 10.41) has been drafted in such a way as to satisfy the requirements of both subsection (1) and subsection (4), and can be used for either.

Section 21 notices to be in a prescribed form (England)

10.41 HA 1988 s21(8), inserted by Deregulation Act 2015 s37, makes provision for the Secretary of State to prescribe the form of a notice under subsection (1) or (4) in relation to an assured shorthold tenancy in England. Section 21(8) does not apply to Wales. The form of notice has been prescribed by the Assured Shorthold Tenancy Notices and Prescribed Requirements (England) (Amendment) Regulations 2015.[68] The notice is listed as Form 6A in the Schedule to the Assured Tenancies and Agricultural Occupancies (Forms) (England) Regulations 2015.[69] Use of the prescribed form is mandatory for all assured shorthold tenancies (other than statutory periodic tenancies) beginning on or after 1 October 2015, and for all tenancies (irrespective of start date) which are in existence on 1 October 2018.[70] See appendix A for a copy of the prescribed form.

Restrictions on the use of section 21 notices (England)

10.42 If the tenancy is one to which HA 1988 s19A applies (ie, it was granted after 28 February 1997 and none of the exceptions in HA 1988 Sch 2A applies), then any possession order granted on the basis of a section 21 notice may not take effect earlier than six months after the grant of the original tenancy.[71] In the case of a replacement tenancy, the order may not take effect earlier than six months after the beginning of the original tenancy. A replacement tenancy is a tenancy which comes into being on the coming to an end of an earlier

67 Other than statutory periodic tenancies which arose on or after 1 October 2015 on the expiry of a fixed-term tenancy which was granted before that date: Deregulation Act 2015 s41(2).
68 SI No 1725. Note that the form of notice set out in the Schedule to these Regulations replaces an earlier, incorrect notice which was annexed to the original Assured Shorthold Tenancy Notices and Prescribed Requirements (England) Regulations 2015 SI No 1646.
69 SI No 620.
70 Deregulation Act 2015 s41(3).
71 HA 1988 s21(5), inserted by HA 1996 s99.

assured shorthold tenancy, where the landlord and tenant are the same as under the earlier tenancy, and the premises let are the same or substantially the same as those let under the earlier tenancy.[72]

10.43   Landlords are also prohibited from relying on section 21 notices in certain situations. In relation to tenancies in England which began on or after 1 October 2015,[73] section 21(4B)[74] provides that a section 21 notice cannot be given within the period of four months from the date when the tenancy began. However, this restriction applies only to the original tenancy, not to a replacement tenancy[75] or to a statutory periodic tenancy.[76]

10.44   For tenancies in England which began before 1 October 2015, however, there is nothing to prevent a section 21 notice from being given during the first four months of a tenancy, subject to the landlord having complied with the rules for protection of tenants' deposits and in relation to statutory licensing, where relevant: see paras 10.56–10.102.

10.45   Until the Deregulation Act 2015, there was no rule that a section 21 notice would lapse or cease to have effect if proceedings were not issued within a certain period after service of the notice. However, in relation to tenancies in England which began on or after 1 October 2015,[77] and also in relation to all assured shorthold tenancies in existence on 1 October 2018,[78] section 21(4D)[79] provides that section 21 notices will only be effective for a period of six months after the notice was *given* (not from the date when it takes effect). The purpose of this provision is to ensure that landlords resort to a section 21 notice only when they genuinely want possession, and that tenants should not have to live with the uncertainty created by a notice which the landlord may not intend to act on for a considerable time.

72 HA 1988 s21(7).

73 Other than statutory periodic tenancies which arose on or after 1 October 2015 on the expiry of a fixed-term tenancy which was granted before that date: Deregulation Act 2015 s41(2).

74 Inserted by Deregulation Act 2015 s36(2).

75 As defined in s21(7): see para 10.42 above. Note, however, that if the original tenancy was for less than four months, the four-month moratorium on giving a section 21 notice runs from the start of the original tenancy.

76 See s21(4C), inserted by Deregulation Act 2015 s36(2).

77 Other than statutory periodic tenancies which arose on or after 1 October 2015 on the expiry of a fixed-term tenancy which was granted before that date: Deregulation Act 2015 s41(2).

78 Deregulation Act 2015 s41(3).

79 Inserted by Deregulation Act 2015 s36(2).

10.46 Section 21(4E) applies where a section 21(4) notice is given and the tenancy is, for example, a two-monthly, three-monthly or six-monthly contractual periodic tenancy. Since the date specified in a section 21(4) notice must not be before the earliest day on which a notice to quit given by the landlord could take effect, the duration of the notice will be longer in those cases than the standard two calendar months. In such cases, the landlord will be able to rely on the notice for a period of four months from the date specified in the notice.

10.47 Where the tenancy began before 1 October 2015, there is no such limit on the 'life' of a section 21 notice, no matter how long ago it was given. However, this transitional position lasts only until 1 October 2018, whereupon, if the same tenancy is still in existence on that date, the six months' limit specified in section 21(4D) or (less commonly) the longer period under section 21(4E) will apply to any section 21 notice given in respect of that tenancy.[80]

Compliance with prescribed legal requirements

10.48 In relation to assured shorthold tenancies which began on or after 1 October 2015,[81] and also in relation to all such tenancies which are in existence on 1 October 2018,[82] HA 1988 s21A[83] provides that a notice under section 21(1) or section 21(4) may not be given in England at a time when the landlord is in breach of a 'prescribed requirement'. Under section 21A, the prescribed requirements will be statutory obligations imposed on landlords which relate to:

(a) the condition of dwelling-houses or their common parts,
(b) the health and safety of occupiers of dwelling-houses, or
(c) the energy performance of dwelling-houses.[84]

Section 21A does not apply to Wales.

10.49 The current prescribed requirements are specified in the Assured Shorthold Tenancy Notices and Prescribed Requirements (England) Regulations 2015.[85] The first is to provide tenants with a copy of the

---

80 Deregulation Act 2015 s41(3). It would appear that the time limit will operate whether the section 21 notice is given before or after 1 October 2018.

81 Other than statutory periodic tenancies which arose on or after 1 October 2015 on the expiry of a fixed-term tenancy which was granted before that date: Deregulation Act 2015 s41(2).

82 Deregulation Act 2015 s41(3).

83 Inserted by Deregulation Act 2015 s38.

84 Housing Act 1988 s21A(2).

85 SI No 1646.

gas safety record in accordance with regulation 36(6) of the Gas Safety (Installation and Use) Regulations 1998.[86] The second requirement is to provide an energy performance certificate in accordance with regulation 6(5) of the Energy Performance of Buildings (England and Wales) Regulations 2012.[87] The failure to provide a gas safety certificate and an energy performance certificate at the time a section 21 notice is given will therefore constitute a defence to any proceedings based on that notice.

10.50   Regulation 36(6) of the Gas Safety (Installation and Use) Regulations 1998 requires the landlord to give:

(a) a copy of the gas safety record to each existing tenant of premises to which the record relates within 28 days of the date of the gas safety check; and

(b) a copy of the last gas safety record made in respect of each appliance or flue to any new tenant of the premises before that tenant occupies those premises.

In relation to (a) above, regulation 2(2) of the Assured Shorthold Tenancy Notices and Prescribed Requirements (England) Regulations 2015 provides:

> For the purpose of section 21A of the Act, the requirement prescribed by paragraph (1)(b) [ie, compliance with the Gas Safety Regulations] is limited to the requirement on a landlord to give a copy of the relevant record to the tenant and the 28-day period for compliance with that requirement does not apply.

The 28-day requirement for giving a copy of the latest gas safety certificate to an existing tenant is therefore disapplied. The landlord will only need to give the gas safety certificate to the tenant at any time after the check and then proceed, if he wishes, to serve a section 21 notice. It is uncertain whether regulation 36(6)(b) (latest gas safety record to be given to any new tenant before he or she occupies) is also intended to be part of the prescribed requirement. If the latest gas safety certificate was not in fact given to the tenant before he or she occupied, this is a breach which cannot be rectified later. However, the regulation as drafted appears to apply to both limbs of regulation 36(6), although this may not have been the legislative intention.

---

86 SI No 2451.
87 SI No 3118.

Requirement for landlord to provide prescribed information

10.51 In relation to assured shorthold tenancies which began on or after 1 October 2015,[88] HA 1988 s21B, inserted by Deregulation Act 2015 s39, provides that regulations may require landlords and their agents to give certain prescribed information about the rights and responsibilities of the landlord and tenant under an assured shorthold tenancy to the tenant under such a tenancy. Section 21B applies only in England. Regulation 3 of the Assured Shorthold Tenancy Notices and Prescribed Requirements (England) Regulations 2015[89] provides that the specific requirement in section 21B is to provide tenants with a copy of the Department for Communities and Local Government booklet *'How to rent: the checklist for renting in England'*.[90]

10.52 The prescribed information may be provided to the tenant in hard copy, or by email where the tenant has notified the landlord or agent of an email address at which he or she is content to accept service of notices and other documents. A landlord who has provided the tenant with the prescribed document is not required to supply a further copy of the document each time a different version of that document is published during the tenancy. This requirement does not apply where the landlord is a housing association or other private registered provider of social housing. Nor does it apply where the tenancy is a replacement tenancy and the landlord provided the tenant with the document under an earlier tenancy, provided that the version of the document provided to the tenant under the earlier tenancy is the same version which is in effect on the first day of the new tenancy.[91]

10.53 This requirement applies *only* to assured shorthold tenancies which began on or after 1 October 2015 (other than statutory periodic tenancies where the fixed term began before that date). It will not apply to any earlier tenancies, even after 1 October 2018.[92]

Repayment of rent where tenancy ends before the end of a period

10.54 HA 1988 s21C, inserted by Deregulation Act 2015 s40, provides that where:

---

88 Other than statutory periodic tenancies which arose on or after 1 October 2015 on the expiry of a fixed-term tenancy which was granted before that date: Deregulation Act 2015 s41(2).

89 SI No 1646.

90 Obtainable at: www.gov.uk.

91 Assured Shorthold Tenancy Notices and Prescribed Requirements (England) Regulations 2015 reg 3(5).

92 Deregulation Act 2015 s41.

- as a result of the service of a section 21 notice a tenancy in England is brought to an end in the middle of a period of the tenancy; and
- the tenant has paid rent in advance for that final period; and
- the tenant was not in occupation of the property at any time during that period,

the tenant is entitled to a proportionate refund of rent from the landlord. If a repayment of rent is due under this provision, and has not been made when the court makes an order for possession under section 21, the court must order the landlord to repay the amount of rent to which the tenant is entitled.

Other restrictions on section 21 notices

10.55   Statute has created restrictions on the giving of section 21 notices in three other scenarios:

1) where the property is required by the HA 2004 to be licensed and is not licensed;
2) where the landlord is in breach of the provisions in the HA 2004 (as amended) relating to the protection of tenancy deposits; and
3) where the section 21 notice is given in retaliation for a complaint made by the tenant and/or in response to local authority action in relation to the defective condition of the property.

Each of these scenarios gives rise to a potential defence to a claim for possession. They will be examined in turn.

Section 21 notices and premises subject to licensing requirements

10.56   HA 2004 ss75 and 98 prevent section 21 notices being valid where a house in multiple occupation (HMO) which is subject to mandatory or additional licensing (section 75) or a property which is subject to selective licensing (section 98), is not licensed. Licensing of HMOs is dealt with in Part 2 of the 2004 Act, while selective licensing of other residential accommodation is dealt with in Part 3 of that Act. The failure to license a property where required to do so will provide the tenant with a complete defence to a claim for possession based on a section 21 notice.

10.57   In relation to HMOs subject to mandatory[93] and additional licensing, HA 2004 section 75(1) provides that 'No section 21 notice may be given in relation to a shorthold tenancy of a part of an unlicensed HMO so long as it remains such an HMO.' An 'unlicensed HMO' is defined in HA 2004 s73 in the following terms:

(1) For the purposes of this section an HMO is an 'unlicensed HMO' if –
    (a) it is required to be licensed under this Part but is not so licensed, and
    (b) neither of the conditions in subsection (2) is satisfied.
(2) The conditions are –
    (a) that a notification has been duly given in respect of the HMO under section 62(1) and that notification is still effective (as defined by section 72(8));
    (b) that an application for a licence has been duly made in respect of the HMO under section 63 and that application is still effective (as so defined).

10.58   The conditions in subsection (2) above apply where:

- the 'person having control' or manager of the HMO 'notifies the local housing authority of his intention to take particular steps with a view to securing that the house is no longer required to be licensed' and the authority issues a temporary exemption notice (HA 2004 s62(1)); and
- a valid application for a licence has been made to the authority (HA 2004 s63).

Any such notification or application must be 'effective', which it will be if it has not been withdrawn and other conditions set out in HA 2004 s72(8) are satisfied. A landlord can therefore escape the HA 2004 s75 prohibition on giving a section 21 notice if he or she has applied for a licence at the time the notice is given. A subsequent application for a licence will not, however, validate a section 21 notice which has already been given.

10.59   Similarly, where a selective licensing scheme is in force,[94] HA 2004 s98(1) provides that 'No section 21 notice may be given in relation to a shorthold tenancy of the whole or part of an unlicensed

---

93 For HMOs subject to mandatory licensing, see HA 2004 s59, together with the Licensing of Houses in Multiple Occupation (Prescribed Descriptions) (England) Order 2006 SI No 371 and the Licensing of Houses in Multiple Occupation (Prescribed Descriptions) (Wales) Order 2006 SI No 1712.
94 For the designation of selective licensing areas, see HA 2004 s80.

house so long as it remains such a house.' An 'unlicensed house' is defined in HA 2004 s96 in the following terms:

(1) For the purposes of this section a house is an 'unlicensed house' if –
   (a) it is required to be licensed under this Part but is not so licensed, and
   (b) neither of the conditions in subsection (2) is satisfied.
(2) The conditions are –
   (a) that a notification has been duly given in respect of the house under section 62(1) or 86(1) and that notification is still effective (as defined by section 95(7));
   (b) that an application for a licence has been duly made in respect of the house under section 87 and that application is still effective (as so defined).

10.60   Where a selective licensing regime is in force, a landlord is not subject to the prohibition on giving a section 21 notice imposed by HA 2004 s98 where:

- the 'person having control' or manager of the property 'notifies the local housing authority of his intention to take particular steps with a view to securing that the house is no longer required to be licensed' and the authority issues a temporary exemption notice under either HA 2004 s62(1) (relating to the mandatory or additional licensing of HMOs) or HA 2004 s86(1) (relating to the selective licensing scheme); or
- a valid application for a licence has been made to the authority under HA 2004 s87.

Any such notification or application must be 'effective', which it will be if it has not been withdrawn and other conditions set out in HA 2004 s95(7) are satisfied. A landlord can therefore escape the HA 2004 s98 prohibition on giving a section 21 notice if he or she has applied for a relevant licence under HA 2004 s87 at the time the notice is given. A subsequent application for a licence will not, however, validate a section 21 notice which has already been given.

Section 21 notices and tenancy deposits

10.61   HA 2004 ss212–215, which came into force on 6 April 2007, introduced a framework for the protection of tenants' deposits. The Act places an obligation on a landlord or agent who receives a tenancy deposit which has been paid in connection with an assured shorthold tenancy to protect that deposit in one of the authorised deposit protection schemes. HA 2004 s212 provides for the establishment of tenancy deposit schemes which 'are available for the purpose of safeguarding tenancy deposits paid in connection with shorthold tenancies'.[95] The dual purpose of such schemes is both to safeguard tenancy deposits and to facilitate the resolution of disputes arising in connection with such deposits. There are two kinds of tenancy deposit scheme: a custodial scheme, which holds the deposit money itself during the tenancy; and an insurance scheme, under which the landlord retains the deposit money and pays a fee or premium to the scheme to ensure the deposit is protected.[96]

10.62 A 'tenancy deposit' is defined as 'any money intended to be held (by the landlord or otherwise) as security for (a) the performance of any obligations of the tenant, or (b) the discharge of any liability of his, arising under or in connection with the tenancy'.[97]

10.63 In *Johnson v Old*,[98] the parties entered into an assured shorthold tenancy for a fixed term of six months, at a monthly rent of £1,000. The landlord required that the total rent for the fixed term should be payable in advance in one payment of £6,000. The tenant contended that the sum of £6,000 was a deposit which the landlord had failed to protect as required by the 2004 Act and that a HA 1988 s21 notice was accordingly invalid under HA 2004 s215 (see para 10.73). The Court of Appeal held that on the facts, the money was clearly paid as advance rent and not as a deposit: it was not security for the performance of any obligation or for the discharge of any liability.

10.64 However, the description of any payment as 'rent in advance' is not necessarily to be taken at face value. If rent is genuinely payable in advance, then the landlord should not expect any further payment until that sum is exhausted. If, for example, a landlord takes three months' rent in advance at the start of a tenancy, he or she should not demand a further payment of rent until the fourth month. If rent is demanded for the second month, then the remainder of the initial payment is being held as security and is therefore a tenancy deposit.

10.65 HA 2004 s212(9)(a) provides that 'references to a landlord or landlords in relation to any shorthold tenancy or tenancies include references to a person or persons acting on his or their behalf in relation to the tenancy or tenancies'. The obligations and liabilities created by the Act are therefore imposed on a landlord's agent who deals with

95 HA 2004 s212(1).
96 The procedures for protection of deposits are set out in HA 2004 Sch 10 and in the Housing (Tenancy Deposit Schemes) Order 2007 SI No 796.
97 HA 2004 s212(8).
98 [2013] EWCA Civ 415.

tenancy deposits just as much as they are imposed on the landlord personally.

10.66   HA 2004 ss212–215C provide as follows:

Tenancy deposit schemes

212(1) The appropriate national authority must make arrangements for securing that one or more tenancy deposit schemes are available for the purpose of safeguarding tenancy deposits paid in connection with shorthold tenancies.

(2) For the purposes of this Chapter a 'tenancy deposit scheme' is a scheme which –

(a) is made for the purpose of safeguarding tenancy deposits paid in connection with shorthold tenancies and facilitating the resolution of disputes arising in connection with such deposits, and

(b) complies with the requirements of Schedule 10.

(3) Arrangements under subsection (1) must be arrangements made with any body or person under which the body or person ('the scheme administrator') undertakes to establish and maintain a tenancy deposit scheme of a description specified in the arrangements.

(4) The appropriate national authority may –

(a) give financial assistance to the scheme administrator;

(b) make payments to the scheme administrator (otherwise than as financial assistance) in pursuance of arrangements under subsection (1).

(5) The appropriate national authority may, in such manner and on such terms as it thinks fit, guarantee the discharge of any financial obligation incurred by the scheme administrator in connection with arrangements under subsection (1).

(6) Arrangements under subsection (1) must require the scheme administrator to give the appropriate national authority, in such manner and at such times as it may specify, such information and facilities for obtaining information as it may specify.

(7) The appropriate national authority may make regulations conferring or imposing –

(a) on scheme administrators, or

(b) on scheme administrators of any description specified in the regulations,

such powers or duties in connection with arrangements under subsection (1) as are so specified.

(8) In this Chapter –

'authorised', in relation to a tenancy deposit scheme, means that the scheme is in force in accordance with arrangements under subsection (1);

'custodial scheme' and 'insurance scheme' have the meaning given by paragraph 1(2) and (3) of Schedule 10);

'money' means money in the form of cash or otherwise;

'shorthold tenancy' means an assured shorthold tenancy within the meaning of Chapter 2 of Part 1 of the Housing Act 1988;

'tenancy deposit', in relation to a shorthold tenancy, means any money intended to be held (by the landlord or otherwise) as security for –

(a) the performance of any obligations of the tenant, or

(b) the discharge of any liability of his,

arising under or in connection with the tenancy.

(9) In this Chapter –

(a) references to a landlord or landlords in relation to any shorthold tenancy or tenancies include references to a person or persons acting on his or their behalf in relation to the tenancy or tenancies, and

(b) references to a tenancy deposit being held in accordance with a scheme include, in the case of a custodial scheme, references to an amount representing the deposit being held in accordance with the scheme.

Requirements relating to tenancy deposits

213(1) Any tenancy deposit paid to a person in connection with a shorthold tenancy must, as from the time when it is received, be dealt with in accordance with an authorised scheme.

(2) No person may require the payment of a tenancy deposit in connection with a shorthold tenancy which is not to be subject to the requirement in subsection (1).

(3) Where a landlord receives a tenancy deposit in connection with a shorthold tenancy, the initial requirements of an authorised scheme must be complied with by the landlord in relation to the deposit within the period of 30 days beginning with the date on which it is received.

(4) For the purposes of this section 'the initial requirements' of an authorised scheme are such requirements imposed by the scheme as fall to be complied with by a landlord on receiving such a tenancy deposit.

(5) A landlord who has received such a tenancy deposit must give the tenant and any relevant person such information relating to –

(a) the authorised scheme applying to the deposit,

(b) compliance by the landlord with the initial requirements of the scheme in relation to the deposit, and

(c) the operation of provisions of this Chapter in relation to the deposit,

as may be prescribed.

(6) The information required by subsection (5) must be given to the tenant and any relevant person –

(a) in the prescribed form or in a form substantially to the same effect, and

    (b) within the period of 30 days beginning with the date on which the deposit is received by the landlord.

  (7) No person may, in connection with a shorthold tenancy, require a deposit which consists of property other than money.

  (8) In subsection (7) 'deposit' means a transfer of property intended to be held (by the landlord or otherwise) as security for –

    (a) the performance of any obligations of the tenant, or

    (b) the discharge of any liability of his,

arising under or in connection with the tenancy.

  (9) The provisions of this section apply despite any agreement to the contrary.

 (10) In this section –

'prescribed' means prescribed by an order made by the appropriate national authority;

'property' means moveable property;

'relevant person' means any person who, in accordance with arrangements made with the tenant, paid the deposit on behalf of the tenant.

Proceedings relating to tenancy deposits

214(1) Where a tenancy deposit has been paid in connection with a shorthold tenancy on or after 6 April 2007, the tenant or any relevant person (as defined by section 213(10)) may make an application to the county court on the grounds –

    (a) that section 213(3) or (6) has not been complied with in relation to the deposit, or

    (b) that he has been notified by the landlord that a particular authorised scheme applies to the deposit but has been unable to obtain confirmation from the scheme administrator that the deposit is being held in accordance with the scheme.

 (1A) Subsection (1) also applies in a case where the tenancy has ended, and in such a case the reference in subsection (1) to the tenant is to a person who was a tenant under the tenancy.

  (2) Subsections (3) and (4) apply in the case of an application under subsection (1) if the tenancy has not ended and the court –

    (a) is satisfied that section 213(3) or (6) has not been complied with in relation to the deposit, or

    (b) is not satisfied that the deposit is being held in accordance with an authorised scheme, as the case may be.

 (2A) Subsections (3A) and (4) apply in the case of an application under subsection (1) if the tenancy has ended (whether before or after the making of the application) and the court –

    (a) is satisfied that section 213(3) or (6) has not been complied with in relation to the deposit, or

    (b) is not satisfied that the deposit is being held in accordance with an authorised scheme, as the case may be.

  (3) The court must, as it thinks fit, either –

     (a) order the person who appears to the court to be holding the deposit to repay it to the applicant, or

     (b) order that person to pay the deposit into the designated account held by the scheme administrator under an authorised custodial scheme,

    within the period of 14 days beginning with the date of the making of the order.

(3A) The court may order the person who appears to the court to be holding the deposit to repay all or part of it to the applicant within the period of 14 days beginning with the date of the making of the order.

  (4) The court must order the landlord to pay to the applicant a sum of money not less than the amount of the deposit and not more than three times the amount of the deposit within the period of 14 days beginning with the date of the making of the order.

  (5) Where any deposit given in connection with a shorthold tenancy could not be lawfully required as a result of section 213(7), the property in question is recoverable from the person holding it by the person by whom it was given as a deposit.

  (6) In subsection (5) 'deposit' has the meaning given by section 213(8).

Sanctions for non-compliance

215(1) Subject to subsection (2A), if (whether before, on or after 6 April 2007) a tenancy deposit has been paid in connection with a shorthold tenancy, no section 21 notice may be given in relation to the tenancy at a time when the deposit is not being held in accordance with an authorised scheme.

  (1A) Subject to subsection (2A), if a tenancy deposit has been paid in connection with a shorthold tenancy on or after 6 April 2007, no section 21 notice may be given in relation to the tenancy at a time when section 213(3) has not been complied with in relation to the deposit.

  (2) Subject to subsection (2A), if section 213(6) is not complied with in relation to a deposit given in connection with a shorthold tenancy, no section 21 notice may be given in relation to the tenancy until such time as section 213(6)(a) is complied with.

  (2A) Subsections (1), (1A) and (2) do not apply in a case where –

     (a) the deposit has been returned to the tenant in full or with such deductions as are agreed between the landlord and tenant, or

     (b) an application to the county court has been made under section 214(1) and has been determined by the court, withdrawn or settled by agreement between the parties.

  (3) If any deposit given in connection with a shorthold tenancy could not be lawfully required as a result of section 213(7), no section 21 notice may be given in relation to the tenancy until such time as the property in question is returned to the person by whom it was given as a deposit.

(4) In subsection (3) 'deposit' has the meaning given by section 213(8).

(5) In this section a 'section 21 notice' means a notice under section 21(1)(b) or (4)(a) of the Housing Act 1988 (recovery of possession on termination of shorthold tenancy).

Statutory periodic tenancies: deposit received before 6 April 2007

215A(1) This section applies where –

  (a) before 6 April 2007, a tenancy deposit has been received by a landlord in connection with a fixed term shorthold tenancy,

  (b) on or after that date, a periodic shorthold tenancy is deemed to arise under section 5 of the Housing Act 1988 on the coming to an end of the fixed-term tenancy,

  (c) on the coming to an end of the fixed-term tenancy, all or part of the deposit paid in connection with the fixed-term tenancy is held in connection with the periodic tenancy, and

  (d) the requirements of section 213(3), (5) and (6) have not been complied with by the landlord in relation to the deposit held in connection with the periodic tenancy.

(2) If, on the commencement date –

  (a) the periodic tenancy is in existence, and

  (b) all or part of the deposit paid in connection with the fixed-term tenancy continues to be held in connection with the periodic tenancy,

section 213 applies in respect of the deposit that continues to be held in connection with the periodic tenancy, and any additional deposit held in connection with that tenancy, with the modifications set out in subsection (3).

(3) The modifications are that, instead of the things referred to in section 213(3) and (5) being required to be done within the time periods set out in section 213(3) and (6)(b), those things are required to be done –

  (a) before the end of the period of 90 days beginning with the commencement date, or

  (b) (if earlier) before the first day after the commencement date on which a court does any of the following in respect of the periodic tenancy –

    (i) determines an application under section 214 or decides an appeal against a determination under that section;

    (ii) makes a determination as to whether to make an order for possession in proceedings under section 21 of the Housing Act 1988 or decides an appeal against such a determination.

(4) If, on the commencement date –

  (a) the periodic tenancy is no longer in existence, or

  (b) no deposit continues to be held in connection with the periodic tenancy, the requirements of section 213(3), (5) and (6) are treated as if they had been complied with by the landlord in relation to any deposit that was held in connection with the periodic tenancy.

(5) In this section 'the commencement date' means the date on which the Deregulation Act 2015 is passed.

Shorthold tenancies: deposit received on or after 6 April 2007

215B(1) This section applies where –

   (a) on or after 6 April 2007, a tenancy deposit has been received by a landlord in connection with a shorthold tenancy ('the original tenancy'),

   (b) the initial requirements of an authorised scheme have been complied with by the landlord in relation to the deposit (ignoring any requirement to take particular steps within any specified period),

   (c) the requirements of section 213(5) and (6)(a) have been complied with by the landlord in relation to the deposit when it is held in connection with the original tenancy (ignoring any deemed compliance under section 215A(4)),

   (d) a new shorthold tenancy comes into being on the coming to an end of the original tenancy or a tenancy that replaces the original tenancy (directly or indirectly),

   (e) the new tenancy replaces the original tenancy (directly or indirectly), and

   (f) when the new tenancy comes into being, the deposit continues to be held in connection with the new tenancy, in accordance with the same authorised scheme as when the requirements of section 213(5) and (6)(a) were last complied with by the landlord in relation to the deposit.

(2) In their application to the new tenancy, the requirements of section 213(3), (5) and (6) are treated as if they had been complied with by the landlord in relation to the deposit.

(3) The condition in subsection (1)(a) may be met in respect of a tenancy even if the tenancy deposit was first received in connection with an earlier tenancy (including where it was first received before 6 April 2007).

(4) For the purposes of this section, a tenancy replaces an earlier tenancy if –

   (a) the landlord and tenant immediately before the coming to an end of the earlier tenancy are the same as the landlord and tenant at the start of the new tenancy, and

   (b) the premises let under both tenancies are the same or substantially the same.

Sections 215A and 215B: transitional provisions

215C(1) Sections 215A and 215B are treated as having had effect since 6 April 2007, subject to the following provisions of this section ...

[*Section 215C(2)–(8) are not set out here, as they relate only to claims settled or proceedings brought before the commencement date, which was 26 March 2015.*]

10.67   In summary, a landlord or agent who receives a tenancy deposit in connection with an assured shorthold tenancy must:

- comply with the 'initial requirements' of an authorised scheme within 30 days of receiving it;[99] and
- give the tenant and any 'relevant person' the prescribed information relating to the scheme and its operation within the same period of 30 days.[100] A 'relevant person' is 'any person who, in accordance with arrangements made with the tenant, paid the deposit on behalf of the tenant'.[101]

10.68   No specific form has been prescribed for the information required to be given to the tenant, despite the reference to a prescribed form in section 213(6)(a). However, the content of the prescribed information is set out in detail in the Housing (Tenancy Deposits) (Prescribed Information) Order 2007,[102] as amended by the Deregulation Act 2015 s30. In *Ayannuga v Swindells*,[103] the Court of Appeal stated that it was clear that the requirements of the Order were of real importance to a tenant, as they defined the circumstances in which tenants could recover their deposits and the means by which disputes regarding deposits could be resolved. The Court rejected the landlord's argument that certain items in the list of information required were procedural matters only, the absence of which did not put the tenant at a substantial disadvantage. Those provisions were not to be regarded as mere matters of procedure or of subsidiary importance.

10.69   Likewise, in *Suurpere v Nice*[104] the Court observed that the list of particulars in the Prescribed Information Order was detailed and specific. The requirement for landlords to provide such detailed information, together with the sanction for non-compliance, demonstrated the importance attached to the giving of information which would enable tenants to understand how the scheme worked and how they should seek the return of their deposit. The requirement that the landlord should certify that the information provided is accurate to

99 HA 2004 s213(3).
100 HA 2004 s213(5) and (6).
101 HA 2004 s213(9).
102 SI No 797.
103 [2012] EWCA Civ 1789, [2013] HLR 9.
104 [2011] EWHC 2003 (QB), [2012] 1 WLR 1224.

the best of his or her knowledge and belief was an essential aspect of the required information.

10.70   HA 2004 imposes sanctions for non-compliance with the procedures for protection of deposits. Section 214 provides for a financial sanction where the landlord fails to protect a deposit and/or to provide the tenant with prescribed information about the chosen scheme within the 30-day period; or where the landlord did originally protect the deposit within the statutory period, but has failed to ensure that the deposit continues to be protected (and the deposit is still not protected by the date of the court hearing). In the event of any such non-compliance, the tenant or any relevant person may make an application to the county court for an order under section 214.

10.71   Where, on such an application, the court is satisfied that:

- the landlord has failed to comply with the initial requirements of an authorised tenancy deposit scheme (ie, to protect the deposit and comply with any additional requirements which the particular scheme may impose) within 30 days of receiving the deposit, or
- the landlord has failed to give the prescribed information to the tenant within the same 30-day period, or
- the deposit is not currently protected,

the court must either order the repayment of the deposit or order the person who appears to be holding the deposit to pay it into an authorised custodial scheme within 14 days.[105] Where the tenancy has already ended, the court must order the person who appears to be holding the deposit to repay all or part of it to the applicant.[106]

10.72   In addition, the court must also order the landlord to pay a penalty award to the tenant within 14 days.[107] The award for non-compliance under section 214 is in the court's discretion, from a minimum of the amount of the deposit to a maximum of three times the deposit.[108] The landlord will not be able to escape the penalty by late

---

105 HA 2004 s214(2) and (3).
106 HA 2004 s214(2A) and (3A).
107 HA 2004 s214(4).
108 At the time this book is published, there is no case-law authority as to whether, in the event of there being more than one breach of the statutory requirements following the grant of a replacement tenancy or tenancies, or upon a fixed-term tenancy becoming statutory periodic, such serial non-compliance is to be treated as a continuing breach giving rise to a single penalty award or as separate breaches incurring multiple penalty awards.

compliance,[109] and the tenant can obtain an award under section 214 while the tenancy is in existence or after the tenancy has ended. A claim under section 214 may be brought by way of counterclaim to a claim for possession, and in a claim based on rent arrears a section 214 award may be set off against such arrears.[110] The court's exercise of its discretion in deciding on the appropriate amount of the award, between one and three times the amount of the deposit, is not constrained by any statutory factors to which it must have regard. Considerations such as the relative culpability or inexperience of the landlord, whether the deposit was eventually fully protected, the length of time for which it remained unprotected, and whether the landlord relied on a reputable letting agent to deal with such matters, may be expected to play a part in assisting the court to determine the appropriate amount.[111] Where a letting agent received the deposit money, a claim can also be brought against the agent, who is likely to find the court less sympathetic to attempts to mitigate the level of the award on the grounds of ignorance or inexperience.[112]

10.73   HA 2004 s215[113] provides a further sanction for a landlord's failure to comply with the section 213 obligations. Section 215(1) provides that if a tenancy deposit has been paid in connection with an assured shorthold tenancy, no section 21 notice requiring possession may be given in relation to the tenancy at any time when:

- the deposit is not being held in accordance with an authorised scheme;[114] or
- (in respect of deposits paid on or after 6 April 2007) the deposit has

---

109 The decision in *Vision EnterprisesLtd (t/a Universal Estates) v Tiensia* [2010] EWCA Civ 1224, [2012] 1 WLR 94 was reversed by the amendments to HA 2004 s214 made by the Localism Act 2011 s184.

110 See *Gladehurst Properties Ltd v Hashemi* [2011] EWCA Civ 604, [2011] HLR 36, in relation to a counterclaim brought by joint tenants, where one of the joint tenants appeared to be conducting the proceedings on his own. The landlord argued that by virtue of CPR 19.3 the claim had to be conducted by both joint tenants unless the court ordered otherwise. It was held that, since the other joint tenant had signed a witness statement affirming that he had agreed to take part in the proceedings, he was a party to the action, despite his failure to sign a statement of truth. See also *Ireland v Norton* July 2012 *Legal Action* 41 (Brighton County Court), in which the court made an order that the joint tenant was not required to be a party for the purposes of the counterclaim.

111 See *Okadigbo v Chan* [2014] EWHC 4729 (QB).

112 See *Draycott v Hannells Letting Limited* [2010] EWHC 217 (QB), [2010] HLR 27.

113 As amended by Localism Act 2011 s184.

114 See HA 2004 s213(4).

not been protected or the initial requirements of such a scheme[115] have not been complied with, within 30 days of receipt; or

- the prescribed information[116] has not been given to the tenant and any relevant person (until such time as the information is given).

10.74 The sanction operates differently, depending on whether the landlord's non-compliance consists, on the one hand, in the failure to protect the deposit or in allowing protection to lapse, or, on the other, in the failure to provide the full prescribed information. In the first situation, where the deposit is not currently protected or where (in the case of deposits paid on or after 6 April 2007) a landlord has failed to protect the tenant's deposit within the time limit of 30 days, the effect of section 215(2A) is that in most cases the landlord will not be able to serve a section 21 notice on the tenant unless he or she returns the deposit, either in full or less any agreed deductions.[117] The landlord cannot avoid these consequences by belatedly arranging to protect the deposit after the 30-day period has passed, except where, following the belated protection, the original tenancy has ended and has been replaced by a new tenancy (including a statutory periodic tenancy) entered into between the same parties in respect of the same premises.[118] The only other situation in which the landlord, having failed to protect the deposit within the 30-day period, may serve a section 21 notice is where the tenant has brought a claim for the financial penalty under section 214 (see para 10.70) and that claim has been determined by the court, withdrawn or settled.[119]

10.75 Whether the landlord's default lies in failure to protect the deposit or failure to provide the prescribed information, the landlord can always avoid the section 215 sanction (preventing the giving of a valid section 21 notice) by returning the deposit to the tenant. Where a landlord takes steps to return the deposit for this purpose, a tenant will not normally be entitled to refuse to accept reimbursement of the money with a view to resisting a subsequent possession claim based on a section 21 notice.[120]

---

115 See HA 2004 s213(4).

116 See para 10.68 above.

117 HA 2004 s215(2A)(a).

118 HA 2004 s215B: see para 10.84. The landlord will nevertheless have become liable to a penalty award under s214 by virtue of having failed to protect the deposit within the initial 30-day period.

119 HA 2004 s215(2A)(b).

120 But, where the landlord did not make it clear that he was intending to return the full deposit, see *Ahmed v Shah*, Bradford County Court, June 2015, noted in *Nearly Legal*, 1 August 2015, available in NL deposits archive.

10.76   Where the landlord has protected the deposit within the 30-day period and complied with any further initial requirements of the chosen scheme, but has failed to give the prescribed information, he or she will only be able to serve a section 21 notice once he or she has belatedly given the correct information[121] or otherwise in any of the circumstances specified in section 215(2A) (see para 10.74 above). Where the landlord has protected the deposit within 30 days of receiving it, but has not given prescribed information, late compliance remains possible, in that once the prescribed information has been given, a section 21 notice can then be served. However, the landlord and/or agent will still be subject to a section 214 penalty as a result of the failure to give the correct information within the 30-day period. Late compliance does not absolve the landlord of liability under section 214.

10.77   Some landlords and agents formerly maintained a practice of giving a section 21 notice to a tenant at the very start of a fixed-term tenancy, dated to take effect at the end of the fixed term. It has been suggested[122] that, where the landlord gave a section 21 notice on the very first day of a tenancy, but subsequently protected the deposit and gave the prescribed information within the initial period of 30 days, section 215 does not afford a defence, since the landlord had complied with the statutory requirements within the period allowed. However, the practice of giving a section 21 notice at the beginning of a tenancy no longer survives in relation to tenancies in England which have commenced on or after 1 October 2015,[123] when section 21(4B), inserted by the Deregulation Act 2015 s36(2), came into force. Section 21(4B) prohibits the giving of section 21 notices within the first four months of a tenancy (other than a replacement tenancy): see para 10.43.

10.78   The legislation concerning tenancy deposits has been substantially amended and supplemented since its inception: once by the Localism Act 2011 and again by the Deregulation Act 2015. As a result, deposits received – or treated as received – at certain times are subject to specific rules. The situations which require special attention may be summarised as follows:

---

121 HA 2004 s215(2).

122 Obiter, by Hamblen J, in *R (Tummond) v Reading County Court* [2014] EWHC 1039 (Admin).

123 Other than statutory periodic tenancies which arose on or after 1 October 2015 on the expiry of a fixed-term tenancy which was granted before that date: Deregulation Act 2015 s41(2).

- deposits received before 6 April 2007 (where there has been no subsequent replacement tenancy);
- deposits received before 6 April 2007 where the tenancy became statutory periodic after that date (and where there has been no subsequent replacement tenancy);
- deposits received on or after 6 April 2007 and before 6 April 2012; and
- deposits received on or after 6 April 2007 which continue to be held in respect of subsequent replacement tenancies.

These differences in treatment are dealt with below. The flowcharts at para 10.106 (relating to section 214 claims) and para 10.107 (relating to potential defences under section 215) may also assist in providing a checklist of the relevant factors.

Deposits received before 6 April 2007 (where there has been no subsequent replacement tenancy)

10.79   In *Charalambous v Ng*[124] a deposit was paid in respect of an assured shorthold tenancy which began in August 2004 and became a statutory periodic tenancy in August 2005. No replacement tenancy had been entered into since the inception of tenancy deposit protection on 6 April 2007, and the deposit had not been protected. The Court of Appeal held that a section 21 notice served in October 2012 was invalid. HA 2004 section 215(1) provided that no section 21 notice could be given 'at a time when the deposit is not being held in accordance with an authorised scheme'.

10.80   The decision in *Charalambous v Ng* was given statutory effect by the Deregulation Act 2015 s31, which amended subsections (1) and (2A) of section 215. The effect is that the prohibition on giving a section 21 notice where the deposit has not been protected applies whether the deposit was paid 'before, on or after 6 April 2007'. Thus, where the current tenancy pre-dated 6 April 2007, even though the landlord is not in breach of any obligation under HA 2004, he or she still cannot give a section 21 notice without first making arrangements to protect the deposit. It is uncertain whether the requirement to give prescribed information applies in these circumstances.[125] However, the landlord is not liable to a penalty award under section

---

124 [2014] EWCA Civ 1604, [2015] HLR 15.
125 Since s215(2) refers back to s213(6), but the 30-day time limit under s213(6)(b) cannot have any application to pre-6 April 2007 tenancies. It is suggested that the subsections should be read purposively, and that the prescribed information must be given.

214 for failure to protect the deposit where the current tenancy began before the onset of deposit protection on 6 April 2007.[126] In practice it will be uncommon that a tenancy which began prior to 6 April 2007 has not since been superseded by a statutory periodic tenancy or a replacement tenancy.

Deposits received before 6 April 2007 where the tenancy became statutory periodic after that date (and where there has been no subsequent replacement tenancy)

10.81   Special provision is also made for the situation where, before 6 April 2007, a tenancy deposit was received by a landlord or agent in connection with a fixed-term assured shorthold tenancy, and the fixed term ended on or after 6 April 2007, and the deposit has continued to be held under the statutory periodic tenancy which followed (there being no subsequent replacement tenancy). In *Superstrike Ltd v Rodrigues*,[127] the Court of Appeal held that it was clear from HA 1988 s5 that a statutory periodic tenancy which comes into being at the end of a fixed-term tenancy is a new tenancy, and that the landlord was therefore at that stage obliged to protect the deposit with an authorised scheme (even though no such obligation existed when the original fixed-term tenancy began). The decision in the specific (and uncommon) factual circumstances which gave rise to *Superstrike* has now been superseded by HA 2004 s215A, inserted by Deregulation Act 2015 s32. Section 215A has the effect that, where the statutory periodic tenancy was still in existence on 26 March 2015,[128] the landlord was required to protect the deposit and give the prescribed information within 90 days, ie by 23 June 2015,[129] failing which the sanctions in section 214 and section 215 would apply. However, if the periodic tenancy was no longer in existence on 26 March 2015, or the deposit had been returned, the landlord is deemed to have complied with the statutory requirements.

126   HA 2004 s214(1), amended by Deregulation Act 2015 s31(2), with the addition of the words 'on or after 6 April 2007').

127   [2013] EWCA Civ 669, [2013] HLR 42. In *Superstrike*, the tenancy was for a fixed term of one year less one day, starting on 8 January 2007.

128   Being the commencement date of the relevant provisions of the Deregulation Act 2015.

129   Or, if earlier, by the date on which the court determined a claim for the s214 penalty (or decided an appeal against such a determination) or made a determination in possession proceedings based on a HA 1988 s21 notice (or decided an appeal against such a determination): HA 2004 s215A(3)(b).

Deposits received on or after 6 April 2007 and before 6 April 2012

10.82 Different rules relating to the sanctions for non-compliance applied under the law prior to 6 April 2012, since the original provisions of HA 2004 ss213–215 were amended by the Localism Act 2011 s184 with effect from that date.[130] However, as a result of transitional provisions,[131] the rules have now been harmonised and the amended sections (including Deregulation Act 2015 amendments) now apply equally to deposits received before 6 April 2012, with the following modification. Where a tenancy was already in existence on 6 April 2012, but the landlord had not protected the tenant's deposit or given the prescribed information, the landlord was given a further period of grace of 30 days from that date, ie until 6 May 2012, within which to protect the tenant's deposit and serve the prescribed information. If the landlord failed to do this, he or she became liable to the penalty award under the amended section 214, and also became subject to the restraints on giving a section 21 notice under the amended section 215 (see paras 10.70 and 10.73).

Deposits received on or after 6 April 2007 which continue to be held in respect of replacement tenancies

10.83 Although the Court of Appeal decision in *Superstrike Ltd v Rodriguez* concerned the specific factual circumstances of a tenancy with a fixed term which began before the commencement date of 6 April 2007 and became a statutory periodic tenancy thereafter, its reasoning created uncertainty in other cases involving deposits which had initially been received *after* 6 April 2007. In such cases, although the landlord had duly complied with the requirements of the legislation on receipt of the deposit, the judgment in *Superstrike* suggested that, where the original tenancy ended and a new tenancy came into being between the same parties,[132] the landlord would need to com-

---

130 Amendments made by the Localism Act 2011 had the effect of reversing the decisions in *Tiensia v Vision Enterprises Ltd (trading as Universal Estates)* [2010] EWCA Civ 1224, [2012] 1 WLR 94 (in which it was held that a landlord could escape the s214 penalty by late compliance) and *Gladehurst Properties Ltd v Hashemi* [2011] EWCA Civ 604, [2011] HLR 36 (in which it was held that a tenant could not apply for a s214 award after the tenancy had come to an end). The landlord's period for compliance with the s213 obligations was also extended from 14 to 30 days.

131 Localism Act 2011 (Commencement No 4 and Transitional, Transitory and Saving Provisions) Order 2012 SI No 628 Sch para 16.

132 ie, where the tenancy was 'renewed' at the expiry of the fixed term, or where it became a statutory periodic tenancy.

ply with the statutory requirements once more. This was because, in the Court's analysis, where the deposit continued to be held by the landlord as security for the performance of the tenant's obligations under the new tenancy, it followed that the tenant should be treated as having notionally paid, and the landlord as having received, the deposit afresh in respect of the new tenancy. The obligations under HA 2004 s213 would therefore apply anew to that notional receipt. Clearly, the landlord is obliged to keep the deposit protected at all times in any event,[133] but it was inferred from the reasoning in *Superstrike* that landlords would need to give the prescribed information afresh whenever a new tenancy carrying the same deposit requirement arose, or, in default, face the sanctions in HA 2004 ss214 and 215.

10.84   However, this issue has been addressed by HA 2004 s215B, inserted by Deregulation Act 2015 s32, with the effect that these consequences of the *Superstrike* decision are avoided. Section 215B(1) and (2) provide that, where a deposit was received on or after 6 April 2007,[134] and the landlord has complied with the section 213 requirements (even if not within the statutory time limit), and the original tenancy has come to an end, the landlord is deemed to have complied with those requirements in relation to any new tenancy which replaces the original tenancy, provided that the deposit continues to be protected with the same authorised scheme as before. A 'replacement tenancy' for these purposes is any new tenancy which follows on immediately from the previous tenancy, is entered into between the same landlord and the same tenant and is a tenancy of the same, or substantially the same, premises.[135] The replacement tenancy may be a new contractual tenancy (whether fixed-term or periodic) or it may be a statutory periodic tenancy which has arisen on expiry of an original fixed-term tenancy. Where a tenancy is expressed to be for a fixed term 'and thereafter from month to month', however, the fixed term and periodic phases are part of the same tenancy, and the later, periodic phase is not therefore a 'replacement tenancy'.

10.85   Where a landlord has protected the deposit late (ie, outside the 30-day period), he or she becomes subject to the section 214 penalty

---

133 See HA 2004 ss214(2)(b), 214(2A)(b) and 215(1).

134 This includes a 'deemed' receipt where the deposit was originally received before 6 April 2007, but the s213 requirements have been complied with on or after that date, following a renewal of the original tenancy: HA 2004 s215B(3).

135 HA 2004 s215B(4). Note that the definition of a tenancy replacing an earlier tenancy is similar, but not identical, to the definition of a 'replacement tenancy' in HA 1988 s21(7).

and is unable to give a section 21 notice in respect of the same tenancy unless (in general) he or she returns the deposit to the tenant. Section 215B has no effect on that position, and the tenant will have a complete defence to a possession claim brought in breach of these provisions.

10.86 It is necessary to analyse the factual background carefully before advising a tenant that he or she may have a defence to possession proceedings, especially where there has been more than one tenancy between the parties and where the deposit has eventually become protected, even if not within the statutory period of 30 days from the date of receipt. Section 215B also has the effect that, where a landlord has protected the deposit late during the 'original tenancy', and has also given the prescribed information within the 'original tenancy' (see para 10.87 below), and a replacement tenancy (as defined) comes into existence, then in relation to the new tenancy (and any subsequent replacement tenancy) the landlord is deemed to have complied with the section 213 requirements. He or she will still be subject to the section 214 penalty for the original breach of obligation, but will not need to return the deposit in order to give a section 21 notice in respect of the later tenancy.

10.87 The term 'original tenancy' in section 215B(1)(a) does not refer only to the first or initial tenancy in a series. Its meaning extends to the first tenancy during which the deposit is protected (even if that is the second, third, fourth, etc tenancy in line). This appears to be the effect of section 215B(3), which provides:

> (3) The condition in subsection (1)(a) may be met in respect of a tenancy even if the tenancy deposit was first received in connection with an earlier tenancy (including where it was first received before 6 April 2007).

This means that once the landlord has complied with the initial requirements of an authorised scheme and given the prescribed information somewhere along the line of tenancies, he or she is deemed to have complied with those requirements in respect of any subsequent replacement tenancy.

10.88 The position is different where the landlord has protected the deposit within the term of the original tenancy, but has not given prescribed information within the same tenancy. Where a replacement tenancy subsequently comes into existence, section 215B does not apply to that tenancy, because the landlord did not fully comply with the section 213 requirements during the original tenancy. But the *Superstrike* principle of a notional fresh payment of the deposit comes to the landlord's aid, because it gives the landlord a new opportunity to comply with the section 213 obligations every time a replacement tenancy arises. Since the deposit is already being held in accordance with an authorised scheme when the new tenancy begins (assuming protection has not lapsed), the section 213(3) obligation is fulfilled in respect of the new tenancy. Once the prescribed information is given (even if not within 30 days of the start of the new tenancy), the landlord avoids the sanction under section 215(1A) and 215(2); and section 215B will then operate to confer deemed compliance in respect of any subsequent replacement tenancy. Alternatively, the landlord can simply return the deposit before serving the section 21 notice. In these circumstances the landlord can give a valid section 21 notice in respect of the current or any replacement tenancy. He or she has not, of course, escaped sanction altogether, because a penalty under section 214 has been incurred because of the earlier failure to comply.

10.89   In other situations, a landlord may also to a limited extent redeem an earlier failure to comply with the protection requirements, at least in relation to the giving of section 21 notices. This is the case where the landlord either:

- did not protect the deposit during the original tenancy or replacement tenancies to date; or
- did protect the deposit during the original or any replacement tenancy, but failed to comply with any other 'initial requirements' of the authorised scheme; or
- did protect the deposit during the original tenancy or any replacement tenancy, but allowed protection to lapse at the end of that tenancy.

In each of these cases it appears that the landlord can avoid the sanction of being unable to give a section 21 notice by protecting the deposit (and complying with any other initial requirements) within the first 30 days of any subsequent tenancy. Once the landlord has done this, and has given the prescribed information (whether within the 30-day period or not), he or she avoids the sanction under section 215(1A) and 215(2); and section 215B then operates to confer deemed compliance in respect of any subsequent replacement tenancy. Alternatively, the landlord can simply return the deposit. In those circumstances, the landlord can serve a valid section 21 notice in respect of the current or any further replacement tenancy. He or she has not, of course, escaped sanction altogether, because a penalty under section 214 has been incurred because of the earlier failure to comply.

10.90 Sections 215A (see para 10.81) and 215B (see para 10.84) are treated as having had effect since 6 April 2007, in order to forestall any claims or defences based on earlier instances of non-compliance which might otherwise have been brought or raised.[136]

10.91 Where a tenancy is renewed or a statutory periodic tenancy arises, the landlord must always ensure that the deposit remains protected with an authorised scheme. Where the landlord has chosen one of the insurance schemes, he or she may need to pay a renewal fee or premium in order to retain protection at the start of a new tenancy, and if protection is allowed to lapse, the sanction in section 215 (together with the section 214 penalty, if protection is not renewed before the hearing of the section 214 application) will come into effect.[137] Tenants should be alerted by the scheme provider itself if their deposit is in danger of becoming unprotected following the expiry of the current fixed term,[138] but they should check with the scheme in any event that the deposit remains protected when a new tenancy (including a statutory periodic tenancy) comes into being.

Retaliatory eviction

10.92 The Deregulation Act 2015 contains measures which are designed to protect assured shorthold tenants from retaliatory eviction, at least for a period of time, where they have made a complaint to the landlord about disrepair or other defects in the rented property. The statutory purpose is to encourage tenants to report poor conditions in their home without fearing that they will immediately receive a section 21 notice requiring them to leave.

10.93 Sections 33 and 34 of the Act came into force on 1 October 2015. They apply to tenancies that began after that date,[139] but after three years, ie from 1 October 2018 onwards, they will apply to all assured shorthold tenancies in existence on that later date.[140]

---

136 HA 2004 s215C, inserted by Deregulation Act 2015 s32.
137 HA 2004 Sch 10 para 5A(9).
138 The scheme must give at least two months' notice to the landlord and the tenant of the date when the deposit will cease to be protected: HA 2004 Sch 10 para 5A(8).
139 Other than statutory periodic tenancies which arose on or after 1 October 2015 on the expiry of a fixed-term tenancy which was granted before that date: Deregulation Act 2015 s41(2).
140 Deregulation Act 2015 s41(3).

Preventing retaliatory eviction

33(1) Where a relevant notice is served in relation to a dwelling-house in England, a section 21 notice may not be given in relation to an assured shorthold tenancy of the dwelling-house –

   (a) within six months beginning with the day of service of the relevant notice, or

   (b) where the operation of the relevant notice has been suspended, within six months beginning with the day on which the suspension ends.

(2) A section 21 notice given in relation to an assured shorthold tenancy of a dwelling-house in England is invalid where –

   (a) before the section 21 notice was given, the tenant made a complaint in writing to the landlord regarding the condition of the dwelling-house at the time of the complaint,

   (b) the landlord –

      (i) did not provide a response to the complaint within 14 days beginning with the day on which the complaint was given,

      (ii) provided a response to the complaint that was not an adequate response, or

      (iii) gave a section 21 notice in relation to the dwelling-house following the complaint,

   (c) the tenant then made a complaint to the relevant local housing authority about the same, or substantially the same, subject matter as the complaint to the landlord,

   (d) the relevant local housing authority served a relevant notice in relation to the dwelling-house in response to the complaint, and

   (e) if the section 21 notice was not given before the tenant's complaint to the local housing authority, it was given before the service of the relevant notice.

(3) The reference in subsection (2) to an adequate response by the landlord is to a response in writing which –

   (a) provides a description of the action that the landlord proposes to take to address the complaint, and

   (b) sets out a reasonable timescale within which that action will be taken.

(4) Subsection (2) applies despite the requirement in paragraph (a) for a complaint to be in writing not having been met where the tenant does not know the landlord's postal or e-mail address.

(5) Subsection (2) applies despite the requirements in paragraphs (a) and (b) not having been met where the tenant made reasonable efforts to contact the landlord to complain about the condition of the dwelling-house but was unable to do so.

(6) The court must strike out proceedings for an order for possession under section 21 of the Housing Act 1988 in relation to a

dwelling-house in England if, before the order is made, the section 21 notice that would otherwise require the court to make an order for possession in relation to the dwelling-house has become invalid under subsection (2).

(7) An order for possession of a dwelling-house in England made under section 21 of the Housing Act 1988 must not be set aside on the ground that a relevant notice was served in relation to the dwelling-house after the order for possession was made.

(8) Subsection (1) does not apply where the section 21 notice is given after –

(a) the relevant notice has been wholly revoked under section 16 of the Housing Act 2004 as a result of the notice having been served in error,

(b) the relevant notice has been quashed under paragraph 15 of Schedule 1 to that Act,

(c) a decision of the relevant local housing authority to refuse to revoke the relevant notice has been reversed under paragraph 18 of Schedule 1 to that Act, or

(d) a decision of the relevant local housing authority to take the action to which the relevant notice relates has been reversed under section 45 of that Act.

(9) Subsection (2) does not apply where the operation of the relevant notice has been suspended.

(10) References in this section and section 34 to a relevant notice served, or complaint made, in relation to a dwelling-house include a relevant notice served, or complaint made, in relation to any common parts of the building of which the dwelling-house forms a part.

(11) But subsection (10) applies only if –

(a) the landlord has a controlling interest in the common parts in question, and

(b) the condition of those common parts is such as to affect the tenant's enjoyment of the dwelling-house or of any common parts which the tenant is entitled to use.

(12) In this section and section 34 a reference to a complaint to a landlord includes a complaint made to a person acting on behalf of the landlord in relation to the tenancy.

(13) In this section and section 34 –

'assured shorthold tenancy' means a tenancy within section 19A or 20 of the Housing Act 1988;

'common parts', in relation to a building, includes –

(a) the structure and exterior of the building, and

(b) common facilities provided (whether or not in the building) for persons who include one or more of the occupiers of the building;

'controlling interest' means an interest which is such as to entitle the landlord to decide whether action is taken in relation to a complaint within this section or a relevant notice;

'dwelling-house'has the meaning given by section 45 of the Housing Act 1988;

'relevant local housing authority', in relation to a dwelling-house, means the local housing authority as defined in section 261(2) and (3) of the Housing Act 2004 within whose area the dwelling-house is located;

'relevant notice' means –

(a) a notice served under section 11 of the Housing Act 2004 (improvement notices relating to category 1 hazards),

(b) a notice served under section 12 of that Act (improvement notices relating to category 2 hazards), or

(c) a notice served under section 40(7) of that Act (emergency remedial action);

'section 21 notice' means a notice given under section 21(1)(b) or (4)(a) of the Housing Act 1988 (recovery of possession on termination of shorthold tenancy).

Further exemptions to section 33

34(1) Subsections (1) and (2) of section 33 do not apply where the condition of the dwelling-house or common parts that gave rise to the service of the relevant notice is due to a breach by the tenant of –

(a) the duty to use the dwelling-house in a tenant-like manner, or

(b) an express term of the tenancy to the same effect.

(2) Subsections (1) and (2) of section 33 do not apply where at the time the section 21 notice is given the dwelling-house is genuinely on the market for sale.

(3) For the purposes of subsection (2), a dwelling-house is not genuinely on the market for sale if, in particular, the landlord intends to sell the landlord's interest in the dwelling-house to –

(a) a person associated with the landlord,

(b) a business partner of the landlord,

(c) a person associated with a business partner of the landlord, or

(d) a business partner of a person associated with the landlord.

(4) In subsection (3), references to a person who is associated with another person are to be read in accordance with section 178 of the Housing Act 1996.

(5) For the purposes of subsection (3), a business partner of a person ('P') is a person who is –

(a) a director, secretary or other officer of a company of which P is also a director, secretary or other officer,

(b) a director, secretary or other officer of a company in which P has a shareholding or other financial interest,

(c) a person who has a shareholding or other financial interest in a company of which P is a director, secretary or other officer,

(d) an employee of P,

(e) a person by whom P is employed, or

(f) a partner of a partnership of which P is also a partner.

(6) Subsections (1) and (2) of section 33 do not apply where the landlord is a private registered provider of social housing.

(7) Subsections (1) and (2) of section 33 do not apply where –

(a) the dwelling-house is subject to a mortgage granted before the beginning of the tenancy,

(b) the mortgagee is entitled to exercise a power of sale conferred on the mortgagee by the mortgage or by section 101 of the Law of Property Act 1925, and

(c) at the time the section 21 notice is given the mortgagee requires possession of the dwelling-house for the purpose of disposing of it with vacant possession in exercise of that power.

(8) In subsection (7) –

(a) 'mortgage' includes a charge, and

(b) 'mortgagee' includes a receiver appointed by the mortgagee under the terms of the mortgage or in accordance with the Law of Property Act 1925.

10.94 Section 33 operates to prevent the landlord from obtaining possession in either of two situations. First, section 33(1) imposes a prohibition on giving a section 21 notice within a period of six months from the date of service of a relevant local authority notice.[141] A 'relevant notice' is an improvement notice served under HA 2004 ss11–12 or a notice of emergency remedial action served under HA 2004 s40(7). There is nothing to prevent the landlord from giving a section 21 notice as soon as the six months' moratorium under section 33(1) expires, even if the landlord's motive is retaliatory and even if the landlord has still not carried out the specified works. Nevertheless, tenants and local authorities will take some encouragement from knowing that service of a relevant notice requiring the landlord to remedy the defects complained of will not give rise to an *immediate* section 21 notice requiring the tenant to leave.

10.95 The second situation is more complex in its operation, but its purpose is clear: that is, to prevent the landlord from responding to a complaint of poor conditions, whether the tenant's initial complaint to the landlord or a later complaint to the local authority, by giving the tenant a section 21 notice requiring possession, in either case before a relevant local authority notice is served.

10.96 Section 33(2) provides that a section 21 notice given to an assured shorthold tenant is invalid where the following conditions apply.

141 Or, where the relevant notice is suspended, within six months of the date on which the suspension is lifted.

First, before the section 21 notice was given, the tenant must have made a complaint in writing to the landlord about the condition of the property in question. The requirement for the notice to be in writing is waived where the tenant does not know the landlord's postal or email address. Second, either the landlord did not respond at all to the tenant's complaint within 14 days; or the landlord provided an inadequate response; or the response consisted of giving the tenant a section 21 notice. An 'adequate response' for this purpose is a response which both describes the action which the landlord proposes to take to address the tenant's complaint and sets out a reasonable timescale within which that action will be taken. A response falling short of those requirements would be an inadequate response. This second condition is also waived if the tenant made reasonable efforts to contact the landlord to make the complaint, but was unable to do so. Third, the tenant must then have made a complaint to the local housing authority about the condition of the property. Complaint should be made to the environmental health department or other department exercising functions under HA 2004 Part 1 (Housing Health and Safety Rating System). Fourth, the landlord then gave a section 21 notice to the tenant (if not already given in response to the initial complaint). Fifth, the local authority must have served a relevant notice on the landlord in response to the complaint. A 'relevant notice' has the same meaning as under section 33(1) (see para 10.94 above).

10.97   Where a section 21 notice has become invalid in these circumstances before a possession order is made, the court must strike out possession proceedings based on the notice.[142] On the other hand, where the court makes a possession order *before* the relevant local authority notice is served, the order may not be set aside on that account.[143] In order to establish a defence to the landlord's possession claim, the tenant must stress to the local authority the importance of serving an improvement notice (or, less commonly, a notice of emergency remedial action) as a matter of some urgency, as the notice must be served before the possession hearing.

10.98   Where a relevant local authority notice has been served, but its operation has been suspended, a section 21 notice which is otherwise valid will not be rendered invalid under Deregulation Act 2015 s33(2).[144] Tenants and their representatives should seek to persuade

142 Deregulation Act 2015 s33(6).
143 Deregulation Act 2015 s33(7).
144 Deregulation Act 2015 s33(9).

the authority not to suspend its notice in these circumstances, and not to come to an informal arrangement with the landlord upon the landlord undertaking to attend to repairs, since in either case this will have the effect of defeating the protection which it is the intention of the Act to afford tenants.

10.99 The reference in section 33(2) to a written complaint to the landlord includes a complaint made to the landlord's agent.[145] The premises which are the subject of the complaint or the relevant notice may include the common parts of the building, provided that the landlord has a 'controlling interest' in the common parts; and that the condition of the common parts affects the tenant's enjoyment of the premises.[146]

10.100 The provisions in Deregulation Act 2015 s33 to combat retaliatory eviction are directed at landlords in the private rented sector. They do not apply where the landlord is a housing association or other private registered provider of social housing.[147] Deregulation Act 2015 s34 also creates a number of exceptions to the operation of section 33. First, there is nothing to stop the landlord serving a valid section 21 notice where the defects that have given rise to the service of the relevant local authority notice have been caused by the tenant's own acts or omissions, in breach of the implied duty to use the property in a tenant-like manner or of an express term of the tenancy to the same effect.[148] Second, the restrictions on giving a section 21 notice do not apply where the property is 'genuinely on the market for sale'.[149] A property is not genuinely on the market for sale where the landlord intends to sell to an 'associated person' (as defined in HA 1996 s178) or a business partner. It is suggested that a landlord seeking to establish this exemption will need to do more than merely show that the property has been placed with an estate agent for sale. It is likely that a court will require evidence, for instance, that the property is being actively marketed, including details of advertising and of approaches from potential buyers. Third, section 33 has no application where the property is subject to a mortgage which was granted before the tenancy began; and, as a result of the landlord's default, the mortgage lender is entitled to exercise a power of sale; and, at the time the section 21 notice is given, the lender, or a receiver appointed to act on its

145 Deregulation Act 2015 s33(12).
146 Deregulation Act 2015 s33(10) and (11).
147 Deregulation Act 2015 s34(6).
148 Deregulation Act 2015 s34(1).
149 Deregulation Act 2015 s34(2).

behalf, requires possession of the property for the purpose of selling it.[150]

10.101   The effectiveness of section 33(2) as a safeguard against retaliatory eviction in these circumstances will depend on the ability of local authority environmental health departments to respond promptly to tenants' complaints, and their willingness to serve a 'relevant notice', where appropriate, before the landlord is able to obtain a possession order. There is a particular difficulty where the landlord uses the paper-based accelerated possession procedure, since the date when the court is to consider the claim for possession will not be known.[151] It is therefore essential that the tenant completes the Defence Form which accompanies the court documents, setting out details of the initial complaint, the landlord's response (or lack of it) and the further complaint to the local authority, and returns the form to the court within the period allowed of 14 days. On receipt of the Defence Form and consideration of the papers by the judge, it is to be expected that the matter will be listed for hearing in the light of the fact that the service of a relevant notice on the landlord before a possession order is made will require the court to strike out the proceedings. The tenant will then need to press the authority to make its decision and to serve the appropriate notice as soon as possible, and in any event before the date of hearing.

Abandoned premises

10.102   When Housing and Planning Act 2016 Part 3 (Recovering abandoned premises in England) is brought into force, a private landlord of an assured shorthold tenant in England (including a private registered provider of social housing) may give the tenant a notice bringing the tenancy to an end (a 'section 57 notice') and recover possession if there has been no response by the tenant to a series of three consecutive warning notices spanning a period of at least eight weeks and where the 'unpaid rent condition' is satisfied.[152] Where a tenancy is brought to an end in this way, the tenant may within six months of the date of the section 57 notice apply to the county court for an order reinstating the tenancy if he or she has a good reason

---

150 Deregulation Act 2015 s34(7).
151 See chapter 22.
152 HPA 2016 ss57–59: see, further, paras 1.188–1.192.

for having failed to respond to the warning notices.[153] If the court finds that the tenant had a good reason for failing to respond to the warning notices, it may make any order it thinks fit for the purpose of reinstating the tenancy.

Application of this chapter to Wales

10.103 At the time of publication of this book, some of the legislative provisions set out in this chapter which derive from the Localism Act 2011, the Deregulation Act 2015 and the Housing and Planning Act 2016 (when in force) apply only to England, and not to Wales. These are:

- The additional requirement of a six months' notice of non-renewal where a tenancy for a fixed term of two years or more was granted by a housing association or other PRPSH: see para 10.25.
- The effect of HA 1988 s21(4ZA) (whereby the requirement in s21(4)(a) for the date specified in the notice to be the last day of a period of the tenancy is omitted) in relation to contractual periodic assured shorthold tenancies in England granted on or after 1 October 2015 and all other contractual periodic assured shorthold tenancies still in existence on 1 October 2018: see paras 10.38–10.40.
- The requirement in HA 1988 s21(8) that a section 21 notice[154] be in a prescribed form: see para 10.41.
- The restriction in HA 1988 s21(4B), to the effect that a section 21 notice[155] may not be given within the first four months from the start of the tenancy (other than a replacement tenancy): see paras 10.43–10.44.
- The restriction in HA 1988 s21(4D), to the effect that a section 21 notice[156] will be effective for a maximum period of six months from the date the notice was given: see paras 10.45–10.47.

---

153 HPA 2016 s60.
154 ie, in relation to tenancies beginning on or after 1 October 2015, and all tenancies in existence on 1 October 2018.
155 ie, in relation to tenancies beginning on or after 1 October 2015, and all tenancies in existence on 1 October 2018.
156 ie, in relation to tenancies beginning on or after 1 October 2015, and all tenancies in existence on 1 October 2018.

- The obligation on landlords[157] under HA 1988 s21A to comply with prescribed requirements relating to the condition of premises, the health and safety of occupiers and energy performance: see paras 10.48–10.50.
- The obligation on landlords[158] under HA 1988 s21B to give prescribed information to tenants: see paras 10.51–10.53.
- The provisions in HA 1988 s21C relating to repayment of rent where the tenancy ends before the end of a tenancy period for which the tenant has paid rent in advance: see para 10.54.
- The provisions in Deregulation Act 2015 ss33 and 34[159] relating to retaliatory eviction: see paras 10.92–10.102.
- The provisions in Housing and Planning Act 2016 ss57–61 relating to abandoned premises:[160] see para 10.101.

10.104 At the date of publication, the remaining parts of this chapter – paras 10.1–10.24; 10.26–10.37; 10.42; and 10.55–10.91 – apply to both England and Wales (except where otherwise indicated), but only until the date on which the Renting Homes (Wales) Act 2016 comes into force. This Act, which was passed by the National Assembly for Wales on 18 January 2016, creates a completely new framework of housing law based on 'occupation contracts' which is derived from the work of the Law Commission.[161] From the date of commencement of the new regime, assured tenancies (including assured shorthold tenancies) are abolished, and existing assured shorthold tenancies become 'converted standard contracts'.[162] From that date, therefore, this chapter ceases to apply to Wales, and the law of rented residential occupation in Wales is governed by the Renting Homes (Wales) Act 2016 and the regulations made thereunder.

---

157 ie, in relation to tenancies beginning on or after 1 October 2015, and all tenancies in existence on 1 October 2018.

158 ie, in relation to tenancies beginning on or after 1 October 2015.

159 ie, in relation to tenancies beginning on or after 1 October 2015, and all tenancies in existence on 1 October 2018.

160 Not in force at the date of publication of this book.

161 See Law Commission, *Renting Homes: The Final Report*, Vol 1: Report, Cm 6781-I, Law Com No 297, 2006; and *Renting Homes: The Final Report*, Vol 2: Draft Bill, Cm 6781-II, Law Com No 297, 2006.

162 Renting Homes (Wales) Act 2016 s240 and Schedule 12.

Flowcharts

10.105 Advising tenants facing section 21 possession proceedings in England

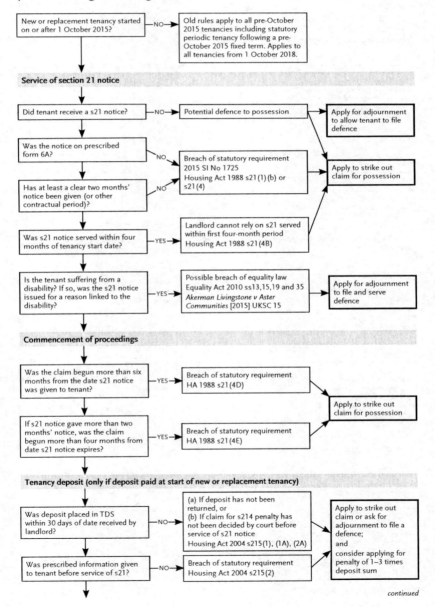

New or replacement tenancy started on or after 1 October 2015? —NO→ Old rules apply to all pre-October 2015 tenancies including statutory periodic tenancy following a pre-October 2015 fixed term. Applies to all tenancies from 1 October 2018.

Service of section 21 notice

Did tenant receive a s21 notice? —NO→ Potential defence to possession → Apply for adjournment to allow tenant to file defence

Was the notice on prescribed form 6A? —NO→ Breach of statutory requirement 2015 SI No 1725 Housing Act 1988 s21(1)(b) or s21(4) → Apply to strike out claim for possession

Has at least a clear two months' notice been given (or other contractual period)? —NO→

Was s21 notice served within four months of tenancy start date? —YES→ Landlord cannot rely on s21 served within first four-month period Housing Act 1988 s21(4B)

Is the tenant suffering from a disability? If so, was the s21 notice issued for a reason linked to the disability? —YES→ Possible breach of equality law Equality Act 2010 ss13,15,19 and 35 *Akerman Livingstone v Aster Communities* [2015] UKSC 15 → Apply for adjournment to file and serve defence

Commencement of proceedings

Was the claim begun more than six months from the date s21 notice was given to tenant? —YES→ Breach of statutory requirement HA 1988 s21(4D)

Apply to strike out claim for possession

If s21 notice gave more than two months' notice, was the claim begun more than four months from date s21 notice expires? —YES→ Breach of statutory requirement HA 1988 s21(4E)

Tenancy deposit (only if deposit paid at start of new or replacement tenancy)

Was deposit placed in TDS within 30 days of date received by landlord? —NO→ (a) If deposit has not been returned, or (b) If claim for s214 penalty has not been decided by court before service of s21 notice Housing Act 2004 s215(1), (1A), (2A) → Apply to strike out claim or ask for adjournment to file a defence; and consider applying for penalty of 1–3 times deposit sum

Was prescribed information given to tenant before service of s21? —NO→ Breach of statutory requirement Housing Act 2004 s215(2)

continued

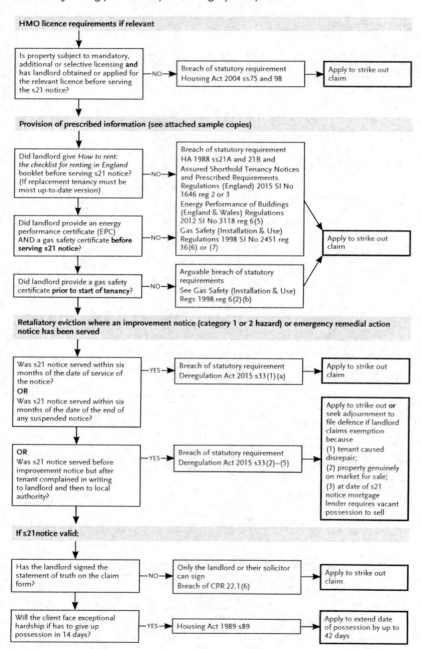

10.106 Tenancy deposit claims under Housing Act 2004 s214

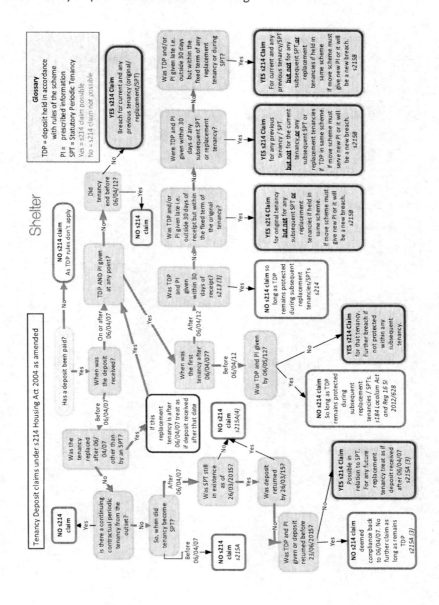

10.107   Tenancy deposits and validity of section 21 notices under Housing Act 2004 s215

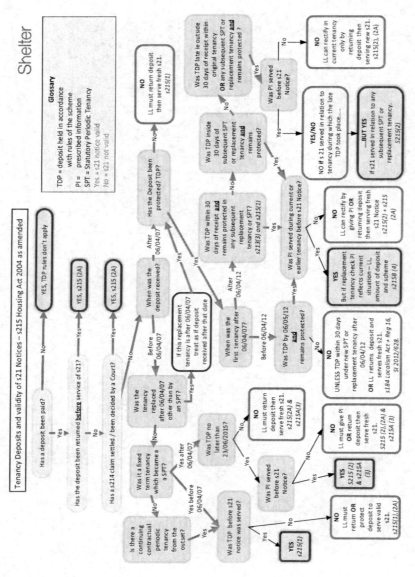

Shelter

Glossary

TDP = deposit held in accordance with rules of the scheme
PI = prescribed information
SPT = Statutory Periodic Tenancy
Yes = s21 notice valid
No = s21 not valid

CHAPTER 11

Other private sector lettings

Introduction

11.1   The predominant form of letting in the private rented sector is the assured shorthold tenancy: see chapter 10. However, a privately renting occupier may for various reasons find that his or her letting is outside the assured tenancy scheme. This may be because:

- the tenancy (or an earlier tenancy) dates back to a time before the assured tenancy regime came into effect[1] and is protected by the Rent Act 1977; or
- the tenancy is a fully assured tenancy with long-term protection; or
- the tenancy is one of a kind which is specifically excluded from being an assured or assured shorthold tenancy; or
- the occupier does not have a tenancy at all, but a licence.

Each of these types of letting is examined below.

Tenancies within the Rent Act 1977

11.2   Tenancies which were granted by private sector landlords before 15 January 1989[2] were generally protected tenancies under the Rent Act 1977. Such tenancies retain their Rent Act protection: see chapter 12. Rent Act protection also applies where a tenancy was granted after 15 January 1989, but followed on immediately from a previous tenancy which was a Rent Act regulated tenancy; and in other limited circumstances (see para 12.7).

Fully assured tenancies

11.3   There are certain limited instances in which a tenant of a private sector landlord may enjoy a fully assured tenancy. The first, and unlikely, instance is where the landlord expressly provides, in accordance with Housing Act (HA) 1988 Sch 2A paras 1–3, that the tenancy is not to be an assured shorthold tenancy. These exceptions apply where the tenancy is granted on or after 28 February 1997 to a person who was not previously a fully assured tenant of the same landlord. That

---

1   That is, before 15 January 1989, the date when the Housing Act (HA) 1988 Part I came into force.

2   That is, the date when HA 1988 Part I came into force, ushering in the regime of assured and assured shorthold tenancies.

tenancy will be an assured shorthold tenancy unless the agreement contains a provision to the effect that it is not an assured shorthold;[3] or unless the landlord serves a notice on the tenant, before or after the commencement of the tenancy, that the tenancy is not to be, or is no longer to be, an assured shorthold tenancy.[4]

11.4   However, where the tenancy began between 15 January 1989 and 27 February 1997 inclusive, that tenancy would be an assured shorthold tenancy only if it was preceded by a notice in the form prescribed under HA 1988 s20, warning the prospective tenant that he or she was about to enter into an assured shorthold tenancy.[5] The burden is on the landlord to prove that a 'section 20' notice in the correct form was served at the appropriate time. If service of such a notice cannot be proved, the tenant will have a fully assured tenancy. Moreover, if one or more further tenancies have been entered into between the same landlord and the same tenant (or to joint tenants at least one of whom was a tenant under the prevous assured tenancy), each replacement tenancy will in most circumstances also be a fully assured tenancy (see paras 10.5 and 10.6).[6]

Mandatory grounds for possession of assured tenancies (private sector only)

11.5   A fully assured tenant can only be lawfully evicted if the landlord follows the correct procedure in serving a notice of seeking possession under HA 1988 s8 and obtains a possession order based on one of the grounds for possession in HA 1988 Sch 2. See chapter 2 for the procedure for recovery of possession and chapter 3 for grounds 6 to 17 of the grounds for possession, which (apart from ground 14A) apply in the same way to private sector assured tenancies and to social sector assured tenancies. However, mandatory grounds 1 to 5 and 7B[7] apply only to private sector tenancies, and they are therefore discussed in this chapter. They will rarely be encountered, even where the tenancy was granted between 15 January 1989 and 27 February 1997, since

3 HA 1988 Sch 2A para 3.
4 HA 1988 Sch 2A paras 1 and 2.
5 See para 10.4.
6 HA 1988 s20(3), where the new tenancy was entered into before 28 February 1997 and HA 1988 Sch 2A para 7 where the new tenancy was entered into on or after 28 February 1997.
7 Not in force until the commencement of Immigration Act 2016 s41(2). See para 11.18.

each of the grounds depends upon a notice having been served at the beginning of the tenancy, and a landlord letting between 1989 and 1997 is more likely to have served a 'section 20' notice of assured shorthold tenancy (see para 11.4 above). The five grounds are as follows.

Ground 1: Owner-occupiers

11.6   HA 1988 Sch 2 ground 1 provides:

> Not later than the beginning of the tenancy the landlord gave notice in writing to the tenant that possession might be recovered on this ground or the court is of the opinion that it is just and equitable to dispense with the requirement of notice and (in either case) –
>
> (a) at some time before the beginning of the tenancy, the landlord who is seeking possession or, in the case of joint landlords seeking possession, at least one of them occupied the dwelling-house as his only or principal home; or
>
> (b) the landlord who is seeking possession or, in the case of joint landlords seeking possession, at least one of them requires the dwelling-house as his, his spouse's or his civil partner's only or principal home and neither the landlord (or, in the case of joint landlords, any one of them) nor any other person who, as landlord, derived title under the landlord who gave the notice mentioned above acquired the reversion on the tenancy for money or money's worth.

11.7   This ground is similar to Case 11 in Rent Act 1977 Sch 15 (see para 12.75), but is wider in its ambit. A landlord must:

- *prove that at, or before, the grant of the tenancy the landlord gave notice in writing that possession might be recovered on this ground.* The notice need not be in any particular form and may be included as a recital in any tenancy agreement provided that the agreement does not operate retrospectively;

or

- *satisfy the court that 'it is just and equitable to dispense with the requirement of notice'.* These words have 'a very wide importance' and mean that the court should take into account all of the circumstances, including questions of greater hardship, and not just the circumstances which surround a failure to give written notice.[8] If the court fails to consider relevant circumstances, any

---

8   *Bradshaw v Baldwin-Wiseman* (1985) 17 HLR 260, CA; *Fernandes v Parvardin* (1982) 264 EG 49, CA; *Boyle v Verrall* (1997) 29 HLR 436, [1997] 1 EGLR 25, CA and *Wynne v Egan* June 1997 *Legal Action* 15, CA.

possession order may be set aside.[9] A tenant's persistent late payment of rent may be a relevant circumstance.[10] If oral notice was given when a tenancy was granted, it may be an important factor favouring dispensation, but it does not follow that oral notice is a prerequisite for such a decision. Absence of oral notice is not a reason for restricting dispensation to circumstances where there is an 'exceptional case'.[11] Courts may consider circumstances affecting the landlord, the landlord's successors in title, the tenant's circumstances and the effect of the failure to give notice.[12] In one Rent Act case, where, prior to the granting of a tenancy, tenants were told orally that the premises were the landlord's home and that the landlord would be returning, and there was no misunderstanding about this, the court considered that oral notice was just as effective as written notice and so dispensed with the formal requirements.[13] However, in another Rent Act case where no formal notice was given at the beginning of the tenancy because at that time the landlord had no intention of returning to the premises, it was not just and equitable to dispense with the requirement.[14] The fact that the parties signed what purported (wrongly) to be a temporary 'licence' agreement is not enough to make it 'just and equitable' to dispense with the need for a notice;[15]

and either

• *at some time before the grant of the tenancy, the landlord, or if there are joint landlords, at least one of them, had occupied the dwelling-house as his or her only or principal home.*[16] A landlord's previous occupation may suffice even if it was only temporary or intermittent.[17] To satisfy this limb, the landlord need not give any reason for requiring possession;

or

---

9 *Hegab v Shamash* June 1998 *Legal Action* 13, CA.

10 *Boyle v Verrall* (1997) 29 HLR 436, [1997] 1 EGLR 25, CA.

11 Ibid. See also *Mustafa v Ruddock* (1998) 30 HLR 495, [1997] EGCS 87, CA.

12 *Bradshaw v Baldwin-Wiseman* (1985) 17 HLR 260, CA.

13 *Fernandes v Parvardin* (1982) 264 EG 49, CA. Cf *White v Jones* (1994) 26 HLR 477, CA.

14 *Bradshaw v Baldwin-Wiseman* (1985) 17 HLR 260, CA.

15 *Ibie v Trubshaw* (1990) 22 HLR 191, CA.

16 Note the contrast with the wording under Rent Act 1977 Sch 15 Case 11 (discussed at 12.78 below).

17 *Naish v Curzon* (1985) 17 HLR 220, CA; *Mistry v Isidore* (1990) 22 HLR 281, [1990] 2 EGLR 97, CA and *Ibie v Trubshaw* (1990) 22 HLR 191, CA.

- *the landlord (or at least one of them) 'requires the dwelling-house as his or his spouse's only or principal home'.* The landlord need not show that the premises are 'reasonably' required, merely that the landlord 'bona fide wants' or 'genuinely has the immediate intention' of occupying the premises.[18] Premises need not be required as a permanent residence and fairly intermittent residence will be sufficient.[19]

11.8   This ground for possession is not available to a new landlord who acquired the premises 'for money or money's worth' from an original landlord who gave a notice that possession might be recovered under this ground. The purpose of this provision is to prevent an outsider buying up tenanted property and then evicting the tenant.[20] In this connection the word 'purchasing' means 'buying'.[21] It does not include 'inheriting',[22] acquiring through a family settlement,[23] a transfer to a family member 'in consideration of mutual love and affection'[24] or the granting of an intermediate lease with no premium.[25] A tenant will have a defence to proceedings under this ground if his or her tenancy was in existence at the date when the premises were bought. The relevant date is the date of exchange of contracts, and not the date of completion.[26] However, owners are entitled to rely on ground 1 if they buy premises with vacant possession and subsequently let to tenants,[27] or if they buy premises with one sitting tenant who leaves and is then replaced by another tenant.[28] If landlords become 'landlords by purchase' they do not acquire the

---

18 Cf, Rent Act 1977 Sch 15 Case 9. See *Kennealy v Dunne* [1977] QB 837.
19 *Naish v Curzon* (1985) 17 HLR 220, CA and *Davies v Peterson* (1989) 21 HLR 63, [1989] 06 EG 130, CA.
20 *Fowle v Bell* [1946] 2 All ER 668 and *Epps v Rothnie* [1945] KB 562, [1946] 1 All ER 146.
21 *Powell v Cleland* [1948] 1 KB 262, [1947] 2 All ER 672.
22 *Baker v Lewis* [1946] 2 All ER 592, CA. Note, though, that where an owner said, before she died, that she wished her executors to offer a property for sale to the plaintiff, who then bought it, he was 'a landlord by purchase' and was not entitled to possession: *Amaddio v Dalton* (1991) 22 HLR 332.
23 *Thomas v Fryer* [1970] 1 WLR 845, [1970] 2 All ER 1, even though money was paid by one beneficiary under the will to the others.
24 *Mansukhani v Stanley* (1992) *Times* 17 April.
25 *Powell v Cleland* [1948] 1 KB 262, [1947] 2 All ER 672.
26 *Emberson v Robinson* [1953] 1 WLR 1129 and *Newton and Wife v Biggs* [1953] 2 QB 211, [1953] 1 All ER 99.
27 *Epps v Rothnie* [1945] KB 562, [1946] 1 All ER 146.
28 *Fowle v Bell* [1947] KB 242, [1946] 2 All ER 668. See also *Newton and Wife v Biggs* [1953] 2 QB 211, [1953] 1 All ER 99 where the former owner sold premises to

right to bring proceedings under ground 1 even if a new contractual tenancy on different terms is created or there are minor changes in the subject matter of the tenancy, for example, by the addition or deduction of rooms.[29] Similarly if a 'landlord by purchase' dies, the person to whom the property is transferred acquires no greater right under ground 1 than the original landlord by purchase.[30]

Ground 2: Possession required by mortgagees

11.9   HA 1988 Sch 2 ground 2 provides:

> The dwelling-house is subject to a mortgage granted before the beginning of the tenancy and –
> (a) the mortgagee is entitled to exercise a power of sale conferred on him by the mortgage or by section 101 of the Law of Property Act 1925; and
> (b) the mortgagee requires possession of the dwelling-house for the purpose of disposing of it with vacant possession in exercise of that power; and
> (c) either notice was given as mentioned in Ground 1 above or the court is satisfied that it is just and equitable to dispense with the requirement of notice;
> and for the purposes of this ground 'mortgage' includes a charge and 'mortgagee' shall be construed accordingly.

11.10   This ground applies if, for example, the landlord/mortgagor has defaulted on instalments of the mortgage. The purpose of this ground is to enable the landlord's mortgagee, who has consented to a borrower letting – or where the mortgage deed does not prohibit letting – to obtain the full vacant possession value when exercising a power of sale. Note, though, the suggestion by Lord Denning MR that the court's equitable powers may prevent a lender from obtaining possession, 'except when it is sought bona fide and reasonably for the purpose of enforcing the security'.[31] In practice, the ground is rarely needed, since the tenant will usually be an assured shorthold tenant rather than a fully assured tenant, though it may be used by a mortgagee who wishes to bring a fixed-term assured shorthold tenancy to an end before the contractual term has expired.

---

the plaintiff on condition that he was granted a tenancy. The new landlord was not a landlord by purchase.

29 *Wright v Walford* [1955] 1 QB 363, [1955] 1 All ER 207.
30 *Littlechild v Holt* [1950] 1 KB 1, [1949] 1 All ER 933.
31 *Quennel v Maltby* [1979] 1 WLR 318, CA, approved in *Albany Home Loans Ltd v Massey* [1997] 2 All ER 609, (1997) 29 HLR 902, CA.

11.11   Note that an 'owner-occupier' notice under ground 1 must be given for this ground to apply. For the principles to be applied when a landlord seeks to persuade the court to dispense with service of a notice prior to commencement of the tenancy see para 11.7.

Ground 3: Tenancy preceded by a 'holiday let'

11.12   HA 1988 Sch 2 ground 3 provides:

> The tenancy is a fixed-term tenancy for a term not exceeding eight months and –
> (a) not later than the beginning of the tenancy the landlord gave notice in writing to the tenant that possession might be recovered on this ground; and
> (b) at some time within the period of twelve months ending with the beginning of the tenancy, the dwelling-house was occupied under a right to occupy it for a holiday.

11.13   This ground was designed to enable landlords who let premises on holiday lets during, for example, the summer, to be able to recover possession if they let them on longer lets during the winter. However, the ground operates in wider circumstances than that. To rely on ground 3, a landlord must prove all the following:

- The premises were occupied at some time during the preceding 12 months for the purpose of 'a holiday'. Even if a landlord produces a copy of a 'holiday let agreement' relating to such a period, it may be possible for the tenant to prove that that agreement was 'a sham' or 'did not reflect the intention of the parties' to it.[32] The burden of proving this lies on the tenant.
- The relevant tenancy was granted for a fixed period of not more than eight months. It is, however, arguable that ground 3 is available even where a tenant who initially agreed to rent the premises for eight months has held over and occupied the premises for a far longer period.
- Not later than the commencement of the tenancy the landlord gave written notice to the tenant that this ground for possession might be relied upon.

The court has no power to dispense with service of the notice required prior to the grant of the tenancy.[33]

---

32 See *Buchmann v May* [1978] 2 All ER 993 and *R v Rent Officer for Camden ex p Plant* (1980) 257 EG 713, (1980) 7 HLR 15, QBD.
33 Cf *Fowler v Minchin* (1987) 19 HLR 224, CA and *Springfield Investments v Bell* (1990) 22 HLR 440, CA.

Ground 4: 'Out of term' letting by specified educational institution

11.14   HA 1988 Sch 2 ground 4 provides:

> The tenancy is a fixed-term tenancy for a term not exceeding twelve months and –
>
> (a) not later than the beginning of the tenancy the landlord gave notice in writing to the tenant that possession might be recovered on this ground; and
>
> (b) at some time within the period of twelve months ending with the beginning of the tenancy, the dwelling-house was let on a tenancy falling within paragraph 8 of Schedule 1 to this Act.

11.15   This ground applies where, during the 12 months preceding the tenancy, the premises were let by a specified educational institution.[34] The term 'specified educational institution' includes universities, any other publicly funded institution providing further education and a number of associations and companies which have been specifically designated as such for Rent Act and Housing Act purposes, and any private registered provider of social housing or registered social landlord.

11.16   As with ground 3 above, notice stating that this ground may be relied upon has to be served before the commencement of the tenancy.

Ground 5: Property required for a minister of religion

11.17   HA 1988 Sch 2 ground 5 provides:

> The dwelling-house is held for the purpose of being available for occupation by a minister of religion as a residence from which to perform the duties of his office and –
>
> (a) not later than the beginning of the tenancy the landlord gave notice in writing to the tenant that possession might be recovered on this ground; and
>
> (b) the court is satisfied that the dwelling-house is required for occupation by a minister of religion as such a residence.

Notice that possession might be required under this ground must be served before the grant of the tenancy, and the landlord must satisfy the court that the property is required for occupation by a minister of religion as a residence. It is similar to Rent Act 1977 Sch 15 Case 15.[35]

---

34 See Assured and Protected Tenancies (Lettings to Students) Regulations 1998 SI No 1967 as amended.

35 See para 12.83.

Ground 7B: Occupier without the right to rent

11.18   HA 1988 Sch 2 ground 7B provides:

Both of the following conditions are met in relation to a dwelling-house in England.

Condition 1 is that the Secretary of State has given a notice in writing to the landlord or, in the case of joint landlords, one or more of them which identifies –

(a) the tenant or, in the case of joint tenants, one or more of them, or

(b) one or more other persons aged 18 or over who are occupying the dwelling-house,

as a person or persons disqualified as a result of their immigration status from occupying the dwelling-house under the tenancy.

Condition 2 is that the person or persons named in the notice –

(a) fall within paragraph (a) or (b) of condition 1, and

(b) are disqualified as a result of their immigration status from occupying the dwelling-house under the tenancy.

For the purposes of this ground a person ('P') is disqualified as a result of their immigration status from occupying the dwelling-house under the tenancy if –

(a) P is not a relevant national, and

(b) P does not have a right to rent in relation to the dwelling-house.

P does not have a right to rent in relation to the dwelling-house if –

(a) P requires leave to enter or remain in the United Kingdom but does not have it, or

(b) P's leave to enter or remain in the United Kingdom is subject to a condition preventing P from occupying the dwelling-house.

But P is to be treated as having a right to rent in relation to a dwelling-house if the Secretary of State has granted P permission for the purposes of this ground to occupy a dwelling-house under an assured tenancy.

In this ground 'relevant national' means –

(a) a British citizen,

(b) a national of an EEA State other than the United Kingdom, or

(c) a national of Switzerland.

At the time of publication of this edition, this ground was not in force. It is inserted into HA 1988 Sch 2 Part 1 by Immigration Act 2016 s41(2). When brought into effect, it will apply to all assured and assured shorthold tenancies, whether entered into before or after the date of commencement. It will apply where at least one of the occupiers does not have the 'right to rent' within the meaning of Immigration Act 2014 s21(2) and that person has been identified in a notice given by the Secretary of State.

By virtue of HA 1988 s10A (inserted by Immigration Act 2016 s41(5), not yet in force at the date of publication), where ground 7B is made out in respect of a joint tenancy, but one of the joint tenants has the 'right to rent', the court may, instead of making a possession order, order that the tenancy be transferred into the sole name of the qualifying joint tenant.

Tenancies excluded from the assured tenancy scheme

11.19 Certain kinds of private sector tenancies are excluded from the assured tenancy scheme altogether and therefore cannot be either assured or assured shorthold tenancies. These are:

- Tenancies at a high rent (ie, £100,000 per annum or more),[36] or, if granted before 1 April 1990, tenancies of premises with high rateable values (ie, over £1,500 in Greater London and over £750 elsewhere).[37]
- Tenancies under which no rent is payable.[38]
- Tenancies at a low rent (ie, at a rent of less than £1,000 per annum in London or less than £250 per annum elsewhere, or, if granted before 1 April 1990, at a rent less than two-thirds of the rateable value).[39]
- Tenancies of business premises which are protected under the Landlord and Tenant Act 1954 Part II.[40]
- Tenancies of properties which are licensed for the supply and consumption of alcohol on the premises, where the dwelling 'consists of or comprises' such premises.[41]
- Tenancies of properties let with agricultural land exceeding two acres.[42]
- Tenancies of properties comprised in agricultural holdings.[43]

36 HA 1988 Sch 1 para 2(1)(b), amended in England by Assured Tenancies (Amendment) (England) Order 2010 SI No 908 and in Wales by Assured Tenancies (Amendment of Rental Threshold) (Wales) Order 2011 SI No 1409.
37 References to Rating (Housing) Regulations 1990 SI No 434.
38 HA 1988 Sch 1 para 3.
39 HA 1988 Sch 1 paras 3A–3C, inserted by the References to Rating (Housing) Regulations 1990 SI No 434.
40 HA 1988 Sch 1 para 4.
41 HA 1988 Sch 1 para 5.
42 HA 1988 Sch 1 para 6.
43 HA 1988 Sch 1 para 7.

- Tenancies of accommodation granted to students by specified educational institutions or by another specified body.[44]
- Holiday lettings where the tenant merely has 'the right to occupy the dwelling-house for a holiday'.[45]
- Tenancies granted by resident landlords.[46] (This exception does not apply to purpose-built blocks of flats.) For the exception to apply, the tenancy must have been granted by a landlord who, both at the time of the grant of the tenancy and at all times since, has had his or her 'only or principal home' elsewhere in the building. An assured tenant cannot be deprived of security of tenure by accepting a new tenancy or moving to another part of the same building *after* a landlord has become a resident landlord. There are periods of disregard after the sale of premises or the death of a resident landlord when the new owner or the personal representatives of the deceased landlord are able to take advantage of the exemption.[47]
- Crown tenancies, but not premises under the management of the Crown Estate Commissioners.[48]
- Tenancies granted by private landlords under arrangements made by local housing authorities in accordance with their functions under HA 1996 ss188, 190, 200 or s204(4) (interim duties towards the homeless). Such tenancies cannot be assured or assured shorthold tenancies before the end of 12 months from the date of notification of the local authority's decision or from the determination of any HA 1996 s202 review or section 204 appeal, unless the landlord notifies the tenant in the meantime that the tenancy is to be an assured or assured shorthold tenancy.[49] Note that there is no similar exception from assured tenancy status where the

---

44 HA 1988 Sch 1 para 8. The specified bodies are listed in the Assured and Protected Tenancies (Lettings to Students) Regulations 1998 SI No 1967, as amended. They include private registered providers of social housing.

45 HA 1988 Sch 1 para 9. But note *Buchmann v May* [1978] 2 All ER 993, CA and *R v Rent Officer for Camden ex p Plant* (1980) 257 EG 713, (1980) 7 HLR 15, QBD (where tenancies which were not genuine holiday lets were found to be Rent Act protected tenancies).

46 HA 1988 Sch 1 para 10.

47 See HA 1988 Sch 1 paras 17–22.

48 HA 1988 Sch 1 para 11. The Crown Tenancies Bill, a private member's bill which would provide that certain Crown tenancies may be assured tenancies, was presented to Parliament on 4 July 2016.

49 HA 1996 s209, as substituted by Homelessness Act 2002 Sch 1 para 19. See paras 8.12–8.13.

accommodation is provided to enable the local authority to perform the main housing duty under HA 1996 s193.

- Tenancies granted by local authorities and other local government bodies.[50]
- Tenancies granted by fully mutual housing associations.[51]
- Tenancies granted under arrangements for the provision of support for asylum-seekers or dependants of asylum-seekers made under section 4 or Part VI of the Immigration and Asylum Act 1999.[52]
- Tenancies granted by private landlords under arrangements for the provision of accommodation to persons with temporary protection.[53]

11.20   If one of these exceptions applies, the tenant has no security of tenure and the landlord does not need to prove a reason or ground for possession. The landlord has to prove only that the contractual tenancy has been terminated. Once a notice to quit has been served and has expired, the tenant has no statutory protection, other than (in some cases) Protection from Eviction Act 1977 s3, which provides that it is unlawful for a landlord to evict such a tenant without obtaining a possession order from the court.[54] Where a court makes an order for the possession of a property in any of these cases, the court cannot postpone the date of possession for longer than 14 days after the date of the order, unless it appears to the court that exceptional hardship would be caused by requiring possession to be given up by that date, in which case the court may postpone possession for a maximum of six weeks. See, further, chapter 15 for the position of tenants with limited protection from eviction.

---

50   HA 1988 Sch 1 para 12.
51   HA 1988 Sch 1 para 12(1)(h). See *Berrisford v Mexfield Housing Co-operative Ltd* [2011] UKSC 52; *Sterling v Cyron Housing Co-Operative Ltd* [2013] EWHC 4445 (QB); and *Southward Housing Co-operative Ltd v Walker* [2015] EWHC 1615 (Ch), [2016] Ch 443. See also paras 8.20–8.26 and 15.1.
52   HA 1988 Sch 1 para 12A, inserted by Immigration and Asylum Act 1999 Sch 14 para 88.
53   HA 1988 Sch 1 para 12B. See the Displaced Persons (Temporary Protection) Regulations 2005 SI No 1379.
54   See para 15.2.

Licences

11.21   Some private sector occupiers do not have the status of a tenant, and therefore cannot qualify for the statutory protection afforded by the Rent Act 1977 or the Housing Act 1988. Where the occupier has entered ino a written agreement which describes itself as a tenancy or acknowledges that a tenancy has been created, it is likely to be a true 'tenancy'. In other cases, however, there may be no written agreement, or there may be an agreement which bears the label of a licence, or occupancy, or similar term. In those cases it is necessary to examine the rights and obligations in the arrangements under which occupation was permitted. Where there is no written agreement, these may have to be inferred from the conduct of the parties.

The tenancy/licence distinction

11.22   A tenancy is a legal interest in property. A licence is merely a personal permission to occupy accommodation. This formal distinction is of little assistance, however, in determining the true nature of a particular arrangement. In practice it can be difficult to establish with certainty which status an occupier has. People who stay in accommodation on a temporary, or casual, or informal basis may be *licensees* eg, hotel guests, most hostel dwellers, or 'lodgers' in someone else's home. The problem of deciding whether a particular arrangement is a tenancy or a licence may be illustrated by comparing, for example, a hostel resident (who is likely to be a licensee) with the occupier of a bedsit in a converted house (who is likely to be a tenant).

11.23   In the leading case of *Street v Mountford*[55] the House of Lords held that, where a landlord granted the right to occupy residential accommodation for a term at a rent, and the occupier obtained exclusive possession of the premises, this normally gave rise to a tenancy. The elements of exclusive possession, a term or period and rent were therefore to be regarded as the 'hallmarks' of a residential tenancy. Payment of rent is normally an essential condition of the existence of a tenancy, though there may be exceptions.[56]

11.24   It is a question of fact whether an occupier has exclusive possession. To determine whether the right to exclusive possession exists, it is necessary to examine both the agreement and the factual

---

55 [1985] 2 All ER 289, HL.
56 *Ashburn Anstalt v Arnold* [1988] 2 WLR 706, CA.

circumstances. Familiar examples of situations where there is, or is likely to be, *no* exclusive possession are:

- where the occupier has a room in the landlord's own home and the landlord[57] retains general control over the room and the premises;
- where the landlord either provides services such as room cleaning or otherwise retains the right of unrestricted access to the occupier's room;
- where the landlord retains the right to move the occupier from room to room (this must be a genuine right, such as is often found in short stay hostels, and not a 'sham' provision);
- hotel accommodation;
- hostel accommodation.

The agreement in the above instances is likely to be a licence. For further discussion of the tenancy/licence distinction, see chapter 1 at paras 1.7–1.19.

No intention to enter into legal relations

11.25   In *Street v Mountford*, the House of Lords recognised that, even where exclusive possession is granted, the arrangement may still be a licence, and not a tenancy, where:

- there is no genuine intention (on both sides) to enter into the legal relationship of landlord and tenant; or
- the letting is a *service occupancy* (ie, accommodation which is tied to a person's employment, where it is necessary to live on the premises to do the job; *or* where the employee is obliged under his or her contract of employment to live on the premises and that requirement is imposed for the 'better performance of duties' under the employment contract).

11.26   Examples of situations where there is no intention to enter into legal relations are:

- accommodation provided as an act of generosity or friendship;[58]
- a family arrangement.[59] However, the fact that the landlord and the occupant are related will not necessarily prevent a tenancy arising;[60]

---

57   The term 'landlord' in this paragraph is used to denote 'landlord or licensor'.
58   *Booker v Palmer* [1942] 2 All ER 674, CA.
59   *Facchini v Bryson* [1952] 1 TLR 1386, CA.
60   *Nunn v Dalrymple* (1989) 21 HLR 569, CA.

- occupation during negotiations subject to contract, eg by a purchaser before completion.[61]

Shared accommodation

11.27　The written agreement will not necessarily determine the nature of the relationship.[62] In the case of *Antoniades v Villiers*,[63] a couple who were living together signed separate 'licence agreements' for a one-bedroom flat. The landlord claimed, in a purported term of the agreement, to be able to permit other people to use the flat. It was held that the agreements were a sham, or a 'pretence', and that the occupiers in reality had a joint tenancy of the flat. Neither the 'label' on an agreement nor even its detailed terms will therefore be conclusive as to the nature of the arrangement. It is necessary to examine closely the terms of the agreement, especially those which purport to deny exclusive possession, and to investigate whether those terms reflect the reality of the arrangement between the parties. Evidence of how the parties have conducted their dealings in practice is relevant to ascertaining whether the written agreement reflects their true intentions.

11.28　In the associated case of *AG Securities v Vaughan*[64] the occupiers were single people who shared a four bedroom flat and who had each signed 'licence agreements'. As one occupier left, he or she was replaced by a different occupier. Each person paid a separate charge. It was held that these were genuine licences, because no one had exclusive possession of a particular room or of any part of the flat. There could not be a joint tenancy because each of the occupiers had arrived at different times and paid a different charge, and so there was no 'unity of interest'.

11.29　Where there is an oral agreement, it may be necessary to look at the way in which the parties have behaved, in order to determine what the terms of the agreement are. If, in practice, the occupier has enjoyed exclusive possession, the likelihood is that a tenancy has been created.

61　*Sopwitch v Stutchbury* (1985) 17 HLR 50, CA.
62　*Street v Mountford* [1985] 2 All ER 289, HL.
63　[1988] 3 All ER 1058, HL.
64　[1988] 3 All ER 1058, HL.

Specific types of licence

11.30 Agreements which claim to be licences or to deny exclusive occupation should be treated with caution. Advisers should analyse their terms to establish whether or not they are genuine licences, or whether in reality they are tenancies, which are likely to be assured shorthold tenancies. Such agreements can take many different forms. An example has been the growth in recent years of so-called 'property guardian' agreements, whereby the contract grants the right to occupation of a building on a temporary or precarious basis, on the understanding that the occupier is fulfilling the purpose of keeping the building secure or otherwise acting as caretaker. Other agreements contain terms which purport to deny exclusive possession of part of the building to the occupier, such as reserving to the landlord the right to place other persons in shared occupation of the property. Even where a particular room is nominated for occupation, the agreement may contain a term requiring the occupier to move to a different room at the discretion of the landlord.

11.31 The same principles derived from the decision in *Street v Mountford* and subsequent case-law apply in such instances. Where a particular room has been offered to the incoming occupier at a specific rent, this may be taken to imply that exclusive possession has been granted and accordingly that a tenancy has been created. In these circumstances, if the agreement does not specify the particular unit of accommodation, but merely purports to grant a right of occupation of the premises as a whole, it may be that the agreement is a 'pretence'.[65] In other circumstances, such as where the occupiers reach agreement between themselves on the allocation of rooms without reference to the landlord, the agreement is likely to be a licence. In all cases, it is necessary to ask whether the terms of the written agreement represent the true nature of the bargain between the parties. Although subsequent conduct does not, of itself, determine the nature of contractual rights, the question is whether the landlord genuinely intended to exercise the terms of the written agreement. Evidence of whether certain terms of the agreement have actually been implemented may be relevant to the question of whether those terms genuinely reflect the parties' common intention.

---

65 See *Antoniades v Villiers* [1988] 3 All ER 1058, HL and para 11.27 above.

Termination of licences

11.32   Licensees in the private sector do not have any potential for long-term security. They may be entitled to basic protection from eviction (ie the right not to be evicted except following a valid notice to quit and a court order for possession).[66] Some licensees, however, will be 'excluded occupiers' and will not be entitled even to this basic protection from eviction. See further, chapter 15.

Unfair terms: tenancies and licences

11.33   Whether the particular agreement is a tenancy or a licence, there may be terms in the agreement which offend the 'unfair terms' provisions in Part 2 of the Consumer Rights Act 2015. Part 2 applies to contracts entered into, and relevant notices issued, on or after 1 October 2015.[67] Unfair terms may include, for example, clauses imposing excessive fees or charges, unfair restrictions on the use of the accommodation, provision for unilateral variation of the agreement by the owner, or provision for termination of licences with unreasonably short notice.[68] Contracts entered into before 1 October 2015 are still governed by the Unfair Terms in Consumer Contracts Regulations 1999 (UTCC Regs).[69] The 'unfair terms' provisions of Part 2 of the 2015

---

66   Under Protection from Eviction Act 1977 s3 (prohibition of eviction without due process of law) and s5 (requirements of valid notice to quit).

67   Relevant guidance has been issued by the Competition and Markets Authority: see *Guidance on the unfair terms provisions in the Consumer Rights Act 2015,* CMA 37, 31 July 2015. The guidance supersedes the general unfair contract terms guidance originally issued by the Office of Fair Trading (OFT), including the specific *Guidance on unfair terms in tenancy agreements* (OFT 356, September 2005). However, the CMA Guidance contains a *Historic Annex A to unfair contract terms guidance,* which preserves examples of fair and unfair terms considered by the OFT, including the 'Grey List' which appeared in Schedule 2 to the UTCC Regs (Indicative and non-exhaustive list of terms which may be regarded as unfair). The CMA considers that the Annex continues to provide practical illustrations of how the principles of contractual fairness have been applied in particular cases. The CMA has also published *Guidance for lettings professionals on consumer protection law,* CMA 31, June 2014, but this pre-dates the Consumer Rights Act 2015.

68   The provisions of other consumer legislation may also have a bearing on letting agreements, notably the Consumer Protection from Unfair Trading Regulations 2008 SI No 1277, the Consumer Contracts (Information, Cancellation and Additional Charges) Regulations 2013 SI No 3134, and the Consumer Protection (Amendment) Regulations 2014 SI No 870.

69   1999 SI No 2083.

Act are substantially the same as those of UTCC Regs 1999, although they have been extended in scope.[70] Because of this continuity in the legislation, case-law under the UTCC Regs is for the most part still relevant under the 2015 Act. In particular, the courts have held that the prohibition of unfair terms applies to tenancy agreements.[71] The origin of these provisions is Council Directive 93/13/EEC.[72]

70 The unfair terms provisions in Consumer Rights Act 2015 Part 2 extend to 'consumer notices' (CRA 2015 s61(7)) as well as to contract terms, including individually negotiated terms (which are excluded from the UTCC Regs 1999). See the useful summary of the two regimes in the *Guidance on the unfair terms provisions in the Consumer Rights Act 2015*, pp5–18.
71 See *R (Khatun) v Newham LBC* [2004] EWCA Civ 55; [2004] HLR 29.
72 See *Brusse and de Man Garabito v Jahani BV*, C-488/11; [2013] HLR 38, 30 May 2013. In this case the ECJ held that the Directive (which deals with unfair terms in consumer contracts), applies to all residential tenancy agreements where the landlord is acting for purposes relating to a 'trade, business or profession', and the tenant is renting the property for use as his or her home (para 34). The Court also held that if, as a matter of domestic law, the national court has power to raise an issue which was not raised by the parties, it is required to assess the fairness of a contractual term and apply the Directive.

CHAPTER 12

Rent Act tenancies

continued

Introduction

12.1 This chapter applies only to tenancies granted before 15 January 1989, or, after that date, in the limited circumstances provided for by Housing Act (HA) 1988 s34 – see para 12.7. There are nevertheless still many Rent Act regulated tenancies still in existence. In this chapter, all references are to the Rent Act (RA) 1977 unless otherwise stated.[1]

12.2 The law relating to these tenants' security of tenure and to possession proceedings brought against them is an amalgam of the common law and protection superimposed on it[2] by the Rent Acts. Before the passing of the first Rent Act,[3] landlords bringing possession proceedings had to prove only that they owned or had an interest in the premises in question and that they were entitled to possession. Usually, this involved proving that any occupant had never had permission to be on the premises or, alternatively, that any such permission had been terminated in accordance with the provisions of the licence or tenancy. Apart from when landlords sought to forfeit fixed-term tenancies for breach of covenant, there was no question of a landlord having to prove any ground or reasons for seeking possession or that it was reasonable for the court to make an order.

12.3 Although landlords' and tenants' rights have been greatly modified by statute, the old common law rules remain highly relevant to residential occupiers who wish to defend possession proceedings. Even where a tenant has full Rent Act protection, a landlord must prove that any occupant's contractual tenancy has been determined properly before relying on the Rent Act grounds for possession.[4] A landlord's failure to determine a contractual tenancy, for example, by serving an invalid notice to quit (see paras 14.8–14.26), provides a complete defence even though there may be unanswerable Rent Act grounds for possession. In the same way, where an occupier is outside full Rent Act or Housing Act protection the only defence that he or she may have to possession proceedings is likely to be that the

1 The major works on the Rent Acts (including the precursors of RA 1977) are R E Megarry, *The Rent Acts*, Stevens & Sons Ltd (11th ed, 1988) and *Blundell's Rent Restriction Cases*, Sweet and Maxwell (3rd ed, 1955).
2 Common law rules have themselves been considerably modified, eg, the restrictions on forfeiture in Law of Property Act 1925 s146 and County Courts Act 1984 s138. See paras 14.51 and 14.63.
3 Increase of Rent and Mortgage Interest (War Restrictions) Act 1915.
4 RA 1977 s98 and Sch 15 (see para 12.31). The position is different for assured and assured shorthold tenants, for whom a specific form of notice is required by the Housing Act 1988. See chapters 1 and 10.

landlord has failed to terminate the tenancy or licence in the proper way. The common law rules relating to determination of tenancies are dealt with in detail in chapter 14.

12.4   The effect of most of the Rent Acts passed between 1915 and 1977 was to provide tenants who enjoyed full Rent Act status with two forms of rights, namely, control over recoverable rents and security of tenure. Rent control takes the form of a 'fair rent' determined by the rent officer in accordance with RA 1977 s70. The Rent Acts (Maximum Fair Rent) Order 1999[5] limits increases in registered fair rents by reference to an arithmetical formula, generally based on the Retail Price Index plus 5 per cent.

Who is entitled to Rent Act protection?

12.5   Tenancies which are regulated by RA 1977 are those which were granted before 15 January 1989[6] by private sector landlords or which replaced such earlier tenancies. It is possible to create a regulated tenancy after 15 January 1989 only in certain exceptional cases such as where the new tenancy follows on immediately from a previous tenancy which was a regulated tenancy and is granted to the same tenant by the same landlord (see para 12.7 below).

12.6   The term 'regulated tenancy' is the general term used to describe a tenancy with full Rent Act protection. It includes both the 'protected' (contractual) and the 'statutory' phases of the tenancy. The term 'regulated tenancy' will be used in this chapter unless it is necessary to distinguish between the protected and statutory phases of the tenancy.

Regulated tenancies commencing on or after 15 January 1989

12.7   HA 1988 s34 provides that no new Rent Act protected tenancies can be created after 15 January 1989, unless one of three exceptions applies:

---

5   SI No 6.
6   That is, the date when Part I of the Housing Act 1988 came into force, ushering in the regime of assured and assured shorthold tenancies.

- the tenancy was entered into in pursuance of a contract made before 15 January 1989 (being the date when the 1988 Act came into force);
- the tenancy was granted to an existing Rent Act regulated tenant by the same landlord. If there are joint tenants or joint landlords, it is sufficient for only one of the joint tenants to have been a regulated tenant and for only one of the joint landlords to have been the landlord of the existing tenant or tenants. Although the wording of the provision is less than clear, it is plain that Parliament's intention was that this exception should apply even if the tenant has moved from other accommodation, provided that the same person is landlord of both properties;[7]
- before the grant of the new tenancy an order for possession was made on the ground of suitable alternative accommodation against a protected or statutory tenant[8] and in the possession proceedings relating to the earlier tenancy, the court directed that the tenancy of the suitable alternative accommodation should be held on a protected tenancy, ie, the contractual phase of a regulated tenancy. The court should consider whether an assured tenancy would 'afford the required security'. If it would not, it may direct that the suitable alternative accommodation should be held on a protected tenancy. It is obviously important that representatives of Rent Act tenants in suitable alternative accommodation cases do all they can to ensure that the court directs that the new tenancy should be held on a protected tenancy. The market rent which would be recoverable under an assured tenancy (as opposed to a 'fair rent' under a regulated tenancy) may mean that the alternative accommodation would not be suitable to the means of the tenant and/or that it would be unreasonable to make a possession order.

---

7 See *Laimond Properties Ltd v Al-Shakarchi* (1998) 30 HLR 1099, (1998) *Times* 23 February, CA; *Kotecha v Rimington* March 1991 *Legal Action* 15; *Singh v Dalby* September 1992 *Legal Action* 22; *Gorringe v Twinsectra* June 1994 *Legal Action* 11; *Secretarial & Nominee Co Ltd v Thomas* [2005] EWCA Civ 1008, [2006] HLR 5; *Bacon v Mountview Estates plc* [2015] UKUT 588 (LC) and *Swanbrae Ltd v Ryder* [2015] UKUT 69 (LC).
8 Under RA 1977 s98(1)(a) or Sch 15 Case 1 or Rent (Agriculture) Act 1976 Sch 4 Case 1.

Conditions of Rent Act protection

12.8   RA 1977 s1 defines a protected tenancy as follows:

> Subject to this Part of this Act, a tenancy under which a dwelling-house (which may be a house or part of a house) is let as a separate dwelling is a protected tenancy for the purposes of this Act.

> Any reference in this Act to a protected tenant shall be construed accordingly.

12.9   The terms 'dwelling-house' and 'let as a separate dwelling' have been extensively considered in case-law and are discussed further in paras 1.22 and 1.26 respectively.

12.10   The opening words of RA 1977 s1 refer to the various exceptions to full Rent Act protection which are listed in RA 1977 Part I. The exceptions (in summary) are as follows:

- dwelling-houses with rateable values above certain limits (if granted before 1 April 1990) or where the rent is more than £25,000 per annum (if granted on or after 1 April 1990) (s4);
- tenancies where no rent is payable or the rent is less than two-thirds of the rateable value (if granted before 1 April 1990) or less than £1,000 per annum in Greater London or £250 elsewhere (if granted on or after 1 April 1990) (s5);
- certain shared ownership leases (s5A);
- certain dwelling-houses let with other land (s6);
- tenancies where the tenant is obliged to pay for board or substantial attendances (s7);
- lettings by certain educational establishments to students (s8);
- holiday lettings (s9);
- agricultural holdings (s10);
- licensed premises (s11);
- some lettings by resident landlords[9] (s12);
- landlord's interest belonging to the Crown, but not where the property is under the management of the Crown Estates Commissioners (s13);[10]

---

9 The conditions for 'resident landlord' status are similar to those relating to the corresponding exception to assured tenancies (see para 11.19), except that under the Rent Act the landlord needs only to occupy as a residence another dwelling in the same building, and not necessarily as his or her 'only or principal home'.

10 The Crown Tenancies Bill, a private member's bill which would provide that certain Crown tenancies may be assured tenancies, was presented to Parliament on 4 July 2016.

- landlord's interest belonging to a local authority or another local government body (s14); and
- landlord's interest belonging to a housing association or housing co-operative (ss15 and 16).

Rent Act tenancies: general principles

12.11 Full Rent Act protection gives residential tenants the right to continue as 'statutory tenants'[11] even after their contractual tenancy has terminated, provided that they continue to occupy the premises 'as a residence'. However, this status of 'virtual irremovability' is qualified – landlords are given various 'grounds for possession'[12] which, if proved, may enable the county court to make a possession order.

12.12 A landlord must always terminate a tenant's contractual tenancy (for example, by serving a valid notice to quit) *before* issuing possession proceedings. Failure by a landlord to terminate the contractual tenancy provides a complete defence, however overwhelming the Rent Act grounds for possession may be. This will not be the case, however, if the contractual tenancy has been terminated at some time in the past and the tenant is already a statutory tenant.

12.13 If statutory tenants cease to 'occupy premises as a residence', they lose their Rent Act protection, and a landlord then has to prove only that the contractual tenancy has, at some stage, been terminated. However, statutory tenants are not treated as ceasing to occupy as a residence (and so may keep Rent Act protection) where they are temporarily absent or, in some circumstances, even where they live in two different homes. For further discussion of statutory residence, see para 12.16 below.

12.14 There are two categories of grounds for possession: 'discretionary grounds'[13] and 'mandatory grounds'.[14] If a landlord proves that a tenant's contractual tenancy has been terminated and that one of the *mandatory* grounds for possession exists, there is an automatic entitlement to an order for possession. However, where a contractual tenancy has been terminated and one of the *discretionary* grounds for possession exists, the landlord must, in addition, satisfy the court

---

11 See RA 1977 s2.
12 The grounds for possession are set out in RA 1977 s98 and Sch 15. See para 12.31 onwards.
13 RA 1977 Sch 15 Cases 1–10 and s98(1), which deals with the availability of suitable alternative accommodation.
14 RA 1977 Sch 15 Cases 11–20.

that it is reasonable to make an order for possession. Even after a possession order has been made, provided that it was made on discretionary grounds, the court may still have power to vary, stay or suspend the order (see chapter 31).

12.15   RA 1977 also provided for an intermediate category of tenants (and some licensees) who had the limited protection of 'restricted contracts'.[15] Tenants who did not have full Rent Act security because they had a resident landlord[16] were restricted contract holders. Other tenants who were not entitled to Rent Act protection[17] but whose rent included payment for the use of furniture or for services were also likely to have restricted contracts. Occupiers with restricted contracts had only minimal rights to delay the operation of a possession order (see RA 1977 ss102A–106A). Very few, if any, restricted contracts still exist (see para 12.95).

Statutory tenancies

12.16   As noted in para 12.6, the term 'regulated tenancy' is used to denote a Rent Act tenancy in either of the phases of its existence: the protected (contractual) phase or the statutory phase. After a protected tenancy has been determined, it becomes a statutory tenancy with continuing Rent Act protection, provided that the tenant occupies the premises 'as his residence'.[18] Although there is no requirement in the Act that a contractual tenant should occupy premises as a residence, this is crucial for statutory tenants.

12.17   RA 1977 s2 provides for the creation of statutory tenancies:

2(1) Subject to this Part of this Act –

(a) after the termination of a protected tenancy of a dwelling-house the person who, immediately before that termination, was the protected tenant of the dwelling-house shall, if and so long as he occupies the dwelling-house as his residence, be the statutory tenant of it; and

(b) Part I of Schedule 1 to this Act shall have effect for determining what person (if any) is the statutory tenant of a dwelling-house or, as the case may be, is entitled to an assured tenancy of a dwelling-house by succession at any time after the death

---

15 RA 1977 ss19 and 20 (repealed by HA 1988 s140 and Sch 18).
16 RA 1977 s12.
17 Usually because their landlord provided board or substantial 'attendances'. RA 1977 s7. See, eg *Otter v Norman* [1989] AC 129, (1988) 20 HLR 594, HL.
18 RA 1977 s2.

of a person who, immediately before his death, was either a protected tenant of the dwelling-house or the statutory tenant of it by virtue of paragraph (a) above.

(2) In this Act a dwelling-house is referred to as subject to a statutory tenancy when there is a statutory tenant of it.

(3) In subsection (1)(a) above and in Part I of Schedule 1, the phrase 'if and so long as he occupies the dwelling-house as his residence' shall be construed as it was immediately before the commencement of this Act (that is to say, in accordance with section 3(2) of the Rent Act 1968).

(4) A person who becomes a statutory tenant of a dwelling-house as mentioned in subsection (1)(a) above is, in this Act, referred to as a statutory tenant by virtue of his previous protected tenancy.

(5) A person who becomes a statutory tenant as mentioned in subsection (1)(b) above is, in this Act, referred to as a statutory tenant by succession.

12.18   As noted in para 12.13, if a statutory tenant ceases to reside in the premises, Rent Act protection is lost completely and a landlord bringing possession proceedings need prove only ownership of the premises, the termination of the contractual tenancy and that the tenant no longer resides in the premises. There is no need in these circumstances to prove a Rent Act ground for possession or that it is reasonable to make an order for possession. On the other hand, if a statutory tenant does not give up possession and continues to live in the premises, the only way in which the landlord can repossess is to prove one of the Rent Act grounds for possession, and, if appropriate, that it is reasonable to make an order for possession.[19]

12.19   There was no express requirement in the first Rent Acts[20] that a statutory tenant reside in the premises. However, in a series of cases it was decided that the protection given to a statutory tenant is 'a personal privilege which ceases when the tenant goes out of occupation'.[21] The object of the Acts was to protect tenants who occupied premises as their home,[22] not absentee tenants. The continuing importance of this principle is recognised by RA 1977 s2(3).

12.20   In determining whether or not a tenant occupies premises as a residence, the first material date is the date of termination of the

---

19 *Boyer v Warbey (No 1)* [1953] 1 QB 234 and *Brown v Draper* [1944] KB 309, [1944] 1 All ER 246.

20 Increase of Rent and Mortgage Interest (War Restrictions) Act 1915 and Increase of Rent and Mortgage (Restrictions) Act 1920.

21 *Middleton v Baldock (TW)* [1950] 1 KB 657, [1950] 1 All ER 708.

22 *Skinner v Geary* [1931] 2 KB 546.

contractual tenancy.[23] Whether or not the tenant was living in the premises during the contractual tenancy is irrelevant. However, if the tenant is not residing in the premises when the contractual tenancy is terminated, a statutory tenancy cannot arise.[24] Even if a former protected tenant resumes residence after the termination of the contractual tenancy, it is impossible to reinstate Rent Act protection as a statutory tenant; it is lost forever. In addition, the tenant must remain in residential occupation throughout the statutory tenancy. Accordingly, if the tenant sublets the whole of premises rented, the protection of a statutory tenancy is lost because it is impossible for the tenant to be in residential occupation.[25] However, it is not necessary for the tenant to reside in all parts of the premises all of the time. A landlord cannot claim that a tenant has ceased to be a statutory tenant of one part only of the premises and recover possession of that part.[26]

12.21   'Residence' in the context of Rent Act statutory tenancies is not interpreted in a narrow sense.[27] A statutory tenant need not occupy premises 24 hours per day, 365 days per year. It is accepted that tenants may be in residence for the purpose of the Rent Act even though they have been physically absent from premises for prolonged periods of 'temporary absence'. Similarly, it is well established that a tenant may maintain residence in two homes at the same time. Each of these alternatives is considered in the following paragraphs.

23 *Skinner v Geary* [1931] 2 KB 546; *John M Brown Ltd v Bestwick* [1951] 1 KB 21, [1950] 2 All ER 338 and *Colin Smith Music Ltd v Ridge* [1975] 1 WLR 463.
24 *Brown v Bestwick* [1951] 1 KB 21, [1950] 2 All ER 338. Cf *Francis Jackson Developments Ltd v Hall* [1951] 2 KB 488.
25 *Brown v Bestwick* [1951] 1 KB 21, [1950] 2 All ER 338 and *Ujima Housing Association v Ansah* (1998) 30 HLR 831, CA. See also RA 1977 Sch 15 Case 6 below and *Regalian Securities Ltd v Ramsden* [1981] 1 WLR 611, (1981–82) 2 HLR 84, HL at 74.
26 *Berkeley v Papadoyannis* [1954] 2 QB 149. Contrast the residence requirement for assured tenancies under the Housing Act 1988 s1 or secure tenancies under the Housing Act 1985 s81, whereby statutory protection depends on occupation as the tenant's 'only or principal home'.
27 *Skinner v Geary* [1931] 2 KB 546.

Temporary absence

12.22   Tenants must show two things to establish that they are still occupying, as a residence, premises from which they are temporarily
absent.[28]

- *Some kind of physical presence.* It is not enough merely to keep
an inward intention to return. This intention must be clothed by
outward and visible signs of the intention to return. Tenants must
leave behind deliberate symbols of their occupation and preserve
the premises for their ultimate homecoming.[29] In some cases
this requirement has been satisfied by tenants leaving behind
furniture,[30] relatives[31] or a caretaker to look after the premises.[32]
In practice, tenants intending to be absent for any length of time
would be well advised to leave behind some personal items such
as books, clothes, crockery and cutlery as well as furniture.

- *The tenant must at all times retain a definite intention to return.*
There must also be a practical possibility of the tenant fulfilling
the intention of returning within a reasonable time.[33] It is not
enough for this intention to be dependent on something else happening, such as the death of a parent.[34] The court should consider
the tenant's intention both at the date of the expiry of the notice to
quit and during the time since its expiry.[35] It should focus on 'the
enduring intention' of the tenant and not on 'fleeting changes of
mind'. This is particularly true of an elderly tenant in poor health
whose intentions 'may well have fluctuated from time to time
and even from day to day'.[36] The reasons for a tenant's absence
may be relevant and it is far easier to prove an intention to return
if the initial absence is due to 'some sudden calamity' such as

---

28   *Brown v Brash* [1948] 2 KB 247.
29   *Brown v Brash* [1948] 2 KB 247.
30   *Gofor Investments Ltd v Roberts* (1975) 29 P&CR 366.
31   *Dixon v Tommis* [1952] 1 All ER 725; *Hammersmith and Fulham LBC v Clarke*
(2001) 33 HLR 77, March 2001 *Legal Action* 28, CA.
32   *Brown v Brash* [1948] 2 KB 247 and *Amoah v Barking and Dagenham LBC* [2001]
All ER (D) 138 (Jan), March 2001 *Legal Action* 28, ChD.
33   *Tickner v Hearn* [1960] 1 WLR 1406.
34   *Cove v Flick* [1954] 2 QB 326 (Note), [1954] 2 All ER 441.
35   The Court of Appeal gave guidance concerning the factors relevant to assessing
the tenant's intention to return in the secure tenancy case of *Islington LBC v
Boyle* [2011] EWCA Civ 1450, [2012] HLR 18.
36   *Hammersmith and Fulham LBC v Clarke* (2001) 33 HLR 77, March 2001 *Legal
Action* 28, CA.

a sentence of imprisonment[37] or a flood.[38] Other reasons given for temporary absence have been illness of the tenant,[39] illness of relatives,[40] disrepair and pregnancy of the tenant's wife.[41]

12.23   It is a question of fact and degree in each case whether the absence is such that the tenant has ceased to occupy premises as a residence. The burden of proof initially lies on the landlord to show that the tenant is absent. Once a landlord has established this, it is for the tenant to show that a physical presence in the premises and an intention to return have been maintained.[42]

12.24   The following cases illustrate how long 'temporary absence' can be:

- *Wigley v Leigh*[43] – tenant's absence from 1940 to 1949. Initially she stayed with relatives because her husband was at war but she was then prevented from returning because she suffered from tuberculosis.
- *Dixon v Tommis*[44] – at the time of the hearing the tenant had been absent for six months and did not intend to return for three years. He left his furniture in the premises while his son and his son's family lived there.
- *Gofor Investments v Roberts*[45] – at the time of the hearing the tenants had been absent for five years and intended to return within 'three to five years'. They had been living in Morocco and Malta and had left their furniture and two sons in the premises.
- *Richards v Green*[46] – the tenant had been absent for two and a half years. He had been living at a house owned by his parents, initially because they had been ill, but after their death because he was clearing up the house and arranging for it to be sold.

---

37 *Brown v Brash* [1948] 2 KB 247 and *Amoah v Barking and Dagenham LBC* (2001) 81 P&CR D12, March 2001 *Legal Action* 28, ChD.
38 *Bushford v Falco* [1954] 1 WLR 672, [1954] 1 All ER 957.
39 *Tickner v Hearn* [1960] 1 WLR 1406.
40 *Richards v Green* (1984) 11 HLR 1, (1983) 268 EG 443, CA.
41 *Atyeo v Fardoe* (1979) 37 P&CR 494.
42 *Roland House Gardens v Cravitz* (1975) 29 P&CR 432 and *Amoah v Barking and Dagenham LBC* March 2001 *Legal Action* 28, ChD.
43 [1950] 2 KB 305, [1950] 1 All ER 73.
44 [1952] 1 All ER 725. See too *Brown v Draper* [1944] 1 All ER 246; *Hallwood Estates v Flack* (1950) 66 TLR (Pt 2) 368.
45 (1975) 29 P&CR 366.
46 (1984) 11 HLR 1, (1983) 268 EG 443, CA.

- *Tickner v Hearn*[47] – absence of five and a half years by a tenant who was in a mental hospital suffering from schizophrenia. The mere fact that she was 'mentally unsound' did not mean that she was incapable of forming an intention to return to the premises.[48]

12.25 On the other hand, in *DJ Crocker Securities (Portsmouth) Ltd v Johal*[49] the Court of Appeal refused to overturn a judge's finding that a tenant had ceased to occupy a flat as his home. The tenant had left to look after his father in Malaysia in 1977. Since then he had lived and worked in Malaysia with his wife and children, and between 1980 and 1988 had only spent between nine and 26 days each year in the flat.

Occupation through other people

12.26 Although the presence of friends and relatives living in premises may be evidence of the absent tenant's intention to return,[50] it is not, as a general rule, possible for a tenant to maintain Rent Act protection through the residence of other people without an intention of returning in person.[51] However, an exception was that a husband was deemed to be continuing to occupy premises as a residence even if he did not intend to return, if his wife was still living in the premises.[52] Statute now makes provision for this situation in the Family Law Act 1996 s30(4) as amended by the Civil Partnership Act 2004. One spouse's or civil partner's occupation is to be treated for the purposes of the Rent Act 1977[53] as occupation by the other spouse (or civil partner) as that spouse's (or civil partner's) residence. If the spouse (or civil partner) who is the tenant moves out and the statutory tenancy continues as a result of the non-tenant spouse's or civil partner's residence, the actual tenant remains liable for the rent, unless an order is made under Family Law Act 1996 Sch 7 para 11.[54]

---

47 [1960] 1 WLR 1406.
48 However, in *Duke v Porter* (1987) 19 HLR 1, [1986] 2 EGLR 101, CA there was an absence of ten years. Held: tenant had ceased to occupy as a residence.
49 [1989] 42 EG 103. See also *Prince v Robinson* (1999) 31 HLR 89, CA.
50 *Dixon v Tommis* [1952] 1 All ER 725; *Roland House Gardens v Cravitz* (1975) 29 P&CR 432 and *Blanway Investments Ltd v Lynch* (1993) 25 HLR 378, CA.
51 *Collins v Claughton* [1959] 1 WLR 145, [1959] 1 All ER 95.
52 *Old Gate Estates v Alexander* [1950] 1 KB 311, [1949] 2 All ER 822.
53 As well as for the purposes of the Housing Act 1985 (secure tenancies) and the Housing Act 1988 (assured tenancies).
54 *Griffiths v Renfree* (1989) 21 HLR 338, [1989] 2 EGLR 46, CA.

There is no 'deemed residence' unless at some time both spouses have lived in the premises as a marital or partnership home.[55]

12.27   Rent Act protection cannot, however, be maintained by the continuing occupation of an ex-spouse of the tenant,[56] although the Family Law Act 1996 Sch 7 does provide for the transfer of tenancies from one spouse or civil partner to another before termination of the relationship.[57] Obviously, none of these problems of continuing occupation arises if the tenancy was originally granted in joint names because occupation by one joint tenant is sufficient to maintain a statutory tenancy.[58]

12.28   A Rent Act protected tenancy does not vest in the trustee in bankruptcy if the tenant is made bankrupt. Accordingly, there is nothing to prevent a statutory tenancy arising in the ordinary way to protect the bankrupt tenant in occupation.[59]

Residence in two homes

12.29   It has been recognised since the early days of the Rent Acts[60] that it is possible for a tenant to occupy two properties as residences at the same time. A tenant may maintain Rent Act protection in both homes or, alternatively, may maintain protection in one while owning the other.

12.30   The classic example is of a tenant who has one home in the town and another in the country.[61] The question 'to be answered by

---

55 Family Law Act 1996 s30(7) and see *Hall v King* (1988) 55 P&CR 307, [1987] 2 EGLR 121, (1987) 19 HLR 440, CA.

56 *Heath Estates v Burchell* (1979) 251 EG 1173; *Crago v Julian* (1992) 24 HLR 306, [1992] 1 All ER 744, CA.

57 See also Matrimonial Causes Act 1973 s24. It is important that any application for a transfer of the tenancy is made promptly if the tenant spouse is not actually residing in the premises and the tenancy is a statutory tenancy. Occupation by a non-tenant spouse ceases to count as residence by the tenant on the making of the decree absolute unless the contrary is specifically ordered. The making of the decree absolute may terminate the statutory tenancy unless the order transferring the tenancy is made simultaneously.

58 *Lloyd v Sadler* [1978] QB 774, [1978] 2 WLR 721, CA. For further discussion of the position of spouses, former spouses and other cohabitants, see chapter 20.

59 Insolvency Act 1986 s283(3)(a). Note, however, that bankruptcy may provide a ground for possession: *Cadogan Estates Ltd v McMahon* [2001] AC 378, [2000] 3 WLR 1555, HL.

60 For example, *Skinner v Geary* [1931] 2 KB 546. See too *Stephens v Kerr* [2006] EWCA Civ 187, [2006] All ER (D) 186 (Feb).

61 For example, *Langford Property Co v Athanassoglou* [1948] 2 All ER 722.

ordinary common sense standards, is whether the particular premises are in the personal occupation of the tenant as his or her home,
or, if the tenant has more than one home, as one of his or her homes.
Occupation merely as a convenience for ... occasional visits'[62] is not
sufficient. It is not merely a question of what a tenant does in particular premises. The court should look at all the circumstances and
the way in which the tenant leads his or her life.[63] Comparatively
limited periods of occupation may be sufficient. In *Langford Property
Co v Athanassoglou*[64] a tenant slept in his 'town house' twice a week
and rarely ate there. In *Bevington v Crawford*,[65] tenants lived mainly
in Cannes and spent approximately two or three months each year
in their rented accommodation in Harrow. It is more difficult for a
tenant to claim to occupy separate premises as residences when they
are close together.[66] For example, in *Hampstead Way Investments Ltd
v Lewis-Weare*,[67] a tenant rented a flat half a mile from a house which
he owned and in which his wife lived. He slept most nights in the
rented accommodation but the House of Lords held that he did not
occupy it as a residence. Similarly, the Rent Act does not provide
protection for premises which are occupied only occasionally when
the tenant is on holiday.[68]

Recovery of possession of Rent Act tenancies

12.31 The starting point for all grounds of possession of regulated tenancies is RA 1977 s98, which provides:

> 98(1) Subject to this Part of this Act, a court shall not make an order for
> possession of a dwelling-house which is for the time being let on a
> protected tenancy or subject to a statutory tenancy unless the court
> considers it reasonable to make such an order and either –

---

62 *Beck v Scholz* [1953] 1 QB 570, [1953] 1 All ER 814 at 816.
63 *Regalian Securities Ltd v Scheuer* (1982) 263 EG 973.
64 [1949] 1 KB 29, [1948] 2 All ER 722.
65 (1974) 232 EG 191.
66 *Regalian Securities Ltd v Scheuer* (1982) 263 EG 973. See also *Swanbrae Ltd v Elliott* (1987) 19 HLR 86.
67 [1985] 1 WLR 164, [1985] 1 All ER 564, HL, though, *Palmer v McNamara* (1991) 23 HLR 168, (1991) 17 EG 88, CA ('occupation as a residence' under RA 1977 s12 satisfied even though there was no cooker and the landlord did not sleep in premises).
68 *Walker v Ogilvy* (1974) 28 P&CR 288.

(a) the court is satisfied that suitable alternative accommodation is available for the tenant or will be available for him when the order in question takes effect, or

(b) the circumstances are as specified in any of the Cases in Part I of Schedule 15 to this Act.

(2) If, apart from subsection (1) above, the landlord would be entitled to recover possession of a dwelling-house which is for the time being let on or subject to a regulated tenancy, the court shall make an order for possession if the circumstances of the case are as specified in any of the Cases in Part II of Schedule 15.

...

12.32   The main distinction between the various grounds for possession is that if landlords rely on one of the 'discretionary' grounds, they must prove not only the existence of the ground for possession but also that it is reasonable to make an order for possession. In deciding whether it is reasonable to make an order, the court must take into account similar factors to those which are discused in relation to secure and assured tenancies: see, for example, paras 3.69–3.76 and 3.171–3.201.

12.33   The discretionary grounds are those set out in Cases 1 to 10 of RA 1977 Sch 15. There is a further discretionary ground in RA 1977 s98(1)(a) (ie, that 'suitable alternative accommodation' is or will be available if and when possession is granted). The 'mandatory' grounds are those set out in Schedule 15 Cases 11 to 20 and there is a further mandatory ground where there is statutory overcrowding.[69] In these cases the landlord has to prove only that the contractual tenancy has been terminated and that a ground for possession is satisfied. In the following paragraphs the discretionary grounds will be considered first.

Suitable alternative accommodation

12.34   This discretionary ground is fulfilled if 'the court is satisfied that suitable alternative accommodation is available for the tenant or will be available for him when the order in question takes effect'.[70]

12.35   Further guidance concerning the suitability of alternative accommodation is given in RA 1977 Sch 15 Part IV paras 3–8, which provide:

3   For the purposes of section 98(1)(a) of this Act, a certificate of the local housing authority for the district in which the dwelling-house

---

69   RA 1977 s101.

70   RA 1977 s98(1)(a).

in question is situated, certifying that the authority will provide suitable alternative accommodation for the tenant by a date specified in the certificate, shall be conclusive evidence that suitable alternative accommodation will be available for him by that date.

4 Where no such certificate as mentioned in paragraph 3 above is produced to the court, accommodation shall be deemed to be suitable for the purposes of section 98(1)(a) of this Act if it consists of either –

(a) premises which are to be let as a separate dwelling such that they will then be let on a protected tenancy (other than one under which the landlord might recover possession of the dwelling-house under one of the Cases in Part II of this Schedule), or

(b) premises to be let as a separate dwelling on terms which will, in the opinion of the court, afford to the tenant security of tenure reasonably equivalent to the security afforded by Part VII of this Act in the case of a protected tenancy of a kind mentioned in paragraph (a) above,

and, in the opinion of the court, the accommodation fulfils the relevant conditions as defined in paragraph 5 below.

5(1) For the purposes of paragraph 4 above, the relevant conditions are that the accommodation is reasonably suitable to the needs of the tenant and his family as regards proximity to place of work, and either –

(a) similar as regards rental and extent to the accommodation afforded by dwelling-houses provided in the neighbourhood by any local housing authority for persons whose needs as regards extent are, in the opinion of the court, similar to those of the tenant and of his family; or

(b) reasonably suitable to the means of the tenant and to the needs of the tenant and his family as regards extent and character; and

that if any furniture was provided for use under the protected or statutory tenancy in question, furniture is provided for use in the accommodation which is either similar to that so provided or is reasonably suitable to the needs of the tenant and his family.

(2) For the purposes of sub-paragraph (1)(a) above, a certificate of a local housing authority stating –

(a) the extent of the accommodation afforded by dwelling-houses provided by the authority to meet the needs of tenants with families of such number as may be specified in the certificate, and

(b) the amount of the rent charged by the authority for dwelling-houses affording accommodation of that extent,

shall be conclusive evidence of the facts so stated.

6   Accommodation shall not be deemed to be suitable to the needs of the tenant and his family if the result of their occupation of the accommodation would be that it would be an overcrowded dwelling-house for the purposes of Part X of the Housing Act 1985.
7   Any document purporting to be a certificate of a local housing authority named therein issued for the purposes of this Schedule and to be signed by the proper officer of that authority shall be received in evidence and, unless the contrary is shown, shall be deemed to be such a certificate without further proof.
8   In this Part 'local housing authority' and 'district' in relation to such an authority have the same meaning as in the Housing Act 1985.

A landlord may prove that alternative accommodation is 'suitable' either by obtaining a certificate that the local authority will provide accommodation or by proving that accommodation is available to the tenant which satisfies the various criteria set out in RA 1977 Sch 15 Part IV paras 4–6, above.

12.36   This ground for possession is very similar to Housing Act (HA) 1988 Sch 2 ground 9 (see para 3.372).

12.37   It should be noted that HA 1988 s34 provides that in possession proceedings against a regulated tenant based on the availability of suitable alternative accommodation, the court should consider whether the grant of an assured tenancy would provide reasonably equivalent security.[71] If 'in the circumstances, the grant of an assured tenancy would not afford the required security', the court may direct that the suitable alternative accommodation should also be held on a Rent Act protected tenancy. Since a regulated tenant is entitled to a registered 'fair rent' and since the grounds for possession against assured tenants are wider than those against regulated tenants, tenants' representatives should try to persuade the court to direct that any tenancy of the alternative accommodation should be a protected tenancy.

12.38   So far as rent is concerned, tenants' representatives should remind the court that if the alternative accommodation is being offered on an assured tenancy, there will be minimal rent control and after a year (or the termination of any fixed-term tenancy, if later), the landlord will be able to serve a notice of increase to a market rent.[72] This is clearly a factor that has a direct bearing on the security which the tenant is entitled to expect. Accordingly, it may be necessary to adduce evidence about market rents in the area. Alternatively, a landlord may

71 HA 1988 s34(1)(c). See para 12.7.
72 HA 1988 s13.

be persuaded to consent to a direction that the alternative accommodation should be held on a protected tenancy.

Discretionary grounds

Case 1: Rent arrears or breach of an obligation of the tenancy

12.39   RA 1977 Sch 15 Case 1 provides:

> Where any rent lawfully due from the tenant has not been paid, or any obligation of the protected or statutory tenancy which arises under this Act, or –
>
> (a) in the case of a protected tenancy, any other obligation of the tenancy, in so far as is consistent with the provisions of Part VII of this Act, or
>
> (b) in the case of a statutory tenancy, any other obligation of the previous protected tenancy which is applicable to the statutory tenancy,
>
> has been broken or not performed.

This is the most common ground for possession used by landlords of Rent Act tenants. The claimant landlord must prove either that there are rent arrears or that there has been a breach of a term or other obligation of the tenancy.

Rent arrears

12.40   A landlord must prove two things: first, that rent was lawfully due from the tenant and, second, that some rent remained unpaid at the date of issue of the claim.[73] This applies only to rent which is due from the actual tenant against whom possession is claimed and not to arrears due from a predecessor of the present tenant (including a deceased tenant whom the present tenant has succeeded).[74] Rent becomes lawfully due at midnight on the day when it is payable.[75] If rent has been tendered to the landlord on a regular basis when it has become due, but has not been accepted by the landlord, there is a complete defence to the proceedings based on alleged rent arrears if the tenant pays into court all the rent which is due,[76] or where the

---

73   *Bird v Hildage* [1948] 1 KB 91.
74   *Tickner v Clifton* [1929] 1 KB 207.
75   *Aspinall v Aspinall* [1961] Ch 526.
76   *Bird v Hildage* [1948] 1 KB 91 and CPR 37.3.

tenant has put the money aside and can tender it. If a landlord refuses to accept rent, it is important that the tenant continues to tender rent regularly (for example, by sending cheques by recorded delivery) and maintains a separate bank account for any rent that has been rejected. If the tenant has not tendered rent regularly and there are arrears outstanding when proceedings are issued, the mere fact that the tenant is able to pay all the rent arrears and fixed costs before the hearing date does not deprive the landlord of the ground for possession under Case 1, but it is unlikely that the court would consider it reasonable to make an order for possession in those circumstances.

12.41   Failure to provide a rent book does not disentitle the landlord from claiming that rent is lawfully due.[77]

12.42   When advising a tenant who faces a claim for possession based on rent arrears, it is important to check exactly what rent is lawfully recoverable, and, in particular, whether the landlord has been claiming too much rent. This may happen where:

- *A landlord has been charging more than a 'fair rent' registered by the rent officer.*[78] A rent registration for furnished premises is binding even if a later tenancy of the same premises is unfurnished, and vice versa. Tenants who have paid more than the registered rent may claim back the difference for a period of up to two years before the claim.[79]

- *A landlord has increased the rent without complying with RA 1977 s51.* In general, any agreement between a landlord and a Rent Act protected tenant to increase the rent (instead of applying to register a fair rent) must comply with the provisions of section 51. Such an agreement must be in writing and contain wording pointing out that a tenant's security of tenure is not affected by refusing to enter into the agreement and referring to the tenant's right to apply to a rent officer to fix a fair rent. If a landlord unilaterally increases the rent or if an agreement does not comply with section 51, the increase is irrecoverable and the tenant can claim back the difference for a period of one year.[80]

- *A landlord has failed to serve a valid notice of increase.* In some situations (for example, where a landlord wants to increase the rent

---

77 *Shaw v Groom* [1970] 2 QB 504.

78 RA 1977 ss44, 45 and 57. See *Rakhit v Carty* [1988] 2 QB 315, (1990) 22 HLR 198, CA. Cf *Metrobarn v Gehring* [1976] 1 WLR 776; *Kent v Millmead Properties Ltd* (1982) 10 HLR 13 and *Cheniston Investments Ltd v Waddock* (1990) 20 HLR 652, CA.

79 RA 1977 s57(3)(b).

80 RA 1977 s57(3)(a).

following a new rent registration) the landlord must serve a formal notice of increase.[81] Failure to do so means that the increase
is not legally recoverable.

- *A landlord has failed to furnish the tenant with an address at which
  notices may be served.* In such circumstances, Landlord and Tenant
  Act 1987 s48 provides that any rent which would otherwise be due
  is to be treated as not being due before the landlord has rectified
  the failure.[82] The tenant should, however, put aside rent in these
  circumstances, since the accumulated sum will fall due as soon as
  the landlord has supplied an address for service.

These provisions may mean that, in some cases, a landlord claiming
rent arrears in fact owes the tenant money rather than vice versa.
A tenant may reclaim the balance by suing (or, if proceedings have
already been issued, by counterclaiming) or by withholding rent until
all sums due have been recovered.[83]

12.43   Advisers should also check whether there is any possibility of a
set-off and counterclaim for breach of repairing obligations (see para
21.44), or whether there has been any failure by the relevant authorities to make payments of housing benefit (see para 16.31) or the
housing costs element of universal credit (see para 16.80). See too
the discussion of the equivalent 'rent arrears' grounds relating to
secure and assured tenants (HA 1985 Sch 2 ground 1; HA 1988 Sch
2 ground 10) at para 3.11.

Breach of any other tenancy obligation

12.44   This limb of Case 1 is similar to HA 1988 Sch 2 ground 12 and to the
second limb of HA 1985 Sch 2 ground 1: see para 3.255.

12.45   The original provisions of the contractual tenancy continue to bind
a statutory tenant so far as they are consistent with the provisions of
the Rent Act 1977.[84] Breach of such obligations is a ground for possession, but see para 12.47 concerning waiver.

12.46   Where a clause in a tenancy agreement gives a landlord a right of
re-entry if the tenant becomes bankrupt and, after termination of the

81 See RA 1977 ss45(2) and 49.
82 See *Dallhold Estates (UK) Pty Ltd v Lindsay Trading Properties Inc* [1994] 17 EG
    148, CA; *Hussain v Singh* [1993] 31 EG 75, CA but cf *Rogan v Woodfield Building
    Services Ltd* (1995) 27 HLR 78, [1995] 20 EG 132, CA (section 48 had been
    complied with where address for service of notices was clear from tenancy
    agreement) and *Drew-Morgan v Hamid-Zadeh* (2000) 32 HLR 316, [1999] 2
    EGLR 13, CA.
83 RA 1977 ss54 and 57.
84 RA 1977 s3(1).

contractual tenancy, the tenant is made bankrupt, the landlord may rely upon Case 1. Tenants in these circumstances are 'obliged' not to become bankrupt if they wish to remain in possession of their home. By becoming bankrupt, tenants break 'an obligation of the previous protected tenancy' within the meaning of Case 1(b).[85]

Waiver

12.47   The acceptance of rent by a landlord who has knowledge of a breach of covenant may amount to a waiver of that breach and thus prevent the landlord from relying on Case 1.[86] If the tenancy is contractual, acceptance of rent is a complete waiver of a breach even if the acceptance is qualified. However, if the tenancy is statutory, it is a question of fact in each case as to whether the breach has been waived. A qualified acceptance of rent from a statutory tenant (for example, acceptance 'without prejudice') may mean that the landlord is still entitled to rely on the breach of covenant,[87] but an unqualified acceptance of rent by the landlord of a statutory tenant is as much a waiver of the breach as if it were a payment by a contractual tenant.[88]

12.48   Acceptance of rent by a landlord's agents, who have knowledge of a breach of covenant, amounts to waiver.[89] The knowledge of a porter that there is someone other than a tenant living in the premises amounts to knowledge of the landlord.[90] See further discussion of waiver at para 14.57.

Case 2: Nuisance or annoyance, user for immoral or illegal purposes

12.49   RA 1977 Sch 15 Case 2 provides:

> Where the tenant or any person residing or lodging with him or any sub-tenant of his has been guilty of conduct which is a nuisance or annoyance to adjoining occupiers, or has been convicted of using the dwelling-house or allowing the dwelling-house to be used for immoral or illegal purposes.

---

85 *Cadogan Estates Ltd v McMahon* [2001] AC 378, (2001) 33 HLR 42, HL.
86 *Carter v Green* [1950] 1 All ER 627. See too para 14.57.
87 *Oak Property Co v Chapman* [1947] KB 886, [1947] 2 All ER 1 and *Trustees of Smith's (Henry) Charity v Willson* [1983] 1 All ER 73.
88 *Carter v Green* [1950] 1 All ER 627, cf *Trustees of Smith's (Henry) Charity v Willson* [1983] 1 All ER 73.
89 *Hyde v Pimley* [1952] 2 QB 506, [1952] 2 All ER 102.
90 *Metropolitan Properties Co Ltd v Cordery* (1979) 251 EG 567.

Nuisance or annoyance

12.50 In this ground, 'nuisance' and 'annoyance' are both used in the natural sense of the words. This ground may be satisfied by drunkenness, abusive behaviour, noise, obstructive behaviour towards other occupiers, or violence.[91] Unknown people coming to the premises at all hours of the day and night may amount to an annoyance.[92] It is not necessary that the act which led to the annoyance should have taken place on the premises. For example, a married tenant who exercised 'undue familiarity' with the landlord's daughter in an alley some 200 yards away from the rented premises was held to be guilty of 'annoyance'.[93] It is possible for the court to infer that annoyance or nuisance has been caused to adjoining occupants without direct evidence from them,[94] but it is more usual for the landlord to call the adjoining occupants to give evidence. The word 'adjoining' does not mean that the premises must be physically touching the tenant's premises. It means that the persons affected by nuisance or annoyance must live near enough to be affected by the tenant's conduct, for example, because they share a common entrance.[95]

Immoral or illegal purposes

12.51 'Immoral purposes' is the statutory formula for prostitution.[96] In relation to illegal purposes, the mere fact that a tenant has been convicted of a crime which took place on the premises may not be sufficient to establish this limb of the ground for possession. It must be shown that:

> ... for the purpose of committing the crime, the premises have been used ...[It is] not enough that the tenant has been convicted of a crime with which the premises have nothing to do beyond merely being the scene of its commission.[97]

12.52 However, the ground may be satisfied even though a tenant has been convicted of an offence which does not specifically refer to 'using

---

91 Per Wood J in *Cobstone Investments Ltd v Maxim* [1985] QB 140, (1984) 15 HLR 113.
92 *Florent v Horez* (1983) 268 EG 807.
93 *Whitbread v Ward* (1952) 159 EG 494.
94 *Platts (Frederick) Co v Grigor* [1950] 1 All ER 941, CA.
95 *Cobstone v Maxim* [1984] 2 All ER 635.
96 *Yates v Morris* [1951] 1 KB 77.
97 Per Scrutton LJ in *Schneiders & Sons v Abrahams* [1925] 1 KB 301 at 311.

premises'.[98] Depending on the circumstances, a conviction for possession of cannabis or some other unlawful drug on the premises may amount to a ground for possession. There may, however, be a difference between tenants having drugs in their immediate possession on the premises (for example, in a pocket or a handbag) and using the premises as a storage or hiding place.[99] Examples of other activities which may satisfy this ground for possession are using premises as a 'coiner's den' or as a deposit for stolen goods.[100]

Case 3: Neglect of or damage to the premises

12.53   RA 1977 Sch 15 Case 3 provides:

> Where the condition of the dwelling-house has, in the opinion of the court, deteriorated owing to acts of waste by, or the neglect or default of, the tenant or any person residing or lodging with him or any sub-tenant of his and, in the case of any act of waste by, or the neglect or default of, a person lodging with the tenant or a sub-tenant of his, where the court is satisfied that the tenant has not, before the making of the order in question, taken such steps as he ought reasonably to have taken for the removal of the lodger or sub-tenant, as the case may be.

This ground is similar to HA 1988 Sch 2 ground 13 (see para 3.274).

12.54   There is no need for a landlord to give advance warning of an intention to issue proceedings relying on this ground,[101] although failure to do so may be relevant when the court considers reasonableness and costs. Where allegations that the tenant has neglected premises have been substantiated, it may be unreasonable to make an order for possession without giving the tenant an opportunity to put matters right.[102]

Case 4: Ill treatment of furniture

12.55   RA 1977 Sch 15 Case 4 provides:

> Where the condition of any furniture provided for use under the tenancy has, in the opinion of the court, deteriorated owing to ill-

---

98 *Abrahams v Wilson* [1971] 2 QB 88.

99 *Abrahams v Wilson* [1971] 2 QB 88, per Widgery LJ. On 'reasonableness' in such cases, see *Bristol CC v Mousah* (1997) 30 HLR 32, CA.

100 *Schneiders & Sons v Abrahams* [1925] 1 KB 301 and *Everett v Stevens* [1957] CLY 3062.

101 *Lowe v Lendrum* (1950) 159 EG 423, CA.

102 *Holloway v Povey* (1984) 15 HLR 104, (1984) 271 EG 195, CA.

treatment by the tenant or any person residing or lodging with him or any sub-tenant of his and, in the case of any ill-treatment by a person lodging with the tenant or a sub-tenant of his, where the court is satisfied that the tenant has not, before the making of the order in question, taken such steps as he ought reasonably to have taken for the removal of the lodger or sub-tenant, as the case may be.

This case is similar to ground 15 in HA 1988 Sch 2 (grounds for possession of dwelling-houses let on assured tenancies): see para 3.279.

Case 5: Notice to quit by tenant

12.56   RA 1977 Sch 15 Case 5 provides:

> Where the tenant has given notice to quit and, in consequence of that notice, the landlord has contracted to sell or let the dwelling-house or has taken any other steps as the result of which he would, in the opinion of the court, be seriously prejudiced if he could not obtain possession.

There must be a valid tenant's notice to quit before a landlord can rely on this ground for possession.[103] The words 'notice to quit' have their normal technical meaning (see para 14.6) and the disappearance of a tenant followed by a return by him of the keys did not amount to a 'notice to quit'.[104] Similarly, an agreement to move out is not sufficient.[105]

12.57   There are few cases on the meaning of 'serious prejudice'. In an old case decided on a section with different wording, it was held that there was no prejudice to a landlord where a proposed sale of the premises 'went off' without any liability for damages on the part of the landlord.[106]

Case 6: Subletting without the landlord's consent

12.58   RA 1977 Sch 15 Case 6 provides:

> Where, without the consent of the landlord, the tenant has, at any time after –
> (a)   ...
> (b)   22nd March 1973, in the case of a tenancy which became a regulated tenancy by virtue of section 14 of the Counter-Inflation Act 1973;

103 *De Vries v Sparks* (1927) 137 LT 441.
104 *Standingford v Bruce* [1926] 1 KB 466.
105 *De Vries v Sparks* (1927) 137 LT 441.
106 *Hunt v Bliss* (1919) 89 LJKB 174.

(bb) the commencement of section 73 of the Housing Act 1980, in the case of a tenancy which became a regulated tenancy by virtue of that section;

(c) 14th August 1974, in the case of a regulated furnished tenancy; or

(d) 8th December 1965, in the case of any other tenancy,

assigned or sublet the whole of the dwelling-house or sublet part of the dwelling-house, the remainder being already sublet.

This ground gives protection to landlords against the risk of finding someone unknown to them installed in the property.[107] The ground applies even if there is no prohibition against assigning or subletting in the tenancy agreement. The word 'assigned' includes a vesting assent (that is, a transfer of a lease made to implement the terms of a will) made by executors of a deceased tenant which takes effect as an assignment.[108] It does not, however, apply unless all of the premises rented have been disposed of by assigning or subletting. In practice the ground applies only to subletting or assignment by a contractual tenant. If a statutory tenant sublets the whole premises, Rent Act protection is lost because the tenant can no longer occupy the premises as a residence (see para 12.20). It is not possible to assign a statutory tenancy.

12.59   Consent to a subletting or assignment may be given implicitly,[109] for example, by accepting rent for some time after acquiring knowledge of the subletting. Consent may be given after the subletting or assignment, at any time up to the issue of proceedings.[110] If the tenancy agreement contains a provision that the tenant cannot assign or sublet without the permission of the landlord, there is an implied proviso that consent cannot be withheld unreasonably.[111]

12.60   It is not necessary for a landlord to prove that a subtenancy or subtenancies have continued to exist right up to the date when proceedings were issued. It is enough that a tenant has at any time sublet or assigned the whole of the premises.[112] However, there are likely to be strong grounds for arguing that it is unreasonable to make an order for possession if there is no subsisting subtenancy at the time when proceedings are issued. This ground for possession can enable a landlord to obtain possession against both the tenant and

---

107 *Hyde v Pimley* [1952] 2 All ER 102.
108 *Pazgate Ltd v McGrath* (1985) 17 HLR 127.
109 *Regional Properties Co v Frankenschwerth* [1951] 1 KB 631, [1951] 1 All ER 178.
110 *Hyde v Pimley* [1952] 2 All ER 102.
111 Landlord and Tenant Act 1927 s19 and Landlord and Tenant Act 1988 s1.
112 *Finkle v Strzelczyk* [1961] 3 All ER 409.

subtenant (notwithstanding the effect of RA 1977 s137), provided that the court is satisfied that it is reasonable to make the order.[113]

Case 7: Controlled off-licences

12.61 Case 7 was repealed by Housing Act 1980 s152 and Sch 26. It related to controlled off-licences.

Case 8: Former employees

12.62 RA 1977 Sch 15 Case 8 provides:

> Where the dwelling-house is reasonably required by the landlord for occupation as a residence for some person engaged in his whole-time employment, or in the whole-time employment of some tenant from him or with whom, conditional on housing being provided, a contract for such employment has been entered into, and the tenant was in the employment of the landlord or a former landlord, and the dwelling-house was let to him in consequence of that employment and he has ceased to be in that employment.

In order to succeed under this ground a landlord must prove that:

- *The tenant was in the employment of the landlord or a former landlord at the time when the premises were let.*[114] 'Tenant' refers to the original contractual tenant. For example, if the spouse or civil partner of the original tenant becomes a statutory tenant by succession,[115] the landlord can rely on this ground for possession if the original tenant was in the landlord's employment at the beginning of the contractual tenancy.[116]

- *Premises were let in consequence of that employment.* This is a question of fact in each case. The questions to be asked are: 'What was the reason for the landlord letting the premises to the tenant?' 'Was it let because of the tenant's employment or was there another reason?'[117] It is possible for premises to be let in consequence of employment even if there is no reference to the premises in the employee's contract of employment. If premises are let some time after an employee originally took the job, the letting may be

---

113 *Leith Properties v Springer* [1982] 3 All ER 731, CA.
114 *Fuggle (RF) v Gadsden* [1948] 2 KB 236.
115 Where the death occurs on or after 15 January 1989, only a spouse or civil partner will succeed to a statutory tenancy. Other members of the family will succeed to an assured tenancy: RA 1977 Sch 1 para 3.
116 *Bolsover Colliery v Abbott* [1946] KB 8.
117 *Braithwaite and Co Ltd v Elliot* [1947] KB 177, [1946] 2 All ER 537 at 539.

in consequence of the employment or it may be treated as a separate 'independent' transaction.[118] If a former employer grants a new contractual tenancy after the tenant has stopped working for that employer, the new tenancy cannot be in consequence of that employment.[119] It is not necessary for it to be shown that the tenancy was granted as a result of any particular type of employment, only that it was in consequence of the relationship of employer and employee.[120]

- *Employment has ceased.* A tenant who has changed jobs (for example, from a farm worker to a laundry machine operator) but who is still employed by the same employer has not ceased to be in employment.[121]
- *The premises are reasonably required by the landlord for occupation as a residence by someone engaged in the whole-time employment of the landlord or someone with whom a contract of employment has been entered into which is conditional on housing being provided.* When the court considers whether or not the proposed new occupant is employed or whether a contract of employment has been entered into, the relevant date is the date of the court hearing.[122] The premises must be reasonably required for occupation by the new employee.[123]

12.63   A tenant may be entitled to compensation if a landlord obtains an order for possession under Case 8 by deceit. See para 12.72.

Case 9: Premises required for occupation by a landlord or landlord's family

12.64   RA 1977 Sch 15 Case 9 provides:

> Where the dwelling-house is reasonably required by the landlord for occupation as a residence for –
> (a) himself, or
> (b) any son or daughter of his over 18 years of age, or
> (c) his father or mother, or
> (d) if the dwelling-house is let on or subject to a regulated tenancy, the father or mother of his *spouse or civil partner,*

---

118 *Long Eaton Co-op v Smith* [1949] 2 KB 144, [1949] 1 All ER 633.
119 *Lever Brothers v Caton* (1921) 37 TLR 664.
120 *Munro v Daw* [1947] 2 All ER 360.
121 *Duncan v Hay* [1956] 1 WLR 1329.
122 *Benninga (Mitcham) Ltd v Bijstra* [1945] 2 All ER 433.
123 See comments on similar wording in Case 9 at para 12.65.

and the landlord did not become landlord by purchasing the dwelling-house or any interest therein after –

(i) 7th November 1956, in the case of a tenancy which was then a controlled tenancy;

(ii) 8th March 1973, in the case of a tenancy which became a regulated tenancy by virtue of section 14 of the Counter-Inflation Act 1973;

(iii) 24th May 1974, in the case of a regulated furnished tenancy; or

(iv) 23rd March 1965, in the case of any other tenancy.

This ground for possession has to be read in conjunction with RA 1977 Sch 15 Part III para 1, which provides:

A court shall not make an order for possession of a dwelling-house by reason only that the circumstances of the case fall within Case 9 in Part I of this Schedule if the court is satisfied that, having regard to all the circumstances of the case, including the question whether other accommodation is available for the landlord or the tenant, greater hardship would be caused by granting the order than by refusing to grant it.

'Reasonably required'

12.65   Case 9 applies where the premises are reasonably required as a residence by the landlord or certain specified members of the landlord's family. The words 'reasonably required' mean more than a 'desire' on the landlord's part, but less than 'absolute necessity'.[124] The court should consider whether this requirement is reasonable on the landlord's part, and in doing so the tenant's interests are not relevant.[125] The tenant's interests should be taken into account when the overall questions of greater hardship and reasonableness are considered: see para 12.69 in relation to greater hardship.

12.66   Matters which are relevant when considering whether the landlord's requirements are 'reasonable' include: the nature and place of the landlord's business; the size of the family; their actual residence or lack of it; their health; and 'innumerable other possible factors'.[126] The requirement need not be an immediate requirement. It is perfectly proper for a landlord to seek possession under Case 9 where the need for accommodation will exist in the ascertainable but not too far

124 *Aitken v Shaw* 1933 SLT (Sh Ct) 21 and *Kennealy v Dunne* [1977] QB 837.
125 *Funnell v Armstrong* [1962] EGD 319.
126 *Chandler v Strevett* [1947] 1 All ER 164 per Bucknill LJ.

distant future.[127] However, possession was refused in a case where a landlord stated that he required a basement for his daughter to live in on her marriage which might take place in two years' time,[128] and in a case where the trial judge had found that premises purportedly let to five surveyors were 'an investment property' which was not required as a residence by the landlord.[129] The landlord must need the premises 'with a view to living there for some reasonable period, definite or indefinite', and not for the purpose of sale[130] or for temporary accommodation while repairs are carried out in the landlord's own accommodation.[131] A landlord can come within this ground for possession even if only part of the premises is required.[132]

12.67   The premises must be required for the landlord, or for the landlord's children, the landlord's parents or parents-in-law.[133] It has been said that this includes 'all normal emanations of' the landlord,[134] including a housekeeper who lived in the same household as the landlord and was paid to look after the landlord's children following his separation from his wife.[135] It does not include someone who would occupy premises as a separate household and not as part of the landlord's household, for example, where it was intended that a couple should live in a separate self-contained flat in the same building as the landlord, in order to look after him.[136] Where premises are owned by joint landlords, they must reasonably be required as a residence for *all* the joint landlords.[137] Personal representatives of the deceased landlord may be a 'landlord' for the purposes of Case 9. Usually, it is necessary for the personal representatives to have a beneficial interest in the premises in order to come within this ground for possession. However, in exceptional cases personal representatives who do not have a beneficial interest may reasonably require possession, for

---

127 *Kidder v Birch* (1983) 265 EG 773. See also *Alexander v Mohamadzadeh* (1986) 18 HLR 90, (1985) 276 EG 1258 (relevant date for deciding whether premises are required is date of hearing, not date of issue of proceedings).

128 *Kissias v Lehany* [1979] CLY 1625.

129 *Ghelani v Bowie* [1988] 42 EG 119, CA.

130 *Rowe v Truelove* (1976) 241 EG 533.

131 *Johnson-Sneddon v Harper* May 1977 *LAG Bulletin* 114.

132 *Kelley v Goodwin* [1947] 1 All ER 810.

133 But not step-children: *Towns v Hole* [1956] CLY 7493 and *Harty v Greenwich LBC and Done* [1956] CLY 7494.

134 *Richter v Wilson* [1963] 2 QB 426.

135 *Smith v Penny* [1947] KB 230.

136 *Richter v Wilson* [1963] 2 QB 426 and *Bloomfield v Westley* [1963] 2 All ER 337.

137 *Baker v Lewis* [1946] 2 All ER 592.

example, so that children of the original, deceased landlord may live in the premises.[138]

Landlord by purchase

12.68 Landlords are not entitled to rely on Case 9 if they became landlords by purchasing the premises after specified dates.[139] See also the explanation of the equivalent wording in HA 1988 Sch 2 ground 1 at para 11.8.

'Greater hardship'

12.69 Tenants have a complete defence to possession proceedings brought under Case 9 if they can prove that greater hardship would be caused to them by a possession order than would be caused to the landlord by refusing to grant the possession order. The burden of proving this lies on the tenant.[140] The court should consider how the balance of hardship will operate at the time when a possession order would take effect.[141] The 'greater hardship test' gives the court a very wide discretion to take into account all factors which may affect both landlord and tenant.[142] Matters which may be taken into consideration include:

- The availability of other accommodation for both landlord and tenant. Judges can apply their own knowledge of the difficulty in finding accommodation[143] but it is always advisable for tenants to be able to give evidence about the unsuccessful attempts which they have made to find other accommodation and any particular local accommodation difficulties. The fact that a tenant has taken no steps to look for other accommodation may be prejudicial.[144]
- The financial means of both parties, for example, the ability or inability of a tenant to buy a house.[145]

---

138 *Patel v Patel* [1982] 1 All ER 68.
139 See para 12.64.
140 *Smith v Penny* [1947] KB 230; *Manaton v Edwards* (1985) 276 EG 1256, (1985) 18 HLR 116, CA.
141 *Wheeler v Evans* [1948] 1 KB 459; *Kidder v Birch* (1983) 265 EG 773.
142 *Robinson v Donovan* [1946] 2 All ER 731.
143 *King v Taylor* [1954] 3 All ER 373 and *Bassett v Fraser* (1981) 9 HLR 105. See also *Manaton v Edwards* (1985) 276 EG 1256.
144 *Kelley v Goodwin* [1947] 1 All ER 810 and *Alexander v Mohamadzadeh* (1986) 18 HLR 90, (1985) 276 EG 1258.
145 *Kelley v Goodwin* [1947] 1 All ER 810.

- The health of the parties, both physical and mental, and the nearness of relatives.[146]
- Hardship which may occur in the future, as well as present hardship.[147]
- The need for a tenant to sell or to store furniture on moving.[148]
- Hardship which may be caused to others who may be affected by the grant or refusal of an order for possession including:

    ... relatives, dependants, lodgers, guests and the stranger within the gates but [the court] should weigh such hardship with due regard to the status of the persons affected and their 'proximity' to the tenant or landlord.[149]

The court should not take into account trivial things such as 'the absence of a view of a neighbouring hill, river, tree or something pleasant of that kind'.[150]

12.70   There is a 'convention' that where the only issues before a court are questions of greater hardship and reasonableness, no order for costs should be made against the party who loses.[151]

12.71   It is hard for a landlord or tenant who is dissatisfied with a trial judge's finding in relation to greater hardship to succeed on appeal. The Court of Appeal takes the view that in all but exceptional cases greater hardship is a matter for the trial judge, and that findings made at first instance should not be upset.[152] Generally, inferences made by judges about greater hardship are based on their findings of fact and no appeal can be made against such findings. There have, however, been successful appeals where tenants argued that the judge's inferences drawn from the facts were wrong and where the judge failed to consider the question of greater hardship properly. It appears that, contrary to the usual rule, the Court of Appeal may be able to take into account material changes in circumstances which have occurred since the original hearing on 'greater hardship' appeals.[153]

---

146 *Thomas v Fryer* [1970] 2 All ER 1 and *King v Taylor* [1954] 3 All ER 373.
147 *Sims v Wilson* [1946] 2 All ER 261; *Wheeler v Evans* [1948] 1 KB 459 and *Bumstead v Wood* (1946) 175 LT 149.
148 *Sims v Wilson* [1946] 2 All ER 261.
149 *Harte v Frampton* [1948] 1 KB 73, [1947] 2 All ER 604.
150 *Coplans v King* [1947] 2 All ER 393.
151 *Funnell v Armstrong* [1962] EGD 319.
152 *Coplans v King* [1947] 2 All ER 393 and *Hodges v Blee* (1988) 20 HLR 32, (1987) 283 EG 1215.
153 *King v Taylor* [1954] 3 All ER 373.

Compensation for misrepresentation or concealment

12.72 Rent Act 1977 s102 provides:

> Where, in such circumstances as are specified in Case 8 or Case 9 in Schedule 15 to this Act, a landlord obtains an order for possession of a dwelling-house let on a protected tenancy or subject to a statutory tenancy and it is subsequently made to appear to the court that the order was obtained by misrepresentation or concealment of material facts, the court may order the landlord to pay to the former tenant such sum as appears sufficient as compensation for damage or loss sustained by the tenant as a result of the order.

This provision is similar to HA 1988 s12 but, unlike HA 1988 s12, it applies to only two grounds for possession: Cases 8 and 9.

Case 10: Overcharging of subtenant

12.73 RA 1977 Sch 15 Case 10 provides:

> Where the court is satisfied that the rent charged by the tenant –
> (a) for any sublet part of the dwelling-house which is a dwelling-house let on a protected tenancy or subject to a statutory tenancy is or was in excess of the maximum rent for the time being recoverable for that part, having regard to ... Part III of this Act, or
> (b) for any sublet part of the dwelling-house which is subject to a restricted contract is or was in excess of the maximum (if any) which it is lawful for the lessor, within the meaning of Part V of this Act to require or receive having regard to the provisions of that Part.

Case 10 applies where a tenant overcharges a subtenant who is also entitled to Rent Act protection. It may come about, for example, by charging more than the registered rent,[154] or where there has been a failure to comply with the statutory provisions relating to agreed increases in rent.[155] This ground for possession does not apply where the interest of the sub-occupant is outside the protection of RA 1977 or where there is merely an arrangement to share the premises with other people.[156] If a subtenant is overcharged, the court may make an order for possession of the whole of the premises rented by the tenant or just that part to which the overcharging relates.[157] There appears to be no reported authority on the position of a subtenant when a

---

154 RA 1977 ss44 and 45.
155 RA 1977 s51. See para 12.42.
156 *Kenyon v Walker* [1946] 2 All ER 595.
157 *Boulton v Sutherland* [1938] 1 All ER 488.

landlord has established that there has been overcharging within the meaning of Case 10. In ordinary circumstances, an order for possession against a tenant also operates against a subtenant, but it would seem that if the subtenancy is lawful, the subtenant would become a direct tenant of the landlord as a result of RA 1977 s137.[158]

Case 10A: Occupiers without the 'right to rent'

12.74   RA 1977 Sch 15 Case 10A provides:

> Both of the following conditions are met in relation to a dwelling-house in England.
>
> Condition 1 is that the Secretary of State has given a notice in writing to the landlord or, in the case of joint landlords, one or more of them which identifies –
> (a) the tenant or, in the case of joint tenants, one or more of them, or
> (b) one or more other persons aged 18 or over who are occupying the dwelling-house,
> as a person or persons disqualified as a result of their immigration status from occupying the dwelling-house under the tenancy.
>
> Condition 2 is that the person or persons named in the notice –
> (a) fall within paragraph (a) or (b) of condition 1, and
> (b) are disqualified as a result of their immigration status from occupying the dwelling-house under the tenancy.
>
> For the purposes of this case a person ('P') is disqualified as a result of their immigration status from occupying the dwelling-house under the tenancy if –
> (a) P is not a relevant national, and
> (b) P does not have a right to rent in relation to the dwellinghouse.
>
> P does not have a right to rent in relation to the dwelling-house if –
> (a) P requires leave to enter or remain in the United Kingdom but does not have it, or
> (b) P's leave to enter or remain in the United Kingdom is subject to a condition preventing P from occupying the dwellinghouse.
>
> But P is to be treated as having a right to rent in relation to a dwelling-house if the Secretary of State has granted P permission for the

---

158 It is debatable whether or not a landlord would be able to rely on this ground against the subtenant: cf *Leith Properties v Springer* [1982] 3 All ER 731, CA, where it was held that a landlord was entitled to rely on Case 6 against a subtenant notwithstanding the effect of RA 1977 s137. Even if that reasoning does apply to proceedings under Case 10, it is hard to imagine circumstances where it would be reasonable for the court to make an order against the tenant which would have the effect of ousting the subtenant.

purposes of this case to occupy a dwelling-house which is for the time being let on a protected tenancy or subject to a statutory tenancy.

In this case 'relevant national' means –
(a) a British citizen,
(b) a national of an EEA State other than the United Kingdom, or
(c) a national of Switzerland.

At the time of publication of this edition, this ground was not in force. It is inserted into RA 1977 Sch 15 Part 1 by Immigration Act 2016 s41(6). When brought into effect, it will apply to all regulated tenancies, whether entered into before or after the date of commencement. It will apply where at least one of the occupiers does not have the 'right to rent' within the meaning of Immigration Act 2014 s21(2) and that person has been identified in a notice given by the Secretary of State.

Mandatory grounds

Case 11: Returning owner-occupier

12.75 RA 1977 Sch 15 Case 11 provides:

Where a person (in this Case referred to as 'the owner-occupier') who let the dwelling-house on a regulated tenancy had, at any time before the letting, occupied it as his residence and –
(a) not later than the relevant date the landlord gave notice in writing to the tenant that possession might be recovered under this Case, and
(b) the dwelling-house has not, since –
    (i)   22nd March 1973, in the case of a tenancy which became a regulated tenancy by virtue of section 14 of the Counter-Inflation Act 1973;
    (ii) 14th August 1974, in the case of a regulated furnished tenancy; or
    (iii) 8th December 1965, in the case of any other tenancy, been let by the owner-occupier on a protected tenancy with respect to which the condition mentioned in paragraph (a) above was not satisfied, and
(c) the court is of the opinion that of the conditions set out in Part V of this Schedule one of those in paragraphs (a) and (c) to (f) is satisfied.

If the court is of the opinion that, notwithstanding that the condition in paragraph (a) or (b) above is not complied with, it is just and equitable to make an order for possession of the dwelling-house, the court may dispense with the requirements of either or both of those paragraphs as the case may require.

The giving of a notice before 14th August 1974 under section 79 of the Rent Act 1968 shall be treated, in the case of a regulated furnished tenancy, as compliance with paragraph (a) of this Case.

Where the dwelling-house has been let by the owner-occupier on a protected tenancy (in this paragraph referred to as 'the earlier tenancy') granted on or after 16th November 1984 but not later than the end of the period of two months beginning with the commencement of the Rent (Amendment) Act 1985 and either –

(i) the earlier tenancy was granted for a term certain (whether or not to be followed by a further term or to continue thereafter from year to year or some other period) and was during that term a protected shorthold tenancy as defined in section 52 of the Housing Act 1980, or

(ii) the conditions mentioned in paragraphs (a) to (c) of Case 20 were satisfied with respect to the dwelling-house and the earlier tenancy,

then for the purposes of paragraph (b) above the condition in paragraph (a) above is to be treated as having been satisfied with respect to the earlier tenancy.

12.76   Like Cases 12 and 20, this ground for possession should be read in conjunction with RA 1977 Sch 15 Part V, which provides:

Provisions applying to Cases 11, 12 and 20

1. In this Part of this Schedule – '
   mortgage' includes a charge and 'mortgagee' shall be construed accordingly;
   'owner' means, in relation to Case 11, the owner-occupier; and
   'successor in title' means any person deriving title from the owner, other than a purchaser for value or a person deriving title from a purchaser for value.

2. The conditions referred to in paragraph (c) in each of Cases 11 and 12 and in paragraph (e)(ii) of Case 20 are that –

   (a) the dwelling-house is required as a residence for the owner or any member of his family who resided with the owner when he last occupied the dwelling-house as a residence;

   (b) the owner has retired from regular employment and requires the dwelling-house as a residence;

   (c) the owner has died and the dwelling-house is required as a residence for a member of his family who was residing with him at the time of his death;

   (d) the owner has died and the dwelling-house is required by a successor in title as his residence or for the purpose of disposing of it with vacant possession;

   (e) the dwelling-house is subject to a mortgage, made by deed and granted before the tenancy, and the mortgagee –
       (i) is entitled to exercise a power of sale conferred on him by

the mortgage or by section 101 of the Law of Property Act 1925; and

(ii) requires the dwelling-house for the purpose of disposing of it with vacant possession in exercise of that power; and

(f) the dwelling-house is not reasonably suitable to the needs of the owner, having regard to his place of work, and he requires it for the purpose of disposing of it with vacant possession and of using the proceeds of that disposal in acquiring, as his residence, a dwelling-house which is more suitable to those needs.

12.77 In Case 11, as with all the other grounds for possession in RA 1977 Sch 15 Part II (ie, Cases 11 to 20) the phrase 'relevant date' is defined by Schedule 15 Part III para 2, which provides:

2. Any reference in Part II of this Schedule to the relevant date shall be construed as follows –

(a) except in a case falling within paragraph (b) or (c) below, if the protected tenancy, or, in the case of a statutory tenancy, the previous contractual tenancy, was created before 8th December 1965, the relevant date means 7th June 1966; and

(b) except in a case falling within paragraph (c) below, if the tenancy became a regulated tenancy by virtue of section 14 of the Counter-Inflation Act 1973 and the tenancy or, in the case of a statutory tenancy, the previous contractual tenancy, was created before 22nd March 1973, the relevant date means 22nd September 1973; and

(c) in the case of a regulated furnished tenancy, if the tenancy or, in the case of a statutory furnished tenancy, the previous contractual tenancy was created before 14th August 1974, the relevant date means 13th February 1975; and

(d) in any other case, the relevant date means the date of the commencement of the regulated tenancy in question.

12.78 The purpose of Case 11 was to allow owner-occupiers who intended to go away and then to return to their homes to let the premises while they were away.[159] To rely on Case 11 a landlord must prove that:

- *Prior to the granting of the tenancy in question, the landlord had at some time in the past occupied the premises as a residence.* It is not necessary for landlords to prove that they occupied the premises immediately before the granting of the tenancy.[160] Residence at any time in the past is sufficient. It is sufficient for such previous

---

159 Griffiths LJ in *Bradshaw and Martin v Baldwin-Wiseman* (1985) 17 HLR 260 at 264, [1985] 1 EGLR 123.

160 Rent (Amendment) Act 1985, reversing the effect of *Pocock v Steel* [1985] 1 WLR 229.

residence to have been temporary and intermittent, although visits to a house by a landlord to stay with a partner who lives there do not count as 'occupation as a residence'.[161] The landlord must previously have occupied the same premises as those which are let to the tenant whom the landlord is seeking to evict: it is not sufficient for the landlord to have lived in other rooms in the same building.

- *Notice of intention to rely on Case 11 was given before the commencement of the tenancy.* The Schedule provides that such notice must be in writing, although no particular form is necessary. It has been said that it is 'of the utmost importance to a tenant that he should appreciate when he takes rented property whether or not he is obtaining security of tenure'.[162] Such notice must actually be received by the tenant, otherwise it has not been given in accordance with the terms of the Schedule. It is not enough for the landlord merely to say that it was sent to the tenant if a tenant's evidence that it was not received is believed.[163] Alternatively, the landlord may satisfy the court that it is just and equitable to dispense with service of the notice. The criteria which apply are the same as under HA 1988 Sch 2 ground 1 (see para 11.7).

- *All tenants to whom the premises have previously been let since the dates specified in Case 11 have been given written notice.* Again there is a provision which entitles the court to dispense with this requirement if it is considered just and equitable to do so.

- *One of the requirements in subparagraphs 2(a), (c), (d), (e) or (f) in RA 1977 Sch 15 Part V is satisfied.* The most important of these is that the premises are 'required as a residence'. All that is required is that the landlord 'bona fide wants [to occupy]' or 'genuinely has the immediate intention' of occupying the premises.[164] The landlord need not require the premises as a permanent residence and fairly intermittent residence will be sufficient.[165] This is a question of fact in each case. It is sufficient if only one of two

---

161 *Naish v Curzon* (1985) 17 HLR 220, [1985] 1 EGLR 117, CA; *Mistry v Isidore* (1990) 22 HLR 281, [1990] 2 EGLR 97, CA and *Ibie v Trubshaw* (1990) 22 HLR 191, CA.

162 *Bradshaw and Martin v Baldwin-Wiseman* (1985) 17 HLR 260, (1985) 49 P&CR 382, [1985] 1 EGLR 123.

163 *Minay v Sentongo* (1983) 45 P&CR 190.

164 *Kennealy v Dunne* [1977] QB 837, cf *Ghelani v Bowie* (1988) 42 EG 119, CA.

165 *Naish v Curzon* (1985) 17 HLR 220, [1985] 1 EGLR 117, where it was argued by the tenant that the landlord required the premises only for holidays and short visits, and *Davies v Peterson* (1989) 21 HLR 63, [1989] 06 EG 130, CA.

joint landlords requires the premises as a residence.[166] Another important use of Case 11 would be where a landlord's place of work has changed and he or she wishes to sell the house with vacant possession in order to buy a new house which is more suitable, bearing in mind the place of work.[167] The other situations in which possession may be obtained under Case 11 arise following the death of the landlord or relate to rights of a mortgagee.

Case 12: Retirement homes

12.79   RA 1977 Sch 15 Case 12 provides:

> Where the landlord (in this Case referred to as 'the owner') intends to occupy the dwelling-house as his residence at such time as he might retire from regular employment and has let it on a regulated tenancy before he has so retired and –
> (a) not later than the relevant date the landlord gave notice in writing to the tenant that possession might be recovered under this Case; and
> (b) the dwelling-house has not, since 14th August 1974, been let by the owner on a protected tenancy with respect to which the condition mentioned in paragraph (a) above was not satisfied; and
> (c) the court is of the opinion that of the conditions set out in Part V of this Schedule one of those paragraphs (b) to (e) is satisfied.
>
> If the court is of the opinion that, notwithstanding that the condition in paragraph (a) or (b) above is not complied with, it is just and equitable to make an order for possession of the dwelling-house, the court may dispense with the requirements of either or both those paragraphs, as the case may require.

This ground for possession is similar in format to Case 11. For the definition of 'relevant date' see RA 1977 Sch 15 Part III para 2 (see para 12.77). Provisions about the giving of written notice and the circumstances in which notice may be dispensed with are also similar to those relating to Case 11.

12.80   Case 12 may be relied on if:

- the owner has retired and requires the premises as 'a retirement home'; or
- the owner has died and the premises are required as a residence for a member of the family ('member of the family' is not defined and is wider than the limited list of relations in in Case 9); or

---

166   *Tilling v Whiteman* [1980] AC 1.

167   There must be a connection within a reasonable time between the proposed sale and purchase: *Bissessar v Ghosn* (1986) 18 HLR 486, CA.

- the owner has died and a successor in title either requires the premises as a residence or wishes to dispose of them with vacant possession; or
- in some circumstances a mortgagee requires the premises for the purpose of disposing of them with vacant possession.

Case 13: Out of season holiday lets

12.81 RA 1977 Sch 15 Case 13 provides:

> Where the dwelling-house is let under a tenancy for a term of years certain not exceeding 8 months and –
> (a) not later than the relevant date the landlord gave notice in writing to the tenant that possession might be recovered under this Case; and
> (b) the dwelling-house was, at some time within the period of 12 months ending on the relevant date, occupied under a right to occupy it for a holiday.
> For the purposes of this case a tenancy shall be treated as being for a term of years certain notwithstanding that it is liable to determination by re-entry or on the happening of any event other than the giving of notice by the landlord to determine the term.

This ground is almost identical to Housing Act 1988 Sch 2 ground 3 (see para 11.12). It is important to note that, unlike Cases 11 and 12, the court has no power to dispense with the requirement for service of notice prior to the grant of the tenancy.[168]

Case 14: Lettings to non-students by educational institutions

12.82 RA 1977 Sch 15 Case 14 provides:

> Where the dwelling-house is let under a tenancy for a term of years certain not exceeding 12 months and –
> (a) not later than the relevant date the landlord gave notice in writing to the tenant that possession might be recovered under this Case; and
> (b) at some time within the period of 12 months ending on the relevant date, the dwelling-house was subject to such a tenancy as is referred to in section 8(1) of this Act.
> For the purposes of this Case a tenancy shall be treated as being for a term of years certain notwithstanding that it is liable to determination

---

168 cf *Fowler v Minchin* (1987) 19 HLR 224, [1987] 1 EGLR 108, CA.

by re-entry or on the happening of any event other than the giving of notice by the landlord to determine the term.

This ground applies to any premises which, during the period of 12 months preceding the current tenancy, were let by a specified educational institution to a student who was pursuing or intended to pursue a course of study provided by that institution or by another specified educational institution.[169] It is almost identical to HA 1988 Sch 2 ground 4 (see para 11.14). Notice in writing must have been given to the current tenant prior to the grant of the tenancy and the court has no power to dispense with service of that notice.

Case 15: Ministers of religion[170]

12.83   RA 1977 Sch 15 Case 15 provides:

Where the dwelling-house is held for the purpose of being available for occupation by a minister of religion as a residence from which to perform the duties of his office and –
(a) not later than the relevant date the tenant was given notice in writing that possession might be recovered under this Case, and
(b) the court is satisfied that the dwelling-house is required for occupation by a minister of religion as such a residence.

This Case is similar to ground 5 in HA 1988 Sch 2 (grounds for possession of dwelling-houses let on assured tenancies): see para 11.17.

Case 16: Agricultural employees

12.84   RA 1977 Sch 15 Case 16 provides:

Where the dwelling-house was at any time occupied by a person under the terms of his employment as a person employed in agriculture, and –
(a) the tenant neither is nor at any time was so employed by the landlord and is not the widow of a person who was so employed, and
(b) not later than the relevant date, the tenant was given notice in writing that possession might be recovered under this Case, and
(c) the court is satisfied that the dwelling-house is required for occupation by a person employed, or to be employed, by the landlord in agriculture.
For the purposes of this Case 'employed', 'employment' and 'agriculture' have the same meanings as in the Agricultural Wages Act 1948.

---

169 See RA 1977 s8 and Assured and Protected Tenancies (Lettings to Students) Regulations 1998 SI No 1967 as amended.
170 cf HA 1988 Sch 2 ground 5, see para 11.17.

The court cannot dispense with the requirement that notice must be served prior to the commencement of the tenancy. A term in a tenancy agreement that the tenant will vacate on 28 days' notice if the premises are required for another farm worker is not sufficient,[171] but a certificate of a fair rent which was handed to the tenant before the commencement of the tenancy and which stated that the tenancy was to be subject to Case 16 has been held to be sufficient.[172]

Case 17: Redundant farmhouses

12.85   RA 1977 Sch 15 Case 17 provides:

> Where proposals for amalgamation, approved for the purposes of a scheme under section 26 of the Agriculture Act 1967, have been carried out and, at the time when the proposals were submitted, the dwelling-house was occupied by a person responsible (whether as owner, tenant, or servant or agent of another) for the control of the farming of any part of the land comprised in the amalgamation and
>
> (a) after the carrying out of the proposals, the dwelling-house was let on a regulated tenancy otherwise than to, or to the widow of, either a person ceasing to be so responsible as part of the amalgamation or a person who is, or at any time was, employed by the landlord in agriculture, and
>
> (b) not later than the relevant date the tenant was given notice in writing that possession might be recovered under this Case, and
>
> (c) the court is satisfied that the dwelling-house is required for occupation by a person employed, or to be employed, by the landlord in agriculture, and
>
> (d) the proceedings for possession are commenced by the landlord at any time during the period of 5 years beginning with the date on which the proposals for the amalgamation were approved or, if occupation of the dwelling-house after the amalgamation continued in, or was first taken by, a person ceasing to be responsible as mentioned in paragraph (a) above or his widow, during a period expiring 3 years after the date on which the dwelling-house next became unoccupied.
>
> For the purposes of this Case 'employed' and 'agriculture' have the same meanings as in the Agricultural Wages Act 1948 and 'amalgamation' has the same meaning as in Part II of the Agriculture Act 1967.

The court cannot dispense with the requirement that notice must be served prior to the commencement of the tenancy.

---

171 See *Fowler v Minchin* (1987) 19 HLR 224, [1987] 1 EGLR 108, CA, where a possession order was refused.

172 *Springfield Investments Ltd v Bell* (1990) 22 HLR 440, [1991] 02 EG 157, CA.

Case 18: More redundant farmhouses

12.86   RA 1977 Sch 15 Case 18 provides:

Where –

(a) the last occupier of the dwelling-house before the relevant date was a person, or the widow of a person, who was at some time during his occupation responsible (whether as owner, tenant, or servant or agent of another) for the control of the farming of land which formed, together with the dwelling-house, an agricultural unit within the meaning of the Agriculture Act 1947, and

(b) the tenant is neither –

(i) a person, or the widow of a person, who is or has at any time been responsible for the control of the farming of any part of the said land, nor

(ii) a person, or the widow of a person, who is or at any time was employed by the landlord in agriculture, and

(c) the creation of the tenancy was not preceded by the carrying out in connection with any of the said land of an amalgamation approved for the purposes of a scheme under section 26 of the Agriculture Act 1967, and

(d) not later than the relevant date the tenant was given notice in writing that possession might be recovered under this Case, and

(e) the court is satisfied that the dwelling-house is required for occupation either by a person responsible or to be responsible (whether as owner, tenant, or servant or agent of another) for the control of the farming of any part of the said land or by a person employed or to be employed by the landlord in agriculture, and

(f) in a case where the relevant date was before 9th August 1972, the proceedings for possession are commenced by the landlord before the expiry of 5 years from the date on which the occupier referred to in paragraph (a) above went out of occupation.

For the purposes of this Case 'employed' and 'agriculture' have the same meanings as in the Agricultural Wages Act 1948 and 'amalgamation' has the same meaning as in Part II of the Agriculture Act 1967.

The court cannot dispense with the requirement that notice must be served prior to the commencement of the tenancy.

Case 19: Protected shorthold tenancies

12.87   This ground for possession is now of historical interest only. Protected shorthold tenancies could only be granted between 1980 and 1989 for a fixed term of between one and five years. All new tenancies granted to former protected shorthold tenants after 15 January 1989 are automatically assured shorthold tenancies.[173]

Case 20: Lettings by armed forces personnel

12.88   RA 1977 Sch 15 Case 20 provides:

> Where the dwelling-house was let by a person (in this Case referred to as 'the owner') at any time after the commencement of section 67 of the Housing Act 1980 and –
>
> (a) at the time when the owner acquired the dwelling-house he was a member of the regular armed forces of the Crown;
> (b) at the relevant date the owner was a member of the regular armed forces of the Crown;
> (c) not later than the relevant date the owner gave notice in writing to the tenant that possession might be recovered under this Case;
> (d) the dwelling-house has not, since the commencement of section 67 of the Act of 1980 been let by the owner on a protected tenancy with respect to which the condition mentioned in paragraph (c) above was not satisfied; and
> (e) the court is of the opinion that –
>> (i) the dwelling-house is required as a residence for the owner; or
>> (ii) of the conditions set out in Part V of this Schedule one of those in paragraphs (c) to (f) is satisfied.
>
> If the court is of the opinion that, notwithstanding that the condition in paragraph (c) or (d) above is not complied with, it is just and equitable to make an order for possession of the dwelling-house, the court may dispense with the requirements of either or both of these paragraphs, as the case may require.
>
> For the purposes of this Case 'regular armed forces of the Crown' has the same meaning as in section 1 of the House of Commons Disqualification Act 1975.

Members of the regular armed forces may rely on this ground for possession only if they were members of the forces at the time when they acquired the premises and at the date when the tenancy began. The provisions relating to the giving of notice are similar to those in Case 11. See para 12.76 for the conditions in subparagraphs (c) to (f) of Part V which may found a claim for possession.

---

173 HA 1980 ss51–55 and HA 1988 s34(3). See *Defending possession proceedings*, 4th edn, 1997, pp232–233.

Other provisions entitling landlords to possession

Statutory overcrowding

12.89 RA 1977 s101 concerns overcrowded dwelling-houses. It provides:

> At any time when a dwelling-house is overcrowded, within the meaning of Part X of the Housing Act 1985 in such circumstances as to render the occupier guilty of an offence, nothing in this Part of this Act shall prevent the immediate landlord of the occupier from obtaining possession of the dwelling-house.

12.90 This section in effect provides an additional mandatory ground for possession. It operates where the number of persons occupying the dwelling contravenes either the 'room standard' or the 'space standard', as defined in HA 1985 ss325 and 326, such that the occupier who causes or permits the overcrowding commits an offence under section 327.[174] The effect of RA 1977 s101 is to deprive the tenancy of its statutory protection, so that the landlord only has to determine the contractual tenancy and obtain a possession order on that basis.

12.91 It has been held that a room with no natural lighting or ventilation was not a room generally used in the locality as a living or a bedroom,[175] and so it could not be taken into account when determining the number of rooms.

12.92 A 'room' is a room which can be used for living or sleeping in.[176] The relevant date when overcrowding must exist is the date of the trial and so a tenant has a complete defence if overcrowding has ceased by the time of the court hearing.[177] It is not necessary for there to be a conviction before a landlord can rely on this 'ground'.[178] All that a landlord needs to do is to prove that the circumstances are such that a conviction for overcrowding could be obtained and that any contractual tenancy has been validly determined, normally by serving a notice to quit.

12.93 Where there is statutory overcrowding, the court has no power to postpone a possession order.[179]

---

174 The provisions of HA 1985 ss324–329 are not set out in detail in this edition. The reader is referred to *Defending possession proceedings*, 7th edn, pp381–384.

175 *Patel v Godal* [1979] CLY 1620.

176 *Patel v Godal* [1979] CLY 1620.

177 *Zbytniewski v Broughton* [1956] 2 QB 673, [1956] 3 All ER 348. Cf *Henry Smith's Charity v Bartosiak-Jentys* (1992) 24 HLR 627, [1991] 2 EGLR 276, CA.

178 *Zbytniewski v Broughton* [1956] 2 QB 673, [1956] 3 All ER 348.

179 *Henry Smith's Charity v Bartosiak-Jentys* (1992) 24 HLR 627, [1991] 2 EGLR 276, CA.

Demolition orders, prohibition orders etc

12.94   Where a prohibition order[180] under HA 2004 or a demolition order[181] under HA 1985 is made in relation to premises let under a regulated tenancy, the effect of such orders is to remove Rent Act protection. This enables the landlord to recover possession on the basis that the tenancy has been reduced to a contractual tenancy. The tenancy must still be terminated in the usual way (which will normally be by notice to quit where the tenancy is periodic), and the landlord will need to obtain a court order for possession.[182] The tenant who is evicted in these circumstances may apply to be rehoused by the local authority under the Land Compensation Act 1973 s39(1). The authority has a duty to secure that the former tenant will be provided with suit-able alternative residential accommodation on reasonable terms. A displaced tenant will also be entitled to claim a home loss payment from the authority.[183]

Restricted contracts

12.95   A significant number of tenants who moved into premises before 15 January 1989, and who did not enjoy full Rent Act protection occu-pied those premises under a form of limited protection known as a 'restricted contract'.[184] Many tenants of resident landlords whose interests were created before 15 January 1989 and who were deprived of full Rent Act protection[185] had restricted contracts. The other prin-cipal classes of tenants who had restricted contracts were those who were excluded from Rent Act protection,[186] but whose rent included payment for the use of furniture or for services. Some licensees who were required to pay for furniture or services also had restricted con-tracts. Occupiers with restricted contracts had only limited rights to delay the period before a possession order took effect.[187]

---

180 See HA 2004 s33.
181 See HA 1985 s270(3).
182 Protection from Eviction Act 1977 s3. See para 15.2.
183 Land Compensation Act 1973 s29.
184 See RA 1977 s19.
185 RA 1977 ss12 and 20.
186 Often because their tenancies included the provision of substantial 'attendances' or small quantities of board by the landlord: see RA 1977 s7 and para 12.10.
187 See RA 1977 ss102A–106A.

12.96   Nowadays, there are virtually no tenants or licensees remaining with restricted contracts. HA 1988 s36 provided not only that no new restricted contracts could be created on or after 15 January 1989, but also that if the rent under a restricted contract was varied by agreement on or after that date, the letting should be treated as a new contract, and could therefore no longer be a restricted contract. Only tenants or licensees whose interests were created before 15 January 1989 and whose rents have not been varied by agreement at any time since that date may still have restricted contracts. (A registration of a rent by a rent tribunal does not count as a variation by agreement.) For this reason this edition no longer deals with restricted contracts.[188]

---

188 See *Defending possession proceedings*, 4th edn, 1997, chapter 16.

Rental purchase agreements

Introduction

13.1   'Rental purchase agreements'[1] are happily now almost of historical interest only. The true rental purchase agreement was, in essence, a contract for the sale of a property with the purchaser allowed into possession paying the purchase price by instalments and with completion of the sale taking place only following payment of the last instalment. It is inaccurate to describe the arrangement as a rental agreement because the purchaser was usually allowed into possession under the terms of the agreement for sale, not as a tenant, but as a licensee.

13.2   For a short analysis of the purchase and rental arrangements entered into within Muslim communities to encourage home purchase, without infringing Islamic principles on the payment and receipt of interest, see chapter 40.

13.3   Usually, 'rental purchase agreements' were in written form, often in a standard template. The agreement provided for a specified sum to be paid before completion could be called for. It usually also specified the interest rate to be charged on the outstanding capital. A fixed weekly or monthly sum was generally specified, which went either directly towards repaying the capital or towards satisfying the accruing interest, buildings insurance and other outgoings, with only part going towards payment of the capital. Some agreements provided for completion to take place before payment of the whole capital sum but with the seller granting a mortgage at the date of completion of the sale for the sum outstanding at that time. There were many permutations.

Rental purchase and the evasion of security of tenure

13.4   Many ostensible rental purchase agreements were prepared not with the intention of selling the property to a willing purchaser but with the sole intention of avoiding the Rent Act (RA) or Housing Act (HA) protection otherwise given to tenants, by the simple device of

1   See generally B Hoggett, 'Houses on the never-never: some legal aspects of rental purchase' (1972) 36 Conv 325; 'Houses on the never-never: some recent developments' (1975) 39 Conv 343; 'How to help the rental purchaser' June 1976 *LAG Bulletin* 133; L Burrows and R Murphy, *Rental purchase – the case for change* (1990); and Shelter and National Consumer Council, *Buying a home on rental purchase; a consumer view* (1989).

not creating a tenancy. Following *Street v Mountford*,[2] it was thought that, where a bona fide rental purchase agreement had been made as intended by the parties, no landlord/tenant relationship would be established. However, after *Bretherton v Paton*,[3] it seems that entering into possession even with the intention of purchasing the property does not bar the application of the *Street* principle that a tenancy arises where the occupier has exclusive possession for making a specified periodic payment. Usually, in such circumstances the tenancy would be an assured shorthold tenancy under HA 1988.

13.5   Where it proves necessary to consider whether an arrangement is a bona fide rental purchase, advisers should consider the following points:

- Was there any expectation that the occupier would in fact purchase the property? If not, then this is likely to be decisive. It will be necessary to check the dealings between the parties *before* the document was signed. How was the property advertised? What conversation took place? Did the owner really want to sell the property?
- Was the sale price inflated above market value or was the interest rate specified in the agreement inflated as compared to the then current mortgage rate?
- Is the term of repayment unduly long, either in itself or when compared with the length of any leasehold interest granted?
- Are there any clauses in the agreement inconsistent with a bona fide contract for sale, for example, a prohibition against assigning, subletting or parting with possession?
- Was there the usual investigation of title and the condition of the property as is customary before a purchase/sale?
- Have the parties' actions since the date of the agreement been more consistent with a tenancy than a bona fide sale?
- Were solicitors instructed by the occupier before entering into the agreement, as would be common for a genuine sale/purchase?

13.6   Where an occupier wishes to dispute his or her description in the agreement (for example, as 'purchaser' rather than as 'tenant') he or she can either apply for a declaration by the county court that he or

2   [1985] AC 809, [1985] 2 WLR 877, HL.
3   (1986) 18 HLR 257, CA; cf *Sharp v McArthur* (1987) 19 HLR 364, CA; see also *Martin v Davies* (1983) 7 HLR 119, [1952] CPL 189, CA and *Francis Jackson Developments Ltd v Stemp* [1943] 2 All ER 601, CA.

she is a tenant with statutory protection[4] or raise that proposition as
a defence to possession proceedings.

Statutory and equitable protection

13.7   Assuming that the agreement in question is a bona fide rental purchase agreement, the court has a statutory discretion to protect the
occupier from eviction. HA 1980 s88(1) provides:

> (1) Where, under the terms of a rental purchase agreement, a person
> has been let into possession of a dwelling-house and, on the ter-
> mination of the agreement or of his right to possession under it,
> proceedings are brought for the possession of the dwelling-house,
> the court may –
> (a) adjourn the proceedings; or
> (b) on making an order for the possession of the dwelling-house,
> stay or suspend execution of the order or postpone the date of
> possession;
> for such period or periods as the court thinks fit.

This is broadly similar to the protection given to mortgage borrowers
in default (see Part V of this book) although there is no requirement
that the occupier clear the arrears within a reasonable period.

13.8   The court can, but is not obliged to, grant relief on the condition that the occupier makes payments towards the arrears. HA 1980
s88(2) provides:

> (2) On any such adjournment, stay, suspension or postponement the
> court may impose such conditions with regard to payments by the
> person in possession in respect of his continued occupation of the
> dwelling-house and such other conditions as the court thinks fit.

The court has specific power to revoke or vary any condition which it
has imposed.[5]

13.9   The definition of 'rental purchase agreement' is quite widely
drafted in HA 1980 s88(4):

> (4) In this section 'rental purchase agreement' means an agreement
> for the purchase of a dwelling-house (whether freehold or lease-
> hold property) under which the whole or part of the purchase price
> is to be paid in three or more instalments and the completion of
> the purchase is deferred until the whole or a specified part of the
> purchase price has been paid.

---

4 RA 1977 s141 or HA 1988 s40.
5 HA 1980 s88(3).

The definition requires the purchase price to be paid in at least three instalments so as not to protect purchasers who are allowed into possession in the more usual transaction after exchange of contracts (where, usually, a ten per cent deposit is paid before completion when the second and final instalment is made).

13.10 The court has some limited equitable jurisdiction to grant relief against forfeiture for breach of any terms of the agreement, although the statutory discretion is much more extensive.[6]

The necessity for possession proceedings

13.11 Where a person is let into possession under a rental purchase agreement (as defined in HA 1980 s88(4) above at para 13.9) and continues to reside in the property after termination of the agreement or his or her right to possession under the agreement, then the provisions of the Protection from Eviction Act 1977 will usually apply so as to require the owner to regain possession by court order.[7] An additional prohibition against eviction without court order is contained in the Consumer Credit Act 1974 s92(2) in respect of regulated conditional sale agreements. It states:

> At any time when the debtor is in breach of a regulated conditional sale agreement relating to land, the creditor is entitled to recover possession of the land from the debtor, or any person claiming under him, on an order of the court only.

Other points

13.12 Payments under 'an agreement for the purchase of a dwelling under which the whole or part of the purchase price is to be paid in more than one instalment and the completion of the purchase is deferred until the whole or a specified part of the purchase price has been paid' qualify as 'rent' for housing benefit purposes.[8]

6 See references at note 1 above and the note at (1974) 37 MLR 705.
7 HA 1980 Sch 25 para 61.
8 Housing Benefit Regulations 2006 SI No 213 reg 12(1)(i).

PART III

Other tenancy issues

CHAPTER 14

Termination of contractual tenancies

continued

Introduction

14.1   This chapter is primarily relevant whenever a landlord is seeking to obtain possession from:

- a Rent Act (RA) protected tenant; or
- an unprotected tenant, that is, a tenant who lacks any statutory security of tenure.

Additionally, the following topics in this chapter are relevant both to the above tenancies and to secure and assured (including assured shorthold) tenancies:

- tenant's notice to quit;
- surrender.

Otherwise, this chapter is mostly not relevant to secure or full assured tenants, or to introductory or demoted tenants, who continue to occupy their homes as their only or principal homes.

14.2   Before a landlord can succeed in obtaining a possession order against an unprotected tenant or a Rent Act protected tenant, the original contractual tenancy must be terminated. If a landlord fails to prove that this has happened, the tenant has a complete defence to possession proceedings,[1] even if the landlord has grounds[2] for possession. Where a tenant has a Rent Act protected tenancy and occupies the premises as his or her residence, the effect of the termination is to convert the tenancy into a statutory tenancy.[3]

14.3   The most common ways in which a contractual tenancy can be terminated are by:

- expiry of a fixed term;
- service of a notice to quit by a landlord or tenant;
- surrender;
- forfeiture; and,
- in some circumstances, service of a notice of increase of rent.

These various methods are considered in more detail in the following paragraphs.

---

1   *Wallis v Semark* [1951] 2 TLR 222, CA.
2   See para 12.34 onwards.
3   RA 1977 s2(1)(a).

Expiry of fixed-term tenancies

14.4   If a tenancy is initially granted for a fixed period ('a fixed term') such as six months or one year, the contractual tenancy usually ends at the expiry of that period by the passage of time. If the tenancy is a Rent Act protected tenancy,[4] any tenant who still occupies the premises as his or her residence at the end of that period automatically becomes a statutory tenant. If a fixed-term tenancy has expired, a landlord usually need not serve a notice to quit before bringing possession proceedings because the contractual tenancy has already been terminated.[5] Occasionally, however, the terms of the original contractual tenancy may be such that it continues even after the expiry of the initial fixed-term period. For example, if the tenancy agreement states that the tenancy is for a term 'of one year, and thereafter from month to month until determined by notice to quit', the landlord will have to terminate the continuing contractual periodic tenancy, after the expiry of the initial year, before bringing possession proceedings.

14.5   Once a fixed-term tenancy has come to an end by the passing of time, the courts generally lean against implying a new contractual periodic tenancy, unless there has been an express agreement for a new tenancy. The fact that a tenant continues to pay rent does not by itself imply a new contractual tenancy.[6] Occasionally, a landlord and a tenant may make an express agreement which will be construed either as commencing a new contractual periodic tenancy or as a variation of the original tenancy, which means that a contractual periodic tenancy continues to exist.[7] In such a case, a landlord has to serve a notice to quit before starting possession proceedings.

Notice to quit by a landlord or tenant

14.6   The most common way of terminating a contractual periodic[8] tenancy is by either the landlord or the tenant serving a notice to quit. Unlike surrender (see para 14.36), when both parties agree to the tenancy coming to an end, a notice to quit operates to terminate the

---

4   See para 12.5.
5   RA 1977 s3(4) and *Morrison v Jacobs* [1945] KB 577.
6   *Morrison v Jacobs* [1945] KB 577; *Westminster City Council v Basson* (1991) 23 HLR 225, [1991] 1 EGLR 277, CA.
7   *Bungalows (Maidenhead) Ltd v Mason* [1954] 1 WLR 769.
8   That is, a tenancy which was not originally granted for a fixed period of time, such as a weekly or monthly tenancy.

contractual tenancy whether or not the other party agrees. If the tenancy has not been terminated in any other way, failure to serve a valid notice to quit is a complete defence to possession proceedings.[9] Similarly tenants have a complete defence to possession claims if court proceedings are issued before the expiry of the notice to quit.[10] A notice to quit should be strictly construed by the court. If invalid, it cannot be amended.[11] It is for a landlord seeking possession to prove that a valid notice to quit has been served.[12] Once a notice to quit has been served, whether by landlord or tenant, it cannot be withdrawn or revoked.[13] Where a tenant has served a notice to quit, but changes his or her mind and wishes to remain, he or she will need to negotiate a new tenancy, or possibly a temporary licence, with the landlord from the date the notice takes effect.

14.7   Notices to quit have no application during a fixed-term tenancy unless the tenancy agreement contains a 'break clause' which expressly provides that the term may be terminated prematurely by a notice. Otherwise, the usual method at common law for a landlord to terminate a fixed-term tenancy before it expires is by forfeiture (see para 14.46). There is no need for a notice to quit where the tenancy has already become a Rent Act statutory tenancy.[14]

Requirements of a notice to quit: Protection from Eviction Act 1977 s5

14.8   A notice to quit must comply both with the statutory requirements of Protection from Eviction Act (PEA) 1977 s5 and with common law requirements. Section 5 provides:

> (1) Subject to subsection (1B) below no notice by a landlord or a tenant to quit any premises let (whether before or after the commencement of this Act) as a dwelling shall be valid unless –
>   (a) it is in writing and contains such information as may be prescribed, and
>   (b) it is given not less than 4 weeks before the date on which it is to take effect.
> (1A) Subject to subsection (1B) below, no notice by a licensor or licensee to determine a periodic licence to occupy premises as a dwelling

---

9 See, eg, *Plaschkes v Jones* (1982) 9 HLR 110.
10 *Beaney v Branchett* (1987) 19 HLR 471, [1987] 2 EGLR 115.
11 *Precious v Reedie* [1924] 2 KB 149.
12 *Lemon v Lardeur* [1946] KB 613.
13 *Fareham BC v Miller* [2013] EWCA Civ 159, [2013] HLR 22.
14 RA 1977 s3(4) and *Morrison v Jacobs* [1945] KB 577.

(whether the licence was granted before or after the passing of this Act) shall be valid unless –

(a) it is in writing and contains such information as may be prescribed, and

(b) it is given not less than 4 weeks before the date on which it is to take effect.

(1B) Nothing in subsection (1) or subsection (1A) above applies to –

(a) premises let on an excluded tenancy which is entered into on or after the date on which the Housing Act 1988 came into force unless it is entered into pursuant to a contract made before that date; or

(b) premises occupied under an excluded licence.

(2) In this section 'prescribed' means prescribed by regulations made by the Secretary of State by statutory instrument, and a statutory instrument containing any such regulations shall be subject to annulment in pursuance of a resolution of either House of Parliament.

(3) Regulations under this section may make different provision in relation to different descriptions of lettings and different circumstances.

Subsections (1A) and (1B) were inserted by the Housing Act (HA) 1988 s32. PEA 1977 s5 does not apply to an agricultural holding, even if it includes a dwelling.[15]

14.9   Section 5 now applies to:

- periodic Rent Act protected tenancies (ie, regulated tenancies which have not already become statutory tenancies by prior service of a notice or expiry of a fixed term);
- unprotected tenancies, apart from 'excluded tenancies';[16] and
- licences, apart from 'excluded licences'.

14.10   Tenancies and licences are excluded from section 5 if:

- *The occupier shares with the landlord or licensor accommodation which is part of his or her 'only or principal home'.* However, a tenancy or licence is not excluded if the accommodation shared consists only of storage areas or means of access, such as corridors or staircases.
- *The occupier lives in the same building as the landlord or licensor and shares accommodation with a member of the landlord's or licensor's*

---

15 *National Trust v Knipe* [1997] 4 All ER 627, (1998) 30 HLR 449, CA.

16 The classes of excluded letting are set out in PEA 1977 s3A: see para 15.5. Where an excluded tenancy began before 15 January 1989, and there has been no increase in rent or other substantial variation of terms after that date, the requirements in section 5 will apply to it: PEA 1977 s5(1B)(a) and s8(5) and (6).

family. The definition of 'member of the family' which appears in HA 1985 s113 applies. This includes spouses or civil partners, people living together as spouses or as civil partners, parents, children, grandparents, grandchildren, siblings, uncles and aunts.

- *The tenancy or licence is granted as a temporary expedient to a person who entered the premises as a trespasser.*
- *The tenancy or licence merely confers the right to occupy for a holiday.*
- *The tenancy or licence is not granted for money or money's worth.*
- *A licensee occupies a room in a hostel provided by a local authority, development corporation, the Regulator of Social Housing, a housing trust, a private registered provider of social housing or a registered social landlord.*[17]
- *The tenancy or licence is granted to provide accommodation to an asylum-seeker under Immigration and Asylum Act 1999 s4 or Part VI.*[18]
- *The tenancy or licence is granted in order to provide accommodation for displaced persons granted temporary protection.*
- *(Under provisions which are not in force at the date of publication) The tenancy or licence is a letting of premises which are subject to a Secretary of State's notice under Immigration Act 2014 s33D identifying occupiers who do not have the 'right to rent'.*

14.11   Case-law has determined that other categories of letting are also excluded from PEA 1977 ss 3[19] and 5. Where a homeless person has been placed in interim accommodation[20] (whether shared or self-contained) pending the local housing authority's decision, or in temporary accommodation for other purposes,[21] such accommodation is considered not to be let or occupied 'as a dwelling'[22] and so does not

---

17 PEA 1977 s3A, as amended by Housing and Regeneration Act 2008 (Consequential Provisions) Order 2010 SI No 866 Sch 2 para 13.

18 Note that section 4 will be repealed by Immigration Act 2016 Sch 11 para 1, when this provision is brought into force.

19 Section 3 prohibits eviction except under an order for possession from the court: see para 15.2.

20 Under HA 1996 s188(1).

21 Such as temporary accommodation provided to a person who is found to have become homeless intentionally under HA 1996 s190(2).

22 *R (CN and ZH) v Newham LBC and Lewisham LBC* [2014] UKSC 62, [2015] HLR 6. See also *Desnousse v Newham LBC, Paddington Churches HA and Veni Properties Ltd* [2006] EWCA Civ 547, [2006] 3 WLR 349; *Brillouet v Landless* (1996) 28 HLR 836, CA; and *Mohammed v Manek and Kensington and Chelsea RLBC* (1995) 27 HLR 439, CA. Where, however, a local authority has accepted a housing duty under HA 1996 s193(2), it is generally accepted that the

attract the limited protection of the Act. Periodic excluded lettings may be terminated by contractual notice only. If the agreement does not specify the length of notice, this will usually be equivalent to the length of the rental period or (in the case of a licence) will consist of reasonable notice.[23] See also paras 15.8–15.9.

14.12   A valid notice to quit must give a date for departure which complies with both common law and statutory requirements. At common law, the period of notice must be at least a full rental period of the tenancy and the notice must generally take effect on either the first day or the last day of a tenancy period (for the common law requirements in full, see paras 14.17–14.22 below). In addition, PEA 1977 s5(1) and (1A) stipulate that the period of the notice should be at least four weeks in length. The period of four weeks does not mean 28 'clear' days. In calculating the four-week period, one should include the day on which the notice to quit is served, but not the last day referred to in the notice to quit. A notice served on a Friday on a tenant under a weekly tenancy complies with PEA 1977 s5 if it expires on a Friday four weeks later (provided that Friday is the first or last day of the tenancy period).[24]

14.13   Section 5 applies to notices served by both landlords and tenants. Tenants' notices to quit must give at least four weeks' notice where the tenancy is a weekly tenancy and at least one month's notice where the tenancy is monthly, and must take effect on the first or last day of a period of the tenancy. The notice must be in writing, but need not follow any particular form.[25]

14.14   The Notices to Quit etc (Prescribed Information) Regulations 1988[26] (see para 14.15 below), which specify certain information which must be included in a notice to quit, apply only to landlords.

14.15   The 'prescribed information' to be included in notices served by landlords is contained in the Schedule to the Notices to Quit etc (Prescribed Information) Regulations 1988. The wording is:

temporary accommodation provided is to be regarded as a 'dwelling' and a notice to quit which complies with the requirements of PEA 1977 s5 will therefore be necessary: *Rogerson v Wigan MBC* [2004] EWHC 1677 (QB), [2005] HLR 10.

23 In *Mehta v Royal Bank of Scotland* (2000) 32 HLR 45, it was held that a reasonable period of notice for a long-term hotel resident would be not less than four months.

24 *Schnabel v Allard* [1967] 1 QB 627, where a notice given on Friday 4 March to expire on Friday 1 April was held to be good.

25 See *Hounslow LBC v Pilling* [1993] 1 WLR 1242, (1993) 25 HLR 305, CA and *Laine v Cadwallader* [2001] L&TR 77, (2001) 33 HLR 397, CA.

26 SI No 2201.

1. If the tenant or licensee does not leave the dwelling, the landlord or licensor must get an order for possession from the court before the tenant or licensee can lawfully be evicted. The landlord or licensor cannot apply for such an order before the notice to quit or notice to determine has run out.

2. A tenant or licensee who does not know if he has any right to remain in possession after a notice to quit or notice to determine runs out can obtain advice from a solicitor. Help with all or part of the cost of legal advice and assistance may be available under the Legal Aid Scheme. He should also be able to obtain information from a Citizens' Advice Bureau, a Housing Aid Centre or a Rent Officer.

14.16   Where a tenant serves a notice to quit which is too short, it has been held that it is possible for a landlord and tenant to waive the requirement of at least four weeks' notice by agreeing on a shorter period of notice. In *Hackney LBC v Snowden*,[27] a sole secure tenant signed a notice to quit which was expressed to take effect three days later and was subsequently re-housed by the council as a result of alleged domestic violence. Her husband sought to defend the council's claim for possession on the basis that the notice had not complied with PEA 1977 s5. The Court of Appeal decided that it was open to the parties to agree to treat the notice as valid. The fact that the tenant's husband had rights of occupation under the Family Law Act 1996 s30 did not restrict the tenant's right to bring the tenancy to an end.

Requirements of a notice to quit: common law

14.17   A valid notice to quit must also comply with certain common law rules. The first such requirement is that the notice must comply with any express provisions relating to service or validity which are contained in the tenancy agreement. Any such express provision usually overrides the general common law rules, but cannot override the provisions of PEA 1977 s5.[28] An express provision may, however, state that a notice to quit should give more notice than usual.[29] Similarly, an express provision may provide that a notice to quit may be validly served in the middle of a rental period.[30]

---

27 *Hackney LBC v Snowden* (2001) 33 HLR 49, CA and *Lewisham LBC v Lasisi-Agiri* [2003] EWHC 2392 (Ch), [2003] 45 EGCS 175.

28 cf *Prudential Assurance Co v London Residuary Body* [1992] 2 AC 386, HL.

29 *Doe d Peacock v Raffan* (1806) 6 Esp 4.

30 *Charles Clay & Sons Ltd v British Railways Board* [1970] 2 All ER 463, Ch D.

Clarity and timing

14.18   The main common law requirement is that a notice to quit should state with certainty when the notice expires. Landlords have a duty:

> ... to give notices in terms which are sufficiently clear and unambiguous in that the right date is either stated or can be ascertained by the tenant by reference to his tenancy agreement with the terms of which he must be taken to be familiar ...[31]

14.19   The time between the date on which notice is served and the date on which it purports to take effect should be at least as long as the rental period of the tenancy.[32] If the tenancy is a monthly tenancy, the notice to quit should give at least one month's notice. If the tenancy is a quarterly tenancy, the notice should give at least three months' notice.[33] However, in addition to giving the correct length of time, it is vital that the notice expires on the correct day. A notice to quit for a weekly tenancy may expire either on the same day as the date on which the tenancy commenced or on the day before[34] (ie, the first or last day of the tenancy period), or in some circumstances on the date on which the rent is paid.[35] In respect of a monthly tenancy, if the tenancy began on the first day of the month or rent is payable on the first day of the month, the notice may validly expire on the first or last day of the month.[36] A notice to quit expiring on any other day is invalid and the tenant will have a complete defence to possession proceedings. As a safeguard against this eventuality, most standard form notices to quit contain a 'saving clause' (see para 14.20). The usual rule is that a contractual tenancy ends at midnight on the date on which the notice to quit expires.[37] The Civil Procedure Rules (CPR) do not apply when calculating time in relation to service of a notice to quit. Possession proceedings cannot be issued until the notice to quit has expired.

31   *Addis v Burrows* [1948] 1 KB 444, [1948] 1 All ER 177 at 182 per Evershed LJ.

32   *Doe d Peacock v Raffan* (1806) 6 Esp 4.

33   *Lemon v Lardeur* [1946] KB 613. A yearly tenancy can be determined by six months' notice.

34   *Newman v Slade* [1926] 2 KB 328 and *Harler v Calder* (1989) 21 HLR 214, [1989] 1 EGLR 88, CA.

35   *Crane v Morris* [1965] 1 WLR 1104 and *Harler v Calder* (1989) 21 HLR 214, [1989] 1 EGLR 88, CA. For a yearly tenancy, see *Sidebotham v Holland* [1895] 1 QB 378.

36   *Precious v Reedie* [1924] 2 KB 149 and *Queen's Club Gardens Estates v Bignell* [1924] 1 KB 117. Note the definition of 'month' in LPA 1925 s61(a).

37   *Bathavon RDC v Carlile* [1958] 1 All ER 801.

14.20   It is usual for landlords to serve notices to quit which, as well as giving a specific date, also include an alternative formula such as the following: '... or at the end of the period of your tenancy which will end next after the expiration of four weeks from the service upon you of this notice'. Such a saving clause is valid[38] provided that proceedings are not issued before the date on which the tenancy could have been validly determined. In spite of the lack of clarity in a notice which gives an incorrect expiry date followed by a saving clause, it has been held that this kind of ambiguity does not invalidate a notice.[39]

14.21   Although the overriding consideration is that a notice to quit must be clear and unambiguous, minor misdescriptions are not usually fatal. Where a notice contains a mistake in the date when it is to become effective, but the reasonable recipient of the notice would have realised the error and understood what the correct date should be, the notice is likely to be valid.[40] The question which a court should ask is: 'Is the notice quite clear to a reasonable tenant reading it? Is it plain that he cannot be misled by it?'[41] For example, a notice referring to 'The Waterman's Arms' which should have referred to 'The Bricklayer's Arms' has been held to be valid.[42] Similarly, a notice served in 1974 stating that the tenant should give up possession in 1973 rather than 1975 has been held to be valid because it was clear to the tenant that there was a clerical error and the landlord intended the notice to refer to 1975.[43]

14.22   There are no common law requirements relating to signature of notices to quit. It is necessary only that a tenant should be able to ascertain who has sent the notice. A notice to quit must include all of the premises let under the particular tenancy agreement. A notice

38 *Addis v Burrows* [1948] 1 All ER 177; *Fletcher v Brent LBC* [2006] EWCA Civ 960, [2007] HLR 12 and *Bradford Community Housing Ltd v Hussain* [2009] EWCA Civ 763, [2010] HLR 16.
39 *Bradford Community Housing Ltd v Hussain* [2009] EWCA Civ 763, [2010] HLR 16. See also *Spencer v Taylor* [2013] EWCA Civ 1600, in which a notice given under HA 1988 s21(4) in relation to an assured shorthold tenancy contained a saving clause as an alternative to an incorrect expiry date. The notice was upheld.
40 *Garston v Scottish Widows Fund* [1998] 1 WLR 1583, CA.
41 *Carradine Properties Ltd v Aslam* [1976] 1 All ER 573 at 576 per Goulding J, approved in *Mannai Investment Co Ltd v Eagle Star Life Assurance Co Ltd* [1997] AC 749, HL.
42 *Doe d Armstrong v Wilkinson* (1840) 1 A & E 743. Cf *Jankovitch v Petrovitch* August 1978 LAG Bulletin 189, CA.
43 *Carradine Properties Ltd v Aslam* [1976] 1 All ER 573.

to quit which purports to terminate a tenant's interest in only part of the property covered by the tenancy is completely ineffective.[44]

Service

14.23   A notice to quit may be served either by a landlord or tenant or by an authorised agent. In some circumstances, a notice to quit may be given in the name of the agent[45] but it is more usual for notice served by an agent to state that it is served 'for and on behalf of' the landlord. One joint owner may validly serve notice to quit on behalf of other joint owners even if they are not named in the notice.[46] Similarly, one joint tenant may serve a notice to quit on the landlord and so determine the contractual tenancy even if the other joint tenant does not agree.[47] A notice to quit served by a landlord on only one out of several joint tenants is sufficient to determine the joint contractual tenancy.[48] It is not possible for a landlord to purport to terminate one joint tenant's interest in the premises without determining the interest of the other joint tenants.[49]

14.24   The notice to quit must be served on or before the date in the notice from which time starts to run, otherwise it is invalid and totally ineffective. It need not be served personally by handing it to the tenant. However, the common law rules on what is valid service are far from clear. There are few recent cases and many of the reported cases appear to conflict. It has been held sufficient to leave a notice to quit with a tenant's wife or servant even though it did not actually come to the tenant's attention before the time started running. The modern view seems to be that, unless the Law of Property Act (LPA) 1925 s196 applies (see para 14.25), a landlord must prove that any notice to quit left at the premises came to the attention of the tenant.[50]

---

44   *Woodward v Dudley* [1954] Ch 283.

45   See *Lemon v Lardeur* [1946] KB 613.

46   *Doe d Aslin v Summersett* (1830) 1 B & Ad 135 and *Annen v Rattee* (1985) 17 HLR 323, CA. Cf *Jacobs v Chaudhuri* [1968] 2 All ER 124; *Featherstone v Staples* [1986] 2 All ER 461, CA and *Leckhampton Dairies Ltd v Artus Whitfield Ltd* (1986) 130 SJ 225.

47   See para 45.33.

48   *Doe d Bradford v Watkins* (1806) 7 East 551 and *Hammersmith and Fulham LBC v Monk* [1992] 1 AC 478, (1992) 24 HLR 206.

49   *Greenwich LBC v McGrady* (1982) 6 HLR 36.

50   *Wandsworth LBC v Atwell* (1995) 27 HLR 536, [1996] 01 EG 100, CA and *Enfield BC v Devonish and Sutton* (1997) 29 HLR 691, (1997) 75 P&CR 288, CA.

14.25   LPA 1925 s196 allows for valid service of a notice to quit (or other notices relating to property) to be made by registered post or recorded delivery, or by personal delivery to the tenant's property, but only when the agreement expressly states that service will be effective where it is carried out in accordance with section 196. Where the tenancy was created by written agreement, the agreement may state that LPA 1925 s196 applies. Section 196 provides that a notice is 'sufficiently served if … left at the last-known place of abode or business in the United Kingdom of the lessee … [or] if it is sent by post in a registered letter addressed to the lessee … at the aforesaid place of abode or business, office or counting-house, and if that letter is not returned by the postal operator … undelivered'.[51] Section 196(5) provides that: 'The provisions of this section shall extend to notices required to be served by any instrument affecting property executed or coming into operation after the commencement of this Act unless a contrary intention appears'. A notice to quit is not a notice 'required to be served' by the instrument, that is, the tenancy agreement. Section 196 therefore does not apply to the service of notices to quit unless the tenancy agreement expressly incorporates it.[52] Where LPA 1925 s196 applies, service is deemed to occur at the time at which the recorded delivery letter would arrive in the ordinary course of the post. Accordingly, a notice may be validly served even though it is not actually received by the addressee.[53] Alternatively, the agreement can provide expressly for service by these methods.

14.26   The notice should be addressed to the tenant of the premises, and not to a subtenant, although the general rule is that it will operate to determine the subtenancy as well as the head tenancy.[54] Where a tenant rents a bed-sitting room, there is no need for the notice to be delivered to or fixed to the door of that room. It is sufficient for it to be

---

51 See s196(3) and (4). The term 'registered post' in s196(4) includes service by recorded delivery: Recorded Delivery Service Act 1962 s1(1). In *Blunden v Frogmore Investments Ltd* [2002] EWCA Civ 573, [2003] 2 P&CR 6, it was held that, where the lease provided for service in accordance with LPA 1925 s196, there had been good postal service despite the fact that the tenant had not received any of the three letters containing the notice and all three letters had been returned by the Post Office.

52 *Wandsworth LBC v Atwell* (1995) 27 HLR 536, [1996] 01 EG 100, CA and *Enfield BC v Devonish and Sutton* (1997) 29 HLR 691, (1997) 75 P&CR 288, CA.

53 *Re 88 Berkeley Road, London NW9, Rickwood v Turnsek* [1971] Ch 648.

54 *Mellor v Watkins* (1874) LR 9 QB 400 per Blackburn J. However, a lawful regulated or assured subtenant may become the tenant of the head landlord following the termination of the intermediate tenancy: RA 1977 s137 and HA 1988 s18.

delivered through the letter box in the main door on the ground floor of the building.[55] If a tenant has died, the notice must be served either on the person who becomes legally entitled to the tenancy under the deceased tenant's will or, if the tenant died without making a will, on the Public Trustee[56] or administrator of the estate (see para 18.1).

Rent Act statutory tenants and notices to quit

14.27   Although there is no need for landlords to serve notices to quit on Rent Act statutory tenants before starting possession proceedings, such tenants remain liable for rent until any statutory tenancy has been validly determined,[57] even if they have moved out of the premises. This liability can be ended only by a possession order, voluntary agreement of landlord and tenant, or a notice to quit served by the tenant.

14.28   Rent Act 1977 s3(3) provides:

> Subject to section 5 of the Protection from Eviction Act 1977 (under which at least 4 weeks' notice to quit is required), a statutory tenant of a dwelling-house shall be entitled to give up possession of the dwelling-house if, and only if, he gives such notice as would have been required under the provisions of the original contract of tenancy, or, if no notice would have been so required, on giving not less than 3 months' notice.

14.29   A tenant cannot unilaterally determine a Rent Act statutory tenancy without serving a notice to quit and the usual strict requirements relating to notices apply (although a landlord may be prepared to agree to waive them).[58] Advisers should therefore caution tenants against simply departing without giving notice or reaching agreement with the landlord. Landlords may be prepared to pay substantial sums in return for the surrender of a statutory tenancy.

---

55 *Trustees of Henry Smith's Charity v Kyriacou* [1989] 2 EGLR 110, (1990) 22 HLR 66, CA.

56 Law of Property (Miscellaneous Provisions) Act 1994 s14 and Public Trustee (Notices Affecting Land) (Title on Death) Regulations 1995 SI No 1330, as amended by the Public Trustee (Notices Affecting Land) (Title on Death) (Amendment) Regulations 2001 SI No 3902. See also *Wirral BC v Smith and Cooper* (1982) 43 P&CR 312, (1982) 4 HLR 81, CA.

57 *Trustees of Smith's (Henry) Charity v Willson* [1983] 1 All ER 73, CA.

58 *King's College Cambridge v Kershman* (1948) 64 TLR 547; *Boyer v Warbey (No 1)* [1953] 1 QB 234 and RA 1977 s5(1).

Acceptance of rent after service of a notice to quit

14.30 Acceptance of rent after a notice to quit has been served does not usually operate to create a new contractual tenancy.[59] In order to establish that a new contractual tenancy has been created, a tenant has to show that this was the intention of both landlord and tenant.[60] Payment and acceptance of rent may, however, operate as a waiver on the landlord's part of any breach of a condition in the tenancy agreement, provided that such breach is not continuing.

Rent Act tenancies: notice of increase of rent

14.31 In some circumstances a notice of increase of rent may terminate a periodic Rent Act protected contractual tenancy in exactly the same way as a notice to quit.[61] RA 1977 s49(4) provides:

> Where a notice of increase is served during a contractual period and the protected tenancy could, by a notice to quit served by the landlord at the same time, be brought to an end before the date specified in the notice of increase, the notice of increase shall operate to convert the protected tenancy into a statutory tenancy as from that date.

14.32 If a landlord wishes to increase the rent to the amount of a new fair rent registered by the rent officer,[62] a notice of increase in the prescribed form must be served.[63] In addition, such an increase can usually take effect only if the tenancy is already a statutory tenancy or if the landlord can convert the contractual tenancy into a statutory tenancy. Rather than requiring the landlord to serve both a notice to quit and a notice of increase, a notice of increase which gives at least as much notice as would be necessary in a notice to quit fulfils both functions.

14.33 If the notice of increase is invalid (for example, because it fails to comply with statutory requirements, purports to operate retrospectively, or does not give sufficient notice), it is ineffective in converting a contractual tenancy into a statutory tenancy. If tenants pay

---

59 *Clarke v Grant* [1950] 1 KB 104; *City of Westminster v Basson* (1991) 23 HLR 225, [1991] 1 EGLR 277. An invalid agreement for an irrecoverable rent increase does not vary an existing tenancy agreement or amount to a new contractual tenancy: *Sopwith v Stutchbury* (1983) 17 HLR 50.

60 *Vaughan Armatrading v Sarsah* (1995) 27 HLR 631, CA.

61 A notice of increase of rent in respect of an assured tenancy under HA 1988 s13 does not have the effect of terminating the contractual tenancy.

62 See RA 1977 s72 and Pt III.

63 RA 1977 s49(2).

increases in rent after the service of invalid notices of increase, they are not estopped from maintaining that there is still a contractual tenancy.[64]

Tenant's notice to quit

14.34   A tenant who wishes unilaterally to terminate a periodic tenancy must also serve a notice to quit on the landlord which complies with the relevant common law and/or statutory requirements concerning the validity and service of notices.[65] Similarly, one joint tenant may serve a notice to quit on the landlord and so determine the contractual tenancy even if the other joint tenant does not agree.[66] However, any material defect in the notice to quit, such as the period of notice being shorter than the minimum requirement of four weeks, will render the notice ineffective, where it is served without the consent of the other joint tenant.[67] In *Sims v Dacorum BC*,[68] the Supreme Court has held that, while the other joint tenant is clearly deprived of his or her tenancy in these circumstances, this does not amount to a breach of Human Rights Act (HRA) 1998 Sch 1 Article 8 or of HRA 1988 Sch 1 Part II Article 1 of the First Protocol. The lower court had considered the proportionality of the proposed eviction in the course of making the possession order. See further chapter 26 on human rights defences.

Termination of agreements under the Immigration Act 2014

14.35   At the time of publication, these provisions were not yet in force. Immigration Act (IA) 2014 s33D (inserted by IA 2016 s40(3)) provides that the landlord under a residential tenancy agreement relating to premises in England may terminate the agreement where the

---

64   *Wallis v Semark* [1951] 2 TLR 222, CA.

65   But see *Hackney LBC v Snowden* (2001) 33 HLR 49, [2001] L&TR 60, CA, in which it was held that the landlord and tenant can agree to treat a notice to quit which was too short as valid and thereby waive the requirement of at least 28 days' notice in PEA 1977 s5. In relation to a tenant's notice to quit generally, see paras 1.115–1.133.

66   *Hammersmith LBC v Monk* [1992] 1 AC 478, (1992) 24 HLR 206, HL; *Greenwich LBC v McGrady* (1982) 6 HLR 36; *Crawley BC v Ure* (1995) 27 HLR 524, CA; *Notting Hill Housing Trust v Brackley* [2001] EWCA Civ 601, [2002] HLR 212 and *Wilson (by her litigation friend, the Official Solicitor) v Harrow LBC* [2010] EWHC 1574 (QB). Cf *Harrow LBC v Johnstone* (1996) 28 HLR 83, CA.

67   *Hounslow LBC v Pilling* [1993] 1 WLR 1242, (1993) 25 HLR 305, CA.

68   *Sims v Dacorum BC* [2014] UKSC 63, [2015] HLR 7.

Secretary of State has given a notice in writing to the landlord identifying the occupier or occupiers of the premises, where all the occupiers are disqualified as a result of their immigration status from occupying premises under such an agreement (that is, they do not have the 'right to rent' within the meaning of IA 2014 s21(2)). The landlord may terminate the agreement by giving at least 28 days' notice in writing in the prescribed form. Such notice is to be treated as a notice to quit where a notice to quit would otherwise be required to bring the residential tenancy agreement to an end. Such agreements are excluded from the requirement to obtain a court order for possession (PEA 1977 s3A(7D), inserted by IA 2014 s33E(5)). A 'residential tenancy agreement' is defined in IA 2014 s20 as a tenancy, lease or licence which grants a right of occupation of premises for residential use, which provides for payment of rent (whether or not a market rent), and which is not an excluded agreement within the meaning of Schedule 3 to the Act. In addition, IA 2014 s33E (also inserted by IA 2016 s40(3)) provides that it is an implied term of a residential tenancy agreement (other than a regulated tenancy under RA 1977, which is subject to a new ground for possession in Schedule 15 Case 10A, or an assured or assured shorthold tenancy under HA 1988, which is subject to a new ground for possession in Schedule 2 ground 7B) that the landlord may terminate the tenancy if the premises are occupied by an adult who does not have the 'right to rent'. IA 2014 s33E is silent as to the notice required to terminate such an agreement, but it is suggested that the provisions of PEA 1977 s5 (validity of notices to quit a periodic tenancy) and s3 (prohibition of eviction without court order) apply in the usual way, except in cases which have been the subject of a Secretary of State's notice under s33D. IA 2014 ss33D and 33E apply in relation to a residential tenancy agreement entered into before or after the coming into force of these provisions.

Surrender

Surrender by express agreement

14.36   A surrender is a voluntary agreement of both landlord and tenant that the tenancy should come to an end without the service of a notice to quit (or where service of a notice is not possible, such as in the case of a fixed-term tenancy without a break clause). An express surrender must state an immediate intention that the tenancy should come to an end. It cannot operate to take effect in the future. Surrenders by express agreement must be made by deed,[69] although in some circumstances an oral agreement may be effective as a surrender by operation of law (see paras 1.102–1.114 above and 14.38–14.45 below).

14.37   If there are joint tenants, all tenants must agree to the surrender.[70] A husband has no implied authority to surrender a tenancy on behalf of his wife.[71]

Surrender by operation of law

14.38   Even if there is no express surrender by deed, the law may consider that the landlord and tenant have behaved in an unequivocal way which is inconsistent with the continuance of the contractual tenancy. In such circumstances, if their behaviour makes it inequitable for one of the parties to claim that the tenancy still exists, the law will imply a surrender. In *Foster v Robinson*,[72] Sir Raymond Evershed MR stated:

> It has been laid down that in order to constitute a surrender by operation of law there must be, first, an act or purported surrender invalid per se by reason of non-compliance with statutory or other formalities, and secondly, some change of circumstances supervening on, or arising from, the purported surrender, which, by reason of the doctrine of estoppel or part performance, makes it inequitable and fraudulent for any of the parties to rely upon the invalidity of the purported surrender.[73]

14.39   In *Mattey Securities Ltd v Ervin*,[74] when considering the circumstances in which a surrender by operation of law may occur, Bracewell J said:

> The conduct of the parties must unequivocally amount to an acceptance that the tenancy is ended for the doctrine to apply. Although a surrender by operation of law does not require that there is an

---

69 See LPA 1925 s52; Law of Property (Miscellaneous Provisions) Act 1989 s2 and *Ealing Family Housing Association v McKenzie* [2003] EWCA Civ 1602, [2004] 36 HLR 21.
70 *Leek and Moorlands Building Society v Clark* [1952] 2 QB 788.
71 *Re Viola's Indenture of Lease, Humphrey v Stenbury* [1909] 1 Ch 244.
72 [1951] 1 KB 149, CA.
73 [1951] 1 KB 149, CA at 155, quoting from Foa, *General Law of Landlord and Tenant*, 7th edn, Hamish Hamilton, 1947, pp617–618. See also *Dibbs v Campbell* (1988) 20 HLR 374, CA.
74 [1998] 34 EG 91, CA. See also *Sable v QFS Scaffolding Ltd* [2010] EWCA Civ 682, [2010] L&TR 30, in which Morgan J set out a series of propositions summarising the doctrine of surrender by operation of law.

intention of the parties to surrender the lease, it does however require that there is some unequivocal act which has the effect of estopping the parties from asserting that the lease is still extant.

14.40   In *Chamberlain v Scalley*,[75] it was held that, for there to be an implied surrender, there must be unequivocal conduct on the part of both the landlord and the tenant which is inconsistent with the continuance of the tenancy. There are three main situations in which there may be an effective surrender by operation of law.

14.41   The **first situation** is where there is an agreement that the tenant should abandon the tenancy and that the landlord should resume possession of the premises.[76] It is necessary for the tenant to hand back the premises to the landlord. In *Hoggett v Hoggett and Wallis*,[77] the tenant tried to surrender premises to the landlord while his wife was still living in them. This was not a valid surrender. Similarly, the mere departure by a tenant from the premises while rent is owing is not an implied surrender unless there is agreement.[78] In *Belcourt Estates Ltd v Adesina*[79] the Court of Appeal stated that there must be either relinquishment of possession and its acceptance by the landlord or other conduct consistent only with the cesser of the tenancy, and the circumstances must be such as to render it inequitable for the tenant or the landlord to dispute that the tenancy has ceased. Mere inaction or omissions cannot be unequivocal conduct. The position may be different if there has been a long absence and there are substantial rent arrears outstanding.[80]

---

75   (1992) 26 HLR 26, CA. See too *Andre v Robinson* [2007] EWCA Civ 1449.

76   *Phene v Popplewell* (1862) 12 CBNS 334.

77   (1980) 39 P&CR 121, CA. See too *Ealing Family Housing Association v McKenzie* [2003] EWCA Civ 1602, [2004] HLR 21 and *Hackney LBC v Ampratum* September 2003 *Legal Action* 25, Central London Civil Trial Centre.

78   *Preston BC v Fairclough* (1982) 8 HLR 70, CA. See also paras 1.178–1.181. When Housing and Planning Act (HPA) 2016 Part 3 (Recovering abandoned premises in England) is brought into force, a private landlord of an assured shorthold tenant in England (including a private registered provider of social housing) may give the tenant a notice bringing the tenancy to an end if there has been no response by the tenant to a series of three consecutive warning notices spanning a period of at least eight weeks and where the 'unpaid rent condition' is satisfied: HPA 2016 ss57–59 (see paras 1.188–1.192 and 10.102).

79   [2005] EWCA Civ 208. Cf *Artworld Financial Corporation v Safaryan* [2009] EWCA Civ 303, [2009] L&TR 20, where Jacob LJ said 'Going in and living in the property is, in effect, taking over it and treating it as your own, which is inconsistent with the continuance of a lease.' (para 25).

80   *Preston BC v Fairclough* (1982) 8 HLR 70, CA; *R v Croydon LBC ex p Toth* (1986) 18 HLR 493 and *Chamberlain v Scalley* (1992) 26 HLR 26, CA.

14.42   The **second situation** is where there is a delivery of the key. Delivery of the key to the premises by the tenant to the landlord, and its
acceptance by the landlord may, depending on the circumstances,
be a surrender by operation of law. In *Furnivall v Grove*,[81] there was
a surrender where a tenant handed back the key and a few days later
the landlord demolished the building. On the other hand, in *Boynton-
Wood v Trueman*,[82] a tenant handed the key of a cottage to his landlord so that repairs could be carried out. The court held that there was
no surrender because there was 'no unequivocal act on the part of
the tenant ... which would indicate that he was surrendering his tenancy'. In *Laine v Cadwallader*,[83] tenants left and put the keys through
the landlord's letter box. The landlord sued, among other things, for
four weeks' rent in lieu of notice. The Court of Appeal held that the
dropping off of the keys was not a surrender, but an offer to surrender. There had been no acceptance of the offer by the landlord.

14.43   The **third situation** is where there is an agreement for a new lease.
The creation of a new lease between landlord and tenant, or between
the landlord and some third party with the agreement of the tenant,
determines the original contractual tenancy.[84] This is the case even
if the new lease is for a shorter period than the old lease[85] or if there
is an agreement that instead of a tenancy the tenant should enjoy a
rent-free licence for the rest of his or her life.[86] If the new lease is for
some reason invalid, there is no surrender of the earlier lease unless

---

81 (1860) 8 CB(NS) 496. See also *Phene v Popplewell* (1862) 12 CBNS 334, where
the tenant delivered the key to the landlord who then painted out the tenant's
name above the premises and instructed an auctioneer to put up a 'To let' sign.

82 (1961) 177 EG 191. See also *Proudreed Ltd v Microgen Holdings* [1996] 12 EG
127, (1995) *Times* 17 July, CA and *Borakat v Ealing LBC* [1996] EGCS 67, QBD.

83 [2001] L&TR 8, CA. See also *Padwick Properties Ltd v Punj Lloyd Ltd* [2016]
EWHC 502 (Ch).

84 eg, *Climping Park Ltd v Barritt* (1989) *Independent* 15 May, CA. In these
circumstances a tenant is estopped from denying the validity of the new lease
and so cannot deny the implied surrender of the old lease, for a landlord
cannot validly grant a new lease without first procuring a surrender of the old
lease: *Jenkin R Lewis & Son Ltd v Kerman* [1970] 1 All ER 833, but cf *Rhyl UDC
v Rhyl Amusements Ltd* [1959] 1 All ER 257 and *Ashton v Sobelman* [1987] 1
WLR 177 (agreement between freeholder and subtenant alone not sufficient).
See also *Sable v QFS Scaffolding Ltd* [2010] EWCA Civ 682, [2010] L&TR 30
(no surrender where negotiations had been taking place between the landlord
and a prospective new tenant, but the existing tenant had not done anything
inconsistent with the continuation of the tenancy).

85 *Phene v Popplewell* (1862) 12 CBNS 334.

86 *Foster v Robinson* [1951] 1 KB 149, [1950] 2 All ER 342, provided that it is a
genuine transaction.

the surrender has been made by deed.[87] The new agreement must be more than a variation of the terms of the existing tenancy,[88] although an agreed increase in rent may, depending on the circumstances, take effect either as an implied surrender and re-grant of a new lease, or as a variation of the terms of the existing lease.[89] A request by the tenant that the landlord should re-let the premises to someone else does not operate as a surrender if his wife is still in occupation of the premises.[90] However, where a sole tenant left the property as a result of domestic violence, obtained alternative accommodation and returned the keys to the housing association landlord, it was held that there had been a surrender by operation of law, despite the fact that her husband was still in occupation. The husband's right of occupation under Family Law Act 1996 s30 could not prevent the tenant from terminating her contractual relationship with the landlord.[91]

14.44   If a tenancy is surrendered, and the tenant moves out with an intention to cease residing at the premises, that is the end of the tenancy. In these circumstances, a surrender by operation of law takes effect irrespective of the parties' intentions[92] and there is no need for the landlord to bring possession proceedings. If, however, a landlord and a Rent Act protected (contractual) tenant agree to the surrender of a tenancy, but the tenant continues to occupy the premises as a residence, the only effect of the surrender is to convert the protected tenancy into a statutory tenancy.[93] The landlord still has to prove a Rent Act ground for possession, and, if appropriate, that it

---

87 *Rhyl UDC v Rhyl Amusements Ltd* [1959] 1 All ER 257 and the cases reviewed by Harman J at 267.

88 *Smirk v Lyndale Developments* [1975] 1 All ER 690. An agreement that a tenant will rent additional land or an extra part of premises and that the total should be held as one parcel with an increased rent operates as an implied surrender and regrant: *Jenkin R Lewis & Son Ltd v Kerman* [1970] 1 All ER 833. Similarly the variation of the term (ie, length) of a lease so that it subsists for a longer period also operates as an implied surrender and regrant: *Re Savile Settled Estates, Savile v Savile* [1931] 2 Ch 210.

89 cf *Jenkin R Lewis & Son Ltd v Kerman* [1970] 1 All ER 833 and *Gable Construction Co Ltd v Inland Revenue Commissioners* [1968] 2 All ER 968.

90 *Hoggett v Hoggett and Wallis* (1979) 39 P&CR 121, CA. See also *Fredco Estates v Bryant* [1961] 1 All ER 34 (where the landlord said that the tenant could use three extra rooms with no increase in rent: it was held there was no surrender) and *Coker v London Rent Assessment Panel* [2006] All ER (D) 297 May.

91 *Sanctuary Housing Association v Campbell* [1999] 1 WLR 1279, (2000) 32 HLR 100, CA.

92 *Jenkin R Lewis & Son Ltd v Kerman* [1970] 1 All ER 833.

93 RA 1977 s2(1)(a) and *R v Bloomsbury and Marylebone CC ex p Blackburne* (1985) 275 EG 1273, CA.

is reasonable for the court to make an order for possession (see para 12.31). This is the case even if the landlord, the tenant and a prospective purchaser all agree that the purchaser will acquire the property with vacant possession and that the tenant will not make any claim to occupy the premises against the purchaser.[94]

14.45   A surrender of a tenancy does not terminate any subtenancy which the tenant has previously created. The subtenant becomes a direct tenant of the landlord[95] on the terms of the subtenancy even if the head tenancy contained a covenant against subletting without the landlord's consent.[96] However, where the tenant terminates the tenancy by serving a notice to quit on the landlord, this will bring any subtenancy to an end.[97]

Forfeiture

Nature of forfeiture

14.46   Forfeiture is the procedure which allows a landlord to bring to an end a contractual fixed-term tenancy or lease before expiry of the fixed period of time for which the tenancy or lease was originally granted. Forfeiture of a fixed-term tenancy has the same effect as a notice to quit on a periodic tenancy (see para 14.6). If the tenancy is outside statutory protection, forfeiture means that the landlord is entitled to repossess the premises.[98] If the tenancy is a Rent Act protected tenancy, forfeiture merely converts the contractual protected tenancy into a statutory tenancy. Forfeiture can take place only if there is an express provision in the lease allowing the landlord to 're-enter' or forfeit. In practice, all fixed-term leases contain such clauses. Forfeiture is not, however, appropriate to terminate a fixed-term assured or assured shorthold tenancy, since HA 1988 s5(1) provides the only means of bringing an assured tenancy to an end (see para 1.41).[99] In respect of a fixed-term secure tenancy or a flexible tenancy, HA 1985 s82(3) provides that where a court would have made an order in

---

94 *Appleton v Aspin and Plane* (1987) 20 HLR 182, CA.
95 *Mellor v Watkins* (1874) LR 9 QB 400; *Parker v Jones* [1910] 2 KB 32; *Cow v Casey* [1949] 1 KB 474 and *Basingstoke and Deane BC v Paice* (1995) 27 HLR 433.
96 *Parker v Jones* [1910] 2 KB 32.
97 *Pennell v Payne* [1995] QB 192, [1995] 2 All ER 592, CA.
98 Subject, where applicable, to any restraint imposed by PEA 1977.
99 See *Artesian Residential Investments Ltd v Beck* [2000] QB 541, (2000) 32 HLR 107, CA.

accordance with a provision in the tenancy for re-entry or forfeiture, it will instead make an order under that section. Such an order has the effect that the fixed term will end, but will be replaced by a periodic tenancy under HA 1985 s86(1): see para 1.73. The effect of these provisions is that each of HA 1985 and HA 1988 provides a statutory means of terminating the relevant type of tenancy on the basis of a ground for possession, so that the tenant cannot apply for relief from forfeiture (see para 14.60).

14.47   At common law, there was no need for a landlord to bring court proceedings to forfeit a lease: an unequivocal act on the part of the landlord sufficed.[100] Most commonly, this consisted of the landlord entering the premises and taking possession. However, PEA 1977 s2 provides:

> Where any premises are let as a dwelling on a lease which is subject to a right of re-entry or forfeiture it shall not be lawful to enforce that right otherwise than by proceedings in the court while any person is lawfully residing in the premises or part of them.

On whether premises are 'let as a dwelling', see *Pirabakaran v Patel*,[101] in which the premises consisted of a ground floor shop and first floor flat. When the tenant fell into rent arrears, the landlords exercised their right of re-entry to take possession of the shop premises. They argued that the premises were not 'let as a dwelling' and, following re-entry, the lease had become forfeit. However, the Court of Appeal held that the premises fell within section 2: for the purposes of the section, 'let as a dwelling' meant 'let wholly or partly as a dwelling'.

14.48   The service of court proceedings claiming forfeiture is an unequivocal act which amounts to forfeiture.[102] In view of the various forms of relief available to lessees (see para 14.60), the lease is not actually terminated until a court order is made, but the effect of an order is that forfeiture takes effect from the date when proceedings were served.[103] However, if proceedings include a claim for an injunction to restrain the lessee from future breaches of covenant, the issue and service of proceedings is not an unequivocal act and so does not give

---

100 An agreement with an existing subtenant that the subtenant will change the locks is not sufficient to forfeit the headlease: *Ashton v Sobelman* [1987] 1 WLR 177.

101 [2006] EWCA Civ 685, [2006] 1 WLR 3112. See also *Belgravia Property Investment and Development Co Ltd v Webb* [2001] EWCA Civ 2075, [2002] L&TR 29 and *Sajjid v Rajan* [2011] EWCA Civ 1180.

102 *Grimwood v Moss* (1872) LR 7 CP 360 and *Canas Property Co v KL Television Services Ltd* [1970] 2 QB 433.

103 *Borzak v Ahmed* [1965] 2 QB 320.

rise to forfeiture.[104] A landlord claiming forfeiture in the county court must use claim form N5 and follow the general rules governing the content of particulars of claim in possession cases.[105] When issuing proceedings, a landlord must notify any person who may be entitled to relief from forfeiture.[106]

14.49   Even before issuing proceedings for forfeiture, a landlord may have to comply with various statutory and procedural requirements. For example, there are special restrictions on the forfeiture of long leases for arrears of rent and service charges which are described in paras 14.56 (service charges) and 14.61 (rent). If the landlord is claiming forfeiture due to rent arrears, the general rule is that there must be a formal written demand before proceedings are issued. In practice, however, this rule is usually excluded by a provision in the lease which gives the landlord a right to re-enter if there are arrears 'whether the rent has been lawfully demanded or not'. In addition, the County Courts Act 1984 s139(1) provides that if six months' rent is owing at the commencement of the action and if there are insufficient goods on the premises to cover the arrears, proceedings may be issued without a formal demand for rent even if there is no corresponding provision in the lease.

14.50   If forfeiture proceedings are issued for breach of any other covenant in the lease, a notice must be served under LPA 1925 s146 before the issue of proceedings.[107] Service of a LPA 1925 s146 notice by sending it to the property in question is effective, even if it does not actually come to the attention of the lessee.[108]

14.51   Section 146 provides:

Restrictions on and relief against forfeiture of leases and underleases
(1) A right of re-entry or forfeiture under any proviso or stipulation in a lease for a breach of any covenant or condition in the lease shall not be enforceable, by action or otherwise, unless and until the lessor serves on the lessee a notice –
    (a) specifying the particular breach complained of; and
    (b) if the breach is capable of remedy, requiring the lessee to remedy the breach; and

---

104 *Moore v Ullcoats Mining Co Ltd (No 1)* [1908] 1 Ch 575.
105 CPR PD 55A para 2. See chapter 21.
106 CPR PD 55A para 2.4 (cf CCR Ord 6 r3(2)).
107 The section 146 notice must give particulars of the breaches of covenant and call upon the lessee to remedy them: *Fox v Jolly* [1916] 1 AC 1, HL. However, it is not necessary to give particulars of every defect: *Adagio Properties v Ansari* [1998] 35 EG 86, CA.
108 *Van Haarlam v Kasner Charitable Trust* [1992] 36 EG 135, ChD (lessee in prison).

(c) in any case, requiring the lessee to make compensation in money for the breach;

and the lessee fails, within a reasonable time thereafter, to remedy the breach, if it is capable of remedy, and to make reasonable compensation in money, to the satisfaction of the lessor, for the breach.

(2) Where a lessor is proceeding, by action or otherwise, to enforce such a right of re-entry or forfeiture, the lessee may, in the lessor's action, if any, or in any action brought by himself, apply to the court for relief; and the court may grant or refuse relief, as the court, having regard to the proceedings and conduct of the parties under the foregoing provisions of this section, and to all the other circumstances, thinks fit; and in case of relief may grant it on such terms, if any, as to costs, expenses, damages, compensation, penalty, or otherwise, including the granting of an injunction to restrain any like breach in the future, as the court, in the circumstances of each case, thinks fit.

(3) A lessor shall be entitled to recover as a debt due to him from a lessee, and in addition to damages (if any), all reasonable costs and expenses properly incurred by the lessor in the employment of a solicitor and surveyor or valuer, or otherwise, in reference to any breach giving rise to a right of re-entry or forfeiture which, at the request of the lessee, is waived by the lessor, or from which the lessee is relieved, under the provisions of this Act.

(4) Where a lessor is proceeding by action or otherwise to enforce a right of re-entry and forfeiture under any covenant, proviso, or stipulation in a lease, or for non-payment of rent, the court may, on application by any person claiming as under-lessee any estate or interest in the property comprised in the lease or any part thereof either in the lessor's action (if any) or in any action brought by such person for that purpose, make an order vesting, for the whole term of the lease or any less term, the property comprised in the lease or any part thereof in any person entitled as under-lessee to any estate or interest in such property upon such conditions as to execution of any deed or other document, payment of rent, costs, expenses, damages, compensation, giving security, or otherwise, as the court in the circumstances of each case may think fit, but in no case shall any such under-lessee be entitled to require a lease to be granted to him for any longer term than he had under his original sub-lease.

(5) For the purposes of this section –

(a) 'Lease' includes an original or derivative under-lease; also an agreement for a lease where the lessee has become entitled to have his lease granted; also a grant at a fee farm rent, or securing a rent by condition;

(b) 'Lessee' includes an original or derivative under-lessee, and the persons deriving title under a lessee; also a grantee under any such grant as aforesaid and the persons deriving title under him;

     (c) 'Lessor' includes an original or derivative under-lessor, and the persons deriving title under a lessor; also a person making such grant as aforesaid and the persons deriving title under him;

     (d) 'Under-lease' includes an agreement for an under-lease where the under-lessee has become entitled to have his under-lease granted;

     (e) 'Under-lessee' includes any person deriving title under an under-lessee.

(6) This section applies although the proviso or stipulation under which the right of re-entry or forfeiture accrues is inserted in the lease in pursuance of the directions of any Act of Parliament.

(7) For the purposes of this section a lease limited to continue as long only as the lessee abstains from committing a breach of covenant shall be and take effect as a lease to continue for any longer term for which it could subsist, but determinable by a proviso for re-entry on such a breach.

(8) This section does not extend –

     (i) To a covenant or condition against assigning, underletting, parting with the possession, or disposing of the land leased where the breach occurred before the commencement of this Act; or

     (ii) In the case of a mining lease, to a covenant or condition for allow-ing the lessor to have access to or inspect books, accounts, records, weighing machines or other things or to enter or inspect the mine or the workings thereof.

(9) This section does not apply to a condition for forfeiture on the bankruptcy of the lessee or on taking in execution of the lessee's interest if contained in a lease of –

     (a) Agricultural or pastoral land;

     (b) Mines or minerals;

     (c) A house used or intended to be used as a public-house or beer-shop;

     (d) A house let as a dwelling-house, with the use of any furniture, books, works of art or other chattels not being in the nature of fixtures;

     (e) Any property with respect to which the personal qualifications of the tenant are of importance for the preservation of the value or character of the property, or on the ground of neigh-bourhood to the lessor, or to any person holding under him.

(10) Where a condition of forfeiture on the bankruptcy of the lessee or on taking in execution of the lessee's interest is contained in any lease, other than a lease of any of the classes mentioned in the last subsection, then –

     (a) if the lessee's interest is sold, within one year from the bank-ruptcy or taking in execution, this section applies to the forfeit-ure condition aforesaid;

(b) if the lessee's interest is not sold before the expiration of that year, this section only applies to the forfeiture condition aforesaid during the first year from the date of the bankruptcy or taking in execution.

(11) This section does not, save as otherwise mentioned, affect the law relating to re-entry or forfeiture or relief in case of non-payment of rent.

(12) This section has effect notwithstanding any stipulation to the contrary.

(13) The county court has jurisdiction under this section.

14.52 Law of Property Act 1925 s146 gives tenants two opportunities to resist forfeiture: first, an opportunity to remedy any breach which is capable of remedy and, second, to apply for relief from forfeiture.[109] It applies to breaches of all covenants except for non-payment of rent.[110] A landlord cannot avoid these provisions by dressing up a forfeiture as a surrender of the lease.[111] There are special provisions relating to service of notices where a landlord alleges that a lessee has been in breach of the lessee's repairing covenant.[112]

14.53 If the notice given under LPA 1925 s146(1) does not state whether or not the breach is capable of remedy or, if it is remediable, does not require the lessee to remedy it within a reasonable time, the notice is invalid.[113] Breaches of 'positive covenants' (for example, to keep premises in repair) are usually capable of remedy if the lessee can comply with them within a reasonable time.[114] This applies even if the lessee is in breach of a continuing positive covenant. However, it is often more difficult to remedy a breach of a negative covenant.[115] For example, a breach of a covenant not to assign, sublet or part with possession is incapable of remedy because the assignment or subletting has already taken place and cannot be undone.[116] Breaches of covenant against immoral user (prostitution) cannot usually be remedied owing to the stigma which attaches to the premises and the

---

109 *Expert Clothing Service and Sales v Hillgate House Ltd* [1986] Ch 340, [1985] 2 All ER 998 per Slade LJ. For relief from forfeiture, see para 14.60.

110 LPA 1925 s146(11).

111 *Plymouth Corporation v Harvey* [1971] 1 WLR 549.

112 Leasehold Property (Repairs) Act 1938.

113 *Expert Clothing Service and Sales v Hillgate House Ltd* [1986] Ch 340, [1985] 2 All ER 998.

114 *Rugby School (Governors) v Tannahill* [1935] 1 KB 87 and *Expert Clothing Service and Sales v Hillgate House Ltd* [1986] Ch 340, [1985] 2 All ER 998.

115 But cf *Savva v Hussein* [1996] 2 EGLR 65, (1997) 73 P&CR 150, CA.

116 *Scala House and District Property Co v Forbes* [1974] QB 575.

possible effect on property values,[117] although this is not an automatic rule,[118] particularly if the tenant does not know about the breach. A breach involving a criminal conviction cannot be remedied.[119]

14.54   Commonhold and Leasehold Reform Act 2002 (CLRA) s168 provides that a landlord under a long lease of a dwelling may not serve a notice under section 146(1) unless:

- it has been finally determined on an application under section 168(4) that the breach has occurred; or
- the tenant has admitted the breach; or
- a court in any proceedings, or an arbitral tribunal in proceedings pursuant to a post-dispute arbitration agreement, has finally determined that the breach has occurred.[120]

A 'long lease' is defined in CLRA 2002 s76. The most common 'long leases' are: shared ownership leases; leases granted for a term of years certain exceeding 21 years; and leases granted under the right to buy provisions of HA 1985 Part V or the right to acquire provisions of HA 1996 s17.

Service charges

14.55   Landlord and Tenant Act (LTA) 1985 ss18–30 impose restrictions on the amount of service charges which can be recovered from a lessee, and on the time and manner of their recovery. 'Service charge' is defined in LTA 1985 s18(1) as: ' an amount payable by a tenant of a dwelling as part of or in addition to the rent (a) which is payable, directly or indirectly, for services, repairs, maintenance improvements or insurance or the landlord's costs of management, and (b) the whole or part of which varies or may vary according to the relevant costs'. The 'relevant costs' are 'the costs or estimated costs incurred or to be incurred by or on behalf of the landlord, or a superior landlord, in connection with the matters for which the service charge is payable'.

---

117 *Rugby School (Governors) v Tannahill* [1935] 1 KB 87; *Egerton v Jones* [1939] 2 KB 702 and *British Petroleum Pension Trust v Behrendt* (1986) 18 HLR 42, (1985) 276 EG 199.

118 *Glass v Kencakes Ltd* [1966] 1 QB 611.

119 *Hoffmann v Fineberg* [1949] Ch 245 (gaming club, no licence); *Ali v Booth* (1966) 110 SJ 708, (1966) 199 EG 641, CA (food hygiene offences) and *Dunraven Securities v Holloway* (1982) 264 EG 709 (Obscene Publications Act offences).

120 CLRA 2002 s168 does not apply to service charges or administrative charges, but a similar restriction on the service of LPA 1925 s146 notices in relation to such charges is imposed by HA 1996 s81 (see para 14.56).

A service charge demand can therefore include the estimated cost of works to be done or services to be provided in the future, where the lease provides for such sums to be payable in advance. LTA 1985 s19(1) permits relevant costs to be taken into account in determining the amount of a service charge (a) only to the extent that they are reasonably incurred, and (b) where they are incurred on the provision of services or the carrying out of works, only if the services or works are of a reasonable standard.

14.56   HA 1996 s81 prevents landlords from exercising a right of re-entry or forfeiture[121] of premises let as a dwelling for failure to pay service charges (including administration charges) unless the amount claimed is either agreed or admitted by the lessee or has been determined by an appropriate tribunal or court or an arbitral tribunal in accordance with Arbitration Act 1996 Part I.[122] This restriction applies to all leases of residential property other than business tenancies and agricultural holdings, and not only to long leases. The importance of this provision is that it prevents freeholders from pressurising lessees who have a genuine dispute about service charges (or their mortgagees) into paying up rather than face forfeiture proceedings. An application may be made to the First-tier Tribunal for a determination as to whether a service charge is payable and, if it is, the amount which is payable.[123] The court has power to transfer a question which the First-tier Tribunal would have jurisdiction to determine (including claims involving the reasonableness of service charges) to the First-tier Tribunal (Property Chamber), or in Wales to the Leasehold Valuation Tribunal.[124]

Waiver of breach

14.57   If landlords waive particular breaches of covenant, they cannot subsequently rely on those breaches in order to bring proceedings for forfeiture. A landlord may waive a breach expressly or by implication. Waiver takes place where the landlord does an unequivocal act which

---

121   The exercise of a right of re-entry or forfeiture includes the service of a notice under LPA 1925 s146(1): HA 1996 s81(4A). For section 146 notices, see para 14.51.

122   See *Mohammadi v Anston Investments* [2003] EWCA Civ 981, [2004] HLR 8. In the county court case of *Church Commissioners for England v Koyale Enterprises*, January 2012 *Legal Action* 20, Central London County Court, it was held that a default judgment is a determination for the purposes of HA 1996 s81.

123   Landlord and Tenant Act 1985 s27A(1).

124   CLRA 2002 s176A.

recognises the continued existence of the lease after having knowledge of the ground for forfeiture. There are certain actions which
amount to waiver of breach irrespective of the landlord's intention,[125]
for example, a demand for or receipt of rent which accrues after
knowledge of a breach giving a right to forfeit[126] even if the demand
is made 'without prejudice'[127] or the commencement of proceedings
seeking access to premises.[128] The knowledge or actions of agents[129]
or employees such as porters[130] are deemed to be equivalent to direct
knowledge of the landlord. Suspicion that there is a breach without
actual knowledge of the facts is not enough to constitute waiver.[131]

14.58   No demand for rent after proceedings have been issued can
amount to waiver because the landlord has already acted unequivocally in issuing those proceedings. Similarly, there is no waiver of a
breach even if the landlord knows about it but merely stands by without interfering while the lessee carries on with the conduct which
amounts to the breach.

14.59   A continuing breach of covenant continually gives rise to new
rights to forfeit and so waiver cannot affect future breaches.[132] Waiver
operates to prevent a landlord from relying on a particular breach
only, and has no effect in relation to subsequent breaches. Subletting
is a 'one off' breach which only occurs at the time when premises
are initially sublet. However, sharing premises may be a continuing
breach which persists even after waiver.[133]

125 *Central Estates (Belgravia) v Woolgar (No 2)* [1972] 1 WLR 148, [1972] 3 All ER
     610.
126 *Blackstone Ltd v Burnetts (West End) Ltd* [1973] 1 WLR 1487; *Van Haarlam v
     Kasner Charitable Trust* [1992] 36 EG 135, ChD; *Iperion Investments Corporation
     v Broadwalk House Residents* [1992] EGLR 235, QBD (ORB) and *Thomas v Ken
     Thomas Ltd* [2006] EWCA Civ 1504, [2006] L&TR 21.
127 *Segal Securities v Thoseby* [1963] 1 QB 887, [1963] 1 All ER 500.
128 *Cornillie v Saha and Bradford and Bingley BS* (1996) 28 HLR 561, (1996) 72
     P&CR 147, CA.
129 *Central Estates (Belgravia) v Woolgar (No 2)* [1972] 1 WLR 1048, [1972] 3 All ER
     610.
130 *Metropolitan Properties Co Ltd v Cordery* (1979) 251 EG 567.
131 *Chrisdell Ltd v Johnson and Tickner* (1987) 19 HLR 406, CA.
132 *Segal Securities v Thoseby* [1963] 1 All ER 500 and *Houghton v Kemp* [1996] 12
     CL 348.
133 *Metropolitan Properties Co Ltd v Crawford and Wetherill* March 1987 *Legal Action*
     20.

Relief from forfeiture

14.60 Even if a landlord establishes that a tenant has breached a covenant, the tenant may still be entitled to apply for relief from forfeiture. If the court grants relief, the tenant's contractual tenancy is restored to full effect and continues as if the landlord had not sought to forfeit.[134] Relief from forfeiture may be expressed to be conditional, for example, on the tenant not committing future breaches of covenant. There are several forms of relief which operate in different ways. The powers of the county court and High Court to grant relief from forfeiture differ.

Arrears of rent – long lessees

14.61 CLRA 2002 s166 provides that a tenant under a long lease[135] is not liable to pay rent unless the landlord has given a notice demanding payment. The notice must specify the amount of the payment and the date on which the tenant is liable to make it. The date on which the tenant is liable to make the payment must not be either less than 30 days or more than 60 days after the day on which the notice is given, or before the date on which payment would have been due under the lease. Any notice must be in the prescribed form, but may be sent by post instead of personal service.[136]

14.62 Landlords of long lessees may not forfeit for failure to pay rent (including service charges or administration charges which are 'reserved as rent' in the lease), unless the total amount unpaid exceeds 'the prescribed sum', or consists of or includes an amount which has been payable for more than 'a prescribed period'.[137] The prescribed sum is currently £350 and the prescribed period is currently three years.[138]

---

134 *Hynes v Twinsectra Ltd* (1996) 28 HLR 183, [1995] 35 EG 136, CA.
135 For the meaning of 'long lease' see CLRA 2002 s76, summarised at para 14.54.
136 See too Landlord and Tenant (Notice of Rent) (England) Regulations 2004 SI No 3096 and Landlord and Tenant (Notice of Rent) (Wales) Regulations 2005 SI No 1355 (W103) which contain additional requirements, namely notes for both lessees and lessors.
137 CLRA 2002 s167(1).
138 See Rights of Re-entry and Forfeiture (Prescribed Sum and Period) (England) Regulations 2004 SI No 3086 and Rights of Re-entry and Forfeiture (Prescribed Sum and Period) (Wales) Regulations 2005 SI No 1352 (W100).

Arrears of rent – county court

14.63 Procedure for forfeiture for non-payment of rent in the county court is governed by County Courts Act (CCA) 1984 s138. The 1984 Act was amended by the Administration of Justice Act 1985 s55, the Courts and Legal Services Act 1990 and the Crime and Courts Act 2013. Section 138, as amended, provides:

Provisions as to forfeiture for non-payment of rent

138(1) This section has effect where a lessor is proceeding by action in the county court (being an action in which the county court has jurisdiction) to enforce against a lessee a right of re-entry or forfeiture in respect of any land for non-payment of rent.

(2) If the lessee pays into court or to the lessor not less than 5 clear days before the return day all the rent in arrear and the costs of the action, the action shall cease, and the lessee shall hold the land according to the lease without any new lease.

(3) If –

(a) the action does not cease under subsection (2); and

(b) the court at the trial is satisfied that the lessor is entitled to enforce the right of re-entry or forfeiture,

the court shall order possession of the land to be given to the lessor at the expiration of such period, not being less than 4 weeks from the date of the order, as the court thinks fit, unless within that period the lessee pays into court or to the lessor all the rent in arrear and costs of the action.

(4) The court may extend the period specified under subsection (3) at any time before possession of the land is recovered in pursuance of the order under that subsection.

(5) ... if –

(a) within the period specified in the order; or

(b) within that period as extended under subsection (4),

the lessee pays into court or to the lessor –

(i) all the rent in arrear; and

(ii) the costs of the action,

he shall hold the land according to the lease without any new lease.

(6) Subsection (2) shall not apply where the lessor is proceeding in the same action to enforce a right of re-entry or forfeiture on any other ground as well as for non-payment of rent, or to enforce any other claim as well as the right of re-entry or forfeiture and the claim for arrears of rent.

(7) If the lessee does not –

(a) within the period specified in the order; or

(b) within that period as extended under subsection (4),

pay into court or to the lessor –

(i) all the rent in arrear; and

(ii) the costs of the action,

the order shall be enforceable in the prescribed manner and so long as the order remains unreversed the lessee shall, subject to subsections (8) and (9A), be barred from all relief.

(8) The extension under subsection (4) of a period fixed by a court shall not be treated as relief from which the lessee is barred by subsection (7) if he fails to pay into court or to the lessor all the rent in arrear and the costs of the action within that period.

(9) Where the court extends a period under subsection (4) at a time when –

(a) that period was expired; and

(b) a warrant has been issued for the possession of the land,

the court shall suspend the warrant for the extended period; and, if, before the expiration of the extended period, the lessee pays into court or to the lessor all the rent in arrear and all the costs of the action, the court shall cancel the warrant.

(9A) Where the lessor recovers possession of the land at any time after the making of the order under subsection (3) (whether as a result of the enforcement of the order or otherwise) the lessee may, at any time within six months from the date on which the lessor recovers possession, apply to the court for relief; and on any such application the court may, if it thinks fit, grant to the lessee such relief, subject to such terms and conditions, as it thinks fit.

(9B) Where the lessee is granted relief on an application under subsection (9A) he shall hold the land according to the lease without any new lease.

(9C) An application under subsection (9A) may be made by a person with an interest under a lease of the land derived (whether immediately or otherwise) from the lessee's interest therein in like manner as if he were the lessee; and on any such application the court may make an order which (subject to such terms and conditions as the court thinks fit) vests the land in such a person, as lessee of the lessor, for the remainder of the term of the lease under which he has any such interest as aforesaid, or for any lesser term.

In this subsection any reference to the land includes a reference to a part of the land.

(10) Nothing in this section or section 139 shall be taken to affect –

(a) the power of the court to make any order which it would otherwise have power to make as respects a right of re-entry or forfeiture on any ground other than non-payment of rent; or

(b) section 146(4) of the Law of Property Act 1925 (relief against forfeiture).

14.64   CCA 1984 s138 provides three different forms of relief from forfeiture in cases of non-payment of rent:

- *If all the rent arrears and costs are paid to the lessor or into court at least five days before the return day, the action automatically ceases* and the lease continues as if no proceedings had been issued.[139] The 'return day' is the date on the claim form even if that hearing is in fact only treated as a directions hearing and the action is adjourned for a full hearing at a later date.[140] If all arrears and costs are paid at least five days before the return day, the tenancy remains a contractual tenancy.

• At the hearing, if there is a claim based on arrears of rent, the court must automatically delay possession for at least four weeks. If during this period the lessee pays to the lessor or into court all the arrears and costs, there is again complete relief from forfeiture[141] and the tenancy continues as a contractual tenancy. The Court of Appeal has held that the words 'the lessee pays into court ... all the rent in arrear' used in CCA 1984 s138(3) do not mean that the court can order payment of the rent in arrears only at the date of issue of the claim form. It is to be assumed that the lease continues after service of the claim, that the tenant remains under an obligation to pay the sum reserved in the lease as rent and that 'all the rent in arrear' means the rent payable up to the date stated in the order.[142] The court may, of its own motion, adjourn the hearing once for enquiry to ascertain the lessee's ability to pay rent, but it is usually wrong for there to be two such adjournments without the lessor's consent.[143] The period of postponement may be extended at any time before possession is actually recovered.[144]

• The lessee may apply to the court within six months of the landlord recovering possession (for example, by sending in the bailiff or otherwise) for relief against forfeiture.[145] Similar applications for relief where there has been peaceable re-entry may be made under CCA 1984 s139(2), although in view of PEA 1977 s2 (see above) this will rarely be applicable to residential premises.

139 CCA 1984 s138(2).
140 *Swordheath Properties Ltd v Bolt* [1992] 38 EG 154, CA. See also CCA 1984 s147.
141 CCA 1984 s138(3).
142 *Maryland Estates v Bar-Joseph* [1999] 1 WLR 83, (1999) 31 HLR 269, CA.
143 *R v A Circuit Judge ex p Wathen* (1976) 33 P&CR 423 (tenant admitted arrears of rent, but said that he had an expectancy of money under a trust at an unknown future date).
144 CCA 1984 s138(4); see para 14.63.
145 CCA 1984 s138(9A) (para 14.63), reversing the effect of *Di Palma v Victoria Square Property Co Ltd* [1986] Ch 150, (1985) 17 HLR 448. Cf *Jones v Barnett* [1984] Ch 500, [1984] 3 All ER 129.

Other breaches of covenants – county court

14.65 Law of Property Act 1925 (LPA) s146(2) (reproduced at para 14.51) provides that a lessee may apply for relief from forfeiture and that the court may grant such relief, subject to whatever conditions it thinks fit. This general discretion to grant relief does not apply where there are arrears of rent.[146] Although the most common way for lessees to apply for relief from forfeiture is to counterclaim in forfeiture proceedings which the landlord has issued, it is possible for lessees themselves to issue proceedings in which they claim relief. Indeed, that is the only way in which relief may be sought if a landlord peaceably re-enters premises which are not 'let as a dwelling' and so not protected by PEA 1977 s2. Lord Templeman summarised the law in *Billson v Residential Apartments*[147] by stating:

> A tenant may apply for ... relief from forfeiture under section 146(2) after the issue of a section 146 notice but he is not prejudiced if he does not do so. A tenant cannot apply for relief after a landlord has forfeited a lease by issuing and serving a writ, has recovered judgment and has entered into possession pursuant to that judgment. If the judgment is set aside or successfully appealed the tenant will be able to apply for relief in the landlord's action but the court in deciding whether to grant relief will take into account any consequences of the original order and repossession and the delay of the tenant. A tenant may apply for relief after a landlord has forfeited by re-entry without first obtaining a court order for that purpose, but the court in deciding whether to grant relief will take into account all the circumstances including delay on the part of the tenant.

14.66 Underlessees have, in all cases, including rent arrears cases, the right to apply for relief and to have leases vested in themselves instead of the lessees.[148] This operates by granting a new lease which comes into effect from the date when relief is given.[149]

14.67 If there are joint lessees of premises, all must apply together for relief under LPA 1925 s146.[150] The court may grant relief in respect of part only of premises if, for example, the breaches of covenant are confined to one distinct part of the building.[151]

---

146 LPA 1925 s146(11); but see paras 14.63–14.64.
147 [1992] 1 AC 494, (1992) 24 HLR 218, HL.
148 LPA 1925 s146(4).
149 *Cadogan v Dimovic* [1984] 1 WLR 609.
150 *Fairclough (TM) and Sons Ltd v Berliner* [1931] 1 Ch 60.
151 *GMS Syndicate Ltd v Gary Elliott Ltd* [1982] Ch 1.

Equitable jurisdiction – county court

14.68 The court has a further equitable jurisdiction, wider than LPA 1925 s146(4), to grant relief to underlessees or mortgagees.[152] This jurisdiction does not, however, extend to lessees in rent arrears cases because of the inclusion of the words 'shall be barred from all relief' in CCA 1984 s138(7) (see para 14.63).[153]

Relief from forfeiture in the High Court

14.69 Proceedings for forfeiture of leases of residential premises are usually brought in the county court, however large the arrears of rent, because of the restrictions contained in the Civil Procedure Rules Part 55.[154] The High Court's powers to grant relief are contained in the Common Law Procedure Act 1852 ss210–212. These provisions state that a lessee must seek relief within six months of the execution of judgment, although it appears that there is an equitable jurisdiction for the court to grant relief outside that period if there has been peaceable re-entry.[155] LPA 1925 s146 (para 14.52) applies equally to High Court proceedings.

Principles on which relief from forfeiture is granted

14.70 The circumstances in which relief is granted vary considerably and the courts are reluctant to lay down general principles.[156] It is clear, however, that courts must take into account all relevant circumstances. The harm caused to a landlord by breach of covenant (for example, its effect on the value of the property[157]) is important. For this reason, relief was frequently refused where an unlawful subletting or assignment led to the creation of a Rent Act statutory tenancy (where there would not otherwise have been one and where it would have been reasonable for a landlord to refuse consent to the sublet-

---

152 *Abbey National BS v Maybeech Ltd* [1985] Ch 190, [1984] 3 All ER 262.
153 *Di Palma v Victoria Square Property Co Ltd* [1986] Ch 150, (1985) 17 HLR 448.
154 CPR 55.3 and PD 55A para 1.1.
155 *Thatcher v Pearce and Sons* [1968] 1 WLR 748.
156 *Leeward Securities Ltd v Lilyheath Properties Ltd* (1983) 271 EG 279, (1983) 17 HLR 35, CA and *Bickel v Duke of Westminster* [1977] QB 517 at 524 per Lord Denning MR.
157 *Central Estates (Belgravia) v Woolgar (No 2)* [1972] 3 All ER 610.

ting or assignment).[158] Similarly, it is rare for relief to be given where the covenant broken is a covenant against immoral user, since the courts take the view that a 'stigma' may attach to the property.[159] If a breach has been brought to an end, or ended some time ago, the court is more likely to grant relief.[160] If the breach complained of would not have been a breach if the landlord had consented, it is relevant to consider whether the landlord could reasonably have withheld consent.[161] Similarly, the intention of the lessee at the time of committing the breach is important. For example, where the lessee had no intention of breaching the lease, but the breach was brought about by a solicitor's mistake, relief was granted.[162] The landlord's conduct is also relevant and, in a case where the court found that the landlord's conduct was unreasonable and that the landlord had engaged in acts of harassment against the lessee, relief was given without hesitation.[163] The tenant's age and health may be relevant. The court must consider the proportionality of forfeiture, and where the leasehold interest has a value, a balance must be struck between allowing the landlord to obtain a windfall benefit and securing the performance of the tenant's covenants.[164]

Forfeiture and Rent Act protection

14.71   A landlord who wishes to evict a Rent Act protected tenant for breach of a covenant during a fixed-term tenancy has to go through two stages, although both may be dealt with at the same hearing. First, the court must consider whether the lease should be forfeited and,

---

158 *Leeward Securities Ltd v Lilyheath Properties Ltd* (1983) 271 EG 279, (1983) 17 HLR 35, CA and *West Layton Ltd v Ford* [1979] QB 593.

159 *British Petroleum Pension Trust v Behrendt* (1986) 18 HLR 42, (1986) 52 P&CR 117.

160 More recently the courts have been prepared to grant relief where forfeiture would produce a 'windfall' gain for the lessor, which should be considered according to the principles of proportionality. In *Freifeld and another v West Kensington Court Ltd* [2015] EWCA Civ 806, [2016] 1 P&CR 5 the Court of Appeal, in allowing the lessees' appeal and granting relief from forfeiture, held that the judge below had failed to consider the question of the windfall the landlord would gain 'as a self-standing consideration ... on its own merits'. The court noted that relief can still be granted even though a breach is deliberate. See also *Patel v K&J Restaurants Ltd* [2010] EWCA Civ 1211, [2011] L&TR 6.

161 *Scala House and District Property Co v Forbes* [1974] QB 575.

162 *Scala House and District Property Co v Forbes* [1974] QB 575.

163 *Segal Securities v Thoseby* [1963] 1 All ER 500.

164 *Freifeld v West Kensington Court Ltd* [2015] EWCA Civ 806, [2016] 1 P&CR 5.

if appropriate, whether relief against forfeiture should be given.[165] If the lease is forfeited, the tenancy becomes a statutory tenancy. The court has then to consider whether a Rent Act ground for possession exists (most commonly under Case 1: see para 12.39) and, if so, whether it is reasonable to make an order for possession.[166]

---

165 *Central Estates (Belgravia) v Woolgar (No 2)* [1972] 1 WLR 1048, [1972] 3 All ER 610. The position is very different if the tenant is an assured tenant – see para 14.46.

166 See *Wolmer Securities v Corne* [1966] 2 QB 243, [1966] 2 All ER 691.

CHAPTER 15

Unprotected tenants and licensees

Introduction

15.1   If a tenant does not come within one of the forms of statutory protection provided by the Housing Act (HA) 1985, Housing Act 1988
or the Rent Act (RA) 1977, a landlord seeking possession need only
commence proceedings and prove that they have an interest in the
premises and that the contractual tenancy has been determined.
In this book such tenants are referred to as 'unprotected tenants'.[1]
Unprotected tenants include Crown tenants,[2] tenants of fully mutual
housing co-operatives,[3] student tenants of university accommodation[4] and tenants of temporary accommodation provided by a local
authority following its acceptance of a homelessness duty.[5] It is likely
that the only defence available to most such tenants is to allege that
the contractual tenancy had not been determined at the date when
proceedings were issued,[6] for example, because a notice to quit was
defective. If the landlord is a public authority, including a 'hybrid'
authority exercising a public function,[7] it may be possible to defend
the claim for possession on public law grounds, or, in exceptional
cases, on 'human rights' grounds. For further discussion of human
rights and public law defences, see chapters 25 and 26. See also
chapter 27 for consideration of defences under the Equality Act 2010,
which may be available against a public or private landlord.

Requirement for a court order: Protection from Eviction Act 1977 s3

15.2   Protection from Eviction Act (PEA) 1977 s3 makes it unlawful for
landlords of many unprotected tenants and licensees to enforce their
right to recover possession 'otherwise than by proceedings in the
court'. Landlords who fail to comply with PEA 1977 s3 commit the

---

1   Although they may have the limited protection of PEA 1977 s3 (requirement of
a possession order): see para 15.3.
2   RA 1977 s13; HA 1988 Sch 1 para 11.
3   But see *Berrisford v Mexfield Housing Co-operative Ltd* [2011] UKSC 52, [2012]
HLR 15 and paras 8.20–8.26.
4   RA 1977 s8; HA 1988 Sch 1 para 8.
5   HA 1985 Sch 1 para 4. See paras 8.12–8.13 and 11.19.
6   For the termination of contractual tenancies, see chapter 14.
7   See *R (Weaver) v London & Quadrant Housing Trust* [2009] EWCA Civ 587,
[2009] HLR 40 and para 25.38.

criminal offence of unlawful eviction under section 1(2) of that Act
and are liable to a claim for damages in tort. Section 3 provides:

Prohibition of eviction without due process of law

(1) Where any premises have been let as a dwelling under a tenancy
which is neither a statutorily protected tenancy nor an excluded
tenancy and –

    (a) the tenancy (in this section referred to as the former tenancy)
has come to an end, but

    (b) the occupier continues to reside in the premises or part of
them,

it shall not be lawful for the owner to enforce against the occupier,
otherwise than by proceedings in the court, his right to recover
possession of the premises.

(2) In this section 'the occupier', in relation to any premises, means
any person lawfully residing in the premises or part of them at the
termination of the former tenancy.

(2A) Subsections (1) and (2) above apply in relation to any restricted
contract (within the meaning of the Rent Act 1977) which –

    (a) creates a licence; and

    (b) is entered into after the commencement of section 69 of the
Housing Act 1980;

as they apply in relation to a restricted contract which creates a
tenancy.

(2B) Subsections (1) and (2) above apply in relation to any premises
occupied as a dwelling under a licence, other than an excluded
licence, as they apply in relation to premises let as a dwelling
under a tenancy, and in those subsections the expressions 'let' and
'tenancy' shall be construed accordingly.

(2C) References in the preceding provisions of this section and section
4(2A) below to an excluded tenancy do not apply to –

    (a) a tenancy entered into before the date on which the Housing
Act 1988 came into force, or

    (b) a tenancy entered into on or after that date but pursuant to a
contract made before that date,

but, subject to that, 'excluded tenancy' and 'excluded licence' shall
be construed in accordance with section 3A below.

(3) This section shall, with the necessary modifications, apply where
the owner's right to recover possession arises on the death of the
tenant under a statutory tenancy within the meaning of the Rent
Act 1977 or the Rent (Agriculture) Act 1976.

15.3   Section 3 applies where a tenancy is 'neither a statutorily protected
tenancy nor an excluded tenancy'. A statutorily protected tenancy is
defined in PEA 1977 s8(1) as:

(a) a protected tenancy within the meaning of the Rent Act 1977 or a tenancy to which Part I of the Landlord and Tenant Act 1954 applies;

(b) a protected occupancy or statutory tenancy as defined in the Rent (Agriculture) Act 1976;

(c) a tenancy to which Part II of the Landlord and Tenant Act 1954 applies;

(d) a tenancy of an agricultural holding within the meaning of the Agricultural Holdings Act 1986 which is a tenancy in relation to which that Act applies;

(e) an assured tenancy or assured agricultural occupancy under Part I of the Housing Act 1988;

(f) a tenancy to which Schedule 10 to the Local Government and Housing Act 1989 applies;

(g) a farm business tenancy within the meaning of the Agricultural Tenancies Act 1995.

It is arguable that section 3 does not therefore confer protection from eviction where the tenancy has formerly been a Rent Act protected tenancy or an assured or assured shorthold tenancy. However, in cases where it is alleged that the tenant has lost statutory protection by ceasing to reside in the premises, the tenancy is (on the landlord's case) no longer a 'statutorily protected tenancy' and accordingly section 3 will apply.

15.4   PEA 1977 s3 therefore applies to tenancies which are not statutorily protected and to licences, apart from those tenancies and licences which are specifically excluded from its scope (see para 15.5 below), provided that the occupier is 'lawfully residing in the premises ... at the termination of the former tenancy'. Where a tenant has created a subtenancy or licence without the landlord's consent in breach of a term of the tenancy agreement, the subtenant or licensee will not be a lawful occupier as against the head landlord; although, as far as his or her own landlord is concerned, he or she will be in lawful occupation.

Excluded lettings

15.5   The categories of tenancies and licences which are 'excluded' from the benefit of PEA 1977 s3[8] are defined in PEA 1977 s3A. A tenancy or licence is excluded if:

---

8   And also from PEA 1977 s5 (notice to quit to be at least 28 days in duration and to contain prescribed information): see para 14.8.

- *The occupier shares with the landlord or licensor accommodation which is part of his or her 'only or principal home'.*[9] However, a tenancy or licence is not 'excluded' if the accommodation shared consists only of storage areas or means of access, such as corridors or staircases.[10]
- *The occupier lives in the same building as the landlord or licensor and shares accommodation with a member of the landlord's or licensor's family.*[11] The definition of 'member of the family' which appears in HA 1985 s113 applies. This includes spouses or civil partners, people living together as husband and wife or as civil partners, parents, children, grandparents, grandchildren, siblings, uncles and aunts.
- *The tenancy or licence is granted as a temporary expedient to a person who entered the premises as a trespasser.*[12]
- *The tenancy or licence merely confers the right to occupy for a holiday.*[13]
- *The tenancy or licence is not granted for money or money's worth.*[14]
- *A licensee occupies a room in a hostel provided by a local authority, development corporation, the Regulator of Social Housing, a housing trust, a private registered provider of social housing or a registered social landlord.*[15]
- *The tenancy or licence is granted to provide accommodation under Immigration and Asylum Act 1999 s4 (for those temporarily admitted or whose asylum claims have been refused) or Part VI (support for asylum seekers).*[16]
- *The tenancy or licence is granted in order to provide accommodation for displaced persons granted temporary protection.*[17]
- (Under provisions which are not in force at the date of publication) *The tenancy or licence is a letting of premises which are subject to a Secretary of State's notice under Immigration Act 2014 s33D*

9 PEA 1977 s3A(2).
10 PEA 1977 s3A(5)(a).
11 PEA 1977 s3A(3).
12 PEA 1977 s3A(6).
13 PEA 1977 s3A(7)(a).
14 PEA 1977 s3A(7)(b).
15 PEA 1977 s3A(8).
16 PEA 1977 s3A(7A), inserted by Immigration and Asylum Act 1999 Sch 14 para 73 and amended by Immigration, Asylum and Nationality Act 2006 s43(4). Note that section 4 will be repealed by Immigration Act 2016 Sch 11 para 1, when this provision is brought into force.
17 PEA 1977 s3A(7C), inserted by the Displaced Persons (Temporary Protection) Regulations 2005 SI No 1379.

identifying occupiers who do not have the 'right to rent' under Immigration Act 2014 s21(2).[18]

15.6   Case-law has determined that other categories of letting are also excluded from PEA 1977 s3. Where a homeless person has been placed in interim accommodation[19] (whether shared or self-contained) pending the local housing authority's decision, or in temporary accommodation for other purposes,[20] such accommodation is considered not to be let or occupied 'as a dwelling'[21] and so does not attract the limited protection of the 1977 Act.

15.7   An unprotected tenant or licensee who is entitled to await a court order under PEA 1977 s3 has a complete defence to possession proceedings if the contractual tenancy or licence has not been lawfully terminated by the time that proceedings are issued,[22] or if a further tenancy or licence has been created. Such unprotected tenancies or licences, if periodic, can be lawfully terminated only by a valid notice to quit, which must comply with PEA 1977 s5 (see para 14.8), and the tenant or licensee can lawfully be evicted only by court order under section 3 of that Act. For the detailed requirements relating to notices to quit, see paras 14.6–14.26.

15.8   If the tenancy is an 'excluded letting', however, a court order is not required for a lawful eviction, subject to the minimal safeguards of section 6 of the Criminal Law Act 1977, which prohibits using or threatening violence to person or property for the purpose of securing entry into any premises, when there is someone present on those premises at the time who is opposed to the entry. At common law, a notice to quit is still required to terminate a periodic excluded tenancy, but the period of the notice will (in the absence of any specific provision in the agreement) be the same as the rental period.[23] Thus,

---

18 PEA 1977 s3A(7D), to be inserted by Immigration Act 2016, s40(5)).

19 Under HA 1996 s188(1).

20 Such as temporary accommodation provided to those who became homeless intentionally under HA 1996 s190(2).

21 *R (CN and ZH) v Lewisham LBC and Newham LBC* [2014] UKSC 62, [2015] HLR 6. See also *Desnousse v Newham LBC, Paddington Churches HA and Veni Properties Ltd* [2006] EWCA Civ 547, [2006] 3 WLR 349; *Brillouet v Landless* (1996) 28 HLR 836, CA and *Mohammed v Manek and Kensington and Chelsea RLBC* (1995) 27 HLR 439. Where, however, a local authority has accepted a housing duty under HA 1996 s193(2), it has been suggested that the temporary accommodation provided is to be regarded as a 'dwelling' and a court order for possession will therefore be required for a lawful eviction: *Rogerson v Wigan MBC* [2004] EWHC 1677 (QB), [2005] HLR 10.

22 *GLC v Jenkins* [1975] 1 WLR 155, [1975] 1 All ER 354.

23 *Doe d Peacock v Raffan* (1806) 6 Esp 4.

an excluded weekly tenancy will require one week's notice to quit which must expire on the first or last day of the rental period.[24] A common law notice to quit need not be in writing unless the tenancy stipulates otherwise.[25]

15.9   In the case of licensees, notice to terminate a licence must also now comply with PEA 1977 s5 (see para 14.8) unless the licence is excluded. If there are joint owners, notice may be given by one of them acting alone.[26] In the case of an excluded licence, the owner must observe any contractual provisions which the licence contains relating to termination. If a licence is excluded, notice may be given orally.[27] Whether or not there are contractual provisions in the licence, a licensee must be given reasonable notice.[28] There is no need for the notice itself to specify the particular time or, indeed, a reasonable time. However, a reasonable time must have elapsed between the giving of the notice and the issue of court proceedings.[29] The notice determines the licence immediately on service,[30] but if the notice specifies a period of time which is too short, it does not become operative until the expiry of such a reasonable time. There are no set rules about what is 'reasonable'. The length of time depends on the circumstances in any particular case, and factors which may be taken into account include the length of time that the licensee has resided in the premises and the periods for which payments have been made.[31]

15.10   A former unprotected tenant or licensee whose letting has been determined but who remains on the premises is a trespasser. Accordingly, owners are entitled to damages for trespass without bringing evidence that they could or would have relet the property if the trespasser had not been there. The measure of damages will be either the amount of loss suffered by the owner or the value to the trespasser

---

24 *Crate v Miller* [1947] KB 946.
25 *Timmins v Rowlinson* (1765) 3 Burr 1603; *Bird v Defonvielle* (1846) 2 C & K 415, 420, n(b).
26 *Annen v Rattee* (1985) 17 HLR 323, (1984) 273 EG 503.
27 *Crane v Morris* [1965] 1 WLR 1104, [1965] 3 All ER 77.
28 *Minister of Health v Bellotti* [1944] KB 298, [1944] 1 All ER 238.
29 *Minister of Health v Bellotti* [1944] KB 298, [1944] 1 All ER 238.
30 *Minister of Health v Bellotti* [1944] KB 298, [1944] 1 All ER 238.
31 In *Mehta v Royal Bank of Scotland* (1999) 32 HLR 45, it was held that a reasonable period of notice for a long-term hotel resident would be not less than four months.

of the use of the property for the period of occupation. Usually this is the ordinary letting value of the property.[32]

Unauthorised tenants of mortgagors

15.11   These are tenants who find themselves threatened with eviction not by their landlord, but by their landlord's mortgage lender. In the typical situation, the landlord will have defaulted in his or her payments under the mortgage, and the lender will have obtained, or be in the course of obtaining, a possession order in mortgage possession proceedings against the landlord. The tenant will usually be an assured shorthold tenant in relation to his or her landlord, but this does not necessarily mean that the tenancy is binding on the lender.

15.12   In these circumstances, tenants' rights depend on whether their tenancies were authorised under the terms of the landlord's mortgage. It is invariably a term of residential mortgage agreements that the borrower is not permitted to let the mortgaged property without the consent of the mortgage lender. A tenancy will normally be authorised either where the landlord has obtained the permission of the lender or where the landlord has a 'buy to let' mortgage and the tenancy complies with any conditions in the mortgage deed. It will also be binding on the mortgagee if it was already in existence when the mortgage was created.

15.13   In the case of an *authorised* tenancy, the lender will be unable to obtain a possession order against a tenant in occupation without taking the appropriate steps to terminate the tenancy. In the absence of such measures, the lender's claim for possession must be dismissed. Where the tenant is an assured shorthold tenant, the lender will need to terminate the assured shorthold tenancy in the standard way, ie, by seeking possession on the basis of a ground for possession (where the fixed term of the tenancy has not yet expired) or (where the tenancy is or has become periodic) by serving a two months' notice under HA 1988 s21. In many cases, the tenant may be able to negotiate with the lender and reach an agreement which will allow him or her to stay in the property for a longer period, on the basis that rent is paid to the lender under the existing agreement.

32   *Swordheath Properties Ltd v Tabet* [1979] 1 WLR 285, [1979] 1 All ER 240; *Ministry of Defence v Thompson* [1993] 40 EG 148, (1993) 25 HLR 552, CA and *Ministry of Defence v Ashman* (1993) 66 P&CR 195, (1993) 25 HLR 513, CA. See chapter 29.

15.14   On the other hand, if the tenant is an *unauthorised* tenant (usually because the landlord has an ordinary residential mortgage and did not have permission to let the property), the lender can apply for a warrant of possession to enforce the mortgage possession order which it has obtained against the landlord and the court bailiff will then be required to evict the tenant. However, at any time the tenant may be able to obtain a two months' stay of possession under the Mortgage Repossessions (Protection of Tenants etc) Act 2010. See also paras 37.26–37.30.

15.15   The effect of the Mortgage Repossessions (Protection of Tenants etc) Act 2010 is that the unauthorised tenant has the right to ask the court to delay the date for possession. The tenant has two opportunities to exercise this right (though it can be exercised only once).

Tenant applies for a delay at the mortgage possession hearing

15.16   At the hearing of the possession claim, on the application of the unauthorised tenant, the court may stay or postpone the date of possession for up to two months (s1(2)). A 'tenancy' means an assured or assured shorthold tenancy or a Rent Act regulated tenancy. Where the tenant knows the date of hearing, he or she can attend court, take part in the hearing and ask the judge to allow a maximum of two months before the possession order takes effect.

Tenant applies for a delay after the possession order, on a refusal of lender to delay possession for two months

15.17   If the tenant does not find out about the impending eviction until after the possession order is made, he or she can still approach the lender and ask it to give a written undertaking not to enforce the order for a period of two months. If the lender will not do so, the tenant may apply to the court for an order staying or suspending execution of the order for up to two months (s1(4)). The tenant's approach to the lender and application to the court can be made at any time up to the date of eviction. Application is made on county court form N244 (Application Notice). The tenant should attach copies of all relevant documents, including: his or her tenancy agreement; any correspondence with the lender; and evidence of payment of rent to the landlord. The Department for Communities and Local Government has issued *Guidance to the Mortgage Repossession (Protection of*

Tenants etc) Act 2010.[33] The Guidance stresses that a written tenancy agreement is not necessary and that courts should accept other evidence such as: a rent book or other proof of payments; housing benefit documentation; correspondence between the borrower and the tenant which refers to a tenancy; or proof that a deposit has been registered with one of the tenancy deposit schemes.

15.18   When considering whether to exercise its power to postpone possession, the court must have regard to the circumstances of the tenant, and to the nature of any breach of a term of the tenancy (such as a failure to pay rent): s1(5). The court may impose a condition that payments be made to the lender by the tenant (s1(6)). The court may not postpone the date of possession if it has already done so once already, even if the earlier postponement was for less than two months.

Lender's notice of execution of possession order

15.19   The lender cannot enforce a mortgage possession order until it has sent a warning notice to the property (s2(2)). The purpose of the notice is to inform any occupiers that the lender has applied or intends to apply for a warrant, and to ensure that they also know what they can do to obtain a postponement. The warning notice must be in a prescribed form.[34] The possession order may not be executed until 14 days after the notice is given.

---

33 Available at www.gov.uk.
34 The prescribed form is set out in the Dwelling Houses (Execution of Possession Orders by Mortgagees) Regulations 2010 SI No 1809.

CHAPTER 16

Welfare benefits for tenants

continued

Introduction

16.1 Many occupiers faced with possession proceedings are in that situation as a result of failure to make rental or other payments to their landlord. The purpose of this chapter is to outline the assistance with housing costs which is available to tenants and other renting occupiers under the two main welfare benefits schemes.

16.2 There are two different schemes which provide assistance for those on low incomes with the payment of rent and certain other housing costs. One is the housing benefit scheme, which is administered by local housing authorities. For many years from 1982 when it was introduced, housing benefit was the only regime which provided support for tenants. Many claimants still receive housing benefit, and will continue to receive it for the foreseeable future. Housing benefit is payable by local authorities even though the claimant is receiving other benefits such as income support or employment and support allowance from the Department of Work and Pensions (DWP). However, many new benefit claimants now receive payment under the second scheme, namely, universal credit. Universal credit is a new form of benefit whereby the DWP makes a single monthly payment to claimants which is intended to cover all their needs, including housing costs. Tenants of working age who are presently in receipt of housing benefit will find themselves increasingly brought within the universal credit regime in the future. Note that the term 'tenants', as used in this chapter, is intended to include licensees and other occupiers paying a periodic rent or occupation charge for their accommodation.

16.3 The first question, therefore, is what type of benefit the tenant is receiving, or is entitled to if he or she has not yet submitted a claim or has not yet received a decision on a claim. In most cases, it will be clear from the kind of benefit or benefits which the occupier is already receiving whether he or she is within the housing benefit or the universal credit scheme. In other cases, the tenant may need specialist welfare benefits advice and assistance in ensuring that he or she makes the correct kind of claim and in pursuing the claim to decision and payment.

Housing benefit

The scheme in outline

16.4   Housing benefit is claimed from, and payable by, the local housing authority for the area in which the property is situated. Housing benefit is not available to owner-occupiers (financial assistance for mortgage borrowers is outlined in chapter 35). If the landlord is the council itself, housing benefit is paid as a rent rebate. In all other cases, housing benefit is paid by the council as a rent allowance, usually to the tenant, although in some cases it can be paid direct to the landlord.

16.5   In outline, the statutory scheme[1] provides that recipients of any of the means-tested 'passport benefits' – namely, income support, income-based jobseeker's allowance, income-related employment and support allowance and guarantee credit or pension credit – and others on low income are eligible for assistance with their housing costs. Such assistance may amount to 100 per cent of these costs, while others with slightly higher incomes may be eligible to receive proportionate help. Those who are not on a passport benefit will have their entitlement assessed in accordance with the amounts of their income and capital. Their housing benefit will be worked out on the basis of their 'applicable amount', which is the amount of money which the state deems sufficient to meet the basic living needs of the particular size and composition of household. For reasons outlined in the following paragraphs, however, many occupiers whose level of income entitles them to the maximum assistance will not have their rent paid in full. Detailed consideration of the housing benefit rules is outside the scope of this book. For a full description of the workings of the housing benefit scheme, see *Help with Housing Costs Volume 2: Guide to Housing Benefit by Sam Lister and Martin Ward,* published jointly by Shelter and the Chartered Institute of Housing, and updated each year. For a comprehensive summary of all welfare benefits, see the *Welfare Benefits and Tax Credits Handbook,* published annually by Child Poverty Action Group (CPAG). This chapter is concerned with those elements of the scheme which touch directly on possession proceedings.

---

1   The scheme is contained in the Social Security Contributions and Benefits Act 1992 and in the Housing Benefit Regulations (HB Regs) 2006 SI No 213. See also the Housing Benefit and Council Tax Benefit Guidance published by the Department of Work and Pensions, together with relevant HB Circulars.

Eligible rent and liability for rent

16.6   A tenant may claim assistance from the housing benefit scheme with payment of rent which he or she is liable to pay (or is treated by the authority as liable to pay) for his or her home. 'Rent' includes rent payable under a tenancy agreement, mesne profits, licence fees or charges, and payments for 'use and occupation' of accommodation. The property for which housing benefit is claimed must be one which the claimant normally occupies as his or her home.[2] A tenant may be able to claim for a period when he or she is absent from the home (whether in the UK or abroad), so long as there is an intention to return to the home and the period of absence does not in most cases exced four weeks.[3]

16.7   A tenant's 'eligible rent' is the amount on which his or her housing benefit entitlement is based. It may be equal to the actual rent, but in many cases it is a lower amount. The rules are complex, and the reader is referred to chapters 7 to 9 of the Shelter/CIH *Guide to Housing Benefit*. In the case of tenants in the private rented sector, housing benefit is paid on the basis of a flat-rate 'local housing allowance', which is often substantially less than than the average level of market rents charged in the locality (see para 16.11).

16.8   Some occupiers may be treated as liable for rent or other occupation charges even though they are not actually liable to the landlord for such payments. A spouse or partner should be treated as liable where for some reason the liable person is not eligible to claim housing benefit or is absent from the property. A former partner or another member of the household should be treated as liable if he or she has to make payments in order to continue living in the home because the person liable to make them is not doing so, and the authority considers it reasonable to treat that person as liable.[4] Thus, for example, a son or daughter of the tenant who has remained in occupation while the tenant has gone away for an uncertain period may apply for housing benefit on this basis.

16.9   In most cases, the eligible rent is determined either on the 'standard basis' or by reference to the local housing allowance (LHA).

---

2   Social Security Contributions and Benefits Act 1992 s130(1)(a). See also HB Regs 2006 reg 7(2).

3   Housing Benefit and State Pension Credit (Temporary Absence) (Amendment) Regulations 2016 SI No 624. There are some exceptions to this general rule: for example, where there is a need to receive medical treatment abroad, in which case entitlement can be extended for up to 26 weeks.

4   HB Regs 2006 reg 8(1).

Where the rent is inclusive of certain ineligible service charges, however, a deduction will be made from the gross rent before the amount
of housing benefit is assessed. Thus, for example, where the rent
payable is inclusive of water and heating charges, amounts attributable to those expenses (other than in respect of communal areas) will
not be payable by housing benefit.

Standard cases

16.10   In standard cases, the eligible rent will usually be the actual rent less
any ineligible service elements such as water charges. The following
cases are dealt with on the standard basis of assessment:

- council tenancies, where housing benefit is paid by way of a rent
  rebate;
- tenancies from a housing association or other registered provider
  of social housing (provided that the local authority accepts that the
  rent and the size of the accommodation are not unreasonable);
- Rent Act protected and statutory tenancies with a registered fair
  rent.

However, this does not necessarily mean that the tenant will have
his or her rent paid in full by housing benefit. A deduction from the
eligible rent may be made if the tenant is considered to be under-
occupying the property by reference to the social sector size criteria;
and deductions from the actual amount of housing benefit may be
made because of non-dependants in the household (see para 16.22)
or because of an earlier overpayment (see para 16.35).

Local housing allowance cases

16.11   The local housing allowance (LHA) is the means by which housing
benefit is paid to most tenants and occupiers of private rented accommodation. The LHA scheme was introduced on 7 April 2008 and
applies where a tenant pays rent to a private landlord. It does not
apply to tenants of councils, housing associations or other registered
providers of social housing, except where the accommodation is let
by a provider at a full market rent. Nor does it apply to Rent Act
protected or statutory tenancies; or to hostels, houseboats, caravans
or other mobile homes, or to shared ownership leases; or to tenants
whose housing benefit claims started before 7 April 2008 and who
have lived at the same address without any break in claim since then;
or where the claimant lives in 'exempt accommodation', notably

where a not-for-profit landlord provides a package of care, support or supervision.

16.12   In LHA cases, the claimant is paid a standard housing allowance, determined according to the size of property which is considered appropriate to his or her household composition.[5] If the contractual rent is higher than the LHA payable for the relevant size of dwelling, the tenant will have to make up the shortfall from other income. The LHA is the maximum rent that will be payable by housing benefit for dwellings of different sizes in a particular area. It is based on the number of bedrooms that each household is deemed to require. The Valuation Service compiles a list of market rents for each size of property within a *broad rental market area* (BRMA).[6] A BRMA is usually more extensive than the area of a single local authority. The LHA for each area is based on the 30th percentile of the rents recorded by the rent officer, that is, on the highest rent paid within the bottom 30 per cent of the private rented sector market. The levels of LHA are set on a yearly basis by the rent officer.[7] The size criteria and bedroom allowances, according to which each household is assessed, are broadly the same as the corresponding rules in the social rented sector (see para 16.15).

16.13   Where an occupier comes within the LHA regime, his or her housing benefit entitlement is based on the relevant LHA figure at the date of claim. That figure continues to apply until the next uprating of LHA rates, normally at the beginning of April each year. The applicable LHA amount will be reviewed, however, and may be increased or reduced where there is a change of circumstances which requires a reassessment. This includes a variation in the number of household members or a material change in age, for example, a child reaching his or her 16th birthday. An increase in the rent actually charged does not qualify for a reassessment unless the previous rent was lower than the relevant amount of LHA. Where the occupier moves home, this will also give rise to an reassessment, although the applicable LHA is likely to remain the same if the move is within the same BRMA unless there is a change in the number of household members.

5   HB Regs 2006 regs 12D and 13C–13E. See also chapter 2 of the DWP's *Local Housing Allowance Guidance Manual*.

6   A BRMA is the area within which a person could reasonably be expected to live having regard to facilities and services for the purposes of health, education, recreation, personal banking and shopping, taking account of the distance of travel, by public and private transport, to and from those facilities and services.

7   LHA amounts are available at https://lha-direct.voa.gov.uk.

Shared accommodation rate

16.14   The amount of LHA applicable to most single people aged under 35 is limited to the shared accommodation rate, which is intended to cover rent payable on one-bedroom shared accommodation.[8] Certain classes of occupier are exempt from the shared accommodation rate and will qualify for one-bedroom self-contained accommodation, These include persons who require overnight care; former care leavers under the age of 22; homeless persons over 25 who have previously slept rough and who have spent three months or more in a homeless hostel; and ex-offenders over 25 who pose a risk of serious harm to the public and who are subject to management under the Multi-Agency Public Protection Arrangements scheme (MAPPA).

The social sector size criteria

16.15   A deduction from housing benefit for council and housing association tenants based on under-occupation of the home (sometimes referred to as the 'bedroom tax' or the 'removal of the spare room subsidy') was introduced by the Housing Benefit (Amendment) Regulations 2012,[9] with effect from 1 April 2013. The policy purpose is to bring size assessments in the social rented sector in line with the local housing allowance regime. The regulations provide that, in calculating the housing benefit entitlement of social sector tenants, their eligible rent will be reduced by 14 per cent if the claimant has one more bedroom than is necessary, and by 25 per cent if there are two or more 'spare' rooms.[10] Where a room has been designated as a bedroom by the landlord, the local authority will count it as such for the purposes of the legislation. It may be possible for the tenant to argue that a room is needed, and has been used, for purposes other than a bedroom, such as for the storage of disability-related equipment, and should not therefore be considered a bedroom. Case-law has held that questions concerning whether a room should be classified as a bedroom would normally be answered by its description,[11] the reason for its classification and how similar rooms are used elsewhere in the area. However, there may be scope for arguments over whether a room or space is suitable as a bedroom for a particular person, depending on particular factors including size, configuration

---

8   See *Local Housing Allowance Guidance Manual* (DWP) para 2.050.
9   SI No 3040.
10   HB Regs 2006 (as amended) reg B13.
11   ie, according to the landlord's designation of the number of bedrooms.

and overall dimensions; access, lighting, ventilation and privacy.[12] If the authority does not accept the tenant's arguments relating to the classification of a room, the tenant may appeal to the tribunal against the decision to implement an under-occupation deduction.

16.16　　The social sector under-occupation deduction applies only to those of working age. No reduction applies if either the claimant or partner has reached pension credit age. Occupiers under shared ownership leases and those in local authority temporary accommodation are also exempt. The size criteria are used to calculate the number of bedrooms that a household requires, according to the number and ages of its members. One bedroom is permitted for each of the following classes:

- every adult couple;
- every other person aged 16 or over, including lodgers;
- any two children aged under 16 of the same sex;
- any two children aged under 10 regardless of their gender; and
- every other child.

16.17　　A claimant or partner who requires regular overnight care from a non-resident carer will be allowed one additional bedroom.[13] It is necessary to provide evidence to the council that the occupier reasonably requires this care; or that he or she is receiving a particular benefit.[14] An extra bedroom will be allowed for a disabled child who would normally be expected to share a bedroom under size criteria rules but is unable to do so owing to their disability.[15] An additional bedroom is also allowed for a foster family (whether or not the foster parent currently has a foster child residing with them) and for a family member in the Armed Forces who will return to the home.

16.18　　The fact that a particular bedroom is actually in use for other purposes is irrelevant if the circumstances do not fall within one of the statutory exemptions. Thus, a bedroom is treated as 'spare' even if the claimant and his or her partner need to sleep apart because of a

---

12　*Secretary of State for Work and Pensions v Nelson and Fife Council* [2014] UKUT 525 (AAC))

13　HB Regs 2006 reg B13(6), inserted by the Housing Benefit and Universal Credit (Size Criteria) (Miscellaneous Amendments) Regulations 2013 SI No 2828 following the decision of the Court of Appeal in *Burnip v Birmingham City Council; Trengove v Walsall MBC; Gorry v Wiltshire CC* [2012] EWCA Civ 629; [2012] HRLR 20.

14　Namely, attendance allowance, the middle or highest rate care component of disability living allowance, or either rate of the daily living component of personal independence payment (PIP).

15　Housing Benefit Regulations 2006 reg 13(5)(ba).

medical condition; or if the claimant is disabled and needs the room for medical appliances or for treatment. The Government's view is that discretionary housing payments should be made to cover these circumstances (see para 16.28). The fact that substantial adaptations have been carried out to the property for the benefit of a disabled member of the household likewise has no effect on the operation of the size criteria. No account is taken of children who stay overnight if they normally reside elsewhere. Where there is shared custody, the child will be treated as residing with the parent who receives child benefit.[16]

16.19   Lodgers count as occupying a room under the size criteria rules for housing benefit. For the purposes of calculating the amount of means-tested benefits, a fixed proportion[17] of the income received from a lodger is disregarded, but the remainder is deducted in full from benefit entitlement.

The benefits cap

16.20   Section 96 of the Welfare Reform Act 2012 introduced the concept of the 'benefits cap', which was implemented by Part 8A (sections 75A–75G)[18] of the Housing Benefit Regulations 2006. The essence of the cap is that a household's total income from mainstream welfare benefits should not exceed a fixed weekly amount. Regulation 75G fixes the 'relevant amount' at £350 per week (£18,200) for a single claimant and £500 per week (£26,000 per annum) for all other households.[19] The effect of this provision is that where a single person or couple's total entitlement to benefits exceeds the cap, they will lose the amount of the excess and will receive only the capped amount. The cap does not apply to persons of pension age; or where the tenant or partner is in receipt of certain benefits, including disability living allowance, personal independence payment or attendance allowance. There is a 'grace period' of 39 weeks after the termination of employment during which the cap will not apply.

16   *MR v North Tyneside Council and Secretary of State for Work and Pensions* [2015] UKUT 34 (AAC).
17   At the time of publication, the amount of the disregard is £20 per week.
18   Inserted by the Benefit Cap (Housing Benefit) Regulations 2012 reg 2(5).
19   With effect from the autumn of 2016, the Government intends to reduce the benefits cap for families and couples to £23,000 per annum in London (£15,410 for single people) and £20,000 per annum (£13,400 for single people) outside London. See Welfare Reform and Work Act 2016 s8(2) amending Welfare Reform Act 2012 s96(5).

16.21   The immediate impact of the benefits cap is borne by the claimant's housing benefit award. The local authority is required to calculate the total income from welfare benefits to which the household would otherwise be entitled, and reduce housing benefit so as to ensure that the cap is not exceeded. The authority may not reduce housing benefit to less than 50 pence per week (so that the claimant will remain eligible to apply for a discretionary housing payment: see para 16.28). Where the cap applies, the likely outcome for many tenants will be that their accommodation will be unaffordable and rent arrears will accrue. Tenants in this position should be encouraged to apply for discretionary housing payments immediately to assist in bridging the shortfall in their rent. Although discretionary housing payments are time limited and may not cover the entire shortfall, they may enable a household to remain in their home.

Non-dependants

16.22   A tenant's eligible rent will be reduced if he or she has a 'non-dependant' living in the same property. A non-dependant is someone who lives with the tenant as a member of the household, but who is not the tenant's partner or dependent child. Often, this will be a grown-up son or daughter. The term does not include joint owners, subtenants or lodgers. A set deduction from the tenant's housing benefit is made for each non-dependant according to their circumstances, irrespective of what contribution the non-dependant actually makes to the household finances. No deduction is made if the claimant or partner receives certain disability benefits. The tenant will often not have realised the obligation to notify the authority, for example, when a young person leaves full-time education and starts work. A failure to declare a non-dependant is a frequent cause of a claim by the local authority for an overpayment of housing benefit.

Making a claim for housing benefit

16.23   A claim for housing benefit can be made in one of the following ways:[20]

- On a housing benefit claim form. Each local authority has its own claim forms, as there is no national template. Some authorities accept claims by telephone or online.

---

20 HB Regs 2006 reg 83.

- When a person makes a claim for income support, income-based jobseeker's allowance, employment and support allowance or pension credit, this is usually done by telephone to the Department of Work and Pensions (DWP), and in the course of the call they should be asked whether they wish to claim housing benefit as well. The DWP then sends an electronic notification to the authority. Where such benefits are claimed otherwise than by telephone, the DWP should send a housing benefit claim form (HCTB1) to the claimant, and this should be completed and sent to the authority. The claimant may be asked to provide further information and/or to complete the authority's standard claim form.
- By letter from the claimant, his or her solicitor or adviser, or someone acting on the claimant's behalf, stating that they wish to claim HB. The local authority should then send out its standard claim form for completion.

16.24   Regulation 86(1) of the Housing Benefit Regulations 2006 provides:

> ... a person who makes a claim, or a person to whom housing benefit has been awarded, shall furnish such certificates, documents, information and evidence in connection with the claim or the award or any question arising out of the claim or the award, as may reasonably be required by the relevant authority in order to determine that person's entitlement to, or continuing entitlement to, housing benefit, and shall do so within one month of the relevant authority requiring him, or the Secretary of State requesting him, to do so, or such longer period as the relevant authority may consider reasonable.

Claimants will be expected to produce evidence of the tenancy or other agreement; the rent or other occupation charge; (except where the claimant is on a 'passport' benefit) full details of income and capital; and details of all household members, their age and financial status. It is necessary to provide a National Insurance number, or evidence that an application for one has been made. Where the claimant fails to provide all the information and evidence reasonably required by the council, the claim will be treated as 'incomplete', or may be regarded as a 'defective' claim.[21] Many instances of rent arrears arise from problems of this kind, as a result of which housing benefit has not been awarded or has been suspended. In such cases, the claimant should be encouraged, and where possible assisted, to

21 The authority must nevertheless make a decision on the claim (Tribunal of Commissioners R(H) 3/05). See also HB/CTB U9/2004, paras 23–26 and HB/CTB G8/2007. The claimant has a right to appeal against a refusal to award housing benefit: Child Support, Pensions and Social Security Act 2000 Sch 7.

provide the missing information, since if the authority accepts that he or she had an entitlement, the outstanding benefit will be paid and will serve to reduce or even clear the rent arrears.

16.25 Once a claim has been submitted, it is essential for the claimant, or someone acting on his or her behalf, to check that it has been received by the authority, that it is being processed and that all necessary evidence of personal and financial circumstances has been provided. Sometimes claims may be 'lost' in the system and it is essential to keep track of them. Where the claimant supplies documents (such as wages slips) in connection with the claim, he or she should ask for a note of receipt from the housing benefit office.

Maximising housing benefit to clear arrears

16.26 If there are arrears of rent or occupation charges and the occupier is presently (or has recently been) on a low income, the starting point should be to check that housing benefit is being paid and/or has been paid and that the correct amount is being, and has been, received. See the common situation outlined in para 16.24 above, in which housing benefit is due, but has not been paid because insufficient evidence has been provided in support of the claim.

Backdating

16.27 Once the appropriate current housing benefit entitlement has been established, it may be possible to make inroads into the outstanding arrears. First, the local authority has power to *backdate benefit for up to one month* if the claimant demonstrates that he or she had 'continuous good cause for failing to make a claim'.[22] 'Good cause' is undefined and may be established by a variety of circumstances ranging from ill-health to earlier inaccurate advice. Lack of awareness of the housing benefit system or of possible entitlement is not of itself good cause, but may be taken into account alongside other factors.

Discretionary housing payments

16.28 Second, the occupier may be able to apply for a *discretionary housing payment*. The scheme for payment of discretionary housing payments (which are strictly not part of the housing benefit scheme)

---

22 HB Regs 2006 reg 83(12A), as amended. Prior to 1 April 2016, the period for which benefit could be backdated was up to six months. For claimants who have reached pension credit age, the maximum period of backdating is three months and good cause need not be shown. See DWP Circular HB A3/2016.

is contained in the Discretionary Financial Assistance Regulations 2001[23] made under the Child Support, Pensions and Social Security Act 2000. Discretionary housing payments may be made for the benefit of those who are entitled to housing benefit, have a liability to pay rent and 'appear ... to require some further financial assistance' in order to meet their housing costs. Guidance[24] issued to local authorities by the DWP sets out both a description of the scheme and an indication of the breadth of the discretion to assist with unmet housing costs. Each authority can decide for itself the circumstances in which it will make a discretionary housing payment, although it must ensure that its decision-making procedures are lawful.

16.29   A discretionary housing payment may be made in respect of rent arrears,[25] or rent in advance or to meet the cost of a deposit. Guidance[26] also confirms that payments may be used to cover reductions in housing benefit or universal credit caused by the effects of the benefit cap (see para 16.20) or rent shortfalls on account of local housing allowance restrictions (see para 16.12) or the social rented sector size criteria (see para 16.15). They may also be awarded to meet a rent shortfall to prevent a household from becoming homeless while the local housing authority explores other options for assisting them, or to cover non-dependant deductions. Discretionary housing payments are awarded on a time-limited basis and, although they may be renewed for a further period, there can be no expectation that they will continue after the current award period expires. There is no appeal against the refusal of a discretionary housing payment, or against the amount awarded, although the authority may be asked to review its decision.

Effect of housing benefit issues on possession proceedings

16.30   The *Pre-action Protocol for possession claims by social landlords* requires social landlords to take active steps to ensure that any difficulties with housing benefit claims are resolved wherever possible without court proceedings. The full text of the Protocol is set out in appendix E. Paragraphs 2.5 and 2.6 of the Protocol are especially relevant:

23   SI 2001 No 1167.
24   *Discretionary Housing Payments Guidance Manual*, DWP, obtainable from government websites.
25   Discretionary Financial Regulations 2001 SI No 1167; *R (Gargett) v Lambeth LBC* [2008] EWCA Civ 1450, [2009] LGR 527.
26   *Discretionary Housing Payments Guidance Manual* para 2.3.

2.5 The landlord should offer to assist the tenant in any claim the tenant may have for housing benefit, discretionary housing benefit or universal credit (housing element).

2.6 Possession proceedings for rent arrears should not be started against a tenant who can demonstrate that –

(a) the local authority or Department for Work and Pensions have been provided with all the evidence required to process a housing benefit or universal credit (housing element) claim;

(b) [they have] a reasonable expectation of eligibility for housing benefit or universal credit (housing element); and

(c) [they have] paid other sums due not covered by housing benefit or universal credit (housing element).

The landlord should make every effort to establish effective ongoing liaison with housing benefit departments and DWP and, with the tenant's consent, make direct contact with the relevant housing benefit department or DWP office before taking enforcement action.

The landlord and tenant should work together to resolve any housing benefit or universal credit (housing element) problems.

As to the consequences of non-compliance with the Protocol, paragraphs 2.13 and 2.14 provide:

2.13 If the landlord unreasonably fails to comply with the terms of the protocol, the court may impose one or more of the following sanctions –

(a) an order for costs; and

(b) in cases other than those brought solely on mandatory grounds, adjourn, strike out or dismiss claims.

2.14 If the tenant unreasonably fails to comply with the terms of the protocol, the court may take such failure into account when considering whether it is reasonable to make possession order.

16.31   Where a possession claim has been started on the basis of a discretionary ground for possession, whether by a social landlord or private landlord, the court may be asked to adjourn the proceedings pending the outcome of an application for housing benefit and/or for a discretionary housing payment if that is a realistic option. It is not generally possible to secure a stay or adjournment where a court is satisfied that mandatory ground 8[27] of the assured tenancy grounds for possession in Housing Act (HA) 1988 Sch 2 is made out in respect of an assured or assured shorthold tenant. In such a case, the court must order possession even if arrears have accumulated

---

27 Ground 8 is satisfied where, both at the date of the service of the notice of seeking possession and at the date of the hearing, at least eight weeks' or two months' rent is unpaid. See para 3.99.

for want of housing benefit to which the tenant is entitled, subject to the possibility of a public law defence (see chapter 25) or an Equality Act defence in appropriate circumstances (see chapter 27); and subject to a counterclaim for damages by the tenant which may be set off against the rent arrears.[28] In some cases, the tenant may need to appeal an unfavourable decision to the First-tier Tribunal. Pending the determination of such an appeal, the court may be requested to grant a stay of the proceedings. In complex cases, advisers should consider asking for a direction to file a defence, which will set out the nature of the housing benefit dispute and will serve to indicate why a stay is justified.

16.32   Once the occupier has made a claim for housing benefit, and has provided all the necessary evidence of means, the local authority should make a decision on the claim within 14 days.[29] If it is not possible to determine a claim for benefit in respect of a private or housing association tenant within the 14-day period, assuming that the claimant has not failed without good cause to provide the required evidence, the authority must make a payment on account of prospective entitlement.[30] The amount of the interim payment shall be such amount as the authority considers reasonable. This duty is capable of enforcement in proceedings for judicial review.[31]

16.33   Where the claimant in such a case is the local authority itself, the tenant may be advised to respond to any possession proceedings based on arrears either by inviting the court to strike out the proceedings as an abuse of process[32] or by entering a defence and counterclaim on the basis of breach of statutory duty. However, the private law duty which forms the basis of the counterclaim arises only after a decision to make a payment of housing benefit has been taken.[33] If the problem is in securing such a decision, the tenant may seek to defend the claim on the basis that for the authority to bring proceedings in these circumstances is unlawful, being a decision made on flawed grounds and/or an improper exercise of power.

---

28   *North British Housing Association v Matthews* [2004] EWCA Civ 1736, [2005] 1 WLR 3133.

29   HB Regs 2006 reg 89(2).

30   HB Regs 2006 reg 93(1).

31   See *R v Liverpool City Council ex p Johnson* 23 June 1994, unreported, QBD, and *R v Haringey LBC ex p Ayub* (1993) 25 HLR 566, QBD.

32   *Lambeth LBC v Tagoe* August 2000 *Legal Action* 24.

33   *Haringey LBC v Cotter* (1997) 29 HLR 682, CA.

16.34   Where the claimant is a private landlord or housing association, the tenant may consider the possibilty of joining[34] the local authority as a third party to the claim (under Part 20 of the Civil Procedure Rules 1998) if there has been an actionable breach of duty. Alternatively, the senior officer responsible for housing benefit could be summonsed[35] to give evidence relating to the occupier's entitlement to housing benefit and reasons for non-payment of it. Either step should ensure that the authority carries out an urgent review of the benefit claim and may prompt payment of any outstanding benefit. If the entire proceedings have been caused by local authority failures in dealing with the defendant's housing benefit claim, that authority could be joined as a third party simply for the purpose of obtaining an order for costs against it.[36]

Overpayments

16.35   Local authorities have the power to recover overpayments of housing benefit from both the claimant *and* any other person to whom such benefit was paid (which may include the landlord: see para 16.43).[37] If recovery is made by deducting an amount from the tenant's future benefit entitlement, the tenant faces the possibility of being unable to pay the rent in full and of subsequent arrears arising. However, many authorities seek to recover the overpayment from the payee in a lump sum. Where the amount of the overpayment is debited to the rent account, the question arises as to whether this sum can constitute 'arrears' in any proceedings for possession. The answer depends on whether the landlord is the local authority.

16.36   An overpayment of housing benefit is defined as

> ... any amount which has been paid by way of housing benefit and to which there was no entitlement under these Regulations (whether on the initial decision or as subsequently revised or superseded ...) and includes any amount paid on account under regulation 93 (payment on account of a rent allowance) which is in excess of the entitlement to housing benefit as subsequently decided.[38]

An overpayment may have been made by way of payment to the claimant, the landlord, the landlord's agent or any other person, or by way

34 Under CPR 19.
35 Under CPR 34.
36 CPR 48.2 and *Asra Greater London Housing Association v Cooke* June 2001 *Legal Action* 31.
37 HB Regs 2006 regs 99–107.
38 HB Regs 2006 reg 99.

of a credit made to a local authority's own rent account by way of rent
rebate where the tenant is a council tenant. Whether the occupier is
a social or private sector tenant or licensee, the authority is required
properly to notify a decision to recover an overpayment. Until such
notification is given the overpayment is not legally recoverable.[39]

16.37   Where claims for overpayments are concerned, tenants may need
advice from a specialist welfare benefits adviser about whether a
particular overpayment is recoverable or not. Local authorities may
sometimes fail to follow proper decision-making procedures, or
omit to notify claimants how their housing benefit award has been
assessed. Overpayments caused by 'official error' are not recoverable,
where the payee could not reasonably have been expected to realise
that the amount received was an overpayment.[40]

16.38   Where an overpayment is recoverable, the authority has a discretion whether or not to recover it. The decision that an overpayment
is recoverable is separate from the decision to recover it; and the fact
that an overpayment is recoverable does not mean that the authority
must recover it. DWP Guidance[41] states that due regard should be
given to the circumstances relating to individual cases, when deciding whether or not recovery is appropriate. There is no right of appeal
against a decision to exercise the discretion to recover, or against the
method of recovery, although an authority which acted unreasonably or irrationally could be subject to judicial review. The powers
of the tribunal in relation to overpayment decisions are limited to
determining whether the occupier has been paid more than his or
her entitlement, and whether the resulting overpayment is legally
recoverable.

16.39   In some circumstances, an overpayment may be reduced by an
'underlying entitlement'.[42] For example, where the reason for the
overpayment is the tenant's absence from the property, it may be that
a spouse, partner or another member of the family would have been
eligible for housing benefit and could have made a claim in his or her
own right. If the family member has not made such a claim, it may
be regarded as an 'underlying entitlement'. In these circumstances,

---

39   *Warwick DC v Freeman* (1995) 27 HLR 616, CA and *R v Thanet DC ex p
    Warren Court Hotels Ltd* (2001) 33 HLR 32, QBD. Procedural deficiences in
    a notification letter may be cured in the course of the appeal process itself:
    Haringey LBC v Awaritefe [1999] EWCA Civ 1491, (1999) 32 HLR 517.

40   HB Regs 2006 reg 100(2).

41   *Housing Benefit Overpayments Guide* paras 2.145–2.147.

42   HB Regs 2006 reg 104(1). See also *Housing Benefits Overpayments Guide*, paras
    3.30–3.45.

where a local authority would otherwise seek to recover an overpayment from the tenant, in calculating the overpayment it must give credit for the underlying entitlement of the household member (which in some cases may cancel out the overpayment).[43]

Council tenants

16.40 Typically, a local authority pays housing benefit to its own tenants by way of credit to the rent account (ie, a rent rebate). The rent due is 'paid'[44] directly in this way in whole or in part, and the occupier's rent liability is met at least to the extent of that credit or payment. Inevitably, there are sometimes errors and tenants are paid benefit to which they are not entitled. The regulations prescribe careful procedures to regulate recovery and ensure notification in such cases.[45] However, local authorities, on discovering an overpayment, sometimes 'seize' back from the occupier's rent account the benefit overpaid and then issue rent statements showing tenants 'in arrears' by that amount. This means of recovery may be unlawful for two reasons. First, before taking recovery action, the authority must issue written notification of the decision that there has been an overpayment and that it should be recovered, together with details of the method selected for recovery.[46] Second, the permitted methods of recovery of overpaid housing benefit do not include debiting the amount of the overpayment to the occupier's rent account. This is because the statutory definition of 'payment' of benefit has the effect that, in the context of council tenancies, the amount of housing benefit awarded by way of rent rebate extinguishes liability for the corresponding amount of rent. The 'rent lawfully due' has therefore been paid in that amount. Unless the tenancy agreement expressly allows for overpayments to be recovered as additional rent, the council cannot resurrect a liability for rent which has been extinguished.[47] The DWP's *Housing Benefit Overpayments Guide* emphasises the distinction between a recoverable overpayment of housing benefit and arrears of rent.[48] An overpayment can, however, be recovered from the tenant by deductions from ongoing housing benefit entitlement.

43 CH/4490/2014; *JM v LB Tower Hamlets (HB)* [2015] UKUT 460 (AAC).
44 See the definition of 'pay' in Social Security Administration Act 1992 s134(2).
45 HB Regs 2006 reg 102.
46 HB Regs 2006 reg 90 and Sch 9 para 15.
47 *R v Haringey LBC ex p Ayub* (1993) 25 HLR 566, QBD.
48 See *Housing Benefit Overpayments Guide* paras 4.90–4.93.

Other tenants

16.41   The position is different when housing benefit payments have been made direct to private landlords or housing associations or other private registered providers of social housing, and benefit is subsequently discovered to have been overpaid. In these circumstances, the local authority has power to seek recovery from the landlord.[49] Where the landlord repays the money to the authority in response to such a request, the effect of the recovery is that the tenant's rent account will be debited with the amount repaid. Regulation 95(2) of the Housing Benefit Regulations 2006 provides that:

> Any payment of rent allowance made to a landlord pursuant to this regulation or to regulation 96 (circumstances in which payments may be made to a landlord) shall be to discharge, in whole or in part, the liability of the claimant to pay rent to that landlord in respect of the dwelling concerned, except in so far as –
>
> (a) the claimant had no entitlement to the whole or part of that rent allowance so paid to his landlord; and
>
> (b) the overpayment of rent allowance resulting was recovered in whole or in part from that landlord.

It is arguable that this provision is ultra vires in so far as it seeks to regulate a contractual liability between landlord and tenant, but the provision (together with its predecessor in the 1987 Regulations)[50] has been in effect for many years without challenge.

16.42   In all cases, whether concerning council tenants or other tenants, local authorities have the power to recover overpaid housing benefit by deduction of an amount from the tenant's ongoing benefit entitlement. This means that the tenant will need to make up the shortfall in current rent to prevent arrears arising on the rent account. Alternatively, authorities may in some circumstances request the Department of Work and Pensions to make deductions from certain DWP benefits to repay an overpayment. Authorities may also apply to the county court to register an overpayment determination as a court order, which can then be enforced by warrant of execution, or by any of the other methods of enforcement available to creditors. Recoverable overpayments of housing benefit may be recovered by deductions from earnings.[51]

---

49 Social Security Administration Act 1992 s75(3)(a) and HB Regs 2006 reg 101.
50 See the former Housing Benefit (General) Regulations 1987 reg 93(1).
51 HB Regs 2006 reg 106A.

Direct payments of housing benefit

16.43 Where housing benefit is in the form of the local housing allowance (LHA), the general rule is that the LHA is paid to the tenant, and not directly to the landlord. However, in some circumstances, the authority *must* make direct payments to the landlord.[52] This is the case where:

- the rent is eight weeks or more in arrears,[53] unless the authority considers it to be in the tenant's overriding interest not to make direct payments; or
- direct payments toward rent arrears are already being made by the DWP by deduction from income support, income-based jobseeker's allowance, pension credit or employment and support allowance.[54]

16.44 In other cases the authority has a discretion to make direct payments to the landlord[55] in circumstances where:

- the tenant has difficulty managing his or her own affairs; or
- direct payment would assist the claimant to secure or retain a tenancy; or
- it is improbable that the tenant will pay the rent; or
- the authority was previously making mandatory direct payments to the landlord, but is no longer obliged to do so (eg, because the tenant's arrears have fallen below eight weeks).

In all cases, the authority must not make direct payments of housing benefit to a landlord who is not a 'fit and proper person', unless it is in the best interests of the tenant to do so.[56]

16.45 The availability of direct payments is clearly relevant to possession proceedings both because it provides a basis for negotiation in the hope of averting the need to take proceedings; and also because failure by a landlord to seek direct payments may be helpful in establishing that it is not reasonable for the court to make a possession

---

52 HB Regs 2006 reg 95(1).
53 Rent is in arrears once the contractual date for payment has passed without payment being made, irrespective of whether rent is due in advance or in arrear (see Circular HB/CTB A26/2009). Thus, where rent is payable monthly in advance and no payment has been made, the tenant will be in two months' arrears after one month and one day. At that stage, the landlord may contact the authority and request a direct payment.
54 See para 16.47.
55 HB Regs 2006 reg 96(3A).
56 HB Regs 2006 reg 95(3).

order in proceedings based on a discretionary ground. A proposal may be made to the court that the tenant or the tenant's advisers will immediately invite the authority to make direct payments, together with an offer of payment of the arrears by instalments, and the court may be requested to adjourn the proceedings accordingly.

16.46   Where direct payments are to be made, both the tenant and the landlord must be informed in writing by the authority.[57] On receipt of the direct payment, the landlord must apply the housing benefit for the purpose for which it is paid, namely in satisfaction of the occupier's current rent liability. Difficulties can arise if subsequently it is discovered that an amount of housing benefit has been overpaid (see para 16.35).

Direct deductions from other benefits

16.47   Direct deductions may be made by the Department of Work and Pensions (DWP) from a tenant's 'passport' benefits, ie from weekly income support, income-based jobseeker's allowance, employment and support allowance or pension credit, and the amounts deducted paid to the landlord towards arrears of rent.[58] The DWP has produced guidance on the 'third party payments' scheme.[59] Where a claimant is in receipt of housing benefit, the DWP also has power to make direct deductions from these benefits to pay water charges and heating charges which are not covered by housing benefit.[60]

16.48   The landlord may request direct deductions if the tenant is in at least four weeks' rent arrears and has been in arrears over a period of at least eight weeks. The DWP may also make its own decision to make direct deductions if the tenant is in at least four weeks' rent arrears, though he or she has been in arrears for less than eight weeks, and in its opinion it is in the overriding interest of the family that direct deductions should be made. The tenant can also make a request to the DWP. The standard weekly deduction is a sum equal to five per cent of the personal allowance for a single claimant aged over 25.

57   HB Regs 2006 reg 90 and Sch 9 para 11.
58   Social Security (Claims and Payments) Regulations 1987 SI No 1968 Sch 9 para 5(1) and (6).
59   *How to Apply for Third Party Payments* and *Third Party Payments creditor/ Supplier Handbook*. See also Housing Benefit and Council Tax Benefit Guidance: Part D, para D1.570 onwards.
60   Social Security (Claims and Payments) Regs 1987 Sch 9 para 5(3).

Decisions, reconsideration and appeals

16.49 When an authority notifies any decision concerning a housing benefit claim, it must inform the claimant of his or her right to a written statement of reasons for its decision, and of the right to ask the authority to reconsider the decision, together with the right to appeal to a tribunal (except where the decision is one which cannot be appealed, such as the exercise of discretion to recover an over-payment). A request for reconsideration (also sometimes called revision or supersession) should normally be made within one month, although the authority can extend this time limit. The claimant may still request a reconsideration of a decision, even though it is not an appealable decision. Where a sanction has been applied to a claim for jobseeker's allowance, this should not affect entitlement to housing benefit.[61]

16.50   Appeals against decisions not to award housing benefit or against other appealable decisions go to the First-tier Tribunal (Social Entitlement Chamber). The time limit for appealing is one month from the date of notification of the authority's decision, or of an unfavourable reconsideration, although either the authority or the tribunal has discretion to accept an appeal out of time. An unsuccessful appellant may appeal further from the decision of the First-tier Tribunal to the Upper Tribunal, but only on the basis of an error of law and only with the permission of either tribunal.

Universal credit

The scheme in outline

16.51 The Welfare Reform Act 2012 laid the foundations for the universal credit scheme. The new scheme is designed to replace the various means-tested benefits in the previous (and still current) system – namely, income support, income-based jobseeker's allowance, income-related employment and support allowance, working tax credit, child tax credit and housing benefit – with a single benefit known as universal credit. The policy intention is to simplify the system, and to make the effect of earned income on benefits more predictable and transparent. By combining the previous in-work benefits into one, the objective is to remove disincentives to work and avoid

61 HB U1/2015.

the 'benefits trap' whereby claimants reap little or no financial advantage from starting work.

16.52   The universal credit scheme began in April 2013, and is being phased in by the Department of Work and Pensions (DWP) over a period of years. During the period when the new system is being gradually introduced, people in similar circumstances may receive benefit under one or other scheme. Whether someone is affected by the introduction of universal credit depends on where he or she lives and whether a new claim is being made or whether claimants are being transferred from an existing benefit that is being phased out. Those over working age will continue to receive pension credit and housing benefit for the foreseeable future, although it is intended that housing benefit for such tenants will eventually be paid as part of pension credit.[62]

16.53   In contrast with the earlier system, whereby most means-tested benefits are claimed from the DWP while housing benefit is administered by local housing authorities, universal credit – which includes an element intended to cover housing costs – is centrally administered. In further contrast with payment arrangements under the system of various DWP benefits and housing benefit, universal credit claimants will receive all their benefit entitlement in a single payment. Universal credit is assessed, calculated and paid on a *monthly* basis. Moreover, whereas council tenants receive housing benefit by way of rent rebate and private and housing association tenants can in some circumstances request the local authority to pay housing benefit direct to the landlord, the housing costs element of universal credit is paid to tenants unless the DWP agrees otherwise.

Making a claim

16.54   A claim for universal credit can be made by a single individual or jointly by a couple.[63] Claims are normally required to be submitted online.[64] With limited exceptions, claims on paper or by telephone are not accepted. Claimants should seek assistance at their local job-

---

62 The timetable for transition of existing benefits to universal credit is available from www.gov.uk. Over time, the benefits replaced by universal credit will be referred to as 'legacy benefits'. Existing claimants of legacy benefits are expected to be transferred to universal credit between July 2019 and March 2022: written statement HCWS96, 20 July 2016.

63 There is no provision for a joint claim in the housing benefit system: only one person in a couple can be the claimant.

64 Applications are made online at https://www.gov.uk/apply-universal-credit.

centre if they do not have access to the internet or if they have diffi-culties in making their claim online.[65] Once a claim has been set up, the claimant is given an 'online account', which he or she will need to use to report any changes of circumstances.

16.55 Once an online claim form has been submitted, the claimant will be required to attend an interview at the local Jobcentre Plus. Claim-ants will need to bring proof of identity and a copy of their tenancy agreement or rent statement. At the interview, claimants will be asked to accept a number of conditions. These conditions comprise the 'claimant commitment'.[66]

16.56 Universal credit is paid in arrears every calendar month. New claimants should receive their first payment of universal credit about five weeks after the date of claim, but the waiting period in practice is frequently longer. Clearly, such delays present major problems for tenants and their landlords.[67] Payments are made directly into a claim-ant's bank account. Couples living together who both claim universal credit will receive a single monthly payment into one account. How-ever, the DWP has power to pay certain claimants more frequently or to make alternative payment arrangements where the circumstances justify it (see para 16.69). Payments cannot be backdated for longer than one month, and only in limited circumstances such as ill health, disability or failure of the system.

16.57 The calculation of a claimant's entitlement to universal credit is based on a *maximum amount*.[68] The appropriate maximum amount is the total of the claimant's *standard allowance* and any additional *elements* or allowances for which he or she qualifies. The standard allowance is the amount which the state provides for the claimant's basic subsistence, including food, clothing and utility bills. A claim-ant is entitled to one of four standard allowances, which are allocated respectively for a single person aged under 25; a single person aged 25 or older; a couple where both are under 25; or a couple of whom at least one is 25 or over.[69] To the standard allowance are added any additional elements which apply to the claimant's circumstances.

65 Assistance can also be obtained from a helpline on 0345-600-0723.
66 See para 16.71.
67 There is a waiting period of seven days for claimants who are subject to all work related requirements and those with limited capacity for work: Universal Credit Regulations 2013 SI No 376 reg 19A(1). In these cases, with some exceptions, such as care leavers and victims of domestic violence, no payment at all is made in respect of the first seven days of the claim.
68 Universal Credit Regulations 2013 reg 23.
69 Welfare Reform Act 2012 s9(1).

There are seven elements, namely, the Child Element; the Disabled Child addition; the Limited Capacity for Work Element; the Limited Capacity for Work Related Activity Element; the Carer Element; the Childcare Costs Element; and the Housing Costs Element.

The Housing Costs Element

16.58   The housing costs element[70] of universal credit replaces housing benefit for tenants and other occupiers who pay rent or periodic charges for their accommodation. It also replaces support for mortgage interest, which is payable to some owner-occupiers in receipt of means-tested benefits (see para 36.18). Once the amount of the housing costs element has been established, it will need to be added to the claimant's standard allowance and any other additional elements for which the claimant qualifies to arrive at the maximum amount.

16.59   In order to claim housing costs, a person must be liable to 'make payments in respect of the accommodation they occupy as their home'.[71] Such payments must be quantified and include rent, payments in respect of a licence, mooring charges and site fees for mobile homes. Certain kinds of liability, including ground rent, service charges and care home fees, are not covered.[72] Where a claimant occupies 'specified accommodation', even though he or she claims universal credit, the housing costs element will not be payable, and the occupier will need to claim housing benefit alongside his or her claim for universal credit. In these cases, any payment of housing benefit will not be included in calculating whether the benefit cap applies. 'Specified' accommodation includes domestic violence refuges and local authority hostels and other kinds of supported accommodation where care, support or supervision is provided to the occupier.

16.60   Certain people may be treated as liable to pay rent, where the liable person is not paying. The partner of a sole tenant is automatically treated as liable, while any other person is to be treated as liable to make payments where (a) the person who is liable to make the payments is not doing so, (b) the claimant has to make the payments in order to continue occupation of the accommodation, (c) the claimant's circumstances are such that it would be unreasonable to expect them to make other arrangements; and (d) it is reasonable in all the

---

70   Universal Credit Regulations 2013 reg 25.
71   Welfare Reform Act 2012 s11(1).
72   See Universal Credit Regulations 2013 Sch 1 para 3.

circumstances to treat the claimant as liable to make the payments.[73] Thus, a member of the tenant's family may be able to claim housing costs where the tenant has gone away or is otherwise not in a position to pay the rent or make a claim.

The size criteria

16.61 The amount of the claimant's housing costs is based on the number of rooms to which the claimant is entitled under the size criteria. For tenants of private rented accommodation, the Local Housing Allowance rules apply in the same way as they do to eligible rent for housing benefit (see para 16.15). The housing costs payable will therefore be a fixed amount according to the number of bedrooms the claimant is entitled to. However, private sector tenants will not be allowed more than four bedrooms even if they qualify for more under the size criteria. For social sector tenants of working age, whether a claimant is under-occupying will depend on his or her household size and composition, and on the number of bedrooms that is deemed appropriate for the needs of the household. The number of bedrooms to which the claimant is entitled will be assessed according to the same size criteria as for the local housing allowance (execpt that there is no four-bedroom overall limit). If the claimant's property has more bedrooms than the size criteria allow, the same restrictions as in housing benefit cases operate to reduce the housing costs by a fixed percentage of 14 per cent (for one excess bedroom) or 25 per cent (for two excess bedrooms).[74] Social sector tenants of pension credit age or above are not subject to the size criteria.

16.62 Under the size criteria,[75] one bedroom is allowed for each of:

- the tenant or joint tenants;
- any other person aged 16 or over;
- any two children aged under 10;
- two children of the same sex aged under 16; and
- any other child.

A separate bedroom is also allowed for an overnight carer where the tenant requires such care[76] and the carer stays overnight 'on a regular

---

73 Universal Credit Regulations 2013 Sch 2 paras 1 and 2.
74 Universal Credit Regulations 2013 Sch 4 para 36.
75 Universal Credit Regulations 2013 Sch 4 paras 8, 10(1).
76 Universal Credit Regulations 2013 Sch 4 para 12(1). The tenant must be in receipt of disability living allowance care component at the higher rate, attendance allowance or the daily living component of personal independence payment.

basis'; a foster parent or adoptive parent with whom a child has been placed for adoption;[77] a child in the armed forces or reservists who is deployed on operations;[78] and a severely disabled child who is not reasonably able to share a room with another child.[79]

16.63   The rules in respect of lodgers are different for universal credit than for housing benefit. For the purposes of housing benefit (including local housing allowance), any room occupied by a lodger counts towards the number of rooms allowed by the size criteria: see para 16.19. However, for the purposes of universal credit, lodgers will not be treated as occupying a room. The size criteria will therefore apply, so that a room is treated as a spare room even though it is occupied by a lodger. In further contrast to housing benefit, however, any income from lodgers will be fully disregarded in calculating the amount of a claimant's universal credit award: universal credit claimants are therefore permitted to keep the full income which they receive from lodgers.

Shared accommodation rate

16.64   Single people under 35 renting accommodation in the private rented sector will only be entitled to the 'shared accommodation rate' of housing costs, which is intended to cover the rent on a room in a shared house. Some classes of under-35 single claimants are exempt from these restrictions, notably care leavers, though only up to their 22nd birthday; people in receipt of the severe disability premium; people with a non-resident carer; former residents of hostels for homeless persons; and ex-offenders subject to Multi Agency Public Protection Arrangements (MAPPA). The rules are the same as for housing benefit (see para 16.14). Single people aged over 35 and couples of any age will not be restricted to the shared accommodation rate.

Discretionary housing payments

16.65   Discretionary Housing Payments (DHPs) may be available to claimants of universal credit in the same way as to housing benefit claimants (see para 16.28).[80] DHPs can be paid to give additional financial

---

77   Universal Credit Regulations 2013 Sch 4 para 12(4).
78   Universal Credit Regulations 2013 Sch 4 para 11(5)(d).
79   Universal Credit Regulations 2013 Sch 4 para 12(6). The child must be eligible for the middle or highest rate of disability living allowance.
80   See the *Discretionary Housing Payments Guidance Manual* (including Local Authority Good Practice Guide) published by DWP.

help with housing costs, including rent (with certain exclusions), rent in advance, deposits or other 'one off' costs associated with a housing need such as removal costs. DHPs can cover rent shortfalls caused by the application of the size criteria in the social rented sector or the size-related Local Housing Allowance restrictions in the private rented sector, or by reductions in universal credit caused by the benefit cap or by housing cost contributions (see para 16.66 below). They may also be used to cover increases in work-related expenditure arising from a move to a cheaper locality, such as higher travel costs. Local authorities have a broad discretion in deciding whether to make a DHP, and as to the amount of any such payment and the period for which it will be paid.

Housing cost contributions

16.66 Housing cost contributions (known as non-dependant deductions for housing benefit purposes: see para 16.22) are also taken into account in the calculation of a claimant's housing costs element. The assumption is that other adult members of the claimant's household should make a contribution to the rent, whether they are in fact doing so or not. Housing costs contributions are payable by anyone who lives with the claimant and is not the claimant's partner, or dependent on him or her, or a lodger.[81] There is a standard monthly deduction for each non-dependant, in contrast to the graduated deductions which are applied in the housing benefit scheme. A couple will count as two non-dependants, and a double deduction will be made. If the total amount of housing costs contributions exceeds the housing cost element of universal credit, the housing costs element will be nil: this will not, however, affect entitlement to the standard element or any other elements. No deduction is made if the claimant or partner receives certain disability benefits.[82] Nor is any contribution payable where the non-dependant is under 21; or is a single parent with a child under 5; or a person in receipt of state pension credit, certain disability benefits[83] or carer's allowance; or a family member who is a member of the armed forces and is away on operations.[84]

81 Universal Credit Regulations 2013 Sch 4 para 9(2).
82 ie, the middle or highest rate care component of disability living allowance, attendance allowance or the daily living component of a personal independence payment.
83 ie, the middle or highest rate care component of disability living allowance, attendance allowance or the daily living component of a personal independence payment.
84 Universal Credit Regulations 2013 Sch 4 para 16.

The benefits cap

16.67   The 'benefits cap' applies to universal credit to similar effect as it does to housing benefit, although its mode of operation is different.[85] The cap is the maximum amount of benefits income which a claimant of working age and his or her household can receive. The cap is applied to the total income received from specified benefits by the claimant, his or her spouse or partner or any dependent children. Claimants who are over the qualifying age for pension credit will not be subject to the benefit cap. If only one of a couple is over the qualifying age for pension credit, the benefit cap will apply until both partners are over pension credit age (whereas if the couple were in receipt of housing benefit and one is over pension credit age, the cap would not apply at all).

16.68   Where the cap applies, the claimant's universal credit entitlement will be reduced so that the amount paid does not exceed the cap. It is open to the claimant to apply for a discretionary housing payment to make up all or part of a rent shortfall or assist with other housing-related expenses.

Alternative Payment Arrangements

16.69   In view of the fact that universal credit is paid monthly in arrears, some occupiers will find it difficult to manage their finances. Where a claimant needs additional support in adapting to universal credit or in dealing with his or her rent or other outgoings, an Alternative Payment Arrangement (APA) may be put in place. There are three possible kinds of APA: 'managed payments', whereby the housing element of universal credit is paid directly to the landlord (whether in the social or private rented sector); a 'frequency' arrangement, whereby claimants can receive payment more often than on a monthly basis; and a 'split' option, whereby payments can be divided between two members of the same household. DWP officers will decide whether a claimant qualifies for APAs in the light of various factors set out in guidance.[86]

16.70   APAs may be requested and implemented at any point during the universal credit claim. The need may be identified at the outset, alongside personal budgeting support, or during the claim, if it is

---

85 Universal Credit Regulations 2013 regs 78–83.

86 Accessible at www.gov.uk/government/uploads/system/uploads/attachment_ data/file/399782/personal-budgeting-support-guidance.pdf. Annex A lists factors that would indicate a need for an APA.

evident that the claimant is struggling with the single monthly payment. Payment to another person may be arranged where it appears necessary to protect the interests of the claimant, his or her partner or child, or of a severely disabled person for whom the claimant has regular and substantial caring responsibilities.[87] Otherwise, where there are rent arrears, direct payments may be requested by the claimant or claimant's adviser, or by the landlord. Landlords may notify the DWP that rent arrears are accruing and ask for the claimant's housing element of universal credit to be paid direct to them in order to preserve the claimant's home. This will normally be agreed where a rent arrears 'trigger' point has been reached. The triggers are where the claimant is currently in two months' rent arrears; or the claimant has continually underpaid rent over a period of time and is in at least one month's arrears; or the claimant has been evicted for rent arrears within the past 12 months; or the claimant has been threatened with repossession. Guidance suggests that, if it is aware that arrears have reached the level of one month's rent, the DWP should hold a review to see whether budgeting support is needed and if direct payments should be made. In addition, up to 20 per cent of the claimant's universal credit can be deducted to pay rent arrears, which is a significantly higher proportion than the level of direct deductions available under income support or other existing means-tested benefits.[88]

Claimant commitment

16.71 Where a claim for universal credit has been made, the claimant will need to accept a 'claimant commitment'.[89] The purpose of the claimant commitment is to set out what the claimant is required to do to find work or prepare for work. For a claimant who is already working, it may describe what steps have to be taken to find better paid work, or more hours of work. Failure to comply may result in disqualification from benefit.

16.72 The concept of 'conditionality' is a core feature of the universal credit scheme. It is based on the premise that in return for receiving benefits, a claimant should keep to his or her claimant commitment and that if he or she does not do so, he or she can be penalised or 'sanctioned', usually in the form of the withdrawal of benefits.

---

87 Universal Credit, Personal Independence Payment, Jobseeker's Allowance and Employment and Support Allowance (Claims and Payments) Regulations 2013 SI No 380 reg 58(1).
88 See para 16.48.
89 Welfare Reform Act 2012 s14.

16.73   In order to determine the kind of claimant commitment which will apply to each individual, the DWP will allocate him or her to a particular level of conditionality. Claimants will be placed in one of four groups, which prescribe different 'work-related requirements'.[90] The group in which the claimant is placed will depend on his or her personal circumstances and will be reviewed on an ongoing basis. The requirements reflect the fact that universal credit is payable to four broad classes of claimant: those who are working but on low pay (for whom it replaces tax credits); those who are unemployed and looking for work (for whom it replaces income-based jobseeker's allowance); those who are not working because they are sick or injured (for whom it replaces income-related employment and support allowance, or in some cases, income support); and those who are not working because they are in other groups such as single parents with young children (for whom it replaces income support).

16.74   The four groups are:

- The 'all work related requirements' group. Persons subject to all work related requirements are given a 'work search' requirement and a 'work availability' requirement. They may also be required to attend work-focused interviews and do work preparation. Claimants subject to the work search requirement are asked to take all reasonable action to find work, and any particular action specified by the DWP. This will include making applications for jobs, obtaining references and 'creating and maintaining an online profile'. The work availability requirement is that claimants are able and willing immediately to take up paid work (or more paid work or better paid work).

- The 'work preparation' group. Persons in this group may be required to attend work-focused interviews and do work preparation. They cannot be required to look for work or be available for work. A work preparation requirement may include any particular action specified by the DWP for the purpose of making it more likely that the claimant will obtain paid work (or more paid work or better paid work).

- The 'work-focused interview only' group. Persons in this group are required to attend a work-focused interview. This is an interview which relates to work or work preparation. Such interviews may help identify work opportunities as well as training or education which may improve the claimant's ability to find work.

90 Welfare Reform Act 2012 ss15–18.

- The 'no work-related requirements' group. Persons subject to no work-related requirements are at the lowest level of conditionality, and do not face any conditions on their claim.

16.75 If at any time the DWP decide that a different set of requirements is appropriate, it will be necessary for the claimant to enter into a new claimant commitment. If claimants fail to meet their work-related requirements, the DWP may apply a sanction to their claim. This will reduce the amount of universal credit which the household will receive for a certain period of time. There are four levels of sanction, and the particular sanction imposed will depend on the nature of the failure and on which of the work-related groups applies to the claimant.

Overpayments

16.76 In contrast with housing benefit, all overpayments of universal credit are recoverable, including those arising from official error.[91] However, the DWP has discretion not to recover an overpayment. Methods of recovery are similar to those applicable to housing benefits overpayments (see para 16.35), including by means of deduction from current benefits. Rates of deduction are substantially higher under universal credit[92] than under the housing benefit system.

Reviews and appeals

16.77 Where a person has received an adverse decision in relation to a claim for universal credit, he or she may apply to the DWP for a revision of the decision. This request must normally be made within one month of receiving the decision, although if the claimant has asked the DWP for a written statement of reasons, the period may be extended. The DWP has power to grant an extension of the time for a revision application. On receipt of the application, the DWP should carry out a mandatory reconsideration of its decision, taking into account any further information or evidence which the claimant has provided in support of the revision.

91 Social Security (Overpayments and Recovery) Regulations 2013 SI No 384 reg 3.
92 The regulations provide for a maximum deduction of 40 per cent from the universal credit standard allowance where there has been a conviction, caution or penalty and 25 per cent or 15 per cent in other cases: Social Security (Overpayments and Recovery) Regulations 2013 SI No 384. See also DWP, *Advice for Decision Making*, chapters D1–D3.

16.78   Where the claimant remains dissatisfied with the decision of the DWP following mandatory reconsideration, he or she can in most instances appeal against the decision to the First-tier Tribunal. Appeals should be submitted on form SSCS1 (obtainable online from government websites) to HMCTS, SSCS Appeals Centre, PO Box 1203, Bradford BD1 9WP. The time limit for appealing is normally one month, but can be extended if the DWP or the Tribunal agree.

Effect of universal credit issues on possession proceedings

16.79   The *Pre-action Protocol for possession claims by social landlords*[93] requires social landlords to take active steps to ensure that any problems with benefit claims are, where possible, resolved without recourse to court proceedings. The Protocol (the full text of which is set out in appendix E) enshrines the principle that the landlord and tenant should work together to resolve any universal credit (housing element) problems. In particular, the social landlord is expected to assist the tenant in any claim which he or she may have for the housing element of universal credit (Protocol, para 2.5). 'Assistance' in this context implies something more active than merely offering information or advice. Possession proceedings for rent arrears should not be started against a tenant who can demonstrate that he or she has provided the DWP with all the evidence it requires to process a universal credit (housing element) claim; and has a reasonable expectation of eligibility for the housing element; and has paid other sums due not covered by universal credit. The Protocol requires the landlord to make every effort to establish effective ongoing liaison with the DWP and, with the tenant's consent, make direct contact with the relevant DWP office before taking enforcement action. If the landlord unreasonably fails to comply with the terms of the Protocol, the court may (in cases other than those brought solely on mandatory grounds) adjourn, strike out or dismiss claims and/or impose an order for costs (Protocol, para 2.13). Conversely, if the tenant unreasonably fails to comply with the terms of the Protocol, the court may take such failure into account when considering whether it is reasonable to make a possession order (Protocol, para 2.14).

16.80   Where a possession claim has been started on the basis of a discretionary ground for possession, whether by a social landlord or

93   See also para 16.30.

private landlord, the court may be asked to adjourn the proceedings pending the outcome of an application for universal credit (housing element) or for a discretionary housing payment if that is a realistic option (see also para 21.52). It is not generally possible to secure such an adjournment where a court is satisfied that mandatory ground 8[94] of the assured tenancy grounds for possession in HA 1988 Sch 2 is made out in respect of an assured or assured shorthold tenant, unless the tenant has an arguable counterclaim for damages (eg, for breach of the landlord's repairing obligation) which may be set off against the rent arrears; or unless the tenant has a public law defence[95] (where the claimant is a registered provider of social housing) or a defence under the Equality Act 2010.[96] In the absence of such a defence, the court must order possession where ground 8 is proved, even if the arrears have accumulated for want of universal credit to which the tenant is entitled.[97]

Council tax reduction

16.81   Most tenants and other occupiers are liable to pay council tax to the local authority, which provides the means whereby local public services are funded. The council tax reduction (or rebate) scheme operates to assist those on a low income with payment of their council tax. Each local authority administers its own council tax reduction scheme, although every scheme must comply with certain 'prescribed requirements'. Thus, most councils operate a national 'default scheme', either in whole or in part, but may vary or modify the scheme in certain respects: for example, some councils reduce the amount of the eligible rebate to 90 per cent of the full council tax liability, whereas others will adopt the default position that the eligible rebate is 100 per cent of the tax charged. Further consideration of council tax reduction schemes is beyond the scope of this book, and the reader is referred to the Shelter/CIH publication *Help with Housing Costs Volume 1: Guide to Universal Credit and Council Tax Rebates*.

---

94 Ground 8 is satisfied where, both at the date of the service of the notice of seeking possession and at the date of the hearing, at least eight weeks' or two months' rent is unpaid. See para 3.99.
95 See chapter 25.
96 See para 27.24.
97 *North British Housing Association v Matthews* [2004] EWCA Civ 1736, [2005] 1 WLR 3133.

CHAPTER 17

Premises occupied by employees

17.1   Employees who occupy residential premises owned by their private sector employers (sometimes called 'tied accommodation') may be either tenants or licensees. Where it is necessary for the employee to live in the premises for the better performance of a job or where it is a term of the employee's contract of employment that he or she is required to live in the premises, it is likely that the employee is merely a licensee of those premises.[1] These are generally employees who have to live in or near their place of work, such as resident caretakers or wardens. Such persons are called 'service occupiers' or 'service licensees'. If it is neither necessary nor a condition of employment that he or she lives in the premises, an employee who has exclusive possession for a term and who pays rent will usually be a tenant.[2] If the tenancy satisfies the usual requirements for Rent Act (RA) or Housing Act (HA) protection[3] there is security of tenure, but subject to the possibility that possession proceedings may be brought under the 'service tenancy' grounds, namely, RA 1977 Sch 15 Case 8 (see para 12.62) or HA 1988 Sch 2 ground 16 (see para 3.397), or (in the case of an assured shorthold tenancy) following a notice requiring possession under HA 1988 s21.

17.2   If, however, employees are licensees, they have no security of tenure. Service licensees have only the limited protection that employers must bring court proceedings to evict them. Protection from Eviction

---

1   *Smith v Seghill Overseers* (1874–75) LR 10 QB 422; *Fox v Dalby* (1874–75) LR 10 CP 285 and *Glasgow Corporation v Johnstone* [1965] AC 609, [1965] 2 WLR 657.

2   *Royal Philanthropic Society v County* (1986) 18 HLR 83, (1985) 276 EG 1068.

3   One particular problem which tenants who are employees sometimes face is that often there is no rent payable and accordingly the tenancy cannot be an assured tenancy because of HA 1988 Sch 1 para 3 or a regulated tenancy because of RA 1977 s5. See *Heslop v Burns* [1974] 1 WLR 1241 and *Montagu v Browning* [1954] 1 WLR 1039.

Act (PEA) 1977 s3(2B) extends the requirement of a court order to licences, other than excluded licences[4]. For good measure, PEA 1977 s8(2) provides:

> For the purposes of Part I of this Act a person who, under the terms of his employment, had exclusive possession of the premises other than as a tenant shall have been deemed to have been a tenant and the expressions 'let' and 'tenancy' shall be construed accordingly.

The effect of section 8(2) is that a service occupier with exclusive possession does not become a trespasser when his or her service licence ends.[5] Consequently, a court is not bound to make a possession order to take effect immediately or 'forthwith', although the court's powers are limited by HA 1980 s89 (see para 28.1).

17.3 This means that both PEA 1977 s1 (unlawful eviction and harassment of occupier) and s3 (prohibition of eviction without due process of law) apply to service licensees. Although a service licensee may not pay a quantified rent for his or her accommodation, it is likely that the value of the accommodation will be reflected in the level of his or her wages. The letting would not therefore be an 'excluded letting' within PEA 1977 s3A, because it would be granted for 'money or money's worth'(see para 15.5).[6]

17.4 Employers need prove only that they own or have an interest in the premises and that the rights of the employee (or ex-employee) to reside in the premises have been determined, in accordance with either the contract of employment or any other agreement relating to the premises. In general, the notice required to determine a service licence is the same as the notice necessary to terminate the employment, and it is not necessary to serve a separate notice to terminate the licence under PEA 1977 s5.[7]

17.5 If service licensees consider that they have been unfairly dismissed, an application may be made to an employment tribunal. Although the tribunal may recommend reinstatement, this is of little assistance in defending possession proceedings for tied accommodation. The tribunal cannot compel re-instatement and the court considering possession proceedings is interested only in ascertaining whether or not the contract has been terminated. It cannot take into account whether the contract has been terminated fairly or unfairly.

4 See para 15.9.
5 See para 28.4.
6 PEA 1977 s3A(7)(b).
7 *Doe d Hughes v Derry* (1840) 9 C & P 494; *Ivory v Palmer* [1975] ICR 340, CA, and *Norris v Checksfield* [1991] 1 WLR 1241, (1991) 23 HLR 425, CA.

Applications for adjournments of possession proceedings in these circumstances, pending the hearing of an application to an employment tribunal, are generally unsuccessful.[8]

17.6   Where a tenant's landlord and employer is a local authority or another public sector body which fulfils the 'landlord condition' in HA 1985 s80(1), and where the tenant is required by his or her contract of employment to occupy the property for the better performance of duties, the tenancy will not be a secure tenancy[9] (see para 1.69). Similar exclusions from security apply where the tenant is a member of a police force living in rent-free accommodation or an employee of a fire and rescue authority.[10] In such cases, where the local authority intends to terminate the employment and seek possession of the accommodation, it must serve notice in accordance with the contract and on expiry of the notice it will usually need to apply for a possession order against the former employee, though no ground for possession is necessary (see para 17.2 above). Where an employee lives in premises which are used mainly for non-housing purposes, but is not obliged by his or her contract of employment to do so, he or she may be a secure tenant, but will be subject to the 'service tenancy' ground for possession[11] when the employment ceases.

17.7   Employees of public authorities may, in some circumstances, be able to defend a claim for possession on public law grounds[12] and/or, in exceptional cases, on 'human rights' grounds[13] (see chapters 25 and 26). See also chapter 27 in relation to defences under the Equality Act 2010 on the basis of disability discrimination:[14] such defences may be available against a public or private landlord.

8 See, eg *Whitbread West Pennines Ltd v Reedy* [1988] ICR 807, (1988) 20 HLR 642, CA (manager of public house dismissed).
9 HA 1985 Sch 1 para 2(1).
10 HA 1985 Sch 1 para 2(2) and 2(3).
11 HA 1985 Sch 2 ground 12 (see para 3.321).
12 For example, where the public body has failed to follow its own policies in relation to the process of terminating the defendant's employment and seeking possession of the premises.
13 For example, where the employee had, after many years' service, become unable to perform his duties because of chronic illness and the public body had failed to offer alternative accommodation.
14 For example, where the landlord/employer had decided to terminate the defendant's employment because of the defendant's mobility problems when reasonable adjustments to working patterns would have enabled him or her to continue doing the job. See also, in relation to the public sector equality duty under Equality Act 2010 s149, *Barnsley MBC v Norton* [2011] EWCA Civ 834, [2011] HLR 46 (see para 27.61).

17.8   Farm workers and other occupiers working in agriculture whose accommodation is provided by their employers and who satisfy the 'agricultural worker condition'[15] may have special protection as protected agricultural occupiers under Rent (Agriculture) Act 1976 s2 or as assured agricultural occupiers under HA 1988 s24. This book does not deal with agricultural occupancies. The reader is referred to specialist works such as Christopher Rodgers, *Agricultural Law*, Bloomsbury Professional, 4th ed, 2016.

15   See Rent (Agriculture) Act 1976 Sch 3 and HA 1988 Sch 3.

CHAPTER 18

Death of the tenant

Termination of contractual tenancies on death

18.1　A contractual tenancy does not terminate on the tenant's death unless the tenancy expressly states that this is to happen.[1] If the tenant leaves a will, the tenancy passes to the tenant's executors. If there is no will and the tenant dies intestate, the tenancy passes to the Public Trustee until such time as letters of administration are taken out.[2] Unless there has been an automatic statutory succession (see paras 18.5–18.10 below), this applies to protected Rent Act (RA) tenancies, assured and assured shorthold tenancies, secure tenancies, flexible tenancies, introductory tenancies, demoted tenancies and family intervention tenancies, but not to Rent Act statutory tenancies.

18.2　Where a tenant has died and there is no statutory successor, but the property is still occupied,[3] the landlord will need to observe specific procedures in order to recover possession of the property. In order to terminate a periodic tenancy, notice to quit must be served on the executors or administrators of the late tenant's estate, as the case may be. If a grant of probate or administration has not yet been taken out, the notice must be addressed to the personal representatives of the deceased tenant and left at or posted to the last known place of residence of the deceased. In addition a copy of the notice, similarly addressed, must be served on the Public Trustee at PO Box 3010, London WC2A 1AX.[4] The notice itself should not be addressed to the Public Trustee. The copy notice sent to the Public Trustee must be accompanied by Form NL1 (application for registration) and the appropriate fee. A Practice Note is available on the Ministry of Justice website. Where the property is occupied at the date of expiry of the notice to quit, the landlord will need to take proceedings to recover possession.[5]

18.3　If a deceased tenant's contractual periodic tenancy is not determined in this way, any occupiers have a complete defence to possession proceedings which are issued before the tenancy has been

---

1　*Youngmin v Heath* [1974] 1 WLR 135. In relation to the position following the death of a tenant, see also paras 1.137–1.149.

2　Law of Property (Miscellaneous Provisions) Act 1994 s14.

3　The occupiers are likely to be members of the deceased tenant's family who do not qualify to be statutory successors.

4　Law of Property (Miscellaneous Provisions) Act 1994 s18 and Public Trustee (Notices Affecting Land) (Title on Death) Regulations 1995 SI No 1330, amended by the Public Trustee (Notices Affecting Land) (Title on Death) (Amendment) Regulations 2001 SI No 3902. See also *Wirral BC v Smith* (1982) 4 HLR 81, (1982) 43 P&CR 312, CA.

5　Protection from Eviction Act 1977 s3.

determined.[6] In the long term, however, there is nothing to stop the landowner serving a valid notice to quit and then bringing new proceedings.

18.4   Further steps may need to be taken where the deceased tenant held an assured or assured shorthold tenancy, and there is no statutory successor to the tenancy.[7] Where there is no one who qualifies to be a statutory successor, assured and assured shorthold tenancies can be inherited by will or on intestacy. Where the tenant died without leaving a will, the tenancy will vest in the Public Trustee, who will hold it subject to a trust in favour of the next of kin who is (or are) beneficially entitled to the deceased's estate.[8] In these circumstances, where the beneficiary is occupying the property as his or her only or principal home, it will not be sufficient for the landlord to serve a notice to quit on the personal representatives and (where applicable) the Public Trustee (see para 18.2 above). The landlord will also need to bring proceedings to terminate the assured or assured shorthold tenancy which has devolved on a beneficiary in occupation. Where the tenancy is a fully assured tenancy, the landlord will need to rely on mandatory ground 7 of Housing Act (HA) 1988 Sch 2 (see para 3.368). Ground 7 can be used whether the tenancy is fixed-term or periodic. Where the tenancy is a periodic assured shorthold tenancy, however, the landlord will be able to bring possession proceedings based on a notice given under HA 1988 s21 (see para 10.7).

Statutory succession on the death of a tenant

18.5   The most important question to be addressed on the death of a tenant is whether any occupier has a statutory right to succeed to the tenancy. The rules governing statutory succession are different, depending on whether the deceased tenant was a Rent Act regulated tenant, a secure or flexible tenant under HA 1985, or an assured or assured shorthold tenant under HA 1988.

---

6 *Wirral BC v Smith* (1982) 4 HLR 81, (1982) 43 P&CR 312, CA.
7 See paras 18.5–18.10 below for the rules of statutory succession.
8 Under Administration of Estates Act 1925 s46(1)(ii).

Statutory succession: secure tenancies

18.6   On the death of a secure tenant, the tenancy will pass to a person who is qualified to succeed to it under HA 1985 s86A[9] (in England only) or s87 (in Wales, and in England in respect of tenancies that began before 1 April 2012).[10] Section 86A, which applies to tenancies which began on or after 1 April 2012, provides that a person is qualified to succeed to the tenancy if:

- he or she occupied the property as an only or principal home and is either:
  - the spouse or civil partner of the deceased tenant; or
  - a person who was living with the tenant as his or her spouse or as if they were civil partners;

or

- where is no such person, an express term of the tenancy makes provision for a person other than such a spouse or civil partner of the tenant to succeed to the tenancy, and the person's succession is in accordance with that term.[11]

Under section 87, which applies generally in Wales, but in England applies only to tenancies which began before 1 April 2012, a person is qualified to succeed to the tenancy if:

- he or she occupied the property as an only or principal home and is either:
  - the spouse or civil partner of the deceased tenant; or
  - another member of the family[12] who resided with the tenant throughout the period of 12 months ending with the tenant's death.

There can be only one succession to a secure tenancy. Where one of two joint tenants dies, and the other becomes a sole tenant by survivorship, this counts as a succession, and there can therefore be no further succession on the death of the survivor.[13] Where a surviving joint tenant no longer occupies the property as his or her only or principal home, it is not possible for another member of the family to succeed, even though the family member occupies the property and has fulfilled the 12-months residence requirement.[14] As a result,

---

9   Inserted by Localism Act 2011 s160.
10   For the transitional provisions, see Localism Act 2011 s160(6).
11   HA 1985 s86A(2).
12   As defined in HA 1985 s113.
13   HA 1985 s88(1)(b).
14   *Solihull MBC v Hickin* [2012] UKSC 39, [2012] HLR 40.

the tenancy loses its secure status and can be terminated by notice to quit.[15]

18.7   In the case of a periodic secure tenancy, where there is a person qualified to succeed the deceased tenant under HA 1985 ss86A or 87, the tenancy vests by virtue of section 89 in that person. Special provision is made under HA 1985 s90 for the devolution of a fixed-term secure tenancy (including a flexible tenancy) where there is a person qualified to succeed. Section 90(1) provides that the tenancy will remain secure during the administration of the deceased tenant's estate, and will continue to be secure when it is vested in the successor.[16] However, where no one is qualified to succeed to the tenancy, the tenancy will cease to be a secure tenancy when it is vested in another person in the course of administration of the estate, or when it becomes known that when the tenancy is so vested, it will not be a secure tenancy. A tenancy which ceases to be secure by virtue of this section cannot subsequently become a secure tenancy again.[17] In these circumstances, the landlord, on giving at least four weeks' written notice to the tenant, may apply to the court for an order for possession, and the court must make an order for possession, which when executed will terminate the fixed-term tenancy.[18]

18.8   Where a person other than the late tenant's spouse or civil partner (as defined) succeeds to a secure tenancy (including a flexible tenancy), and the accommodation afforded by the property is more extensive than is reasonably required by the tenant, the landlord may seek possession on HA 1985 Sch 2 ground 15A (in England) or ground 16 (in Wales). The court must be satisfied both that suitable alternative accommodation is available to the tenant and that it is reasonable to make an order for possession.[19]

Statutory succession: introductory and demoted tenancies

18.9   HA 1996 Part V provides for succession to introductory and demoted tenancies. In the case of an introductory tenancy, a person is qualified to succeed to the tenancy if he or she occupied the property as

15 See para 18.2 above.
16 The tenancy will also remain secure when it is vested in pursuance of an order made in proceedings for divorce or dissolution of civil partnership or in other family proceedings: see HA 1985 s90(3)(a).
17 HA 1985 s90(4).
18 HA 1985 s90(6)–(10).
19 See para 3.338.

an only or principal home at the time of the tenant's death and is either the spouse or civil partner of the deceased tenant, or is another member of the family[20] who resided with the tenant throughout the period of 12 months ending with the tenant's death.[21] The qualifying conditions mirror HA 1985 s87 in relation to secure tenancies, and were not altered by the Localism Act 2011, so they continue to apply irrespective of the date when the tenancy began. There can be no succession if the deceased tenant was already a successor. Where there is no person qualified to succeed the tenant, the tenancy ceases to be an introductory tenancy when it is vested or otherwise disposed of in the course of the administration of the tenant's estate,[22] or when it is known that the tenancy will cease to be an introductory tenancy when so vested or disposed of.[23] Similar provisions exist in relation to succession to demoted tenancies.[24]

Statutory succession: assured and assured shorthold tenancies

18.10   On the death of a periodic assured or assured shorthold tenant, the tenancy will pass by statutory succession to the deceased tenant's spouse or civil partner or anyone living with the original tenant as spouse or civil partner, provided that immediately before the death, that person was occupying the dwelling as his or her only or principal home. Where there is such a successor, the tenancy vests in that person and, accordingly, does not devolve under the tenant's will or intestacy.[25] The list of potential successors may effectively be extended by contract if there is specific provision in the tenancy agreement for other members of the family to 'succeed' in the absence of a statutory successor. Such a provision does not give rise to a true succession, but generally operates by way of a contractual obligation on the landlord to grant a new tenancy. This is often the case where the landlord is a housing association which acquired the property by stock transfer from a local authority, whereupon the former secure tenants of the authority became assured tenants on the transfer of ownership.[26]

---

20 As defined in HA 1985 s113.
21 HA 1996 ss131–133.
22 Otherwise than in pursuance of an order made in matrimonial, civil partnership or Children Act proceedings: see HA 1996 s133(3)(a).
23 HA 1996 s133(3)(b).
24 HA 1996 ss143H–143J, inserted by Anti-social Behaviour Act 2003 Sch 1 para 1.
25 HA 1988 s17(1).
26 HA 1988 s38(3).

There can be only one succession to an assured tenancy. Where one of two joint tenants dies, and the other becomes a sole tenant by survivorship, this counts as a succession, and there can therefore be no further succession on the death of the survivor, except in the unlikely event that a second succession is permitted by the tenancy agreement.[27] See para 18.4 above for the procedure which the landlord must follow to regain possession following the death of an assured or assured shorthold tenant where the occupier is not qualified to succeed to the tenancy, but has inherited it under the late tenant's will or on intestacy.

18.11   Special provision is made for certain assured or assured shorthold tenancies (other than statutory periodic tenancies) granted on or after 1 April 2012 by housing associations in occupation or other private registered providers of social housing.[28] Where the tenancy is for a fixed term of two years or more, and the deceased tenant leaves in England a spouse or civil partner or anyone who lived with the tenant as his or her spouse or civil partner, provided that such person was occupying the dwelling as his or her only or principal home, then, on the death, the tenancy vests in the spouse or civil partner and, accordingly, does not devolve under the tenant's will or intestacy.[29] Where the tenancy is a periodic tenancy or a tenancy for a fixed term of two years or more, and

- immediately before the death, the dwelling was not occupied by a spouse or civil partner of the deceased tenant as his or her only or principal home;
- but an express term of the tenancy makes provision for a person other than a spouse or civil partner of the tenant to succeed to the tenancy;
- and there is a person who satisfies the conditions for succession in the tenancy agreement,

then, on the death, the tenancy vests in that person,[30] and, accordingly, does not devolve under the tenant's will or intestacy.[31] These provisions do not apply to shared ownership leases.[32]

---

27 HA 1988 s17(2)(b).
28 Localism Act 2011 s161(7).
29 HA 1988 s17(1B), inserted by Localism Act 2011 s161.
30 Provided that the deceased tenant was not already a successor: HA 1988 s17(10).
31 HA 1988 s17(1A) and (1C).
32 HA 1988 s17(7).

Statutory succession: Rent Act regulated tenancies

18.12   In the ordinary course of events, a Rent Act statutory tenancy comes to an end on the death of the tenant.[33] As a statutory tenancy is only a personal right it cannot be left to another person through the deceased tenant's will.[34] However, RA 1977 s2(1)(b) and Sch 1 Part I, as amended by the Housing Act (HA) 1988 s39, provide that a spouse or civil partner who was living with the tenant at the time of death can succeed to the tenancy. A spouse or civil partner who 'inherits' a tenancy in this way is called a 'statutory tenant by succession' and acquires a statutory tenancy. 'Spouse' is defined as including any person living with the deceased tenant as wife or husband, and 'civil partner' is defined as including any person living with the deceased as if a civil partner.[35] If there was no spouse or civil partner, a member of the tenant's family who had been living with the tenant for two years immediately before the death is entitled to succeed to the tenancy. Any such member of the family who succeeds to a tenancy as a result of the death of a tenant on or after 15 January 1989 acquires an assured tenancy. The succession provisions apply to both protected (contractual) and statutory tenancies.[36] RA 1977 Sch 1 provides that any tenancy can be passed on twice only if the first successor is a spouse or civil partner, as defined. A second succession will always be to an assured tenancy.

Conflict between inheritance and statutory succession

18.13   It is possible for a tenant to leave a contractual tenancy by will to one person, but for another to be entitled to succeed to the tenancy under the relevant statutory provisions. In this situation, the statutory successor prevails. Where the deceased tenant held a Rent Act protected tenancy, any person who would be entitled to succeed to the tenancy acquires a statutory tenancy by succession and the contractual tenancy goes into 'abeyance' until the statutory tenancy

33   RA 1977 s2. See chapter 12 and *Skinner v Geary* [1931] 2 KB 546.
34   *John Lovibond and Sons Ltd v Vincent* [1929] 1 KB 687.
35   RA 1977 Sch 1 para 2(2), as amended by Civil Partnership Act 2004 Sch 8 para 13.
36   *Moodie v Hosegood* [1952] AC 61, [1951] 2 All ER 582, HL.

comes to an end.[37] The problem does not occur with periodic assured and assured shorthold tenancies, because HA 1988 s17(1) specifically provides that, where there is a statutory succession to a spouse or civil partner,[38] the tenancy vests in the successor, and accordingly does not devolve under the tenant's will or intestacy. Certain fixed-term assured tenancies granted by private registered providers of social housing also vest automatically in the statutory successor.[39] Where a person qualifies to succeed a periodic secure tenant under HA 1985 ss86A or 87, the tenancy also vests in that person by virtue of HA 1985 s89(1).[40]

Rent arrears and succession

18.14   A person who acquires a tenancy by succession takes the tenancy free from any rent arrears which existed at the late tenant's death. Such arrears become a liability of the deceased tenant's estate and cannot be carried over to the successor's rent account.[41] However, where the tenancy was subject to a postponed or suspended possession order, such order will continue to have effect, so that in these circumstances the successor may in practice become responsible for the late tenant's arrears as a result of the need to comply with the terms of the order.[42] In these circumstances, the successor may wish to apply to be joined as a party to the proceedings in which the order was made; and, in the light of the succession, for a variation or discharge of the order.

37 *Moodie v Hosegood* [1952] AC 61, [1951] 2 All ER 582, HL, overruling *Smith v Mather* [1948] 2 KB 212, [1948] 1 All ER 704 and *Thynne v Salmon* [1948] 1 KB 482, [1948] 1 All ER 49.
38 See para 18.10.
39 See para 18.11.
40 See para 18.7.
41 *Tickner v Clifton* [1929] 1 KB 207.
42 *Sherrin v Brand* [1956] 1 QB 403.

CHAPTER 19

Possession proceedings and the bankrupt tenant

19.1   For the effect of bankruptcy on the home of an owner-occupier, see chapter 43.

19.2   Insolvency Act (IA) 1986 s283 provides that, with very limited exceptions, tenancies which carry statutory security of tenure do not vest in the trustee in bankruptcy. Consequently, a secure or assured or Rent Act protected tenant is able to preserve statutory security of tenure, which would otherwise be lost because the trustee would not be occupying the property.

19.3   Section 283 provides:

> (1) Subject as follows, a bankrupt's estate ... comprises –
>   (a) all property belonging to or vested in the bankrupt at the com- mencement of the bankruptcy, and
>   (b) any property which by virtue of any of the following provisions of this Part is comprised in that estate or is treated as falling within the preceding paragraph.
>
> ...
>
> (3A) Subject to section 308A ..., subsection (1) does not apply to –
>   (a) a tenancy which is an assured tenancy or an assured agricul- tural occupancy within the meaning of Part I of the Housing Act 1988, and the terms of which inhibit an assignment as mentioned in section 127(5) of the Rent Act 1977, or
>   (b) a protected tenancy, within the meaning of the Rent Act 1977, in respect of which, by virtue of any provision of Part IX of that Act, no premium can lawfully be required as a condition of assignment, or
>   (c) a tenancy of a dwelling-house by virtue of which the bankrupt is, within the meaning of the Rent (Agriculture) Act 1976, a protected occupier of the dwelling-house, and the terms of which inhibit an assignment as mentioned in section 127(5) of the Rent Act 1977, or

(d) a secure tenancy, within the meaning of Part IV of the Housing Act 1985, which is not capable of being assigned, except in the cases mentioned in section 91(3) of that Act.

19.4 The trustee in bankruptcy can elect to have such tenancies vest in him or her by serving a notice under IA 1986 s308A. Such notice must ordinarily be served within 42 days of the trustee becoming aware of the tenancy, although the court may extend the period. There would usually be no reason for the trustee to make such an election, and every reason why the tenant's home should be preserved, except in the rare instances where the tenancy may lawfully be assigned for money or where the trustee wishes to disclaim the tenancy. It appears, however, that introductory tenancies, demoted tenancies and family intervention tenancies are not excluded from the bankrupt's estate and therefore vest in the trustee in bankruptcy.

19.5 Rent arrears are a debt which is provable in the bankruptcy. The question arises whether the landlord's remedy of claiming possession on the ground of rent arrears is affected by the tenant's bankruptcy. IA 1986 s285 provides:

Restriction on proceedings and remedies

(1) At any time when proceedings on a bankruptcy application are ongoing or proceedings on a bankcruptcy petition are pending or an individual has been made bankrupt the court may stay any action, execution or other legal process against the property or person of the debtor or, as the case may be, of the bankrupt.

(2) Any court in which proceedings are pending against any individual may, on proof that a bankruptcy application has been made or a bankruptcy petition has been presented in respect of that individual or that he is an undischarged bankrupt, either stay the proceedings or allow them to continue on such terms as it thinks fit.

(3) After the making of a bankruptcy order no person who is a creditor of the bankrupt in respect of a debt provable in the bankruptcy shall –

(a) have any remedy against the property or person of the bankrupt in respect of that debt, or

(b) before the discharge of the bankrupt, commence any action or other legal proceedings against the bankrupt except with the leave of the court and on such terms as the court may impose.

This is subject to sections 346 (enforcement procedures) and 347 (limited right to distress).

(4) Subject as follows, subsection (3) does not affect the right of a secured creditor of the bankrupt to enforce his security.

(5) Where any goods of an undischarged bankrupt are held by any person by way of pledge, pawn or other security, the official receiver

may, after giving notice in writing of his intention to do so, inspect the goods.

Where such a notice has been given to any person, that person is not entitled, without leave of the court, to realise his security unless he has given the trustee of the bankrupt's estate a reasonable opportunity of inspecting the goods and of exercising the bankrupt's right of redemption.

(6) References in this section to the property or goods of the bankrupt are to any of his property or goods, whether or not comprised in his estate.

19.6   Case-law has considered the question whether, where a tenant is an undischarged bankrupt, IA 1986 s285(3)(a) restricts the landlord from obtaining possession on a rent arrears ground. This depends upon whether a claim for possession is, in the terms of the subsection, a remedy against the person or property of the bankrupt in respect of a debt which is provable in the bankrutpcy.

19.7   In *Ezekiel v Orakpo*,[1] which concerned a fixed-term business lease, it was held that an action for possession following forfeiture of the lease was not a 'remedy against ... the property of the bankrupt in respect of [a] debt'.[2] Where it is necessary for the landlord to obtain a possession order before exercising a right of re-entry following forfeiture of a lease,[3] it is not the possession order which terminates the lease, since this is already forfeit. There was, accordingly, no 'property' against which the landlord could claim a remedy. By contrast, however, assured, secure and Rent Act regulated tenancies do not come to an end until execution of the order, or until possession is otherwise delivered up.

19.8   In *Harlow DC v Hall*,[4] the Court of Appeal accepted that Mr Hall's secure tenancy was, while it lasted, 'property' within the meaning of IA 1986 s285(1).[5] On the facts, however, section 285(3)(a) had no application, since (under the law prior to the implementation of the Housing and Regeneration Act 2008 Sch 11: see para 28.16) the defendant's secure tenancy had ended by the date when the

---

1   [1977] QB 260.
2   Within Bankruptcy Act 1914 s7(1), the predecessor of IA 1986 s285(3). See also *Razzaq v Pala* (1997) 38 EG 157.
3   See para 14.46. Protection from Eviction Act 1977 s2 provides that 'where any premises are let as a dwelling on a lease which is subject to a right of re-entry or forfeiture it shall not be lawful to enforce that right otherwise than by proceedings in the court while any person is lawfully residing in the premises or part of them'.
4   [2006] EWCA Civ 156, [2006] 1 WLR 1216.
5   [2006] EWCA Civ 156, [2006] 1 WLR 1216 para 14.

bankruptcy order was made. However, the Court of Appeal also considered whether the position would be different if the bankruptcy order had been made *before* the date when the tenancy ended. In the court's view, it would have made no difference, and the possession order could still be enforced. Chadwick LJ said:

> It would, I think, be unfortunate if the outcome in cases of this nature turned on whether the bankruptcy order was made just before or just after the possession order ... I am satisfied that that is not the position.

19.9   The question of the effect of bankruptcy and debt relief orders (see para 19.10 below) on rent arrears as a ground for possession proceedings has been resolved in two Court of Appeal cases decided together, namely, *Sharples v Places for People Ltd* and *Godfrey v A2 Dominion Homes Ltd*.[6] In the former case, Ms Sharples was an assured tenant. She fell into rent arrears and her landlord issued proceedings for possession on the basis of ground 8 of HA 1988 Sch 2 ground 8 (two months' rent arrears: see para 3.99). Before the possession hearing she was declared bankrupt. It was argued for the tenant that under IA 1986 s285(3)(a) it was not open to the court to make an order for possession against her on the ground of rent arrears because this would be a remedy against her property in relation to a debt that was provable in the bankruptcy. However, the Court of Appeal held that 'neither forfeiture, nor a court order for possession, nor recovery of possession by the landlord, nor an order for bankruptcy, eliminates the personal indebtedness constituted by the rent arrears'.[7] An order for possession was not a 'remedy in respect of' the rent arrears debt and the making of a possession order did not fall within the restrictions in section 285(3). This was the case irrespective of the tenant's security of tenure. Etherton LJ stated:

> An order for possession is not obtained with a view to payment of arrears of rent at all. Its object is to restore to the landlord the right to full possession and enjoyment of the landlord's property.[8]

19.10   Similar issues have arisen in relation to debt relief orders (DROs) under IA 1986 Part 7A, inserted by the Tribunals, Courts and Enforcement Act 2007. A DRO is made by the official receiver upon an application made through an approved intermediary (IA 1986 s251B). The

---

6 Both cases have the same citation: [2011] EWCA Civ 813, [2011] HLR 45.
7 Per Etherton LJ, para 63.
8 Para 65.

effect of the making of a DRO is to impose a moratorium on enforcement of the relevant debts by creditors. IA 1986 s251G provides:

(1) A moratorium commences on the effective date for a debt relief order in relation to each qualifying debt specified in the order ('a specified qualifying debt').

(2) During the moratorium, the creditor to whom a specified qualifying debt is owed –

    (a) has no remedy in respect of the debt, and

    (b) may not –

        (i) commence a creditor's petition in respect of the debt, or

        (ii) otherwise commence any action or other legal proceedings against the debtor for the debt,

    except with the permission of the court and on such terms as the court may impose.

(3) If on the effective date a creditor to whom a specified qualifying debt is owed has any such petition, action or other proceeding as mentioned in subsection (2)(b) pending in any court, the court may –

    (a) stay the proceedings on the petition, action or other proceedings (as the case may be), or

    (b) allow them to continue on such terms as the court thinks fit.

(4) In subsection (2)(a) and (b) references to the debt include a reference to any interest, penalty or other sum that becomes payable in relation to that debt after the application date.

(5) Nothing in this section affects the right of a secured creditor of the debtor to enforce his security.'

19.11   In *Godfrey v A2 Dominion Homes Ltd*,[9] which was heard and decided with *Sharples v Places for People Ltd* (above, para 19.9), Mr Godfrey was an assured tenant. He fell into rent arrears and the landlord issued possession proceedings on HA 1988 Sch 2 grounds 10 and 11. Before the possession hearing the Insolvency Service had approved a DRO in respect of the tenant which included the rent arrears. At the possession hearing, it was argued for the tenant that section 251G prevented the court from making an order for possession in respect of the arrears. The county court disagreed and made a suspended possession order conditional on payments of the current rent plus £5 per week off the arrears. The Court of Appeal held that its analysis in *Sharples*[10] of the meaning of the phrase 'remedy in respect of [a] debt' in IA 1986 s285 was equally applicable to section 251G and the DRO regime. Again, this was the case irrespective of the tenant's security of tenure. However, it would not be reasonable for the Court to make

9 [2011] EWCA Civ 813, [2011] HLR 45.
10 See para 19.9 above.

an order for possession which required the tenant to pay an amount off the arrears which had been included in the DRO. Such an order would be inconsistent with the policy behind a DRO, namely, a one-year moratorium on the enforcement of debts included in the DRO followed by the elimination of the indebtedness. It was open to the court, however, to make a possession order suspended on payment of current rent and of any arrears which were not included in the DRO. The county court had therefore been wrong to make a suspended possession order conditional on payment by the tenant of the arrears included in the DRO. The possession order was varied so that it was suspended on payment of the current rent plus £5 per week off the costs.

19.12   The Court further held that where possession proceedings are taken against a bankrupt tenant on discretionary grounds, it would be inconsistent with the purpose of a bankruptcy order to make a suspended or postponed possession order which required payment of arrears provable in the bankruptcy. However, the obligation to pay current rent due after the bankruptcy is not affected. An order could therefore be suspended on payment of the current rent and of any arrears which had accrued since the bankruptcy.

19.13   The Court of Appeal in *Sharples* and *Godfrey* rejected the argument that a landlord was required by IA 1986 s285(3)(b) (in respect of a bankrupt tenant) or s251G(2)(b) (in respect of a tenant subject to a DRO) to obtain the court's permission before bringing possession proceedings where no money claim is made in respect of arrears which were provable in the bankruptcy or specified in the DRO. Nor should such proceedings be stayed, whether under section 285(1) or (2) or under section 251G(3).

19.14   Accordingly, the Court of Appeal in *Sharples* and *Godfrey* summarised its conclusions as follows:

> (1) an order for possession of property subject to a tenancy, including an assured tenancy, on the ground of arrears of rent, which are provable in the bankruptcy of the tenant, is not a 'remedy ... in respect of that debt' within IA 1986 s285(3)(a);
> (2) that is so, whether the order is an outright order for possession or is a conditional suspended possession order;
> (3) IA 1986 s285(3)(b) is implicitly limited to legal proceedings against the bankrupt 'in respect of that debt'; that is to say, it is qualified in the same way as IA 1986 s285(3)(a);
> (4) accordingly, proceedings for an order for possession of property subject to a tenancy, including an assured tenancy, on the ground of rent arrears, in which no claim is made for arrears provable in the

tenant's bankruptcy, are not subject to the automatic stay in IA 1986 s285(3)(b);

(5) an order for possession of property subject to a tenancy, including an assured tenancy, on the ground of arrears of rent, which are the subject of the tenant's DRO, is not a 'remedy in respect of the debt' within IA 1986 s251G(2)(a), whether the order is an outright order for possession or is a conditional suspended possession order;

(6) proceedings for possession of property subject to an assured tenancy on the ground of rent arrears, which are provable in the tenant's bankruptcy or are the subject of the tenant's DRO, should not normally be stayed under IA 1986 s285(1) or (2) or IA 1986 s251G(3);

(7) on the hearing of such proceedings, no order can be made for payment of such arrears; nor should a suspended order for possession be made conditional on payment of such arrears, but it should be made conditional on payment of any other arrears (ie those not provable in the bankruptcy or subject to the DRO) and current rent.[11]

19.15   Following the decision in *Sharples* and *Godfrey*, it is clear that a landlord can apply for a possession order against a tenant in rent arrears who has been made bankrupt or who has entered into a DRO, regardless of the tenant's security of tenure. Rent arrears accrued at the date of the bankruptcy order or DRO are provable debts or qualifying debts respectively. However, while a landlord can rely on pre-bankruptcy or pre-DRO arrears as evidence that a ground for possession is made out, any suspended or postponed possession order made on a discretionary ground cannot require repayment of any arrears which have been included in the bankruptcy or DRO. Therefore, the bankrupt tenant, or tenant with a DRO, will not have to make payment of those arrears as a condition of the order. The landlord, as a creditor, will lose his or her rights to recover the arrears, except by way of distribution in the bankruptcy or DRO. A tenant in these circumstances may, however, be ordered to pay the current (future) rent together with an amount for arrears which have accrued since the bankruptcy order or which were not included in the DRO, together with costs. See *Irwell Valley Housing Association Ltd v Docherty*,[12] in which a postponed possession order had been made before the DRO. The DRO had expunged only the judgment debt, but the arrears had increased because the tenant had not paid the current rent during the moratorium period.

19.16   It follows that a possession order suspended *prior to* the making of the bankruptcy order or DRO may be varied after the making of

11 Per Etherton LJ, para 95.
12 [2012] EWCA Civ 704.

the order to exclude payment of the rent arrears from the judgment debt.[13] In these circumstances, a tenant should be advised to apply to the court for a variation so that the rent arrears included in the bankruptcy or DRO are no longer subject to the suspended order.

13 See The Insolvency Service, *Intermediary Guidance Notes* (V14.0), October 2015, p9.

CHAPTER 20

Domestic relationship breakdown in a rented home

Introduction

20.1   This chapter outlines briefly the steps which may be taken to maintain occupation of the family home where there has been a breakdown of the domestic relationship between the adult occupiers – most commonly between spouses or other cohabitants – and the home is rented. (For the parallel position on relationship breakdown where the family home is held on a mortgage, see chapter 39.) These few pages are only intended to highlight some of the issues.

20.2   Often a crisis in relation to occupation of the rented home (for example, the service of possession proceedings) arises at the same time as, or shortly after, a breakdown in the domestic relationship between occupiers. For example, as a result of the relationship breakdown one partner may have moved out, jeopardising security of tenure and/or leaving the other facing financial difficulties in paying the rent, which will put the home at risk.

20.3   Where the landlord has not yet threatened possession proceedings there is usually time to get advice about immediate entitlement to remain in the home and any rights to obtain a transfer of the tenancy. Where very urgent action is needed (for example, to prevent violence or to prevent the loss of the tenancy), the client should be immediately directed to a source of specialist advice on family law.

Preserving the tenancy

20.4   The following paragraphs are concerned with the situation in which not only has the relationship broken down but also one of the partners has *left* the family home.

Sole tenant in occupation

20.5   If the partner remaining in the family home is the sole tenant there should be little difficulty in preserving the home until the issues arising from the relationship breakdown are resolved. Where the breakdown of the relationship has caused financial difficulties this may trigger an entitlement for the tenant to housing benefit or to higher payments of such benefit. If, however, possession proceedings are threatened or have been launched, the appropriate chapters of this book should assist in avoiding dispossession.

Sole tenant has left

20.6   In this scenario there are twin concerns for the partner remaining in possession. The first is to prevent the departed tenant from ending the tenancy. The second is to ensure that the tenancy retains any security of tenure and survives any possession proceedings brought by the landlord. In the longer term, once those matters have been addressed, the partner remaining may seek to have the tenancy transferred into his or her sole name as part of the legal arrangements made to resolve the consequences of the relationship breakdown.

20.7   If the remaining occupier is a *spouse* or *civil partner* of the sole tenant he or she enjoys legal rights of occupation (and associated benefits) by virtue of the 'home rights' conferred by the Family Law Act 1996 s30 for as long as the marriage or civil partnership lasts. Any question of occupation thereafter should be addressed in the legal proceedings to end the marriage or partnership.

20.8   The *cohabitant* of the departed tenant, who remains in occupation, by contrast, has no such automatic rights to continue to occupy the home but can apply to the court for an 'occupation order' under the Family Law Act 1996 s36. If granted, that confers rights equivalent to the home rights enjoyed by a spouse or civil partner.[1]

20.9   If there is any risk that the departed sole tenant may end the tenancy without other arrangements being in place for the continued occupation of the former family home, the non-tenant partner may need to move very quickly to obtain a court order to prevent the tenant from either giving notice to quit or surrendering the tenancy. Such a pre-emptive injunction is, for obvious reasons, usually sought without notice to the tenant until after the injunction is granted. Where the partners are married, the family court has jurisdiction to grant such an injunction under the Matrimonial Causes Act 1973 s37(2)(a). Where the partners are unmarried, the jurisdiction will be based on the court's power to grant interim relief in proceedings under the Family Law Act 1996 or the Children Act 1989 (brought to obtain an occupation order or to achieve a transfer of the tenancy from the tenant partner).[2]

20.10   If no such protection is obtained from the court, the sole tenant could simply end the tenancy by giving notice to quit or by agreeing a surrender with the landlord (although the latter would be unusual as the presence of the former partner will prevent the tenant giving

---

1   *Gay v Enfield LBC* [2000] 1 WLR 673, (1999) 31 HLR 1126, CA.
2   *Greenwich LBC v Bater* [1999] 4 All ER 944, (2000) 32 HLR 127, CA and *Re F (Minors)* [1994] 1 WLR 370, (1993) 26 HLR 354, CA.

vacant possession).[3] This may happen very fast, for example, because the landlord is prepared to waive any requirements as to length or formality of the notice to quit.[4] Once the tenancy has been ended it will plainly not be available for the purpose of being transferred from one partner to the other. It will also be too late for even a spouse or civil partner to set aside the termination of the tenancy.[5] The owner would be able to seek possession against the remaining former partner as a trespasser.

20.11   If the departed tenant's tenancy is continuing, the remaining partner needs to ensure that the tenancy is safeguarded until other arrangements can be made. For example, if the tenant's rent is not being paid, the remaining partner could pay it. If the remaining partner is a spouse or civil partner, any payments he or she makes are treated by law as though they had been made by the tenant and must be accepted as such.[6] Likewise, a payment of rent made by a cohabitant with an occupation order is treated as being made by the tenant.[7] Housing benefit may be claimed by the occupying partner if the person legally liable to pay for the family home is not paying.[8]

20.12   Although the sole tenant is not physically present, the continued occupation by the former partner may operate to preserve any security of tenure that the tenant enjoyed. Where the remaining occupier is the tenant's spouse or civil partner, his or her own occupation is deemed to be occupation by the tenant for the purposes of preserving security of tenure as a protected, assured, secure, demoted or introductory tenant.[9] The same 'deemed occupation' arises if the remaining partner is a cohabitant who has successfully applied for an occupation order.[10]

20.13   The remaining partner may also have to intervene in any possession proceedings taken against the sole tenant in order to preserve the home.

20.14   If those possession proceedings are based on the proposition that any security of tenure has been lost by failure of the sole tenant –

---

3   But see *Sanctuary Housing Association v Campbell* [1999] 1 WLR 1279, (2000) 32 HLR 100, CA.

4   *Hackney LBC v Snowden* (2001) 33 HLR 554, [2001] L&TR 6, CA.

5   *Harrow LBC v Johnstone* [1997] 1 WLR 459, (1997) 29 HLR 475, HL and *Newlon Housing Association v Al-Sulaimen* [1999] 1 AC 313, (1998) 30 HLR 1132, HL.

6   Family Law Act 1996 s30(3).

7   Family Law Act 1996 s36(13).

8   Housing Benefit Regulations 2006 SI No 213 reg 8.

9   Family Law Act 1996 s30(4).

10   Family Law Act 1996 s36(13).

who has left – to occupy the premises as his or her home, the remaining partner may be able to be joined as a party to the proceedings and then defend successfully on the basis that there is continuing deemed occupation by a spouse or civil partner with home rights or by a cohabitant with an occupation order (see para 20.12).

20.15   If the possession proceedings are based on one of the grounds for possession which requires the court to be satisfied that suitable alternative accommodation is available, this may involve (consequent on a relationship breakdown) the provision of separate units of housing for the tenant and his or her partner. Any spouse, civil partner or cohabitant anxious that he or she should be adequately housed if possession is ordered against the tenant in these circumstances should apply to be joined as a party to the proceedings.[11]

Joint tenant remaining in occupation[12]

20.16   The first priority for the joint tenant who remains in occupation of a family home held on a joint tenancy is to ensure that the other joint tenant does not bring the joint tenancy to an end. Although the other joint tenant, acting alone, cannot end the joint tenancy by means of a surrender, a joint tenancy can be ended by that tenant giving the landlord a notice to quit. The other joint tenant need not even inform or consult the one in occupation before giving such notice.[13] The effect of a valid notice to quit is to bring the whole joint tenancy to an end,[14] which obviously leaves the former partner in occupation as a trespasser and entitles the landlord to possession.[15]

20.17   If there is any risk that the departed joint tenant may end the tenancy without other arrangements being in place for the continued occupation of the former family home, the joint-tenant partner may need to move very quickly to obtain a court order to prevent the other joint tenant from giving notice to quit. Such a pre-emptive injunction is, for obvious reasons, usually sought without notice to the other joint tenant until after the injunction is granted. Where the

---

11   *Wandsworth LBC v Fadayomi* [1987] 1 WLR 1473, (1987) 19 HLR 512, CA. See CPR 19.4.

12   Jenrick and Bretherton, 'Joint tenancies: continuing implications for housing and family law' [2000] JHL 8.

13   *Notting Hill Housing Trust v Brackley* [2001] EWCA Civ 601, [2002] HLR 10, CA.

14   *Hammersmith and Fulham LBC v Monk* [1992] 1 AC 478, [1990] 3 WLR 1144, HL; *Crawley BC v Ure* [1996] QB 13, (1995) 27 HLR 524 and *Sims v Dacorum BC* [2014] UKSC 63, [2015] HLR 7.

15   *Greenwich LBC v McGrady* (1983) 81 LGR 288, (1982) 6 HLR 36, CA.

partners are married, the family court potentially has jurisdiction to grant such an injunction under the Matrimonial Causes Act 1973 s37(2)(a).[16] Where the partners are unmarried, the jurisdiction may be based on the court's power to grant interim relief in proceedings under the Family Law Act 1996 or the Children Act 1989 (brought to obtain an occupation order or to achieve a transfer of the tenancy from joint to sole names).[17]

20.18   If a joint tenant has already given a notice to quit, it should be checked for validity. A notice not complying with the relevant contractual or statutory requirements is not effective to terminate the tenancy (because the agreement of all joint tenants is needed to waive any defect).[18] If it is a valid notice, it terminates the tenancy and cannot be set aside, even in matrimonial proceedings.[19] See para 14.17 onwards for further discussion concerning the validity of notices to quit.

20.19   Of course, if the landlord is prepared to grant the remaining party a new sole tenancy with equivalent security of tenure, there is no difficulty caused by either partner giving notice to quit.

20.20   It may be possible for the two joint tenants to 'regularise' matters either by the departed tenant completing a deed of release or by both joint tenants assigning the tenancy into the sole name of one of them. In either case, the remaining joint tenant becomes the sole tenant. However, these options may not be available in respect of some tenancies. There have been particular difficulties with secure joint tenancies in this regard.[20]

20.21   If the departing joint tenant fails to make any contribution towards the rent, the remaining joint tenant may obtain assistance from the housing benefit scheme both towards his or her own 'share' of the rent and towards the share of the former partner (see chapter 16).

20.22   The joint tenant may rely on his or her own occupation as meeting any necessary conditions of residence for retention of security of tenure (for example, the continued occupation by one of several

---

16 See *Newlon Housing Trust v Alsulaimen and Another* [1998] UKHL 35, [1999] AC 313.

17 *Greenwich LBC v Bater* [1999] 4 All ER 944, (2000) 32 HLR 127, CA.

18 *Hounslow LBC v Pilling* [1993] 1 WLR 1242, (1993) 25 HLR 305, CA. Cf *Ealing Family Housing Association Ltd v McKenzie* [2003] EWCA Civ 1602, [2004] HLR 21 and *Fletcher v Brent LBC* [2006] EWCA Civ 960, [2007] HLR 12.

19 *Harrow LBC v Johnstone* [1997] 1 WLR 459, (1997) 29 HLR 475, HL and *Newlon Housing Association v Al-Sulaimen* [1999] 1 AC 313, (1998) 30 HLR 1132, HL.

20 *Burton v Camden LBC* [2000] 2 AC 399, (2000) 32 HLR 625, HL and Blandy, 'Secure Tenancies and Relationship Breakdown Revisited' [2000] JHL 47.

joint secure tenants maintains the 'security of tenure' of a secure or assured tenancy).[21]

20.23   In any possession proceedings, the joint tenant may defend in just the same way as a sole tenant.

Transferring the tenancy[22]

20.24   In the longer term, the sensible outcome following a relationship breakdown is often the making of a court order for transfer of the tenancy (if that is needed) into the sole name of the partner remaining in the home. Jurisdiction to make such orders is available both in the Matrimonial Causes Act 1973 s24 (for spouses) and in the Family Law Act 1996 s53 (for spouses, civil partners and cohabitants). Alternatively, where the parties are parents, an order can be made for a transfer of the tenancy for the benefit of a child.[23] Procedural rules make provision for notice to be given to the landlord. The housing statutes themselves make provision for the consequences of such transfer orders being made (see, for example, HA 1985 s91(3)(b) in relation to orders for transfer of secure tenancies). Any competent family law specialist should be familiar with the process involved in securing an order for the transfer of the tenancy.

21 HA 1985 s81 and HA 1988 s1.
22 See Bridge, 'Transferring tenancies of the family home' [1998] Fam Law 26.
23 Children Act 1989 Sch 1 para 1(2)(e).

Possession procedure

Procedure in possession proceedings

continued

The need for possession proceedings

21.1 In relation to mortgaged property, it is not strictly necessary at common law for lenders to obtain a possession order in order to take possession. In practice, however, in order to ensure that they are able to sell the property as mortgagees in possession, it is necessary for lenders to take possession proceedings.[1] In most situations involving residential occupiers of rented premises it is necessary for landlords who wish to evict occupiers to take possession proceedings through the courts. In other cases, it is usual for landlords to take proceedings, even though they are not obliged to do so (see para 21.5 below). In many circumstances, landlords who take the law into their own hands by evicting people without first obtaining court orders risk prosecution under the Protection from Eviction Act (PEA) 1977, together with a possibility of a fine and/or imprisonment and/or a claim for substantial damages for breach of covenant for quiet enjoyment, trespass and/or unlawful eviction under the Housing Act (HA) 1988 ss27 and 28.[2] However, there are exceptions which advisers should bear in mind.

Trespassers

21.2 See chapter 23 for the specific procedural rules relating to possession proceedings against trespassers. However, court proceedings are not always necessary to evict trespassers. See paras 21.3–21.6 below.

Excluded licences and tenancies[3]

21.3 PEA 1977 s3[4] prohibits eviction without due process of law, ie, without a court order, for lawful occupiers who do not have security of tenure. However, PEA 1977 s3A[5] creates categories of 'excluded' tenancies and licences to which the protection of section 3 does not apply. The combined effect of these sections is that if there is an excluded tenancy or licence, a landlord who evicts without a court order may not be committing a criminal offence under PEA 1977 s1 (unlawful eviction and harassment) and, if the tenancy or licence has

---

1 See chapters 33 and 34.
2 See Arden, Chan and Madge-Wyld *Quiet enjoyment*, 7th edn, LAG, 2012.
3 See also paras 15.5–15.10.
4 See para 15.2.
5 See para 15.5.

been properly terminated (for example, by service of a valid notice to quit), the occupier has no civil redress.

21.4   A tenancy or licence is excluded if:

- under its terms the occupier shares any accommodation with the landlord or licensor and immediately before the tenancy or licence was granted and also at the time it comes to an end, the landlord or licensor occupied as his or her only or principal home 'premises of which the whole or part of the shared accommodation formed part';
- the tenant or licensee shares accommodation with a member of the family of the landlord or licensor and the landlord or licensor has his or her only or principal home in the building where the shared accommodation is situated;
- it was granted as a temporary expedient to someone who entered the premises as a trespasser;
- it confers on the tenant or licensee the right to occupy premises for a holiday only;
- it is granted otherwise than for money or money's worth;
- it is a licence of a room in a hostel[6] provided by a social sector landlord, such as a local authority, housing association or other registered provider of social housing; or
- it is granted to provide accommodation to asylum-seekers under the Immigration and Asylum Act 1999 Part VI; or to provide accommodation under the Displaced Persons (Temporary Protection) Regulations 2005;[7] or
- (Under provisions which are not in force at the date of publication) it is a letting of premises which are subject to a Secretary of State's notice under Immigration Act 2014 s33D identifying occupiers who do not have the 'right to rent'.

Case-law has determined that other categories of letting are also excluded from section 3. Where a homeless person has been placed in interim accommodation[8] pending the local housing authority's decision, or in certain other kinds of temporary accommodation

---

6 A 'hostel' means 'a building in which is provided, for persons generally or for a class or classes of persons – (a) residential accommodation otherwise than in separate and self-contained sets of premises, and (b) either board or facilities for the preparation of food adequate to the needs of those persons, or both' (HA 1985 s622).

7 SI No 1379: see reg 5. The class applies to persons granted 'temporary protection', meaning limited leave to enter or remain granted pursuant to Part 11A of the Immigration Rules HC 395.

8 Under HA 1996 s188(1).

under HA 1996 Part 7, such accommodation is not considered to be 'occupied as a dwelling' and so does not attract the protection of section 3. The Supreme Court has rejected the argument that eviction without a court order in these circumstances amounted to a violation of Human Rights Act 1998 Sch 1 Article 8.[9]

21.5   From the point of view of landlords, it may be wise to take possession proceedings even if they believe that there is an excluded tenancy or licence. This is because there is not only the risk that the tenancy or licence may not, in fact, be excluded, but also, if the occupants are on the premises at the time of eviction, the possibility of a prosecution under the Criminal Law Act 1977 s6 (using or threatening violence to secure entry to premises where there is someone present on the premises who is opposed to the entry). Prosecutions can be brought under the Criminal Law Act 1977 s6 even if the occupiers are trespassers. An offence may be committed under section 6 of that Act 'whether the violence in question is directed against the person or against property'.[10]

21.6   If a landlord is threatening to evict without obtaining a possession order, and the occupiers believe that they enjoy some form of security of tenure, the occupiers could seek an injunction from the county court and apply for a declaration concerning their status. However, while legal aid is available, subject to financial eligibilty, to enable an occupier to defend a possession claim, it is no longer available in relation to claims for an injunction or a declaration in these circumstances unless the occupier has been unlawfuly evicted.[11]

Possession procedure

21.7   Civil Procedure Rules 1998 (CPR) Part 55 applies to most claims for possession. The procedure set out in CPR 55 Part I (General Rules) must be used where the claim includes a possession claim brought:

- by a landlord (or former landlord);
- by a mortgagee;
- by a licensor (or former licensor); or
- against trespassers.[12]

9 *R (CN and ZH) v Lewisham LBC and Newham LBC* [2014] UKSC 62, [2015] HLR 6.
10 Criminal Law Act 1977 s6(4)(a).
11 See chapter 24 and Legal Aid, Sentencing and Punishment of Offenders Act 2012 Sch 1 para 33.
12 CPR 55.2.

21.8   The General Rules do not apply to:

- accelerated proceedings for possession of assured shorthold tenancies. These are dealt with in Part II of CPR 55 (see chapter 22).
- claims against squatters for an interim possession order under the Criminal Justice and Public Order Act 1994. These are dealt with in Part III of CPR 55 (see chapter 23).
- claims for a demotion order[13] only. These are governed by Part III of CPR 65.
- claims for possession of business premises, including tenancies of mixed business and residential premises.[14]

The full text of CPR Part 55 and its Practice Directions is set out in appendix F.

Before commencing possession proceedings, social landlords must ensure that they have complied with the *Pre-action Protocol for possession claims by social landlords.*[15] Lenders must similarly comply with the *Pre-action Protocol for possession claims based on mortgage or home purchase plan arrears in respect of residential property.*[16]

Issue of proceedings – which court?

21.9   Possession proceedings may be started at any county court hearing centre. If a claim is started in a hearing centre which is not the centre for the district where the property is situated, the claim will be transferred to the hearing centre which serves the address of the property.[17] A claimant may start proceedings in the High Court only if there are exceptional circumstances[18] such as:

- complicated disputes of fact;
- points of law of general importance; or
- where, in a claim against trespassers, there is a substantial risk of public disturbance or of serious harm to people or property which properly require immediate determination.

---

13 See chapter 6.
14 Such cases will usually fall within Part II of the Landlord and Tenant Act 1954: *Patel v Pirabakaran* [2006] EWCA Civ 685, [2006] 1 WLR 3112.
15 See appendix E and paras 3.77–3.80.
16 See appendix E and paras 37.3–37.14.
17 CPR 55.3(1). See also PD 55A para 1.1.
18 PD 55A para 1.3.

21.10 The value of the property and the amount of any financial claim may be relevant circumstances, but they alone do not usually justify starting the claim in the High Court. Practice Direction (PD) 55A sets out the consequences of issuing in the High Court when not justified:

> If a claimant starts a claim in the High Court and the court decides that it should have been started in the county court, the court will normally either strike the claim out or transfer it to the county court on its own initiative. This is likely to result in delay and the court will normally disallow the costs of starting the claim in the High Court and of any transfer.[19]

21.11 If a claim is issued in the High Court it must be accompanied by a certificate stating the reasons for bringing the claim in the High Court, verified by a statement of truth.[20]

21.12 In addition, statute provides that landlords who initiate proceedings in the High Court may be prohibited from recovering some or all of their costs.[21]

Starting proceedings

21.13 The landlord, as the person in whom title to the property is vested, is the only person entitled to be claimant. If there are joint landlords, both or all of them must be claimants unless the court orders otherwise.[22] An agent of the landlord has no standing to bring proceedings in his or her own name.[23]

21.14 Claim forms and particulars of claim in possession actions must be in the prescribed form.[24] They must be verified by a statement of

---

19 PD 55A para 1.2. See *Enfield LBC v Phoenix* [2013] EWHC 4286 (QB), in which it was held that the human rights contentions raised by the defendants were not so complex as to justify issuing proceedings in the High Court and that there was no present substantial risk of public disturbance of a nature that would require immediate determination of the possession claim. See also *Crompton v Woodford Scrap Metal Ltd* [2014] EWHC 1260 (QB).

20 CPR 55.3(2). See *Crompton v Woodford Scrap Metal Ltd* [2014] EWHC 1260 (QB), in which the absence of such a certificate resulted in the case being transferred to the county court.

21 RA 1977 s141(4), HA 1985 s110(3) and HA 1988 s40(4).

22 CPR 19.3.

23 *Chesters Accomodation Agency v Abebrese* [1997] EWCA Civ 2137, (1997) *Times* 28 July.

24 PD 55A para 1.5. The forms are listed in Table 1 of CPR Practice Direction 4. They are forms N5 (claim form for possession of property); N5A (claim form for relief against forfeiture); N5B (claim form for possession of property (accelerated procedure) (assured shorthold tenancy); N119 (particulars of claim

truth.[25] CPR 22.2(1) provides that without a statement of truth the proceedings remain effective, but the claimant's case will need to be supported by evidence given subsequently (either in person or by witness statement). Alternatively, the court may strike out a statement of case which is not verified by a statement of truth. It is essential that statements of case should be properly verified. For details of who may sign a statement of truth, generally, see PD 22.3. The requirement in CPR 22.1(a) for the statement of case to be signed is not a mere technicality or a matter of form. It has been held, at first instance,[26] that a statement of truth in a possession claim form which had not been signed personally, but which bore the rubber stamp of a signature of an employee in the claimant's legal services department who had no personal knowledge of the case, had not been 'signed' within the meaning of CPR 22.1.

21.15   In a claim against trespassers, if the claimant does not know the names of all the people in occupation, the claim must be brought against 'persons unknown' in addition to any named defendants.[27]

Particulars of claim

21.16   Particulars of claim must be filed and served with the claim form.[28] Except where the accelerated possession procedure is used, or the claimant is applying for an interim possession order against trespassers, particulars of claim must take one of the following forms:

- Form N119 (claims in respect of rented residential property);
- Form N120 (claims in respect of mortgaged residential property);
- Form N121 (claims against trespassers).

Particulars of claim in the standard form are reproduced in the precedents in appendix B.[29]

---

for possession of rented residential premises); N120 (particulars of claim for possession of mortgaged residential premises) and N121 (particulars of claim for possession: claim against trespassers).

25 CPR 22.1.
26 *Birmingham City Council v Hosey* December 2002 *Legal Action* 20, Birmingham County Court (HHJ MacDuff QC).
27 CPR 55.3(4). See chapter 23.
28 CPR 55.4.
29 Forms can be downloaded at www.justice.gov.uk/courts/procedure-rules/civil/forms.

21.17 All particulars of claim in possession cases must:

- identify the land or property to which the claim relates;[30]
- state whether it is residential property;[31]
- state the ground on which possession is claimed;[32]
- give full details of any mortgage or tenancy agreement;[33]
- give details of every person who, to the best of the claimant's knowledge, is in possession of the property;[34] and
- comply with CPR 16, ie the particulars must contain a concise statement of the facts relied upon, and, if interest is sought, give details of the claim for interest.

21.18 There are additional requirements for particulars of claim where the claim relates to a tenancy of residential premises.[35] If the claimant alleges that there has been non-payment of rent, the particulars of claim must state:

- the amount due at the start of proceedings;
- in schedule form:
  - the dates when arrears of rent arose;
  - all amounts of rent due;
  - the dates and amounts of all payments made; and
  - a running total of the arrears.

  In general, the schedule should cover the preceding two years, or if the first date of default occurred less than two years before the date of issue, it should cover the period from the first date of default. However, if the claimant wishes to rely on a history of arrears which is longer than two years, this should be stated in the particulars and a full schedule should be exhibited to a witness statement;[36]
- the daily rate of any rent and interest;
- any previous steps taken to recover arrears, with full details of any court proceedings; and
- any relevant information about the defendant's circumstances, including whether the defendant is in receipt of social security benefits and whether any such benefits are paid direct to the landord.

---

30 PD 55A para 2.1(1).
31 PD 55A para 2.1(2).
32 PD 55A para 2.1(3).
33 PD 55A para 2.1(4).
34 PD 55A para 2.1(5).
35 PD 55A para 2.3.
36 PD 55A, para 2.3A.

21.19 If the claim for possession relates to the conduct of the tenant, the particulars of claim must state details of the conduct alleged.[37] If the possession claim relies on a statutory ground or grounds for possession, the particulars of claim must specify the ground or grounds relied on.[38]

21.20   The particulars of claim should also give the name of any person known to be entitled to apply for relief from forfeiture. In those circumstances, the claimant must file a copy of the particulars of claim for service on any person who is entitled to apply for relief from forfeiture.[39]

21.21   If the claimant is a mortgage lender who is seeking possession of residential premises, the particulars of claim must state:[40]

- details of the mortgage account, including:
  - the amount of the advance, any periodic repayments and payments of interest required to be made;
  - the amount required to redeem the mortgage, including any solicitors' costs and administration charges payable;
  - if the loan secured by the mortgage is a regulated consumer credit agreement, the total amount outstanding under the terms of the agreement; and
  - the rate of interest payable (i) at the commencement of the mortgage, (ii) immediately before any arrears accrued, and (iii) at the commencement of proceedings;
- relevant information about the defendant's circumstances, in particular, details of any social security benefits and whether direct payments of benefit are made to the claimant;
- previous steps taken by the claimant to recover money secured by the mortgage and details of any court proceedings;
- whether the loan secured by the mortgage is a regulated consumer credit agreement and, if so, the date when notice was given under section 76 (notice of intention to recover possession) or section 87 (default notice) of the Consumer Credit Act 1974;
- whether a Class F land charge has been registered or a notice under the Matrimonial Homes Act 1983 has been entered, and whether a notice under the Family Law Act 1996 has been registered (and if any of these things have been done, the claimant

37 PD 55A para 2.4A.
38 PD 55A para 2.4B.
39 PD 55A para 2.4. For further details as to forfeiture, see para 14.46.
40 PD 55A para 2.5.

must serve notice of proceedings upon the person named in the charge or notice).

21.22 If the claim is based on mortgage arrears, the particulars of claim must set out:

- a schedule of the dates when the arrears arose, all amounts due and paid and a running total of arrears;
- details of any other payments required to be made under the terms of the agreement, such as insurance premiums, penalties, legal costs and administrative charges;
- details of any other sums claimed; and
- whether or not any of these payments is in arrears and whether or not it is included in the amount of any periodic payment.[41]

If the claimant wishes to rely on a history of arrears which is longer than two years, it should state this in its particulars of claim and exhibit a full (or longer) schedule to a witness statement.[42]

21.23 In mortgage possession proceedings brought against the landlord of an unauthorised tenant[43] by the landlord's lender, the tenant may in some circumstances apply to the court under Mortgage Repossessions (Protection of Tenants etc) Act 2010 for the order for possession to be suspended for two months.[44]

21.24 There are additional requirements for particulars of claim where the claim is against trespassers.[45] The particulars of claim must state the claimant's interest in the land or the basis of his right to claim possession, together with the circumstances in which the land was occupied without licence or consent.

21.25 The effect of a failure by a claimant to comply with these rules depends on the circumstances. CPR 3.10 provides that, where there has been an error of procedure, such as a failure to comply with a rule or practice direction, the error does not invalidate any step taken unless the court so orders and the court may make an order to remedy the error. If information is missing, it will be necessary for the claimant to seek permission to amend the particulars under CPR 17.1(3), either at the hearing or (depending on whether the defendant needs further time to prepare his or her case as a result of receiving the information) following an adjournment. On the other hand,

---

41 PD 55A para 2.5.
42 PD 55A para 2.5A.
43 ie, where the lender has not consented to the creation of the tenancy by its borrower (the landlord).
44 CPR 55.10(4A). See paras 15.11–15.19.
45 PD 55A para 2.6. See chapter 23.

if the failure to comply with the rules has been deliberate, with the intention of obtaining an unfair advantage against the defendant, the court has power to strike out the claim.[46]

Possession Claims Online (PCOL)

21.26   Practice Direction 55B[47] enables landlords and mortgagees to start certain possession claims under CPR 55 by requesting the issue of a claim form electronically via the PCOL website. Where a claim has been started electronically, the claimant, the defendant and their representatives may then take further steps in the claim electronically, using PCOL. Parties may communicate with the court using the messaging service facility, available on the PCOL website.[48]

21.27   A possession claim may be started online if:

- it is brought under Section I of CPR Part 55; and
- it includes a possession claim for residential property by a landlord against a tenant, solely on the ground of arrears of rent (but not a claim for forfeiture of a lease); or
- it is brought by a mortgagee against a mortgagor, solely on the ground of default in the payment of sums due under a mortgage; and
- it does not include a claim for any other remedy except for payment of arrears of rent or money due under a mortgage, interest and costs.[49]

21.28   Landlords and mortgagees may request the issue of proceedings by completing an online claim form at the PCOL website and paying the appropriate issue fee electronically via PCOL or by some other means approved by Her Majesty's Courts and Tribunals Service (HMCTS). The particulars of claim must be included in the online claim form and may not be filed separately. It is not necessary for the landlord or mortgagee to file a copy of the tenancy agreement, mortgage deed or mortgage agreement with the particulars of claim. The particulars of claim must include a history of the rent or mortgage account in schedule form, setting out:

---

46 CPR 3.4.
47 Reproduced in appendix F.
48 Details and a User Guide are available at www.possessionclaim.gov.uk/pcol.
49 CPR PD 55B para 5.1.

- the dates and amounts of all payments due and payments made under the tenancy agreement, mortgage deed or mortgage agreement, either from the first date of default if that date occurred less than two years before the date of issue or otherwise for a period of two years immediately preceding the date of issue; and
- a running total of the arrears.[50]

21.29 When the court issues the claim, it should serve a printed version of the claim form and a defence form on the defendant by post in the usual manner. The claim form should have printed on it a unique customer identification number or a password by which the defendant may access the claim on the PCOL website. Tenants may file defences (and, if appropriate, counterclaims) in the ordinary way, by filing the document with the court.[51] Alternatively, they may complete the relevant online form at the PCOL website, and, if, making a counterclaim, pay the appropriate fee electronically via PCOL or by some other means approved by HMCTS.[52]

21.30 All statements of case (including online claims, defences and application notices) must be verified by a statement of truth.[53] Some applications may also be made electronically.[54] Landlords may request the issue of warrants of possession electronically.[55] Tenants may apply electronically for the suspension of warrants,[56] by completing an online application for suspension at the PCOL website and paying the appropriate fee electronically or by some other means approved by HMCTS. When an online application for suspension is received, an acknowledgment of receipt should automatically be sent to the defendant by the court, but that acknowledgment does not constitute a notice that the online application has been served.

---

50 CPR PD 55B para 6.3. Alternatively, if the claimant has, before commencing proceedings, provided the defendant with a full schedule of the arrears, it is sufficient to include in the particulars of claim a summary of the arrears, provided that the claimant complies with the requirements of CPR PD 55B paras 6.3A–6.3C.
51 See paras 21.35 (Defences) and 21.42 (Counterclaims).
52 CPR PD 55B para 7.1.
53 CPR PD 55B para 8.1. For the form of a statement of truth, see CPR PD 22 paras 2 and 3.
54 CPR PD 55B para 11.1.
55 See para 31.35.
56 CPR PD 55B para 13.1. See para 31.56.

Date of hearing

21.31   On the issue of a possession claim form, the court should fix a date for the first hearing.[57] The hearing date will be not less than 28 days from the date of issue[58] but the standard period between issue of the claim and the hearing will be not more than eight weeks.[59] The defendant must be served with the claim form and particulars of claim not less than 21 days before the hearing date.[60] Shorter periods apply to claims against trespassers (see para 21.33 below).

Service of the claim form

21.32   The standard Civil Procedure Rules on service apply to ordinary possession claims. CPR Part 6 allows the court to arrange personal service, delivery by first class post, for the claim form to be left at the defendant's last known address, or service via the document exchange. Alternatively, the claimant may arrange service. Special rules apply to service of claims brought against trespassers.[61]

21.33   The period between service and hearing must be at least:

- two days where there is a claim against trespassers for possession of non-residential land;
- five days where there is a claim against trespassers for possession of residential premises; or
- 21 days for all other possession claims.[62]

21.34   However, those periods may be shortened.[63] Practice Direction 55A states that particular consideration should be given to shortening the period where:

- the defendant, or a person for whom the defendant is responsible, has assaulted or threatened to assault the claimant, a member of the claimant's staff, or another tenant;
- there are reasonable grounds for fearing such an assault; or

---

57 CPR 55.5(1).
58 CPR 55.5(3)(a).
59 CPR 55.5(3)(b).
60 Subject to the court's power to extend or shorten the time for compliance with any rule: CPR 3.1(2)(a): see para 21.34.
61 See CPR 55.6 and chapter 23.
62 CPR 55.5(2) and (3).
63 CPR 3.1(2)(a).

- the defendant, or a person for whom the defendant is responsible, has caused serious damage or threatened to cause serious damage to the property or to the home or property of another resident.[64]

Defences

21.35 Parts I, II and IV of this book set out the substantive and technical defences which may be raised in response to an action for possession of residential property. The reader should refer to the main text for consideration of the issues which must always be reviewed in drafting defences.

21.36 A defendant who wishes to defend a possession claim must file a defence with the court and serve a copy on the claimant within 14 days of service of the claim form.[65] A defendant to a possession claim who fails to file or serve a defence may still take part in the proceedings, but the failure to file or serve a defence may be taken into account when the court decides what costs order to make.[66] For example, if the first hearing is not effective and has to be adjourned because the tenant turns up without having filed or served a defence but obtains an adjournment by telling the court about a defence to the claim, the court may order the tenant to pay the wasted costs of the adjourned hearing.

21.37 Defences to possession claims must be in the prescribed form set out in Table 1 of CPR Practice Direction 4.[67] It is open to defendants to file a fully pleaded defence, but strictly the relevant prescribed form must also be filed.[68]

21.38 CPR Part 10 does not apply to possession claims and there is therefore no need for the defendant to file an acknowledgment of service.[69] Similarly, CPR Part 12 (default judgment) does not apply to possession claims.[70] This means that it is not possible for a claimant

---

64 PD 55A para 3.2.
65 CPR 15.2. However, this rule does not apply to claims against trespassers: see CPR 55.7(2).
66 CPR 55.7(3).
67 PD 55 para 1.5. The defence forms listed in CPR PD 4 are forms N11 (general defence form); N11B (accelerated possession procedure); N11D (demotion of tenancy); N11R (rented residential premises) or N11M (mortgaged residential premises): obtainable at https://www.justice.gov.uk/courts/procedure-rules/civil/forms.
68 CPR PD 55 para 1.5.
69 CPR 55.7(1).
70 CPR 55.7(4).

to obtain a possession order by default if the defendant fails to file or serve a defence.

21.39   In Consumer Credit Act cases, the borrower may apply for a time order in the defence or by making an application in the proceedings.[71]

21.40   The defence should answer each of the substantive points raised in the particulars of claim, because failure to respond to a point made is taken as admission of it. Moreover, any defence and, if appropriate, counterclaim must be sufficiently accurately drafted to withstand the test of a full trial. It is not sufficient for the defence to comprise a blank denial of the claimant's case. If the defendant disputes the claimant's account of the facts, the defendant will be expected to set out a summary of his or her version of events in the defence, together with, if appropriate, the legal basis for the defendant's case (eg that he or she has security of tenure). Where the claim is brought on a discretionary ground for possession and the defendant wishes to assert that it is not reasonable for the court to make an order for possession, it is necessary to say so expressly in the defence and to give details (or 'particulars') of why it is not reasonable to make a possession order. A defence must be verified by a statement of truth.[72]

Challenging the decision to bring proceedings

21.41   Tenants and other occupiers may in some circumstances seek to challenge the decision by a social landlord to bring possession proceedings – for example, where the decision infringes principles of public law or human rights. For an explanation of the circumstances in which such defences may be raised, see chapters 25 and 26. The principles on which defences of this kind may be available are set out in the judgments of the Supreme Court in *Manchester CC v Pinnock*[73] and *Hounslow LBC v Powell*.[74] Such challenges may be raised in the county court by way of a public law defence, provided that the claim is genuinely disputed on substantial grounds, or a 'human rights' defence, provided that the basis of the defence contended for is 'seriously arguable'.[75] If there are disputes of fact, evidence may be heard

---

71   PD 55 para 7.1.
72   PD 22 paras 2 and 3.
73   [2010] UKSC 45, [2011] HLR 7.
74   [2011] UKSC 8, [2011] HLR 23.
75   For the procedure relating to public law and human rights defences, see chapter 25 and 26.

in the course of the county court proceedings. Where, however, the court has a discretion concerning the making of a possession order, a county court judge is able to take into account an argument that the institution of proceedings is unlawful when considering the issue of reasonableness.[76]

Counterclaims

21.42 Often the defendant will wish to raise a grievance arising from the breach of some duty by, or misconduct on the part of, the landlord/owner. Most frequently this occurs in cases of non-compliance with the law relating to protection of tenancy deposits, disrepair and harassment. As such a complaint arises out of the subject matter of the proceedings, usually a lease or tenancy, it may be raised by way of a counterclaim. For details of the law applicable to counterclaims for disrepair, readers are referred to Luba, Forster and Prevatt, *Repairs: tenants' rights*,[77] and for counterclaims for harassment to Arden, Chan and Madge-Wyld, *Quiet enjoyment*.[78] However, it should be noted that the following heads of claim appear most commonly in counterclaims to possession proceedings (particularly those brought for rent arrears).

Failure to comply with tenancy deposit requirements

21.43 Breach of the requirement to protect the tenant's deposit with an authorised scheme and to give the prescribed information to the tenant concerning the scheme and its operation, each within 30 days from the date on which the deposit was received.[79]

Disrepair

21.44 • Breach of an express repairing covenant in the tenancy agreement (see the terms of the tenancy agreement).

---

76 *Castle Vale Housing Action Trust v Gallagher* [2001] EWCA Civ 944, (2000) 33 HLR 72 and *R (Mills) v Airways Housing Society Ltd* [2005] EWHC 328 (Admin).
77 5th edn, LAG, 2016.
78 7th edn, LAG, 2012.
79 The claim is brought under HA 2004 s214(4) and is for an award of not less than the amount of the deposit and not more than three times that amount. See paras 10.70–10.72.

- Failure to repair the structure or exterior of the premises or the common parts (including drains, gutters and external pipes).[80]
- Failure to repair (or maintain in proper working order) installations in the dwelling or serving the dwelling for the supply of water, gas and electricity and for sanitation (including basins, sinks, baths and sanitary conveniences).[81]
- Failure to take reasonable care of the tenant and the tenant's property to prevent injury to either.[82]
- Negligence in the construction of the dwelling, performance of repairing works or treatment of infestation, etc.
- Nuisance (where the disrepair is caused by a problem emanating from property retained by the landlord).

Harassment

21.45
- Trespass to land/trespass to the person/trespass to goods (tort).
- Breach of the covenant for quiet enjoyment (contract).
- Breach of the Protection from Eviction Act 1977 s3 (for unprotected tenants and licensees).
- Intimidation (tort).
- Breach of the Housing Act 1988 ss27 and 28 (unlawful eviction).

21.46 It is advisable for any counterclaim to be included in the same document as the defence. If that is done, the court's permission to bring a counterclaim against a claimant is not needed. However, if a tenant wishes to bring a counterclaim at a later stage, the court's permission is required.[83] Any counterclaim should contain full particulars of the matters complained of. Counterclaims are governed by CPR Part 20. A court fee must be paid on filing the counterclaim, which is based on the same sliding scale as that governing standard money claims, according to the value or limit of the counterclaim.

21.47   If the defendant recovers damages on his or her counterclaim, these may be set off against the claimant's money claim, eg for rent arrears, so as to reduce in whole or in part monies claimed by the claimant. In the case of counterclaims for disrepair, in particular, the application of a full set-off may amount to a complete defence to an action for arrears of rent. Accordingly, the body of the defence itself

---

80 Landlord and Tenant Act 1985 s11, as amended.
81 Landlord and Tenant Act 1985 s11, as amended.
82 Defective Premises Act 1972 s4.
83 CPR 20.4.

should plead the set-off, even though it is seeking to set off an as yet unquantified claim for damages in the counterclaim.[84]

21.48   An example of a defence (including counterclaims as appropriate) is given in appendix B.

Preparation for the hearing

21.49   Except where the claim is against trespassers, claimants should file and serve all witness statements at least two days before the hearing.[85] In arrears cases these should include evidence of the arrears up to the date of the hearing, if necessary by including a daily rate. However, this does not prevent a landlord or mortgagee bringing the position up to date at the hearing itself.[86] Consideration should be given to issuing requests for witness summonses to secure the attendance of witnesses if necessary. Where rent arrears are due to the failure of the local authority to pay housing benefit (assuming that the defendant has provided all the necessary information to enable entitlement to be assessed), it may be appropriate to require the attendance of a senior housing benefit officer. CPR 34 provides that a party or the court may issue a witness summons. Application must be made in the prescribed form (N20). The summons must be served at least seven days before the hearing at which the witness is to attend.[87] The witness can also be required to bring documents to court.

21.50   In mortgage possession claims, the claimant must, within five days of receiving notice of the hearing, send a notice to 'The Tenant or Occupier' of the property. Notices must also be sent to the housing department of the local authority and to any other lender who has a registered charge over the property. The notice must give details of the parties to the proceedings and of the date and place of the hearing. The claimant must produce a copy of each of the notices and evidence of service at the hearing.[88] The lender's representative must also bring to the hearing two copies of a completed Mortgage Pre-action Protocol checklist (court form N123) which shows

---

84 *British Anzani (Felixstowe) Ltd v International Marine Management (UK) Ltd*
    [1980] QB 137, [1979] 3 WLR 451.
85 CPR 55.8(4).
86 PD 55 para 5.2.
87 CPR 34.5.
88 CPR 55.10. See para 37.24.

how the lender has sought to comply with the requirements of the Protocol.[89]

21.51 Where the claimant has served the claim form and particulars of claim, the claimant must produce a certificate of service at the hearing.[90]

Adjournments

21.52 In view of the fact that some tenants do not seek legal advice, or are unable to obtain advice, until just before a hearing, it is often necessary for their advisers to seek an adjournment at the initial hearing. Whether or not such an application is successful will depend on the particular circumstances of the case. If it is possible to draft a defence which shows that the tenant has a real prospect of successfully defending the claim, the court is far more likely to adjourn. The court may want to know why (if it is the case) the tenant delayed seeking advice. If the case is one of many listed in court and there is insufficient time to hear the matter, practical list management may mean that the judge has no alternative but to adjourn. Where the claim has been brought on a discretionary rent arrears ground, the court will often grant an adjournment to enable the defendant to pursue an outstanding claim for housing benefit or universal credit or to investigate whether the correct amount of benefit has been paid. On the other hand, if the tenant's adviser/representative is not able to point to any defence, or only to a very weak defence, the court may choose to deal with the case at the first hearing.

21.53 In some cases brought on discretionary grounds for possession, it may be appropriate to ask the court to grant either a general adjournment or an 'adjournment on terms'. The most common example of this kind of adjournment is in rent arrears or mortgage arrears cases, where the defendant is already bringing the arrears down gradually by regular instalments and/or is offering to make payments by standing order or by direct deduction from benefits. In these circumstances, assuming that payments are maintained without fail, the court may accept that it is not necessary to make any kind of possession order at all at the present time. It will be open to the claimant to ask the court to restore the case for hearing if the defendant defaults on the terms of the order granting the adjournment. Likewise, in relatively low

---

89 CPR PD 55A para 5.5. See also para 37.12 and appendix E.
90 CPR 55.8(6).

level 'behaviour' cases, if there have been no recent complaints about the defendant's behaviour or if the defendant is willing to sign an 'acceptable behaviour contract' or to give an undertaking to the court concerning his or her future conduct, the court may find it acceptable to adjourn the case on specified terms.

21.54 In light of the Court of Appeal decision in *North British Housing Association Limited v Matthews*,[91] there are limitations on courts' powers to adjourn where landlords are seeking possession under mandatory grounds. See para 3.106. However, these limitations do not apply where possession is sought on a discretionary ground.

21.55 Factors which should be borne in mind in seeking an adjournment include:

- The overriding objective, ie, the importance of dealing with cases justly. This includes ensuring that the parties are on an equal footing, saving expense, dealing with cases proportionately, ensuring that cases are dealt with expeditiously and fairly and allocating the appropriate share of the court's resources.[92]
- Whether there has been non-compliance with the rules, practice directions or previous orders.
- Whether or not legal aid has been granted to the defendant, or whether a legal aid application is pending.
- The risk of prejudice to either party.
- The extent to which the party applying for the adjournment has been responsible for creating the difficulty.[93]

21.56 In *Bates v Croydon LBC*,[94] a tenant facing a possession claim alleging 53 complaints of nuisance to neighbours sought an adjournment to obtain legal aid. It was refused. The hearing date was then moved forward, with the result that she was given three days to read witness statements produced by the council and to prepare for the hearing. The Court of Appeal set aside the possession order. The defendant had been put on very short notice to deal with the documentation, exhibits and witness statements. She was required to respond in writing to lengthy allegations and then conduct her own case in person. While the court accepted the desirability of conducting litigation with proper dispatch, and was reluctant to review case management decisions of district judges, the decision reached in this case was wrong.

91 [2004] EWCA Civ 1736, [2005] HLR 17.
92 CPR 1.1.
93 See, eg *McShane v William Sutton Trust* (1997) 1 L&T Rev D67, December 1997 *Legal Action* 13: a pre-CPR case.
94 [2001] EWCA Civ 134, (2001) 33 HLR 70.

An adjournment was appropriate for Ms Bates to finalise her legal aid application and enable her to be represented.

21.57   Where the claimant opposes an adjournment, the adviser will need to show that the defendant has a potential defence to the proceedings which has a reasonable prospect of success, and that the claim must be adjourned to ensure that the defendant is able to secure a fair hearing of his or her case. The adviser may in appropriate cases propose that the court gives case management directions and adjourns the case pending compliance with those directions: see para 21.59.[95]

At the hearing

21.58   Possession claims are usually listed before a district judge at the county court hearing centre. A typical possession list may contain twenty cases or more, to be dealt with in a single morning or afternoon. District judges may therefore have an average of five minutes to deal with each case. If the defendant can show that there is insufficient time to deal with the issues in the case and/or that he or she needs further time to obtain evidence relevant to his or her defence, it is likely that the court will grant an adjournment of that hearing.

21.59   At the first hearing, or any adjourned hearing, the court may either decide the claim or give case management directions.[96] Where the claim is genuinely disputed on grounds which appear to be substantial, case management directions will include allocation of the claim to a particular track or enable it to be allocated.[97]

21.60   Where factual matters are in dispute, and evidence is required to resolve those matters, the claim should not be dealt with summarily at the initial hearing.[98]

21.61   If it is clear from correspondence or other communications between the parties that there is a genuine dispute or that the defendant needs more time to prepare his or her case, to avoid the expense of the hearing the claimant should seek to agree case management directions with the defendant. If a list of agreed directions is submitted to the court in good time, with a request that the hearing be

95 CPR 55.8(1).
96 CPR 55.8(1).
97 CPR 55.8(2).
98 *Benesco Charity Ltd v Kanj and Persons Unknown* [2011] EWHC 3415 (Ch). Compare, however, in relation to human rights defences, *Thurrock Borough Council v West* [2012] EWCA Civ 1435, [2013] HLR 5: see chapter 26.

vacated, the judge may agree to adjourn the case and make an order in the agreed terms without the need for the parties to attend. The court may require the request to be framed as an application for a consent order, which will attract a court fee.

21.62   By way of example, where the defendant wishes to defend the claim for possession and to counterclaim for breach of the landlord's repairing obligations, directions may include some or all of the following, where applicable:

- Defendant to file and serve a fully pleaded Defence and Counterclaim by [date and time].
- Case to be allocated to the Fast Track.[99]
- The parties to agree a single joint expert and to have permission to rely on the written evidence of that expert.
- The parties to make standard disclosure of documents by list by [date and time].
- Inspection of documents by [date and time].
- The parties to exchange witness statements of all witnesses of fact on whose evidence they intend to rely by [date and time].
- The parties to file pre-trial checklists by [date and time].
- Matter to be listed for trial thereafter [with time estimate].
- Costs in the case (meaning that the costs of the directions hearing will follow the costs order to be made at the final hearing).

A specific date and time will be allocated to each direction as the deadline for compliance with it.

21.63   It is essential to give careful consideration to the claimant's list of documents. If the defendant has reason to believe that the list is not complete, a request should be made for the documents or class of documents which are missing. If the claimant refuses to disclose a particular document, an application may be made for an order for specific disclosure under CPR 31.12. Witness statements should only be completed after disclosure and should include comments, if appropriate, on any of the documents disclosed. Witness statements will normally be exchanged simultaneously, by prior arrangement.

Hearings in private

21.64   Human Rights Act 1998 Sch 1 Article 6[100] usually requires a public hearing. However, CPR 39.2(3)(c) provides that a hearing may be in

---

99 The usual track for possession proceedings. See para 21.66.
100 See para 22.15.

private if it involves confidential information (including information relating to personal financial matters) and publicity would damage that confidentiality. The Practice Direction to CPR Part 39, paras 1.1 to 1.5, states that the decision as to whether a hearing is held in public or private must be made by the judge, having regard to representations (para 1.4) and Article 6(1) (para 1.4A). Mortgage possession claims, possession claims based on rent arrears and applications to suspend warrants should, in the first instance, be listed as hearings in private (para 1.5). Such provisions do not amount to a breach of Article 6 because, like many other Convention provisions, Article 6 does not provide an absolute right. It has to be balanced against other rights, such as the right to privacy given by Article 8. CPR 39.2 and the Practice Direction to CPR Part 39 have been drafted specifically with Article 6 in mind. They leave a discretion to the judge in each case. If that discretion is exercised reasonably, in accordance with the spirit of the Convention, it is unlikely to be criticised. Indeed, taking into account the provisions of Articles 8 and 14, it is possible that a tenant defending a rent arrears case would have been able to challenge the pre-CPR position, where claims against tenants were held in public and claims by lenders against borrowers based on mortgage arrears were held in private.

21.65   The legality of CPR 39.2(3)(c) and the Practice Direction to CPR Part 39, paras 1.5 to 1.7, was challenged unsuccessfully in *R (Pelling) v Bow County Court (No 2)*.[101] Dr Pelling claimed that these provisions were ultra vires and breached Article 6. The Divisional Court held that the general rule that hearings are to be in public[102] is not absolute. CPR 39.2(3) is facultative and permits certain limited exceptions. Accordingly, CPR 39.2 is not unlawful or ultra vires and does not breach Articles 6 or 10.

Allocation to track

21.66   Many possession claims are decided without ever having been allocated to one of the usual 'tracks' available for civil cases. Possession claims should be allocated to the small claims track only if all the parties agree.[103] If a possession claim is allocated to the small claims track, the fast track costs regime applies, but the trial costs are in

101 [2001] UKHRR 165, [2001] ACD 1, QBD.
102 See *Scott v Scott* [1913] AC 417, HL.
103 CPR 55.9(2).

the discretion of the judge and should not exceed the amount of fast track costs allowable in CPR 45.38 if the value were up to £3,000 (currently £485).[104]

21.67   In considering the appropriate track for a possession claim, the court should take into account:

- CPR 26.8, which refers to: the financial value of the claim; the nature of the remedy sought; the likely complexity of facts, law or evidence; the number of parties; the value of any counterclaim; the amount of oral evidence; the importance of the claim to people who are not parties; the views expressed by the parties; and the circumstances of the parties;
- the amount of any arrears of rent or mortgage instalments;
- the importance to the defendant of retaining possession;
- the importance of vacant possession to the claimant; and
- if applicable, the alleged conduct of the defendant.[105]

The financial value of the claim is not necessarily the most important factor. A possession claim may be allocated to the fast track, whatever the value of the property. Complex cases, or those requiring a trial of longer than one day, will usually be assigned to the multi-track.

Evidence at the hearing

21.68   Where the claim is based on rent or mortgage arrears, the claimant's evidence should include the amount of any arrears outstanding. Such evidence may be brought up to date orally or in writing on the day of the hearing if necessary. The defendant should where possible give evidence of any outstanding benefit payments relevant to rent or mortgage arrears; and about the status of any benefit claims about which a decision has not yet been made, including any pending reviews or appeals.[106]

21.69   If a possession claim has not been allocated to track, or has been allocated to the small claims track, any fact that needs to be proved may be proved by evidence in writing, ie, by a witness statement or a claim form with a statement of truth.[107] However, if that evidence is disputed and the maker of the witness statement is not present,

104 CPR 55.9(3).
105 PD 55 para 6.1.
106 PD 55A para 5.3.
107 CPR 55.8(3).

the court will usually adjourn the claim so that oral evidence can be given.[108]

21.70　　If the claim has been allocated to the fast track or the multi-track, the usual rules of evidence at trial, including the rules about hearsay evidence, contained in CPR Parts 32–35 apply. Oral evidence will therefore be required,[109] although it may well be that witness statements will be treated as evidence in chief and oral evidence will consist largely of cross-examination.

21.71　　For the general procedural rules about the admissibility of hearsay evidence and the requirement (in some circumstances) to give notice of intention to rely on hearsay evidence, see the Civil Evidence Act 1995 ss1–4 and CPR 33.1–33.5.

21.72　　In *Moat Housing Group-South Ltd v Harris and Hartless*[110] the Court of Appeal reviewed the use of hearsay evidence in possession claims based on anti-social behaviour and gave guidance to the lower courts. It is now well established that hearsay evidence can be given at the trial of a possession action, but 'the willingness of a civil court to admit hearsay evidence carries with it inherent dangers'. It is much more difficult for judges to assess the truth of what they are being told if the original makers of statements are not present in court to be cross-examined on their evidence. Where hearsay evidence is to be relied on, the Court stressed the importance of a landlord giving a tenant prompt notice of any complaints that are made about his or her behaviour, so that the tenant is not faced in court with serious complaints made by anonymous or absent witnesses. In this case, the large volume of hearsay evidence presented the court with an unusually difficult problem. The Court of Appeal considered that more attention should be paid by claimants to the need to state, by convincing direct evidence, why it was not reasonable and practicable to produce the original makers of statements as witnesses. If statements involve multiple hearsay, the route by which the original statement came to the attention of the person attesting to it should be identified as far as practicable.[111]

21.73　　Anonymous hearsay evidence may be admissible, provided that the court is satisfied that it is consistent with the first-hand or direct

108　PD 55A para 5.4.
109　CPR 32.2.
110　[2005] EWCA Civ 287, [2005] HLR 33. See too *Washington Housing Company Ltd v Morson* [2005] EWHC 3407 (Ch) and *Wear Valley DC v Robson* [2008] EWCA Civ 1470, [2009] HLR 27.
111　Civil Evidence Act 1995 s4 sets out the factors which are relevant to the weighing of hearsay evidence.

evidence which is before the court. In *Boyd v Incommunities Ltd*,[112] a social landlord issued proceedings against a tenant, relying on allegations of anti-social behaviour directed at his neighbours, including noise nuisance and intimidating requests for money. Evidence of the various incidents was contained in anonymous hearsay statements from three neighbours which were summarised in the witness statement of the landlord's tenancy enforcement officer. The officer stated that the neighbours did not wish to give direct evidence, as they were too frightened of reprisals to be identified. The Court of Appeal rejected the tenant's argument that the trial judge had placed undue weight on the anonymous evidence. It accepted that the practice of admitting anonymous hearsay evidence in litigation of this type was well-established. The defendant had a history of criminal convictions, including offences of dishonesty, violence and intimidation, and the hearsay evidence was consistent with his record.[113]

Interim rent

21.74 While awaiting the hearing or trial of the claim for possession, a landlord may apply for an order for interim rent.[114] Such applications are rare. If one is made, the tenant may respond with an undertaking to pay current rent pending trial. No order for interim rent should be made, however, if there is a genuine dispute over the sum due or if a counterclaim is being pursued.[115] Failure to make payments under an order for interim rent, coupled with breach of an order to file a list of documents, where there is no realistic prospect of the tenant ever paying current rent or arrears may justify striking out

---

112 [2013] EWCA Civ 756, [2013] HLR 44. See too *Solon South West Housing Association Ltd v James* [2004] EWCA Civ 1847, [2005] HLR 24, which also concerned the admissibility of anonymous hearsay evidence.

113 See also *Welsh v Stokes* [2007] EWCA Civ 796, [2008] 1 WLR 1224 (a road accident case), in which Dyson LJ said: 'The decision what weight (if any) to give to hearsay evidence involves an exercise of judgment. The court has to reach a conclusion as to its reliability as best it can on all the available material. Where a case depends entirely on hearsay evidence, the court will be particularly careful before concluding that it can be given any weight. But there is no rule of law which prohibits a court from giving weight to hearsay evidence merely because it is uncorroborated and cannot be tested or contradicted by the opposing party'. [para 23]

114 CPR 25.6–25.9.

115 *Old Grovebury Manor Farm v Seymour* [1979] 1 WLR 263, [1979] 1 All ER 573.

a defence and making a possession order.[116] In cases involving discretionary grounds, the court should still consider the question of 'reasonableness'.

21.75   In practice, it is more common for courts to make an order for payment of current rent under their general case management powers,[117] for example, as a term of any adjournment.[118] Where financial terms are imposed as a condition of an adjournment, the onus lies on tenants to satisfy the court that they cannot comply with any condition before it is imposed.

21.76   Also, if a possession claim against a secure, assured, or Rent Act regulated tenant is adjourned, the court must, unless it considers that to do so would cause exceptional hardship or would otherwise be unreasonable, impose conditions with regard to the payment of rent and arrears of rent (if any).[119]

---

116 *Tower Hamlets LBC v Ellson* July 2000 *Legal Action* 28, CA.
117 eg, CPR 3.1(3).
118 See, under the old rules, *Agyeman v Boadi* (1996) 28 HLR 558, [1996] EGCS 14, CA.
119 RA 1977 s100(3), HA 1985 s85(3) and HA 1988 s9(3).

Accelerated possession proceedings

Accelerated possession proceedings

22.1   Part 55 of the Civil Procedure Rules 1998 (CPR) provides for accelerated possession claims where property is let on an assured shorthold
tenancy[1] following service of a 'no fault' Housing Act (HA) 1988 section 21 notice. The procedure was introduced on 1 November 1993[2]
and was subsequently incorporated into CPR Part 55. The possession
procedure available to landlords against full assured tenants is the
standard one contained in CPR 55 Part I: see chapter 21.

22.2   The accelerated possession procedure applies only to claims
brought under HA 1988 s21 to recover possession against assured
shorthold tenants.[3] The conditions set out in CPR 55.12 must be met.
The procedure can be used only where:

- the tenancy (including any agreement for the tenancy) was entered
  into on or after 15 January 1989;
- the only purpose is to recover possession: the accelerated procedure cannot be used to claim rent arrears or to make any other
  claim;
- the tenancy did not immediately follow an assured tenancy which
  was not an assured shorthold tenancy;
- there has been an assured shorthold tenancy in accordance with
  either HA 1988 s19A (ie, 'automatic' shorthold tenancies granted
  on or after 28 February 1997) or HA 1988 s20(1)(a)–(c) (pre-28
  February 1997 fixed-term tenancies granted for a term certain of
  not less than six months where a 'section 20' notice[4] of assured
  shorthold tenancy was given prior to the grant of the tenancy);
- the tenancy is subject to a written agreement, or follows a tenancy
  where there was a written agreement; and
- a HA 1988 section 21(1) or section 21(4) notice has been given.[5]

22.3   Where the tenancy is a demoted assured shorthold tenancy, the only
conditions that need to be satisfied are that the sole purpose of the
claim is to recover possession and that a HA 1988 s21 notice has
been given.

Readers should refer to chapter 10 for a detailed analysis of the
rules governing assured shorthold tenancies.

---

1   For assured shorthold tenancies generally, see chapter 10.
2   In the former County Court Rules (CCR) Ord 49 r6A.
3   CPR 55.11.
4   See para 10.4.
5   See para 10.7 onwards.

22.4   Claims under the accelerated possession procedure may be brought in any county court hearing centre and will be issued by that centre.[6] Where the claim has not been brought in the county court hearing centre which serves the address of the property, and the judge directs that a date be fixed for a hearing, the proceedings will be transferred after issue to that hearing centre.[7] The claim form must:

- be in the form set out in the Practice Direction (Form N5B);
- contain the information and be accompanied by the documents required in that form; and
- have all sections completed.

Defending accelerated possession claims

22.5   A blank defence form (N11B) should accompany every claim form issued under the accelerated procedure. It is crucially important that tenants who wish to defend proceedings brought under the accelerated procedure return the defence form to the court within 14 days after service of the claim form.[8] Form 11B should be used for this purpose, even though Practice Direction 55A does not actually specify the form. If the defence form is not returned, the claim for possession will be treated as unopposed and a possession order may be made without any hearing.

22.6   Common mistakes by landlords using the accelerated procedure include:

- an agent acting as claimant instead of the landlord;[9]
- an agent signing the statement of truth on the claim form;
- failure to exhibit the HA 1988 section 21 notice (notice requiring possession): the court has no power to dispense with this requirement;
- failure to exhibit (if applicable) the HA 1988 s20 notice (ie, notice required before the grant of an assured shorthold tenancy commencing before 28 February 1997): again, the court has no power to dispense with this;
- seeking to include a claim for rent arrears;

---

6 CPR 55.11(2).
7 CPR 55.16(1A).
8 CPR 55.14.
9 See *Chesters Accommodation Agency Ltd v Abebrese* (1997) 94(33) LSG 27, (1997) 141 SJLB 199, (1997) *Times* 28 July, CA and CPR 22.1(6).

- defects in the HA 1988 s20 notice[10] (see para 10.4 and the cases referred to there);
- defects in the HA 1988 s21 notice (see para 10.28).

For details of possible defences which may be raised in response to 'no fault' section 21 claims for possession of assured shorthold tenancies, see chapter 10.

22.7   Accelerated possession claims should be referred to a district judge, either on receipt of a defence, or on the claimant making a request for an order for possession after the expiry of 14 days from service of the claim form.[11] The judge can still consider any defence if it is received out of time but before the landlord's request is considered. If the defendant does not file a defence, and no request for possession is received from the claimant within three months after service, the claim will be stayed automatically.[12]

22.8   When considering accelerated possession claims, district judges should either:[13]

- make an order for possession without a hearing; or
- if they are not satisfied that the claim was served or that the claimant is entitled to possession, fix a hearing date and give case management directions – at least 14 days' notice of the hearing must be given; or
- strike out the claim if it discloses no reasonable grounds for bringing the proceedings.

If the claim is struck out, reasons must be given with the order. In those circumstances, the claimant landlord may apply to restore the claim within 28 days.

22.9   The Court of Appeal has stated that if the tenant's defence form or reply raises a case which, if true, would constitute an arguable defence, the judge has no discretion to make a possession order without a hearing:

> [The accelerated possession procedure] is a robust machinery. It depends upon district judges rigorously considering the documents which have been filed. Some replies may be little more than a plea, however genuine, for mercy. But if, on the face of the reply, a matter has been raised which, if true, might arguably raise a defence; or if the

---

10 The requirement for a HA 1998 s20 notice applies only if the tenancy was granted before 28 February 1997.
11 CPR 55.15.
12 CPR 55.15(4).
13 CPR 55.16.

documents filed by the claimant might arguably disclose a defect in his claim, then the district judge must necessarily be 'not satisfied' ...[14]

22.10   It is usual for the court to order that the tenant pay the landlord's fixed costs on the claim form. If the tenant wishes to pay costs by instalments, the appropriate box on the form N11B should be completed.[15]

22.11   In some cases, the tenant may have made a homelessness application to the local housing authority under HA 1996 Part 7. The Homelessness Code of Guidance recommends that local authorities should accept a household as statutorily homeless when the section 21 notice expires.[16] In spite of this, many local housing authorities insist on the landlord taking possession proceedings to evict the household and refuse to regard them as homeless until they have actually been evicted from the home. Such policies cause expense to landlords and distress to occupiers. The tenant will normally be ordered to pay the landlord's costs. In such circumstances, the tenant may wish to ask the court to consider making a costs order against the local housing authority under CPR 46.2. This would require the authority to be joined as a party and in that event the authority would be given the opportunity to attend a hearing at which the issue of costs would be further considered. Alternatively, the homeless applicant could make a formal complaint to the authority and request reimbursement of the costs awarded.

Postponement of possession

22.12   Where a landlord is entitled to a possession order under the accelerated procedure, the court must make an order to take effect within 14 days, unless exceptional hardship would be caused to the tenant, in which case the court may delay the date for the giving up of possession for a maximum of six weeks.[17] Claimants may indicate, in response to the relevant question in the claim form, that they are content for the judge to consider postponing the date for possession without a hearing. In those cases judges may fix the date for possession up to six weeks ahead without a hearing.

---

14   *Manel v Memon* (2001) 33 HLR 24, [2000] 33 EG 74, CA. Although this was a case decided under the former CCR Ord 49 r6A, the same principles apply to the accelerated possession procedure under CPR 55 Part II.

15   CPR 55.18.

16   Homelessness Code of Guidance for Local Authorities, DCLG/DoH, July 2006, para 8.32.

17   HA 1980 s89.

22.13   Otherwise, if a defendant seeks postponement of the date for giving up possession on the ground of exceptional hardship, the judge must make an order for possession within 14 days, but direct a hearing on the issue of postponement. The hearing must be before the date on which possession is to be given up. If, at the hearing, the judge is satisfied that exceptional hardship would be caused by requiring possession to be given up by the date already fixed, he or she may vary the order to specify a later date. However, that later date may be no more than six weeks after the date on which the original order was made.[18]

22.14   Where the court has made a possession order under the accelerated procedure, CPR 55.19 provides that the tenant may make an application to set aside or vary the order within 14 days of service. The court also has power to set aside or vary the order on its own initiative.[19] If the tenant did not receive the court papers or was unable to return the defence form within 14 days, or was not aware that he or she had grounds to defend the claim, there is an opportunity to have the court reconsider its decision. Application should be made on notice in court form N244.

Accelerated possession and human rights

22.15   It has been suggested that the accelerated possession procedure might fall foul of Human Rights Act 1998 Sch 1 Article 6. Article 6 provides:

> In the determination of his civil rights and obligations or of any criminal charge against him, everyone is entitled to a fair and public hearing within a reasonable time by an independent and impartial tribunal established by law ...

However, in view of the firm line taken by the Court of Appeal in *Manel v Memon*[20] it is unlikely that this view will prevail. Article 6 only comes into play if the proceedings in question are decisive of private rights and obligations.[21] If the tenant accepts (or, by not returning the defence form, is deemed to accept) that there is no defence, there are no civil rights to be determined. If the tenant claims that there is a defence, there is an entitlement to a public hearing.

18   PD 55A para 8.4 and HA 1980 s89.
19   CPR 55.19(b).
20   (2001) 33 HLR 24, [2000] 33 EG 74, CA. See para 22.9.
21   *Ringeisen v Austria (No 1)* (1979–80) 1 EHRR 455, ECtHR.

CHAPTER 23

Possession proceedings against trespassers and other unlawful occupiers

The meaning of 'trespasser'

23.1   The term 'trespasser' carries different meanings. In its commonly understood sense, it means a squatter, ie a person who enters on land or property without the consent of the owner (or other person with an immediate right to possession) and remains there. In its wider, common law sense, the term also extends to former tenants and licensees who have been lawfully occupying the property, but whose contract has ended and who have no statutory security or right to remain.

23.2   Historically, there was no need for landowners to bring court proceedings to evict trespassers. They were entitled to use 'self-help' and to evict trespassers (in the wider sense) without a court order.[1] However, in the words of Lord Denning, this was a course 'not to be recommended' to landowners because of the 'possible disturbance' which might be caused.[2] In addition, a landowner risks prosecution under the Criminal Law Act (CLA) 1977 s6 if violence to people or property is used or threatened for the purpose of securing entry to premises when there is someone present on those premises.[3] Alternatively, if the trespassers are former tenants or licensees who are entitled to rely on the Protection from Eviction Act (PEA) 1977 s3,[4] a landlord using self-help also risks prosecution. Advisers should, however, note CLA 1977 s7, which creates a criminal offence where a trespasser (meaning in this context a squatter) fails to leave the premises if required to do so by or on behalf of a displaced residential occupier[5] or a protected intending occupier[6] of those premises. Legal Aid, Sentencing and Punishment of Offenders Act 2012 s144 also creates an offence of squatting in a residential building.[7]

---

1   *R v Blankley* [1979] Crim LR 166; *McPhail v Persons, Names Unknown* [1973] Ch 447, [1973] 3 All ER 393, CA.

2   *McPhail v Persons, Names Unknown* [1973] Ch 447, [1973] 3 All ER 393, per Lord Denning MR at 396.

3   Unless the landowner is a displaced residential occupier or protected intending occupier: see below and Criminal Law Act 1977 ss7, 12 and 12A.

4   PEA 1977 as amended by HA 1988 ss30 and 31. See para 15.2.

5   As defined in Criminal Law Act 1977 s12(3).

6   As defined in Criminal Law Act 1977 s12A.

7   The offence is committed when (a) a person is in a residential building as a trespasser, having entered it as a trespasser; (b) the person knows, or ought to know, that he or she is a trespasser; and (c) the person is living in the building or intends to live there for any period.

Possession claims against trespassers

23.3   In possession proceedings against trespassers, landowners need prove only their title and an intention to regain possession.[8] If occupiers wish to claim some right of occupation which amounts to a defence (for example, a continuing licence or tenancy), the burden of proving its existence lies on them. The main defences likely to be advanced by people who face possession proceedings brought by landowners who claim that they are trespassers are:

- They have a tenancy or licence which has not been determined.[9]
- Although the people in occupation of land do not themselves have a tenancy or licence granted by the claimant landowner, someone else, other than the landowner, has an intermediate tenancy or licence which has not been determined. Landowners are not entitled to orders for possession unless they can prove that they have an immediate right to possession. This is not the case if there is an intermediate undetermined tenancy or licence. This situation most commonly arises where a tenant moves away or dies and someone else is living in the property without the landowner's permission.
- The landowner has failed to comply with the necessary procedural requirements, for example, as to service of proceedings (see para 21.32). Sometimes this may succeed in delaying matters, giving occupiers time to find other accommodation, but it will not provide a long-term defence.
- The decision by a public body, such as a local authority, to bring possession proceedings can be challenged on public law grounds (for example, that it has failed to take into account relevant factors or has misdirected itself in law) or on human rights grounds. See chapters 25 and 26.
- The former trespassers have acquired possessory title as a result of adverse possession (Limitation Act 1980 s15(1)) or have rights under the Land Registration Act 2002 (see para 23.21).

---

8   *Portland Managements v Harte* [1977] QB 306, [1976] 1 All ER 225.
9   See *Garwood v Bolter* [2015] EWHC 3619 (Ch), [2016] BPIR 367, in which a claim for possession by the landlord's trustee in bankruptcy failed where there were assured shorthold tenants in occupation who had not been named in the proceedings or given notice of the hearing.

23.4   Proceedings may be issued as ordinary possession claims. Alternatively, they may be issued as 'a claim against trespassers' in accordance with CPR 55.1.[10] CPR 55.1(b) provides that:

> a 'possession claim against trespassers' means a claim for the recovery of land which the claimant alleges is occupied only by a person or persons who entered or remained on the land without the consent of a person entitled to possession of that land but does not include a claim against a tenant or sub-tenant whether his tenancy has been terminated or not.

The 'possession claim against trespassers' under CPR 55 is therefore not available to be used against unlawful subtenants. It can, however, be used against former licensees.

23.5   The differences between a standard CPR 55 Part I[11] possession claim and a claim against trespassers are that in a claim against trespassers:

- Proceedings may be issued in the High Court if there is a substantial risk of public disturbance or of serious harm to people or property which properly require immediate determination.[12]
- The particulars of claim must state the claimant's interest in the land or the basis of the right to claim possession, and the circumstances in which it was or is occupied without licence or consent.[13]
- If the claimant does not know the name of a person in occupation, the claim must be brought against 'persons unknown' in addition to any named defendants.[14] Service of the claim form, particulars of claim and any witness statements must be effected against 'persons unknown' by attaching them to the main door of the property or some other part of the premises so that they are clearly visible and through the letter box in a sealed transparent envelope addressed to 'The Occupiers'; or, where the property consists of land, by placing stakes on the land. If these methods are to be used, the claimant must supply the court with sufficient stakes and transparent envelopes.[15]

---

10 The summary procedure against those who entered into or remained in occupation without licence or consent contained in the former County Court Rules (CCR) Ord 24 or the Rules of the Supreme Court (RSC) Ord 113 no longer exists.

11 See chapter 21.

12 PD 55A para 1.3(3).

13 PD 55A para 2.6.

14 CPR 55.3(4).

15 PD 55A para 4.1.

- The normal rule that a defendant who wishes to defend must file a defence within 14 days does not apply.[16]
- The time between service and the hearing must be at least two days (non-residential land) or at least five days (residential premises).[17]

23.6 A claimant which is itself a licensee of premises (such as a short-life housing association) may bring a claim against trespassers provided that it has a right of effective control over land.[18]

23.7 Occasionally, landowners are concerned that, following eviction, trespassers may move on to neighbouring land. In *Secretary of State for the Environment, Food and Rural Affairs v Meier and others*,[19] the defendants had set up an unauthorised encampment in woodland owned by the Secretary of State and managed by the Forestry Commission. The Secretary of State sought a possession order not only in respect of the land occupied by the defendants, but also in respect of other publicly owned woods in the area. The Supreme Court held that a possession order could not extend to land not yet occupied by the defendants. It was not possible to recover possession of land not occupied by another because the owner already enjoyed uninterrupted possession of it.

23.8 However, in *Meier*, the Supreme Court did uphold the grant of an injunction prohibiting the defendants from occupying the other woods, in spite of the possible difficulties of enforcement. There was no evidence in the particular case that an injunction would prove to be an ineffective remedy. If necessary, such an injunction can be granted against 'persons unknown'.[20]

23.9 Under the old summary procedure (the former County Court Rules Ord 24 and Rules of the Supreme Court Ord 113), all that landowners could claim was an order for possession and costs. They could not make any claim for mesne profits or damages. In view of the fact that claims against trespassers now come within CPR Part 55, there is no apparent reason why financial claims should not also

---

16 CPR 55.7(2).

17 CPR 55.5(2).

18 *Manchester Airport v Dutton* [2000] QB 133, [1999] 3 WLR 524, CA; *Countryside Residential (North Thames) Ltd v Tugwell* [2000] 34 EG 87, CA. See also *Harper v Charlesworth* (1825) 4 B & C 574.

19 [2009] UKSC 11, [2010] HLR 15.

20 For other examples of injunctions granted to prevent trespass, see *Hampshire Waste Services Ltd v Persons Unknown* [2003] EWHC 1738 (Ch), September 2003 *Legal Action* 27 and *Northampton BC v Connors* [2003] All ER (D) 196, August 2003 *Legal Action* 31.

be brought, although the concept of a money judgment against persons unknown is clearly problematic.

23.10   Under the old summary procedure, a body of case-law grew up to determine what might amount to a triable issue.[21] However, none of these cases applies to the procedure under CPR Part 55 because it is not a summary procedure. If a defendant wishes to defend a claim, the court will either try the case at the first hearing or give case management directions.[22]

23.11   At the hearing, anyone who is not a named party to the proceedings may apply to be joined and added as a defendant.[23] Unless occupiers have a defence to the proceedings, however, there is no point in applying to be joined as a defendant since it merely opens up the likelihood of an order for costs. Orders for costs cannot be made against 'persons unknown', only against named defendants.

Possession orders

23.12   When dealing with claims against trespassers courts should usually make an order for possession to take effect 'forthwith' (ie, immediately).[24] The court can make an order for possession to take effect on a specified later date only if all parties consent, or if the defendants are licensees under a rental purchase agreement or are former service occupiers[25] (see paras 13.7 and 17.2).

Damages for trespass

23.13   Landowners are entitled to seek orders for damages for trespass. There is no need for them to prove that they would have re-let the premises. Damages are assessed according to the loss suffered by the landowner or the value of the premises to the trespassers, and in

---

21   eg, *Henderson v Law* (1985) 17 HLR 237; *Cooper v Varzdari* (1986) 18 HLR 299 and *Filemart v Avery* [1989] 46 EG 92, CA.

22   CPR 55.8(1). See para 21.59 and *Benesco Charity Ltd v Kanj and Persons Unknown* [2011] EWHC 3415 (Ch).

23   CPR 19.4.

24   *McPhail v Persons, Names Unknown* [1973] Ch 447, [1973] 3 All ER 393, CA; *Swordheath Properties Ltd v Floydd* [1978] 1 WLR 550, [1978] 1 All ER 721 and *Mayor and Burgesses of Camden LBC v Persons Unknown* [1987] CLY 2183, June 1987 *Legal Action* 19, CA.

25   *McPhail v Persons, Names Unknown* [1973] 3 All ER 393, CA.

the absence of other evidence, this will usually be the ordinary letting value.[26]

Public law defences

23.14 As explained in more detail in chapter 25, the decision of a public body, such as a local authority, to bring a possession claim may be challenged on the grounds that:

- the decision is so unreasonable that no reasonable public authority could have come to such a decision;
- the authority failed to take into account relevant material when reaching its decision;
- the authority took into account irrelevant material in coming to the decision;
- in making the decision the authority misdirected itself in law;
- the authority has fettered its discretion by adopting a blanket policy without regard to the facts of the individual case; or
- the authority has breached its obligations under the Human Rights Act 1998.

23.15 A secure or assured tenant may challenge a decision to bring proceedings for possession on a discretionary ground as an aspect of reasonableness in the proceedings themselves.[27] Even where the defendant is a trespasser with no private law or contractual rights, it may be possible to challenge the decision to evict on public law grounds. Formerly, this could be done only by seeking an adjournment of the possession proceedings in order to bring a claim for judicial review.[28] However, it is now established that such challenges may be brought in the county court by way of a public law defence to the possession claim, unless there are particular reasons for seeking judicial review in the Administrative Court (such as where it is intended

---

26 *Swordheath Properties v Tabet* [1979] 1 WLR 285, [1979] 1 All ER 240, CA; *Ministry of Defence v Thompson* [1993] 40 EG 148, (1993) 25 HLR 552, CA and *Ministry of Defence v Ashman* (1993) 25 HLR 513, [1993] 40 EG 144, CA.

27 *Wandsworth LBC v Winder (No 1)* [1985] AC 461, HL; *Bristol DC v Clark* [1975] 1 WLR 1443, [1975] 3 All ER 976 and *Cannock Chase DC v Kelly* [1978] 1 WLR 1, [1978] 1 All ER 152, CA.

28 *Avon CC v Buscott and others* [1988] QB 656, [1988] 1 All ER 841, CA and *Waverley BC v Hilden* [1988] 1 WLR 246, [1988] 1 All ER 807. See also *R v Southwark LBC ex p Borrow* December 1988 *Legal Action* 17, but cf *Hackney LBC v Lambourne* (1993) 25 HLR 172, CA, where the Court of Appeal struck out the tenant's 'administrative law defence'.

to ask the court to make a declaration of incompatibility under the Human Rights Act 1998). If there are disputes of fact, evidence may be heard in the course of the county court proceedings. The principles on which public law and human rights defences may be based were confirmed by the Supreme Court in *Manchester CC v Pinnock*[29] and *Hounslow LBC v Powell*.[30] In *Leicester City Council v Shearer*,[31] the Court of Appeal upheld a decision by the county court judge dismissing the claim for possession. The council had rejected the occupier's request to remain in the former family home following the suicide of her estranged husband despite the fact that it would have had power to consider granting a direct let of the property to her under its housing allocation scheme. The facts of the case were exceptional. The council had acted unlawfully in failing to identify the powers available to it and in notifying the occupier that there was no question of her being able to remain at the property. In *Thurrock BC v West*,[32] the grandson of a deceased council tenant did not qualify to succeed to the secure tenancy because there had already been a prior succession. He argued that since he and his own family had lived with his grandparents in the property for four years, it would be disproportionate to evict him. His defence was, however, rejected by the Court of Appeal. The Court held that the threshold for establishing an arguable case that a local authority was acting in breach of Article 8 rights is a high one which will be met in only a small proportion of cases. The Article 8 defence in this case did not even reach the threshold of being reasonably arguable. There was nothing exceptional about the housing needs of a couple with a small child and limited financial means. The defence should have been struck out summarily at the earliest opportunity.

23.16   It has been held, however, that trespassers who have occupied land or property without lawful permission are unlikely to be able to show that a decision to evict them engages rights under Article 8. In *Birmingham City Council v Lloyd*,[33] it was held that it would only be in very highly exceptional circumstances that it would be appropriate for the court to consider a proportionality argument on behalf of some-

29 [2010] UKSC 45, [2011] HLR 7.
30 [2011] UKSC 8, [2011] HLR 23.
31 [2013] EWCA Civ 1467, [2014] HLR 8.
32 [2012] EWCA Civ 1435, [2013] HLR 5. See also *Fareham BC v Miller* [2013] EWCA Civ 159, [2013] HLR 22.
33 [2012] EWCA Civ 969, [2012] HLR 44.

one who had entered as a trespasser.[34] For a more detailed discussion of public law and human rights defences, see chapters 25 and 26.

23.17   Courts dealing with possession proceedings will not be sympathetic to applications for adjournments to enable a public law or human rights defence to be filed, or for judicial review procedings to be brought, unless it can be shown at the first hearing that there is a seriously arguable case. Courts are particularly reluctant to allow squatters to use such arguments merely to delay proceedings. Trespassers who have an arguable defence should seek legal representation and apply for legal aid as soon as possible after it is known that a decision to take proceedings has been made.

23.18   The fact that a local authority is in breach of its statutory obligations (for example, to provide accommodation to homeless people under HA 1996 Part 7) does not necessarily provide a defence to possession proceedings.[35] However, breach of such statutory obligations may be important in support of a submission that a local authority has acted unreasonably.[36]

Enforcement of possession orders

23.19   A possession order made against trespassers in a county court may be enforced either in the High Court or in a county court.[37] See para 31.49. In the High Court, no notice is required to be given of an

---

34 See *Malik v Fassenfelt* [2013] EWCA Civ 798, [2013] 3 EGLR 99, in which the majority declined to express a view as to whether an Article 8 defence could be raised in a claim made by a private landlowner against trespassers, but in any event it was proportionate to make a possession order, and *Manchester Ship Canal Developments Ltd v Persons Unknown* [2014] EWHC 645 (Ch). But see also *McDonald v McDonald* [2016] UKSC 28, [2016] HLR 28, in which the Supreme Court rejected the argument that a court should, when entertaining a claim for possession by a private sector owner (in this case a claim against an assured shorthold tenant) against a residential occupier, be required to consider the proportionality of evicting the occupier.

35 *Southwark LBC v Williams* [1971] Ch 734, [1971] 2 WLR 467; *Kensington and Chelsea RLBC v Wells* (1973) 72 LGR 289 and *R v Barnet LBC ex p Grumbridge* (1992) 24 HLR 433, DC.

36 See, eg, *West Glamorgan CC v Rafferty* [1987] 1 WLR 457, (1986) 18 HLR 375; *Tower Hamlets LBC v Rahanra Begum* [2005] EWCA Civ 116, [2006] HLR 9; *Sharp v Brent LBC* [2003] EWCA Civ 779, [2003] HLR 65 and *R v Brent LBC ex p McDonagh* (1989) 21 HLR 494, DC.

37 Article 8B, High Court and County Courts Jurisdiction Order 1991, inserted by the High Court and County Courts Jurisdiction (Amendment No 2) Order 2001. See CPR 83.13 and para 31.46 for enforcement in the High Court.

application for, or execution of, a writ of possession against trespassers, including former licensees.

'Adverse possession' defences

23.20　The Limitation Act 1980 s15(1) provided that no action could be
brought to recover any land after the expiration of the limitation
period of 12 years. 'Limitation ... extinguishes the right of the true
owner to recover the land, so that the squatter's possession becomes
impregnable, giving him a title superior to all others.'[38] Time ran
from the commencement of the adverse possession. That required
a degree of occupation or physical control, coupled with an intention to possess without the consent of the paper owner.[39] After 12
years' adverse possession, the paper proprietor of the land held it on
trust for the squatter, who might apply to be registered at HM Land
Registry as proprietor of a new estate, where the registered land was
freehold, or as proprietor of the registered estate where that estate
was leasehold.[40]

23.21　　However, where the title to land is registered, the old law of
adverse possession has been replaced by the Land Registration Act
(LRA) 2002. Under that Act, with effect from 13 October 2003, adverse
possession of itself, for however long, does not bar the owner's title
to a registered estate in land.[41] A squatter is entitled to apply to the
Land Registry to be registered as proprietor after ten years' adverse
possession.[42] If the application is not opposed by any of those notified, the squatter should be registered as proprietor of the land. Otherwise, adverse possession for ten years does not by itself give a right
to registration. If any of the people notified opposes the application
it should be rejected, unless the adverse possessor can bring him
or herself within one or more of three conditions contained in LRA
2002 Sch 6 para 5. If the squatter's application for registration is
refused but the squatter remains in adverse possession for a further

---

38　*Buckinghamshire CC v Moran* [1990] Ch 623, 635, [1989] 3 WLR 152, CA.
39　*JA Pye (Oxford) Ltd v Graham* [2002] UKHL 30, [2003] 1 AC 419. But see *Smart
v Lambeth LBC* [2013] EWCA Civ 1375, [2014] HLR 7 in which it was held that
the defendant's occupation of the properties had been with the express or
implied permission of the council, and therefore did not constitute adverse
possession at all.
40　LRA 1925 s75.
41　LRA 2002 s96.
42　See LRA 2002 s97 and Sch 6 and Land Registration Rules 2003 SI No 1417.

two years, he or she is entitled to apply once again to be registered and should this time be registered as proprietor whether or not the registered proprietor objects. The purpose of the two-year period is to enable the paper owner to evict the squatter.[43]

23.22   Where the registered proprietor brings proceedings to recover possession from a squatter in that intervening period, LRA 2002 s98 allows the squatter to establish certain limited defences. Ten years' adverse possession by itself is not a defence. However, if a landowner obtains judgment for possession against someone who has been in adverse possession for ten years, that judgment ceases to be enforceable two years after the date of the judgment.[44] If a court determines that a squatter has a defence under section 98 or that a judgment for possession ceases to be enforceable under the same section, the court must direct the Land Registrar to register that person as proprietor of the estate.[45]

23.23   The LRA 2002 did not affect the position of those who had already acquired possessory title prior to its implementation on 13 October 2003. Schedule 12 para 18 provides that where a registered estate in land was held in trust for a person by virtue of LRA 1925 s75(1) immediately before that date, that person is entitled to be registered as the proprietor of the estate. Similarly, a person has a defence to any action for the possession of land if he or she is entitled under Sch 12 para 18 to be registered as the proprietor of an estate in the land.

23.24   LRA 2002 Sch 12 para 7 provided that for a period of three years after 13 October 2003 the squatter's unregistered interest would be an overriding interest whether or not he or she was in actual occupation and so would be binding on purchasers. However, after that period any squatter who has not been registered as owner will only

---

43 In *Best v Chief Land Registrar* [2015] EWCA Civ 17, [2015] HLR 17 the Court of Appeal allowed an appeal against a decision of the Chief Land Registrar that the occupier's application to register title to a property on the basis of ten years' adverse possession should be rejected. The reason for the rejection was that the effect of the Legal Aid, Sentencing and Punishment of Offenders Act 2012 s144, which created a criminal offence of squatting in a residential building, was to prevent a person from relying on any period of adverse possession which involved a criminal offence. However, the Court of Appeal held that Parliament must be taken to have accepted that, bearing in mind the public policy advantages of adverse possession at common law, the mere fact that possession begins with criminal trespass should not preclude a successful claim to adverse possession.

44 LRA 2002 s98(2).

45 LRA 2002 s98(5).

continue to have an overriding interest if he or she remains in occupation and Sch 3 para 2 applies.

Interim possession orders

23.25   The Criminal Justice and Public Order Act (CJPOA) 1994 ss75 and 76 created a form of interim possession order (IPO) which can only be granted against trespassers (meaning, in this instance, squatters). Failure to comply with an IPO is a criminal offence (see below). The procedure for obtaining IPOs is now contained in CPR Part 55.

23.26   The IPO procedure applies only in limited circumstances. It can be used if:

- *The landowner is claiming possession only.* An applicant cannot seek an IPO if there is a claim for another remedy (for example, damages).[46]
- *The applicant has an immediate right to possession and has had such a right throughout the period of unlawful occupation.*[47]
- *The defendants entered premises as trespassers.*[48] It cannot be used against former tenants, subtenants or licensees. The Criminal Law Act 1977 s12(1)(a) defines 'premises' as 'any building, any part of a building under separate occupation, any land ancillary to a building, the site comprising any building or buildings together with any land ancillary thereto ...'.
- *The application is issued within 28 days of the date when the owner first knew, or ought reasonably to have known, that the defendants were in occupation.*[49]

23.27   Landowners seeking IPOs should use forms N5 (claim form)[50] and N130, which comprises both the application and the statement in support of the application. The written evidence (ie, the statement) must be made personally by the claimant (not by a solicitor or agent) unless the claimant is a corporate body in which case an authorised officer may make it. It includes an undertaking to re-instate the defendant and to pay damages if so ordered by the court.

23.28   The court should fix a hearing date as soon as possible after the documents have been filed, but not less than three days after the date

---

46   CPR 55.21(1)(a).
47   CPR 55.21(1)(b).
48   CPR 55.21(2).
49   CPR 55.21(1)(c).
50   See PD 55.13.

on which the application for an IPO is issued. 'Three days' means three clear days and Saturdays, Sundays, Bank Holidays, Christmas Day and Good Friday do not count.[51]

23.29   Service of form N5, the completed form N130 and a blank form of defendant's witness statement (form N133) must take place within 24 hours after issue of proceedings. This should be done by fixing a copy to the main door or other conspicuous part of the premises, and if practicable, inserting a copy in a sealed and transparent envelope addressed to the occupiers through the letter-box in accordance with CPR 55.6. Failure to do so provides a defence to the proceedings.

23.30   In deciding whether or not to grant an IPO, the court should have regard to whether or not the owner has given the undertakings in the prescribed form N130 to reinstate the occupier and pay damages if the court subsequently finds that the IPO should not have been made. Before making an order, the court should have regard to whether or not the claimant has undertaken not to damage the premises or the defendant's belongings and not to grant a right of occupation to any other person pending the final hearing.[52]

23.31   The court must make an IPO if:

- it is satisfied as to service;[53]
- the claimant is only seeking possession, has an immediate right to possession and has had such a right throughout the period of unlawful occupation and the defendant entered the premises as a trespasser;[54] and
- adequate undertakings have been given.[55]

23.32   If an IPO is made in form N134, it must be served on the trespassers with copies of the claimant's forms N5 and N130 within 48 hours of its being sealed.[56] Under CJPOA 1994 s76 it is a criminal offence to be 'present on the premises as a trespasser at any time during the currency of the order' but no offence is committed if the trespasser leaves the premises within 24 hours and does not return. Similarly, no offence is committed if a copy of the order is not fixed to the premises.

---

51 CPR 2.8.
52 CPR 55.25.
53 See CPR 55.25(2)(a) and CPR 55.6(a).
54 See CPR 55.21.
55 See CPR 55.25(1).
56 CPR 55.26.

23.33   If an IPO is made, the court fixes a return day which is not less than seven days after the initial hearing.[57] The IPO lapses on the return day. This means that once the return day has arrived, it is no longer a criminal offence for trespassers to be on the premises. At the return day hearing, the court may either make a final possession order or dismiss the claim or give further directions or enforce any of the claimant's undertakings. A final order for possession is made in form N136.

23.34   Where the court does not make an IPO, the court will set a date for the hearing of the claim, and may give directions for the future conduct of the claim. Subject to any such directions, the case will proceed as a standard possession claim. If the occupiers have vacated the premises they may apply before the return day on grounds of urgency to set aside an IPO which has been made. Any such application should be supported by a witness statement.[58]

23.35   CJPOA 1994 s77 gives local authorities power to direct the removal of vehicles and their occupants from land or highway. Section 77(1) provides:

> If it appears to a local authority that persons are for the time being residing in a vehicle or vehicles within that authority's area –
> (a) on any land forming part of a highway;
> (b) on any other unoccupied land; or
> (c) on any occupied land without the consent of the occupier,
> the authority may give a direction that those persons and any others with them are to leave the land and remove the vehicle or vehicles and any other property they have with them on the land.

'Vehicle' is defined as including a caravan. Where an authority has made a removal direction, occupiers of the vehicle must, as soon as practicable, leave the land or remove from the land any vehicle or other property which is the subject of the direction, and must not re-enter on the land for a period of three months. Failure to comply with the direction is a summary offence, for which enforcement action may be taken in the magistrates' court. Where, on a complaint made by a local authority, the court is satisfied that persons and vehicles in which they are residing are present on land within that authority's area in contravention of a direction given under section 77, it may make an order requiring the removal of any vehicle and occupier present on the land.

23.36   Local authorities, at the initial stage of deciding whether and to whom to give a removal direction under CJPOA 1994 s77, have to consider the relationship of their proposed action to other statutory and humanitarian considerations and make their decision accordingly. Such decisions should be reviewed by local authorities if there is a change in circumstances. They must strike a balance between the competing and conflicting needs of those encamped illegally and of residents in the area. A removal direction can only apply to people who were on the land at the time when the direction was made and, therefore, can only be contravened by such people.[59]

23.37   It is arguable that the IPO procedure does not constitute access to a fair hearing within the meaning of Human Rights Act 1998 Sch 1 Article 6. Key elements of a fair hearing such as the right to participate effectively, equality of arms, the right to an adversarial hearing and the right to be present are all missing. Defendants have no right to be present unless a witness statement has been served in reply. Under the IPO procedure defendants are at a substantial disadvantage and do not have a proper opportunity to present their case or to comment upon the other party's evidence.[60] However, the procedure is rarely used, and its compatibility with Article 6 remains untested.

---

59 *R v Lincolnshire CC ex p Atkinson* (1996) 8 Admin LR 529, [1995] NPC 145, QBD. See also *R v Wolverhampton MBC ex p Dunne* (1997) 29 HLR 745, [1997] COD 210, QBD and *R (Ward) v Hillingdon LBC* [2001] EWHC 91 (Admin), [2001] HRLR 40.

60 But see *R (Ward) v Hillingdon LBC* [2001] EWHC 91 (Admin), [2001] HRLR 40.

CHAPTER 24

Public funding to defend possession proceedings

Introduction

24.1   In April 2013, responsibility for the provision of public money to assist litigants of low income passed from the Legal Services Commission to the Legal Aid Agency (LAA) which is an executive agency of the Ministry of Justice. Under Legal Aid, Sentencing and Punishment of Offenders Act 2012 (LASPO) the Lord Chancellor is obliged to secure that legal aid is made available in accordance with that Act.[1] 'Legal aid' includes both criminal legal aid and 'civil legal services'. LASPO provides for the appointment of the Director of Legal Aid Casework who is responsible for the provision of legal aid services through the LAA. Detailed transitional arrangements were made to deal with the statutory change in legal aid which was previously regulated under the Access to Justice Act 1999.[2] The fundamental difference in the legislation is that under LASPO-only work which is specifically within scope as defined in that legislation is capable of being funded. The only exception is where in a particular individual's case the LAA can be persuaded to grant 'exceptional funding' which in practice is numerically insignificant.

24.2   The Funding Code issued under the Access to Justice 1999 has been replaced by the Legal Aid (Merits Criteria) Regulations 2013[3] (the 'Merits Regs') and Legal Aid (Procedure) Regulations 2012 (the 'Procedure Regulations').[4] The Funding Code Decision-Making Guidance has been replaced by Lord Chancellor's Guidance[5] ('Guidance'). LAA also publishes 'Frequently Asked Questions Civil Legal Aid Reforms' which gives an insight into LAA thinking on various issues and interpretation.[6]

24.3   The terms under which 'providers' contract with the LAA for the provision of civil legal services are currently contained in the Standard Civil Contracts 2013 and 2014. Public funding for assistance in a housing dispute is provided through the 2013 Contract and its

---

1   LASPO s1(1).

2   The Legal Aid, Sentencing and Punishment of Offenders Act 2012 (Consequential, Transitional and Saving Provisions) Regulations 2013 SI No 534 and the Legal Aid, Sentencing and Punishment of Offenders Act 2012 (Consequential, Transitional and Saving Provisions) (Amendment) Regulations 2013 SI No 621.

3   SI No 104.

4   SI No 3098.

5   www.gov.uk/government/uploads/system/uploads/attachment_data/file/332795/legal-aid-lord-chancellors-guidance.pdf.

6   http://legalaidhandbook.files.wordpress.com/2013/04/legal-aid-reform-faq-v3.pdf.

'Housing and Debt Specification'. Advisers will be required to have easy access to the myriad of documents regulating legal aid work and these are most readily accessed through the *Legal Aid Handbook* and its associated website which contains everything that is relevant in one location.[7]

24.4   In the context of housing litigation there are in effect three possible levels of service. These are: Legal Help, Help at Court and Legal Representation. Legal Help and Help at Court are services provided by solicitors and not-for-profit organisations who contract with the LAA and provide advice and assistance to a predetermined number of clients by reference to the number of 'matter starts' a 'provider' has contracted to undertake during the year. The LAA funds a separate and distinct scheme to assist defendants to possession proceedings in certain courts. The 'Housing Possession Court Duty Scheme' forms part of a provider's contract in those courts approved for the scheme by the LAA.[8] Legal Help and Help at Court are both described as 'Controlled Work'. Legal Representation, by contrast, is 'Licensed Work' provided to a client by a solicitor under a 'legal aid certificate' which is applied for and awarded on a case-by-case basis. Legal Representation may take the form of either Investigative Representation or Full Representation and a solicitor can apply for either level depending on whether, at the time of the application, it is possible to estimate the prospects of successfully defending the proceedings. See para 24.12 below. The most important difference between the levels of service is between Legal Help/Help at Court and Legal Representation under a certificate. There is often a significant overlap between work which can be carried out at either of these levels.

Using the Legal Help and Help at Court schemes

24.5   The availability of Legal Help and Help at Court is separate from the availability of Legal Representation. The Lord Chancellor's Guidance states 'Legal help cannot cover advocacy before any court … Help at Court covers only informal advocacy usually by way of mitigation at individual court hearings (typically this will be in possession proceedings where the client has no defence to possession but seeks to influence the discretion of the court in relation to postponing possession

---

7   www.legalaidhandbook.com/laspo-resources/.
8   www.gov.uk/government/publications/housing-possession-court-duty-schemes-hpcds.

or suspending eviction)'.[9] Cases involving possession claims for mortgage arrears and applications for orders for sale are required to be dealt with through the 'Gateway' scheme. See para 24.26 below.

24.6   Part 3 of the Procedure Regulations 2012 makes provision for the making and withdrawal of applications for assistance through Legal Help and Help at Court.

24.7   The same form (Controlled Work 1) is used for the Legal Help and Help at Court schemes. If an adviser has been providing advice under the Legal Help scheme and it then proves necessary to represent at a hearing which falls within the criteria of cases for Help at Court, no further paperwork is necessary.

Using the Legal Representation scheme

24.8   Legal Representation is available to take or defend proceedings and in the context of possession proceedings is designed to provide for the defendant the full range of services available from a solicitor when defending proceedings. This includes not just the services of the solicitor but also, where relevant, the cost of experts and counsel. Legal Representation can be authorised by the LAA either for Investigative Representation or for Full Representation. Where the prospects of success are clear then it is appropriate to apply for Full Representation.

24.9   Part 4 of the Procedure Regulations makes provision for the making and withdrawal of determinations in respect of Legal Representation. An application for Legal Representation is made to the LAA, which will consider whether to make a determination as to the grant of a 'legal aid certificate'. This decision is made having regard to the Civil Legal Aid (Merits Criteria) Regulations 2013[10] and the Guidance.

24.10   The Merits Regs provide that Legal Representation can be either by way of 'Legal Representation' or 'Investigative Representation'.[11] Legal Representation means the provision of civil legal services to a person who is a party to proceedings, who wishes to be joined as a party to those proceedings or is contemplating issuing proceedings.[12] Investigative Representation means legal representation limited to

9   Lord Chancellor's Guidance (see note 5 above) at para 6.9(b).
10 SI No 104.
11 Merits Regs 2013 reg 18(1).
12 Merits Regs 2013 reg 18(2).

investigation of the strength of the contemplated proceedings and includes the issuing and conducting of proceedings but only so far as necessary to obtain disclosure of information relevant to the prospects of success of the proceedings *or* to protect the position of the individual applying for investigative representation in relation to an urgent hearing or the time limit for the issue of the proceedings.[13] Investigative Representation may only be granted where substantial investigative work is required before prospects can be determined.[14] The Guidance defines such work as being where the solicitor will reasonably need to carry out at least six hours of fee earner investigative work *or* disbursements together with any counsel's fees would cost £400 or more excluding VAT.[15] Application can, and should, be made at the outset for Investigative Representation where it is clear that the criteria are met. It is not necessary to carry out work at Legal Help level first. Providers will want to avoid unnecessarily using a 'case start' and in any event the work is charged at hourly rates rather than at a fixed fee.

24.11   The Merits Regulations set out specific criteria for determining whether Full Representation should be granted in possession proceedings relating to an individual's home:[16]

Criteria for determinations for full representation in relation to court orders for possession

61(1) For the purposes of a determination for full representation in relation to any matter described in paragraph 33(1)(a) of Part 1 of Schedule 1 to the Act (court orders for sale or possession of the individual's home), to the extent that it relates to court orders for possession of the individual's home, the criteria in –

(a) regulation 39 (standard criteria for determinations for legal representation) and regulation 43 (prospects of success criterion for determination of full representation) apply;

(b) regulations 41, 42 and 44 (criteria for determinations for full representation) do not apply; and

(c) paragraph (2) apply.

(2) The Director must be satisfied that the following criteria are met –

(a) if the individual is the defendant to a claim for possession, the individual has a defence to the claim; and

(b) ...

(c) the proportionality test is met.

---

13 Merits Regs 2013 reg 18(3).
14 Merits Regs 2013 reg 40(1).
15 Para 6.11.
16 Merits Regs 2013 reg 61(1).

24.12   'Moderate' is defined as having a 50 per cent or more (but less than 60 per cent) chance of obtaining a successful outcome; 'borderline' is where it is not possible by reason of disputed law, fact or expert evidence to decide that the chance of obtaining a successful outcome is 50 per cent or more, or to classify the prospects that the individual is unlikely to obtain a successful outcome; 'marginal' means a 45 per cent or more chance , but less than a 50 per cent chance of obtaining a successful outcome.

24.13   Regulation 39 sets out the standard criteria applicable before legal representation maybe approved in any case:

> **39** An individual may qualify for legal representation only if the Director is satisfied that the following criteria are met –
> (a) the individual does not have access to other potential sources of funding (other than a conditional fee agreement) from which it would be reasonable to fund the case;
> (b) the case is unsuitable for a conditional fee agreement;
> (c) there is no person other than the individual, including a person who might benefit from the proceedings, who can reasonably be expected to bring the proceedings;
> (d) the individual has exhausted all reasonable alternatives to bringing proceedings including any complaints system, ombudsman scheme or other form of alternative dispute resolution;
> (e) there is a need for representation in all the circumstances of the case including –
> (i)   the nature and complexity of the issues;
> (ii) the existence of other proceedings; and
> (iii) the interests of other parties to the proceedings; and
> (f) the proceedings are not likely to be allocated to the small claims track.

24.14   Regulation 41 provides:

> **41** An individual may qualify for full representation only if the Director is satisfied that the criteria in regulation 39 (standard criteria for determinations for legal representation) and the following criteria are met –
> (a) the cost benefit criteria in regulation 42;
> (b) the prospects of success criterion in regulation 43; and ...

24.15   Regulation 42 provides:

> **42**(1) The cost benefit criteria are as follows.
> ...
> (3) If the case is –
> (a) not primarily a claim for damages or other sum of money; and
> (b) not of significant wider public interest,

the Director must be satisfied that the reasonable private paying individual test is met.

(4) If the case is of significant wider public interest, the Director must be satisfied that the proportionality test is met.

24.16 Regulation 44 is irrelevant in the context of possession proceedings as it applies only to multi-party damages action.

24.17 Regulation 8 sets out the Proportionality Test:

For the purposes of these Regulations, the proportionality test is met if the Director is satisfied that the likely benefits of the proceedings to the individual and others justify the likely costs, having regard to the prospects of success and all the other circumstances of the case.

24.18 LASPO Sch 1 Pt 1 para 33 deals with the 'Loss of Home' and permits for civil legal services to be provided to an individual in relation to court orders for sale or possession of their home or the eviction from the individual's home of the individual or others. 'Home' is defined as meaning the individual's house, caravan, houseboat or other vehicle or structure (including the land on which it is located or to which it is moored) where that is the individual's only or main residence.[17] However, this definition of 'home' does not include a vehicle or structure occupied by the individual if there are no grounds on which it can be argued that occupation of the vehicle or structure is and began otherwise than as a trespasser.[18] In this context, individuals occupying a vehicle or structure as a trespasser include individuals who do so by virtue of title derived from a trespasser or a licence or consent given by a trespasser or a person deriving title from a trespasser.[19] A person who is occupying a vehicle or structure as a trespasser does not cease to be a trespasser by virtue of being allowed time to leave the vehicle or structure. Where there are good grounds for bringing a human rights or public law challenge to the decision to bring or progress eviction proceedings, public funding for judicial review might be available.

24.19 It is the LAA's view that it is not necessary for possession proceedings to be issued before assistance through the Legal Help scheme can be given provided the client has received formal written notification that proceedings will be issued (such as a HA 1988 s8 or section 21 notice) unless there is some intervention. An application for Legal Representation will not be granted before proceedings have

17 LASPO Sch 1 Pt 1 para 33(9) and (11).
18 Para 33(10).
19 Para 33(12).

been issued at court by the opponent.[20] In mortgage and rent arrears cases, Legal Representation cannot be granted without a full or partial defence. There is no such requirement for Legal Help.[21] Demotion of tenancy cases are out of scope.[22]

24.20   It is important for advisers, when applying for Legal Representation, to identify the nature of the evidence or legal argument that needs to be presented to the court. This should be set out in a covering letter or witness statement prepared to support the legal aid application. Copies of relevant documents should be provided. It may be possible to obtain from a barrister, who is prepared to advise informally, a preliminary advice in the form of an email which can be submitted in support of an application for a legal aid certificate. In possession claims based on discretionary grounds for possession, it is important to point out the need for the claimant to prove reasonableness before *any* order for possession can be granted (outright or postponed) and to identify any factors which will be relied on in opposition to the proposition that it is reasonable for a possession order to be made.

24.21   Public funding is also available to an individual in relation to a bankruptcy order where the bankruptcy petition was presented by a person other than the individual and the individual's estate includes their home. This includes legal services provided in relation to a statutory demand.[23] Funding is available for services relating to proceedings brought by a trustee in bankruptcy for an order under Trusts of Land and Appointment of Trustees Act 1996.[24] Funding is also available to an individual in relation to court orders for sale or possession or eviction from the home or in relation to a bankruptcy order where the home is included in the individual's estate and where the issues involved relate to a proposal by that individual to establish a business, the carrying on of a business by that individual (whether or not the business is being carried on at the time the services are provided) or the termination or transfer of a business that was being carried on by that individual.[25]

---

20 Legal Aid Agency Frequently Asked Questions on legal aid reform version 3, FAQ Q98.
21 FAQ Q99.
22 FAQ Q106.
23 Para 33(2).
24 Para 33(5).
25 Para 33(3).

24.22   Since 1 April 2016 it has been mandatory for applications for legal aid certificates to be made online using the LAA Client and Cost Management System (CCMS).

24.23   In urgent cases, Emergency Representation can be authorised either by a solicitor provider (if the firm has been granted authority to do so as a delegated function by the LAA) or directly from the LAA. Emergency Representation is a form of Legal Representation and authorises work which needs to be done as an emergency before a Full Representation public-funding certificate can be obtained. The scope of an emergency certificate should only cover work that is urgently required. The default financial limit in an emergency certificate is £1,350 (inclusive of counsel's fees and disbursements). Where a provider has granted emergency legal aid the provider must within five business days notify the LAA of this and provide to the LAA the necessary supporting documents.[26] Failure to do so can cause a delay in the issuing of a substantive certificate. Payment will not be made by the LAA for work carried out during the period from the end of the emergency certificate and prior to the date of the substantive certificate.

Advice to applicants for public funding

24.24   When assisting people who are considering applying for public funding it is important to advise them about any likely financial contribution which they may be required to pay to the LAA each month.[27] This is particularly important when applying for an emergency certificate because the applicant undertakes to accept any offer of public funding which is made to him or her. Not to accept the offer will result in the LAA revoking the emergency certificate and looking to the applicant to pay all of the costs which are paid to the solicitor and counsel by the LAA.

24.25   Similarly, it is essential to advise the applicant to co-operate at all times with the LAA, both before the grant of the full public funding certificate (if an emergency certificate has been granted) and where a substantive public funding certificate has been issued. A client should also be advised of the requirement that he or she notifies the LAA of any change in his or her financial circumstances or that of

---

26 SI No 3098 reg 39.
27 Civil Legal Aid (Financial Resources and Payment of Services) Regs 2013 SI No 480 reg 44.

any person whose resources are aggregated with the client which might affect the terms on which funding is provided.[28] Failure to co-operate with the LAA can result in the certificate being revoked. If the certificate is revoked the client must pay to the LAA all costs paid or payable under the certificate and is liable to pay to the provider the difference between the amount paid or payable by the LAA and the full amount of the provider's costs payable on the indemnity basis under CPR 44.3.[29] In recent times the LAA has been much more active in seeking to recover costs paid on revocation of a certificate than was previously the case. This advice to the client must be set out in the 'client care' letter sent to the applicant at the time of the legal aid application, but there is no substitute for talking to the client about this.

Public funding in possession proceedings involving home owners

24.26   As a result of the changes to legal aid introduced in 2013, the availability of assistance to persons facing mortgage repossession or an application for an order for sale is restricted. Such cases are now 'debt matters' and those wishing to apply for Legal Help or Help at Court are required to be dealt with through the Civil Legal Advice (CLA) telephone line known as 'The Gateway'. Part 2 of the Procedure Regulations sets out the Gateway requirements. The LAA has also published specific guidance in *Civil Legal Advice and the gateway – Guidance for Civil Contracted Providers*.

24.27   Any person seeking assistance through Legal Help and Help at Court must apply to the Gateway unless that person is an 'exempted' person. Application can be made by phone, post, email or other approved electronic format. The phone number is 0845 345 4 345 and the opening hours are Monday to Friday 9am to 8pm and Saturday 9am to 12.30pm. To book a call back applicants are invited to go to callmeback.justice.gov.uk or to text 'legalaid' and their name to 80010.

24.28   A person is 'exempt', and so entitled to make application to a provider face to face, if he or she is a child or a prisoner. Additionally, an individual is exempt if he or she is a previously assessed person with a linked problem. This is defined as someone who in the previous

28   Reg 18.
29   Reg 47.

12 months has qualified for Gateway work provided by a face to face provider and requires further help arising out of or related to a matter in relation to which Gateway work was provided by a face to face provider.

24.29   CLA will assess callers as to their financial eligibility for assistance and to determine whether a remote service is appropriate for the individual. A client's preference for face to face assistance is not a determining factor. A person who requires Legal Representation under a certificate will always be offered access to a face to face provider. Where a person is unhappy about a decision made by CLA following the assessment for suitability for remote advice. they can ask for a review of that decision.[30] Where a client is referred by CLA to a face to face provider, they will be allocated a CLA reference number which the provider must record as evidence of the fact that the client has been assessed as requiring face to face assistance. Face to face providers should check the reference number by phoning 0845 124 7447.

24.30   It is important to recognise that referral to the Gateway in a mortgage repossession or order for sale case is not necessary where Legal Representation ('licensed work') is immediately required. The Lord Chancellor's Guidance states:

> 8.12 Part 2 of the Procedure Regulations do not apply to applications for licensed work. A provider will therefore be able to make an application for licensed work in Gateway areas of law on behalf of a client. However, an application for licensed work should not be made until all work which could have been carried out under legal help has been completed. Unless, therefore, the matter is urgent and legal representation is immediately required it would usually be expected that an application for the initial legal help should be made through the Gateway. If not, the application for licensed work may be premature.[31]

Housing Possession Court Duty Scheme

24.31   Alongside mainstream services offered by providers under the 2013 Contract and the CLA Gateway the LAA also funds face to face services through the Housing Possession Court Duty Scheme. This scheme operates throughout England and Wales and offers 'on the day' emergency face to face advice and advocacy at court to anyone facing possession proceedings. Anyone facing eviction or having

30 LAA Frequently Asked Questions Version 3, Q139.
31 *Lord Chancellor's Guidance on Civil Legal Aid* para 8.12.

property repossessed can get free legal advice and representation on the day of their hearing, regardless of their financial circumstances. Full details of the Scheme are given in the LAA's 'Housing Possession Court Duty Scheme – Guidance for Service Providers'.

24.32   Under the Scheme providers who hold a specific contract with the LAA operate a 'duty desk' at the county court during times when the court schedules possession hearings. Cases covered include private rented and social rented and mortgage possession proceedings, applications to stay warrants for possession and applications for sale based on charging orders. Possession claims based on nuisance or unauthorised occupation are outside the scope of the Scheme. The Scheme 'may assist repeat clients if they are in genuine need of it and it is appropriate to do so.'

24.33   The fee paid to providers (currently £71.55 or £75.60 in London exclusive of VAT per individual seen) covers any work done at the initial session at court. The Scheme does not cover advice given at court to people who do not have a hearing listed on that day even if they have a hearing listed in the future or are making an application to suspend a warrant. If the client has a defence which warrants full funding under a Legal Representation certificate, the provider at court can arrange to see the defendant subsequently. If, however, the provider intends to open a Legal Help case than a fee cannot be claimed under the Scheme. However, the time spent at court can be counted towards the Legal Help case.

Remuneration from the Legal Aid Agency

24.34   The rates of payment to suppliers are set out in the Civil Legal Aid (Remuneration) Regulations 2013.[32] Under the Legal Help and Help at Court scheme 'providers' are paid a fixed fee of £157 (exclusive of VAT) for each 'matter start'. However, where the provider incurs costs in excess of three times the fixed fee, a claim can be made for payment as an Escape Fee Case. Payment in such cases will be made on the basis of specified hourly rates.[33] Currently, the hourly rates are £45.95 (£48.74) for preparation, attendance and advocacy, £25.74 (£25.74) for travel and waiting and £3.65 (£3.78) for routine letters out and telephone calls. The sums in brackets are for providers in London. Higher rates of remuneration are payable where the

32   SI No 422.
33   Unified Contract Civil Specification para 7.19.

client is a defendant to possession proceedings in the county court. The relevant figures are £52.56 (£56.16), £27.05 (£27.81) and £3.78 (£4.05).[34] The sums are exclusive of VAT and disbursements (other than counsel's fees) can be claimed in addition.

24.35   Payment for work carried out under a Legal Representation certificate is made on the basis of time spent rather than a fixed fee. · The hourly rates are higher than under the Legal Help and Help at Court schemes and for that reason it is advisable to obtain a certificate as soon as possible. The relevant hourly rates for work in the county court are currently £59.40 (£63.00 in London) for preparation and attendance, £29.25 attending court or conference with counsel, £59.40 for advocacy, £26.28 travel and waiting, £5.94 per item for routine letters out and £3.29 for routine telephone calls.

24.36   In appropriate cases it is possible to claim an increased rate of payment for work done by way of a percentage enhancement to the hourly rates which cannot exceed 50 per cent for work in the county court and 100 per cent in the higher courts.[35]

24.37   The LAA 'Escape Cases Electronic Handbook'[36] contains useful guidance to its caseworkers providing clarification on specific issues relating to funding. Most usefully, however, it contains an electronic link to LAA documents dealing with all aspects of LAA funding.

The Legal Aid Agency's statutory charge

24.38   Advice to clients on the possible application of the statutory charge is important because failure properly to advise about public funding is one of the greatest causes of complaints about solicitors. It is necessary to advise mortgage borrowers, in particular, of the possible application of the LAA's statutory charge. In summary, the statutory charge arises in favour of the LAA whenever any property is preserved or recovered in any proceedings in which a publicly funded litigant takes part, except so far as regulations provide otherwise.[37] The Civil Legal Aid (Statutory Charge) Regulations 2013[38] set out the details of its operation and enforcement.

---

34 Or £75.60 in London.
35 Reg 6(3).
36 www.gov.uk/government/uploads/system/uploads/attachment_data/ file/438774/escape-cases-guidance.pdf.
37 LASPO s25.
38 SI No 503.

24.39   Where a mortgage-borrower is successful in preserving the home, the charge arises unless he or she is awarded costs which are recovered and as a result no claim is made against the legal aid fund. In *Parkes v Legal Aid Board*,[39] the Court of Appeal held that where the right to possession of property is retained or extended, the statutory charge attaches to that property notwithstanding that the beneficial interests in the property were never in issue. Certainly, the LAA's practice is now to apply the statutory charge in virtually all cases where a mortgage-borrower has been successful in preventing loss of the home in litigation where a Legal Representation certificate has been granted.

24.40   The LAA's *Statutory Charge Manual* provides further guidance on its thinking concerning the charge. This covers its definition, the valuation of property preserved, calculation of the statutory charge, enforcement (and, importantly, postponement of enforcement) and registration of the charge at the Land Registry.

24.41   In relation to *Parkes* the Manual observes:

Preservation of Possession (*Parkes v Legal Aid Board* [1996] 4 All ER 271)

6. The charge arises if, as a result of the proceedings, the legally aided individual prevents property from being sold. The decision of the Court of Appeal in *Parkes v Legal Aid Board* [1996] 4 All ER 271 demonstrates that the statutory charge applies in all cases where possession is either recovered or preserved.

...

9. In these cases the property to which the statutory charge attaches is the avoidance of a sale so that the legally aided individual has possession of property for a substantial period of time, or that the legally aided individual obtains the benefit of being able to dispose of the property themselves.

24.42   While *Parkes* was a case involving an application for an order for sale under what is now the Trusts of Land and Appointment of Trustees Act 1996 s14, which was successfully defended, the court in that case went on to discuss the general application of the statutory charge in possession proceedings. In *McPherson v Legal Services Commission*,[40] a court concluded that because a compromise of possession proceedings brought by a mortgage lender had resulted in the borrower preserving possession of the security, that property had been preserved and accordingly the statutory charge arose. In *McPherson* the court

39 [1997] 1 WLR 1547, [1996] 4 All ER 271, CA. See also M Thompson, 'The Legal Aid Charge' [1997] Conv 47.
40 [2008] EWHC 2865 (Ch).

observed that if a court refused 'to make an early order for possession' but stayed possession on terms then the charge would arise.
It was, however, doubted that the charge arose where, at the date of
settlement, there was negative equity.[41] There may, however, be grey
areas where advisers will need to be careful about how court orders
should be worded and diligent in subsequently disputing the LAA's
view that the statutory charge applies.

24.43   Regulations provide that, in the context of a possession claim, the
statutory charge does not arise in respect of the cost to the LAA of
work undertaken under the Legal Help or Help at Court scheme.[42]

24.44   Where the LAA has funded Legal Representation in proceedings
which it considers to have significant wider public interest and where
the statutory charge would apply, the LAA has discretion to waive
some, or all, of the amount of the statutory charge if it considers it
equitable to do so.[43]

24.45   If, after getting Legal Help or Help at Court, the client goes on
to receive help with Legal Representation under a Legal Representation certificate, the statutory charge will arise in favour of the LAA
in relation to the work carried out under Legal Help in addition to
work under the certificate providing it is in connection with the same
proceedings or dispute.[44]

24.46   In enforcing the statutory charge, the LAA has the same rights
as are available to a chargee in respect of a charge given between
parties.[45]

24.47   Where the statutory charge does apply the LAA may postpone
enforcement if:

(a) by order of the court or agreement it relates to property to be used
    as a home by the legally aided party or his dependents ...;
(b) the LAA is satisfied that the property in question will provide
    appropriate security for the statutory charge; and
(c) the LAA considers that it would be unreasonable for the legally
    aided party to repay the amount of the charge.[46]

Where the statutory charge is postponed, the LAA must – as soon as
it is possible – register a charge under the Land Registration Act 2002
to secure the amount of the charge or take equivalent steps (whether

---

41 Para [90] of the judgment.
42 Civil Legal Aid (Statutory Charge) Regulations 2013 SI No 503 reg 4(1).
43 Reg 9.
44 Reg 4(2).
45 Reg 21.
46 Reg 22(1).

in England and Wales or in any other jurisdiction) to protect its interests in the property.[47]

24.48   The LAA has only very limited discretion in relation to postponement of the enforcement of the statutory charge. Unless the property preserved is adequate security for the sums to be deferred, it would appear that the client will be at risk of the LAA seeking to enforce the monies secured by the statutory charge. The LAA may review the decision to defer enforcement and again, unless it considers that the criteria for postponement still apply, must enforce the charge.[48] If the LAA continues to defer enforcement of the charge it may do so on such terms and conditions as to repayment of the amount of the charge by way of interim payments of either capital or interest or both, as appears to the LAA to be appropriate.[49]

24.49   Where enforcement of the statutory charge is postponed, interest accrues for the benefit of the LAA.[50] Interest is recoverable at the rate of eight per cent per annum from the date when the charge is first registered and continues to accrue until the amount of the statutory charge is paid. The capital sum, on which interest is calculated, is the lesser of the amount of the statutory charge outstanding from time to time (ignoring any interest that has accrued) and the value of the property recovered at the time of its recovery.[51] The legally aided party may make interim payments of either capital or interest but no payment may be used to reduce the capital outstanding while any interest remains outstanding.[52]

24.50   The adviser must notify the LAA of the preservation or recovery of property using form CIV ADMIN1 or, in the case of post-April 2016 certificates, using CCMS at the 'reporting outcome' stage. Where the LAA cannot agree to postpone enforcement of the charge the legally aided party will be asked to pay enough money to redeem the charge. If this is not paid, the LAA Debt Recovery Unit will decide whether to take enforcement proceedings or steps to register a charge on the home. The Manual states that the LAA will take a commercial approach to deciding what is the most cost effective way to secure the LAA's interests.[53] In the context of deciding whether to postpone enforcement of the charge, the Manual notes: 'A common sense

---

47   Reg 22(2).
48   Reg 24(1).
49   Reg 24(2).
50   Reg 22(5)(a).
51   Reg 25 (1).
52   Reg 25(2).
53   Statutory Charge Manual para 6.5.

approach should be used to determine whether it is unreasonable for the client to repay the statutory charge. A sensible test is 'can they borrow from a high street lender?' In the majority of cases, legally aided individuals are going to be on low incomes or benefits and will be in no position to repay the statutory charge at the conclusion of their case, and will not be able to borrow from a high street lender.[54]

24.51   The Manual deals with reviews as to continued postponement of the charge. It observes that immediate enforcement may be appropriate where: 'For example, the charge was postponed a long time ago, and now the legally aided individual can repay the charge but has refused to do so.' Continued postponement may be appropriate if: 'For example the client is on a subsistence benefit and has no other household income or client is retired or has a long term illness'. A requirement for interim payments may be considered if: 'For example, the client is better off than they were at conclusion of their case and is able to make regular repayments of say, £40 a month to clear their liability.' The instalment amount that clients repay towards their charges should be set at an amount higher than the monthly interest which accrues; otherwise the client will not see their charge reduce in amount with each payment.[55]

24.52   Advisers are reminded of the duty to notify the LAA immediately of any property preserved so that the LAA can consider whether there are steps which need to be taken at that stage to safeguard the fund.[56] Unfortunately, this obligation is not always recognised and advisers put themselves at risk if, ultimately, money subject to the statutory charge cannot be recovered because of delay in the LAA being advised about property being preserved. In such circumstances it is the LAA's view that it has the power to defer payment of a solicitor's costs.[57]

24.53   The statutory charge will still arise where property is preserved in cases where a certificate has been discharged or revoked but where the client (or his or her personal representative or trustee in bankruptcy) has continued to defend the proceedings.[58]

24.54   Theoretically, the statutory charge may apply to contractual tenancies preserved (though not to a Rent Act statutory tenancy which is no more than a personal right), given that the charge attaches to any

---

54 Para 7.1.4.
55 Statutory Charge Manual para 7.6.
56 Reg 15(1).
57 Statutory Charge Manual para 6.2.
58 Reg 10.

'property'. The Manual notes that the 'charge can attach to anything of value including ... real property, which means land or an interest in land, including leases, land or property abroad.[59] In practice, there would seem to be little point in the LAA seeking to enforce the statutory charge against the vast majority of assisted tenants.

59   Para 3.1.

Public law defences

The public law defence: an introduction

25.1   This chapter is about a particular form of defence available when the claimant in possession proceedings is a 'public' body (such as a government department or a local authority) or a private organisation carrying out a 'public' function.[1] The defence cannot be used where the claimant is a private individual (or private company or private trust) which is seeking to recover possession for their (or its) own benefit.

25.2   The defence is available to homeowners, tenants, subtenants, licensees and even trespassers. The particular situations in which the defence can be relied upon by trespassers are dealt with in chapter 23. This chapter is about its availability in all other cases.

25.3   In short summary, the defence 'works' by the application of the following principles. Public bodies must respect the rule of law. They must not act unlawfully or seek to give effect to their unlawful actions or unlawful decisions. When they try to recover possession based on an unlawful decision or unlawful act, the defendant can defend the possession claim by arguing that the court should refuse a possession order because granting it would be to give effect to the public body's unlawful conduct or unlawful decision.

25.4   In the context of a claim for possession, a public body must act lawfully throughout the process by which it seeks to gain possession. That means that a public body must not reach an unlawful decision to terminate a tenancy or licence or give an occupier a notice to leave based on that unlawful decision. It must not unlawfully decide to issue a possession claim or later unlawfully decide to press it to trial. It must not make an unlawful decision to execute (that is, enforce) a possession order that it has obtained.[2]

25.5   The courts have long had a supervisory jurisdiction to ensure that public bodies act lawfully. In doing so, they apply a body of principles known as 'public' or 'administrative' law to check the legality of the actions of public authorities. Those principles are now the underpinning of a distinct branch of civil law and the subject of many (large) textbooks.[3] Most of the principles were established by cases in which

---

1   See para 25.34 for a fuller description of the cases in which a public law defence can be deployed and the meaning of 'public' body and 'public' function.

2   For further discussion of the range of decisions that may be challenged see para 25.46.

3   For examples see: Wade and Forsyth *Administrative Law*, OUP, 11th edition, 2014; Woolf, Jowell, Le Sueur, Donnelly and Hare *De Smith's Judicial Review*,

challenges were brought *against* alleged unlawful action. But in possession claims, the same principles can be relied on – by way of *defence* – where the claimant is itself a public body.

25.6   For present purposes, it is sufficient to identify the following basic parameters of public or administrative law regarding what a public body may or may not lawfully do:

a) it must not act beyond the powers given to it;[4]
b) if it has been given a discretion whether to do or not to do something, it must not constrain that discretion by adopting absolute rules;[5]
c) it must act fairly and in accordance with the rules of natural justice;
d) when making a decision about exercising its powers or performing its duties, it must take into account all relevant considerations[6] and must exclude any irrelevant considerations;
e) it must not allow its decisions to be tainted by bias, bad faith, corruption or unlawful discrimination;
f) where there is an express or implied duty to do so, it must give reasons for what it is doing;
g) if it is under a duty to do something, it must carry out that duty;
h) if it has indicated that in particular circumstances it will act in a certain way, it will usually be required to meet a 'legitimate expectation' that it will act in the way it has indicated;
i) it must correctly interpret and apply any relevant laws; and
j) it must not reach a decision which is perverse or irrational, ie a decision so unreasonable that no public body properly directing itself could have reached that decision.[7]

Sweet & Maxwell, 7th edition, 2013; Craig, *Administrative Law*, Sweet & Maxwell, 7th edition, 2012 or Endicott *Administrative Law*, OUP, 3rd edition, 2015.

4 In Latin, acting beyond one's powers is to act 'ultra vires'.

5 Known as 'fettering a discretion'.

6 For example, in taking a decision to terminate a tenancy originally granted to a tenant to provide a home for himself and the children, a relevant consideration would be the likelihood of the children (through another adult) applying to the courts for a transfer of the tenancy to them for their benefit: *R v Hammersmith & Fulham LBC ex p Quigley* (2000) 32 HLR 379, (1999) *Independent* 24 May, QBD.

7 Often (without great accuracy) described as the '*Wednesbury* test' derived from *Associated Provincial Picture Houses Ltd v Wednesbury Corporation* [1948] 1 KB 223, CA.

25.7   Of course, the public body will also be acting unlawfully if it infringes the criminal law or any statutory provision of civil law rendering particular conduct unlawful. The specific issues which arise where a public body has unlawfully discriminated against an occupier on grounds relating to their disability, and then sought possession, are discussed in chapter 27. The same issues would arise where the public body had unlawfully discriminated against an occupier on any other prohibited grounds.

25.8   An increasingly common contention is that the act or decision of the public body is unlawful because it represents an infringement of the occupier's rights protected by the Human Rights Act (HRA) 1998. Section 6 of that Act provides that it is unlawful for a public body to act incompatibly with a Convention right. Section 7(1)(b) enables the 'victim' of such infringement to rely on the Convention right in 'any legal proceedings'. That provision puts beyond doubt the availability of the 'public law defence' to a defendant in a possession claimwhere the alleged unlawful act of the public body is a breach of a Convention right. This is quite distinct from the 'human rights defence' described in chapter 26. That involves no assertion of any unlawfulness on the part of the claimant public body. However, there are many cases in which the defendant may wish to advance both of these defences and chapter 26 contains an outline of the Convention rights which may prove useful in framing a public law defence based upon them.

25.9   It is not yet clear whether the principles available to be deployed in a public law defence (set out at para 25.6 above) can now be treated as sufficiently enlarged to include the requirement that a public body's actions must always be 'proportionate' in order to be lawful. That requirement is presently a feature of the 'human rights' defence described in chapter 26. It seems likely that it will be recognised as an available limb of a public law defence in possession claims because 'proportionality' is a feature brought into our law by principles of the law of the European Convention on Human Rights (ECHR) and almost all possession claims will engage the right to 'respect for a home' protected by HRA 1998 Sch 1 Article 8.

25.10   The usual method of obtaining judicial scrutiny of the lawfulness or otherwise of the actions of a public body, measured against the above principles, is by bringing a claim for 'judicial review'. That involves the victim of unlawful administrative action or inaction *taking a claim* against a public body in the civil courts.

25.11   The procedure for seeking judicial review is set out in the Civil Procedure Rules (CPR) Part 54. Claims for judicial review are heard in the Administrative Court which is a branch of the High Court. It now sits in London and at several regional centres.[8] Cases are heard by specially 'nominated' High Court judges or deputy judges. To prevent public bodies being troubled by vexatious and stale cases, the rules require that claims are made promptly following alleged unlawful action and that the permission of the court is obtained to bring the claim.[9] If a claim ultimately succeeds, the Administrative Court has power to make special orders to stop a public body doing something (a prohibition order), or to require it to do something (a mandatory order[10]) or to quash its decision (a quashing order[11]). In certain circumstances, the court can even take for itself the decision that the public body should lawfully have taken.[12]

25.12   Historically, a defendant to a possession claim, having identified alleged unlawful action by the public body bringing that claim, would have invited the judge dealing with the possession proceedings to adjourn the claim to enable an application for judicial review to be made in the Administrative Court. That would obviously lead to delay and, since further and separate proceedings would be involved, additional expense. The legal burden of the proceedings would switch from the claimant in the county court to the claimant in the Administrative Court. The result was significant disruption and inconvenience.

25.13   As a result, even in the years before tenants of public bodies obtained security of tenure, the courts recognised that defendants in possession proceedings brought by public bodies should be able to rely on public law principles as a ground of *defence* to the possession claim itself.

25.14   For example, in *Bristol CC v Clark*,[13] a council tenant fell into arrears of rent as a result of unemployment and illness. The council gave notice to quit and brought a possession claim. The tenant argued that, before bringing the claim, the council had failed to take into account relevant considerations – a government circular on dealing with rent arrears and/or the possibility of suing for the arrears and then seeking an attachment of earnings order to recover the rent. Although that defence failed on its facts, and a possession order was

8 Birmingham, Cardiff, Leeds and Manchester.
9 CPR 54.4 and 54.5.
10 In old cases, known as 'mandamus'.
11 In old cases, known as 'certiorari'.
12 CPR 54.19.
13 [1975] 1 WLR 1443, [1975] 3 All ER 976, CA and see also *Bristol CC v Rawlins* (1977) 76 LGR 166, (1977) 34 P&CR 12, CA.

made, the Court of Appeal had no difficulty with accepting the availability and application of public law principles in the defence of the
possession claim.

25.15   Any suggestion that this decision may have been a 'one-off' was
dispelled on its re-affirmation by the Court of Appeal shortly afterwards in a case involving another council tenant: *Cannock Chase DC
v Kelly*.[14]

25.16   In the mid-1980s the House of Lords confirmed this line of Court
of Appeal cases by explicitly holding that a council tenant in a rent
arrears case could – as part of his or her defence – raise a public law
challenge to an essential ingredient of the council's possession claim.
In *Wandsworth LBC v Winder (No 1)*,[15] the tenant was in rent arrears.
He was allowed to raise the point that a rent increase – which he
had refused to pay – had been imposed by the council acting beyond
its powers. Although that defence ultimately failed on its facts,[16] the
public law defence – or *'Winder'* defence – to possession claims was
firmly established.

25.17   With the general extension of security of tenure to most tenants
of social housing by the Housing Act (HA) 1980 and by later consolidating legislation (as described in Part I of this book), the public law
defence largely fell into abeyance. There was no real need to raise
such a defence where the tenant enjoyed such a high degree of security of tenure that the public body which was the landlord was in any
event required to prove a statutory ground for possession and also,
usually, that it would be reasonable for the court to make a possession order. For the next 20 years, the public law defence remained in
occasional use, mainly by those who enjoyed no security of tenure,
for example, Gypsies and other Travellers[17] on council sites and a
small number of other non-secure tenants and licensees.[18]

25.18   The public law defence also suffered something of a temporary
setback[19] when the Court of Appeal developed a line of authority

14 [1978] 1 WLR 1, [1978] 1 All ER 152, CA and see also *Sevenoaks DC v Emmott*
    (1979) 78 LGR 346, (1979) 39 P&CR 404, CA.
15 [1985] AC 461, (1984) 17 HLR 196, HL.
16 *Wandsworth LBC v Winder (No 2)* (1987) 20 HLR 400, CA.
17 *West Glamorgan CC v Rafferty* [1988] 1 WLR 45, (1986) 18 HLR 375, CA.
18 *Cleethorpes BC v Clarkson* (1978) 128 NLJ 860, July 1978 *LAG Bulletin* 166; *R
    v Wear Valley DC ex p Binks* [1985] 2 All ER 699, QBD; *Kensington & Chelsea
    RLBC v Haydon* (1984) 17 HLR 114, CA and see generally *Wandsworth LBC v A*
    [2000] 1 WLR 1246, [2000] BLGR 81, CA.
19 More fully described in N Nicol, 'Public Law Defences in Possession
    Proceedings' [2010] JR 85.

limiting its availability only to those occupiers who (like Mr Winder) had a continuing private law right to remain in occupation under the tenancies they had been granted.[20]

25.19   However, in a more recent decision of the House of Lords,[21] concerned with occupiers who had no private law rights, this area of controversy was 'swept aside by the House without further ado. All seem to have accepted it as settled law ... that 'conventional' judicial review grounds can be raised by way of defence to possession proceedings in the county court'.[22]

25.20   The Court of Appeal later rejected a suggestion that the 'sweeping aside' of this limitation was accidental or that it is not bound to follow the House of Lords on the point.[23]

25.21   With an increasing number of occupiers living in accommodation owned by public bodies but *not* enjoying full security of tenure (for example, non-secure tenants, introductory tenants, demoted tenants, assured shorthold tenants, failed successors, and the like) the public law defence had begun to enjoy a renaissance by the end of the last decade.

25.22   The House of Lords clearly sanctioned the use of public law defences to possession claims in *Doherty v Birmingham CC*.[24] That was a claim for possession of a pitch on an official Gypsy caravan site. The trial judge held that any public law challenge to the council's decision to evict could only be brought by judicial review. The House of Lords set aside his order and remitted the public law defence for trial in the possession claim.

25.23   More recently, in *Manchester CC v Pinnock*,[25] the Supreme Court held that a public law defence *is* available in possession proceedings, even where the statutory jurisdiction of the court hearing the possession claim seems to be limited by statute to merely checking whether the procedural requirements for the making of a possession order are satisfied.[26]

---

20 See *Avon CC v Buscott* [1988] QB 656, (1988) 20 HLR 385, CA and *Manchester CC v Cochrane* [1999] 1 WLR 809, (1999) 31 HLR 810, CA.
21 *Lambeth LBC v Kay* [2006] UKHL 10, [2005] HLR 31.
22 *Doherty v Birmingham CC* [2006] EWCA Civ 1739, [2007] HLR 32 at [36].
23 *Salford CC v Mullen* [2010] EWCA Civ 336, [2010] HLR 35 at [47]–[49].
24 [2008] UKHL 57, [2008] HLR 45.
25 [2010] UKSC 45, [2011] HLR 7.
26 The decision in *Manchester CC v Cochrane* [1999] 1 WLR 809, (1999) 31 HLR 180, CA, to the contrary effect, should no longer be followed – see *Manchester CC v Pinnock* paras [82]–[87].

25.24   The judgment contains a useful summary of the earlier House of Lords cases on the availability of the public law defence. Lord Neuberger said at [27]–[28]:

> 27. ... In *Kay v Lambeth LBC* [2006] 2 AC 465 at para [110] ... Lord Hope explained that, following *Wandsworth London Borough Council v Winder* [1985] AC 461, in principle, it would be open to a defendant 'to challenge the decision of a local authority to recover possession as an improper exercise of its powers at common law' on the traditional judicial review ground 'that it was a decision that no reasonable person would consider justifiable.
>
> 28. In *Doherty v Birmingham CC* [2009] 1 AC 367 the law as stated in para [110] of *Kay* was substantially reaffirmed ... The law on the judicial review point was affirmed by Lord Hope, Lord Walker, and Lord Mance, at paras 56, 123 and 157 respectively ...

25.25   The same judgment later restates the law on the availability of public law defences in these terms at [81]:

> ... where a tenant contends that the decision of a local authority landlord to issue, or indeed to continue, possession proceedings can in some way be impugned, the tenant should be entitled to raise that contention in the possession proceedings themselves, even if they are in the County Court. This seems to us to follow from the decision of the House of Lords in *Wandsworth v Winder* [1985] AC 461, as cited and approved in the present context in *Kay v Lambeth* [2006] 2 AC 465, para 110, and again in *Doherty v Birmingham* [2009] 1 AC 367, paras 56, 123 and 157 (see para 28 above). This approach also derives strong support from the observations of Lord Bingham in *Kay v Lambeth* [2006] 2 AC 465, para 30.

25.26   These principles must now be regarded as well settled. Where the claimant for possession is a body which would be amenable to a judicial review of its decision-making in the Administrative Court, the defendant to a possession claim can in principle deploy a public law defence in the county court. Whether such a defence is, in practice, available will depend on the facts of the case.

25.27   In *Pinnock*, the claim for possession was brought against a demoted[27] tenant. The tenant had received notice of intention to seek possession and there had been an oral hearing – by a panel of council officers – of an application for a review of that decision. Lord Neuberger said at [72]:

> Rightly, in our view, it is common ground that a court has jurisdiction, under normal judicial review principles, to satisfy itself that the local authority and panel have indeed acted reasonably and have

27 See chapter 6 of this book.

investigated the relevant facts fairly, when deciding to bring possession proceedings. From this it must follow that any decision by the local authority to continue possession proceedings is similarly susceptible to judicial review. At the same time, it is right to emphasise that it would almost always require a marked change of circumstances following a panel's decision to approve the proceedings, before an attempt could properly be made to judicially review the continuance of proceedings which were initially justified.

25.28   In a more recent group of Supreme Court cases, reported under the name *Hounslow LBC v Powell*,[28] the Supreme Court additionally held that:

- the decision to bring possession proceedings was one in respect of which *reasons* should normally be provided to the prospective defendant, not later than the point in time at which a tenant would need to frame their defence;[29] and
- a public law defence in the county court could not only challenge the decision to bring the proceedings but also any prior decision on which the possession claim was founded eg the decision to serve a notice to quit.[30]

25.29   These recent cases emphasise the point that the public law defence is about challenging the decision-making by the claimant public body at any of the stages up to and including the decision to press the claim at a trial. It has nothing to do with an evaluation by the court of the factual circumstances of the claim. That sort of evaluation will be undertaken either as part of the court's consideration of 'reasonableness' (if the tenant has full security of tenure) or in the course of determining a proportionality defence advanced in reliance on human rights, as discussed in chapter 26 (where the occupier does not enjoy full security of tenure).

25.30   It is important to raise two notes of caution:

- It will be for the occupier to prove the public law defence on the balance of probabilities. The court will presume that the public body has acted lawfully until the contrary be shown (known as the 'presumption of regularity').
- Some care must be exercised in ensuring that the public law defence is only deployed in *appropriate* cases.

---

28 [2011] UKSC 8, [2011] 2 AC 186.
29 Per Lord Phillips at [114]–[117].
30 Per Lord Phillips at [120].

25.31   On the latter point, the Court of Appeal has granted permission to appeal in a possession case specifically to enable it to discourage the taking of frivolous public law defences.[31] In later giving judgment dismissing the appeal, it said:

> The only reason we granted permission is that we considered it important to make it absolutely clear that public law attacks of the technical and over-theoretical sort advanced here have no merit whatsoever in this sort of case ... .

and

> ... They were hopeless from the outset. Such defences should only be raised when they have real and obvious substance: it is not appropriate to construct intellectual edifices of public law without any proper foundations in reality.[32]

25.32   Although the courts dealing with possession claims do not have an explicit filter to weed out plainly unmeritorious public law defences, equivalent to the requirement of 'permission' in judicial review proceedings,[33] a public law defence should not be allowed to go to trial unless it is 'seriously arguable'.[34] The county court will not usually direct any defence to a possession claim to go for trial unless it is satisfied that the claim 'is genuinely disputed on grounds that appear to be substantial'.[35]

25.33   The following examples of 'public law defence' cases in the High Court and Court of Appeal may be helpful in indicating the sorts of situations in which the defence might assist an occupier:

- In *Welwyn Hatfield DC v McGlynn*,[36] the defendant was a non-secure tenant. Following complaints of anti-social behaviour the council served notice to quit. In correspondence, the council made it clear that if any further anti-social behaviour occurred, it would seek possession. On receipt of further complaints, it issued a possession claim. The public law defence was that the requirements of natural justice, seen in the light of the correspondence, required the defendant at least to be told the nature of the allegations and have an opportunity to deny or respond to them before the claim was launched. The Court of Appeal held that defence to be seriously arguable and remitted the case for trial.

31 *London Borough of Brent v Corcoran* [2010] EWCA Civ 774, [2010] HLR 43.
32 At paras [12] and [26].
33 CPR 54.4.
34 *Lambeth LBC v Kay* [2006] UKHL 10, [2006] 2 AC 465 per Lord Hope at [110].
35 CPR 55.8(2).
36 [2009] EWCA Civ 285, [2010] HLR 10.

- In *Croydon LBC v Barber*,[37] a non-secure tenant was violent and abusive towards a resident caretaker. The council served notice to quit and issued a possession claim. In the course of the proceedings, an expert medical report was obtained which indicated that the defendant had significant mental health problems and that the violent incident had been a manifestation of his disability. The public law defence was that, in deciding to press on with the possession claim, the council had failed to have regard to its own policies and procedures relating to management of anti-social behaviour by vulnerable occupiers. The Court of Appeal upheld that defence and dismissed the possession claim.
- In *Eastlands Homes Partnership Ltd v Whyte*,[38] the landlord served notice seeking possession on an assured shorthold tenant for reasons of rent arrears and anti-social behaviour. It then began a possession claim. The public law defence was that the landlord had: failed to follow its own policy in relation to rent arrears; offered an appeal against its decision but failed to disclose the evidence put before the appeal panel and/or broadened the matters considered on appeal beyond the case summary it had prepared; and, having stated that it would offer a second or further appeal, failed to do so. The judge upheld the defence and dismissed the possession claim.
- In *Leicester City Council v Shearer*,[39] the tenant had died and notice to quit had been served on the public trustee to bring his tenancy to an end. The council sought possession from his widow, who had no right to succeed to the tenancy. She defended the claim on the basis that the council had wrongly and unlawfully failed to give proper consideration to the possibility of making her a direct offer of a new tenancy under a power available in its housing allocation scheme. The Court of Appeal upheld the dismissal of the possession claim on that ground.
- In *Beech v Birmingham CC*,[40] an elderly and frail tenant had given notice to quit. The council sought possession from those remaining in possession. The public law defence was that the council, in resolving to take possession proceedings in reliance on the notice to quit, failed to take into account – or sufficiently into account – its omission to comply with a statutory requirement or to take

---

37 [2010] EWCA Civ 51, [2010] HLR 36.
38 [2010] EWHC 695 (QB).
39 [2013] EWCA Civ 1467, [2014] HLR 8.
40 [2014] EWCA Civ 830, [2014] HLR 38.

precautionary steps which Parliament considered it ought to take as a matter of public policy for the support and protection of vulnerable people. The Court of Appeal said 'a public law defence based on *Wednesbury* unreasonableness would be bound to fail. It is inconceivable that, on a judicial review of the council's decision to commence possession proceedings for possession of the property, the court would grant a quashing order.'

- In *Fareham BC v Miller*[41] the council served a notice to quit to end a non-secure tenancy. It initially decided to give the defendant a further chance to retain his home but, on hearing that he had been imprisoned, it then brought a claim for possession. The Court of Appeal affirmed rejection of a public law defence. It said: 'A *Wednesbury* challenge depends not on whether the decision to continue the possession claim was objectively reasonable but whether it was a decision which no reasonable authority could have taken in the light of all the relevant circumstances.' On the facts, that public law defence failed.

- In *Mohamoud v Kensington & Chelsea RLBC*[42] the council served notice to quit to determine a non-secure tenancy of accommodation provided in performance of its homelessness duties. The public law defence was that, prior to serving the notice, the council had failed to make an assessment of the needs of the tenant's children and have regard to their best interests, as required by Children Act 2004 s11. The Court of Appeal held that no such assessment had been required and upheld the making of a possession order.

Put shortly, a public law defence will only succeed – and a possession claim only be dismissed – if, had the same point been taken in a claim for judicial review under the procedure described above at para 25.11, the occupier would have succeeded in having the unlawful decision, or act, quashed.[43]

The cases in which it can be deployed

25.34   The whole premise of a public law defence is that the claimant is a *public* body which has failed to act in accordance with the public law

---

41 [2013] EWCA Civ 159, [2013] HLR 22.
42 [2015] EWCA Civ 780, [2015] HLR 38.
43 *Barnsley Metropolitan Borough Council v Norton* [2011] EWCA Civ 834, [2011] HLR 4.

principles described above in para 25.6. There is no obligation on a *private* individual or company when carrying out private functions to follow or apply such principles. So the public law defence cannot usually be raised in answer to a possession claim made by a private owner or landlord. The claimant must be a *public* body or at very least a body exercising a *public* function when seeking possession.

25.35   There is no exhaustive list of those bodies which are subject to the public law principles described above. Although local authorities and other statutorily-created landlords and landowners are plainly covered, it has been left to the courts to work out, almost on a case-by-case basis, whether quasi-public landlords and landowners – particularly social landlords such as housing associations – are subject to public law principles when seeking possession.

25.36   In *Poplar HARCA v Donoghue*,[44] the Court of Appeal rejected the proposition that all such social landlords were automatically to be treated as public authorities. However, it found that Poplar HARCA (which had been set up by the local housing authority to take over parts of its housing stock in a small scale stock-transfer) was a public authority in so far as it carried out the function of making arrangements for the provision of short-term accommodation to those homeless households (such as the defendant) that the council would previously have accommodated.[45] In the event, the human rights defence in that case failed (for reasons explored more fully in para 26.31).

25.37   Whether a particular social housing provider is or is not a 'public' body accordingly falls to be decided in each case and turns on both the nature of the provider itself and on whether the particular function in which it is engaged is public as opposed to 'private'. The correct approach has been considered in a series of recent cases.

25.38   In *R (Weaver) v London & Quadrant Housing Trust*,[46] the trust served a notice seeking possession on an assured tenant relying on mandatory ground 8 (rent arrears). She sought judicial review of that decision, contending that the giving of the notice breached her Convention rights. An issue was raised as to whether the trust was a 'public authority' and whether the giving of the notice had been a private

---

44 [2001] EWCA Civ 595, (2001) 33 HLR 73.

45 The decision was disapproved by members of the House of Lords in a later case on the basis that the Court of Appeal had relied too heavily on the historical connection between the council and the housing association, rather than on the 'public' nature of the function (managing social housing) that Poplar HRCA was undertaking: *YL v Birmingham CC* [2007] UKHL 27, [2007] HLR 44.

46 [2009] EWCA Civ 587, [2009] HLR 40.

or public act. By a majority, the Court of Appeal upheld a Divisional Court decision that – for most social landlords – the functions of letting and terminating tenancies were functions of a public nature. The majority found that:

> ... the following features in particular are highly relevant to the question whether the functions of the Trust are public functions (although none of them on its own is in any sense conclusive): the substantial public subsidy which enables the Trust to achieve its objectives; the way in which the allocation agreements [for nominations by local authorities] circumscribe the freedom of the Trust to allocate properties; and the nature of the regulation to which the Trust is subject. In addition, the vast majority of RSL [registered social landlord] tenants enjoy statutory protection as regards the circumstances in which a social housing tenancy may be terminated.[47]

The court was also influenced by the fact that the housing trust was a social landlord able to use special statutory powers to address anti-social behaviour which were not available to private landlords. In the event, the claim failed on its facts.

25.39   These propositions were later directly applied in a possession claim: *Eastlands Homes Partnership Ltd v Whyte*.[48] There the landlord conceded that the court was bound by the decision of the Court of Appeal in *Weaver*. The judge said, having considered the evidence of the status and functioning of the claimant social landlord, that: 'The Claimant is in no better position than London and Quadrant, and accordingly is to be regarded as a public authority and a public body.'[49]

25.40   It should not be assumed that the question of whether a social landlord seeking possession is engaged in a private or public act is finally settled. Although the Supreme Court refused permission to the trust to appeal in the *Weaver* case, it expressly recognised in its reasons for refusal that the point was of general importance. Permission was refused only on the special facts of the case (that the Trust had succeeded in defeating Ms Weaver's claim on the facts and she had pursued no appeal from the dismissal of her claim).

25.41   In *R (McIntyre) v Gentoo Group*,[50] the Administrative Court held that a decision of a housing association to grant or refuse a mutual exchange was a public function for the purposes of applying public law principles. It said that:

47 At para [101].
48 [2010] EWHC 695 (QB).
49 At para [5].
50 [2010] EWHC 5 (Admin).

... the decision in Weaver is directly applicable. The declaration granted by the Divisional Court in that case, that the defendant was amenable to judicial review on conventional public law grounds in respect of decisions taken in the performance of its function of managing and allocating its housing stock (or perhaps more accurately, as the majority of the Court of Appeal thought, its stock of social housing), applies not merely to decisions concerning the termination of a tenancy of social housing but also to those concerned with the mutual exchange of such tenancies.[51]

25.42   In *R (Macleod) v Governors of the Peabody Trust*[52] the claimant was an assured tenant. He notified his landlord, Peabody, that he wished to exchange his tenancy with the tenant of a social housing property in Edinburgh. Peabody declined to approve such an exchange. He said that Peabody was amenable to judicial review as a public body in relation to the decision it made in respect of the proposed exchange. He claimed that Peabody had failed to follow its own policy in relation to mutual exchange and that it did not take account of its duty under Equality Act 2010 s149. By reason of those matters, it was argued that Peabody had unlawfully fettered its discretion and that its decision was irrational. The Administrative Court dismissed the claim. The judge considered *Weaver* and *McIntyre* and said at [20] and [21]:

> 20. It is important to note that the general principles enunciated by Lord Justice Elias in *Weaver* have to be applied to the facts of each particular case. *Weaver* did not decide that all RSLs are public bodies. On the facts of this case I am not satisfied that Peabody was exercising a public function in relation to the tenancy of Mr Macleod. I take into account the following factors.
>
> - Peabody purchased the properties ... using funds raised on the open market, not via any public subsidy or grant.
> - Although the properties were not let a full market rent, it is not clear that they were pure social housing. The key workers for whom the property was reserved included those with a family income of up to £60,000 per annum. ... The provision of below market rent properties for such workers does not fall within the definition of social housing in the Housing and Regeneration Act 2008: see section 69.
> - Unlike the RSL in *Weaver* Peabody had no allocation relationship with any local authority. It was not acting in close harmony with a local authority to assist the local authority to fulfil its statutory duty.

---

51 At para [27].
52 [2016] EWHC 737 (Admin), {2016] HLR 27.

- Rents for the properties ... are not subject to the same level of statutory regulation as social housing in general.

21. True it is that some public function was fulfilled by the provision of homes for key workers in London. However, in my judgment the cumulative effect of the various factors in the circumstances of this case does not have the sufficiency of public flavour which Lord Justice Elias found in *Weaver*. In *Weaver* Lord Justice Elias noted that it will not follow that all tenants of an RSL will be able to claim the benefit of a public law remedy just because the RSL is exercising a public function in relation to some or even most of its tenants.

25.43   There has, as yet, been no decision from the Supreme Court on which public bodies are subject to public law principles in possession claims. Meanwhile, the court decisions described above effectively mean that the possession claims of all private registered social housing providers and registered social landlords (mainly, housing associations) may be met by a public law defence but perhaps only in respect of claims relating to their 'social housing' properly so-called as opposed to claims relating to stock they lease or rent on market terms.[53]

25.44   Given the parallel obligation on public bodies to respect the Convention rights of occupiers (see para 25.8 above), public law defences are often run in parallel with defences based on alleged infringement of Conventions rights (ie the 'human rights defence' described in chapter 26). For an example of an early county court decision in a case in which both defences were advanced see *Brighton and Hove CC v Alleyn*.[54]

The decisions that can be challenged

25.45   The most obvious decision to be subjected to a challenge by way of a public law defence will be the decision to file a possession claim. If the defendant can demonstrate that *that* decision was unlawful, the proceedings will not have been lawfully brought and will fall to be dismissed. Dismissal of the claim is usually inevitable in such circumstances because the court will not allow its processes to be used unlawfully.[55]

---

53 See the discussion of this point in *R (Macleod) v Peabody Trust Governors* [2016] EWHC 737 (Admin), [2016] HLR 27.

54 [2011] EW Misc 6 (CC).

55 See *Lewisham LBC v Malcolm* [2008] UKHL 43, [2008] HLR 41 and *Doherty v Birmingham CC* [2008] UKHL 57, [2008] HLR 45. But see also para 25.63 below.

25.46   However, as indicated above, a public body seeking possession may make a sequence or series of decisions in respect of any claim for possession. These can include decisions: to give a notice to quit; to serve a notice seeking possession; to review or not to review those decisions; to issue the claim; to press on to trial having seen the defendant's defence; to press for a possession order having heard the defendant give evidence or in the light of written evidence; and (later) to seek to execute the possession order.

25.47   In *Salford CC v Mullen*,[56] the Court of Appeal decided that, in the light of earlier and modern authority, a public law defence could be raised and 'apply to *any* decision of the [claimant public body] relevant to seeking possession which could be the subject of judicial review.'[57]

25.48   This has added particularly useful dimensions to the public law defence. First, the defence is now available even where the initial decisions to serve notice and bring proceedings were lawful, if a subsequent decision (for example, to press for a possession order) was unlawful. Second, the fact that the last challengeable decision before the making of a possession order will be the decision to seek an order from the judge at the close of the evidence means that the lawfulness of the decision-making will be tested on the most up-to-date facts rather than the facts as they were known to the public body at some much earlier stage.

25.49   This has the added advantage of enabling the court that is dealing with the possession claim to adjudicate on a public law defence *after* it has considered and resolved (during the trial) any factual disputes. In contrast, the Administrative Court would not usually be engaged in fact-finding and would treat the relevant facts as being the facts as they had appeared to the public body at the time of its (often much) earlier decision.

25.50   The defendant's defence and argument at trial will need to identify precisely which decisions are being subjected to a public law challenge. That is because the effects of success will be different depending upon which decision is unlawful. For example, if the decision to give notice was lawful but the subsequent decision to bring proceedings was unlawful, the result may be that the claim is dismissed but that the original lawful notice could be used to found another claim. In *McGlynn* (see para 25.33 above), the only pleaded challenge in the defence was to the decision to bring the claim. On

---

56   [2010] EWCA Civ 336, [2010] HLR 35.
57   [2010] EWCA Civ 336, [2010] HLR 35 at [74].

appeal, the defendant sought permission to amend the grounds of appeal (and the defence) so as to challenge the earlier decision to give notice to quit. That was refused as being too late.

25.51   Success in a challenge to the decision to bring the proceedings will sometimes leave the occupier in a legal 'limbo'. This is particularly common in situations where a notice to quit is lawfully given to end a tenancy but the subsequent possession claim is dismissed on public law grounds. The occupier will simply remain in possession as a trespasser until the public body can make a lawful decision to recover possession or agrees to grant a fresh tenancy. It is, for example, often wrongly assumed that success for the defendants in *McGlynn* and *Barber* (see para 25.33 above) meant that they remained tenants. Yet, in those cases, the only success was to achieve a state of 'tolerated' trespass until another – but this time lawful – decision could be made to issue possession claims against them. In other cases, the decision successfully challenged will be the decision to serve a notice to quit. In such a case, the notice will not, presumably, have lawfully determined the tenancy and it will continue.

When the defence is not available

25.52   Given that the public law defence most commonly strikes at the very root of the claimant's decision to launch the possession proceedings, it might have been thought that it would be available to the defendant in each and every possession claim brought by a public body.

25.53   However, a particular difficulty arose in the context of modern statutory schemes which expressly or by implication make the grant of a possession order 'mandatory', if the court is satisfied that certain conditions are made out. The most obvious is the statutory scheme relating to *introductory* tenancies which provides that, unless the court is satisfied that the notice provisions have not been complied with, it shall make an order.[58] Another more recent example is the availability of *'automatic'* possession grounds against some secure tenants under HA 1985 s84A.

25.54   The courts initially held that the effect of such statutory provisions was to 'oust' the ability of the defendant to take a public law defence in the possession claim. Instead, the defendant had to persuade the court to adjourn the possession claim so that a claim for judicial review could be made in the Administrative Court. Although

---

58   HA 1996 s127(2) and see, generally, chapter 5.

the courts recognised the consequent delay, expense and administrative inconvenience involved in such a procedure as described at para 25.12 above (and called for Parliament to reconsider),[59] the requirement for that procedure to be followed was initially applied not only to the *introductory* tenancy regime[60] but also to *demoted* tenancy cases.[61]

25.55 However, the Supreme Court has swept away this qualification on the availability of the public law defence, even where the relevant statutory provision otherwise requires that the court hearing the possession claim 'shall' or 'must' order possession.[62]

25.56 It does not follow that the public law defence is now available in every possession claim brought by a public body. As already emphasised (see para 25.31 above), the defence as drafted – or at least as outlined to the judge at the initial hearing of the possession claim – must demonstrate that there is a real possibility of the defence, if tried, successfully defeating the possession claim.

The procedure relating to public law defences

25.57 A public law defence should usually be raised at the earliest opportunity and be properly pleaded and particularised in a written defence that is filed and served before the first return date on the possession claim. That statement of case should enable the court to see that the claim is genuinely disputed on 'substantial' grounds.

25.58 The later the point is taken, the more difficult it will be to establish. For example, in one case the Court of Appeal said:[63]

> The submission that [it was] *Wednesbury* unreasonable for the Council to rely on the Notice to Quit was not made orally before or at the trial. It was made for the first time in clear terms in ... the appellants' written closing submissions filed nearly two weeks after the close of evidence. The Council's lawyers did not appreciate the precise nature of the argument and therefore did not address it in their written closing submission. I am not at all surprised in those circumstances that the Judge did not refer to that submission in his judgment. ... The

59 Expressed most starkly in the judgments in *Manchester CC v Cochrane* [1999] 1 WLR 809, (1999) 31 HLR 810.
60 See *Manchester CC v Cochrane* [1999] 1 WLR 809, (1999) 31 HLR 810, CA; *R (McLellan) v Bracknell Forest DC* [2001] EWCA Civ 1510, (2001) 33 HLR 86 and *Salford CC v Mullen* [2010] EWCA Civ 336, [2010] HLR 35.
61 *Manchester CC v Pinnock* [2009] EWCA Civ 852, [2010] HLR 7.
62 *Manchester CC v Pinnock* [2010] UKSC 45, [2011] HLR 7.
63 *Beech v Birmingham CC* [2014] EWCA Civ 830, [2014] HLR 38 at [77]–[78].

Judge was entitled to ignore the new submission. It was never formally part of the appellants' pleaded defence. No evidence was led on it. The appellants never had permission to raise it as a new un-pleaded defence. No opportunity was given to the Council at the trial to call oral evidence on the point. ... It seems to me to be obvious as a matter of basic fairness that the provisions relied upon by the appellants should have been put to the Council's witnesses in cross-examination and that the Council itself should have had the opportunity to call its own written and oral evidence on the relevance and application [of the material documents] both generally and in this specific case.

However, shortly after the Supreme Court had again franked the general availability of the public law defence in *Pinnock*, the courts started to find that defendants in possession claims were taking public law points much more readily and even in cases where those points appeared weak. Additionally, public bodies bringing possession claims were sometimes 'ambushed' by public law points being raised at the first hearing of seemingly undefended possession claims and, not having come prepared to meet those points, saw their cases being readily adjourned.[64]

25.59   To meet these perceived difficulties, the *Pre-action Protocol for possession claims by social landlords* was expanded in April 2015 to incorporate new provisions with the intention of ensuring both that public authority claimants not only acted fairly but also that they were not taken by surprise by public law defences. The new Protocol provides that:

3.2 In cases where the court must grant possession if the landlord proves its case then before issuing any possession claim social landlords –

(a) should write to occupants explaining why they currently intend to seek possession and requiring the occupants within a specified time to notify the landlord in writing of any personal circumstances or other matters which they wish to take into account. In many cases such a letter could accompany any notice to quit and so would not necessarily delay the issue of proceedings; and

(b) should consider any representations received, and if they decide to proceed with a claim for possession give brief written reasons for doing so.

64 'There has been a proliferation of public law and/or Human Rights Act defences raised in possession claims and frequently in those cases in which there would not otherwise be a defence': Kerry Bretherton and Laura Tweedy, 'The impact of public law in property cases', Property Law Bar Association, 2009.

3.3 In these cases, the social landlord should include in its particulars of claim, or in any witness statement filed under CPR 55.8(3), a schedule giving a summary –

(a) of whether it has (by statutory review procedure or otherwise) invited the defendant to make representations of any personal circumstances or other matters which they wish to be taken into account before the social landlord issues proceedings;

(b) if representations were made, that they were considered;

(c) of brief reasons for bringing proceedings; and

(d) copies of any relevant documents which the social landlord wishes the Court to consider in relation to the proportionality of the landlord's decision to bring proceedings.

If the Protocol is followed, the court should be in a position to resolve at an early stage whether the possession claim is genuinely disputed on grounds that appear to be substantial[65] and, if so satisfied, to give directions for trial of the public law defence or other case management directions.

The powers of the court

25.60   For the reasons explained above (at para 25.45), the ordinary result of successful deployment of the public law defence will be the dismissal of the possession claim. Indeed, the court has very little room for manoeuvre. If the claim was unlawfully brought, it will ordinarily be dismissed.

25.61   The county court cannot grant any of the orders usually available to the Administrative Court and described at para 25.11 above.[66] Although that could be rectified by regulations enabling those orders to be available in possession cases, no such regulations have been made.[67]

25.62   The county court cannot, for example, quash a notice to quit or a notice seeking possession which a public body has unlawfully given. It cannot grant an order prohibiting the public body from bringing another possession claim on the same facts nor direct it to act in a particular way. Although the county court has power to make 'binding declarations',[68] the scope for making such declarations in respect of successful public law defences has yet to be fully explored.

65 CPR 55.8(2).
66 County Courts Act 1984 s38(3).
67 County Courts Act 1984 s38(4).
68 CPR 40.20.

25.63   It might be thought that there is no 'broad discretion' of the type
that the Administrative Court has in deciding whether to grant relief
(and what relief to grant) to a claimant who has successfully established unlawful conduct on the part of a public body. However, in
Barnsley MBC v Norton [69] the Court of Appeal was dealing with a case
of established breach of a public law duty but upheld the making of
a possession order. It said that 'given that a breach of a public law
duty is relied on by way of defence in the present case, it seems to me
that it is open to the court in this situation to take the view that, if the
decision would *not* have been set aside on an application for judicial
review, it should *not* provide a basis for a defence to the proceedings
for possession' (emphasis added)

Public law points at the warrant stage

25.64   If a public sector defence fails (or is not identified and pursued at
a hearing) and a possession order is granted, the public authority
claimant will normally apply for a warrant to execute the possession
order.

25.65   If, at that stage, it is identified that the occupier had a public law
defence but the point was not taken, it may be possible – depending
upon the circumstances – to seek to set aside the possession order
and secure permission to put in a late defence. Applications to set
aside possession orders are discussed in chapter 31.

25.66   Alternatively, it may be that the public body's decision to seek the
execution of the possession order can itself be identified as unlawful.
It is not yet clear whether, in that situation, the defendant can:

- apply in the possession proceedings to stay or suspend execution
  on the grounds that the application for the warrant was based on
  an unlawful decision to seek one;[70]
  or must instead:
- apply in the Administrative Court for judicial review of the decision to apply for a warrant and seek an interim order in those
  proceedings for a stay of any enforcement of the possession
  order.

---

69 [2011] EWCA Civ 834, [2011] HLR 4.
70 This will be particularly difficult to assert where HA 1980 s89 operates to fetter
    the power of the court which is dealing with the possession claim in relation to
    enforcement. See *R (JL) v Secretary of State for Defence* [2013] EWCA Civ 449,
    [2013] HLR 27.

25.67 By analogy with *R (JL) v Secretary of State for Defence*[71] (a case turning on HRA 1998 Sch 1 Article 8) it may be possible to contend that, in exceptional cases, the court dealing with the possession claim could examine the lawfulness of the decision to seek to enforce the possession order at the warrant stage. However, such a contention would break new ground and it may be sensible at least to lodge a judicial review claim as a fall-back.

---

71 [2013] EWCA Civ 449, [2013] HLR 27. For a fuller discussion of this case see chapter 31 at para 31.42.

CHAPTER 26

Human rights defences

The 'human rights defence': an introduction

26.1   The 'human rights defence' is a relatively new phenomenon in the landscape of possession proceedings. It is available because the Human Rights Act ('HRA') 1998[1] makes it unlawful for a public authority to act in a way which is incompatible with a Convention right[2] and *also* renders every court – including one dealing with a possession claim – a 'public authority'.[3] As a result, a defendant to a possession claim can raise a defence that it would be unlawful for the court to grant a possession order (or a particular form of possession order) where such an order would be incompatible with a Convention right.

26.2   This chapter describes the background to the 'human rights defence', identifies each of the Convention rights on which defendants to possession claims most commonly rely, illustrates the sorts of cases in which the defence might be used, and concludes with a discussion of the relevance of human rights at the warrant stage.

26.3   Although the human rights defence is relatively 'new', the Convention rights are not. For over 60 years, the United Kingdom has guaranteed – to those within its jurisdiction – the basic protection of fundamental human rights provided by the European Convention on Human Rights (ECHR/'the Convention'). The UK is not only a signatory to the ECHR but was one of the first state signatories to allow individual complaints of infringement to be presented to the European Court of Human Rights (ECtHR).

26.4   These Convention rights might have theoretically been available to be relied on by tenants and other occupiers facing possession proceedings during the second half of the 20th century. But they were of limited usefulness in practice to people in the UK. The procedure for complaint to the ECtHR in Strasbourg was not well known and the delays at that court were such that any occupier seeking to rely on the provisions of the Convention would long since have been evicted, by operation of the possession proceedings in the domestic courts, before their case in Strasbourg was heard. Accordingly, there were relatively few applications to the ECtHR, asserting a breach of the relevant rights, made by occupiers who were defending possession proceedings. Nevertheless, some UK possession cases did successfully complete that process.

---

1   Which was only brought into force in October 2000.
2   HRA 1998 s6(1).
3   HRA 1998 s6(3)(a).

26.5   *Connors v UK*[4] provided a particularly good early example of how the Convention rights could be used in a possession case. The Connors were a Gypsy family who had lived for many years on a local authority Gypsy caravan site. When the council received complaints of anti-social behaviour, it gave notice terminating their licence to occupy their pitch. It sought and obtained an outright possession order on the grounds that the Connors were trespassers. An attempt to stop the eviction by a claim for judicial review failed and the family were (in unpleasant circumstances) evicted from the site and onto the highway.

26.6   They complained to the ECtHR of breaches of a series of Convention rights:

- Article 6,[5] because they had had no forum in which to dispute the allegations made against them;
- Article 8,[6] because no respect had been shown for their long-standing homes by the summary process of eviction;
- Article 14,[7] because only *Gypsy* caravan sites were excluded from the protection of the Caravan Sites Act 1968 and the occupiers of such sites had none of the statutory rights of tenants and licensees of local authorities; and
- Article 1 of Protocol 1,[8] because items of their personal property had been interfered with, retained and later dumped in the course of the eviction.

26.7   The court focused on the Article 8 complaint. It held that such serious interference with Article 8 rights as summary eviction from a longstanding home required particularly weighty reasons of public interest by way of justification. The ECtHR was not persuaded that the necessity for a scheme which permitted the summary eviction of the Connors family, without any investigation of the merits, had been sufficiently demonstrated. It found that the eviction process was not attended by the requisite procedural safeguards, namely, the requirement to establish proper justification for the serious interference with Article 8 rights, and consequently could not be regarded as justified by a 'pressing social need' or proportionate to the legitimate aim being pursued. There was, accordingly, a violation of Article 8.

---

4 [2004] ECHR 223, [2004] HLR 52.
5 See para 26.107.
6 See para 26.30.
7 See para 26.119.
8 See para 26.125.

The complaints of breaches of most other Articles were subsumed in that finding. Mr Connors was awarded compensation.

26.8   Although the Connors family were ultimately successful, their case exemplified the weakness of the pre-HRA 1998 arrangements. They had been unable to rely directly on their rights in the UK courts. They had been unable to stop their eviction. Their compensation came through only many years after the relevant events and only on a complaint to the Strasbourg court.

26.9   The function of the HRA 1998 was to 'bring rights home' by enabling the Convention rights to be enforced in the domestic courts. This chapter cannot provide a detailed description of the content of the HRA 1998 or of its application to housing cases generally. The reader is referred to other texts for that.[9] The focus here is exclusively on how the HRA 1998 may be relied upon by an occupier in defending a possession case.

26.10   In short summary, the HRA 1998 'works' by making it unlawful for any public authority to act incompatibly with an individual's Convention rights.[10] The Convention rights are those set out in Schedule 1 of the Act. The individual who is an alleged victim of an unlawful infringement of Convention rights may rely on those rights in any proceedings brought against him or her.[11] In applying and interpreting the Convention rights in such cases, our courts must take account of any relevant decisions of the ECtHR.[12]

26.11   From that short description it will be seen that a defendant to a possession claim might contend that, in his or her particular case, a possession order (or a particular form of order), or an actual eviction, would be a breach of his or her individual Convention rights.

26.12   Of course, although this chapter has its focus on the European Convention on Human Rights and the HRA 1998, the UK is a signatory to many other international instruments addressing housing rights. They cannot be explored in this text.[13] None of them is covered by the HRA 1998 and none will furnish a freestanding defence to a possession claim.

---

9   Baker and Carter, *Housing and Human Rights Law*, LAG, 2001 and Luba, *Housing and the Human Rights Act: a special bulletin*, Jordans, 2000.

10   HRA 1998 s6(1).

11   HRA 1998 s7.

12   HRA 1998 s2.

13   See generally Nik Nicol's helpful articles: 'Applying the Right to Housing' [2002] JHL 11; 'The Other Human Rights' [2001] *Human Rights* 156 and 'A Right to Housing' July 1998 *Legal Action* 8. See also Dr P Kenna, *Housing Rights and Human Rights* (FEANTSA, 2005).

The cases in which it can be deployed

All cases?

26.13 Every possession claim will be brought in a court. Every court is a 'public authority' for the purposes of the HRA 1998 s6. The 'human rights defence' (that the court would be acting incompatibly with a Convention right in making a possession order – or a particular form of order) is therefore potentially available in every possession claim.

26.14 Unlike the 'public law defence', described in chapter 25, the 'human rights defence' is not usually concerned with the legality of the conduct of the claimant. It is invoked because *the court* itself is a public authority and the defendant is seeking to ensure that the court does not infringe his or her Convention rights in the possession proceedings.

26.15 Accordingly, it would be wrong to assume that human rights defences based on the HRA 1998 are only available in possession claims where the claimant is itself a public body or public authority.

Cases brought by private individuals and private bodies

26.16 Historically, some commentators suggested that human rights issues were not relevant at all in claims for possession against occupiers of *privately* owned property or land where the claimant was not a public authority. Yet, in any and every possession case, even in a case between private landlord and private tenant or between private mortgage lender and mortgage borrower, the court is obliged to *interpret* any relevant statutory scheme, wherever possible, in accordance with Convention rights.

26.17 For example, in *Ghaidan v Godin-Mendoza*,[14] a dispute arose between a private landlord and an occupier as to whether the occupier had succeeded to the Rent Act tenancy of his late same-sex partner. Although the Rent Act provided such a right only to persons living as 'husband or wife' of the deceased, the House of Lords held that in order to avoid infringement of Article 14, read with Article 8, the Act should be interpreted so as to give the same right to a partner in a same-sex couple.

26.18 Therefore, where one reading of a statutory scheme would give rise to a defence in a possession claim but another would not, the occupier will obtain the benefit of that defence if the former interpretation is the one that is compatible with Convention rights

14 [2004] UKHL 30, [2004] HLR 46.

and the other is not. That applies just as much in a case between 'private' parties as in a claim brought by a 'public authority'.

26.19   Nevertheless, most of the initial cases in which the 'human rights defence' was deployed in order to defeat a possession claim *did* involve public authority claimants. Indeed, in the Supreme Court case which recognised the availability of the 'human rights defence' to possession proceedings in domestic courts,[15] that court specifically left open for decision in a later case the question of whether it could be equally well invoked in proceedings brought by other claimants.[16]

26.20   This reticence did not reflect the general approach of the Strasbourg Court. Even in cases brought between private parties, in which a domestic court had to decide whether or not to grant an order leading to the recovery of possession, the ECtHR expected the domestic court itself to apply and protect the Convention rights of the occupiers.[17] The availability of Convention rights to those facing possession claims brought by private bodies and individuals, as much as in claims brought by public authorities, was most recently restated[18] by the ECtHR in these terms:

> An analogy may also be drawn with cases concerning evictions from properties previously owned by the applicants but lost by them as a result of civil proceedings *brought by a private person*, civil proceedings brought by a public body, or tax enforcement proceedings'.[19] [Emphasis added]

As authority for that proposition, the court referred to *Zehentner v Austria*[20] (proceedings brought by a creditor); *Brežec v Croatia*[21] (proceedings brought by the true owner of premises); *Gladysheva v Russia*[22] (proceedings brought by a municipal body); and *Rousk v Sweden*[23] (tax enforcement proceedings).

26.21   In our domestic courts, at least one Lord Justice of Appeal, when faced with the issue, expressed the view that the human rights

15 *Manchester CC v Pinnock* [2010] UKHL 45, [2011] HLR 7.

16 At para [50].

17 See, for example, *Zehentner v Austria* [2009] ECHR 1119, (2011) 52 EHRR 22; *Belchikova v Russia* [2010] ECHR 2266; *Zrilic v Croatia* [2013] ECHR 921; and *Brežec v Croatia* [2013] ECHR 705, [2014] HLR 3.

18 See N Madge 'Small earthquake in Bulgaria: not many dead' [2016] 19 JHL 61.

19 *Ivanova and Cherkezov v Bulgaria* [2016] ECHR 373, [2016] HLR 21.

20 [2009] ECHR 1119, (2011) 52 EHRR 22.

21 [2013] ECHR 705, [2014] HLR 3.

22 [2011] ECHR 2021, [2012] HLR 19.

23 [2013] ECHR 746. See too *Lemo and others v Croatia* [2014] ECHR 755.

defence could be advanced in answer to a private claimant's case.[24] But a full division of the Court of Appeal later held that it could not be.[25]

26.22　　That decision was faithfully followed by the lower courts.[26] A further authoritative review by the Supreme Court was needed.

26.23　　Eventually, in *McDonald v McDonald*[27] the Supreme Court decided in June 2016 that although a claim for possession of a home would engage the Convention right protected by HRA 1998 Sch 1 Article 8 (see para 26.30), if the claimant was not a public authority or a body exercising a public function, the court could treat the question of the necessity or proportionality of the interference with that right as already concluded by the underlying statutory scheme regulating the recovery of possession. In that case, a private landlord relied on the right to recover possession available following service of a Housing Act 1988 s21 notice. The Supreme Court held that this statutory regime left no room for an individual assessment of the necessity or proportionality of the recovery of possession based on the circumstances of the particular defendant. The court dealing with the possession claim should treat the balance between the competing Convention rights of the parties as already struck by the legislature The current position is therefore that a human rights defence is in principle available in any and every possession claim, irrespective of the type of claimant but that a human rights defence will not be available where the occupier seeks to resist the claim of a private landlord or landowner by reliance only on the personal circumstances of his or her household. So, for example, there will be no interference with a Convention right where an occupier has entered into a contract or a legal charge putting their home at risk if a rental payment or mortgage instalment is not paid and then a claim for possession is brought by the private landlord or lender simply as the means of enforcing rights arising from that contract or charge.[28]

24　Ward LJ in *Malik v Fassenfelt* [2013] EWCA Civ 798, [2013] 3 EGLR 99.
25　*McDonald v McDonald* [2014] EWCA Civ 1049, [2014] HLR 43.
26　For example, in a case brought by a private mortgage lender, *Southern Pacific Mortgage Ltd v V* [2015] EW Misc B42 (CC); in a case brought by a private landowner, *Dutton v Persons Unknown* [2015] EWHC 3988 (Ch) and in a claim by a housing co-op, *Southward Housing Co-Operative Ltd v Walker* [2015] EWHC 1615 (Ch), [2016] Ch 443 at [165(3)].
27　[2016] UKSC 28, [2016] HLR 28.
28　*Vrzic v Croatia* [2016] ECHR 642, September 2016 *Legal Action* 33 at [68]–[72].

Cases in which the court has a wide discretion

26.24   Reliance on the 'human rights defence' is rarely needed in the sort of possession case in which the court is required to consider whether granting a possession order would be 'reasonable' in the circumstances and where it has a wide discretion in relation to the form of order made and the enforcement of it.

26.25   That is not to say that Convention rights are irrelevant in such cases. For example, in *Lambeth LBC v Howard*,[29] Sedley LJ said that, while Article 8 should not carry county courts to materially different outcomes from those which they had been arriving at in applying the condition of reasonableness, 'it can do no harm, and may often do a great deal of good, if the exercise is approached for what it is, an application of the principle of proportionality'.

26.26   Similarly, in *Kay v Lambeth LBC; Leeds CC v Price*,[30] Lord Brown said that:

> 203. ... where the domestic law requires the court to make a judgment (most notably perhaps in those cases under Schedule 2 to the Housing Act 1985 where repossession can only be ordered if the court considers it reasonable), or to exercise a discretion, the judge will bear in mind that he is performing this task in the context of the defendant's Article 8 right to respect for his home. ...

26.27   In *Gallagher v Castle Vale Housing Action Trust*,[31] an outright possession order was made against a secure tenant following complaints of nuisance. She argued that she was not personally to blame for the offensive conduct and had not acquiesced in it; the disturbance was caused by members of the family who were about to move out, and the nuisance would therefore cease. The Court of Appeal considered that the test of 'reasonableness' takes into account most of the issues that might be raised in an attempt to show that a possession order is a 'proportionate' remedy. Nonetheless, an outright order should only be made in a very clear-cut case and only where it was 'proportionate' to do so. The outright order was set aside and a two-year suspended possession order was substituted. The court reinforced the importance, given Article 8, of making an order depriving someone of his or her home only where a clear case was made out for doing so.

---

29   [2001] EWCA Civ 468, (2001) 33 HLR 636.
30   [2006] UKHL 10, [2006] HLR 22.
31   [2001] EWCA Civ 944, (2001) 33 HLR 72.

26.28   Most recently, in *Manchester CC v Pinnock* the Supreme Court said of this class of case (where the court must be satisfied as to the 'reasonableness' of making the order sought):[32]

> 55. ... Any factor which has to be taken into account, or any dispute of fact which has to be resolved, for the purpose of assessing proportionality under Article 8(2), would have to be taken into account or resolved for the purpose of assessing reasonableness under section 84 of the 1985 Act. Reasonableness ... like proportionality under Article 8(2), requires the court to consider whether to order possession at all, and, if so, whether to make an outright order rather than a suspended order, and, if so, whether to direct that the outright order should not take effect for a significant time.
>
> 56. Moreover, reasonableness involves the trial judge 'tak[ing] into account all the relevant circumstances ... in ... a broad common-sense way': *Cumming v Danson* [1942] 2 All ER 653, 655, per Lord Greene MR. It therefore seems highly unlikely, as a practical matter, that it could be reasonable for a court to make an order for possession in circumstances in which it would be disproportionate to do so under Article 8.

The most relevant human rights

26.29   The Convention rights upon which a defendant can rely in a possession claim are those set out in HRA 1998 Sch 1. The following paragraphs identify those most commonly relied upon by such defendants.

Article 8

26.30   Article 8 reads:

Right to respect for private and family life
(1) Everyone has the *right to respect for* his private and family life, *his home* and his correspondence. [Emphasis added]
(2) There shall be no interference by a public authority with the exercise of this right except such as is in accordance with the law and is necessary in a democratic society in the interests of national security, public safety or the economic well-being of the country, for the prevention of disorder or crime, for the protection of health or morals, or for the protection of the rights and freedoms of others.

26.31   Because Article 8 establishes the right to respect for an individual's 'home', it is obviously the right most often relied upon in possession

32 [2010] UKSC 45, [2011] HLR 7.

proceedings against occupiers who are residing in a building, or on land, in respect of which possession is claimed.

26.32   The ECtHR, the ultimate authority on the interpretation of the Convention, has placed considerable emphasis on the importance of avoiding an eviction which would infringe Article 8 rights.[33] It has repeatedly stated that:

> ... the loss of one's home is a most extreme form of interference with the right to respect for the home.[34]

In consequence it has held that:

> Any person at risk of an interference of this magnitude should in principle be able to have the proportionality and reasonableness of the measure determined by an independent tribunal in the light of the relevant principles under Article 8 of the Convention, notwithstanding that, under domestic law, his or her right of occupation has come to an end.[35]

26.33   Accordingly, it is now well settled that a possession claim in respect of a home will 'engage' the Article 8 right and that if the defendant raises an arguable 'human rights defence' the court will need to be satisfied that the terms of Article 8(2) are met before an order for possession can be made.

26.34   That will involve the court dealing, in turn, with the issues of:

- whether the claim relates to a defendant's 'home';
- if so, whether the claim constitutes an actual or threatened interference with 'respect' for the home;
- if so, whether the claim is brought in accordance with the law;
- if so, whether the making of a possession order would serve one of the prescribed purposes (the interests of national security, public safety, the economic well-being of the country, the prevention of disorder or crime, the protection of health or morals, or the protection of the rights and freedoms of others); and

---

33   For a modern restatement of the principles governing the ECtHR's approach to Article 8 in housing cases see *Garib v The Netherlands* [2016] ECHR 211, 2016 April *Legal Action* 39 at [116] and for a modern example of the application of each element of Article 8 to a housing case see *Ivanova v Bulgaria* [2016] ECHR 373, [2016] HLR 21 at [49]–[54].

34   For use of this rubric see: *Connors v UK* [2004] ECHR 223, [2004] HLR 52 at [83]; *McCann v UK* (2008) 47 EHRR 40, [2008] HLR 40 at [49]–[50]; *Paulić v Croatia* [2009] ECHR 1614 at paras [43]–[45]; *Kay v UK* (2012) 54 EHRR 30, [2011] HLR 2 at [68]; *Buckland v UK* (2013) 56 EHRR 16, [2013] HLR 2 at [65] and *Rousk v Sweden* Application [2013] ECHR 746 at [137].

35   *Ćosić v Croatia* [2009] ECHR 80, (2011) 52 EHRR 39.

- if so, whether any form of possession order is 'necessary' in the sense of being a proportionate response to the purpose it is intended to vindicate.

Each of these issues requires consideration in turn.

Home

26.35   In *Qazi v Harrow London Borough Council*[36] Lord Bingham said that it was unsurprising that Article 8 protects the home 'since few things are more central to the enjoyment of human life than having somewhere to live'.[37]

26.36   There will seldom be an issue as to whether the possession claim is brought in respect of a 'home'. A person may have a home for the purposes of Article 8 without having any proprietary right in the land or building, and may have a right to respect for that home even if occupation of the land or building is not lawful.[38] As the High Court has recently held:

> 165. (1) 'Home' is an autonomous concept under Article 8. It requires that the individual have *'sufficient continuing links'* with the place in question (*Gillow v UK* (1986) 11 EHRR 335 at [46]), but does not require that the individual have a legal right under domestic law to occupy the place (*Buckley v UK* (1996) 23 EHRR 101, [63]).[39]

26.37   The existence of a home in Strasbourg jurisprudence is identified with 'sufficient and continuing links' in terms of the social and psychological attachment, or 'bond', that develops between a person and their accommodation or neighbourhood, rather than simply with the concept of 'a roof over one's head'.[40]

26.38   Put simply,

> on a straightforward reading of the Convention, its use of the expression 'home' appears to invite a down-to-earth and pragmatic consideration whether (as Lord Millett put it in *Uratemp Ventures Ltd v Collins*[41]) the place in question is that where a person 'lives and to which he returns and which forms the centre of his existence', since

---

36 [2003] UKHL 43, [2003] HLR 75.

37 [2003] UKHL 43, [2003] HLR 75 at [8].

38 *Kryvitska v Ukraine* [2010] ECHR 1850 and *Petolas v Croatia* Application no 74936/12, 28 April 2016, ECtHR at [60].

39 *Southward Housing Co-Operative Ltd v Walker and another* [2015] EWHC 1615 (Ch), [2016] 443 at [165](1).

40 See *Harrow LBC v Qazi* [2001] EWCA Civ 1834, [2002] HLR 14 reversed on other grounds at [2003] UKHL 43, [2003] HLR 75.

41 [2001] UKHL 43, (2001) 33 HLR 85 at [31].

'home' is not a legal term of art and Article 8 is not directed to the protection of property interests or contractual rights.[42]

26.39   In *Powell*, *Hall* and *Frisby*, Lord Hope said that the obligation to consider proportionality only arises if the property constitutes the occupant's *home* – the individual has to show sufficient and continuing links with a place to show that it is his or her home for the purposes of Article 8 but 'in most cases it can be taken for granted that a claim by a person who is in lawful occupation to remain in possession will attract the protection of Article 8.'[43]

26.40   Most recently, the Supreme Court has said:

> 61. ... In Article 8 the concept of 'home' is autonomous and does not depend on classification under domestic law. It is concerned with occupation in fact, and it is not limited to premises which are lawfully occupied or have been lawfully established. It is concerned with 'the existence of sufficient and continued links with a specific place'. See among others *Hounslow LBC v Powell* [2011] 2 AC 186, Lord Hope para 33; *Prokopovich v Russia* (2006) 43 EHRR 10, para 36; *Kryvitska and Kryvitskyy v Ukraine* App No 30856/03, para 40. Thus premises may not be 'let as a dwelling' ... and yet be a home for the purposes of Article 8 of the ECHR.'[44]

26.41   This can mean that if the defendant's occupation is merely transient, it may not constitute a home. It has been said that:

> 33. This issue is likely to be of concern only in cases where an order for possession is sought against a defendant who has only recently moved into accommodation on a temporary or precarious basis. The Leeds appeal in *Kay v Lambeth LBC* [2006] 2 AC 465, where the defendants had been on the recreation ground in their caravan for only two days without any authority to be there, provides another example of a situation where it was not seriously arguable that Article 8 was engaged.[45]

The issue arises most commonly in relation to short term occupation of land by members of travelling communities[46] and in respect of protest encampments on privately owned land.

---

42   Lord Bingham in *Harrow LBC v Qazi* [2003] UKHL 43, [2003] HLR 75 at [8].
43   [2011] UKSC 8, [2011] HLR 23 at [33].
44   *R (ZH and CN) v Newham LBC and Lewisham LBC* [2014] UKSC 62, [2015] HLR 6 at [61] and see to like effect *Lemo v Croatia* [2014] ECHR 755 at [30].
45   *Hounslow LBC v Powell* [2011] UKSC 8, [2011] HLR 23 at [33]
46   For example, *Leeds CC v Price* [2006] UKHL 10, [2006] HLR 22 and *R (O'Brien) v Bristol CC* [2014] EWHC 2423 (Admin).

26.42   In one of the latter cases, proposals to undertake exploratory drilling with a view to possible fracking for shale gas led to the establishment of a protest camp which had been occupying land for some 16 months before a possession claim came to trial. The High Court judge said

> 33. ... I would have had no hesitation in saying that there is a genuine dispute on the issue of whether the Protection Camp is the home of the second and third defendants. On that issue, I accept [the] submission that if the Protection Camp is not their home, it is very difficult to see what else is. ...[47]

26.43   In *O'Rourke v UK*[48] the Strasbourg Court made no final decision on whether a few nights accommodation in a hostel could amount to a 'home', but rejected the Article 8 claim on other grounds.

26.44   If defendants are no longer in occupation but have established that premises were, in the past, their residence, the court dealing with the possession claim will need to consider whether sufficient links with it have been maintained for it to properly remain capable of being described as their 'home'.[49]

26.45   An Article 8 defence cannot be maintained in respect of possession of premises that were merely the intended or potential 'home' of the defendant but which he or she has never occupied.[50] A 'home' can be in premises in combined residential and business use but would not usually cover separate industrial units.[51] Possession claims relating to mobile homes set up on pitches or plots of land raise interesting questions as to whether the 'home' for Article 8 purposes is that mobile home, or the plot or pitch or both. It had been hoped those questions might be addressed in *Stokes v United Kingdom*[52] in which they were expressly raised by the Strasbourg Court. In the event, that case was settled.

---

47   *Dutton v Persons Unknown* [2015] EWHC 3988 (Ch) at [33] and see *Jones v Persons Unknown* [2014] EWHC 4691 (Ch) for the eviction of another 'fracking' encampment.

48   Application no 39022/97, 26 June 2001.

49   See *Gillow v UK* (1989) 11 EHRR 335, (1986) *Times* 29 November and *Blečić v Croatia* [2004] ECHR 397, (2006) 43 EHRR 48.

50   *Globa v Ukraine* [2012] ECHR 1375.

51   *Khamidov v Russia* (2009) 49 EHRR 13, [2007] ECHR 928.

52   [2010] ECHR 1862

Interference

26.46   The Strasbourg Court has repeatedly said that:

> 68. ... the loss of one's home is the most extreme form of *interference* with the right to respect for the home. Any person *at risk of* an interference of this magnitude should in principle be able to have the proportionality of the measure determined by an independent tribunal in light of the relevant principles under Article 8 of the Convention.[53] [Emphasis added]

There will not normally be even a potential infringement of an Article 8 right arising simply from a change in the contractual relationship for occupancy of a 'home' (eg the expiry of a tenancy term or the taking effect of a notice to quit). Those things do not of themselves put occupation of a home in issue.

26.47   The Supreme Court has very recently re-emphasised that Article 8 is not engaged by the service of a notice to quit in accordance with the terms of the tenancy, even though such service may only be possible because a particular protection (whether statutory or at common law) has not been afforded to the tenant.[54] As Lord Neuberger observed in *Sims* (giving the judgment of the court) 'no judgment of the Strasbourg court begins to justify such a proposition'.[55]

26.48   But an actual or prospective possession order will amount to an 'interference', even if its effect is delayed or postponed.[56] As a result, possession proceedings themselves – whatever the form of order sought – interfere with Article 8 rights.

Requirement of legality

26.49   If the subject of the claim is a 'home', the next question is whether the possession claim which may constitute an interference with the right to respect for it is brought 'in accordance with the law', in the sense of meeting the legal requirements necessary to make good the particular form of possession claim. If it is not, it should be dismissed by the court in any event without the need to embark upon examination of a 'human rights defence'.

---

53   See, for example, *Kay v UK* [2010] ECHR 1322, [2011] HLR 2 at [68].

54   *Sims v Dacorum BC (Secretary of State for Communities and Local Government intervening)* [2014] UKSC 63, [2015] HLR 7 at [22].

55   *Southward Housing Co-Operative Ltd v Walker & Another* [2015] EWHC 1615 (Ch), [2016] Ch 443 at [165(5)].

56   *Bjedov v Croatia* [2012] ECHR 886; *Buckland v UK* [2012] ECHR 1710, (2013) 56 EHRR 16 and *Petolas v Croatia* Application no 74936/12, 28 April 2016, ECtHR at [62].

26.50   If the claimant is a public authority and it is said not to have been acting 'in accordance with the law' (whether by acting in breach of the defendant's Convention rights or otherwise) that contention should be addressed through a 'public law defence' (see chapter 25) rather than in a 'human rights defence'. If the public law defence succeeds, the claimant's claim will not be in 'accordance with the law' and granting a possession order would infringe the Article 8 right.

26.51   Of course, if the claimant obtains a possession order in respect of a person's home, or secures execution of it, by abusing the process of the court or by trick or deception, a breach of Article 8 will occur because the claimant has not acted 'in accordance with the law'.

26.52   In one case, a local authority landlord carried out an eviction which was unlawful in a number of different respects.[57] A warrant was issued without first obtaining the permission of a judge in circumstances where such permission was required. The eviction policy of the council was infringed. The bailiff did not surrender possession to the council but to a carpenter employed by an independent contractor who had no authority to sign the warrant. The tenant's application to stay or suspend the warrant was defended by the council in an abusive and unfair manner. A breach of Article 8 was established and led to an award of damages.

Serving the prescribed interests

26.53   It will usually be relatively easy for the court to be satisfied that the claim is brought to protect one of the listed 'interests' (for example, in an anti-social behaviour case, the interests of 'public safety' or 'prevention of crime and disorder' and, in a rent arrears case, 'the economic well-being of the country').

26.54   In most cases, the court will simply assume or presume that the possession claim is being advanced for a legitimate reason falling within one of the prescribed categories.

26.55   In *Manchester CC v Pinnock*, the Supreme Court said that:[58]

> 52. ... Where a person has no right in domestic law to remain in occupation of his home, the proportionality of making an order for possession at the suit of the local authority will be supported not merely by the fact that it would serve to vindicate the authority's ownership rights. It will also, at least normally, be supported by the fact that it would enable the authority to comply with its duties in relation to

---

57   *AA v London Borough of Southwark* [2014] EWHC 500 (QB).
58   [2011] UKSC 6, [2011] HLR 7 at [52]–[53].

the distribution and management of its housing stock, including, for example, the fair allocation of its housing, the redevelopment of the site, the refurbishing of sub-standard accommodation, the need to move people who are in accommodation that now exceeds their needs, and the need to move vulnerable people into sheltered or warden-assisted housing. Furthermore, in many cases (such as this appeal) other cogent reasons, such as the need to remove a source of nuisance to neighbours, may support the proportionality of dispossessing the occupiers.

53. ... In other words, the fact that the authority is entitled to possession and should, in the absence of cogent evidence to the contrary, be assumed to be acting in accordance with its duties, will be a strong factor in support of the proportionality. ...

26.56   The same point was subsequently cast in these terms in *Hounslow LBC v Powell*:[59]

36. ... the next question is what legitimate aims within the scope of Article 8(2) may the claimant authority rely on for the purposes of the determination of proportionality and what types of factual issues will be relevant to its determination. The aims were identified in *Pinnock*, para 52. The proportionality of making the order for possession at the suit of the local authority will be supported by the fact that making the order would (a) serve to vindicate the authority's ownership rights; and (b) enable the authority to comply with its public duties in relation to the allocation and management of its housing stock. Various examples were given of the scope of the duties that the second legitimate aim encompasses – the fair allocation of its housing, the redevelopment of the site, the refurbishing of sub-standard accommodation, the need to move people who are in accommodation that now exceeds their needs and the need to move vulnerable people into sheltered or warden-assisted housing. In *Kryvitska and Kryvitskyy v Ukraine* (Application No 30856/03) (unreported) given 2 December 2010, para 46 the Strasbourg court indicated that the first aim on its own will not suffice where the owner is the State itself. But, taken together, the twin aims will satisfy the legitimate aim requirement.

37. So, as was made clear in *Pinnock*, para 53, there will be no need, in the overwhelming majority of cases, for the local authority to explain and justify its reasons for seeking a possession order. It will be enough that the authority is entitled to possession because the statutory prerequisites have been satisfied and that it is to be assumed to be acting in accordance with its duties in the distribution and management of its housing stock. ...

59   [2011] UKSC 8, [2011] HLR 23 at [36]–[37].

26.57 In some circumstances, a public authority claimant will want to draw the court's attention to the particular 'legitimate aim' it relies upon. In such a case 'if it wishes to do so, it must plead the reason that it proposes to found upon and it must adduce evidence to support what it is saying. The particular grounds on which it relies can then be taken into account in the assessment. No point can be taken against the local authority, however, if it chooses not to take this course and to leave it to the tenant to raise such points as she wishes by way of a defence'.[60]

26.58 If the claimant is not a public authority, the position will usually be even more straightforward. The lawful recovery of possession of land or property a person owns is self-evidently a 'legitimate' aim and sufficient of itself. Indeed, the vindication of the claimant's right to possession may be necessary to give effect to the claimant's own Convention rights under Article 1 of Protocol 1 (see para 26.125).

Is making a possession order 'necessary' (ie proportionate)

26.59 If the subject of a lawfully brought claim is possession of a 'home', the crucial issue in a human rights defence based on Article 8 will usually be whether the possession order and subsequent eviction of the defendant is 'necessary' within the terms of Article 8(2). This requirement is interpreted by the ECtHR as requiring that the proposed action is 'proportionate', that is, no more than is reasonably necessary to achieve the legitimate aim being pursued.

26.60 In this sense, Article 8 operates at two levels: procedural and substantive.

26.61 At the *procedural* level, it requires that, before a possession order is made or an eviction is carried out, the occupiers have had an opportunity to raise the question of the necessity (or otherwise) of their eviction and to have an independent determination of that issue. If there is a factual dispute about whether a possession order is 'necessary', a court or tribunal must be able to address and resolve that dispute. So this 'procedural' dimension to Article 8 has three limbs:[61]

(a) Any person at risk of being dispossessed of his home at the suit of a local authority should in principle have the right to raise the question of the proportionality of the measure, and to have it determined by an independent tribunal in the light of Article 8, even if his right of occupation under domestic law has come to an end: ...

(b) A judicial procedure which is limited to addressing the proportionality of the measure through the medium of traditional judicial

60 [2011] UKSC 8, [2011] HLR 23 at [43].
61 *Manchester CC v Pinnock* [2011] UKSC 45, [2011] HLR 7 at [45].

review (ie one which does not permit the court to make its own assessment of the facts in an appropriate case) is inadequate as it is not appropriate for resolving sensitive factual issues: ...

(c) Where the measure includes proceedings involving more than one stage, it is the proceedings as a whole which must be considered in order to see if Article 8 has been complied with ... .

26.62 Most recently, the ECtHR has put it in this way:[62]

53. Under the Court's well-established case-law ... the assessment of the necessity of the interference in cases concerning the loss of one's home for the promotion of a public interest involves *not only issues of substance but also a question of procedure*: whether the decision-making process was such as to afford due respect to the interests protected under Article 8 of the Convention ... Since the loss of one's home is a most extreme form of interference with the right to respect for the home, any person risking this – whether or not belonging to a vulnerable group – should in principle be able to have the proportionality of the measure determined by an independent tribunal in the light of the relevant principles under that Article. [Emphasis added]

26.63 The second dimension of Article 8 is *substantive* ie it operates to ensure that the court or tribunal, dealing with the question – raised by the occupier – as to whether eviction is 'necessary', will not make a possession order or authorise an eviction unless satisfied that to do so is 'necessary', ie reasonable and proportionate having regard to the facts of the particular case.

26.64 When the HRA 1998 first came into force, some initially supposed that, in any and every housing possession case, the court would – as a result of the substantive element of Article 8 – need to be satisfied that the claimant could establish sufficient justification for the making of a possession order in Article 8(2) terms.

26.65 For example, in the early post-HRA 1998 case of *Harrow LBC v Qazi*, once the Court of Appeal was satisfied that the defendant occupied the premises as his 'home', and that Article 8 was therefore engaged by the claim for possession, it remitted the Article 8(2) question of 'necessity' or justification for trial in the county court.[63]

26.66 However, it took the domestic courts almost a decade finally to conclude that a human rights defence relying on Article 8 *would* require the court to be satisfied, on the particular facts of the case, that the making of a possession order was 'necessary' in the substantive sense.

---

62 *Ivanova and Cherkezov v Bulgaria* [2016] ECHR 373, [2016] HLR 21 at [53].
63 [2001] EWCA Civ 1834, [2002] HLR 14.

26.67   Paragraphs 26.68 to 26.79 trace the course of the decision-making over that period. The reader interested only in the *current* position should go straight to para 26.80.

The initial (now superseded) position of the domestic courts

26.68   The successful appeal by the claimant landlord in the *Qazi* case triggered three successive decisions of the House of Lords which left many landlords, tenants and judges in a state of uncertainty about how and when Article 8(2) operated in the domestic courts in those cases where the general law (whether statutory or common law) stipulated that on proof of certain requirements, for example, termination of an unprotected tenancy by notice to quit, a possession order should be made.

26.69   The first of the three cases was *Harrow LBC v Qazi* itself.[64] The council brought a possession claim against a former joint secure tenant whose wife had terminated the tenancy by serving a notice to quit (see para 1.128). The House of Lords held by a majority that the law which enables a public authority landlord to exercise its unqualified right to recover possession with a view to making the premises available for letting to others on its housing list does not violate Article 8. The result was that contractual and property rights to possession could not be defeated by a defence based on Article 8.[65] On 11 March 2004 the ECtHR decided – without giving specific reasons – that Mr Qazi's application to that court was inadmissible.

26.70   The second decision of the House of Lords was on the appeals in *Kay v Lambeth LBC* and *Leeds CC v Price*.[66] In *Kay*, the council had licensed 'short life' premises to a trust which purported to grant licences to those allowed into occupation. In fact those 'licences' created a relationship of landlord and tenant as between the trust and the sub-occupants.[67] However, Lambeth LBC gave notice to terminate the interest of the trust and brought possession proceedings against Mr Kay and other occupiers as trespassers. Defences based on Article 8 were struck out and possession orders were made. The defendants appealed, relying on the ECtHR decision in *Connors* (see para 26.5), but the Court of Appeal[68] dismissed the appeal and held

---

64 [2003] UKHL 43, [2003] HLR 75.
65 See also *Newham LBC v Kibata* [2003] EWCA Civ 1785, [2004] HLR 28 and *Bradney v Birmingham CC; Birmingham CC v McCann* [2003] EWCA Civ 1783, [2004] HLR 27, each applying the *Qazi* decision.
66 [2006] UKHL 10, [2006] HLR 22.
67 *Bruton v London and Quadrant Housing Trust* [1999] UKHL 26, (1999) 31 HLR 902.
68 [2004] EWCA Civ 926, [2004] HLR 56.

that *Connors* was only of assistance to the domestic courts in relation to cases involving Gypsies. In *Price*, the council sought possession of land which had been unlawfully occupied by the defendant trespassers, who were Gypsies. The claim was transferred to the High Court for determination of the preliminary issue of whether the defendants could rely on Article 8. The judge, applying *Harrow LBC v Qazi* (see para 26.69), held that they could not and made a possession order. On appeal[69] the Court of Appeal held that:

1) *Qazi* and *Connors* were inconsistent decisions;
2) the Court of Appeal had been wrong in *Lambeth LBC v Kay* to suggest that the decision in *Connors* applied only in Gypsy cases; and
3) the domestic courts should follow and apply *Qazi* until it had been reconsidered by the House of Lords in the light of *Connors*;

and granted leave to appeal to the House of Lords.

26.71   The two appeals were joined and heard together by seven law lords. They reconsidered *Qazi* in the light of *Connors*. The appeals were dismissed in both cases. It was unanimously agreed that Article 8 does not in terms give a right to be provided with a home and does not guarantee the right to have one's housing problem solved by the state authorities. But the House of Lords was divided on whether the HRA 1998 would, in exceptional cases, permit an occupier to defend the claim on the basis that a possession order would be disproportionate. Lord Hope, giving the leading speech of the majority, rejected that possibility. He said that:

> 109. ... Judges in the county courts, when faced with such a defence [based on Article 8 principles], should proceed on the assumption that domestic law strikes a fair balance and is compatible with the occupier's Convention rights.[70]
>
> 110. But, in agreement with [the majority] I would go further. Subject to what I say below, I would hold that a defence which does not challenge the law under which the possession order is sought as being incompatible with Article 8, but is based only on the occupier's personal circumstances, should be struck out ... [If] the requirements of the law have been established and the right to recover possession is unqualified, the only situations in which it would be open to the court to refrain from proceeding to summary judgment and making the possession order are these: (a) if a seriously arguable point is raised that the law which enables the court to make the possession order is incompatible with Article 8, the county court in the exercise of its jurisdiction under the HRA 1998 should deal with the argument in

69 [2005] EWCA Civ 289, [2005] HLR 31.
70 [2006] UKHL 10, [2006] HLR 22 at [109].

one or other of two ways: (i) by giving effect to the law, so far as it is possible to do so under section 3, in a way that is compatible with Article 8, or (ii) by adjourning the proceedings to enable the compatibility issue to be dealt with in the High Court; (b) if the defendant wishes to challenge the decision of a public authority to recover possession as an improper exercise of its powers at common law on the ground that it was a decision that no reasonable person would consider justifiable, he should be permitted to do this provided again that the point is seriously arguable: *Wandsworth LBC v Winder* [1985] AC 461. ...[71]

26.72   The decision of the majority in *Kay* and *Price* effectively nullified any potential the HRA 1998 might have to furnish a substantive defence based on the facts of a particular case. The first part of para [110] extracted above did no more than re-state the mechanisms provided by HRA 1998 ss3 and 4 in relation to potentially incompatible statutory schemes (see para 26.152). The second part, which became known as 'gateway (b)', was nothing more than a statement of the availability of the existing public law defence available on conventional administrative law principles (see chapter 25).

26.73   The third case to reach the House of Lords was *Doherty v Birmingham CC*.[72] In that claim the council sought possession of a plot on an official Gypsy caravan site. The case seemed on all fours with *Connors* (see para 26.5) in which it had been held that the statutory scheme of summary eviction of travellers from such sites without examination of the merits otherwise than in a claim for judicial review was incompatible with Article 8. The defence accordingly addressed both the gateways (a) and (b) identified by Lord Hope in *Kay* and contended that, on the specific facts, an eviction would be disproportionate. The House of Lords held that the underlying statutory scheme was incompatible with Article 8 and that the 'gateway (b)' defence should be remitted for trial. Although the majority were agreed that the terms of para [110] of *Kay* had to be enlarged, they were not entirely clear about how.

26.74   There were two almost immediate consequences of the decision in *Doherty*. The first was a rash of cases in the High Court[73] and

---

71   [2006] UKHL 10, [2006] HLR 22 at [110].
72   [2008] UKHL 57, [2008] HLR 45.
73   *Hillingdon LBC v Collins* [2008] EWHC 3016 (Admin), [201] BLGR 54; *Wandsworth LBC v Dixon* [2009] EWHC 27 (Admin), [2009] L&TR 28; *Defence Estates v JL* [2009] EWHC 1049 (Admin) and *Stokes v London Borough of Brent* [2009] EWHC 1426 (QB).

Court of Appeal[74] each seeking to identify how, if at all, a proportionality approach could be forced into the 'enlarged' gateway (b) and
then applied in individual cases. For reasons explained below, nothing is to be gained from now detailing those cases here.[75]

26.75   Second, it became even clearer than it had been before *Doherty*
that the decisions of the UK courts were out of step with the approach
being taken on the same issue by the ECtHR. In *McCann v UK*,[76] the
Strasbourg court firmly and clearly held that where a proportionality
defence was raised to a claim for a possession order in respect of an
occupier's home, the terms of Article 8(2) required that the court
seized of the possession claim be satisfied, having regard to the aim
pursued by the claimant and the circumstances of the defendant,
that eviction would be proportionate. It has followed and applied that
approach in a series of subsequent cases.[77]

26.76   While proceedings in the House of Lords continued, the Stras-
bourg Court had to deal with the complaint made to it by Mr Kay.
That Court initially posed the following question for the parties in
Kay v UK:[78]

> Did the applicants have the opportunity to have the proportionality of
> their evictions determined by an independent tribunal in light of the
> relevant principles under Article 8? (*McCann v the United Kingdom*
> Application no 19009/04, 13 May 2008)

26.77 In its determination on the merits, the ECtHR found that UK law
did not enable an examination of the proportionality of an eviction
on its individual facts and thus violated Article 8.[79] The ECtHR welcomed the increasing tendency of the domestic courts to develop and
expand conventional judicial review grounds in the light of Article

---

74 *Smith v Evans* [2007] EWCA Civ 1318, [2008] 1 WLR 661; *Doran v Liverpool CC*
[2009] EWCA Civ 146, [2009] 1 WLR 2365; *Central Bedfordshire v Taylor* [2009]
EWCA Civ 613, [2010] HLR 12; *Manchester CC v Pinnock* [2009] EWCA Civ 852,
[2010] HLR 7 and *Salford CC v Mullen* [2010] EWCA Civ 336, [2010] HLR 35.

75 For a review of how the domestic decisions have unfolded and what might have
been done to reconcile the approach of the domestic courts and Strasbourg see
N Madge, 'Article 8: La Lutta Continua?' [2009] JHL 43 and for an analysis of
how the cases might be applied in the then state of the jurisprudence see M
Robinson, 'Declaration of rights' [2010] 137 *Adviser* 17.

76 [2008] ECHR 978, [2008] HLR 40.

77 See *Ćosić v Croatia* [2009] ECHR 80, (2011) 52 EHRR 39; *Zehentner v Austria*
[2009] ECHR 1119, (2011) 52 EHRR 22; *Paulić v Croatia* [2009] ECHR 1614 and
Belchikova v Russia [2010] ECHR 2266.

78 [2008] ECHR 1193.

79 [2010] ECHR 1322, [2011] HLR 2.

8. It noted that in *Birmingham CC v Doherty*,[80] the House of Lords had referred to the possibility of challenges on conventional judicial review grounds encompassing more than just traditional *Wednesbury* grounds and stated that the gateway (b) test[81] set out by Lord Hope in *Kay* should in future be applied in a more flexible manner, allowing for personal circumstances to be relevant to the county court's assessment of the reasonableness of a decision to seek a possession order. The ECtHR noted that the widening of gateway (b) occurred after the end of the *Kay* case. It found a breach of Article 8 in its procedural aspect because the decision by the county court to strike out the occupants' Article 8 defences meant that the procedural safeguards required by Article 8 for the assessment of the proportionality of the interference were not met. The occupants were dispossessed of their homes without any possibility of having the proportionality of the measure determined by an independent tribunal. Modest compensation was ordered to be paid.

26.78   In summary, the ECtHR decided that the substantive law, allowing a land owner to obtain a possession order against occupants who had become trespassers did not breach Article 8. The problem, at the time of *Kay* in the domestic courts, was procedural. The courts were not able to consider the proportionality of the decision to bring the possession claim. The ECtHR has repeatedly required that the court determining the possession claim must be able to decide the proportionality of the proposed eviction and it has re-affirmed that again since its decision in *Kay*.[82]

26.79   Inevitably, the newly established UK Supreme Court was faced with a number of appeals inviting it to sort out the difficulties the domestic courts were having in applying the trio of House of Lords cases described above and was invited to find a means of reconciling them with the decisions coming from Strasbourg.

---

80   [2008] UKHL 57, [2008] HLR 45.
81   '... if the requirements of the law have been established and the right to recover possession is unqualified, the only situations in which it would be open to the court to refrain from proceeding to summary judgment and making the possession order are these: (a) if a seriously arguable point is raised that the law which enables the court to make the possession order is incompatible with Article 8 ['gateway (a)'], ... (b) if the defendant wishes to challenge the decision of a public authority to recover possession as an improper exercise of its powers at common law on the ground that it was a decision that no reasonable person would consider justifiable ['gateway (b)'] ...': *Kay v Lambeth LBC; Price v Leeds CC* [2006] UKHL 10, [2006] HLR 22 per Lord Hope at [110].
82   *Kryvitska v Ukraine* [2010] ECHR 1850.

The current position

26.80   In July 2010 the Supreme Court deployed nine of its 12 justices to hear, over four days, the appeal by the tenant in *Manchester CC v Pinnock*.[83] Seven of those same justices were assigned to hear appeals arising from *Salford CC v Mullen*[84] in late November 2010. The cases raised again the questions of:

- whether alleged infringement of Article 8 rights could be raised in a county court possession claim; and
- how the court was to satisfy itself – in cases where no judgment otherwise fell to be made about reasonableness – whether an order would be proportionate.

Collectively, the decisions made in those appeals confirm that an Article 8 human rights defence is in principle available in possession proceedings in the domestic courts.

26.81   In *Manchester CC v Pinnock*,[85] after considering the growing body of ECtHR jurisprudence on Article 8 and possession clams in general, the Supreme Court held that if UK 'law is to be compatible with Article 8 ... the court must have the power to assess the proportionality of making the order, and, in making that assessment, to resolve any relevant dispute of fact.'[86]

26.82   After referring to the decisions of the House of Lords in *Qazi*,[87] *Kay*,[88] and *Doherty*,[89] Lord Neuberger, giving the judgment of the Court, stated that it was 'unnecessary to consider them in any detail'. As there was 'now [an] unambiguous and consistent approach' of the ECtHR, the Supreme Court had to consider whether it was appropriate to depart from those decisions.

26.83   Although the Supreme Court was not bound to follow Strasbourg decisions,

> Where ... there is a clear and constant line of decisions whose effect is not inconsistent with some fundamental substantive or procedural aspect of our law, and whose reasoning does not appear to overlook or misunderstand some argument or point of principle, we consider that it would be wrong for this Court not to follow that line.[90]

---

83   [2009] EWCA Civ 852, [2010] HLR 7.
84   [2010] EWCA Civ 336, [2010] HLR 35.
85   [2010] UKSC 45, [2011] HLR 7.
86   [2010] UKSC 45, [2011] HLR 7 at [49].
87   [2003] UKHL 43, [2003] HLR 75.
88   [2006] UKHL 10, [2006] HLR 22.
89   [2008] UKHL 57, [2008] HLR 45.
90   [2010] UKSC 45, [2011] HLR 7 at [48].

Lord Neuberger said that even before the decision in *Kay v UK*,

> we would, in any event, have been of the opinion that this Court should now accept and apply the minority view of the House of Lords in those cases. In the light of *Kay v UK*, that is clearly the right conclusion.[91]

26.84 In *Pinnock*, in relation to demoted tenants, Lord Neuberger stated that:

> 78. ... an occupier who is the defendant in possession proceedings in the County Court and who claims that it would be incompatible with his Article 8 Convention rights for him to be put out of his home must be able to rely on those rights in defending those proceedings.[92]

On the face of it, the breadth of the decision of principle upheld in *Pinnock* appeared to apply to all kinds of occupiers lacking full security of tenure, not just demoted tenancies, and even where the relevant housing legislation – or landlord and tenant legislation – seemingly required the court to make a possession order.

26.85 The matter was put beyond all doubt in *Powell, Hall and Frisby* in which Lord Hope held that:

> 3. ... this proposition applies to all cases where a local authority seeks possession in respect of a property that constitutes a person's home for the purposes of Article 8.[93]

So, what was said in *Pinnock* applies to all other kinds of occupancy lacking full security of tenure and even where a court would otherwise be compelled by some statutory provision or common law rule to grant possession.[94]

26.86 This approach subsequently gained statutory recognition when Housing Act 1985 section 84A[95] was enacted. It provided additional 'mandatory' or 'absolute' grounds for possession against secure tenants but recognised that they had to operate subject to Article 8 rights. Section 84A(1) expressly stipulates that the new grounds are 'subject ... to any available defence based on the tenant's Convention rights'.

The question for the court

26.87 When an Article 8 defence is raised, and ultimately comes before the court for trial, the question for the court is relatively simple on the

---

91 [2010] UKSC 45, [2011] HLR 7 at [49].
92 [2010] UKSC 45, [2011] HLR 7 at [78].
93 [2011] UKSC 8, [2011] HLR 23 at [3].
94 For a contemporary account of the importance of this decision see N Madge *The Game of Ping Pong is Over* [2011] L&TR 3.
95 Introduced by Anti-social Behaviour, Crime and Policing Act 2014.

necessity/proportionality issue. The question is 'whether the eviction is a proportionate means of achieving a legitimate aim.'[96] or, slightly more fully, 'whether making an order for the occupier's eviction is a proportionate means of achieving a legitimate aim.'[97]

26.88   Answering this question requires a focus on the facts of the particular case and, usually, a balancing of the interests of the claimant against the individual personal circumstances of the defendant. An Article 8 defence cannot be defeated by simple reliance on a rule (whether of common law or statute) that requires the making of a possession order in a particular class of case because:

> 54. ... given that the right to respect for one's home under Article 8 of the Convention touches upon issues of central importance to the individual's physical and moral integrity, maintenance of relationships with others and a settled and secure place in the community, the balancing exercise under that provision in cases where the interference consists in the loss of a person's only home is of a different order, with particular significance attaching to the extent of the intrusion into the personal sphere of those concerned (see *Connors v UK* Application no 66746/01, [2004] ECHR 223). This can normally only be examined *case by case*. ...'[98] [Emphasis added]

26.89   By the time it reaches this question, the court should already have been satisfied that the case for possession is lawfully brought and that making a possession order would pursue a legitimate aim (eg the control of harmful anti-social behaviour). Indeed, 'in virtually every case where a residential occupier has no contractual or statutory protection, and the [claimant] is entitled to possession as a matter of domestic law, there will be a very strong case for saying that making an order for possession would be proportionate. However, in some cases there may be factors which would tell the other way'.[99]

26.90   So, the critical issue at this stage is usually whether there is something about the factual scenario – most centrally the personal circumstances of the occupants – which 'tells the other way' and enables the court to say that the making of a possession order (or a particular form of order) would not be proportionate on the facts of a particular case.

26.91   Successful defences are most likely 'in respect of occupants who are vulnerable as a result of mental illness, physical or learning

---

96 *Manchester CC v Pinnock* [2010] UKSC 45, [2011] HLR 7 at [52].
97 *Hounslow LBC v Powell* [2011] UKSC 8, [2011] HLR 23 at [33].
98 *Ivanova and Cherkezov v Bulgaria* [2016] ECHR 373, [2016] HLR 21.
99 [2010] UKSC 45, [2011] HLR 7 at [54].

disability, poor health or frailty'.[100] Indeed, those sorts of cases may also require a claimant, which is a public authority, 'to explain why it is not securing alternative accommodation'.[101]

26.92   In *Pinnock*, the Supreme Court declined to give further guidance about how particular factual scenarios should be handled, stating that 'the wide implications of the obligation to consider the proportionality of making a possession order are best left to the good sense and experience of judges sitting in the County Court.'[102]

26.93   Subsequently, the Court of Appeal made it clear that provided the trial judge asks and answers the question of proportionality by applying the law to the facts found, an appellate court will be very reluctant to disturb his or her final assessment.[103]

26.94   It is important to stress that at this stage – the trial on the merits – the court is not looking for something 'exceptional'. It would be 'both unsafe and unhelpful to invoke exceptionality as a guide. ... [E]xceptionality is an outcome and not a guide'.[104]

26.95   Instead, the court should simply be directing itself to the particular facts of the case. It can usually treat the lawful pursuit of a legitimate aim in the making of a possession order as a 'given' and ask itself whether turning the defendant out of his or her home would be a reasonable and proportionate thing to do on the facts of the particular case.

26.96   However, where the claim is brought by a private landlord or landowner, or by a lender which is a private company or a private individual, the court is not required to engage with the question of whether a possession order would represent a necessary or proportionate interference with the Article 8 right on the facts of the particular case because the statutory arrangements relating to the recovery of possession in such claims have already struck the balance between the interests of the parties (see para 26.23 above).

26.97   Given the procedural difficulties (described at 26.133 below) of getting an Article 8 defence to the trial stage, it is little surprise that only very few Article 8 defences have so far succeeded in defeating possession claims. The majority fail either on a summary determination or at trial.

---

100 [2010] UKSC 45, [2011] HLR 7 at [64].
101 [2010] UKSC 45, [2011] HLR 7 at [64].
102 [2010] UKSC 45, [2011] HLR 7 at [57].
103 *Southend on Sea BC v Armour* [2014] EWCA Civ 231, [2014] HLR 23 but see also *Fareham BC v Miller* [2013] EWCA Civ 159, [2013] HLR 22 in which a dismissal of a possession claim on Article 8 grounds was reversed on appeal.
104 [2010] UKSC 45, [2011] HLR 7 at [51].

26.98   The leading example of a successful Article 8 defence is *Southend on Sea BC v Armour*.[105] In that case, the defendant was an introductory tenant. In the early months of his tenancy there were incidents of anti-social behavior and the council began a claim for possession. For various reasons, the claim did not come to trial for over a year. In that time, the tenant had overcome various mental health issues and demonstrated his capacity to maintain his tenancy in a proper way. He had established a settled home in the property for himself and his dependent daughter. The trial judge decided that, on those facts, even if it would have been proportionate to have made a possession order had the facts remained as they were when the claim was launched, it was no longer proportionate to do so at the date of trial. The claim was dismissed. Appeals by the council were rejected in turn by the High Court and Court of Appeal.

26.99   There have also been a handful of successful Article 8 defences at first instance. Examples include the following:

- *Chesterfield BC v Bailey*:[106] Mr and Mrs Bailey were joint council tenants. Their relationship ended. Mr Bailey left and five years later served notice to quit to bring the joint tenancy to an end. After it expired, the council sought possession. The claim was dismissed. The judge decided that, even if the notice to quit had been valid, it would not have been proportionate to make a possession order having regard to the defendant's rights under Article 8. He said:

  65. ... This defendant had lived in this property since 2002, had lived in a previous council property since 1996, and had moved from that property mainly at the behest of the council ... She has spent money on this property and any move involves further expenditure of money. In a case such as this, where her husband had given the present notice in circumstances where she could do nothing about it (and did not even have notice of it until either it had taken effect or possibly very shortly before) I do not find it reasonable for the council without more to rely on that notice. Where a tenant is without blame it seems to me that the council should look and see whether otherwise they might be entitled to obtain possession ... Where there are no statutory grounds available to them (as here), and where there is no fault on the part of the defendant, and the defendant had previously had and enjoyed security of tenure without complaint, an order for possession would in my view breach the defendant's Article 8 rights.[107]

105 [2014] EWCA Civ 231, [2014] HLR 23.
106 [2011] EW Misc (CC) 18, Recorder Tidbury.
107 [2011] EW Misc (CC) 18 at [65].

- *Lambeth LBC v Caruana:*[108] Ms Caruana and her daughter lived in adjacent properties. Both were former 'short-life' occupiers. Ms Caruana's daughter had a young child. Lambeth sought possession to sell the properties on the open market. Ms Caruana's daughter suffered from a number of mental health problems and at times required the care of her mother. When unwell, Ms Caruana's daughter was unable to care for her own child. Ms Caruana often had to assume responsibility for her granddaughter at short notice. Lambeth offered an undertaking that it would not enforce a possession order until it had made the family a final offer of suitable alternative accommodation in accordance with its allocation scheme. Several days before the trial, an offer was made, but Ms Caruana and her daughter were unable to view the accommodation. Ms Caruana and her daughter maintained that it would be disproportionate, and a breach of Article 8, to make a possession order. The trial judge agreed and dismissed both claims for possession. While he did not prejudge the suitability of any offered accommodation or dictate what would be considered suitable, he acknowledged that the family's circumstances were unusual and that the council had so far made limited efforts to find somewhere suitable for them. Therefore, it was not proportionate to make a possession order at this time. Lambeth's application for permission to appeal to the Court of Appeal was later dismissed.
- *Affinity Sutton Homes Ltd v Cooper:*[109] Mr Cooper was granted a secure tenancy by Bromley Council. There was then a large-scale transfer of Bromley's housing stock to Affinity. As a result, Mr Cooper became an assured tenant. Accordingly, there was no statutory right for any family member other than a spouse to succeed, but his new tenancy agreement contained a contractual option for a new tenancy to be granted to any family member who resided with the tenant throughout the 12-month period before his or her death. It stated: 'all claims to succeed to the tenancy must be made ... in writing within six months of the death of the tenant'. Mr Cooper died in March 2009. His son Colin Cooper, who had been living with him for 37 years, did not make a claim within six months of his father's death but Affinity was aware during the six-month period that he wanted to succeed to the tenancy. Affinity did not ask him to give a written request for a new tenancy, but served a notice to quit and began a possession claim. Colin

---

108 May 2014 *Legal Action* 21, County Court.
109 January 2013 *Legal Action* 38, County Court.

Cooper was sectioned under the Mental Health Act 1983 in October 2009. The judge dismissed the possession claim finding that it would be disproportionate to deny him the right to continue to reside in a home where he has been for 37 years.

- *River Clyde Homes Ltd v Woods:*[110] Ms Woods was a vulnerable alcoholic and had been provided with social housing following domestic abuse. Before her tenancy obtained security of tenure she had engaged in an act of anti-social behaviour and allowed a third party to live with her (in each case contrary to her tenancy agreement). The landlord gave notice to quit and sought possession without needing to rely on statutory grounds. At an initial hearing, a court decided that an Article 8 defence should be considered on its merits, rather than summarily determined, because the tenant disputed the allegations and the landlord's case was being advanced without reliance on particular grounds or reasons.[111] At trial, the court considered that an eviction would not be proportionate. There had been no repetition of the incidents, no further complaints, the tenant had brought her drinking under control and an eviction would significantly exacerbate her vulnerability.

26.100 A full human rights defence might also succeed on facts such as these:

a) A council grants a tenancy to Mr B. He lives in the flat until he dies. His wife succeeds to the tenancy but she too dies. The council then serves a notice to quit on her estate to end the tenancy. Mr B's son who has lived in the property for 50 years has no statutory right to succeed, and has known no other home, faces a claim for possession.

b) Ms C is a sole tenant, living in social housing with her 25-year-old son who is disabled. He has never lived anywhere else. She abandons the tenancy, leaving him in occupation. The claimant serves notice to quit and brings a possession claim.

c) A housing association brings a possession claim against Mr D, an assured tenant, under mandatory HA 1988 Sch 2 Ground 8. Mr D defends saying he has made a housing benefit claim which, through no fault of his own, has not yet been determined by the local council. If it is granted, the housing benefit will clear the

---

110 December 2015 *Legal Action* 44, Sheriff Court.
111 [2015] HLR 33, September 2015 *Legal Action* 49.

arrears.[112] (Or a housing association seeks possession on the same facts against an assured shorthold tenant relying upon a HA 1988 s21 notice.)

d) Ms E, an elderly occupier, is terminally ill (or about to undergo major surgery) but the claimant seeks immediate possession.

26.101 It is worth emphasising again that the question for the court is not 'did the claimant consider proportionality' but rather 'is it proportionate for the court' to order possession. The key difference between the human rights defence described in this Chapter and the public law defence (described in chapter 25) is that conventional public law defences focus upon the claimant's decision-making process and the procedure followed by the claimant. In contrast, human rights or 'proportionality' defences focus upon court-generated outcomes. As Lord Bingham said in *R (Begum) v Denbigh High School Governors*[113] 'what matters in any Convention rights case is the practical outcome, not the quality of the decision making process that led to it.[114]

26.102 In dealing with a human rights defence the court is deciding for itself on the facts as agreed (or as found at trial), whether the making of a possession order would be proportionate. In a public law defence, the court is simply deciding whether the claim is lawfully brought to the court by the claimant.

26.103 However, as explained at 26.50 above, occupants defending possession claims may well be able to rely on both traditional administrative law grounds in a public law defence and 'proportionality' arguments in a human rights defence. If that happens, courts will have to consider both the decision-making process by the claimant and then the impact of the occupier's personal circumstances on the issue of proportionality. In appropriate cases, a defence might also be advanced in reliance on the Equality Act 2010 (see chapter 27) in addition to a 'human rights' and/or 'public law' defence.

26.104 When dealing with the human rights defence at trial, the court may be required to resolve *disputed facts*. In *Pinnock*, Lord Neuberger said:

- 'ECtHR jurisprudence requires the court considering such a challenge to have the power to make its own assessment of any *relevant facts* which are in dispute.' [73]

112 See *North British Housing Association Limited v Matthews* [2004] EWCA Civ 1736, [2005] HLR 17.

113 [2006] UKHL 15, (2007) 1 AC 100.

114 [2006] UKHL 15, (2007) 1 AC 100 at [31].

- 'Where it is required in order to give effect to an occupier's Article 8 Convention rights, the court's powers of review can, in an appropriate case, extend to reconsidering for itself the facts found by a local authority, or indeed to *considering facts* which have arisen since the issue of proceedings, by hearing evidence and forming its own view.' [74]
- 'a County Court judge who is invited to make an order for possession against a demoted tenant ... can consider whether it is proportionate to make the order sought, and can investigate and determine any *issues of fact* relevant for the purpose of that exercise.' [104]

26.105 These should not simply be findings of fact as to the position when the claim was brought. In *Powell, Hall* and *Frisby*, Lord Hope stated at [53] that the 'court's powers of review can, in an appropriate case, extend to reconsidering for itself the facts found by a local authority, or indeed to considering the *facts which have arisen since the issue of proceedings*, by hearing evidence and forming its own view.'

26.106   For a discussion of the likely outcomes if a human rights defence based on Article 8 succeeds, see para 26.159

Article 6

26.107 Article 6 is in the following terms:

Right to a fair trial
In the determination of his civil rights and obligations ... everyone is entitled to a fair and public hearing within a reasonable time by an independent and impartial tribunal established by law ...

26.108 In effect, the Article provides an underpinning of the requirements, of the Civil Procedure Rules (CPR) and our common law, that legal proceedings, including possession proceedings, are conducted fairly, openly and expeditiously.

26.109   Where the claim is for possession of a 'home', Article 6 adds little if anything to the procedural aspect of Article 8 described above at 26.61.

26.110   In one case, it was suggested by the occupier that Article 6 required an automatic hearing by a court *before* a possession order, that a court had earlier granted, was executed. The Court of Appeal rejected that contention. It said:[115]

115 *St Brice v Southwark LBC* [2001] EWCA Civ 1138, [2002] HLR 26.

19. ... The routine enforcement of court orders, made after a hearing in compliance with Article 6, should not normally entail a separate hearing. In order to safeguard and make best use of resources housing and court administration needs to be flexible and efficient as well as fair, and the present procedure, as it worked in this case, meets those needs. As Lord Bingham said in *Brown v Stott* [2001] 2 WLR 817 at 825B –

> 'What a fair trial requires cannot ... be the subject of a single, unvarying rule or collection of rules. It is proper to take account of the facts and circumstances of particular cases, as the European Court has consistently done.'

26.111 In other cases, Article 6 may be invoked as a back-stop if, unusually, there is unreasonable delay[116] or other unfairness in the conduct of a possession claim or other housing-related dispute.[117]

26.112 Indeed, Article 6 is most often invoked by *claimants* in possession proceedings who assert that it takes too long to obtain or enforce possession orders.[118]

26.113 For a discussion of the likely outcomes if a human rights defence based on Article 6 succeeds, see para 26.159

Articles 9, 10 and 11

26.114 These Articles protect a variety of personal freedoms which might be engaged by aspects of possession claims.

26.115 They provide as follows:

Article 9

Freedom of thought, conscience and religion

(1) Everyone has the right to freedom of thought, conscience and religion; this right includes freedom to change his religion or belief and freedom, either alone or in community with others and in public or private, to manifest his religion or belief, in worship, teaching, practice and observance.

---

116 In *Anderson v UK* [2010] ECHR 145, the ECtHR said 'reasonableness of the length of proceedings must be assessed in the light of the circumstances of the case and with reference to the following criteria: the complexity of the case, the conduct of the applicant and the relevant authorities and what was at stake for the applicant in the dispute' at [24]. In *Korelec v Slovenia* Application no 28456/03, 12 May 2009, the ECtHR found breach of Article 6 where a dispute involving succession rights – and a landlord's possession claim – took eight years to resolve.

117 *Tsfayo v UK* [2007] ECHR 656, [2007] HLR 19.

118 See, for example, *Palumbo v Italy* [2000] ECHR 649; *Mirzayev v Azerbaijan* [2009] ECHR 1986 and *Panteleeva v Ukraine* [2007] ECHR 562.

(2) Freedom to manifest one's religion or beliefs shall be subject only to such limitations as are prescribed by law and are necessary in a democratic society in the interests of public safety, for the protection of public order, health or morals, or for the protection of the rights and freedoms of others.

Article 10

Freedom of expression

(1) Everyone has the right to freedom of expression. This right shall include freedom to hold opinions and to receive and impart information and ideas without interference by public authority and regardless of frontiers. This Article shall not prevent States from requiring the licensing of broadcasting, television or cinema enterprises.

(2) The exercise of these freedoms, since it carries with it duties and responsibilities, may be subject to such formalities, conditions, restrictions or penalties as are prescribed by law and are necessary in a democratic society, in the interests of national security, territorial integrity or public safety, for the prevention of disorder or crime, for the protection of health or morals, for the protection of the reputation or rights of others, for preventing the disclosure of information received in confidence, or for maintaining the authority and impartiality of the judiciary.

Article 11

Freedom of assembly and association

(1) Everyone has the right to freedom of peaceful assembly and to freedom of association with others, including the right to form and to join trade unions for the protection of his interests.

(2) No restrictions shall be placed on the exercise of these rights other than such as are prescribed by law and are necessary in a democratic society in the interests of national security or public safety, for the prevention of disorder or crime, for the protection of health or morals or for the protection of the rights and freedoms of others. This Article shall not prevent the imposition of lawful restrictions on the exercise of these rights by members of the armed forces, of the police or of the administration of the State.

26.116 These Articles are most usually relied upon by demonstrators and protestors who are occupying land in order to advance their cause or draw attention to it.[119] Most such defences fail to pass the summary

---

119 See, for example, *City of London v Samede* [2012] EWCA Civ 160, [2012] HLR 14 (occupation of St Paul's Cathereral churchyard); *Mayor of London v Hall* [2010] EWCA Civ 817, [2011] 1 WLR 504 (occupation of Parliament Square gardens) and *Manchester Ship Canal Developments v Persons Unknown* [2014] EWHC 645 (Ch) (protest camp on road verges).

assessment stage for the procedural handling of a possession claim (see para 26.136).

26.117 But these Articles can also be invoked in the domestic residential premises context. In one case, a landlord sought and obtained possession for breach of a clause in a tenancy agreement which prohibited the tenant from erecting or keeping a satellite dish on the outside of their flat. The tenants needed the satellite dish to receive communications in their languages of Farsi and Arabic. The ECtHR held that their eviction had been an unlawful infringement of their Article 10 rights.[120]

26.118 For a discussion of the likely outcomes if a human rights defence based on Article 9, 10 or 11 succeeds, see para 26.159.

Article 14

26.119 Where other Convention rights are engaged (or an issue arises within the ambit of a Convention right) Article 14 is intended to ensure that no one is a victim of unjustified discrimination. The Article is in these terms:

Prohibition of Discrimination

The enjoyment of the rights and freedoms set forth in this Convention shall be secured without discrimination on any ground such as sex, race, colour, language, religion, political or other opinion, national or social origin, association with a national minority, property, birth or other status.

26.120 It is most unlikely that there will be any suggestion that the court itself will be guilty of unjustified discrimination if it makes a possession order (or a particular form of order).

26.121 If it is said that the bringing of the possession claim, or acts leading up to it, amount to unjustified discrimination by a *public authority* claimant, that will be addressed through a 'public law defence' (see chapter 25) or by a defence based on infringement of the prohibitions on discrimination contained in the Equality Act 2010 (see chapter 27).

26.122 If it is said that the bringing of the possession claim, or acts leading up to it, amount to unjustified discrimination by a *private* claimant, that will normally be addressed through a defence based on infringement of the prohibitions on discrimination contained in the Equality Act 2010 (see chapter 27).

120 *Mustafa v Sweden* [2008] ECHR 1710, (2011) 52 EHRR 24.

26.123   The only remaining category of Article 14 argument likely to be in play is one which asserts that the court's application of a particular statutory provision would result in discrimination, ie, that there is something wrong with the underlying law.[121] For that situation see para 26.152.

26.124   For a discussion of the likely outcomes if a human rights defence based on Article 14 succeeds, see para 26.159.

Article 1 of the First Protocol

26.125 Article 1 is the Convention right concerned with the protection of an individual's possessions. It provides:

> **Protection of Property**
> Every natural or legal person is entitled to the peaceful enjoyment of his possessions. No one shall be deprived of his possessions except in the public interest and subject to the conditions provided for by law and by the general principles of international law.

26.126 For the purposes of Article 1, 'possessions' include tenancies, leases, licences and other rights to occupy land.

26.127   This means that this Convention right can be invoked in a 'human rights defence' even where the property subject of the claim is not occupied and is not anyone's home (ie, where Article 8 cannot be relied upon).

26.128   In some cases, the making of a possession order will itself serve to end a tenancy or other right and thus 'deprive' the defendant of a 'possession' (in which case Article 1 may be engaged).

26.129   But more commonly, the underlying legal right (eg the lease or tenancy which amounts to a 'possession') will have been ended by expiry of a term or by a notice to quit taking effect before the possession claim is brought.

26.130   No defence under Article 1 will arise in that more common case. The Court will not be infringing the Convention right by granting possession because it will not be taking away or restricting the enjoyment of any remaining 'possession'.[122] Of course, if the claimant in the possession claim is a *public authority* which has acted in breach of the Article 1 right, the defendant could raise either a 'public law' defence or a 'human rights' defence relying on that breach.

---

121 See, for example, *Michalak v Wandsworth LBC* [2002] EWCA Civ 271, [2002] HLR 39.

122 *Dacorum BC v Sims* [2014] UKSC 63, [2015] HLR 7 and *R(CN and ZH) v Lewisham and Newham LBC* [2014] UKSC 62, [2015] HLR 6.

26.131   Where the defence is able to rely on Article 1, it is likely to provide a less powerful shield than a defence based on Article 8; certainly in a case where the claimant would otherwise have an unqualified right to possession in domestic law. In particular, the Article cannot be used to assert that there must be an individual assessment of the merits of an eviction of a particular occupier. For example, in a case in which domestic law provided for the demolition, in all cases, of buildings improperly erected without planning consent, the ECtHR set out these principles:[123]

> 72. The salient issue is whether the interference would strike a fair balance between the first applicant's interest to keep her possessions intact and the general interest to ensure effective implementation of the prohibition against building without a permit.
>
> 73. According to the Court's settled case-law, the second paragraph of Article 1 of Protocol No 1 must be read in the light of the principle set out in the first sentence of the first paragraph: that an interference needs to strike a fair balance between the general interest of the community and the individual's rights. This means that a measure must be both appropriate for achieving its aim and not disproportionate to that aim ... However, the High Contracting Parties enjoy a margin of appreciation in this respect, in particular in choosing the means of enforcement and in ascertaining whether the consequences of enforcement would be justified ... When it comes to the implementation of their spatial planning and property development policies, this margin is wide ...
>
> 74. For that reason, unlike Article 8 of the Convention, Article 1 of Protocol No 1 does not in such cases presuppose the availability of a procedure requiring an individualised assessment of the necessity of each measure of implementation of the relevant planning rules. It is not contrary to the latter for the legislature to lay down broad and general categories rather than provide for a scheme whereby the proportionality of a measure of implementation is to be examined in each individual case ... There is no incongruity in this, as the intensity of the interests protected under those two Articles, and the resultant margin of appreciation enjoyed by the national authorities under each of them, are not necessarily co-extensive ... Thus, although the Court has in some cases assessed the proportionality of a measure under Article 1 of Protocol No 1 in the light of largely the same factors as those that it has taken into account under Article 8 of the Convention ... this assessment is not inevitably identical in all circumstances.
>
> 75. In the first applicant's case, the house was knowingly built without a permit ... and therefore in flagrant breach of the domestic building regulations. In this case, regardless of the explanations that the

123 *Ivanova and Cherkezov v Bulgaria* [2016] ECHR 373, [2016] HLR 21.

first applicant gave for this failure, this can be regarded as a crucial consideration under Article 1 of Protocol No 1. The order that the house be demolished, which was issued a reasonable time after its construction ... simply seeks to put things back in the position in which they would have been if the first applicant had not disregarded the requirements of the law. The order and its enforcement will also serve to deter other potential lawbreakers ... which must not be discounted in view of the apparent pervasiveness of the problem of illegal construction in Bulgaria (see paragraphs 41–43 above). In view of the wide margin of appreciation that the Bulgarian authorities enjoy under Article 1 of Protocol No. 1 in choosing both the means of enforcement and in ascertaining whether the consequences of enforcement would be justified, none of the above considerations can be outweighed by the first applicant's proprietary interest in the house.

76. The implementation of the demolition order would therefore not be in breach of the first applicant's rights under Article 1 of Protocol No 1.

26.132   For a discussion of the likely outcomes if a human rights defence based on Article 1 of Protocol 1 succeeds, see para 26.159.

The procedure relating to human rights defences

26.133   The court dealing with a possession claim is under no obligation to identify for itself any available human rights defence.

26.134   Defendants wishing to rely on their Convention rights must raise the point[124] and set it out in a properly pleaded and particularised defence,[125] or (if there has not been an opportunity to file and serve a defence) be able to outline the prospective defence and indicate when a proper pleading will be filed.

26.135   Human rights defences are relatively easy to assert (because in most cases, particularly when relying on Article 8, the defendant will simply be outlining their contentions on any disputed facts and giving detailed particulars of their personal circumstances) but very rarely succeed.

---

124 *Hounslow LBC v Powell* [2011] UKSC 8, [2011] HLR 23 at [33]; *Brogan v UK* Application no 74946/10, 13 May 2014, ECtHR at [54]; *Budimir v Croatia* (2016) 62 EHRR SE11, March 2016 *Legal Action* 29 and *South Lanarkshire Council v McKenna* [2014] Scots SC 1 at [35]. The issue of proportionality does not arise 'automatically' in every housing possession case: *Petolas v Croatia* Application no 74936/12, 28 April 2016, ECtHR at [72].

125 *Thurrock BC v West* [2012] EWCA Civ 1435, [2013] HLR 5 at [29].

26.136　　In *Pinnock*, Lord Neuberger said:

> If an Article 8 point is raised, the court should initially consider it summarily, and if, as will no doubt often be the case, the court is satisfied that, even if the facts relied on are made out, the point would not succeed, it should be dismissed. Only if the court is satisfied that it could affect the order that the court might make should the point be further entertained.[126]

26.137　In *Powell, Hall and Frisby*, Lord Hope said that a 'court should initially consider [the human rights defence] summarily and if it is satisfied that, even if the facts relied upon are made out, the point would not succeed, it should be dismissed'.[127]

26.138　　The ECtHR decision in *McCann v UK* refers to occupiers 'raising an arguable case which would require a court to examine the issue; in the great majority of cases, an order for possession could continue to be made in summary proceedings'.[128]

26.139　　Because most possession claims are initially issued with a return date which allows only a summary hearing of a few minutes, the Court will at that hearing have to consider whether to dispose of a human rights defence summarily, there and then (or perhaps at an adjourned hearing fixed for the purpose), or given directions for its trial.

26.140　　The correct approach now to be adopted in the UK courts was identified in *Birmingham CC v Lloyd*.[129] The Court of Appeal said:

> 26. In *Pinnock*, the Supreme Court explained that, when an Article 8 defence is raised in a case coming before the District Judge in the possession list, the District Judge should identify the grounds on which the Article 8 right is said to be based, so that it can be assessed whether there is a real prospect of the Article 8 defence succeeding. This involves taking the facts on which the Article 8 argument is based as being correct and deciding whether, if faced with those facts, a judge could reasonably decide that an Article 8 defence would justify refusing a possession order.

26.141　The test to be applied by the district judge on such a summary consideration was set out by the Supreme Court itself in *Hounslow LBC v Powell*:[130]

> 33. ... The court will only have to consider whether the making of a possession order is proportionate if the issue has been raised by the

126 [2010] UKSC 45, [2011] HLR 7 at [61].
127 [2011] UKSC 8, [2011] HLR 23 at [34]. See too [92].
128 [2008] ECHR 285, [2008] HLR 40 at [54].
129 [2012] EWCA Civ 969, [2012] HLR 44.
130 [2011] UKSC 8, [2011] HLR 23.

occupier and it has crossed the high threshold of being seriously arguable. ...

35. [Counsel for the occupiers] accepted that the threshold for raising an arguable case on proportionality was a high one which would
succeed in only a small proportion of cases. I think that he was right
to do so: see also *Pinnock*, para 54. Practical considerations indicate
that it would be demanding far too much of the judge in the county
court, faced with a heavy list of individual cases, to require him to
weigh up the personal circumstances of each individual occupier
against the landlord's public responsibilities. Local authorities hold
their housing stock, as do other social landlords, for the benefit of the
whole community. It is in the interests of the community as a whole
that decisions are taken as to how it should best be administered. The
court is not equipped to make those decisions, which are concerned
essentially with housing management. This is a factor to which great
weight must always be given, and in the great majority of cases the
court can and should proceed on the basis that the landlord has sound
management reasons for seeking a possession order.

The result of this guidance has been that most human rights defences
will be disposed-of in a short summary hearing at an early stage of
a possession claim. The appeal courts have repeatedly made it clear
that that is the expectation. It will only be 'rare cases' that survive the
initial scrutiny and go forward for full trial.[131]

26.142   In *Riverside Group Ltd v Thomas*[132] the landlord granted the defendant an assured shorthold (starter) tenancy. Following complaints
about her anti-social behaviour, the landlord served a notice under
HA 1988 s21 and claimed possession. The claim was transferred to
the High Court. While waiting for trial of that claim, the landlord was
granted an anti-social behaviour injunction. The defendant, acting in
person, sought a full trial of the issue of whether possession would
be proportionate under Article 8 and whether the section 21 mandatory possession scheme was compatible with HRA 1998 (as to which
see para 26.157 below)

26.143   The judge stated that 'this possession claim is plainly one in
which a possession order ought to be granted summarily since there
is no proper basis to conclude that the threshold for more detailed
consideration is justified' (para 41). He made an immediate possession order.

---

131 *McDonald v McDonald* [2016] UKSC 28, [2016] HLR 28 at [73].
132 [2012] EWHC 169 (QB), Ryder J.

26.144   In *Corby BC v Scott* (heard with *West Kent Housing Association Ltd v Haycraft*)[133] the defendants were, respectively, an introductory tenant of a council and an assured shorthold ('starter') tenant of a housing association. In each case, the landlord claimed possession on the basis that the legal requirements for notice had been satisfied and that, as a matter of property law, they were entitled to possession. In each case, the tenant raised a defence based on Article 8. Ms Scott said that she had been subjected to a murderous attack in July 2010. HHJ Hampton refused to make a possession order. Mr Haycraft denied the allegation made against him and relied on ill-health. HHJ Simpkiss dismissed an appeal against a possession order granted to West Kent.

26.145   On appeal, Lord Neuberger MR said:

> 18. The effect of the reasoning in *Pinnock* [2011] 2 AC 104 ... at least in relation to demoted and introductory tenancies, [is that] it will only be in 'very highly exceptional cases' that it will be appropriate for the court to consider a proportionality argument', although exceptionality is an outcome and not a guide. ...

The facts in *Scott* got 'nowhere near justifying the contention that it would be disproportionate for the council to obtain possession'. The 'murderous attack' was 'simply irrelevant to the issue of Article 8 proportionality' (para 24). It was a case 'which should not have gone to trial' (para 26). In relation to *Haycraft*, the initial allegation was properly investigated by the reviewing panel. Its conclusion was clearly articulated and well-reasoned. Mr Haycraft had not come up with any new points which called the finding into question, or any challenge to the procedure or reasoning involved in the review. There was no good evidence that his health problems would be exacerbated by eviction. HHJ Simpkiss was entitled to conclude that Mr Haycraft's pleaded case was not strong enough to justify a hearing on the issue of proportionality.

26.146   Lord Neuberger said:

> 35. ... a judge (i) should be rigorous in ensuring that only relevant matters are taken into account on the proportionality issue, and (ii) should not let understandable sympathy for a particular tenant have the effect of lowering the threshold identified by Lord Hope in [*Hounslow LBC v Powell* [2011] UKSC 8 at [33] and [35]] ...

He emphasised:

> 39. ... the desirability of a judge considering at an early stage (normally on the basis of the tenant's pleaded case on the issue) whether the

133 [2012] EWCA Civ 276, [2012] HLR 23.

tenant has an arguable case on Article 8 proportionality, before the issue is ordered to be heard. If it is a case which cannot succeed, then it should not be allowed to take up further court time and expense to the parties, and should not be allowed to delay the landlord's right to possession.

The court allowed *Corby*'s appeal and dismissed *Haycraft*'s appeal.

26.147   The relevant authorities on the correct approach to human rights defences at the summary assessment stage were brought together in *Thurrock Borough Council v West*[134] in which the Court of Appeal identified a range of applicable principles including these:

> 29. Sixthly, an Article 8 defence on the grounds of lack of proportionality must be pleaded and sufficiently particularised to show that it reaches the high threshold of being seriously arguably: Powell at [33] and [34] (Lord Hope).

> 30. Seventhly, unless there is some good reason not to do so, the Court must at the earliest opportunity summarily consider whether the Article 8 defence, as pleaded, and on the assumption that the pleaded facts relied upon are correct, reaches that threshold: *Pinnock* at [61], *Powell* at [33]and [34] (Lord Hope) and [92] (Lord Phillips), *Corby BC* at [39], *Birmingham City Council v Lloyd* at [26] and [27] (Lord Neuberger MR). If the pleaded defence does not reach that threshold, it must be struck out or dismissed: ibid. The resources of the court and of the parties should not be further expended on it.

26.148   Although several of the authorities refer to the need for a human rights defence to be 'exceptional' or 'highly exceptional' on its merits to survive scrutiny at the summary assessment stage, the correct test is to identify whether the defence – on the assumption that the pleaded facts are decided in the defendant's favour – has a real prospect of bringing the court to any other conclusion than the making of an outright order for possession or, to put it in the language of CPR 55.8(2) (which specifies when the court in a possession claim may give case management directions for trial), whether the human rights defence appears 'to be substantial'.

26.149   One judge has recently described the exercise in these terms, when faced with a human right defence:

> 16. ... I accept [the] submission that I should not make a possession order unless I am satisfied that there is no genuine dispute in answer to this claim on grounds which appear to this court to be substantial. If the claim is genuinely disputed on grounds which appear to be substantial, I should do no more than give case management directions for the future conduct of the case. I should grant possession

134 [2012] EWCA Civ 1435, [2013] HLR 5.

only if I am satisfied that the defendants have failed to demonstrate that they have a realistically arguable defence to the claim. If satisfied that the defendants do demonstrate a realistically arguable defence to the claim, then I should do no more than give directions for the trial of that claim.[135]

26.150 In recent years, the courts have increasingly been required to make summary assessments of human rights defences advanced 'at the last minute' (sometimes by possession day duty representatives) at the first hearings of possession claims. To guard against the prospect of both the claimant and the court being faced at such a hearing with a late human rights defence to what would otherwise be an unanswerable possession claim, the *Pre-action Protocol for possession claims by social landlords* (reproduced in full in appendix E) has been modified to 'flush out', at an early stage, the sort of points that might be raised by a defendant in a human rights defence.

26.151 Part 3 of the new Pre-action Protocol states:

> 3.2 In cases where the court must grant possession if the landlord proves its case then before issuing any possession claim social landlords –
> (a) should write to occupants explaining why they currently intend to seek possession and requiring the occupants within a specified time to notify the landlord in writing of any personal circumstances or other matters which they wish to take into account. In many cases such a letter could accompany any notice to quit and so would not necessarily delay the issue of proceedings; and
> (b) should consider any representations received, and if they decide to proceed with a claim for possession give brief written reasons for doing so.
>
> 3.3 In these cases the social landlord should include in its particulars of claim, or in any witness statement filed under CPR 55.8(3), a schedule giving a summary –
> (a) of whether it has (by statutory review procedure or otherwise) invited the defendant to make representations of any personal circumstances or other matters which they wish to be taken into account before the social landlord issues proceedings;
> (b) if representations were made, that they were considered;
> (c) of brief reasons for bringing proceedings; and
> (d) copies of any relevant documents which the social landlord wishes the Court to consider in relation to the proportionality of the landlord's decision to bring proceedings.

---

135 *Dutton v Persons Unknown* [2015] EWHC 3988 (Ch) at [16], HHJ Hodge QC.

Human rights defences based on a challenge to the underlying law

26.152   The defendant may take the point, in defence of any possession claim, that the underlying law (statute or common law) which enables the claimant to seek a possession order, or appears to require the court to grant one, is itself incompatible with a Convention right. This sort of defence was discretely identified by Lord Hope at para 110(a) of his speech in *Lambeth LBC v Kay*.[136]

26.153   If it can be seriously argued that legislation relied on by the claimant in a possession claim, or falling to be applied by the court in such a claim, appears incompatible with a Convention right, the first task of the court dealing with the possession claim will be to construe the legislation compatibly with the relevant Convention right if it is possible to do so.[137]

26.154   If such a construction seems impossible, the court should transfer the proceedings to the High Court so that it can consider making a declaration of incompatibility under HRA 1998 s4.

26.155   However, this is likely only to delay rather than prevent, eviction for the defendant occupier. That is because, even if a declaration of incompatibility is made, it is not binding on the parties to the proceedings in which it is made.[138] So, for example, if the High Court declares that a mandatory statutory ground for possession is incompatible with Convention rights, the parties' rights are unaffected by the declaration.

26.156   To date, no defendant has succeeded in obtaining a declaration that a statutory provision concerned with possession orders is incompatible with the Convention – although a declaration would have been granted in *Doherty v Birmingham CC*[139] in respect of the legislation concerned with possession of official Gypsy caravan sites if parliament had not already passed (but not yet brought into force) amending legislation which repealed the incompatible provision.[140]

26.157   The unsuccessful challenges which have so far been made, to legislation relating to possession proceedings, on the ground that it is incompatible include:

---

136 [2006] UKHL 10, [2006] HLR 22.
137 HRA 1998 s3.
138 HRA 1998 s4(6)(b).
139 [2008] UKHL 57, [2008] HLR 45.
140 Housing and Regeneration Act 2008 s318.

- *Poplar Housing and Regeneration Community Association Ltd v Donoghue.*[141] The case concerned a possession claim against an assured shorthold tenant following service of a HA 1988 s21 notice. The Court of Appeal held that, notwithstanding its mandatory terms, the right to possession contained in section 21(4) did not conflict with the tenant's rights under Article 8. The section was clearly necessary in a democratic society in so far as there had to be a procedure for recovering possession of property at the end of a tenancy. The court said that it would defer to parliament as to whether the restricted power of the court in relation to possession orders sought under that section was legitimate and proportionate. The Court of Appeal has recently held itself bound by this decision, even after *Pinnock* and *Powell.*[142]

- *R (McLellan) v Bracknell Forest DC.*[143] This case concerned a possession claim against an introductory tenant (see chapter 5). It was held that the statutory procedure for recovery of possession against introductory tenants contained in the HA 1996 was compliant with Convention rights. The Supreme Court reached the same conclusion in *Powell.*

- *Reigate & Banstead DC v Benfield* was heard with *McLellan* (above). The Court of Appeal rejected a proposition that the HA 1980 s89 – which restricts the court's discretion about the time it can allow for possession to be given – was incompatible with the Convention rights. The Supreme Court reached the same conclusion in *Powell.*

- *Sheffield CC v Smart.*[144] The council claimed possession against non-secure tenants being accommodated under homelessness legislation following service of notices to quit. The Court of Appeal held that the balance of interests arising under Article 8(2) had in all its essentials been struck by the legislature when enacting the statutory scheme for the housing of homeless persons and their eviction. The legislation was not incompatible with the Convention rights. The Supreme Court reached the same conclusion in *Powell.*

- *Michalak v Wandsworth LBC.*[145] This was a possession claim brought against a relative of a deceased secure tenant who did not

141 [2001] EWCA Civ 595, (2001) 33 HLR 73.
142 *McDonald v McDonald* [2014] EWCA Civ 1049, [2014] HLR 43 upheld on appeal at [2016] UKSC 28, [2016] HLR 28.
143 [2001] EWCA 1510, (2001) 33 HLR 86.
144 [2002] EWCA Civ 4, [2002] HLR 34.
145 [2002] EWCA Civ 271, [2002] HLR 39.

qualify to succeed to the secure tenancy because his relationship with the deceased was not in the list of 'members of a family' contained in the HA 1985 s113. The Court of Appeal held that, although the provision was discriminatory in relation to a matter within the scope of Article 8, and so Article 14 was engaged, there was an objective justification for establishing a 'closed' list in section 113, that is, the need for certainty in determining which members of a secure tenant's family were eligible to succeed. The scheme was not incompatible.[146] However, this may not be the last word on challenges to discriminatory succession schemes.[147]

- *Southwark LBC v St Brice.*[148] The defendant applied to set aside a warrant which had been executed. The Court of Appeal held that the rules of procedure which allowed the issue of a warrant for possession and arrangements for execution following non-compliance with a suspended possession order did not infringe Articles 6, 8 or 14. Proportionality had been considered when the possession order was made.

- *R (Gilboy) v Liverpool CC.*[149] The Court of Appeal rejected a claim made in judicial review proceedings that the demoted tenancy scheme (see chapter 6) was incompatible with Convention rights because it made grant of a possession order mandatory if the claimant had served a notice and conducted a review, irrespective of the merits of the possession claim and in the absence of any independent scrutiny of those merits. The Supreme Court reached the same conclusion in *Pinnock*.

- *Waltham Forest LBC v Coombes.*[150] Following the death of his parents who were secure tenants, the defendant wished to remain in the family home. The council served notice to quit on the personal representatives and sought possession. The High Court dismissed a claim that the Protection from Eviction Act 1977 s3 was incompatible with Convention rights.

- *Sims v Dacorum BC.*[151] Mr and Mrs Sims were joint secure council tenants. Mrs Sims left the home and served a notice to quit which brought the tenancy to an end. The council then sought possession from Mr Sims. The Supreme Court rejected the contention

146 See also *Sharp v Brent LBC* [2003] EWCA Civ 779, [2003] HLR 65 and *R (Gangera) v Hounslow LBC* [2003] EWHC 794 (Admin), [2003] HLR 68.
147 See I Loveland, 'Housing: succession' May 2016 *Legal Action* 24.
148 [2001] EWCA Civ 1138, [2002] HLR 26.
149 [2008] EWCA Civ 751, [2009] HLR 11.
150 [2010] EWHC 666 (Admin), [2010] 2 All ER 940.
151 [2014] UKSC 63, [2015] HLR 7.

that the rule enabling one joint tenant unilaterally to determine a joint period tenancy by valid notice was incompatible with Article 8 or Article 1 of Protocol 1.

- *Secretary of State for Transport v Blake*[152] and *Nicholas v Secretary of State for Defence*.[153] These cases both concerned the statutory provisions exempting tenants of the Crown from security of tenure. The Court of Appeal declined to make declarations of incompatibility.

26.158 Despite these unsuccessful challenges, there are so many statutory provisions relating to possession proceedings that there may yet be a declaration of incompatibility to be made in respect of one of them. Indeed, in *Pinnock*, Lord Neuberger stated that 'the conclusion that the court must have the ability to assess the Article 8 proportionality of making a possession order in respect of a person's home may require certain statutory and procedural provisions to be revisited', eg Housing Act 1980 s89 and some of the provisions of CPR 55, which appear to mandate a summary procedure in some types of possession claim'.[154]

Potential outcomes

26.159 If the court is satisfied, on considering a human rights defence, that a possession order (or particular form of order) would be incompatible with Convention rights it must decline to make that order, or that form of order. Likewise, if authorising execution of a warrant would have that effect, authority must be withheld by the court.

26.160 As Lord Neuberger stated in *Pinnock* 'if domestic law justifies an outright order for possession, the effect of Article 8 may, albeit in exceptional cases, justify (in ascending order of effect) granting an extended period for possession, suspending the order for possession on the happening of an event, or even refusing an order altogether'.[155]

26.161 The flexibility of a court dealing with a human rights defence is limited by HA 1980 s89 which, in many cases, limits the period for which a possession order can be postponed to 14 days (unless there is exceptional hardship, in which case up to 42 days can be allowed).

152 [2013] EWHC 2945 (Ch).
153 [2015] EWCA Civ 53, [2015] HLR 25.
154 [2010] UKSC 45, [2011] HLR 7 at [63].
155 [2011] UKSC 8, [2011] HLR 23 at [62].

In *Pinnock*, Lord Neuberger said that this provision 'may present difficulties in relation to cases where Article 8 claims are raised'.[156]

26.162   However, the Supreme Court later considered HA 1980 s89 in *Powell, Hall and Frisby*. Notwithstanding what was said in *Pinnock*, it stated that no evidence had been put before it to show that, in practice, the maximum period of six weeks was insufficient to meet the needs of cases of exceptional hardship.[157]

26.163   The Supreme Court went on to hold that section 89 does not 'take away from the court its ordinary powers of case management. It would be perfectly proper for it, for example, to defer making the order for possession pending an appeal or to enable proceedings to be brought in the administrative court which might result in a finding that it was not lawful for a possession order to be made.'[158]

26.164   However, if a trial of the human rights defence has taken place, it seems that the court has limited options – either finding that it is disproportionate to make a possession order at all and dismissing the claim or finding that the claimant is entitled to possession and that it is proportionate to make a possession order to take effect in a maximum of six weeks (assuming exceptional hardship). Lord Neuberger has recently identified the four available options for the court hearing the possession claim as:

(a) make an immediate order for possession;
(b) make an order for possession on a date within 14 days;
(c) in cases of exceptional hardship make an order for possession on a date within six weeks; or
(d) decline to make an order for possession at all.

But he added that:

The cases in which it would be justifiable to refuse, as opposed to postpone, a possession order must be very few and far between, even when taken as a proportion of those rare cases where proportionality can be successfully invoked. They could only be cases in which the landlord's interest in regaining possession was heavily outweighed by the gravity of the interference in the occupier's right to respect for her home.[159]

26.165   The upholding of a human rights defence simply reflects the court's assessment of the particular facts as they stand at the date of trial or hearing. The effect of dismissal of the claim, or the refusal of

---

156 [2010] UKSC 45, [2011] HLR 7 at [63].
157 [2011] UKSC 8, [2011] HLR 23 at [62].
158 [2011] UKSC 8, [2011] HLR 23 at [63].
159 *McDonald v McDonald* [2016] UKSC 28, [2016] HLR 28 at [73].

authority to execute a possession order, will not create any new contractual relationship between the claimant and defendant or restore an earlier one. For example, if a tenancy has been ended by notice to quit, the dismissal of a claim for possession will not restore it. The defendant will be liable to pay damages for use and occupation during any period while they remain in possession as a trespasser.

26.166   If – following the dismissal of a possession claim – the factual matrix changes, the claimant will be free to bring another claim or application.

Human rights at the warrant stage

26.167 Once a possession order has been granted, it may be executed by warrant obtained under an essentially administrative procedure (as described in chapter 31). Nothing in the Convention rights requires a court to arrange a further hearing before the issue or execution of a warrant.[160]

26.168   By this stage, unless the possession order is set aside and the claim is remitted for re-hearing, it will be too late for a human rights *defence* to the possession claim to be invoked.

26.169   But, as explained above, Article 8 contains a procedural dimension which applies to the proceedings as a whole (see para 26.61). That means that it must be possible for the occupier to contend, at very least, that some development that has arisen since the possession order was made would now render an eviction incompatible with the right to respect for a home. In most cases, if that point were raised in the county court, the fetter on delaying eviction imposed by HA 1980 s89 would deprive the court of an ability to respond.

26.170   Instead, if the claimant *is a public authority* (such as a social landlord) the occupier will need to apply in the Administrative Court for a judicial review of the decision to apply for the warrant and establish either that: (1) the decision to apply for a warrant was unlawful; or (2) it would not be 'proportionate' for the eviction to go ahead.[161] Only exceptionally would the Administrative Court hearing such a claim allow the claimant to take points that could and should have been advanced in an earlier defence to the possession claim itself.

---

160 *Southwark LBC v St Brice* [2001] EWCA Civ 1138, [2002] HLR 26.
161 *R (JL) v Secretary of State for Defence* [2013] EWCA Civ 449, [2013] HLR 27 and see *JL v The United Kingdom* Application no 66387/10, 30 September 2014.

26.171   The Court of Appeal has recently said this about the timing of an Article 8 defence in a claim for possession of residential property:[162]

> 89. ... As was made clear in the judgment of Briggs LJ in R *(JL) v Secretary of State for Defence* [2013] EWCA Civ 449, [2013] PTSR 1014, with which the other members of the Court of Appeal agreed, save in exceptional circumstances an Article 8 defence ought to be raised during the possession proceedings and in particular at the trial. *To raise an Article 8 argument at the enforcement stage, when it could and should have been raised earlier, will almost always be an abuse of process.* In the present case, there were exceptional circumstances, namely that (1) an Article 8 argument was in fact advanced by the appellants in their closing submissions at the trial but Judge May either declined to hear it or peremptorily dismissed it but in either case she gave no reasons for doing so in her formal judgment, and (2) Arden LJ, on the application for permission to appeal, took the view that rather than granting permission to appeal it would be better for the appellants, then acting in person, to pursue their Article 8 point at the enforcement stage. ... [Emphasis added]

The inclusion of 'almost always' in that formulation may enable a defendant to a claim to make good an application to have his or her Convention rights examined by a court before a properly obtained possession order is executed. It remains to be seen how the courts will accommodate such applications.

---

162 *Lawal v Circle 33 Housing Trust* [2014] EWCA Civ 1514, [2015] HLR 9 at [89].

Disability discrimination defences

Possession proceedings and the Equality Act 2010

27.1   Where a tenant or occupier or a member of their household has a disability, and there is a link between the disability and the landlord's decision to seek possession of the premises, the possibility of invoking the Equality Act (EA) 2010 by way of defence to possession proceedings should be considered. The occupier in these circumstances may be able to argue that his or her eviction would be unlawful under the Act. The cornerstone of this argument lies in EA 2010 s35(1), which makes it unlawful for a person managing premises to discriminate against a person occupying those premises on the basis of a 'protected characteristic',[1] by evicting them or taking steps for the purpose of securing their eviction, or by subjecting them to any other detriment.[2] This chapter deals specifically with those cases in which the protected chacteristic is disability because of the special protection given to disabled persons by the legisation and its particular relevance to housing possession cases.

27.2   EA 2010 repealed the Disability Discrimination Act (DDA) 1995. The 1995 Act[3] provided a basis for a defence to possession proceedings where the defendant occupier could show that, for a reason relating to disability, the claimant landlord was treating him or her less favourably than the landlord would treat others to whom that reason would not apply.[4] Case-law under the 1995 Act may still be relevant in some instances, although care must be taken in relying on it in view of the significant differences between the provisions of the respective Acts.

27.3   Under EA 2010, 'disability' is one of the 'protected characteristics', which also comprise: age, gender reassignment, marriage and civil partnership, pregnancy and maternity, race, religion or belief, sex, and sexual orientation.[5] Where a landlord discriminates (directly or indirectly) against an occupier on the basis of a protected characteristic (apart from age, or marriage or civil partnership)[6] by seeking

---

1   See para 27.3.
2   EA 2010 s35(1)(b) and (c). See para 27.22.
3   DDA 1995 s24(1).
4   Under the DDA 1995, the landlord would nevertheless be able to resist such a defence if he or she could justify treating the disabled person less favourably, in circumstances where the landlord considered that the action was necessary in order not to endanger the health or safety of any person and it was reasonable to hold that opinion: DDA 1995 s24(3).
5   EA 2010 s4.
6   See para 27.20.

to evict that person or by subjecting him or her to a detriment on account of that characteristic, the occupier may be able to establish a defence or seek a remedy under the 2010 Act. Among the protected characteristics, special provision is made for disabled persons. In the leading case of *Akerman-Livingstone v Aster Communities Limited*,[7] Lady Hale said:

> ... this case is concerned with the protected characteristic of disability, which can raise different equality issues from those raised by a claim of, say, sex or race discrimination. Whereas treating a man equally with a woman usually means treating him in the same way as a woman is treated, treating a disabled person equally with a non-disabled person may mean treating him differently from a non-disabled person. This is in order to ensure that he can play a full part in society despite his disabilities.[8]

27.4   In the same case, the nature of that special provision was described in the following terms:

> The scheme of the Equality Act 2010 is to define what is meant by discrimination and then to define the circumstances in which such discrimination is unlawful. The Act prohibits both direct and indirect discrimination against disabled persons in the same way that it prohibits discrimination against persons with the other characteristics protected by the Act. But it also contains two types of discrimination which are specific to persons with a disability. It is discrimination to fail to comply with the specific duties to make the reasonable adjustments which are required by the Act in particular contexts (section 21(2)) There is also a more general concept of 'disability discrimination' defined by section 15 ...[9]

27.5   EA 2010 s6 defines 'disability' in the same terms as it was defined in DDA 1995:

> (1) A person (P) has a disability if –
>
> > (a) P has a physical or mental impairment, and
> >
> > (b) the impairment has a substantial and long-term adverse effect on P's ability to carry out normal day-to-day activities ...

27.6   A 'substantial' effect is one which is 'more than minor or trivial'.[10] The definition of disability is amplified by EA 2010 Sch 1, by the

---

7 [2015] UKSC 15, [2015] HLR 20.

8 *Akerman-Livingstone* para [2].

9 *Akerman-Livingstone* para [15]. In respect of section 21(2) (duty to make reasonable adjustments), see para 27.43; and in respect of disability discrimination under section 15, see para 27.11.

10 EA 2010 s212(1).

Equality Act 2010 (Disability) Regulations 2010,[11] and by Guidance issued by the Office for Disability Issues.[12] The Act provides that the effect of an impairment is 'long-term' if: (a) it has lasted for at least 12 months; or (b) it is likely to last for at least 12 months; or (c) it is likely to last for the rest of the life of the person affected.[13] Even where an impairment ceases to have a substantial adverse effect on a person's ability to carry out normal day-to-day activities, it is to be treated as continuing to have that effect if that effect is likely to recur. An impairment is to be treated as having a substantial adverse effect even though measures are being taken to treat or correct it, including medical treatment and the provision of aids.[14]

27.7   Guidance states that the term 'physical or mental impairment' should be given its ordinary and natural meaning. However, it is clear that impairment may result from an illness or it may consist of an illness:

> The Act contemplates (certainly in relation to mental impairment) that an impairment can be something that results from an illness as opposed to itself being the illness ... It can thus be cause or effect. No rigid distinction seems to be insisted on and the blurring which occurs in ordinary usage would seem to be something the Act is prepared to tolerate.[15]

Certain medical conditions, namely cancer, HIV infection[16] and multiple sclerosis are each recognised as a disability, so that there is no need to prove the effect of the impairment.[17] A person is deemed to have a disability, and hence to be a disabled person for the purposes of the Act, where that person is certified as blind, severely sight impaired, sight impaired or partially sighted by a consultant ophthalmologist.[18]

27.8   Addiction to alcohol, nicotine or any other substance is to be treated as not amounting to an impairment for the purposes of the

---

11 SI No 2128.
12 'Equality Act 2010 Guidance: Guidance on matters to be taken into account in determining questions relating to the definition of disability', Office for Disability Issues, May 2011.
13 EA 2010 Sch 1 para 2.
14 Except for aids such as spectacles or contact lenses used to correct sight impairment.
15 *College of Ripon and York St John v Hobbs* [2001] UKEAT 585/00/1411, [2002] IRLR 185 para [32].
16 Defined as infection by a virus capable of causing the Acquired Immune Deficiency Syndrome.
17 EA 2010 Sch 1 para 6.
18 Equality Act 2010 (Disability) Regulations 2010 SI No 2128 reg 7.

Act unless the addiction was originally the result of administration of medically prescribed drugs or other medical treatment.[19] Other conditions which are not to be treated as an impairment are a tendency to set fires; a tendency to steal; a tendency to physical or sexual abuse of other persons; exhibitionism; and voyeurism.[20]

27.9   EA 2010 ss13–27 set out the prohibited conduct that constitutes unlawful discrimination, encompassing the duty to make reasonable adjustments. Section 13 prohibits direct discrimination. It provides:

> (1) A person (A) discriminates against another (B) if, because of a protected characteristic, A treats B less favourably than A treats or would treat others.
>
> ...
>
> (3) If the protected characteristic is disability, and B is not a disabled person, A does not discriminate against B only because A treats or would treat disabled persons more favourably than A treats B.

Where the landlord can be shown to have directly discriminated against a tenant on grounds of his or her disability, this would afford a defence to a possession claim. The reference to less favourable treatment 'because of a protected characteristic' is clearly wide enough to cover a person who is treated less favourably not because he or she has a protected characteristic, but because he or she is associated with someone who has such a characteristic, eg the parent of a disabled child.

27.10   EA 2010 s19(1) prohibits indirect discrimination, defined in the following terms:

> (1) A person (A) discriminates against another (B) if A applies to B a provision, criterion or practice which is discriminatory in relation to a relevant protected characteristic of B's.
>
> (2) For the purposes of subsection (1), a provision, criterion or practice is discriminatory in relation to a relevant protected characteristic of B's if –
>
> (a) A applies, or would apply, it to persons with whom B does not share the characteristic,
>
> (b) it puts, or would put, persons with whom B shares the characteristic at a particular disadvantage when compared with persons with whom B does not share it,
>
> (c) it puts, or would put, B at that disadvantage, and
>
> (d) A cannot show it to be a proportionate means of achieving a legitimate aim.
>
> ...

---

19 Equality Act 2010 (Disability) Regulations 2010 reg 3.
20 Equality Act 2010 (Disability) Regulations 2010 reg 4.

By way of example, if a landlord required all tenants in rent arrears to complete a statement showing full details of their financial circumstances before it would entertain an offer of payment, this practice would be likely to discriminate against a tenant who was unable to provide such a statement without assistance because of a learning disability.

27.11   In addition to the instances of direct and indirect discrimination defined in sections 13 and 19 respectively, EA 2010 s15 creates a wider concept of discrimination arising from disability:[21]

> (1) A person (A) discriminates against a disabled person (B) if –
>   (a) A treats B unfavourably because of something arising in consequence of B's disability, and
>   (b) A cannot show that the treatment is a proportionate means of achieving a legitimate aim.
> (2) Subsection (1) does not apply if A shows that A did not know, and could not reasonably have been expected to know, that B had the disability.

27.12   The purpose of section 15 is to ensure that treatment which is unfavourable because of 'something arising in consequence of' a person's disability may amount to discrimination even where the reason for the treatment is not the disability itself. The section was enacted in order to address certain issues identified in a line of cases under DDA 1995, which culminated in the House of Lords decision in *Lewisham LBC v Malcolm*.[22] The way in which the section operates was explained by the Supreme Court in *Akerman-Livingstone v Aster Communities Limited*.[23] Where a defence under section 15 is raised, then assuming that the defendant is in fact disabled within the meaning of the Act, the Court held that there are two key questions:

> (a) whether the eviction is 'because of something arising in consequence of B's disability'; this was a reformulation from that in the Disability Discrimination Act 1995, intended to make it clear that where something arising in consequence of the disability was the reason for the unfavourable treatment, the landlord (or other provider) would have to justify that treatment; there was no need for a comparison with how it would treat any other person; it might have to behave differently towards a disabled tenant from the way in which it would behave towards a non-disabled tenant; and if so
> (b) whether the landlord can show that the unfavourable treatment is a proportionate means of achieving a legitimate aim.[24]

---

21   Section 15 has no counterpart in the DDA 1995.
22   [2008] UKHL 43, [2008] HLR 41.
23   [2015] UKSC 15, [2015] HLR 20.
24   Per Lady Hale, para [18].

27.13   The test of 'unfavourable treatment' under section 15 is different from that of 'less favourable treatment' in section 13 and from that of placing another person at a 'particular disadvantage' in section 19, and does not require a comparison with the way in which another person who is not disabled would have been treated. Nor does it require a direct causal link between the unfavourable treatment and the disability itself, only that there is a link between the treatment and 'something arising in consequence of' the disability. In possession proceedings based on a statutory ground for possession, the 'something arising' will be the facts or allegations that underlie the ground, such as rent arrears, anti-social behaviour or a breach of tenancy conditions. In other circumstances, such as introductory tenancies, the 'something arising' may be found in the reasons given in the notice of intended proceedings. Where no reason is required to be given, as in Housing Act (HA) 1988 s21 notices in respect of assured shorthold tenancies, it is necessary to show that the landlord's actual reason for seeking possession is associated with the disability of the tenant or with that of a household member. The 'something arising' need not be the sole cause of the decision to evict. Discrimination may be made out if that reason is 'a cause, the activating cause, a substantial and effective cause, a substantial reason, an important factor'.[25]

27.14   Any conduct or neglect or omission that arises as a result, effect or outcome of a person's disability will constitute 'something arising in consequence of' the disability. In the context of possession claims, this may include rent arrears associated with depression or learning disability leading to an inability to manage finances or engage with the benefits system.[26] Nuisance behaviour associated with a mental illness may also be 'something arising' from a disability.

27.15   A landlord who serves a notice to quit (or other notice requiring possession) or brings possession proceedings against a disabled tenant is treating that person 'unfavourably'. A tenant may therefore have a defence to the subsequent possession proceedings (whatever the type of tenancy) or may be able to restrain the landlord from behaving unfavourably towards him or her where the reason for the landlord's action is 'something arising in consequence of [the tenant's] disability'; and the landlord cannot show that his or her actions are a proportionate means of achieving a legitimate aim. In many cases, an act of discrimination may be both section 15 discrimination

---

25 Per Lord Nicholls in *Nagarajan v London Regional Transport* [1999] UKHL 36, [2000] 1 AC 501.

26 See *Wright v Croydon LBC* [2007] EWHC 3465 (QB), [2007] All ER (D) 95.

arising from disability and indirect discrimination under section 19 and the defence should be pleaded accordingly.

27.16   Section 15 does not apply, however, unless the landlord knows, or can reasonably be expected to know, that the occupier (or the relevant member of the household) is a disabled person. A social landlord may well have knowledge of the existence of a disability as this may be recorded on the housing file, even if the housing officer currently dealing with the tenancy is not aware of it. Moreover, social landlords are likely to be public authorities for the purposes of the public sector equality duty under EA 2010 s149 (see para 27.54) and are thereby required to have due regard to the need to eliminate discrimination and advance equality of opportunity. The need to have 'due regard' carries an enhanced duty of enquiry as to whether a disability exists and, if so, whether it is relevant to the landlord's decision, especially if some feature of the evidence raises a real possibility that the person concerned is disabled in a sense relevant to the question being decided.[27] In some cases the landlord may not know of the existence of the disability, or of its relevance to the breach of tenancy, when proceedings are issued, but becomes aware of the full circumstances in the course of the proceedings. To continue with the proceedings or to enforce a possession order in these circumstances would amount to 'taking steps for the purpose of securing [the tenant's] eviction'[28] with the necessary knowledge and would become unlawful from that point, unless the landlord can justify the discriminatory action.

27.17   Case-law has stressed the importance of a party who seeks to rely on a disability discrimination defence making clear the nature of the impairment on which the defence is advanced, and of both parties obtaining expert medical evidence.[29] Medical evidence will be required to deal with the nature and degree of the impairment, and whether the impairment has a substantial and long-term adverse effect on the ability of the individual to carry out normal day-to-day activities, together with the specific relevance of the disability to the landlord's reasons for wanting possession. It is essential that the defence should: set out in detail the nature of the impairment; identify the unfavourable treatment in question (usually the service of a notice to quit or other notice, followed by issuing a possession claim); and explain how the landlord's decision to bring the proceedings is

27 *Pieretti v Enfield LBC* [2010] EWCA Civ 1104, [2011] HLR 3.
28 See EA 2010 s35(1)(b) and para 27.22.
29 *Swan Housing Association Ltd v Gill* [2013] EWCA Civ 1566, [2014] HLR 18. And see Mummery LJ in *McNicol v Balfour Beatty Rail Maintenance Ltd* [2002] EWCA Civ 1074, [2002] ICR 1498.

a consequence of 'something arising' from the occupier's disability. The defendant's witness statement, together with any other witness statements made in support, must contain the evidence necessary to substantiate all aspects of the defence. Where a tenant relies upon the disability of another member of the household in order to raise a defence under section 15, it appears that the disabled person must be made a party to the claim.[30]

27.18　　Where the reason for the possession claim is caused by an impairment which is excluded under the Equality Act 2010 (Disability) Regulations 2010 (such as substance addiction or a tendency to physical abuse), even though the impairment is itself caused by a disability, the occupier will not be 'disabled' for the purposes of the Act.[31] In other situations, an occupier may be disabled as a result of depression or other pre-existing mental health condition, but he or she may also be prone to substance abuse or a tendency to react violently. Where the reason for the possession action is the nuisance behaviour of the occupier, it will often be difficult to know whether the ultimate cause is the disability or the excluded condition. Expert medical opinion will be necessary to address the issue. The courts have taken the approach that 'if the legitimate impairment was a reason and thus an effective cause of the less favourable treatment, then prima facie discrimination is made out notwithstanding that the excluded condition also forms part of the ... reason for that treatment'.[32] It follows that the admissible impairment need not be the sole cause of the possession proceedings or other unfavourable treatment.

27.19　　A claim or counterclaim on the basis of discrimination under the Act may include a claim for damages, which may extend to compensation for injured feelings.[33] The county court must not make an award of damages unless it first considers whether to make any other disposal.[34]

30　*Hainsworth v Ministry of Defence* [2014] EWCA Civ 763, [2014] IRLR 728.
31　*X v Governors of a School* [2015] UKUT 0007 (AAC).
32　*P v Governors of a Primary School* [2013] UKUT 154 (AAC) at para 52, quoting Lloyd Jones J in *Governors of X Endowed Primary School v Special Educational Needs and Disability Tribunal and others* [2009] EWHC 1842 (Admin), [2009] IRLR 1007.
33　EA 2010 s119(4).
34　EA 2010 s119(6).

Discrimination in relation to premises

27.20   EA 2010 Part 4 (Premises) applies the above instances of unlawful discrimination (direct and indirect discrimination, and discrimination arising from disability) to lettings and other disposals of property, and to the management of premises. Part 4 applies to controllers and managers of premises, which include private and social landlords and letting agents. These provisions apply to discrimination on the basis of any of the protected characteristics *other than* age, and marriage and civil partnership.

27.21   EA 2010 s33 deals with the 'disposal' of premises. A person who has the right to dispose of premises (which includes a right to let or sub-let) must not – whether by the terms on which he offers to dispose of the premises, by declining to dispose of the premises, or in his treatment of a person seeking the premises – unlawfully discriminate against any person on the basis of any relevant protected characteristic. Further protection is provided against harassment and victimisation by controllers and managers of premises in relation to the disposal and occupation of those premises.[35]

Management of premises

27.22   EA 2010 s35 prohibits any form of discrimination in the management of premises on the basis of any relevant protected characteristic. Section 35 provides:

> **Management**
> (1) A person (A) who manages premises must not discriminate against a person (B) who occupies the premises –
>   (a) in the way in which A allows B, or by not allowing B, to make use of a benefit or facility;
>   (b) by evicting B (or taking steps for the purpose of securing B's eviction);
>   (c) by subjecting B to any other detriment.
> (2) A person who manages premises must not, in relation to their management, harass –
>   (a) a person who occupies them;
>   (b) a person who applies for them.
> (3) A person (A) who manages premises must not victimise a person (B) who occupies the premises –
>   (a) in the way in which A allows B, or by not allowing B, to make use of a benefit or facility;

---

35   EA 2010 s33(3) and (4).

(b) by evicting B (or taking steps for the purpose of securing B's eviction);

(c) by subjecting B to any other detriment.

27.23 Section 35(1) therefore identifies the kinds of activity which may amount to prohibited discrimination in the context of the management of premises. The tests of discrimination to be applied to the various management activities described in section 35 are those found in sections 13, 15 and 19 (see paras 27.9–27.11 above).

Defences to possession proceedings

27.24 In appropriate cases, EA 2010 may provide a defence to a claim for possession. In particular, where the reason for the possession proceedings derives from, or is associated with, the tenant's disability, section 15 provides the basis for a defence. It is not necessary to show less favourable treatment in order to make good a section 15 defence. A defence may be established where it can be shown that the landlord is seeking to evict a tenant or occupier 'because of something arising in consequence of [the tenant's] disability', and the landlord is unable to satisfy the court that eviction is a proportionate means of achieving a legitimate aim. Where a possession claim is brought against a Rent Act protected tenant or a secure tenant under HA 1985 or an assured tenant under HA 1988, and the ground for possession relied on is a discretionary ground, Equality Act arguments may be subsumed under submissions in relation to reasonableness, although an Equality Act defence should still be pleaded in the alternative. A specific Equality Act defence will be required where the court would otherwise have no discretion in the making of an order (see further paras 27.39–27.40).

27.25 EA 2010 s136 deals with the burden of proof in equality and discrimination cases. It provides:

(1) This section applies to any proceedings relating to a contravention of this Act.

(2) If there are facts from which the court could decide, in the absence of any other explanation, that a person (A) contravened the provision concerned, the court must hold that the contravention occurred.

(3) But subsection (2) does not apply if A shows that A did not contravene the provision.

If, therefore, there are facts from which the court could conclude that an eviction was discriminatory under section 15 'because of something arising in consequence of a person's disability', it would be for the landlord to prove that it was not. If the landlord could not show that the eviction was not discriminatory, the landlord would then have the burden of showing that eviction was nevertheless a proportionate means of achieving a legitimate aim (see, further, para 27.34 below).

27.26   In *Akerman-Livingstone v Aster Communities Limited*,[36] the occupier suffered from complex post-traumatic stress disorder, and it was accepted that his chronic mental health condition amounted to a disability. Having become homeless, he applied to Mendip District Council for assistance. The Council accepted that it owed him a duty[37] to secure that accommodation was available to him. It therefore arranged for the landlord, a private registered provider of social housing, to provide him with temporary accommodation. For reasons associated with his disability, the occupier declined a number of offers of alternative accommodation. The Council considered its final offer of accommodation to be suitable. Following the occupier's refusal to accept the property offered, the Council notified him that it considered that its duty was now discharged. Accordingly, the landlord served notice to quit and issued a claim for possession. The occupier sought to defend the proceedings on Equality Act grounds, in addition to human rights and public law grounds (see chapters 25 and 26 respectively for these grounds).

27.27   In relation to the discrimination defence, it was argued on behalf of the landlord that, in relation to a claim for possession of residential premises, a court should take the same approach to a defence raising an argument of unlawful discrimination under EA 2010 s35(1)(b) as it would to a defence based on human rights. The latter approach derives from the Supreme Court decisions in the cases of *Manchester City Council v Pinnock*[38] and *Hounslow London Borough Council v Powell*[39] (see paras 26.30–26.106). As Lord Hope explained in *Powell*, '[T]he court will only have to consider whether the making of a possession order is proportionate if the issue has been raised by the occupier and it has crossed the high threshold of being seriously arguable'. The threshold for raising an arguable case on proportionality was a high one which would succeed in only a small proportion of cases.[40]

---

36 [2015] UKSC 15, [2015] HLR 20.
37 Under HA 1996 s193(2) (the 'full' housing duty under Part VII of the 1996 Act (homelessness)).
38 [2010] UKSC 45, [2011] HLR 7.
39 [2011] UKSC 8, [2011] HLR 23.
40 *Powell* at paras [33] and [35].

27.28   In *Akerman-Livingstone*, the landlord's argument was successful in the county court, the High Court and the Court of Appeal.⁴¹ It was, however, rejected in the Supreme Court. Lord Wilson set out the correct approach in discrimination cases:

a) The normal procedure of the court in addressing a defence under section 35(1)(b) of the 2010 Act to an action for possession should not be equated with its normal procedure in addressing a defence to such an action under Article 8 of the Convention.

b) Where a defence is raised under section 35(1)(b) to an action for possession, there should be no presumption that the action is fit for summary disposal. On the contrary rule 55.8(2) of the CPR calls for a careful evaluation at that initial stage whether the claim is genuinely disputed on grounds which appear to be substantial.

c) Where such a defence is raised, the court should adopt a four-stage structured approach to the claimant's attempt to show, pursuant to section 15(1)(b) of the 2010 Act, that the steps which it is taking for the purpose of securing the defendant's eviction are a proportionate means of achieving a legitimate aim.⁴²

27.29   Lord Neuberger explained that the protection afforded by EA 2010 s35(1)(b) was an additional, more specific and stronger right afforded to disabled occupiers over and above the Article 8 right:

More specifically, although both types of defence involve the court considering the proportionality of making an order for possession, the protection afforded by section 35(1)(b) is plainly stronger than the protection afforded by Article 8. Section 35(1)(b) provides a particular degree of protection to a limited class of occupiers of property, who are considered by Parliament to deserve special protection. The protection concerned is founded on a desire to avoid a specific wrong in a number of fields, not just in relation to occupation of property, namely discrimination against disabled persons. Further, once the possibility of discrimination is made out, the burden of proof is firmly on the landlord to show that there was no discrimination contrary to section 15(1)(a) , or that an order for possession is proportionate under section 15(1)(b), of the 2010 Act – see section 136 of that Act. Additionally, the proportionality exercise under section 15(1)(b) involves focussing on a very specific issue, namely the justification for discrimination.⁴³

27.30   The Supreme Court observed that there were a number of differences between Article 8 and EA 2010 which indicated that a different approach to discrimination cases was necessary. The most obvious

41 [2014] EWCA Civ 1081, [2014] HLR 44.

42 *Akerman-Livingstone* para [64]. As to the four-stage structured approach mentioned by Lord Wilson, see further para 27.32.

43 *Akerman-Livingstone* para 55.

difference was that EA 2010 s35 applied to both private and social landlords, whereas only public authorities were obliged by section 6(1) of the Human Rights Act 1998 to act compatibly with Convention rights. But the substantive rights were also different. All occupiers have a right to respect for their home under Article 8, but in EA 2010 Parliament had expressly provided for an *extra* right to equal treatment in terms of protection against direct or indirect discrimination in relation to eviction. Parliament had further expressly provided, in sections 15 and 35, for disabled people to have rights in respect of the accommodation which they occupy which are different from, and extra to, the rights of non-disabled people. Landlords may be required to accommodate, or to continue to accommodate, a disabled person when they would not be required to accommodate, or continue to accommodate, a non-disabled person.[44]

27.31   On the other hand, this is not an absolute obligation. A landlord is entitled to serve notice, bring a possession claim or take other steps to evict a disabled tenant if it can be shown that this is a proportionate means of achieving a legitimate aim. While section 15 differs in its terms from Article 8 (where the public authority has to show that its interference is 'necessary in a democratic society'), the concept of proportionality has come to be interpreted in the same way.[45]

27.32   In *Akerman-Livingstone*, the Supreme Court accepted that in cases of this kind it was necessary for courts to adopt the structured approach to the assessment of proportionality developed through the case-law of the past two decades.[46] This involves four incremental stages represented by the following questions:

1) What are the claimant's aims or objectives in taking steps for the purpose of securing the defendant's eviction?
2) Is there a rational connection between the claimant's objectives and the defendant's eviction?
3) Is the eviction of the defendant no more than is necessary to accomplish those objectives?[47]

---

44 *Akerman-Livingstone* para [25], per Lady Hale.
45 See *Akerman-Livingstone* para [27], per Lady Hale.
46 See *Bank Mellat v Her Majesty's Treasury (No 2)* [2013] UKSC 39, [2014] 1 AC 700; *R (Elias) v Secretary of State for Defence* [2006] EWCA Civ 1293, [2006] 1 WLR 3213 and *De Freitas v Permanent Secretary of Ministry of Agriculture, Fisheries, Lands and Housing* [1998] UKPC 30, [1999] 1 AC 69.
47 The first three elements were explained by Mummery LJ in *R (Elias) v Secretary of State for Defence* [2006] EWCA Civ 1293, [2006] 1 WLR 3213 at para [165]: 'First, is the objective sufficiently important to justify limiting a fundamental

4) Is the eviction proportionate in the wider sense, or, in other words, does the eviction strike a fair balance between the claimant's need to accomplish its objectives and the disadvantages thereby caused to the defendant as a disabled person?[48]

27.33 In relation to the first of the structured questions, one aim of a possession action would be the vindication of the claimant's ownership rights, while a second aim of a possession claim brought by a housing association would usually be to enable it to comply with its housing management functions and to assist the local housing authority with its duties to homeless persons and in the operation of its allocation scheme. Accordingly, in carrying out the proportionality assessment for EA 2010 purposes, where possession actions are brought by social landlords against tenants who otherwise have no right to remain in the property, it can generally be taken for granted without the need for specific proof, that the social landlord is acting in pursuance of those twin aims;[49] and further, that those aims are entitled to weigh heavily in a proportionality exercise. Likewise, the second question, as to the existence of a rational connection between those aims and the defendant's eviction, will almost invariably be answered in the affirmative. To that extent, the proportionality exercise is similar to that in Article 8 cases. However, that is not by itself enough to counter a discrimination defence. Drawing a comparison with Article 8 cases, Lady Hale in *Akerman-Livingstone* said, 'It simply does not follow that, because those twin aims will almost always trump any right to respect which is due to the occupier's home, they will also trump the occupier's equality rights'.[50]

right? Secondly, is the measure rationally connected to the objective? Thirdly, are the means chosen no more than is necessary to accomplish the objective?'.

48 Whereas in *Pinnock* and *Powell*, the Supreme Court rejected the structured approach to proportionality in considering Article 8 defences. See *Hounslow LBC v Powell*, per Lord Hope at para [41].

49 See *Manchester City Council v Pinnock* [2010] UKSC 45, [2011] HLR 7 at paras [52]–[53], per Lord Neuberger. See also Lord Hope in *Hounslow London Borough Council v Powell* [2011] UKSC 8, [2011] HLR 23 at para [35]: 'Local authorities hold their housing stock, as do other social landlords, for the benefit of the whole community ... This is a factor to which great weight must always be given, and in the great majority of cases the court can and should proceed on the basis that the landlord has sound management reasons for seeking a possession order'.

50 *Akerman-Livingstone*, para [30]. See also para [29]: 'In the great majority of [Article 8] cases, the court is simply not equipped to judge the weight of an individual's right to respect for her home against the weight of the interests of the whole community for whom the authority has to manage its limited housing resources'.

27.34   The third and fourth limbs of the 'structured approach' (see para 27.32) focus on, respectively, whether eviction is no more than is necessary to achieve the legitimate aim, or whether there is some less intrusive means of doing so; and whether eviction is proportionate, bearing in mind the nature of the defendant's disability and his or her personal circumstances.[51] Referring to the fourth limb, Lady Hale said in *Akerman-Livingstone*: 'This is the importance, at the end of the exercise, of the overall balance between the ends and the means: there are some situations in which the ends, however meritorious, cannot justify the only means which is capable of achieving them.'[52] Further guidance in applying the elements of proportionality was given by the Supreme Court in the following terms:

> No landlord is allowed to evict a disabled tenant because of something arising in consequence of the disability, unless he can show eviction to be a proportionate means of achieving a legitimate aim. He is thus obliged to be more considerate towards a disabled tenant than he is towards a non-disabled one. The structured approach to proportionality asks whether there is any lesser measure which might achieve the landlord's aims. It also requires a balance to be struck between the seriousness of the impact upon the tenant and the importance of the landlord's aims. People with disabilities are 'entitled to have due allowance made for the consequences of their disability' (*Malcolm*, para 61). It certainly cannot be taken for granted that the first of the twin aims will almost invariably trump that right. Even where social housing is involved, the general considerations involved in the second of the twin aims may on occasions have to give way to the equality rights of the occupier and in particular to the equality rights of a particular disabled person. The impact of being required to move from this particular place upon this particular disabled person may be such that it is not outweighed by the benefits to the local authority or social landlord of being able to regain possession.[53]

27.35   In applying the third and fourth tests in the structured exercise, it is essential to bear in mind the burden of proof in Equality Act cases (see para 27.25). In any proceedings relating to a contravention of EA 2010, if there are facts from which the court could decide, in the absence of any other explanation, that a person contravened the provision concerned, the court must hold that the contravention occurred, unless the person shows that he or she did not contravene the provision. The landlord is therefore required to show not merely that he

---

51 For an explanation of the four tests and their application to the facts of the *Akerman-Livingstone* case, see Lord Wilson's speech at paras [68]–[75].
52 See *Akerman-Livingstone* para [28].
53 Per Lady Hale at para [31].

or she had considered any alternatives to eviction that would have met the legitimate objective, but that, as a matter of evidence and judgment, no such alternative was reasonably possible. The issue of whether any other measure would have sufficed and the question of proportionality in the round are matters for the court to decide.[54] In respect of the burden of proof, the Supreme Court in *Akerman-Livingstone* gave further guidance:

> Once facts are established that could give rise to a discrimination claim, the burden shifts to the landlord to prove otherwise. This will depend upon the particular type of discrimination alleged. If it is a claim (or defence) of direct discrimination, for example that a disabled person has been evicted when a non-disabled person in the same or similar circumstances has not, then the landlord would have to show that the disability was not the reason for the difference in treatment. If it is a claim of indirect discrimination, for example that the landlord has imposed a requirement upon its tenants which puts disabled tenants at a particular disadvantage, then the landlord would have to show that there was a good independent reason for the requirement. If it is a claim of disability discrimination under section 15, then the landlord would have to show that there was no less drastic means of solving the problem and that the effect upon the occupier was outweighed by the advantages. The express burden of proof provisions in the Equality Act cannot simply be ignored because there are some elements in the proportionality exercise which can be taken for granted.[55]

27.36   It is now clear that a defence to a possession claim under EA 2010 ss15 and 35 is not equivalent, either in substance or procedurally, to a defence under Article 8. In the words of Lord Neuberger in *Akerman-Livingstone*:

> Provided that a defendant establishes that the landlord is (or at a summary stage, may well be) seeking to evict him 'because of something arising in consequence of [his] disability', the landlord faces a

---

54 See, for example, *The Ralph & Irma Sperring Charity v Tanner* January 2013 *Legal Action* 39, Bristol County Court, in which the landlord of an assured shorthold tenant brought a claim for possession because of the poor condition of the property and the garden. A report from a clinical psychologist indicated that the state of the property and garden was ultimately attributable to the tenant's learning disability. The judge found that that there had been improvement over time and the property was currently at an acceptable standard; the relevant breaches of the tenancy had now been addressed and there was a low risk of the tenancy terms and conditions not being met in the future; and there would plainly be considerable distress involved in the eviction, particularly to the defendant's 11-year-old daughter, who had never known any other home. It was not proportionate to make a possession order.

55 Per Lady Hale at para [34].

significantly more difficult task in having to establish proportionality than does a landlord who faces an Article 8 defence.[56]

27.37   This does not mean that a landlord cannot seek or obtain summary judgment for possession. Under Civil Procedure Rules (CPR) 55.8, at the first hearing the court may decide the case summarily, or may give case management directions where the claim is genuinely disputed on grounds which appear to be substantial. It is therefore open to the court to order possession summarily if the landlord is able to establish that the defendant has no real prospect of establishing that he or she is under a disability; or that it is clear that the reason for possession is not 'something arising in consequence of [the] disability'; or that the claim is plainly 'a proportionate means of achieving a legitimate aim'. However, such instances are likely to be uncommon:

> The problem for a landlord seeking summary judgment for possession in such a case would not be one of principle, but one of practice. Each of the three types of issue referred to ... [above] would often give rise to disputed facts or assessments, eg whether the defendant suffers from a physical or mental disability, whether it has led to the possession claim, and where the proportionality balance comes down. Summary judgment is not normally a sensible or adequate procedure to deal with such disputes, which normally require disclosure of documents, and oral and/or expert evidence tested by cross-examination. There will no doubt be cases where a landlord facing a section 35(1)(b) defence may be well advised to seek summary judgment, but they would, I suspect, be relatively rare.[57]

27.38   It is clear from case-law under the DDA 1995 that discrimination under EA 2010 may operate as a free-standing defence. There is no need to plead discrimination as a counterclaim.[58] However, the defendant may wish to make a counterclaim for damages in respect of the harm he or she has suffered as a result of the discrimination. In this context, it will be important to deal specifically in the defendant's witness statement with the effect on him or her of the proceedings and of the discriminatory conduct, including any failure to make reasonable adjustments.[59] Equality Act counterclaims

---

56   At para [58]
57   Per Lord Neuberger, para [60].
58   *Manchester CC v Romano; Manchester CC v Samari* [2004] EWCA Civ 834, [2004] HLR 47.
59   See para 27.43.

are within scope of legal aid, like other counterclaims in possession proceedings.[60]

27.39   Where possession is sought against a Rent Act protected, secure or assured tenant on a discretionary ground, the defendant's disability, and its effect (if any) on the reason for seeking possession, are clearly matters relevant to the court's exercise of its discretion as to whether it is reasonable in all the circumstances to make a possession order.[61] It is nevertheless advisable to plead an Equality Act defence, where appropriate, as an alternative. In such cases, Equality Act arguments should also be pleaded as matters which should inform the court's determination of reasonableness, notably in the context of what alternatives there may be to possession action or what measures may be taken to assist the tenant to preserve his or her tenancy.

27.40   On the other hand, a specific Equality Act defence may be important, and indeed determinative, in those cases where the court has no statutory discretion and the landlord would otherwise be entitled to possession, eg, where possession is sought against:

- an assured shorthold tenant following service of a HA 1988 s21 notice; or
- an assured or assured shorthold tenant on ground 8 of the mandatory grounds for possession in HA 1988 Sch 2; or
- a non-secure or non-assured tenant; or
- an introductory or demoted tenant.

Where the claim for possession is based upon a procedural step such as a HA 1988 s21 notice, the claimant may argue that a defence on Equality Act grounds has no prospect of success because a landlord is not required to give any reason for requiring possession under the section 21 notice procedure. But, where the evidence indicates that the landlord's decision is in fact motivated by issues associated with the tenant's disability, it may well be possible to establish the defence. In arguing a discrimination defence under EA 2010 s15, it is necessary to demonstrate the causal link between the disability and the possession claim in order to satisfy the court that the landlord's decision to evict the defendant has been made 'because of something arising' in consequence of the occupier's disability. To establish a

60 Legal Aid, Sentencing and Punishment of Offenders Act 2012 (LASPO) Sch 1 para 33(6)(a). Free-standing claims under the Equality Act are also in scope: LASPO Sch 1 para 43.

61 See, in relation to the corresponding provisions of the DDA 1995, *North Devon Homes Ltd v Brazier* [2003] EWHC 574 (QB), [2003] HLR 59 and *Manchester CC v Romano; Manchester CC v Samari* [2004] EWCA Civ 834, [2004] HLR 47.

defence under section 19 (indirect discrimination), it is necessary to show that the landlord has applied to the defendant a provision, criterion or practice which is discriminatory in relation to the defendant's disability and which places the defendant at a particular disadvantage when compared with persons who are not disabled. In either case, and bearing in mind the burden of proof,[62] the defendant's own evidence will be central to the argument. Care must therefore taken in drafting his or her witness statement, which should set out in detail: the nature and effects of the disability; the issues of causation or of the disadvantage experienced by the defendant; how it is proposed to deal with any complaints of breach of tenancy obligations; how the measures envisaged would be effective; and the desired outcome of the proceedings.

27.41   Where the claimant is a public body, there may be an overlap between Equality Act and public law defences, and the possibility of a complementary public law defence should always be considered. Such a defence may well be available where it appears that the landlord has not followed its own policies or procedures on disability (see chapter 25). In *Barber v Croydon LBC*,[63] where the council sought possession following a single act of assault by a vulnerable tenant, it was held that the council was acting in breach of its own anti-social behaviour policy, which required it to consult specialist agencies and to consider the needs of vulnerable persons. The evidence established that the incident was associated with the tenant's medical condition. In that case, the Court of Appeal rejected an argument of unlawful discrimination under the DDA 1995. It held, however, that the council had acted unlawfully in failing to liaise with relevant support services and to consider a less intrusive remedy than eviction, such as an acceptable behaviour contract. The council's approach was wrong in principle and led to a decision which no authority could reasonably have taken.

27.42   Certain accommodation services are expressly excluded from the scope of EA 2010 Part 4 relating to premises, notably where the provision of accommodation is generally for the purpose of short stays by individuals who live elsewhere;[64] or where accommodation is provided for the purpose only of exercising a public function or providing a service to the public or a section of the public (eg overnight accommodation in a guesthouse provided under homelessness func-

---

62 See paras 27.25 and 27.35.
63 [2010] EWCA Civ 51, [2010] HLR 26.
64 EA 2010 s32(3(a).

tions or accommodation provided in prison for the purpose of carry-ing out the public function of detaining convicted offenders).[65] In such cases, some protection may be available under EA 2010 Part 3 (Services and public functions).[66]

Duty to make reasonable adjustments

27.43 The duty to make 'reasonable adjustments' for disabled persons, which is found in EA 2010 s20 and Sch 21, may also have a bear-ing on possession proceedings. Specifically, the duty may be relevant to the question of reasonableness, where a discretionary ground is concerned; or to the issue of justification under sections 15 or 19, in terms of whether the landlord can show that his or her actions amount to a proportionate response to a legitimate aim. It may also be relevant to compliance with the public sector equality duty (see para 27.54). In the context of disability discrimination and housing, a duty to make reasonable adjustments is imposed on those provid-ing services or performing public functions[67] and on those involved in the disposal and management of premises.[68] However, the duty to make adjustments in relation to physical features is significantly less onerous for those engaged in the disposal and management of premises than for other service providers or those exercising public functions.

27.44 The duty to make reasonable adjustments is founded on the prin-ciple of equal treatment through the creation of a level playing field for disabled persons and those who do not have a disability. Each of the three elements of the duty is designed to address situations where a disabled person is placed at a 'substantial disadvantage' in compari-son with someone who is not disabled. The duty may require that dis-abled people are treated differently from others or more favourably than others. There is no provision for 'justification' where a breach of this duty has been found to exist, and proportionality does not therefore provide a defence as such, although it is clearly an aspect of the duty 'to take such steps as is reasonable'. But breach of the duty to make reasonable adjustments would make it difficult for an owner or landlord to succeed in an argument of justification in response to a defence under section 15 or section 19.

65 EA 2010 s32(3)(b).
66 EA 2010 s29.
67 EA 2010 s29(7) and Sch 2.
68 EA 2010 s38.

27.45   EA 2010 s20 provides:

Duty to make adjustments

(1) Where this Act imposes a duty to make reasonable adjustments on a person, this section, sections 21 and 22 and the applicable Schedule apply; and for those purposes, a person on whom the duty is imposed is referred to as A.

(2) The duty comprises the following three requirements.

(3) The first requirement is a requirement, where a provision, criterion or practice of A's puts a disabled person at a substantial disadvantage in relation to a relevant matter in comparison with persons who are not disabled, to take such steps as it is reasonable to have to take to avoid the disadvantage.

(4) The second requirement is a requirement, where a physical feature puts a disabled person at a substantial disadvantage in relation to a relevant matter in comparison with persons who are not disabled, to take such steps as it is reasonable to have to take to avoid the disadvantage.

(5) The third requirement is a requirement, where a disabled person would, but for the provision of an auxiliary aid, be put at a substantial disadvantage in relation to a relevant matter in comparison with persons who are not disabled, to take such steps as it is reasonable to have to take to provide the auxiliary aid.

(6) Where the first or third requirement relates to the provision of information, the steps which it is reasonable for A to have to take include steps for ensuring that in the circumstances concerned the information is provided in an accessible format.

(7) A person (A) who is subject to a duty to make reasonable adjustments is not (subject to express provision to the contrary) entitled to require a disabled person, in relation to whom A is required to comply with the duty, to pay to any extent A's costs of complying with the duty.

(8) A reference in section 21 or 22 or an applicable Schedule to the first, second or third requirement is to be construed in accordance with this section.

(9) In relation to the second requirement, a reference in this section or an applicable Schedule to avoiding a substantial disadvantage includes a reference to –

(a) removing the physical feature in question,

(b) altering it, or

(c) providing a reasonable means of avoiding it.

(10) A reference in this section, section 21 or 22 or an applicable Schedule (apart from paragraphs 2 to 4 of Schedule 4) to a physical feature is a reference to –

(a) a feature arising from the design or construction of a building,

(b) a feature of an approach to, exit from or access to a building,

(c) a fixture or fitting, or furniture, furnishings, materials, equipment or other chattels, in or on premises, or
(d) any other physical element or quality.
(11) A reference in this section, section 21 or 22 or an applicable Schedule to an auxiliary aid includes a reference to an auxiliary service.
(12) A reference in this section or an applicable Schedule to chattels is to be read, in relation to Scotland, as a reference to moveable property.
(13) The applicable Schedule is, in relation to the Part of this Act specified in the first column of the Table, the Schedule specified in the second column.

27.46 Section 20(2) provides that the duty comprises three requirements, which may apply where a disabled person is placed at a substantial disadvantage in comparison with non-disabled people:

1) Where a provision, criterion or practice puts a disabled person at a substantial disadvantage in relation to a relevant matter in comparison with persons who are not disabled, the *first requirement* is to take such steps as it is reasonable to have to take to avoid the disadvantage.[69]

2) Where a physical feature puts a disabled person at a substantial disadvantage in relation to a relevant matter in comparison with persons who are not disabled, the *second requirement* is to take such steps as it is reasonable to have to take to avoid the disadvantage. However, the second requirement does *not* apply to landlords or those involved in letting or disposing of premises. It may only, under provisions which have not as yet been brought into force, apply in relation to common parts, where the landlord is a responsible person in relation to the common parts.[70]

3) Where a disabled person would, but for the provision of an auxiliary aid, be put at a substantial disadvantage in relation to a relevant matter in comparison with persons who are not disabled, the *third requirement* is to take such steps as it is reasonable to have to take to provide the auxiliary aid.

Section 21(1) provides that a failure to comply with the first, second or third requirement is a failure to comply with a duty to make reasonable adjustments. A person who fails to comply with the duty in relation to a disabled person discriminates against that person.[71]

---

69 The terminology of 'provision, criterion or practice' has replaced the equivalent formulation of "practice, policy or procedure' used in the DDA 1995.
70 EA 2010 Sch 4 paras 5–7.
71 EA 2010 s21(2).

27.47   The ways in which the duty to make reasonable adjustments is to be applied to rented premises are set out in EA 2010 s36 and Sch 4 para 2. The duty to make reasonable adjustments applies to the 'controller' of premises to let or of let premises. The term 'controller' includes a person by whom premises are let or a person who manages them. However, only the first and third requirements apply to the letting and management of rented property. The words 'provision, criterion or practice' in the first requirement are not defined in the Act, but include the terms of a tenancy, or of any agreement relating to a tenancy.[72] A reference to a disabled person in this context means a disabled person who is either a tenant of the premises or who is otherwise entitled to occupy them. The obligation to make reasonable adjustments applies only if the controller receives a request to take steps to avoid the disadvantage or provide the auxiliary aid.

27.48   In all cases, the disabled person must be placed at a substantial disadvantage, and the 'relevant matters' are: (a) the enjoyment of the premises; and (b) the use of a benefit or facility, entitlement to which arises as a result of the letting.[73] 'Substantial' is defined as 'more than minor or trivial'.[74] The test as to whether the disabled person is enabled to 'enjoy' premises is whether the adjustment would enable him or her to live in the ordinary way, as would any other tenant in the premises.[75]

Reasonable adjustments for disabled persons in respect of premises

27.49   It is important to note that the second requirement, concerning physical features which create the substantial disadvantage, does not

---

72   In *Lalli v Spirita Housing Ltd* [2012] EWCA Civ 497, [2012] HLR 30, it was held that a decision to apply for an injunction to restrain a resident of sheltered accommodation from entering the communal lounge was not a 'provision, criterion or practice' which discriminated against him. In any event, the discontinuance of proceedings following the assessment of disability amounted to a reasonable adjustment. See also *Drum Housing Association Ltd v Thomas-Ashley* [2010] EWCA Civ 265, [2010] P&CR 17, a case under the DDA 1995, in which the tenant, who suffered from bipolar mood disorder, kept a dog in breach of the terms of the tenancy. This was also a breach of a prohibition in the head lease. The Court of Appeal held that it was not open to the landlord to change the terms of her tenancy, since this would have provoked forfeiture of its own lease from the head lessor.
73   EA 2010 Sch 4 para 2(5).
74   EA 2010 s212(1).
75   *Beedles v Guinness Northern Counties* [2011] EWCA Civ 442, [2011] HLR 31.

apply to those who rent out, dispose of or manage premises.[76] Those disposing of and managing premises are therefore only required to make reasonable adjustments in respect of a 'provision, criterion or practice' and auxiliary aids (ie, the first and third requirements under section 20(2)).[77] Even in relation to those requirements, it is never reasonable for the controller to have to take a step which would involve the removal or alteration of a physical feature.[78]

27.50   Where the need for adjustments has been identified, whether the adjustments are required to be made will depend upon a number of considerations. The Code of Practice on Services, Public Functions and Associations[79] gives guidance as to the matters which may be relevant to consideration of what is reasonable, at least as far as services are concerned. These include: the costs of making the adjustment; the extent to which it is practicable to take the steps requested; the impact of the adjustment on the landlord and its management practices, and on others; and the financial and other resources available to the landlord.

27.51   In relation to possession proceedings taken on account of rent arrears or other breach of the tenancy, the duty to make reasonable adjustments may provide the basis for an argument that steps should have been taken to provide support for the tenant which would have assisted him or her to comply with tenancy terms. Alternatively, it might be argued that some measure short of possession action would suffice to deal with the problem, such as facilitating a care assessment, consulting other specialist agencies or offering an anti-social behaviour contract. The provision of support with benefit claims and debt may enable the defendant to regain control of his or her finances, maintain payments of current rent and comply with arrangements for payment of arrears. Where a tenant with a learning disability cannot understand written materials, a reasonable adjustment might provide for the landlord to make personal contact, by telephone or home visit, in the event that the tenant falls into rent arrears. The duty is not discharged until the disabled person is no longer at a substantial disadvantage.[80] It has been established in employment law that it is not necessary for the disabled person to

76 EA 2010 Sch 4 paras 2(2) and 3(2). Note that the second requirement will apply in relation to common parts, if para 5 of Sch 4 is brought into force.

77 EA 2010 s38 and Sch 4.

78 EA 2010 Sch 4 para 2(8).

79 *Services, public functions and associations: Statutory Code of Practice*, Equality and Human Rights Commission, 2011, available at www.equalityhumanrights.com.

80 *Archibald v Fife Council* [2004] UKHL 32, [2004] IRLR 651.

show that the adjustment would definitely have eliminated the disadvantage: it is enough if there is some prospect of removing it.[81]

27.52   The duty to make reasonable adjustments can therefore be used in support of other arguments based on discrimination. It provides a different perspective from which to approach the case. In some cases, it may prove conclusive where the defendant is otherwise unlikely to succeed on the basis of reasonableness or proportionality. The defendant's witness statement should be carefully drafted to explain the nature of the reasonable adjustments required and how they would assist, or would have assisted, him or her, and what the defendant hopes the outcome of the proceedings will be. Where conditions for an adjournment on terms or for a suspended or postponed possession order are being negotiated, advisers should seek to include a request for reasonable adjustments in a recital to the order or in a covering letter, to whch reference may subsequently be made in the event of a breach of the order.

27.53   Special provision is made in relation to the duty to make reasonable adjustments in those cases which are not covered by EA 2010 Part 4 (Premises), but where accommodation is provided in exercise of a public function.[82] In this case, the service provider must comply with the first, second and third requirements.[83] The duty under this head is to 'disabled persons generally' and the 'relevant matter' is the provision of the service or the exercise of the function. In the context of being subjected to a detriment such as eviction or possession action, being placed at a substantial disadvantage means 'suffering an unreasonably adverse experience when being subjected to the detriment'.[84] The statutory purpose is to ensure that those exercising public functions anticipate the particular needs of disabled people by developing policies and practices which address those needs.

---

81 *Cumbria Probation Board v Collingwood* UKEAT/0079/08/JOJ.
82 See para 27.42 above.
83 EA 2010 Sch 2 para 2.
84 EA 2010 Sch 2 para 2(5)(b).

Public Sector Equality Duty

27.54   The public sector equality duty (PSED) is contained in EA 2010 s149:

(1) A public authority must, in the exercise of its functions, have due regard to the need to –

    (a) eliminate discrimination, harassment, victimisation and any other conduct that is prohibited by or under this Act;

    (b) advance equality of opportunity between persons who share a relevant protected characteristic and persons who do not share it;

    (c) foster good relations between persons who share a relevant protected characteristic and persons who do not share it.

(2) A person who is not a public authority but who exercises public functions must, in the exercise of those functions, have due regard to the matters mentioned in subsection (1).

(3) Having due regard to the need to advance equality of opportunity between persons who share a relevant protected characteristic and persons who do not share it involves having due regard, in particular, to the need to –

    (a) remove or minimise disadvantages suffered by persons who share a relevant protected characteristic that are connected to that characteristic;

    (b) take steps to meet the needs of persons who share a relevant protected characteristic that are different from the needs of persons who do not share it;

    (c) encourage persons who share a relevant protected characteristic to participate in public life or in any other activity in which participation by such persons is disproportionately low.

(4) The steps involved in meeting the needs of disabled persons that are different from the needs of persons who are not disabled include, in particular, steps to take account of disabled persons' disabilities.

(5) Having due regard to the need to foster good relations between persons who share a relevant protected characteristic and persons who do not share it involves having due regard, in particular, to the need to –

    (a) tackle prejudice, and

    (b) promote understanding.

(6) Compliance with the duties in this section may involve treating some persons more favourably than others; but that is not to be taken as permitting conduct that would otherwise be prohibited by or under this Act.

    ...

27.55   The PSED[85] is 'not a duty to achieve a result', but a duty 'to have due regard to the need' to achieve the aims identified in section 149(1).[86] It is not necessary to establish a causal link between the disability and the decision or action complained of, as is necessary under sections 13 and 19 (direct and indirect discrimination) or under section 15 (discrimination arising from disability). In this context, the public authority is required to consider the impact of a particular decision on those with protected characteristics, as opposed to the cause of, or reason for, that decision. The question is whether the authority has had due regard, or has given appropriate weight, to the potentially discriminatory effects of its policies or decisions; and whether it has considered how such adverse effects could be avoided in order to advance equality of opportunity. The PSED applies to a wider set of protected characteristics than those to which the provisions in respect of premises apply, in that age is included (s149(7)).

27.56   Section 149(4) specifically requires public bodies to 'take steps to take account of disabled person's disabilities', while s149(6) makes it clear that this may involve treating some people more favourably than others.

27.57   The PSED applies to all public authorities.[87] It also applies to any person who is not a public authority but who is exercising public functions. A public function is a function of a public nature for the purposes of the Human Rights Act 1998.[88] It is likely that most housing associations and other registered providers of social housing and registered social landlords will be considered to be exercising public functions when they make decisions concerning the management and allocation of their housing stock, including the decision to terminate a tenancy, under the principles in *R (Weaver) v London & Quadrant Housing Trust.*[89]

27.58   In *R (Brown) v Secretary of State for Work and Pensions,*[90] a case concerned with the closure of post offices, the Administrative Court set out a number of factors which are relevant to the duty to have

---

85 See *The Essential Guide to the Public Sector Equality Duty*, Equality and Human Rights Commission, available at www.equalityhumanrights.com.

86 Per Dyson LJ in *R (Baker) v Secretary of State for Communities and Local Government* [2008] EWCA Civ 141, [2009] PTSR 809, at para 31 (concerning an earlier form of the duty in Race Relations Act 1976 s71). '"Due regard" means the regard that is "appropriate in all the circumstances"'.

87 As defined by EA 2010 s150 and specified in Sch 19.

88 EA 2010 ss149(2) and 150(5), and see Human Rights Act 1998 s6(3)(b).

89 [2009] EWCA Civ 587, [2010] 1 WLR 363. See para 25.38.

90 [2008] EWHC 3158 (Admin), [2009] PTSR 1506 per Aikens LJ at paras 90–96.

regard to the statutory objectives under section 149.[91] Those in public authorities who have to take decisions which affect or might affect disabled people must be aware of their duty to have due regard to the identified aims. The duty to have regard involves a conscious approach and state of mind. It is not satisfied by 'ticking boxes'. The duty must be integrated within the discharge of the authority's public functions. It must be exercised in substance, with rigour and with an open mind. The duty is not limited to a particular point in time and is a continuing one. The Court noted that it is good practice for those exercising public functions to keep an adequate record showing that they had actually considered their disability equality duties and addressed relevant questions. Proper record-keeping encourages transparency and the conscientious attention of decision-makers to their equality duties. If records are not kept it may be more difficult, in evidential terms, for a public authority to persuade a court that it has fulfilled the duty.[92]

27.59   The fact that the authority has not made specific reference to the section 149 duty in carrying out the particular function does not necessarily indicate that the duty under the Act has not been performed. But it is good practice for the decision maker to make express reference to the statutory provision and to any code or other guidance in all cases where the PSED is in play.[93] In that way the decision maker is more likely to ensure that the relevant factors are taken into account.

27.60   Provided that a court is satisfied that there has been proper consideration of the duty, and that the provider has had a proper appreciation of the potential impact of its decision on the equality objectives and the desirability of achieving them, then it is for the decision maker to decide how much weight should be given to the various factors informing the decision. There must be a proper and conscientious focus on the statutory criteria, but if that is demonstrated, the court cannot interfere with the decision simply because it would have given greater weight to the equality implications.[94]

---

91 In this case, under DDA 1995 s49A, the precursor of EA 2010 s149.

92 See *R (Brown) v Secretary of State for Work and Pensions* [2008] EWHC 3158 (Admin), [2009] PTSR 1506 per Atkins J at para 96.

93 *Brown*, para 93.

94 For a distillation of various points drawn from the case-law, see the judgment of McCombe LJ in *Bracking v Secretary of State for Work and Pensions* [2013] EWCA Civ 1345, [2014] Eq LR 40 at para 26, citing in particular dicta of Elias LJ in *R (Hurley & Moore) v Secretary of State for Business, Innovation and Skills* [2012] EWHC 201 (Admin), [2012] Eq LR 447 paras 77–78 and 89.

27.61   In *Barnsley MBC v Norton*[95] the defendant was a caretaker at a local school. He lived in non-secure accommodation on site with his wife and daughter, who suffered from cerebral palsy. When his employment ended, the council sought possession in order to offer the house to a new caretaker. The defendant argued that the council was in breach of the public sector equality duty.[96] The Court of Appeal accepted that the council was under a duty to have due regard to the need to take steps to take the defendant's daughter's disability into account. It had taken no account of the fact that possession proceedings would have an impact on the daughter. It was in breach of the PSED by failing to address the duty before commencing proceedings or at any later stage. Despite this, the court held that, however much consideration had been given to the daughter's disability, the council would inevitably have concluded that it should nevertheless seek possession because of its need for the accommodation. The court considered that the daughter's needs would be addressed in the course of the family's application for assistance under HA 1996 Part 7 (Homelessness).

27.62   Despite the outcome in the *Norton* case, the Court of Appeal affirmed that the council was required to consider the PSED as part of the eviction process. It could not avoid addressing the implications of possession proceedings for an occupant known to be severely disabled, relying on the assumption that in the event of eviction her disability would fall to be considered under homelessness duties.[97] While the existence of HA 1996 Pt 7 duties was clearly a relevant factor, it did not follow that the duty to consider the daughter's disability 'allows the Council to leave the question of her future accommodation and provision over to be coped with under Part 7 ... if it comes to that'. However, on the facts of the case, it was a question of looking to the future, since there was an imperative that the house be made available for a new caretaker. The PSED would, however, continue up to the eviction. The council was in control of the timing of eviction, and any decision to enforce the possession order would itself be subject to the duty. In some cases, the duty might lead to an offer of suitable alternative accommodation.[98]

95 [2011] EWCA Civ 834, [2011] HLR 46.
96 In this case, under DDA 1995 s49A, the precursor of EA 2010 s149.
97 *Norton* paras 28–30.
98 In this context, the Court drew by analogy on the judgment of the Supreme Court in *Manchester City Council v Pinnock* [2010] UKSC 45, [2011] HLR 7, in which Lord Neuberger approved the proposition that Article 8 proportionality is more likely to be a relevant issue in respect of occupants who are vulnerable

27.63   The importance of the PSED has also been recognised in the context of homelessness decision-making, in ways which have a bearing on possession proceedings. In *Pieretti v Enfield London Borough Council*,[99] a case relating to an intentional homelessness decision, the Court of Appeal rejected the argument that the predecessor duty in DDA 1995 s49A was a generalised duty relating only to the formulation of policy, and held that it was also a duty to be implemented in relation to decisions or actions taken by a public authority in specific cases. Wilson LJ stated that if some feature of the evidence raised a real possibility that the person concerned was disabled in a sense relevant to the question being decided, the authority was required to make enquiries sufficient to satisfy itself as to whether a disability existed and if so whether it was relevant to the decision under consideration.[100]

27.64   In the context of the assessment of whether a homeless person is 'vulnerable' within the meaning of HA 1996 s189(1)(c), and hence in priority need of accommodation, the Supreme Court has emphasised that the PSED requires an authority to demonstrate that those who make decisions on its behalf focus sharply on the nature and effects of disability:

> More specifically, each stage of the decision-making exercise as to whether an applicant with an actual or possible disability or other 'relevant protected characteristic' falls within section 189(1)(c), must be made with the equality duty well in mind, and 'must be exercised in substance, with rigour, and with an open mind'. There is a risk that such words can lead to no more than formulaic and high-minded mantras in judgments and in other documents ... It is therefore appropriate to emphasise that the equality duty, in the context of an exercise such as a section 202 review, does require the reviewing officer to focus very sharply on (i) whether the applicant is under a disability (or has another relevant protected characteristic), (ii) the extent of such disability, (iii) the likely effect of the disability, when taken together

---

and that 'the issue may also require the local authority to explain why they are not securing alternative accommodation in such cases' (para [64]).

99 [2010] EWCA Civ 1104, [2011] HLR 3.
100 *Pieretti* para 36. See also *R (Tiller) v East Sussex CC* [2011] EWCA Civ 1577, a case under DDA 1995 s49A concerning an unsuccessful challenge to a decision to discontinue the provision of an on-site 24-hour warden service in a sheltered housing scheme, and *Swan Housing Association Ltd v Gill* [2013] EWCA Civ 1566, [2014] HLR 18, in which it was held that the court itself was not a public authority for the purposes of the PSED.

with any other features, on the applicant if and when homeless, and (iv) whether the applicant is as a result 'vulnerable'.[101]

27.65　Where a housing provider exercising public functions brings possession proceedings on a discretionary ground for possession, the PSED may be advanced as a major factor in informing the court's decision in relation to the reasonableness of making an order. It is clearly relevant to the question of reasonableness that the claimant provider should have had due regard to the disability of an occupier in deciding to evict the household. Where proceedings are brought on a mandatory ground, or where no ground for possession is required (including where a local authority has decided not to renew a flexible tenancy, or where a social housing provider is seeking to terminate an assured shorthold tenancy following a notice under HA 1988 s21), the adviser will first need to consider whether a defence of discrimination may be raised under EA 2010 s15 (or under either of sections 13 and 19). If there is no causal link between the disability and the reason for the decision to evict, it will then be necessary to consider whether the PSED may provide a defence to the proceedings. This requires an investigation into whether the housing provider has had due regard to the extent and effects of the occupier's disability in determining whether it is appropriate to pursue the possession claim. Where there are complaints of nuisance or anti-social behaviour, and one of the occupiers is disabled, again the provider will be expected to have considered whether other measures, such as the provision of suitable alternative accommodation, might be adopted. Where serious anti-social behaviour has occurred, however, the court is unlikely to be convinced that a proportionate response is other than eviction.[102] Where the defendant has failed to pay rent, the provider should consider whether its policies in dealing with disabled tenants might have provided greater support to facilitate benefits claims or money management, or whether sufficient attention has been given to other possible solutions which would have enabled rent to be paid.

101　*Hotak v Southwark LBC; Kanu v Southwark LBC; Johnson v Solihull MBC* [2015] UKSC 30, [2015] HLR 23 per Lord Neuberger at para 78.
102　*Brent LBC v Corcoran* [2010] EWCA Civ 774, [2010] HLR 43. This was a case concerning a claim for possession against a licensee of a plot on a travellers' site on account of criminal conduct including drug dealing and selling stolen goods. The Court of Appeal was dismissive of a defence under DDA 1995 s49A on the basis that the licensee's aged and terminally ill mother was living on the pitch, although it acknowledged that some consideration would need to be given to the mother's situation when it came to execution of the order.

CHAPTER 28

Possession orders

The effect of possession orders

Occupiers without full statutory protection

28.1   At common law judges had a discretion to allow occupiers (other than trespassers) a reasonable time in continued occupation before a possession order took effect, even if they had no security of tenure.[1] However, this discretion was largely taken away by the Housing Act (HA) 1980. With various exceptions, orders for possession must now take effect not later than 14 days after the making of the order unless that would cause exceptional hardship, in which case the order can be postponed to a date which is not more than six weeks after the making of the order. There is no definition of 'exceptional hardship'. HA 1980 s89 provides:

> **Restriction on discretion of court in making orders for possession of land**
>
> (1) Where a court makes an order for the possession of any land in a case not falling within the exceptions mentioned in subsection (2) below, the giving up of possession shall not be postponed (whether by the order or any variation, suspension or stay of execution) to a date later than fourteen days after the making of the order, unless it appears to the court that exceptional hardship would be caused by requiring possession to be given up by that date; and shall not in any event be postponed to a date later than six weeks after the making of the order.
>
> (2) The restrictions in subsection (1) above do not apply if –
>
>   (a) the order is made in an action by a mortgagee for possession; or
>
>   (b) the order is made in an action for forfeiture of a lease; or
>
>   (c) the court had power to make the order only if it considered it reasonable to make it; or
>
>   (d) the order relates to a dwelling-house which is the subject of a restricted contract (within the meaning of section 19 of the 1977 Act); or
>
>   (e) the order is made in proceedings brought as mentioned in section 88(1) above.

---

1   *Air Ministry v Harris* [1951] 2 All ER 862 (six months was too long); *Sheffield Corporation v Luxford* [1929] 2 KB 180 (one year was too long) and *Jones v Savery* [1951] 1 All ER 820 (one month was reasonable).

HA 1980 s89 applies as much to orders made in the High Court as to those made in the county court.[2] Where the defendant is applying for permission to appeal, however, section 89 does not limit the court's power to grant a stay of execution of the possession order.[3]

28.2   In *London Borough of Hounslow v Powell*[4] the Supreme Court considered whether a longer period than six weeks might be required in some cases to satisfy a test of proportionality under Human Rights Act (HRA) 1998 Sch 1 Article 8. The court rejected the argument that HA 1980 s89 could be read subject to HRA 1998 s3(1), so as to allow the court to postpone possession for a longer period than six weeks. Section 89 imposed a precise timetable in limiting the court's power to postpone.[5] The Court observed that section 89 did not take away the court's ordinary powers of case management, so that the court might adjourn for more information or to enable the defendant to bring proceedings for judicial review.

28.3   Gathering together all possible variations (including those not referred to in HA 1980 s89), the position is as follows.

Trespassers

28.4   Courts must make an order to take effect immediately[6] unless the trespassers are former service occupiers[7] or former occupiers under

2   *Hackney LBC v Side by Side (Kids) Ltd* [2003] EWHC 1813 (QB), [2004] 1 WLR 363. The earlier decision of Harman J in *Bain and Co v Church Commissioners for England* [1989] 1 WLR 24, (1989) 21 HLR 29, ChD, that 'a court' meant 'a county court', was wrong.
3   *Admiral Taverns (Cygnet) Ltd v Daniel and Daly* [2008] EWHC 1688 (QB), [2009] 4 All ER 71.
4   [2011] UKSC 8, [2011] HLR 23.
5   In *McDonald v McDonald* [2016] UKSC 28, [2016] HLR 28, in relation to the operation of HA 1980 s89 where the occupier has raised a 'human right' defence, Lord Neuberger and Lady Hale said: 'The cases in which it would be justifiable to refuse, as opposed to postpone, a possession order must be very few and far between, even when taken as a proportion of those rare cases where proportionality can be successfully invoked. They could only be cases in which the landlord's interest in regaining possession was heavily outweighed by the gravity of the interference in the occupier's right to respect for her home ... Were a proportionality defence to be available in section 21 [HA 1988] claims, it is not easy to imagine circumstances in which the occupier's Article 8 rights would be so strong as to preclude the making, as opposed to the short postponement, of a possession order.' [73]
6   *McPhail v Persons, Names Unknown* [1973] Ch 447, [1973] 3 All ER 393, CA.
7   Protection from Eviction Act 1977 s8(2).

a rental purchase agreement[8] or unless both parties consent to a longer period (see para 23.12).

Proceedings brought by a mortgagee for possession

28.5   Courts have a wide discretion to adjourn the proceedings, or to suspend or postpone a possession order (see para 34.12 onwards). For discussion of the general procedure in mortgage possession actions, see chapter 37.

Forfeiture of a lease

28.6   In rent arrears cases any order forfeiting a lease must be suspended for at least 28 days.[9] In proceedings for forfeiture based on other breaches of covenant, courts have a wide discretion to grant relief from forfeiture or to postpone the order (see para 14.60 onwards).

Rental purchase agreements

28.7   In rental purchase cases, the court has a wide discretion to adjourn, or stay or suspend a possession order.[10]

Mandatory grounds against Rent Act, secure and assured tenants, and proceedings against assured shorthold, demoted and introductory tenants

28.8   If the court is satisfied that a landlord is entitled to possession on one of the mandatory grounds or because a HA 1988 s21 notice served on an assured shorthold tenant has expired, the court must make a possession order to take effect within 14 days unless exceptional hardship would be caused, in which case six weeks may be allowed[11] (see para 28.1). The same applies to possession claims against introductory and demoted tenants (see chapters 5 and 6).

---

8   HA 1980 s88(1).
9   County Courts Act 1984 s138(3). See para 14.63.
10   HA 1980 s88(1); see para 13.7.
11   HA 1988 s9(6) and HA 1980 s89.

Discretionary grounds within Rent Act 1977, Housing Act 1985 and Housing Act 1988

28.9   Where possession has been sought on a discretionary ground, courts have a wide discretion to adjourn the possession claim or to postpone the date for possession or to stay or suspend execution of the order (see below, paras 28.11–28.13).

All other cases

28.10   The county court's discretion is limited by HA 1980 s89 to a maximum of 14 days unless exceptional hardship would be caused by eviction within 14 days, in which case up to six weeks may be allowed.

Tenants with security of tenure: possession on discretionary grounds

28.11   Even if a landlord of a regulated (Rent Act) or assured or secure tenant proves that one of the discretionary grounds for possession is made out, the court may consider that it is not reasonable to make any order for possession.[12] For example, in rent arrears cases, if the arrears are low, the court may adjourn generally with liberty to restore on terms that the tenant shall pay current rent and a weekly or monthly sum towards the arrears, or merely make a money judgment order with a direction that the tenant pay off the arrears by instalments. Alternatively, if the court is not satisfied that it is appropriate to make an absolute order, it may make a postponed or suspended possession order. Rent Act (RA) 1977 s100, HA 1985 s85 and HA 1988 s9(2), which are in almost identical terms, give the court a wide discretion to postpone the date on which possession should be given or to stay or suspend the execution of an order.

28.12   HA 1985 s85 provides:

> **Extended discretion of court in certain proceedings for possession**
> (1) Where proceedings are brought for possession of a dwelling-house let under a secure tenancy on any of the grounds set out in Part I or Part III of Schedule 2 (grounds 1 to 8 and 12 to 16: cases in which the court must be satisfied that it is reasonable to make a possession order), the court may adjourn the proceedings for such period or periods as it thinks fit.

---

12 See, eg *Woodspring DC v Taylor* (1982) 4 HLR 95, CA and paras 3.69–3.76.

(2) On the making of an order for possession of such a dwelling-house on any of those grounds, or at any time before the execution of the order, the court may –

(a) stay or suspend the execution of the order, or

(b) postpone the date for possession,

for such period or periods as the court thinks fit.

(3) On such an adjournment, stay, suspension or postponement the court –

(a) shall impose conditions with respect to the payment by the tenant of arrears of rent (if any) and rent, unless it considers that to do so would cause exceptional hardship to the tenant or would otherwise be unreasonable, and

(b) may impose such other conditions as it thinks fit.

(4) If the conditions are complied with, the court may, if it thinks fit, discharge or rescind the order for possession.[13]

28.13   Housing Act 1988 s9 provides:

Extended discretion of court in possession claims

(1) Subject to subsection (6) below, the court may adjourn for such period or periods as it thinks fit proceedings for possession of a dwelling-house let on an assured tenancy.

(2) On the making of an order for possession of a dwelling-house let on an assured tenancy, or at any time before the execution of such an order, the court, subject to subsection (6) below, may –

(a) stay or suspend execution of the order, or

(b) postpone the date of possession,

for such period or periods as the court thinks just.

(3) On any such adjournment as is referred to in subsection (1) above or any such stay, suspension or postponement as is referred to in subsection (2) above, the court, unless it considers that to do so would cause exceptional hardship to the tenant or would otherwise be unreasonable, shall impose conditions with regard to payment by the tenant of arrears of rent (if any) and rent and may impose such other conditions as it thinks fit.

(4) If any such conditions as are referred to in subsection (3) above are complied with, the court may, if it thinks fit, discharge or rescind any such order as is referred to in subsection (2) above.[14]

...

(6) This section does not apply if the court is satisfied that the landlord is entitled to possession of the dwelling-house –

(a) on any of the grounds in Part I of Schedule 2 to this Act; or

---

13 Section 85(4) was amended by Housing and Regeneration Act (H&RA) 2008 Sch 11 para 3(3), but the amendment has not been brought into force. See para 31.33.

14 Section 9(4) was amended by H&RA 2008 Sch 11 para 8(3), but the amendment has not been brought into force. See para 31.33.

(b) by virtue of subsection (1) or subsection (4) of section 21 below.

Status of the tenant after the possession order takes effect

28.14   Absolute (or outright) orders for possession take effect on the date on which the order states possession is to be given up, but tenancies with statutory protection do not end until the order is executed, ie until the tenant is evicted, or leaves in compliance with the order.[15]

28.15   For many years, the courts held in a series of cases that secure tenancies terminated on the date for possession specified in the order and that the tenant became a 'tolerated trespasser' from that date onwards, subject to variation or discharge of the order. Likewise, many tenants with *suspended* possession orders became tolerated trespassers either when they breached the terms of the order or when the date for possession in the order expired (since, as the law then stood, possession itself had been lost and what was suspended was enforcement of the order).[16] Where the court made a *postponed* possession order, however, the tenancy would continue unless or until the court made a further order. In the event of the tenant breaching the terms of postponement, it would be necessary for the landlord to apply to the court to fix a date for possession. As a result of the twilight status of the tolerated trespasser, many people lost their tenancy rights, including rights to repair and the right to buy and, on the death of a tolerated trespasser, a family member would find that there was no tenancy to which he or she could succeed.

28.16   Tenants no longer become tolerated trespassers when the date for possession in a court order expires or on breach of a suspended possession order. In *Knowsley Housing Trust v White*,[17] the House of Lords held that assured tenancies did not terminate until the date of execution of the order (following Rent Act authority in *Sherrin v Brand*[18]) and cast doubt on the judicial reasoning that had produced

---

15   See para 28.16, notably footnote 15.
16   See *Thompson v Elmbridge* [1987] 1 WLR 1425; *Burrows v Brent LBC* [1996] 1 WLR 1448; *Greenwich LBC v Regan* (1996) 28 HLR 469, (1996) 72 P&CR 507, CA; *Lambeth LBC v Rogers* (2000) 32 HLR 361; *Harlow DC v Hall* [2006] EWCA Civ 156, [2006] 1 WLR 2116 and *Bristol CC v Hassan* [2006] EWCA Civ 656, [2006] 1 WLR 2582.
17   [2008] UKHL 70, [2009] 1 AC 636.
18   [1956] 1 QB 403.

the doctrine of the tolerated trespasser.[19] Then, following the coming into force of the Housing and Regeneration Act (H&RA) 2008 Sch 11 on 20 May 2009, the Housing Acts 1985, 1988 and 1996 were amended to provide that tenancies falling within those Acts do not end until the possession order is executed, ie, until actual eviction.[20] It is, of course, entirely possible for such a tenancy to be terminated voluntarily by surrender or by a tenant's notice to quit. Where a tenant leaves in accordance with a possession order, but before eviction, it is likely that the tenancy ends by implied surrender.

28.17   For any tenant who had already become a tolerated trespasser before 20 May 2009, and who still occupied the same premises as his or her only or principal home on that date, H&RA 2008 provides that he or she, as from that date, acquired a 'replacement tenancy', provided that the parties had not already entered into another tenancy. Any outstanding liability for rent owed by the tenant to the landlord before the commencement date was treated as a liability in respect of rent under the new tenancy. Likewise, the possession order under which the original tenancy ended was to be treated as if it applied to the new tenancy.

28.18   An agreement that an occupier may remain in premises after an absolute (or outright) possession order has been made (for example, that occupation may continue on terms that payments of rent and instalments towards arrears are made) was characterised in *Burrows v Brent LBC*[21] as a forbearance by the landlord from executing the order. After a period of compliance with the terms of forbearance, the tenant may apply to the court for a variation of the order (assuming that it was made on a discretionary ground). There may be circumstances in which such an agreement might be construed as the creation of a new tenancy, but the existence of the outright order

---

19 [2008] UKHL 70, [2009] HLR 17 at paras [90]–[93]. Further doubt on the judicial reasoning which gave rise to the concept of the tolerated trespasser was expressed by the Supreme Court in *Austin v Southwark LBC* [2010] UKSC 28, [2011] 1 AC 355, but the Court declined to reverse the earlier case-law which had been assumed to be right and had been acted on in many tens of thousands of cases.

20 See HA 1985 s82(2), substituted by H&RA 2008 Sch 11 para 2(3), in relation to secure tenancies; new HA 1988 s5(1A), inserted by Sch 11 para 6(2) (assured tenancies); HA 1988 s21(3), as amended by Sch 11 para 9(2) and s21(4A), inserted by Sch 11 para 9(3) (assured shorthold tenancies); HA 1996 s127(1A), inserted by Sch 11 para 12(3) (introductory tenancies) and HA 1996 s143D(1A), inserted by Sch 11 para 13(3) (demoted tenancies).

21 [1996] 1 WLR 1448, (1997) 29 HLR 167.

means that such an inference is unlikely, in the absence of clear evidence that this was the intention of the parties.

Conditional (postponed or suspended) possession orders

28.19 When postponing or suspending possession orders against assured, secure or Rent Act regulated tenants, the court must impose conditions with regard to the repayment of arrears (if any) unless this would cause exceptional hardship or would otherwise be unreasonable. The court may impose such other conditions as it thinks fit.[22]

28.20 The effect of a conditional possession order (ie a postponed or 'suspended' order which is conditional upon the defendant's complying with certain terms) depends upon the particular form in which the order is expressed (see paras 28.27–28.44).

Criteria for postponing or suspending possession orders

28.21 The approach which the court must adopt in dealing with a claim for possession on a discretionary ground has been described as follows:

> Where, as here, the landlord relies on ... [discretionary grounds] the court has potentially three issues, although a determination of one issue in favour of the tenant may make further issues academic: first, to decide whether grounds for possession are made out, which is an issue of fact; secondly, to decide whether it is reasonable to make an order for possession, which involves the exercise of judicial discretion, but with a substantial element of judgment as to whether or not the making of the order is reasonable; and thirdly, to decide whether to postpone the date for possession or to stay or suspend execution, which involves a further exercise of judicial discretion.[23]

28.22 The court's powers under RA 1977 s100(2), HA 1985 s85(2) and HA 1988 s9(2) must be exercised judicially. Except in cases of serious anti-social behaviour or drug dealing, where a postponed or suspended order is the exception,[24] the court has a wide discretion in deciding whether to make an outright possession order or a postponed or suspended order, and in determining the factors which should influence the exercise of its discretion. In principle, an outright order

---

22 RA 1977 s100(3); HA 1985 s85(3)(b); HA 1988 s9(3).
23 *West Kent Housing Association v Davies* (1998) 31 HLR 415, per Robert Walker LJ at 418.
24 *Bristol City Council v Mousah* (1997) 30 HLR 32, CA and other cases referred to in para 3.176.

should be made only where no lesser alternative would realistically make sense.[25] In two cases involving 'cannabis farms',[26] the Court of Appeal has given tentative guidance in relation to cases involving the commission of criminal offences at the property, notably in assessing whether there was 'cogent evidence providing a real hope that the defendant had mended his ways'.[27] Factors which the court may consider include: the degree of co-operation with the landlord; the extent and duration of the behaviour complained of; honesty and full disclosure of previous bad behaviour; early acceptance of culpability; and genuine remorse. Tenants who have lied in their evidence run the risk that the court will not accept assurances from them about future behaviour. Nevertheless, dishonesty in giving evidence is not an automatic bar to the making of a suspended possession order. The willingness of the tenant to consent to a condition such as unannounced inspections by the landlord may be a relevant factor.

28.23   In rent arrears cases, the fundamental purpose of a postponed or suspended possession order is to enable any arrears to be paid off within a reasonable time. In a case involving a private landlord, the Court of Appeal has expressed the view that any postponement or suspension should enable the arrears to be cleared within a period which does not extend into the mists of time.[28]

28.24   In practice, unless there are large rent arrears, on the first occasion that a tenant is brought to court in possession proceedings, it is usual, if the grant of an order is appropriate at all, for a possession order to be postponed or suspended on condition that the tenant pays the current rent when due *and* a regular amount towards the arrears.[29] Even if rent arrears are high, the court may take the view that the landlord has contributed to some extent to the problem (eg, in allowing large arrears to accrue without taking earlier action or in failing to comply with the *Pre-action Protocol for possession claims by social landlords* (see para 3.77 and appendix E)) and that, accordingly, the tenant should be given the chance to pay off the arrears by instal-

---

25 *CDS Housing v Bellis* [2008] EWCA Civ 1315, February 2009 *Legal Action* 28.

26 *City West Housing Trust v Massey and Manchester & District HA v Roberts* [2016] EWCA Civ 704: see para 3.194.

27 *Sandwell MBC v Hensley* [2008] HLR 22, per Gage LJ.

28 *Taj v Ali* (2001) 33 HLR 26, [2000] 43 EG 183, CA (judge wrong to make suspended possession order where arrears of £14,503 to be paid off at £5 per week) but cf *Lambeth LBC v Henry* (2000) 32 HLR 874, CA and para 28.25 below.

29 *Laimond Properties Ltd v Raeuchle* (2001) 33 HLR 113, [2000] L&TR 319, CA. See too the *Pre-action Protocol for possession claims by social landlords*, see paras 3.77–3.80.

ments under a conditional possession order. Where, however, a landlord brings a claim for possession against an assured (including an assured shorthold) tenant who owes eight weeks' or two months' rent on the basis of HA 1988 Sch 1 ground 8 (whether as a sole ground or in addition to other grounds), and the terms of the ground are made out,[30] the grant of possession is mandatory.

28.25   It is not uncommon for courts to make postponed or suspended orders which provide for arrears to be paid off over several years.[31] The Court of Appeal has said that court practice is to be merciful to tenants and to give them a realistic opportunity to pay arrears. The question of whether it is appropriate for a tenant who owes substantial arrears to have the threat of losing his or her home hanging over him or her for years is a political question and does not go to the correctness of making an order.[32] Some judges take the realistic view that if a possession order is postponed or suspended, there is a greater likelihood of the landlord recovering arrears, whereas if an absolute possession order is made, it is unlikely in reality that the landlord will ever recover the arrears. Courts are generally more prepared to postpone or suspend an order against a tenant with substantial arrears if the landlord is a local authority or other social landlord, rather than a private individual.

28.26   When considering what form of order should be made, the length of time the defendants have been tenants, their previous conduct, their age and health are all relevant factors.[33] The court should also take into account the level of arrears and the tenant's income and expenditure. Again, there is little guidance about determining the level or amount of such payments, but there is a strong argument that, for tenants in receipt of means-tested subsistence benefits such as income support or income-based jobseeker's allowance, no suspended order should require the tenant to pay more than five per cent[34] of the personal allowance for a single claimant aged 25 or over towards the arrears. This is the maximum amount which the Department of Work and Pensions (DWP) can deduct from those benefits

30 See para 3.99
31 See, eg *Lambeth LBC v Henry* (2000) 32 HLR 874, CA, where the Court of Appeal refused to criticise a suspended possession order which provided for payment of arrears over a period of 23 years. Cf para 28.23 and *Taj v Ali* (2001) 33 HLR 26, [2000] 43 EG 183, CA.
32 *Lambeth LBC v Henry* (2000) 32 HLR 874, CA.
33 *Woodspring DC v Taylor* (1982) 4 HLR 95, CA.
34 Currently (from April 2016), £3.70 per week or thereabouts.

and pay direct to the landlord towards satisfaction of arrears.[35] The basis of the argument is that those responsible for welfare benefits legislation consider that, taking into account the subsistence needs of claimants and their families, no more than 5 per cent of their benefit should be deducted when direct payments are made to the landlord; and therefore that it would be unreasonable and contrary to RA 1977 s100(3), HA 1985 s85(3) and HA 1988 s9(3) for the court to order the payment of a greater sum. Indeed, if the DWP is already making direct deductions which are reducing the arrears, it may well be unreasonable for the court to make any possession order at all because the landlord's interests are already being adequately pro-tected.[36] With the advent of universal credit (see chapter 16), however, higher direct deductions from benefit entitlement are available. The maximum amount that may be deducted from a person's universal credit entitlement is 40 per cent of the standard allowance.[37] The regulations establish a priority list of debts and no more than three separate deductions can be made. Guidance states that deductions for rent shall be no less than 10 per cent and no more than 20 per cent of the standard allowance. It is nevertheless open to tenants' representatives to argue that a payment arrangement which would take the household income substantially below the standard subsist-ence level of benefit cannot be a reasonable basis for an order.

Postponed possession orders

28.27   Two alternative forms of conditional possession order are in use by the courts in relation to assured, secure and Rent Act regulated ten-ancies, where an order is made on discretionary grounds. One is the *postponed* possession order, whereby the date for possession is not fixed by the original order. This involves a two-stage process. Follow-ing the making of a postponed possession order, the landlord will need to apply again to the court to fix the possession date, but cannot do so as long as the tenant is complying with the terms of the order. In a rent arrears case, the terms will comprise payment of current rent together with regular payments off the arrears. In a behaviour case, the terms will usually require the tenant to cease committing

---

35 Social Security (Claims and Payments) Regulations 1987 SI No 1968 Sch 9 para 5(3) as amended.

36 *Woodspring DC v Taylor* (1982) 4 HLR 95, CA; *Second WRVS Housing Society v Blair* (1987) 19 HLR 104 and *Brent LBC v Marks* (1999) 31 HLR 343, CA.

37 The Universal Credit, Personal Independence Payment, Jobseeker's Allowance and Employment and Support Allowance (Claims and Payments) Regulations 2013 SI No 380 Sch 6 paras 4, 6 and 7.

the acts complained of and abide by the conditions of the tenancy agreement. Court form N28A provides a template for the postponed possession order (see appendix B).

28.28   Where the court makes a postponed possession order in respect of a secure or assured tenancy, the procedure to fix a date for possession following a breach of the order is governed by CPR Practice Direction 55A para 10. At least 14 days and not more than three months before applying to the court to fix a possession date, the landlord must give written notice to the tenant. In a rent arrears case this notice must:

- state that the landlord intends to apply for an order fixing the date on which the tenant is to give up possession;
- record the current arrears and, by reference to a rent statement, state how the tenant has failed to comply with the postponed order;
- request the tenant to reply to the landlord within seven days agreeing or disputing the stated arrears; and
- inform the tenant of his or her right to apply to the court for a further postponement of the order, or to stay or suspend enforcement.[38]

28.29   In the tenant's reply to such a notice, he or she must provide details of payments or credits to the account if the stated arrears are in dispute. Otherwise, he or she must explain why payments have not been made.[39] If the landlord applies to the court for a date to be fixed, he or she must do so by filing an application notice (court form N244) under CPR Part 23. The application must state whether or not there is any outstanding claim for housing benefit by the tenant. With the application the landlord must file:

- a copy of the letter to the tenant warning of the intention to apply for a date to be fixed;
- a copy of the tenant's reply, if any, and copies of any subsequent correspondence;
- a statement of the rent account showing the arrears that have accrued since the first failure to pay in accordance with the order

38 PD 55A para 10.4.
39 Where the procedure is adapted to anti-social behaviour cases, Sedley LJ in *Wandsworth LBC v Whibley* [2008] EWCA Civ 1259, [2009] HLR 26 gave guidance on the content of the tenant's reply to the landlord's notice. It is not sufficient for the tenant to issue a bare denial of a breach. The court will expect a detailed response in order that it may establish whether there is a real triable issue concerning the alleged breach. Since the tenant has already, by definition, breached the terms of the agreement, he or she will need to have a cogent answer once there is prima facie evidence of repetition.

or the arrears that have accrued during the period of two years immediately preceding the date of the application notice, where the first such failure to pay occurs more than two years before that date.[40]

28.30 The landlord's application is then referred to a district judge, who will usually make a decision on the papers, ie, without a hearing, by fixing the date for possession as the next working day. If the tenant has responded to the landlord's notice, explaining his or her difficulties, it is likely that the district judge will wish to refer the application to a hearing at which the tenant's circumstances may be fully considered. If the judge considers that a hearing is necessary, a date should be set for the application to be heard and the tenant should be served with the application notice and supporting evidence.

28.31 Where a date for possession is fixed and expires, the landlord can request the court to issue a warrant of possession and the court bailiff will set a date for eviction. At all times, the court retains its wide discretion under RA 1977 s100, HA 1985 s85(2) and HA 1988 s9(2). The tenant may still apply, at any time up to the date of eviction, to vary the possession order or to stay or suspend the warrant of possession on terms.

Suspended possession orders

28.32 The 'suspended possession order' is something of a misnomer, since what is suspended under the standard form of the order is not possession itself, but enforcement of the order. However, the term is in common use and will be used here. Under the standard court form of suspended possession order, which has been in use since October 2001 (form N28), a date is fixed for possession, but the order provides that:

> ... this order is not to be enforced so long as the defendant pays the claimant the rent arrears and the amount for use and occupation [and costs] totalling £.... by the payments set out below in addition to the current rent.

28.33 In the event of a breach of the order, the landlord may apply for a warrant of possession.[41] In that event, the tenant will need to apply to stay or suspend the warrant, if eviction is to be averted. In the same notice of application, the tenant may also apply for a variation of the terms of the possession order, if appropriate (see para 31.21). There

40 PD 55A para 10.7.
41 For more detailed consideration of the enforcement process, see para 31.36.

is no requirement for the landlord to give notice to the tenant of its intention to apply for a warrant, although the court is likely to disapprove of a landlord applying for a warrant following a single missed payment or without warning the tenant about the default and inviting him or her to make up the missing payment(s). In county court proceedings,[42] the only notice which the tenant receives is notice of the date of eviction itself, in court form N54 delivered in advance of the eviction date by the bailiff. Use of this form is not mandatory under the Civil Procedure Rules, but it is clearly necessary to alert the tenant to the imminence of eviction. The N54 notice also notifies the tenant of his or her right to apply to the court to vary the possession order or to seek a suspension of the warrant (where the order is based on discretionary grounds). In *Southwark LBC v St Brice*,[43] Kennedy LJ said:

> It is important that so far as possible tenants should receive such notice in time to enable them to take advice and, if so advised, bring the matter back to the court before the date fixed for eviction.

Postponed or suspended?

28.34 The N28A form of postponed possession order was introduced in July 2006 in response to an invitation issued to judges by the Court of Appeal in *Bristol City Council v Hassan*[44] to use a two-stage order as a means of avoiding the creation of 'blameless tolerated trespassers', which at that time was the effect of breach of a suspended possession order made in form N28 following the expiry of the possession date. In that case, Brooke LJ stated that the form of the order used was a matter of discretion for the judge.

28.35 Although 'tolerated trespassers' are no longer a common phenomenon, there is still a place for the postponed possession order, where the court has decided to make a conditional order.[45] Postponed orders are not favoured by landlords (or by mortgagees), since they require a further application to the court. It is suggested that the postponed order is in many cases preferable to a suspended order. It is of course a matter for the discretion of the court in the circumstances of each case.[46] If a tenant has a poor record of payment, and has not

---

42 For the position in relation to enforcement in the High Court, see para 31.46.
43 [2001] EWCA Civ 1138, [2002] HLR 26.
44 [2006] EWCA Civ 656, [2006] HLR 31.
45 For a full discussion of this issue, see Robert Latham, 'Conditional possession orders after *Knowsley Housing Trust v White*' March 2009 *Legal Action* 27.
46 *Bristol City Council v Hassan* [2006] EWCA Civ 656, [2006] HLR 31.

kept to agreements to pay off arrears, the court is likely to make a suspended order in form N28. In other cases, the postponed possession order may be the more reasonable and proportionate method of disposal. A postponed order enables the court to supervise the process of enforcement in a way which does not happen with a suspended possession order, where the landlord only has to ask the court to issue a warrant of possession as an administrative act. The use of postponed orders should also result in a reduction in the number of last-minute applications to suspend warrants.

28.36   In *Leicester City Council v Aldwinckle*,[47] in which a suspended possession order was executed while the tenant was away from her flat for health reasons, Leggatt LJ unfavourably contrasted the county court procedure with that in the High Court, in which notice of the landlord's decision to apply for a writ of possession to execute an order was required to be given to the tenant and the court's permission was required for enforcement. He expressed the view that the county court procedure should be brought into line with that of the High Court. The requirement under a postponed possession order for the landlord to apply to fix a date enables the court to exercise judicial scrutiny of the process, and to take account of any changes in the tenant's circumstances since the date of the order. In some cases, the landlord may be applying for a warrant some time after the original possession order was made, and the tenant's circumstances may be very different from before. Yet, where the possession order is suspended, there is no opportunity for the court to examine whether it is still reasonable and proportionate for the landlord to proceed to eviction, other than on the tenant's application for a suspension of the warrant. Depending on the circumstances, the court may consider that, in the event of a breach of a conditional order, it should take a further look at the situation before a warrant of possession is issued.[48]

28.37   Form N28A (postponed possession order) contains a provision that 'this order shall cease to be enforceable when the total judgment debt is satisfied'. Once the tenant has paid off the arrears and any costs in full, the order will cease to have effect and it will be necessary for the landlord to issue fresh proceedings if the tenant falls into arrears again. Form N28 (suspended possession order) does not

---

47 [1992] 24 HLR 40.
48 In *Southwark LBC v St Brice* [2001] EWCA Civ 1138, [2002] HLR 26, the Court of Appeal nevertheless held that the existing procedure, whereby a warrant of possession can be obtained as an administrative act is not incompatible with HRA 1998 Sch 1 Articles 6, 8 and 14. See further para 31.44.

contain such a provision. The court may be asked to add a clause of this kind to the standard order. Alternatively, once the money judgment under a suspended order has been satisfied, it will be necessary at that time to ask the court to discharge the order (see para 31.34), failing which it may be re-activated if the tenant later falls into new arrears. In *Zinda v Bank of Scotland*,[49] the court had made a suspended possession order on the basis that the borrower should pay a monthly sum of £96.02 towards the mortgage arrears in addition to the contractual monthly instalments (CMIs). Several years after the order was made, the Bank agreed to consolidate the arrears. As a result, the arrears were cleared, but the borrower now had to pay a higher CMI. He fell into arrears again and the Bank applied for a warrant of possession. The Court of Appeal rejected the borrower's argument that the suspended possession order had ceased to be enforceable once the arrears had been consolidated. The terms of the order still required the CMI to be paid, and the Bank was therefore entitled to apply for a warrant on the first occasion that the borrower defaulted in payment of the revised CMI. It was not necessary for the Bank to issue fresh possession proceedings. In the same way, a suspended possession order in respect of rented property would continue in effect after the tenant had cleared the rent arrears[50] since it would continue to apply to the payment of ongoing current rent, unless the tenant makes a successful application to the court to discharge the order. If more than six years have elapsed since the possession order was made, it cannot be enforced without the permission of the Court.[51]

28.38   Where a tenancy which is subject to a postponed or suspended possession order is transferred from one spouse or civil partner to another under the Family Law Act 1996 Sch 7 (formerly the Matrimonial Homes Act 1983 Sch 1 para 3(1)), the new tenant will take the tenancy under the terms of the postponed or suspended order. However, in the event of a subsequent breach of those terms, it has been held that the landlord would not be entitled to enforce that order against the new tenant.[52] If landlords wish to evict in such circumstances, they would have to bring fresh proceedings against the new tenant.

---

49 [2011] EWCA Civ 706, [2011] HLR 40.
50 Unless the order contained a 'proleptic' provision to the effect that it would be discharged automatically on full payment of the arrears and costs: see para 31.32.
51 See para 31.41.
52 *Church Commissioners v Al-Emarah* [1996] 3 WLR 633, (1997) 29 HLR 351, CA.

28.39   Spouses and civil partners of tenants (who are not joint tenants) have the same rights as tenants themselves to seek the suspension or postponement of orders in possession proceedings, provided that they are still living in the premises.[53] These rights continue to subsist until the making of a decree absolute of divorce or until dissolution of a civil partnership.

28.40   Although in many cases a suspended or postponed possession order will be a favourable outcome for the tenant, it should be remembered that it is still a possession order and that if a tenant subsequently fails to comply with its conditions it can be difficult to argue that those conditions were not reasonable at the time they were imposed. In all circumstances where a tenant or borrower is making an offer of payment, it is essential to ensure that he or she will be able to afford to make any proposed payments before reaching an agreement for payment of arrears by a particular amount.

Conditional orders in anti-social behaviour cases

28.41   The templates in court forms N28 and N28A are designed specifically for rent arrears cases. There are no templates for conditional possession orders based on the grounds of nuisance or anti-social behaviour. Such orders may follow a similar pattern, being based either on the postponement of the date for possession (whereby a further application to the court is needed to fix the date for possession) or on the suspension of enforcement. In both cases the nature of the conditions will be that the tenant must abide by the terms of the tenancy and refrain from acts of a certain kind.

28.42   There is conflicting judicial guidance on which of these options is the more appropriate to nuisance cases. In *Knowsley Housing Trust v McMullen*,[54] a case concering a suspended possession order, the Court of Appeal held that in the particular circumstances of that case (in which the tenant had learning difficulties and the complaints were of nuisance committed by her son) there should be a clause in the order requiring the landlord to apply for permission to issue a warrant. The Court suggested, however, that this course would be appropriate only in exceptional cases. In this case, the defendant's disability rendered her 'peculiarly deserving of the protection of the court'.[55]

53 See Family Law Act 1996 s30(3)and (4) and para 20.11.
54 [2006] EWCA Civ 539, [2006] HLR 43.
55 [2006] EWCA Civ 539, [2006] HLR 43 at para [66].

28.43   In contrast, in *Wandsworth LBC v Whibley*,[56] Sedley LJ approved the approach of adapting the form of postponed possession order (Form N28A) and CPR PD 55A para 10 to cases of nuisance, noting that in rent arrears cases a breach is likely to be a matter of record, while in nuisance cases there is more likely to be a dispute on the facts over whether a breach has occurred:

> In a nuisance case there is obvious good sense in following a similar procedure: if, on being notified of the impending application and invited to respond, the defendant remains silent or puts in a plainly spurious or irrelevant response, an order may properly be made summarily. But if, as is more probable in nuisance cases, an issue is raised which is capable of affecting the court's decision, justice will require the defendant to be given an opportunity to put his or her case. The court will of course be astute not to let merely factitious or obstructive responses impede a summary disposal; but, inconvenient though it will be for the lessor and for a time nightmarish for the neighbours, it is not permissible for a tenant who has a possible tenable answer to lose his or her home unheard.

28.44   In respect of conditional orders based on behaviour, it is suggested that a postponed order with no date fixed for possession should be the norm, since a suspended order enables the landlord to apply for a warrant on the basis of the landlord's own assessment that a breach has occurred. Where allegations of anti-social behaviour are in dispute, or where there are questions about the seriousness of the alleged acts or the degree of culpability, it is arguably essential that the court should have the opportunity to review the matter before the bailiff is instructed to evict. It is, of course, open to the tenant to apply for suspension of the warrant; but it is preferable that the court should be able to consider the issues without the pressure of an imminent eviction date. While landlords may object to postponed orders on the basis that the requirement to apply to fix a possession date introduces a further stage in the process, this must be weighed against the overwhelming importance to the tenant of not losing the roof over his or her head. In the alternative, a suspended order could be made subject to a requirement that a warrant should not issue without the permission of the court.

Consent orders

28.45   It is a well-established principle that landlords and tenants cannot 'contract out' of the statutory protection provided by RA 1977, HA

56 [2008] EWCA Civ 1259, [2009] HLR 26.

1985 or HA 1988.[57] This rule can have important consequences where occupiers with security of tenure decide to compromise possession proceedings by agreeing to a 'consent order'. The court cannot make a 'consent order' against a secure, assured or Rent Act protected tenant unless there is either a concession by express admission on the part of the tenant that Housing Act or Rent Act protection does not apply or, alternatively, it is established that a ground for possession exists and, if appropriate, that it is reasonable to make an order for possession.[58] Any order made without such a concession or without the establishment of a ground for possession and consideration of reasonableness, is a nullity and can be challenged by judicial review, even if both parties were legally represented and consented to it.[59] It may well be that a 'consent order' could be set aside at a later date if it were established that a concession that statutory protection did not apply was not made bona fide.[60] It will often be acceptable, however, where the terms of an order have been agreed, to include a recital in the order whereby the tenant admits the existence of a ground for possession and that it is reasonable for a possession order to be made.

28.46   In *R v Bloomsbury and Marylebone County Court ex p Blackburne*,[61] possession proceedings based on rent arrears were settled on the basis that the tenant would consent to a possession order in return for payment of £11,000 plus costs. Both parties were legally represented. Subsequently, the tenant changed his mind and successfully applied for judicial review to quash the possession order.

28.47   In *Plaschkes v Jones*,[62] an unrepresented tenant went to court intending to defend possession proceedings. However, at court he agreed to a possession order, being under the impression that he would be able to obtain a council house. He later found that he was not able to get a council house and the Court of Appeal allowed his

---

57 *Barton v Fincham* [1921] 2 KB 291 and *Mouat-Balthasar v Murphy* [1967] 1 QB 344, [1946] 2 All ER 595.

58 *R v Bloomsbury and Marylebone County Court ex p Blackburne* (1985) 275 EG 1273, CA; *R v Newcastle upon Tyne County Court ex p Thompson* (1988) 20 HLR 430, QBD; *Wandsworth LBC v Fadayomi* [1987] 1 WLR 1473, (1987) 19 HLR 512, CA; *Hounslow LBC v McBride* (1999) 31 HLR 143, CA (see para 28.48 below) and *R v Birmingham CC ex p Foley* March 2001 *Legal Action* 29, QBD.

59 *R v Bloomsbury and Marylebone County Court ex p Blackburne* (1985) 275 EG 1273, CA.

60 See, eg, Atkins LJ's references to bona fides in *Barton v Fincham* [1921] 2 KB 291.

61 (1985) 275 EG 1273, CA.

62 (1982) 9 HLR 110.

subsequent appeal because the county court had not considered the question of reasonableness.

28.48　　In *Hounslow LBC v McBride*,[63] a claim against a secure tenant based on non-payment of rent and serious criminal conduct causing nuisance or annoyance, the parties agreed that a suspended possession order should be made. At a brief hearing lasting no more than five minutes which was attended by solicitors, but not by the defendant, the district judge made the order sought. Before making the order she checked that the figure for the arrears was agreed and that the defendant understood the implications of the order. However, there was no evidence or concession on the part of the tenant. In a later affidavit it was stated that both solicitors 'assumed that the district judge would simply rubber stamp the order'. Later, the council alleged that the defendant had broken the conditions of the suspended order and applied for a warrant of possession. Both the possession order and the warrant were set aside. Simon Brown LJ said that 'an order such as this is not in law capable of being consented to unless the terms of the Act are satisfied'. A distinction has to be drawn between a form of order which contains an admission about those matters on which the jurisdiction to make the order rests (for example, reasonableness) and an order, such as this one, which did not.

28.49　　However, in *R v Worthing BC ex p Bruce*,[64] an occupier unsuccessfully appealed against the refusal of his application for judicial review of the making of a consent order in possession proceedings. He had compromised his claim for a declaration and the council's counterclaim for possession when the action was part heard on terms that he would withdraw a 'right to buy' claim and give up possession. The Court of Appeal held that the implied admission in the consent order, that the tenant was not a secure tenant, taken together with the fact that the order was made by the judge after hearing at least some evidence, enabled the order to stand.

63　(1999) 31 HLR 143, CA.

64　[1994] 24 EG 149, (1994) 26 HLR 223, CA. See also *Morris v Barnet LBC* December 1995 *Legal Action* 18, CA.

CHAPTER 29

Mesne profits and damages for trespass

29.1   If someone is in wrongful occupation of land, the owner of that land is entitled to damages. These may be referred to as damages for trespass or for 'use and occupation', or, if the occupier is a former tenant whose tenancy has been terminated, as mesne profits. However, where the occupier is a subtenant or a licensee of a tenant, there can be no liability for mesne profits or damages for use and occupation until the (head) tenancy has been determined. Until that time the tenant is liable to the landlord for rent. It is only after the tenancy has been terminated that any sub-occupier can become liable for damages for use and occupation.[1]

29.2   It has always been standard practice for landlords to claim mesne profits against former tenants from the date of termination of the tenancy until possession is given up. They are generally assessed as a lump sum figure for the period from termination of the tenancy until the date of the possession hearing and then as a daily sum until possession is actually delivered up. Secure, assured and Rent Act regulated tenancies do not end until the tenant is actually evicted,[2] or leaves voluntarily at the end of a fixed term or following a surrender or on the expiry of a tenant's notice to quit, so that rent, rather than mesne profits, is usually payable until the tenant's departure.[3]

---

1 *Braintree DC v Vincent* [2004] EWCA Civ 415. So, if a suspended possession order or a postponed possession order is made, in view of *Knowsley Housing Trust v White* [2008] UKHL 70, [2009] 1 AC 636 and Housing and Regeneration Act 2008 Sch 11, the order should refer to 'rent at the daily rate of £X', rather than 'mesne profits at the daily rate of £X'.
2 See para 28.16.
3 In view of *Knowsley Housing Trust v White* [2008] UKHL 70, [2009] 1 AC 636 and the Housing and Regeneration Act 2008 Sch 11, orders should now refer to 'rent at the daily rate of £X', rather than 'mesne profits at the daily rate of £X'.

29.3   A claim for damages for use and occupation can be included in a possession claim against trespassers.[4]

29.4   The owner of land may either claim for the loss which has been suffered or for the value of the benefit which the occupier has received.[5] If the owner is claiming for the loss suffered, damages or mesne profits are calculated according to the 'fair value of the premises'. In the absence of special circumstances, this may be assessed according to the ordinary letting value,[6] ie the market value. In relation to mesne profits, the rent paid by the tenant before the tenancy was terminated may be the best evidence of this. It is not necessary for landowners to prove that they would have re-let the premises if the defendant had not been in occupation.[7]

29.5   The position may be more complicated if the former rent does not represent a fair value for the premises. In those circumstances, the open market value may not be the appropriate rate for mesne profits where there are special circumstances, for example, where the property is not usually let on the open market.[8]

4 See para 23.13.
5 *Ministry of Defence v Thompson* [1993] 40 EG 148, (1993) 25 HLR 552, CA and *Ministry of Defence v Ashman* (1993) 66 P&CR 195, (1993) 25 HLR 513, CA.
6 *Swordheath Properties v Tabet* [1979] 1 WLR 285, [1979] 1 All ER 240.
7 *Swordheath Properties v Tabet* [1979] 1 WLR 285, [1979] 1 All ER 240, CA and *Viscount Chelsea v Hutchinson* (1996) 28 HLR 17, [1994] 43 EG 153, CA. See also *Shi v Jiangsu Native Produce Import & Export Corporation* [2009] EWCA Civ 1582, in which it was held that mesne profits should have been assessed in a sum representing the loss suffered by the landowner as a result of being deprived of vacant possession of the property.
8 See, eg *Ministry of Defence v Ashman* (1993) 66 P&CR 195, (1993) 25 HLR 513, CA, where the defendants would probably never have occupied the premises if they had had to pay the full market rent and the value to the wife (after her husband had left) was no more than she would have had to pay for suitable local authority housing if she could have been immediately rehoused.

Costs

Costs in possession claims

30.1   In general, and with the important exception of mortgage possession claims, the usual rules about costs in the Civil Procedure Rules
(CPR) apply to possession claims. This chapter accordingly considers rules relating to costs in landlord and tenant possession claims,
but not the costs in mortgage possession claims – for those see para
37.80.[1]

30.2   The starting point is CPR 44.2 which states:

(1) The court has discretion as to –
  (a) whether costs are payable by one party to another;
  (b) the amount of those costs; and
  (c) when they are to be paid.
(2) If the court decides to make an order about costs –
  (a) the general rule is that the unsuccessful party will be ordered
  to pay the costs of the successful party; but
  (b) the court may make a different order.

So, if a defendant tenant has defeated a landlord's claim, the tenant
should always seek an order that the landlord pays the costs. In deciding about costs, the court must have regard to all the circumstances,
including the conduct of the parties, whether a party has succeeded
on part of his or her case, even if he or she has not been totally successful, and any payment into court or offer.[2]

30.3   'Conduct' includes conduct before the issue of proceedings, as
well as conduct during the case. For example, failure to send a letter
before action, which would have informed the tenant about the landlord's concerns and enabled him or her to respond without the need
for litigation, may justify refusing an award of costs to the landlord.[3]

30.4   A pre-CPR example of circumstances in which a successful party
was ordered to pay the losing party's costs occurred in *Ottway v Jones*.[4]
The claimant landlord established grounds for possession based on
nuisance and annoyance but failed to satisfy the court that it was
reasonable to make an order for possession, with the result that judgment on the claim was entered for the defendant. However, in view
of the finding of nuisance, the judge held that the successful defendant should pay the plaintiff's costs and this order was not disturbed

---

1   Detailed consideration of the law of costs is outside the scope of this book. See
CPR Parts 44 to 48 and the *Practice Direction relating to Costs*.
2   CPR 44.2(4).
3   *Brent LBC v Aniedobe* January 2000 *Legal Action* 25, CA. See too the *Pre-action
Protocol for possession claims by social landlords* (see para 3.77 and appendix E).
4   [1955] 1 WLR 706, [1955] 2 All ER 585.

by the Court of Appeal. There is no reason why that case would be decided any differently under the CPR.

30.5   Costs may be awarded on either the standard basis or on the indemnity basis.[5] Where costs are awarded on the *standard* basis, the court should allow only those costs which are reasonable and proportionate to the matters in issue. Any doubt which the court may have about whether costs have been reasonably incurred or are reasonable and proportionate in amount should be resolved in favour of the paying party. Where costs are assessed on the *indemnity* basis, the court need be satisfied only that they are reasonable. Issues of proportionality do not apply. Any doubt should be resolved in favour of the receiving party.[6]

30.6   When awarding costs the court may order detailed or summary assessment. If *detailed* assessment is ordered, the receiving party's solicitor (or costs draughtsman) prepares a detailed bill which is served on the paying party. If the costs are disputed and agreement is not reached, a detailed assessment hearing should be listed for a costs judge to decide the amount of costs.

30.7   If *summary assessment* is ordered, the judge who has heard the case immediately assesses costs, by considering the Statement of Costs in Form N260 that the receiving party's solicitor should have served at least 24 hours before the hearing. Summary assessment is the norm for fast-track trials and for other hearings lasting not more than a day.[7] There are fixed advocacy costs in fast-track trials, depending on the value of the claim.[8] Where, in possession proceedings, there is no claim for payment of money, fast track advocacy costs are currently fixed at £690 unless the court orders otherwise.[9] In addition to the advocacy costs, the court may award an additional sum (currently £345) in respect of a legal representative attending the trial if the court considers that it was necessary for that person to attend to assist the advocate.[10] Summary assessment of costs is not possible where the receiving party is publicly funded.[11] It is common

---

5 CPR 44.3.

6 CPR 44.3.

7 PD 44 para 9.2.

8 CPR 45.38. Currently £485 for claims up to £3,000; £690 for claims of more than £3,000 but not more than £10,000; £1,035 for claims of more than £10,000 but less than £15,000; and £1,650 for claims in excess of £15,000, where the claim was issued after 6 April 2009.

9 CPR 45.38(4).

10 CPR 45.39(2).

11 PD 44 para 9.8.

for judges when making a possession order against a defendant who is publicly funded, either to make no order for costs or to make an order for costs but to provide that the order should not be enforced until such time as a determination of the defendant's liability has been made in accordance with Legal Aid, Sentencing and Punishment of Offenders Act 2012 (LASPO) s26 which restricts the court's powers to make a costs order against a publicly funded litigant.

Fixed costs

30.8 Fixed costs apply to certain types of possession claims unless the court orders otherwise. CPR 45.1 provides that fixed costs apply where:

- the defendant gives up possession and pays the amount claimed (if any) and the fixed commencement costs (CPR 45.1(2)(c));
- one of the grounds for possession is arrears of rent, the court gave a fixed date for hearing, a possession order is made (whether suspended or not) and the defendant has either failed to deliver a defence or the defence is limited to specifying proposals for payment of arrears (CPR 45.1(2)(d));
- the claim is brought under the accelerated procedure (CPR Part 55 section 2) against an assured shorthold tenant, a possession order is made and the defendant has neither delivered a defence nor otherwise denied liability (CPR 45.1(2)(e)); or
- the claim is a demotion claim under section 3 of CPR Part 65 or a demotion claim is made in the same claim form in which a claim for possession is made under CPR Part 55 and that demotion claim is successful (CPR 45.1(2)(f)).

30.9 The court has power to depart from fixed costs although the presumption is that fixed costs will apply.[12] The amounts of fixed costs are set out in CPR 45.5 Table 3. They are presently as follows:

---

12 CPR 45.1.

TABLE 3		
Fixed costs on commencement of a claim for the recovery of land or a demotion claim		
Where the claim form is served by the court or by any method other than personal service by the claimant	Where – • the claim form is served personally by the claimant; and • there is only one defendant	Where there is more than one defendant, for each additional defendant personally served at separate addresses by the claimant
£69.50	£77.00	£15.00

Costs on entry of judgment in a claim for the recovery of land or a demotion claim

45.6(1)Where –

    (a) the claimant has claimed fixed commencement costs under rule 45.5; and

    (b) judgment is entered in a claim to which rule 45.1(2)(d) or (f) applies, the amount to be included in the judgment for the claimant's solicitor's charges is the total of –

        (i) the fixed commencement costs; and

        (ii) the sum of £57.25.[13]

  (2)Where an order for possession is made in a claim to which rule 45.1(2)(e) applies, the amount allowed for the claimant's solicitor's charges for preparing and filing –

    (a) the claim form;

    (b) the documents that accompany the claim form; and

    (c) the request for possession,

  is £79.50.

Proceedings begun in the High Court

30.11   If proceedings are issued in the High Court against a Rent Act protected tenant, a Housing Act assured tenant or a Housing Act secure tenant, a landlord is not entitled to recover any costs.[14]

---

13 The total (in 2016) is generally £481.75, ie issue fee of £355(or £325 if PCOL is used) plus costs on issue of £69.50 and £57.25 on judgment.

14 RA 1977 s141, HA 1985 s110 and HA 1988 s40.

Small claims track cases

30.12   It is rare for possession claims to be allocated to the small claims track.[15] However, if a possession claim is allocated to the small claims track, the fast track costs regime applies but the trial costs are in the discretion of the judge and should not exceed the amount of fast track costs allowable in CPR 46.2 if the value were up to £3,000, ie currently £485.[16]

---

15 See para 21.66.
16 CPR 55.9(3).

CHAPTER 31

After the possession order

Appeals

31.1   If a possession order is made or refused by a district judge, an appeal lies to a circuit judge.[1] Permission to appeal is required. If permission is refused by the district judge, a further application for permission to appeal can be made to a circuit judge. Permission to appeal should be given only where the appeal has a real prospect of success or there is some other compelling reason why the appeal should be heard.[2] The Appellant's Notice[3] attaching grounds of appeal must be filed within 21 days of the date on which the order appealed against was made, unless the court extends or shortens that period.[4]

31.2   Permission to appeal to a High Court judge against an order of a circuit judge should be sought from the trial judge. If permission is refused by the trial judge, it may be sought from a High Court judge. However, if a possession order is made in a claim allocated to the multi-track, an appeal will go directly to the Court of Appeal.[5] Permission for such an appeal may be given by the trial judge or the Court of Appeal.

31.3   There is no right of appeal on any question of fact if the court could grant possession only on being satisfied that it was reasonable to do so.[6] However, this does not exclude, in a proper case, the possibility of an appeal against a finding of reasonableness.[7] But, as indicated in the text of this book relating to each of the main statutory schemes for security of tenure, it is generally difficult to overturn any order where the issue is whether it was reasonable to award possession to the claimant.

31.4   Appeals should be allowed only where the decision of the lower court was 'wrong' or was unjust because of a serious procedural or other irregularity in the proceedings in the lower court'.[8] Appeals are therefore limited to a review of the decision of the lower court,

---

1   See generally CPR Part 52. Practice Direction (PD) 52B deals with the procedure for appeals in the county court and High Court. PD 52C deals with appeals to the Court of Appeal.
2   CPR 52.3(6).
3   Court form N161.
4   CPR 52.4(2).
5   PD 52A para 3.5.
6   County Courts Act 1984 s77(6). For the basis of the court's discretion, see RA 1977 s98(1), HA 1985 s84(2)(a) and HA 1988 s7 as it applies to grounds 9–17.
7   *Gallagher v Castle Vale Housing Action Trust* [2001] EWCA Civ 944, (2001) 33 HLR 72 and *Hounslow LBC v McBride* (1999) 31 HLR 143, CA.
8   CPR 52.11(3).

although exceptionally the appeal court may consider that in the circumstances of an individual appeal it would be in the interests of justice to hold a re-hearing.[9]

31.5   Pending an appeal, an application should be made for a stay of the order for possession, because the mere lodging of an appeal does not act as a stay.[10] If a stay is refused by the judge whose decision is being appealed, application for a stay may be made to the appeal judge or the appeal court.

31.6   Different provisions apply to second appeals – for example, against a High Court judge's dismissal of an appeal from a circuit judge. They are outside the scope of this book: reference should be made to Access to Justice Act 1999 s55 and CPR 52.13.

Setting aside the possession order

31.7   The circumstances in which a party who fails to attend a trial may apply to set aside an order are set out in CPR 39.3(3)–(5):

> (3) Where a party does not attend and the court gives judgment or makes an order against him, the party who failed to attend may apply for the judgment or order to be set aside.
> (4) An application made under ... paragraph (3) must be supported by evidence.
> (5) Where an application is made under paragraph ... (3) by a party who failed to attend the trial, the court may grant the application only if the applicant –
>   (a) acted promptly when he found out that the court had exercised its power to strike out or to enter judgment or make an order against him;
>   (b) had a good reason for not attending trial; and
>   (c) has a reasonable prospect of success at the trial.

31.8   There has been some divergence of judicial opinion as to whether the court's powers to set aside an order are limited to the conditions in CPR 39.3(5), or whether the court has a more general discretion based on its case management powers in CPR Part 3. In *Forcelux Ltd v Binnie*,[11] a long leaseholder was away from his flat when proceedings for forfeiture took place. He did not receive notification of the hearing at which a possession order was made and the order was executed in his

---

9 See CPR 52.11(1)(b) and *Ealing LBC v Richardson* [2005] EWCA Civ 1798, [2006] HLR 13.
10 CPR 52.7.
11 [2009] EWCA Civ 854, [2010] HLR 20.

absence. Some four months after first becoming aware of the order, the leaseholder applied to set aside the possession order and for relief from forfeiture. The landlord contended that CPR 39.3 governed the application to set aside the order, and that the leaseholder could not succeed because he had not acted promptly when he discovered that an order had been made against him. The Court of Appeal held that CPR 39.3 applies where the hearing in question is a 'trial'. A hearing in a busy undefended possession list could not be considered a trial, even if it resulted in a possession order being made. However, the court did have jurisdiction to deal with the matter under its general management powers in CPR Part 3, and in particular CPR 3.1(2)(m), under which the court may:

> ... take any other step or make any other order for the purpose of managing the case and furthering the overriding objective.

On the facts of the case, it was appropriate to set aside the possession order and grant relief from forfeiture.

31.9   A different approach was subsequently taken in *Hackney LBC v Findlay*[12] in which the council landlord obtained an outright order for possession against a secure tenant in his absence, on the basis of rent arrears. Following his eviction, the defendant applied to set aside the order and be readmitted to the property. The district judge granted the application and set aside the possession order. The Council's appeal to the circuit judge was dismissed. Both judges dealt with the case under CPR 3.1 rather than CPR 39.3, and did not consider whether the defendant had a good reason for not attending the hearing. The Court of Appeal held that the decision in *Forcelux v Binnie* did not mean that a court hearing an application to set aside a possession order should disregard the requirements of CPR 39.3(5). The correct approach was for the court to consider the factors listed in both CPR 39.3(5) and CPR 3.9 (relief from sanctions).[13] In the absence of unusual and compelling circumstances, the provisions of CPR 39.3(5) should take precedence. The case was remitted to a district judge for a finding of fact to be made as to whether the defendant had a good reason for not attending the hearing at which the possession order was made.

31.10   Further guidance has been given by the Court of Appeal in *Bank of Scotland plc v Pereira*[14] both as to the correct approach to applications

---

12 [2011] EWCA Civ 8, [2011] HLR 15.

13 CPR 3.9 has been substantially amended since this judgment by the Civil Procedure (Amendment) Rules 2013 SI No 262.

14 [2011] EWCA Civ 241, [2011] HLR 26.

to set aside possession orders and as to whether the appropriate course of action is to apply to set aside an order or to appeal. The case concerned a 'sale and rent back' transaction, in which the purchaser Ms Pereira failed to make mortgage payments and the bank sought possession against the tenants and former owners. At the trial, which Ms Pereira did not attend, an order was made whereby the tenants were permitted to re-register themselves as proprietors at the Land Registry, subject to the bank's mortgage. Ms Pereira's application under CPR 39.3 to set aside the order was dismissed, on the grounds that she had failed to act promptly and did not have a good reason for not attending trial, since she had clearly been aware of the hearing date and of the judgment. Ms Pereira appealed to the Court of Appeal against both the order made at trial and the later decision refusing her application to set aside that order. The appeal was dismissed. The judge had been right to dismiss the application to set aside the order made at trial. The evidence showed that the appellant had been aware of that hearing and of its outcome. Nor was there any basis for granting permission to appeal out of time against the original order.

31.11   The Court of Appeal identified certain principles which it considered would apply to the vast majority of cases. Where a party seeks to set aside an order on the grounds that he or she did not attend the trial, he or she should usually proceed under CPR 39.3. Earlier case-law authorities on setting aside possession orders under CPR 39.3 are therefore still relevant.[15] If, on the other hand, a party could not demonstrate a good reason for not attending the trial and/or that he or she made his or her CPR 39.3 application promptly, but it was clear that he or she had grounds to appeal against the judge's decision, he or she was still entitled to seek permission to appeal and it should not matter whether or not he or she was present at trial. In practice, however, a party who did not attend the trial is likely to face greater difficulties in pursuing an appeal, not only because the appeal is likely to be brought out of time but also because evidence that was not raised at trial cannot be adduced on appeal unless the court gives permission.[16]

31.12   The court also stated that a party who has made a CPR 39.3 application which failed, on the basis that he had no prospect of success at

15 *Governors of Peabody Donation Fund v Hay* (1987) 19 HLR 145, CA; *Southwark LBC v Joseph* March 2000 *Legal Action* 29 and *Lewisham LBC v Gurbuz* [2003] EWHC 2078 (Ch).

16 See CPR 52.11(2) and the three-part test for deciding whether a party should be granted permission to adduce fresh evidence following trial which was laid down in *Ladd v Marshall* [1954] 1 WLR 1489, CA (see para 31.19).

trial, should not normally be permitted to bring an appeal against the original decision but should appeal the decision made on the CPR 39.3 application. While much would depend on the factual context, the appellate court would nevertheless take a great deal of persuading to depart from the conclusion reached by the judge hearing the application under CPR 39.3.

31.13   An application to set aside a possession order should be made on Form N244. The applicant must either give all necessary factual material in paragraph 10 of the application notice (continuing on a separate sheet if necessary) or prepare a separate witness statement. The statement should: give the precise reason why he or she did not attend the court hearing, attaching any evidence of the reason, such as a medical note; give the date on which he or she became aware of the order; and explain why, if the court which made the order had known the full circumstances (including the prospect of any new evidence or later developments which might have been anticipated at that time), the outcome is likely to have been different. Every effort should be made, by way of witness statements and in submissions, to relate the circumstances of the case to the overriding objective in CPR 1 and to demonstrate how setting the possession order aside would promote the purpose of a just resolution.

31.14   The mere fact that an application has been made to set aside a possession order or to suspend its operation does not automatically prevent a court from enforcing a warrant for possession. In some courts, bailiffs may agree not to evict if an application to set aside or suspend a possession order has been made, although as a matter of law a landlord may insist on the execution of a warrant unless a judge has ordered a stay. In the absence of clear written confirmation from the landlord or the court that a warrant will not be executed, tenants should apply to stay the warrant if eviction is likely to take place before the hearing of the application to set aside or suspend the order. CPR 3.1(2)(f) gives the court jurisdiction to stay execution. In addition, County Courts Act 1984 s88 provides that:

> If at any time it appears to the satisfaction of the court that any party to any proceedings is unable from any cause to pay any sum recovered against him ... or any instalment of such a sum, the court may, in its discretion, stay any execution issued in the proceedings for such time and on such terms as the court thinks fit, and so from time to time until it appears that the cause of inability has ceased.

Applications to set aside possession orders can be made even after execution has resulted in the eviction of the tenant, provided that they are made promptly.[17]

31.15   Non-service of the claim form is a ground for setting aside any possession order.[18] Posting a document to the tenant's 'usual or last known residence'[19] is good service, even if the tenant does not receive it. In *Nelson v Clearsprings (Management) Limited,*[20] a case decided under CPR 39.3 (see para 31.7), as a result of the landlord's error in completing the claim form, the proceedings were posted to the property next door to the defendant's residence. The Court of Appeal held that, where a defendant had not been served with the claim form and had no knowledge of the proceedings, he or she would usually be entitled as of right to an order setting aside the judgment and for the costs of the application, provided that he or she had acted without undue delay on becoming aware of the judgment. On the other hand, if a claimant is served with an application to set aside a judgment in these circumstances, and believes that he can show that the defendant has no real prospect of successfully defending the claim, then he may apply to the court for an order dispensing with service.

31.16   In possession proceedings against secure tenants, evidence that a local authority has failed to credit housing benefit and that, if this had been done, arrears would have been significantly lower at the time when the possession order was made should give good grounds for applying to set aside a possession order. Non-compliance by social landlords with the *Pre-action Protocol for possession claims by social landlords* will also provide a basis for the argument that the defendant would have had a reasonable prospect of success at the hearing.

31.17   An application to set aside a possession order does not operate automatically as a stay of execution. If a warrant is likely to be executed before the hearing of the application to set aside, a separate

---

17 See *Governors of Peabody Donation Fund v Hay* (1987) 19 HLR 145, CA; *Grimshaw v Dunbar* [1953] 1 QB 408, CA; *Ladup Ltd v Siu* (1984) 81 LSG 283, (1983) *Times* 24 November, CA and *Tower Hamlets LBC v Abadie* (1990) 22 HLR 264. In *Ahmed v Mahmood* [2013] EWHC 3176 (QB), a writ of possession was set aside after execution, and even after re-letting, as a result of a false statement made by the landlord in his application for permission to issue the writ. See para 31.66.

18 *White v Weston* [1968] 2 QB 647, [1968] 2 WLR 1459, but see *Akram v Adam* [2004] EWCA Civ 1601, [2005] 1 WLR 2782 and *Hackney LBC v Driscoll* [2003] EWCA Civ 1037, [2004] HLR 7.

19 CPR 6.9(2).

20 [2006] EWCA Civ 1252, [2007] 1 WLR 962.

application for a stay of execution must be made pending the hearing (see paras 31.14 and 31.56).

31.18   If a possession order is set aside, the effect is the same as if the order had never been made.[21] Usually, the court will give directions about the filing of a defence and other procedural matters.

31.19   If the basis for the request to set aside an order is the availability of fresh evidence, the principles enumerated by Lord Denning in *Ladd v Marshall*[22] should be borne in mind:

> In order to justify the reception of fresh evidence for a new trial, three conditions must be fulfilled: first it must be shown that the evidence could not be obtained with reasonable diligence for use at the trial: second the evidence must be such that, if given, it would probably have an important influence on the result of the case, although it need not be decisive: third the evidence must be such as is presumably to be believed, or in other words, it must be apparently credible, although it need not be incontrovertible.

31.20   Where a defendant is applying to set aside a possession order made on a discretionary ground for possession, it will often be advisable to include in the application notice an alternative application to vary the order and/or to suspend the warrant of possession (if one has been issued) on terms, in the event that the 'set aside' application is not successful.

Variation of orders

31.21   If occupiers have no prospect of having a possession order set aside, the court may have power to vary the order (for example, from an outright to a postponed or suspended order) or to suspend execution of the order. Where tenants enjoy statutory security of tenure and a possession order has been made under a discretionary ground, courts have wide powers to stay or suspend execution of any possession order or to postpone the date of possession (see chapter 28). Housing Act (HA) 1985 s85(2) gives such powers in the case of secure tenants, while HA 1988 s9(2) gives similar rights to assured tenants. Rent Act (RA) 1977 s100(2) applies in the case of Rent Act regulated tenants. These powers can be exercised after the making of a possession order 'at any time *before the execution* of such an order', even if an absolute

---

21   See *Governors of Peabody Donation Fund v Hay* (1987) 19 HLR 145, CA and *Tower Hamlets LBC v Abadie* (1990) 22 HLR 264.
22   [1954] 3 All ER 745 at 748, CA.

possession order was originally made[23] or if the original order was made by consent.[24] Such an application

> is not in any way affected or fettered by the reasons given by [the district judge who heard the possession claim] ... on such an application the district judge can take all relevant circumstances into account as they appear at the time of the application. Those will include any medical evidence which is before the court, any evidence as to the defendant's behaviour since the original order and the effect of an immediate order for possession which is not suspended upon the likelihood of the applicant being rehoused under the Housing Act 1996. ... There is a continuing remedy in the county court.[25]

31.22 However, in view of the words 'at any time before the execution of the order' in RA 1977 s100(2), HA 1985 s85(2) and HA 1988 s9(2), such an application cannot be granted if tenants have already given up possession without the need for execution of the order. The words 'at any time before the execution of the order' in section 85(2) have to be read subject to the qualification 'and for so long as execution is required to give effect to that order'.[26] Nor can such an application be used to obtain a complete rehearing of the case.[27] Where the court has made an absolute order under, for example, HA 1988 Sch 2 ground 16 (service tenancy) or ground 17 (tenancy induced by false statement), the power can be used to delay possession so that the tenant has more time to find other accommodation, but it cannot be used to delay indefinitely the date when possession should be given up, even if the circumstances of landlord and tenant have changed.[28]

31.23 It is possible for landlords to apply to 'convert' suspended or postponed possession orders obtained on one ground, such as rent arrears, into absolute or outright possession orders where there have been other breaches of the tenancy such as anti-social behaviour. In

---

23 *Plymouth CC v Hoskin* [2002] EWCA Civ 684; August 2002 *Legal Action* 32; *Payne v Cooper* [1958] 1 QB 174, [1957] 3 WLR 741 and *Ujima Housing Association v Smith* October 2001 *Legal Action* 21, ChD, where, by the time of the application to suspend, the defendant had accepted her legal responsibility for serious damage to a shared kitchen and had offered to pay £150 in compensation. This was a change of circumstances that justified suspension.
24 *Rossiter v Langley* [1925] 1 KB 741.
25 Per Clarke LJ, *Plymouth City Council v Hoskin* [2002] EWCA Civ 684, August 2002 *Legal Action* 32.
26 *Dunn v Bradford MDC, Marston v Leeds City Council* [2002] EWCA Civ 1137, [2003] HLR 15.
27 *Goldthorpe v Bain* [1952] 2 QB 455, [1952] 2 All ER 23 at 25.
28 *Goldthorpe v Bain* [1952] 2 QB 455, [1952] 2 All ER 23.

Manchester City Council v Finn,[29] the Court of Appeal referred to the words 'at any time' in HA 1985 s85(2) and stated that a purposive construction has to be adopted. If a suspended order is still running, liberty to apply to the court is implicit, without the need to start new proceedings for possession. Courts can make a new order, even if the old order has not expired or if the new order would provide for possession to be given up forthwith. On such an application, the court has to bear in mind the guidance given in cases such as *Sheffield City Council v Hopkins*[30] on the exercise of its discretion in such a situation, and should be astute to ensure that tenants are not taken by surprise. However, that does not necessarily extend to insisting that the proceedings be delayed by the equivalent of the extra time that would have been taken if the landlord had had to begin new proceedings. The court can ensure that any notice of application gives the grounds and particulars which put the tenant to no greater disadvantage than envisaged by HA 1985 s84(3). Courts should determine any application to vary a possession order in exactly the same way as they would determine an original claim.

31.24   In view of the references to applications being made at any time before the execution of the possession order and to suspension or postponement for such period or periods as the court thinks fit or just in HA 1988 s9(2), HA 1985 s85(2) or Rent Act 1977 s100(2), it is clear that more than one application under those sections can be made.[31]

31.25   When postponing, suspending or staying possession orders against assured, secure or Rent Act regulated tenants, the court must impose conditions with regard to the repayment of arrears (if any), unless this would cause exceptional hardship or would otherwise be unreasonable.[32] Spouses and civil partners of tenants (who are not themselves joint tenants) have the same rights as the actual tenant to seek the suspension or postponement of orders, provided that they are still living in the premises, and those rights continue to subsist until the making of a decree absolute of divorce or dissolution of civil partnership.[33]

---

29 [2002] EWCA Civ 1998, [2003] HLR 41.
30 [2001] EWCA Civ 1023, [2002] HLR 12. See para 31.62.
31 *Sherrin v Brand* [1956] 1 QB 403, [1956] 1 All ER 194 at 204 per Birkett LJ;
    Vandermolen v Toma (1982–83) 9 HLR 91 and *Ealing LBC v Richardson* [2005]
    EWCA Civ 1798, [2006] HLR 13.
32 See, eg HA 1988 s9(3).
33 See chapter 20.

31.26   The court has a comparable jurisdiction where other statutory safe-guards apply. For example, where a lease has been forfeit on grounds of non-payment of rent, a lessee may apply for relief even after eviction,[34] provided that the application is made within six months of the date on which the landlord recovered possession. The lessee cannot apply for relief following eviction where forfeiture is on grounds of non-payment of service charges or other breach of condition,[35] unless the landlord has not actually re-entered in pursuance of the order[36] or unless the landlord has forfeited by peaceable re-entry.[37] In the case of mortgage borrowers, the Administration of Justice Act 1970 s36 provides that the court may stay or suspend execution or postpone the date for delivery of possession 'at any time before the execution of [the] judgment or order'. That power may be exercised only if 'it appears to the court that ... the mortgagor is likely to be able within a reasonable period to pay any sums due'.[38]

31.27   There is no statutory power to stay, suspend or postpone the making of a possession order where there is no security of tenure.[39]

31.28   The court has only very limited power to suspend or delay the date for giving possession where the order is made under a mandatory ground[40] or where the tenancy is an assured shorthold tenancy[41] or introductory tenancy[42] or demoted tenancy,[43] or where the landlord has declined to renew a flexible tenancy.[44] Where an order for possession is made under a mandatory ground, that ground should be stated on the face of the order. It is not proper for the judge (even the same judge who made the order) to determine at a later date whether the order was made on a mandatory ground or some other

---

34 County Courts Act 1984 s138(9A) (county court; cf *Di Palma v Victoria Square Property Co Ltd* [1986] Ch 150, [1985] 3 WLR 207, CA) or Common Law Procedure Act 1852 s210 (High Court). See para 14.63.

35 *Rogers v Rice* [1892] 2 Ch 170.

36 *Egerton v Jones* [1939] 2 KB 702

37 *Billson v Residential Apartments Ltd* [1992] 1 All ER 141, HL.

38 See *Western Bank Ltd v Schindler* [1977] Ch 1, [1976] 3 WLR 341 and *Cheltenham and Gloucester BS v Norgan* [1996] 1 WLR 343, (1996) 28 HLR 443, CA. See para 34.30.

39 See HA 1980 s89 (see para 28.1).

40 HA 1980 s89. See, eg RA 1977 Sch 15 Cases 11–19, HA 1985 Sch 2 grounds 9–11 and HA 1988 Sch 2 grounds 1–8.

41 HA 1988 s21.

42 HA 1996 s127.

43 HA 1996 s143D and HA 1988 ss20C and 21(5A).

44 HA 1985 s107D.

ground.[45] Accordingly, where an order for possession made on a particular ground fails to state the ground on the face of the order, it should be regarded as having been granted on uncertain grounds, leading to the assumption that the court had retained a discretion. In such circumstances, a court can revisit the exercise of discretion by the previous judge.[46]

31.29   An application to suspend or postpone possession should be made on either Form N244 or N245. It should be supported by evidence. This means that the tenant must either complete paragraph 10 of Form N244 as fully as possible or prepare a witness statement dealing with all matters relied on. Form N245 is headed 'Application for suspension of a warrant and/or variation of an order'. It therefore seems designed for this kind of application. However, the form is framed as a detailed financial statement. While in some cases it may be helpful to set out the defendant's financial circumstances in this way, the form gives no space for a witness statement or for any other evidence. In most cases the defendant will wish to explain to the court why he or she has been unable to comply with the existing order and include other information relevant to his or her personal circumstances. It is suggested that it is generally preferable to use Form N244 for this purpose.

Discharge of possession orders

31.30   HA 1985 s85(4) provides that if the conditions of a stay or of a postponed or suspended order are complied with, the court may, if it thinks fit, discharge or rescind the order for possession.[47] HA 1988 s9(4), in relation to assured tenancies, is in similar terms. Before the House of Lords' judgment in *Knowsley Housing Trust v White*,[48] case-law had insisted that the court's power to discharge or rescind an order was dependent on the defendant's absolute compliance with its terms, so that even a single breach would prevent the court

45 *Diab v Countrywide Rentals 1 plc* October 2001 *Legal Action* 15, (2001) *Independent* 5 November, 10 July 2001, unreported, ChD.

46 *Diab v Countrywide Rentals 1 plc* October 2001 *Legal Action* 15, (2001) *Independent* 5 November, 10 July 2001, unreported, ChD. See also *Capital Prime Plus plc v Wills* (1999) 31 HLR 926, CA.

47 See para 31.33 for the (as yet) unimplemented replacement of HA 1985 s85(4) and HA 1988 s9(4) by the Housing and Regeneration Act 2008.

48 [2008] UKHL 70, [2009] 1 AC 636.

from discharging the order.[49] Yet, under the Rent Act, the courts had accepted more general powers in relation to such orders.[50]

31.31 Since *Knowsley*, it is now clear that the court has a much wider discretion. Lord Neuberger, giving the judgment of the House, stated, in relation to HA 1988 s85:

> The section should be construed, as far as permissible, to confer as much flexibility as possible on the court, and in such a way as to minimise future uncertainty and need for further applications ... The wording of section 85(4), particularly if read with the practicalities in mind, does not preclude the court from effectively committing itself in advance to discharging a suspended order, provided that (a) certain conditions are complied with, and (b) neither the landlord (by applying for a warrant of possession) nor the tenant (by applying under section 85(2)) seeks, in the meantime, reconsideration of the terms of the discharge provision.[51]

31.32 There is nothing to prevent the court from including a 'proleptic' discharge provision (ie, one that anticipates the discharge of the order in the event of compliance) in a postponed or suspended possession order. It is for the court to decide the extent to which compliance with the strict terms of the order will or will not be required for the order to be discharged.[52] In practice, the court is likely to make discharge conditional on full payment of the arrears and any other sums due under the order, even though all payments under the order may not have been made on the due dates. It must follow that, where the order does not provide in advance for its own discharge, a tenant can apply to the court to discharge the order (under HA 1985 s85(4) or HA 1988 s9(4)) when the arrears have been paid off, on the basis that the court can decide that full payment represents compliance with the conditions of the order. Lord Neuberger also drew attention to the scope of the court's general powers of management under CPR Part 3:

> Quite apart from the wording of section 85(4), it appears to me that there is a strong argument for saying that, particularly with the advent of the CPR, it would in any event be open to a court to make an order which includes a provision that, in certain events, the order would

---

49 See *Marshall v Bradford MDC* [2001] EWCA Civ 594, [2002] HLR 428 and *Swindon BC v Aston* [2002] EWCA Civ 1850, [2003] HLR 610.
50 *Sherrin v Brand* [1956] 1 QB 403 and *Payne v Cooper* [1958] 1 QB 174.
51 *Knowsley Housing Trust v White* [2008] UKHL 70, [2009] 1 AC 636 at para [97].
52 Para [107].

automatically be discharged ... In this connection, it appears to me that CPR 3.1(2)(a) may be particuarly in point.[53]

31.33   The Housing and Regeneration Act (H&RA) 2008[54] proposed to replace section 85(4) by the following provision:

> (4) The court may discharge or rescind the order for possession if it thinks it appropriate to do so having had regard to –
> (a) any conditions imposed under subsection (3), and
> (b) the conduct of the tenant in connection with those conditions.

The Act contains a similar re-enactment of HA 1988 s9(4). However, neither of these subsections has yet been brought into force since, following the judgment in *Knowsley Housing Trust v White*, it was considered that the courts already have sufficiently wide powers under the existing statutory provisions.

31.34   The courts' powers to vary or discharge possession orders were critical at a time (prior to 20 May 2009, the date of implementation of H&RA 2008 Sch 11) when tenants who became 'tolerated trespassers' could revive their tenancies by one of these means.[55] Although the tolerated trespasser is no more, and secure and assured tenancies do not end until execution of the possession order, there is still a purpose in seeking to discharge an order. This is because, even if the arrears are cleared, a suspended possession order in form N28 will continue to apply to current rent and may be enforced if new arrears accrue.[56] An alternative to discharge, however, is for an order to contain a provision such as the following:

> This order shall cease to be enforceable when the total judgment debt is satisfied.

31.35   The above clause appears in the standard court form N28A (postponed possession order). It does not appear in the standard form of suspended possession order (court form N28), but the court may be willing to add such a term to the order if requested to do so. CPR 4 provides that 'a form may be varied by the court or a party if the variation is required by the circumstances of a particular case'.

---

53   Para [100].
54   Sch 11 para 3(3); see also Sch 11 para 8(3) in relation to the proposed replacement of HA 1988 s9(4).
55   See para 28.15.
56   See *Zinda v Bank of Scotland* [2011] EWCA Civ 706, [2011] HLR 40, in relation to a suspended order made in mortgage possession proceedings.

Execution of a warrant of possession

31.36   If a tenant fails to give up possession as required by an absolute order, the landlord's usual remedy is to apply to the county court for a warrant of possession.[57] Landlords will follow the same procedure if they wish to enforce a suspended order for possession following a tenant's failure to comply with the terms of that order. A warrant cannot be issued before the date on which it is ordered that possession be given. If a warrant is issued in such circumstances, it is a nullity.[58]

31.37   The procedure in relation to warrants is governed by CPR Part 83 (Writs and Warrants: General Provisions).[59] CPR 83.26 deals with warrants of possession in the county court. An application for a warrant may be made without notice to the defendant and must be made to the county court hearing centre where the possession order was made or to which the proceedings have been transferred.[60] Application is made by the landlord completing court form N325.[61] A lender applying to enforce a mortgage possession order must certify that notice has been given to the occupier of the property under the Dwelling Houses (Execution of Possession Orders by Mortgagees) Regulations 2010.[62] A warrant of possession against a trespasser cannot be issued after three months from the date of the possession order without the permission of the court.

31.38   Where a tenant fails to comply with the terms of the suspension, a landlord cannot enforce a suspended possession order without

---

57   CPR 83.26(1).

58   *Tuohy v Bell* [2002] EWCA Civ 423, [2002] 1 WLR 2703.

59   Introduced, with effect from 6 April 2014, by the Civil Procedure (Amendment) Rules 2014 SI No 406. The former CCR 26 r17 and RSC Order 45 r3, which were originally preserved in Schedules 1 and 2 of the Civil Procedure Rules 1998, have been abolished.

60   CPR 83.26(2).

61   Note that the form must be completed properly. Failure to specify the amount of arrears currently outstanding may lead to the request for the warrant being refused or, if a warrant has been issued, to the warrant being set aside: *Westminster City Council v Mbah* June 1995 *Legal Action* 19; *South London Housing Association v Raxworthy* March 1996 *Legal Action* 11 (following *Hackney LBC v White* (1995) 28 HLR 219, CA); *Lambeth LBC v Johnson* December 1996 *Legal Action* 14 and *Westminster CC v Thomas* March 1997 *Legal Action* 12, but cf *Tower Hamlets LBC v Azad* (1998) 30 HLR 241, CA and *Abbey National v Gibson* September 1997 *Legal Action* 15, CA.

62   SI No 1809. See CPR 83.26(5) and see also para 15.19.

making an application for a warrant,[63] but (unless the original order specified that no warrant was to be issued without the permission of the court) a warrant in the county court is issued without any prior notice to the tenant and without a hearing.[64] In this respect the county court procedure differs from that in the High Court, where CPR 83.13(3) provides that, with limited exceptions, a writ of possession will not be issued without the permission of the court.[65] CPR 83.13(8) provides that permission will not be granted unless every person in actual occupation of the land is given such notice as the court considers sufficient to enable him to apply to court for any relief to which he may be entitled. In cases involving a tenancy, therefore, permission to issue a writ of possession to enforce a suspended order for possession on the grounds of an alleged breach of the terms of that order must not be given without allowing the tenant the opportunity to be heard.[66]

31.39   Tenants who fail to comply with possession orders theoretically commit a contempt of court. In extreme or exceptional cases landlords may apply to the court for penal notices to be attached to possession orders and, after re-service, apply to commit those who still refuse to give up possession to prison for contempt of court.[67]

31.40   A county court warrant can be executed at any time within one year after it has been issued. If landlords wish to rely on a warrant after that period an application must be made for it to be renewed.[68] Although tenants are not notified in advance of landlords' applications for warrants of possession in the county court, the court bailiffs should notify occupiers of the time and date of eviction, using form

---

63   *R v Ilkeston County Court ex p Kruza* (1985) 17 HLR 539 and *Hanif v Robinson* (1994) 26 HLR 386, CA.

64   In relation to the differences between the standard form of suspended possession order (N28) and the postponed possession order (N28A), see further paras 28.27–28.44. For criticism of the county court procedure, see comments by the Court of Appeal in *Leicester CC v Aldwinkle* (1992) 24 HLR 49, CA.

65   The exceptions, where the court's permission is not required, are where a writ of possession is issued (1) against trespassers (unless more than three months have expired since the date of the order) and (2) against a borrower in proceedings to enforce a mortgage or charge. See para 31.48.

66   See *Nicholas v Secretary of State* October 2015 *Legal Action* 40. See further, para 31.48.

67   *Tuohy v Bell* [2002] EWCA Civ 423, [2002] 1 WLR 2703; *De Grey v Ford* [2005] EWCA Civ 1223 and *Trustee in Bankruptcy of Canty v Canty* [2007] EWCA Civ 241, [2007] BPIR 299.

68   CPR 83.3(3).

N54 (Notice of Eviction).[69] The notice points out that in some circumstances the court can decide to suspend the warrant and explains the procedure to be followed.[70] For a discussion of warrants for possession in mortgage actions, see paras 37.65–37.73.

31.41   Permission to issue a warrant of possession in the county court is required if six years have elapsed since the date of the possession order.[71] Failure to obtain permission is an abuse of process and any warrant obtained in such circumstances should be set aside.[72] Applications for permission are normally made without notice with a witness statement in support, although the court may direct that the application should be served and heard on notice. However, permission should not be granted unless the claimant can show that the circumstances justify departing from the general rule. In *Patel v Singh*[73] the Court of Appeal refused permission to issue a writ of execution. Peter Gibson LJ said:

> In my judgment, therefore ... the court must start from the position that the lapse of six years may, and will ordinarily, in itself justify refusing the judgment creditor permission to issue the writ of execution, unless the judgment creditor can justify the granting of permission by showing that the circumstances of his or her case takes it out of the ordinary.

69 Although there is no requirement in the CPR to give notice of the eviction date, the importance of serving the Form N54 cannot be over-stated: see *London and Quadrant Housing Association v Watson* May 2015 *Legal Action* 44, Central London County Court, in which a warrant of possession was set aside after eviction where the defendant was in the process of applying to suspend the warrant and had not received any notice of the eviction. See also para 31.71.

70 See para 31.56 in relation to staying or suspending warrants of possession.

71 CPR 83.2(3)(a). While there is no equivalent provision in the High Court, in most cases it is necessary to apply for permission to issue a writ of possesson in any event: see para 31.48.

72 *Hackney LBC v White* (1996) 28 HLR 219, CA. The six-year limitation applies even if the order has been suspended by a judge on terms that had not been complied with in the intervening period. See also *AA v Southwark LBC* [2014] EWHC 500 (QB), in which eviction was held to be unlawful and an abuse of process both because the warrant had been issued without the prior permission of the court and because of the manner in which it was executed (the entire contents of the defendant's flat, including his passport, laptops, papers, personal belongings and furniture, having been removed, taken to a refuse disposal facility and destroyed).

73 [2002] EWCA Civ 1938, [2003] CPLR 149.

The burden is on the claimant to prove that it is 'demonstrably just' to grant permission.[74]

Warrants and human rights

31.42   Where a local authority or other social landlord is seeking to enforce a possession order by warrant of possession, and where the court would ordinarily have no discretion other than to delay eviction for a maximum of six weeks, the question may arise as to whether the defendant may rely on HRA 1998 Sch 1 Article 8 to prevent his or her eviction at that stage. In *R (JL) v Secretary of State for Defence*,[75] the defendant was registered disabled and a wheelchair user. She had formerly been married to an army officer and lived in forces accomodation, but because of his violence she had been granted a licence of other accommodation. She sought judicial review of the Secretary of State's decision to enforce the possession order against her. The Court of Appeal held that it would normally be an abuse of process to re-litigate the Article 8 issue at the enforcement stage where it had already been considered by way of a proportionality review during the possession proceedings themselves, or to litigate it for the first time when it could have been raised as a defence in the possession proceedings. However, there are exceptional cases in which to raise an Article 8 argument at the enforcement stage is not an abuse. One example would be a fundamental change in the occupier's personal circumstances, such as the recent diagnosis of a terminal illness. Because the court's discretion to postpone the execution of possession orders in such cases is limited to six weeks under HA 1980 s89, a defence of disproportionate inteference with the occupier's Article 8 rights does not give the court power to stay or suspend the warrant for a longer period.[76] The only way of preventing an eviction at the warrant stage is by way of judicial review, whereby the occupier requests the Administrative Court to quash the decision to apply for the warrant.

31.43   The failure of the Civil Procedure Rules to provide a requirement for automatic notification to a tenant of an application to issue a warrant for possession in the county court might be considered to be

---

74   *Duer v Frazer* [2001] 1 WLR 919. Permission to issue a warrant of possession was refused in *Kensington & Chelsea RLBC v Scarlett* November 2005 *Legal Action* 20, Central London County Court.

75   [2013] EWCA Civ 449, [2013] HLR 27.

76   See *McDonald v McDonald and others* [2016] UKSC 28, [2016] 3 WLR 45 paras [72]–[73].

a breach of HRA 1998 Sch 1 Articles 6 and 8 and Article 1 of the First Protocol. There is no apparent justification for the discrepancy between the different procedures in the High Court and county court appearing in CPR 83.13 and 83.26. Enforcement proceedings are certainly within the ambit of Article 6.[77] The European Court of Human Rights has stated, albeit in a case involving rather different issues, that applicants are:

> ... entitled to expect a coherent system that would achieve a fair balance between the authorities' interests and [their] own; in particular, [they] should have ... a clear, practical and effective opportunity to challenge an administrative act that was a direct interference with [any] right of property.[78]

31.44 It was argued in *Southwark LBC v St Brice*[79] that the absence of any requirement that the tenant be given notice of an application to issue a warrant deprives him or her of a fair hearing within the meaning of Article 6. That may not be significant if the warrant is issued shortly after a possession hearing and there has been no change of circumstances. However, if a considerable time has passed since the order was made, the defendant's circumstances have often changed to an extent which is relevant to the decision to execute the order. Similar arguments were deployed in relation to Article 8 and Article 1 of the First Protocol, together with Article 14 (prohibition of discrimination).

31.45 However, in *St Brice*, the Court of Appeal held that the procedure which allows the issue of a warrant of possession and the arrangements for execution following breach of a suspended possession order does not infringe tenants' rights under Article 6, 8 or 14. Tenants' rights to possession of premises are determined when suspended possession orders are made. The issue of the warrant of possession is simply a step authorised to be taken to enforce that order. It does not alter the legal status of the tenant or make any kind of decision in relation to his or her rights, and so is not required to be the subject of a separate hearing. Furthermore, although possession proceedings may interfere with tenants' right to respect for their homes, they are clearly in accordance with the law and are a legitimate and proportionate response to proof of a ground for possession.

---

77 See, eg *Immobiliare Saffi v Italy* (2000) 30 EHRR 756, ECtHR.
78 *De La Pradelle v France* (1992) A 253-B.
79 [2001] EWCA Civ 1138, [2002] HLR 26.

Enforcement of a county court possession order in the High Court

31.46   In some cases, a landlord or lender may wish to arrange for the enforcement of a county court possession order by High Court enforcement officers (HCEOs). Usually, this is because they perceive that enforcement will be quicker in the High Court. County Courts Act 1984 s42 provides that where proceedings for the enforcement of any order of a county court are transferred to the High Court, the order may be enforced as if it were an order of the High Court.[80] Following the making of a possession order, the claimant may apply to the county court for an order under section 42 transferring the proceedings to the High Court. Such an application should be made on notice to the defendant, supported by evidence as to why the claimant is unwilling to have the order executed in the normal way by the county court bailiffs.

31.47   The county court judge has a wide discretion in deciding whether or not to grant the application. In response to an application to 'transfer up', it may be argued that claimants should produce evidence of how long the High Court process is likely to take, as compared with county court bailiffs, bearing in mind that in tenancy cases the claimant will need to apply for permission to issue a writ of possession in the High Court. A defendant's reasons for opposing a transfer may include: the difficulties he or she will face in making an application to stay or suspend enforcement in the High Court; that the costs involved in using a HCEO are disproportionate; and that the HCEO does not need to give notice of the eviction.[81] A borrower may argue that the fact that the lender can issue a writ of possession without permission places him or her at a particular disadvantage in seek-

---

80 County Courts Act 1984 s42(5). The High Court itself may also order a transfer of proceedings: County Courts Act 1984 s41. Where the possession order has been made against trespassers, it is not necessary to apply for a transfer of the proceedings to the High Court. The order may be enforced in the High Court or the county court: High Court and County Courts Jurisdiction Order 1991 article 8B. See para 31.49.

81 In deciding whether to 'transfer up', the court should consider various factors, in particular, the overriding objective in CPR 1.1; the amount of the rent or mortgage arrears; and whether there is a likelihood that a warrant or writ of possession might be suspended by any court before eviction took place. The court should also look for adequate assurances that the tenant would not be prejudiced by the transfer, and may impose conditions on the transfer for the tenant's protection: per District Judge Salmon in *Birmingham City Council v Mondhlani* [2015] EW Misc B41 (CC), Birmingham County Court, 6 November 2015.

ing a stay or suspension, and that the proceedings should therefore remain in the county court.

31.48　　If the court makes an order for transfer, the claimant must then apply to the High Court for permission to issue a writ of possession, except that permission is not required where a writ of possession is issued against trespassers (unless more than three months have expired since the date of the possession order) or against a borrower in mortgage possession proceedings.[82] In cases where permission is required, the landlord must apply to the High Court for permission and give notice of the application to the defendant. This gives the occupier a final opportunity to prevent eviction by making an application to set aside or vary the possession order or to stay or suspend the writ of possession.[83] In cases involving a tenancy, permission to issue a writ of possession to enforce an outright possession order or a suspended possession order following a breach of its terms must not be given without allowing the tenant the opportunity to be heard.[84]

31.49　　Where an order for possession has been made against trespassers, the claimant may use an abbreviated procedure in applying for a writ of possession. In these circumstances, claimants may make an application using court form N293A (combined certificate of judgment and request for writ of possession). The landowner must certify that the certificate is required for the purpose of enforcing a judgment against goods or against trespassers. On payment of the appropriate fee, the county court will seal the form and send it to the High Court for enforcement.

82　CPR 83.13(2). See para 31.38 above. A former licensee whose licence has been terminated is a trespasser, and is not entitled to notice of the application for a writ of possession: *Fineland Investments Ltd v Pritchard (No 3)* [2011] EWHC 113 (Ch).

83　CPR 83.13(8) provides that permission will not be granted unless every person in actual occupation of the land is given such notice as the court considers sufficient to enable him to apply to court for any relief to which he may be entitled. This is similar to the position under the former RSC Order 46, and case-law under that provision is likely to remain relevant. See also *Fleet Mortgage and Investment Co Ltd v Lower Maisonette 46 Eaton Place Ltd* [1972] 2 All ER 737.

84　See *Nicholas v Secretary of State* October 2015 *Legal Action* 40, in which the Secretary of State for Defence had applied without giving notice to the defendant for permission to issue a writ of permission. It was held that permission should not have been granted and that the writ of possession should be set aside. The court noted that, by failing to give notice, the claimant deprives the occupier of an opportunity to apply to the court to stay or suspend the writ of possession, and that failure may justify setting aside a writ even after it has been executed.

31.50   In the county court case of *Birmingham City Council v Mondh-lani*,[85] which concerned a claim for possession by a local authority against a secure tenant, it became evident that a practice had developed among claimant landlords of using form N293A to apply for a writ of possession without seeking permission to do so or giving notice to the tenants concerned. The court expressed alarm at the way the procedural rules had been 'side-stepped'.[86] In the wake of this decision, a Practice Note[87] has been issued by the Senior Master which emphasises that

- Form N293A is intended for enforcement of possession orders against trespassers only;
- CPR 83.13(2) requires the permission of the High Court before a High Court Writ of Possession can be issued; and
- CPR 83.13(8)(a) requires sufficient notice to be given to all occupants of the premises to enable them to apply to the court for any relief to which they may be entitled.

The Practice Note further provides that:

- The Queen's Bench Division Enforcement Section will not accept Form N293A for transfer to the High Court for enforcement of a possession order of the county court other than for possession orders against trespassers.
- The Queen's Bench Masters will not accept applications under County Courts Act 1984 s41 for transfer of a county court possession claim for enforcement. Such applications must be made under County Courts Act 1984 s42 to a judge at the hearing centre of the county court where the possession order was made, so that judges can satisfy themselves that the appropriate notice has been given under CPR 83.13(8).

31.51   In cases where the court has a discretion as to whether to make a possession order (under HA 1988 s9(2), HA 1985 s85(2) or Rent Act 1977 s100(2), or in mortgage possession proceedings under Administration of Justice Act 1970 s36), a tenant or borrower may wish

---

85 [2015] EW Misc B41 (CC), Birmingham County Court, 6 November 2015.

86 In *Ahmed v Mahmood* [2013] EWHC 3176 (QB), the claimant applied for a High Court writ of possession by completing form N293A, in which she certified that there was no application or other procedure pending, although the defendant had appealed the possession order. The writ of possession was set aside after eviction: the 'falsification' of the form N293A was an abuse of process.

87 Applications for transfers for enforcement of possession orders to the High Court: Senior Master Practice Note, 21 March 2016. See also Nearly Legal, nearlylegal.co.uk/2016/03: 'Righting wrong writs. High Court enforcement'.

to apply to the court to stay or suspend enforcement. Alternatively, whether or not there is a discretion, a defendant may wish to apply to set aside[88] the possession order. County Courts Act 1984 s42(6) provides:

> Where proceedings for the enforcement of any judgment or order of a county court are transferred under this section –
> (a) the powers of any court to set aside, correct, vary or quash a judgment or order of a county court, and the enactments relating to appeals from such a judgment or order, shall continue to apply;
> ...

31.52 It seems therefore that, where an order for transfer of proceedings has been made, an application to set aside or vary the possession order may still be made in the county court, while an application to stay or suspend enforcement must be made to the High Court. The usual form of Application Notice (court form N244) should be used. Where application is to be made to the High Court, a tenant (but not a mortgagor) should have received notice of the claimant's application for permission to issue a writ of possession, and this will contain details of the High Court district registry and case reference number. Otherwise, it will be necessary to contact the district registry in order to ascertain the stage which has been reached in the process of transfer and (where required) permission. Where mortgage borrowers are concerned, as the claimant lender does not need to obtain permission for a writ of possession or to give notice of the eviction date, defendants or their representatives will need to act with speed to secure a court hearing before the HCEO arrives to evict. If a stay of enforcement is granted, it is essential that the HCEO (if known) is informed of the stay immediately.

31.53 Once permission has been given (where necessary) and a writ of possession has been issued, there is no requirement on HCEOs to notify the tenant of the date when they will come to evict.[89] Some HCEOs will give notice to the tenant as a matter of good practice, but the notice period is likely to be short. However, where a HCEO is seeking to seize goods as well as recover possession, the occupier must be given seven days' notice.[90]

---

88 See para 31.7.
89 *Pritchard and others v Teitelbaum and others* [2011] EWHC 1063 (Ch), [2011] 2 EGLR 1.
90 Taking Control of Goods Regulations 2013 SI No 1894 reg 6.

Effect of a warrant

31.54   When the bailiffs come to execute a county court warrant, or the sheriffs or High Court enforcement officers execute a writ of possession, they can evict anyone they find on the premises, even if they were not a party to the possession proceedings or they moved in after the possession order was made.[91] The only remedy for someone in the premises who was not a party to possession proceedings is to apply to be joined to the action and to set aside the order for possession. Obviously, this is likely to be successful only if there would have been a defence to the proceedings which has a real prospect of success.

31.55   At common law anyone entitled to possession, or anyone acting on his or her behalf, was entitled to use reasonable force to eject a trespasser.[92] While tenants with statutory security do not become trespassers when the date for possession in the order has passed, bailiffs are entitled to use reasonable force to execute the warrant.[93]

Staying and suspending warrants

31.56   In cases where the possession order was made on discretionary grounds (under HA 1988 s9(2), HA 1985 s85(2) or Rent Act 1977 s100(2), or in mortgage possession proceedings (subject to the discretion under Administration of Justice Act 1970 s36), and a warrant of possession has been issued, a tenant or borrower may apply to the court to stay or suspend the warrant.

31.57   Generally applications to suspend county court warrants for possession are heard by district judges. Form N245 appears to be intended for such an application, but as it consists mainly of financial information, in practice Form N244 is more often used with a

---

91   *R v Wandsworth County Court ex p Wandsworth LBC* [1975] 3 All ER 390.
92   *McPhail v Persons Unknown* [1973] Ch 447, [1973] 3 WLR 71, CA. However, it is now a criminal offence to evict any occupier, including a trespasser, by using or threatening violence to secure entry (Criminal Law Act 1977 s6) unless the person carrying out the eviction is a 'displaced residential occupier' or a 'protected intending occupier': see para 23.2.
93   For a case in which the Court of Appeal held that an occupier may authorise the police to evict a trespasser, see *Porter v Commissioner of Police of the Metropolis* 20 October 1999, unreported, CA. See also dictum of Cockburn CJ in *R v Roxburgh* (1871) 12 Cox CC 8.

witness statement in support.[94] There is no limit to the number of applications that can be made to suspend a warrant.[95]

31.58   In accordance with the usual procedure governing applications, an application for a stay should be made on at least three days' notice[96] to the landlord, unless it is particularly urgent (for example, the warrant is about to be executed). If possible, it is better for time to be abridged under CPR 3.1(2)(a), allowing short notice to the landlord, than for the application to be made without notice.[97]

31.59   If there is a substantial dispute over the amount of rent claimed to be owing and the tenant's compliance with a conditional possession order, the application should be adjourned so that the up-to-date position can be established.[98] One particular cause of tenants' failures to comply with the financial provisions of suspended or postponed orders may be delays in receiving housing benefit or the housing costs element of universal credit, or the fact that the tenant has not, for whatever reason, claimed or received all the benefits that are due to them. Where there is reason to believe that the tenant may be entitled to benefits which would have paid or contributed towards the rent, the court will not be in a position to decide whether it is reasonable to suspend the warrant until the possibility of an under-payment of benefit has been explored, and an adjournment of the application should be sought on that basis. It is essential to ask the court also to order that the warrant be stayed pending the final hearing of the application.

31.60   Where the claimant is in breach of its own obligations towards the defendant, it may be possible to raise a counterclaim at the

---

94 See para 31.29 above.

95 In *Ealing LBC v Richardson* [2005] EWCA Civ 1798, [2006] HLR 13, the tenant succeeded in a further application after eight previous applications to suspend warrants.

96 CPR 23.7(1).

97 In practice, the defendant may apply to suspend a warrant at any time up to execution, including on the day of eviction itself, provided that application is made before possession is taken by the bailiff. See *Royal Bank of Scotland v Bray* January 2012 *Legal Action* 20, Halifax County Court, in which the bailiff confirmed that he had received a telephone call from the court informing him that the defendant borrower was at the court asking to see the judge while he was still at the property and before it had been fully secured and the locks changed. The district judge found that the warrant had not been executed at the time that the defendant attended court and issued her application. Accordingly, the court still had its normal discretion under the Administration of Justice Acts 1970 and 1973 to suspend the warrant on terms.

98 *Haringey LBC v Powell* (1996) 28 HLR 798, CA.

enforcement stage. In *Rahman v Sterling Credit Ltd*[99] a lender obtained a possession order on the grounds of mortgage arrears, but the order remained unexecuted. Eight years later, the borrower applied for permission to file a counterclaim alleging for the first time that the loan was an extortionate credit bargain.[100] The Court of Appeal held that the fact that the possession order had been made did not affect the power of the court to permit the making of a counterclaim at this stage. The question was whether the proceedings were at an end. This was not the case. In the light of the overriding objective, it was appropriate to grant permission to bring a counterclaim rather than direct that the claim be brought by separate action, because the counterclaim was related to the original claim and savings of time and expense would be made.

31.61   The same reasoning would apply to counterclaims against landlords for breach of repairing obligations. There is no reason why such counterclaims should not be raised after a possession order has been made, including at the warrant stage, whether they relate to matters that occurred before the date of the possession order or whether the defects complained of arose subsequent to the possession order. It will, of course, be necessary to seek the court's permission and application should be made under CPR 20. It should be submitted on the tenant's behalf that the subject matter of the counterclaim is closely related to the original claim, since both issues arise out of the same tenancy agreement and it is convenient that they should be determined in the course of the same proceedings. While there cannot be a set-off in these circumstances,[101] the fact that the tenant is successful in recovering damages on his or her counterclaim which will reduce the rent arrears may well have a direct bearing on the outcome of the tenant's application to stay or suspend the warrant.[102] If permission is granted, the court will give directions on the counterclaim, which may include provision for expert evidence, and the warrant should be stayed pending the completion of directions and a final hearing.

---

99 [2001] 1 WLR 496, CA. See also *British Anzani (Felixstowe) Ltd v International Marine Management (UK)* [1980] QB 137.

100 The 'extortionate credit bargain' provisions in the Consumer Credit Act 1974 have been replaced by the 'unfair relationship' provisions in ss140A–140D of the Act: see para 34.83 onwards.

101 Since judgment for the rent arrears has already been given.

102 See *Midland Heart Ltd v Idawah* [2014] EW Misc B48, October 2014 *Legal Action* 47, Birmingham County Court, with commentary on *Nearly Legal*, 2 August 2014.

31.62 When exercising its discretion to stay or suspend execution or postpone the date for possession under RA 1977 s100(2), HA 1985 s85 or HA 1988 s9(2), the court may, subject to the necessary procedural safeguards, take account of matters other than those relied on as grounds for making the original possession order, for example, breaches of the terms of the tenancy agreement or anti-social behaviour.[103] In such cases, while not attempting to fetter the discretion of district judges, the Court of Appeal has stated[104] that the following points are relevant:

- The discretion should be used so as to further the policy of the legislation, reinforced by HRA 1998 Sch 1 Article 8. The policy is to evict only after a serious breach of an obligation, where it is reasonable to do so, and where the tenant is proved to have breached any condition of suspension.
- The overriding objective of the CPR, especially the need for applications to be dealt with in a summary and proportionate way, means that it may not be possible to deal with wider issues on an application to suspend or vary. They may need to be dealt with in some other way.
- The discretion to consider other allegations should generally be exercised more readily in respect of matters occurring after commencement of the proceedings.
- The fact that the landlord had or had not included the allegations as part of the original proceedings is relevant.
- However, the tenant should have clear evidence of what is alleged against him or her, especially where the allegations were not contained in the original proceedings.
- The court should also consider the practicalities of dealing with matters on the execution of a warrant.
- The fact that the tenant is at the mercy of the court, together with the responsibilities of a social landlord to its other tenants.

31.63 The above factors are not exhaustive. District judges have to exercise their discretion, bearing in mind the importance of the issue to the tenant, who is at risk of losing his or her home, and the responsibilities of social landlords to their other tenants. However, the court

---

103 *Sheffield City Council v Hopkins* [2001] EWCA Civ 1023, [2002] HLR 12; *Manchester City Council v Finn* [2002] EWCA Civ 1998, [2003] HLR 41. Cf *Hammersmith and Fulham LBC v Brown* [2000] 5 CL 350 and *Islington LBC v Reeves* [1997] CLY 2715. See also para 31.23 above.
104 *Sheffield CC v Hopkins* [2001] EWCA Civ 1023, [2002] HLR 12.

cannot take into account allegations which have not been proved or admitted by the tenant.

31.64   Tenants outside the protection of the Rent Act 1977, the Housing Act 1985 and the Housing Act 1988, or tenants against whom a possession order was made on a mandatory ground for possession, cannot apply to stay or suspend the execution of a warrant for possession once it has been issued, other than to delay the time for possession to the maximum period of six weeks from the date of the order.[105]

After eviction

31.65   If execution has taken place, former tenants are unable to rely on the county court's general powers to suspend or stay judgments or orders[106] or to extend time or to allow for payment by instalments.[107]

31.66   Similarly, once eviction has taken place, the court no longer has any power to stay, suspend or set aside a warrant under RA 1977 s100(2), HA 1985 s85(2) or HA 1988 s9(2), since those powers are expressly limited by the words 'at any time before the execution of the order'.[108] An application to set aside a warrant in these circumstances can only succeed if the possession order itself is set aside (see para 31.7 above), or the warrant has been obtained by fraud or there has been an abuse of process or oppression in its execution. In *Hammersmith and Fulham LBC v Hill*,[109] the Court of Appeal held that there was an arguable case of oppression where representations by a housing officer deterred the tenant from seeking legal help or advice

---

105   HA 1980 s89. See para 28.1.

106   County Courts Act 1984 s71.

107   CPR 3.1(2)(a) and (f). See *Moore v Registrar of Lambeth County Court* [1969] 1 All ER 782.

108   See *Scott-James v Bass Chehab* [1988] 41 EG 75, CA; *Leicester City Council v Aldwinkle* (1991) 24 HLR 40, CA; *Hammersmith and Fulham LBC v Hill* (1994) 27 HLR 368, [1994] 35 EG 124, CA and *Tower Hamlets LBC v Azad* (1998) 30 HLR 241, CA. But cf *Islington LBC v Harridge* (1993) *Times* 30 June, CA, where it was held that an application was 'made' on the day before eviction when the application was lodged with the court and accordingly the court had power to hear it even though eviction had taken place prior to the hearing. Cf also *Haringey LBC v Innocent* June 1995 *Legal Action* 19 (bailiffs executing warrant gained entry to the former secure tenant's home, but tenant re-entered using her back door key and resumed possession. Held: the warrant had not been executed and the court still had power to stay or suspend the warrant).

109   (1995) 27 HLR 368.

or otherwise from making application to stay the warrant before execution.[110]

31.67 In relation to 'oppression' in the execution of a warrant, the Court of Appeal has stated that:

> [O]ppression may be very difficult if not impossible to define, but it is not difficult to recognise. It is the insistence by a public authority on its strict rights in circumstances which make that insistence manifestly unfair. The categories of oppression are not closed because no-one can envisage all the sets of circumstances which could make the execution of a warrant oppressive.[111]

31.68 Case-law provides guidance as to what amounts to, and what does not amount to, 'oppression'. For example, in *Saint v Barking and Dagenham LBC*,[112] a secure tenant failed to comply with the terms of a suspended possession order during a short period while he was held on remand in custody. Although he had notified the council about his detention and whereabouts, without notice to him, the council applied for a warrant which was executed during his absence. The Court of Appeal set aside the warrant and directed his reinstatement. Peter Gibson LJ held that the conduct of the council in obtaining and executing the warrant had, in the circumstances, been 'oppressive'. First, the council had been under a duty 'promptly' to invite the defendant to renew his claim for housing benefit. That obligation required the council to send the renewal form to an address where it was likely to come to his attention (ie, his prison address). The council was relying on its own wrong-doing in obtaining the warrant to the extent that non-payment of housing benefit had caused the suspended order to be breached. Secondly, before the applicant's arrest his level of arrears had fallen below the level required to comply with the suspended order, and when the warrant was applied for, his outstanding debt was small (£336). In these circumstances, if he

---

110 See also *Hackney LBC v Gabriel* December 1994 *Legal Action* 14 (warrant executed more than a year after issue); *Lewisham LBC v Clarke* December 1994 *Legal Action* 14 (where the council had misrepresented correspondence from the Department of Social Security which had affected payment of housing benefit); *Greenwich LBC v Minnican* December 1994 *Legal Action* 14 (local authority failed to arrange direct deductions from income support payments, as envisaged when the suspended possession order was made) and *Westminster CC v Mbah* June 1995 *Legal Action* 19 (warrant set aside because application failed to state the amount of money remaining due: this requirement is now found in CPR 83.26(7)).

111 *Southwark LBC v Sarfo* (2000) 32 HLR 602 at 609, CA, per Roch LJ.

112 (1999) 31 HLR 620, CA.

had been given an opportunity to apply to suspend the warrant of possession, he would have succeeded.

31.69   Other examples of oppressive behaviour have included:

- Continuing with execution of a warrant even though the tenant had paid the full amount of the arrears to the housing officer who attended with the bailiffs to execute the warrant.[113]
- Execution of a warrant when the tenant was entitled to believe that no further step would be taken until her housing benefit applications had been decided, against a background of maladministration that had been manifestly unfair.[114]
- A housing officer not telling the defendant that a warrant had been applied for, even though the tenant had said that she was going abroad and had paid court costs and provided evidence of the renewal of her housing benefit claim.[115]
- Eviction of a tenant amounted to oppression taking into account: (a) a letter claiming that the defendant was behind with his payments under the court order when he was in fact ahead of schedule; (b) the issue of a warrant of possession one day before the expiry of the time allowed for the defendant to produce documents in support of his claim for housing benefit; (c) the issue of a warrant for possession at a time when the arrears which had accrued on the account were simply the result of an administrative decision to suspend the defendant's housing benefit; and (d) the failure to inform the defendant of his right to apply to the court under section 85(2) at the time when the warrant was applied for.[116]
- Eviction of a tenant who was making irregular payments towards the arrears, which stood at £274. The council had failed to have regard to its own rent arrears policy requiring it to use eviction only as a last resort. In particular, it had failed to consider applying for an attachment of earnings order against the tenant, who was in work.[117]

31.70   In some circumstances, misleading information from a third party, such as a member of the court staff, which deprives a tenant of the chance of taking steps to have execution of a warrant for possession

113   *East Staffs BC v Brady* January 1999 *Legal Action* 26.
114   *Southwark LBC v Sarfo* (2000) 32 HLR 602, CA.
115   *William Sutton HT v Breen* March 2000 *Legal Action* 29.
116   *Barking and Dagenham LBC v Marquis* October 2002 *Legal Action* 28, Ilford County Court.
117   *Southwark LBC v Augustus* February 2007 *Legal Action* 29, Lambeth County Court.

stayed may equally amount to oppression, thereby entitling the court
to set aside execution of the warrant.[118]

31.71   On the other hand, in *Jephson Homes Housing Association v
Moisejevs*,[119] the Court of Appeal decided that if a possession warrant is obtained and executed against a secure tenant without fault
on anyone's part, it cannot properly be set aside as oppressive or an
abuse of process. Oppression cannot exist without the unfair use of
court procedures. An eviction cannot be regarded as oppressive or
abusive merely because it is appreciated, after the event, that the tenant might have applied to stay or suspend execution of the warrant.
There is no requirement that a tenant should be given notice of a
request for the issue of a possession warrant.[120] The absence of such
a requirement in the county court[121] has been noted above (see para
31.38). However, cases may arise when the landlord can properly be
held to have acted oppressively if the tenant received no notice whatever of the impending eviction and could not reasonably have been
expected to anticipate it.

31.72   Other examples where it has been held that execution of a warrant
has *not* been oppressive include cases where:

- Shortly before the council made an application for a warrant, the
tenant took a lump sum of £400 to the council. A housing officer
received it with the words 'That will do for now'. The tenant took
no further step and made no further payment because he thought
that the council would be in touch with him. The court found it
'difficult to believe' in all the circumstances that the tenant had
genuinely formed the belief that he had simply to wait for the

118 *Hammersmith and Fulham LBC v Lemeh* (2001) 33 HLR 231, [2001] L&TR
423, CA (tenant who attended court to apply for suspension wrongly told by
court staff that there was no warrant) and *Lambeth LBC v Hughes* (2001) 33
HLR 350, CA (council wrote to the defendant stating that the only way to stop
eviction would be to pay all the arrears in full; bailiff's letter giving date of
eviction sent by second-class post arrived as the eviction was taking place).
119 [2001] 2 All ER 901, (2001) 33 HLR 594, CA. See too *Circle 33 Housing Trust v
Ellis* [2005] EWCA Civ 1233, [2006] HLR 7.
120 Although once the date for eviction has been set, the court bailiffs' office
should send form N54 (Notice of Eviction), referred to at para 31.40. See also
London and Quadrant Housing Association v Watson May 2015 *Legal Action* 44,
Central London County Court, in which a warrant of possession was set aside
after eviction where the defendant had not received any letter or other notice
of the eviction. HHJ Saggerson considered that the circumstances in which
oppression could arise included the lack of service of notices.
121 See CPR 83.26(2) and, in relation to the former County Court Rules, *Peachey
Property Corp v Robinson* [1967] 2 QB 543, [1966] 2 WLR 1386 and *Leicester CC
v Aldwinkle* (1992) 24 HLR 40, CA.

council to contact him. The judge preferred the evidence of the housing officer and rejected the allegation of 'oppressive' conduct. The Court of Appeal dismissed the tenant's appeal.[122]

• There was a dispute over housing benefit. The tenant had a poor rent record and there had been substantial non-compliance with a possession order.[123]

Warrants of restitution

31.73   Sometimes, particularly in trespasser cases, occupiers move into premises after a warrant has been executed or the claimant has in some other way regained possession in accordance with an order for possession. Unless there is some connection between the new occupiers and the people who were originally evicted, the landlord cannot apply for a further warrant in the same proceedings, but must issue further proceedings for possession. Once an order has been executed the proceedings are over and cannot be reactivated.[124]

31.74   The position is different if there is a 'close nexus' between the new occupiers and any people who were dispossessed in earlier proceedings. If the further occupation is 'part and parcel of the same transaction'[125] the landlord is entitled to apply without notice for a warrant of restitution in the county court or a writ of restitution in the High Court.[126] The effect of a warrant of restitution is to enable the bailiff or sheriff to evict any person in unlawful occupation of premises again without the landowner having to issue new proceedings. A warrant of restitution may be issued even though not all of the new occupiers of the land were among the original defendants.[127] It is theoretically possible for a landowner to apply to court to commit for contempt a person who has re-entered premises unlawfully after an earlier eviction, but such an order should be made in only the most exceptional circumstances.[128]

---

122 *Camden LBC v Akanni* (1997) 29 HLR 845, CA.

123 *Hackney LBC v Asik,* March 2000 *Legal Action* 29, CA.

124 *Thomas v Metropolitan Housing Corp* [1936] 1 All ER 210; *Ratcliffe v Tait* (1664) 1 Keble 216; *Lovelace v Ratcliffe* (1664) 1 Keble 785; *Doe d Pait v Roe* (1807) 1 Taunton 55; *Clissold v Cratchley* [1910] 2 KB 244 and *Brighton BC v Persons Unknown* June 1991 *Legal Action* 13.

125 *Wiltshire CC v Frazer (No 2)* [1986] 1 WLR 109, [1986] 1 All ER 65 per Simon Brown J.

126 CPR 83.26(8) (county court) and 83.13(5) (High Court).

127 *Wiltshire CC v Frazer (No 2)* [1986] 1 WLR 109, [1986] 1 All ER 65.

128 *Alliance Building Society v Austen* [1951] 2 All ER 1068, where such an order was, in fact, granted.

Mortgages

Mortgages

Introduction

32.1   In 1904, a law lord said, 'No one, I am sure, by the light of nature ever understood an English mortgage of real estate'.[1] In 1986, the Law Commission, in more reserved tone, commented in its introduction to Working Paper No 99 on the reform of land mortgages:[2]

> The English law of land mortgages is notoriously difficult. It has never been subjected to systematic statutory reform, and over several centuries of gradual evolution it has acquired a multi-layered structure that is historically fascinating but inappropriately and sometimes unnecessarily complicated.

32.2   The current state of the English law of mortgages is inadequate. This was recognised by the Law Commission as long ago as November 1991 when it published its recommendations for the reform of the law regulating land mortgages.[3] In July 2009 in a white paper, *A better deal for consumers – delivering real help now and change for the future,*[4] the then government indicated that the Law Commission had been asked to conduct a review of the fundamental principles of residential mortgage law with a view to bringing it up to date.

32.3   The defects in the law have become all the more important given the great social impact of its subject matter. In 2014, 14.3 million households in England lived in owner-occupied accommodation. This represents 63 per cent of all homes (down from 69 per cent in 2001). Of those, 6.9 million homes were subject to a mortgage.[5] Between 1980 and 2008 the number of mortgage possession actions started in the county courts in England and Wales rose from 27,105 to 142,741. Since then they have fallen to 19,853 in 2015.[6] However, 23,218 possession warrants were issued in 2015 by mortgage lenders. The number of repossessions by members of the Council of Mortgage Lenders (CML), which comprises all the major lenders, in 2015 was 10,200.[7]

---

1   *Samuel v Jarrah Timber and Wood Paving Corporation* [1904] AC 323 at 326, per Lord MacNaughten.
2   *Land Mortgages,* Law Commission Working Paper No 99, HMSO, 1986.
3   *Transfer of Land – Land Mortgages,* Law Com No 204 HC5, HMSO, 1991.
4   www.berr.gov.uk/files/file52072.pdf.
5   English Housing Survey Headline Report 2013/14, DCLG, February 2015 (revised October 2015).
6   *Mortgage and Landlord Possession Statistics Quarterly, England and Wales: October to December 2015,* Ministry of Justice, 11 February 2016.
7   Council of Mortgage Lenders Press Release, 11 February 2016.

32.4   It is against this backdrop that this Part is written, to try to explain the law and practice of mortgage possession actions and how advisers can help prevent loss of occupation by borrowers and their families.

The nature of legal mortgages

32.5   A lender that has secured its loan on property by way of a mortgage has a considerable advantage over an unsecured lender and is not solely dependent on the solvency of the borrower to recover the money loaned. A mortgagee (ie lender) has a number of options for enforcing the mortgage debt. The lender may: sue the borrower on the personal covenant in the mortgage deed; appoint a receiver to collect rent due from any tenants in the property; or seek a foreclosure order from a court. However, in practice, large institutional lenders usually seek to obtain possession of the property and sell with vacant possession to recover the money owed to them.[8] Part V of this book primarily deals with the law and practice related to this last method of enforcement. Throughout, the terms 'lender' and 'borrower' will be used in place of the more technical terms, respectively 'mortgagee' and 'mortgagor', except where a term of art is to be used. The lender will almost invariably be a bank, building society or similar institution rather than an individual.

32.6   Since 1925, legal mortgages have been capable of being made in only one of two ways.[9] The first is the granting of a lease by the freehold owner to the lender for a term of 3,000 years. Where the property is leasehold, the lease granted in favour of the lender is for a term equivalent to the owner's interest, less one day. In both cases there is included a provision for 'cesser on redemption', that is for the lease to terminate on redemption of the loan. The second (and much more usual) way is a charge by deed expressed to be by way of legal mortgage. This is commonly known as a legal charge. Although the borrower remains the holder of the legal estate, with the lender obtaining no legal term as such, the lender is by statute given the

---

8 See *Alliance & Leicester plc v Slayford* [2000] EWCA Civ 257, [2001] 1 All ER (Comm) 1 and M Thompson, 'The cumulative range of mortgagee's remedies' [2002] Conv 53 for a discussion of the interrelationship between the different remedies open to a lender.

9 Law of Property Act 1925 ss85(1) and 86(1). See also *Lavin v Johnson* [2002] EWCA Civ 1138 and C McNall, 'Truth suppressed? "Purported conveyance by way of mortgage"' [2003] Conv 326.

same powers and remedies as a lender whose loan is protected by the creation of a lease in the lender's favour.[10]

32.7   In practice, modern institutional lenders invariably rely on mortgages by way of legal charge because they are simpler to use. The legal charge is an agreement whereby a particular property is used as security to ensure that a borrower complies with the terms of a loan from the lender without the transfer of possession or title by the borrower to the lender. In the event of default by the borrower, the lender is given various statutory powers in respect of the property and, generally, additional contractual powers are reserved to the lender in the mortgage deed. The borrower is usually made responsible in the charge deed for the maintenance and insurance of the building, and is made personally liable for payment of the mortgage money and the lender's legal costs and expenses in enforcing the security. Advisers should look at the terms of the charge deed (and any collateral agreement) for the details in each case. In the cases of loans from secondary lenders, it is essential to obtain a copy of the loan agreement as well as the legal charge so that all the terms of the loan are clear. Usually, a copy can be obtained on request.

Types of mortgage

32.8   There are two different forms of modern mortgage commonly used by individuals for the securing of a loan, whether for the initial purchase of a property or for a subsequent loan. It is important for advisers to clarify which form of loan the borrower has entered into.

32.9   The first is the *capital repayment* (or annuity) mortgage. This usually requires a monthly repayment to the lender, part of which is repayment of the capital borrowed and the balance of which is interest. In this way the capital is repaid gradually over the term of the loan.

32.10   The second form of mortgage is the *interest-only* or 'endowment' mortgage in which, usually, two monthly payments are required: one is to the lender and comprises interest on the capital borrowed, and the other is to a financial institution which, over the term of the mortgage (through investment), accumulates a lump sum payment which should be adequate to pay off the capital sum borrowed. An interest-only mortgage is now not normally granted to owner occupiers but is much more usually taken out by 'buy to let' mortgage landlords.

10 Law of Property Act 1925 s87(1).

32.11   Historically, the most common of these 'capital vehicles' was the endowment insurance policy. During the term, the benefit of the policy is sometimes formally assigned to the lender and it is a condition of the loan that the premiums are paid on the policy. However, the policy may not have been the subject of a deed of assignment when the mortgage was taken out and as a result the policy remains the borrower's and can be disposed of at the borrower's discretion. Some endowment insurance policies are 'with profits' and are designed to give the borrower a small additional lump sum at the end of the term, over and above the money needed to pay off the loan and redeem the mortgage. A 'with profits' endowment mortgage requires higher monthly instalments.

32.12   An alternative is the *pension* mortgage, where the owner's private retirement pension is used as security for repayment of the capital borrowed. Individual savings accounts (ISAs) can also be used as an investment 'wrapper' to secure a mortgage. In such cases, the capital needed to repay the mortgage is paid out of the lump sum which becomes payable to the borrower when the pension plan matures or when the ISA is cashed in. No formal assignment of the pension or ISA can be made, and so lenders are really relying on their right to possession as security in the event of the capital not being repaid at the end of the agreed term. As with endowment mortgages, the borrower is required to pay interest on the outstanding capital throughout the term.

32.13   Many interest-only mortgages are taken out with no 'repayment vehicle' in place from the outset of the loan. Usually, the borrower will rely on an increase in the value of the security as a basis for their later ability to make repayment of the loan. Often, the loan will have started as an interest-only loan with an endowment or other similar facility in place. Commonly, this is often the first thing which the borrower stops paying when money becomes tight.

32.14   In 2006/07 33 per cent of all residential mortgages advanced in the UK (excluding buy-to-let mortgages) were sold on an interest-only basis, up from 13 per cent in 2002. The share was even higher in the credit-impaired segment where 50 per cent of mortgages were estimated to have been on an interest-only basis.[11] Since then the number of new interest-only mortgages has declined significantly other than in the 'buy-to-let' sector where interest-only loans are the norm. Advisers will need to identify whether a 'repayment vehicle' was taken out at the start of the mortgage and, if so, whether that is

11 FSA *Mortgage market review* DP09/03 October 2009 para 4.90.

still available. In 2013, the Financial Conduct Authority recognised that a significant number of borrowers with 'interest-only' mortgages were going to be unable to repay the mortgage advance at the end of the term and issued its finalised guidance 'Dealing fairly with interest-only mortgage customers who risk being unable to repay their loan'.[12]

32.15   A further variant is the *flexible* or *off-set* mortgage, which seeks to blur the distinction between capital repayment and interest-only loans. In essence, this is usually an interest-only mortgage which allows the borrower to make capital payments ostensibly at any time, with the capital payment instantly reducing the balance due and on which interest payments are calculated. Some of these 'flexible' mortgage 'products' are designed to combine the borrower's other personal finances with the mortgage debt, in effect so that the mortgage is used as a bank account. The aim is to ensure maximum financial benefit for the borrower. However, in this way all of the borrower's indebtedness is secured in favour of the lender by the mortgage. Such mortgages commonly also include provisions whereby the borrower is permitted to have mortgage payment 'holidays' where no payments are required for a specified period.

32.16   Traditionally, banks and building societies have been responsible for mortgage lending for people to be able to buy their own homes. More recently, the banks in particular have been advancing significantly in the 'buy-to-let' mortgage market. This is where the loan is specifically given for the purpose of a landlord letting the property to tenants. At the end of 2009 there were 1.2 million 'buy-to-let' mortgages representing 11 per cent of the residential mortgage market.[13] With effect from 21 March 2016, the Mortgage Credit Directive Order 2015[14] introduced significant changes to the regulation of 'buy-to-let' mortgage lending to consumers, including the compulsory registration of consumer 'buy-to-let' mortgage firms.

---

12 www.fca.org.uk/static/documents/finalised-guidance/fg13-07.pdf.
13 CML Press Release, 12 November 2009.
14 SI No 910.

CHAPTER 33

The lender's common law right to possession

33.1   At common law because a legal charge gives the lender a notional lease of the property, the lender is, subject to any agreement to the contrary in the deed, entitled to take possession of the property as soon as the deed has been executed.[1] It is not necessary for the borrower to be in default. However, if someone other than the borrower has a right to possession in priority to that of the lender, the latter would be prevented from taking possession (see para 41.1). The fact that a borrower may have entered into a sub-charge does not strip the lender, as principal chargee, of its right to possession. Both principal chargee and sub-chargee have rights to possession.[2]

33.2   Obviously, modern institutional lenders do not want possession of the property as they would prefer that they receive the regular repayments agreed with the borrower. The exercise of this right to possession is usually only a preliminary step to enforcing the security by way of sale with vacant possession in case of financial or other default under the mortgage.

33.3   Unless the mortgage deed requires it, at common law, notice of proceedings for possession need not be given.[3] Depending on the terms of the mortgage deed, before issuing the claim the lender may send a 'calling-in' letter (see para 34.35). This specifies the amount required to be paid by the borrower to redeem the loan. The mortgage deed may require the lender to make such a formal demand for the outstanding loan before it becomes payable in whole. Alternatively, the mortgage deed may provide that the whole outstanding

---

1   Law of Property Act 1925 s95(4). See *Four-maids Ltd v Dudley Marshall (Properties) Ltd* [1957] Ch 317, [1957] 2 All ER 35 and generally R J Smith 'The mortgagee's right to possession – the modern law' [1979] Conv 266.

2   *Credit & Mercantile plc v Marks* [2004] EWCA Civ 568, [2005] Ch 81.

3   *Jolly v Arbuthnot* (1859) 4 De G & J 224.

loan becomes due immediately on default in which case the calling-in letter is not necessary. However, lenders must have regard to the *Pre-action Protocol for possession claims based on mortgage or home purchase plan arrears in respect of residential property*, see paras 37.3–37.14 and appendix E. It is not strictly necessary at common law for lenders to obtain a possession order in order to take possession.[4] However, a land mortgage securing a regulated mortgage contact or a Consumer Credit Act regulated agreement is enforceable only on the order of a court.[5]

33.4   The exercise of the power of sale by receivers acting on behalf of the lender (which enables a lender to sell the security without first seeking a possession order) does not amount to a deprivation of a possession contrary to Human Rights Act 1998 Sch 1 Article 1 of the 1st Protocol.[6]

33.5   Where, however, it can be shown that the lender's claim for possession has been brought for reasons not in any way related to recovery of the mortgage debt then the claim is improperly brought. The claim would be an abuse of process and could be struck out. There will, however, be very real evidential difficulties in showing that the possession proceedings have been brought for some 'collateral purpose'.[7]

33.6   At common law, any occupier of the security can be evicted as a trespasser. However, where a property is occupied, a lender would be guilty of an offence under the Criminal Law Act 1977 s6 if it recovered possession using force. In practice, to ensure an ability to sell as mortgagees in possession, lenders do seek orders for possession. The extent to which parliament has modified this common law right to possession is discussed in chapter 34.

33.7   Some charge deeds contain a clause effectively creating a notional tenancy between the lender and the borrower. Such a clause is called an 'attornment clause'. If the agreement contains such a clause, then the lender must first terminate the tenancy before exercising its right to possession.[8] Such clauses are not commonly used in modern

---

4   *Ropaigealach v Barclays Bank plc* [2000] QB 263, (2000) 32 HLR 234, CA.
5   Consumer Credit Act 1974 s126 as amended by the Financial Services and Markets Act 2000 (Regulated Activities) (Amendment) (No 2) Order 2013 SI No 1881 art 20(38).
6   *Horsham Properties Group Ltd v Clark and Others* [2008] EWHC 2327 (Ch), [2009] 1 P&CR 8.
7   See generally *Co-operative Bank plc v Phillips* [2014] EWHC 2862 (Ch), [2014] Costs LR 830, paras 38–50.
8   *Hinckley and Country Building Society v Henny* [1953] 1 WLR 352.

institutional lenders' mortgage deeds. The legal charge may expressly state when the lender is able to seek possession from the borrower.

33.8   A lender's right to possession of the security will become statute barred under the Limitation Act 1980 where a borrower has remained in possession for more than 12 years from the date when the lender's right to possession arose. Advisers will need to check the terms of the legal charge to assess when the right to possession arose and also whether there have been any part payments or written acknowledgment[9] which might have restarted the 12-year limitation period.

9 *National Westminster Bank plc v Ashe* [2008] EWCA Civ 55, [2008] 1 WLR 710.

CHAPTER 34

Courts' powers to allow borrowers to remain in their homes

Legal and regulatory control of mortgages – overview

34.1   On 31 October 2004 major changes were made to the legal regulation of residential mortgages. The Financial Services and Markets
Act (FSMA) 2000 brought significant elements of mortgage lending under the administrative regulatory control of the Financial
Services Authority (FSA). In April 2014 the FSA was dissolved and
its functions taken over by the Financial Conduct Authority (FCA).
Regulations issued under FSMA 2000 introduced the concept of the
'regulated mortgage contract'. FSMA 2000 also set up the Financial
Ombudsman Service (FOS) as a dispute resolution body whose function is to investigate and resolve complaints about regulated activities
as an adjunct to the courts, including those relating to the sale, granting and administration of mortgages. Initially, only first charges were
capable of qualifying as 'regulated mortgage contracts'. As a result of
the transposition of the European Mortgage Credit Directive, Directive 2014/17/EU into domestic law on 21 March 2016, the Mortgage
Credit Directive Order 2015[1] brought second and subsequent mortgages within regulation as 'regulated mortgage contracts'.

34.2   Regulation of residential mortgages is provided through a combination of regulatory measures operated by the FCA under the FSMA
2000 and in the context of possession claims though the court's powers under the Consumer Credit Act (CCA) 1974 and the Administration of Justice Acts (AJA) 1970 and 1973.

34.3   Mortgages which fall within the definition of a 'regulated mortgage contract' are administratively controlled by the FCA. This now
includes the majority of first, second and subsequent mortgages
entered into prior to 21 March 2016 providing they were regulated by
the 1974 Act and the agreement would have been a regulated mortgage contract if entered into after 21 March 2016.[2] In the event of
possession proceedings, the courts have in relation to those loans,
the powers available in the AJA 1970 and 1973. Since 1 April 2014 the
courts have also had the various powers set out in CCA 1974 Part 9.

34.4   In the case of first charges entered into prior to 31 October 2004
these remain outside the definition of regulated mortgage contracts
and are outside regulatory control by the FCA under FSMA 2000. In

---

1   SI No 910.
2   The Financial Services and Markets Act 2000 (Regulated Activities) Order
2001 SI No 544 art 61(5), inserted by Financial Services and Markets Act 2000
(Regulated Activities) (Amendment) Order 2016 SI No 392 art 2(18)(b).

the context of possession claims the courts have the powers available under AJA 1970 and 1973 in relation to these mortgages. Where the loan agreement in question falls within the now very narrow category of agreements within scope of CCA 1974, as a consumer credit regulated agreement, the powers of the court are those available under CCA 1974 Act.

34.5   The first and essential question for advisers to determine is whether the borrower has a regulated mortgage contract. For a full analysis of the provisions relating to regulated mortgage contracts see para 35.4 and following. For discussion of the consumer credit legislation see para 34.61 and following. This chapter will deal with the powers available to the court when considering a possession claim by a mortgage lender. The following chapter will consider in more detail the regulatory control of residential mortgage loans and how these may impact on how a mortgage lender deals with a borrower in arrears with their mortgage and how an adviser can assist a borrower.

Inherent powers and equitable relief

34.6   As has been indicated above (see chapter 33), the lender has an immediate legal right to possession of the mortgaged property. The court, when considering an application by the lender for an order for possession, has only limited inherent and statutory powers to prevent the lender from obtaining possession or to delay repossession.

34.7   The High Court has an inherent discretion in possession proceedings to grant a short adjournment only (for example, 28 days) so as to allow any default to be remedied or for the loan to be paid off.[3] This is in distinction to the general power available to the court to adjourn proceedings in exercise of its case management functions under CPR 3.1.[4]

The court's equitable jurisdiction

34.8   It has also been stated that the court's equitable powers extend to preventing a lender from taking possession 'except when it is sought bona fide and reasonably for the purpose of enforcing the security

---

3   *Birmingham Citizens Permanent Building Society v Caunt* [1962] Ch 883. See too *Cheltenham & Gloucester plc v Booker* (1997) 29 HLR 634, CA.

4   See also *Cheval Bridging Finance Ltd v Bhasin* [2008] EWCA Civ 1613.

and then only subject to such conditions as the court thinks fit to impose'.[5]

34.9   This is a proposition of equity articulated by Lord Denning MR in 1979, which has since been approved in the Court of Appeal.[6] The extent of this equitable jurisdiction has yet to be fully assessed.

34.10   The courts have also accepted an equitable jurisdiction, which potentially may assist borrowers, through the doctrine of 'unconscionable bargain'. Under this jurisdiction, the court can set aside the legal charge or clauses within a charge on the basis that they are 'unconscionable', 'unfair' or 'unreasonable', where the lender 'has imposed the objectionable terms in a morally reprehensible manner ... in a way which affects his conscience'.[7] Browne-Wilkinson J gave as the classic example of such a bargain, a case 'where advantage has been taken of a young, inexperienced or ignorant person to introduce such a term which no sensible well-advised person or party would have accepted'.[8]

34.11   It seems that there has to be some element of morally reprehensible behaviour, involving abusive inequality of bargaining power such as to 'shock the conscience of the court'.[9] While of obviously limited application, in appropriate cases this equitable jurisdiction may prove to be an additional basis of defence to a possession claim.[10]

5   *Quennell v Maltby* [1979] 1 WLR 318, [1979] 1 All ER 568, CA at 571e.
6   *Albany Homes Loans v Massey* [1997] 2 All ER 609, (1997) 29 HLR 902, CA. Cf *Sadiq v Hussain* [1997] NPC 19, (1997) 73 P&CR D 4 (where a judge had been wrong to rely on *Quennell v Maltby* as there had been no collusion meaning that the transaction had been unconscionable) and *Co-operative Bank plc v Phillips* [2014] EWHC 2862 (Ch), [2014] Costs LR 830 (where proceedings were not an abuse of process and had not been brought for a collateral purpose). See also M P Thompson, 'The Powers and Duties of Mortgagees' [1998] Conv 391.
7   *Multiservice Bookbinding Ltd v Marden* [1979] Ch 84 at 110F.
8   *Multiservice Bookbinding Ltd v Marden* [1979] Ch 84.
9   See *Creswell v Potter* [1978] 1 WLR 255; *Backhouse v Backhouse* [1978] 1 All ER 1158; *Lloyds Bank Ltd v Bundy* [1974] 3 All ER 757, CA and *Alec Lobb (Garages) Ltd v Total Oil GB Ltd* [1983] 1 All ER 944.
10   See *Credit Lyonnais Bank Nederland v Burch* [1997] 1 All ER 144, CA. Cf *Portman Building Society v Dusangh* [2000] 2 All ER (Comm) 221, CA. See also L McMurty, 'Unconscionability and undue influence: an interaction?' [2000] 64 Conv 573.

Statutory powers

34.12 Historically, so far as powers available to the courts to assist borrowers in arrears was concerned, the default statutory regime was that of the AJA 1970 and 1973. Where the loan secured a consumer credit agreement, as defined in the CCA 1974, the wider powers available to the courts under CCA 1974 applied instead. However, this all changed on 1 April 2014 in respect of regulated mortgage contracts with the courts then being given the additional and wider powers within CCA 1974 Part 9 which up to then had only been available in respect of CCA 1974 loans. See 34.61 below.

In the case of mortgages which are not regulated mortgage contracts and which do secure consumer credit agreements within the definition of CCA 1974 the courts powers are as provided for under that Act. In relation to mortgages which are outside the regulated mortgage contract regime and also not regulated by CCA 1974 the court has only the more limited powers under AJA 1970 and 1973.

Administration of Justice Acts 1970 and 1973

34.13 Administration of Justice Act (AJA) 1970 Part 4, together with AJA 1973 s8, sets out the court's principal powers to assist borrowers who are in default.[11] It has been said that AJA 1970 represents a form of 'social legislation' in which 'Parliament has attempted to give legislative shelter to a wide class of owner-occupiers'.[12]

AJA 1970 s36(1) provides:

Where the mortgagee under a *mortgage* of land which consists of or includes a *dwelling-house* brings an action in which he claims possession ... not being an action for *foreclosure* in which a claim for possession ... is also made, the court may exercise any of [its] powers ... if it appears to the court that in the event of its exercising the power the mortgagor *is likely* to be able within a *reasonable period* to pay any *sums due* under the mortgage or to remedy a default consisting of a breach of any other obligation arising under or by virtue of the mortgage. [Authors' emphasis: the italicised phrases are considered below.]

34.14 AJA 1970 s36(2) provides that the court:

(a) may adjourn the proceedings, or

---

11 See generally R J Smith, 'The mortgagee's right to possession – the modern law' [1979] Conv 266 and A Clarke, 'Further implications of s36 of the Administration of Justice Act' [1983] Conv 293.

12 *Centrax Trustees Ltd v Ross* [1979] 2 All ER 952 at 955f per Goulding J.

(b) on giving judgment, or making an order, for delivery of possession ... or at any time before execution of such judgment or order
may:
  (i) stay or suspend execution of the judgment or order, or
  (ii) postpone the date for delivery of possession,
for such period or periods as the court thinks reasonable.

34.15 By AJA 1970 s36(3) any order made in exercise of any section 36(2)
powers may be made:

... subject to such conditions with regard to payment by the mortgagor
of any sum secured by the mortgage or the remedying of any default
as the court thinks fit.

The court is empowered by AJA 1970 s36(4) to vary or revoke any
condition imposed under section 36(3) but not the period of any postponed possession order.[13]

34.16 AJA 1970 s36 is qualified by AJA 1973 s8(2) which states:

A court shall not exercise ... the powers conferred by section 36 ...
unless it appears to the court not only that the mortgagor is likely to
be able within a reasonable period to pay any amounts regarded ...
as due on account of the principal sum secured, together with the
interest on those amounts, but also that he is likely to be able by the
end of that period to pay any further amounts that he would have
expected to be required to pay by then on account of that sum and of
interest on it ...

34.17 In effect, before exercising any of its powers it must appear to the
court not only that the borrower is likely to be able to pay off the
missed monthly payments within a reasonable period, but also that
it is likely that by the end of that reasonable period the borrower will
also have paid off the payments which will have fallen due during that
period. This will usually mean being able to show that the borrower
can resume payment of the current instalments and can also make
regular additional payments towards the arrears so that at the end of
the reasonable period all the arrears will have been discharged. However, section 36 would also be satisfied if the borrower can pay off the
arrears over the reasonable period and discharge the payments that
have fallen due over that period by a payment made at the end of that
period,[14] for example, by way of a lump sum payment. Similarly, section 36 applies where the borrower can show that he or she can pay

---

13 *Secured Residential Funding v Greenhill* noted at *Current Law Week* 22 October
1993, Bournemouth County Court, HHJ Darwell-Smith.
14 *Governor & Company of the Royal Bank of Scotland v Elmes* April 1998 *Legal
Action* 11.

the monthly instalments as they fall due with the arrears only being discharged by the end of the mortgage term. It is not a requirement of section 36 that payment towards discharge of the arrears needs to be made each month.[15]

34.18   The court's powers apply equally to endowment mortgages,[16] where there is no obligation to repay the capital originally borrowed until the end of the loan period, as they do to annuity (or capital repayment) mortgages,[17] where part of each monthly repayment is capital and part interest.[18] By analogy, interest-only loans would also be included. AJA 1970 s36 powers can also be exercised whether or not there is default under the mortgage deed itself, for example, breach of some collateral agreement.[19]

34.19   AJA 1970 s38A, inserted by CCA 1974,[20] provides:

> This Part of this Act shall not apply to a mortgage securing an agreement which is a regulated agreement within the meaning of the Consumer Credit Act 1974.

34.20   Clearly the legislative intent was to have mutually exclusive statutory regimes under the two Acts. However, since 1 April 2014 the court, when dealing with a regulated mortgage contract, has available to it the powers under CCA 1974 Part 11. See para 34.61 below. Such agreements do not fall within the definition of a regulated agreement in CCA 1974 and therefore AJA 1970 powers are not disapplied although, in practice, this is academic in that the powers under Part 11 are more extensive than under AJA 1970.

'Mortgage'

34.21   As indicated in chapter 32, there is no significant practical difference between a legal mortgage and a legal charge. AJA 1970 s39(1) confirms that the expression 'mortgage' includes a 'charge' and that 'mortgagor' and 'mortgagee' should be similarly construed.

---

15 *Paratus AMC Ltd v Sobey and another* April 2014 *Legal Action* 29, Bristol CC.
16 Para 32.10 above.
17 Para 32.9 above.
18 *Bank of Scotland v Grimes* [1985] QB 1179, [1985] 3 WLR 294, CA.
19 *Western Bank Ltd v Schindler* [1977] Ch 1, [1976] 3 WLR 341, CA and generally C Harpum, 'A mortgagee's right to possession and the mischief rule' (1977) 40 MLR 356.
20 Consumer Credit Act 1974 s192(4).

'Dwelling-house'

34.22   AJA 1970 s39(1) defines 'dwelling-house' as including 'any building or part thereof which is used as a dwelling'. Section 39(2) amplifies this by expressly providing that: 'The fact that part of the premises comprised in a dwelling-house is used as a shop or office or for business, trade or professional purposes shall not prevent the dwelling-house from being a dwelling-house for the purposes of this Part of this Act'. The relevant time for determining whether land consists of, or includes, a dwelling-house is the date the lender claims possession.[21] The fact that the property may be used as a dwelling for someone other than the borrower does not prevent the security from being a dwelling-house and so within scope of AJA 1970. However, if the non-borrower occupier is in occupation in breach of a term of the mortgage, this itself amounts to a breach within the meaning of AJA 1970 s36(1).

'Foreclosure'

34.23   Although it is often said that a property is being 'foreclosed' by a lender for mortgage default, in practice the common form of enforcement is that of obtaining possession and subsequent sale. The court's powers are not available where the lender's claim includes a claim for foreclosure.

34.24   Foreclosure of residential mortgages is very rare as it is more complex than enforcement by possession and sale. The latter is usually sufficient as a method of enforcement. Foreclosure is technically quite different from the obtaining of possession and subsequent sale in that it involves the extinction of the borrower's equitable right to redeem the mortgage on the property and the vesting of the legal estate absolutely in the lender. An example will illustrate the difference.

Example

X borrows £220,000 by way of a mortgage from C Ltd. X repays £40,000 before C Ltd obtains possession and sells for £240,000. X would receive £60,000 after redemption of the existing mortgage of £180,000. If C Ltd foreclosed on the property, instead of taking possession and selling, X would lose the equity of £60,000. C Ltd would become the absolute owner of the property worth £240,000 and X would receive nothing.

---

21   *Royal Bank of Scotland v Miller* [2001] EWCA Civ 344, [2002] QB 255. See also *Bank of Scotland plc v Brennan* [2014] NICh 1.

34.25 In view of the draconian nature of foreclosure, the courts are reluctant to grant foreclosure orders and there are procedural obstacles in the way of a lender seeking such an order. Briefly, the procedure to obtain such an order is as follows. Once repayment of the mortgage money has fallen due, for example, on breach of any term in the mortgage or after calling-in by the lender (ie, an express and unconditional demand is made for payment) and it remains unpaid, the lender can apply for a foreclosure decree nisi in Form N299. This order directs the taking of accounts between the lender and the borrower as to money paid during the term of the mortgage, and provides that if the borrower pays the remaining outstanding money by a particular date then the mortgage is redeemed and the debt discharged. If the mortgage is not redeemed by that date, then the lender can apply for a foreclosure order *absolute*. The lender then becomes the legal owner and the property is transferred to it. At the request of any person interested, the court has the power[22] to order sale of the property instead of foreclosure. Usually, such an order for 'judicial sale' would be granted so as to ensure that the borrower receives the balance of the sale price once the lender has been paid off. The court's dislike of foreclosure is such that, on occasion, even after a foreclosure order absolute has been made, it will 'open' the foreclosure. As a result of this, and the efficacy of other methods of enforcement, fore-closure is rarely used by lenders[23] although it may be pleaded as part of the lender's claim for relief in addition to claims for sale and/or possession. The remedy of foreclosure may amount to a breach of the borrower's rights under Human Rights Act 1998 Sch 1, Article 1 of Protocol No 1.

34.26 It seems likely that foreclosure is no longer possible in the case of 'regulated agreements' within the meaning of CCA 1974 (see para 34.45) because section 113(1) of that Act prevents a lender from obtaining any greater benefit by enforcing any security provided in relation to a regulated agreement than would be the case if no such security had been given. No authority on the point has been found but, in view of the very restricted use of foreclosure, the point may remain academic.

34.27 The Administration of Justice Acts add, to some limited degree, to the court's powers in cases where foreclosure is claimed. In effect, where foreclosure alone is claimed, the only statutory (as opposed to

---

22 Law of Property Act 1925 s91(1) and (2).
23 For a note on foreclosure in commercial mortgages, see E Bannister, 'Foreclosure – a remedy out of its time?' (1992) *Estates Gazette* 28 March.

common law or inherent) power is adjournment. If the claim is for foreclosure and possession, there appears to be power to adjourn the foreclosure claim and then to adjourn the possession claim or stay, suspend execution or postpone any order for possession.[24]

'Is likely'

34.28   The question of whether a borrower is likely to be able to pay any sums due within a reasonable time is one of fact for the judge on the evidence before him or her, whether in a witness statement or given by way of oral evidence.[25] The Court of Appeal has observed:

> It must be possible for [judges] to act without evidence, especially where, as here, the mortgagor was present in court and available to be questioned and no objection to the reception of informal material is made by the mortgagee. Clearly, it will sometimes be prudent for the mortgagor to put in an affidavit before the hearing.[26]

For this reason, it is essential that the borrower(s) attend the possession hearing. Otherwise it is likely that there will be no evidence before the district judge to allow him or her to exercise the court's statutory powers, although the district judge may of his or her own volition ask about the last payments or in some other way seek evidence from the lender's representative. It may be reasonable to adjourn proceedings in order to determine, at a later date, whether there has emerged, in the interim, any prospect of the borrower being able within a reasonable period to pay sums due under the mortgage, for example, where a student borrower is studying for qualifications which would result in employment adequate to enable the borrower to discharge the arrears.[27] The court cannot suspend an order for possession, however hard the circumstances, if there is no prospect of the borrower reducing the arrears.[28]

---

24   AJA 1970 s36 and AJA 1973 s8(3). See generally S Tromans, 'Mortgages: possession by default' [1984] Conv 91.

25   *Royal Trust Company of Canada v Markham* [1975] 1 WLR 1416, [1975] 3 All ER 433, CA and *Western Bank Ltd v Schindler* [1977] Ch 1, [1976] 2 All ER 393, CA.

26   Nourse LJ in *Cheltenham & Gloucester Building Society v Grant* (1994) 26 HLR 703 at 707.

27   *Skandia Financial Services Ltd v Greenfield* [1997] CLY 4248, Horsham County Court.

28   *Abbey National Mortgages v Bernard* [1995] NPC 118, (1996) 71 P&CR 257, CA.

'Reasonable period'

34.29　One crucial question which has to be asked in each case, is: what is the 'reasonable period'? It has been stated, obiter, that in making the assessment the court must 'bear in mind the rights and obligations of both parties, including [the lender's] right to recover the money by selling the property, if necessary, and the whole past history of the security'.[29] More important, however, is the approach to the length of the period during which arrears are to be cleared.

34.30　In *Cheltenham & Gloucester Building Society v Norgan*,[30] the Court of Appeal reviewed the authorities and concluded that, when assessing a 'reasonable period', it was appropriate for the court to take account of the whole of the remaining part of the original term of the mortgage. The court stated that in determining the 'reasonable period' the court 'should take as its starting point the full term of the mortgage and pose at the outset the question: would it be possible for the mortgagor to maintain payment-off of the arrears by instalments over that period?'[31] The court listed a number of considerations which are likely to be relevant when establishing what is a reasonable period. They are:

- How much can the borrower reasonably afford to pay, both now and in the future?
- If the borrower has a temporary difficulty in meeting his obligations, how long is the difficulty likely to last?
- What was the reason for the arrears which have accumulated?
- How much remains of the original term?
- What are the relevant contractual terms, and what type of mortgage is it, ie when is the principal due to be repaid?
- Is it a case where the court should exercise its power to disregard accelerated payment provisions (AJA 1973 s8)?
- Is it reasonable to expect the lender, in the circumstances of the case, to recoup the arrears of interest: (1) over the whole of the original term, or (2) within a shorter period, or even (3) within a longer period, ie by extending the repayment period? Is it reasonable to expect the lender to capitalise the interest or not?

29　*Centrax Trustees v Ross* [1979] 2 All ER 952 at 957, per Goulding J.
30　[1996] 1 WLR 343, (1996) 28 HLR 443, CA. See also J Morgan, 'Mortgage arrears and the family home' (1996) 112 LQR 553 and M Thompson, 'Back to square two' [1996] Conv 118. See too *First Middlesbrough Trading and Mortgage Co Ltd v Cunningham* (1974) 28 P&CR 69, CA and *Western Bank v Schindler* [1977] Ch 1, [1976] 3 WLR 341.
31　[1996] 1 All ER 449 at 458.

- Are there reasons affecting the security which should influence the length of the period for payment?[32]

34.31   It is clear from the judgment that the level of equity in the security to protect the lender is a significant factor in determining whether the court will exercise its discretion in the borrower's favour. No doubt mindful of certain obiter dicta in *Norgan*, to the effect that the court should be less sympathetic if a borrower has once failed to meet payments calculated by reference to the balance of the contractual term, it is not universal practice to use the balance of the term as the starting point in assessing the reasonable period. In the case of regulated mortgage contracts (for which see para 35.6) the FCA's stated position is that in appropriate cases the remaining term of the mortgage will be the reasonable repayment period.[33]

34.32   Where there is sufficient equity in the property (ie the surplus value of the property arrived at after deducting the money outstanding under any mortgages), it is hard to see what risk there is to the lender in deferring possession. It can be useful to clarify with the lender before the hearing whether it accepts that there is equity or to produce evidence to prove the amount of equity to show that the lender is not at risk. An estate agent's valuation may be helpful as a guide although the Court of Appeal has commented that such valuations should be treated with 'reserve'.[34] Institutional lenders may have property valuations which bear little relationship to a genuine valuation based, as they are, on general statistics relating to market trends or even 'drive by' valuations. It may be helpful for advisers to do a search on Zoopla or a similar website to try to identify the rough value of the security although this is no substitution for a professional valuation. Where there is likely to be a dispute about the value of the property, and therefore the level of equity, this of itself may be sufficient to persuade the Legal Aid Agency to grant a public funding certificate for legal representation (see chapter 24). In such cases it should be pointed out that, in practice, the courts are influenced greatly by the valuation evidence.

34.33   Where, however, there is no equity (ie, there would be a shortfall if the property were sold) it is possible to argue that the lender's interests are better served by a delay in possession being given up,

---

32 [1996] 1 All ER 449 at 463a.

33 Mortgages and Home Finance: Conduct of Business Sourcebook (MCOB) 13.3.6, see para 35.37.

34 *Bristol & West Building Society v Ellis* (1997) 29 HLR 282, (1996) 73 P&CR 158, CA.

particularly where there is some prospect of the market improving. The contrary view is that on a falling market it is in the lender's interest to allow sale to proceed at the earliest opportunity so that the loss to the lender is minimised.

34.34   See chapter 43 for the situation where the borrower wishes to sell the property in order to pay off the loan.

'Sums due'

34.35   Most mortgage deeds enable the lender to 'call in' the loan at any time or else provide that the capital money in total becomes immediately payable in the event of any default. As originally drafted, AJA 1970 s36 enabled the court to give relief to the borrower only if it were likely that he or she could pay any sums due under the mortgage. The court's power to give relief was therefore available in such cases only if the borrower could pay off any arrears *and* the outstanding capital which had invariably also become payable. To resolve this anomaly, AJA 1973 s8(1) redefined 'sums due' to make it clear that in the case of instalment mortgages or mortgages where payment was deferred in whole or part, the financial default to be considered at the hearing was limited to the normal instalments due but unpaid and that the provision for earlier repayment of capital contained in the mortgage deed was to be ignored.

34.36   AJA 1973 s8(1) provides:

> (1) Where by a mortgage of land which consists of or includes a dwelling-house, or by any agreement between the mortgage under such a mortgage and the mortgagor, the mortgagor is entitled or is to be permitted to pay the principal sum secured by instalments or otherwise to defer payment of it in whole or in part, but provision is also made for earlier payment in the event of any default by the mortgagor or of a demand by the mortgagee or otherwise, then for purposes of section 36 of the Administration of Justice Act 1970 (under which a court has power to delay giving a mortgagee possession of the mortgaged property so as to allow the mortgagor a reasonable time to pay any sums due under the mortgage) a court may treat as due under the mortgage on account of the principal sum secured and of interest on it only such amounts as the mortgagor would have expected to be required to pay if there had been no such provision for earlier payment.

34.37   The purpose of the sub-section is to permit borrowers to seek protection from the court where the loan was taken out on an instalment repayment basis so as to enable the court to allow the borrower time to pay off arrears and not the capital debt, which has fallen due and immediately repayable as a result of an 'accelerated payment clause' or on demand.

34.38   Section 8(1) will not apply where deferral is granted as a mere indulgence by the lender, lacking contractual force, unless it is enforceable by estoppel.[35] Where an agreement to secure a bank overdraft provides that money owed shall become payable only on demand, then there is no agreement to defer payment and so the agreement falls outside the scope of AJA 1973 s8.[36] These are sometimes described as 'all monies' charges. In such cases, the court retains the more limited power under AJA 1970 s36 to suspend enforcement of a possession order to enable the borrower to pay off the entire debt (ie principal, interest and any other sums due) over a reasonable period.[37] However, in such cases, the court has no contractual term to consider by way of guidance as to what the reasonable period should be and therefore will have to determine this in isolation. An 'all monies' charge cannot be relied on as security for monies due under a regulated consumer credit agreement where the legal charge expressly disapplies it as security for that debt.[38]

34.39   A reasonable time must be given to the borrower to comply with a demand for repayment before the lender is permitted to claim possession unless it is clear that, even if given a reasonable period, the borrower will not be able to pay off the mortgage debt.[39] The court retains its AJA 1970 s36 powers despite the fact that the original mortgage term may have expired.[40]

34.40   In Northern Ireland a Chancery Master has held that it is not legitimate for a lender to capitalise arrears and then bring possession proceedings asserting that those arrears can be relied on as arrears which require to be repaid when the court is considering whether to exercise AJA 1970 s36 discretion in the borrower's favour.[41]

34.41   Normally a suspended possession order is not automatically discharged by the repayment or capitalisation of the arrears. Suspended orders for possession usually require two elements to be satisfied for the order to remain unenforceable. The first is payment of the

---

35 *Rees Investments Ltd v Groves* [2002] 1 P&CR DG9, 27 June 2001, unreported, ChD, Neuberger J, noted at April 2002 *Legal Action* 22.

36 See *Habib Bank Ltd v Tailor* [1982] 1 WLR 1218, [1982] 3 All ER 561, CA.

37 See *Habib Bank v Tailor* [1982] 1 WLR 1218, [1982] 3 All ER 561, CA and *Santander (UK) plc v McAtamney* [2013] NI Master 15.

38 *Northen Bank Ltd v McKinstry & Ant* [2001] NICh 130.

39 *Sheppard & Cooper v TSB Bank plc (No 2)* [1996] 2 All ER 654, ChD.

40 *LBI HF v Stanford & Another* [2015] EWHC 3131 (Ch).

41 *Bank of Scotland plc v Rea* [2014] NI Master 11.

accruing instalments as they fall due. The second is further instalment payments towards reducing the arrears. Repayment of the arrears will have no effect on the requirement for the borrower to continue to maintain the accruing instalments for the order to remain suspended. Where a borrower discharges the arrears but fails to maintain payment of the accruing monthly instalments the lender can take steps to enforce the possession order.[42] It is still open to a borrower in such circumstances to apply to vary or revoke any condition in the possession order or, as an alternative, to apply to suspend the warrant.

Administration of Justice Acts and human rights

34.42 Self-evidently, the making and enforcement of a possession order in respect of a borrower's home will engage Human Rights Act 1998 Sch 1 Article 8 and Article 1 of the First Protocol. *Fisher & Lightwood's Law of Mortgage* at paragraph 26.63 observes:

> Where the mortgaged property is the mortgagor's home, a possession order if made and executed will constitute an interference by a public authority with the right conferred by Article 8. However, there is no inconsistency between the common law, as mitigated by section 36 of the 1970 Act and section 8 of the 1973 Act, and the Convention rights under Article 8 or Article 1 of the First Protocol.
>
> In exercising its discretion as to whether or not to grant an Order for sale of a mortgagor's home, the court should bear in mind the provisions of Article 8, and the need in any democratic society to balance the claims of creditors against the interests and rights of debtors, and not give automatic precedence to the interests of creditors.[43]

34.43 The Court of Appeal has held that AJA 1970 s36 strikes the right balance between the rights of the borrower to remain in his or her home and the rights of the lender to repayment within a reasonable period. There is no breach of Article 8 or Article 1 of the First Protocol.[44] Where the borrower is unable to rely on AJA 1970 s36 then Article 8 may enable the court as a public body to provide limited relief to a borrower.[45] However, there would need to be some exceptional

---

42 *Zinda v Bank of Scotland plc* [2011] EWCA Civ 706, [2011] HLR 40.

43 14th Edition, Lexis Nexis, 2014.

44 *Barclays Bank plc v Alcorn* [2002] EWCA Civ 817, October 2002 *Legal Action* 29.

45 For a discussion of this in the context of the law in Northern Ireland see *Swift Advances plc v Heaney* [2013] NI Master 18. See *Southern Pacific Mortgages Ltd v Green* [2015] EW Misc B42 (CC), 19 November 2015.

circumstances before this would be viable.[46] See generally, chapter 26 on 'human rights defences'.

Consumer Credit Act 1974

34.44   The 1974 Act regulates agreements under which credit is given to an individual. Section 8(1) defines a consumer credit agreement as being 'an agreement between an individual ('the debtor') and any other person ('the creditor') by which the creditor provides the debtor with credit of any amount'. While the initial definition is wide in scope, it is subject to significant exemptions.

34.45   Section 8(3)[47] now provides:

> (3) A consumer credit agreement is a regulated credit agreement within the meaning of this Act if it –
> (a) is a regulated credit agreement for the purposes of Chapter 14A of Part 2 of the Regulated Activities Order;
> *and* [Emphasis added]
> (b) if entered into on or after 21 March 2016 is not an agreement of the type described in Article 3(1)(b) of Directive 2014/17/EU of the European Parliament and of the Council of 4th February 2014 on credit agreements for consumers relating to residential immovable property.

Financial Services and Markets Act (Regulated Activities) Order 2001 and EU Directive 2014/17/EU

34.46   The Financial Services and Markets Act (Regulated Activities) Order 2001 article 60B[48] defines 'regulated credit agreement'. In summary this is an agreement entered into after 1 April 2014 whereby an individual is provided with credit of any amount which is not an 'exempt agreement'. For agreements entered into prior to 1 April 2014, the agreement must either previously have been regulated or have become regulated by CCA 1974 to fall within the definition.

34.47   Articles 60C to 60H of the 2001 Order lists a number of agreements which are exempt agreements for the purposes of the regulated credit agreement provisions. The most significant is an agreement

---

46 *McDonald v McDonald* [2016] UKSC 28, [2016] HLR 28. See also *Vrzic v Croatia* Application no 43777/13, 12 July 2016, ECHR.
47 See the Mortgage Credit Directive 2015 SI No 910 Sch 1 Pt 1 art 2(2), as revised by 2016 SI No 392 art 3(2).
48 SI No 544 as inserted by the Financial Services and Markets Act 2000 (Regulated Activities) (Amendment) (No 2) Order 2013 SI No 1881 art 6 and 2016 SI No 392 art 2(10).

relating to a *regulated mortgage contract.*[49] See para 35.6 for description of regulated mortgage contract.

34.48 Article 3 of EU Directive 2014/17/EU[50] is intended to bring into regulation the majority of orthodox loans for the purchase of individual's homes. Article 3(1)(b) of the Directive defines the agreements to which it applies as:

> (a) credit agreements which are secured either by mortgage or by another comparable security commonly used in a Member State on residential immovable property or secured by a right related to residential immovable property; and
> (b) credit agreements the purpose of which is to acquire or retain property rights in land or in an existing or projected building.

34.49 By virtue of (1) the exclusion from the provisions of CCA 1974 for regulated mortgage contract holders and (2) the exclusion of loans taken out for the purchase or retention of rights in land, the application of CCA 1974 is likely to be limited.

34.50 However, advisers will need to be aware, when advising a mortgage borrower whose loan does not constitute a regulated mortgage contract, of the nature of those loans which are outside scope of CCA 1974. The FCA Handbook gives guidance in this area.[51] The exempted agreements within article 60[52] are as follows:

Article 60C Exemptions relating to the nature of the agreement

34.51 This article excludes loans with credit exceeding £25,000 where the agreement is entered into wholly or predominately for the purposes of a business carried on, or intended to be carried on, by the borrower. If the agreement contains a declaration made by the borrower acknowledging that the agreement is entered into for business purposes, the declaration complies with Rules provided by the FCA for the purposes of this article, the agreement is presumed to have been entered into for the borrower's business purposes.[53] This presumption is disapplied if when the lender (or if there is more than one lender, any of the lenders) entered into the agreement or any person who has acted on behalf of the or any lender has or has reasonable cause

---

49 Art 60C(2) inserted by 2015 SI No 1863 art 2(2).
50 Directive 2014/17/EU of the European Parliament and of the Council of 4 February 2014 on credit agreements for consumers relating to residential immovable property and amending Directives 2008/48/EC and 2013/36/EU and Regulation (EU) No 1093/2010.
51 Perimeter Guidance Manual (PERG) 2.7.19CG.
52 As inserted by 2013 SI No 1881 art 6.
53 Art 60C(5).

to suspect that the agreement is not entered into by the borrower wholly or predominately for the purposes of a business carried on, or intended to be carried on, by the borrower.[54]

Article 60D Exemption relating to the purchase of land for non-residential purposes

34.52   This exemption applies if, at the time the agreement was entered into, any sums due under it are secured by legal charge on condition that less than 40 per cent of the land is used, or is intended to be used, as or in connection with a building (a) by the borrower or a 'related person' of the borrower, or (b) in the case of credit provided to trustees, by an individual who is a beneficiary of the trust or a related person of a beneficiary.[55]

34.53   For the purposes of calculating the 40 per cent, the area of any land which comprises a building or other structure containing two or more storeys is to be taken to be the aggregate of the floor areas of each of those storeys. Article 60D(3)(b) provides:

> (3)(b)   A 'related person' in relation to a person ('B') who is the borrower or (in the case of credit provided to trustees) a beneficiary of the trust, means –
> (i)   B's spouse or civil partner,
> (ii)   a person (whether or not of the opposite sex) whose relationship with B has the characteristics of the relationship between husband and wife, or
> (iii)   B's parent, brother, sister, child, grandparent or grandchild.

Article 60E Exemption relating to the nature of the lender

34.54   This exemption applies where the agreement is for the purchase of land and the lender is a local authority or a lender specified, or of a description specified, in rules made by the FCA. Certain other categories of prescribed lenders are also exempted in this article.

Article 60F Exemptions relating to the number of repayments to be made

34.55   This exemption relates to a limited number of different agreements where usually repayment of the loan is to be made within a 12-month period, where the number of payments is restricted and where no interest or other significant charges are payable.

---

54   Art 60C(6) and *Wood v Capital Bridging Finance Ltd* [2015] EWCA Civ 451, [2015] ECC 17.
55   Art 60D(1) and (2).

Article 60G Exemptions relating to the total charge for credit

34.56 This exemption relates to specialist loans made where the amount of interest and charges levied is restricted.

Article 60H Exemptions relating to the nature of the borrower

34.57 This exemption applies to a borrower who is an individual where the agreement is secured on land (or unsecured where credit exceeds £60,260) and the agreement includes a declaration made by the borrower which provides that the borrower agrees to forego the protection and remedies that would be available to the borrower if the agreement were a regulated agreement which complies with rules made by the FCA. Prior to the agreement being entered, into the borrower must have provided the lender with a statement made in relation to the income or assets of the borrower and that statement and the connection between the statement and the agreement complies with rules made by the FCA. This exemption is sometimes described as the 'high net worth individual' exemption.

Article 60HA Exemptions not permitted under the mortgages directive[56]

34.58 This withdraws exemption in some loans within articles 60E, 60F and 60H in relation to agreements of a kind described in EU Directive Article 3(1) (ie to acquire or retain property rights) where under the EU Directive they are taken out of scope by virtue of Article 3(2) of that Directive or where the agreement relates to a bridging loan or a 'restricted public loan' offered to limited members of the public.

34.59 The 1974 Act initially had jurisdictional financial thresholds. Loans in excess of £5,000 were taken out of regulation. This limit was increased to £25,000 in 1998. With effect 6 April 2008, the limit was removed entirely.[57]

34.60 The provisions of CCA 1974 are notoriously complicated, dealing as they do with a multitude of different types of credit transaction. The Act seeks to prescribe the way in which regulated agreements are entered into. Failure to observe any of these rules renders the agreement 'improperly executed' and so unenforceable without a court order.[58] In addition, the loan agreement must be in a prescribed

---

56 Inserted by 2015 SI No 910 Sch 1 Pt 2 art 4(19).
57 Consumer Credit Act 2006 (Commencement No 4 and Transitional Provisions) Order 2008 SI No 831.
58 CCA 1974 s65.

form[59] and there is a requirement for copies of the unexecuted agreement be given to the borrower and a prescribed procedure for the execution of the agreement.[60] The sanction for non-compliance with the formality provisions is that the agreement is deemed not to have been 'properly executed' and is enforceable only by way of a court order under CCA 1974 s127.[61] A lender seeking to enforce an agreement which breaches these formality requirements must apply for an enforcement order. The court has discretion to allow enforcement but only if it is considered just to do so.[62] The provisions of CCA 1974 are not simple and reference should be made to the standard works on consumer credit law for more details.[63]

Judicial Control under Consumer Credit Act 1974 Pt 9

34.61   CCA 1974 Part 9 entitled 'Judicial Control' sets out the court's powers available to assist borrowers. These include:

- enforcement orders where an agreement has not been properly executed (s127);
- time orders (s129);
- powers to suspend orders (s135); and
- power to vary agreements and securities (s136).

34.62   Originally these powers were only available when the court was dealing with legal charges securing 'consumer credit regulated agreements'. On 1 April 2014 the provisions of CCA 1974 Part 9 were applied to regulated mortgage contracts by an amendment to CCA 1974 s126 relating to enforcement of land mortgages. The Financial Services and Markets Act 2000 (Regulated Activities) (Amendment) Order 2014[64] inserted a new CCA 1974 s126(2):

> Subject to section 140A(5) (unfair relationships between creditors and debtors), for the purposes of subsection (1) and Part 9 (judicial control), a regulated mortgage contract which would, but for Article 60C(2) of the Financial Services and Markets Act 2000 (Regulated

---

59   CCA 1974 s60 and Consumer Credit (Agreements) Regulations 1983 SI No 1553

60   CCA 1974 ss58, 61, 61A, 62 and 63.

61   CCA 1974 s65(1).

62   CCA 1974 s127, as amended by CCA 2006 s15.

63   See Goode, *Consumer credit law & practice* (5 Vols), Butterworths, and Goode, *Consumer credit reports* (3 vols), Butterworths and Alexander Hill-Smith, *Consumer Credit: Law and Practice*, Routledge, 2015.

64   Financial Services and Markets Act 2000 (Regulated Activities) (Amendment) Order 2014 SI No 366 art 3(3).

Activities) Order 2001, be a regulated agreement is to be treated as if it were a regulated agreement.

34.63 The FCA has confirmed the extension of the court's powers by this measure in its Handbook:

> Section 126(2) of the CCA (as inserted by the Financial Services and Markets Act 2000 (Regulated Activities) (Amendment) Order 2014) provides, however, that for the purposes of section 126(1) of the CCA (a land mortgage securing a regulated mortgage contract enforceable (so far as provided in relation to the agreement) on an order of the court only) and Part 9 of the CCA (judicial control) a regulated mortgage contract which would, but for the exemption in PERG 2.7.19CG(1), be a regulated mortgage contract is to be treated as if it were a regulated mortgage contract. This is subject to section 140A (5) of the CCA (unfair relationships between creditors and debtors), which provides that an order under section 140B of the CCA (powers of court in relation to unfair relationships) shall not be made in connection with a credit agreement which is an exempt agreement under PERG 2.7.19C G. It therefore follows that, for example, the CCA provisions relating to time orders apply to regulated mortgage contract.[65]

34.64 The importance of this amendment should not be understated given its application to all regulated mortgage contracts. It extended significantly the powers available to the court to assist borrowers in default. The statutory limitations, in particular within AJA 1970 to suspend orders only where arrears could be paid off within a reasonable period, were removed. It remains to be seen to what extent the court's discretion based on case-law determined under Part 9 when dealing with second and subsequent charges will be applied when considering main stream first charge regulated mortgages.[66]

34.65 It is important to emphasise to district judges hearing possession claims relating to regulated mortgage contracts that these powers are distinct from, and much wider than, those under the Administration of Justice Acts with which they may be more familiar. In particular, the absence of any requirement to clear arrears within a 'reasonable period' should be stressed. District judges may be used to time order considerations in relation to second and subsequent charges but not in relation to first charges which are regulated mortgage contracts.

---

65 PERG 4.17.2 G.
66 See R Rosenberg 'Calling Time on Time Orders?' *Quarterly Account*, Spring 2016, issue 40.

Time orders under section 129

34.66   Receipt of an 'arrears notice' under CCA 1974 ss86B or 86C or a default notice under CCA 1974 s76 entitles the borrower to apply to the court for a time order. Application for a time order is made by way of a CPR Part 8 claim. Alternatively, the borrower can seek a time order in any possession claim, either in his or her defence or by application notice in the proceedings.[67] In most cases, it will be advisable to seek a time order at the earliest possible opportunity.

34.67   In respect of a loan secured within CCA 1974 a lender must serve an arrears notice under CCA 1974 ss86B or 86C where, in effect, the borrower has failed to missed two contractual payments. A lender is not entitled to enforce the agreement during the period of non-compliance. Before a borrower is entitled to apply for a time order, he or she is obliged, in relation to a regulated agreement:

- to give notice indicating that an application for a time order is to be made;
- within that notice to indicate that he or she wants to make a proposal for payment; and
- to give details of that proposal.

The application cannot be made until at least 14 days have elapsed after the date when the notice was given to the lender.

34.68   A lender is not entitled to recover possession of land for a loan secured by an agreement to which CCA 1974 applies unless a default notice has been served. The default notice must be in a prescribed form and specify the nature of the breach of the agreement being alleged.[68] If the borrower complies with the notice, the breach is treated as never having occurred.[69] The contents of the default notice must be accurate. If the amount claimed by the creditor to remedy non-payment is inaccurate, the default notice is invalid and any subsequent proceedings liable to be struck out.[70]

34.69   Assuming that the borrower does not pay off the arrears, or remedy other default, within the period specified in the default notice, the lender can issue a possession claim. A mortgage securing a regulated agreement is specifically enforceable only by an order of the court.[71] The time order provisions, together with the supplementary powers

---

67   CPR PD 55A para 7.1.
68   CCA 1974 ss87 and 88 and Consumer Credit (Enforcement, Default and Termination Notices) Regulations 1983 SI No 1561.
69   CCA 1974 s89.
70   *Worcester Lease Management Services Ltd v Swain & Co* [1999] 1 WLR 263, CA.
71   CCA 1974 s126.

contained in CCA 1974 ss135 and 136, give the court powers to assist the borrower significantly in excess of those in the Administration of Justice Acts.

34.70   CCA 1974 s129(1) provides:

> If it appears to the court just to do so –
> (a) on an application for an enforcement order, or
> (b) on an application made by a debtor ... after service on him of –
>   (i) a default notice, or
>   ...
> (ba) on an application made by a debtor ... after he has been given notice under section 86B or 86C; or
> (c) in an action brought by a creditor ... to enforce a regulated agreement or security, or recover possession of any ... land to which a regulated agreement relates,
> the court may make an order under this section (a 'time order').

The court has the discretion to make a time order even if the borrower has not sought one or even if the borrower is not present in court. The only requirement is that it should appear to the court 'just to do so'. Form N440 in CPR Part 4 may be used to make a time order application. See the precedent at appendix B for a consumer credit defence and Part 20 claim.

34.71   CCA 1974 s129(2) provides:

> A time order shall provide for one or both of the following, as the court considers just –
> (a) the payment by the debtor ... of any sum owed under a regulated agreement or a security by such instalments, payable at such times, as the court, having regard to the means of the debtor ... and any surety, considers reasonable;
> (b) the remedying by the debtor ... of any breach of a regulated agreement (other than non-payment of money) within such period as the court may specify.

34.72 If it wishes to make a time order, the court is required by the section to order payment of any money owed by instalments or the remedying of other default. However, having determined to exercise its discretion to make a time order, the court must have regard only to the means of the debtor (and any surety) when considering the size and rate of instalments. It is not legitimate to look to possible hardship caused to the lender. Equally, there is no requirement that the arrears or any other monies owed be paid off within a 'reasonable period' or even by the end of the original contractual loan period. The court is given very wide discretion.

34.73   The court's power under CCA 1974 s129(2)(a) enables it to order payment by instalments of 'any sum owed', ie already owed. Only in the cases of hire-purchase and conditional sale agreements may the courts deal with sums which fall due for payment in the future.[72]

34.74   This seemed to rule out the rescheduling of anything other than the total of instalments missed by the date of the hearing. However, many legal charges provide that, as soon as default occurs, the whole loan becomes immediately payable. Alternatively, lenders may have 'called-in' the loan before issuing proceedings. In other words, demand by letter for immediate payment of the outstanding loan. This 'calling-in' letter is distinct from the statutory default notice. If the whole loan has been called in by any of these means, a time order can deal with the total debt.

Suspending enforcement under section 135

34.75   Allied to the time order provisions is the related but distinct power to impose conditions or to suspend operation of any order the court makes. CCA 1974 s135 provides:

> (1) If it considers it just to do so, the court may in an order made by it in relation to a regulated agreement include provisions –
> (a) making the operation of any term of the order conditional on the doing of specified acts by any party to the proceedings;
> (b) suspending the operation of any term of the order either –
> (i) until such time as the court subsequently directs, or
> (ii) until the occurrence of a specified act or omission.

34.76   This subsection empowers the court to suspend enforcement of an order for possession, whether conditionally on payment of specified instalments by the borrower or until a particular event (for example, default in an instalment order, or the date the property is sold or the borrower rehoused by a local authority). Where a court finds it appropriate to make a time order, the enforcement of any possession order can be suspended so long as payment of the instalments under the time order is made.

34.77   Any person, 'affected by a time order'[73] or 'affected by a provision'[74] included in an order under CCA 1974 s135 may apply to the court for a variation or revocation in the case of a time order or a variation in the case of a section 135 order. These are particularly useful provisions because they allow a lender to make application to the

---

72   CCA 1974 s130(2).
73   CCA 1974 s130(6).
74   CCA 1974 s135(4).

court for a variation of the terms of a time order where, for example, a time order has been granted on favourable terms to allow the borrower to overcome temporary difficulties. It can be argued that the lender is not prejudiced by the granting of a time order on terms generous to the borrower, as the lender would be able to come back to court to have those terms varied.

Power to vary agreement under section 136

34.78   Finally, CCA 1974 contains a rather cryptic provision in section 136 under the heading 'Power to vary agreements and securities'. The section reads:

> The court may in an order made by it under this Act include such provision as it considers just for amending any agreement or security in consequence of a term of the order.

34.79   In *Southern & District Finance plc v Barnes*,[75] the Court of Appeal (in hearing three linked appeals and in reviewing conflicting county court decisions) gave general guidance on the time order provisions:

- When a time order is applied for, the court must first consider whether it is just to make it. This involves consideration of all of the circumstances of the case, including the position of the lender as well as that of the borrower.
- When a time order is made it should usually be made only for a stipulated period on account of temporary financial difficulty.
- The court must consider what instalments would be reasonable, both in amount and their timing, having regard to the borrower's means.
- If, despite being given more time, the borrower will be unable to resume payment of the total indebtedness by at least the amount of the contractual instalments, no time order should be made. In such circumstances it is more equitable to allow the regulated agreement to be enforced.
- When a time order is made following financial default, the 'sum owed' means every sum which is due and owing; in the context of possession proceedings, that usually comprises the total indebtedness (for the reasons given in para 34.74).
- The court may vary the contractual interest rate under CCA 1974 s136.

---

75   (1995) 27 HLR 691, [1995] Con Cred LR 62, CA. See also A Dunn, 'Footprints on the sands of time: sections 129 and 136 Consumer Credit Act 1974' [1996] 60 Conv 209 and R Rosenberg, 'Calling Time' *Quarterly Account* Issue 63 p11.

- Where a time order is made governing the whole of the outstanding balance due under the loan, there will be consequences for the term of the loan, the rate of interest or both.
- If justice requires the making of a time order, the court should suspend any possession order so long as the terms of the time order are complied with.

34.80   Further guidance can be gleaned from the judgments. Once it is accepted that it is just to make a time order, it appears to be legitimate to assess what the borrower can afford in the temporary period of relief which he or she is being given and to fix this as the rate of payment due to the lender. Variation of the interest rate to give efficacy to this rate of payment is permissible. It is worth noting that the Court of Appeal in *Barnes*[76] expressly approved the approach of one circuit judge who reduced the interest rate under the loan agreement to nil and ordered the total indebtedness to be repaid over a period exceeding the original contractual term. In *Director General of Fair Trading v First National Bank plc*,[77] the circuit judge's approach was approved. However, it was also observed that 'time orders extending over long periods of time are usually better avoided'.

34.81   It is important to recognise that the time order provisions are distinct from the 'unfair relationship' provisions contained in CCA 1974 ss140A–140C (described at para 34.83). It is possible for the 'unfair relationship' provisions to be used in addition to an application for a time order in the same proceedings or independently from a time order application.

34.82   Advisers have historically only looked to the time order provisions within the context of CCA 1974 regulated agreements. It remains to be seen how the courts apply these provisions in the context of first charge regulated mortgage contracts. It is anticipated that a less restrictive interpretation will be given in respect of these powers in relation to the wider category of loans constituting regulated mortgage contracts.

Unfair relationships

34.83   The 'extortionate credit bargain' provisions of the CCA 1974, as originally enacted, were replaced by the 'unfair relationship' provisions of

---

76   *Southern & District Finance plc v Barnes* (1995) 27 HLR 691, [1995] Con Cred LR 62, CA.
77   [2001] UKHL 52, [2002] 1 AC 481.

the CCA 2006 and are found at CCA 1974 ss140A–140D. CCA 1974 s140A provides:

Unfair relationships between creditors and debtors

(1) The court may make an order under section 140B in connection with a credit agreement if it determines that the relationship between the creditor and the debtor arising out of the agreement (or the agreement taken with any related agreement) is unfair to the debtor because of one or more of the following –

    (a) any of the terms of the agreement or of any related agreement;

    (b) the way in which the creditor has exercised or enforced any of his rights under the agreement or any related agreement;

    (c) any other thing done (or not done) by, or on behalf of, the creditor (either before or after the making of the agreement or any related agreement).

(2) In deciding whether to make a determination under this section the court shall have regard to all matters it thinks relevant (including matters relating to the creditor and matters relating to the debtor).[78]

(3) For the purposes of this section the court shall (except to the extent that it is not appropriate to do so) treat anything done (or not done) by, or on behalf of, or in relation to, an associate or former associate of the creditor as if done (or not done) by, or on behalf of, or in relation to, the creditor.

(4) A determination may be made under this section in relation to a relationship notwithstanding that the relationship may have ended.

(5) An order under section 140B shall not be made in connection with a credit agreement which is an exempt agreement for the purposes of Chapter 14A of Part 2 of the Regulated Activities Order by virtue of article 60C (2) of that Order (regulated mortgage contracts and regulated home purchase plans).[79]

34.84 The court's powers to make an order under CCA 1974 s140B are available in respect of 'any agreement between an individual (the 'debtor') and any other person (the 'creditor') by which the creditor provides the debtor with credit of any amount'[80] other than regulated mortgage contracts or regulated home purchase plans.

---

78 Deceit by the debtor or non-disclosure of all relevant facts tends to be fatal to any possible challenge: *First National Securities Ltd v Bertrand* [1980] Con Cred LR 5 and *Premier Finance Co v Gravesande* [1985] Con Cred LR 22.

79 Section 140A(5) was amended by 2013 SI No 1881 art 20(39).

80 CCA 1974 s140C(1).

34.85   CCA 1974 s140B provides:

Powers of court in relation to unfair relationships

(1) An order under this section in connection with a credit agreement may do one or more of the following –

   (a) require the creditor, or any associate or former associate of his, to repay (in whole or in part) any sum paid by the debtor or by a surety by virtue of the agreement or any related agreement (whether paid to the creditor, the associate or the former associate or to any other person);

   (b) require the creditor, or any associate or former associate of his, to do or not to do (or to cease doing) anything specified in the order in connection with the agreement or any related agreement;

   (c) reduce or discharge any sum payable by the debtor or by a surety by virtue of the agreement or any related agreement;

   (d) direct the return to a surety of any property provided by him for the purposes of a security;

   (e) otherwise set aside (in whole or in part) any duty imposed on the debtor or on a surety by virtue of the agreement or any related agreement;

   (f) alter the terms of the agreement or of any related agreement;

   (g) direct accounts to be taken, or (in Scotland) an accounting to be made, between any persons.

(2) An order under this section may be made in connection with a credit agreement only –

   (a) on an application made by the debtor or by a surety;

   (b) at the instance of the debtor or a surety in any proceedings in any court to which the debtor and the creditor are parties, being proceedings to enforce the agreement or any related agreement; or

   (c) at the instance of the debtor or a surety in any other proceedings in any court where the amount paid or payable under the agreement is relevant.

(3) An order under this section may be made notwithstanding that its effect is to place on the creditor, or any associate or former associate of his, a burden in respect of an advantage enjoyed by another person ...

34.86   If the borrower or surety alleges that the relationship is unfair it is for the lender to prove to the contrary.[81] CCA 1974 also entitles a party to any proceedings mentioned in section 140B(2) to have any person who might be the subject of an order under CCA 1974 s140B made a party to the proceedings.[82] An application by the borrower or

---

81   CCA 1974 s140B(9).
82   CCA 1974 s140B(8).

surety under CCA 1974 s140B(2)(a) may be made only in the county court.[83]

34.87 The 'unfair relationship' provisions were introduced with effect from 6 April 2007 when the previous 'extortionate credit bargain' provisions were repealed.[84] It is thought that, as with the previous extortionate credit bargain provisions, the borrower will need to show much more than the transaction was 'unwise.'[85] It may also be the case, as before, that there is a need to show 'at least a substantial imbalance in bargaining power of which one party has taken advantage'.[86] Under the unrevised 1974 Act the rate of interest charged was highly relevant and will clearly remain an issue.[87] The amended 1974 Act does, however, allow the court to take into account events and circumstances which occurred after the transaction was entered into, effectively side-stepping *Paragon Finance plc v Nash*,[88] which had concluded that in assessing the 'credit bargain' it was permissible to look at the original terms only. Under the unfair relationship provisions the court is entitled to assess the fairness of the relationship between the borrower and lender as at the date of trial or, if the relationship has ended, as at that date. The fact that a loan agreement was entered into more than 12 years earlier is not a bar.[89]

34.88 The unfair relationship provisions have, it would seem, been deliberately drafted in a way which gives the county court considerable discretion and it remains to be seen how the courts will develop the jurisprudence.[90] The Office of Fair Trading issued some guidance on 'unfair relationships'.[91]

34.89 Practice Direction 7B, entitled *Consumer Credit Act 2006 – Unfair Relationships* which supplements CPR r7.9 contains a CCA procedure which must be used when a debtor or a surety makes an

---

83 CCA 1974 s140B(2) and (4).

84 CCA 2006 s19 and Consumer Credit Act 2006 (Commencement No 2 and Transitional Provisions and Savings) Order 2007 SI No 123.

85 *Wills v Wood* [1984] Con Cred LR 7 and *Paragon Finance plc v Nash* [2002] 1 WLR 685.

86 See *Wills v Wood* [1984] Con Cred LR 7.

87 *Davies v Directloans Ltd* [1986] 1 WLR 823 and *Patel v Patel* [2009] EWHC 3264 (QB), [2010] 1 All ER (Comm) 864.

88 [2002] 1 WLR 685.

89 *Patel v Patel* [2009] EWHC 3264 (QB), [2010] 1 All ER (Comm) 864.

90 *Deutsche Bank (Suisse) SA v Khan and others* [2013] EWHC 452 (Comm) contains a helpful summary of relevant case-law.

91 See *Unfair relationships: enforcement action under Part 8 of the Enterprise Act 2002* OFT, May 2008 (updated August 2011).

application for an order relating to an unfair relationship under CCA 1974 s140B(2)(a). PD 7B para 10 states that where a debtor or surety intends to seek an order relating to an unfair relationship between a creditor and that debtor, the debtor or surety must serve written notice of intention on the court and every other party to the claim within 14 days of service of the claim form. PD 55A para 7.1 entitled *Consumer Credit Act claims relating to the recovery of land* provides that any application by the defendant for a time order under CCA 1974 s129 may be made in his or her defence or by application notice in the proceedings.

CHAPTER 35

Regulation of mortgage lending by the Financial Conduct Authority

Introduction

35.1   The Financial Services Authority (FSA) was established by the Financial Services and Markets Act (FSMA) 2000 to regulate the activities
of persons involved in financial services in the UK. In January 2000
it was announced that the FSA would be responsible for mortgage
regulation and in 2001 this was extended to cover those advising and
arranging mortgages as well as the conduct of lenders. The regime
set up by the FSA for the regulation of residential mortgages came
into effect on 31 October 2004.[1] FSMA 2000 also set up the Financial Ombudsman Service[2] (FOS) for the resolution of some types of
dispute 'quickly and with a minimum of formality'.[3] In April 2014,
responsibility for the regulation of mortgage loans was transferred
from the FSA and the Office of Fair Trading (OFT) to the Financial
Conduct Authority (FCA). For the first time, responsibility for financial regulation was vested in one body.

35.2   The regulatory role of the FCA and the FOS is not a simple alternative to the use of the courts. Advisers will need to have regard to
the statutory regimes of the Administration of Justice Acts (AJA)
1970 and 1973 and the Consumer Credit Act (CCA) 1974 which set
out the courts' powers in relation to possession claims by lenders.[4]
The authority of the FSA and the power of the FOS may, however,
be an important adjunct when seeking to challenge the way that a
mortgage lender is responding to a borrower whose loan falls within
the scope of FSMA 2000.

35.3   FSMA 2000 ss19 and 22 impose a 'general prohibition' on any
person from carrying on an activity regulated by the Act without
appropriate authorisation from the FCA. An activity is a 'regulated
activity' within the meaning of the 2000 Act if it is carried on by way
of a business and if it is a 'specified' activity. FSMA 2000 empowers
the FCA to issue Rules and Guidance in respect of the conduct of
persons authorised under FSMA 2000.[5] Advisers should accordingly
be aware of the provisions of the Rules and Guidance to ensure that
negotiations with lenders can take place in the context of the relevant
ground rules. While breach of the Rules does not deprive a lender

1   Mortgages: Conduct of Business Sourcebook (Amendment) Instrument 2004
and Financial Services and Markets Act (FSMA) 2000 ss138, 145, 156 and
159(1).
2   FSMA 2000 Part XVI.
3   FSMA 2000 s225.
4   See chapter 34.
5   FSMA 2000 s137A and s139A.

of its right to claim possession a borrower or, indeed any person, who suffers loss as a result of a contravention may bring an action for damages. Furthermore such a breach could found a complaint to the FOS. In an appropriate case, a defendant in possession proceedings, could apply for a stay of that claim to enable the complaint to be determined. See paras 35.16 and 35.64 below.

35.4 The Financial Services and Markets Act 2000 (Regulated Activities) Order 2001 Chapter 14A defines as a specified activity the entering into of a 'regulated credit agreement' by a lender.[6] See para 34.46 above. In turn, this is defined as the giving of credit of any amount to an individual which is not in turn exempted by the 2001 Order.

35.5 Chapter 15 of the 2001 Order deals with 'Regulated Mortgage Contracts'. Entering into a 'regulated mortgage contract' as a lender is a 'specified' activity.[7] 'Administrating' a regulated mortgage contract is also a specified kind of activity.[8] In practice, the vast majority of residential mortgages will fall within the definition as being a loan made to an individual to enable that person to buy a home for themselves, where the loan is secured on that home.

35.6 Article 61 of the 2001 Order, as amended, defines the regulated mortgage contract:

Regulated mortgage contracts

61(1) Entering into a regulated mortgage contract as lender is a specified kind of activity.

(2) Administering a regulated mortgage contract is also a specified kind of activity, where –

(a) the contract was entered into by way of business on or after 31 October 2004; or

(b) the contract –

(i) was entered into by way of business before 31 October 2004, and

(ii) was a regulated credit agreement immediately before 21 March 2016.

(3) In this Chapter –

(a) subject to paragraph (5), a contract is a 'regulated mortgage contract' if, at the time it is entered into, the following conditions are met –

---

6 Financial Services and Markets Act 2000 (Regulated Activities) Order 2001 SI No 544 art 60B–60Q as inserted by Financial Services and Markets Act 2000 (Regulated Activities) (Amendment) (No 2) Order 2013 SI No 1881.

7 FSMA 2000 (Regulated Activities) Order 2001 art 61(1).

8 FSMA 2000 (Regulated Activities) Order 2001 art 61(2).

(i)   the contract is one under which a person ('the lender') provides credit to an individual or to trustees ('the borrower');

(ii) the contract provides for the obligation of the borrower to repay to be secured by a mortgage on land in the EEA;

(iii) at least 40% of that land is used, or is intended to be used –

(aa) in the case of credit provided to an individual, as or in connection with a dwelling; or

(bb) in the case of credit provided to a trustee which is not an individual, as or in connection with a dwelling by an individual who is a beneficiary of the trust, or by a related person;

but such a contract is not a regulated mortgage contract if it is a regulated home purchase plan'[9]

(b) 'administering' a regulated mortgage contract means either or both of –

(i)   notifying the borrower of changes in interest rates or payments due under the contract, or of other matters of which the contract requires him to be notified; and

(ii) taking any necessary steps for the purposes of collecting or recovering payments due under the contract from the borrower;

but a person is not to be treated as administering a regulated mortgage contract merely because he has, or exercises, a right to take action for the purposes of enforcing the contract (or to require that such action is or is not taken);

(c) 'credit' includes a cash loan, and any other form of financial accommodation.

(4) For the purposes of paragraph (3)(a)(ii) –

(a) a 'mortgage' includes a charge and (in Scotland) a heritable security;

(b) the area of any land which comprises a building or other structure containing two or more storeys is to be taken to be the aggregate of the floor areas of each of those storeys;

(c) 'related person', in relation to the borrower or (in the case of credit provided to trustees) a beneficiary of the trust, means –

(i)   that person's spouse;

(ii) a person (whether or not of the opposite sex) whose relationship with that person has the characteristics of the relationship between husband and wife; or

(iii) that person's parent, brother, sister, child, grandparent or grandchild;

9 Mortgage Credit Directive Order 2015 SI No 910 Sch 1 art 4(21) and the Financial Services and Markets Act 2000 (Regulated Activities) (Amendment) (No 2) Order 2006 SI No 2383 art 17.

(5) In this Chapter, a contract entered into before 21 March 2016 is a 'regulated mortgage contract' only if –

    (a) at the time it was entered into, entering into the contract was an activity of the kind specified by paragraph (1), or

    (b) the contract is a consumer credit back book mortgage contract within the meaning of article 2 of the Mortgage Credit Directive Order 2015.

35.7   The Mortgage Credit Directive Order 2015[10] art 2 defines 'consumer credit back book contract' as a contract which –

    (a) (i)   is entered into before 21 March 2016,

       (ii) immediately before 21 March 2016 is a regulated credit agreement within the meaning of article 60B (3) of the Regulated Activities Order,

       (iii) would not be an exempt agreement within the meaning of article 60B (3) of the Regulated Activities Order by virtue of article 60D of that Order (exempt agreements: exemption relating to the purchase of land for non-residential purposes) if it were entered into immediately before 21 March 2016, and

       (iv) would be a regulated mortgage contract if it were entered into on or after 21 March 2016; or

    (b) (i)   is entered into on or after 21 March 2016 in the circumstances described in Article 28,

       (ii) would be a regulated credit agreement within the meaning of article 60B (3) of the Regulated Activities Order if it had been entered into immediately before 21 March 2016, and

       (iii) is a regulated mortgage contract immediately after it is entered into; ...

35.8   It is by virtue of article 2(a) that existing consumer credit regulated loans which met the criteria became regulated mortgage contracts on 21 March 2016. This is confirmed by the FCA Handbook which sets out its views on various issues. The suggestion is made in the Handbook that this also applies to loans entered into prior to 31 October 2004.[11]

35.9   The FCA's Handbook observes that, if at the time the agreement was entered into, all of the requirements to constitute a regulated mortgage contract are satisfied, then the agreement remains regulated throughout the mortgage term even if, subsequently, not all of the requirements remain satisfied.[12] Similarly, there may be instances

10 SI No 910.

11 Perimeter Guidance Manual (PERG) 4.4A.1C G.

12 PERG 4.4.3 G.

where an existing contract which is not a regulated mortgage contract is replaced as a result of variation (whether initiated by the borrower or the lender) and that the new contract will constitute a regulated mortgage contract.[13]

35.10   The most obvious example of a regulated mortgage contract is a loan made to an individual to enable the individual to buy a home for themselves, where the loan is secured on that home. However, there is no requirement that the borrower should occupy the property. There is a requirement that at least 40 per cent of the land should be used as a house, but there is no requirement that it is the borrower who uses it as a house. So, for example: (1) a loan may be a regulated mortgage contract if the property on which it is secured is to be occupied by the borrower's relatives as their home; or (2) a loan may be a regulated mortgage contract if the borrower does not occupy the property on which the loan is secured and instead intends to sell the property to a third party, with the mortgage remaining on the house until then. However, if the borrower is acting on a commercial basis, the loan in (2) may be excluded as a loan to a commercial borrower.[14]

35.11   The expression 'as or in connection with a dwelling' within article 61(3) means that loans to buy a small house with a large garden would in general be covered. However, if at the time of entering into the contract the intention was for the garden to be used for some other purpose – for example, if it was intended that a third party was to have use of the garden – the contract would not constitute a regulated mortgage contract.[15]

35.12   The definition of regulated mortgage contract contains no reference to the purpose for which the loan is being made. So, in addition to loans made to individuals to purchase residential property, the definition is wide enough to cover other loans secured on land, such as loans to consolidate debts, or to enable the borrower to purchase other goods and services.[16]

13 PERG 4.4.4 G.
14 PERG 4.4.6A G.
15 PERG 4.4.7 G.
16 PERG 4.4.10 G.

Loans that are not regulated mortgage contracts

35.13   Article 61A[17] lists a number of mortgage contracts which are not regulated mortgage contracts. It is important that advisers are able to identify particular loans which fall outside the definition of the regulated mortgage contract as different and less extensive powers are available to the court when dealing with a possession claim. It provides:

Mortgage contracts which are not regulated mortgage contracts

61A(1) A contract falls within this paragraph if it is –

(a) a regulated home purchase plan;

(b) a limited payment second charge bridging loan;

(c) a second charge business loan;

(d) an investment property loan;

(e) an exempt consumer buy-to-let mortgage contract;

(f) an exempt equitable mortgage bridging loan; or

(g) an exempt housing authority loan.

(2) A contract falls within this paragraph if –

(a) it is a limited interest second charge credit union loan;

(b) the borrower receives timely information on the main features, risks and costs of the contract at the pre-contractual stage; and

(c) any advertising of the contract is fair, clear and not misleading.

(3) For the purposes of this article, if an agreement includes a declaration which –

(a) is made by the borrower, and

(b) includes –

(i) a statement that the agreement is entered into by the borrower wholly or predominantly for the purposes of a business carried on, or intended to be carried on, by the borrower,

(ii) a statement that the borrower understands that the borrower will not have the benefit of the protection and remedies that would be available to the borrower under the Act if the agreement were a regulated mortgage contract under the Act, and

(iii) a statement that the borrower is aware that if the borrower is in any doubt as to the consequences of the agreement not being regulated by the Act, then the borrower should seek independent legal advice,

the agreement is to be presumed to have been entered into by the borrower wholly or predominantly for the purposes specified in sub-paragraph (b) (i) unless paragraph (4) applies.

17 Inserted by Mortgage Credit Directive Order 2015 SI No 910 Sch 1 Pt 2 art 4(22) and amended by 2015 SI No 1863 art 2(5) and 2016 SI No 392 art 2(19).

(4) This paragraph applies if, when the agreement is entered into –

  (a) the lender (or, if there is more than one lender, any of the lenders), or

  (b) any person who has acted on behalf of the lender (or, if there is more than one lender, any of the lenders) in connection with the entering into of the agreement,

knows or has reasonable cause to suspect that the agreement is not entered into by the borrower wholly or predominantly for the purposes of a business carried on, or intended to be carried on, by the borrower.

(5) For the purposes of this article a borrower is to be regarded as entering into an agreement for the purposes of a business carried on, or intended to be carried on, by the borrower if the agreement is a buy-to-let mortgage contract and –

  (a) (i) the borrower previously purchased, or is entering into the contract in order to finance the purchase by the borrower of, the land subject to the mortgage;

    (ii) at the time of the purchase the borrower intended that the land would be occupied as a dwelling on the basis of a rental agreement and would not at any time be occupied as a dwelling by the borrower or by a related person, or where the borrower has not yet purchased the land the borrower has such an intention at the time of entering into the contract; and

    (iii) where the borrower has purchased the land, since the time of the purchase the land has not at any time been occupied as a dwelling by the borrower or by a related person; or

  (b) the borrower is the owner of land, other than the land subject to the mortgage, which is –

    (i) occupied as a dwelling on the basis of a rental agreement and is not occupied as a dwelling by the borrower or by a related person; or

    (ii) secured by a mortgage under a buy-to-let mortgage contract.

(6) For the purposes of this article –

'borrower' and 'lender' have the meaning set out in article 61(3) (regulated mortgage contracts);

'borrower-lender agreement', 'borrower-lender-supplier agreement', 'credit union' and 'total charge for credit' have the meanings set out in article 60L (interpretation of Chapter 14A);

'bridging loan' has the meaning given by Article 4(23) of the mortgages directive;

'buy-to-let mortgage contract' has the meaning given in article 4 of the Mortgage Credit Directive Order 2015 (interpretation of Part 3);

'exempt consumer buy-to-let mortgage contract' is a contract that, at the time it is entered into, is a consumer buy-to-let mortgage contract within the meaning of article 4 of the Mortgage Credit Directive Order 2015 and –

    (a) is of a kind to which the mortgages directive does not apply by virtue of Article 3(2) of that directive; or

    (b) is a bridging loan;

'investment property loan' is a contract that, at the time it is entered into, meets the conditions in paragraphs (i) to (iii) of article 61(3)(a) and the following conditions –

    (a) less than 40% of the land subject to the mortgage is used, or intended to be used, as or in connection with a dwelling by the borrower or (in the case of credit provided to trustees) by an individual who is a beneficiary of the trust, or by a related person; and

    (b) the agreement is entered into by the borrower wholly or predominantly for the purposes of a business carried on, or intended to be carried on, by the borrower;

'exempt equitable mortgage bridging loan' is a contract that –

    (a) is a bridging loan;

    (b) is secured by an equitable mortgage on land; and

    (c) is an exempt agreement within the meaning of article 60B (3) (regulated credit agreements) by virtue of article 60E (2) (exempt agreements: exemptions relating to the nature of the lender).

'exempt housing authority loan' is a contract that –

    (a) provides for credit to be granted by a housing authority within the meaning of article 60E (exempt agreements: exemptions relating to the nature of the lender); and

    (b) if it is entered into on or after 21st March 2016 –

        (i)   is of a kind to which the mortgages directive does not apply by virtue of Article 3(2) of that directive,

        (ii) is a bridging loan, or

        (iii) is a restricted public loan within the meaning of article 60HA (exempt agreements: exemptions not permitted under the mortgages directive), in respect of which the borrower receives timely information on the main features, risks and costs at the pre-contractual stage, and any advertising is fair, clear and not misleading.

'limited payment second charge bridging loan' is a contract that, at the time it is entered into, meets the conditions in paragraphs (i) to (iii) of article 61(3)(a) and the following conditions –

    (a) it is a borrower-lender-supplier agreement financing the purchase of land;

    (b) it is used by the borrower as a temporary financing solution while transitioning to another financial arrangement for the land subject to the mortgage;

    (c) the mortgage ranks in priority behind one or more other mortgages affecting the land in question; and

(d) the number of payments to be made by the borrower under the contract is not more than four;

'limited interest second charge credit union loan' is a contract that, at the time it is entered into, meets the conditions in paragraphs (i) to (iii) of article 61(3)(a) and the following conditions –

(a) it is a borrower-lender agreement;

(b) the mortgage ranks in priority behind one or more other mortgages affecting the land in question;

(c) the lender is a credit union; and

(d) the rate of the total charge for credit does not exceed 42.6 per cent;

'payment' has the meaning set out in article 60F (8) (exempt agreement: exemptions relating to number of repayments to be made);

'regulated home purchase plan' has the meaning set out in article 63F(3)(a) (entering into and administering regulated home purchase plans);

'related person' in relation to the borrower or (in the case of credit provided to trustees) a beneficiary of the trust, means –

(a) that person's spouse or civil partner;

(b) a person (whether or not of the opposite sex) whose relationship with that person has the characteristics of the relationship between husband and wife; or

(c) that person's parent, brother, sister, child, grandparent or grandchild;

'second charge business loan' is a contract that, at the time it is entered into, meets the conditions in paragraphs (i) to (iii) of article 61(3)(a) and the following conditions –

(a) the lender provides the borrower with credit exceeding £25,000;

(b) the mortgage ranks in priority behind one or more other mortgages affecting the land in question; and

(c) the agreement is entered into by the borrower wholly or predominantly for the purposes of a business carried on, or intended to be carried on, by the borrower.

35.14   The Financial Services and Markets Act 2000 (Regulated Activities) Order 2001[18] also engages with 'home purchase plans'[19] which are in nature similar to mortgages but are designed not to contravene Islamic law against payment of *riba* or interest (see chapter 40). In essence, a home purchase plan is where a purchaser buys a property on the basis that it will be held on trust for the purchaser and an individual(s) as beneficial tenants in common. The transaction must

18   SI No 544 art 63F(3).
19   See FCA Handbook PERG 14.4.

also provide that the individual(s) or a 'related person' is entitled to occupy more than 40 per cent of the property in question and that there is an obligation on the individual(s) to purchase the property during the course of or at the end of a specified period.

35.15　　FSMA 2000 Pt 3 sets up a requirement for persons engaged in mortgage lending activities to be authorised by the FCA. Part V enables the FCA to regulate the performance of authorised persons. An agreement entered into in relation to a regulated activity by a person when not authorised is unenforceable by that person and the other party is entitled to recover any money paid or property transferred and compensation for any loss sustained as a result of having parted with it.[20]

35.16　　The FCA is charged with regulatory control of a myriad of different financial services and has issued a *Handbook*[21] which contains over 30 'sourcebooks' setting out the rules governing regulated persons in different fields. The *Handbook* and its regulations are issued pursuant to powers given to the FCA under FSMA 2000.[22] If a lender fails to comply with the rules it runs the risk of regulatory and disciplinary action by the FCA. A borrower (or, indeed, any person) who can show that he or she has suffered loss as a result of a contravention of a rule may sue the authorised person for damages.[23] Breach of the Mortgage Conduct of Business Rules is not of itself a defence which deprives the lender of its right to possession. The availability of such a claim for damages may enable a borrower to argue that he or she has a right of set off such that the claim for damages justifies the court exercising its discretion to suspend any possession order.[24] However, subject to any rules which may be made by the FCA, such a contravention does not render the transaction void or unenforceable.[25]

35.17　　In the *Handbook*, *The Rules* issued by the FCA are identified by a suffix 'R' to a particular paragraph. *Guidance* issued by the FSA is identified by a suffix 'G'. Guidance is generally designed to throw light on a particular aspect of regulatory requirement but is not of itself binding. The *Handbook* also contains commentary which

---

20　FSMA 2000 s26.
21　www.handbook.fca.org.uk.
22　FSMA 2000 ss138, 139, 145, 149, 156 and 157(1).
23　FSMA 2000 s150 and s138D as substituted by Financial Services Act 2012 s24.
24　See *Thakker v Northern Rock plc* [2014] EWHC 2107 (QB).
25　FSMA 2000 s138E.

identifies evidential provisions which tend to show compliance with a particular rule. These paragraphs contain suffix 'E'.[26]

35.18   The Handbook contains three distinct sourcebooks relevant to secured loans. The *Perimeter Guidance Manual* (abbreviated to PERG) contained within the Handbook's Regulatory Guides provides general advice as to the application of the FCA regulation and in particular chapter PERG 4 provides 'Guidance on regulated activities connected with mortgages'. This sets out the FCA view of the law and is a helpful introduction to the issues. While not legally determinative it must be given considerable weight when assessing the legal implications of any transaction. The *Consumer Credit sourcebook* (abbreviated to CONC) deals with issues relating to consumer credit lending and now is of limited application dealing only with those mortgage loans which fall outside the definition of, or are excluded from, the *regulated mortgage contract* regime.

35.19   The most relevant sourcebook in the context of residential mortgage loans is the *Mortgages and Home Finance: Conduct of Business sourcebook* (abbreviated to MCOB). MCOB is contained within the Business Standards section of the Handbook. This governs the relationships between the lender and borrower including any intermediaries. This sourcebook applies to activities carried out in respect of regulated mortgage contracts, equity release transactions, home purchase plans and regulated sale and rent back agreements.[27] It consists of 14 chapters governing every facet of the life of a mortgage. Chapter 13 of MCOB deals with arrears and repossession.

The Mortgage Conduct of Business (MCOB) rules

35.20   The MCOB rules cover all aspects of the mortgage lender/borrower relationship effectively from the cradle to the grave and, indeed, beyond, since they also regulate mortgage shortfalls. Significant changes were made to MCOB with effect from 26 April 2014 consequent on the *Mortgage Market Review* which had been undertaken by the FSA.[28] The changes were intended to tighten mortgage regulation. Transitional provisions allow lenders greater flexibility when dealing with regulated mortgage contracts and home purchase plans

---

26   See generally chapter 5 'status of provisions' of the FCA's *Reader's Guide: an introduction to the Handbook*, November 2015.

27   MCOB 1.2.2 G.

28   www.fca.org.uk/your-fca/documents/policy-statements/fsa-ps12-16.

already in existence at that date.[29] Advisers should create a link to the MCOB sourcebook as a web 'favourite' for easy access. The most relevant chapters in relation to mortgage repossession cases are: chapter 11, which deals with 'Responsible lending'; chapter 12 on 'Charges'; and, most importantly, chapter 13, which deals with 'Arrears, payment shortfalls and repossessions'.

35.21   MCOB 11.6.20 R deals in detail with the requirements for a 'responsible lending policy'. A lender must put in place, and operate in accordance with, a written policy setting out the factors it will take into account in assessing a customer's ability to pay. Further, more detailed, guidance is given in MCOB 11.6.2 to 11.6.19 as to the evidence needed to satisfy a lender that the borrower has the ability to repay the loan being sought. This requires a lender to undertake a forensic examination of a prospective borrower's financial history and existing and likely future expenditure. This includes a stress test to see if the borrower is able to meet payments in the event of interest rate rises. Specific guidance is given where the loan is for the purposes of debt consolidation where the prospective borrower has an 'impaired' credit history.[30]

35.22   MCOB 12 seeks to regulate 'early repayment charges', 'arrears charges' and 'excessive charges'. Guidance at 12.2.1 G reaffirms earlier obligations in MCOB about appropriate disclosure at pre-application stage, at offer stage and general product disclosure to make charges transparent to customers. Paragraph 12.2.1 is expressly intended to reinforce 'these requirements by preventing a [lender] from imposing unfair and excessive charges'.

35.23   MCOB 12.3.1 R deals with 'early repayment charges'. It requires a lender to 'ensure that any regulated mortgage contract that it enters into does not impose, and cannot be used to impose, an early repayment charge other than one that is (1) able to be expressed as a cash value and (2) a reasonable pre-estimate of the costs as a result of the customer repaying the amount due under the regulated mortgage contract before the contract has terminated'.

35.24   MCOB 12.4.1 R regulates 'arrears charges'. It provides:

> [A lender] must ensure that any regulated mortgage contract that it enters into does not impose, and cannot be used to impose, a charge or charges for a payment shortfall on a customer unless the firm is objectively able to justify that the charge is equal to or lower than

29 MCOB 11.7.1 R and 11.6.3 R.
30 MCOB 11.6.16 R.

a reasonable calculation of the cost of the additional administration required as a result of the customer having a payment shortfall.

The levying of a charge where the lender and borrower have come to an agreement about repayment of the arrears, which is being met by the borrower, would tend to be taken by the FCA as breach of MCOB 12.4.1 R.[31] In addition, lenders are required to allocate payments received from the borrower towards payment of arrears rather than towards any interest or charges on the arrears.[32]

35.25   MCOB 12.5.1 R requires a lender 'to ensure that any regulated mortgage contract that it enters into does not impose, and cannot be used to impose, excessive charges upon a customer'.

35.26   MCOB 13 deals with 'Arrears and repossessions'. The chapter seeks to control both the administration of a regulated mortgage contract during its lifetime and also the recovery of any mortgage shortfall debt after repossession and sale.

MCOB 13.1 'Dealing fairly with customers in arrears: policy and procedures'

35.27   A lender is obliged to 'deal fairly with any customer who (a) has a payment shortfall on a regulated mortgage contract or home purchase plan; (b) has a sale shortfall; or (c) is otherwise in breach of a home purchase plan.'[33] A lender must also 'put in place, and operate in accordance with, a written policy (agreed by its governing body) and procedures for complying with [its duty to deal fairly]'.[34]

35.28   Lenders are required to 'establish and implement clear, effective and appropriate policies and procedures for the fair and appropriate treatment of [borrowers] whom the [lender] understands, or reasonably suspects, to be particularly vulnerable'.[35]

35.29   Guidance observes that borrowers 'who have mental health difficulties or mental capacity limitations may fall into the category of particularly vulnerable customers'.[36]

35.30   The MCOB sourcebook requires that:

A *firm* must, when dealing with any *customer* in payment difficulties:

---

31 MCOB 12.4.1A E.
32 MCOB 12.4.1B R.
33 MCOB 13.3.1R (1).
34 MCOB 13.3.1 R (2).
35 MCOB 13.3.1C R.
36 MCOB 13.3.1D R (1).

(1) make reasonable efforts to reach an agreement with a *customer* over the method of repaying any payment shortfall or *sale shortfall*, in the case of the former having regard to the desirability of agreeing with the *customer* an alternative to taking possession of the property;

(2) liaise, if the *customer* makes arrangements for this, with a third party source of advice regarding the payment shortfall or *sale shortfall*;

(3) allow a reasonable time over which the payment shortfall or *sale shortfall* should be repaid, having particular regard to the need to establish, where feasible, a payment plan which is practical in terms of the circumstances of the *customer*;

(4) grant, unless it has good reason not to do so, a *customer's* request for a change to:

    (a) the date on which the payment is due (providing it is within the same payment period); or

    (b) the method by which payment is made;

    and give the *customer* a written explanation of its reasons if it refuses the request;

(5) where no reasonable payment arrangement can be made, allow the *customer* to remain in possession for a reasonable period to effect a sale; and

(6) not repossess the property unless all other reasonable attempts to resolve the position have failed.[37]

35.31 The duty to have an adopted policy to deal with arrears and mortgage shortfall debts 'does not oblige a [lender] to provide customers with a copy of the written policy and procedures. Nor, however, does it prevent a [lender] from providing customers with either these documents or a more customer-orientated version'.[38]

35.32 In relation to the obligation not to seek repossession unless all other reasonable attempts to resolve the position have failed:

(1) a firm must consider whether, given the individual circumstances of the customer, it is appropriate to do one or more of the following in relation to the regulated mortgage contract or home purchase plan with the agreement of the customer:

    (a) extend its term; or

    (b) change its type; or

    (c) defer payment of interest due on the regulated mortgage contract or of sums due under the home purchase plan (including, in either case, on any sale shortfall); or

---

37 MCOB 13.3.2A R.
38 MCOB 13.3.3 G.

(d) treat the payment shortfall as if it was part of the original amount provided but a firm must not automatically capitalise a payment shortfall where the impact would be material; or

(e) make use of any Government forbearance initiatives in which the firm chooses to participate;

(2) a firm must give customers adequate information to understand the implications of any proposed arrangement; one approach may be to provide information on the new terms in line with the annual statement provisions.[39]

35.33 The impact of capitalisation is considered to be material if, either on its own or taken together with previous automatic capitalisations, it increased:

(1) the interest payable over the term of the regulated mortgage contract by £50 or more; or

(2) the contractual monthly repayment amount under the regulated mortgage contract by £1 or more.[40]

35.34 A firm must make customers aware of the existence of any applicable Government schemes to assist borrowers in payment difficulties in relation to regulated mortgage contracts.[41]

35.35 In relation to capitalisation of arrears it is noted that:

In the FCA's view, in order to comply with Principle 6, which states 'A firm must pay due regard to the interests of its customers and treat them fairly', firms should not agree to capitalise a payment shortfall save where no other option is realistically available to assist the customer.[42]

35.36 Lenders are advised that these options are not exhaustive and that the FCA would expect lenders to be able to justify a decision to offer a particular option.[43]

35.37 In terms of the requirement to adopt a reasonable approach to the length of time a borrower should be given to clear arrears, MCOB guidance provides:

... The FCA takes the view that the determination of a reasonable repayment period will depend upon the individual circumstances. In appropriate cases this will mean that repayments are arranged over the remaining term.[44]

39 MCOB 13.3.4A R.
40 MCOB 13.3.4AA R.
41 MCOB 13.3.4B R.
42 MCOB 13.3.4D G.
43 MCOB 13.3.4C G.
44 MCOB 13.3.6 G.

35.38   Lenders are advised that, if they intend to outsource aspects of customer relationships (including debt collection), the FCA will hold
them responsible for the way in which this work is carried out.[45]

MCOB 13.3 'Record keeping: payment shortfalls and repossessions'

35.39   A lender which is also involved in the administration of a regulated
mortgage contract is obliged to make and retain an adequate record
of its dealings with borrowers in arrears (or who have a mortgage
shortfall debt) to enable it to show that it has complied with the obligations imposed by MCOB chapter 13. A lender is required to retain
a record of its dealings with the borrower in arrears[46] for three years,
including a recording of all telephone conversations between the
lender and borrower where the arrears are discussed.

> The record should contain, or provide reference to, matters such as:
> (1) the date of first communication with the customer after the
>   account was identified as being in arrears;
> (2) in relation to correspondence issued to a customer in arrears, the
>   name and contact number of the employee dealing with that cor-
>   respondence, where known;
> (3) ... [*This paragraph deals with business mortgages*]
> (4) information relating to any new payment arrangements
>   proposed;
> (5) the date of issue of any legal documents;
> (6) the arrangements made for the sale after the repossession –
>   (whether legal or voluntary);
> (7) the date of any communication summarising the customer's out-
>   standing debt after sale of the repossessed property and
> (8) the date and time of each call for the purposes of MCOB 13.3.9
>   R(1).[47]

MCOB 13.4.1 R 'Arrears: provision of information to the customer'

35.40   A lender is required to provide a comprehensive package of information to a borrower in arrears. The rule provides:

> If a customer falls into arrears on a regulated mortgage contract, a
> [lender] must as soon as possible, and in any event within 15 business

---

45   MCOB 13.3.8 G.
46   MCOB 13.3.9 R.
47   MCOB 13.3.10 G.

days of becoming aware of that fact, provide the customer with the following in a durable medium:

(1) the current Money Advice Service information sheet *Problems Paying Your* Mortgage;
(2) a list of the due payments either missed or only paid in part;
(3) the total sum of the payment shortfall;
(4) the charges incurred as a result of the payment shortfall;
(5) the total outstanding debt, excluding charges that may be added on redemption; and
(6) an indication of the nature (and where possible the level) of charges the customer is likely to incur unless the payment shortfall is cleared.[48]

MCOB 13.4.5 R 'Steps required before action for repossession'

35.41   Before issuing possession proceedings a lender must:

1) provide the information listed in para 35.40;
2) ensure that the borrower is informed of the need to contact the local housing authority to establish whether he or she is 'eligible' for local authority housing if the property is repossessed; and
3) 'clearly state the action that will be taken with regard to repossession'.[49]

It is far from clear what this last requirement means in practice.

MCOB 13.5 R 'Statements of charges'

35.42   Some lenders have adopted punitive policies of levying additional charges on borrowers in arrears and the MCOB seeks to ensure that at least, the borrower is made aware of the extent of the charging. It states:

> Where an account is in arrears, and the payment shortfall or sale shortfall is attracting charges, a [lender] must provide the customer with a regular written statement (at least once a quarter) of the payments due, the actual payment shortfall, the charges incurred and the debt.[50]

35.43   Charges that trigger the requirement for regular statements include all charges and fees levied directly as a result of the account falling into arrears. This includes charges such as monthly administrative

48   MCOB 13.4.1 R.
49   MCOB 13.4.5 R.
50   MCOB 13.5.1 R.

charges, legal fees and interest. If interest is applied to the amount of the arrears, as it is applied to the rest of the mortgage, a lender need not send a written statement, unless other charges are also being made. If interest is applied to the amount of the arrears in a different manner to the rest of the mortgage, then a written statement will be required.[51]

MCOB 13.5 R 'Pressure on customers'

35.44 MCOB also seeks to protect borrowers from the more unpleasant forms of debt collection: The Rules state 'a [lender] must not put pressure on a customer through excessive telephone calls or correspondence, or by contact at an unreasonable hour'.[52] Guidance suggests that a reasonable hour will usually fall between 8 am and 9 pm. Putting pressure on a borrower includes the use of documents which resemble a court summons or other official documents, or are intended to lead the borrower to believe that they have come from or have the authority of a court. It also includes the use of documents containing unfair, unclear or misleading information intended to coerce the borrower into paying.[53]

MCOB 13.6 R 'Repossessions'

35.45 Lenders are required to dispose of repossessed properties and to deal with the consequences of sale in a reasonable manner. The rule provides:

> A [lender] must ensure that, whenever a property is repossessed (whether voluntarily or through legal action) and it administers the regulated mortgage contract or home purchase plan in respect of that property, steps are taken to:
> (1) market the property for sale as soon as possible; and
> (2) obtain the best price that might reasonably be paid, taking account of factors such as market conditions as well as the continuing increase in the amount owed by the customer.[54]

35.46 Guidance suggests that:

> ... it is recognised that a balance has to be struck between the need to sell the property as soon as possible, to reduce or remove the

---

51 MCOB 13.5.2 G (1).
52 MCOB 13.5.3 R.
53 MCOB 13.5.5 G.
54 MCOB 13.6.1 R.

outstanding debt, and other factors which might prompt the delay of the sale. These might include market conditions ... but there may be other legitimate reasons for deferring action. This could include the expiry of a period when a grant is repayable on re-sale, or the discovery of a title defect that needs to be remedied if the optimal selling price is to be achieved.[55]

35.47   Guidance further provides that a lender is not required to recover a shortfall on sale and may not wish to recover a shortfall in some situations 'for example where the sums involved make action for recovery unviable'.[56] It then deals with two scenarios:

'If the proceeds of sale are less than the amount due'

35.48   A lender is obliged to ensure that, as soon as possible after the sale of a repossessed property, the borrower is informed in a 'durable medium' of the size of the mortgage shortfall and, where relevant, whether the debt might be pursued by another person, for example a mortgage indemnity insurer.[57] Durable medium is defined as paper or electronic medium such as a floppy disc, CD Rom or DVDs.

35.49   If a lender intends to seek to recover the shortfall the borrower must be told of this fact and this notification must take place within six years of the date of sale.[58]

'If the proceeds of sale are more than the debt'

35.50   A lender is obliged to ensure that reasonable steps are taken, as soon as possible after the sale, to inform the borrower, in a durable medium of the surplus and, subject to the rights or any other lender, to pay the surplus to the borrower.[59]

Consumer Credit sourcebook

35.51   The Consumer Credit sourcebook (CONC) is one of the FCA's specialist sourcebooks. It is intended to regulate lenders' responses to both secured and unsecured consumer credit lending in respect of credit lending outside the context of regulated mortgage contracts or home

---

55 MCOB 13.6.2 G.
56 MCOB 13.6.5 G.
57 MCOB 13.6.3 R.
58 MCOB 13.6.4 R.
59 MCOB 13.6.6 R.

purchase plans. Many of the sentiments in MCOB are replicated in CONC.

Arrears, default and recovery (including repossessions) (CONC 7)

35.52 CONC 7.3.3 G deals with 'Forbearance and due consideration'. Rule 7.3.4 requires a lender to '... treat customers in default or in arrears difficulties with forbearance and due consideration.

35.53 CONC 7.3.5 G provides:

Examples of treating a customer with forbearance would include the firm doing one or more of the following, as may be relevant in the circumstances:

(1) considering suspending, reducing, waiving or cancelling any further interest or charges (for example, when a customer provides evidence of financial difficulties and is unable to meet repayments as they fall due or is only able to make token repayments, where in either case the level of debt would continue to rise if interest and charges continue to be applied);

(2) allowing deferment of payment of arrears:

(a) where immediate payment of arrears may increase the customer's repayments to an unsustainable level; or

(b) provided that doing so does not make the term for the repayments unreasonably excessive;

(3) accepting token payments for a reasonable period of time in order to allow a customer to recover from an unexpected income shock, from a customer who demonstrates that meeting the customer's existing debts would mean not being able to meet the customer's priority debts or other essential living expenses (such as in relation to a mortgage, rent, council tax, food bills and utility bills).

35.54 Guidance continues: 'Where a customer is in default or in arrears difficulties, a firm should allow the customer reasonable time and opportunity to repay the debt.'[60]

35.55 In relation to 'Enforcement of debts', CONC provides:

7.3.17 R A firm must not take steps to repossess a customer's home other than as a last resort, having explored all other possible options.

7.3.18 R A firm must not threaten to commence court action, including an application for a charging order or (in Scotland) an inhibition or an order for sale, in order to pressurise a customer in default or arrears difficulties to pay more than they can reasonably afford.

60 CONC 7.3.6 G.

7.3.19 G Firms seeking to recover debts under regulated credit agreements secured by second or subsequent charges in England and Wales should have regard to the requirements of the relevant pre-action protocol (PAP) issued by the Civil Justice Council. The aims of the PAP are to ensure that a firm and a customer act fairly and reasonably with each other in resolving any matter concerning arrears, and to encourage more pre-action contact in an effort to seek agreement between the parties on alternatives to repossession. The Pre-Action Protocol on Possession Proceedings applies to all mortgage repossession cases in Northern Ireland. The Home Owner and Debtor Protection (Scotland) Act 2010 provides for pre-action requirements to be placed on secured lenders in Scotland.

The FCA refers back in this context, with approval, to the two publications from the Office of Fair Trading *Debt collection guidance* (published in July 2003) and *Irresponsible lending – OFT Guidance for creditors* (published in March 2010 and updated February 2011).

Secured lending

35.56   CONC 15.1.1 R states:

> This chapter applies to:
> (1) a firm with respect to consumer credit lending in relation to regulated credit agreements secured on land; and
> (2) a firm with respect to credit broking in relation to credit agreements secured on land.

35.57   CONC 15.1.2 G observes:

> Firms which carry on consumer credit lending or credit broking should comply with all rules which apply to that regulated activity in CONC and other parts of the Handbooks. For example, CONC 7 applies to matters concerning arrears, default and recovery (including repossession) and applies generally to agreements to which this chapter applies. This chapter sets out specific requirements and guidance that apply in relation to agreements secured on land. Regulated mortgage contracts and home purchase loans are not regulated credit agreements and are excluded, to the extent specified in article 36E of the Regulated Activities Order from credit broking.

Sale and rent back

35.58   The FCA also regulates agreements whereby a home owner sells his or her property and simultaneously rents it back from the buyer. An interim regulatory regime was introduced on 1 July 2009 with the 'full regime' effective on 30 June 2010.[61] The provisions bring under FCA control persons who carry on the business of arranging or advising in relation to a 'regulated sale and rent back agreement.[62] This is an arrangement whereby:

- a person ('the agreement provider') buys all or part of a 'qualifying interest' in land from an individual or trustees ('the agreement seller') and
- the 'agreement seller' or an individual who is the beneficiary of the trust (if the 'agreement seller' is a trustee) or a related person is entitled under the arrangement to occupy at least 40 per cent of the land in question as or in connection with a dwelling and intends to do so.[63]

35.59   The definition of a 'related person' is:

'related person' in relation to the agreement seller or, where the agreement seller is a trustee, a beneficiary of the trust, means –
(i) that person's spouse or civil partner;
(ii) a person (whether or not of the opposite sex) whose relationship with that person has the characteristic of the relationship between husband and wife;
(iii) that person's parent, brother, sister, child, grandparent or grandchild.[64]

The FCA prohibits exploitative advertising and cold calling, provides for a 14-day cooling off period to provide owners time to reflect on the proposed transaction, provides for a minimum five-year tenancy and ensures that the risks associated are made clear to the owner.

35.60   Where a homeowner facing eviction by their lender sells their property to a third party and is then granted rights to occupy under a rent back arrangement, the seller's rights under that arrangement do not constitute an overriding interest binding on a mortgage lender who advances monies to enable the third party to purchase the property from the homeowner.[65]

---

61 FCA Handbook MCOB 6.9 and PERG 14.4A.
62 Financial Services and Markets Act 2000 (Regulated Activities) Order 2001 art 63J.
63 Financial Services and Markets Act 2000 (Regulated Activities) Order 2001 art 63J (3)(a).
64 Financial Services and Markets Act 2000 (Regulated Activities) Order 2001 art 63J(4)(c).
65 *Scott v Southern Pacific Mortgages Ltd* [2014] UKSC 52, [2014] HLR 48. Cf *Mortgage Express v Lambert* [2016] EWCA Civ 555.

Dispute resolution

35.61   The Financial Services and Markets Act 2000 Part 16 provides for the setting up of the Financial Ombudsman Service (FOS) to investigate complaints about lenders (although it also covers those involved in the administration of regulated mortgage contracts). Complaints are to be determined according to what the Ombudsman considers to be 'fair and reasonable in all the circumstances of the case'.[66] The FCA Handbook sets out an elaborate complaints dispute resolution procedure entitled 'Dispute Resolution: Complaints' which is contained within the Redress section of the Handbook.

35.62   The procedure provides that a complainant must first seek redress through the lender's internal complaint's procedure. The FOS cannot look into a complaint until either the lender has issued its final response to the complaint or eight weeks have elapsed from the date the complaint was received by the lender.[67] The complaint can be lodged online or the FOS complaint form can be downloaded from the FOS website.[68] There is a specific Appendix to the complaints procedure dealing with Payment Protection Insurance issues.[69] If the FOS upholds a complaint, it may make a money award, an interest award, a costs award against the lender or a direction that the lender takes such steps in relation to the complaint as the FOS considers just and appropriate (whether or not a court could order those steps to be taken) or both.[70] The FOS can make a money award (up to a maximum of £150,000) of such amount as is considered to be fair compensation for one or more of the following;

- financial loss (including consequential or prospective loss); or
- pain and suffering; or
- damage to reputation; or
- distress; or
- inconvenience

whether or not a court would award compensation.[71]

If the FOS considers that a larger financial award is required the FOS can recommend that the lender pays the balance. In respect of costs it is noted that 'In most cases complainants should not need to have

---

66 FSMA 2000 s228.
67 DISP 3.2.2 R.
68 www.financial-ombudsman.org.uk.
69 DISP App 3.1.1.
70 DISP 3.7.
71 DISP 3.7.2 R.

professional advisers to bring complaints to the Financial Ombuds-man Service, so awards of costs are unlikely to be common'.[72]

35.63   The FOS is unable to consider a complaint 'more than six months after the date the lender's final response was sent to the complain-ant or more than (a) six years after the event complained of, or (if later) (b) three years from the date on which the complainant became aware (or ought reasonably to have become aware) that he had cause for complaint'.[73] The FOS retains discretion to consider a complaint outside these time limits where failure to comply was 'as a result of exceptional circumstances'.[74] Expressly, the FOS guidance provides that the six-month time limit is only triggered by a response which is a final response. The final response must tell the complainant about the six-month time limit that the complainant has to refer a com-plaint' to the FOS.[75]

35.64   Unfortunately, the FOS does take time to determine complaints to it, with investigations taking months rather than weeks. It remains to be seen to what extent the court dealing with possession will itself grant a stay of proceedings, under CPR 26.4(2)(b), to allow negoti-ations to take place between the parties or to allow the FOS time to investigate a complaint. In *Derbyshire Home Loans Ltd v Keaney*,[76] a stay on proceedings was granted to enable a complaint to the FOS to be processed if necessary, given the claimant's failure to deal with proposals put to it by the borrowers. It is worth noting in this context that the *Pre-action Protocol for possession claims based on mortgage or home purchase plan arrears in respect of residential property* provides at paragraph 8.1:

> The lender should consider whether to postpone the start of a posses-sion claim where the borrower has made a genuine complaint to the Financial Ombudsman Service (FOS) about the potential possession claim.[77]

35.65   The FOS website can be found at www.financial-ombudsman.org.uk. The FOS operates a technical advice desk which is the ombudsman's information resource for business and consumer advisers. The web-site suggests that the advice desk '... can give an informal steer on how the ombudsman might approach a particular complaint – or answer

---

72 DISP 3.7.10 G.
73 DISP 2.8.2 R.
74 DISP 2.8.2 R.
75 DISP 2.8.3 G.
76 April 2007 *Legal Action* 28, Bristol County Court.
77 DISP 3.9.11 G.

more general questions about our rules and how we work'. The advice desk can be contacted on tel: 020 7964 1400 (open 9am to 6pm Monday to Friday) and by email at: technical.advice@financial-ombudsman.org.uk.

35.66   Advisers will need to ensure that where a lender does not comply with a Rule or Guidance that this is taken up with the lender as quickly as possible. In the context of a threatened or actual possession claim this should also be raised by identifying any breach of the *Pre-action Protocol for possession claims based on mortgage or home purchase plan arrears in respect of residential property* with which many of the MCOB provisions are comparable.

CHAPTER 36

Preventing the lender from obtaining possession

Introduction

36.1   In practice, mortgage possession actions can usually be successfully defended only by raising enough money to satisfy the lender or, failing that, by persuading the court that it is right to exercise one of the statutory powers to deny possession or restructure the loan, described in chapter 34. In common with most debt cases, this involves minimising the borrower's expenditure and maximising the borrower's income.

36.2   Where the borrower is working, the question of income maximisation is largely one of ensuring that he or she is in receipt of any possible relevant additions to salary or wages, in-work benefits, working tax credit, child tax credit, maintenance and child support payments, child benefit, etc. If the borrower is unemployed, it is important to ensure that: benefit payments are correct and complete; any potential tax rebates have been claimed; and any unfair dismissal, redundancy or discrimination claims have been considered.

36.3   It is also worth checking whether the borrower is protected by any payment protection insurance (PPI) (where an insurance company has agreed to make part or all of the mortgage repayments for a limited period of time following the borrower becoming sick or unemployed). Detailed consideration of these options is really outside the scope of this chapter and readers seeking such assistance are encouraged to go online to National Debtline,[1] which has a range of leaflets and advice on all aspects of debt. However, a brief synopsis of options relating to cutting mortgage costs and increasing relevant income is provided in the following paragraphs.

Reducing mortgage costs

36.4   Although most lenders have quite wide-ranging powers to lend money as they wish, lenders often say that options for rescheduling the loan, so as to reduce the borrower's payments, are not available, possible or practical. It will be necessary to persevere and show the lender that by reducing the current mortgage costs by rescheduling over a longer term or by altering the level and/or frequency of repayment, it will be possible for the borrower to meet future commitments.

---

1   www.nationaldebtline.org; tel: 0808 808 4000.

Reduction of repayments

36.5   Lenders can be expected to agree to accept interest-only payments, and defer capital repayments within repayment mortgages at least in the short term. This should prevent further arrears accruing providing payments are made. The lender may require that the unpaid capital elements be paid off when normal repayments are resumed. In relation to regulated mortgage contracts (see para 35.6), the Financial Conduct Authority (FCA) requires lenders to deal fairly with any borrower in arrears.[2] Lenders must also operate within their written policy for complying with this obligation. FCA guidance suggests that lenders may wish to defer payment of interest due on a regulated mortgage contract or treat any arrears as if they were part of the original amount borrowed.[3] An unreasonable response to such a request might found the basis for a complaint to the Financial Ombudsman Service (FOS): see para 35.61.[4] Many financial institutions are also sensitive to bad media publicity where the lender is obviously acting insensitively.

36.6   Where the borrower took out payment protection insurance (PPI) to pay the mortgage instalments in the event of unemployment or sickness, it is important to lodge the necessary claim form with insurers as soon as possible. Many of these policies set a very short timescale within which a claim should be made. Do not be put off lodging the claim after the time specified, because the insurers can extend the time at their discretion. PPI is commonly taken out with second mortgages or 'secured loans'. Payments received under PPI, which are then used by a claimant receiving income support or income-based jobseeker's allowance to pay housing costs not covered by the Department for Work and Pensions (DWP), are not treated as the claimant's income.[5] Similarly, payments which these claimants receive from other sources (rather than being paid directly by a third party to the lender), which are actually used to make payments towards a secured loan which does not qualify for assistance under the benefit regulations, are ignored unless the claimant has used insurance policy payments for the same purpose.[6]

---

2 Mortgage: Conduct of Business sourcebook (MCOB) 13.3.1 R (1)(b).
3 MCOB 13.3.4 G (1)(c) and (d).
4 www.financial-ombudsman.org.uk.
5 Income Support (General) Regulations (IS Regs) 1987 SI No 1967 Sch 9 para 29 and Jobseeker's Allowance Regulations (JSA Regs) 1996 SI No 207 Sch 7 para 30.
6 IS Regs 1987 Sch 9 para 30(a)–(d) and JSA Regs 1996 Sch 7 para 31.

36.7   It is now well recognised that many people were mis-sold PPI. Often, this only comes to light when a claim is made under the policy and then refused. Sometimes, borrowers are unaware of the fact that part of the loan they took out included an up-front single premium which they recognise they did not want or was not suitable for them. Complaint can be made where payment was made for a PPI policy was taken and only a small refund is paid when the loan is redeemed early. It is worth assessing whether a complaint can be made to the company with whom the policy was taken out and, if needs be, subsequently to the FOS. The FCA and the FOS can provide further information about this issue.

Extension of the mortgage term

36.8   In any 'repayment mortgage' case, it may be possible to extend the term of the loan so as to reduce the capital element and, in consequence, the amount of the monthly repayment. This option need not be pursued if the lender is prepared to accept interest-only payments for a period. Extending the term of the loan involves entering into a new mortgage arrangement. It may be possible, as part of that process, to have the existing arrears 'capitalised' by the lender wiping out the arrears and increasing the outstanding capital by an equivalent amount. In this way, the borrower can be given a fresh start.

36.9   Again the FCA encourages lenders, in relation to regulated mortgage contracts,[7] to consider extending the term of the regulated mortgage contract.[8]

Changing the type of mortgage

36.10   Where the mortgage is a capital repayment mortgage, it is worth considering whether it is possible to switch to an 'interest-only' mortgage. In this way, the monthly payments would only be of the interest and none of the capital. FCA policy is to discourage lenders from granting interest-only mortgages so many lenders will be hesitant to agree to the switch.

36.11   In the case of an endowment mortgage, it is worth considering whether there would be a reduction in monthly payments by

7   See para 35.6 above.
8   MCOB 13.3.4 G (1)(a).

switching to a repayment mortgage. The amount of interest paid each month would remain the same but the monthly repayments of the capital (over the remainder of the term or over an extended term) may be less than the payments of the endowment insurance premium. The amount of capital originally borrowed from the lender could be reduced by the surrender or sale value of the endowment policy. If the endowment policy has been going for some years, more will be raised by selling the policy to an endowment policy investor. The borrower should contact a reputable insurance broker for details of how the policy could be sold on. It can be difficult to sell policies which have been in existence for only a few years. If the lender agrees to a new loan, a mortgage protection policy may have to be taken out to cover the possibility of the borrower's death before the end of the loan term.

36.12 Where an endowment mortgage borrower is told by the endowment policy insurance company that the sums likely to be realised at the end of the term of the policy are less than the amount needed to pay off the mortgage loan, the borrower would probably be better advised to negotiate with the lender to make additional payments towards the shortfall rather than taking out an additional endowment or similar policy to pay off the shortfall. Borrowers who have been advised that their endowment policy is unlikely to be enough to pay off the capital borrowed and who feel that they may have been mis-sold the policy should contact the FCA.[9]

36.13 The *Pre-action Protocol for possession claims based on mortgage or home purchase plan arrears in respect of residential property* (see paras 37.3–37.14 and appendix E) expressly identifies four options for consideration by the lender and borrower, namely extending the term of the mortgage, changing the type of mortgage, deferring payment of interest and capitalising the arrears.

Remortgaging

36.14 Where there are two or more mortgages (one of which may well be with a 'fringe' mortgage company which charges high rates of interest), or even where there is one high interest rate loan, it is worth trying to persuade one of the mainstream lenders (such as a bank or building society) to 'remortgage' the loan. This involves redemption of the existing loan(s) and replacement with a new mortgage agreement.

9 See www.fca.org.uk.

It is easier to persuade a building society or bank to remortgage the property if, at the time of the new mortgage, the borrower's local housing authority agrees to enter into a form of mortgage guarantee which would indemnify the lender in the event of the bank or building society suffering a loss because of any default.[10] It is worth arguing that the lender has, in the future, nothing to lose, as the money will be recovered either following repossession and sale or, if there is any shortfall, by the local authority meeting the shortfall under the terms of the guarantee. Unfortunately, such 'guarantees' from local authorities are not common in practice.

36.15   Extreme caution should be exercised when considering whether to remortgage with institutions other than mainstream mortgage lenders because the terms offered may well be disadvantageous over a period of time. The fees for remortgaging may also be considerable, as they include not only surveyors' and solicitors' fees but also the commission charged by the mortgage broker who arranges the remortgage. However, it is worth seeking specialist advice from a reputable mortgage broker as some lenders are keen to attract new customers, often on initially advantageous terms.

36.16   Where a borrower is 'threatened with homelessness', ie it is 'likely that he will be homeless within 28 days',[11] it is useful to remind the housing authority of its duty[12] to 'take reasonable steps to secure that accommodation does not cease to be available for [the borrower's] occupation'. This duty may extend to requiring the authority to use one or more of its powers in Housing Act (HA) 1996 Part 7 to try to prevent dispossession. This duty arises only where the local housing authority is satisfied that the borrower is in priority need and is not intentionally threatened with homelessness.

Repurchase by local authorities

36.17   In practice, it is quite common for a defaulting borrower who has purchased his or her previously council-owned property to ask the local authority to buy the property back. Local authorities purchasing properties which have previously been bought under the 'right to buy' provisions of HA 1985 receive government subsidy.[13]

---

10   See HA 1985 s442.
11   HA 1996 s175(4).
12   HA 1996 s195(2).
13   Local Authorities (Capital Finance) (Amendment) Regs 1999 SI No 501.

Financial help from the Department for Work and Pensions

36.18 For a detailed analysis of the rules relating to mortgage interest payments by the DWP for people eligible for income support, income-based jobseeker's allowance (JSA), income-related employment and support allowance and pension credit, reference should be made to the current year's edition of the Child Poverty Action Group's *Welfare benefits and tax credit handbook.* In May 2016 the House of Commons Library published *Support for mortgage interest scheme* (often referred to as SMI) which provides a helpful synopsis and history of the scheme.[14]

36.19 The DWP is required, in most cases, to pay interest on loans taken out for the purchase or repair or improvement of the home, where the borrower is in receipt of income support or income-based JSA.[15] Claimants receiving income-related employment and support allowance and pension credit can also receive assistance.[16] There is no obligation on the DWP to pay the capital element in the monthly loan repayment or the monthly premium on the insurance policy in endowment mortgages, or to assist in maintaining the private pension contribution in cases of pension mortgages.

36.20 Since 5 January 2009, the waiting period before benefit will be paid has in most cases been 13 weeks for new working age claimants. Prior to this, longer periods of 26 or 39 weeks for full SMI applied, depending when the loan was taken out. Receipt of SMI is indefinite except for JSA claimants to whom it is only paid for two years. The maximum loan on which mortgage interest is met was increased in January 2009 from £100,000 to £200,000

36.21 Interest is payable by the DWP by reference to a standard interest rate. Since October 2010 this has been based on the average mortgage rate published by the Bank of England.[17] It currently is, and has since then been, 3.63 per cent. Payments are made to the lender every four weeks in arrears even if the contractual payments are due monthly.

---

14 Briefing Paper 06618, 3 May 2016.
15 IS Regs 1987 regs 17(e) and 18(f) and Sch 3 paras 7 and 8; JSA Regs 1996 reg 83(f) and Sch 2 paras 14 and 15.
16 Employment and Support Allowance Regulations 2008 SI No 794 Sch 6 and State Pension Credit Regulations 2002 SI No 1792 Sch 2.
17 Social Security (Housing Costs) (Standard Interest Rate) Amendment Regulations 2010 SI No 1811.

36.22   The Welfare Reform and Work Act 2016 received Royal Assent on 16 March 2016. Section 18 gives the Secretary of State power to make regulations providing for loans to be made in respect of a person's liability to make owner-occupier payments in respect of accommodation occupied by the person as that person's home. The 2016 Act empowers the Secretary of State to replace the current statutory regime of SMI payments made to home owner benefit recipients with repayable loans. The regulations to be made may include provisions as to when and how the loans are to be repaid and allow for administrative costs to be charged. Section 21 enables the Secretary of State to make what transitional provisions or savings he or she considers necessary or expedient.

Procedure and tactics

Venue for possession proceedings

37.1   Proceedings for possession of a dwelling-house may be brought by a mortgage lender in any county court hearing centre.[1] Where the loan is one regulated by the Consumer Credit Act (CCA) 1974, proceedings must be brought in the county court.[2] The claim for possession in a non-CCA case may be brought in the High Court if the claimant files, with the claim form, a certificate stating the reasons for bringing the proceedings in the High Court verified by a statement of truth. Circumstances may, in an appropriate case, justify a mortgage lender starting a claim in the High Court if:

- there are complicated disputes of fact;
- there are points of law of general importance.[3]

The value of the property and the amount of any financial claim may be relevant circumstances but these factors alone will not usually justify starting the claim in the High Court.[4]

37.2   If a claimant starts a claim in the High Court and that court decides that it should have been started in the county court, the court will usually either strike out the claim or transfer it to the county court of its own initiative. The court will usually disallow the costs of starting the claim in the High Court or of any transfer.[5] In practice, proceedings are usually brought in the county court and the procedure and tactics discussed in this chapter apply to proceedings in that court unless otherwise indicated.

Mortgage arrears protocol

37.3   On 18 November 2008 the *Pre-action Protocol for possession claims based on mortgage or home purchase plan arrears in respect of residential property*[6] ('Mortgage Arrears Protocol') came into effect. It was revised on 6 April 2015. The full text is set out in appendix E. The aims of the protocol are to ensure that the lender and borrower 'act fairly and reasonably with each other' in resolving any matter concerning mortgage arrears and to 'encourage greater pre-action contact' in order to

---

1   Civil Procedure Rules (CPR) 55.3(1)(a).
2   CCA 1974 s141(1).
3   CPR (PD) 55 para 1.3.
4   PD 55 para 1.4.
5   PD 55 para 1.2.
6   www.justice.gov.uk/civil/procrules_fin/contents/protocols/prot_mha.htm.

seek agreement between the parties and, where agreement cannot be reached, to enable efficient use of the court's time and resources. The protocol aims also to encourage lenders to check who is in occupation of the relevant property before issuing proceedings.

37.4 The protocol applies to first charge residential mortgages regulated by the Financial Conduct Authority (FCA) under the Financial Services and Markets Act (FSMA) 2000, second charge mortgages and other secured loans regulated under the CCA 1974 and 'unregulated residential mortgages'. The Protocol expressly states that it does not apply to 'buy to let' mortgages.

37.5 The lender 'must respond promptly' to any proposal for payment of the arrears made by a borrower and, if the lender does not agree to such a proposal, it should give written reasons within ten business days of the proposal.[7] If the borrower fails to comply with an agreement, the lender should warn the borrower, by giving the borrower 15 business days' notice in writing, of its intention to start a possession claim unless the borrower remedies the breach of the agreement.[8]

37.6 The Protocol, at para 6.1, counsels against the issuing of proceedings in three sets of circumstances relating to a borrower who is seeking to pay the arrears:

> A lender must not consider starting a possession claim for mortgage arrears where the borrower can demonstrate to the lender that the borrower has–
> (a) submitted a claim to
>   (i) the Department for Work and Pensions (DWP) for Support for Mortgage Interest (SMI) or, if appropriate, Universal Credit; or
>   (ii) an insurer under a mortgage payment protection policy; or
>   (iii) a participating local authority for support under a Mortgage Rescue Scheme, or other means of homelessness prevention support provided by the local authority;
>   (iv) and has provided all the evidence required to process a claim;
> (b) a reasonable expectation of eligibility for payment from the DWP or from an insurer or support from the local authority or welfare or charitable organisation such as the Veterans Welfare Scheme or Royal British Legion;
> (c) an ability to pay a mortgage instalment not covered by a claim to the DWP or the insurer in relation to a claim under paragraph 6.1(1)(a) or (b);

7 Para 5.6.
8 Para 5.8.

(d) difficulty in respect of affordability or another specific personal or financial difficulty, and requires time to seek free independent debt advice, or has a confirmed appointment with a debt adviser and

(e) a reasonable expectation, providing evidence where possible, of an improvement in their financial circumstances in the foreseeable future (for example a new job or increased income from a lodger).

37.7 The second set of circumstances where proceedings could be deferred is set out in the Protocol at para 6.2 and deals with the situation of a borrower seeking time to sell:

> If a borrower can demonstrate that reasonable steps have been or will be taken to market the property at an appropriate price in accordance with reasonable professional advice, the lender must consider postponing starting a possession claim to allow the borrower a realistic period of time to sell the property. The borrower must continue to take all reasonable steps actively to market the property where the lender has agreed to postpone starting a possession claim.

Protocol para 6.3 specifies that where, notwithstanding paragraphs 6.1 and 6.2, the lender has agreed to postpone starting a possession claim because the borrower proposes to sell, the borrower should provide the lender with a copy of the particulars of sale, the Energy Performance Certificate (EPC) or proof that an EPC has been commissioned and (where relevant) details of purchase offers received. The borrower should give the lender details of the estate agent and the conveyancer instructed to deal with the sale. The borrower should also authorise the estate agent and the conveyancer to communicate with the lender about the progress of the sale and the borrower's conduct during the process.

37.8 The third situation where the Protocol advises forbearance by a lender is where the borrower has complained about the lender's conduct. Paras 8.1 and 8.2 provide:

> The lender must consider whether to postpone the start of a possession claim where the borrower has made a genuine complaint to the Financial Ombudsman Service (FOS) about the potential possession claim.

> Where a lender does not intend to await the decision of the FOS, it must give notice to the borrower, with reasons, that it intends to start a possession claim.

37.9 Protocol para 6.4 provides that where the lender decides not to postpone the start of a possession claim, it must inform the borrower of the reasons for this decision at least five business days before starting proceedings.

37.10 Emphasis is placed on alternative dispute resolution. The Protocol provides, at para 7.1, that 'Starting a possession claim should be a last resort and must not normally be started unless all other reasonable attempts to resolve the situation have failed'.

37.11 According to Protocol para 7.1, the parties should consider whether, given the individual circumstances of the borrower and the form of the agreement, it is reasonable and appropriate to do one or more of the following:

- extend the term of the mortgage;
- change the type of mortgage;
- defer payment of interest due under the mortgage;
- capitalise the arrears; or
- make use of any Government forbearance initiative in which the lender chooses to participate.

37.12 If proceedings are issued, the lender must bring to court two completed copies of form N123, which is a checklist requiring the lender to identify how it has in the previous three months complied with the Protocol.[9] A blank copy of form N123 is at appendix A.

37.13 While the Protocol does not contain specific sanctions for non-compliance, the general 'Practice Direction – Pre-action Conduct and Protocols'[10] states at para 13:

> The court may take into account the extent of a party's compliance with a relevant pre-action protocol when giving directions for the managements of claims and when making costs orders.

37.14 If in the opinion of the court there has been non-compliance with the Protocol or the 'Practice Direction – Pre-action Conduct and Protocols' that Protocol provides at para 15 that the court may order that:

> (a) the parties are relieved of the obligation to comply or further comply with the pre-action protocol or the Practice Direction;
> (b) the proceedings are stayed while particular steps are taken to comply with the pre-action protocol or the Practice Direction;
> (c) sanctions are to be applied.

This can include an order that the party at fault pays the costs of the proceedings or part of the costs of the other party.[11]

---

9 PD 55A para 55.8.
10 www.justice.gov.uk/courts/procedure-rules/civil/pdf/preview/pre-action-protocol-amendments-6-april.pdf.
11 Para 16.

Claim form

37.15   Mortgage possession proceedings are brought by claim form with attached particulars of claim. The claim form is normally endorsed by the court with the hearing date fixed.[12] However, if the claim is not brought at the country court hearing centre which serves the address where the land is situated, the date will be fixed for hearing when the claim is received by that hearing centre.[13] The hearing date cannot be less than 28 days from the date of issue[14] and the standard period between the issue of the claim form and the hearing should not be more than eight weeks.[15] The defendant must be served with the claim form and the particulars of claim not less than 21 days before the hearing.[16] The stage of borrower default at which lenders issue proceedings varies but can be when as little as two months' arrears have accrued. In practice, proceedings are brought to enforce payment with the deterrent that failure to pay will result in possession being lost. The proceedings are in the same form whether the claimant is a first or subsequent mortgagee.

37.17   The particulars of claim attached to the claim form are required[17] to set out certain details relating to the loan including, among others, the amount of the loan; any periodic payment and any payment of interest required to be made; and, in schedule form, to show the dates and amounts of all payments due and payments made under the mortgage agreement for the period of two years immediately preceding the date of issue of the proceedings.[18] If the lender wishes to rely on a history of arrears which is longer than two years, this must be stated in the particulars of claim and a full (or longer) schedule exhibited to a witness statement.[19]

37.18   In the case of claims issued using 'Possession Claims Online'[20] (PCOL) the lender does not need to provide a schedule showing the arrears from the date of default or for two years if default exceeds that period, provided that such a schedule has been served before issue. Instead, the lender need only provide a summary of the arrears in

12 CPR 55.4 and 55.5.
13 CPR 55.5(1A).
14 CPR 55.5(3)(a).
15 CPR 55.5(3)(b).
16 CPR 55.5(3)(c).
17 PD 55A para 2.5 and form N120.
18 PD 55A para 2.5(3).
19 PD 55A para 2.5A.
20 www.possessionclaim.gov.uk/pcol/.

the claim form but must, not more than seven days from the issue of proceedings, serve on the defendant a schedule of arrears if they exceed two years or from the date of default if less than two years. In a PCOL case, a lender which has only provided a summary of arrears in the claim form must also make a witness statement or provide oral evidence at the hearing that the appropriate schedule was served on the defendant before the proceedings were issued.[21]

37.19 Details of any other payments required to be made as a term of the mortgage (such as for insurance premiums, legal costs, default interest, penalties, administrative or other charges) must also be specified, as must details of any other sums claimed, stating the nature and amount of any such charge. The lender must also specify whether any of those payments are in arrears and whether these are included in the amount of any periodic payment. However, failure to provide the required information may not justify refusal to grant a possession order.[22] The claim form must be verified by a statement of truth.[23] In the usual way, the defendant(s) has 14 days within which to file any defence. An acknowledgment of service is not required.[24]

37.20 Generally, the only defence available will be to seek the benefit of the court's powers under the Administration of Justice Acts (AJA) 1970 and 1973 or the CCA 1974 (see chapter 34). See appendix B for a precedent defence. Although it is important to file a formal defence if any unusual point is to be argued, the courts should allow a defendant to be heard without any formal pleadings being served.[25] CPR 55.7(3) expressly provides that where a borrower has not filed a defence he or she 'may take part in any hearing' although the court may take the default into account on the question of costs. Arguably, this provision would entitle a borrower who is in breach of a directions order to be heard and he or she need not apply for relief from sanctions. It remains to be seen to what extent the courts will stay proceedings under CPR 26.4 to allow any complaint concerning a regulated mortgage contract (see para 35.6) to be investigated by the Financial Ombudsman Service. See para 37.8 above.

37.21 It is not possible to obtain a default judgment in mortgage possession proceedings.[26] Form N11M, the defence form which is sent

21 PD 55B para 6.3–6.3C.
22 *Nationwide Anglia Building Society v Shillibeer* [1994] CLY 3295.
23 CPR 22.1.
24 CPR 55.7.
25 See *Redditch Benefit Building Society v Roberts* [1940] Ch 415, [1940] 1 All ER 342, CA and CPR 55.7(3).
26 CPR 55.7(4).

out by the court with the possession claim form, must be used by the defendant.[27] This enables the borrower to give a complete picture of his or her finances because the form is really little more than an income and expenditure statement. An application for a time order under CCA 1974 s129 may be made in the defence or by application notice in the proceedings.[28]

37.22   Where, after proceedings have been issued, the borrower pays off the arrears, it may be appropriate to adjourn the proceedings generally so that the lender can apply to reinstate the proceedings if further arrears accrue. This saves further legal costs which are likely to be added to the borrower's mortgage debt.[29] However, discharging the arrears may well not relieve the borrower from an obligation under a suspended possession order to continue to pay the monthly instalments as they fall due if the possession order is to remain suspended.[30] If the arrears have been cleared, the borrower should apply to the court to discharge the order.

Parties to proceedings

37.23   The claimant must join as defendants not only the borrower(s) but also those people in occupation who are known to claim a right to remain.[31] An occupier who is not a legal owner (the property being in the sole name of the borrower) does not have the absolute right to be joined as defendant. Where a spouse or civil partner has registered a Class F land charge, or a notice or caution pursuant to the Family Law Act 1996 s31, he or she has the right to be notified of the action being brought by the lender against his or her spouse, and should be sent a copy of the particulars of claim.[32] He or she does not have to be joined as defendant by the lender from the outset. Whether or not any such charge, notice or caution has been registered, a 'connected person' who is not a defendant may apply to be joined as a defendant 'at any time before the action is finally disposed of in that court' and shall be made a defendant with a view to meeting the borrower's

---

27 PD 55A para 1.5.
28 PD 55A para 7.1. See also form N440.
29 *Halifax plc v Taffs* April 2000 *Legal Action* 15, [2000] CLY 4385, CA. See also *Greyhound Guaranty Ltd v Caulfield* [1981] CLY 1808 approved in *Zinda v Bank of Scotland plc* [2011] EWCA Civ 706, [2011] HLR 40.
30 *Zinda v Bank of Scotland plc* [2011] EWCA Civ 706, [2011] HLR 40.
31 *Brighton and Shoreham Building Society v Hollingdale* [1965] 1 All ER 540.
32 Family Law Act 1996 s56.

liabilities provided that the court 'does not see any special reason against it' and the court is satisfied that he or she may be able to persuade the court to exercise any of its powers under AJA 1970.[33] The expression 'connected person' in relation to any person means that person's spouse, former spouse, civil partner, former civil partner, cohabitant or former cohabitant.[34] In the case of a former spouse, former civil partner or former cohabitant, the right to apply to be joined as a defendant applies only where that person has the benefit of a court order conferring rights of occupation. In such circumstances, the court can only refuse the application to be joined if there are 'special reasons' against the applicant being joined in the claim. Where a person has registered his or her rights of occupation under the Family Law Act 1996 as a land charge or at the Land Registry then the lender is also obliged to serve notice of the claim on that person.[35]

37.24   It is quite possible that a deserted spouse or civil partner may not hear about the proceedings until the bailiffs come to execute a warrant for possession, but it would be possible for him or her to apply at that stage to be joined as a defendant and to claim relief. Occupiers (such as tenants) who wish to be joined as defendants should apply by letter to the court and attend the hearing.[36] Alternatively, they could simply attend the hearing and ask to be joined as a defendant then. CPR 55.10(2) requires the lender, within five days of being notified by the court of the hearing date, to send to the mortgaged property a notice addressed to the 'tenant or the occupier' as well as to the local housing authority for the district where the property is located, and to the registered proprietor of any other legal charge, stating that possession proceedings have been issued and giving details of the parties to the proceedings the court venue and the hearing date. The lender is also required to produce, at the hearing, a copy of the notice and evidence that the notice has been served.[37]

37.25   An occupying tenant (who may well have no right to remain as against the lender) may need to apply to be joined as defendant so as to obtain a possession order which names him or her as a party for the purpose of application to the local housing authority for assistance under the homelessness provisions of the Housing Act

---

33 Family Law Act 1996 s55.
34 Family Law Act 1996 s54(5).
35 Family Law Act 1996 s56.
36 CPR 19.4.
37 CPR 55.10(4).

(HA) 1996 Pt 7. Advisers should consider the practice of the local housing authority before making any application because a tenant renders himself or herself at risk as to costs by becoming a party to the claim. However, a lender would not usually take steps to recover costs against the tenant but would rely on recovery of costs against the security of the property (see para 37.80). A tenant wishing to be joined in the proceedings, as a named defendant, should be advised of this theoretical risk.

37.26   The Mortgage Repossessions (Protection of Tenants etc) Act 2010 gives the court power to suspend an order for possession on applica-tion by a tenant. Where a mortgage lender brings a possession claim in respect of a property which consists of or includes a dwelling-house and there is an unauthorised tenancy of all or part of the property, the court may *on making an order for possession*, on the application of the tenant, postpone delivery of possession for up to two months.[38]

37.27   There is an 'unauthorised tenancy' only if:

(a) an agreement has been made which, as between the parties to it (or their successors in title) is or gives rise to –
   (i) an assured tenancy (within the meaning of the Housing Act 1988), or
   (ii) a protected or statutory tenancy (within the meaning of the Rent Act 1977), and
(b) the lender's interest in the property is not subject to the tenancy. (s1(8)).

37.28   Subsequently, the court may, on the application of the tenant, *stay or suspend execution of the order* for a period not exceeding two months if –

(a) the court did not exercise its powers to suspend on application of the tenant when making the order for possession or if it did the tenant applicant was not the tenant when it exercised those powers,
(b) the tenant has asked the lender to give an undertaking in writing not to enforce the order for two months beginning with the date the undertaking is given, and
(c) the lender has not given such an undertaking. (s1(4))

The court's powers under section 1(4) arise only where an order for possession has been made but not executed.[39]

37.29   In considering whether to exercise its powers, the court must have regard to:

---

38 Mortgage Repossessions (Protection of Tenants etc) Act 2010 s1(1) and (2) and CPR 55.10 (4A).
39 Mortgage Repossessions (Protection of Tenants etc) Act 2010 s1(3).

    (a) the circumstances of the tenant, and
    (b) if there is an outstanding breach by the tenant of a term of the
        unauthorised tenancy –
        (i) the nature of that breach, and
        (ii) whether the tenant might reasonably be expected to have
            avoided breaching that term or to have remedied the breach.[40]

37.30   Any postponement, stay or suspension may be made conditional on
the making of payments to the lender in respect of occupation of the
property.[41] The making of these payments, pursuant to an undertaking given by a lender under Mortgage Repossessions (Protection of
Tenants etc) Act 2010 s1(4)(c) or a condition imposed by the court
on the tenant, is not to be regarded as creating (or as evidence of the
creation of) any tenancy or other rights to occupy the property.[42]

37.31   Enforcement of a possession order by a lender in respect of a
dwelling-house may take place only following the service of a prescribed form giving the tenant/occupier no less than 14 days' notice
of the date for the eviction.[43]

37.32   The *Pre-action Protocol for possession claims based on mortgage or
home purchase plan arrears in respect of residential property* deals with
the situation where there is an 'authorised' tenant in occupation of
the property. In this context, an 'authorised tenant' is a tenant whose
tenancy is authorised between the borrower and the lender.[44] It is
assumed that this is intended to deal with the tenant under a buy to
let mortgage. The protocol provides that in such cases the court will
consider whether: (a) further directions are required; (b) to adjourn
the possession claim until possession has been recovered against the
tenant; or (c) to make an order conditional upon the tenant's right of
occupation.[45]

37.33   The fact that the borrower is bankrupt does not mean that he or
she has no right or power to address the court in possession proceedings. Both the order and warrant are directed to the named defendants and as such they have the right to raise issues which are relevant
to the exercise of any AJA 1970 or 1973 discretion.[46] The trustee in

---

40 Mortgage Repossessions (Protection of Tenants etc) Act 2010 s1(5).
41 Mortgage Repossessions (Protection of Tenants etc) Act 2010 s1(6).
42 Mortgage Repossessions (Protection of Tenants etc) Act 2010 s1(7).
43 Mortgage Repossessions (Protection of Tenants etc) Act 2010 s2(2).
44 Para 1.1(e).
45 Para 7.2.
46 *Nationwide Building Society v Purvis* [1998] BPIR 625, CA.

bankruptcy of a bankrupt borrower should be joined as a party only if the court so directs.[47]

Evidence

37.34   A claim for possession is heard in private (unless the court directs to the contrary).[48] The evidence in support of the claim will be set out in the particulars of claim and verified by a statement of truth.[49] Additional evidence may be given by witness statement without specific court order except where the case is allocated to the fast track or multi-track or the court otherwise orders.[50] Usually, institutional lenders make use of this facility as it is easier and more cost-effective to give evidence by witness statement than to incur the expense of attendance at court of management personnel. Pro forma witness statements are generally produced, which do little more than confirm the contents of the particulars of claim. The mortgage deed is usually exhibited to the witness statement, as is any calling-in letter. Where relevant, an up-to-date search certificate of HM Land Registry or Land Charges Department will also be exhibited to indicate whether any notice, caution or Class F land charge has been registered to protect a civil partner or spouse's rights of occupation under family legislation.

37.35   However, it is possible on the application of any party to obtain an order requiring the maker of the witness statement to attend court for cross-examination. If the maker of a witness statement does not attend the hearing and the borrower 'disputes material evidence in the statement, the court will normally adjourn the hearing so that oral evidence can be given'.[51] The borrower may wish to require attendance of the maker of the witness statement where, for example, the lender is claiming arrears of payments which include separate interest charges on missed monthly payments so as to have this clarified for the court. Advisers can then argue that only bona fide missed payments should be taken into account in considering whether to postpone an order or not. Borrowers should seek the attendance of the makers of witness statements only if there is some good reason,

---

47   *Alliance Building Society v Shave* [1952] Ch 581.
48   PD 39 para 1.5.
49   CPR PD 55A para 5.1.
50   CPR 55.8(3).
51   PD 55A para 55.8.5.4.

in view of the formidable position which lenders have in connection with costs and expenses.[52] The witness statement is usually sent by post to the borrower before the hearing and must be served at least two days before the hearing.[53] However, this does not prevent evidence about the level of arrears being brought up to date orally or in writing on the day of the hearing if necessary.[54]

37.36   The court is entitled to accept material adduced as evidence informally by the borrower or his or her representative even if that does not strictly comply with the laws of evidence.[55] If the lender disputes what the borrower has said then formal evidence would need to be called.

37.37   Advisers may wish to request, instead of the attendance of the maker of the witness statement, an order from the court that the claimant file a detailed witness statement setting out all sums claimed to be due and a copy of the loan account from the inception of the loan so as to indicate to the court the full details of the claim.

Hearings and orders for possession

37.38   The hearing of the claim is usually in private and before a district judge.[56] Given the number of possession claims being listed for hearing, the court may well expect to be able to spend only a matter of minutes on each case. If any substantive argument is raised, then it is likely that the hearing will be adjourned to another date. In such cases, the borrower should offer to make some payment towards the mortgage in the interim. If the case is to be defended the court should either proceed to deal with the case or give case management directions to include, 'where the claim is disputed on grounds which appear to be substantial', allocating to track.[57]

37.39   In deciding allocation to track, the matters to which the court shall have regard include, under CPR 26.8, the level of arrears, the importance to the defendant of retaining possession and the importance

---

52 See para 37.80.

53 CPR 55.8(4).

54 PD 55A para 55.8.5.2.

55 *Cheltenham & Gloucester Building Society v Grant* (1994) 26 HLR 703, CA. See also M Thompson, 'A very wide discretion?' [1995] Conv 51.

56 Originally Administration of Justice Act 1970 s38(3) (repealed by County Courts Act 1984 s148(3)) and now CPR PD 39 para 1.5.

57 CPR 55.8(1) and (2).

of vacant possession to the claimant.[58] In practice, it is rare for an 'undefended' claim to be allocated to a track.

37.40   With many hearings in private, practice and procedure vary. Usually, the lender's solicitor outlines the history of the case and advises on any change in circumstances since the date of the witness statement. The representative may hand to the judge an informal note specifying the level of the arrears, the current monthly instalment and the balance and indicating the date and the amount of the last payment made into the account. The original legal charge and a search for the purpose of identifying any rights registered under the Family Law Act 1996 may be produced for examination by the district judge and a certificate of service will be produced if, unusually, the claimant has served the claim form and particulars of claim.[59] There is strictly no need for the *original* charge certificate to be produced because office copies of the register and documents filed at the Land Registry are admissible under the Land Registration Act 2002 s67.[60] The lender is obliged to produce at the hearing a copy of the 'Dear Occupier' notice as well as evidence that the notice has been served.[61] Failure to produce these can be grounds for an adjournment. Where no valid search has been made it is for the claimant to satisfy the court that there are no people who should be notified in accordance with the Family Law Act 1996 s56. The lender's representative should present form N123 Mortgage Pre-action Protocol checklist completed in accordance with that form's guidance notes. It is essential, before the hearing starts, for the lender's representative to be asked for a copy of the N123. Advisers will need to take immediate instructions from the borrower on what is asserted there about compliance with the Protocol (see para 37.3).

37.41   The borrower should then be asked to comment on the lender's case and to justify the court's exercise of any statutory power to postpone the giving up of possession. It is important to ensure that the court has the essential information needed to assess the case, including:

- the current balance outstanding;
- the arrears;
- the monthly instalment;
- the remaining term of the mortgage;

58 CPR 55.9.
59 CPR 55.8(6).
60 Civil Evidence Act 1995 s9.
61 CPR 55.10(4)(b).

- the last payment made and the amount of it; and
- the '*Norgan* figure' (being the monthly payment required to pay off the arrears by the end of the mortgage term).

Where there is equity available to protect the lender, then this should be made clear. It is obviously essential that the borrower attends the hearing so as to give evidence to support any claim for statutory relief. Useful evidence includes:

- a letter of confirmation from the Department for Work and Pensions concerning payment of mortgage interest;
- evidence of future regular employment from a new employer;
- a loan from friends or relatives;
- proof of remortgage facilities; or
- an estate agent's valuation of the property.

Where relief by way of a time order is being sought (see para 34.69), realistic statements of income and expenditure should be available if not provided in N11M.

37.42   If, when arranging the mortgage, the borrower was required to pay for a mortgage indemnity policy, taken out by the lender to protect it in the event of a shortfall on sale following the borrower's eviction, this should be made clear to the district judge if there is any doubt about the extent of the security. Since such a policy indemnifies the lender (either entirely or to a pre-set figure), the lender will not usually be prejudiced by the court giving any benefit of the doubt to the borrower in deciding whether to delay possession. The existence of such a policy should be clear from the mortgage offer letter which would have been sent to the borrower at the time the loan was taken out (as paying for the policy would have been one of the 'special' conditions of the advance).

37.43   When considering possible orders for postponed possession, advisers should obviously seek to argue for as long a period as is viable so that the amount of money required to be paid monthly towards the arrears is minimised. That said, advisers need to bear in mind observations in the judgment in *Norgan* that if the borrower is given the period most favourable to the borrower and then defaults, it will be easier for the lender to argue against the borrower being given a further postponement, in any future application by the borrower.[62]

37.44   In the case of a regulated mortgage contract (see para 35.6), it is important to ensure that the district judge is aware that, when

---

62 *Cheltenham & Gloucester Building Society v Norgan* [1996] 1 All ER 449 at 459, although in *Norgan*, the Court of Appeal granted a fourth suspension.

considering an application for a possession order, there is no statutory restriction requiring the arrears to be paid off within a 'reasonable period' (see para 34.62) as the court has discretion under CCA 1974 ss129 and 135. In addition, it is important also to ask the district judge to consider making a time order (see para 34.66) as well as suspending any order for possession granted in favour of the lender.

37.45   Any order giving statutory relief is likely to require the borrower to pay a stated amount per month in addition to the normal monthly instalment. The usual postponed order for possession in mortgage cases is set out as county court form N31. Effectively, the number of months it will take to clear off the arrears at £X per month is the 'reasonable period' being identified by the court for the purposes of the AJA 1970 s36(1).

37.46   Courts generally lean against making outright orders for possession unless the borrower either fails to attend the hearing or is unable to make any proposals which meet the statutory criteria. Usually, the court will, unless the security is insufficient or threatened, be concerned not to grant an outright order in favour of the lender unnecessarily. Where the court does not feel able to exercise its discretion, then an order for possession in 28, or possibly 56, days is given in favour of the lender.

37.47   Where the borrower's financial position is uncertain (for example, where he or she has recently applied for a job or where a fresh claim has been made for income support and the amount of help to come from the Department for Work and Pensions is not clear), it is possible to ask the court to exercise its general case management powers under CPR 3.1 to adjourn for a short period to allow the issues to be clarified. Borrowers should, if at all possible, offer to make some payments in the interim.

37.48   Where an 'interest only' mortgage borrower has defaulted in maintaining payments under the policy intended for the repayment of the capital it is common for lenders, where they become aware of this, to 'switch' the mortgage from an interest-only loan to a capital and interest loan. Particularly where the mortgage has been running for some time, this results in a substantial increase in the monthly payments expected from the borrower. Advisers must check carefully whether the legal charge provides for this. In any event it is arguable that, even if there is no 'capital vehicle' in place to repay the original loan, the loan could be repaid from the sale of the security if there were insufficient funds available to the borrower at the end of the mortgage term. It would be open to the lender to make application to the court if there was a change in circumstances such as to put the lender at risk.[63]

37.49   If the borrower is not able to persuade the district judge to grant a postponed order for possession because the borrower is not able to meet the current payments and clear the arrears over a reasonable time, some district judges have adopted a practice of granting an order for possession effective sometime in the future. This might be, for instance, an order for possession in three months' time. The rationale would seem to be that this gives a borrower, who is not able to meet the statutory criteria for relief, a period of time in order to improve his or her situation. If their situation improves, the borrower can apply to the court at that stage for a variation of the order for possession so that it is then postponed on terms. Alternatively, the court may direct that there be a review hearing in, say, three months to ensure that the case is reassessed automatically.

37.50   In general, an order for possession should not be made against only one of two borrowers where it would not advantage the lender because the other borrower is entitled to remain in possession. For example, where a husband has no defence to the claim but where the wife has an arguable defence based on her consent to the charge being obtained by undue influence (see chapter 42). In such circumstances, the court should not grant a possession order against the husband alone but should adjourn the proceedings with liberty to restore should the wife leave the property or an order for possession be made against her.[64]

37.51   Where it is clear that some form of statutory relief is to be given to the borrower, advisers should argue for an adjournment on terms as to the making of specified monthly payments by the borrower instead of a suspended order for possession. The advantage is that, in the event of default, a further hearing would be required if an adjournment was originally ordered; whereas a lender would be able to apply immediately for a warrant for possession without further hearing if the terms of a postponed or suspended order were breached. Many district judges are unwilling to adjourn on terms as they feel that this is insufficient by way of incentive to the borrower to pay and/or that by building in this extra step in the proceedings all that is being

---

63 See *Household Mortgage Corporation plc v Etheridge* April 1997 *Legal Action* 13.
64 *Albany Home Loans Ltd v Massey* [1997] 2 All ER 609, (1997) 29 HLR 902, CA. See also M P Thompson, 'The powers and duties of mortgagees' [1998] 62 *Conv* 391.

done is to increase the legal costs which will usually be added to the mortgage debt.

37.52   By contrast, in the High Court, execution of an order for possession because of a breach of a suspensory term cannot take place without the defendant being given an opportunity to be heard.[65]

37.53   In a mortgage claim, the court should not usually attach to a postponed order for possession a requirement that the warrant for possession should not be executed without permission of the court,[66] although in practice it is not unknown for such a requirement to be added.

37.54   A borrower is not barred from making an application for a further postponement of an order or warrant just because a similar application has been refused before, although the court can dismiss such an application if it is an abuse of process.[67] It is important to be able to point to some change of circumstances since the time the previous order was made.

37.55   Where a borrower is not able to satisfy the court that it should grant him or her any statutory relief, then the lender is entitled to possession of the property. This may put the borrower in practical difficulty if some time is required to obtain alternative accommodation (either privately or from the local housing authority) and the lender is not willing to defer, by consent, the obtaining of physical possession. The county court has sufficient jurisdiction to postpone execution of the warrant for possession for a limited period.[68] However, this power must be used judicially and the limits of this jurisdiction are unclear. Advisers will note that the limitations imposed on the court by HA 1980 s89 in respect of the implementation of the possession order (14 days or six weeks in case of exceptional hardship) is disapplied in a claim for possession by a mortgage lender.[69]

65 *Fleet Mortgage and Investment Co v Lower Maisonette 46 Eaton Place Ltd* [1972] 2 All ER 737 and *Practice Direction* [1972] 1 All ER 576.
66 *Royal Trust Co of Canada v Markham* [1975] 3 All ER 433, CA.
67 *Abbey National Mortgages v Bernard* (1996) 71 P&CR 257, [1995] NPC 118, CA.
68 See *Kelly v White, Penn Gaskell v Roberts* [1920] WN 220.
69 HA 1980 s89(2)(a).

Counterclaims

37.56 The making of a counterclaim for damages against a lender does not prevent the latter from exercising its common law right to possession. Even where a meritorious counterclaim exists (for example, for negligence or breach of warranty arising out of a survey report on the condition of the mortgaged property), this does not allow, for instance, the court to exercise its statutory discretion any differently, because damages received by virtue of the counterclaim would not necessarily extinguish arrears by the end of a 'reasonable period'.[70] The position may be different where the counterclaim against the lender is pleaded by way of a set-off and if the existence and prospects of success can be regarded as enabling the sums due to be paid within a reasonable period[71] or where the counterclaim is for rescission of the mortgage.[72] An action for damages (see para 35.16), for example, for breach of the *Mortgages and Home Finance: Conduct of Business sourcebook* (see para 35.19) may result in the borrower being able to argue for discretion to be exercised under AJA 1970 or 1973.[73] The situation for mortgages governed by CCA 1974 may be different, in that the court's power to assist the borrower is not qualified by having to be satisfied that the arrears and accruing payments will be paid up to date by the end of a 'reasonable period'.

Money judgments

37.57 The practice of the major institutional lenders varies but some lenders include, as part of the relief claimed, a request for judgment for the entire debt due at the date of the hearing. The particulars of claim and the witness statement in support form the evidence for that claim as well as for the order for possession. The rationale is that a money judgment makes it easier for the lender to take subsequent enforcement action (if, for example, the property is sold for less than the

---

70 See *National Westminster Bank plc v Skelton* [1993] 1 All ER 242, CA; *Citibank Trust v Ayivor* [1987] 1 WLR 1157; *Barclays Bank plc v Tennet* CAT 242, 6 June 1984, noted at [1985] CLY 5; *Midland Bank plc v McGrath* [1996] EGCS 61, CA and *Barclays Bank plc (t/a The Woolwich) v Boyd* [2015] NICH 16.

71 See *Ashley Guarantee plc v Zacaria* [1993] 1 All ER 254, CA and *Royal Bank of Scotland v O'Shea* April 1998 *Legal Action* 11, CA.

72 See *Barclays Bank plc v Waterson* (1988) Manchester County Court, noted at [1989] CLY 2505.

73 See *Thakker v Northern Rock plc* [2014] EWHC 2107 (QB).

money judgment obtained). However, the court has the discretion under the County Courts Act 1984 s71(2) to suspend payment of the entire debt. In the usual case, the money judgment is postponed on the same terms as the order for possession.[74]

37.58   There are instances where it would be right to depart from the practice of granting a money judgment (for example, if the borrower produces evidence of the sale of the mortgaged property taking place within a reasonable period).[75] The money judgment, in cases where a postponed order for possession is also obtained, does not appear on the judgment register as a county court judgment unless and until the terms of the suspension are breached and the lender takes steps to enforce the order for possession. The Register of Judgments, Orders and Fines Regulations 2005[76] reg 9(d) exempts from registration as a county court judgment 'an order for the payment of money arising from an action for the recovery of land (whether for costs, payments due under a mortgage, arrears of rent or otherwise) until the creditor takes any step to enforce the order ...'.

37.59   It is not an abuse of process for a lender to seek possession first before subsequently choosing the further remedy of seeking a money judgment.[77] Accordingly, it is not improper for a lender who has been met with a successful *Barclays Bank v O'Brien*[78] defence (for which, see para 42.4) to choose after disclaiming the security of the legal charge to sue on the personal covenant in the legal charge with a view, as an unsecured creditor, to bankrupt the mortgage borrower, even if this might result in the trustee in bankruptcy applying for an order for sale.[79]

37.60   A lender's claim for a money judgment is not to be struck out as an abuse simply because no money judgment was requested in previous unopposed proceedings in which a possession order was obtained where, in those proceedings, a money claim was made.[80] However, a claimant who had obtained a money judgment as well as a possession order based on an 'all monies' legal charge cannot subsequently issue fresh proceedings against the defendant seeking a money judgment in relation to a guarantee entered into by the

---

74 *Cheltenham & Gloucester Building Society v Grattidge* (1993) 25 HLR 454, CA.
75 *Cheltenham & Gloucester Building Society v Johnson* (1996) 28 HLR 885, CA.
76 SI No 3595.
77 *Zandfarid v BCCI* [1996] 1 WLR 1420.
78 [1994] 1 AC 180, HL.
79 *Alliance & Leicester plc v Slayford* [2000] EWCA Civ 257, (2001) 33 HLR 66.
80 *UCB Bank plc v Chandler* (2000) 79 P&CR 270, [1999] EGCS 56, CA.

defendant before the previous proceedings. In such circumstances, the claimant's cause of action merges in the earlier judgment.[81]

37.61   *The Pre-action Protocol for possession claims based on mortgage or home purchase plan arrears in respect of residential property* provides that, where a potential claim includes a money claim and a possession claim, then the Protocol's provisions apply to both claims.[82]

Appeals

37.62   Appeals from a district judge generally lie to a circuit judge.[83] The procedure is set out in CPR Part 52 and Practice Direction 52. Appeals from the circuit judge lie to the High Court in most cases (but not where the circuit judge has heard an appeal). CPR 52.11(3) provides that:

> [t]he appeal court will allow an appeal where the decision of the lower court was (a) wrong or (b) unjust because of a serious procedural or other irregularity in the proceedings in the lower court.

However, an appeal court will be reluctant to interfere with an exercise of discretion unless it can be shown that the judge had:

- applied the wrong legal principle;
- reached a conclusion that no reasonable tribunal, properly informed as to the law and facts, could have reached;
- had regard to factors that were irrelevant; or
- failed to have regard to factors which were relevant.[84]

37.63   An application for permission to appeal may be made to the lower court at the hearing at which the decision to be appealed was made or to the appeal court in an appellant's notice.[85] Permission to appeal may be given only where (a) the court considers that the appeal would have a real prospect of success or (b) there is some other compelling

---

81   *Lloyds Bank plc v Hawkins* [1998] Lloyd's Rep Bank 379, CA. See also P Mostyn, 'No interest for mortgagees after money judgment' [1998] NLJ 1728 for a discussion of the case and an argument that lenders are, post-judgment, restricted to interest on the judgment debt at the statutory judgment rate rather than any contractual rate. See also *Director General of Fair Trading v First National Bank plc* [2001] UKHL 52, [2002] 1 AC 481.

82   Para 4.2.

83   See Access to Justice Act 1999 (Destination of Appeals) Order 2000 SI No 1071, paras 3, 4 and 5.

84   *City West Housing Trust v Massey* [2016] EWCA Civ 704, para 8.

85   CPR 52.3(2) and (3).

reason why the appeal should be heard.[86] The appeal must be filed within 21 days of the making of the order under appeal, in Form N161. The lodging of an appellant's notice does not stay enforcement of the order under appeal unless the appeal court or the lower court orders otherwise.[87] An undertaking not to seek to enforce the order under appeal should be sought from the claimant or a stay should be sought from the district judge or the circuit judge pending appeal. There are special rules relating to second appeals, that is an appeal from a circuit judge hearing a case on appeal from the district judge.[88]

37.64   It has been held at circuit judge level that where a borrower has unsuccessfully applied to a district judge for the suspension of a warrant and has been evicted, a circuit judge has no jurisdiction to hear an appeal even if the appellant's notice was filed within the 21-day period for lodging the appeal.[89] A contrary position has been taken by another circuit judge under CCR Ord 37 r6.[90]

Warrants for possession

Pre-execution

37.65   In the county court, where an immediate order for possession has been made at a hearing, or any period of postponement has expired, or where the terms of any postponed order have been broken, the lender is free to apply without notice for the issue and execution of a warrant for possession. No further hearing is required and this does not breach Human Rights Act 1998 Sch 1 Article 6.

37.66   It is often only when the occupiers receive notification of the proposed eviction by the bailiffs that advice is sought. At this stage, where there has been a hearing, advisers should consider applying to set aside the original possession order, if there are grounds for doing so under CPR 39.3, before execution of the warrant. For example, where the borrower did not attend the hearing because of non-receipt of the claim form or illness. Applications should be made in form N244, preferably with a supporting witness statement and if

---

86 CPR 52.3(6).
87 CPR 52.7.
88 CPR 52.13.
89 *Jayashankar v Lloyds TSB plc* [2011] EW Misc 9 CC.
90 *Hyde Park Funding Ltd v Ioannou* [1999] CLY 4382.

possible with a draft defence to the original claim (see precedent at appendix B).

37.67   The Mortgage Repossessions (Protection of Tenants etc) Act 2010 requires lenders seeking to enforce a possession order to serve notice at the property before the eviction.[91] This legislation was intended to give unauthorised tenants (see paras 37.26–37.31) the right to apply to the court to defer eviction by their landlord's lender. However, the provisions go wider than affecting tenants and put in place a further step for lenders wishing to enforce a possession order in respect of residential premises. Execution of a possession order may take place:

(a) only if the lender gives notice at the property of any prescribed step taken for the purpose of executing the order, and

(b) only after the end of the prescribed period beginning with the day on which such notice is given.[92]

37.68   Regulations provide that the prescribed period is 14 calendar days and the prescribed step is the service on the tenant or occupier of a prescribed form advising of the lender's intention to enforce the possession order no fewer than 14 days before the date for the eviction. A copy of the notice is contained in appendix A to this book. While the 2010 Act enables 'unauthorised tenants' to make application to the court, it does not widen the legal options open to other occupiers although, confusingly, the statutory notice is addressed to 'tenant/occupier'.

37.69   Where occupiers are not parties to the proceedings, they may wish to make applications to be joined as defendants, as well as applying to have the order for possession set aside. An application to be joined as a party may be made on notice using form N244 and should also be supported by evidence setting out the occupier's interest in or connection with the claim.[93] Where a tenant occupies part of the property he or she may be able to have judgment set aside only in respect of the part he or she occupies.

37.70   A borrower in breach of a conditional postponed order for possession can apply to have the order itself further postponed and/or the condition varied, or alternatively to have the warrant for possession suspended on terms. AJA 1970 s36 may be used to stay or suspend execution of an order for possession 'at any time before execution

---

91 Dwelling Houses (Execution of Possession Orders by Mortgagees) (England and Wales) Regulations 2010 SI No 1809.

92 s2(2).

93 PD 19 paras 1.3 and 1.4.

of such ... order'.[94] Similar scope is given to the court in respect of regulated agreements within the meaning of the CCA 1974.[95] Any application for such a further stay or suspension should usually be made on notice to the lender on form N244. It is advisable to make such an application (see precedent at appendix B) pending negotiations if there is any doubt as to whether a lender will agree to a stay or execution of the order.

Post-execution

37.71 Once the bailiff has executed the warrant and the borrower has been displaced, the court's statutory powers are exhausted.[96] However, the court's power to set aside judgment granting the order for possession and the subsequent warrant for possession may still be of assistance.[97] See para 31.66 for a discussion of the circumstances where the warrant for possession may be set aside on grounds of fraud, oppression or abuse of process by the lender. A party to proceedings who, through no fault of his or her own, did not have notice of a hearing until after it had already commenced, but who then made no attempt to apply to have the hearing recommenced could not later expect the court to set aside judgment given against him or her.[98] Where the borrower can raise the money to redeem the mortgage prior to exchange of contracts on the lender's sale, the court may restrain the lender from selling.

37.72 The borrower's equity of redemption is extinguished when the lender enters into a contract for sale, rather than at the time of completion, although it is unclear what the situation would be where the borrower has grounds to have the original order set aside or where the warrant was obtained by fraud or there has been abuse of the process or oppression in its execution such as to justify the warrant being set aside.[99] Where a lender is concerned about the risk of a

---

94 See *R v Bloomsbury and Marylebone County Court ex p Villerwest Ltd* [1976] 1 All ER 897, CA; *R v Ilkeston County Court ex p Kruza* (1985) 17 HLR 539 and *Hawtin v Heathcote* [1976] CLY 371, Altrincham County Court.

95 Consumer Credit Act 1974 s135.

96 *Cheltenham & Gloucester Building Society v Obi* (1996) 28 HLR 22, CA; *Mortgage Agency Services Number Two Ltd v Bal* [1998] EWCA Civ 1186, (1998) 95(28) LSG 31 and *Jayashankar v Lloyds TSB plc* [2011] EW Misc 9 (CC).

97 CPR 39.3. See also *Governors of Peabody Donation Fund v Hay* (1987) 19 HLR 145, CA; *Hammersmith and Fulham LBC v Hill* (1995) 27 HLR 368, CA and *Cheltenham & Gloucester Building Society v Obi* (1996) 28 HLR 22, CA.

98 CPR 39.3 and *National Counties Building Society v Antonelli* [1995] NPC 177, CA.

99 *National Provincial Building Society v Ahmed* [1995] 38 EG 138, CA.

borrower making some sort of application to the court which would have the effect of putting off a prospective buyer, the appropriate step is for the lender to apply for an order for sale under the Law of Property Act 1925 s91 where taking the property by virtue of the court order would protect the buyer absolutely.[100]

37.73   Where, however, an occupier is evicted by the bailiff and claims to have an independent right to remain as against the lender, for example, as an occupier with a tenancy binding on the lender or as an occupier with a superior equitable interest (for which see chapters 38 and 41), he or she may apply to have judgment set aside or stayed so far as he or she is concerned and to be allowed to defend the proceedings.[101]

Responsibilities of the mortgagee in possession

37.74   In the context of residential mortgages, the lender will be seeking possession of the borrower's home with a view to evicting the borrower and selling with vacant possession. For a discussion on the responsibilities imposed on the lender when selling, see para 43.14. A borrower will be concerned about the time it takes for the sale to be concluded and the fact that interest continues to accrue until the final payment of the mortgage following sale. The common law 'Duty to account' imposed on a mortgagee in possession may be of some assistance to borrowers in these circumstances. The extent of this liability has not been considered recently by the courts, and many of the old cases do not readily lend themselves to giving guidance on the position where modern institutional lenders take possession for the sole purpose of selling with vacant possession. The duty to account operates in the borrower's favour by allowing the borrower, on redeeming the mortgage, to set off against monies due to the lender under the mortgage any rent or other profits received during the period of the lender's possession of the mortgaged property. If necessary, the court can order the taking of accounts in redemption proceedings.

37.75   A lender who goes into possession of the mortgaged property, and thereby excludes the borrower from control of it, is bound to account to the borrower, not only for the rents and profits which it actually receives, but also for the rents and profits which, but for its

---

100   *Arab Bank plc v Mercantile Holdings* [1994] Ch 71.
101   *Minet v Johnson* (1890) 63 LT 507 and *Hawtin v Heathcote* [1976] CLY 371.

wilful default or neglect, might have been received, ie for everything received, or which might or ought to have been received, while the lender is in possession.[102]

37.76   A lender which fails to rent out the property will be liable to account for rent that could have been received. In the seventeenth-century case of *Anon*[103] it was held that the lender's liability to account arose on a failure to let to a tenant who was capable of paying the going rent for the property. The short note of the case states:

> A Mortgagee shall not account according to the value of the land, viz. He shall not be bound by any proof that the land was worth so much, unless you can likewise prove that he did actually make so much of it or might have done so, had it not been for his wilful default: as if he turned out a sufficient tenant, that held it at so much rent, or refused to accept a sufficient tenant that would have given so much for it.

The burden of proof is on the person alleging 'wilful default' in not letting the property.[104] The onus shifts to the lender where the borrower shows that the property can be let or has been let. Then it is up to the lender to show that it has been vigilant in attempts to let the property.

37.77   The courts have been more restrictive in terms of imposing obligations on a mortgagee in possession in relation to repair of the property. It appears that there is some general obligation not to be negligent in relation to protection of the repossessed property, with the lender being under a duty to take reasonable steps to protect the property against vandalism.[105]

37.78   Where a borrower leaves personal property in the property repossessed, the lender owes a limited duty towards the borrower as involuntary bailee.[106] Reference will need to be had to the terms of the mortgage in question. However, subject to those terms, the obligation on an involuntary bailee is only to do what is right and reasonable.[107]

---

102 *Halsbury's Laws* Vol 32 para 698.

103 (1682) 1 Vern 45.

104 *Brandon v Brandon* (1862) 10 WR 287.

105 See generally P Morgan, M Hyland and W Clark, *Fisher and Lightwood's law of mortgage*, 14th edn, Butterworths, 2014; *Norwich General Trust v Grierson* [1984] CLY 2306 and H Markson, 'Liability of lenders in possession' (1979) 129 NLJ 334.

106 *Da Rocha Afodu and Another v Mortgage Express Ltd and Another* [2014] EWCA Civ 454.

107 See *Scotland v Solomon* [2002] EWHC 1886 and *Campbell v Redstone Mortgages Ltd* [2014] EWHC 3081 Ch.

37.79   One of the practical problems which can be a cause of further ani-
mosity between the lender and borrower is in deciding what items in
the property are fixtures, and as a result should be left in situ when
the borrower leaves, and what items are the borrower's and can lawfully be removed when the borrower gives up possession. In *TSB
Bank plc v Botham*,[108] the Court of Appeal gave guidance on whether
tap fittings, extractor fans, mirrors, 'white goods' and the like were
part of the fixtures and as such the lender's to dispose of with the
security on sale or were the borrower's to remove.

Costs

37.80   Advisers assisting borrowers should be aware of the advantageous
position which lenders have concerning legal and other costs. In
other types of litigation, the usual rule is that costs follow the event. In
mortgage cases, the lender is at common law entitled to all its 'costs,
charges and expenses' reasonably and properly incurred in preserving the security or recovering the mortgage debt, including the costs
of possession proceedings.[109] Costs of possession proceedings themselves will be allowed as being part of these 'just allowances',[110] even
without mention of an order for costs in the court order.

37.81   Usually the lender's position is strengthened by express contractual terms in the mortgage deed. CPR 44.5 deals with assessment of
costs where they are payable under a contract. It provides:

44.5(1) Subject to paragraphs (2) and (3), where the court assesses
(whether by summary or detailed assessment) costs which are
payable by the paying party to the receiving party under the terms
of a contract, the costs payable under those terms are, unless the
contract expressly provides otherwise, to be presumed to be costs
which –
(a) have been reasonably incurred; and
(b) are reasonable in amount,
and the court will assess them accordingly.
(2) The presumptions in paragraph (1) are rebuttable. Practice Direction 44 – General rules about costs – sets out circumstances where
the court may order otherwise.
(3) ...

---

108 [1996] EGCS 149, (1996) 73 P&CR (D) 1, CA. See also S Elwes, 'When do
    chattels form part' (1995) 11 IL & P 141.
109 *Drydon v Frost* (1838) My & C 670; *National Provincial Bank of England v Games*
    (1886) 31 Ch D 582, CA and *Sandon v Hooper* (1843) 6 Beav 246.
110 *Wilkes v Saunion* (1877) 7 Ch D 188.

37.82   PD 44.7.1 refines this:

7.1 Rule 44.5 only applies if the court is assessing costs payable under a contract. It does not –

(a) require the court to make an assessment of such costs; or

(b) require a mortgagee to apply for an order for those costs where there is a contractual right to recover out of the mortgage funds.

37.83   PD 44.7.2 sets out various principles which apply in mortgage possession claims:

7.2 (1) The following principles apply to costs relating to a mortgage.

(2) An order for the payment of costs of proceedings by one party to another is always a discretionary order: section 51 of the Senior Courts Act 1981 ('the section 51 discretion').

(3) Where there is a contractual right to the costs, the discretion should ordinarily be exercised so as to reflect that contractual right.

(4) The power of the court to disallow a mortgagee's costs sought to be added to the mortgage security is a power that does not derive from section 51, but from the power of the courts of equity to fix the terms on which redemption will be allowed.

(5) A decision by a court to refuse costs in whole or in part to a mortgagee may be –

(a) a decision in the exercise of the section 51 discretion;

(b) a decision in the exercise of the power to fix the terms on which redemption will be allowed;

(c) a decision as to the extent of a mortgagee's contractual right to add the mortgagee's costs to the security; or

(d) a combination of two or more of these things.

(6) A mortgagee is not to be deprived of a contractual or equitable right to add costs to the security merely by reason of an order for payment of costs made without reference to the mortgagee's contractual or equitable rights, and without any adjudication as to whether or not the mortgagee should be deprived of those costs.

7.3 (1) Where the contract entitles a mortgagee to –

(a) add the costs of litigation relating to the mortgage to the sum secured by it; or

(b) require a mortgagor to pay those costs,

the mortgagor may make an application for the court to direct that an account of the mortgagee's costs be taken.

(Rule 25.1(1)(n) provides that the court may direct that a party file an account.)

(2) The mortgagor may then dispute an amount in the mortgagee's account on the basis that it has been unreasonably incurred or is unreasonable in amount.

(3) Where a mortgagor disputes an amount, the court may make an order that the disputed costs are assessed under rule 44.5.

The court has no authority to assess the lender's costs unless: (1) it is requested to do so by the lender;[111] or (2) it determines that they have not been reasonably incurred or are unreasonable in amount.[112]

37.84   In practice, lenders usually seek a specific order that there be 'no order as to costs' (or 'costs to be added to security') or simply make no reference to the costs at the hearing, relying on a mortgagee's right to add costs to the security.

37.85   While it is clear that a lender is in a strong position as regards costs, the borrower can ask the court to restrict the lender's claim for costs in a number of ways. CPR 44.5 effectively restates the decision in the leading case of *Gomba Holdings (UK) Ltd v Minories Finance Ltd (No 2)*[113] and sets out the principles which apply. The lender's entitlement to the costs of the possession proceedings does not exclude the court's jurisdiction to regulate the payment of litigation costs. Even where the mortgage deed provides for the lender's costs to be paid on the indemnity basis, the court has the discretion to override that contractual provision and to disentitle the lender from receiving those costs. This can be done where the costs claimed by the lender have been unreasonably incurred or where they are unreasonable in amount.

37.86   Walton J put it this way:

> The court might very well take the view that, in the circumstances of any particular case, [the contractual right to costs on an indemnity basis] was a contractual provision which it ought to overlook and it ought not to give effect to.[114]

37.87   The court may order that the disputed costs are assessed under CPR 44.5 and PD 44.7.2.

37.88   Where the lender has acted unreasonably in relation to the bringing of proceedings or in relation to some aspect of the proceedings, it is advisable to ask at the hearing for the court expressly to direct, as part of the order, that the lender 'be not at liberty to add any costs to the security' in relation to the proceedings or the particular hearing in question. Where it is clear that the lender has flouted the *Pre-action Protocol for possession claims based on mortgage or home purchase*

---

111 *Principality Building Society v Llewellyn* [1987] CLY 2940 and *Bank of Ireland Home Mortgages Ltd v Bissett* [1999] 11 CL 53.

112 *Gomba Holdings (UK) Ltd v Minories Finance Ltd (No 2)* [1993] Ch 171, [1992] 3 WLR 723, CA.

113 [1993] Ch 171, [1992] 3 WLR 723, CA.

114 *Bank of Baroda v Panessar* [1987] Ch 335, [1987] 2 WLR 208 at 224D. See also *Gomba Holdings (UK) Ltd v Minories Finance Ltd (No 2)* [1993] Ch 171, [1992] 3 WLR 723, CA and C Evans, 'The new rules are working!' [2000] *Adviser* 79.

plan arrears in respect of residential property advisers should seek such an order.

37.89   In addition, the borrower, as the paying party in the proceedings, is entitled to ask the court to subject the lender's solicitor's costs to detailed assessment under the Solicitors Act 1974 s70. In practice, borrowers are better advised to issue an application within the proceedings or, alternatively, a Part 8 claim against the lender for an account of sums due under the mortgage and in this way to challenge the sums recouped from the borrower in respect of the lender's costs.[115]

37.90   On 22 April 2014 the county court's equity jurisdiction was increased to £350,000 and so the county court is the usual venue for applications contesting lender's legal costs.[116]

37.91   Under the Solicitors Act 1974, the party asking for the assessment of the costs will have to pay for the costs of the assessment proceedings unless he or she is able to persuade the court to reduce the amount of the costs to be paid by one-fifth of the sum claimed.[117] However, it is possible to identify a part only of the bill for scrutiny by the court and so restrict the risk of the consequences of the 'one-fifth rule'. It would seem that the district judge has some discretion, under Solicitors Act 1974 s70(10), to disregard the one-fifth rule where there are 'any special circumstances'. It seems likely that a similar approach would apply in applications made by borrowers for an account in respect of the lender's solicitors costs.

37.92   It is advisable to ask the lender to provide details of its bill of costs, itemising the number of letters written and received, phone calls made and received, the time spent, the status of the fee earner in the case and the hourly rate claimed as well as the work undertaken. Details of the amount of the disbursements involved should also be provided.

37.93   Subject to the terms of the mortgage deed, a borrower is not personally liable for such costs[118] and does not have to pay them directly. They will be added to the security as part of the mortgage and paid out of the proceeds of the sale.[119] Lenders are entitled to add costs to the security even against a borrower with a public funding certificate

115 *Tim Martin Interiors Ltd v Akin Gump LLP* [2011] EWCA Civ 1574, [2012] 1 WLR 2946.
116 County Courts Act 1984 s23 as amended by Crime and Courts Act 2013 s17(5) and County Court Jurisdiction Order 2014 SI No 503 art 3.
117 Solicitors Act 1974 s70(9).
118 *Sinfield v Sweet* [1967] 3 All ER 479, [1967]1 WLR 1489.
119 *National Provincial Bank of England v Games* (1886) 31 Ch D 582, CA.

and this will not be contrary to Legal Aid, Sentencing and Punishment of Offenders Act 2012 s26 which normally restricts awards of costs against publicly funded parties.[120] This is because, technically, the costs are recovered from the security and not the borrower.

120 *Saunders v Anglia Building Society (No 2)* [1971] 1 All ER 243, HL.

CHAPTER 38

Tenants of borrowers

Introduction

38.1 At common law, a borrower had no power to grant a tenancy which was binding on the mortgage lender. Since 1925, borrowers have had statutory power to grant certain types of lease.[1] However, this statutory power can be excluded by the terms of the mortgage deed and, in practice, the power to grant tenancies is invariably excluded either absolutely or on terms that the property cannot be let without prior written approval. Where a borrower seeks consent from the lender to let out the security, it may in exceptional circumstances be possible to imply a term that the lender's consent would not be unreasonably refused.[2]

38.2 Providing a borrower remains in control of the property, and does not get into arrears, the lender may not be interested in any third party occupation. In recent years, many institutional lenders have advanced money under 'buy-to-let' mortgages specifically to enable their borrowers to rent out properties. It is clear that, irrespective of whether the tenancy is binding on the lender, as between the borrower/landlord and the tenant, the tenancy will be binding on the former, if only by estoppel.[3] However, when a lender seeks possession, the position of a tenant is usually dependent on whether the tenancy was granted before or after the mortgage deed was executed.[4]

Tenancies granted before the date of the mortgage

Registered land

38.3 In common with any other purchaser of a legal interest, a mortgagee takes the property subject to any interests which qualify as 'overriding interests' within the meaning of the Land Registration Act 2002 Sch 3 para 2. Some tenancies qualify as overriding interests.

---

1   Law of Property Act 1925 s99 and *Habib Bank AG Zurich v Utocroft 2 Ltd* [2015] EWHC 3481 (Ch).
2   *Starling v Lloyds TSB Bank plc* [2000] EGLR 101, CA and *Citibank International plc v Kessler* [1999] Lloyd's Rep Bank 123.
3   *Dudley and District Benefit Society v Emerson* [1949] 2 All ER 252, CA and *Chatsworth Properties v Effiom* [1971] 1 All ER 604, CA.
4   *Berkshire Capital Funding Ltd v Street* (2000) 32 HLR 373, CA and *Woolwich Building Society v Dickman* [1996] 3 All ER 204, (1996) 28 HLR 661, CA.

38.4   A lease granted for a term not exceeding three years, where the tenant is in possession, is effective to create a legal interest.[5] Such a tenancy need not be registered at HM Land Registry to bind the lender and will qualify as an overriding interest, being the right of a person in actual occupation, unless enquiries have been made and these rights are not disclosed.[6] The fact that a tenant may have signed a form of consent subordinating his or her rights as tenant to those of the lender to enable the borrower landlord to obtain the mortgage, does not prevent the tenant subsequently relying on his or her tenancy as an overriding interest which binds the lender.[7]

38.5   In addition, a lease for a term not exceeding seven years also qualifies as an overriding interest[8] and, provided it is in writing, will be valid and binding on the lender whether or not the tenant is in occupation. In the case of registered land, the mortgage is completed and becomes effective on the date it is executed, although tenancies which are created after completion of the advance but before registration at HM Land Registry will be binding on the lender.[9] This applies even if the tenancy is granted in breach of a term of the legal charge.[10] See para 35.60 for the position of owners who become tenants after entering into 'sale and rent back' agreements.

Unregistered land

38.6   The tenancy of a person who went into occupation before the mortgage was granted will be binding on the lender if validly created. That means either: (1) the tenancy was created formally by deed; or (2) it was one capable of being created orally, ie, for a term not exceeding three years taking effect in possession at the best rent which can be reasonably obtained without taking a fine.[11] This will include weekly and monthly tenancies. Given the provisions of the Land Registration

---

5 Law of Property Act 1925 s54(2).
6 Land Registration Act 2002 Sch 3 para 2; *Barclays Bank Ltd v Stasek* [1957] Ch 28; *Bolton Building Society v Cobb* [1965] 3 All ER 814, [1966] 1 WLR 1; *Woolwich Equitable Building Society v Marshall & Long* [1952] Ch 1, [1951] 2 All ER 769, ChD and *Barclays Bank plc v Zaroovabli* [1997] Ch 321, [1997] 2 All ER 19, ChD.
7 *Woolwich Building Society v Dickman* [1996] 3 All ER 204, CA.
8 Land Registration Act 2002 Sch 3 para 1.
9 *Abbey National Building Society v Cann* [1991] 1 AC 56, [1990] 1 All ER 1085, HL and *Pourdanay v Barclays Bank plc* [1997] Ch 321, ChD.
10 *Barclays Bank plc v Zaroovabli* [1997] Ch 321, [1997] 2 All ER 769.
11 Law of Property Act 1925 s54(2) and *Universal Permanent Building Society v Cooke* [1952] Ch 95, CA.

Act 2002 in relation to compulsory registration of land, in practice it is uncommon to find unregistered titles.

38.7   Although it is conceivable that a borrower may have been able to allow tenants into a property in anticipation of the completion of the initial purchase, in practice cases where a tenant has an interest binding on a lender are more likely to arise with second or subsequent mortgages. The effect of a binding tenancy is that the lender cannot take possession as against the tenant who can rely on the legal interest created by the tenancy. So long as the borrower is allowed to retain the property as against the lender, he or she is entitled to claim the rent and to sue for possession against the tenant.[12] If the lender claims possession in accordance with its common law right, then the tenant is bound to pay the rent to the lender.[13] This includes any rent due but unpaid to the borrower at the time of the lender's demand.[14] Where the lender takes possession and gives notice to the tenant requiring rent to be paid to it, the tenant cannot set off against the rent a personal claim he or she has against the borrower.[15] A borrower executing a second mortgage deed, after the granting of a tenancy, to correct the terms of an earlier deed entered into before the granting of the tenancy does not replace the earlier deed so as to result in the tenancy being binding on the lender.[16]

Tenancies granted after the date of the mortgage

38.8   As indicated above (see para 38.1), most mortgage deeds exclude the borrower's statutory power to grant leases, either absolutely or without the lender's specific permission. It has been held that a tenancy granted under the Rent Act 1977, in breach of such a term in the mortgage deed, is not binding on the lender although it remains binding as such on the borrower.[17] The principle applies equally to tenancies under the Housing Act 1988. The statutory tenant's 'status of irremovability' granted to a Rent Act protected tenant on the ending of the contractual tenancy does not bind the lender if the original contractual tenancy was granted in breach of a term in the mortgage

---

12 Law of Property Act 1925 ss99 and 141 and *Trent v Hunt* (1853) 9 Exch 14.
13 *Rogers v Humphreys* (1835) 4 Ad & El 299.
14 *Moss v Gallimore* (1779) 1 Doug KB 279.
15 *Reeves v Pope* [1914] 2 KB 284.
16 *Walthamstow Building Society v Davies* (1990) 22 HLR 60, CA.
17 *Dudley and District Benefit Society v Emerson* [1949] Ch 707, [1949] 2 All ER 252, CA. Cf *Abbey National plc v Yusuf* June 1993 *Legal Action* 12.

deed.[18] As a result, the occupying tenant has no claim to remain once the lender exercises its right to possession. Unless and until something takes place to change the relationship, the tenant is, as against the lender, a trespasser. Since 1 October 2010, unauthorised tenants have had the right to apply to the court for an order postponing enforcement of a possession order for up to two months. See paras 37.26–37.31. Where a tenant is required by the lender to pay rent to it, the tenant can raise this recognition of a tenancy as a defence to any claim by the borrower for the payment of rent.[19]

38.9   The fact that the lender knew that a borrower was proposing to rent out the property for which mortgage finance was being sought does not prevent the lender from relying on a clause prohibiting the granting of a tenancy.[20] See para 37.32 above in relation to the impact of the Mortgage Arrears Protocol on tenants in such situations.

38.10   The occupier's tenancy, however, becomes binding on the lender if the lender does something expressly or by implication to recognise the tenant as its tenant.[21] As the original tenancy between the borrower and the tenant is a nullity so far as the lender is concerned, any tenancy created between the tenant and the lender must take effect as a new tenancy. An example of this arose where a lender's solicitor wrote to the borrower's tenant informing him that he should not pay any more rent to his 'former landlords' and making new arrangements for payment of rent.[22] The test is not one of intention but of objectivity – what would a reasonable person understand the relationship to be? In this case, the court held that, by writing to the borrower's tenant in such terms, the lender was estopped from denying that it had accepted him as its tenant.

38.11   Mere knowledge of an unauthorised post-mortgage tenancy, coupled with a failure to take steps to evict the tenant, does not have the effect of creating a new tenancy with the lender.[23] Acceptance of rent by the lender from the borrower's tenant creates a tenancy between the two parties, although the terms of the tenancy are not necessarily the same as the tenancy from the borrower but are such

18 *Britannia Building Society v Earl* [1990] 2 All ER 469, (1990) 22 HLR 98, CA. For a commentary see S Bridge, 'The residential tenant and the mortgaged reversion' [1990] Conv 450. See also *Mann v Nijar* (2000) 32 HLR 223, CA and *Sadiq v Hussain* [1997] NPC 19, CA.
19 *Underhay v Read* (1888) 20 QBD 209, CA.
20 *Lloyds Bank plc v Doyle* April 1996 *Legal Action* 17, CA.
21 See *Stroud Building Society v Delamont* [1960] 1 All ER 749.
22 *Chatsworth Properties v Effiom* [1971] 1 All ER 604, CA.
23 *Taylor v Ellis* [1960] Ch 368 and *Parker v Braithwaite* [1952] 2 All ER 837.

as are agreed or inferred from conduct.[24] Receipt by a lender of payments made by a tenant in the absence of evidence from which it could be inferred that the payments were coming from the occupier does not bind the lender.[25] A lender's requirement that payment of rent should in future be made to a receiver appointed under a legal charge as a formal agent for the borrower (as is usually the case with receivers) does not create a landlord and tenant relationship between tenant and lender.[26]

38.12   The mere fact, however, that a receiver has been appointed does not in an appropriate factual context prevent a court from concluding that a tenancy has arisen with the lender as landlord.[27] Where a first mortgagee has acted in such a way as to have created a tenancy between itself and occupying tenants, a second mortgagee in possession proceedings is entitled to a possession order but subject to the rights of the tenants until such time as those rights are determined.[28]

38.14   The definition of 'mortgagor' in the Administration of Justice Acts 1970 and 1973 as including 'any person deriving title under the original mortgagor'[29] does not include the borrower's tenant so as to enable that tenant to seek the protection of the Acts as if he or she were the borrower.[30] Where, however, a tenant does pay the rent to the lender to avoid eviction, he or she may deduct the amount actually paid to the lender from any future rental payments to the borrower.[31]

38.15   Under the Consumer Credit Act 1974, it would be open to a tenant who is joined as a defendant to seek to persuade the court to exercise its discretion to make a time order and to postpone any order for possession. The court is empowered[32] to make a time order and to postpone a possession order of its own volition where it is 'just to do so' in actions brought for possession of land to which a regulated agreement relates. It is clear that a time order must be directed at

---

24   *Keith v R Gancia & Co Ltd* [1904] 1 Ch 774, CA.
25   *Paratus AMC Ltd v Fosuhene* [2013] EWCA Civ 827, [2014] HLR 1.
26   *Lever Finance Ltd v Needleman's Property Trustee* [1956] Ch 357 and Law of Property Act 1925 s109(2).
27   *Mann v Nijar* (2000) 32 HLR 223, CA.
28   *Berkshire Capital Funding Ltd v Street* (1999) 78 P&CR 321, CA.
29   Administration of Justice Act 1970 s39(1).
30   See *Britannia Building Society v Earl* [1990] 2 All ER 469, (1990) 22 HLR 98, CA.
31   *Johnson v Jones* (1839) 9 Ad and El 809 and *Underhay v Read* (1887) 20 QBD 209, CA.
32   Consumer Credit Act 1974 ss129(1) and (2) and 135

the borrower, requiring payment by the borrower. However, in the face of potential proceedings by the tenant for breach of covenant for quiet enjoyment, the borrower may be persuaded to meet the payments required under the time order.

38.16　A tenant whose tenancy is invalid as against the lender is still, during the period of a contractual as opposed to a statutory tenancy, a person interested in the equity of redemption and has the right to take a transfer of the mortgage on paying off the loan.[33] Similarly, as a person entitled to redeem the mortgage, the tenant can ask the court to order sale of the property with a view to buying it.[34]

38.17　Where occupiers are occupying the property under a tenancy which is not binding on the lender, it has been held to be inappropriate for the lender to claim that they are trespassers for the purposes of CPR 55 to obtain an order for possession. The correct procedure is by way of an orthodox possession claim.[35]

38.18　A tenant evicted by a lender as a result of possession being obtained against the borrower may be able to sue the borrower/landlord for breach of the covenant for quiet enjoyment ordinarily implied into the tenancy agreement.[36] A similar right to claim damages for breach of an express covenant for quiet enjoyment may arise where there is a written lease.[37] However, there may well be practical difficulties in enforcing a monetary judgment against the borrower/landlord unless other assets can be identified.

38.19　Tenants threatened with eviction in these circumstances should consider applying to be joined as defendants to the possession proceedings with a view to claiming damages against the borrower/landlord within those proceedings under CPR 19.1. Where an expedited hearing resulting in judgment can be arranged, or where it is possible to obtain judgment in default, it would be possible to register a charging order against the title. Assuming that there is sufficient equity, the judgment would be satisfied on the lender selling the property.

38.20　The Council of Mortgage Lenders (CML) has issued advice to its members on appropriate practice involving 'buy-to-let' tenants, unauthorised tenants and repossessions see *Industry guidance on*

33　*Tarn v Turner* (1888) 39 Ch D 456, CA as considered in *Britannia Building Society v Earl* [1990] 2 All ER 469, [1990] 1 WLR 422, CA.

34　Law of Property Act 1925 s91(2) and *National Westminster Home Loans v Riches* [1995] 43/95 CLW 2.

35　*London Goldhawk Building Society v Eminer* (1977) 242 EG 462. See CPR 55.5.

36　*Stalker v Karim* June 1994 *Legal Action* 12 and *Sutherland v Wall* [1994] CLY 1448.

37　*Carpenter v Parker* (1857) 3 CBNS 206.

buy-to-let arrears and possessions (June 2009 – reviewed March 2016). The CML has also issued *Buy-to-let: statement of practice* which deals with all aspects of administration of buy-to-let mortgages (updated December 2015).

Assured tenancies

38.21   The Housing Act (HA) 1988 introduced a mandatory ground for possession available to a borrower/landlord or a lender against assured tenants.[38] There is no corresponding ground under the Rent Act 1977. The ground provides that the court must make an order for possession where:

- the mortgage was granted before the beginning of the tenancy;
- the lender is entitled to exercise a power of sale conferred by the deed or under the Law of Property Act 1925 s107;
- the lender requires possession of the dwelling-house for the purpose of disposing of it with vacant possession;

and either:

- notice was given by the landlord not later than the beginning of the tenancy that possession might be required under this ground; or
- the court considers it is just and equitable to dispense with the requirement of notice.

For further discussion see chapter 10.

38.22   Assured tenancies created after the mortgage, and in breach of a prohibition on the granting of tenancies, are not binding on the lender but are, however, binding on the borrower (see para 38.8). This ground for possession specifically envisages a lender permitting a borrower to create a tenancy without running the risk of the tenant claiming security of tenure by virtue of the lender's permitting the tenancy to arise.

38.23   From 1 October 2010, unauthorised tenants have had the right to apply to the court for a postponement of enforcement of a possession order for up to two months. See paras 37.26–37.31.

---

38   HA 1988 Sch 2 ground 2: see para 11.9.

CHAPTER 39

Domestic relationship breakdown in mortgaged homes

Introduction

39.1   The two most common causes of mortgage default are reduction of income following loss of employment and relationship breakdown. Where partners separate, it may be inevitable that the home has to be sold if neither can afford to maintain the property on his or her sole income. However, where it is possible for one partner to maintain the property there are two additional problems for the remaining partner to consider over and above the continuing problem of paying for any existing mortgage. The first is preventing the sale of the property by the other party and the second is preventing the property from being used as security for further loan finance, with the corresponding increased risk of eviction by a new lender.

Sole ownership

39.2   Where the property is in the sole legal ownership of the departed partner, he or she is free to sell the property or raise further mortgage finance on it. As a result, where the couple are married or have entered into a civil partnership, it is important for the remaining spouse or civil partner to register his or her statutory right to occupy the home ('home rights') under the Family Law Act (FLA) 1996 s30 as soon as possible. The statutory 'home rights' are quite distinct from any rights of occupation which a person may have as a beneficiary under any trust of land under the Trusts of Land and Appointment of Trustees Act (TLATA) 1996.

39.3   In the case of registered land, this should be done by way of a notice registered at HM Land Registry; or if the title is unregistered, a class F land charge. If in doubt, an index map search should be made to check if the property is registered or not. This is done by sending District Land Registry Form SIM to the Land Registry for the area in which the property is situated. Land Registry Practice Guide 10, 'Official Searches of the Index Map', provides more information on the process.[1] No fee is payable on filing Form SIM. Land Registry Practice Guide 11 deals with obtaining a copy of the register in relation to any title.

39.4   Application for the registration of home rights is made on form HR1. No fee is payable. HM Land Registry practice is automatically to notify the registered proprietor that an entry relating to the family

---

1   See www.landreg.gov.uk.

home has been made. This is, according to HM Land Registry, to ensure compliance with the registered proprietor's rights under the Human Rights Act 1998 Sch 1, Article 1 or Protocol 1. Advisers must therefore ensure that people registering home rights are aware of this process.

39.5   The effect of registration of home rights is, in practice, that the legal owner is unable to sell or mortgage the property until the notice or charge is vacated. Taking this step has no effect on any prior mortgage and any arrears which may accrue under that loan. However, where such home rights have been registered, a lender is required: to give notice to the remaining spouse or civil partner of any possession proceedings brought;[2] to name that person in the particulars of claim; and to file at court a copy for service on that person. Such a person may then apply to be joined as a defendant with a view to persuading the court to exercise its statutory powers.[3]

39.6   A 'connected person' has the right to make the mortgage repayments to the lender in respect of the home and should do so if he or she can, in order to avoid loss of possession.[4] 'Connected person' in relation to the borrower means that person's spouse, former spouse, civil partner, former civil partner, cohabitant or former cohabitant.[5] He or she has the right to seek to be joined as a party to any possession proceedings 'at any time before the action is finally disposed of in that court'[6] and will be made a party if the court does not see 'a special reason' against him or her being joined and is satisfied that he or she may be able to meet the legal owner's mortgage liabilities either with or without the court exercising its Administration of Justice Act (AJA) 1970 and 1973 powers. The connected person does not need to have registered any home rights in order to be able to have the benefit of these provisions.

39.7   An occupier who does not fall within the definition of 'connected person' has no right to contest the possession proceedings or to pay the mortgage instalments on behalf of the legal owner. Where, however, he or she has an equitable interest in the property which has priority over the interest of the lender, this protects him or her against dispossession (see chapter 41) and possession proceedings

---

2 FLA 1996 s56.
3 FLA 1996 s55.
4 FLA 1996 s30(3).
5 FLA 1996 s54(5).
6 FLA 1996 s55(3).

brought by a lender can be defended on this basis. Likewise, if the occupier is a tenant (see chapter 40).

Joint ownership

39.8   Where the property is in joint legal ownership, the departed partner obviously cannot lawfully sell or obtain further mortgage finance without the remaining partner's agreement because that partner would have to execute the necessary mortgage deed or transfer form. It would, however, be open to the departed partner to seek a court order requiring sale of the property or, indeed, any other order that the court may think fit to make in relation to the property.[7] Given the abolition, by TLATA 1996[8] of the previous historical presumption of a trust for sale where land is owned jointly, the court is given wide discretion as to whether, on any application following relationship breakdown, the home should be sold or its occupation regulated. For an analysis of the law on this topic see para 43.29.

39.9   In the case of married couples, the court has the usual wide-ranging power to transfer property as part of its matrimonial jurisdiction on divorce or judicial separation and similar powers are available to civil partners under the Civil Partnership Act 2004.[9] As joint owners, both partners remain equally liable under the mortgage deed and are usually both joined as defendants in any proceedings brought by a lender.

39.10   Difficulties can arise where one joint legal owner forges the signature of the other on a deed creating a legal charge. In the case of registered land, the legal charge is effective if registration at HM Land Registry is completed. The innocent joint legal owner's beneficial interest may, however, qualify as an overriding interest if he or she is in actual occupation. With unregistered land, the beneficial interest of the owner who has created the forgery passes to the lender, leaving the legal estate being held on trust by the joint legal owners for the innocent legal owner and the lender. The lender would be able to seek a court order for sale under TLATA 1996. For further detail reference should be made to one of the major works on land law.[10]

---

7   TLATA 1996 s14.
8   TLATA 1996 ss4 and 5 and Sch 2.
9   Civil Partnership Act 2004 ss66 and 72 and Sch 5.
10   See K Gray and S Gray, *Elements of land law* 5th edn, Oxford University Press, 2008.

CHAPTER 40

Islamic property finance

40.1   Shariah law prohibits the charging or receipt of interest. As a result, followers of Islam have had to devise ways of being able to purchase properties with the assistance of loans from commercial lenders without the requirement to pay interest. This chapter is intended to give an overview of the types of transaction available to assist in house purchase consistent with Islamic principles. There are three main types of financial arrangement.

40.2   Under the *Murabaha*, a customer agrees the purchase with a seller. The provider (usually a bank) buys the property and then re-sells it to the customer at an agreed higher price, ie the original purchase price plus an agreed profit margin. The total cost to the customer and the repayment term are agreed at the outset, although provision may be made for the customer to discharge the debt at any time. The higher price depends on: the purchase price paid by the provider; the amount of any initial contribution made by the customer; and the repayment term. The provider takes a first charge on the property. The customer takes possession and starts making fixed monthly payments to the provider. This transaction has the approval of Shariah scholars in that this amounts to trading (ie the buying and selling of houses at a profit) and not lending. Under this scheme it is usual for the customer to have to provide a significant down payment, usually 20 per cent of the higher price. In this model, because the customer is the home owner subject to a mortgage, the usual powers available to the court will apply in case of default and possession proceedings.

40.3   Under the *Ijara* scheme, the provider buys the property that the customer wants to acquire. The property is then leased to the customer by the provider for a specified period at an agreed rent. During the period of the lease, the title remains with the provider. The customer enters into a 'promise to purchase' agreement under which the property is transferred to the tenant at the end of the lease. There is also a tenancy agreement which regulates the rights of occupation. The customer makes fixed monthly payments during the term of the lease, calculated so that part of the payment is rent and part goes towards the purchase price. The rental element is calculated based on the amount of the property that has not been 'bought' through the customer's initial down payment. The monthly payments are reassessed usually every six months, with the rental element being recalculated with reference to market interest rates. The customer is usually allowed to repay the purchase price early and to make payments in excess of the agreed monthly instalment. Title to the property is transferred to the customer at the end of the agreed term when the agreed purchase price has been paid. While this arrangement has all the hallmarks of a 'shared ownership' arrangement (see chapter 9), the customer would be either an assured or an assured shorthold tenant and would appear to have the protection available to rental purchasers. See para 13.7.

40.4   The third variant is the *Ijara with diminishing Musharaka*. Under this model, the customer agrees a price for the purchase of a property. The customer puts down a significant deposit, for example, 20 per cent, with the provider paying the balance. The title is acquired in the provider's name with the property being held on express trust for the customer and the provider. The customer enters into a 'promise to purchase' agreement and a tenancy agreement. The provider's share is divided into smaller units (for example, eight units worth 10 per cent of the higher purchase price) and over the agreed term the customer buys these units. As the provider's share in the property diminishes, so do the customer's rental payments. At the end of the term the title is transferred to the customer. Again, the customer would be either an assured or an assured shorthold tenant until the title is transferred on final payment of the purchase price. However, it would appear that application could be made to the court under the Trusts of Land and Appointment of Trustees Act 1996 for orders in relation to the property because it is held on trust.

40.5   These financial home purchase arrangements fall within the definition of the Financial Conduct Authority's (FCA's) regulated *home purchase plan* and are regulated under the Financial Services and Markets Act 2000.[1] However, regulated home purchase plans

---

1   Financial Services and Markets Act 2000 (Regulated Activities) Order 2001 SI No 544 art 63F(3) inserted by Financial Services and Markets Act 2000 (Regulated Activities) (Amendment) (No 2) Order 2006 SI 2383 art 18.

are excluded from falling within the definition of regulated mortgage contracts.[2] Whilst the *Murabaha* scheme has always fallen within the control of the FCA, regulation of *Ijara* 'home purchase plans' was brought within the control of the FCA with effect from 6 April 2007.[3] The *Pre-action Protocol for possession claims based on mortgage or home purchase plan arrears in respect of residential property* applies in relation to any possession proceedings brought in respect of a 'home purchase plan' which it defines as a 'method of purchasing a property by way of a sale and lease arrangement that does not require the payment of interest'.[4]

40.6   The result is that a borrower under any of these three arrangements faced with a possession claim can expect the lender to comply with the Protocol in advance of any possession claim being issued. See para 37.3.

2 Financial Services and Markets Act 2000 (Regulated Activities) Order 2001 SI No 544 art 61(3)(a) inserted by Financial Services and Markets Act 2000 (Regulated Activities) (Amendment) (No 2) Order 2006 SI No 2383 art 17.
3 Financial Services and Markets Act 2000 (Regulated Activities) (Amendment) (No 2) Order 2006 SI No 2383.
4 Mortgage Arrears Protocol para 1.1(b).

CHAPTER 41

Rights of equitable owners

Introduction

41.1   This chapter considers those cases in which the legal title to a property is vested in the name of one or more people (the legal owner or owners) but where another person has an interest in the property which is recognised in equity but falls short of being a legal interest. The most common example is where a matrimonial home (or a home shared by unmarried partners) is in the sole legal ownership of one spouse (or partner) but where the other has an equitable interest. Such an occupier, who is not a legal owner, may defeat a mortgage lender's possession claim by relying on an equitable interest.

41.2   A legal charge is treated as a legal interest in land. So a mortgage lender who advances money secured by a legal charge is treated as a purchaser of a legal interest in the property which is being used as the security. In the case of *registered* land, a purchaser takes the property subject to entries on the land register and any 'overriding interests', which can include the rights of people in actual occupation except where enquiry is made of those people and they do not disclose their rights in circumstances where they could reasonably have been expected to do so.[1] In the case of *unregistered* land, it is a basic principle of English land law that a bona fide purchaser for value of a legal estate (which includes a mortgage lender) takes that estate subject to any equitable interests in the property of which the lender has notice, whether actual or constructive.[2] The application of these general principles in the context of residential mortgages is considered in more detail below. In certain circumstances, occupiers who are not legal owners but who have some form of equitable interest in the property can effectively prevent the lender from obtaining possession. In this way, the defaulting legal owner may retain occupation under the protection of the equitable owner, without even making any further financial payments. However, advisers should be aware that a lender is likely to respond to continued non-payment by applying for an order for sale and possession under the Trusts of Land and Appointment of Trustees Act (TLATA) 1996. The following is a brief outline only of what is a complicated area of residential land law.

---

1   Land Registration Act 2002 Sch 3 para 2(b).
2   Law of Property Act 1925 ss199(1) and 205(1).

Creation of equitable interests

41.3 The courts have found it difficult to be consistent when deciding whether an occupying non-owner has acquired an equitable interest in a property. However, recent decisions of the House of Lords and the Supreme Court in *Stack v Dowden*[3] and *Jones v Kernott*[4] have resulted in some welcome guidance as to how to approach identification and quantification of beneficial interests in land.

41.4 No apology is made for not analysing the extensive case-law in detail. For a full explanation, reference must be made to the standard works on land law as well as family law (many of the decisions have been reached in the context of relationship breakdown). However, by way of example only, the courts have held that a non-legal owner can acquire an equitable interest by:

- paying directly for the purchase of a property which was conveyed into the legal owner's sole name;[5]
- contributing towards the deposit paid on the purchase;[6]
- helping with the construction of the house;[7] or
- making regular and substantial direct financial contributions to the mortgage.[8]

41.5 Great weight is attached to the making of a financial contribution or a direct contribution of money's worth.[9] Indirect financial contribution to the purchase of the property may result in the acquisition of an equitable interest. For example, where the non-owner has contributed to the pooling of resources from which payments for the property are made or has in some other way relieved the legal owner from expenditure on the property.[10] Alternatively, where the non-

---

3   [2007] UKHL 17, [2007] 2 AC 432.

4   [2011] UKSC 53, [2012] HLR 14.

5   *Pettitt v Pettitt* [1970] AC 777, [1969] 2 All ER 385, HL. A resulting trust does not, however, arise from the fact that money was lent to facilitate a purchase: see *Hussey v Palmer* [1972] 1 WLR 1286, CA and *Pettitt v Pettitt* [1970] AC 777, [1969] 2 All ER 385, HL. See also *Midland Bank plc v Cooke* [1995] 4 All ER 562, (1995) 27 HLR 733, CA, where the court held that, where an equitable owner had established an interest by direct contribution, the court will assess the size of the beneficial proportion by investigating the whole course of dealings between the parties.

6   See *Gissing v Gissing* [1971] AC 886, HL and *Burns v Burns* [1984] Ch 317, [1984] 1 All ER 244, CA at 264.

7   *Cooke v Head (No 1)* [1972] 1 WLR 518, [1972] All ER 38, CA.

8   *Gissing v Gissing* [1971] AC 886, [1970] 3 WLR 255, HL.

9   See *Lloyds Bank plc v Rosset* (1990) 22 HLR 349, [1991] 1 AC 107, HL.

10 *Grant v Edwards* [1986] Ch 638, [1986] 2 All ER 426, CA.

legal owner has acted to his or her detriment on the basis of assumed joint ownership, then the court may be prepared to recognise some equitable interest under a constructive trust.[11] In *Stack v Dowden*,[12] the House of Lords determined that, where the legal title to a property is held jointly, the presumption is that the joint owners also hold the property jointly for themselves in equity. That presumption can be displaced by evidence that the owners' common intention was different at the time of purchase or that it changed over time.[13]

Nature of equitable interests

41.6   The courts have not always been consistent in defining the nature of the interest accruing to the occupying non-owner who successfully argues that he or she has some form of equitable interest. The court may hold that the occupier is a beneficiary under a resulting or constructive trust. If this is the case, the legal owner holds the property jointly on his or her behalf and on behalf of the non-legal owner.[14] An alternative basis for granting relief may be to find that the non-legal owner has rights under an irrevocable licence conferring some form of interest that is binding on the legal owner and lender.[15]

Binding equitable interests

Legal ownership in one name

41.7   Whether an equitable owner's interest in a property (which is vested legally in another person) binds third parties depends on whether the land is registered or unregistered.

---

11   *Midland Bank Ltd v Dobson* [1986] 1 FLR 171; *Coombes v Smith* [1986] 1 WLR 808, [1987] 1 FLR 352 and *Re Basham (decd)* [1986] 1 WLR 1498, [1987] 1 All ER 405, ChD. See also *Drake v Whipp* (1996) 28 HLR 531, [1996] 1 FLR 826, CA.
12   [2007] 2 AC 432.
13   *Jones v Kernott* [2011] UKSC 53, [2012] HLR 14.
14   *Oxley v Hiscock* [2004] EWCA Civ 546, [2004] 3 WLR 715; 'Resulting and constructive trusts of land: the mist descends and rises' [2005] Conv 79; *Kingsnorth Finance Co v Tizard* [1986] 1 WLR 783, [1986] 2 All ER 54 and *Grant v Edwards* [1986] Ch 638, [1986] 2 All ER 426.
15   *Re Sharpe* [1980] 1 WLR 219 and see *Bristol and West Building Society v Henning* [[1985] 1 WLR 778, 1985] 2 All ER 606, CA, and noted at [1985] Conv 361.

41.8   In the case of *registered* land, a lender taking a legal charge takes it subject to the interests specified in the Land Register and to any overriding interests.[16]

41.9   Land Registration Act 2002 Sch 3 para 2 defines which interests that have *not* been specified in the Land Register can constitute an overriding interest of a person in occupation, and includes:

Interests of persons in actual occupation

2 An interest belonging at the time of the disposition to a person in actual occupation, so far as relating to land of which he is in actual occupation, except for –

(a) ...

(b) an interest of a person of whom inquiry was made before the disposition and who failed to disclose the right when he could reasonably have been expected to do so;

(c) an interest –

(i) which belongs to a person whose occupation would not have been obvious on a reasonably careful inspection of the land at the time of the disposition, and

(ii) of which the person to whom the disposition is made does not have actual knowledge at that time.

41.10   The wording differs slightly from the comparable provision in the previous legislation.[17] The aim of the legislation is to protect occupiers of property where the fact of their occupation would alert a purchaser to the possibility of unrecorded interests on the Land Register and, as a result, the necessity to make further enquiry. It follows that the interests of an actual occupier 'override' the legal charge taken by the lender except in cases where either: (1) the actual occupier has unreasonably failed, on enquiry, to disclose his or her own entitlement; or (2) the relevant occupation was neither reasonably discoverable by nor actually known to the lender. The inclusion of the wording 'could reasonably have been expected to do so', which did not appear in the previous legislative definition of 'overriding interest', would seem to suggest that there is now some duty of candour on an occupier to assert a right (but only if enquiry is made).

41.11   In *Williams & Glyn's Bank Ltd v Boland*,[18] the House of Lords held that the beneficial interest under a trust of an occupying spouse, acquired by way of substantial contribution to the initial purchase

16 Land Registration Act 2002 s29(1) and (2) and Sch 3.

17 Land Registration Act 1925 s70(1)(g). In March 2016 the Law Commission published a consultation paper 'Updating the Land Registration Act 2002' in contemplation of revision of the law in this area.

18 [1981] AC 487, [1980] 3 WLR 138, HL.

price of the house, is an overriding interest capable of binding a lender. Whether someone is in 'actual occupation' is a question of fact.[19] Occupation must not only be actual but should be apparent or patent such as to 'put a person inspecting the land on notice that there was some person in occupation'.[20] Vicarious occupation through, for example, a spouse or other relative or even a limited company[21] qualifies.[22] Protection only applies to the part actually occupied although in the context of residential mortgages this restriction might have limited impact. A child cannot be a person in occupation for this purpose.[23] The relevant date for considering whether someone is in occupation is the date of execution of the mortgage, not the date of its registration at HM Land Registry.[24]

41.12   Where the mortgage financed the initial purchase of the property and the purchase and the mortgage were simultaneous, the courts have been loath to allow an equitable owner's rights to take precedence over the lender's legal interest where the equitable owner knew, at the time, that the mortgage was being taken out. In such circumstances, the courts have concluded that the equitable owner intended that his or her interest be postponed to that of the lender and so is estopped from claiming priority.[25] This postponement of the equitable owner's interest applies even to a subsequent remortgage taken out by the legal owner without the equitable owner's knowledge but limited to the extent of the original mortgage.[26] Where, however, the mortgage was genuinely granted, after the property's acquisition, to a borrower in whom the legal estate had already vested, where the beneficial owner was unaware of the creation of the legal charge, then that occupier's equitable interest binds the lender.[27]

---

19 *Lloyds Bank plc v Rosset* [1989] Ch 350, (1990) 22 HLR 349, CA and *Link Lending Ltd v Bustard* [2010] EWCA Civ 424.

20 *Malory Enterprises Ltd v Cheshire Homes Ltd* [2002] Ch 216.

21 *Stockholm Finance Ltd v Garden Holdings Inc* [1995] NPC 162.

22 *Abbey National Building Society v Cann* [1991] 1 AC 56, 1990) 22 HLR 360, HL.

23 *Hypo-Mortgage Services Ltd v Robinson* [1997] 2 FLR 71, [1997] 2 FCR 422, CA.

24 See Land Registration Act 2002 Sch 3 para (2)(i) and *Abbey National Building Society v Cann* [1991] 1 AC 56, (1990) 22 HLR 360, HL.

25 See *Paddington Building Society v Mendelsohn* (1985) 50 P&CR 244, CA; M P Thompson, 'The retreat from Boland' [1986] Conv 57; *Bristol and West Building Society v Henning* [1985] 1 WLR 778, (1985) 17 HLR 432, CA and *Scott v Southern Pacific Mortgages Ltd* [2014] UKSC 52, [2014] HLR 48.

26 *Equity Home Loans Ltd v Prestridge* [1992] 1 WLR 137, (1992) 24 HLR 76, CA and *Locobail (UK) Ltd v Waldorf Invstment Corpn* (1999) *Times* 31 March.

27 *Williams and Glyns Bank v Boland* [1981] AC 487, [1980] 3 WLR 138, HL and *HSBC v Dyche* [2009] EWHC 2954 (Ch).

41.13   In the case of *unregistered* land, a mortgage lender advancing money on land by way of legal charge takes the security subject to any equitable interests in the property of which it has notice, whether actual, constructive or imputed.[28] Actual notice is self-explanatory. Constructive notice is notice which the lender would have obtained 'if such enquiries and inspections had been made as ought reasonably to have been made' by the lender.[29] Imputed notice is the actual or constructive notice of the lender's agent, although only so far as notice was received by the agent in the case of the lender granting the mortgage.[30] It is not clear when a lender is fixed with constructive notice or the lengths to which a lender has to go to discharge its duty to make reasonable enquiry. It seems that the courts require considerable enquiries to be made. In one case it was held that a lender's agent visiting the property at a prearranged time was insufficient enquiry to discharge an obligation to find out whether a matrimonial home was occupied by a spouse who might have an equitable interest.[31] As with registered land, the courts have proved unwilling to allow a beneficial owner to bind a lender where he or she knowingly was to benefit from the legal owner's borrowing money by way of mortgage, although the courts' reasoning is open to question.[32]

41.14   In practice, however, the question of whether an equitable owner's interest or right binds a lender is most likely to arise in cases of mortgages entered into *after* the initial purchase of the property.

41.15   Where a lender has granted a mortgage on a property which is subject to equitable rights in priority to its rights under the mortgage, that lender will often dispute the assertion that there is a binding equitable interest – on the assumption that the claim is being fabricated in an attempt to prevent eviction.[33] Advisers should therefore test the evidence supporting the claim of the equitable interest at an early stage.

41.16   Similarly advisers will need to assess whether there would be any basis for a lender to be able to argue that the beneficial owner's conduct constitutes an estoppel so as to resurrect the lender's rights.[34]

---

28 Law of Property Act 1925 s199.
29 Law of Property Act 1925 s199(1)(ii)(a).
30 Law of Property Act 1925 s199(1)(ii)(b).
31 *Kingsnorth Finance Co v Tizard* [1986] 2 All ER 54, [1986] 1 WLR 783. See also *Lloyds Bank plc v Carrick* [1996] 4 All ER 630, (1996) 28 HLR 707, CA.
32 See *Bristol and West Building Society v Henning* [1985] 1 WLR 778, [1985] 2 All ER 606, CA.
33 *Midland Bank plc v Dobson* [1986] 1 FLR 171.
34 *Barclays Bank plc v Goff* [2001] EWCA Civ 685, [2001] 2 All ER (Comm) 847.

If these are not applicable, it would remain open to the lender to apply for an order for sale under TLATA 1996 s14.[35] Alternatively, it is open to the lender to sue the legal owner for repayment of the loan by virtue of any covenant to repay contained in the mortgage deed. If the borrower is made bankrupt, his or her trustee in bankruptcy could seek a court order for sale of the property under TLATA 1996 s14.[36] See para 43.29.

Legal ownership in several names

41.17   Different legal considerations apply where the title to the mortgaged property is held legally in joint names. Although there was initially some doubt, following the decision in *Williams & Glyn's Bank Ltd v Boland*,[37] the House of Lords, in *City of London Building Society v Flegg*,[38] confirmed that a lender who advances money on the security of a property where the legal title is vested in two or more people as trustees or a trust corporation, is free from the concern of whether or not other people may have equitable interests under such a trust.[39] As a result of the 'overreaching' provisions of the Law of Property Act 1925,[40] such a lender takes its interest under the mortgage free from all beneficial claims. The value of an equitable owner's interests theoretically attach to the capital money realised when the property is sold. Notice of beneficial interests in unregistered land and actual occupation in registered land is irrelevant. Equitable owners under a trust of registered land are generally entitled to register a 'restriction' on the relevant register of title but this will not prevent those rights being 'overreached' by the sale of the property or the grant of a mortgage.

Mortgage consent forms

41.18   In an effort to avoid the risk of being landed with a binding equitable owner, most lenders now require adult occupiers (intending

---

35 *Bank of Baroda v Dhillon* (1997) 30 HLR 845, [1998] 1 FLR 524, CA.
36 See *Alliance & Leicester plc v Slayford* [2000] EWCA Civ 257, (2001) 33 HLR 66 and M P Thompson, 'The cumulative range of a mortgagee's remedies' [2002] Conv 53.
37 [1981] AC 487, [1980] 3 WLR 138, HL.
38 [1988] AC 54, (1987) 19 HLR 484, HL.
39 Law of Property Act 1925 ss2 and 27.
40 Law of Property Act 1925 s36(1) and *Re Sharpe* [1980] 1 WLR 219.

or actual) who are not to be joined as parties to the mortgage deed to execute forms of consent or undertaking prior to completion of the mortgage. These are intended to postpone any legal or equitable rights they may have, until after those of the lender. Executing such a form may act either as an estoppel, preventing the equitable owner from seeking to rely on his or her interest, or have the effect of postponing such rights to those of the lender.[41]

---

41 *Woolwich Building Society v Plane* [1997] EWCA Civ 2372; *Woolwich Building Society v Dickman* [1996] 3 All ER 204, (1996) 28 HLR 661, CA; *Le Foe v Le Foe and Woolwich plc* [2001] 2 FLR 970 and *Skipton Building Society v Clayton* (1993) 25 HLR 596, (1993) 66 P&CR 223, CA.

CHAPTER 42

Undue influence

Introduction

42.1   Historically, the courts have sought to protect people who have acted to their detriment because of undue pressure put on them. In recent years, there has been a burgeoning trend of borrowers (or sureties, namely, persons allowing their own property to be used as security for the borrower's liabilities) claiming that a mortgage is voidable, and hence unenforceable. This is commonly based on a claim of misrepresentation or because of 'undue influence' put on them, either by the lender directly or, more commonly, by a third party for whose benefit finance is being sought. The wrongdoing which is relevant is any conduct which has 'misled' the surety as to relevant facts of a proposed transaction or has caused the surety's will to be overborne or coerced. In this context, the expression 'surety' is intended to include joint owners who allow their interest in property to be used as security for another joint owner for whose benefit a loan is taken out, as well as a person who puts up property as security for another where that person is not him or herself putting anything forward as security for the loan.

42.2   Litigation in this field has been extensive since the 1980s. The House of Lords considered the law on two separate occasions in the leading cases of *Barclays Bank v O'Brien* and *CIBC Mortgages v Pitt*[1] in 1994 and *Royal Bank of Scotland v Etridge (No 2)*[2] in 2001. This chapter is simply designed to introduce advisers to the issues. For a comprehensive analysis of the law, reference should be made to leading texts on land law and mortgages.[3]

Lender misconduct

42.3   The instances where a surety will allege that a bank or other mortgage lender has misrepresented or pressured a borrower or surety into signing a legal charge are limited. Before the transaction will be set aside, it will be necessary to show that unfair advantage has been taken in the sense that the transaction was to the manifest

---

1   [1994] 1 AC 180, [1993] 4 All ER 417 and [1994] 1 AC 200, [1993] 4 All ER 433, HL.

2   [2002] AC 773, [2002] HLR 4, HL.

3   K Gray and S Gray, *Elements of land law*, 5th edn, Oxford University Press, 2008 and P Morgan, M Hyland and W Clark, *Fisher and Lightwood's law of mortgage*, 14th edn, Butterworths, 2014.

disadvantage of the victim.[4] Where, however, there is actual undue influence (as contrasted with constructive undue influence, for which see below) then manifest disadvantage does not need to be shown.[5] There is no general duty on a bank to advise a potential surety as to the nature of a relevant transaction although the situation is likely to be different where the surety is an existing customer.[6] Where the lender is taken to be under a duty, and its explanation is inadequate, the security may not be enforceable.[7] Where the principal debtor was acting as the lender's agent, the lender is fixed with the misrepresentation or undue influence practised by him or her.[8] However, cases are rare in which the lender simply leaves the principal debtor to extract a signature from the surety by whatever means he or she may choose.

Misconduct of the principal debtor

42.4   In recent years, the courts have in some cases sought to impose liability on lenders for the misconduct of a principal debtor where that person could reasonably have been expected to have had influence over a prospective mortgage borrower or surety. Most of the cases have involved wives being prevailed upon to enter into second mortgages of the matrimonial home, with the principal debtor being their husband. In the leading cases of *Barclays Bank plc v O'Brien*[9] and *CIBC Mortgages v Pitt*.[10] The House of Lords sought to define the circumstances in which a lender will be deemed to be on notice of undue influence or misrepresentation perpetrated in order to induce a borrower to enter into the mortgage or a joint owner to put up his or her interest as surety, such as to enable the borrower or surety to apply to the court to have the transaction declared ineffective to charge that person's interest in the property used as security. While,

---

4   *National Westminster Bank plc v Morgan* [1985] AC 686, (1985) 17 HLR 360, HL.
5   *O'Hara v Allied Irish Banks Ltd* [1985] BCLC 52.
6   *Cornish v Midland Bank plc* [1985] 3 All ER 513, CA. *Barclays Bank v Khaira* [1992] 1 WLR 623, [1996] 5 Bank LR 196, ChD; *Midland Bank v Perry* [1988] 1 FLR 161, (1987) Fin LR 237, CA and *Verity v Lloyds Bank* [1995] NPC 148, [1995] CLC 1557, QBD.
7   *Barclays Bank plc v O'Brien* [1994] 1 AC 180, [1993] 4 All ER 417, HL.
8   *Kings North Trust Ltd v Bell* [1986] 1 WLR 119 and *Barclays Bank plc v Kennedy* (1989) 21 HLR 132, (1989) 58 P&CR 221, CA.
9   [1994] 1 AC 180, [1993] 4 All ER 417, HL.
10 [1994] AC 200, (1994) 26 HLR 90, HL.

commonly, such cases involve second mortgages on jointly owned property, the principles apply equally where a sole owner or a beneficial co-owner is prevailed on by a principal debtor to secure finance made available to that person.

42.5   Where the lender is taken to be on notice of the principal debtor's misconduct, the lender is not able to enforce the mortgage. However, the lender's rights against the principal debtor remain unaffected. In this way, the surety may be able to resist possession proceedings by the lender. Advisers should be aware that where the surety and the principal debtor are joint owners then, ultimately, possession is at risk if the principal debtor is bankrupted and an order for sale sought by the trustee in bankruptcy or where the lender may be able independently to seek an order for sale under TLATA 1996.[11] See para 43.29.

42.6   The following is an attempt to summarise the situation following *O'Brien* and *Pitt* in the light of the refinements of the principles by the House of Lords in *Etridge (No 2)*.[12] A mortgage may be unenforceable against the innocent party for misrepresentation by the principal debtor to the innocent party so long as the misrepresentation would have been sufficient to make a contract voidable if that misrepresentation had been made by the lender. An innocent misrepresentation suffices.[13]

42.7   The mortgage may also be unenforceable or set aside if there has been undue influence exercised resulting in the surety entering into the transaction. Undue influence is unacceptable behaviour which 'arises out of a relationship between two persons where one has acquired over another a measure of influence, or ascendancy, of which the ascendant person takes unfair advantage'.[14] Undue influence may be actual undue influence (for example, threats) or presumed undue influence which is treated as tainting a transaction either because of a particular type of relationship (for example, solicitor and client) or because of an actual relationship where the surety trusted and relied on the abuser. A lender having actual knowledge of the facts entitling the surety to apply to set aside is very rare. A lender is put on enquiry wherever a person offers to stand as surety for the debts of a spouse or any other person involved in some

11 *First National Bank plc v Achampong* [2003] EWCA Civ 487, [2004] 1 FCR 18, CA.
12 *Royal Bank of Scotland v Etridge (No 2)* [2002] 2 AC 773, [2002] HLR 4, HL.
13 *TSB v Camfield* [1995] 1 All ER 951, (1995) 27 HLR 206, CA.
14 *Royal Bank of Scotland v Etridge (No 2)* [2002] 2 AC 773, [2002] HLR 4, HL at [8].

non-commercial relationship (whether heterosexual, homosexual or platonic, whether or not involving cohabitation[15]) of which the lender is aware. The relationship of employer/employee falls within this definition.[16] The transaction must not appear to be to the surety's advantage.[17]

42.8   The requirement that the transaction is not to the innocent borrower/surety's financial advantage will often be fulfilled in the case where the borrower is being asked to stand as surety for the principal debtor's debts and where no direct financial gain is being obtained by the surety. This was the case in *O'Brien* and such cases are described in the case-law as 'surety cases'. Where, however, the transaction is ostensibly a joint borrowing by the borrower/surety and the principal debtor, then there will be no constructive notice to the lender even if the stated purpose (as in *Pitt*) was false.[18] These are called 'joint loan cases'. Cases where a spouse becomes surety for the debts of a company whose shares are held by her and her husband, even when the surety is a director or secretary, cannot be equated with joint loans.[19]

42.9   A lender may be put on notice, even if the loan being sought is ostensibly a joint borrowing, if the advantage to be gained by the borrower/surety is out of proportion to the risk being undertaken.[20] Knowledge possessed by solicitors acting for a lender, the principal debtor and surety in a remortgage (as to the purpose for which monies were to be used) is not imputed to the lender.[21]

42.10   Where the lender is put on enquiry, it must take 'reasonable steps' to bring home to the surety the risks involved in the transaction proposed.[22] The usual way to disprove undue influence is for the lender to ensure that the surety had full access to independent professional advice. However, the essential question is not whether

---

15 *Massey v Midland Bank plc* [1995] 1 All ER 929.

16 *Credit Lyonnais Bank Nederland NV v Burch* [1997] 1 All ER 144, (1997) 29 HLR 513, CA.

17 *Royal Bank of Scotland v Etridge (No 2)* [2002] AC 773, [2002] HLR 4, HL.

18 See for example *The Mortgage Business plc v Green and another* [2013] EWHC 4243 (Ch).

19 *Royal Bank of Scotland v Etridge (No 2)* [2002] AC 773, [2002] HLR 4, HL.

20 *Goode Durrant Administration v Biddulph* (1994) 26 HLR 625; *Barclays Bank v Sumner* [1996] EGCS 65 and *Bank of Scotland v Bennett* [1997] 1 FLR 801, [1997] 3 FCR 193, ChD.

21 *Halifax Mortgage Services Ltd v Stepsky* [1996] Ch 207, (1996) 28 HLR 522, CA; *Scotlife Home Loans (No 2) v Hedworth* (1996) 28 HLR 771; *National Westminster Bank plc v Beaton* (1997) 30 HLR 99, CA; *Woolwich plc v Gomm* (2000) 79 P&CR 61, CA and *Northern Rock Building Society v Archer* (1999) 78 P&CR 65, CA.

22 *Royal Bank of Scotland v Etridge (No 2)* [2002] 2 AC 773, [2002] HLR 4, HL.

the surety understood the implications of what was being proposed but whether he or she was free of pressures which might threaten to override independent judgment.[23] In *Etridge (No 2)*, the House of Lords drew a distinction between transactions entered into before the ruling in that case (ie 11 October 2001) and those after.

42.11   In pre-*Etridge* transactions, Lord Nicholls, in *Etridge (No 2)*, indicated that the duty on lenders was as set out in *O'Brien*. Reasonable steps would have been taken if the lender had received from a solicitor confirmation that the surety had been advised of the risks involved in the transaction. The lender would also have satisfied the requirement by advising that the surety obtain independent legal advice or by insisting that the surety attend a private meeting (without the principal debtor being present) with a representative of the lender at which the surety was warned about the risks. However, the lender cannot simply rely on an honest belief that the surety was advised by a solicitor. The lender must have taken active steps not only to ensure that a solicitor was retained but also that the solicitor was instructed to give the surety independent advice on the transaction.[24]

42.12   In post-*Etridge (No 2)* transactions, a more taxing protocol is required to be followed, involving again the requirement for advice from a solicitor. The steps to be taken by a lender are:

- The lender must make direct contact with the surety to identify the solicitor whom the surety will instruct and to advise that the role of that solicitor will be to ensure that any later consent to the transaction cannot be disputed.
- The lender must receive the surety's nomination of a solicitor.
- The lender must disclose to the solicitor all relevant information in respect of the principal debtor's financial position and the extent, purpose and terms of the proposed transaction. A copy of the loan application form should be provided to the solicitor.
- The solicitor and the surety must meet in the absence of the principal debtor. At that meeting, the solicitor must advise, in suitably non-technical language, about the nature and implications of the transaction. The relevant documents must be explained, as must the implications if the lender has to take enforcement action – for example, repossession and/or bankruptcy. The advice must cover the extent of the surety's liability under the transaction and the fact that the transaction is optional. The solicitor must check that

23 *Royal Bank of Scotland v Etridge (No 2)* [2002] 2 AC 773, [2002] HLR 4 at [20] and *Niersmans v Pesticcio* [2004] EWCA Civ 372 at [23].
24 *Yorkshire Bank v Tinsley* [2004] EWCA Civ 816, [2004] 1 WLR 2380 at [29].

the surety wishes to proceed and indicate to the surety that the lender will be advised that these issues have been covered and that the transaction is being entered into in the knowledge of this.

42.13 Receipt by the lender of written confirmation from the solicitor in question that these steps have been taken protects the lender from any future allegation of undue influence or misrepresentation. Clearly, however, the solicitor involved in this process runs the risk of a claim of negligence if the surety suffers loss as a result of the transaction because he or she will owe a duty of care to the surety.

The relief available to the surety

42.14 A surety who successfully raises an *O'Brien* defence will be able to resist the claim for possession based on the legal charge.

42.15 It is not possible to 'partly' escape from the consequences of a transaction where, for example, a surety knew that he or she was guaranteeing a certain sum whereas the mortgage which he or she was induced to enter into secured a much larger debt.[25] In such circumstances, the whole transaction must be set aside. Where, however, a loan arrangement comprises several transactions, for example, a loan agreement with a separate later side letter, it is possible to sever the objectionable transaction leaving the other uncontaminated part enforceable.[26] A lender granting a remortgage which would otherwise be voidable by the surety has a 'right of subrogation' in relation to a previous charge which was not voidable and can claim possession based on the element of the remortgage referable to the previous mortgage.[27] Where a further remortgage takes place, that lender is also protected on the principle of 'sub-subrogation'.[28] A remortgaging lender in such circumstances is entitled to the same security as the original lender but cannot be subrogated to an amount greater than the mortgage which has been discharged by the remortgage.[29] Where a mortgage which is voidable because of undue influence is

---

25 *TSB Bank plc v Camfield* [1995] 1 WLR 430, [1995] 1 All ER 951, CA.

26 *Barclays Bank plc v Caplan* [1998] 1 FLR 532, ChD.

27 *Halifax plc v Omar* [2002] EWCA Civ 121, [2002] 2 P&CR 377 and *Halifax Mortgage Services Ltd v Muirhead* (1997) 76 P&CR 418, CA.

28 *UCB Group Ltd v Hedworth* [2003] EWCA Civ 1717.

29 *Cheltenham & Gloucester plc v Appleyard* [2004] EWCA Civ 291, [2004] 13 EGCS 127. See also *Anfield (UK) Ltd v (1) Bank of Scotland plc (2) Siddiqui (3) London Scottish Finance Ltd* [2010] EWHC 2374 (Ch), [2011] 1 WLR 2414.

discharged and a new mortgage is created between the same parties, the new mortgage is itself voidable.[30]

The lender's response

42.16   A surety who delays asserting an *O'Brien* defence (for example, by acknowledging the legal charge in matrimonial ancillary relief proceedings) may be barred from raising it in subsequent possession proceedings brought by the lender.[31] There is nothing improper in a lender, met with an *O'Brien* defence, seeking a money judgment against the principal debtor with a view to bankruptcy of the principal debtor and subsequent sale by the trustee in bankruptcy of the security.[32]

Taking instructions from the innocent borrower/ surety

42.17   Much will depend on the circumstances of each case, but there are a number of common issues which will need to be addressed when considering an *O'Brien* defence:

- Was the mortgage granted before or after 11 October 2001, ie pre- or post-*Etridge (No 2)*?
- Did the principal debtor exert real pressure or misrepresent matters to the borrower/surety? What exactly was said and done? Did the borrower/surety rely on the principal debtor for financial decisions and rely unquestioningly on him or her?
- What educational or business background does the borrower/ surety have?
- How was the transaction explained by the principal debtor? Were half-truths or inaccuracies involved?
- Where, when, how and before whom was the document signed?
- Is there a certificate confirming that the implications were made known to the borrower/surety?

---

30 *Yorkshire Bank plc v Tinsley* [2004] EWCA Civ 816, [2004] 1 WLR 2380.
31 *First National Bank plc v Walker* [2001] 1 FCR 21, CA.
32 *Alliance & Leicester plc v Slayford* [2000] EWCA Civ 257, [2001] 1 All ER (Comm) 1. See M P Thompson, 'The cumulative range of a mortgagee's remedies' [2002] Conv 53.

- Did the client have any advice from the lender or from anyone else? If so, who and what was the advice? Was the extent of present and prospective future financial liability made clear? Was the principal debtor present when the advice was given? Did the borrower/surety understand the advice?
- Did the lender insist on legal advice being obtained as a precondition to the loan?
- Did the borrower/surety receive legal advice, and, if so, from whom and what was that advice?
- Did the borrower/surety understand the nature of the transaction?
- Was the transaction in relation to a guarantee or a joint loan? What did the lender believe it to be for and what did the loan application say it was for?
- Advisers should obtain on disclosure the correspondence between the lender and the solicitor/adviser to clarify who, and in relation to what, any solicitors were expected to advise.

42.18 Armed with this information, advisers will be able to make a clearer judgment of the strengths of the potential defence. It is open to the disadvantaged surety to take the initiative and, as a claimant, seek a declaration that the mortgage was voidable as against him or her. There is no need to wait for the lender to seek possession. Indeed, there may be potential problems for a surety who delays taking action based on discretionary bars to the setting aside of the charge such as delay, acquiescence or affirmation.[33]

---

33 See *Barclays Bank plc v Goff* [2001] EWCA Civ 635, [2001] All ER (Comm) 847.

CHAPTER 43

Sale of the home

Introduction

43.1   For the vast majority of borrowers in difficulty with their mortgage, the aim will be to try to preserve their occupation of the home. In possession proceedings, the lender will usually be looking to force the borrower into making increased payments to pay off arrears with the sanction that eviction will follow if sufficient payments are not made. Very often, this threat will be backed by an order for possession postponed for as long as the stipulated payments are made.

43.2   However, where it is clear that dispossession is inevitable, a borrower may seek the opportunity of selling the home, ie the property mortgaged to the lender. Alternatively, where the borrower has given up possession, either voluntarily in the face of possession proceedings or following eviction after proceedings, the borrower will be concerned about the sale of the home by the lender. This would be either because there may be a surplus due to the borrower after the mortgage has been redeemed or because the lender will wish to recover the amount of any shortfall if the sale proceeds are not sufficient to discharge the mortgage debt in total. Occupiers of a mortgaged property may also face a claim by the lender for a specific order from the court for the property to be sold. This may arise where the lender is unable to rely on the mortgage in order to obtain possession with a view to sale as mortgagee in possession. This may occur where, for instance, the lender is faced with an occupier who has successfully raised a *Barclays Bank v O'Brien*[1] defence (for which see para 42.4) or where a joint owner has forged the signature of the other joint owner.[2] In such a case, the lender will be seeking an order for sale and possession under the Trusts of Land and Appointment of Trustees Act (TLATA) 1996. Such an order may be sought, as an alternative, in possession proceedings.

Sale by the borrower

43.3   As the owner of the mortgaged property, the borrower is at liberty to sell the property at any time. The lender's consent is not required. However, the buyer will not usually complete the purchase until the seller's solicitors give a formal undertaking that they will provide either the receipted legal charge in the case of unregistered land

---

1 [1994] 1 AC 180, [1993] 3 WLR 786, HL.
2 *First National Securities Ltd v Hegerty* [1985] QB 850.

or, where the title is registered, a form DS1 duly receipted by the lender. In turn, the seller's solicitors will not give such an undertaking, for which the partners of the solicitor's firm in question would be personally liable, until they are satisfied that the sale proceeds will be sufficient to redeem the mortgage or, if there is more than one mortgage, all the mortgages secured against the property. Where the seller is acting in person, the buyer will want to ensure that some other arrangement is in place so that any mortgage debt is paid off on completion.

43.4   It is usually in both the lender's and the borrower's interests for the borrower to remain in occupation until the home is sold. In this way it is likely that the sale price will be higher than would be obtained by the lender if the home is empty following the borrower leaving. In addition, any income support or other benefits payable on account of mortgage interest will continue to be paid direct to the lender while the borrower is in occupation, reducing the ultimate mortgage debt.

Where the whole mortgage debt can be paid from the sale proceeds

43.5   Where, before proceedings have been started, it is clear to the borrower that sale of the home is inevitable, the borrower should advise the lender of the decision to sell. The lender should be asked to agree to delay issuing proceedings on the basis of the borrower showing that reasonable steps are being taken to sell the home at the appropriate market price as advised by an estate agent. The borrower should agree to keep the lender advised about progress. The *Pre-action Protocol for possession claims based on mortgage or home purchase plan arrears in respect of residential property* requires the lender in these circumstances to consider delaying proceedings and, if it decides nonetheless to issue proceedings, to give the borrower its reasons at least five business days before starting proceedings.[3] This might entitle the borrower to refer the lender's decision by way of a complaint to the Financial Ombudsman Service (see para 35.61) or to apply for a stay of possession proceedings under CPR 26.4(2)(6).

43.6   If the sale proceeds will be sufficient to pay off the whole mortgage debt, it is open to the borrower to argue, where possession proceedings are issued, that the arrears would be paid off out of the sale proceeds and that therefore Consumer Credit Act 1974 s129 or the Administration of Justice Act (AJA) 1970 s36 can assist the borrower

---

3 Mortgage Arrears Protocol paras 6.2 and 6.4.

providing that the court is satisfied that the sale would take place within a reasonable timescale. In the context of AJA 1970 it is a question of fact for the court in each case whether the borrower will be able to sell within a reasonable period.[4] It is important to produce some evidence to support the assertion that a sale is likely within the proposed period.[5] In the initial stages of the sale process a simple letter from an estate agent as to the likely time-scale should be sufficient. There is no reason why the reasonable period should not be six or nine or even 12 months, but in one case the Court of Appeal postponed a possession order for only three months to enable the borrowers to try to sell.[6]

43.7   The length of time which the borrower might expect to be given by the court will obviously depend on the particular circumstances. The Court of Appeal has given some general guidance.[7] Where the home was already on the market and there was some indication of delay on the part of the borrower, it might be that a short period of postponement of only a few months would be reasonable. Where there was likely to be considerable delay in selling the property and/ or its value was close to the total of the mortgage debt and arrears (so that the lender was at risk as to the adequacy of the security), immediate possession or only a short period of postponement might be reasonable. Where there had already been considerable delay in realising a sale and/or the likely sale proceeds were unlikely to cover the mortgage debt and arrears, or there was simply not sufficient evidence about the sale value, the usual order would be for immediate possession. The level of equity is of considerable significance.

43.8   It remains unclear whether the courts discretionary powers can be relied upon in order to stay enforcement in relation to part of the security where, for instance, part of the property can be sold to pay off the mortgage.[8]

4 *National and Provincial Building Society v Lloyd* [1996] 1 All ER 630, (1996) 28 HLR 459, CA.
5 *Bristol & West Building Society v Ellis* (1997) 29 HLR 282, (1997) 73 P&CR 158, CA.
6 *Target Home Loans v Clothier* [1994] 1 All ER 439, (1993) 25 HLR 48, CA.
7 *Bristol & West Building Society v Ellis* (1997) 29 HLR 282, (1997) 73 P&CR 158, CA.
8 *Barclays Bank plc v Alcorn* [2002] EWHC 498 (Ch), October 2002 *Legal Action* 29.

Where the whole mortgage debt cannot be paid from the sale proceeds

43.9 Where the sale price is likely to be insufficient to discharge the mortgage debt in total then, in practice, the lender can prevent a sale by the borrower from proceeding. This is because the seller will be unable to redeem the legal charge on completion. In such circumstances, it is open to the borrower to apply to the court for an order directing, at the court's instigation, the sale of the property under the Law of Property Act (LPA) 1925 s91.[9] Section 91(2) provides:

> In any action, whether for foreclosure, or for redemption, or for sale, or for the raising and payment in any manner of mortgage money, the court, on the request of the mortgagee, or of any person interested either in the mortgage money or in the right of redemption, and, notwithstanding that –
> (a) any other person dissents; or
> (b) the mortgagee or any person so interested does not appear in the action;
> and without allowing any time for redemption or for payment of any mortgage money, may direct a sale of the mortgaged property, on such terms as it thinks fit, including the deposit in court of a reasonable sum fixed by the court to meet the expenses of sale and to secure performance of the terms.

43.10 The court is given wide discretion whether to direct a sale and, if so, on what terms. Under LPA 1925 s91 the court has the discretion to order sale and to allow the borrower to remain in occupation pending sale, even where there is a negative equity.[10] However, where the sale proceeds would fall substantially below the amount of the mortgage debt, an order for sale will not be made save in exceptional circumstances.[11] The court is not limited to considering purely financial matters when exercising its discretion and is fully entitled to take into account the pressing social needs of the borrower.[12] In cases where the lender is pressing for possession with a view to it conducting a sale, the county court has no discretion to suspend a warrant for possession to enable an application to be made in the court for an order for sale under LPA 1925 s91 except where there are funds

9 *Palk v Mortgage Services Funding plc* [1993] Ch 330, (1993) 25 HLR 56, CA. See also *Polonski v Lloyds Bank Mortgages Ltd* [1998] 1 FLR 896, (1999) 31 HLR 721, ChD.

10 *Barrett v Halifax Building Society* (1996) 28 HLR 634, ChD.

11 See *Palk v Mortgage Services Funding plc* [1993] Ch 330, (1993) 25 HLR 56, CA and *Pearn v Mortgage Business plc* (1998) LSG 4 February, ChD.

12 *Polonski v Lloyds Bank Mortgages Ltd* [1998] 1 FLR 896, (1999) 31 HLR 721, ChD.

available to the borrower to make up the shortfall on sale.[13] A borrower wishing to seek an order for sale must ensure that the application is determined before the lender seeks to enforce a possession order.

43.11   The county court has discretion, in appropriate cases, to give conduct of the sale to the lender while postponing the execution of a warrant for possession and so allowing the borrower to remain in possession pending sale, even where there is little (if any) equity in the property.[14] This can be done where the court is satisfied that:

- possession would not be required by the lender pending completion of the sale but only by the purchasers on completion;
- the presence of the borrowers pending completion would enhance, or at least not depress, the sale price;
- the borrowers would co-operate in the sale; and
- they would give possession to the purchasers on completion.

43.12   Both those claiming to have a beneficial interest in the security[15] and tenants[16] have been held to have the right to apply for an order for sale under LPA 1925 s91.

43.13   Where the amount owing under the mortgage is in excess of £350,000 the county court has no jurisdiction to consider an application under LPA 1925 s91 and the application must be made in the High Court.[17] However, the High Court is likely to transfer the case to the county court for a hearing.

Sale by the lender

43.14   Borrowers will be concerned about a sale by the lender in two circumstances. The first is where the lender has taken possession and is seeking (as mortgagee in possession) to sell and to recoup the outstanding mortgage debt from the sale proceeds. The second is where the occupier has raised a defence which prevents the lender from

13 *Cheltenham & Gloucester plc v Krausz* [1996] 1 WLR 1558, [1997] 1 All ER 21, CA. See A Kenny, 'No postponement of evil day' [1998] Conv 223 and M Dixon, 'Combating the mortgagee's right to possession: new hope for the mortgagor in chains?' [1998] *Legal Studies* 279.

14 *Cheltenham & Gloucester plc v Booker* (1997) 73 P&CR 412, (1997) 29 HLR 634, CA.

15 *Halifax Building Society v Stansfield* [1993] EGCS 147, CA.

16 *National Westminster Home Loans v Riches* [1995] CLW 43/95. See chapter 38.

17 County Courts Act 1984 s23 and County Court Jurisdiction Order 2014 SI No 503 art 3.

obtaining an order for possession. In such circumstances, the lender has the option of applying to the court for an order for sale.

Lender selling as a mortgagee in possession

43.15 In the context of residential mortgages, the lender will be seeking possession of the borrower's home with a view to evicting the borrower and selling with vacant possession. As a disincentive to the taking of possession, the common law imposes some fairly ill-defined obligations on the lender after possession has been taken. In practice, particularly in a depressed property market, disputes between the lender and the borrower tend to arise over, first, the timing of the sale and, second, the sale price.

43.16 As mortgagee in possession, the common law imposes an obligation on the lender to 'take reasonable precautions to obtain the true market value of the mortgaged property at the date on which he decides to sell'.[18] It is clear that while there is an obligation to obtain the best price at the date of sale, the timing of that sale is left to the judgment of the lender,[19] although in choosing the time a reasonable degree of care must be exercised.[20]

43.17 The lender must ensure that the property is fairly and properly exposed to the market.[21] This duty is owed both to the borrower and any guarantor[22] although it does not extend to people claiming as beneficiaries under constructive, resulting or other trusts.[23] The borrower may bring an action for breach of duty against the lender, but a separate action in negligence may lie also against the lender's selling agents.[24] The lender cannot discharge the duty of care by merely putting the sale in the hands of apparently competent estate agents and the lender will be liable for the negligence of the agents even if

18 *Cuckmere Brick Co Ltd v Mutual Finance Ltd* [1971] Ch 949, CA at 968H; *Meftah v Lloyds TSB Bank plc (No 2)* [2001] 2 All ER (Comm) 741, ChD and *Michael v Miller* [2004] EWCA Civ 282, [2004] 2 EGLR 151.

19 *Bank of Cyprus v Gill* [1979] 2 Lloyd's Rep 508, CA.

20 *Standard Chartered Bank Ltd v Walker* [1982] 1 WLR 1410, [1982] 3 All ER 938, CA.

21 *Silven Properties Ltd v Royal Bank of Scotland plc* [2004] 1 WLR 997.

22 *Standard Chartered Bank Ltd v Walker* [1982] 1 WLR 1410, [1982] 3 All ER 938, CA and *American Express International Banking Corp v Hurley* [1985] 3 All ER 564. See also *Skipton Building Society v Stott* [2001] QB 261, [2000] 3 WLR 1031, CA.

23 *Parker-Tweedale v Dunbar Bank plc (No 1)* [1991] Ch 26, [1990] 2 All ER 588, CA.

24 See *Garland v Ralph Pay and Ransom* (1984) 271 EG 106 and *Minah v Bank of Ireland* [1995] EGCS 144.

the lender may be able to recover damages payable to the borrower from the agents.[25] Provisions in a legal charge purporting to exclude the lender's duty to take reasonable care do not exempt the lender if loss arises from the lender's failure to take such reasonable care.[26]

43.18   In the case of a 'regulated mortgage contract' (see para 35.6) where a property is repossessed (either voluntarily or through legal action) a lender must take steps to market the property for sale as soon as possible and obtain the best price that might reasonably be paid, taking account of factors such as market conditions as well as the continuing increase in the amount owed by the borrower to the lender.[27] Where a lender chooses to sell by auction, it is under a duty to ensure that the auction is preceded by appropriate advertisement.[28]

43.19   Where the lender has sold at an undervalue, the borrower's usual remedy will be a claim for damages based on the estimated undervalue.[29] In most cases, such damages will be sought in counterclaim in an action by the lender for a money judgment against the borrower for the shortfall on sale.[30] It would be possible in the alternative, where the property has still to be sold, to seek an injunction to prevent the sale. It is open to a borrower to seek such an injunction even after exchange of contracts but before completion.[31]

43.20   Borrowers concerned about a sale at a possible undervalue will wish to consider a number of issues, including:

- Was the property sold at auction? Sale at an auction is legitimate but the property must be properly described in sale particulars, sufficient notice of the auction should be given and the reserve price should not be unusually low.
- How does the sale price compare with earlier valuations? What can the borrower say about other similar properties being sold in the area?
- Where was the sale advertised? Was this adequate exposure?
- Who was the buyer and was the property then resold soon afterwards?
- Did the sale price just cover the mortgage debt?

---

25   *Tomlin v Luce* (1890) 43 ChD 191, CA.
26   See *Bishop v Bonham* [1988] 1 WLR 742, CA.
27   MCOB 13.6.1 R.
28   *Pendlebury v Colonial Mutual Life Assurance Society Ltd* (1912) 13 CLR 676.
29   Law of Property Act 1925 s104(2). See *Michael v Miller* [2004] EWCA Civ 282, [2004] 2 EGLR 151 and *Mortgage Express v Mardner* [2004] EWCA Civ 1859.
30   *Platts v TSB Bank plc* [1998] 2 BCLC 1.
31   *Shercliff v Engadine Acceptance Corporation Pty Ltd* [1978] 1 NSWLR 729.

- Did the lender sell following one or more competent surveyor's recommendations about the method of sale?
- In the case of a specialised property, was expert advice taken as to how and where to market the property?

43.21 In any case where litigation is contemplated, it will be essential to obtain an expert's report on the value of the property. This should be done as soon as possible. Whether there is the possibility of successful litigation against the lender will ultimately depend on the strength of the expert evidence available.

43.22 On completion of the sale, the borrower will be entitled to be paid the balance of the purchase monies after the mortgage(s) has been redeemed. For that reason, the borrower should notify the lender of his or her whereabouts so that any balance can be forwarded to him or her where there are surplus proceeds of sale.

43.23 In the case of a 'regulated mortgage contract', a lender is obliged to take reasonable steps (as soon as possible after the sale) to inform the borrower of the surplus and, subject to the rights of any other secured lender, to pay it to the borrower.[32]

43.24 However, where the sale proceeds are insufficient to pay off the mortgage in full, there is nothing to prevent the lender suing the borrower for the shortfall on the personal covenant in the mortgage deed.[33] If this is likely, it is important to try to identify whether a mortgage indemnity guarantee policy was taken out at the time of the initial mortgage advance. A mortgage indemnity guarantee policy is simply an insurance policy taken out by the lender (although paid for by the borrower) to protect itself, in part, from any financial loss suffered when a mortgaged property is repossessed and sold.

43.25 The relevant limitation period for the recovery of the outstanding balance on the mortgage is 12 years (and six years for the interest) from the date of the accrual of the lender's right to the debt.[34] It is essential to consider the terms of the legal charge in question, to assess when the right arose.[35] A written acknowledgment of, or part payment towards, the debt will restart the 12-year limitation period.[36]

---

32 MCOB 13.6.6 R.
33 *Gordon Grant and Co Ltd v Boos* [1926] AC 781, PC.
34 *Bristol & West plc v Bartlett* [2002] EWCA Civ 1181, [2002] 4 All ER 544.
35 *West Bromwich Building Society v Wilkinson* [2005] UKHL 44, [2005] 1 WLR 2303.
36 Limitation Act 1980 s29(5). See *Ashcroft v Bradford & Bingley PLC* [2010] EWCA Civ 223, [2010] 2 P&CR 13.

43.26   In the case of a 'regulated mortgage contract', a lender is obliged, as soon as possible after the sale of the repossessed property, to inform the borrower of the amount of the shortfall, and (where relevant) that the debt may be pursued by another company (for example, a mortgage indemnity insurer).[37] Any decision to recover the mortgage shortfall must be notified to the borrower within six years.[38] In addition, members of the Council of Mortgage Lenders have agreed that (with effect from 11 February 2000) no enforcement action will be taken unless, within six years from the sale of a property at a shortfall, a borrower has been contacted about recovery of the outstanding debt.[39]

43.27   In relation to 'regulated mortgage contracts', the FCA expects a lender to treat a mortgage shortfall debt as it would an arrears debt.[40] See para 35.48 and following.

43.28   There is no need to obtain an order from the court authorising sale of the property after possession is obtained. The lender's right to sell the property will have arisen either under the terms of the mortgage deed or under LPA 1925.

Lender seeking an order for sale

43.29   Where land is held on trust (for example, by the defaulting borrower and a person with an overriding beneficial interest), TLATA 1996 enables the court, among other things, to order its sale and the eviction of any occupiers. 'Trust of land' is widely defined and comprises 'any trust of property which consists of or includes land' irrespective of the date of creation or origin of that trust.[41] This will include express, implied, resulting or constructive trusts.

43.30   TLATA 1996 s14(1)–(2) give the court jurisdiction to make such order as it 'thinks fit' in resolution of any dispute over whether trust land should be sold or retained for occupation by the trust beneficiaries. A mortgage lender, having an interest in the trust property, is able to apply to the court for an order for sale. The matters to which the court is expressly to have regard, when determining whether to make an order for sale, include:

---

37 MCOB 13.6.3 R. See para 35.48.
38 MCOB 13.6.4 R. See para 35.49.
39 *Debt following mortgage possession*, see www.cml.org.uk/cml/consumers/guides/debt#3.
40 MCOB 13.1.5 G.
41 TLATA 1996 s1(2).

- the intention of the person(s) who created the trust;
- the purposes for which the trust property is held;
- the welfare of any minor who occupies or might reasonably be expected to occupy the trust property as a home; and
- the interests of any secured creditor of any beneficiary.[42]

43.31   Early case-law was unsympathetic to occupiers notwithstanding the clear policy change introduced by TLATA 1996 abolishing the statutory 'trust for sale'. A lender in possession proceedings faced with a binding overriding interest is able to apply for an order for sale.[43] In *Mortgage Corporation Ltd v Shaire*,[44] the court observed that the presumption of sale contained within the concept of the trust for sale had been abolished by TLATA 1996. TLATA 1996 s15(1) contains four factors (see para 43.30) to be taken into account with the interests of the secured lender being but one. There is no suggestion that those interests should be given any greater weight than the interests of children residing in the house. The court in *Shaire* concluded that parliament had intended to relax the law so as to enable the courts to have more discretion in favour of families and against banks and other chargees. On the facts of the case, an order for sale was made but was suspended on Ms Shaire paying interest on the sum effectively charged on the property in favour of the claimant. While her signature had been forged on the legal charge, the claimant had a valid charge on the other joint owner's interest in the property. Providing the claimant was compensated in interest, the family's occupation of the home could be preserved and the lender was adequately protected pending the eventual sale of the property.

43.32   Whether, in any particular case, an order for sale will be refused or postponed depends on the extent to which a secured creditor is at risk and if it can be compensated financially pending sale of the property[45] and repayment of the monies secured at that time. Case-law since *Shaire* has seen a hardening in judicial attitudes. Issues such as ill health may be relevant when considering the duration of any period of postponement of sale but may be irrelevant (in the

---

42   TLATA 1996 s15(1).

43   *Bank of Baroda v Dhillon* [1998] 1 FLR 524, CA.

44   [2001] Ch 743, [2001] 4 All ER 364, ChD.

45   *Bank of Ireland Home Mortgages Ltd v Bell* [2000] EWCA Civ 426, [2001] 2 All ER (Comm) 920; *Edwards v Lloyds TSB Bank plc* [2004] EWHC 1745 (Ch), [2005] 1 FCR 139 and *First National Bank plc v Achampong* [2003] EWCA Civ 487, [2005] 1 FCR 18. See R Probert, 'Creditors and section 15 of the Trusts of Land and Appointment of Trustees Act 1996: first among equals?' [2002] Conv 61.

absence of any compensatory payments to the lender) when considering whether to allow a lender's application for sale.[46]

---

46 *Bank of Ireland Home Mortgages Ltd v Bell* [2001] 2 All ER (Comm) 920, [2001] 2 FLR 809; *Edwards v Lloyds TSB Bank plc* [2004] EWHC 1745 (Ch), [2005] 1 FCR 139 and *Edwards v Bank of Scotland* [2010] EWHC 652 (Ch).

CHAPTER 44

Possession claims by unsecured creditors

Introduction

44.1   Owner-occupiers are, in certain circumstances, at risk of possession claims by creditors who were, at least initially, unsecured creditors. Advisers should be alert to these possible claims when advising owner-occupiers in relation to their debts. Owners can be evicted by way of a successful application for an order for sale: (1) following a creditor obtaining a charging order; and (2) on the application of the owner's trustee in bankruptcy. The two possibilities are looked at separately in this chapter.

Charging orders

44.2   Under the Charging Orders Act (COA) 1979 a creditor may, after obtaining a money judgment against a debtor, apply to the court for a charging order and then register a charge in relation to property owned beneficially by a judgment debtor, whether alone or jointly with others.[1] The procedure is regulated by the Civil Procedure Rules (CPR) Part 73.

44.3   The relevant court for an application for a charging order is the county court except where the judgment debt is a High Court judgment in excess of £5,000,[2] in which case the judgment creditor has the option of using either the High Court or county court.

44.4   Following the judgment for the debt, application is made without notice to the county court for an interim charging order (previously known as a charging order nisi). This is done using Practice Form N379.[3] An application for an interim charging order in respect of an interest in land must to be made to the County Court Money Claims Centre.[4] Usually the interim order is made without a hearing by a court officer and not a judge.[5] A party may request that a decision by a court officer be reconsidered by a district judge by filing a request within 14 days of the date of service of the interim order.[6] Reconsideration will take place without a hearing.[7]

---

1   COA 1979 s2(1).
2   COA 1979 s1(2) and County Court Jurisdiction Order 2014 SI No 503.
3   CPR Practice Direction (PD) 73.3.
4   CPR 73.4(1).
5   CPR 73.4(2) and (3).
6   CPR 73.5(1) and (2).
7   CPR 73.5(3).

44.5   Where the charge relates to *registered* land held both legally and beneficially by the judgment debtor, the creditor can enter a 'notice' in the charges register of the debtor's title or, in the case of *unregistered* land, a charge under the Land Charges Act 1972. Where the order relates to the debtor's beneficial interest under a trust of land, a 'restriction' can be entered in the proprietorship register of the registered title.[8] It appears that no similar protection is available to a creditor in relation to unregistered land where the debtor has only a beneficial interest.

44.6   Copies of the interim charging order, the application notice and any documents filed in support must be served by the judgment creditor on the judgment debtor within 21 days of the date of the interim charging order.[9] The judgment creditor must also serve these documents on any co-owner and the judgment debtor's spouse or civil partner.[10]

44.7   If any person objects to the court making a final charging order, that person must file and serve on the judgment creditor written evidence stating the grounds of objection, not later than 28 days after service on that person of the application notice and interim order.[11] If grounds of objection to the making of a final charging order are filed, the court must transfer the application for hearing to the judgment debtor's home court.[12]

44.8   Unless the application has been transferred to the judgment debtor's home court, the application for the final order will be considered by a district judge. When considering the application, the court may make a final charging order, discharge the interim order and dismiss the application, decide any issues in dispute, direct a trial of such issues and, if necessary, give directions or make such other order as the court considers appropriate.[13] Where a final charging order is made without a hearing, any application to vary or discharge that charging order must be made to the County Court Money Claims Centre. That application must be transferred for a hearing to the judgment debtor's home court.[14]

---

8 See Land Registry Practice Guide 76: charging orders, updated June 2016.
9 CPR 73.7(1).
10 CPR 73.7(7).
11 CPR 73.10(2).
12 CPR 73.10(3).
13 CPR 73.10(7).
14 CPR 73.10B(1) and (2).

44.9   The onus is on the debtor to show cause why the order should not be made final.[15]

44.10   The court has a discretion whether to grant the charging order and is required to take into account:

> all the circumstances of the case and, in particular, any evidence before it as to ... (a) the personal circumstances of the debtor, and (b) whether any other creditor of the debtor would be likely to be unduly prejudiced by the making of the order.[16]

The fact that there has been no default under an order requiring a judgment debtor to pay a sum of money by instalments does not prevent a charging order being made in respect of that sum. However, the fact that there has been no default under that order must be taken into account by the court when considering its discretion whether to make a charging order.[17]

44.11   *Enforcement* of the charging order cannot take place unless there has been default in payment under an instalment order.[18]

44.12   The court should not grant the charging order where the size of the debt is small compared with the value of the property.[19] The mere fact that other creditors would be prejudiced will not of itself amount to exceptional circumstances such that the charging order should not be made final. In the absence of something about the judgment creditor's conduct, which would cause undue prejudice where there are a number of competing creditors, the 'first past the post' principle applies.[20]

44.13   Where the charging order is being sought against the legal estate of a sole owner or of all the joint legal owners, advisers should point out the limited powers described below (para 44.18) that the court has to prevent an order for sale on the creditor's application. In practice, however, it is not difficult for a creditor to obtain a final charging order.

---

15   *Roberts Petroleum Ltd v Bernard Kenny Ltd* [1983] 2 AC 192, [1982]1 WLR 305, HL and *United Overseas Bank Ltd v Iwuanyanwu* [2001] All ER (D) 40, ChD.

16   COA 1979 s1(5); *Harman v Glencross* [1985] Fam 49, [1986] 1 All ER 545, CA and *Roberts Petroleum Ltd v Bernard Kenny Ltd* [1983] 2 AC 192, HL. For the exercise of the court's powers in the context of simultaneous divorce proceedings see also *Harman v Glencross* (above) and *Austin-Fell v Austin-Fell and Midland Bank plc* [1990] Fam 172, [1990] 3 WLR 33.

17   COA 1979 s1(7) and (8) inserted by Tribunals, Courts and Enforcement Act 2007 s93 with effect 1 October 2012.

18   COA 1979 s3(4C).

19   *Robinson v Bailey* [1942] 1 All ER 498.

20   *British Arab Commercial Bank plc and others v Algosaibi and Brothers Company and others* [2011] EWHC 2444 (Comm), [2011] BPIR 1568.

44.14 The court-imposed charge made by a charging order 'shall have the like effect and be enforceable in the same courts and in the same manner as an equitable charge created by the debtor by writing under his hand'.[21] Variation or discharge of a charging order is possible on application by 'the debtor or any person interested in any property to which the order relates'.[22] Where a final charging order has been obtained by a creditor before a judgment debtor is made bankrupt, it is not open to the trustee in bankruptcy to apply to discharge the charging order.[23]

44.15 Proceedings to enforce a charging order by sale of the property are regulated by CPR 73.10C and PD 73. The court may, upon application by a person who has obtained a charging order over an interest in property, order sale of the property to enforce the charging order.[24] Where the charging order was made at the County Court Money Claims Centre, a claim for an order for sale must be made to the judgment debtor's home court.[25] The claimant for an order for sale must use the Part 8 procedure.[26]

44.16 Where a charging order has been granted against the beneficial interest of only one of two or more joint owners, the judgment debtor will need to apply under the Trusts of Land and Appointment of Trustees Act (TLATA) 1996 for an order for sale.[27] It has been held that the power to enforce a charging order under TLATA 1996 is compliant with the European Convention on Human Rights.[28]

44.17 The Lord Chancellor is given powers to specify, by regulations, the sum below which it is not possible to impose or to enforce a charging order.[29] From 6 April 2013, this sum has been set at £1,000 in respect of loans which are regulated agreements within the meaning of the Consumer Credit Act 1974 and where an order for sale is sought.[30] The House of Commons Library's Standard Note SN/HA/6614 'Enforcing a Charging Order' provides a helpful summary of the law in this area.

21 COA 1979 s3(4). See *Bland v Ingrams Estates Ltd* [2001] Ch 767.
22 COA 1979 s3(5).
23 *Nationwide Building Society v Wright* [2009] EWCA Civ 811, [2010] 2 WLR 1097.
24 CPR 73.10C(1).
25 CPR 73.10C(2).
26 CPR 73.10C(4).
27 *Midland Bank v Pike* [1988] 2 All ER 434 (ChD).
28 *National Westminster Bank plc v Rushmer* [2010] EWHC 554 (Ch), [2010] 2 FLR 362.
29 COA 1979 s3A.
30 Charging Orders (Orders for Sale: Financial Thresholds) Regulations 2013 SI No 491.

44.18   Where the charging order made is against the legal estate of either a sole owner or of all the joint owners the court has none of the discretion available under TLATA 1996. There is no trust of land in this situation. The court is simply dealing with an application by a creditor who has the benefit of an equitable charge.

44.19   Under CPR 73.10C, the creditor can apply for an order for sale and for an order for possession using a Part 8 claim form with supporting witness statement, setting out the charging order which it is sought to enforce, the amount still outstanding to the creditor, details of prior mortgagees, the sums outstanding and the estimated sale price.[31] This application has to be made by issuing a new claim and cannot be made in existing proceedings. An application for an order for sale based on a charging order is an application to enforce an equitable charge. The county court has jurisdiction where the sum owing is under £350,000.[32] Otherwise, the application must be made in the High Court, although it is likely that the High Court will transfer the case to the county court even if the sum involved exceeds the county court financial limit.[33] Appendix A to PD 73 contains optional forms of orders for sale in respect of both properties owned solely by the judgment debtor and by the judgment debtor jointly with others. The application is heard in the county court by a district judge. In practice, district judges are often unwilling to grant the creditor's application for sale and possession because they consider that the security of the charging order is adequate protection for a creditor who was originally unsecured.

44.20   When seeking to resist the application for sale, it is important to emphasise the fact that the creditor is already well protected and to point out the detriment which will result to innocent members of the family if the sale is allowed to proceed, particularly where the sale would result in insufficient funds to enable the family to be rehoused.[34] If the debtor is able to offer alternative ways of discharging the judgment debt, these should be put forward.

44.21   When a judgment creditor obtains a charge on a property as security for a judgment debt, the creditor's security extends also to interest on the debt even if interest is not expressly mentioned in the order. In equity, the creditor is also entitled to add the costs of enforcing the

31 PD 73.4.3.
32 County Courts Act 1984 s23 and County Court Jurisdiction Order 2014 SI No 503.
33 *National Westminster Bank plc v King* [2008] EWHC 280 (Ch).
34 See generally *Harman v Glencross* [1985] Fam 49, [1984] 2 All ER 577, CA.

charge to the security. The amount of interest recoverable under the charging order is not restricted by the Limitation Act 1980.[35] Similarly, the judgment creditor is entitled to the costs of enforcing the charging order including the costs of fending off claims by third parties that they had beneficial interests in the proceeds of sale of the property subject to the charging order.[36]

44.22   The rights of a creditor who has a charging order are not statute barred after 12 years under the Limitation Act 1980 because the holder does not have a right to possession such that time can run against it under section 15 and extinction of title cannot therefore occur under section 17.[37]

Trustees in bankruptcy

44.23   When a person becomes bankrupt, his or her property vests in the trustee in bankruptcy as soon as that person is appointed. The property is vested in the trustee without the necessity of any deed of transfer.[38] The trustee's duty is then 'to get in, realise and distribute'[39] the bankrupt's assets and to distribute the estate in accordance with the Insolvency Act (IA) 1986.

44.24   Where the legal and beneficial estate is in the sole name of the bankrupt, then the trustee is at liberty to dispose of that asset without the need to consider the position of others. However, where the legal estate is in the joint names of the bankrupt and a third party, or where the bankrupt and a third party have beneficial interests, then the trustee is a 'person interested' who can apply under TLATA 1996 s14 for an order for sale. The bankruptcy of a 'beneficial joint tenant' operates as an act of severance, resulting in the property being held by the owners on a 'tenancy in common'.[40] Where there is a spouse or civil partner in occupation (but not a mere cohabitant) who has no legal or beneficial interest, he or she will have to rely on any rights of occupation under the Family Law Act 1996. A cohabitant who has neither a legal nor beneficial interest in the property will not

---

35 *Ezekiel v Orakpo* [1997] 1 WLR 340, CA.
36 *Holder v Supperstone* [2000] 1 All ER 457, ChD.
37 *Yorkshire Bank Finance Ltd v Mulhall* [2008] EWCA Civ 1156, [2009] 2 All ER (Comm) 164.
38 IA 1986 s306(1) and (2).
39 IA 1986 s305(2).
40 *Re Gorman* [1990] 1 WLR 616, [1990] 1 All ER 717.

be able to resist an application for an order for possession in advance of sale.

44.25   Insolvency Act 1986 s335A[41] provides that, when considering applications for sale and possession of property by the trustee under TLATA 1996 s14, the court shall make such order as it thinks just and reasonable having regard to:

(a) the interests of the bankrupt's creditors;

(b) where the application is made in respect of land which includes a dwelling-house which is or has been the home of the bankrupt or the bankrupt's spouse or civil partner or former spouse or former civil partner –

(i)   the conduct of the spouse, civil partner, former spouse or former civil partner, so far as contributing to the bankruptcy,

(ii) the needs and financial resources of the spouse, civil partner, former spouse or former civil partner, and

(iii) the needs of any children; and

(c) all the circumstances of the case other than the needs of the bankrupt.[42]

44.26   The usual criteria by which the court assesses an application for sale under the TLATA 1996 are expressly excluded where the trustee in bankruptcy is the claimant.[43] The application for an order for sale is made to the bankruptcy court.[44]

44.27   IA 1996 provides for a statutory presumption in favour of making the order for possession and sale for the benefit of the creditors *after* a 12-month period:

> ... after the end of the period of one year beginning with the first vesting ... of the bankrupt's estate in a trustee, the court shall assume, unless the circumstances of the case are exceptional, that the interests of the bankrupt's creditors outweigh all other considerations.[45]

44.28   While this statutory presumption would seem to favour the creditors 12 months after the bankruptcy, it does not prevent an application for sale/possession by the trustee during that period. However, faced with the prospect of a defended application during the initial period, many trustees will prefer to wait for this statutory period to elapse before making the application. It is, however, arguable that this statutory presumption that the property is to be sold after the end of the

---

41 Inserted by TLATA 1996 s25(1) and Sch 3 para 23.

42 IA 1986 s335A (2).

43 TLATA 1996 s15(4).

44 IA 1986 s335A(1).

45 IA 1986 s335A(3).

12 months infringes Human Rights Act 1998 Sch 1 Article 8 (and Article 1 of the First Protocol).[46]

44.29   The Insolvency Act 1986, therefore, allows for the enforcement of the interests of creditors to be delayed, but not indefinitely. The statutory period of 12 months will, in most cases, allow a breathing space for the third party to seek alternative accommodation. However, the IA 1986, in effect, does allow this period to be exceeded where there are 'exceptional circumstances'. The fact that innocent third parties will be made homeless is not such an 'exceptional circumstance' as to prevent a sale being ordered.[47] In *Re Citro*,[48] it was held, by a majority, that the interests of the creditors will usually prevail over the interests of a spouse and children, and that more than the ordinary consequences of debt and improvidence would be necessary before the court would be able to postpone sale for a substantial period.

44.30   Where relevant, it is important to emphasise the personal circumstances of the debtor's family, including, for example, the effect on the children's education, particularly if they are shortly to take examinations. If this is the case, it may be possible to have the order for possession postponed until after the examination date.[49] In cases where there is severe ill health, it may be possible to argue that this is an exceptional circumstance such as to enable the court to delay sale of the property until either death of the family member or his or her departure from the home.[50]

44.31   Advisers are often left with little scope for manoeuvre when advising the bankrupt or other occupiers affected by the bankruptcy. It is, however, worth arguing that it is open to the trustee to apply under IA 1986 s313 for a charging order over property in favour of the bankrupt's estate. If made, then such a charging order becomes subject to COA 1979 s3, and the court will have the power to impose conditions as to when the charge becomes enforceable. In addition, the bankrupt

---

46 *Jackson v Bell* [2001] EWCA Civ 387, [2001] BPIR 612 and *Barca v Mears* [2004] EWHC 2170, [2005] 2 FLR 1. See also 'Trusts of land, bankruptcy and human rights' [2005] Conv 161.

47 *Re Lowrie* [1981] 3 All ER 353.

48 [1991] Ch 142, [1990] 3 WLR 880, CA. Cf *Re Holliday* [1981] Ch 405, [1981] 2 WLR 996.

49 See generally D Brown, 'Insolvency and the matrimonial home – the sins of the fathers: *In re Citro (A Bankrupt)*' (1992) 55 MLR 284.

50 See *Re Bremner (A Bankrupt)* [1999] 1 FLR 912, ChD and *Claughton v Charalambous* [1999] 1 FLR 740, [1998] BPIR 558, ChD. See also *In the matter of Haghighat (a bankrupt) sub nom Brittain (Trustee of the property of the bankrupt) v Haghighat* [2009] EWHC (Ch) Case no 189 of 2002, [2009] 1 FLR 1271. Cf *Nicholls v Lan* [2006] EWHC 1255 (Ch).

may be allowed to remain living in the property notwithstanding the bankruptcy, conditionally on him or her making payments towards the mortgage and the other outgoings. The bankrupt would not, however, by virtue of this acquire any interest in the property.[51]

44.32   A joint owner who remains in the property following the date of the other owner's bankruptcy is entitled to be repaid (out of the bankrupt's share) for half of the mortgage payments made by him or her but this sum must be set off against an 'occupation rent' in favour of the bankrupt's trustee.[52]

44.33   Since 1 April 2004, where the property which vested in the trustee was the home of the bankrupt or his or her spouse or previous spouse, the trustee has had three years from the date of bankruptcy to start an action to realise the interest by sale or the property automatically revests in the bankrupt.[53] During that period, the trustee must either realise the interest or apply for an order for sale or possession to avoid the revesting in the bankrupt.

44.34   The court must dismiss a trustee's application for sale or possession where the net value of the bankrupt's interest in the property is below an amount prescribed in secondary legislation,[54] currently £1,000.[55] The value of the bankrupt's interest is calculated after deducting the value of any loans secured by mortgage or any other third party interests and the reasonable costs of sale.[56]

44.35   The procedure for applying for an order for sale is as set out above dealing with charging orders in the text (see para 44.19).

44.36   When ordering sale, the court has the power to impose conditions on the sale, including a requirement to reimburse the joint beneficial owner who has paid the instalments to a mortgage lender (so preventing earlier eviction and the sale of the property) to recompense

---

51 IA 1986 s338.
52 *Re Byford; Byford v Butler* [2003] EWHC 1267 (Ch), [2004] 1 FLR 56. See also H Conway, 'Co-ownership, equitable accounting and the trustee in bankruptcy' [2003] Conv 533.
53 IA 1986 s283A, inserted by Enterprise Act 2004 s261(1) and Enterprise Act 2004 (Commencement No 4 and Transitional Provisions & Savings) Order 2003 SI No 2093.
54 IA 1986 s313A, inserted by Enterprise Act 2004 s261 and Enterprise Act 2004 (Commencement No 4 and Transitional Provisions and Savings) Order 2003 SI No 2093.
55 Insolvency Proceedings (Monetary Limits) (Amendment) Order 2004 SI No 547 art 2.
56 Insolvency Proceedings (Monetary Limits) (Amendment) Order 2004 SI No 547 art 3.

him or her for the increase in the house value during the period in which he or she has repaid the loan.[57]

APPENDICES

Statutory notices[1]

This section contains the following notices and forms:

---

1   Forms 1 and 4 are reproduced for illustrative purposes only by kind permission of Oyez Professional Services Limited. Oyez's range of legal forms can be ordered at www.oyezstore.co.uk. Forms 2, 3, 5 and 6 © Crown Copyright.

1   Notice seeking possession of a property let on a secure tenancy

Secure Tenancies (Notices) Regulations 1987,
Schedule, Part I as amended.

This Notice is the first step towards requiring you to give up possession of your dwelling. You should read it very carefully.

HOUSING ACT 1985

Section 83

Notice of Seeking Possession

(1) Name(s) of
Secure Tenant(s).

1. To (1)

If you need advice about this Notice, and what you should do about it, take it as quickly as possible to a Citizens' Advice Bureau, a Housing Aid Centre, or a Law Centre, or to a Solicitor. You may be able to receive Legal Aid but this will depend on your personal circumstances.

(2) Insert name.

2. The landlord (2)
    intends to apply to the Court for an Order requiring you to give up possession of:

(3) Address of
property.

(3)

If you are a secure tenant under the Housing Act 1985, you can only be required to leave your dwelling if your landlord obtains an order for possession from the Court. The order must be based on one of the Grounds which are set out in the 1985 Act (see paragraphs 3 and 4 below).

If you are willing to give up possession without a Court order, you should notify the person who signed this Notice as soon as possible and say when you would leave.

(4) Give the text
in full of each Ground
which is being
relied on.

3. Possession will be sought on Ground(s)
    of Schedule 2 to the Housing Act 1985 which read(s) (4):

Whatever Grounds for possession are set out in paragraph 3 of this Notice, the Court may allow any of the other Grounds to be added at a later stage. If this is done, you will be told about it so you can argue at the hearing in Court about the new Ground, as well as the Grounds set out in paragraph 3, if you want to.

[P.T.O.

HA1/1

(5) Give a full explanation of why each Ground is being relied upon.

4. Particulars of each Ground are as follows (5):

Before the Court will grant an order on any of the Grounds 1 to 8 or 12 to 16, it must be satisfied that it is reasonable to require you to leave. This means that, if one of these Grounds is set out in paragraph 3 of this Notice, you will be able to argue at the hearing in Court that it is not reasonable that you should have to leave, even if you accept that the Ground applies.

Before the Court grants an order on any of the Grounds 9 to 16, it must be satisfied that there will be suitable alternative accommodation for you when you have to leave. This means that the Court will have to decide that, in its opinion, there will be other accommodation which is reasonably suitable for the needs of you and your family, taking into particular account various factors such as the nearness of your place of work, and the sort of housing that other people with similar needs are offered. Your new home will have to be let to you on another secure tenancy or a private tenancy under the Rent Act of a kind that will give you similar security. **There is no requirement for suitable alternative accommodation where Grounds 1 to 8 apply.**

If your landlord is not a local authority, and the local authority gives a certificate that it will provide you with suitable accommodation, the Court has to accept the certificate.

One of the requirements of Ground 10A is that the landlord must have approval for the redevelopment scheme from the Secretary of State (or, in the case of a landlord of a property in England which is a private registered provider of social housing, from the Regulator of Social Housing). The landlord must have consulted all secure tenants affected by the proposed redevelopment scheme.

[P.T.O.

HA1/2

(6) Cross out this paragraph if possession is being sought on Ground 2 of Schedule 2 to the Housing Act 1985 (whether or not possession is also sought on another Ground)

(7) Give the date after which Court proceedings can be brought.

(8) Cross out this paragraph if possession is not being sought on Ground 2 of Schedule 2 to the Housing Act 1985

(9) Give the date by which the tenant is to give up possession of the dwelling-house.

5. (6) **The court proceedings for possession will not be begun until after** (7)

- Court proceedings cannot be begun until after this date, which cannot be earlier than the date when your tenancy or licence could have been brought to an end. This means that if you have a weekly or fortnightly tenancy, there should be at least 4 weeks between the date this Notice is given and the date in this paragraph.

- After this date, Court proceedings may be begun at once or at any time during the following twelve months. Once the twelve months are up this Notice will lapse and a new Notice must be served before possession can be sought.

5. (8) **Court proceedings for possession of the dwelling-house can be begun immediately. The date by which the tenant is to give up possession of the dwelling-house is** (9)

- Court proceedings may be begun at once or at any time during the following twelve months. Once the twelve months are up this Notice will lapse and a new Notice must be served before possession can be sought.

- Possession of your dwelling-house cannot be obtained until after this date, which cannot be earlier than the date when your tenancy or licence could have been brought to an end. This means that if you have a weekly or fortnightly tenancy, there should be at least 4 weeks between the date this Notice is given and the date possession is ordered.

Signed

On behalf of

Address

Tel No.

Date

HA1/3

2 Notice seeking possession of a property let on an assured shorthold tenancy (where possession will be sought under HA 1988 s21)[1]

FORM 6A

Notice seeking possession of a property let on an Assured Shorthold Tenancy

Housing Act 1988 section 21(1) and (4) as amended by section 194 and paragraph 103 of Schedule 11 to the Local Government and Housing Act 1989 and section 98(2) and (3) of the Housing Act 1996

- Please write clearly in black ink. Please tick boxes where appropriate.

- This form should be used where a no fault possession of accommodation let under an assured shorthold tenancy (AST) is sought under section 21(1) or (4) of the Housing Act 1988.

- There are certain circumstances in which the law says that you cannot seek possession against your tenant using section 21 of the Housing Act 1988, in which case you should not use this form. These are:

    (a)   during the first four months of the tenancy (but where the tenancy is a replacement tenancy, the four month period is calculated by reference to the start of the original tenancy and not the start of the replacement tenancy – see section 21(4B) of the Housing Act 1988);

    (b)   where the landlord is prevented from retaliatory eviction under section 33 of the Deregulation Act 2015;

    (c)   where the landlord has not provided the tenant with an energy performance certificate, gas safety certificate or the Department for Communities and Local Government's publication "How to rent: the checklist for renting in England" (see the Assured Shorthold Tenancy Notices and Prescribed Requirements (England) Regulations 2015);

    (d)   where the landlord has not complied with the tenancy deposit protection legislation; or

    (e)   where a property requires a licence but is unlicensed.

Landlords who are unsure about whether they are affected by these provisions should seek specialist advice.

- This form must be used for all ASTs created on or after 1 October 2015 except for statutory periodic tenancies which have come into being on or after 1 October 2015 at the end of fixed term ASTs created before 1 October 2015. There is no obligation to use this form in relation to ASTs created prior to 1 October 2015, however it may nevertheless be used for all ASTs.

What to do if this notice is served on you

- You should read this notice very carefully. It explains that your landlord has started the process to regain possession of the property referred to in section 2 below.

- You are entitled to at least two months' notice before being required to give up possession of the property. However, if your tenancy started on a periodic basis without any initial fixed term a longer notice period may be required depending on how often you are required to pay rent (for example, if you pay rent quarterly, you must be given at least three months' notice, or, if you have a periodic tenancy which is half yearly or annual, you must be given at least six months' notice (which is the maximum)). The date you are required to leave should be shown in section 2 below. After this date the landlord can apply to court for a possession order against you.

- Where your tenancy is terminated before the end of a period of your tenancy (e.g. where you pay rent in advance on the first of each month and you are required to give up possession in the middle of the month), you may be entitled to repayment of rent from the landlord under section 21C of the Housing Act 1988.

- If you need advice about this notice, and what you should do about it, take it immediately to a citizens' advice bureau, a housing advice centre, a law centre or a solicitor.

1   © Crown Copyright. Form reproduced in original form from www.legislation.gov. uk: Assured Shorthold Tenancy Notices and Prescribed Requirements (England) (Amendment) Regulations 2015 SI No 1725 Sch.

1. To:

Name(s) of tenant(s) (Block Capitals)

_____

_____

2. You are required to leave the below address after [   ]¹. If you do not leave, your landlord may apply to the court for an order under section 21 (1) or (4) of the Housing Act 1988 requiring you to give up possession.

Address of premises

_____

_____

3. This notice is valid for six months only from the date of issue unless you have a periodic tenancy under which more than two months' notice is required (see notes accompanying this form) in which case this notice is valid for four months only from the date specified in section 2 above.

4. Name and address of landlord

To be signed and dated by the landlord or their agent (someone acting for them). If there are joint landlords each landlord or the agent should sign unless one signs on behalf of the rest with their agreement.

Signed   *Date*

_____   _____

Please specify whether: landlord ☐ joint landlords ☐ landlord's agent ☐

Name(s) of signatory/signatories (Block Capitals)

_____

_____

Address(es) of signatory/signatories

_____

_____

Telephone of signatory/signatories

_____

---

¹ Landlords should insert a calendar date here. The date should allow sufficient time to ensure that the notice is properly served on the tenant(s). This will depend on the method of service being used and landlords should check whether the tenancy agreement makes specific provision about service. Where landlords are seeking an order for possession on a periodic tenancy under section 21(4) of the Housing Act 1988, the notice period should also not be shorter than the period of the tenancy (up to a maximum of six months), e.g. where there is a quarterly periodic tenancy, the date should be three months from the date of service.

3 Notice seeking possession of a property let on an assured tenancy, an assured agricultural occupancy or an assured shorthold tenancy where possession is sought on one of the grounds in HA 1988 Sch 2[1]

FORM No. 3

Housing Act 1988 section 8, as amended by section 151 of the Housing Act 1996 and section 97 of the Anti-social Behaviour, Crime and Policing Act 2014

FORM 3

Notice seeking possession of a property let on an Assured Tenancy or an Assured Agricultural Occupancy

Housing Act 1988 section 8 as amended by section 151 of the Housing Act 1996 and section 97 of the Anti-social Behaviour, Crime and Policing Act 2014

- Please write clearly in black ink.
- Please cross out text marked with an asterisk (*) that does not apply.
- This form should be used where possession of accommodation let under an assured tenancy, an assured agricultural occupancy or an assured shorthold tenancy is sought on one of the grounds in Schedule 2 to the Housing Act 1988.
- Do not use this form if possession is sought on the "shorthold" ground under section 21 of the Housing Act 1988 from an assured shorthold tenant where the fixed term has come to an end or, for assured shorthold tenancies with no fixed term which started on or after 28th February 1997, after six months has elapsed. There is no prescribed form for these cases, but you must give notice in writing.

1 To:...

Name(s) of tenant(s)/licensee(s)*

2 Your landlord/licensor* intends to apply to the court for an order requiring you to give up possession of:..........
....
....

Address of premises

3 Your landlord/licensor* intends to seek possession on ground(s) .... in Schedule 2 to the Housing Act 1988 (as amended), which read(s):..
....
....

Give the full text (as set out in the Housing Act 1988 (as amended) of each ground which is being relied on. Continue on a separate sheet if necessary.

4 Give a full explanation of why each ground is being relied on:...
....
....

Continue on a separate sheet if necessary.

Notes on the grounds for possession

- If the court is satisfied that any of grounds 1 to 8 is established, it must make an order (but see below in respect of fixed term tenancies).
- Before the court will grant an order on any of grounds 9 to 17, it must be satisfied that it is reasonable to require you to leave. This means that, if one of these grounds is set out in section 3, you will be able to suggest to the court that it is not reasonable that you should have to leave, even if you accept that the ground applies.
- The court will not make an order under grounds 1, 3 to 7, 9 or 16, to take effect during the fixed term of the tenancy (if there is one) and it will only make an order during the fixed term on grounds 2, 8, 10 to 15 or 17 if the terms of the tenancy make provision for it to be brought to an end on any of these grounds.
- Where the court makes an order for possession solely on ground 6 or 9, the landlord must pay your reasonable removal expenses.

1 © Crown Copyright. Form reproduced in original form from www.legislation.gov.uk: Assured Tenancies and Agricultural Occupancies (Forms) (England) Regulations 2015 SI No 620 Sch.

5   The court proceedings will not begin until after: ....
....

Give the earliest date on which court proceedings can be brought

Notes on the earliest date on which court proceedings can be brought

- Where the landlord is seeking possession on grounds 1, 2, 5 to 7, 9 or 16 (without ground 7A or 14), court proceedings cannot begin earlier than 2 months from the date this notice is served on you and not before the date on which the tenancy (had it not been assured) could have been brought to an end by a notice to quit served at the same time as this notice. This applies even if one of grounds 3, 4, 8, 10 to 13, 14ZA, 14A, 15 or 17 is also specified.

- Where the landlord is seeking possession on grounds 3, 4, 8, 10 to 13, 14ZA, 14A, 15 or 17 (without ground 7A or 14), court proceedings cannot begin earlier than 2 weeks from the date this notice is served. If one of 1, 2, 5 to 7, 9 or 16 grounds is also specified court proceedings cannot begin earlier than two months from the date this notice is served.

- Where the landlord is seeking possession on ground 7A (with or without other grounds), court proceedings cannot begin earlier than 1 month from the date this notice is served on you and not before the date on which the tenancy (had it not been assured) could have been brought to an end by a notice to quit served at the same time as this notice. A notice seeking possession on ground 7A must be served on you within specified time periods which vary depending on which condition is relied upon:

  o Where the landlord proposes to rely on condition 1, 3 or 5: within 12 months of the conviction (or if the conviction is appealed: within 12 months of the conclusion of the appeal);

  o Where the landlord proposes to rely on condition 2: within 12 months of the court's finding that the injunction has been breached (or if the finding is appealed: within 12 months of the conclusion of the appeal);

  o Where the landlord proposes to rely on condition 4: within 3 months of the closure order (or if the order is appealed: within 3 months of the conclusion of the appeal).

- Where the landlord is seeking possession on ground 14 (with or without other grounds other than ground 7A), court proceedings cannot begin before the date this notice is served.

- Where the landlord is seeking possession on ground 14A, court proceedings cannot begin unless the landlord has served, or has taken all reasonable steps to serve, a copy of this notice on the partner who has left the property.

- After the date shown in section 5, court proceedings may be begun at once but not later than 12 months from the date on which this notice is served. After this time the notice will lapse and a new notice must be served before possession can be sought.

6   Name and address of landlord/licensor*.

To be signed and dated by the landlord or licensor or the landlord's or licensor's agent (someone acting for him). If there are joint landlords each landlord or the agent must sign unless one signs on behalf of the rest with their agreement.

Signed .... Date ....
....

Please specify whether: landlord/licensor/joint landlords/landlord's agent

Name(s) (Block Capitals)..
....

Address ....
....

Telephone: Daytime .... Evening ....

What to do if this notice is served on you

- This notice is the first step requiring you to give up possession of your home. You should read it very carefully.

- Your landlord cannot make you leave your home without an order for possession issued by a court. By issuing this notice your landlord is informing you that he intends to seek such an order. If you are willing to give up possession without a court order, you should tell the person who signed this notice as soon as possible and say when you are prepared to leave.

- Whichever grounds are set out in section 3 of this form, the court may allow any of the other grounds to be added at a later date. If this is done, you will be told about it so you can discuss the additional grounds at the court hearing as well as the grounds set out in section 3.

- If you need advice about this notice, and what you should do about it, take it immediately to a citizens' advice bureau, a housing advice centre, a law centre or a solicitor.

4 Notice to quit

NOTICE TO QUIT

(BY LANDLORD OF PREMISES LET AS A DWELLING)

Name and
Address of
Tenant.

To

of

Name and
Address of
Landlord.

[I] [We] [as] [on behalf of] your landlord[s],

of

*Me/them or as
appropriate.

give you **NOTICE TO QUIT** and deliver up possession to*

† Address of
premises.

of†

‡ Date for
possession.

on‡   , or the day on which a complete period of your

tenancy expires next after the end of four weeks from the service of this notice.

Date of notice.

Dated

Signed

Name and
Address of
Agent if Agent
serves notice.

_____

INFORMATION FOR TENANT
(See Note 2 overleaf)

1.   If the tenant or licensee does not leave the dwelling, the landlord or licensor must get an
order for possession from the court before the tenant or licensee can lawfully be evicted. The
landlord or licensor cannot apply for such an order before the notice to quit or notice to
determine has run out.

2.   A tenant or licensee who does not know if he has any right to remain in possession after
a notice to quit or a notice to determine runs out can obtain advice from a solicitor. Help with
all or part of the cost of legal advice and assistance may be available under the Legal Aid
Scheme. He should also be able to obtain information from a Citizens' Advice Bureau, a
Housing Aid Centre or a Rent Officer.

[P.T.O.

Oyez 7 Spa Road, London SE16 3QQ
© Crown copyright.

5.1999 MM
L&T61/1

Landlord and Tenant 61

NOTES

1. Notice to quit premises let as a dwelling must be given at least four weeks before it takes effect, and it must be in writing (Protection from Eviction Act 1977, s. 5 as amended).

2. Where a notice to quit is given by a landlord to determine a tenancy of any premises let as a dwelling, the notice must contain this information (The Notices to Quit etc. (Prescribed Information) Regulations 1988).

3. Some tenancies are excluded from this protection: see Protection from Eviction Act 1977, ss. 3A and 5(1B).

L&T61/2

5   Notice under Mortgage Repossessions (Protection of Tenants etc) Act 2010[1]

Notice that your home is at risk

If you are paying rent to live in this property, please read the following carefully.
If you are an owner occupier, please seek advice on your
position as different rules apply

This notice is given under Section 2(4) of the Mortgage Repossessions (Protection of Tenants etc) Act 2010.

I give you notice that the Lender/the Lender's Agent has applied/will apply (delete as appropriate) to the court for a warrant for possession against this property on:.....................................

(Insert the date on which the application for the warrant for possession was made or will be made. The order will only be executed after the end of the 14 day prescribed period.)

At:...

Tel:..

Address:..
....
(Insert the name, address and telephone number of the court at which the application has been or will be made.)

1. This notice advises you that **you could be evicted from your home**. For tenants, be advised that your landlord's Lender has obtained an order for possession against the property. It is now seeking to enforce that order through the courts. Please read this notice carefully. If you need advice you should contact any of the following:

—a Citizens' Advice Bureau;
—a housing advice organisation, or charity such as Shelter;
—a housing aid centre;
—a Law Centre;
—a solicitor.

2. The law gives certain tenants the right to apply to the Lender to ask it not to enforce the order for a period of two months. You should contact the Lender or its Agent on the number given to ask for this delay if you require it. This is to give you time to find somewhere else to live. If you are unsure whether you may qualify, you should seek advice immediately from one of the organisations listed, or a similar organisation. If the Lender agrees to your request, they must confirm this to you in writing. If the Lender refuses your request, or if you receive no reply, you may be able to make an application to court for a similar delay. The Lender may make any agreement with you conditional on you continuing to pay to live at the property. An application to the Lender or to the court should be accompanied by any evidence you have to prove the existence of your tenancy.

3. This notice is not directed at owner occupiers. If you pay a mortgage to live at the property, you should urgently seek advice on your position as you have different rights.

4. If you do not ask for a delay, the Lender can go ahead to obtain possession of this property. Although the warrant for possession cannot be executed earlier than 14 days after the date on which the Lender sent you this notice **you must act quickly if you are seeking the delay, otherwise you may run out of time.**

1   © Crown Copyright. This form can be found in the Schedule to the Dwelling Houses (Execution of Possesssion Orders by Mortgagees) Regulations 2010 SI No 1809.

Served on:...
(Insert address of the property. Address to: "Tenant/Occupier" or name of tenant(s) if known).

Served by::...("the Lender")

Tel:...

Address:..
....
....
(Insert full name of Lender, telephone number and address where enquiries about this notice can be made.)

If served by Lender's Agent:

Served on:...
(Insert address of the property. Address to: "Tenant/Occupier" or name of tenant(s) if known).

Served by:...("the Lender's Agent")

On behalf of:...("the Lender")

Tel:...

Address:..
....
....
(Insert full name of Lender's Agent, telephone number and address where enquiries about this notice can be made.)

Signed... Date.......................................

To be signed and dated by the Lender or the Lender's Agent

6   Mortage Pre-action Protocol checklist

	Click here to reset form	Click here to print form

N123	In the		Claim no.	
Mortgage pre-action protocol checklist				
	Name of claimant			
	Name of defendant			
	Mortgage account number			

You must produce two copies of the Checklist on the day of the hearing.

Checklist

1. Is the possession claim within the scope of the Protocol? ☐ Yes ☐ No

2. Have you provided the defendant with the information/notice in the Protocol —

    (a) paragraph 5.1(a) ☐ Yes ☐ No   If Yes, date provided: ☐☐/☐☐/☐☐☐☐

    (b) paragraph 5.1(b) ☐ Yes ☐ No   If Yes, date provided: ☐☐/☐☐/☐☐☐☐

    (c) paragraph 5.1(c) ☐ Yes ☐ No   If Yes, date of notice: ☐☐/☐☐/☐☐☐☐

    (d) paragraph 5.8 ☐ Yes ☐ No   If Yes, date of notice: ☐☐/☐☐/☐☐☐☐

3. Do you have evidence that the defendant has made a claim for —

    • support for Mortgage Interest (SMI), or if appropriate Universal Credit, or ☐ Yes ☐ No

    • mortgage Rescue Scheme (MRS), or other means of homelessness prevention support, or ☐ Yes ☐ No

    • mortgage payment protection. ☐ Yes ☐ No

    If Yes, please explain why possession proceedings are continuing.

4. Is there an unresolved complaint by the defendant to the Financial Ombudsman Service that could justify postponing the possession claim? ☐ Yes ☐ No

    If Yes, please explain why possession proceedings are continuing.

5. Summarise the number and dates, in the three months prior to the date of this checklist, you attempted to discuss with the defendant ways of repaying the arrears.

N123 Pre-action protocol for possession claims based on mortgage or home purchase plan arrears in respect of residential property (09.15)   © Crown copyright 2015

6. In the three months prior to the date of this checklist have you rejected any proposals □ Yes □ No
   by the defendant to change the date or method of regular payments?

   If Yes, did you respond in accordance with paragraph 5.5 of the Protocol? □ Yes □ No

   If No, please explain why.

7. Please explain what steps the mortgagee has taken to check whether there is a tenant
   of the borrower in occupation, whether that tenant was authorised by the mortgagee,
   and what order the mortgagee is seeking in the light of the information obtained.

8. Have you rejected a proposal for repayment by the defendant in the three months □ Yes □ No
   prior to the date of this checklist?

   If Yes, have you responded in accordance with paragraph 5.6 of the Protocol? □ Yes □ No

   If No, please explain why.

9. Has the defendant indicated that the property will be or is being sold? □ Yes □ No

   If Yes, explain why possession proceedings are proceeding.

Statement of Truth

*I believe that the facts stated in this Checklist are true.

*I am duly authorised by the claimant to sign this statement.

Signed _____   Date _____

Full name

Name of claimant's legal
representative firm

Position or office held
*Delete as appropriate

| **Click here to print form** |

Guidance for the mortgage pre-action protocol checklist

The Checklist

This guidance is provided for those using the Mortgage Pre-Action Protocol Checklist. Use of the Checklist came into effect on 1 October 2009 for all claims issued on or after that date in order to provide a uniform format for the provision of information to demonstrate compliance with the Protocol.

This guide must be read with the Mortgage Pre-Action Protocol, the Civil Procedure Rules and Practice Direction 55.

The Checklist (form N123), must be completed by all claimants (lenders) or their representatives making a possession claim. The claimant or their representative should be able to explain to the court the actions taken or not by the claimant, and the reason for issuing a possession claim.

Once the claimant and defendant (borrower) have been notified by the court of the date of the hearing, a Checklist must be completed indicating the action taken by the claimant within the previous three months to reach an agreement with the defendant, and comply with the Protocol.

The claimant must present two copies of the Checklist on the day of the hearing. No additional documents are necessary unless an issue arises.

Claimants can copy this form onto their systems but the form must not go beyond two sides.

Scope

The following mortgages fall within the scope of the Protocol and Checklist –

(i) first charge residential mortgages and home purchase plans regulated by the Financial Conduct Authority under the Financial Services and Markets Act 2000 as amended by the Financial Services Act 2012;

(ii) second charge mortgages over residential property and other secured loans regulated under the Consumer Credit Act 1974 on residential property; and

(iii) unregulated residential mortgages.

Where a potential claim includes a money claim and a claim for possession, these are also within scope.

Q1 – requires confirmation of the type of mortgage and whether it is within scope of the Protocol as indicated above. If the answer is No, there is no need to compete the rest of the form. However, you must be prepared to explain to the court why you consider that the mortgage does not fall within the scope of the Protocol.

If the answer to Q1 is Yes, all the remaining questions must be answered in full.

Q2 – answer the questions Yes or No, as appropriate, and insert the dates where relevant. Where you have not complied with one or more of these requirements, you must be prepared to explain to the court in full why that is the case.

Q3 – answer the questions Yes or No, as appropriate. Where you have evidence of a claim, you must set out clearly and succinctly why you are proceeding with a claim for possession.

Q4 – answer the question Yes or No, as appropriate. If the defendant has an unresolved complaint you must set out clearly and succinctly why you are proceeding with a claim for possession.

Q5 – you should provide here a list of dates and details of the associated media (for example, letter, telephone, etc). Where use has been made of automated diallers, which do not necessarily keep an individual record of each attempted call, you should confirm the number of attempts and frequency that your system is programmed to make.

Q6 – answer the question Yes or No, as appropriate. Where you have answered:

- No, then no further information is required.
- Yes, you must also confirm whether or not you have complied with the requirements of paragraph 5.4 of the protocol when notifying the defendant of your decision. If the answer to that question is:

  o Yes – then no further information is required on the Checklist but you must be prepared to explain to the court what action you took if requested to do so.

  o No – you should set out your reasons for non-compliance clearly and succinctly.

Q7 – ask the lender to check the status of the tenant in properties where the borrower is in arrears before issuing.

Q8 – answer the question Yes or No, as appropriate. Where you have answered:

- No, then no further information is required.
- Yes, you must also confirm whether or not you have complied with the requirements of paragraph 5.6 of the protocol when notifying the defendant of your decision. If the answer to that question is:
  - o Yes – then no further information is required on the Checklist but you must be prepared to explain to the court what action you took if requested to do so.
  - o No – you should set out your reasons for non-compliance clearly and succinctly.

Q9 – answer the question Yes or No, as appropriate. Where the defendant is trying to sell their property you need to explain clearly and succinctly why you are bringing proceedings including, specifically, whether or not the defendant has complied with the requirements of paragraphs 6.2 and 6.3 of the Protocol.

The statement of truth

The statement of truth must be signed and completed by the claimant or representative. This section must be completed in order to validate the information provided.

Service of the Checklist

Two copies of the Checklist must be brought to the hearing.

APPENDIX B

Statements of case and applications

This section contains the following statements of case and applications:

1 Claim form for possession of property (form N5)

<table>
<tr>
<td colspan="2">Claim form for possession of property</td>
<td>In the
County Court at Anytown</td>
</tr>
<tr>
<td colspan="2"></td>
<td>Claim No.   AN16 09601</td>
</tr>
</table>

Claimant
(name(s) and address(es))

Rainbow District Council
Town Hall
Anytown AN1 1DA

SEAL

Defendant(s)
(name(s) and address(es))

Wayne Ross
32 Small Street
Anytown AN1 7DG

The claimant is claiming possession of :

32 Small Street
Anytown AN1 7DG

which (includes) (~~does not include~~) residential property. Full particulars of the claim are attached.
(The claimant is also making a claim for money).

This claim will be heard on: 21 July   2016   at   10   am/~~pm~~

at County Court at Anytown, Castle Street, Anytown AN1 2GH

At the hearing
• The court will consider whether or not you must leave the property and, if so, when.
• It will take into account information the claimant provides and any you provide.

What you should do
• Get help and advice immediately from a solicitor or an advice agency.
• Help yourself and the court by **filling in the defence form** and **coming to the hearing** to make sure the court knows all the facts.

Defendant's name and address for service

Wayne Ross
32 Small Street
Anytown AN1 7DG

Court fee	£ 325.00
Solicitor's costs	£ 69.50
Total amount	£ 394.50

Issue date	12 June 2016

N5 Claim form for possession of property (05.14)

HMCS

Claim No.	AN16 09601

Grounds for possession

The claim for possession is made on the following ground(s):

- ☑ rent arrears
- ☐ other breach of tenancy
- ☐ forfeiture of the lease
- ☐ mortgage arrears
- ☐ other breach of the mortgage
- ☐ trespass
- ☐ other *(please specify)* _____

Anti-social behaviour

The claimant is alleging:

- ☐ actual or threatened anti-social behaviour
- ☐ actual or threatened use of the property for unlawful purposes

Is the claimant claiming demotion of tenancy?   ☐ Yes   ☑ No

Is the claimant claiming an order suspending the right to buy?   ☐ Yes   ☑ No

See full details in the attached particulars of claim

Does, or will, the claim include any issues under the Human Rights Act 1998?   ☐ Yes   ☑ No

Statement of Truth

*(I believe)(The claimant believes) that the facts stated in this claim form are true.
* I am duly authorised by the claimant to sign this statement.

signed _____ date 6 June 2016

*(Claimant)(Litigation friend *(where the claimant is a child or a patient)*)(Claimant's solicitor)
*delete as appropriate

Full name John Smith

Name of claimant's solicitor's firm Legal Services, Rainbow District Council

position or office held Head of Legal Services
        (if signing on behalf of firm or company)

Claimant's or claimant's solicitor's address to which documents or payments should be sent if different from overleaf.

John Smith
Legal Services
Rainbow District Council
Town Hall
Anytown

Postcode AN1 1DA

	if applicable
Ref. no.	
fax no.	
DX no.	
e-mail	
Tel. no.	

2   Particulars of claim for rented residential premises (form N119)

**Particulars of claim
for possession**
(rented residential premises)

Name of court County Court at Anytown	Claim No. AN16 09601
Name of Claimant Rainbow District Council	
Name of Defendant Wayne Ross	

1. The claimant has a right to possession of:
   32 Small Street Anytown AN1 7DG

2. To the best of the claimant's knowledge the following persons are in possession of the property:
   The Defendant, his wife Ann Ross and their children.

About the tenancy

3. (a) The premises are let to the defendant(s) under a(n) secure   tenancy
   which began on 7 July 2014   .

   (b) The current rent is £98   and is payable each (week) (fortnight) (month).
   (other   )

   (c) Any unpaid rent or charge for use and occupation should be calculated at £ 13.96   per day.

4. The reason the claimant is asking for possession is:
   (a) because the defendant has not paid the rent due under the terms of the tenancy agreement.
   (Details are set out below)(Details are shown on the attached rent statement)
   Rent Arrears at 7 November 2015 - £912.62
   Rent Arrears at 6 March 2016 - £1103.16

   (b) because the defendant has failed to comply with other terms of the tenancy.
   Details are set out below.

   (c) because: (including any (other) statutory grounds)

5. The following steps have already been taken to recover any arrears:
   Repeated correspondence with the Defendant and a Home Visit

6. The appropriate (~~notice to quit~~) (~~notice of breach of lease~~) (notice seeking possession) (~~notice seeking a demotion order~~) (*other*   ) ~~~~was served on the defendant on 8 November 2015 .

About the defendant

7. The following information is known about the defendant's circumstances:
   The Defendant is believed to be working and in receipt of tax credit.

About the claimant

8. The claimant is asking the court to take the following financial or other information into account when making its decision whether or not to grant an order for possession:
   The Claimant is a local authority responsible for the management of its housing stock upon which there are considerable demands. There are 11,500 families awaiting accommodation and identified as living in housing need.

Forfeiture

9. (a) There is no underlessee or mortgagee entitled to claim relief against forfeiture.

~~or (b)~~   ~~of~~

~~is entitled to claim relief against forfeiture as underlessee or mortgagee.~~

What the court is being asked to do:

10. The claimant asks the court to order that the defendant(s):

(a) give the claimant possession of the premises;

(b) pay the unpaid rent and any charge for use and occupation up to the date an order is made;

(c) pay rent and any charge for use and occupation from the date of the order until the claimant recovers possession of the property;

(d) pay the claimant's costs of making this claim.

11. In the alternative to possession, is the claimant asking the court to make a demotion order or an order suspending the right to buy?

☐ Yes   ☑ No

Demotion/Suspension claim
This section must be completed if the claim includes a claim for demotion of tenancy or suspension order in the alternative to possession

12. The (demotion) (suspension) claim is made under:

☐ section 82A(2) of the Housing Act 1985

☐ section 6A(2) of the Housing Act 1988

☐ section 121A of the Housing Act 1985

13. The claimant is a:

☑ local authority   ☐ housing action trust

☐ registered social landlord   ☐ other please specify (suspension claims only)

(Demotion claims only)
14. Has the claimant served on the tenant a statement of express terms of the tenancy which are to apply to the demoted tenancy?

☐ Yes   ☐ No

If Yes, please give details:

15. The claimant is claiming delete as appropriate (demotion of tenancy) (and) (an order suspending the right to buy) because: *State details of the conduct alleged and **any** other matters relied upon.*

Statement of Truth

*(I believe)(The claimant believes) that the facts stated in these particulars of claim are true.

* I am duly authorised by the claimant to sign this statement.

signed _____ date 9 June 2016 _____

(Claimant)(Litigation friend(where claimant is a child or a patient)*)(Claimant's solicitor)
delete as appropriate

Full name John Smith _____

Name of claimant's solicitor's firm Legal Services, Rainbow District Council _____

position or office held Head of Legal Services _____
            (if signing on behalf of firm or company)

3 Defence form for rented residential premises (form N11R) with additional defence form

Defence form
(rented residential premises)

Name of court	Claim No.
County Court at Anytown	AN16 09601
Name of Claimant	
Rainbow District Council	
Name of Defendant	
Wayne Ross	
Date of hearing	
21 July 2016	

Personal details

1. Please give your:

Title ☑Mr ☐Mrs ☐Miss ☐Ms ☐Other Wayne

First name(s) in full
Wayne

Last name
Ross

Date of birth | 2 | 7 | 1 | 0 | 1 | 9 | 8 | 8 |

Address *(if different from the address on the claim form)*

Postcode

Disputing the claim

2. Do you agree with what is said about the premises and the tenancy agreement?   ☑Yes   ☐No

If No, set out your reasons below:

Did you receive the notice from the claimant referred to at paragraph 6 of the particulars of claim?   ☐Yes   ☑No

3. If Yes, when: _____

4. Do you agree that there are arrears of rent as stated in the particulars of claim?

☐ Yes   ☑ No

If No, state how much the arrears are:

£_____   ☑ None

5. If the particulars of claim give any reasons for possession other than rent arrears, do you agree with what is said?

☐ Yes   ☐ No

If No, give details below:

6. Do you have a money or other claim (a counterclaim) against your landlord?

☑ Yes   ☐ No

If Yes, give details:

Arrears

7. Have you paid any money to your landlord since the claim was issued?

☐ Yes   ☑ No

If Yes, state how much you have paid and when:

£_____   date_____

8. Have you come to any agreement with your landlord about repaying the arrears since the claim was issued?

☐ Yes   ☑ No

I have agreed to pay £_____ each (week)(month)

9. If you have not reached an agreement with your landlord, do you want the court to consider allowing you to pay the arrears by instalments?

☑ Yes   ☐ No

10. How much can you afford to pay in addition to the current rent?

£3.65_____ per (week)(month)

About yourself

State benefits

11. Are you receiving Income Support?   ☑ Yes   ☐ No

12. Have you applied for Income Support?   ☐ Yes   ☑ No

   If Yes, when did you apply?   _____

13. Are you receiving housing benefit?   ☐ Yes   ☑ No

   If Yes, how much are you receiving?   £_____ per (week)(month)

14. Have you applied for housing benefit?   ☐ Yes   ☑ No

   If Yes, when did you apply?   _____

15. Is the housing benefit paid   ☐ to you   ☐ to your landlord

Dependants *(people you look after financially)*

16. Have you any dependant children?   ☑ Yes   ☐ No

   If Yes, give the number in each age group below:

   [2] under 11   [ ] 11-15   [ ] 16-17   [ ] 18 and over

Other dependants

17. Give details of any other dependants for whom you are
   financially responsible:

   Partner and two children

Other residents

18. Give details of any other people living at the premises for
   whom you are not financially responsible:

Money you receive

19. Usual take-home pay or income if self-employed *including overtime, commission, bonuses*

		Weekly	Monthly
Usual take-home pay or income if self-employed *including overtime, commission, bonuses*	£_____	☐	☐
Job Seekers allowance	£_____	☐	☐
Pension	£_____	☐	☐
Child benefit	£ 34.40	☑	☐
Other benefits and allowances	£ 198.32	☑	☐
Others living in my home give me	£_____	☐	☐
I am paid maintenance for myself (or children) of	£_____	☐	☐
Other income	£_____	☐	☐
Total income	£ 232.72	☐	☐

Bank accounts and savings

20. Do you have a current bank or building society account? ☑ Yes ☐ No

    If Yes, is it

        ☐ in credit? If so, by how much? £_____

        ☑ overdrawn? If so, by how much? £ 500.00

21. Do you have a savings or deposit account? ☐ Yes ☑ No

    If Yes, what is the balance? £_____

Money you pay out

22. Do you have to pay any court orders or fines?

Court	Claim/Case number	Balance owing	Instalments paid
Anytown Magistrates	ATN 01611	£870.00	£20.00
		Total Instalments paid £20.00	per month

23. Give details if you are in arrears with any of the court payments or fines:

    Not applicable

24.   Do you have any loan or credit debts?   ☐ Yes   ☑ No

Loan/credit from	Balance owing	Instalments paid
	Total Instalments £	per month

25.   Give details if you are in arrears with any loan / credit repayments:

Regular expenses

(Do not include any payments made by other members of the household out of their own income)

26.   What regular expenses do you have?
(List below)

		Weekly	Monthly
Council tax	£ 15.00	☑	☐
Gas	£ 30.00	☑	☐
Electricity	£ 40.00	☑	☐
Water charges	£ 20.00	☑	☐
TV rental & licence	£ 12.00	☑	☐
Telephone	£ 25.00	☑	☐
Credit repayments	£	☐	☐
Mail order	£	☐	☐
Housekeeping, food, school meals	£ 70.00	☑	☐
Travelling expenses	£ 20.00	☑	☐
Clothing	£ 5.00	☑	☐
Maintenance payments	£	☐	☐
Other	£	☐	☐
Total expenses	£ 237.00	☑	☐

Priority debts

27. This section is for **arrears** only. **Do not**
include regular expenses listed at Question 26.

		Weekly	Monthly
Council tax arrears	£_____	☐	☐
Water charges arrears	£_____	☐	☐
Gas account	£_____	☐	☐
Electricity account	£_____	☐	☐
Maintenance arrears	£_____	☐	☐
Others *(give details below)*			
	£ 20.00	☐	☑
	£_____	☐	☐
	£_____	☐	☐

28. If an order for possession were to be made, would you have
somewhere else to live? ☐ Yes   ☑ No

If Yes, say when you would be able to move in: _____

29. Give details of any events or circumstances which have led to your being in arrears of rent *(for example divorce, separation, redundancy, bereavement, illness, bankruptcy)* or any other particular circumstances affecting your case. If there are any reasons why the date any possession order takes effect should be delayed, give them here. If you believe you would suffer exceptional hardship by being ordered to leave the property immediately, say why.

See attached additional defence form.

You need only answer question 30 if the claim form includes a claim for demotion or suspension of
right to buy.

30. Do you agree with what is said about your conduct or use of   ☐ Yes   ☐ No
     the property?

     If No, set out your reasons below:

Statement of Truth

*(I believe)(~~The defendant(s) believe(s)~~) that the facts stated in this defence form are true.
* I am duly authorised by the defendant(s) to sign this statement.

signed _____ date 18 July 2016 _____
*(Defendant)(~~litigation friend~~(*where defendant is a child or a patient*))(~~Defendant's solicitor~~)
**delete as appropriate*

Full name Wayne Ross _____

Name of defendant's solicitor's firm Rainbow Law Centre _____

position or office held _____
                        (if signing on behalf of firm or company)

IN THE COUNTY COURT AT ANYTOWN   CASE NO: AN16 09601

BETWEEN

RAINBOW DISTRICT COUNCIL   Claimant

and

WAYNE ROSS   Defendant

ADDITIONAL DEFENCE FORM

1. This Additional Defence Form is filed to supplement the Defence Form filed in this claim by the Defendant.
2. The Defendant admits that he occupies 32 Small Street Anytown ('the property') with his family under a secure tenancy within the meaning of the Housing Act 1985. The Defendant denies that the Claimant is entitled to termination of that tenancy and possession of the property as claimed.
3. The Defendant denies being served with the Notice Seeking Possession referred to at paragraph 6 of the Particulars of Claim.
4. The Defendant admits that he has failed to make some rent payments as they have fallen due but is not able to comment on the level of underpayment. The Claimant is put to strict proof as to the level of any rent underpayments. The Defendant asserts that in any event he is entitled to set off against any rent otherwise due the sums Counterclaimed as set out below.
5. In the alternative, the Defendant claims the protection of Housing Act 1985 s84 and denies that in all the circumstances it would be reasonable for an Order for Possession to be made.

COUNTERCLAIM

6. The Defendant repeats paragraphs 1 to 5 above.
7. The Defendant is entitled to the benefit of the repairing covenant implied by Landlord and Tenant Act 1985 s11 in respect of which the Claimant is in breach. Further and in the alternative, the Claimant is in breach of the express repairing obligations set out in paragraph 5 of the Tenancy Agreement.
8. In breach of these covenants the Claimant has since, in or about January 2015, failed to keep the property in repair.

PARTICULARS OF DISREPAIR

(i)   Roof leak to main roof
(ii) Rot to kitchen windowsill
(iii) Defective pointing to front wall
[........ *Set out the detail of the other defects complained about*]
9. The Claimant has had notice of these defects by reason of numerous verbal

complaints to its employees since January 2015, a complaint made to the Local Government Ombudsman by the Defendant in October 2015 and by visits by various employees of the Claimant on various dates.

10.   Because of the breaches of covenant, the Defendant has suffered loss, damage, injury and inconvenience.

PARTICULARS

(i)   Due to damp penetration, the Defendant has been unable to use the first floor rear bedroom since March 2015.

(ii)   Decorations have been ruined in the front first floor bedroom because of damp penetration with the result that the Defendant has spent £750 on decorating materials.

(iii)   By reason of the dampness, the Defendant spent additional sums on heating which he estimates at £500 for each Winter quarter.

(iv)   The Defendant's wife has been depressed and a strain has been placed on their marriage.

[*Set out the detail of other consequences of the defects complained about*]

11.   Further and in the alternative, the Claimant is in breach of the Defective Premises Act 1972 s4.

PARTICULARS OF BREACH OF DUTY

---

12.   The Defendant repeats the Particulars set out in paragraph 10 above.

13.   The Defendant claims interest pursuant to County Courts Act 1984 s69 at such rate and for such period as the Court will allow.

14.   The Defendant Counterclaims for:

(1)   Damages limited to £5000.

(2)   A Mandatory Order or Order for specific performance to remedy such of the defects mentioned above as are outstanding at the date of the trial.

(3)   Interest pursuant to County Courts Act 1984 s69.

(4)   Costs.

Dated   18 July 2016

STATEMENT OF TRUTH

I believe that the facts stated in this Defence and Part 20 Counterclaim are true.

W.Ross
....
WAYNE ROSS

c/o Jenny Brown, Rainbow Law Centre, 1 Lavender Close, Anytown

To the Court Manager
And to the Claimant

4 Particulars of claim for mortgaged residential premises (form N120)

Particulars of claim for possession
(mortgaged residential premises)

In the

County Court at Anytown

Equitable Secured Home Loan Ltd

Stephen and Josie Neill

Claim No.

AN16 09615

Claimant

Defendant

1. The claimant has a right to possession of:

    1 Cedar Street Anytown

About the mortgage

2. On 19 February 2010   the claimant(s) and the defendant(s) entered into a mortgage of the above premises.

3. To the best of the claimant's knowledge the following persons are in possession of the property:
    The Defendants

[Delete (a) or (b) as appropriate]

4   (a) The agreement for the loan secured by the mortgage (or at least one of them) is a
    regulated consumer credit agreement. Notice of default was given to the defendant(s)
    on 9 December   2011

    ~~(b) The agreement for the loan secured by the mortgage is not (or none of them is) a regulated consumer credit agreement.~~

5. The claimant is asking for possession on the following ground(s):

    (a) the defendant(s) ~~(has)~~(have) not paid the agreed repayments of the loan and interest.
    Give details (as required under paragraph 2.5 of Practice Direction accompanying Part 55 of the Civil Procedure Rules):
    The arrears amount to £2100.06. See attached schedule of arrears.

N120 Particulars of claim for possession (mortgaged residential premises)(09.15)   HMCS

(b) because:

6. (a) The amount loaned was £ 18,000.00

    (b) The current terms of repayment are: *(include any current periodic repayment and any current payment of interest)*
Monthly payments of £450.00 are payable on the 8th of each month.

    (c) The total amount required to pay the mortgage in full as at 19 June   2016 (not more than 14 days after the claim was issued) would be £ 21,080.99   taking into account any adjustment for early settlement. This includes £ 750.00   payable for solicitor's costs and administration charges.

    (d) The following additional payments are also required under the terms of the mortgage:

£	for	[not] included in 6(c)
£	for	[not] included in 6(c)
£	for	[not] included in 6(c)

    (e) Of the payments in paragraph 6(d), the following are in arrears:

        arrears of £

        arrears of £

        arrears of £

    [(f) The total amount outstanding under the regulated loan agreement secured by the mortgage is £   ]

    (g) Interest rates which have been applied to the mortgage:

        (i) at the start of the mortgage   8.00 % p.a.

        (ii) immediately before any arrears were accrued   12.00 % p.a.

        (iii) at the start of the claim   12.00 % p.a.

7.　The following steps have already been taken to recover the money secured by the mortgage:

Letters sent to the Defendants, telephone calls and a home visit by a debt counsellor.

About the defendant(s)

8.　The following information is known about the defendant's circumstances:
(in particular say whether the defendant(s) (is)(are) in receipt of social security benefits and whether any payments are made directly to the claimant)

The Defendants are believed to be employed.

[Delete either (a) or (b) as appropriate]

9.　(a) There is no one who should be given notice of these proceedings because of a registered interest in the property under section 31(10) of the Family Law Act 1996 or section 2(8) or 8(3) of the Matrimonial Homes Act 1983 or section 2(7) of the Matrimonial Homes Act 1967.

~~(b) Notice of these proceedings will be given to~~　　　　　　　　　　　　　~~who has a registered interest in the property.~~

Tenancy

[Delete if inappropriate]

~~10.　A tenancy was entered into between the mortgagor and the mortgagee on~~

~~A notice was served on~~

What the court is being asked to do

11.   The claimant asks the court to order that the defendant(s):

(a) give the claimant possession of the premises;

(b) pay to the claimant the total amount outstanding under the mortgage.

Statement of Truth

*(I believe)(The claimant believes) that the facts stated in these particulars of claim are true.
* I am duly authorised by the claimant to sign this statement.

signed _____ date _____

*(Claimant)(Litigation friend *where claimant is a child or a patient*)(Claimant's solicitor)
delete as appropriate

Full name   Jayne Osborne

Name of claimant's solicitor's firm   Mammon & Co

position or office held   Solicitor
                              (if signing on behalf of firm or company)

5 Defence form for mortgaged residential premises (form N11M) with additional defence form

---

Defence form
(mortgaged residential premises)

Name of court	Claim No.
County Court at Anytown	AN16 09615

Name of Claimant
Equitable Secured Home Loan Ltd

Name of Defendant
Stephen and Josie Neill

Date of hearing
21 July 2016

Personal details

1. Please give your:

   Title   ☑Mr ☐Mrs ☐Miss ☐Ms ☐Other

   First name(s) in full
   Stephen

   Last name
   Neill

   Date of birth 1 8 0 5 1 9 8 5

   Address *(if different from the address on the claim form)*

   Postcode

Disputing the claim

2. Do you agree with what is said about the property and the mortgage agreement in the particulars of claim? ☑Yes ☐No

   If No, set out your reasons below:

3. Do you agree that there are arrears of mortgage repayments as stated in the particulars of claim? ☑Yes ☐No

   If No, state how much the arrears are: £_____ ☐None

N11M Defence form (mortgaged residential premises) (04.06)   HMCS

4. If the particulars of claim give any reasons for possession other than arrears of mortgage repayments, do you agree with what is said? ☐ Yes   ☐ No

   If No, give details below:

   (Only answer these questions if the loan secured by the mortgage (or part of it) is a regulated consumer credit agreement)

5. Do you want the court to consider whether or not the terms of your original loan agreement are fair? ☑ Yes   ☐ No

6. Do you intend to apply to the court for an order changing the terms of your loan agreement (a time order)? ☑ Yes   ☐ No

Arrears

7. Have you paid any money to your mortgage lender since the claim was issued? ☑ Yes   ☐ No

   If Yes, state how much you have paid and when: £ 150.00   date 2 July 2016

8. Have you come to any agreement with your mortgage lender about repaying the arrears since the claim was issued? ☐ Yes   ☑ No

   I have agreed to pay £ _____ each (week)(month).

9. If you have not reached an agreement with your mortgage lender, do you want the court to consider allowing you to pay the arrears by instalments? ☑ Yes   ☐ No

10. How much can you afford to pay in addition to the current instalments?   £ 100.00   per (week)(month)

About yourself

State benefits

11. Are you receiving Income Support? ☐ Yes ☑ No

12. Have you applied for Income Support? ☐ Yes ☑ No

  If Yes, when did you apply? _____

13. Does the Department of Social Security pay your mortgage interest? ☐ Yes ☑ No

Dependants (people you look after financially)

14. Have you any dependant children? ☑ Yes ☐ No

  If Yes, give the number in each age group below:

  [2] under 11 [ ] 11-15 [ ] 16-17 [ ] 18 and over

Other dependants

15. Give details of any other dependants for whom you are financially responsible:

  Partner and two children

Other residents

16. Give details of any other people living at the premises for whom you are not financially responsible:

Money you receive

		Weekly	Monthly
17. Usual take-home pay or income if self-employed *including overtime, commission, bonuses*	£ 1,100.00	☐	☑
Job Seekers allowance	£	☐	☐
Pension	£	☐	☐
Child benefit	£ 149.06	☐	☑
Other benefits and allowances	£ 463.33	☐	☐
Others living in my home give me	£	☐	☐
I am paid maintenance for myself (or children) of	£	☐	☐
Other income	£	☐	☐
Total income	£ 1,712.39	☐	☐

Bank accounts and savings

18. Do you have a current bank or building society account?   ☑ Yes   ☐ No

If Yes, is it

☐ in credit? If so, by how much?   £_____

☑ overdrawn? If so, by how much? £ 800.00

19. Do you have a savings or deposit account?   ☐ Yes   ☑ No

If Yes, what is the balance?   £_____

Money you pay out

20. Do you have to pay any court orders or fines?   ☑ Yes   ☐ No

Court	Claim/Case number	Balance owing	Instalments paid
Anytown Magistrates	ATN 65491	£500	£80

Total instalments paid £80.00   per month

21. Give details if you are in arrears with any of the court payments or fines:

22. Do you have any loan or credit debts?   ☑ Yes   ☐ No

Loan/credit from	Balance owing	Instalments paid
Better Furnishings Ltd	£1300	£100

Total instalments paid £ 100.00   per month

23. Give details if you are in arrears with any loan / credit repayments:

Regular expenses
(Do not include any payments made by other members of the household out of their own income)

24. What regular expenses do you have?
(List below)

		Weekly	Monthly
Council tax	£ 125.00	☐	☑
Gas	£ 80.00	☐	☑
Electricity	£ 60.00	☐	☑
Water charges	£ 50.00	☐	☑
TV rental & licence	£ 100.00	☐	☑
Telephone	£ 100.00	☐	☑
Credit repayments	£ 280.00	☐	☐
Mail order	£	☐	☐
Housekeeping, food, school meals	£ 600.00	☐	☑
Travelling expenses	£ 180.00	☐	☑
Clothing	£	☐	☐
Maintenance payments	£	☐	☐
Other mortgages	£	☐	☐
Other	£	☐	☐
Total expenses	£ 1,575.00	☐	☑

Priority debts

25. This section is for arrears only. Do not include regular expenses listed at Question 24.

		Weekly	Monthly
Council tax arrears	£	☐	☐
Water charges arrears	£	☐	☐
Gas account	£	☐	☐
Electricity account	£	☐	☐
Maintenance arrears	£	☐	☐

Others (give details below)

£	☐	☐
£	☐	☐
£	☐	☐

26. If an order for possession were to be made, would you have somewhere else to live?   ☐ Yes   ☑ No

    If Yes, say when you would be able to move in: _____

27. Give details of any events or circumstances which have led to your being in arrears with your mortgage (for example divorce, separation, redundancy, bereavement, illness, bankruptcy). If you believe you would suffer exceptional hardship by being ordered to leave the property immediately, say why.

    See Additional Defence Form attached.

Statement of Truth

*(I believe)(The defendant believes) that the facts stated in this defence form are true.
* I am duly authorised by the defendant to sign this statement.

signed_____   date _____
*(Defendant)(Litigation friend(where defendant is a child or a patient))(Defendant's solicitor)
*delete as appropriate

Full name   John Dobson

Name of defendant's solicitor's firm   Rainbow Law Centre

position or office held   Solicitor
                        (if signing on behalf of firm or company)

IN THE COUNTY COURT AT ANYTOWN

BETWEEN

EQUITABLE SECURED HOME LOAN LIMITED   Claimant

and

STEPHEN and JOSIE NEILL   Defendant

ADDITIONAL DEFENCE FORM

---

1. This Additional Defence Form is filed to supplement the Defence Form filed in this claim by the Defendants.
2. The Defendants admit that the agreement for the loan secured by the mortgage in favour of the Claimant is one regulated by the Consumer Credit Act 1974. The Defendants claim the protection of the provisions of that Act and in particular the provisions relating to Time Orders contained in Consumer Credit Act 1974 ss129–136.
3. The Defendants do not dispute the information provided in the Particulars of Claim relating to the mortgage and to the Defendants.

COUNTERCLAIM

---

4. The Defendants repeat their Defence set out above.
5. In November 2015, the Defendant Josie Neill was dismissed from her employment because of ill health. Because of the loss of her salary the Defendants were unable to meet the payments under the agreement with the Claimant. The Defendants expect Josie Neill to return to work in October 2016. Attached to this Defence Form is a letter from the employer confirming that as soon as she is fit to resume work she will be re-employed on the same terms as previously. At that time the Defendants would then be able to resume payments in accordance with the terms of the agreement with the Claimant.
6. The Defendants ask that the Court make a 'Time Order' providing for the monthly instalments due under the agreement to be reduced to £140 with effect from August 2016 until November 2016 and that pursuant to that Time Order the interest rate provided for in the agreement be reduced to an annual rate of 8%.
7. The Defendants Counterclaim for:
   (1) Relief pursuant to Consumer Credit Act 1974 ss129–136.
   (2) Further or other relief.

Dated   18 July 2016

STATEMENT OF TRUTH

We believe that the facts stated in this Defence and Part 20 Counterclaim are true.

....
STEPHEN & JOSIE NEILL
c/o Rainbow Law Centre, 1 Lavender Close, Anytown

To the Court Manager
And to the Claimant

6 Application notice (form N244) to set possession order aside

Application notice

For help in completing this form please read
the notes for guidance form N244Notes.

Name of court	County Court at Anytown
Claim no.	AN16 09601
Warrant no. (if applicable)	
Claimant's name (including ref.)	Rainbow District Council
Defendant's name (including ref.)	Wayne Ross
Date	3 August 2016

1. What is your name or, if you are a solicitor, the name of your firm?

   Wayne Ross

2. Are you a ☐ Claimant ☑ Defendant ☐ Solicitor

   ☐ Other *(please specify)*

   If you are a solicitor whom do you represent?

3. What order are you asking the court to make and why?

   The Order for Possession dated 21 July 2016 be set aside as it was obtained in my absence and I have a good reason for not attending the hearing.

4. Have you attached a draft of the order you are applying for? ☐ Yes ☑ No

5. How do you want to have this application dealt with? ☑ at a hearing ☐ without a hearing

   ☐ at a telephone hearing

6. How long do you think the hearing will last? ☐ Hours 15 Minutes

   Is this time estimate agreed by all parties? ☐ Yes ☑ No

7. Give details of any fixed trial date or period None

8. What level of Judge does your hearing need? District Judge

9. Who should be served with this application? The Claimant

N244 Application notice (06.16)   1   © Crown copyright 2016

10. What information will you be relying on, in support of your application?

☑ the attached witness statement

☐ the statement of case

☐ the evidence set out in the box below

If necessary, please continue on a separate sheet.

Statement of Truth

(I believe) (~~The applicant believes~~) that the facts stated in this section (and any continuation sheets) are true.

Signed _____   Dated 3 August 2010

Applicant('s ~~Solicitor~~)('s litigation friend)

Full name Wayne Ross

Name of applicant's solicitor's firm Rainbow Law Centre

Position or office held _____
(if signing on behalf of firm or company)

11. Signature and address details

Signed _____   Dated 3 August 2016

Applicant('s ~~Solicitor~~)('s litigation friend)

Position or office held _____
(if signing on behalf of firm or company)

Applicant's address to which documents about this application should be sent

Rainbow Law Centre 1 Lavender Close Anytown		If applicable	
	Phone no.	
	Fax no.	
Postcode	DX no.	
	Ref no.	

E-mail address	

2

7 Witness statement in support of application to set possession order aside

Defendant;
W Ross
First

3 August 2016

IN THE COUNTY COURT AT ANYTOWN   CASE NO: AN16 09601

BETWEEN

RAINBOW DISTRICT COUNCIL Claimant

and

WAYNE ROSS Defendant

WITNESS STATEMENT OF WAYNE ROSS

I Wayne Ross of 32 Small Street Anytown, currently unemployed, will say as follows:

1. I am the Defendant in this claim and make this statement in support of my application to have the Order for Possession dated 21 July 2016 set aside having been obtained in my absence. The facts set out in this statement are within my own knowledge or are based on information provided to me by my Solicitors and which I believe to be true.

2. I am the tenant of 32 Small Street Anytown which I rent from the Claimant.

3. On 31 July 2016 I received a copy of the Order for Possession that had been granted to the Claimant on 21 July 2016. This was the first that I had heard about the proceedings that had been brought against me. At no stage have I received any Claim for Possession from the Court nor have I been told by anyone on the Claimant's behalf that proceedings had been started. I should add that I have experienced other problems with postal deliveries. In May and June 2016 a series of letters sent to me at home went missing in the post. My local sorting office accepted that this was their mistake.

4. I can only assume that if the Claim for Possession was posted by the Court (which I understand from my Solicitor is the usual practice) and that the envelope has gone missing somewhere in the postal system.

5. I wish to defend the proceedings brought against me and to Counterclaim against the Claimant for damages for breach of repairing obligation and for a Mandatory Order to require the Claimant to undertake repairs for which it is responsible. I refer to the draft Defence and Counterclaim marked WR 1 which is attached to this statement.

[Alternatively, a brief synopsis of the Grounds for Possession and Counterclaim should be set out]

6. I would respectfully suggest that I have shown that I had a good reason for not attending the hearing and that I have a good defence to the claim brought against me by the Claimant. I would ask that the Possession Order dated 21 July 2016 be set aside and that the Court give Case Management Directions for the service of my Statement of Case and consequential Directions for the disposal of this claim.

7. I believe the facts stated in this Witness Statement are true.

W.Ross
....   Date.....*3 August 2016*..............................
WAYNE ROSS

To the Court Manager
And to The Claimant

8 Application notice (form N244) to suspend warrant for possession

Application notice

For help in completing this form please read
the notes for guidance form N244Notes.

Name of court	
County Court at Anytown	
Claim no.	AN16 09601
Warrant no. (if applicable)	TR 2978N
Claimant's name (including ref.)	Rainbow District Council
Defendant's name (including ref.)	Wayne Ross
Date	27 August 2016

1. What is your name or, if you are a solicitor, the name of your firm?

2. Are you a ☐ Claimant   ☑ Defendant   ☐ Solicitor

   ☐ Other *(please specify)*

   If you are a solicitor whom do you represent?

3. What order are you asking the court to make and why?

   The warrant for possession due to be enforced on 3 September 2016 be suspended on terms.

4. Have you attached a draft of the order you are applying for?   ☐ Yes   ☑ No

5. How do you want to have this application dealt with?   ☑ at a hearing   ☐ without a hearing
   ☐ at a telephone hearing

6. How long do you think the hearing will last?   [ ] Hours   15 Minutes
   Is this time estimate agreed by all parties?   ☐ Yes   ☑ No

7. Give details of any fixed trial date or period   None

8. What level of Judge does your hearing need?   District Judge

9. Who should be served with this application?   Claimant

N244 Application notice (06.16)   1   © Crown copyright 2016

10. What information will you be relying on, in support of your application?

☑ the attached witness statement

☐ the statement of case

☐ the evidence set out in the box below

If necessary, please continue on a separate sheet.

Statement of Truth

(I believe) (The applicant believes) that the facts stated in this section (and any continuation sheets) are true.

Signed _____ Dated 27 August 2016

Applicant(‘s Solicitor)(‘s litigation friend)

Full name Wayne Ross

Name of applicant's solicitor's firm _____

Position or office held _____
(if signing on behalf of firm or company)

11. Signature and address details

Signed _____ Dated 27 August 2016

Applicant(‘s Solicitor)(‘s litigation friend)

Position or office held _____
(if signing on behalf of firm or company)

Applicant's address to which documents about this application should be sent

32 Small Street Anytown	If applicable	
	Phone no.	
	Fax no.	
Postcode	DX no.	
A N 1 7 D G	Ref no.	
E-mail address		

2

9 Witness statement in support of application to suspend warrant

IN THE COUNTY COURT AT ANYTOWN   Claim No: AN10 09601

BETWEEN

RAINBOW DISTRICT COUNCIL   <u>Claimant</u>

and

WAYNE ROSS   Defendant

WITNESS STATEMENT

I, WAYNE ROSS, of 32 Small Street Anytown will say as follows:

1. I am the Defendant in this matter. I make this Witness Statement in support of my application for a suspension of the warrant and for a variation of the suspended possession order granted to the Claimant by this Court on 21 July 2016.

2. Under that order, the Court granted possession of 32 Small Street Anytown to the Claimant on 18 August 2016, but suspended enforcement of the order on terms that I should pay the current weekly rent plus the sum of £3.70 per week towards the arrears, which at that date stood at £1,599.93.

3. Following the order of 21 July 2016, I requested the Department for Work and Pensions to deduct the sum of £3.70 from my weekly income support entitlement and to make these payments directly to the Claimant. I understood that this arrangement would come into effect immediately, but I realised that this was not the case when my housing officer wrote to me informing me that no payments had been received. I contacted the Department for Work and Pensions, and was informed that they had no record of the arrangement. I therefore had to complete another form of request. I understand that direct deductions came into operation several weeks later, and that they have continued to be paid at four weekly intervals in arrear.

4. At all times since the order was made, I have been in receipt of income support. I have also claimed housing benefit throughout, but my contributions towards the rent have changed frequently. At first, my full rent was covered by housing benefit, apart from the sum of £6.50 in respect of water rates and service charges. I have paid at least this sum every week, with the exception of six weeks in August/September 2015. I missed those payments because I was under extreme financial pressure at the time. The electricity company were threatening to cut off my supply because of an outstanding bill of £224. I incurred other debts to friends and family in borrowing the money to pay off that account.

5. Difficulties have also arisen because my son James Ross, who is aged 20 and who now lives with me, started employment in August 2015, and has had three different jobs in the last two months. This has led to a non-dependant deduction being applied to my housing benefit entitlement, resulting in my

weekly contribution to the rent increasing at intervals. I did not realise at first that James's wages would affect my housing benefit, so I did not understand the need to provide evidence of his income to the Claimant's housing benefit office. This resulted in an overpayment of benefit of £324, and this is being recovered from me by deductions of £8.00 each week from my ongoing - benefit.

6. James has been in and out of work during this period. On each occasion that he has started work again, I have declared his income to the housing benefit office, but it has taken several weeks for them to inform me how much I should be paying towards the rent because of the non-dependant deduction.

7. I am currently paying a total of £29.30 towards my weekly rent, together with the weekly instalments of £3.70 off the arrears which are paid by direct deduction.

8. I have not always understood the correspondence which I have received from the housing benefit office, and in particular I did not understand at first that a deduction was being made from my housing benefit because of James's employment.

9. I was informed by my housing officer that unless I made up the shortfall in my payments under the order, a warrant for possession of my flat would be issued. I could not afford to make up these payments in a lump sum.

10. My household now consists of myself, together with James, my other son Jon, who is aged 9, and my daughter Kate, who is aged 10. I suffer from agora-phobia and depression and I am unable to work. I have done my best to comply with the terms of the court order

11. In the circumstances, I respectfully ask the Court to suspend the warrant of possession on terms that I will continue to pay the current rent plus the sum of £3.70 off the arrears.

I believe that the facts set out in this Statement are true.

Dated: *17 October 2016*

Signed   *W. Ross*
          Wayne Ross
          Defendant

To the Court and to the Claimant

Housing Act 1985 Sch 2A: The meaning of 'serious offence' for the purposes of the absolute grounds for possession for anti-social behaviour

SCHEDULE 2A

ABSOLUTE GROUND FOR POSSESSION FOR ANTI-SOCIAL BEHAVIOUR: SERIOUS OFFENCES[1]

Violent offences

1 Murder.

2 Manslaughter.

3 Kidnapping.

4 False imprisonment.

5 An offence under any of the following sections of the Offences against the Person Act 1861–

   (a)   section 4 (soliciting murder),

   (b)   section 16 (threats to kill),

   (c)   section 18 (wounding with intent to cause grievous bodily harm),

   (d)   section 20 (malicious wounding),

   (e)   section 21 (attempting to choke, suffocate or strangle in order to commit or assist in committing an indictable offence),

   (f)   section 22 (using chloroform etc. to commit or assist in the committing of any indictable offence),

   (g)   section 23 (maliciously administering poison etc. so as to endanger life or inflict grievous bodily harm),

   (h)   section 24 (maliciously administering poison etc. with intent to injure, aggrieve or annoy any other person),

   (i)   section 27 (abandoning or exposing children whereby life is endangered or health permanently injured),

   (j)   section 28 (causing bodily injury by explosives),

   (k)   section 29 (using explosives etc. with intent to do grievous bodily harm),

   (l)   section 30 (placing explosives with intent to do bodily injury),

   (m) section 31 (setting spring guns etc. with intent to do grievous bodily harm),

---

1   Inserted by Anti-social Behaviour, Crime and Policing Act 2014 Sch 3.

(n)   section 38 (assault with intent to resist arrest),

(o)   section 47 (assault occasioning actual bodily harm).

6 An offence under any of the following sections of the Explosive Substances Act 1883–

(a)   section 2 (causing explosion likely to endanger life or property),

(b)   section 3 (attempt to cause explosion, or making or keeping explosive with intent to endanger life or property),

(c)   section 4 (making or possession of explosive under suspicious circumstances).

7 An offence under section 1 of the Infant Life (Preservation) Act 1929 (child destruction).

8 An offence under section 1 of the Children and Young Persons Act 1933 (cruelty to children).

9 An offence under section 1 of the Infanticide Act 1938 (infanticide).

10 An offence under any of the following sections of the Public Order Act 1986–

(a)   section 1 (riot),

(b)   section 2 (violent disorder),

(c)   section 3 (affray).

11 An offence under either of the following sections of the Protection from Harassment Act 1997–

(a)   section 4 (putting people in fear of violence),

(b)   section 4A (stalking involving fear of violence or serious alarm or distress).

12 An offence under any of the following provisions of the Crime and Disorder Act 1998–

(a)   section 29 (racially or religiously aggravated assaults),

(b)   section 31(1)(a) or (b) (racially or religiously aggravated offences under section 4 or 4A of the Public Order Act 1986),

(c)   section 32 (racially or religiously aggravated harassment etc.).

13 An offence under either of the following sections of the Female Genital Mutilation Act 2003–

(a)   section 1 (female genital mutilation),

(b)   section 2 (assisting a girl to mutilate her own genitalia).

14 An offence under section 5 of the Domestic Violence, Crime and Victims Act 2004 (causing or allowing the death of a child or vulnerable adult).

Sexual offences

15 An offence under section 33A of the Sexual Offences Act 1956 (keeping a brothel used for prostitution).

16 An offence under section 1 of the Protection of Children Act 1978 (indecent photographs of children).

17 An offence under section 160 of the Criminal Justice Act 1988 (possession of indecent photograph of a child).

18 An indictable offence under Part 1 of the Sexual Offences Act 2003 (sexual offences).

Offensive weapons

19 An offence under either of the following sections of the Prevention of Crime Act 1953–
   (a) section 1 (prohibition of the carrying of offensive weapons without lawful authority or reasonable excuse),
   (b) section 1A (threatening with offensive weapon in public).
20 An offence under any of the following provisions of the Firearms Act 1968–
   (a) section 16 (possession of firearm with intent to endanger life),
   (b) section 16A (possession of firearm with intent to cause fear of violence),
   (c) section 17(1) (use of firearm to resist arrest),
   (d) section 17(2) (possession of firearm at time of committing or being arrested for offence specified in Schedule 1 to the Act of 1968),
   (e) section 18 (carrying a firearm with criminal intent),
   (f) section 19 (carrying a firearm in a public place),
   (g) section 20 (trespassing with firearm),
   (h) section 21 (possession of firearms by persons previously convicted of crime).
21 An offence under either of the following sections of the Criminal Justice Act 1988–
   (a) section 139 (having article with blade or point in public place),
   (b) section 139AA (threatening with article with blade or point or offensive weapon).

Offences against property

22 An offence under any of the following sections of the Theft Act 1968–
   (a) section 8 (robbery or assault with intent to rob),
   (b) section 9 (burglary),
   (c) section 10 (aggravated burglary).
23 An offence under section 1 of the Criminal Damage Act 1971 (destroying or damaging property).
24 An offence under section 30 of the Crime and Disorder Act 1998 (racially or religiously aggravated criminal damage).

Road traffic offences

25 An offence under section 35 of the Offences against the Person Act 1861 (injuring persons by furious driving).
26 An offence under section 12A of the Theft Act 1968 (aggravated vehicle-taking involving an accident which caused the death of any person).
27 An offence under any of the following sections of the Road Traffic Act 1988–
   (a) section 1 (causing death by dangerous driving),
   (b) section 1A (causing serious injury by dangerous driving),
   (c) section 3A (causing death by careless driving when under influence of drink or drugs).

Drug-related offences

28 An offence under any of the following provisions of the Misuse of Drugs Act
   1971–

   (a) section 4 (restriction of production and supply of controlled drugs),

   (b) section 5(3) (possession of controlled drugs with intent to supply),

   (c) section 8(a) or (b) (occupiers etc. of premises to be punishable for permit-
       ting unlawful production or supply etc. of controlled drugs there).

29 An offence under section 6 of that Act (restrictions of cultivation of cannabis
   plant) where the cultivation is for profit and the whole or a substantial part of
   the dwelling-house concerned is used for the cultivation.

Inchoate offences

30(1) An offence of attempting or conspiring the commission of an offence speci-
      fied or described in this Schedule.

   (2) An offence under Part 2 of the Serious Crime Act 2007 (encouraging or assist-
       ing) where the offence (or one of the offences) which the person in question
       intends or believes would be committed is an offence specified or described
       in this Schedule.

   (3) An offence of aiding, abetting, counselling or procuring the commission of
       an offence specified or described in this Schedule.

Scope of offences

31 Where this Schedule refers to offences which are offences under the law of
   England and Wales and another country or territory, the reference is to be
   read as limited to the offences so far as they are offences under the law of
   England and Wales.

Instructions checklist

Social housing and private rented sector occupiers
Occupiers
Full name, address, dates of birth, phone number, occupation, income and savings, national insurance numbers, relationships between.

Name of tenant(s)
Name and address and relationship to occupier.

Status
Protected/statutory/secure/assured tenant/assured shorthold/demoted/introductory/unprotected/successor tenant/assignee/family intervention/post 2016 Act.

Details of accommodation
Room/flat/house, shared facilities, location in house.

Landlord/agent/solicitor
Name, address, telephone number, DX, e-mail, reference number.

Deposit
Amount/protected/returned.

Rent
Amount (inclusive/exclusive of services), rent registration, any irrecoverable rent, arrears, agreement as to level of arrears, is landlord accepting rent, method of payment.

Documents
Tenancy agreement, rent receipts, rent book.

Date of commencement of tenancy

Date of commencement of occupancy

Housing benefit
Amount received/date of claim/possible backdated claim/paid to tenant or landlord/housing benefit shortfall.

Notice to quit/notice of intention to seek possession
Date received/method of service.

Court proceedings
Previous proceedings, current proceedings, hearing date, date of receipt of claim form.

Causes of action against landlord or other
Set-off for disrepair and evidence of landlord's knowledge of disrepair, third party action against local authority over housing benefit.

Correspondence

Details of any previous arrangements to remedy default

Proposals to pay off arrears
Amount/method of payment.

Regular financial commitments
Maintenance, court orders, credit agreement, etc.

Rehousing obligations
Children, pregnancy, vulnerability, community care issues.

Mortgage borrowers

Occupiers
Full name, address, dates of birth, phone number, occupations, income and savings, relationships between, date of commencement of occupation.

Legal owner
Name and address, relationship to occupier.

Mortgagee/solicitors
Name, address, telephone and reference numbers, priority (first, second, etc).

Type of mortgage
Regulated mortgage contract/repayment/endowment/pension/other.

Date of mortgage

Legal title
Freehold/leasehold, registered/unregistered land.
Joint owner/sole/trustee.

Payments
Monthly instalments (interest and capital/endowment), arrears, date of last payment.

Date of commencement of occupancy

Equitable owners
Previous properties occupied as such, details of contribution to purchase or mortgage payments, financial/other detriment.

Correspondence

Court proceedings
Previous/current proceedings, hearing dates, date of receipt of summons.

Details of any previous arrangements to remedy default

Amount required to redeem mortgage

Value of property with vacant possession

Insurance cover
Mortgage indemnity policy, mortgage protection policy.

Regular financial commitments
Maintenance, court orders, credit agreement etc.

Rehousing obligations
Children, pregnancy, vulnerability, community care issues.

Causes of action against lender or other
Misrepresentation, negligence against surveyor/solicitor.
Undue influence.

Mortgage interest payments from Department for Work and Pensions

APPENDIX E

Pre-action Protocols for possession claims[1]

Pre-action Protocol for possession claims by social landlords[2]

PART 1: AIMS AND SCOPE OF THE PROTOCOL

1.1 This Protocol applies to residential possession claims by social landlords (such as local authorities, Registered Social Landlords and Housing Action Trusts) and private registered providers of social housing. Part 2 relates to claims which are based solely on claims for rent arrears. Part 3 relates to claims where the Court's discretion to postpone possession is limited by Housing Act 1980 s89(1). The protocol does not apply to claims in respect of long leases or to claims for possession where there is no security of tenure.

1.2 Part 3 of the protocol applies to cases brought by social landlords solely on grounds where if the case is proved, there is a restriction on the Court's discretion on making an order for possession and/or to which Housing Act 1980 s89 applies.

1.3 Part 2 of the protocol reflects the guidance on good practice given to social landlords and private registered providers in the collection of rent arrears. It recognises that it is in the interests of both landlords and tenants to ensure that rent is paid promptly and to ensure that difficulties are resolved whenever possible without court proceedings.

1.4 Part 3 seeks to ensure that in cases where Article 8 of the European Convention on Human Rights is raised the necessary information is before the Court at the first hearing so that issues of proportionality may be dealt with summarily, if appropriate, or that appropriate directions for trial may be given.

1.5 The aims of the protocol are:

(a) to encourage more pre-action contact and exchange of information between landlords and tenants;

(b) to enable the parties to avoid litigation by settling the matter if possible; and

(c) to enable court time to be used more effectively if proceedings are necessary.

1.6 Courts should take into account whether this protocol has been followed when considering what orders to make. Social Landlords and private registered providers of social housing should also comply with guidance issued from time to time by the Homes and Communities Agency, the Department for Communities and Local Government and the Welsh Ministers.

(a) If the landlord is aware that the tenant has difficulty in reading or understanding information given, the landlord should take reasonable steps to ensure that the tenant understands any information given. The landlord should be able to demonstrate that reasonable steps have been taken to ensure that the information has been appropriately communicated in ways that the tenant can understand.

(b) If the landlord is aware that the tenant is under 18 or is particularly vulnerable, the landlord should consider at an early stage–

---

2   Available at www.justice.gov.uk. Updated at 28 July 2015.

i) whether or not the tenant has the mental capacity to defend possession proceedings and, if not, make an application for the appointment of a litigation friend in accordance with CPR 21;

ii) whether or not any issues arise under Equality Act 2010; and

iii) in the case of a local authority landlord, whether or not there is a
need for a community care assessment in accordance with National
Health Service and Community Care Act 1990.

PART 2: POSSESSION CLAIMS BASED UPON RENT ARREARS
Initial contact

2.1 The landlord should contact the tenant as soon as reasonably possible if the
tenant falls into arrears to discuss the cause of the arrears, the tenant's financial circumstances, the tenant's entitlement to benefits and repayment of the
arrears. Where contact is by letter, the landlord should write separately to
each named tenant.

2.2 The landlord and tenant should try to agree affordable sums for the tenant to
pay towards arrears, based upon the tenant's income and expenditure (where
such information has been supplied in response to the landlord's enquiries).
The landlord should clearly set out in pre-action correspondence any time
limits with which the tenant should comply.

2.3 The landlord should provide, on a quarterly basis, rent statements in a comprehensible format showing rent due and sums received for the past 13
weeks. The landlord should, upon request, provide the tenant with copies
of rent statements in a comprehensible format from the date when arrears
first arose showing all amounts of rent due, the dates and amounts of all payments made, whether through housing benefit, discretionary housing payments or by the tenant, and a running total of the arrears.

2.4 If the tenant meets the appropriate criteria, the landlord should arrange for
arrears to be paid by the Department for Work and Pensions from the tenant's benefit.

2.5 The landlord should offer to assist the tenant in any claim the tenant may
have for housing benefit, discretionary housing benefit or universal credit
(housing element).

2.6 Possession proceedings for rent arrears should not be started against a tenant
who can demonstrate that–

(a) the local authority or Department for Work and Pensions have been provided with all the evidence required to process a housing benefit or universal credit (housing element) claim;

(b) a reasonable expectation of eligibility for housing benefit or universal
credit (housing element); and

(c) paid other sums due not covered by housing benefit or universal credit
(housing element).

The landlord should make every effort to establish effective ongoing liaison
with housing benefit departments and DWP and, with the tenant's consent,
make direct contact with the relevant housing benefit department or DWP
office before taking enforcement action.

The landlord and tenant should work together to resolve any housing benefit
or universal credit (housing element) problems.

2.7 Bearing in mind that rent arrears may be part of a general debt problem, the landlord should advise the tenant to seek assistance from CAB, debt advice agencies or other appropriate agencies as soon as possible. Information on debt advice is available on the Money Advice Service website www.moneyadviceservice.org.uk/en/tools/debt-advice-locator.

After service of statutory notices

2.8 After service of a statutory notice but before the issue of proceedings, the landlord should make reasonable attempts to contact the tenant, to discuss the amount of the arrears, the cause of the arrears, repayment of the arrears and the housing benefit or universal credit (housing element) position and send a copy of this protocol.

2.9 If the tenant complies with an agreement to pay the current rent and a reasonable amount towards arrears, the landlord should agree to postpone issuing court proceedings so long as the tenant keeps to such agreement. If the tenant ceases to comply with such agreement, the landlord should warn the tenant of the intention to bring proceedings and give the tenant clear time limits within which to comply.

Alternative dispute resolution

2.10 The parties should consider whether it is possible to resolve the issues between them by discussion and negotiation without recourse to litigation. The parties may be required by the court to provide evidence that alternative means of resolving the dispute were considered. Courts take the view that litigation should be a last resort, and that claims should not be issued prematurely when a settlement is still actively being explored.

2.11 The Civil Justice Council and Judicial College have endorsed The Jackson ADR Handbook by Susan Blake, Julie Browne and Stuart Sime (2013, Oxford University Press). The Citizens Advice Bureaux website also provides information about ADR: http://www.adviceguide.org.uk/england/law_e/law_legal_system_e/law_taking_legal_action_e/alternatives_to_court.htm. Information is also available at: www.civilmediation.justice.gov.uk/

Court proceedings

2.11 Not later than ten days before the date set for the hearing, the landlord should–

(a) provide the tenant with up to date rent statements; and

(b) disclose what knowledge it possesses of the tenant's housing benefit or universal credit (housing element) position to the tenant.

2.12 (a) The landlord should inform the tenant of the date and time of any court hearing and provide an up to date rent statement and the order applied for. The landlord should advise the tenant to attend the hearing as the tenant's home is at risk. Records of such advice should be kept.

(b) If the tenant complies with an agreement made after the issue of proceedings to pay the current rent and a reasonable amount towards arrears, the landlord should agree to postpone court proceedings so long as the tenant keeps to such agreement.

(c) If the tenant ceases to comply with such agreement, the landlord should warn the tenant of the intention to restore the proceedings and give the tenant clear time limits within which to comply.

2.13 If the landlord unreasonably fails to comply with the terms of the protocol, the court may impose one or more of the following sanctions–

(a) an order for costs; and

(b) in cases other than those brought solely on mandatory grounds, adjourn, strike out or dismiss claims.

2.14 If the tenant unreasonably fails to comply with the terms of the protocol, the court may take such failure into account when considering whether it is reasonable to make possession orders.

PART 3: MANDATORY GROUNDS FOR POSSESSION

3.1 This part applies in cases where if a social landlord proves its case, there is a restriction on the Court's discretion on making an order for possession and/or to which Housing Act 1980 s89 applies (eg non-secure tenancies, unlawful occupiers, succession claims, and severing of joint tenancies).

3.2 In cases where the court must grant possession if the landlord proves its case then before issuing any possession claim social landlords–

(a) should write to occupants explaining why they currently intend to seek possession and requiring the occupants within a specified time to notify the landlord in writing of any personal circumstances or other matters which they wish to take into account. In many cases such a letter could accompany any notice to quit and so would not necessarily delay the issue of proceedings; and

(b) should consider any representations received, and if they decide to proceed with a claim for possession give brief written reasons for doing so.

3.3 In these cases the social landlord should include in its particulars of claim, or in any witness statement filed under CPR 55.8(3), a schedule giving a summary–

(a) of whether it has (by statutory review procedure or otherwise) invited the defendant to make representations of any personal circumstances or other matters which they wish to be taken into account before the social landlord issues proceedings;

(b) if representations were made, that they were considered;

(c) of brief reasons for bringing proceedings; and

(d) copies of any relevant documents which the social landlord wishes the Court to consider in relation to the proportionality of the landlord's decision to bring proceedings.

Pre-action Protocol for possession claims based on mortgage or home purchase plan arrears in respect of residential property[3]

I INTRODUCTION
Definitions
1.1 In this Protocol–

 (a) 'possession claim' means a claim for the recovery of possession of property under Part 55 of the Civil Procedure Rules 1998;

 (b) 'home purchase plan' means a method of purchasing a property by way of a sale and lease arrangement that does not require the payment of interest;

 (c) 'bank holiday' means a bank holiday under the Banking and Financial Dealings Act 1971;

 (d) 'business day' means any day except Saturday, Sunday, a bank holiday, Good Friday or Christmas day; and

 (e) 'authorised tenant' means a tenant whose tenancy is authorised as between the borrower and the lender.

Preamble
2.1 This Protocol describes the behaviour the court will normally expect of the parties prior to the start of a possession claim within the scope of paragraph 3.1 below.

2.2 This Protocol does not alter the parties' rights and obligations.

2.3 It is in the interests of the parties that mortgage payments or payments under home purchase plans are made promptly and that difficulties are resolved wherever possible without court proceedings. However in some cases an order for possession may be in the interest of both the lender and the borrower.

Aims
3.1 The aims of this Protocol are to–

 (a) ensure that a lender or home purchase plan provider (in this Protocol collectively referred to as 'the lender') and a borrower or home purchase plan customer (in this Protocol collectively referred to as 'the borrower') act fairly and reasonably with each other in resolving any matter concerning mortgage or home purchase plan arrears;

 (b) encourage greater pre-action contact between the lender and the borrower in order to seek agreement between the parties, and where agreement cannot be reached, to enable efficient use of the court's time and resources; and

 (c) encourage lenders to check who is in occupation of the property before issuing proceedings.

---

3   Available at www.justice.gov.uk. Updated at 15 June 2015.

3.2 Where either party is required to communicate and provide information to the other, reasonable steps should be taken to do so in a way that is clear, fair and not misleading. If the lender is aware that the borrower may have difficulties in reading or understanding the information provided, the lender should take reasonable steps to ensure that information is communicated in a way that the borrower can understand.

Scope

4.1 This Protocol applies to arrears on–

    (a) first charge residential mortgages and home purchase plans regulated by the Financial Conduct Authority under the Financial Services and Markets Act 2000 (as amended by the Financial Services Act, 2012);

    (b) second charge mortgages over residential property and other secured loans regulated under the Consumer Credit Act 1974 on residential property; and

    (c) unregulated residential mortgages.

4.2 Where a potential claim includes a money claim and a possession claim, this protocol applies to both.

4.3 The protocol does not apply to Buy To Let mortgages.

II ACTIONS PRIOR TO THE START OF A POSSESSION CLAIM
Initial contact and provision of information

5.1 Where a borrower falls into arrears, the lender must provide the borrower with–

    (a) where appropriate, the required regulatory information sheet or the National Homelessness Advice Service/Shelter/Cymru booklet on mortgage arrears;

    (b) information on the current monthly instalments and the amounts paid for the last 2 years; and

    (c) information on the amount of arrears, which should include–

        (i) the total amount of the arrears;

        (ii) the total outstanding of the mortgage or the home purchase plan; and

        (iii) whether interest or charges have been or will be added, and, where appropriate, details or an estimate of the interest or charges that may be payable.

5.2 The lender should also seek information about whether the property is occupied by an authorised tenant.

5.3 The lender must advise the borrower to make early contact with the housing department of the borrower's Local Authority and, should, where relevant refer the borrower to appropriate sources of independent debt advice.

5.4 The parties, or their representatives, must take all reasonable steps to discuss with each other the reasons for the arrears, the borrower's financial circumstances and proposals for repayment of the arrears (see paragraph 7.1). For example, parties should consider whether the reasons for the arrears are temporary or long-term, and whether the borrower may be able to pay the arrears in a reasonable time.

5.5 The lender must consider a reasonable request from the borrower to change the date of regular payment (within the same payment period) or the method by which payment is made. The lender must either agree to such a request or, where it refuses such a request, it must, within a reasonable period of time, give the borrower a written explanation of its reasons for the refusal.

5.6 The lender must respond promptly to any proposal for payment made by the borrower. If the lender does not agree to such a proposal it should give reasons in writing to the borrower within 10 business days of the proposal.

5.7 If the lender submits a proposal for payment, the borrower must be given a reasonable period of time in which to consider such proposals. The lender must set out the proposal in sufficient detail to enable the borrower to understand the implications of the proposal.

5.8 If the borrower fails to comply with an agreement, the lender should warn the borrower, by giving the borrower 15 business days notice in writing, of its intention to start a possession claim unless the borrower remedies the breach in the agreement.

Postponing the start of a possession claim

6.1 A lender must not consider starting a possession claim for mortgage arrears where the borrower can demonstrate to the lender that the borrower has–

  (a) submitted a claim to–

    (i) the Department for Works and Pensions ('DWP') for Support for Mortgage Interest (SMI) or if appropriate Universal Credit; or

    (ii) an insurer under a mortgage payment protection policy; or

    (iii) a participating local authority for support under a Mortgage Rescue Scheme, or other means of homelessness prevention support provided by the local authority,

    (iv) and has provided all the evidence required to process a claim;

  (b) a reasonable expectation of eligibility for payment from the DWP or from an insurer or support from the local authority or welfare or charitable organisation such as the Veterans Welfare Scheme or Royal British Legion;

  (c) an ability to pay a mortgage instalment not covered by a claim to the DWP or the insurer in relation to a claim under paragraph 6.1(1)(a) or (b);

  (d) difficulty in respect of affordability or another specific personal or financial difficulty, and requires time to seek free independent debt advice, or has a confirmed appointment with a debt adviser and

  (e) a reasonable expectation, providing evidence where possible, of an improvement in their financial circumstances in the foreseeable future (for example a new job or increased income from a lodger).

6.2 If a borrower can demonstrate that reasonable steps have been or will be taken to market the property at an appropriate price in accordance with reasonable professional advice, the lender must consider postponing starting a possession claim to allow the borrower a realistic period of time to sell the property. The borrower must continue to take all reasonable steps actively to market the property where the lender has agreed to postpone starting a possession claim.

6.3 Where, notwithstanding paragraphs 6.1 an 6.2, the lender has agreed to postpone starting a possession claim, the borrower should provide the lender with a copy of the particulars of sale, the Energy Performance Certificate ('EPC') or proof that an EPC has been commissioned and (where relevant) details of purchase offers received within a reasonable period of time specified by the lender. The borrower should give the lender details of the estate agent and the conveyancer instructed to deal with the sale. The borrower should also authorise the estate agent and the conveyancer to communicate with the lender about the progress of the sale and the borrower's conduct during the process.

6.4 Where the lender decides not to postpone the start of a possession claim, it must inform the borrower of the reasons for this decision at least 5 business days before starting proceedings.

Further matters to consider before starting a possession claim

7.1 Starting a possession claim should be a last resort and must not normally be started unless all other reasonable attempts to resolve the situation have failed. The parties should consider whether, given the individual circumstances of the borrower and the form of the agreement, it is reasonable and appropriate to do one or more of the following–

(a) extend the term of the mortgage;

(b) change the type of mortgage;

(c) defer payment of interest due under the mortgage;

(d) capitalise the arrears; or

(e) make use of any Government forbearance initiatives in which the lender chooses to participate.

7.2 Where there is an authorised tenant in occupation of the property, at the possession hearing the court will consider whether–

(a) further directions are required;

(b) to adjourn the possession claim until possession has been recovered against the tenant; or

(c) to make an order conditional upon the tenant's right of occupation.

Complaints to the Financial Services Ombudsman

8.1 The lender must consider whether to postpone the start of a possession claim where the borrower has made a genuine complaint to the Financial Ombudsman Service ('FOS') about the potential possession claim.

8.2 Where a lender does not intend to await the decision of the FOS, it must give notice to the borrower, with reasons, that it intends to start a possession claim.

APPENDIX F

CPR Part 55 and Practice Directions[1]

CPR Part 55: Possession claims

55.1 Interpretation
In this Part–
(a) 'a possession claim' means a claim for the recovery of possession of land (including buildings or parts of buildings);
(b) 'a possession claim against trespassers' means a claim for the recovery of land which the claimant alleges is occupied only by a person or persons who entered or remained on the land without the consent of a person entitled to possession of that land but does not include a claim against a tenant or sub-tenant whether his tenancy has been terminated or not;
(c) 'mortgage' includes a legal or equitable mortgage and a legal or equitable charge and 'mortgagee' is to be interpreted accordingly;
(d) 'the 1985 Act' means the Housing Act 1985;
(e) 'the 1988 Act' means the Housing Act 1988;
(f) 'a demotion claim' means a claim made by a landlord for an order under section 82A of the 1985 Act or section 6A of the 1988 Act ('a demotion order');
(g) 'a demoted tenancy' means a tenancy created by virtue of a demotion order; and
(h) 'a suspension claim' means a claim made by a landlord for an order under section 121A of the 1985 Act.

I   General rules

55.2 Scope
(1) The procedure set out in this Section of this Part must be used where the claim includes –
(a) a possession claim brought by a –
  (i)   landlord (or former landlord);
  (ii) mortgagee; or
  (iii) licensor (or former licensor);
(b) a possession claim against trespassers; or
(c) a claim by a tenant seeking relief from forfeiture.
(Where a demotion claim or a suspension claim (or both) is made in the same claim form in which a possession claim is started, this Section of this Part applies as modified by rule 65.12. Where the claim is a demotion claim or a suspension claim only, or a suspension claim made in addition to a demotion claim, Section III of Part 65 applies).
(2) This Section of this Part
(a) is subject to any enactment or practice direction which sets out special provisions with regard to any particular category of claim;
(b) does not apply where the claimant uses the procedure set out in Section II of this Part; and
(c) does not apply where the claimant seeks an interim possession order

under Section III of this Part except where the court orders otherwise or that Section so provides.

55.3 Starting the claim

(1) In the County Court–
  (a) the claimant may make the claim at any County Court hearing centre, unless paragraph (2) applies or an enactment provides otherwise;
  (b) the claim will be issued by the hearing centre where the claim is made; and
  (c) if the claim is not made at the County Court hearing centre which serves the address where the land is situated, the claim will be sent to the hearing centre serving that address when it is issued.
  (Practice Direction 55A includes further direction in respect of claims which are not made at the County Court hearing centre which serves the address where the land is situated.)
(2) The claim may be started in the High Court if the claimant files with his claim form a certificate stating the reasons for bringing the claim in that court verified by a statement of truth in accordance with rule 22.1(1).
(3) Practice Direction 55A refers to circumstances which may justify starting the claim in the High Court.
(4) Where, in a possession claim against trespassers, the claimant does not know the name of a person in occupation or possession of the land, the claim must be brought against 'persons unknown' in addition to any named defendants.
(5) The claim form and form of defence sent with it must be in the forms set out in Practice Direction 55A.

55.4 Particulars of claim

The particulars of claim must be filed and served with the claim form.
(Part 16 and Practice Direction 55A provide details about the contents of the particulars of claim)

55.5 Hearing date

(1) Subject to paragraph (1A), the court will fix a date for the hearing when it issues the claim form.
(1A) If the claim is not made at the County Court hearing centre which serves the address where the land is situated, a date will be fixed for hearing when the claim is received by that hearing centre
(2) In a possession claim against trespassers the defendant must be served with the claim form, particulars of claim and any witness statements –
  (a) in the case of residential property, not less than 5 days; and
  (b) in the case of other land, not less than 2 days,
  before the hearing date.
(3) In all other possession claims –
  (a) the hearing date will be not less than 28 days from the date of issue of the claim form;

(b) the standard period between the issue of the claim form and the hearing will be not more than 8 weeks; and

(c) the defendant must be served with the claim form and particulars of claim not less than 21 days before the hearing date.

(Rule 3.1(2)(a) provides that the court may extend or shorten the time for compliance with any rule)

55.6   Service of claims against trespassers

Where, in a possession claim against trespassers, the claim has been issued against 'persons unknown', the claim form, particulars of claim and any witness statements must be served on those persons by –

(a) (i) attaching copies of the claim form, particulars of claim and any witness statements to the main door or some other part of the land so that they are clearly visible; and

   (ii) if practicable, inserting copies of those documents in a sealed transparent envelope addressed to 'the occupiers' through the letter box; or

(b) placing stakes in the land in places where they are clearly visible and attaching to each stake copies of the claim form, particulars of claim and any witness statements in a sealed transparent envelope addressed to 'the occupiers'.

55.7   Defendant's response

(1) An acknowledgment of service is not required and Part 10 does not apply.

(2) In a possession claim against trespassers rule 15.2 does not apply and the defendant need not file a defence.

(3) Where, in any other possession claim, the defendant does not file a defence within the time specified in rule 15.4, he may take part in any hearing but the court may take his failure to do so into account when deciding what order to make about costs.

(4) Part 12 (default judgment) does not apply in a claim to which this Part applies.

55.8   The hearing

(1) At the hearing fixed in accordance with rule 55.5(1) or at any adjournment of that hearing, the court may –

(a) decide the claim; or

(b) give case management directions.

(2) Where the claim is genuinely disputed on grounds which appear to be substantial, case management directions given under paragraph (1)(b) will include the allocation of the claim to a track or directions to enable it to be allocated.

(3) Except where –

(a) the claim is allocated to the fast track or the multi-track; or

(b) the court orders otherwise,

any fact that needs to be proved by the evidence of witnesses at a hearing referred to in paragraph (1) may be proved by evidence in writing.

(Rule 32.2(1) sets out the general rule about evidence. Rule 32.2(2) provides that rule 32.2(1) is subject to any provision to the contrary)

(4) Subject to paragraph (5), all witness statements must be filed and served at least 2 days before the hearing.

(5) In a possession claim against trespassers all witness statements on which the claimant intends to rely must be filed and served with the claim form.

(6) Where the claimant serves the claim form and particulars of claim, he must produce at the hearing a certificate of service of those documents and rule 6.17(2)(a) does not apply.

55.9 Allocation

(1) When the court decides the track for a possession claim, the matters to which it shall have regard include –

(a) the matters set out in rule 26.8 as modified by the relevant practice direction;

(b) the amount of any arrears of rent or mortgage instalments;

(c) the importance to the defendant of retaining possession of the land;

(d) the importance of vacant possession to the claimant; and

(e) if applicable, the alleged conduct of the defendant

(2) The court will only allocate possession claims to the small claims track if all the parties agree.

(3) Where a possession claim has been allocated to the small claims track the claim shall be treated, for the purposes of costs, as if it were proceeding on the fast track except that trial costs shall be in the discretion of the court and shall not exceed the amount that would be recoverable under rule 45.38 (amount of fast track costs) if the value of the claim were up to £3,000.

(4) Where all the parties agree the court may, when it allocates the claim, order that rule 27.14 (costs on the small claims track) applies and, where it does so, paragraph (3) does not apply.

55.10 Possession claims relating to mortgaged residential property

(1) This rule applies where a mortgagee seeks possession of land which consists of or includes residential property.

(2) Within 5 days of receiving notification of the date of the hearing by the court, the claimant must send a notice to –

(a) the property, addressed to 'the tenant or the occupier';

(b) the housing department of the local authority within which the property is located; and

(c) any registered proprietor (other than the claimant) of a registered charge over the property.

(3) The notice referred to in paragraph (2)(a) must –

(a) state that a possession claim for the property has started;

(b) show the name and address of the claimant, the defendant and the court which issued the claim form; and

(c) give details of the hearing.

(3A) The notice referred to in paragraph 2(b) must contain the information in paragraph (3) and must state the full address of the property.

(4) The claimant must produce at the hearing –
    (a) a copy of the notices; and
    (b) evidence that they have been sent.
(4A) An unauthorised tenant of residential property may apply to the court for the order for possession to be suspended.

55.10A Electronic issue of certain possession claims

(1) A practice direction may make provision for a claimant to start certain types of possession claim in certain courts by requesting the issue of a claim form electronically.

(2) The practice direction may, in particular –
    (a) provide that only particular provisions apply in specific courts;
    (b) specify –
        (i)   the type of possession claim which may be issued electronically;
        (ii) the conditions that a claim must meet before it may be issued electronically;
    (c) specify the court where the claim may be issued;
    (d) enable the parties to make certain applications or take further steps in relation to the claim electronically;
    (e) specify the requirements that must be fulfilled in relation to such applications or steps;
    (f) enable the parties to correspond electronically with the court about the claim;
    (g) specify the requirements that must be fulfilled in relation to electronic correspondence;
    (h) provide how any fee payable on the filing of any document is to be paid where the document is filed electronically.

(3) The Practice Direction may disapply or modify these Rules as appropriate in relation to possession claims started electronically.

II   Accelerated possession claims of property let on an assured shorthold tenancy

55.11 When this section may be used

(1) The claimant may bring a possession claim under this Section of this Part where –
    (a) the claim is brought under section 21 of the 1988 Act to recover possession of residential property let under an assured shorthold tenancy; and
    (b) subject to rule 55.12(2), all the conditions listed in rule 55.12(1) are satisfied.

(2) The claim –
    (a) may be brought in any County Court hearing centre; and
    (b) will be issued by the hearing centre where it is brought.

(3) In this Section of this Part, a 'demoted assured shorthold tenancy' means a demoted tenancy where the landlord is a registered social landlord or a private registered provider of social housing.

(By virtue of section 20B of the 1988 Act, a demoted assured shorthold tenancy is an assured shorthold tenancy)

55.12 Conditions

(1) The conditions referred to in rule 55.11(1)(b) are that –
   (a) the tenancy and any agreement for the tenancy were entered into on or after 15 January 1989;
   (b) the only purpose of the claim is to recover possession of the property and no other claim is made;
   (c) the tenancy did not immediately follow an assured tenancy which was not an assured shorthold tenancy;
   (d) the tenancy fulfilled the conditions provided by section 19A or 20(1)(a) to (c) of the 1988 Act;
   (e) the tenancy –
      (i) was the subject of a written agreement;
      (ii) arises by virtue of section 5 of the 1988 Act but follows a tenancy that was the subject of a written agreement; or
      (iii) relates to the same or substantially the same property let to the same tenant and on the same terms (though not necessarily as to rent or duration) as a tenancy which was the subject of a written agreement; and
   (f) a notice in accordance with sections 21(1) or 21(4) of the 1988 Act was given to the tenant in writing.
(2) If the tenancy is a demoted assured shorthold tenancy, only the conditions in paragraph (1)(b) and (f) need be satisfied.

55.13 Claim form

(1) The claim form must –
   (a) be in the form set out in Practice Direction 55A; and
   (b) (i) contain such information; and
      (ii) be accompanied by such documents,
      as are required by that form.
(2) All relevant sections of the form must be completed.
(3) The court will serve the claim form by first class post (or an alternative service which provides for delivery on the next working day).

55.14 Defence

(1) A defendant who wishes to –
   (a) oppose the claim; or
   (b) seek a postponement of possession in accordance with rule 55.18,
   must file his defence within 14 days after service of the claim form.
(2) The defence should be in the form set out in Practice Direction 55A.

55.15 Claim referred to judge

(1) On receipt of the defence the court will –

(a) send a copy to the claimant; and

(b) refer the claim and defence to a judge.

(2) Where the period set out in rule 55.14 has expired without the defendant filing a defence –

(a) the claimant may file a written request for an order for possession; and

(b) the court will refer that request to a judge.

(3) Where the defence is received after the period set out in rule 55.14 has expired but before a request is filed in accordance with paragraph (2), paragraph (1) will still apply.

(4) Where –

(a) the period set out in rule 55.14 has expired without the defendant filing a defence; and

(b) the claimant has not made a request for an order for possession under paragraph (2) within 3 months after the expiry of the period set out in rule 55.14,

the claim will be stayed.

55.16 Consideration of the claim

(1) After considering the claim and any defence, the judge will –

(a) make an order for possession under rule 55.17;

(b) where the judge is not satisfied as to any of the matters set out in paragraph (2) –

(i)   direct that a date be fixed for a hearing; and

(ii) give any appropriate case management directions; or

(c) strike out the claim if the claim form discloses no reasonable grounds for bringing the claim.

(1A) If–

(a) the judge directs that a date be fixed for hearing in accordance either with paragraph (2) or rule 55.18(1); and

(b the claim has not been brought in the County Court hearing centre which serves the address where the land is situated,

the judge will direct that the proceedings should be transferred to that hearing centre.

(2) The matters referred to in paragraph (1)(b) are that –

(a) the claim form was served; and

(b) the claimant has established that he is entitled to recover possession under section 21 of the1988 Act against the defendant.

(3) The court will give all parties not less than 14 days' notice of a hearing fixed under paragraph (1)(b)(i).

(4) Where a claim is struck out under paragraph (1)(c) –

(a) the court will serve its reasons for striking out the claim with the order; and

(b) the claimant may apply to restore the claim within 28 days after the date the order was served on him.

55.17 Possession order
Except where rules 55.16(1)(b) or (c) apply, the judge will make an order for possession without requiring the attendance of the parties.

55.18 Postponement of possession
(1) Where the defendant seeks postponement of possession on the ground of exceptional hardship under section 89 of the Housing Act 19801, the judge may direct a hearing of that issue.
(2) Where the judge directs a hearing under paragraph (1) –
  (a) the hearing must be held before the date on which possession is to be given up; and
  (b) the judge will direct how many days' notice the parties must be given of that hearing.
(3) Where the judge is satisfied, on a hearing directed under paragraph (1), that exceptional hardship would be caused by requiring possession to be given up by the date in the order of possession, he may vary the date on which possession must be given up.

55.19 Application to set aside or vary
The court may
  (a) on application by a party within 14 days of service of the order; or
  (b) of its own initiative,
set aside or vary any order made under rule 55.17.

III Interim possession orders

55.20 When this section may be used
(1) This Section of this Part applies where the claimant seeks an Interim Possession Order.
(2) In this section –
  (a) 'IPO' means Interim Possession Order; and
  (b) 'premises' has the same meaning as in section 12 of the Criminal Law Act 1977.
(3) Where this Section requires an act to be done within a specified number of hours, rule 2.8(4) does not apply.

55.21 Conditions for IPO application
(1) An application for an IPO may be made where the following conditions are satisfied –
  (a) the only claim made is a possession claim against trespassers for the recovery of premises;
  (b) the claimant –
    (i) has an immediate right to possession of the premises; and
    (ii) has had such a right throughout the period of alleged unlawful occupation; and

(c) the claim is made within 28 days of the date on which the claimant first knew, or ought reasonably to have known, that the defendant (or any of the defendants), was in occupation.

(2) An application for an IPO may not be made against a defendant who entered or remained on the premises with the consent of a person who, at the time consent was given, had an immediate right to possession of the premises.

55.22 The application

(1) Rules 55.3(1) and (4) apply to the claim.

(2) The claim form and the defendant's form of witness statement must be in the form set out in Practice Direction 55A.

(3) When he files his claim form, the claimant must also file –
   (a) an application notice in the form set out in Practice Direction 55A; and
   (b) written evidence.

(4) The written evidence must be given –
   (a) by the claimant personally; or
   (b) where the claimant is a body corporate, by a duly authorised officer.
   (Rule 22.1(6)(b) provides that the statement of truth must be signed by the maker of the witness statement)

(5) The court will –
   (a) issue –
      (i)   the claim form; and
      (ii) the application for the IPO; and
   (b) set a date for the hearing of the application.

(6) The hearing of the application will be as soon as practicable but not less than 3 days after the date of issue.

55.23 Service

(1) Within 24 hours of the issue of the application, the claimant must serve on the defendant –
   (a) the claim form;
   (b) the application notice together with the written evidence in support; and
   (c) a blank form for the defendant's witness statement (as set out in Practice Direction 55A) which must be attached to the application notice.

(2) The claimant must serve the documents listed in paragraph (1) in accordance with rule 55.6(a).

(3) At or before the hearing the claimant must file a certificate of service in relation to the documents listed in paragraph (1) and rule 6.17(2)(a) does not apply.

55.24 Defendant's response

(1) At any time before the hearing the defendant may file a witness statement in response to the application.

(2) The witness statement should be in the form set out in Practice Direction 55A.

55.25 Hearing of the application

(1) In deciding whether to grant an IPO, the court will have regard to whether the claimant has given, or is prepared to give, the following undertakings in support of his application –

    (a) if, after an IPO is made, the court decides that the claimant was not entitled to the order to –

        (i) reinstate the defendant if so ordered by the court; and

        (ii) pay such damages as the court may order; and

    (b) before the claim for possession is finally decided, not to –

        (i) damage the premises;

        (ii) grant a right of occupation to any other person; and

        (iii) damage or dispose of any of the defendant's property.

(2) The court will make an IPO if –

    (a) the claimant has –

        (i) filed a certificate of service of the documents referred to in rule 55.23(1); or

        (ii) proved service of those documents to the satisfaction of the court; and

    (b) the court considers that –

        (i) the conditions set out in rule 55.21(1) are satisfied; and

        (ii) any undertakings given by the claimant as a condition of making the order are adequate.

(3) An IPO will be in the form set out in the relevant practice direction and will require the defendant to vacate the premises specified in the claim form within 24 hours of the service of the order.

(4) On making an IPO the court will set a date for the hearing of the claim for possession which will be not less than 7 days after the date on which the IPO is made.

(5) Where the court does not make an IPO –

    (a) the court will set a date for the hearing of the claim;

    (b) the court may give directions for the future conduct of the claim; and

    (c) subject to such directions, the claim shall proceed in accordance with Section I of this Part.

55.26 Service and enforcement of the IPO

(1) An IPO must be served within 48 hours after it is sealed.

(2) The claimant must serve the IPO on the defendant together with copies of

    (a) the claim form; and

    (b) the written evidence in support, in accordance with rule 55.6(a).

(3) Rules 83.2, 83.3 and 83.26(1)–(9) do not apply to the enforcement of an IPO.

(4) If an IPO is not served within the time limit specified by this rule, the claimant may apply to the court for directions for the claim for possession to continue under Section I of this Part.

55.27 After IPO made

(1) Before the date for the hearing of the claim, the claimant must file a certificate of service in relation to the documents specified in rule 55.26(2).

(2) The IPO will expire on the date of the hearing of the claim.

(3) At the hearing the court may make any order it considers appropriate and may, in particular –

  (a) make a final order for possession;

  (b) dismiss the claim for possession;

  (c) give directions for the claim for possession to continue under Section I of this Part; or

  (d) enforce any of the claimant's undertakings.

(4) Unless the court directs otherwise, the claimant must serve any order or directions in accordance with rule 55.6(a).

(5) Rule 83.26(10) to (12) applies to the enforcement of a final order for possession.

55.28 Application to set aside IPO

(1) If the defendant has left the premises, he may apply on grounds of urgency for the IPO to be set aside before the date of the hearing of the claim.

(2) An application under paragraph (1) must be supported by a witness statement.

(3) On receipt of the application, the court will give directions as to –

  (a) the date for the hearing; and

  (b) the period of notice, if any, to be given to the claimant and the method of service of any such notice.

(4) No application to set aside an IPO may be made under rule 39.3.

(5) Where no notice is required under paragraph (3)(b), the only matters to be dealt with at the hearing of the application to set aside are whether –

  (a) the IPO should be set aside; and

  (b) any undertaking to re-instate the defendant should be enforced, and all other matters will be dealt with at the hearing of the claim.

(6) The court will serve on all the parties –

  (a) a copy of the order made under paragraph (5); and

  (b) where no notice was required under paragraph (3)(b), a copy of the defendant's application to set aside and the witness statement in support.

(7) Where notice is required under paragraph (3)(b), the court may treat the hearing of the application to set aside as the hearing of the claim.

Practice Direction 55A: Possession claims

This Practice Direction supplements Part 55

Section I – General rules

55.3 Starting the claim

1.1 (1) Except where the county court does not have jurisdiction, possession claims should normally be brought in the county court. Only exceptional circumstances justify starting a claim in the High Court.

(2) In the County Court, the claim will be issued by the County Court hearing centre where the claim is made, but will then be sent to the County Court hea ring centre which serves the address where the land is situated. A claimant should consider the potential delay which may result if a claim is not made at the appropriate hearing centre in the first instance.

1.2 If a claimant starts a claim in the High Court and the court decides that it should have been started in the county court, the court will normally either strike the claim out or transfer it to the county court on its own initiative. This is likely to result in delay and the court will normally disallow the costs of starting the claim in the High Court and of any transfer.

1.3 Circumstances which may, in an appropriate case, justify starting a claim in the High Court are if –

(1) there are complicated disputes of fact;

(2) there are points of law of general importance; or

(3) the claim is against trespassers and there is a substantial risk of public disturbance or of serious harm to persons or property which properly require immediate determination.

1.4 The value of the property and the amount of any financial claim may be relevant circumstances, but these factors alone will not normally justify starting the claim in the High Court.

1.5 The claimant must use the appropriate claim form and particulars of claim form set out in Table 1 to Part 4 Practice Direction. The defence must be in form N11, N11B, N11M or N11R, as appropriate.

1.6 High Court claims for the possession of land subject to a mortgage will be assigned to the Chancery Division.

1.7 A claim which is not a possession claim may be brought under the procedure set out in Section I of Part 55 if it is started in the same claim form as a possession claim which, by virtue of rule 55.2(1) must be brought in accordance with that Section.

(Rule 7.3 provides that a claimant may use a single claim form to start all claims which can be conveniently disposed of in the same proceedings)

1.8 For example a claim under paragraphs 4, 5 or 6 of Part I of Schedule 1 to the Mobile Homes Act 1983 may be brought using the procedure set out in Section I of Part 55 if the claim is started in the same claim form as a claim enforcing the rights referred to in section 3(1)(b) of the Caravan Sites Act 1968 (which, by virtue of rule 55.2(1) must be brought under Section I of Part 55).

1.9 Where the claim form includes a demotion claim, the claim must be started in the county court for the district in which the land is situated.

55.4 Particulars of claim

2.1 In a possession claim the particulars of claim must:

(1) identify the land to which the claim relates;

(2) state whether the claim relates to residential property;

(3) state the ground on which possession is claimed;

(4) give full details about any mortgage or tenancy agreement; and

(5) give details of every person who, to the best of the claimant's knowledge, is in possession of the property.

Residential property let on a tenancy

2.2 Paragraphs 2.3 to 2.4B apply if the claim relates to residential property let on a tenancy.

2.3 If the claim includes a claim for non-payment of rent the particulars of claim must set out:

(1) the amount due at the start of the proceedings;

(2) in schedule form, the dates and amounts of all payments due and payments made under the tenancy agreement for a period of two years immediately preceding the date of issue, or if the first date of default occurred less than two years before the date of issue from the first date of default and a running total of the arrears;

(3) the daily rate of any rent and interest;

(4) any previous steps taken to recover the arrears of rent with full details of any court proceedings; and

(5) any relevant information about the defendant's circumstances, in particular:

(a) whether the defendant is in receipt of social security benefits; and

(b) whether any payments are made on his behalf directly to the claimant under the Social Security Contributions and Benefits Act 1992

2.3A If the claimant wishes to rely on a history of arrears which is longer than two years, he should state this in his particulars and exhibit a full (or longer) schedule to a witness statement.

2.4 If the claimant knows of any person (including a mortgagee) entitled to claim relief against forfeiture as underlessee under section 146(4) of the Law of Property Act 1925 (or in accordance with section 38 of the Senior Courts Act 1981, or section 138(9C) of the County Courts Act 1984):

(1) the particulars of claim must state the name and address of that person; and

(2) the claimant must file a copy of the particulars of claim for service on him.

2.4A If the claim for possession relates to the conduct of the tenant, the particulars of claim must state details of the conduct alleged.

2.4B If the possession claims relies on a statutory ground or grounds for possession, the particulars of claims must specify the ground or grounds relied on.

Land subject to a mortgage

2.5 If the claim is a possession claim by a mortgagee, the particulars of claim must also set out:

(1) if the claim relates to residential property whether:

    (a) a land charge of Class F has been registered under section 2(7) of the Matrimonial Homes Act 1967;

    (b) a notice registered under section 2(8) or 8(3) of the Matrimonial Homes Act 1983 has been entered and on whose behalf; or

    (c) a notice under section 31(10) of the Family Law Act 1996 has been registered and on whose behalf; and if so, that the claimant will serve notice of the claim on the persons on whose behalf the land charge is registered or the notice or caution entered.

(2) the state of the mortgage account by including:

    (a) the amount of:

        (i) the advance;

        (ii) any periodic repayment; and

        (iii) any payment of interest required to be made;

    (b) the amount which would have to be paid (after taking into account any adjustment for early settlement) in order to redeem the mortgage at a stated date not more than 14 days after the claim started specifying the amount of solicitor's costs and administration charges which would be payable;

    (c) if the loan which is secured by the mortgage is a regulated consumer credit agreement, the total amount outstanding under the terms of the mortgage; and

    (d) the rate of interest payable:

        (i) at the commencement of the mortgage;

        (ii) immediately before any arrears referred to in paragraph (3) accrued;

        (iii) at the commencement of the proceedings.

(3) if the claim is brought because of failure to pay the periodic payments when due:

    (a) in schedule form, the dates and amounts of all payments due and payments made under the mortgage agreement or mortgage deed for a period of two years immediately preceding the date of issue, or if the first date of default occurred less than two years before the date of issue from the first date of default and a running total of the arrears;

    (b) give details of:

        (i) any other payments required to be made as a term of the mortgage (such as for insurance premiums, legal costs, default interest, penalties, administrative or other charges);

        (ii) any other sums claimed and stating the nature and amount of each such charge; and

        (iii) whether any of these payments is in arrears and whether or not it is included in the amount of any periodic payment.

(4) whether or not the loan which is secured by the mortgage is a regulated consumer credit agreement and, if so, specify the date on which any notice required by sections 76 or 87 of the Consumer Credit Act 1974 was given;

(5) if appropriate details that show the property is not one to which section 141 of the Consumer Credit Act 1974 applies;

(6) any relevant information about the defendant's circumstances, in particular:

   (a) whether the defendant is in receipt of social security benefits; and

   (b) whether any payments are made on his behalf directly to the claimant under the Social Security Contributions and Benefits Act 1992;

(7) give details of any tenancy entered into between the mortgagor and mortgagee (including any notices served); and

(8) state any previous steps which the claimant has taken to recover the money secured by the mortgage or the mortgaged property and, in the case of court proceedings, state:

   (a) the dates when the claim started and concluded; and

   (b) the dates and terms of any orders made.

2.5A If the claimant wishes to rely on a history of arrears which is longer than two years, he should state this in his particulars and exhibit a full (or longer) schedule to a witness statement.

Possession claim against trespassers

2.6 If the claim is a possession claim against trespassers, the particulars of claim must state the claimant's interest in the land or the basis of his right to claim possession and the circumstances in which it has been occupied without licence or consent.

Possession claim in relation to a demoted tenancy by a housing action trust or a local housing authority

2.7 If the claim is a possession claim under section 143D of the Housing Act 1996 (possession claim in relation to a demoted tenancy where the landlord is a housing action trust or a local housing authority), the particulars of claim must have attached to them a copy of the notice to the tenant served under section 143E of the 1996 Act.

55.5 Hearing date

3.1 The court may exercise its powers under rules 3.1(2)(a) and (b) to shorten the time periods set out in rules 55.5(2) and (3).

3.2 Particular consideration should be given to the exercise of this power if:

(1) the defendant, or a person for whom the defendant is responsible, has assaulted or threatened to assault:

   (a) the claimant;

   (b) a member of the claimant's staff; or

   (c) another resident in the locality;

(2) there are reasonable grounds for fearing such an assault; or

(3) the defendant, or a person for whom the defendant is responsible, has

caused serious damage or threatened to cause serious damage to the property or to the home or property of another resident in the locality.

3.3 Where paragraph 3.2 applies but the case cannot be determined at the first hearing fixed under rule 55.5, the court will consider what steps are needed to finally determine the case as quickly as reasonably practicable.

55.6 Service in claims against trespassers

4.1 If the claim form is to be served by the court and in accordance with rule 55.6(b) the claimant must provide sufficient stakes and transparent envelopes.

55.8 The hearing

5.1 Attention is drawn to rule 55.8(3). Each party should wherever possible include all the evidence he wishes to present in his statement of case, verified by a statement of truth.

5.2 If relevant the claimant's evidence should include the amount of any rent or mortgage arrears and interest on those arrears. These amounts should, if possible, be up to date to the date of the hearing (if necessary by specifying a daily rate of arrears and interest). However, rule 55.8(4) does not prevent such evidence being brought up to date orally or in writing on the day of the hearing if necessary.

5.3 If relevant the defendant should give evidence of:

(1) the amount of any outstanding social security or housing benefit payments relevant to rent or mortgage arrears; and

(2) the status of:

(a) any claims for social security or housing benefit about which a decision has not yet been made; and

(b) any applications to appeal or review a social security or housing benefit decision where that appeal or review has not yet concluded.

5.4 If:

(1) the maker of a witness statement does not attend a hearing; and

(2) the other party disputes material evidence contained in his statement,

the court will normally adjourn the hearing so that oral evidence can be given.

5.5 The claimant must bring 2 completed copies of Form N123 to the hearing.

Consumer Credit Act claims relating to the recovery of land

7.1 Any application by the defendant for a time order under section 129 of the Consumer Credit Act 1974 may be made:

(1) in his defence; or

(2) by application notice in the proceedings.

Enforcement of charging order by sale

7.2 A party seeking to enforce a charging order by sale should follow the procedure set out in rule 73.10 and the Part 55 procedure should not be used.

Section II – Accelerated possession claims of property let on an assured shorthold tenancy

55.18 Postponement of possession

A8.1 In the County Court, the claim will be issued by the County Court hearing centre where the claim is made, but will then be sent to the County Court hearing centre which serves the address where the land is situated. A claimant should consider the potential delay which may result if a claim is not made at the appropriate hearing centre in the first instance.

8.1 If the judge is satisfied as to the matters set out in rule 55.16(2), he will make an order for possession in accordance with rule 55.17, whether or not the defendant seeks a postponement of possession on the ground of exceptional hardship under section 89 of the Housing Act 1980.

8.2 In a claim in which the judge is satisfied that the defendant has shown exceptional hardship, he will only postpone possession without directing a hearing under rule 55.18(1) if –

(1) he considers that possession should be given up 6 weeks after the date of the order or, if the defendant has requested postponement to an earlier date, on that date; and

(2) the claimant indicated on his claim form that he would be content for the court to make such an order without a hearing.

8.3 In all other cases if the defendant seeks a postponement of possession under section 89 of the Housing Act 1980, the judge will direct a hearing under rule 55.18(1).

8.4 If, at that hearing, the judge is satisfied that exceptional hardship would be caused by requiring possession to be given up by the date in the order of possession, he may vary that order under rule 55.18(3) so that possession is to be given up at a later date. That later date may be no later than 6 weeks after the making of the order for possession on the papers (see section 89 of the Housing Act 1980).

Section III – Interim possession orders

9.1 The claim form must be in form N5, the application notice seeking the interim possession order must be in form N130 and the defendant's witness statement must be in form N133.

9.2 The IPO will be in form N134 (annexed to this practice direction).

Section IV – Orders fixing a date for possession

10.1 This paragraph applies where the court has made an order postponing the date for possession under section 85(2)(b) of the Housing Act 1985 (secure tenancies) or under section 9(2)(b) of the Housing Act 1988 (assured tenancies).

10.2 If the defendant fails to comply with any of the terms of the order which relate to payment, the claimant, after following the procedure set out in paragraph

10.3, may apply for an order fixing the date upon which the defendant has to give up possession of the property. Unless the court further postpones the date for possession, the defendant will be required to give up possession on that date.

10.3 At least 14 days and not more than 3 months before applying for an order under paragraph 10.2, the claimant must give written notice to the defendant in accordance with paragraph 10.4.

10.4 The notice referred to in paragraph 10.3 must –
(1) state that the claimant intends to apply for an order fixing the date upon which the defendant is to give up possession of the property;
(2) record the current arrears and state how the defendant has failed to comply with the order referred to in paragraph 10.1 (by reference to a statement of the rent account enclosed with the notice);
(3) request that the defendant reply to the claimant within 7 days, agreeing or disputing the stated arrears; and
(4) inform the defendant of his right to apply to the court :
   (a) for a further postponement of the date for possession; or
   (b) to stay or suspend enforcement.

10.5 In his reply to the notice, the defendant must –
(1) where he disputes the stated arrears, provide details of payments or credits made;
(2) where he agrees the stated arrears, explain why payments have not been made.

10.6 An application for an order under paragraph 10.2 must be made by filing an application notice in accordance with Part 23. The application notice must state whether or not there is any outstanding claim by the defendant for housing benefit.

10.7 The claimant must file the following documents with the application notice:
(1) a copy of the notice referred to in paragraph 10.3;
(2) a copy of the defendant's reply, if any, to the notice and any relevant subsequent correspondence between the claimant and the defendant;
(3) a statement of the rent account showing:
   (a) the arrears that have accrued since the first failure to pay in accordance with the order referred to in paragraph 10.2; or
   (b) the arrears that have accrued during the period of two years immediately preceding the date of the application notice, where the first such failure to pay occurs more than two years before that date.

10.8 Rules 23.7 (service of a copy of an application notice), and 23.10 (right to set aside or vary an order made without service of the application notice) and paragraphs 2.3, 2.4 and 2.5 of Practice Direction 23A do not apply to an application under this section.

10.9 On being filed, the application will be referred to the District Judge who –
(1) will normally determine the application without a hearing by fixing the date for possession as the next working day; but
(2) if he considers that a hearing is necessary:
   (a) will fix a date for the application to be heard; and

   (b) direct service of the application notice and supporting evidence on the defendant.

10.10 The court does not have jurisdiction to review a decision that it was reasonable to make an order for possession.

Practice Direction 55B: Possession claims online

This Practice Direction supplements CPR rule 55.10A.

Scope of this practice direction

1.1 This practice direction provides for a scheme ('Possession Claims Online') to operate in specified county courts –

(1) enabling claimants and their representatives to start certain possession claims under CPR Part 55 by requesting the issue of a claim form electronically via the PCOL website; and

(2) where a claim has been started electronically, enabling the claimant or defendant and their representatives to take further steps in the claim electronically as specified below.

1.2 In this practice direction –

(1) 'PCOL website' means the website which may be accessed via the Business Link website and through which Possession Claims Online will operate.

Security

3.1 Her Majesty's Courts and Tribunals Service will take such measures as it thinks fit to ensure the security of steps taken or information stored electronically. These may include requiring users of Possession Claims Online –

(1) to enter a customer identification number or password;

(2) to provide personal information for identification purposes; and

(3) to comply with any other security measures,

before taking any step online.

Fees

4.1 A step may only be taken using Possession Claims Online on payment of the prescribed fee where a fee is payable. Where this practice direction provides for a fee to be paid electronically, it may be paid by –

(1) credit card;

(2) debit card; or

(3) any other method which Her Majesty's Courts and Tribunals Service may permit.

4.2 A defendant who wishes to claim exemption from payment of fees must do so through an organisation approved by Her Majesty's Courts and Tribunals Service before taking any step using PCOL which attracts a fee. If satisfied that the defendant is entitled to fee exemption, the organisation will submit the fee exemption form through the PCOL website to Her Majesty's Courts and Tribunals Service. The defendant may then use PCOL to take such a step.

(Her Majesty's Courts and Tribunals Service website contains guidance as to when the entitlement to claim an exemption from payment of fees arises. The PCOL website will contain a list of organisations through which the defendant may claim an exemption from fees).

Claims which may be started using Possession Claims Online

5.1 A claim may be started online if –

(1) it is brought under Section I of Part 55;

(2) it includes a possession claim for residential property by –

(a) a landlord against a tenant, solely on the ground of arrears of rent (but not a claim for forfeiture of a lease); or

(b) a mortgagee against a mortgagor, solely on the ground of default in the payment of sums due under a mortgage,

relating to land within the district of a specified court;

(3) it does not include a claim for any other remedy except for payment of arrears of rent or money due under a mortgage, interest and costs;

(4) the defendant has an address for service in England and Wales; and

(5) the claimant is able to provide a postcode for the property.

5.2 A claim must not be started online if a defendant is known to be a child or patient.

Starting a claim

6.1 A claimant may request the issue of a claim form by –

(1) completing an online claim form at the PCOL website;

(2) paying the appropriate issue fee electronically at the PCOL website or by some other means approved by Her Majesty's Courts and Tribunals Service.

6.2 The particulars of claim must be included in the online claim form and may not be filed separately. It is not necessary to file a copy of the tenancy agreement, mortgage deed or mortgage agreement with the particulars of claim.

6.2A In the case of a possession claim for residential property that relies on a statutory ground or grounds for possession, the clamant must specify, in section 4(a) of the online claim form, the ground or grounds relied on.

6.3 Subject to paragraphs 6.3A and 6.3B, particulars of claim must include a history of the rent or mortgage account, in schedule form setting out –

(1) the dates and amounts of all payments due and payments made under the tenancy agreement, mortgage deed or mortgage agreement either from the first date of default if that date occurred less than two years before the date of issue or for a period of two years immediately preceding the date of issue; and

(2) a running total of the arrears.

6.3A Paragraph 6.3B applies where the claimant has, before commencing proceedings, provided the defendant in schedule form with –

(1) details of the dates and amounts of all payments due and payments made under the tenancy agreement, mortgage deed or mortgage account –

(a) for a period of two years immediately preceding the date of commencing proceedings; or

(b) if the first date of default occurred less than two years before that date, from the first date of default; and

(2) a running total of the arrears.

6.3B Where this paragraph applies the claimant may, in place of the information required by paragraph 6.3, include in his particulars of claim a summary only of the arrears containing at least the following information –

(1) The amount of arrears as stated in the notice of seeking possession served under either section 83 of the Housing Act 1985 or section 8 of the Housing Act 1988, or at the date of the claimant's letter before action, as appropriate;

(2) the dates and amounts of the last three payments in cleared funds made by the defendant or, if less than three payments have been made, the dates and amounts of all payments made;

(3) the arrears at the date of issue, assuming that no further payments are made by the defendant.

6.3C Where the particulars of claim include a summary only of the arrears the claimant must –

(1) serve on the defendant not more than 7 days after the date of issue, a full, up-to-date arrears history containing at least the information required by paragraph 6.3; and

(2) either –

  (a) make a witness statement confirming that he has complied with sub-paragraph (1) or (2) of paragraph 6.3A as appropriate, and including or exhibiting the full arrears history; or

  (b) verify by way of oral evidence at the hearing that he has complied with sub-paragraph (1) or (2) of paragraph 6.3A as appropriate and also produce and verify the full arrears history.

(Rule 55.8(4) requires all witness statements to be filed and served at least 2 days before the hearing.)

6.4 If the claimant wishes to rely on a history of arrears which is longer than two years, he should state this in his particulars and exhibit a full (or longer) schedule to a witness statement.

6.5 When an online claim form is received, an acknowledgment of receipt will automatically be sent to the claimant. The acknowledgment does not constitute notice that the claim form has been issued or served.

6.6 When the court issues a claim form following the submission of an online claim form, the claim is 'brought' for the purposes of the Limitation Act 1980 and any other enactment on the date on which the online claim form is received by the court's computer system. The court will keep a record, by electronic or other means, of when online claim forms are received.

6.7 When the court issues a claim form it will –

(1) serve a printed version of the claim form and a defence form on the defendant; and

(2) send the claimant notice of issue by post or, where the claimant has supplied an e-mail address, by electronic means.

6.8 The claim shall be deemed to be served on the fifth day after the claim was issued irrespective of whether that day is a business day or not.

6.9 Where the period of time within which a defence must be filed ends on a day when the court is closed, the defendant may file his defence on the next day that the court is open.

6.10 The claim form shall have printed on it a unique customer identification number or a password by which the defendant may access the claim on the PCOL website.

6.11 PCOL will issue the proceedings in the appropriate county court by reference to the post code provided by the claimant and that court shall have jurisdiction to hear and determine the claim and to carry out enforcement of any judgment irrespective of whether the property is within or outside the jurisdiction of that court.

(CPR 30.2(1) authorises proceedings to be transferred from one county court to another.)

Defence

7.1 A defendant wishing to file –

(1) a defence; or

(2) a counterclaim (to be filed together with a defence) to a claim which has been issued through the PCOL system,

may, instead of filing a written form, do so by –

(a) completing the relevant online form at the PCOL website; and

(b) if the defendant is making a counterclaim, paying the appropriate fee electronically at the PCOL website or by some other means approved by Her Majesty's Courts and Tribunals Service.

7.2 Where a defendant files a defence by completing the relevant online form, he must not send the court a hard copy.

7.3 When an online defence form is received, an acknowledgment of receipt will automatically be sent to the defendant. The acknowledgment does not constitute notice that the defence has been served.

7.4 The online defence form will be treated as being filed –

(1) on the day the court receives it, if it receives it before 4 pm on a working day; and

(2) otherwise, on the next working day after the court receives the online defence form.

7.5 A defence is filed when the online defence form is received by the court's computer system. The court will keep a record, by electronic or other means, of when online defence forms are received.

Statement of truth

8.1 CPR Part 22 requires any statement of case to be verified by a statement of truth. This applies to any online claims and defences and application notices.

8.2 CPR Part 22 also requires that if an applicant wishes to rely on matters set out in his application notice as evidence, the application notice must be verified by a statement of truth. This applies to any application notice completed online that contains matters on which the applicant wishes to rely as evidence.

8.3 Attention is drawn to –

(1) paragraph 2 of the practice direction supplementing CPR Part 22, which stipulates the form of the statement of truth; and

(2) paragraph 3 of the practice direction supplementing CPR Part 22, which provides who may sign a statement of truth; and

(3) CPR 32.14, which sets out the consequences of making, or causing to be made, a false statement in a document verified by a statement of truth, without an honest belief in its truth.

Signature

9.1 Any provision of the CPR which requires a document to be signed by any person is satisfied by that person entering his name on an online form.

Communication with the court electronically by the messaging service

10.1 If the PCOL website specifies that a court accepts electronic communications relating to claims brought using Possession Claims Online the parties may communicate with the court using the messaging service facility, available on the PCOL website ('the messaging service').

10.2 The messaging service is for brief and straightforward communications only. The PCOL website contains a list of examples of when it will not be appropriate to use the messaging service.

10.3 Parties must not send to the court forms or attachments via the messaging service.

10.4 The court shall treat any forms or attachments sent via the messaging service as not having been filed or received.

10.5 The court will normally reply via the messaging service where –
   (1) the response is to a message transmitted via the messaging service; and
   (2) the sender has provided an e-mail address.

Electronic applications

11.1 Certain applications in relation to a possession claim started online may be made electronically ('online applications'). An online application may be made if a form for that application is published on the PCOL website ('online application form') and the application is made at least five clear days before the hearing.

11.2 If a claim for possession has been started online and a party wishes to make an online application, he may do so by –
   (1) completing the appropriate online application form at the PCOL website; and
   (2) paying the appropriate fee electronically at the PCOL website or by some other means
approved by Her Majesty's Courts and Tribunals Service.

11.3 When an online application form is received, an acknowledgment of receipt will automatically be sent to the applicant. The acknowledgment does not constitute a notice that the online application form has been issued or served.

11.4 Where an application must be made within a specified time, it is so made if the online application form is received by the court's computer system within that time. The court will keep a record, by electronic or other means, of when online application forms are received.

11.5 When the court receives an online application form it shall –

(1) serve a copy of the online application endorsed with the date of the hearing by post on the claimant at least two clear days before the hearing; and

(2) send the defendant notice of service and confirmation of the date of the hearing by post; provided that

(3) where either party has provided the court with an e-mail address for service, service of the application and/or the notice of service and confirmation of the hearing date may be effected by electronic means.

Request for issue of warrant

12.1 Where –

(1) the court has made an order for possession in a claim started online; and

(2) the claimant is entitled to the issue of a warrant of possession without requiring the permission of the court

the claimant may request the issue of a warrant by completing an online request form at the PCOL website and paying the appropriate fee electronically at the PCOL website or by some other means approved by Her Majesty's Courts and Tribunals Service.

12.2 A request under paragraph 12.1 will be treated as being filed –

(1) on the day the court receives the request, if it receives it before 4 pm on a working day; and

(2) otherwise, on the next working day after the court receives the request.

(Rule 83.2 sets out certain circumstances in which a warrant of execution may not be issued without the permission of the court.)

Application to suspend warrant of possession

13.1 Where the court has issued a warrant of possession, the defendant may apply electronically for the suspension of the warrant, provided that:

(1) the application is made at least five clear days before the appointment for possession; and

(2) the defendant is not prevented from making such an application without the permission of the court.

13.2 The defendant may apply electronically for the suspension of the warrant, by –

(1) completing an online application for suspension at the PCOL website; and

(2) paying the appropriate fee electronically at the PCOL website or by some other means approved by Her Majesty's Courts and Tribunals Service.

13.3 When an online application for suspension is received, an acknowledgment of receipt will automatically be sent to the defendant. The acknowledgment does not constitute a notice that the online application for suspension has been served.

13.4 Where an application must be made within a specified time, it is so made if the online application for suspension is received by the court's computer system within that time. The court will keep a record, by electronic or other means, of when online applications for suspension are received.

13.5 When the court receives an online application for suspension it shall –

(1) serve a copy of the online application for suspension endorsed with the date of the hearing by post on the claimant at least two clear days before the hearing; and

(2) send the defendant notice of service and confirmation of the date of the hearing by post; provided that

(3) where either party has provided the court with an e-mail address for service, service of the application and/or the notice of service and confirmation of the hearing date may be effected by electronic means.

Viewing the case record

14.1 A facility will be provided on the PCOL website for parties or their representatives to view –

(1) an electronic record of the status of claims started online, which will be reviewed and, if necessary, updated at least once each day; and

(2) all information relating to the case that has been filed by the parties electronically.

14.2 In addition, where the PCOL website specifies that the court has the facility to provide viewing of such information by electronic means, the parties or their representatives may view the following information electronically –

(1) court orders made in relation to the case; and

(2) details of progress on enforcement and subsequent orders made.

Index